Commercial Arbitration

KV-501-641

The Law and Practice of Commercial Arbitration in England

Second Edition

SIR MICHAEL J. MUSTILL
One of Her Majesty's Lords Justices of Appeal
of St. John's College Cambridge
and Gray's Inn

STEWART C. BOYD
of Trinity College, Cambridge
and of the Middle Temple
One of Her Majesty's Counsel

COLLEGE OF LAW
LIBRARY
NOT TO BE REMOVE!

Butterworths
London and Edinburgh
1989

United Kingdom	Butterworth & Co (Publishers) Ltd, 88 Kingsway, LONDON WC2B 6AB and 4 Hill Street, EDINBURGH EH2 3JZ
Australia	Butterworths Pty Ltd, SYDNEY, MELBOURNE, BRISBANE, ADELAIDE, PERTH, CANBERRA and HOBART
Belgium	Butterworth & Co (Publishers) Ltd, BRUSSELS
Canada	Butterworths Canada Ltd, TORONTO and VANCOUVER
Ireland	Butterworth (Ireland) Ltd, DUBLIN
Malaysia	Malayan Law Journal Sdn Bhd, KUALA LUMPUR
New Zealand	Butterworths of New Zealand Ltd, WELLINGTON and AUCKLAND
Puerto Rico	Equity de Puerto Rico, Inc, HATO REY
Singapore	Butterworths Asia, SINGAPORE
USA	Butterworths Legal Publishers, AUSTIN, Texas; BOSTON, Massachusetts; CLEARWATER, Florida (D & S Publishers); ORFORD, New Hampshire (Equity Publishing); ST PAUL, Minnesota; and SEATTLE, Washington

All rights reserved. No part of this publication may be reproduced or transmitted in any form or by any means (including photocopying and recording) without the written permission of the copyright holder except in accordance with the provisions of the Copyright Act 1956 (as amended) or under the terms of a licence issued by the Copyright Licensing Agency Ltd, 90 Tottenham Court Road, London, England W1P 9HE. The written permission of the copyright holder must also be obtained before any part of this publication is stored in a retrieval system of any nature. Applications for the copyright holder's written permission to reproduce, transmit or store in a retrieval system any part of this publication should be addressed to the publisher.

Warning: The doing of an unauthorised act in relation to a copyright work may result in both a civil claim for damages and criminal prosecution.

© Sir Michael J. Mustill and Stewart C. Boyd 1989
Reprinted 1991, January and September 1992

A CIP Catalogue record for this book is available from the British Library.

ISBN 0 406 31124 2

Printed and bound in Great Britain by Antony Rowe Ltd, Chippenham, Wiltshire

Preface

When the first edition of this work was published in 1982 the law of arbitration was at a watershed. The Arbitration Act 1979 was beginning to exert its influence. The landmark decision of the House of Lords in *The Nema* had laid down guidelines for the future course of arbitration which indicated a bold change in direction for the principles governing appeals from an award, but without clearly describing where the guidelines were to lead. Two further decisions of the House of Lords in the *Bremer Vulkan* case and *The Hannah Blumenthal* had opened up entirely new territory in examining the contractual relationships involved in an arbitration, but had left many parts of the territory unexplored. It was clear, as we wrote at the time, that 'the law of arbitration is on the move, but in precisely what direction it is impossible to say'.

Six and a half years later, the pace of progress has slackened but not faltered, and its general direction can now be more clearly perceived. The contractual analysis has been explored further in a number of decisions, notably *The Leonidas D* and *The Antclizo*, and valuable theoretical work has been done along the way, which is reflected in Chapter 32 of the present edition. But as a solution to the practical problem to which it was principally addressed, that of killing off moribund references, the contractual analysis has led to a virtual dead-end, from which the way forward can only be through legislation.

In contrast, the stream of authority flowing from *The Nema* has flowed through more fertile territory. The guidelines for appeals have been more fully worked out in decided cases and in amendments to the Rules of Court. In consequence, the principles and practice governing appeals from arbitrators' decisions have become reasonably well settled. This has enabled us to remove much speculative material from Chapter 36 (Appeals), and to give a clearer and more concise picture of the procedure and how it works in practice. A number of decisions have clarified the scope of the arbitrator's duty to give reasons for his award and what those reasons should contain: this topic, formerly discussed in Chapter 36, is now dealt with in Chapter 25 (Types of Award). The power of the Court to order further reasons for the purposes of an appeal is discussed, as previously, in Chapter 36.

As the number of successful applications for leave to appeal from arbitrators' decisions has dwindled to a trickle, attention has been focused on other means of challenging awards. Consistently with the spirit underlying the 1979 Act, these challenges have been firmly resisted by the courts, except in those very few cases indeed where intervention has been necessary to remedy a real injustice. Attention has focused on topics such as bias, real or apparent (see pp. 249 et seq.), correcting mistakes in the award (see pp. 558–561), and adducing fresh evidence after the award (pp. 561–562). Little resort has been had to the other possible means of challenging an unappealable award which we mentioned in Chapter 37, no doubt because no case has arisen in which there has been a sufficiently serious disregard of the law to warrant invoking any of the procedures which we there suggested. Moreover, attempts to treat certain types of error as going to the arbitrator's jurisdiction have been resisted as 'driving a juggernaut through the philosophy of the 1979 Act' (p. 555). The discussion of alternative remedies may, however, still be of value, if only to demonstrate their very limited sphere of application, and is retained in Chapter 37 under the new title 'Recourse against unappealable awards'.

In keeping with the spirit of the 1979 Act, the courts have continued to favour a benevolent approach to the construction of arbitration clauses, preferring if possible to give them a wide rather than a restricted meaning (see pp. 117–121). A similarly benevolent approach has been followed with regard to the construction of awards (pp. 570–571), to clauses excluding the possibility of an appeal on a question of law (p. 365), and towards the use of 'equity clauses' (Chapter 4).

There have been a number of important developments in the field of international commercial arbitration, and in consequence Chapter 4, formerly entitled 'Foreign arbitral law', has been substantially recast, and much new material added, under the new title 'The applicable law and the jurisdiction of the Court'. The reader will now find in this Chapter a discussion of the questions whether the arbitrator must apply the law to the substance of the dispute or to the procedure to be followed, and if so what law, whether English law (including the law of the EEC), foreign law, or some system of law derived from some international or transnational source; whether these questions are affected by the presence of an 'equity clause' or a provision for 'amiable composition'. (Some of this material was formerly in Chapter 37, where it was likely to be hidden from the reader by the unhelpful title – 'Procedures not by way of appeal' – with which the Chapter was previously labelled.) Important changes in the Rules of Court regarding service out of the jurisdiction of proceedings affecting arbitration have enabled a fuller account to be given of the jurisdiction of the English courts over international arbitrations, and the circumstances in which the courts will exercise or abstain from exercising jurisdiction.

We have taken account of the legislation, mainly fragmentary in character, which has touched on the law of arbitration since the previous edition. The most significant is the Civil Jurisdiction and Judgments Act 1982, which affects arbitration in a number of ways (pp. 87, 92, 394–341, 483–484). There has been new legislation concerning the powers of an arbitrator to award interest: this is discussed, together with the somewhat wider powers which may in some cases exist under the common law. Section 10(3) of the Arbitration Act 1985 was passed to fill a gap in the powers with regard to default appointments of arbitrators which we identified in the first edition. Note has also been taken of the Companies Act 1985 and the Insolvency Act 1986 (Chapter 11), as well as of the Supply of Goods and Services Act 1982 (p. 229). We have also considered whether to include discussion of the Consumer Arbitration Agreements Act 1988, but have concluded that it lies outside the scope of a work concerned with commercial arbitration.

Space does not permit us to enumerate the many other changes which will be found in the text. These have tended to increase the length of the book. To compensate for this, some of the Appendices have not been reproduced, namely Appendix 1, Part 1 (Statutes no Longer in Force), Appendix 3 (Special case), Appendix 4 ('Manifest disregard' under United States law), and Appendix 5

(Fact and law). On the other hand Appendix 1 has been enlarged to include the Arbitration (International Investment Disputes) Act 1966, not only for the inherent interest of its provisions, but also because of its developing practical importance in the field of international commercial arbitration. A new Appendix 3 contains the text of the UNCITRAL Model Law, whose influence on the development of arbitration law in the United Kingdom and elsewhere is likely to be far-reaching. A new Appendix 4 contains the text of the principal Arbitration Rules in common use in commercial arbitration in England, namely the Rules of Conciliation and Arbitration of the International Chamber of Commerce, the UNCITRAL Arbitration Rules, the London Maritime Arbitrators' Association Terms (1987), the Rules of the London International Court of Arbitration, and the Institute of Civil Engineers' Arbitration Procedure (1983).

Of the very large number of decisions concerning arbitration which have been reported since the first edition, not all have merited attention in the text. So far as possible, however, we have noted every case which has served to enlarge a proper understanding of the law of arbitration. Inevitably there may be accidental omissions, as there were in the previous edition, and we extend our gratitude to all those readers who have brought to our attention cases or topics deserving of mention in the text, as well as some manifest errors, in the hope and expectation that others will continue to do so in the future.

We also wish to express our gratitude to our publishers for their kindness in agreeing to the preparation of a new index, and for their unfailing support and patience throughout the preparation of the manuscript for publication.

The law is stated on the basis of cases reported and legislation published on or before 1 January 1989.

M.J.M.
S.C.B.

Contents

Chapter 18 Capacity, qualifications, and impartiality of the arbitrator 247

Chapter 19 The arbitrator advocate: the umpire: disagreement 258

Chapter 20 Judicial arbitrators 265

PART V THE CONDUCT OF THE REFERENCE 277

Chapter 24 The course of the reference: the hearing and after   345

Chapter 37 Recourse against unappealable errors of law   638

Appendices

Appendix 1 Legislation affecting arbitration   653

Appendix 2 Convention on the recognition and enforcement of foreign arbitral awards. Done at New York, on 10 June 1958   725

Appendix 3 UNCITRAL Model Law   730

Table of statutes

References in this Table to *Statutes* are to Halsbury's Statutes of England (Fourth Edition) showing the volume and page at which the annotated text of the Act may be found. Page references printed in **bold** type indicate where the Act is set out in part or in full.

Table of cases

PAGE

N

PAGE

PART I
Preliminary

PART 1

Preliminary

CHAPTER 1

Descriptive introduction

In this opening chapter we set out, mainly for the benefit of the reader with no prior knowledge of the English law of arbitration, a synopsis of the most important and distinctive features of the English system. Reasons of brevity dictate that many points of detail are omitted, with the result that much of what follows could reasonably be described as an over-simplification. Nevertheless, it may be found useful to start with a view of the whole subject, and the reader may then turn to later chapters for a more accurate account of matters of detail.

A. THE ENGLISH SYSTEM

1 General

The law of private arbitration[1] is concerned with the relationship between the courts and the arbitral process[2].

In theory, a legal system could be envisaged which adopted an attitude of indifference to private arbitration. Whilst recognising the right of parties to agree that their disputes should be decided by arbitration, the law would do nothing to enforce the agreement, to reinforce the procedure at its points of potential weakness, or to protect the parties against the risk of procedural or substantive injustice. English law came close to taking up this position in late

---

[1] Many procedures referred to as arbitration lie outside the scope of the present work. For example, statutory arbitrations, which are conducted before tribunals whose jurisdiction derives from the statute under which the dispute has arisen; pay arbitrations, where the jurisdiction of the tribunal derives from consent, but which are not usually intended to create legally enforceable obligations. Conversely, there are procedures by which a person chosen by consent makes a binding adjudication on private rights, but which are not arbitrations. The problem of identifying what is, and is not, an arbitration for the purposes of the legislation and the common law is discussed in Chapter 2, p. 30, post.

[2] This statement, which was not meant to be controversial, has attracted some criticism. We had at first planned a response to the critics, but now believe that this would be pointless, given the limited scope of this work, which is two fold. First, to delineate in the light of the statutes and decisions of the courts what the parties and the arbitrator must do, may do and may not do in the conduct of the dispute. Secondly, to explain the ways in which arbitrations are in practice conducted, and may with better advantage be conducted, within the framework of the duties and liberties thus created. In a work devoted to a single domestic system of arbitration the first objective cannot rationally be carried out otherwise than by reference to a relationship between the process of arbitration and the courts which, in the event of disputes, will decide whether the procedural rights of the parties to an arbitration have been infringed, and which will administer remedies if an infringement is found to have occurred. The second objective is concerned with activities which are by definition permissive. Whether it is possible to have practices which are normative, albeit independent of enforcement by any legal process, is a question worthy of serious consideration, but it is not one which can arise in the context of a treatise such as the present.

3

mediaeval times; but no modern developed state[3] can afford such a detached attitude. Arbitration is an important part of commercial life, and every legal system must in some degree be concerned with it. Where the systems differ is in regard to the nature of the relationship between the court and the arbitrator, and the extent to which the court concerns itself is the conduct of the reference.

Essentially, those who devise a law of arbitration may choose between two alternative views of the relationship. First, they may regard arbitration as an aspect of public law. The arbitrator is a delegate of judicial powers which are essentially the property of the State. The powers of enforcement or control are attached to the arbitral process because that process belongs to the state, even if called into existence by a private bargain. The State has the right and duty to ensure, through the medium of the courts, that the reference is conducted in accordance with procedural norms which the State itself lays down.

Alternatively, the legal system may treat arbitration as a branch of private law. Recognising the value of the institution, the State will lend its own coercive powers to reinforce the process at points of weakness. Nevertheless, the formulation of the rights, duties and powers of the arbitrator, and the mutual obligations of the parties in relation to the conduct of the reference, are created and regulated by the private bargain between the parties, and are no concern of the State.

It is essential to an understanding of the English[4] law of arbitration to recognise that throughout its history the law has approached the relationships between the parties and the arbitrator, and between the parties and each other, unequivocally in terms of private law. At every stage in the development of the law of arbitration, the courts have begun by studying the arbitration agreement, so as to ascertain what it says expressly about the problem in issue, and what relevant terms may reasonably be implied. The arbitration law of England is dominated by the law of contract. Once the arbitration agreement has been construed, the courts will recognise any procedure which conforms with it, and will endeavour to enforce whatever positive rights it may be held to create.

2 Sources of law

Anyone coming for the first time into contact with an English arbitration, and wishing to acquaint himself with the relevant principles of law, might reasonably look to the current Arbitration Acts (those of 1950, 1975 and 1979) for a coherent exposition of the central principles of arbitration law. If so, he would be disappointed. There are two reasons for this.

First, because the statutes say little about the powers of the arbitrator, and nothing at all about the conduct of the reference. This is left to the individual contract, construed in the first instance by the arbitrator, and in some cases of controversy, by the Court.

Second, because the Acts are the product of a course of legislation extending over three centuries, whereby the courts have from time to time been given individual extra powers to cure individual weaknesses inherent in a system

---

[3] We are here speaking only of those states which give such recognition to the concept of individual proprietary and contractual rights as to invest the idea of a private arbitration with any meaning.

[4] For brevity, we refer to England, rather than England and Wales. The arbitration law of Scotland differs in important respects from that of England.

based on private contract. The Acts do not purport to provide a complete or methodical exposition of the law.

Thus, the question 'where do I find English arbitration law' receives different answers, according to the subject matter of the enquiry. In summary one may say that—

1 Questions as to the powers of the court to enforce, support, supervise and intervene in arbitral proceedings are largely governed by the Acts. To a limited extent, where the powers exist independently of statute, they are the creation of the common law: viz. that body of previously decided cases, which by virtue of English doctrines of precedent, lays down principles which determine or guide the decisions of courts in subsequent cases.

2 Questions as to the way in which the powers of the court should be exercised in the individual case are governed by the common law.

3 Questions as to the powers of the arbitrator, as to the way in which those powers should be exercised, and as to the proper conduct of the reference are governed by the arbitration agreement, construed by the courts in the light of the common law.

3 The relationship with the Court

Although the Court has wide statutory powers, its instinct is to use them only to support the arbitration, not to interfere in it. The Court will freely grant orders to stay actions commenced in breach of an arbitration agreement, or to constitute or re-constitute the tribunal, or to enforce the award. By contrast, it is very rare to find an intervention in a pending reference; indeed the Court has renounced any claim to a general inherent jurisdiction to do so. Again, although the powers to remit or set aside an award on the ground of a procedural defect are virtually unlimited, they will not be used simply because it is considered that the reference could have been better conducted in some other way. The parties have contracted to have their disputes decided by the arbitral tribunal which they have selected, or which has been selected by a method which the parties have chosen, and that it what they are entitled to receive, and bound to accept.

The right of appeal on a question of law falls into a separate category. Originally introduced by consent, it was progressively given statutory force because it was felt to be useful. Recently, a different opinion was expressed. The procedure was felt to be a possible source of delay, and hence of injustice. The response was to alter the statute, so as to limit the possibility of an appeal. But this was not all: the Court also spontaneously reacted, by imposing on itself a restraint as to the circumstances in which an appeal would be permitted, so as to safeguard the efficacy and autonomy of the arbitral process.

It used occasionally to be suggested that the English courts were hostile to the process of arbitration. Whether this was ever true, in the distant past, is a matter of opinion. What must be clear, to anyone reading the judgments delivered during the past 60 years, is that this is now a complete misconception. Arbitration is not always the best way of deciding a dispute, and the judges have occasionally said so. Nevertheless, they recognise that the process is often more efficient than litigation; and they also recognise that, efficient or not, it is in very many cases the procedure which the commercial man prefers. The courts respect, and give effect to, this preference by abstaining from intervention even in the face of the widest deviation from the conventional procedural norms: always provided that the procedures actually followed conform with those which the parties have expressly or impliedly chosen to accept.

B. THE ARBITRATION AGREEMENT

1 Nature and effect of the agreement

Agreements to arbitrate are of two kinds: those which refer an existing dispute to arbitration, and those which relate to disputes which may arise in the future. Agreements which refer existing disputes, often called 'ad hoc submissions', present few theoretical problems, but they are comparatively rare. For present purposes, we will deal only with the second type of agreement, which usually takes the shape of a clause inserted in the contract which creates those rights and duties which, in the event of dispute, will be the subject of the intended arbitration. (It is convenient to call this 'the substantive contract'.)

English law prescribes no formal requirements for a valid arbitration agreement. It need not even be in writing. An oral arbitration agreement, if followed by completed arbitration proceedings, can be the foundations of an enforceable award, although the agreement will not be an 'arbitration agreement' for the purposes the Arbitration Acts and the proceedings will not be subject to the important processes of the Court to provide support and supervision which those Acts confer. There is no need for the original arbitration agreement to be followed by a formal submission to arbitration once the dispute has arisen. If the dispute falls within the scope of the arbitration clause, and a tribunal has been called into existence to adjudicate upon it, the original agreement coupled with a valid notice of appointment is sufficient to cloak the tribunal with authority to bind the parties by its award, without any further document in the nature of a 'terms of reference' or '*compromis*'[5].

The agreement to arbitrate need not be set out in a single document. Thus it may validly be contained in an exchange of letters or telex messages. Similarly, it is enough for an arbitration clause to be incorporated by reference into the substantive contract, and indeed it is common to see a clause incorporated at two removes: the substantive contract refers to the terms of the contract form of a specified trade association, and the form in turn refers to the arbitration rules of the association.

The question whether a particular dispute between the parties may and must be referred to arbitration depends upon the wording of the agreement, and various forms of arbitration clause in common use differ substantially as to their effect. At their widest, they can be sufficient to give the arbitrator jurisdiction over claims which are not based on the substantive contract: for example, claims in tort which are closely connected with the subject matter of the contract. There are, however, limits to what can be done by even the widest language. If the arbitration clause forms an integral part of the substantive contract, a dispute as to the original validity of the contract must also call in question the validity of the clause, and hence the jurisdiction of the arbitrator. In the eyes of

---

[5] Formal submissions are not infrequently made in practice, particularly if the award may have to be enforced abroad. They serve to make it clear what issues are referred, and to record agreement on any special procedural powers conferred on the arbitrator.

English law it is a logical absurdity to hold that the arbitrator can ask himself a question which, if answered in the negative, implies that he had no jurisdiction to ask it. Accordingly, the courts have held that no clause, however widely drawn, can give the arbitrator jurisdiction to decide upon issues which go to the essential validity of the substantive contract: such as, for example, whether it is void for mistake or for lack of consensus or consideration. A doctrine has, however, been evolved which leads to a different conclusion where the question is whether the contract, acknowledged to have been binding at inception, has been discharged by subsequent events. This doctrine treats the arbitration clause as having a life of its own, severable from the substantive contract[6], and capable of surviving it so as to give the arbitrator continuing jurisdiction not only over disputes arising from events happening whilst the contract was still in existence, but also upon whether the contract has come to an end, and if so with what consequences to the parties. Thus, an arbitrator can hold that the contract has been discharged by frustration or repudiation, or has been rescinded on the ground of misrepresentation or non-disclosure, without casting any doubt upon his own status as arbitrator.

2 Enforcing the arbitration agreement

When it comes to the enforcement of the agreement against a party who has started an action in respect of a claim which ought to have been submitted to arbitration, the usual remedies for breach of contract are of little or no value. An order for the specific performance of the arbitration agreement cannot in practice be enforced. Damages are a possible remedy, but it would be rare for any to be proved. For technical reasons, an injunction is not the correct method of bringing an action in England to a halt. Instead the legislature has intervened by empowering the Court to order that the future conduct of the action shall be stayed, thus leaving the claimant with the choice between referring the dispute to arbitration, or abandoning his claim. This power arises in two distinct situations.

The first relates to domestic arbitration agreements. Essentially these are agreements made between nationals or residents of, or companies registered in or controlled in, the United Kingdom, which provide for the arbitration of disputes in the United Kingdom: it is immaterial whether the agreement was made in England or governed by English law or to be performed in England. Here the Court has a discretion whether or not to stay the action. There is a presumption in favour of granting the stay and so enforcing the agreement to arbitrate, unless there are strong grounds for considering that the dispute can be better dealt with in the High Court. The defendant must apply promptly for the stay, before he has taken any step in the action such as delivering a defence. He must also demonstrate that he is ready and willing to do all things necessary to the proper conduct of the arbitration.

The Court also has power to grant a stay, where the agreement is of a non-

---

[6] The doctrine of the separability of the arbitration clause has not been espoused in the wider form in which it is known in other jurisdictions. But the narrower English form leads in many cases to the same result.

domestic character, under section 1(1) of the 1975 Act[7]. The position is, however, radically different: once called upon by the defendant to do so, the Court is obliged to stay the action, however obvious it may seem that on the grounds of efficiency, economy and convenience the particular dispute is better suited for disposal by a trial in court rather than by arbitration. The Court has, however, no jurisdiction to grant a stay if satisfied that the arbitration agreement is 'null and void or inoperative or incapable of being performed', or that there is not any dispute between the parties with regard to the matter agreed to be referred.

Since an arbitration agreement does not, under English law, deprive the court of jurisdiction, but merely forms a reason why the Court should decline to exercise that jurisdiction, the result of a successful application by the defendant under either Act is not that the Court declares itself to be without jurisdiction, or orders the action to be dismissed. Instead, the action is merely halted until further order. In the ordinary way, if the arbitration goes ahead in a satisfactory manner, the stay will never come to an end, but there are circumstances in which the Court will lift the stay, and the action will proceed.

Under neither Act does the Court intervene of its own volition: it is for the defendant to ask for a stay. In practice, many disputes are allowed to continue in the High Court which could, if the defendant had wished, have been referred to arbitration.

C. THE TRIBUNAL

1 Composition of the tribunal

English arbitral practice tends to prefer a tribunal consisting of one arbitrator[8]. This preference is given statutory recognition in section 6 of the Act, where it is provided that in the absence of an express provision to the contrary, every arbitration agreement shall be deemed to include a provision that the reference shall be to a single arbitrator. The choice of arbitrator is to be made by agreement. If the parties are unable to concur in the appointment, the Court has power to make an appointment.

It is, of course, open to the parties to agree upon a tribunal of more than one arbitrator. Unlike other legal systems, English law does not forbid the appointment of a tribunal consisting of an even number of arbitrators. Indeed, until comparatively recently, a tribunal of two arbitrators was common. Arbitration clauses often provided that each party should nominate an arbitrator, and that in the event of disagreement the reference should be entrusted to an umpire of their choice. If the arbitrators were able to agree on a joint award, the umpire played no part in the decision. If, on the other hand, the arbitrators did not agree, then the umpire became the sole member of the

---

[7] Which gives effect to the 1958 New York Convention on the Recognition and Enforcement of Foreign Arbitral Awards.

[8] It is less expensive to pay the fees of one arbitrator than of three; and easier for one person to find time for the hearing, than for three; and the hearing will usually proceed more quickly if conducted by one person alone. The traditional English system does impose a heavy responsibility on the arbitrator sitting alone, and it takes away the opportunity for an exchange of views within the tribunal. It is felt by many that these disadvantages are more than compensated by the gain in speed and economy: also, perhaps, by the absence of pressure for a compromise between the views of all three members.

tribunal, and the powers of the two original arbitrators came to an end. This practice was so widespread that a provision for an umpire became implied by statute into every agreement for a reference to two arbitrators. Furthermore, the law until recently provided that even where the agreement was for a reference to three arbitrators, of whom the third was to be appointed by the two existing arbitrators, the appointee should act as umpire and not as third arbitrator.

One aspect of this practice seemed anomalous to many foreign observers. Since the arbitrators became functus officio, once they had disagreed and the umpire had entered on the reference, it was conceived that each was thereafter free to act as advocate for the party who had appointed him, in presenting the case to the umpire. Doctrinally, there were obvious objections to a practice whereby the same person was under successive obligations to act impartially in the interests of both parties, and then to act on behalf of one party alone. Nevertheless, the institution of the 'arbitrator/advocate' had great practical advantages[9] and for more than 60 years the court acknowledged that the system worked, that instances of injustice were very rare, and that however anomalous they might seem in principle the proceedings were of the type which satisfied the parties. This being so, the courts held that, provided that the dispute concerned a trade in which this form of arbitration was customary, there was no reason to interfere simply because of the apparent identification of each arbitrator with the party who had appointed him.

This is still the law today. The institution of the arbitrator/advocate has, however, come to occupy a rather less prominent role in London commercial arbitration, because of a change in the law whereby a clause stipulating for two arbitrators, one appointed by each side, with a third arbitrator to be chosen by the two already appointed, is now understood as meaning what it says[10]. The third arbitrator is not an umpire, but is part of the tribunal from the start, and there is no longer any question, under a clause in this form, of the arbitrators changing their status upon disagreement. The parties may still employ the old system if they wish, either by stipulating for two arbitrators and an umpire, or simply by providing that there shall be two arbitrators, one appointed by each side.

Occasionally, there is provision for a tribunal consisting of more than three members. These are almost always the appeal boards of trade associations, which exist for the purpose of rehearing disputes originally decided by two arbitrators or an umpire.

2 Qualifications

English law has little to say about the formal qualifications of the arbitrator.

---

[9] See pp. 258–264, post.
[10] The change was made, not because a tribunal of three arbitrators was thought to be more efficient than a panel of two followed if necessary by an umpire, but simply because parties who had contracted for a tribunal of three should be entitled to that, rather than something different. English practice has not yet fully accommodated itself to panels of three arbitrators, and arrangements are still being made by consent, in the interests of economy and speed, to keep the third arbitrator out of active proceedings, until there is a real possibility that the two arbitrators will disagree.

Any natural person may be an arbitrator, and it is generally speaking no objection that the person nominated is unsuitable for the office.

The law will, however, enforce any express agreement as to the qualifications of the arbitrator, for example, that he shall be a merchant engaged in a particular trade. Where the appointed arbitrator does not possess the required qualifications, the appointment is ineffective, and any award which he may make is void. The objection can, however, be waived, especially if the other party continues with the reference after the ground of objection is known. In practice, therefore, once it is discovered that the appointee is unqualified, the opposing party applies to the court either for a declaration that the arbitrator has no jurisdiction, or for an order removing him from office.

It is also a ground of objection that the nominee lacks impartiality, in that he is so closely associated with one of the parties or with the subject matter of the dispute, as to cast a doubt over his ability to conduct the reference judicially. The Court proceeds on the basis that 'justice must be seen to be done': even if the arbitrator is in fact disposed to act fairly, his appointment and any proceedings in the arbitrator will be set aside. The appointment is, however, valid until revoked, and the objection does not form a ground for alleging that the arbitrator has no jurisdiction. Nor is it a ground of objection to the jurisdiction that the arbitrator is in fact conducting the reference unfairly. Here, the remedies available are those appropriate to cases of misconduct: see pp. 22–23, post.

3 Constituting the tribunal

An arbitral tribunal may be constituted, or completed, in various ways: by the parties themselves, by the nomination of a third party, or by the Court. In the great majority of cases the appointment is made by the parties themselves. No special formalities are required. Where the tribunal consists of a sole arbitrator, all that is required is that they shall agree upon the choice of a person who has consented to act. Where the tribunal consists of two arbitrators, one to be appointed by each side, the claimant must not only choose an arbitrator and obtain his agreement to act, but most also notify the appointment to his opponent. An agreement in this form naturally contemplates that each party will make a nomination in this way. If, however, the claimant makes an appointment and receives no response from his opponent, he may after an appropriate interval give notice that his own appointee will act as sole arbitrator in respect of the dispute.

The appointment of an arbitrator may be made by a third party if the agreement so provides. Very commonly, the power of nomination is entrusted to a trade association, which will make the choice from a panel of members of the association; or to the president of a professional institution, who will often exercise a wider power of choice, very commonly in the light of suggestions made by the parties.

Occasionally, the power of nomination will be conferred by the agreement on the High Court[11], or on the holder of a particular judicial office. In most cases, the assistance of the Court is invoked independently of the agreement, in

---

[11] The Court does not maintain an official list of arbitrators. Instead, each party will propose one or more names, from whom the Court will select.

cases where some impediment has arisen either to the creation or to the continued existence of the tribunal[12].

4 Rights and duties of the arbitrator

Once validly appointed, the arbitrator enters into a complex relationship with the parties, which confers on him various powers, rights and duties.

So far as concerns his powers, the position is reasonably clear. The tribunal has a mandate from both parties alike, whether it consists of a sole arbitrator or of two arbitrators, one appointed by either party. This mandate enables the tribunal to bind the parties to the terms of an award, by virtue of an implied term in the arbitration agreement that each party will honour the award. The mandate cannot be revoked by either party without the leave of the Court, even in respect of the arbitrator whom he has himself appointed.

As regards the rights of the arbitrator, the position is clear where the reference has been concluded by the making of a valid award. The arbitrator is entitled to receive whatever fee may have been agreed, together with his out-of-pocket expenses. If none has been agreed, he is entitled to a reasonable fee, having regard to matters such as his skill, experience and prestige, the difficulty of the issues, the amount in dispute, and the time spent by him at the hearing and in the preparation of the award. In theory, the procedures for fixing the amount of the fee, and for recovering payment, are rather complicated. In practice, what very often happens is this. The arbitrator decides for himself what he regards as a reasonable sum; he states the figure in the award; and he goes on to prescribe which of the parties shall bear the ultimate liability for the fee. He then makes it known that the award is available for collection, upon payment of his fee. If the person who pays the amount demanded, and thereby obtains delivery of the award, is found to be the losing party, he bears the amount of the fee directly. If he proves to be the winning party, he recovers from his opponent the amount which he has paid the arbitrator. In the unusual event of a party disputing the sum decided by the arbitrator, delivery of the award can be obtained pending the determination by the Court of what is a reasonable fee.

The position is less clear where the arbitration has come to an end before the publication of an award. It seems that the arbitrator would be entitled to remuneration for work done, at least where the termination is not due to his own fault, but that he has no remedy for the loss of his opportunity to earn further remuneration by completing the reference[13]. The position as regards the duties of the arbitrator is also unclear. Undoubtedly, the arbitrator is under a moral obligation to use skill, diligence and care in his duties. Failure to comply with this obligation may result in the vacation of his appointment. Whether there is an additional sanction, in the shape of a liability in damages to a party who has suffered loss through his failure to act with the necessary skill, diligence and care has not been finally determined, but it is probable that there is not, except conceivably in extreme cases, amounting in effect to bad faith[14].

---

[12] See Chapter 15, p. 171, post.
[13] The problem is sometimes dealt with by agreement when the arbitrator is appointed, or by express provision in certain standard rules of arbitration.
[14] See the discussion in Chapter 17, pp. 224–232, post.

5 Judicial arbitration

The great majority of arbitrations take place before tribunals composed of individuals who hold no public judicial office. There are, however, two exceptions to this.

First, there is an arbitration held before an official referee, a judge whose usual function is to try matters requiring prolonged examination of documents or accounts, or technical or other matters which cannot conveniently be dealt with by the judge sitting in court in the ordinary way. An official referee also has a separate jurisdiction to hear any reference to arbitration, where the arbitration agreement expressly so provides.

Second, there is a procedure whereby a judge of the commercial court may accept an appointment as sole arbitrator or umpire, in matters of a commercial character.

For certain types of dispute, these procedures have advantages which deserve to be more widely known: see pp. 266–267 and 274, post.

D. BEGINNING AN ARBITRATION

English law regards an agreement to refer future disputes to arbitration as an irrevocable option, enabling the claimant to compel the defendant to submit to arbitration. The option becomes capable of exercise whenever a dispute arises, which falls within the scope of the agreement. The option is exercised when one party takes the appropriate steps to appoint an arbitrator. The valid exercise of the option calls into existence a new contractual relationship, stemming from but independent of the original agreement to arbitrate.

The following comments may be made on this rather complex theoretical model.

First, since most arbitration clauses express the right and obligation to arbitrate in terms of 'disputes'[15], the claimant cannot ordinarily give a valid notice of arbitration unless his claim is disputed. Moreover, in the absence of a 'dispute' (which has been understood as meaning a *genuine* dispute) the Court will not order that the action should be stayed so that the matter can be referred to arbitration. The procedural consequences are important, for this principle opens the way for the plaintiff, even in a case governed by an arbitration clause, to employ the summary mechanisms of the Court where the defendant has no defence at all to the claim, or only a spurious defence. What happens is this. The claimant commences an action in the High Court, and states on affidavit his belief that there is no defence to the claim. The defendant must then respond, also on affidavit, showing reasons why he does have a defence. If the Court accepts the contention of the plaintiff, it will refuse to stay the proceedings and will instead give immediate judgment for the plaintiff[16]. This abbreviated procedure, which is based entirely on documentary evidence, and which

---

[15]   The word 'difference' is sometimes employed in place of 'dispute'. The meaning is for all practical purposes the same. Other forms of clause use the word 'claim', and here the position may be different: see p. 129, post.

[16]   The availability of summary remedies in the arbitration itself is discussed in Chapter 31, p. 487, post, together with the question whether it is possible to employ a summary procedure to protect the defendant from being harassed by spurious claims.

eliminates not only the usual preliminary steps in the action, but also the trial itself, provides a valuable means of obtaining relief by way of an alternative to a speedy arbitration.

Next, there is the notice of arbitration, by which the claimant invokes the option to arbitrate. The notice of arbitration, read in conjunction with the arbitration agreement, determines the scope of the dispute referred to arbitration, and hence the jurisdiction of the arbitrator. It also forms part of the mechanism for constituting the tribunal. If the reference is to a sole arbitrator, the claimant gives notice to his opponent calling upon him to concur in the choice of a nominee[17]. If the agreement contemplates a tribunal of two arbitrators, one appointed by each side, with an umpire or third arbitrator chosen by the two appointees, the claimant: (i) invites a person to act as arbitrator; (ii) obtains the assent of that person; (iii) notifies the appointment to the other party.

In addition to its functions as a means of calling an arbitration into existence, defining its scope, and appointing the tribunal, the notice of arbitration serves also to stop time from running against the claimant under any period of limitation which may apply to the claim, by virtue of a statute or an express provision in the substantive contract. The fact that a notice is not given until after the expiry of the time will not under most forms of arbitration clause[18] deprive the arbitrator of jurisdiction over the claim. Instead, it will form a ground of defence in the arbitration and, in the absence of reasons to the contrary, entitle the respondent to an award in his favour. The expiry of a contractual time limit is not, however, necessarily fatal to the claim. In particular, the Court has jurisdiction to extend a limit imposed by the arbitration agreement, if it considers that 'undue hardship' would be caused by treating the claim as time-barred: section 27. Such hardship is held to exist if the consequences of holding the claim to be lost would be out of proportion to the claimant's fault in allowing the time to expire without taking the simple step of giving notice to arbitrate and to any prejudice suffered by the respondent in consequence of the claimant's delay.

Finally, there is the effect of exercising the option to arbitrate. By commencing the arbitration, the claimant calls into existence a new contractual relationship between himself and the respondent, relating specifically to the disputes entrusted to the arbitrator and involving mutual promises to obey the directions of the arbitrator and to cooperate in the expeditious conduct of the reference. Just as the arbitration clause is a severable agreement, which can survive the termination of the contract in which it is embodied, so also does the new contract have a life of its own. It is governed by some, if not all, of the general principles of the law of contract. In particular, it is capable in principle of being terminated by events which would bring to an end a more ordinary type of contract, such as repudiatory breach, frustration and mutual discharge. The practical utility of this concept is at present uncertain[19].

---

[17] If the parties are unable to agree, the appointment is made by the court.
[18] Some clauses may be construed as barring the right to exercise the remedy of arbitration as a means of enforcing the claim, rather than extinguishing the claim in its entirety.
[19] See pp. 503 et seq., post.

E. THE JURISDICTION OF THE COURT

Where the parties have agreed to submit their differences to arbitration, the Court is usually concerned only with the procedural aspects of the dispute. But on occasion the Court may be required to decide upon the substantive merits; for the existence of an arbitration agreement is not an objection to the jurisdiction of the Court, but merely a reason why the Court may, and in certain circumstances must, abstain from exercising that jurisdiction. This has a number of consequences. The most important is that an action may properly be commenced in an English court in respect of a dispute falling within a valid and subsisting agreement to arbitrate. Moreover, since the presence of an English arbitration clause will ordinarily justify the inference that the parties wish the dispute to be governed by English law, the Court will in principle often have jurisdiction[20] to entertain an action against a party resident abroad.

Just as an arbitration agreement does not found an objection to the jurisdiction of the Court, so also does it not constitute a defence to the action, or a ground for not honouring any resulting judgment. Even the existence of a pending arbitration does not constitute a defence to the action, so long as it does not reach the stage of a valid award. If the defendant wishes to rely upon the arbitration agreement, his remedy is to invite the court to abstain from exercising its undoubted jurisdiction, and to stay the action[21].

Another consequence of the general principle is that where an action has been brought in breach of an agreement to arbitrate, and the Court has consented to stay its own proceedings, so that the matter may be determined by arbitration, the cesser of jurisdiction is only provisional; if the arbitration breaks down, the Court can in certain circumstances resume its jurisdiction, and take the merits of the dispute into its own hands.

Again, even if there is pending action, the Court may be enabled, if an arbitration has broken down, to carry on the proceedings itself, once the jurisdiction has been invoked by the claimant instituting a new action[1].

There is one apparent exception to the rule that an arbitration agreement does not constitute a defence to an action in Court. For nearly 150 years the courts have recognised the validity of clauses[2] which make it a condition precedent to the enforcement of a claim under a contract that the claimant shall have taken the matter to arbitration and obtained a favourable award. Such a clause does not bar the jurisdiction of the Court, but it does provide a defence to the action, where there has been no arbitration and no award. In theory, the defendant is entitled to let the action run on, and use the clause to defeat the claim at the trial. This is rarely done in practice, and the usual course is to employ the clause as a ground for obtaining a stay.

---

[20]   Under RSC Ord. 11, r. 1(1), which gives the court jurisdiction where the action is brought under a contract expressly or impliedly governed by English law, unless jurisdiction is excluded by the terms of the European Judgments Conventions.

[21]   See p. 7, ante.

[1]   This more controversial question is discussed at p. 154, post.

[2]   Known as '*Scott v Avery*' clauses.

F. THE REFERENCE

1 Variety of procedures

The arbitrator is entitled to adopt whatever procedure he thinks fit, provided that it does not conflict with the express or implied terms of the arbitration agreement. It may be said that there is a further constraint on the arbitrator's freedom of choice, namely that he must not infringe the rules of public policy. It is, however, questionable whether English law recognises any rules of procedure which can be characterised as public policy. There are, it is true, certain procedural requirements which are usually regarded as fundamental, such as the principle that the arbitrator should not hear one party in the absence of the other, but even these will yield to express consent, or waiver.

In many cases the procedure to be followed is expressly agreed by the parties in advance. Usually this happens in one of three ways. In the first, the parties agree the substantive terms which apply to their own individual transaction, and for the rest they merely state that the provisions of a standard form of contract are to apply. In many trades, these stipulate that disputes shall be settled in accordance with the rules for arbitration of the trade in question, such rules specifying with a greater or less particularity how the reference is to be conducted. In other cases, the contract will call for the arbitration to take place under the auspices of a named arbitration institution, which has its own procedural rules. Alternatively, the contract may not refer to a trade association or to an institution, but simply provide that the arbitrator shall apply a particular published body of rules.

In situations such as these the general shape of the arbitration is predetermined by the rules, and the arbitrator merely has to exercise his procedural discretion within the framework which they supply. There are, however, many cases where the contract makes no reference to institutions or forms, but simply provides that disputes shall be resolved in (say) London, or that there shall be arbitration according to English law. It might be thought that in such a case the arbitrator is free to exercise a complete discretion as to the manner in which the arbitration is conducted, subject to any procedural directions which the parties may see fit to agree once the arbitration has been commenced. In the great majority of cases this is indeed what happens. The parties and the arbitrators know well enough what to expect of each other, and the arbitrator proceeds to give detailed instructions for the conduct of the dispute without any question being raised about whether some quite different format would be appropriate. In theory, however, the position is different. Although of course it is for the arbitrator to decide upon individual aspects of the proceedings if the parties cannot agree, for example, to what extent they shall be required to give discovery of documents, or how long each party shall be allowed for furnishing its statement of case, nevertheless he is bound to adopt whatever type of procedure the parties have agreed: for his mandate derives from the agreement of the parties to submit their dispute to arbitration, coupled with their appointment of him to act accordingly, and his agreement so to act. If there is an express agreement on procedure there is no problem, but if there is not the arbitrator is bound to follow the implied agreement of the parties. Implication could never, of course, yield detailed rules. Nevertheless, it is possible to say that, for example, an arbitrator charged with a simple dispute about the conformity of delivered goods with the sample according to which they were sold would not be acting in accordance with his mandate if he were to set in motion an elaborate formal procedure, involving discovery of documents, evidence from expert witnesses, cross-examination by lawyers and so on; any more than an arbitrator seized of a large and complex dispute turning on issues of technical expertise and disputed fact would be fulfilling his mandate if he chose to deal with the entire dispute on documents without oral evidence or argument.

These are extreme examples, and where procedures are not laid down by agreement it is always easier to say what is obviously wrong than to prescribe the limits of what is right. The implied terms of the arbitrator's mandate must be arrived at by taking into account the nature of the contract, its express terms, the whole of the commercial background, including any common practices in the trade as regards the resolution of disputes, the choice of tribunal[3] and in some instances, if the parties have already taken the first steps before the arbitrator is appointed, the way in which they have begun to conduct the reference. Since these and other relevant factors vary widely from case to case, there is an equally wide variety in the procedures which the courts have treated as acceptable. At the one extreme can be found a procedure which is virtually indistinguishable from that which would be followed in a High Court action. At the other is a procedure involving a degree of abbreviation and informality wholly repugnant to all the principles on which an English trial is conducted. Between these extremes there are all manner of different procedures, each of which may, in appropriate circumstances, be regarded by the courts as acceptable.

Given this wide variety of different procedures, it would be pointless to look for clear-cut and detailed procedural norms. In the first edition of this work we suggested that two general propositions could be advanced with reasonable confidence: namely that (i) in the absence of express or implied terms to the contrary the arbitrator should adopt a procedure which is adversarial in nature, and (ii) that this procedure should be on broadly the same lines as those followed in a High Court action.

Each of these presumptions—and we emphasise that this is all they are, since they yield to a contrary express or implied term—has been questioned, and we have taken the opportunity to reconsider them. To the first we adhere: partly because it has the high authority of the House of Lords behind it, and partly because it conforms to what we believe to be the practice, so long as the word 'adversarial' is properly understood. Like all labels, it lacks precision, but it usefully points the contrast with an 'inquisitorial' system. The essence of the latter is that the tribunal takes the initiative, in an endeavour to find the truth. Under the adversarial procedure, the arbitrator plays a less active role. Naturally, he wishes to ascertain the truth, but instead of searching for it, he allows it to evolve from a kind of dialectic between the parties, the assumption being that if it is left to the parties to present the alternative versions of the true position, they will between them furnish the arbitrator with sufficient material upon which to base an informed decision.

Bearing this distinction in mind, it may be said that the adversarial system as practised in England has three main characteristics.

---

[3] Thus, if the parties have appointed a prominent lawyer to act as sole arbitrator it is unlikely that they will be expecting a procedure characterised by extreme informality.

The first is that the procedural initiative lies mainly with the parties. If one of the parties desires that a step should be taken to move the arbitration forward, then he takes it himself; if he wishes his opponent to do something, he applies to the arbitrator for an order to that effect. Unless invited to decree what is to happen next, the arbitrator need not do anything at all. The responsibility for maintaining the momentum of the reference rests with the parties. The position is the same at the hearing. Each party decides what evidence to call; he examines his witnesses to adduce this evidence, and tenders them for cross-examination by his opponent. The arbitrator does not and cannot call witnesses himself; he may ask them questions, but the eliciting of the evidence is primarily a matter for the parties.

This is not to suggest that the role of the arbitrator is merely supine. On the contrary, a good arbitrator will stamp his personality on the proceedings in such a way as to ensure that the proceedings are conducted with the minimum of effort, delay and expense. Nevertheless it remains broadly true that his task is to make a choice between alternatives presented to him, rather than to strike out on a course of his own.

The second characteristic of the adversarial system is that in principle the whole of the evidence and argument are presented at a single hearing[4]. There may be preliminary hearings, at which the arbitrator is called upon to give rulings as to the future conduct of the reference, but these are purely procedural, and are not the occasion for evidence or argument. Equally, the parties do not adduce their evidence in advance of the hearing. It is true that, more often than formerly, they reduce the essence of their evidence to writing, and communicate it to the arbitrator as well as to their opponents. In one sense therefore the arbitrator may well have a substantial file of documents by the time the oral proceedings begin. Nevertheless, this does not have the characteristic of a *dossier*, built up by the contributions of the parties, and kept under continuous review by the arbitrator. Nor will there be a series of individual hearings, during which the merits of the dispute are progressively investigated. Instead, the presumption is that the effective business of the arbitration will be done at a single hearing at the conclusion of which the arbitrator will reach his decision on the basis of what has then been laid before him, and nothing else.

Third, the adversarial system as practised in England is predominantly oral in character[5]. Most evidence is given by witnesses who attend in person, although in certain circumstances it is permissible to use written statements in substitution. Although a practice is undoubtedly developing whereby the arbitrator makes himself familiar with the documents in advance of the oral hearing, this is by no means invariably the practice, and in virtually all instances where the dispute is of any complexity the arguments are presented orally, and are often the subject of considerable discussion with the arbitrator.

Our second proposition was that in the absence of contrary provision, the procedure should be on broadly the same lines as in a High Court action. Whatever its merits when written, we doubt whether this can now be sustained

---

[4] Except of course in those cases where the issues are formally separated: as, for example, where the parties agree, or the arbitrator rules, that the issue of liability shall be tried before the arbitrator decides what damages will be awarded if the claimant has proved his case.

[5] Recent developments in the practice of the Commercial Court and commercial arbitrators have tended to increase the written element of the procedure: see p. 321, post. It remains nevertheless the case that the whole procedure is focussed towards an oral hearing.

as a general principle. It is true that in many arbitrations involving lawyers the proceedings do have many features in common with trials at law, but this is because the lawyers and very often the arbitrator are used to this way of conducting disputes and adopt them as a matter of habit. Thus it is common to find, for example, that there will be formal written pleadings, rather than full statements of case; that the arbitrator will order discovery of documents in the English mode; that the hearing will begin with an opening address by the claimant's lawyer; that the evidence will be entirely oral and will be tested by cross-examination; and so on. It is another matter altogether to hold that an arbitrator is obliged to make the reference imitate a civil action or risk having his award set aside for misconduct.

It is, we believe, still right to say that, when used in disputes for which it is suitable, the formal adversarial system provides a method of investigating factual and legal issues which in terms of thoroughness and structural impartiality could reasonably be claimed as second to none. But it has come to be felt in quarters by no means hostile to the general philosophy of the adversarial system, that in complex cases these advantages are bought at an excessive price in time and expense, particularly because every hour occupied at a hearing attended by lawyers, experts, witnesses, shorthand writers and employees of the parties may prove extremely costly. This has brought about a movement, in recent years, towards reducing the oral element in the proceedings. Without any intention to compromise the essentially adversarial character of the proceedings, changes in practice are being made in, for example, the exchange of documents, in advance of the hearing, of a nature which will give the parties and the arbitrator a more explicit idea of the parties' cases on fact, law and evidence than is conveyed by pleadings in the traditional form; the preparation of a 'core bundle' of the principal documents, which the tribunal can usually be expected to have read before the hearing; the use of witness statements as the basis of their evidence, with each witness tendered for cross-examination; and the use of written propositions as the foundation of, although not a substitute for, oral argument on fact and law. Furthermore, an increased awareness on the part of arbitrators of their discretion to abstain from ordering full discovery of documents can lead to notable reductions in the time and cost wasted in the disclosure and copying of useless documents.

These are all ways of making the adversarial system more efficient. If brought about by consent and carried through with discrimination, we see no reason why they should be regarded as infringing any essential principle of English arbitration law, consistently with the traditional tolerance displayed by the English courts towards departures from the strict procedural norm.

These innovations are all aimed at improving a system which, in its essence, takes the same shape as proceedings in a High Court action. There have, however, existed for many years methods of conducting an arbitration which bear no resemblance to such a procedure. There are no pleadings, discovery or other pre-trial exchanges; no oral evidence; often no hearing at all, as distinct from a meeting between the two arbitrators; and if they disagree, the most informal of debates before the umpire.

In some arbitrations, there is even less than this. If the dispute concerns, for example, the quality of goods, the arbitrators (or, if they disagree, the umpire) meet to inspect the goods, and reach a conclusion upon them. There is no argument, and no hearing. In truth, there is nothing adversarial about the proceedings at all.

Between these extreme forms of procedure, there is room for numerous other methods, all of which are acceptable, if they are not in conflict with the express or implied terms of the agreement to arbitrate. It is therefore impossible to furnish a party, unfamiliar with English arbitration, with a guide to the procedure which he will have to follow. For reliable information he must consult his lawyer, or else ask the arbitrator to tell him precisely what the procedure will be.

2 Conciliation: duty to apply the law

English law does not recognise conciliation as a formal institution, in the context of private arbitration, and in practice it is rarely encountered.

Nor is it usual to find that the arbitrator is empowered to act as amiable compositeur or to decide according to 'equity and good conscience'. It is indeed far from clear whether a reference conducted under an agreement containing such a provision is an arbitration at all, for the purpose of the acts and the principles established by the common law[6-10]. What is clear is that in the absence of such a provision the arbitrator is obliged to decide the dispute according to law. The fact that the dispute is being resolved by arbitration rather than an action gives the arbitrator considerable latitude in matters of procedure, but none at all as regards the substance of the dispute. He must apply the rules of law in the same manner as a judge, and must give effect to the contract according to its terms.

3 Foreign law

If the application of the rules governing the conflict of laws indicate that the contract is governed by a foreign law, it is that law which in principle the arbitrator is bound to apply. In practice, the occasions on which foreign law plays a part in the decision are rendered much less frequent by the rule of English procedure that foreign law is assumed to be the same as English law unless the contrary is alleged and proved. The terms and effect of the foreign law are regarded as matters of fact, so that the decision of the arbitrator upon them is not susceptible of appeal.

4 Procedural reinforcement by the Court

Since the rights, duties and powers of the arbitrator are regarded by English law as exclusively the creation of the arbitration agreement and of the mandate by which the parties authorise the arbitrator to conduct the reference and bind them by his award, his procedural powers are subject to the same constraints as apply to any other rights created by private contracts. In particular, the arbitration agreement cannot give the arbitrator any power to make orders which compel performance by third parties; and it cannot confer on him those coercive powers of a public nature which belong only to the court. This is a source of weakness, and the courts have been given by statute, and have

---

[6-10] For a discussion of this difficult topic, see pp. 74 et seq., post.

developed of their own accord, various ancilliary powers by which the conduct of the reference can be made more effective.

In the first place, there is a miscellaneous group of statutory powers, developed in an unsystematic way over the years, which is now to be found in section 12 of the Act. Thus, for example, the Court has power to order the giving of evidence and the production of documents by persons other than the parties to the reference, and can compel them to give evidence on oath before the arbitrator or, in exceptional circumstances, before the officer of the Court. As regards the parties themselves, the Court has power to make procedural orders which, in extreme cases, can lead to the exercise of the remedies for contempt of court, in order to ensure compliance. In particular, the Court can order (a) the discovery of documents to be verified by affidavit; (b) interrogatories to be answered on oath; (c) the preservation or sale of the subject-matter of the reference, and the preservation of any fund in issue in the arbitration; (d) the appointment of a receiver; (e) the grant of an injunction.

In addition, the Court has recently developed an important jurisdiction, whereby claimants can obtain security for their demands by detaining assets of the opposing party. This remedy, known as the 'Mareva' injunction, is similar to procedures such as *saisie conservatoire*, which are features of many legal systems. The purpose of the remedy is to prevent the defendant from taking his assets abroad before the claimant can obtain an award and proceed to enforce it. The defendant's assets are not brought into the custody of the plaintiff or of the court, but are simply made the subject of an injunction to restrain their removal abroad. The order may be directed at assets in any form, and is commonly employed to block movements of credit balances on bank accounts. It is obtained by private application to the High Court, usually without prior notice to the parties affected, who have the right to make a subsequent application to the Court to have the order discharged.

5 Procedural control by the Court

The Court has power to intervene both before and after the award is published, if the reference is not conducted fairly, and in accordance with the express and implied terms of the arbitration agreement. There is, however, a profound difference both as to the nature of the remedies available, and as to the freedom with which they are employed, according to whether the assistance of the Court is invoked before or after the conclusion of the reference.

(a) Intervention during the reference

The Court has no general power to intervene in a pending reference. Instead, there is a miscellaneous collection of specific remedies which may be divided into those which enable the Court to change the condition of the reference by means of active intervention, and those by which the Court merely issues a declaration as to the current state of the agreement to arbitrate[11]. The first group is entirely the creation of statute. The second results from an application of orthodox contractual principles to the relationship constituted by the arbitration agreement.

---

[11] This is an over-simplification. A full list of the remedies is set out in Chapter 32, p. 497, post.

The statutory remedies, created by legislation over a period of many years, are unsystematic and overlapping. They aim primarily at the arbitration agreement and the arbitrator. The most extreme power is that which enables the court to order that the arbitration agreement shall cease to have effect, thus leaving the claimant to pursue his claim by litigation, if at all. Less drastic are those powers which, whilst allowing the arbitration agreement to remain in force, revoke the authority of the particular arbitrator, or remove him from office, or replace him by someone else. The difference between these various remedies is not of major practical importance. Where the tribunal consists of more than one arbitrator, the power may be exercised in relation to an individual arbitrator, or to some of the arbitrators, or to the whole tribunal. Any resulting vacancy will be filled by a fresh nomination, either by the parties themselves or by the court, depending on the circumstances.

These remedies are very sparingly employed. In principle, the remedies are open to objection because they cut across the right of the parties, jealously protected by the English Court, to have the dispute decided by a tribunal of their choice according to a procedure of their choice. The remedies bear harshly on both parties, since they almost inevitably entail that the parties will have to start the dispute again from the beginning. Moreover, it is difficult to be sure, whilst the arbitration is still in progress, that matters are going so badly wrong that real injustice will in the end be found to have been caused. The Court is therefore strongly inclined to abstain from intervention, to let the reference run its course, and then to consider after the award has been published whether it is really necessary to take action.

The remedies in the second group are of a quite different character. They depend on the analysis of the relationships in an arbitration in terms of express or implied contract. As previously stated, it has long been recognised that the arbitration agreement possesses an existence independent from that of the substantive contract in which it is usually embodied. This concept has recently been developed to the extent of holding that the arbitration agreement is capable of premature termination, before the completion of the reference, in consequence of events such as would bring to an end the more ordinary type of contract: for example, repudiatory breach, frustation, or discharge by consent. The implications of this doctrine have been examined in some detail by the courts in situations where there has been such delay in the conduct of the reference that a fair decision is no longer possible. The result has not been satisfactory, and it is probable that legislation will be needed to deal with this particular problem. Whether the doctrine will find a use in other spheres has yet to be decided. When the court applies the contractual analysis, it does not itself act to bring the reference to an end (as it does when exercising its statutory powers), but merely delivers a declaratory judgment to the effect that the reference has already come to an end, together with the contract to arbitrate upon which it was founded. Any further relief, in the shape of an injunction to restrain the claimant and the arbitrator from taking further steps in the reference, is purely ancilliary in nature, and is designed to preserve the status quo.

(b) Intervention after the award

Once the award has been made, the remedies just discussed have no function, for the arbitration agreement has been fully performed, and the arbitrator is functus officio. Any remedies must therefore be aimed at the award itself. Two remedies are available.

First, the Court may set the award aside, under powers conferred by section 23(2) of the Act. The effect is that the parties cease to be bound by the award, and the issues in dispute are entirely reopened. Rather surprisingly, the courts have never had occasion to analyse fully the further consequences of such an order, but if called upon to do so would probably decide that the whole of the proceedings in the reference are annulled, leaving a dispute which is still arbitrable, but before a new tribunal in fresh proceedings, unless it is possible to separate the valid from the invalid portion of the award.

The second, and much less far-reaching remedy, is that of remission, under section 22(1) of the Act. Here, there is no question of the arbitrator being disseized of jurisdiction, or of the proceedings in the arbitration being nugatory; nor does it follow that the award is rendered totally and finally invalid. What happens is that the dispute is sent back to the arbitrator for reconsideration, in the light of the judgment delivered by the court. If remission is ordered because there has been a procedural error, the order has the effect of reinvesting the arbitrator with the jurisdiction which he lost when he became functus officio upon the publication of the award. He is thereupon obliged to resume the reference; to conduct once again that part of it which was the subject of criticism; and then to make a new or supplementary award in the light of what has taken place. If the complaint relates to the award itself (e.g. if it is incomplete) the arbitrator reconsiders the matter and acts appropriately, without necessarily convening a further hearing. Whilst an order for remission is in force, the original award becomes ineffective, until it is confirmed, varied or replaced when the arbitrator has reconsidered the matter in accordance with the directions of the Court.

Originally, setting aside was the primary remedy for procedural default, and remission was reserved for cases where the defect was comparatively trivial. This is no longer so. The courts will save the arbitration if at all possible, and will not make an order which involves the entire proceedings being recommenced, unless satisfied that the hearing cannot safely be left in the hands of the original arbitrator. In those cases where the Court does feel it necessary to intervene, the result is almost always an order for remission rather than setting aside.

It is impossible to set out a complete list of the circumstances in which one or other of the two remedies will be employed. Indeed, it would be useless to try, for although there still exist certain technical constraints on the exercise of the jurisdiction, in practice the Court is moving towards a position where it would be free to intervene in any case where it is shown that the proceedings have been conducted in a manner which is unfair, or which gives the appearance of being unfair, or which does not comply with the express or implied terms of the agreement to arbitrate. These situations are all grouped together under the general description of 'misconduct'. The use of this word is sometimes believed to have connotations of personal impropriety on the part of the tribunal. This is a misapprehension: the word simply means that the reference has not been conducted in the appropriate manner. This may be due to discreditable behaviour on the part of the arbitrator, but it is much more likely to be the result of an honest mistake, from whose consequences the parties ought in fairness to be relieved.

In addition, there are two specific instances which do not fit readily into this general formulation. First, the Court has in recent years asserted a jurisdiction to order remission even in cases where the arbitrator has done nothing wrong, but where a misunderstanding between one party and the arbitrator, or between the two parties themselves has brought about a situation where one party has been unable to present his case to the best advantage.

Second, there are occasions when the complaint upon which the order for remission if founded relates not to the conduct of the reference, but to the award itself: in particular, where the award fails to comply with the substantive requirements summarised at p. 25, post. The most common cause of remission under this heading is that the award fails to deal with all the matters referred to arbitration and where the award is sent back so that the omission can be repaired. It is essential to note that the power to intervene is concerned only with procedural defects in the award. Errors of substance in the decision embodied in the award cannot be corrected by these means: indeed in most cases they cannot be corrected at all. Thus, the courts have repeatedly held that it is not misconduct for the arbitrator to reach a wrong conclusion on an issue of fact, either because he has not properly understood the evidence or the arguments addressed to him, or through carelessness, or lack of ability, or for any other reason. By submitting their disputes to arbitration the parties consent to run the risk that the chosen tribunal will prove unequal to its task. The position is the same as regards errors of law. Whatever the position may have been in the past, it is now quite clear that it is not misconduct to make an error of law, and that the court will not order remission or setting aside, even where it is quite obvious from the terms of the award that the arbitrator has made a mistake. If the losing party has any remedy, it must take the shape of an appeal (see pp. 26–28, post) and this will be available only if it has not been validly excluded by consent.

Of the two groups of remedies by which the Court supervises the procedures in the arbitration, viz. those available during the reference and those which are directed to a published award, those in the second group are much more readily employed. It must, however, be repeated that even these are very sparingly exercised in practice, however wide the jurisdiction may be in theory. The Court will not act unless the matter complained of has created a real risk of injustice; and the injustice is measured, not against some ideal procedural norm, but against the justice which the parties have contracted to accept. Since, as we have seen, agreements to arbitrate are construed as tolerating a high degree of procedural informality and unorthodoxy, the prospect of establishing that there has been a sufficient deviation to justify an intervention by the Court is comparatively small. Furthermore, the attitude of the Court is not such as to encourage their use. For at least 60 years judges have emphasised that traders who have chosen arbitration must reconcile themselves to the consequences of their choice and that it is no use for them to complain after the event that the dispute might have been more thoroughly or skilfully investigated by some procedures closer to those adopted in court. All this being so, it is not surprising that applications to set aside or remit awards are very rare, and that successful applications are rarer still.

G. THE AWARD

1 Types of award

At the conclusion of the reference the arbitrator makes his award. He must begin by taking two decisions as to the form of the award[12].

First, he must consider whether the award should be interim or final. Most awards are final, in that they contain decisions on all the issues submitted to arbitration. There are, however, cases where the dispute raises a series of entirely distinct issues, a decision on one or some of which will dispose of the entire controversy. Thus, for example, an arbitration may raise the question whether the respondent is liable in damages and, if so, what the amount of damage should be. It may be sensible to deal with the issue of liability first, leaving over the question of damages; for unless the claim succeeds on liability, a trial of the remaining issues will be a waste of time and money. Where the issues are divided in this way, the arbitrator is entitled to make an interim award.

The second decision which the arbitrator must make is whether to give reasons for his award. Until quite recently, it was a distinctive, and much criticised, feature of English arbitration practice that arbitrators had either published awards which contained a bare statement of the decision without any account of how it was arrived at, or had given reasons in a separate document expressly declared not to form part of the award. The law on this topic has been somewhat altered by the 1979 Act, and the position may now be summarised as follows: (i) the arbitrator still has no obligation to state the reasons for his findings of fact; (ii) if notified before the making of the award that one party intends to appeal on a question of law, he must state in his award sufficient reasons for his decision to enable the Court to determine the question, if it gives leave to appeal; (iii) for this purpose, the 'reasons' are the findings of fact upon which the arguments of law will be based, not the grounds upon which the arbitrator has arrived at the findings of fact; (iv) the reasons can properly take the shape of an informal narrative, without being set out in any prescribed form; (v) even in cases where he is not obliged to do so, the arbitrator is free to give reasons for his decision, whether of law or fact, if he desires to do so[13].

It is perhaps questionable whether the new legislation has greatly altered the law as to the giving of reasons, but it has undoubtedly created a new psychological atmosphere. Reasoned awards are now much more common than before.

2 The decision

The next step is for the arbitrator to arrive at a decision on the issues in the arbitration. This must be his own decision; he cannot delegate any part of it. He is, however, entitled to consult a third party for an expert opinion on any individual issue, so long as he exercises his own judgment in accepting or rejecting the opinion which he receives. In addition, an arbitrator may retain a

---

[12] Unless the arbitration agreement makes express provision for the time within which the award must be made, which is unusual, the award may be made at any time; except where the award is remitted under s. 22 of the 1950 Act, or s. 1(2) of the 1979 Act, in which event it must be made within three months from the order for remission.

[13] In order to avoid the possibility of an appeal when neither party has requested reasons for this purpose, it is usual for the arbitrator to stipulate that the reasons shall not be shown to the court.

lawyer to help him draw up the award, and to advise him on legal issues; but once again, the decision must be his own, and not that of the lawyer.

Where the tribunal consists of more than one person, all the arbitrators must take part in the reference, and in arriving at the decision. If they are not unanimous, the decision of the majority will stand as the award of them all.

3 Form and substance

English law prescribes no formal requirements for an award. Even an award communicated by word of mouth is binding on the parties. Such awards are not altogether uncommon where an urgent decision is required, but it is the invariable practice for the arbitrator to confirm an oral award in writing.

The award must, however, satisfy a number of substantive requirements. It must contain an adjudication, not merely an expression of expectation, hope or opinion. Unless it is intended to be an interim award, it must be complete, in that it contains an adjudication on all the matters in dispute. It must be certain, so that it is possible to ascertain from the award precisely what the decision is that the arbitrator has reached in relation to the matters in dispute. It must also be final, in the sense that it should not leave any of the issues to be decided by a third party, or (unless it is an interim award) by the arbitrator himself.

4 Interest and costs

The arbitrator has power to make an order for the payment of interest up to the date of his award, on the principal sum awarded. This power is usually exercised so as to make interest run from the date when the principal sum fell due. The rate of interest is in the discretion of the arbitrator, and is usually fixed at a level somewhat above the inter-bank borrowing rate or rates prevailing during the period of indebtedness. The arbitrator has, however, no jurisdiction to make any order as to the payment of interest after the moment when his award is published. Such interest is governed by section 20 of the Act, which provides that interest on the sum awarded shall be charged at the same rate as on a judgment debt. This rate is fixed from time to time by statutory instrument to reflect, in a very broad way, changes in the current cost of borrowing money.

We have already referred to the power of the arbitrator to direct who shall be responsible for paying his fees and expenses. He also has the important function of making an order as to the costs of the reference: that is, the expenditures made by the parties for the purpose of conducting the arbitration. These include the fees of lawyers, the expenses of witnesses, the parties' own disbursements in travelling, copying documents, and so on. If the award makes no provision for the costs of the reference, either party may apply to the arbitrator for an amendment to the award, so as to direct by and to whom the costs shall be paid.

The arbitrator is obliged to exercise his discretion on costs according to the same principles as are applied in the High Court[14]. The primary rule is that the

---

[14] The parties cannot validly agree, *before* the dispute has arisen, that whatever the outcome of the arbitration the parties shall bear their own costs, but an agreement to this effect is permissible *after* the dispute has arisen.

loser should be ordered to pay the costs of the successful party. This rule is, however, subject to various exceptions[15].

The arbitrator has a discretion not only to decide who shall pay the costs, but also to fix their amount. This is, however, not usually done except in simple cases. The usual practice is for the arbitrator to order that the costs shall be 'taxed if not agreed'. With the help of their lawyers, the parties are usually able to reach agreement on an appropriate figure for costs, but if they cannot do so they take steps to have the costs taxed (i.e. formally investigated and fixed) by a judicial officer of the High Court. Taxation is not intended[16] to give the successful party a full indemnity in respect of his outgoings.

5 The effect of an award

A valid award confers on the successful claimant a new right of action, in substitution for the right on which his claim was founded. Every submission to arbitration contains an implied promise by each party to abide by the award of the arbitrator, and to perform his award. It is on this promise that the claimant proceeds, when he takes action to enforce the award.

In addition to this positive effect of conferring a new right on the successful claimant, a valid award has two negative consequences.

First, the successful claimant is precluded by the award from bringing the same claim again in a fresh arbitration or action. In particular, the rule requires that damages resulting from one and the same cause of action, including anticipated future damages, must be assessed once and for all in one proceeding. If the claimant finds that he has suffered more damage than he claimed in the arbitration, he will not usually be permitted to start a further arbitration to recover his further loss.

The publication of a valid award also makes a radical change in the position of the arbitrator. His powers to make procedural orders, and his authority to bind the parties by his decisions comes to an end: he is said to be *functus officio*. Nothing which he does thereafter can have any effect on the rights of the parties. In particular, he has no power to alter his award, except for the very limited purpose of correcting 'any clerical mistake or error arising from any accidental slip or omission'. This allows the arbitrator to correct clerical errors but not to alter the substance of what he has decided, if he has changed his mind after publishing the award.

H. APPEALS ON QUESTIONS OF LAW

For a period of about 60 years, a balance was struck in English arbitration law between the procedural and substantive aspects of judicial control. The great commercial judges who sat in the Court of Appeal during the 1920s stamped the law indelibly with the concept that parties who contract for arbitration can expect neither more nor less than the procedures for which they have contracted, and that where the arbitration agreement was made in the context of a trade where informal procedures were customary, it was these procedures, rather than

---

[15] See Chapter 26, pp. 394–403, post.
[16] Except in the rare case where the arbitrator orders a full indemnity for costs.

those of a formal judicial contest, which the arbitrator was entitled and obliged to employ. At the same time, it was the same judges who also insisted that the arbitrator must apply the rules of substantive law when arriving at his decision, and who established the rule that the parties could not validly agree to exclude their right of recourse to the Court when the arbitrator had arrived at a conclusion which was not in accordance with the law. The reason essentially was this, that if there was no mechanism whereby his decision could be brought into conformity with the law, the arbitrator would feel himself free either to apply his own appreciation of what, in the general estimation of persons engaged in the trade, the law ought to be, or to depart entirely from any general view of the law, so as to give effect to his own ideas as to the justice of the individual case. This risk was considered to be unacceptable for two reasons. First, because there seemed no room for the co-existence of parallel laws of contract in matters of commerce, one applied by the courts, and the other by the individual trades. Second, because parties who had expressly or impliedly contracted to have their disputes decided according to English substantive law were entitled to be sure that this is how the arbitrator will proceed.

Through much of the modern history of English arbitration law there was preserved this balance between a highly permissive attitude on matters of procedure, and a strict insistence on orthodox norms as regards the legal substance of the dispute. The maintenance of judicial control over the legal content of the award was achieved by the procedure of the special case. Essentially, this was a form of appeal, whereby the Court was invited to supply the answer to a question or questions of law set out in the award, on the basis of facts found by the arbitrator. For all practical purposes, the losing party had an absolute right of appeal in all cases where a genuine question of law was involved. The importance of the procedure lay not so much in its use, which was infrequent[17], but in the fact that it was known to be available. For more than a century the procedure appeared to serve well enough, and indeed received statutory reinforcement as recently as 1934. More recently, however, it came under criticism in several quarters, and eventually the 1979 Act saw the establishment of a new system of appeals[18], which went some but not all of the way towards meeting the demands of those who believed that the parties should be free to withdraw their disputes entirely from judicial control on questions of law, whilst still retaining the right to invoke the powers of the Court to enforce the arbitration agreement, and to promote the efficient conduct of the reference[19].

The new system has three main features. First, it enables the parties in certain circumstances to exclude by agreement the right of appeal on a question of law. An 'exclusion agreement' entered into after the commencement of the arbitration is effective in every case, irrespective of the nature of the substantive contract. But an exclusion agreement made before the commencement of the arbitration

---

[17] Until the burst of activity brought about by the United States soya bean meal disputes of 1973, the number of arbitrations taken to the High Court on special case averaged about a dozen, out of a total of thousands of arbitrations each year.

[18] The special case procedure is now virtually obsolete.

[19] A brief account of the history of the 1979 Act is contained in Chapter 29, p. 431, post.

is not effective in the case of a domestic arbitration agreement. Nor does it exclude the right of appeal where the substantive contract falls into one of the special categories established by the 1979 Act. Briefly, these consist of maritime, insurance and commodity contracts. Subject to these exceptions, a prior exclusion agreement is valid.

The second feature of the new system is that the losing party is no longer entitled to appeal as of right. Instead, he must obtain the leave of the Court. The application is made at an oral hearing, at which the parties present their arguments briefly, but in sufficient depth to enable the judge to form an impression as to whether the appeal would be likely to succeed, if leave were granted. A much stronger case for saying that the award was wrong will be required where the issues of law are limited to the circumstances of the particular dispute, than where they are of general practical or theoretical importance.

A further restriction on the right of appeal created by the 1979 Act is that no appeal lies from the decision of the High Court judge to the Court of Appeal unless the judge or the Court of Appeal gives leave, and it is certified by the judge that the question of law is one of general public importance or for some other reason ought to be considered by the Court of Appeal.

A third feature of the new system concerns the form in which the appeal is brought to the High Court. Instead of the special case, with its question of law and the rather frigid statement by the arbitrator of his findings of fact, there is the reasoned award, which the court may, upon the hearing of the appeal decide to uphold, vary, set aside or remit to the reconsideration of the arbitrator. The reasons which the arbitrator is to furnish still consist of his findings of fact. But the courts have emphasised that the arbitrator need not feel inhibited by the formality which used to be associated with the special case. The arbitrator can make his own assessment of the facts which the Court will need, and set out his findings in his own words, without the need for cumbersome submissions by the parties as to what should go into the award, and without the feeling that legal assistance is needed in the drafting of the award.

The purpose of the 1979 Act was to create a new system, not to lay down how it should be operated. It has, however, become plain that the courts feel, and give effect to, a marked reluctance to differ from the opinions of arbitrators on those matters which lie within their own particular fields of practical skill and experience. Moreover, on questions which involve a judicial assessment of the facts of the individual case in the context of established principles (for example, on a question whether a particular interval was a reasonable time), the Court will not interfere, if no error of law by the arbitrator is demonstrable, merely because the judge would himself have arrived at a different conclusion from the arbitrator. The appeal will be allowed only where the judge is satisfied that the conclusion is one at which no reasonable arbitrator, properly directing himself on the legal principles, could have arrived. The 1979 Act has not only meant that there are fewer appeals than previously, but also that there are markedly fewer successful appeals. It is now possible to say that the 1979 legislation marked the occasion of a profound psychological change in the relationship between the courts and the arbitral process.

I. ENFORCEMENT

An award does not immediately entitle the successful party to levy execution against the assets of the unsuccessful party. It is necessary first to convert the award into a judgment or order of the Court.

Where the award is made in England, there are two different methods of enforcement. The first is to bring an action in the High Court, founded on the promise implied in every arbitration agreement, to honour the award of the arbitrator. This action proceeds in the same way as any other action. The plaintiff must allege and prove the existence of a valid arbitration agreement; that the dispute was within the terms of the agreement; that the arbitrator was duly appointed; and that the award sued upon was the award of the arbitrator. The Court will not enter into the merits of the award. A judgment in this action can then be enforced against the assets of the defendant. It is a good defence to such an action that the award is void for failure to comply with some formal or substantive requirement of a valid award, or that it has already been set aside or remitted, or that it was made in excess of jurisdiction. It is, however, important to note that it is not a ground of defence to allege that the proceedings were vitiated by procedural misconduct, for such a defect renders the award voidable, not void. The right course is for the losing party to take the initiative by applying promptly for an order for remission or setting aside, and to invite the Court to stay the action on the award whilst the complaint is investigated.

The other method of enforcement takes the shape of an order for summary relief under section 26 of the Act. In a case where the right to enforcement appears unquestionable, the successful party applies to the court by means of an affidavit verifying the arbitration agreement and the making of the award, and also the failure to comply with it. The Court then has power to order the direct enforcement of the award against the defendant's assets. In addition, the Court has power to enter a formal judgment in favour of the plaintiff.

The summary procedure under section 26 has advantages over an action in terms of speed and cost; but it is not suitable for cases where it is known that there is or may be an objection to the award which cannot properly be disposed of without a trial, or if it is known that proceedings to set aside the award are in hand.

Where the arbitration has been conducted abroad, the award may be enforced by action or by summary proceedings under section 26, in the same manner as an English award. It is, however, more usual for such awards to be enforced under those provisions of the Acts of 1950 and 1975 which give effect, respectively, to the 1927 Geneva Convention on the Execution of Foreign Arbitral Awards and the 1958 New York Convention on the Recognition of Foreign Arbitral Awards.

CHAPTER 2

What is an arbitration?

A. WHY DOES IT MATTER?

1 Relationship of arbitration to other types of process

It could reasonably be expected that a treatise on the law of arbitration would begin with a definition of the subject matter of the work. Such a definition would have a theoretical value, because it would provide a starting point from which it might be possible to develop detailed propositions as to the principles governing the conduct and regulation of the arbitral process. It would also be useful in practice, because it would enable the reader to decide, in relation to a particular process of decision, contracted for or in the course of being conducted, whether the process was subject to the very special relationship with the ordinary courts of law which is peculiar to private arbitrations in England.

In every developed state there exists a variety of persons, groups and institutions who possess, either continuously or for the purposes of a specific occasion, the authority to make decisions affecting the rights of private persons. In every such society there exists a body of law which prescribes how such persons, groups and bodies (who may conveniently be called tribunals, although in many instances the word is a misnomer) should exercise their decision-making functions, and how these functions may be supervised and controlled from outside. In some legal systems, the power to control such tribunals is entrusted to courts or other institutions specially created for the purpose. In England, however, there are no superior administrative courts of general jurisdiction, and it is the ordinary courts of law which possess this power: sometimes in consequence of a specific statutory mandate, but very often because they have, over the centuries, simply assumed for themselves the right and duty to ensure that inferior tribunals operates only within their proper spheres of competence, and in accordance with broad principles of justice.

Inevitably, in a complex modern state there is an immense variety of tribunals, differing fundamentally as regards their composition, their functions, and the sources from which their powers are derived. English law has not yet achieved a formal code of administrative law which can be applied directly to a tribunal of whatever nature and which defines precisely the powers of the supervisory courts. There is no single set of rules, applicable to all tribunals, concerning matters such as the susceptibility of the tribunal's decisions on questions of law or fact to review by the supervising court; the nature of the factual and evidentiary materials upon which such a review is based; the manner in which the jurisdiction of the tribunal is ascertained and steps are taken to see that the tribunal remains within it; the extent to which the tribunal is required to comply with those procedural norms which are usually regarded as characteristic of the judicial process, and the way in which impermissible departures from those norms can be corrected; and the nature of the remedies which are available if the supervising court decides to intervene. This lack of formal rigour is not wholly a disadvantage. It gives the law an adaptability which is absent from more structured systems, and in particular enables the English judge to deploy an armoury of remedies more extensive than that which is available to his counterpart abroad. Nevertheless, it does mean that where there is a complaint that a particular tribunal has stepped outside its proper functions, or has exercised them unfairly, or has arrived at an unfair or unjust result, it is particularly important to identify the tribunal accurately, so that if the relationship between the courts and tribunals of that type has already been defined by judicial decision, the right body of law can be chosen and applied.

This is especially important where the process is said to be an arbitration, for an arbitral tribunal is in a unique category as regards its relationship with the courts. Approaching the matter a priori, one might say that arbitration lies somewhere on a line embodying the following points –

1 Tribunals established by or under the auspices of the state[1], to whose jurisdiction the individual is subject by compulsion not consent, having the power to affect the public legal rights of the individual, and arriving at its decisions by a process which may loosely be called judicial. (For example, the inspector and subsequently the Secretary of State when determining planning appeals.)

2 Tribunals established by or under the auspices of the state, not being courts of law, but intended to act judicially, whose jurisdiction does not derive from consent, and whose decisions have the power to affect the private legal rights of individuals. (For example, certain forms of employment and workmen's compensation tribunals.)

3 Tribunals whose origin lies in consent, but whose jurisdiction in the particular case is compulsory, such tribunals having the power to determine in a judicial manner the public rights of the individual. (For example, the disciplinary tribunals of professional and trade associations.)

4 Tribunals whose jurisdiction derives from consent, having the power to affect the economic but not the legal rights of the individual. (For example, standing or ad hoc pay arbitration tribunals.)

5 Tribunals whose jurisdiction derives from consent, having the power to affect the social or religious, but not the legal, rights of the individual. (For example, disciplinary bodies of a club or a church.)

6 Tribunals, whose jurisdiction may or may not derive from consent, having no power directly to affect the public or private rights of the individual, but to perform functions which may result in such rights being affected. (For example, commissions of enquiry.)

7 Persons (not properly called tribunals) entrusted by consent with the power to affect the legal rights of two parties inter se, in a manner creating legally enforceable rights, but intended to do so by a procedure of a ministerial, and not judicial, nature. (For example, persons appointed by contract to value property, or to certify the compliance of building works with a specification.)

---

[1] Or two or more states, as in the case of the Iranian claims tribunal, which seems to lie somewhere between points 1 and 2: *Dallal v Bank Mellat* [1986] QB 441, [1986] 2 WLR 745.

8 Tribunals with a consensual jurisdiction whose decisions are intended to affect the private rights of two parties inter se, but not in a manner which creates legally enforceable remedies. (For example, the arbitration or conciliatory tribunals of local religious communities, or persons privately appointed to act as mediators between two disputing persons or groups.)

By composing a line of these and similar points, and then placing the private arbitral process somewhere along its length, it should be possible to decide on the general nature of the relationship between the process and the courts. For example, if arbitration were placed somewhere in the area of points 1 to 5, the supervision and control of the tribunal could be effected by the processes now grouped under the title of 'judicial review'. Defects such as an excess of jurisdiction, failure to act fairly, manifest error of law, omission to take account of relevant factual or evidential materials and so on, could all be dealt with by existing remedies of certiorari, mandamus, and prohibition, coupled if necessary with declaratory or injunctive relief.

Alternatively, arbitration could be assimilated to the processes of valuation and certification. On this basis, the controlling court would act through the medium of the law of contract, applying orthodox remedies to infractions of the agreement to value in accordance with the contract and to honour a valuation so made. The full apparatus of judicial review would not be required, and the court would need to intervene under its inherent jurisdiction only in cases of manifest bias or bad faith. Finally, the court could place arbitration in category 8, and treat the review of the arbitral process as lying entirely outside the competence of the courts.

2 Separate historical origins of arbitration

In the event, the English law of arbitration never set off in any of these directions. There are historical reasons for this.

In the first place, there was the influence continually imposed on voluntary arbitration by the existence of the parallel system of arbitration pursuant to an order of the court. In this procedure, the reference to arbitration sprang from an action in court, and always remained part of it, albeit conducted before a tribunal chosen by the parties, and pursuant to a procedure which was in some degree chosen by the parties. The court therefore retained throughout the reference those inherent powers of control and sanction which it possessed in relation to its own proceedings. The procedural advantages which this entailed, by comparison with the fallibility of voluntary agreements to arbitrate, vulnerable as they were to a party who broke his agreement by refusing to arbitrate at all, or to co-operate in a reference once commenced, encouraged the progressive statutory development of a right to have a voluntary arbitration treated as if it originated in a rule of court[2]. Ultimately, the development of other statutory aids to the practical efficacy of voluntary arbitration has made obsolete this assimilation of voluntary arbitration into the parallel system of court-based arbitration, and proceedings in arbitration can no longer be treated as if they were aspects of proceedings in court[3]. Nevertheless, the long period

---

[2] Only as regards questions of procedure. For the residual jurisdiction of the courts over the substance of disputes submitted to arbitration, see p. 154, post.
[3] The link was formally broken by the repeal, by the 1950 Act, of s. 1 of the 1889 Act.

during which the court supervised arbitration proceedings as if they were its own has left its mark, not only on the methods and remedies by which the supervision is exercised, but also on the attitude of the court to the process of voluntary arbitration. The court has always felt itself to stand in a relation to arbitration much closer than exists in respect of other, apparently similar, processes for resolving questions or disputes. It is therefore not surprising to find that the courts have declined to apply the ordinary mechanisms of judicial review to references in voluntary arbitration, but have preferred to utilise and foster, with the aid of the legislature, a special code of procedure adapted to arbitration alone.

Second, it has been recognised for centuries that commercial men prefer to use arbitration rather than the courts to resolve their business disputes. It is true that the courts and text-writers have repeatedly expressed doubts as to the wisdom of this preference[4], but these have reflected a current opinion that arbitration was an inefficient procedure, not that it was undesirable in itself. It came to be seen that since, come what may, the commercial community would insist on the right to arbitrate, the system should be made to work as well as possible. This led to repeated statutory intervention to remedy what were currently seen as the weakest features of the process. The resulting patchwork of statutory reinforcement has no counterpart in other fields of extra-curial procedure. From it, we derive the irrevocability of the arbitrator's mandate without leave of the court; the various provisions which enable the court to complete or to re-constitute the tribunal if consensual methods have failed; and the powers of the court to exercise coercive measures, and measures aimed at third parties, which the parties themselves could not confer on the arbitrator by consent.

Third, the expansion of international and domestic commerce during the nineteenth century carried in its train an almost explosive development of English commercial law, and this in turn stimulated efforts to improve the practical worth of extra-judicial tribunals established to resolve commercial disputes. The great masters of the common law, who created and enriched English commercial jurisprudence between 1840 and 1880, used the concept of the contractual implied term as a principal instrument of innovation. It was therefore natural that since an arbitration clause could be regarded not merely as a mandate to the arbitrator to bind the parties by his award, but also as a contract between the parties to concur in referring the dispute to arbitration, the courts and the legislature should look for terms to imply into this special procedural agreement. The obvious place to begin the search was the practice of parties who drew up formal written submissions, and one therefore finds in the 1854 and 1889 Acts various provisions which were essentially consensual in origin. Some of these concerned the establishment of the tribunal and the conduct of the reference (e.g. those contained in the First Schedule to the 1889 Act). Others affected the relationship between the parties and the court, such as the powers of the court to remit an award, and of the arbitrator to permit an appeal on a question of law by stating a special case for the decision of the High court. This device of developing remedies from the contractual nature of a submission to arbitration has recently come into prominence again, with the

---

[4] For example at the beginning of the nineteenth century, in the 1920s, in the 1950s and in the 1970s.

assertion by the court of a jurisdiction to terminate arbitrations which are being carried forward with excessive delay. One of the foundations relied upon to support this new power is the notion that the arbitration clause is a severable contract, capable (like any other contract) of being brought to an end by repudiation, frustration or mutual agreement. Arbitration is unique in being subjected to this particular form of analysis. No attempt has been made, so far as we are aware, to work out in contractual terms a supervisory jurisdiction in respect of tribunals such as those identified at items 3 to 8 of the list set out above.

Finally, it may be noted that the modern law of arbitration, so far as it concerns the way in which the court exercises control over the arbitrator's conduct of the reference, was shaped during a period when the courts attached paramount importance to freedom of contract. The idea therefore became current that instead of expecting the proceedings in a reference to conform with requirements imposed from outside, and based more or less on the practices of litigation, the procedures should spring from the submission itself, so that the parties should be entitled to expect, and be bound to accept, a mode of conducting the arbitration which fell within the express or implied terms of the contract to arbitrate. Since this contract rarely contained express provisions as to the details of the procedure to be implied, much weight was put on implication; and the natural source of the implication was the practice currently followed in references of a similar type, or in a similar trade. These practices often bore little resemblance to an ordinary judicial process, and the result has been that the court has come to tolerate a remarkable variety of arbitral procedures, deviating from the ordinary procedural norms to a degree which might well prove unacceptable in relation to other kinds of tribunal. Allied to this contractual analysis of the arbitral process there has prevailed at least until very recently a marked tendency for the courts to say that since the parties have contracted for a process which is isolated from the courts[5], this is what they ought to get: so that the less the courts meddle in the process, the better. This permissive attitude is not a feature of the relationship between the courts and any other form of tribunal having power to issue a legally binding decision.

3 Distinctive features of arbitration

The result of all these various historical influences has been to place arbitration in a category completely on its own. In a curious way, it is at the same time dependent on, and independent of, the central judicial system. A decision on whether or not a particular way of resolving a dispute is, or at least is intended to be, an arbitration[6] will thus provide the answers to a number of fundamental procedural questions, amongst which the following are the most important –

(i) Can the supervising court intervene upon proof that the tribunal has made an error of fact, or has reached a conclusion of fact for which there is no evidence, or has misunderstood the effect of the evidence? In an arbitration, the answer is undoubtedly – 'No'[7].

---

[5] Although it has not in fact been isolated from them for at least a century, as we have already suggested.

[6] This must be coupled with the subordinate question whether, if the procedure is an arbitration, it is of a type which falls within the Arbitration Acts: see p. 50, post.

[7] See pp. 558–561, post.

Where the tribunal is of a type which is amenable to judicial review, the answer may in certain circumstances be – 'Yes'[8].

(ii) Can the supervising court intervene if the tribunal has proceeded upon an incorrect view of the law? In relation to arbitrations, as to many[9] other forms of extra-judicial process, the answer is in principle a qualified – 'Yes'; but the qualifications are quite different. In certain types of arbitration[10], the parties can by consent exclude in advance the right to appeal to the High Court on a question of law. In relation to those tribunals invested with a quasi-judicial function to make decisions directly affecting the legal rights of the individual, a statutory (not consensual) exclusion of the right of judicial review is a theoretical possibility[11], but this is not effective in cases where there is an excess of jurisdiction, a concept which has in recent times been very widely applied[12]. In relation to those decision-making bodies or persons, such as valuers or certifiers, who do not exercise a judicial function, the court can intervene in the case of an error of law affecting the basis of the valuation, and it would seem that a clause purporting to exclude this power would be invalid[13].

(iii) If the supervising court can intervene in the event of an error of law, what form does the intervention take, and upon what materials does the court base its decision? Here again there are substantial distinctions between arbitrations and other processes. Where the tribunal is one which is subject to judicial review, the remedy in the event of error is to quash the decision, or make a declaration of invalidity[14]. In the case of arbitration, the remedy now takes the form of a true appeal[15], in which the court can substitute its own decision for that of the tribunal, thus obviating the need for the tribunal to make a fresh decision in substitution for the one which had been quashed[16]. Where the decision is that of a valuer or similar person, the remedy springs directly from the contract itself, for if the valuation, etc., is not made in conformity with the contract, properly applied, the court will decline to enforce the rights which purport to arise from it.

The materials at which the court permits itself to look, when deciding whether an error of law has been established, also vary according to the nature of the

---

[8] There is no need for present purposes to enter with this difficult question of administrative law, a discussion of which is contained in de Smith, *Judicial Review of Administrative Action* (4th edn, 1980) pp. 118 et seq.

[9] Presumably, there is no supervision on questions of law where the tribunal is not one whose decisions do not purport directly to affect the legal rights of the parties: e.g. those in categories 5, 6 and 8, above.

[10] Viz. those prescribed by ss. 3 and 4 of the 1979 Act. For a discussion of the possible limitations on the right to exclude all recourse on questions of law, see Chapter 37, post.

[11] See de Smith, *op. cit.*, pp. 364 et seq.

[12] As in *Anisminic Ltd v Foreign Compensation Commission* [1969] 2 AC 147.

[13] So submitted as a matter of principle. If the contract expressly or impliedly requires the valuation or certification to be made in accordance with the contract, a clause purporting to exclude the right of the court to intervene if it is made otherwise than in accordance with the contract (as properly construed and applied in accordance with the law) should be rejected as inconsistent or else the party would be bound otherwise than in accordance with his agreement. (Alternatively it might be held that a purported contract for a valuation including such a provision is not a legally enforceable contract at all.)

[14] Except in those instances where the statute creating the tribunal creates a special right of appeal to the court, or to some other supervisory body.

[15] For a discussion of the nature of the appeal, see pp. 587–596, post.

[16] The old procedure of setting aside an award for 'error on the face', which was a form of *cassation*, and which still exists in relation to the decisions of other tribunals, was abolished by s. 1(1) of the 1979 Act.

tribunal. Formerly the power of review in the case of extra-judicial tribunals was confined to those cases where an error of law was apparent on the face of the decision. More recently, however, the courts have become increasingly willing to regard an error of law as an excess of jurisdiction; and since the excess may be alleged on the basis of materials not appearing on the face of the decision, the scope for intervention has been greatly enlarged. In an arbitration, an appeal is only feasible where the arbitrator has spontaneously made a reasoned award, or has been ordered to do so by the court, and even then the argument on the appeal cannot step outside the facts stated in the award[17]. The decisions of a valuer, etc., are different again, for an error of law, which in this context amounts to a failure to comply with the terms of the contract pursuant to which the valuer is appointed, can be ascertained by reference to all the facts in the case, in the same way as any other breach of contract.

(iv) What is the effect of procedural misconduct, and in what manner will the court interfere if misconduct is proved? There is substantial modern authority[18] for the view that in relation to extra-curial tribunals other than arbitrations, certain types of misconduct render a decision void; they have no legal effect, cannot be enforced and can safely be ignored. By contrast, the effect of misconduct in an arbitration is to make an award voidable; it remains enforceable, and effective to declare the legal rights of the parties, until and unless it is set aside[19]. There are also jurisdictional differences concerning the right to intervene. Judicial review is primarily the creature of the inherent jurisdiction of the court. The power to intervene in arbitrations by setting aside and remission is the creation of statute[20]. Until recently, these and other theoretical grounds of distinction were reflected by important practical differences between the manner in which the supervising court could intervene. These have now been considerably eroded, although they still exist, notably in relation to the powers of the court to remove, or reconstitute the tribunal, and to annul the agreement to arbitrate, in the event of serious misconduct or delay during an arbitration[1]. The valuable power to remit to the tribunal, as an alternative to quashing its decision, is now available in the course of judicial review, as well as in regard to arbitrations[2]. Moreover, the court may possess an inherent power to intervene by injunction and declaration whilst a reference to arbitration is still in progress, in a manner similar to that practised in relation to other tribunals, instead of waiting until the publication of the award makes it timely to invoke the statutory remedies of remission and setting aside[3]. Neither judicial review[4] nor the statutory powers

---

[17] This is an oversimplification. The court can intervene, even in the absence of reasons, where there is an excess of jurisdiction in the narrower (not the *Anisminic*) sense of the term: see pp. 571–576, post. And there may perhaps be some scope for the deployment of the wider notion of an excess of jurisdiction, in the context of the review of arbitral decisions on questions of law: see pp. 641–643, post.

[18] Cited in de Smith, *op. cit.*, pp. 151 et seq.

[19] See pp. 546–547, post.

[20] Judicial review does not apply to arbitrations.

[1] Where the tribunal is created by the state, the court can prevent it from acting in an individual case, by an order of prohibition; but it cannot abolish or reconstitute the tribunal. Where the decision-making person is a valuer etc., the court has no power to alter the agreement of the parties by removing him and appointing someone else.

[2] RSC Ord. 53, r. 9.

[3] See pp. 503–517, post.

[4] In the shape of certiorari and mandamus.

to set aside and remit created by the Arbitration Acts, apply to the proceedings of valuers and similar persons. Presumably, however, the court will exercise a power to intervene in cases of serious misconduct, by way of injunction and perhaps also by granting declaratory relief.

(v) In respect of what kinds of procedural misconduct will the court intervene? The types of extra-curial tribunal are so various that there would be no point in attempting to list the circumstances which entitle the court to intervene by judicial review, and then to compare them with the reported instances in which the court has held an arbitration to have been vitiated by misconduct. Nor would a comparison between arbitrators and valuers be fruitful, since in each case the choice of procedure depends largely upon the expressed or implied terms of the individual contract. We have, however, already drawn attention to the much more permissive attitude which the court adopts in relation to proceedings in arbitration, and in practice the prospects of persuading it to interfere in an arbitration on the grounds of procedural misconduct are much less than in respect of other tribunals.

(vi) To what extent can the court repair defects in the constitution of the tribunal? Where the tribunal is established by the state, this question does not arise. It is, however, of some importance in relation to consensual tribunals. Here again, arbitration is in a favoured position. If the consensus breaks down either when an attempt is first made to constitute the tribunal, or when it is necessary to replace the tribunal or one of its members, in the event of death, incapacity, refusal to act, or excessive delay, the court has a statutory power (although not a common law power) to repair the agreement by assuming for itself the right of appointment. These powers rarely have a counterpart in relation to other consensual tribunals[5].

(vii) To what extent will the court make available its own coercive powers in order to give efficacy to the process? This is an important aspect of the law of arbitration. The court has statutory powers to make orders in an arbitration which the parties cannot by consent confer on the arbitrator. These are of two kinds: (i) coercive orders directed to the parties themselves, backed by sanctions appropriate to a contempt of court directed against the person or property of a party who fails to comply, and (ii) orders directed to persons who are not parties to the agreement to arbitrate, and have therefore not consented to abide by the directions of the arbitrator. The statutory powers[6] to order, for example, discovery of documents, interrogatories, security for costs, interim preservation of property and examination on oath, and to issue subpoenas compelling persons to give evidence before the arbitrator, have no counterpart in relation to other consensual tribunals. Their availability is also very restricted in relation to extra-curial tribunals established by the state, although in particular instances the tribunal itself may by statute be given certain procedural powers of a coercive nature[6a]. Again, the court will not intervene to protect the process if third parties are

---

[5] *Collins v Collins* (1858) 26 Beav 306; *Bos v Helsham* (1866) LR 2 Exch 72; *Vickers v Vickers* (1867) LR 4 Eq 529.

[6] Discussed in Chapter 21, post.

[6a] We are speaking here of the powers which the tribunal itself may employ. Where an application is made for the tribunal's decision to be judicially reviewed, the supervising court has power to reinforce its own proceedings by orders for discovery, interrogatories and cross-examination: RSC Ord. 53, r. 8.

guilty of conduct which would amount to contempt of court if the proceedings had been conducted in court[7].

(viii) By what means can the decision of the tribunal be enforced? Where the decision is made by a tribunal appointed by the state, it is self-enforcing, in the sense that the coercive powers of the state automatically attach to it, even though further procedures may have to be gone through in order to compel compliance. This is not the case with tribunals established by consent. Some of those listed above give decisions which do not purport directly to affect the legal rights of the parties, and these are naturally not capable of legal enforcement at all. Other decisions, such as those of valuers, do have legal effect, and can be enforced through the courts by enforcing the contracts of whose mechanisms they form part[8]. More direct methods of enforcement are available in an arbitration. Under section 26 of the 1950 Act, the court can give leave to enforce the award in the same manner as a judgment, thus eliminating the need to bring a separate action on the implied term of the arbitration agreement to honour the award of the arbitrator. Again, the Geneva Convention of 1927 and the New York Convention of 1958 (given statutory effect in the United Kingdom by the Acts of 1950 and 1975) provide for the mutual enforcement of foreign awards by the courts of contracting states. These apply only to the awards of arbitrators, and not to the decisions of other consensual tribunals[9].

(ix) Do the members of the tribunal incur a civil liability if they fail to perform their duties with appropriate skill, care or despatch? We deal elsewhere with the immunity from suit in negligence which is probably, but not yet certainly, enjoyed by arbitrators[10], and with the distinction which exists in this respect between arbitrators and valuers. Whether there exists a class of persons who are not arbitrators, but who nevertheless enjoy judicial immunity from suit is an interesting question, which lies outside the scope of this work[11].

B. DEFINING AN ARBITRATION

1 General

For all the above (and other) reasons, therefore, it may be of great practical

---

[7] We do not know of any decision to this effect, but it must follow from *A-G v BBC* [1981] AC 303, [1980] 3 All ER 161 that an arbitral tribunal is not an 'inferior court' for the purposes of Order 52, r. 1. The fact that in some instances there may be an appeal from the arbitrator to the Court makes no difference: see *Shell Co of Australia Ltd v Federal Comr of Taxation* [1931] AC 275 at 296–297. In former times, when there was provision for a submission to be made a rule of court, proceedings for contempt could be instituted against a party who sought to revoke the authority of the arbitrator or who failed to honour the award. This procedure no longer exists, and in any event it had no bearing on a 'contempt of arbitrator' by a third party.

[8] E.g. if the contract is to purchase property at a price to be fixed by a valuer, once a valuation is made and the property transferred, the vendor can sue for the amount fixed by the valuer. By doing so, he enforces the contract to pay, not the valuation itself.

[9] See *Re Hammond and Waterton* (1890) 62 LT 808; *Re Colman and Watson* [1908] 1 KB 47.

[10] See pp. 234–230, post.

[11] We do not have in mind the supposed category of 'quasi-arbitrators', so much as a possible category of persons who act judicially, but in a manner which is not intended directly to affect the legal rights of the parties: e.g. those in category 8, above. If the keynote of judicial immunity is the application of a judicial process, then logically the public interest ought to accord the same immunity to these persons as to arbitrators.

importance to know whether an agreement to have a particular question investigated or decided by a tribunal chosen by consent or by an agreed method is an agreement to arbitrate, or something else; and whether a process which is in the course of reaching, or has reached, a decision is or is not an arbitration. Unfortunately, English law[11a] does not provide a comprehensive answer to the question, 'What is an arbitration?'. There is no code of arbitration law, of which Article 1 would contain an exclusive definition of the arbitral process; the Arbitration Acts contain a patchwork of individual provisions, introduced over the years to buttress a system, the general nature of which is taken for granted; and it is characteristic that although the Acts of 1889, 1930, 1934, 1950 and 1975 contain definitions of 'submissions' and 'arbitration agreement', there is no statute which defines 'arbitrate', 'arbitrator' or 'arbitration'.

This is not in itself a grave objection, for there exist many concepts and institutions which can immediately be recognised in the light of intuition or experience, even if a complete definition adequate to suit all circumstances cannot succinctly be formulated[12]. It would be enough if a list could be made of those characteristics which a method of deciding questions must (or must not) possess if it is to be an arbitration. Unfortunately, even after centuries of judicial involvement in the arbitral process it is still not possible to set out such a list with any degree of confidence. There are two principal reasons for this.

First, there have been very few cases in which the Court has been concerned to decide in general terms whether or not a procedure was, or was intended to be, an arbitration. Instead, the question was whether the process or the tribunal had those characteristics of an arbitration or an arbitrator which carried with them a particular legal consequence of being an arbitration or an arbitrator. Thus, the cases in the House of Lords[13], which at first sight appear to be concerned with the classification of a particular process as arbitration or something else, were in reality concerned with a different question: namely, whether the process shared with arbitration sufficient of those characteristics of an arbitration which confer on the arbitrator an immunity from suit (viz. those which give it a judicial character) for it to be possible to say that the person conducting the process shared in the immunity of the arbitrator. Decisions such as this therefore strike only a glancing blow at the nature of the arbitral process. Moreover, even in those cases where the identification of the process as an arbitration was a central issue, attention was focused on one crucial feature, which was regarded as providing a key to the solution, and the reported decisions are not numerous enough to enable a list of such features to be built up which can be relied upon as complete.

Second, the courts have usually been concerned with the classification of a process at a time when either the outcome of the process or the mode of arriving at it is under attack: i.e. when the process has either reached the stage of a decision, or is at least well under way. In consequence, the courts have been led to involve in the exercise of classification a consideration of the way in which

---

[11a] English law is, of course, far from being alone in this. No doubt in countries with developed laws of arbitration the courts can recognise an arbitration when they see one, without the need for a formal definition. It is, however, notable that the UNCITRAL Model Law, which sets out to cater for all jurisdictions, does not contain a definition.

[12] Cf. the celebrated observation of Scrutton LJ on the definition of an elephant.

[13] *Sutcliffe v Thackrah* [1974] 1 Lloyd's Rep 318, [1974] AC 727; *Arenson v Arenson and Casson, Beckman, Rutley & Co* [1976] 1 Lloyd's Rep 179, [1977] AC 405.

the process was carried out in practice. This is understandable, but not theoretically sound. Arbitration is a process which is carried out pursuant to an agreement to arbitrate. If the agreement is not to arbitrate, but to do something else, the resulting process cannot be an arbitration, however many of the characteristics of an arbitration it may appear to possess, unless the parties can be said by their conduct to have made a consensual variation of the original contract[14]. The converse is also true. The fact that the procedure actually carried out omits features which are characteristic of an arbitration, or indeed possesses features inconsistent with an arbitration, does not necessarily mean that the process is not an arbitration; the position may simply be that the process of arbitration for which the parties contracted has not been properly carried out[15]. Another possibility if the procedure differs fundamentally from that which is appropriate to an arbitration is that the arbitration agreement remains an arbitration agreement, but the parties have decided to ignore the agreement, and resolve their dispute in a different way. Perhaps the view that the actual conduct of the process can be considered when deciding upon its nature can sometimes be justified on the ground that if a particular procedure is adopted without complaint, this is an indication of the parties' original intention when making the agreement to refer; but this is hardly consistent with the well-established general rule that the subsequent conduct of the parties is not admissible to construe a contract. The criterion of subsequent conduct is, we suggest, to be applied with some caution.

Next, there is an element of circularity in some of the tests proposed for identifying a reference to arbitration. If, for example, in order to answer the objections suggested in the preceeding paragraphs, the question 'How was the procedure conducted?' is replaced by 'How does the agreement contemplate that the procedure will be conducted?', the absence of any express indication in the agreement may compel the answer 'Well, that depends upon whether the agreement is for an arbitration or something else'. The problem is most obvious in relation to the criterion of the contemplated procedure, but it arises in relation to other tests as well.

Finally, there is the problem of distinguishing between the questions – (i) is the procedure an arbitration?; (ii) is it an arbitration which falls within the Arbitration Acts?; and (iii) is it an arbitration to which particular provisions of the Acts are applicable?[16] These three questions are not necessarily the same, for a process may be an arbitration without falling within the Acts; yet there are traces in some reported cases that the distinction has become obscured.

---

[14] This will not often happen, and still less frequently will the parties contrive to convert (say) a valuation into a reference which is subject to the Arbitration Acts: for these only apply to references conducted pursuant to an 'arbitration agreement', i.e. a written agreement to submit present or future differences to arbitration. See *Imperial Metal Industries (Kynoch) Ltd v Amalgamated Union of Engineering Workers* [1979] 1 All ER 847. So far as we are aware, the courts have never had occasion to consider the way in which the various statutory and common law procedures for supervision by, and appeal to, the High Court are to be applied to processes of decision which have changed their character in this way.

[15] To take an obvious example, it is a characteristic of an arbitration agreement that the parties contract that the dispute shall be decided fairly. If in practice it is conducted unfairly, it is still an arbitration, and the Court is possessed of the remedies for misconduct conferred by the 1950 Act: any other conclusion would lead to absurd results.

[16] The second and third questions are discussed at pp. 50–52, post.

2 Relevant factors: summary

In spite of these difficulties, it is possible to suggest a list, almost certainly incomplete, of those factors which are material to the question whether a particular process qualifies as an arbitration. This list may be divided into two parts. First, those qualities which are necessary, although not in themselves sufficient[17], if the process is to be considered an arbitration. Second, certain other considerations which are relevant to the question, although not conclusive upon it.

(a) Attributes which must be present

(i) The agreement pursuant to which the process is, or is to be, carried on ('the procedural agreement') must contemplate that the tribunal which carries on the process will make a decision which is binding on the parties to the procedural agreement.

(ii) The procedural agreement must contemplate that the process will be carried on between those persons whose substantive rights are determined by the tribunal.

(iii) The jurisdiction of the tribunal to carry on the process and to decide the rights of the parties must derive either from the consent of the parties, or from an order of the court or from a statute the terms of which make it clear that the process is to be an arbitration.

(iv) The tribunal must be chosen, either by the parties, or by a method to which they have consented.

(v) The procedural agreement must contemplate that the tribunal will determine the rights of the parties in an impartial manner, with the tribunal owing an equal obligation of fairness towards both sides.

(vi) The agreement of the parties to refer their disputes to the decision of the tribunal must be intended to be enforceable in law.

(vii) The procedural agreement must contemplate a process whereby the tribunal will make a decision upon a dispute which is already formulated at the time when the tribunal is appointed.

(b) Other factors which are relevant[17a]

(i) Whether the procedural agreement contemplates that the tribunal will

---

[17] In *Sutcliffe v Thackrah* [1974] 1 Lloyd's Rep 318, [1974] AC 727 and *Arenson v Arenson and Casson, Beckman, Rutley & Co* [1976] 1 Lloyd's Rep 179, [1977] AC 405, various factors were considered and rejected as indicia of that type of process which attracts for the tribunal the judicial immunity of an arbitrator. This did not mean that the Law Lords considered the factors to be irrelevant to the questions whether the tribunal was immune, and whether the process was an arbitration; merely that the possession of a particular quality did not ipso facto make the process an arbitration. For example, the question whether the tribunal has to act fairly as between the parties is not irrelevant; on the contrary, it is crucial. If answered in the negative, the process cannot be an arbitration. But an affirmative answer does not mean that it is an arbitration.

[17a] In the first edition, this list had included as a relevant factor the question whether the procedural agreement conferred the right to call for a decision by the tribunal on both parties or upon one alone. This factor, inserted in deference to views expressed in *Baron v Sunderland Corpn* [1966] 2 QB 56, 64, has now been deleted in the light of *Pittalis v Sherefettin* [1986] QB 868.

receive evidence and contentions, or at least give the parties the opportunity to put them forward.

(ii) Whether the wording of the agreement is consistent or inconsistent with the view that the process was intended to be an arbitration.

(iii) Whether the identity of the chosen tribunal, or the method prescribed for choosing the tribunal, shows that the process was intended to be an arbitration.

(iv) Whether the procedural agreement requires the tribunal to decide the dispute according to law.

3 Relevant factors: detailed discussion

We now offer various comments on these various factors.

(a) Attributes which must be present

(i) **Decision intended to be binding.** The essence[18] of a submission to arbitration is that it comprises a contract to honour the decision of the arbitrator, and a mandate to the arbitrator to make a binding determination of the legal rights of the parties[19]. The converse proposition must also be true, although not so well supported by direct authority, that a procedure which is not intended to result in a decision, or which is intended to result in a decision not enforceable by legal process[20], is not an arbitration governed by the statutory and common law principles which constitute the English law of arbitration[1]. Procedures which are intended to yield an opinion[2], or a recommendation as to future action[3], or a summary of the facts relevant to a disputed issue, are not arbitrations in this sense; nor are procedures which are intended to result in decisions which in practice will be regarded as binding, but which can, if disregarded, be enforced only by extra-judicial means.

(ii) **The parties to the process.** The first two propositions, taken together, amount to this: that the persons who are parties to the procedural agreement, those who are parties to the process, those whose rights and obligations are in

---

[18] It is a necessary condition that the award shall be intended to be binding. But it is not in itself a sufficient condition: see *Arenson v Arenson and Casson, Beckman, Rutley & Co*, supra.

[19] See pp. 417–418, post.

[20] There is no reason why an agreement which contemplates the possibility that the tribunal will, as a preliminary to or substitute for an award, produce something other than a decision, should not lead to proceedings which constitute an arbitration and to an ultimate award, if the circumstances in which the proceedings take place are such as to show that an arbitration is what the proceedings are intended to be. Thus, the agreement may require the parties to attempt conciliation, under the auspices of the tribunal, before going forward with an arbitration. If conciliation fails, the subsequent proceedings will be an arbitration. Equally, the proceedings may contemplate that the award of the tribunal may contain a decision together with something else – for example a recommendation for future action. Such proceedings would, we suggest, be an arbitration, although part of the award would be without legal effect.

[1] See, for example, *Goodyear v Simpson* (1846) 15 M & W 16; *Re Dawdy and Hartcup* (1885) 15 QBD 426.

[2] For example, a decision which is enforceable only by political, religious or commercial sanctions, or by public opinion. The parties to a pay arbitration contemplate that they will abide by the result, and there may be pressures which ensure that they do so. But they rarely if ever make an enforceable contract to this effect.

[3] See *FF Ayriss & Co v Board of Industrial Relations of Alberta* (1960) 23 DLR (2d) 584.

issue and those who are bound by the decision must all be the same. The propositions are not, perhaps, as obvious as they seem. There is no reason in principle why the question raised for the decision of the arbitrator should not be an issue of fact or law unaccompanied by any claim for substantive relief: and indeed claims for a declaration are by no means uncommon in arbitrations. Logically, there should equally be no objection to an arbitrator being called on to decide, as between A and B, an issue concerning the legal rights or liabilities of X, although of course it would not be binding on X[4]. There is, however, some authority to the contrary[5].

(iii) **Consensual resolution of the dispute.**   The essence of a private arbitration, of the kind with which this book is concerned, is that the power of the tribunal to bind the parties by its decision derives from the consent of the parties themselves, and not from some external source[6].

This proposition must, however, be qualified in one respect, namely that where disputes are referred to the decision of an independent tribunal, pursuant to the provisions of a statute, the proceedings may amount to an arbitration, if the statute makes it clear that this is intended[7]. Plainly, not every statutory provision for the resolution of disputes by a tribunal other than the court contemplates an arbitration. Whether the procedure in question is or is not an arbitration is of fundamental procedural significance, for the reasons which we have already stated. But even if it is an arbitration, it does not follow that the

---

[4] Such questions do arise in practice. For example, the right of A to recover substantial damages from B may depend upon whether A has himself incurred liability to X. Or the liability of B for professional negligence may depend upon whether a contract between A and X is valid. Claims of this kind may give rise to practical problems (see p. 141, post) but we have never heard it suggested that a process called into being to decide upon them is not an arbitration merely because X is not a party.

[5] In *Imperial Metal Industries (Kynoch) Ltd v Amalgamated Union of Engineering Workers* [1979] 1 All ER 847 a contract between a government department and a supplier incorporated the 'Fair Wages Clause', which made provision for the resolution by an independant tribunal of disputes as to whether the supplier was paying his employees in accordance with the requirements of the clause. Such a dispute did arise, and the matter was referred to a tribunal, before whom the matter was argued by the suppliers and a trade union representing the workers. The Court of Appeal held that the Act did not apply to the proceedings, and that accordingly the tribunal could not be required to state a case under s. 21(1). Undoubtedly, one ground for the decision was that s. 21(1) applies only to arbitration conducted pursuant to an 'arbitration agreement', as defined by s. 32. Another basis upon which the same conclusion could have been (and perhaps was: see p. 855d) arrived at was that the decision was not intended to be binding on the parties to the reference or on the parties to the substantive contract, and that accordingly the reference was not an arbitration. The Court also took into account the fact that the reference was not invoked by the union, which was not a party to the substantive contract, and indeed could have been raised by a stranger, against the wishes of both parties to the substantive contract (see p. 851b). There are, however, traces in the judgments of the broader proposition that there cannot be an arbitration unless the parties to the reference are the same as the parties to the contract which created the substantive rights and duties in issue. Whilst not doubting the correctness of the decision itself, we venture to question whether this proposition can be accepted without qualification.

[6] It is implicit in the decision in *Dallal v Bank Mellat* [1986] QB 441, [1986] 2 WLR 745, that the Iranian claims tribunal was not a private law arbitration because its competence to rule on claims derived from international treaty and not from the will of the parties. In every other respect it resembled a private law arbitration, but could not be recognised as such because the consent to arbitrate resulted in an agreement which was a nullity under its proper law. The decisions of the tribunal are recognised in England and can presumably be enforced by action, not as arbitral awards, but as judgments of a competent foreign tribunal.

[7] See *Racecourse Betting Control Board v Secretary for Air* [1944] Ch 114.

reference stands in the same relationship to the courts as a private arbitration[8]. In particular –

(i) Whereas certain provisions of the Arbitration Acts, if not all of those provisions[9] apply to all private arbitrations, the 1950 Act applies to statutory arbitrations only in so far as the Act is not inconsistent[10] with the statute pursuant to which the reference takes place, or with any rules or procedures authorised or recognised thereby[11]. Many statutes which provide for disputes to be referred to arbitration exclude the Act in whole or in part. This may well have the effect of taking away the statutory powers of the court to correct errors of procedure or law, whilst leaving it uncertain whether the reference is susceptible to that power of control which is normally exercised over the transactions of inferior tribunals by the procedure now known as 'judicial review'.

(ii) If the courts continue to pursue the strategy of developing their control over proceedings in private arbitrations by applying to the arbitrations agreement some of the concepts of the general law of contract[12], a fundamental divergence will develop between private and statutory arbitrations: for since the latter are not consensual in origin, concepts such as frustrations or repudiation can have no application.

(iv) A consensual tribunal.   It is also of the essence of a private arbitration that the tribunal shall be appointed as the result of agreement between the parties. It is not, of course, necessary that the agreement to arbitrate shall name the arbitrator, or that the parties shall subsequently concur in a choice. The agreement may contemplate that persons will be appointed without the parties' wishes being consulted – as for example, where the right to nominate the tribunal is placed in the hands of a third party, or where the two chosen arbitrators are themselves to choose the umpire, or where the agreement provides for a reference to (say) the president of a stipulated body. Again, if a party is in default in making an appointment, or if a vacancy in the tribunal occurs after appointment, the choice may be made by the court, rather than by the parties, by virtue of powers conferred by the Act. Nevertheless, one can say that in every case of private arbitration the parties have consented, if not to the individual choice, at least to the way in which the choice is made.

(v) An impartial tribunal.   The requirement that the tribunal shall act impartially is so obvious as to require no elaboration. Moreover, it is of little practical importance, for it is hard to imagine the parties to a contract agreeing, either expressly or by implication, that the chosen tribunal should be permitted

---

[8] The differences are so important that many statutory arbitrations cannot be regarded as arbitrations at all, in any real sense of the word.
[9] See pp. 50–52, post.
[10] See *R and W Paul Ltd v Wheat Commission* [1937] AC 139.
[11] S. 31(1).
[12] See pp. 503–517, post.

to act unfairly[13]. An intention that the tribunal shall act fairly is a necessary condition, before an agreement to refer disputes can be characterised as an arbitration agreement. But it is not a sufficient characteristic. Many agreements for the impartial determination of rights are not arbitration agreements[14].

(vi) Enforceable agreement to refer.   At first sight it may seem obvious that if an arbitration necessarily involves the parties in an enforceable contractual obligation to honour the award of the tribunal in respect of their dispute, there can be no arbitration unless there is an enforceable contractual obligation on each party to submit the dispute to the tribunal. In fact, this is not so plain, since throughout the early history of arbitration, agreements to refer which undoubtedly contemplated that the reference would take the shape of an arbitration were at best imperfectly enforceable, in that a party could with impunity frustrate the intended procedure either by refusing to appoint an arbitrator at all, or by revoking his appointment, or by bringing an action in breach of the agreement[15]. More recently, by virtue of sections 1 and 4 of the 1950 Act[16], a substantial measure of enforceability has been conferred on those agreements to refer which fall within the Act: viz. written agreements to submit present or future agreements to arbitration. One could therefore legitimately say that, in the case of written agreements to refer, only those which are intended to attract the measures of enforcement contemplated by sections 1 and 4 can be regarded as agreements to refer: and that only those proceedings which take place pursuant to such an agreement can be regarded as arbitrations[17].

There is, however, a problem in relation to references which follow upon agreements which are not written. It must now be regarded as established law[18] that the Act does not apply to such references[19]. Thus, the test of an intention to give the agreement the benefit of statutory enforceability cannot apply. Nevertheless, there is a difference between an agreement to refer which is intended to be binding in honour only and one which the parties mean to be enforced by whatever legal sanctions may exist, however imperfect they may

---

[13] Contracts to resolve a dispute otherwise than by means of a reasoned decision, arrived at impartially, can readily be conceived: e.g. an agreement to settle an issue by the spin of a coin. The procedure would not be an arbitration: but not specifically because the proceedings were 'unfair'. Statistics are not partial. Conversely, it is possible to visualise a bargain containing gaps which the parties intended to be filled by means which would not necessarily involve a conscious balancing of the conflicting interests of the parties. For example, a contract could simply provide that the consideration for the promise was to be fixed by a third party, without stating any criteria by which he was to judge, or conveying any inference that he was to act without partiality. Here again, the process would not be an arbitration: but not simply through the absence of any requirement of fairness.

[14] The point was forcefully made in *Sutcliffe v Thackrah*, ante, and *Arenson v Arenson and Casson, Beckman, Rutley & Co*, ante. A 'valuer' may owe a duty only to his principal, not to the party with whom his principal has contractual relations. Nevertheless, that duty involves striking a fair balance between the parties: for otherwise the value will not be correct.

[15] See p. 436, post.

[16] Relating respectively to the irrevocability of the appointment of an arbitrator, without leave of the Court, and to the staying of proceedings.

[17] The definition is probably circular, but this is not necessarily a fatal objection.

[18] As a result of *Imperial Metal Industries (Kynoch) Ltd v Amalgamated Union of Engineering Workers* [1979] 1 All ER 847.

[19] See pp. 50–52, post.

be. Such sanctions do exist. We believe that even if section 4 does not apply, a court would enforce an oral submission by staying an action brought in breach of the submission, by exercising its inherent jurisdiction to stay proceedings which are an abuse of its process[20]. Again, although the history of arbitration has been dogged by the notion that a reference to arbitration involves a revocable mandate, we believe that the Court should and will sweep away this outmoded idea, and hold that an oral agreement to refer is subject to an implied undertaking not to revoke the appointment of the tribunal – even if this means the implication of a term to a similar, although not indentical, effect in respect of oral submissions to that which is imposed by statute in regard to written submissions. It does therefore make sense to ask, as one step in deciding whether the contemplated procedure is an arbitration, whether an oral agreement to have a dispute dealt with by an impartial tribunal is intended to have the backing of some form of legal sanction.

It does not, however, follow that the agreement to refer to arbitration must necessarily be unconditional. Commercial contracts occasionally provide for the reference of disputes to a specified court, with an option on either party to call for arbitration. Whether such a provision is initially an 'arbitration agreement' within section 32 of the Act is perhaps an interesting question, but is of no practical importance. If the option is not exercised, there will be no reference, so that the status of the reference can never come in issue. If, conversely, one party does exercise the option[1], both parties are bound to submit the dispute to arbitration; the agreement is then brought within section 32; and the proceedings thereafter constitute a reference to arbitration.

(vii) A formulated dispute.   It now appears[2] to be settled law that a procedure cannot be an arbitration unless there is a formulated dispute in

---

[20] By analogy with *Racecourse Betting Control Board v Secretary of State for Air* [1944] Ch 114.

[1] Which we suggest that he can do even after an action is commenced.

[2] We add this note of qualification because the issue in *Sutcliffe v Thackrah* [1974] 1 Lloyd's Rep 318, [1974] AC 727 and *Arenson v Arenson and Casson, Beckman, Rutley & Co* [1977] AC 405 was not whether the proceedings amounted to an arbitration, or whether the defendant was an arbitrator, but whether he enjoyed a similar immunity from suit to that which (it was assumed) is enjoyed by an arbitrator. There does, however, appear to be a common reasoning which runs through the various speeches, on the following lines – (a) an arbitrator enjoys judicial immunity because he performs a judicial function; (b) therefore a 'quasi-arbitrator' cannot enjoy a similar immunity unless he performs a judicial function; (c) one of the indicia of such a function is that the tribunal is called on to decide a formulated dispute, and since the architects and valuers whose immunity was in issue were not appointed to decide upon disputes, it followed that they could not be immune. This line of reasoning, and indeed the whole tenor of the speeches, indicates that if the House had been called on to decide whether the existence of a dispute was a precondition to the existence of an arbitration, there would have been no doubt about the answer. There is substantial authority, besides *Sutcliffe* and *Arenson*, to support the view expressed in the text. *Collins v Collins* (1858) 26 Beav 306; *Bos v Helsham* (1866) LR 2 Exch. 72; *Re Hopper* (1867) LR 2 QB 367; *Vickers v Vickers* (1867) LR 4 Eq 529; *Thomson v Anderson* (1870) LR 9 Eq 523; *Re Evans, Davies and Caddick* (1870) 22 LT 507; *Re Carus-Wilson v Greene* (1886) 18 QB D 7; *Re Hammond and Waterton* (1890) 62 LT 808; *Chambers v Goldthorpe* [1901] 1 KB 624, per Romer LJ (dissenting); *Re Colman and Watson* [1908] 1 KB 47; *Sutcliffe v Thackrah* [1974] 2 WLR 295, per Lord Reid at 298, Lord Morris at 314, and Viscount Dilhorne at 318. *Tharisis Sulphur and Copper Co Ltd v Loftus* (1872) LR 8 CP 1 (average adjuster held entitled to judicial immunity) may be explicable on the ground that the referee was appointed to resolve a dispute (see Lord Morris in *Sutcliffe v Thackrah* at 309) or it may have been wrongly decided (see per Lord Salmon, ibid., at 322–323). See also, *Aaby's (EB) Rederi A/S v Union of India, The Evje* [1974] 2 Lloyd's Rep 57, per Lord Morris at 63.

existence at the time when the arbitrator is appointed; nor, equally, can an agreement be an arbitration agreement (either within the Act or at common law) unless it contemplates that a dispute will already exist when the appointment is made. The precise juridical basis of the requirement is, perhaps, not entirely clear. Moreover, in theory it may produce some rather surprising results. For example, an agreement for the sale of goods at a price to be fixed by agreement or in default of agreement by X would, it seems, be capable of being an arbitration agreement[3], whereas an agreement at a price to be fixed by X would not. Again, even if the agreement were in the latter form, a disagreement between the parties prior to a decision by the valuer, such as might very often happen, would convert what would otherwise have been a valuation, into something which would at least potentially[4] be an arbitration, with all the fundamental procedural consequences which that would involve.

It is often said that the distinction between an arbitration on the one hand and valuation and kindred proceedings on the other is that the object of one is to resolve disputes, and of the other to prevent disputes from arising.

This formulation is neat, but unhelpful. In many instances where the reference undoubtedly constitutes a valuation, a third person is appointed to fix the value precisely because the parties foresee that they may be unable to agree; and if in fact they do agree, it will be the agreement, not the decision of the valuer, which prevents the dispute arising. We suggest that a more useful distinction can be drawn between a reference which is intended to take place automatically, as part of the agreed mechanism for completing the substantive contract and bringing it into effect, and one which is held in reserve as a means of working out the legal and factual implications of an already complete agreement. Thus, if goods are sold at a price to be fixed by valuation, the agreement is incomplete until the valuation has taken place. The parties may forestall the valuation by reaching a prior agreement; but there must, in every case, be either an agreement or a valuation. This is not so with an arbitration agreement. The occasion for a dispute, or an agreed settlement of a dispute, may never arise; and in the absence of a dispute, the arbitrator has no power to act.

One may observe that the existence of a dispute between the parties is material, not only to the classification of the agreement to refer, but also to the rights of the parties to put the agreement into effect. Thus, if one party to an arbitration agreement makes a claim which the other party admits, this cannot usually be made the subject of arbitration; not because the agreement is any the less an agreement to arbitrate, but simply because under the usual form of agreement the right to call for arbitration does not arise unless there is a dispute.

It may be noted that quite apart from any general requirement of a dispute as a pre-condition for proceedings qualifying as an arbitration at all, an agreement to refer cannot be an 'arbitration agreement' for the purposes of the Act unless it relates to 'differences' between the parties[5], and the proceedings

---

[3] It would not necessarily be an arbitration agreement. That would depend on the presence or absence of other factors.

[4] Other factors would of course be relevant to the question whether the proceedings changed their character in this way.

[5] S. 32.

cannot be an arbitration to which the Act applies unless they take place pursuant to such an agreement[6].

(b) Other factors which are relevant

(i) Evidence and contentions.   There is high authority for the view that a procedure is not an arbitration unless it is intended that the arbitrator shall perform a judicial function; and this has been explained as meaning that he must hear evidence and contentions brought forward by the parties, or at least give them the opportunity of bringing them forward[7]. There are, however, serious difficulties in the way of accepting this as a requirement, as distinct from a relevant factor[8]: for a large majority of procedures which are beyond question arbitrations are conducted without any 'contentions' being addressed to the tribunal, in the sense of a formal reasoned argument. In particular –

(i) In many quality disputes, the arbitrator studies the samples which the parties have furnished, or goes down to the warehouse and inspects the goods, and then forms an opinion on the basis of his own expertise. The idea of the parties bringing forward their own experts to prevail on him to come to a different conclusion would be regarded as eccentric and perhaps even subversive: for the whole purpose of choosing arbitration for a quality dispute is that the parties can with the minimum of time and expense obtain a decision from someone in whose independence and expertise they have faith[9].

(ii) Many London arbitrations[10] have in the past proceeded upon the basis that the dispute will be dealt with by the two arbitrators chosen by the parties themselves, without invoking the assistance of the umpire or third arbitrator. In such cases, each arbitrator simply receives from the party appointing him a file of documents, which he then proceeds to discuss with his co-arbitrator. Very often the nature of the dispute, and of the parties' views upon it, appear so clearly from the files that no further exposition is needed. On other occasions, a covering letter may elaborate the views of the appointing party. But there is nothing in the nature of a confrontation between the parties or their advocates in the presence of the tribunal. Even in those cases where the arbitrators disagree and an umpire is called in, it often happens that the arbitrators assume the role of 'arbitrator/advocates', and present to the umpire the arguments of those who appointed them. This bears no resemblance to the manner in which evidence and argument is advanced in the course of an orthodox judicial process. Yet it

---

6 See p. 51, post. This point was not referred to in *Sutcliffe* or *Arenson*, no doubt because the status of the proceedings as an arbitration (as distinct from a 'quasi-arbitration') was not directly in issue.

7 *Sutcliffe v Thackrah* [1974] AC 727, per Lord Salmon at 763, citing *Re Hopper* (1867) LR 2 QB 367 at 372–373 and *Turner v Goulden* (1873) LR 9 CP 57 at 59; *Arenson v Arenson and Casson, Beckman, Rutley & Co* [1977] AC 405 at 424 and 428, per Lord Simon and Wheatley, respectively. See also, for example, *Re Hopper* (1867) LR 2 QB 367 at 370 and 373, and *Palacath v Flanagan* [1985] 2 All ER 161.

8 See Lords Kilbrandon and Fraser, in *Sutcliffe* at 430 and 442 respectively.

9 It must, however, be accepted that there is a difference between the question whether the parties in practice expect to call evidence (and do so) and the question whether they can insist on doing so if they wish. (See *Bottomley v Ambler* (1877) 38 LT 545.) (See pp. 352–354, post.) The practical problem with the latter question is that it starts a circular enquiry. Perhaps the parties can insist on calling evidence if the proceedings are an arbitration: and they are more likely to be an arbitration if the party can insist on calling evidence. In practice, the agreement to refer rarely says anything about the question of evidence.

10 S. 6(2) of the 1979 Act has brought about an important change of practice: see pp. 173–174, post.

has for decades been sanctioned as a proper, and indeed (if correctly used), valuable aspect of English arbitration procedures.

In these circumstances we suggest that the presence in, or absence from, the agreement of any provision requiring the tribunal to receive evidence and contentions is at most some indication of the intended nature of the proceedings.

(ii) The wording of the agreement.   The way in which the reference is described in the agreement to refer is not conclusive as to the character of the proceedings. Thus, even an explicit agreement that a matter shall be dealt with by 'arbitration' does not necessarily mean that the parties intend the proceedings to be the type of arbitration which is the subject of the Arbitration Acts or of the common law of arbitration[11]. For example, the use of this word is consistent with an intention to invoke a process which involves a decision by an impartial body, but not one which is to be binding in law. Or the other terms of the agreement may show that something in the nature of a valuation was foreseen. Conversely, the use of the word 'valuer' does not inevitably preclude the contract from being interpreted as an arbitration agreement[12].

Nevertheless, common sense suggests that even if the language of the agreement is not necessarily decisive, it will often provide a clear enough impression of what the parties intended. Thus, for example, if an agreement –

(i) provides for the appointment of an 'umpire'[13]; or

(ii) stipulates that the reference shall take place subject to the provisions of the Arbitration Acts[14]; or

(iv) calls for a procedure which is relevant only in regard to arbitrations (for instance if there is an 'exclusion agreement' pursuant to section 3 of the 1979 Act)[15]

one would need to find clear language indicating that one or more of the essential features of an arbitration is missing, before the agreement could be construed as providing for anything other than arbitration.

Conversely, provisions purporting to exclude the Arbitration Acts, or providing that the tribunal shall 'sit as experts not as arbitrators', could not (in the absence of very strong indication to the contrary) be regarded as consistent with an intention to refer disputes to arbitration[15a].

(iii) The choice of tribunal.   The identity of the tribunal named in the agreement, or the method prescribed for choosing the tribunal, may indicate the type of proceedings which are contemplated. A reference to a tribunal chosen from the arbitral panel of a trade association points in one direction; a

---

[11] See *Charles v Cardiff Collieries Ltd* (1928) 44 TLR 448. The case is very obscurely reported in the Court of Appeal, and the point was not raised in the House of Lords.

[12] See, for example, *Re Evans, Davies and Caddick* (1870) 22 LT 507; *Taylor v Yielding* (1912) 56 Sol Jo 253.

[13] See *Re Hopper* (1867) LR 2 QB 367, and cf. *Taylor v Yielding*, supra.

[14] *Pittalis v Sherefettin* [1986] QB 868, [1986] 2 WLR 1003 (rent reviews).

[15] Even a reference to an obsolete procedure might suffice. Although it is nearly a century since s. 1 of the 1889 Act prohibited a submission being made a rule of court, and 30 years since the 1950 Act repealed the existing provision that a submission should have the same effect as if it had been made a rule of court, one still occasionally sees in standard rules of arbitrations which have not been brought up to date a provision that the submission (or the award) may be made a rule of court.

[15a] *Palacath v Flanagan*, supra.

reference to a firm of estate agents or accountants may point in the other. The choice of a lawyer as the tribunal suggests that a more formal procedure is looked for, and that accordingly an arbitration is intended[16]. The status of the persons upon whom the responsibility is conferred may also be a guide[17].

(iv) Obligation to apply the law.   As we shall later suggest[18], it is impossible now to be sure whether an arbitrator is in all cases obliged to decide the dispute according to the substantive law governing the contract, and whether, if such a duty does exist, it can effectively be excluded by express agreement without depriving the process of its character as an arbitration. This being so, it cannot be said that if it is possible to extract from the procedural agreement an intention that the decision shall be (or conversely need not be) made in accordance with the law, this is conclusive as to the status of the reference. Nevertheless, we suggest that if the agreement stipulates that the law need not be applied – e.g. if the tribunal is to decide 'according to equity and good conscience' – this is at least some indication that the procedure is not to be that type of arbitration which is subject to the statutes and common law governing private arbitrations[19].

C. WHICH ARBITRATIONS ARE SUBJECT TO THE ACTS?

The question whether proceedings amount to an arbitration is not the same as the question whether they attract the powers of supervision and reinforcement conferred on the court by the Acts. Nor is it necessarily the same as the question whether *all* the provisions of the 1950 Act apply to the proceedings.

Until recently, it had seemed that the law of arbitration, whether arising by statute or common law, could be divided into three parts –

(i) those statutory provisions which applied to all arbitrations;

(ii) those statutory provisions which applied only to an arbitration conducted pursuant to an arbitration agreement – viz. 'a written agreement to submit present or future differences to arbitration';

(iii) rules of common law applicable to all arbitrations.

The distinction between categories (i) and (ii) was founded on the difference in language between those sections of the 1950 Act which expressly referred to

---

[16] Lawyers are, however, often chosen to act as the tribunal, or the chairman of a tribunal, to conduct proceedings which are not arbitrations: either because they are not of a consensual nature (e.g. the innumerable tribunals established under the auspices of the state to deal with disputes arising from the activities of public bodies), or because they are not intended to utter decisions which are binding in law (e.g. tribunals of inquiry, boards of conciliation, and so on).

[17] It is unlikely to be an arbitration if the task is fulfilled by persons who are 'merely servants employed to add up sums': *Carr v Smith* (1843) 5 QB 128.

[18] Pp. 68–71, post.

[19] If the agreement provides that the tribunal *shall* apply the law, this creates a strong presumption that the proceedings are to be an arbitration. In practice, this is much less common than an agreement relieving the arbitration from the duty to apply the law, although it is not entirely unknown (for instance, where the issue referred to arbitration is defined in terms of a specific statute). Sometimes the issue is stated in a manner so redolent of legal terminology that a decision according to law is plainly intended.

an arbitration agreement[20] and those which did not[1]. The distinction was important, because proceedings which unquestionably amounted to an arbitration might yet fail to qualify as arbitrations pursuant to an arbitration agreement, because although they were consensual in origin, the consensus was not expressed *in writing*[2]. It was hard to find any logical distinction between those provisions which related to all arbitrations, and those which concerned only arbitrations pursuant to written submissions. The difference in language between the two groups of sections plainly derived from the fact that the 1950 Act consolidated a number of previous statutes. That part of the 1889 Act which found its way into Part 1 of the 1950 Act was expressed throughout as applying to arbitrations pursuant to a 'submission' (a word having the same statutory definition as an 'arbitration agreement'). The other consolidated legislation was not, however, consistently expressed in this way. Some provisions of the 1934 Act referred to an arbitration agreement, others did not. Equally, the terms of the 1854 Act were distributed between those which applied only to submissions which could be made a rule of court (i.e. arbitration agreements in writing) and those which were not expressly so limited. Nevertheless, although the historical origins of the 1950 Act accounted for its unsystematic form, the distinction in language between the two groups of sections was conspicuous, and it had seemed very distinctly arguable that effect must be given to it by holding that some provisions of the Act were applicable to oral as well as to written submissions. These included the sections relating to special case, remission and setting aside.

It has, however, now been decided[3] that this view is incorrect, and that no parts of the 1950[4] Act (and presumably of the other arbitration statutes currently in force) apply to references conducted otherwise than pursuant to an 'arbitration agreement'[5]. These references will, however, continue to be subject to the fast-developing powers of the court at common law to supervise consensual arbitrations[6]. The decision is unlikely to be of great practical importance in relation to proceedings where no part of the submission has been reduced to writing. These are in any event rare, and there is nothing anomalous in finding that arbitrations which are so informal that the parties have not troubled to write out the arbitration agreement are not subject to the statutory powers of reinforcement and control applicable to more formal proceedings. Much more

---

[20] Ss. 1 to 9, 10(a), 12(1) to (4), 14–17, 18(1) and (13); 24; 26; 27.

[1] Ss. 12(5) and (6), 13, 18(2), (4) and (5); 19; 20; 21; 22; 23; 25; 28.

[2] Arbitrations which are in toto based on oral submissions must be very rare, although they may have been commonplace two centuries ago. But an ad hoc oral submission of a new aspect of an existing dispute may be tacked on to that dispute in a way which does not constitute an 'arbitration agreement', even if the prior dispute is being carried on pursuant to such an agreement.

[3] *Imperial Metal Industries (Kynoch) Ltd v Amalgamated Union of Engineering Workers* [1979] 1 All ER 847.

[4] Apart of course from those sections referred to in s. 31, which apply to statutory arbitrations unless inconsistent with the statute.

[5] All three members of the Court agreed with Slynn J in this conclusion, which therefore constitutes the ratio decidendi of the case, whatever the precise juristic status of the other questions to which we have already referred. Unfortunately, the arguments of counsel are not reported, so that the historical analysis which formed the basis of the decision cannot now be precisely ascertained.

[6] See pp. 503–517, post.

significant is the potential impact of this decision on those references, originally founded on a written submission, which have been enlarged by oral agreement, or by some form of waiver or estoppel, to comprise new items of dispute. Here, there is now a risk that part of the proceedings may fall outside the ordinary framework of the relationship between arbitration and the court[7].

---

[7] It was not necessary for the Court to go so far as it did in order to hold that the tribunal could not be required to state a special case. For more than one reason it could have been, and indeed was, decided that the proceedings either did not amount to an arbitration at all, or at least not to an arbitration conducted pursuant to an agreement to arbitrate. This would have been sufficient to sustain the conclusion; for apart from the special position of statutory arbitrations, the Acts apply only to voluntary arbitrations. The question whether the 1950 Act applies only to *written* submissions was not in issue, on the facts of the particular case. Again, the Court could have proceeded on the basis of a more narrow historical rationalisation, aimed specifically at the jurisdiction of the arbitrator to state a case. This originated in s. 5 of the 1854 Act, which expressly applied only to compulsory references and to those consensual references which might be made a rule of court: namely, by virtue of s. 17, references which were founded on a submission contained in a deed or other written instrument. There would thus have been no great difficulty in showing that the jurisdiction originally conferred by the 1854 Act, and subsequently expanded by the Acts of 1889 and 1934, was never intended, when the legislation was consolidated in 1950, to govern references founded on an oral submission. This conclusion could have been arrived at without touching upon the more complicated question whether *any* provision of the consolidating Acts applies to such references. The Court did, however, embark on this question, and the views expressed by all the judges must now be regarded as settled law.

CHAPTER 3

Sources of arbitration law

The rules which govern the conduct of arbitrations under English law are derived from four distinct sources: A. the common law; B. statute; C. the express agreement of the parties; and D. the practice of merchants and arbitrators.

A. THE COMMON LAW

By far the most important source of English arbitration law is the common law – viz. the body of law established by the decisions of the courts, and set out in the reported cases. The reason is that England does not possess a comprehensive code of arbitration. The Arbitration Acts of 1950, 1975 and 1979 lay down certain statutory rules for the initiation, conduct and supervision of arbitrations. But there are a number of reasons why the Acts rarely if ever provide a complete solution to the problems which arise in the course of a reference.

In the first place, there are certain arbitrations to which the Acts do not apply: viz. those which are not derived from an 'arbitration agreement', as defined in section 32 of the 1950 Act[1] or section 7(1) of the 1975 Act.

Second, and more important, the Acts do not purport to establish a complete system of procedure. Parts of the arbitration process are dealt with only in outline, and others are not mentioned at all. Most notably, the Acts give no guidance on the numerous problems of procedure which face the arbitrator when he comes to conduct the reference[2].

Finally, the Acts confer on the Court and on the arbitrator certain discretionary powers, but lay down no principles by which they should be exercised. Thus, for example, the Acts empower the Court to appoint and remove arbitrators; to stay proceedings; to revoke an arbitration agreement; and to set aside or remit an award. Similarly, the arbitrator has the power to make an interim award, and to make an award as to costs. Yet if it is desired to know how and when these powers should be exercised, reference to the Acts will yield no guidance.

Thus, it is to the reported cases rather than to the Act that reference must be made for an exposition of the law on arbitral procedure; and it is from this source that most of the statements of principle set out in this book are derived.

This body of law cannot, however, be exploited uncritically. Quite apart

---

[1] See p. 668, post. The definition is applied to the 1979 Act by s. 7(1)(e) thereof.
[2] Apart from s. 12(1), (2), (3) of the 1950 Act which deal with oaths, s. 12(4) of that Act which is concerned with the power to issue a subpoena, and s. 5 of the 1979 Act, which deals with default proceedings.

from alterations in the statutes, which may render previous decisions obsolete[3], the law of arbitration is not a field in which the value of a reported case is proportional to its age. Certainly so far as concerns commercial arbitrations, any nineteenth century decision or dictum should be approached with caution, and even comparatively recent authorities may be unreliable, in the light of changes in circumstances and practice[4].

Furthermore, when considering a reported case it is necessary always to bear in mind the type of arbitration with which it was concerned. Decisions and statements of principle which were perfectly valid at the time, and remain good law today, may nevertheless yield completely false results if applied in a different context. A commodity arbitration on quality and a formal reference pursuant to statutory powers are both examples of arbitration, but they are barely recognisable as the same process, and attempts to transfer principles from one to the other will inevitably lead to error.

B. STATUTE

1 Scope of the legislation

The Arbitration Acts 1950, 1975 and 1979 continue the piecemeal process of expansion, amendment and consolidation which began with the Arbitration Act 1889[5]. But the legislation only applies to arbitrations which derive from an 'arbitration agreement'[6] and this expression is defined in the various Acts in such a way as to exclude agreements which are not in writing. Thus an 'arbitration agreement' is defined in section 32 of the 1950 Act as:

'A written agreement to submit present or future differences to arbitration, whether an arbitrator is named therein or not'. This definition applies to the 1979 Act[7]. The 1975 Act contains a similar definition, viz.:

'An agreement in writing (including an agreement contained in an exchange of letters or telegrams) to submit to arbitration present or future differences capable of settlement by arbitration'[8].

Although the general import of these definitions is clear, certain points call for comment.

In the first place, there are the words 'written', and 'in writing'. It is, we

---

[3] Thus, for example, the statements in *CT Cogstad & Co v H Hewsum Sons & Co* [1921] 2 AC 528 as to the nature of a consultative case, require modification in the light of the power to make an interim award conferred for the first time by the Act of 1934. Failure to recognise this fact caused confusion in the earlier stages of *Fidelitas Shipping Co Ltd v V/O Exportchleb* [1966] 1 QB 630: see p. 371, post.

[4] See the warning given by McNair J in *Henry Bath & Son Ltd v Birgby Products* [1962] 1 Lloyd's Rep 389 at 399.

[5] For an account of the previous legislation relating to arbitration see Hogg, *The Law of Arbitration* (1936) pp. 3 et seq. It has been said that the 1950 Act is a technical statute, which provides for the ousting of the jurisdiction of the Court, so that accordingly the language of it has to be carefully observed: *Re Franklin and Swathling's Arbitration* [1929] 1 Ch 238 at 241. A more liberal approach, which is in accordance with the modern trend, was indicated by Singleton LJ in *Kiril Mischeff Ltd v British Doughnut Co Ltd* [1954] 1 Lloyd's Rep 237 at 246.

[6] *Imperial Metal Industries (Kynoch) Ltd v Amalgamated Union of Engineeering Workers (TASS)* [1979] ICR 23. See p. 51, ante.

[7] S. 7(1)(e) of the 1979 Act.

[8] S. 7(1) of the 1975 Act.

submit, quite clear that the agreement need not be set out in extenso in any written document. Provided that the reference is sufficiently clear to avoid uncertainty[9], all that is needed is a written direction to a place where the terms of the arbitration agreement can be found[10]. Equally clearly, the contract need not make a specific mention of arbitration at all, provided that it can be read together with another contract or document which contains an agreement to arbitrate.

It was at one time doubtful whether the words 'written' or 'in writing' involved a requirement that the agreement shall be signed[11]. But it is now settled that no signature is necessary provided there is a document or documents recognising the existence of an arbitration agreement between the parties[12], and numerous arbitrations have been conducted in accordance with the Act of 1950 without objection, notwithstanding that the contractual documents had not been signed[13].

In almost every case, a commercial arbitration will be based on an arbitration agreement in writing within the meaning of the Acts. There is, however, one situation where an arbitration may take place to which the Acts may not apply, namely where the jurisdiction of an arbitrator who has already been appointed is enlarged or confirmed by an informal submission. This can happen when an arbitrator, who is already seized of a dispute under a written agreement to arbitrate, is given jurisdiction to deal with other disputes by means of an informal ad hoc submission[14]. Less commonly, it can also occur where there is an issue as to the existence of the underlying contract, and hence of the arbitration agreement, and the arbitrator is given a special jurisdiction to determine this issue[15]. Such ad hoc submissions are often set out in writing, but this is not always so; and there may never be an explicit submission at all, since the enlargement of the arbitrator's jurisdiction may result simply from the conduct of the parties[16].

The problem of the informal ad hoc submission is not readily solved, but we believe that the Court will be reluctant to avoid a decision that part of an arbitration is conducted under the Acts and the remainder is not. We suggest that the most satisfactory solution is to regard a written agreement, orally varied, as still remaining a written agreement; so that the jurisdiction of the

---

[9] See p. 105, post.

[10] *Hattersley v Hatton* (1862) 3 F & F 116; *Morgan v William Harrison Ltd* [1907] 2 Ch 137; *Jager v Tolme and Runge and London Produce Clearing House Ltd* [1916] 1 KB 939 at 953; *Wyndham Rather Ltd v Eagle Star and British Dominions Insurance Co Ltd* (1925) 21 Ll L Rep 214 and *Excomm Ltd v Bamaodah, The St Raphael* [1985] 1 Lloyd's Rep 403, CA are amongst many examples. See also *The Al Faiha* [1981] 2 Lloyd's Rep 99 at 101.

[11] It was said, however, that the Court could if necessary compel a party to execute a signed submission, presumably on the grounds of an implied agreement to do so: *Baker v Yorkshire Fire and Life Assurance Co* [1892] 1 QB 144 at 146.

[12] *The St Raphael*, supra. All that is necessary is that there shall be evidence which satisfies the Court that the written terms of the arbitration agreement form part of the agreement between the parties. The assent to the written arbitration agreement may itself be oral, or inferred from the conduct of the parties: *Zambia Steel and Building Supplies Ltd v James Clark & Eaton Ltd* [1986] 2 Lloyd's Rep 225, CA.

[13] Such as arbitrations conducted under bills of lading not signed by the cargo-owner, and under contracts made by exchange of telex messages.

[14] See pp. 133–134, post.

[15] See p. 574, post.

[16] See p. 133, post.

arbitrator, as extended, may be regarded as founded on the original agreement to arbitrate[17].

2 Commencement of 1979 Act

The 1979 Act (including the amendments which it makes to the 1950 Act) only applies to arbitrations commenced on or after 1 August 1979, unless the parties to a reference commenced before that date have agreed in writing that the 1979 Act shall apply to that arbitration, in which case the Act applies to that arbitration from 1 August 1979 or the date of the agreement, whichever is the later[18]. Subsections (2) and (3) of section 29 of the 1950 Act apply to determine when an arbitration is deemed to be commenced for the purposes of the 1979 Act. These subsections are in all material respects the same as subsections (3) and (4) of section 34 of the Limitation Act 1980 which are discussed in a later chapter[19].

C. EXPRESS AGREEMENT

The parties to a commercial transaction frequently make express provision in their contract regarding the procedure which is to be followed. Many standard forms of contract contain not only an agreement to refer disputes to arbitration, but also elaborate provisions as to the way in which the arbitration is to be conducted.

Furthermore, even if the contract itself does not contain a procedural code, it is not uncommon for parties to enter into an agreement as to procedure after a dispute has arisen. This may occur either at or before the time when the arbitrator is appointed, or in the course of subsequent interlocutory proceedings[20].

Since arbitration is a consensual process, the parties should in principle be free to prescribe the rules by which the process is to be operated. The courts have recognised this, in numerous reported cases. There are, however, limits to the parties' power to prescribe their own rules of procedure.

In the first place, there are the limits imposed by the Acts. Not all of the provisions of the statutes are mandatory, and several sections yield to a contrary intention expressed in the arbitration agreement[1]. On the other hand, there are other provisions which the parties are not free to modify. Almost all of these are

---

[17] By analogy with the decisions on the Statute of Frauds. This solution will not, however, serve for the situation where the arbitrator never had jurisdiction at all, because there was no contract: see *Altco Ltd v Sutherland* [1971] 2 Lloyd's Rep 515, per Donaldson J at 519.

[18] Arbitration Act 1979 (Commencement) Order 1979 (S.I. 1979 No. 750): See Appendix 1.

[19] See post, p. 198.

[20] For the obligations of the arbitrator in relation to such a procedure, see p. 281, post.

[1] They are in the Act of 1950, ss. 1 (authority of arbitrator irrevocable except by leave of Court), 6 (reference to sole arbitrator), 7 (supplying of vacancies), 8 (umpire), 9 (amended by the Act of 1979) (three arbitrators), 10(2) (appointment by third party), 12(1), (2) and (3) (evidence on oath), 13 (time for award), 14 (power to make interim awards), 15 (power to order specific performance), 16 (awards to final), 17 (power to correct slips), 18 (costs in the discretion of the arbitrator), 20 (interest on awards).

concerned with the supervisory powers of the Court: including in particular the power to remit or set aside an award[2].

In addition to the limits imposed by statute, the power of the parties to agree upon their own procedure is also limited by considerations of public policy.   The only clear example of such a limitation relates to what is often called 'ouster of the jurisdiction of the Court'. This expression refers to the principle that a party cannot contract out of his right to enforce his rights by instituting proceedings in Court. An action commenced under a contract which contains an arbitration clause is neither irregular nor a nullity, although it may in appropriate circumstances be stayed with a view to arbitration[3]. No provision purporting to exclude a right to sue in Court will be recognised[4]. Nor can the Court's statutory powers of intervention be excluded by agreement, save in the case of a valid exclusion agreement under the 1979 Act[5]. Thus an agreement to exclude the Court's power under section 12 to order security for costs is invalid, although it may tell against the power being exercised[6]; and the parties cannot validly agree between themselves or with the arbitrator that reasons given off the face of the award shall not be shown to the Court in support of an application to set aside or remit the award[7].

This principle of 'ouster' derives from the insistence of the courts in maintaining control over their own procedural powers. It is probable, however, that this is not the only limitation on the right of the parties to fix their own procedure, and that the Court will if necessary intervene even when its own powers are not directly implicated. The courts have gone surprisingly far in recognising agreed procedural codes which differ radically from those of the ordinary legal process[8], but is it likely that in extreme cases the Court will conclude that the agreement is so contrary to fundamental principles that it must be treated as contrary to public policy, and invalid[9].

D. PRACTICE OF MERCHANTS AND ARBITRATORS

Many trades have developed their own, often idiosyncratic, ways of conducting arbitrations. The courts have shown themselves consistently willing, subject always to the dictates of natural justice, to recognise and sanction these individual practices[10], by implying a term in the arbitration agreement that the reference will be conducted in accordance with the practice usual in the trade[11]. It is submitted that this is the correct explanation for the recognition of such special procedures. Some authorities use the word 'custom', but this is misleading.

---

[2] They are: ss. 2; 3; 4(1); 5; 8(3); 9 (in its unamended form, as it applies to arbitrations not conducted under the Act of 1979), 10; 12(4), (5), (6); 18(3); 19 and 21 to 27.

[3] See Chapter 30, post.

[4] *Doleman & Sons v Osset Corpn* [1912] 3 KB 257.

[5] See pp. 631–635, post.

[6] See pp. 335–337, post.

[7] See pp. 562–563, post.

[8] See pp. 289–291, post.

[9] This topic is more fully discussed at pp. 283–286, post.

[10] See, for example, *E E and Brian Smith (1928) Ltd v Wheatsheaf Mills Ltd* (1939) 63 Ll L Rep 237, where the Court recognised a practice which greatly modified the application of the doctrine of res judicata.

[11] This topic is more fully discussed at pp. 286–288, post.

Custom is a species of localised law. The practices followed by the various trade tribunals are recognised by the courts, not because they are part of the law relating to that trade, but because the parties are taken to have agreed that their disputes shall be resolved according to the procedures usual in the trade.

Strictly, the usual trade practice should be proved by evidence. But certain aspects of commercial arbitration in particular trades have become so familiar to the courts that they will in effect take judicial notice of them: such as for example, the use of arbitrator/advocates, the absence of full discovery, and the omission of a hearing. The practices of individual trades have thus become gradually accommodated into the general framework of the law of arbitration.

CHAPTER 4

The applicable law and the jurisdiction of the court

A. INTRODUCTION

This book is concerned with the English law of arbitration, as applied in the courts of England and Wales. In many cases it is necessary to look no further than English law in order to ascertain the nature of the legal relationships which arise out of an arbitration agreement, or to decide the merits of the dispute between the parties. But this is not always so. Commercial arbitration in England has long had an important international element, and in recent years this has been much accentuated. Increasingly it has become necessary to take account of the international character of many commercial arbitrations, not simply because so many of the parties to such arbitrations come from the wider international community, but also because commercial arbitration tends more and more to require arbitrators, the Courts, and even the legislature to look at the practice of commercial arbitration against the perspective of a broader international horizon.

In this Chapter we consider the various ways in which an arbitration may come to be regulated by a foreign[1] system of law. We begin by describing the circumstances in which various aspects of an arbitration may come to be governed by a system of law other than the law of the country in which the arbitration is held. It has long been recognised that the parties to a contract may choose to subject the substance of their relationship to a law other than the law of the place where the arbitration is held. More recently it has come to be recognised that a similar choice exists in respect of the legal incidents arising out of the agreement to arbitrate, in respect of the relationship which arises when a particular dispute is referred to arbitration, and in respect of the procedure to be followed during the reference[2]. These different aspects of the arbitration may, in theory at least, be governed by different systems of law.

At the same time as considering these topics, we also discuss the extent to which English law affords recognition to a choice of procedural law unconnected with any particular system of national law, or to an arbitration agreement which allows the arbitrator to decide the merits of the dispute in accordance with universal legal principles, rather than principles derived from the legal

---

[1] It is difficult to know how to avoid this somewhat parochial expression. 'International' is a possible substitute, but not wholly accurate, since from the perspective of English law, 'foreign' does not mean 'not of the United Kingdom' nor 'not British' but 'not English'. For the English courts, foreign law includes not only the law of other states, but the law of Scotland, Northern Ireland, the Isle of Man and the Channel Islands.

[2] *James Miller & Partners Ltd v Whitworth Street Estates (Manchester) Ltd* [1970] 1 Lloyd's Rep 269, [1970] AC 583; and see also per Lord Diplock in *Compagnie d'Armement Maritime SA v Cie Tunisienne de Navigation SA* [1970] 2 Lloyd's Rep 99 at 116.

system of any one state, or without reference to any legal principles and in accordance with some broader principle of equity or conscience.

Where the merits of the dispute are governed by English law, it may sometimes be necessary to look beyond the domestic principles of English law to the law of the European Communities: the way in which Community law touches the law of arbitration is here briefly discussed.

Lastly, we consider the circumstances in which the English courts will assume jurisdiction over arbitrations containing some foreign element.

B.   LAWS GOVERNING THE ARBITRATION

1. Introduction

An agreed reference to arbitration involves two groups of obligations. The first concerns the mutual obligations of the parties to submit future disputes, or an existing dispute to arbitration, and to abide by the award of a tribunal constituted in accordance with the agreement. It is now firmly established[3] that the arbitration agreement which creates these obligations is a separate contract, distinct from the substantive agreement in which it is usually embedded, capable of surviving the termination of the substantive agreement and susceptible of premature termination by express or implied consent, or by repudiation or frustration, in much the same manner as in more ordinary forms of contract. Since this agreement has a distinct life of its own, it may in principle be governed by a proper law of its own, which need not be the same as the law governing the substantive contract.

The second group of obligations, consisting of what is generally referred to as the 'curial law' of the arbitration, concerns the manner in which the parties and the arbitrator are required to conduct the reference of a particular dispute. According to the English theory of arbitration, these rules are to be ascertained by reference to the express or implied terms of the agreement to arbitrate. This being so, it will be found in the great majority of cases that the curial law, i.e. the law governing the conduct of the reference, is the same as the law governing the obligation to arbitrate. It is, however, open to the parties to submit, expressly or by implication, the conduct of the reference to a different law from the one governing the underlying arbitration agreement. In such a case, the court looks first at the arbitration agreement to see whether the dispute is one which should be arbitrated, and which has validly been made the subject of the reference; it then looks to the curial law to see how that reference should be conducted; and then returns to the first law in order to give effect to the resulting award.

The possibility that the different aspects of the arbitral relationship may be governed by different laws will also exist where the arbitration is conducted in a country other than the one whose laws govern the agreement to arbitrate. Here, the *lex fori* may be relevant not only because the choice of country A as the location of the reference may justify the inference that the parties wish the law of country A to govern the conduct of the dispute, but also because the law

---

[3] *Bremer Vulkan Schiffbau und Maschinenfabrik v South India Shipping Corpn* [1981] 1 Lloyd's Rep 253, [1981] 2 WLR 141, carrying through an analysis which was first developed in *Heyman v Darwins Ltd* [1942] AC 356. See pp. 110–111, post.

of that country may have imperative provisions which the courts will apply to the reference, irrespective of any choice by the parties as to the law governing the contract or the rules which are to be followed.

It may therefore be seen that problems arising out of an arbitration may, at least in theory, call for the application of any one or more of the following laws —

1 The proper law of the contract, i.e. the law governing the contract which creates the substantive rights of the parties, in respect of which the dispute has arisen.

2 The proper law of the arbitration agreement, i.e. the law governing the obligation of the parties to submit the disputes to arbitration, and to honour an award.

3 The curial law, i.e. the law governing the conduct of the individual reference.

Unfortunately, even this analysis appears to be an over-simplification. It is now established that when a dispute arises within the scope of an agreement to arbitrate future disputes, and when that agreement is put into effect by the giving of a notice of arbitration, a new set of contractual relationships comes into existence, requiring the parties to arbitrate the individual dispute. Although this obligation springs from the continuous agreement to arbitrate future disputes, it is distinct from it, at least in the sense that events which terminate one group of relationships do not necessarily terminate the other[4]. Thus, the question — 'Has something happened which means that the parties are no longer obliged to submit *any* of their disputes to arbitration?' is to be answered by reference to different contractual terms from those which govern the question — 'Has something happened which means that the parties are no longer obliged to submit *this* dispute to *this* reference?'. Since the questions are different, it would appear to follow that in theory they may have to be answered by reference to different laws. Thus, in order to give a full account of the position, one must add to the list —

4 The proper law of the reference, i.e. the law governing the contract which regulates the individual reference to arbitration[5].

In practice, it is scarcely conceivable that a situation will arise in which the Court or arbitrator may have to consider four different laws at the same time. Laws 2, 3 and 4 will almost always be the same; and if there is, in a rare instance, any divergence between them, laws 2 and 4 will very rarely be found to differ[6].

---

[4] See per Lord Diplock in the *Bremer Vulkan* case, supra.

[5] A discussion on these lines was attempted in *Black Clawson International Ltd v Papierwerk Waldhof-Aschaffenburg AG* [1981] 2 Lloyd's Rep 446. The result is not attractive. The need for such a laboured analysis may suggest that either the *Black Clawson* case, or *Miller v Whitworth Street Estates*, or both, have been misunderstood. Still further elaboration may be required, since the curial law may on occasion represent the outcome of a collision between two laws: the law whose choice is the logical result of applying the English theories of arbitration, and the imperative rules of the *lex fori*. Enthusiasts may care to note the opportunities for *renvoi* and similar complications, if the application of the English idea of a severable contract to arbitrate leads to the choice of a law which has a different theory of arbitration. We think it best to leave these problems to more specialised works.

[6] Moreover, so far as we can see, the only occasion on which the proper law of the reference will come into play is where it is suggested that the agreement to refer the individual dispute has come to an end leaving intact the continuous agreement to refer future disputes—as was argued in the *Black Clawson* case, ante. (Perhaps questions relating to the validity and enforcement of the award are also referable to this law. It seems more likely, however, that they belong to the proper law of the arbitration agreement, which contains the original promise to honour the award.)

When the court is faced with a problem in this field, questions of classification will have to be considered: for the court cannot identify the relevant law, without first asking whether it is looking for law 2, 3 or 4. It is unnecessary to take up space with a full discussion of this problem[7], but a classification on the following lines would seem to be indicated —

1   The proper law of the arbitration agreement governs the validity of the arbitration agreement[8], the question whether a dispute lies within the scope of the arbitration agreement[9]; the validity of the notice of arbitration; the constitution of the tribunal[10]; the question whether an award lies within the jurisdiction of the arbitrator; the formal validity of the award; the question whether the parties have been discharged from any obligation to arbitrate future disputes.

2   The curial law governs: the manner in which the reference is to be conducted; the procedural powers and duties of the arbitrator; questions of evidence; the determination of the proper law of the contract.

3   The proper law of the reference governs: the question whether the parties have been discharged from their obligation to continue with the reference of the individual dispute.

2   The proper law of the arbitration agreement

The proper law of the arbitration agreement is determined in accordance with the same principles as apply for the determination of the proper law of any ordinary contract[11].

1   The first step is to inquire whether the parties have expressly chosen the law which is to apply to the agreement. If so, this choice of law will prevail, even if the chosen law differs from: (a) the proper law of the underlying contract or (b) the curial law[12].

---

7   Chapter 16 of Dicey & Morris, *The Conflict of Laws* (11th edn) contains a most valuable discussion of the conflicts of laws regarding arbitration. The classification proceeds on rather different lines, but in respect of the individual problems discussed it arrives at conclusions with which in general we would venture to agree.

8   See s. 5(2)(b) of the Arbitration Act 1975, s. 37(1)(a) of the Arbitration Act 1950; *Norske Atlas Insurance Co Ltd v London General Insurance Co Ltd (1927) 28 Ll L Rep 104; Dallal v Bank Mellat* [1986] QB 441.

9   See s. 5(2)(d) of the Arbitration Act 1975, and s. 37(2)(b) of the Arbitration Act 1950. This includes the question whether the arbitrator can rule on the validity of the arbitration agreement: *Dalmia Dairy Industries Ltd v National Bank of Pakistan* [1978] 2 Lloyd's Rep 223.

10   Including the question whether the Court has power under s. 27 of the 1950 Act to extend the time for appointing the tribunal: *International Tank and Pipe SAK v Kuwait Aviation Fuelling Co KSC* [1975] 1 Lloyd's Rep 8 [1975] QB 224. Lord Denning suggested in this case that the reason for this was that s. 27 was in effect an additional statutory term of the agreement. However, the 1950 Act treats as implied terms of the agreement many rules (e.g. as to examination of witnesses) which are plainly governed by the curial law. See also *Bankers and Shippers Insurance Co of New York v Liverpool Marine and General Insurance Co Ltd* (1925) 24 Ll L Rep 85 where, however, the proper law of the arbitration agreement and the curial law were the same; *Gola Sports Ltd v General Sportcraft Co Ltd* [1982] Com LR 51; *Gort of Swaziland Central Transport Administration and Alfko Aussenhandels GmbH v Leila Maritime Co Ltd, The Leila* [1985] 2 Lloyd's Rep 172, 177.

11   See pp. 71–74, post for a discussion of the principles involved.

12   *Hamlyn & Co v Talisker Distillery* [1894] AC 202. See Dicey and Morris *Conflict of Laws* (8th edn) p. 1047, cited with approval by Viscount Dilhorne and Lord Wilberforce in *James Miller and Partners Ltd v Whitworth Street Estates (Manchester) Ltd* [1970] 1 Lloyd's Rep 269, [1970] AC 583. It must be unusual for an arbitration clause in a contract to stipulate for a choice of law which is to apply to the clause and nothing else. No doubt the learned authors had in mind cases in which the arbitration agreement is contained in a separate document, independent of the underlying contract.

2 Where there is no express choice of law, it is necessary to consider whether there is an implied choice of law, in which case the arbitration agreement will be governed by the law impliedly chosen by the parties.

3 If there is no express or implied choice of law, the arbitration agreement will be governed by the law with which the agreement has its closest and most real connection.

Stages 2 and 3 tend to involve exactly the same factual enquiry, and as a result the distinction between the two stages, although sound in theory, is frequently of little practical importance.

The starting point is to determine the proper law of the contract in which the arbitration is embodied. As a general rule the arbitration agreement will be governed by the same law, since it is part of the substance of the underlying contract[13]. But this is not an absolute rule[14], since other factors may point clearly to some other system of law. Thus if the arbitration is to be held in the territory of a state which is a party to the New York Convention on the Recognition and Enforcement of Awards, section 5(2)(b) of the Arbitration Act 1975 appears to give rise to a rebuttable presumption that the law governing the validity of the arbitration agreement is the law where the award is to be made[15]. The presumption would we submit readily be rebutted in favour of the proper law of the underlying contract[16].

If the choice lies between two systems of law, under one of which the arbitration agreement would be invalid, this is a factor in favour of choosing the other[17].

3 The proper law of the reference

The possibility that the law governing the contractual relationship between the parties arising out of the reference of a particular dispute to arbitration may differ from the law governing their obligation to refer disputes to arbitration is discussed above[18]. Although it is possible to envisage circumstances where the parties might expressly choose two different laws to govern the different aspects of their relationship, such an agreement would be extremely unusual. In the absence of an express choice of the proper law of the individual reference, we submit that the ordinary inference would be that the parties intended individual

---

[13] *Hamlyn & Co v Talisker Distillery*, supra. See also *National Gypsum Co Inc v Northern Sales Ltd* [1963] 2 Lloyd's Rep 499.

[14] See the *Black Clawson* case, ante, at p. 455.

[15] The section provides that enforcement of a Convention award may be refused if 'the arbitration agreement was not valid under the law to which the parties subjected it or, failing any indication thereon, under the law of the country where the award was made'. This is intended to operate as a choice of law rule for Convention awards: there are, however, difficulties of a practical and theoretical nature in applying the rule where the agreement does not indicate where the award is to be made. Until this question has been resolved, it cannot be said whether or not the arbitration will result in a Convention award. But it may not be possible to resolve the question without first determining the proper law of the arbitration agreement. The problem is circular: there seems to be no solution which does not involve a *petitio principii.*

[16] See *Cia Maritima Zorroza SA v Sesostris SAE, The Marques de Bolarque* [1984] 1 Lloyd's Rep 652, where it was conceded that the proper law was that of the underlying contract (Spanish) although the arbitration was to be held in London. Cf. *Dallal v Bank Mellat* [1986] QB 441 where an agreement to refer an existing dispute was held to be governed by the law of the seat of arbitration.

[17] *Hamlyn & Co v Talisker Distillery*, ante, at 208.

[18] See pp. 60–62, ante.

references to be governed by the same law that governed the agreement to arbitrate under which the reference is to take place.

4 The curial law

(a) Determining the curial law

The choice of curial law may be made expressly[19], and such a choice is effective, even though the law chosen is neither the proper law of the arbitration agreement nor the law of the country where the arbitration is to take place. An express choice of curial law different from that of the proper law of the arbitration agreement is not particularly unusual and does not give rise to any particular problems. An express choice of curial law different from the law of the country in which the arbitration is to be held is however almost unknown. This is no doubt because of the formidable conceptual and practical problems which are likely to arise should it be necessary to invoke the powers of a court in relation to the reference[20]. Which court or courts has jurisdiction? If the local court has jurisdiction, how is it to regulate an arbitral procedure which is unfamiliar to it and possibly based on quite different procedural concepts? If the courts of the curial law have jurisdiction, how in practice is it to be effectively exercised over an arbitration outside its territory?[1]

In the absence of express agreement, there is a strong prima facie presumption that the parties intend the curial law to be the law of the 'seat'[2] of the arbitration[3], i.e. the place at which the arbitration is to be conducted, on the ground that that is the country most closely connected with the proceedings[4]. So in order to determine the curial law in the absence of an express choice by the parties it is first necessary to determine the seat of the arbitration, by construing the agreement to arbitrate.

Not infrequently the choice of seat is made expressly, and even when this is not so the choice of seat may be inferred without difficulty from other factors, such as the fact that the parties have chosen a set of arbitration rules associated with a particular country or place. The reported cases give little guidance on the principles to be applied in more doubtful cases. Many factors will come into

---

[19] For this purpose, it is not enough to stipulate that the Arbitration Act 1950 will apply, for this has been held to be only an indication that the arbitration agreement is one which gives rise to a compulsory stay of an action brought in the English Court. *Radio Publicity (Universal) Ltd v Compagnie Luxembourgeoise de Radiodifusion* [1936] 2 All ER 721; the *Black Clawson* case, ante.

[20] See *Naviera Amazonica Peruana SA v Compania Internacional de Seguros del Peru* [1988] 1 Lloyd's Rep 116, at 120.

[1] These questions are discussed at pp. 86–92, post. There may be other practical problems: see per Hobhouse J in *The Marques de Bolarque*, supra, at 655.

[2] This expression is interchangeable in this context with 'locus arbitri' or 'forum'. Apart from the fact that it is an English and not a Latin word, it has the merit that it is unlikely to give rise to misunderstanding by being used in contexts where it means something different.

[3] There is a similar presumption with regard to the proper law of the underlying contract: see post, pp. 71–74. This may in turn have a bearing on the proper law of the arbitration agreement: see pp. 62–63, ante.

[4] The possibility that the presumption may be rebutted by something short of an express choice of another law is left open by the formulation approved in the *Miller v Whitworth Streets Estates* case: see per Kerr LJ in *Naviera Amazonica Peruana SA v Compania Internacional de Seguros del Peru* [1988] 1 Lloyd's Rep 116, 119. However, in *Bank Mellat v Helleniki Techniki SA* [1984] QB 291 at 301, Kerr LJ described the rule as a 'fundamental principle . . . in the absence of any contractual provision to the contrary.' A powerful argument in favour of the view that the curial law should always be that of the forum was developed by Dr F A Mann in [1969] ICLQ 997.

play, such as the proper law of the arbitration agreement[5], the nationality of the parties, the practices of a particular trade, and in cases involving state parties or nationalised corporations the probability that the parties would have chosen a neutral seat of arbitration unconnected with either of them if they had thought to deal with the matter expressly.

A choice of curial law may be made at the outset, before any dispute arises, the choice being expressed in the arbitration agreement itself or inferred from the choice of seat or from the other terms and circumstances of the transaction[6]. It is, however, also possible for the parties to make a choice of curial law after the dispute has arisen[7]. One way in which this may happen is by changing the seat of the arbitration. Here, however, a distinction must be drawn between the seat of the arbitration and the place or places at which it is geographically convenient to hold meetings or even the hearing itself. Thus the parties may expressly agree upon arbitration in one country but find it convenient to hold some or even the whole of the hearing in another, perhaps for the convenience of witnesses, or for the convenience of the participants. This will not of itself lead to the inference that the parties intend to change the seat of the arbitration, particularly as such a change may well entrain unforeseen implications with regard to the procedure to be followed, and the identity of the courts having jurisdiction over the reference[8].

(b) Foreign curial law and English public policy

Thus far the discussion of the choice of a foreign curial law has proceeded on the basis of the broad proposition that it is legitimate for the parties to choose such a curial law despite the fact that the arbitration is to take place in England or that the proper law of the arbitration and of the reference is English law. We now move on to consider whether there are any limits to this broad proposition: in other words, whether there may not come a point where the English court will refuse to allow a choice of curial law which involves a fundamental departure from English procedural norms.

Such a collision between English law and the foreign curial law may in practice give rise to a problem in two different situations. Where the arbitration is proceeding in England, the problem will present itself in the guise of an application to the Court to intervene during or after the reference by one of the range of procedures available to correct serious procedural irregularities. Where the arbitration takes place abroad, the problem is most likely to present itself in the guise of a defence to proceedings for enforcement[9]. In either case the party challenging the validity of the procedure will have to resort to some concept of

---

[5] See per Lord Wilberforce in the *Miller v Whitworth Estates* case, supra, at 616.

[6] *James Miller & Partners Ltd v Whitworth Street Estates (Manchester) Ltd*, ante.

[7] The 'actings' of the parties subsequent to the contract can be used to determine the choice of curial law, but not that of the proper law: *Miller v Whitworth Street Estates (Manchester) Ltd*, supra. Probably the situation in this case was that the Court was not concerned with an *initial* choice of the proper law, but with a possible *change* in the curial law, to be inferred from the conduct of the parties.

[8] *Naviera Amazonica Peruana SA v Compania Internacional de Seguros del Peru*, supra, at 120–121, citing with approval Redfern and Hunter, *The Law and Practice of Commercial Arbitration*, p. 69.

[9] The possibility of intervention in an arbitration abroad is discussed at pp. 90–91, post.

English public policy as a source of procedural norms which cannot be ousted by agreement between the parties to an arbitration.

That the English court would in principle reserve to itself the right to inhibit the employment of repugnant procedures, or to refuse to recognise such procedures as giving rise to an arbitration or an enforceable award, seems to us not open to doubt. But at what point would the English court draw the line? There appear to be a number of possibilities.

First, it might be said that the Arbitration Acts provide an answer. We believe that this is not an acceptable solution. The Acts have virtually nothing to say about procedures in an arbitration, as distinct from the remedies which are available to the court in cases where the proper procedure has not been followed, or where the arbitration is for some reason breaking down. The Acts are not a source of *ordre publique*.

Nor in our view is it satisfactory to look for procedures which are invariably followed when arbitrations are conducted in England, and to say that these are so deeply embedded in the English law of arbitration, that an English court could not allow them to be infringed. A procedure which involves, for example, the hearing of evidence from one party in the absence of another is objectionable under English law, not because it infringes some fundamental norm of English arbitration law, applied without discrimination to all arbitrations taking place within the territorial jurisdiction of the English court, but because the common law conceives it to be an implied term of all contracts to arbitrate in accordance with English law that the proceedings should take place in the presence of both parties. It does not follow that the same principle applies, where the parties have chosen to carry on within the jurisdiction an arbitration which is not subject to English law.

In these circumstances it seems to us that one must tackle the question by asking whether there are any rules of procedure which the parties cannot validly exclude by express agreement, in relation to an arbitration conducted under English law. If there are such rules, then the English court would insist upon them where a foreign procedural law is applied: for an exclusion of specific terms which is not permitted by English law, cannot be permissible simply because it is effected through a general reference of the entire arbitral code to the law of the foreign country. We discuss this rather difficult question elsewhere[10]. It is sufficient for present purposes to say that the occasions on which English notions of *ordre publique* impinge upon procedures in an English arbitration conducted according to a foreign curial law are likely to be very few indeed.

(c) 'Transnational' procedural law

The question has been much debated by learned writers and in the jurisprudence of other systems of law whether a situation may exist in which there is no curial law, in the sense that the rules of procedure governing the arbitration are to be derived from a 'transnational' source, owing no allegiance to any municipal

---

[10] See pp. 283–286, post.

system of law[11]. Two benefits are perceived as flowing from the recognition of such a source of procedural rules.

First, the arbitrator would not be fettered by the procedural norms of any particular system of law, but would be free to give effect to the procedure chosen by the parties and to make good any deficiencies in the rules which they have expressly chosen by reference to transnational concepts[12]. In view of the benevolence shown by English law to a wide variety of procedures differing from one another and from the procedure adopted by the superior courts and its readiness to recognise awards made with the minimum of formality, this aspect of the transnational concept would appear to be of relatively little practical importance in relation to arbitrations conducted in England[13].

Second, by freeing the curial law from allegiance to any system of municipal law, it is supposed that the transnational concept would put it beyond the jurisdiction of any national court to intervene[14], to correct what it considers unacceptable procedures[15]. This aspect of the transnational theory has not been accepted, at least not to its fullest extent, by the English courts[16]. The general rule is that the jurisdiction of the English courts cannot be ousted by agreement between the parties. In this sense the transnational concept is not part of English law[17]. If the procedure adopted by the parties retains the features which in English law characterise it as an arbitration, the Court retains jurisdiction over it[18]. It does not follow, however, that the jurisdiction will be exercised. Thus the fact that the parties have purported to exclude the Court's jurisdiction to grant

---

[11] For a select bibliography of the literature on the subject, see Dicey and Morris, *Conflict of Laws* (11th edn) p. 542.

[12] Cf Article 10 of the Rules of Arbitration of the International Chamber of Commerce: 'The rules governing the proceedings before the arbitrator shall be those resulting from these Rules, and where these Rules are silent, any rules which the parties, (or, failing them, the arbitrator) may settle, and whether or not reference is thereby made to a municipal procedural law to be applied to the arbitration.'

[13] It may however be relevant to the recognition of foreign judgments relating to arbitration: see pp. 424–426, post.

[14] The mischief perceived by the proponents of the transnational concept is, we believe, that the existence of the jurisdiction invites unwarranted applications to the court to intervene. We doubt whether this is so in England. Applications to set aside or remit awards occur in a tiny proportion of the total number of references. An even smaller proportion succeed, and only when intervention is necessary to correct genuine procedural injustice. The fact that a number of such cases are regularly reported reflects the scale on which commercial arbitration is conducted in England, rather than a mischief requiring correction.

[15] But without, it seems, putting the arbitration beyond those powers of the court which are regarded as benevolent, such as staying proceedings brought in breach of the arbitration agreement, appointing arbitrators when the agreed machinery breaks down, and enforcing the award.

[16] Similarly the court has rejected the possibility of a proper law of the arbitration agreement unrelated to any system of municipal law: *Dallal v Bank Mellat* [1986] QB 441.

[17] *Bank Mellat v Helleniki Techniki SA* [1984] QB 291, per Kerr LJ at 301: '... our jurisprudence does not recognise the concept of arbitral procedures floating in the transnational firmament, unconnected with any municipal system of law'. Despite this, the English courts recognise that the jurisdiction which they possess has to be exercised with a proper regard for the transnational character of certain types of arbitration, as the actual decision in the case demonstrates (no security for costs ordered in an arbitration under the Rules of the ICC).

[18] If it does not retain those features it does not necessarily follow that it may not be recognised by the courts as giving rise to legal obligations which can be recognised and enforced, e.g. as a valuation or compromise or as the judgment of a competent foreign tribunal: e.g. *Dallal v Bank Mellat* [1986] QB 441 (Iranian claims tribunal): see p. 43, ante. But the powers of the courts to control and give effect to the procedure will be different from those available in an arbitration.

a particular kind of relief, whether expressly or by implication from the nature of the arbitral procedure which they have chosen, is a factor which may well lead the Court, in the exercise of its discretion, not to grant that remedy in the particular case[19]. Moreover the jurisdiction will not ordinarily be exercised so as to intervene in the conduct of references outside the territorial jurisdiction of the Court, i.e. outside England and Wales, nor in references conducted within the jurisdiction under the curial law of another country[20].

C.   THE LAW APPLICABLE TO THE MERITS

The international nature of many commercial transactions makes it inevitable that from time to time an arbitrator will be called upon to consider whether he should determine the rights and liabilities of the parties according to some law other than English law. But, if any question of foreign law does arise, the arbitrator should not attempt to solve it unassisted. He can reasonably expect full legal argument on the choice of the law; and the parties are obliged to tender expert evidence on the content of the chosen law. This being so, there would be no point in attempting here a full discussion of the branch of learning known as conflict of laws. It may, however, be helpful to indicate in outline some of the questions which may arise, of which the following are involved in a determination of the law governing the rights and liabilities of the parties—

1   Which law governs the substantive rights of the parties under the contract: i.e. what is the 'proper law' of the contract?

2   Which particular aspects of the dispute are to be governed by the proper law, and which of them must be determined by the procedural law of the arbitration?

3   What are the relevant provisions of the proper law?

1 The duty to apply the law

Any enquiry into these questions should logically begin by addressing the question whether an award ought in principle to conform with English law[1], in the absence of some express provision to the contrary. The question itself raises certain conceptual problems. In the first place, it is essentially circular in form. If one starts with the idea that an award ought to conform with the law, then some means should be devised to ensure that it does so[2]. If on the other hand attention is first paid to the remedy, and it is found that none exists, then the proposition that the award should be in accordance with law is devoid of any

---

[19] *Bank Mellat v Helleniki Techniki SA*, supra, and p. 89–92, post.

[20] This topic is discussed in more detail later in this Chapter, at pp. 86–92, post.

[1] For the purpose of the discussion, it is assumed that, if there is a duty to apply any law at all, the application of the English rules of private international law results in English law being the proper law of the contract. Any discussion of the duty to apply a foreign system of law would have to start from the proposition that in England foreign law is regarded is a question of fact, albeit of a rather special kind.

[2] The question of possible remedies otherwise than by way of appeal is discussed in Chapter 37.

practical meaning[3]. Second, the answer to the question depends in some degree upon the way in which it is stated. Thus, it may be asked either—

1 Does the arbitrator have a mandate to bind the parties by an award which is not in accordance with the law? or

2 Does the arbitrator have a duty to apply the law when making his award? The answer to these two questions is not necessarily the same[4].

Nevertheless, whether the question is circular or not, one must start somewhere, and a sensible point at which to begin is to see whether there are grounds for saying that an award ought in principle to comply with English law. If the matter is approached in terms of the contractual relationships between the two parties and the arbitrator, there can be little doubt that an affirmative answer is required. By their contract, the parties have agreed that their substantive rights shall be governed by English law. By their arbitration agreement, they have agreed that a dispute about these rights shall be determined by arbitration. By the mandate to the arbitrator, they have instructed him to decide upon their rights. Logically, it must follow that his task is to ascertain those rights in accordance with English law.

Authority for this proposition is rather difficult to supply. This is not surprising. For about 175 years, before the legislation of 1979, the courts had worked out a balance between the interests of finality in the arbitral process, and the desire to ensure that there were no jurisdictions which claimed to draw strength from the law, and yet escaped entirely from its requirements. This balance, essentially pragmatic in nature, took effect as follows—

1 The substantive aspects of the award could be brought into line with the principles of law, if the arbitrator could be detected in error.

2 For this purpose, the error had to be apparent from the terms of the award, or of the documents incorporated into it. In practice, the error could be demonstrated only in two cases: if the arbitrator spontaneously exposed his reasons on the face of the award, or if he was compelled to do so by the mechanism, originally contractual but ultimately mandatory, of the special case.

The very existence of this limited power of control presupposed that the proper exercise of the mandate involved compliance with the law: for if he could please himself what law he applied, or did not apply, there could never be an error of law which called for correction. The courts very rarely, however, found it necessary to say this. Either the admissible material led to the detection of an error, or it did not. If it did, then the courts proceeded straight to a remedy. If it did not, then no question could arise. Nevertheless, one can find scattered over the decades a few isolated statements to the effect that the arbitrator is

---

[3] A striking example of the circular nature of the problem can be seen in *Eagle Star Insurance Co Ltd v Yuval Insurance Co Ltd* [1978] 1 Lloyd's Rep 357 at 362, where the reasoning proceeds from authorities supporting the premise that it is bad policy for the courts to intervene for error, to the conclusion that a contractual provision can validly oust the requirement to decide in accordance with law.

[4] The answer to the first may be—'No, the arbitrator has no power to bind the parties by such an award'. This is perfectly consistent with an answer to the second question such as—'No, the only duty is to take reasonable care, or to do his best, to follow the law'.

indeed obliged[5] to apply the law[6], and during the years between 1800 and 1979 there are few indications that the existence of such a duty was ever seriously doubted[7].

There was, however, one apparent exception to this principle, namely that the arbitrator has never in recent years been conceived to have a duty of following the legal rules of procedure. This is not surprising, for the duties come from quite different sources. The obligation to follow the law, or the limited extent of the arbitrator's mandate, or however else one expresses the idea that the award should conform with the law, comes from the fact that the arbitrator's function is to decide the rights created by the substantive contract. The procedural powers of the arbitrator, on the other hand, are derived from the agreement to arbitrate, not the substantive agreement; and although the arbitration agreement may expressly or by implication call for compliance with legal procedural norms, equally well it may not. The matter is one of construction, which has nothing to do with the obligations and powers which belong to the arbitrator at the moment when he comes to make his decision[8].

Returning to matters of substantive law, it must next be considered whether the 1979 Act, by abolishing the two existing mandatory methods of judicial review and creating another, which is subject in some instances to exclusion by consent, has carried away the previous obligation to comply with the law, thereby giving the arbitrator a power to bind the parties by his own ideas of what appears just. It is, we suggest, quite clear that the enactment of the legislation cannot in itself have had this effect. No trace of an intention to bring about this fundamental change can be seen in the words of the Act, or in those preliminary works which are publicly available. Moreover, quite apart from what the legislature may or may not have intended, a release of the arbitrator from his duty to follow the law is not a necessary implication from the change in the law relating to judicial control over arbitrators. The power of control has not been abolished. On the contrary, it has been expressly preserved in an altered form, subject only to the right in certain cases to exclude the power by consent. It would seem an absurd consequence to say that the absence or presence of a duty to follow the law depends upon whether the substantive

---

[5] There are two qualifications to this principle. First, the parties are free to choose that their dispute shall be decided according to the substantive law of a foreign country: or indeed by a mixture of foreign laws. Second, the arbitrator is entitled, and indeed bound, to recognise such contractual modifications of the parties' prima facie rights and duties as would be recognised in courts of law: so that the parties have considerable latitude to modify their legal position whilst still acting within the framework of the law.

[6] For example, *Jager v Tolme and Runge and London Produce Clearing House Ltd* [1916] 1 KB 939, at 953, 957 and 961, CA; *Re Astley and Tyldesley Coal and Salt Co and Tyldesley Coal Co* (1899) 68 LJ QB 252; *Cottage Club Estates Ltd v Woodside Estate Co (Amersham) Ltd* (1927) 44 TLR 20 at 21; *Ramdutt Ramkissen Das v ED Sassoon & Co* (1929) 98 LJPC 58; *Naamlooze Vennootschap Handels en Transport Maatschappij Vulcaan v J Ludwig Mowinckels Rederi A/S* (1938) 60 Lloyd's Rep 217, 43 Com Cas 252, PC; *Board of Trade v Cayzer, Irvine & Co Ltd* [1927] AC 610 at 614, 628–629, HL; *Tehno-Impex v Gebr Van Weelde Scheepvaartkantoor BV* [1981] 1 Ll L Rep 587 at 59, CA; *President of India v La Pintada Compania Navigacion* [1985] AC 104 at 119.

[7] Before the end of the nineteenth century, one can find decisions, of which *Knox v Symmonds* (1791) 1 Ves 369 is an example, to the effect that an arbitrator need not apply the law where it produces a harsh result. But this line of authority was never followed up.

[8] Although the distinction between substantive and procedural law is often difficult to draw in practice, the fact that there is a difference is so well recognised that it is unnecessary to cite authority. The *Tehno-Impex* case provides a recent example.

contract is or is not one which, according to section 3(1) of the 1979 Act, may contain a valid exclusion agreement.

Rather more persuasive is the argument that when the parties in fact make an exclusion agreement they demonstrate an intention to displace the inferences which have hitherto been made as to the arbitrator's duties and the extent of his mandate[9]. The problem is not capable of discussion at length. We can only say that we see no basis for such an implication, particularly in the case where the contract contains an express choice of law. If the contract expressly states that the obligations which it creates shall be those determined by English law, and that in case of dispute those rights shall be ascertained by the arbitrator, the Court should not imply a term that the arbitrator should when making his ascertainment be at liberty to determine them by some other law, or no law at all.

2 The proper law of the contract

(a) The choice of proper law

In many of the standard forms of contract the parties expressly state their choice of the law which is to govern their rights and obligations. In such a case, it is the duty of the arbitrator to respect the choice, and to apply the provisions of the law in question, if and to the extent that the parties allege and prove them to be different from those of English law.

Where the contract contains no express choice of a proper law, the arbitrator must try to find out what law the parties intended to be applied: their intention must be inferred objectively, from the terms of the contract and the circumstances of the transaction. Various criteria have been suggested for the ascertainment of the proper law[10]. The test which probably represents the law as it now stands requires the tribunal to identify the system of law with which the transaction has its closest and most real connection[11]. Whilst this test is easy to understand and to state, it is often far from simple to apply. In essence, the process involves the identification and weighing-up of the various national characteristics of the contract. If there is an English arbitration clause, this carries great weight[12]. The arbitrator must also consider the nationality of the parties; the place where

---

[9] The argument that the making of an exclusion agreement impliedly relieves an arbitrator from the duty to follow the law takes as its starting point the assumption that an express agreement to this effect would be effective, and yet would leave the arbitration contract still enforceable, and the proceedings conducted by the chosen tribunal still an arbitration. (Whatever else may be said about the aims of the 1979 Act, it quite clearly contemplates that proceedings under a contract containing an exclusion agreement will be an arbitration, and an arbitration within the 1950 Act). The correctness of this assumption is by no means obvious: see pp. 83–85 post. The argument is particularly difficult to sustain if the only legitimate express provision is one which permits deviations only where the law is 'strict' or 'technical': an implied licence to this effect seems wholly unconvincing.

[10] The law stated in the text is a summary of the rules of English private international law, and assumes that these rules are applicable because the curial law is English. Where the curial law is not English the arbitrator must look elsewhere for guidance on the rules to be applied for determining the proper law.

[11] Dicey and Morris, *Conflict of Laws* (10th edn.) p. 145.

[12] Although it is not conclusive: *Compagnie d'Armement Maritime SA v Compagnie Tunisienne de Navigation SA v* [1970] 2 Lloyd's Rep 99.

the contract was made; the place or places where it was to be performed; the language and terminology of the contract; and so on. The inference to be drawn from these factors is, in the last resort, a matter of judgment; and in a commercial arbitration, the judgment of a lay arbitrator will carry great weight with the Court. Indeed it has been said with high authority that 'the expertise of City of London arbitrators (which motivates the use of London arbitration clauses) suggests that these considerations are best left to them'[13].

In spite of this, the identification of the proper law is in the end itself a matter of law, and it is a subject upon which the arbitrator can, and should if the parties so request[14], invoke the assistance of the High Court[15]. It will plainly be desirable, in most instances, for the matter to be decided by the Court at an early stage of the reference; for there will be little point in exposing the parties to the considerable expense of argument and expert evidence on the content of the foreign law, if that law is ultimately to be ruled out as inapplicable.

(b) Issues governed by the proper law

The choice of a foreign law as the proper law of a contract does not necessarily mean that all of the disputes emanating from the contract are regulated by the foreign law. Under the English principles of the conflict of laws, a distinction is drawn between substantive and procedural issues: the former being governed by the proper law, and the latter being in general governed by the curial law[16]. The terminology of this distinction is misleading, for some of the issues which are classed as procedural may have a significant impact on the substantive rights of the parties. Any attempt at a full list of such issues would be out of place in a work of this kind, but the arbitrator may find it helpful to note that whatever his conclusion on the proper law, he may well find that if the dispute raises issues of liability in tort, or of the quantification of damages, or of matters which are procedural in character, he may find himself required to apply the rules of English law.

(C) Proof of foreign law

It is a rule of English procedure that the tribunal must assume the foreign law to be the same as English law, except so far as the contrary is alleged and proved. The arbitrator should give full weight to this presumption, in both its aspects.

First, the arbitrator should recall that it is for the parties to allege that the foreign law differs from English law. If they are content to have their disputes

---

[13] Per Lord Wilberforce in *Compagnie Tunisienne de Navigation SA v Compagnie d'Armement Maritime SA*, supra, at 114. See also the observations of the same learned Lord on the desirability of restricting appeals from the Commercial Court on questions of the choice of law. Presumably, the observations of Lord Wilberforce apply with much less force, if they apply at all, to arbitrations conducted by lawyers; and it is common, where possible issues on the conflicts of law appear on the horizon, for lay arbitrators to appoint a lawyer as umpire. It does not appear from the speeches whether the opinion of Lord Wilberforce was shared by the other members of the Appellate Committee.

[14] Unless the answer is obvious.

[15] There was no suggestion in the *Compagnie Tunisienne* case that the arbitrators were in any way at fault in stating a case. The power to invoke the assistance of the Court can, however, be excluded by a valid exclusion agreement under s. 3 of the 1979 Act.

[16] See pp. 64–68, ante, for a fuller discussion.

decided according to English law, it is no part of his function to multiply trouble and expense by suggesting that the two laws may differ[17]. Furthermore, when it has become plain that one or other party has raised a serious issue as to foreign law, the arbitrator will be well advised to adopt a rigorous attitude towards the particularisation of the claim, however informal the remainder of the proceedings may be. The party who alleges that foreign law is different from English law should be required to state precisely where the difference lies, and precisely what is the effect of the foreign law on the facts of the case in question. The arbitrator should not hesitate to order further particulars of the allegations of foreign law, if he considers that a party genuinely is not sure what propositions are being raised against him.

Second, the arbitrator should bear in mind that it is for the party who alleges a difference between foreign law and English law to prove that the difference exists. Here again, the arbitrator would be well advised to adopt a strict procedure, even if the remainder of the reference is proceeding informally. The foreign law should be proved by oral evidence from persons sufficiently qualified in the relevant law to be able to give an expert opinion, and the evidence should be tested by cross-examination. The arbitrator should decline, so far as possible, to base any part of his decision on documentary material, such as translations of statutes, reported cases or works of reference, except to the extent that this material has been expounded by oral evidence. Documentary material of this kind is very often misleading, unless set against a background of foreign law and procedure; and this is not something which the arbitrator can achieve unaided.

If the evidence of foreign law is unsatisfactory or unconvincing, the right course is for the arbitrator to find as a fact that the party who alleged the difference between the foreign law and the English law has failed to satisfy the burden of proof. The arbitrator should not, of course, attempt to add to the material on foreign law by carrying out his own researches. Nor should he obtain for himself an expert opinion, without the permission of the parties[18]. Even where the parties make no objection to the obtaining of an opinion, the arbitrator should invite them to agree to be bound by its contents; for otherwise they may try to point out mistakes in the opinion, and evidence which is challenged but not made the subject of cross-examination is rarely satisfactory. Since an issue as to the substance and effect of a foreign law is a question of fact[19] the decision of the arbitrator upon it is final. It is not a matter which he should, or indeed can, refer to the High Court.

(d) EEC law

An arbitrator may from time to time be faced with a dispute involving the law of the European Economic Community. If this situation arises, does the arbitrator have the power or the duty to refer a question of EEC law to the

---

[17] This is not to say that there could never be circumstances in which the arbitrator could properly take the lead: if, for example, the application of English law might work an injustice (as in the reinsurance cases under the Stamp Act).

[18] The rules relating to the obtaining of legal advice on English law, as to which see p. 360, post, do not apply in this situation, since foreign law is a question of fact.

[19] *Prodexport State Co for Foreign Trade v ED and F Man Ltd* [1972] 2 Lloyd's Rep 375 at 383.

European Court of Justice for a preliminary ruling[20]? The answer depends on the construction of Article 177 of the Treaty of Rome, the relevant provisions of which read as follows—

> 'Where such a question is raised before any court or tribunal of a Member State that court or tribunal may, if it considers that a decision on the question is necessary to enable it to give judgment, request the Court of Justice to give a ruling thereon. Where any such question is raised in a case pending before a court or tribunal of a Member State, against whose decisions there is no judicial remedy under national law, that court or tribunal shall bring the matter before the Court of Justice'.

It is now clear that an arbitral tribunal whose jurisdiction is based solely on the agreement of the parties is not a 'Court or tribunal of a Member State' for the purposes of Article 177[1]. These words connote an official organ of the state rather than a body which owes its existence to an agreement freely entered into between private individuals or organisations[2]. It follows that an arbitrator appointed pursuant to an arbitration agreement has no power, and correspondingly no duty, to request the Court of Justice to give a ruling on a question of EEC law: that is the function of the ordinary courts of law. In order to invoke a decision of the Court of Justice on a question arising in an arbitration it is therefore necessary first to bring the question before the High Court. Apart from the more obvious ways of doing so, such as by means of an appeal[3] or a preliminary question of law under the 1979 Act[4], it appears that any point of EEC law which is in the realm of public policy or 'ordre publique' may be raised by way of defence to proceedings to enforce the award; or, if it impugns the validity of the arbitration agreement, by way of any of the procedures designed to test the arbitrator's jurisdiction: and in this way the High Court may be enabled to initiate a reference under Article 177.

3 'Equity' clauses: amiable composition

Earlier we have considered whether an arbitrator has a duty to decide the dispute in accordance with the law, if the arbitration agreement is silent as to the manner in which the decision is to be made. It does, however, occasionally happen that the agreement purports expressly to dispense the arbitrator from applying the law either wholly or in part, by some such provision as:

> 'The arbitrator shall be entitled to decide according to equity and good conscience and shall not be obliged to follow the strict rules of law'.

Or the clause may say:

> 'The arbitrator shall be entitled to act as *amiable compositeur.*'

---

[20] For the practice of the English courts, see *Löwenbräu München v Grünhalle Lager International Ltd* [1974] 1 CMLR 1; *Yvonne Van Duyn v Home Office* [1974] CMLR 347; *HP Bulmer Ltd v J Bollinger SA* [1974] 2 CMLR 91, [1974] Ch 401.

[1] *'Nordsee' Deutsche Hochseefischerei GmbH v Reederei Mond Hochseefischerei Nordstern AG & Co KG* Case 102/81, [1982] ECR 1095.

[2] Contrast *Vaassen-Göbbels v Beambtenfonds voor het Mijnbedrijf* Case 61/65 [1966] ECR 261; and *Broekmeulen v Huisarts Registratie Commissie* Case 246/80 [1981] ECR 2311.

[3] See, for example *Bulk Oil (Zug) AG v Sun International Ltd and Sun Oil Trading Co* [1983] 2 Lloyd's Rep 587.

[4] If not excluded by a valid exclusion agreement.

Provisions of this type, which we shall call 'equity' clauses[5], raise theoretical questions of great difficulty. Few English cases touch on the problem, and there has been little academic discussion of the matter in the context of English law and practice. Moreover, if one turns for guidance to literature originating in the continent of Europe, where clauses of this kind are much more common, it is seen that opinions are sharply divided on many questions as to the meaning of such clauses, and the limits of their efficacy[6]. Furthermore the problems are of necessity tackled to a great extent against the background of contractual and procedural laws which are in some respects very different from those of England. Thus, although it is certainly to be hoped that when the matter comes up for explicit decision in England, the Court will be furnished with at least a sample of the relevant foreign writings, it seems likely that in the end the Court will have to work out its own solution to the matter[7]. When doing so, the Court will have to consider the following questions—

1 What does the clause mean? Properly construed, how far does it permit the arbitrator to disregard the ordinary rules of law, and the terms of the contract?

2 What does the clause require, as distinct from permit, the arbitrator to do?

3 Can the clause co-exist with a legally enforceable substantive contract?

4 Can an agreement containing such a clause amount to an arbitration agreement for the purpose of the 1950 Act?

5 What rights of recourse by way of appeal, or otherwise, exist in relation to the substantive basis of the award?

A full discussion of these questions would be an elaborate business, well beyond the scope of this work. Moreover, it is (at least for the time being) unlikely that the question will often arise in England. Equity clauses are not usually found in the type of contract which forms the staple of English arbitration practice[8]. Perhaps the situation will change in the future[9], between international companies or state corporations of the kind which has become

---

[5] We are not here concerned with clauses requiring the arbitrator to apply the rules developed by the costs of equity, but only to clauses requiring the arbitrator to decide otherwise than by reference to legally recognisable criteria: see the distinction drawn by Hobhouse J in *Didymi Corpn v Atlantic Lines and Navigation Co Inc* [1987] 2 Lloyd's Rep 166 at 170.

[6] In a work of the present nature, it would be pointless to attempt a survey of the copious literature on the subject. A select bibliography is to be found in Mustill, *The New Lex Mercatoria: The First Twenty-five years*, in *Liber Amicorum for Lord Wilberforce* (1987), at p. 150. See also E Loguin, *L'Amiable Composition en Droit Comparé et International* (1980), and P. Lalive in *Revue de l'Arbitrage* (1980) pp. 651 and 688.

[7] This has not always happened when the English Court has been invited to develop new rules and procedures by analogy with those existing in civil law countries. The development of the common law by these means is certainly laudable in principle, but the results will not be satisfactory unless the Court is provided with full information; not always the easiest task, since it must be informed through argument, not evidence.

[8] Equity clauses have for many years featured in reinsurance treaties—but more from a wish to evade certain inconvenient provisions (now repealed) of the Stamp Acts, rather than from a decision to subject this particular sort of contract to a system of abstract justice. We do not know of any other field of English commercial law where such clauses are habitually used.

[9] European ideas continue to make an impression on English concepts of arbitral law. The UNCITRAL Arbitration Rules, Article 33 of which permits the parties to empower the arbitrator to act as amiable compositeur 'if the law applicable to the arbitral procedure permits such arbitration', may one day give place to international legislation less solicitous of the local law.

known as 'one-off' contracts[10]. These will mostly incorporate an exclusion agreement under section 3 of the 1979 Act, and although this will not in theory foreclose all possibility of judicial control, in practice it is likely to put the matter almost entirely out of Court[11]. In the circumstances, we shall not seek to do more than indicate some of the considerations which may have to be taken into account, and some of the answers which may possibly be given. The discussion may perhaps serve a useful purpose in drawing the attention of those who contemplate including such a clause in their agreements to the doubts and procedural turmoil which may ensue. Equity clauses are best reserved for transactions where the parties are contracting for a long relationship, in which the maintenance of commercial trust between the parties is reasonably assured. Equity clauses are a recipe for trouble in cases where the contract establishes sharply defined mutual obligations between parties who are briefly drawn together by a single transaction, and who have no ambitions for a continuing business relationship. For this sort of relationship, certainty is preferable to a harmonious vagueness.

(a) The meaning of the clause

Here, we are faced with a circular problem. If the court decides that as a matter of commercial policy it should uphold the validity of the substantive contract and of the arbitration agreement, notwithstanding the presence of an equity clause, it will have to interpret the clause in a way which enables this result to conform with the law of contract and of arbitration. If, on the other hand, the Court decides that commercial policy requires the clause to be given the meaning which the parties themselves intended, it may be constrained to hold that the effectiveness of the substantive contract or the arbitration agreement, or both, must yield to this paramount intention. It is hard to predict where the Court will choose to break into the circle[12]. We suggest, however, that the following are amongst the interpretations which will have to be considered—

1 The clause empowers the arbitrator to adjust the bargain in the light of changed circumstances. This power may be exercised as regards future obligations, in addition to those which are the subject of dispute. The powers extend to a revision of the express terms of the contract, as well as those which are imposed or implied by law.

2 Once the arbitrator is seized of a dispute as to obligations existing or said to have existed in the past, the clause frees him from any duty to respect the rules of law when deciding upon the merits of the dispute.

3 The clause has the same effect as set out in 2, above, except that the arbitrator is obliged to give effect to rules of public policy.

---

[10] Disputes under such contracts form a much higher proportion of those arbitrated abroad than is the case in England, which probably accounts for their greater prominence in the Continental literature.

[11] See the discussion at 648, post.

[12] This problem receives little attention in the foreign literature. Many codes of procedure expressly recognise the power of the arbitrator and of the Court to act as *amiable compositeur* if the contract so provides. The validity of an equity clause, and its compatibility with a binding contract, are therefore not in doubt, so that the Court and the jurists are under no pressure to force an artificial meaning on the clause in order to save the contract.

4 The clause has the same effect as set out in 2 or 3, above, except that the arbitrator cannot depart from the express terms of the contract.

5 The clause empowers (and indeed requires) the arbitrator to apply a system of law, but not a system which is that of any individual state.

6 The clause enables the arbitrator to ignore technicalities and strict constructions.

7 The purpose of the clause is only to ensure that the arbitrator need not conform with ordinary legal procedures when conducting the reference.

(i) Power to adjust the bargain.   We suggest that interpretation 1 is unlikely to be adopted by the English Court. It is most improbable that á general power to reformulate an explicit bargain would be incorporated into anything but a long-term contract, regarded by the parties as exceptionally vulnerable to changes in economic circumstances. Such a contract would only be entered into after the most careful advice, and the advisers would be bound to know of the problems which would be likely to arise if the contract were subjected to English law, or to an arbitration in England. Moreover, if they wished to give the arbitrator a power to adjust the bargain prospectively, they would be sure to employ one of the well-established formulae[13]. Again, most of the equity clauses which are encountered in practice are not expressed in such a way as to suggest that they are intended to deal with the future of the relationship, as distinct from existing disputes.

(ii) No duty to apply the law.   Interpretation 2 may well be thought to correspond best with what the parties truly intend, and in many cases it will also correspond with what the clause actually says. If asked, the parties might even maintain that the decision should be free from the constraints of public policy, and some commentators go far towards accepting this view. Founding partly on Article V(2) of the New York Convention, and partly on the concept of a transnational arbitration entirely free from the constraints of any local system of law, they contend that the only relevant rules of ordre publique are those of the country in which the award is enforced. From a practical point of view, this seems a wholly unacceptable solution. If it is sound, it must follow that at the moment of publication the award has no objective validity. Everything will depend upon the chance of where the plaintiff believes that he can find the defendant's assets. This surely cannot be right. A conscientious arbitrator wishes to decide correctly; if this involves the application of public policy, he needs to know which public policy to apply; and the one thing which he cannot do is to forecast where the award will be enforced. The proposition also ignores the fact that most awards are not enforced through the courts but are honoured spontaneously. The losing party must be entitled to consider before he satisfies the award whether it is in accord with the relevant law. This he cannot do if the law is ascertained in terms of a forecast enforcement which, ex hypothesi will not take place. Again, the status of the award as making the issues res judicata

---

[13] Such as one of the variants of the 'undue hardship' clause.

between the parties must be capable of assessment when it is made, not at some later date when, if at all, it comes forward for enforcement[14].

In addition, it is hard to see any practical basis on which one can achieve a distinction between those arbitrations which are and those which are not isolated from all contact with state laws: and some distinction must be made, since even the most enthusiastic proponents of the theory could hardly assert that all arbitrations involving parties from two different countries take place in a territorial and judicial vacuum.

Furthermore, the hypothesis does not appear soundly based in theory. Article V does not permit the Court to refuse enforcement only if the award is contrary to its own public policy. There is also the case, envisaged by Article V(1)(e), of the award which is set aside or suspended by the Court of the country in which it was made. Plainly, a prime example of such a setting aside or suspension will exist where the award is contrary to the public policy of the *lex fori.* Whatever the attitude of English courts to a foreign award which is alleged to be contrary to the public policy of the foreign law, we find it impossible to conceive that if the arbitration takes place in England the Court will renounce all rights to intervene, however obnoxious to English statute or concepts of morality the award may appear, simply because the parties have written into the contract an arbitration clause and an equity clause.

Whilst this conclusion is, we suggest, virtually irresistible, it is not so easy to be sure what type of legal rule will be treated as overriding an express choice of 'non-law'. In relation to an individual legal system, the problem of distinguishing between 'règles imperatives' and 'règles de droit supplétives' is well known, and notoriously difficult to draw. The problem is, however, rather more complicated in the present case, because it seems that a distinction must be made between foreign and English rules of public policy. Where English law is concerned, the public policy to which the Court must have regard will include at least the rules of the criminal law and those statutory provisions of the civil law out of which it is impossible to contract. But where foreign law is concerned, we suggest that the English courts would have regard only to those rules which make a transaction 'illegal', under those systems of law to whose criminal law the English court, according to English principles of the conflicts of law, will have regard when called on to enforce a contract[15]. These include those rules which are created by the law of the place of performance.

---

[14] Perhaps what the proponents of this theory are really saying is that the award itself is not subject to any rules of public policy at all, and that such rules only come into play when the successful party attempts to enforce in a particular forum an award which is, in the abstract, detached from any national law. (It must be acknowledged that there is always some degree of uncertainty whenever an agreement contains no express choice of law, for until the forum is known there is no way to identify the system of conflicts of laws by which the proper law is to be ascertained. But it is going a long way to suppose that the parties wished their rights to be incapable of final ascertainment even at the moment when the award was published.)

[15] If the equity clause involves a choice of 'non-law' it must also involve a renunciation of the provisions of the *lex fori* relating to conflicts of laws: for although these are sometimes referred to as Private International Law, they are in fact part of the private law of the individual state. The principle that an English court will not enforce a contract which is illegal by the *lex loci solutionis* is however in a quite different category. This is a rule of public policy, founded on considerations of comity, and is not simply concerned with the working out of a private contractual relationship. The parties cannot force the English law to recognise an illegal transaction merely by saying, indirectly, that this is what they want to happen.

(iii) The terms of the contract. The next question is whether a further constraint must be imposed on the operation of the clause, to the extent that the decision must not be inconsistent with the terms of the contract[16]. At first sight it seems that an affirmative answer is inevitable. The substantive terms are just as much part of the contract as the equity clause, and there is no logic in treating the arbitrator as bound by the latter but not the former. On the other hand, it is hard to find a justification for treating the arbitrator as entirely free from the law and entirely bound by the contract, since the English law of contract consists to a great extent of implied terms: viz. those terms which the parties would undoubtedly have included in the contract if they had chosen to deal expressly with the matter. To give a different treatment to express and implied terms seems strange[17], and this suggests that some compromise will need to be found between the two extreme readings of the clause. Once such compromise, which would we believe correspond with the parties' own unformulated ideas of what the clause was intended to achieve, would be to construe the clause as conferring on the arbitrator a duty to use the contract as a starting point for his decision, but not to treat it as compelling him inexorably to a conclusion logically derived from the language of its express terms. Such an interpretation would leave the arbitrator free to adopt one of the following alternatives—

(a) To read the provisions of the contract in the sense which he believes the parties to have intended, even though this would be inconsistent with (i) a literal reading of them, and (ii) the meaning given to them by decisions of the courts[18].

(b) To give relief where, because they have not foreseen the impact of their agreement on the particular problem which has arisen, the contract does not reflect the true intention of the parties.

(c) To decide whether, in the light of events occurring when the contract was made, the true structure of the bargain would be distorted if the contract were to be enforced in full, according to its express terms.

Whether the Court would go further, and allow the following additional liberty is impossible to predict with any confidence—

(d) Even without any intervening circumstance, to depart from a strict interpretation of the contract if it could be seen that the bargain originally made was operating unfairly towards one of the parties[19].

---

[16] Some clauses expressly provide that the arbitrator, even if *amiable compositeur*, must give effect to the contract: see for example, Article 33.3 of the UNCITRAL Rules.

[17] Although this distinction will have to be made if the clause is one which requires the arbitrator to apply 'the contract': for the latter surely means 'the express terms of the contract'. (This must be so, for otherwise the Court would have to distinguish between those rules of law which operate via implied terms, and those which operate directly, which would be quite unworkable.)

[18] We believe that many parties would regard this as one of the prime functions of the clause. Businessmen often complain that the courts read contracts in a perversely literal way, and also that they lack the commercial background necessary to discern the true intentions masked by an inexact use of language. It must, however, be recognised that whilst traders may be unanimous that the Court has chosen the wrong meaning, they find it hard to agree which is right. This was strikingly demonstrated, some years ago, when it became the practice to include in charter-parties a provision to the effect that a particular clause was to be construed as it had been commonly understood before a certain decision of the Court of Appeal. Investigation showed that whilst opinion amongst brokers was unanimous that the clause did not mean what the Court had said, there were at least six different opinions as to what it actually did mean.

[19] This interpretation would not face the arbitrator with an impossible task, for it is one which the judge is required to perform by the consumer protection laws of many countries, including the United Kingdom.

This may not be a problem of real practical importance. Equity clauses are very rarely encountered outside the field of long-term contracts, specially drafted, between parties of approximately equal bargaining power. It would be in only the rarest case that an arbitrator could justifiably think it fair to impose a retrospective modification of such a bargain. Pausing for a moment, it is, we think, possible to say that the modified version of interpretation 4, suggested in the previous paragraphs, is one which may be regarded as having some reasonable relation to the presumed intention of the parties. It is not, we believe, inconsistent with any reported decision on the meaning of an equity clause[20].

(iv) Custom and usage.   It is convenient at this stage to mention a point which has exercised some commentators, namely whether the arbitrator can properly decide contrary to a custom of the trade[1]. To an English lawyer, this seems one of the less formidable problems. Custom and usage form part of the substance of the bargain. The arbitrator can therefore depart from them only in those cases where he can properly override the terms of the contract; and in practical terms it is unlikely that such overriding will often occur, since the customary result is one which, almost by definition, a businessman would treat as fair and reasonable.

(v) International law: lex mercatoria.   We now turn to interpretation 5, namely that the clause empowers the arbitrator to decide according to a system of law which is not the law of any individual state. This is an attractive notion, since it avoids the awkwardness of accepting that the parties have agreed to subject their relationship to the personal views of an arbitrator as to the justice of the case, largely unfettered by any objective norms: the more so since very often the identity of the arbitrator will not be known at the time when the contract is made. If, however, both state law and 'non-law' are to be rejected then something must be put in their place. Various suggestions have been made, of which three may briefly be mentioned.

First, it is said that the arbitrator should decide according to 'international law'. Taking this to mean public international law, the suggestion offers no practical solution, since international law has little or nothing to say about the content of private bargains[2]. The only circumstance in which international law

---

[20] We have been able to find only two English cases in which the effect of such a clause is mentioned. In *Rolland v Cassidy* (1888) 13 App Cas 770, a contract governed by Canadian law expressly required the arbitrators to act as *amiables compositeurs*. The Code of Civil Procedure enabled such arbitrators so to decide otherwise than in accordance with rules of law. The Earl of Selborne LC, delivering the advice of the Privy Council, said: 'Their Lordships would, no doubt, hesitate much before they held that to entitle arbitrators named as *amiables compositeurs* to disregard all law, and to be arbitrary in their dealings with the parties; but the distinction must have some reasonable effect given to it, and the least effect which can reasonably be given to the words is, that they dispense with the strict observance of those rules of law the non-observance of which, as applied to awards, results in no more than irregularity'. We refer below to *Eagle Star Insurance Co Ltd v Yuval Insurance Co Ltd* [1978] 1 Lloyd's Rep 357, in relation to interpretation 6.

[1] The UNCITRAL Rules and the ICC Rules require the arbitrator to 'take into account' the usages of the trade.

[2] We do not understand Hobhouse J in *Dallal v Bank Mellat* [1986] QB 441 as saying that an express choice of public international law would be invalid, but merely that in the absence of such a choice international law can only become part of the proper law by virtue of having been absorbed into some system of municipal law. It is to be noted that the judge was considering the proper law of the arbitration agreement, not the law governing the merits.

might come into play is where the contract is made between States or between one State and a corporate body, and where the obligations which it creates are of an essentially public character[3].

Second, it has been suggested that the *amiable compositeur* should decide according to international arbitration law. We can only say in response to this suggestion that if such a law exists, it is nowhere to be found.

Third, it has been proposed that the clause empowers the arbitrator to decide according to the *lex mercatoria*. With all deference to those who support it, we find this idea hard to accept. Indeed, we doubt whether a *lex mercatoria* even exists, in the sense of an international commercial law divorced from any State law: or, at least, that it exists in any sense useful for the solving of commercial disputes. It is undeniable that a *lex mercatoria* did once prevail in certain fields of law, particularly where there was already a body of ancient law upon which to build[4]. Here, the law was primarily to be derived from the writings of scholars. But all this has long been swamped by legislation and by the flood of reported decisions. So far as the old *lex mercatoria* now exercises any influence on the course of commercial business, it does so by virtue of having been received into the laws of individual states through the medium of judicial decision, and to a lesser degree through being embodied in legislation. What is therefore proposed is a new *lex mercatoria*, growing afresh alongside the highly complex and explicit systems developed over the years by individual states. But what constitutes this body of law, and where is it to be found? So far as concerns general principles, it may be possible to say that the conduct of business men is governed by certain rules, and that these rules are reflected in the laws of all trading nations. For example, it may be said that contracts are made on the presumption that *pacta sunt servanda*, and that they are to be enforced only *rebus sic stantibus*. But this is not enough to solve any but the simplest problem. As soon as one tries to make the principles more particular, it is seen that there is no unanimity as to the way in which they should be applied[5]. The further he descends into the details which will be necessary to enable a commercial dispute to be resolved, the more the searcher for the *lex mercatoria* is driven into a kind of harmonisation of the existing developed systems of mercantile law. If he ever succeeds in achieving his object he will be left with a series of rules which are just as rigid as those of the individual states, and probably a good deal less easy to operate in a consistent

---

[3] Certain agreements whereby sovereign states conferred oil or mineral concessions, entered into at a time when the states in question possessed no developed system of commercial law, have provided that the arbitrator is to decide according to the local law and the 'general principles of law recognised by civilised nations'. (This is not necessarily the same as *public* international law.) Such an agreement makes sense, since there is no collision between the general principles and the individual law, and the need to invoke the general principles is mitigated by the great particularity with which such contracts are usually drawn. An agreement to decide according to international law may be recognised as valid; see per Megaw J in *Orion Compania Espanola de Seguros v Belfort Maatschappij voor Algemene Verzekgringeen* [1962] 2 Lloyd's Rep 257 at 264, a passage not, we suggest, affected by *Eagle Star v Yuval*, ante. We find it hard to accept, however, that the parties to an ordinary commercial contract can ever intend to substitute a body of law relating to relationships between states, for all the state systems of private law which have highly developed rules to deal with precisely the type of contract, and the type of problem, with which the arbitrator will have to contend.

[4] For example the laws of admiralty and of bailment. The laws of bills of exchange and marine insurance also had a particularly international flavour, until comparatively modern times.

[5] As witness the wide divergence between Anglo Saxon and Continental laws on the concept of force majeure.

and satisfactory manner. Having once identified this new code of rules, the arbitrator will be bound to apply it, for this is what (according to the interpretation now being considered) the contract empowers and binds him to do. He will not be permitted to give any effect at all to his own ideas of what is just and equitable, even if he finds that the *lex mercatoria*, once identified, produces a result with which he does not agree. To depart from the new body of law will be a departure from his mandate. Whatever else the party may be taken to wish when they include an equity clause, we find it hard to accept that this is the desired result.

(vi) Freedom from technicalities.   An alternative and substantially narrower reconciliation of these two factors is provided by interpretation 6: namely that the clause only ousts 'technicalities and strict constructions'. These words are a quotation from the principal English authority in which the meaning of an equity clause has been directly in issue[6]. It has never, however, been necessary for the Court to decide exactly how the clause so construed should be applied in practice, and the words themselves are not self-explanatory[7]. Presumably the expression 'strict constructions' indicates that the arbitrator is given the kind of latitude in relation to the application of the contract which was mentioned in relation to interpretation 4. The word 'technicalities' poses more problems. We believe that this does not refer only to the way in which the arbitration is conducted, but that it was intended also to embrace those rules of law which produce the result that because a party has acted or not acted in a particular way, he loses rights which, according to the true commercial content of the bargain, he ought to possess and which, in the circumstances of the case, the arbitrator considers that justice would allow him to enforce[8]. There may, however, be problems here, where the rule derives from an English statute which is mandatory in effect and is based on considerations of public policy. Here, consistently with the view expressed above, it would seem that an English arbitrator has no latitude, even under an equity clause.

Furthermore, it must be noted that a power to disregard technicalities is not the same as a general power to arrive at a fair result. Many instances of unfairness can result from rules of law, or express stipulations in the contract, which are far from technical.

---

[6] *Eagle Star Insurance Co v Yuval*, ante. This definition is part of the ratio decidendi, since it was the choice of this narrow reading which led to the conclusion that the clause was not, as had been decided in *Orion Compania Espanola de Seguros v Belfort Maatschappij voor Algemene Verzekgringeen* [1962] 2 Lloyd's Rep 257, inconsistent with the existence of a binding contract.

[7] In *Home Insurance Co v Administration Aseguraridor de Stat* [1983] 2 Lloyd's Rep 674 the Court found it sufficient to hold, following the *Eagle Star* case, that the clause was intended to free the arbitrator to some extent from strict rules; and in *Overseas Union Insurance Ltd v AA Mutual International Insurance Co Ltd* [1988] 2 Lloyd's Rep 63, Evans J treated the effect of an equity clause as not clearly settled, although it emphasised the fact that arbitrators may draw upon their own expertise and commercial knowledge without formal proof. This is no doubt true, but we suggest that on any view the equity clause must mean more than this, for otherwise it would be superfluous. See also *Home & Overseas Insurance Co Ltd v Mentor Insurance Co (UK) Ltd*, (9 December 1988, unreported), CA.

[8] The right to terminate a contract for a minor breach of conditions might be one example; the strict rules relating to the right to reject goods might be another. So also as regards the rigid rules governing disclosure and misrepresentation in the law of insurance. (By contrast, the general principle that a contract of insurance should be performed in the utmost good faith in not one which, under a businesslike interpretation of the clause, the arbitrator should feel free to ignore.)

Finally, we must mention interpretation 7, namely that the clause does no more than give the arbitrator a free hand in matters of procedure. This is, we believe, too unambitious an assessment of the parties' intentions. The position may perhaps be otherwise in countries where the local law subjects arbitrations to irreducable procedural norms. In England, the courts look to the contract in order to ascertain how the arbitration is to be conducted. A clause cannot, we suggest, properly be construed as allowing the arbitrator to depart from the express or implied terms of the contract as to procedure; and he needs no clause to dispense him from rules imposed by the courts—for none in fact exist[9].

(b) The duty of the arbitrator

One question discussed in the literature is whether the arbitrator not only may but must exercise the latitude conferred on him by the equity clause. The point is of little importance in practice. It is scarcely conceivable that an arbitrator would explicitly announce in his award that he had left equity and good conscience entirely aside. If the award is merely silent on the subject, the Court may legitimately assume that the arbitrator has not just ignored or overlooked the clause, but has tested his conclusion against the requirement of fairness, and has decided that a strict application of the contract and the rules of law will, in the circumstances, yield the most equitable result. Such a procedure is, we suggest, entirely proper even in those cases where the clause is expressed so as to require, and not merely permit, the arbitrator to decide according to equity and good conscience.

(c) The effect on the contract

The question whether an equity clause is consistent with a binding substantive contract will depend to a great extent on the meaning which the Court gives to the clause.

If the clause is interpreted in one of the first four of the ways indicated above, or a variant of them, three possibilities will be open to the Court. First, to hold that the clause is repugnant to the other terms of the bargain, that it must accordingly be rejected, and that the bargain stands as a valid contract. Second, that there is a valid contract to honour whatever award the arbitrator may make. Third, that there is no contract at all.

At first sight, the second proposition appears attractive. After all, a contract may validly provide that (for example) the price of goods is to be fixed by a third party. Cannot the arbitrator be given an equally free hand in relation to the terms of the contract as a whole? We think not. In the first place, it is questionable whether the third party does have an entirely free hand when fixing the price[10]. Second, the function of the third party is to fill a gap in an executory contract. The arbitrator, by contrast, does not come on the scene until the time for performance has already passed, so that whilst the contract still remains executory the parties will not know the extent of their respective rights

---

[9] The arbitrator is, of course, required to observe the basic principle of natural justice expressed in the maxim *audi alterem partem*. We do not believe that it could ever be 'just and equitable' for him to disregard these principles.

[10] A discussion of this point is beyond the scope of the present work.

and duties. Third, there is a fundamental difference between filling a gap in a contract which is otherwise fully ascertained, and leaving the whole of the contractual relationship without final definition until such time, if any, as the arbitrator makes his award.

Accordingly, it seems to us that the choice must lie between the first and third propositions. The clause and the contract cannot co-exist, if the clause is to be read in the wider of the various meanings suggested above[11].

Three arguments may be advanced in support of the view that it is the clause which ought to yield. First, that the clause is contrary to public policy. This argument proceeds by parity of reasoning with the decision of the Court of Appeal in *Czarnikow v Roth, Schmidt & Co*[12]. We suggest that the analogy is unsound. The *Czarnikow Case* was concerned with a clause purporting to oust the right of appeal by way of special case. Quite apart from the fact that in the light of the 1979 Act it cannot now be maintained that there is something inherently objectionable in the contractual exclusion of an appeal, there is no true resemblance between a stipulation that the bargain shall not be governed by law, and one which says that although the contract is governed by law, the Court shall have no power to ensure that the law is properly applied. Stipulations that a bargain is to be binding in honour are recognised by the courts[13], and there is no reason why recognition should be denied to a clause which has the same practical result, even if it proceeds indirectly by modifying the basis on which disputes are to be decided, rather than directly by excising the legal content of the contract.

Second, it may be said that the clause is void for uncertainty. This is unattractive. If the clause itself is void for uncertainty, the consequence would appear to be that the whole contract is void for uncertainty. Once the clause is struck down what remains is a contract without any mechanism for ascertaining the legal content of the parties' rights and obligations. To make good the deficiency by resort to the ordinary principles of English law would be to impose a bargain on the parties different from the one they had attempted to achieve. The alternative is to hold that they have failed in law to achieve any bargain at all. Neither alternative is likely to be viewed with much favour by the Court. The answer may lie in assuming that the uncertainty can be cured by the decision of the arbitrator[14]. This solution rescues the clause and the contract, but does nothing to tell the arbitrator how he should apply the clause.

Third, it may be argued that the parties do not by including an equity clause

---

[11] It must be acknowledged that there are cases in which clauses of this nature have been mentioned without any suggestion that they might render the contract unenforceable. For example, *Rolland v Cassidy* (1888) 13 App Cas 770 at 772; *Jager v Tolme and Runge and London Produce Clearing House* [1916] 1 KB 939 at 953, 957; *Board of Trade v Cayzer, Irvine & Co* [1927] AC 610 at 628–629; *River Thames Insurance Co Ltd v Al Ahleia Insurance Co SAK* [1973] 1 Lloyd's Rep 2 at 7. (We believe that in *Maritime Insurance Co Ltd v Assecuranz-Union Von 1865* (1935) 52 Ll L Rep 16, Goddard J was saying, not that the 'honour' clause made the contract invalid, but that when the parties inserted it they knew that the contract was already unenforceable for want of a stamped policy.) The Court did not, however, necessarily give the clause one of its wider meanings: see especially *Rolland v Cassidy*, ante.

[12] [1922] 2 KB 478.

[13] *Jones v Vernon's Pools Ltd* [1938] 2 All ER 626; *Rose and Frank Co v JR Crompton & Bros Ltd* [1925] AC 445.

[14] As in *Deutsche Schachtbau und Tiefbohrgesellschaft GmbH v Ras al Khaimah National Oil Co* [1987] 2 Lloyd's Rep 246 at 254.

demonstrate an intention to make a bargain which is binding in honour only[15]. What they want is a contract which is rather blurred at the edges, and if the courts will not interpret their clause in this sense, the parties would rather have a binding contract and no clause, than the other way round[16]. It seems, however, that the courts will go to considerable lengths to uphold both the clause and the contract[17], even if constrained to interpret the clause in one of its wider senses[18].

The general question which we have just discussed does not arise if the clause is given a more restricted meaning. Here, there is direct authority[19] for the proposition that the clause and the contract are each enforceable. There will, however, still be problems of some nicety when the Court comes to decide how far it can go in recognising the arbitrator's freedom of choice, whilst still maintaining the enforceability of the contract. Unless the clause is in a very explicit form, this problem need not be faced where the contract is executory at the moment when the question comes before the Court, since it will not be necessary to go beyond saying that the clause gives the arbitrator some degree of liberty. The position will be the same where the contract has been performed, but no dispute has arisen or is capable of arising on which the equity clause would have any practical impact. If, however, the arbitrator has gone ahead in reliance on the clause, and has in some degree substituted his own conclusion for that which would have followed from a strict application of the law, the Court will have to arrive at a conclusion on the matter. We believe that in most cases the Court will try to hold that the contract, the arbitration clause and the decision, are all enforceable. If this proves impossible, the Court is likely to give the clause a meaning which is just narrow enough to save the contract. This may mean that the award is invalid[20] but this seems less objectionable than holding that the claim is not capable of enforcement at all.

(d) The clause and the arbitration

Next, it must be considered whether a contract which contains both an arbitration clause and an equity clause can be regarded as an 'arbitration agreement' for the purposes of the Acts.

It seems that if the clause is so expressed, or construed, as to prevent a binding

---

[15] Except, of course, where the equity clause says (as it sometimes does) that the contract is not intended to be legally binding.

[16] For a possible alternative route to the same conclusion, see Professor Glanville Williams, 60 LQR 69 at 79–80.

[17] *Home Insurance Co v Administration Asigurarilor de Stat* [1983] 2 Lloyd's Rep 674, 677. This part of the judgment is obiter, since Parker J had already decided to give the clause a more restricted meaning. In *Deutsche Schachtbau-und Tiefbohrgesellschaft mbH v Ras Al Khaimah National Oil Co* [1987] 2 Lloyd's Rep 246, the choice of law in an arbitration in Switzerland was left to the arbitrators, who decided to apply 'internationally accepted principles of law governing contractual relations'. The Court of Appeal held that this did not lead to the conclusion that the parties did not intend to create legally enforceable rights and obligations, nor that it was void for uncertainty or contrary to public policy. It was unnecessary to decide what the choice of law involved: there was uncontested evidence that it was valid in Switzerland.

[18] In *Eagle Star Insurance Co Ltd v Yuval Insurance Co Ltd*, ante, the Court of Appeal did not disagree with the conclusion expressed in *Orion v Belfort*, ante, that a wide clause and a contract could not co-exist, but rather with the assumption in *Orion v Belfort* that the clause in question gave the arbitrator a complete discretion.

[19] *Eagle Star v Yuval*, ante; *Home Insurance Co v Administratia Asigurarilor de Stat*, supra.

[20] If in principle the decision is susceptible of attack, see p. 648–649, post.

contract from coming into existence, the answer must be in the negative[1]. If, on the other hand, the presence of the clause can be reconciled with a substantive contract which creates legal rights, there seems no reason why the proceedings should not amount to an arbitration[2].

D. JURISDICTION

1 Introduction: jurisdiction and discretion

We now turn to consider the rules which govern the exercise of jurisdiction over the conduct of arbitrations. Given the importance attached by English law to the seat of the arbitration in the choice of the curial law and to a lesser but still important extent in the choice of the proper law of the contract and thus indirectly of the proper law of the arbitration agreement, it might be thought that English law would have adopted one simple governing rule: that the English court exercises jurisdiction and recognises the jurisdiction of a foreign court if, but only if, the seat of the arbitration is within the territory where that court exercises jurisdiction.

However, as we shall see, this formulation, while acceptable as a rough statement of the effect of the English rules with regard to jurisdiction, is something of an oversimplification. Although there is a good deal to be said, on practical grounds, for basing jurisdiction simply on the seat of the arbitration, English law has not adopted one simple rule of jurisdiction conforming to this model.

The basic rule of English jurisdiction is that it may be invoked as a matter of right against persons[3] who can properly be served with proceedings within the territorial limits of the Court's jurisdiction, i.e. within England and Wales. It cannot be invoked as of right in any other case. There are, however, circumstances, laid down by Rules of Court, in which the Court may as a matter of discretion allow the jurisdiction to be invoked by service of proceedings on persons outside the territorial limits of the jurisdiction[4].

Just as jurisdiction may be invoked as of right against person properly served within the jurisdiction, so also certain types of remedy may be invoked as of right if the plaintiff pleads and proves the ingredients of a cause of action which entitles him to a particular remedy. Thus in the majority of cases an award of debt or damages will flow as a matter of course once the plaintiff has made good

---

[1] This is not as obvious as it might seem. It could be argued that although there can be no arbitration unless the parties intend the award to create legally enforceable rights (see pp. 83–85, ante), this is not the same as saying that the substantive contract must itself create such rights. If the arbitration agreement can be severed from the substantive contract (see pp. 108–111, ante) why should not the one be capable of creating legal rights even if the other does not? This argument raises a question on the law of contract which is too complex to be argued here. We shall only say that we doubt whether the courts will find it convincing.

[2] The point is not discussed in the foreign literature, no doubt because most codes of procedure expressly permit the arbitrator to act as *amiable compositeur*, if the agreement so provides.

[3] We are not here concerned with the exercise of jurisdiction *in rem* which plays no part in the Court's powers in relation to arbitrations, save in the cases mentioned at pp. 339–341, post.

[4] The rules require qualification in cases falling within the European Judgments Conventions: see p. 87, post.

his case. But this is not always so. Equitable remedies, such as injunctions or declarations, and statutory remedies, such as the power to appoint an arbitrator, to set aside an award or to give leave to appeal on a question of law, are almost always discretionary. In the field of arbitration most of the Court's powers fall into the category of discretionary powers[5].

There may thus be two stages at which the Court has a discretion whether to assume jurisdiction or to exercise it by granting a particular remedy. First, when deciding whether to allow service out of the jurisdiction, and second, when deciding whether or not to grant a discretionary remedy[6]. At each stage the fact that the arbitration has its seat abroad or is governed by a foreign law is relevant to the exercise of the discretion.

With these preliminary observations in the background we now turn to consider the circumstances in which the English Court assumes and exercises jurisdiction over arbitration, particularly those conducted in England under a foreign curial law and those conducted abroad, and the circumstances in which an English court will recognise the jurisdiction of a foreign court to make orders in respect of an arbitration.

2 The European Judgments Conventions

Before doing so it is convenient at this point to discuss briefly the impact of the European Judgments Conventions on matters of arbitration. These Conventions have the force of law in the United Kingdom by virtue of section 2 of the Civil Jurisdiction and Judgments Act 1982. However, Article I of the principal Convention[7] provides that the Convention shall not apply to arbitration.

The effect of this is to withdraw from the scope of the Convention matters such as proceedings to set aside or enforce an award[8] or proceedings ancillary to arbitration, e.g. proceedings concerning the validity of an arbitration agreement or for the purpose of appointing or removing an arbitrator[9]. There is a controversy as to whether the effect of Article I is also to render invalid a judgment given despite a valid agreement to arbitrate, but apart from this one case, which is discussed in Chapter 30, post, the Conventions have no bearing on questions of jurisdiction in matters relating to arbitration.

3 Jurisdiction of the English Court

The jurisdiction of the English Court may be invoked as of right by service of

---

[5] The few that do not are referred to specifically below. They are: stay under s. 1 of the 1979 Act, enforcement of the award by action, and damages for breach of the agreement to arbitrate.

[6] The likely outcome at the second stage may also be relevant at the first.

[7] The Convention on Jurisdiction and the Enforcement of Judgments in Civil and Commercial Matters signed at Brussels on 27 September 1968.

[8] Reports by Mr P Jenard on the 1968 Convention and the 1971 Protocol: OJ 1979 No C59 p. 13. Such matters are already dealt with in other international conventions, e.g. the New York Convention: see Appendix 2, post.

[9] Report by Prof Peter Schlosser on the Accession Convention: OJ 1979 No C59, paras 64 and 65. This report and the report cited in the previous footnote, derive their authority from s. 3(3) of the Civil Jurisdiction and Judgments Act 1982.

proceedings on a defendant present within the jurisdiction[10]. In proceedings arising in connection with an arbitration either the respondent or the claimant will be the defendant[11]. So long as the defendant is served within the jurisdiction, the right of the plaintiff to invoke the jurisdiction of the court is not affected by the fact that the seat of the arbitration may not be in England or that the parties may have chosen to arbitrate in England under a foreign curial law.

The position is different where the defendant cannot be served in England. Here the Court may allow proceedings to be served abroad in two categories of case.

The first category consists of proceedings falling within Order 73, rule 7 of the Rules of the Supreme Court. This provides so far as is material to the present discussion, that—

'(1) Service out of the jurisdiction—
   (*a*) of an originating summons for the appointment of an arbitrator or umpire, or
   (*b*) of notice of an originating motion to remove an arbitrator or umpire or to remit or set aside an award, or
   (*c*) of an originating summons or notice of an originating motion under the Arbitration Act 1979, or
   (*d*) of any order made on such a summons or motion as aforesaid,
is permissible with the leave of the Court provided that the arbitration to which the summons, motion or order relates is governed by English law or has been, is being, or is to be held within the jurisdiction.
(1A) Service out of the jurisdiction of an originating summons for leave to enforce an award is permissible with the leave of the Court whether or not the arbitration is governed by English law.'

Rule (1) covers most of the more common types of application. There are, however, a number of exceptions—

1 An application for leave to revoke the authority of an arbitrator or umpire under section 1 of the 1950 Act[12].
2 An order under section 8(3) of the 1950 Act that the umpire shall enter upon the reference as if he were a sole arbitrator.
3 Orders for interim measures under section 12 of the 1950 Act.
4 An order under section 27 extending the time for the commencement of arbitration proceedings.
5 An action to enforce an award[13].
6 Actions relating to the agreement to arbitrate, such as a claim for damages for breach of the agreement, or for a declaration that the agreement has come to an end and an injunction restraining further proceedings.
7 Interlocutory orders under section 5 of the 1979 Act.

Some of these exceptions, however, fall within the second category of cases where the court may give leave to serve proceedings outside the jurisdiction.

---

[10] In the case of an application to stay proceedings brought in breach of an arbitration agreement the jurisdiction will already have been invoked by the plaintiff; so the court will always have jurisdiction to grant a stay.

[11] It is sometimes also necessary to serve the arbitrator if the relief claimed affects him, but we do not believe that the arbitrator is ever the sole defendant to proceedings.

[12] And the powers under s. 25(2) which are consequential on such an order.

[13] As distinct from enforcement under s. 26, which is within Order 73, rule 7(1).

This consists of claims for relief falling within Order 11, rule 1(1) of the Rules of the Supreme Court. The types of claim which are of relevance to arbitration fall within the following subrules, where in the action—

> '(*a*) relief is sought against a person domiciled within the jurisdiction,[14]
>
> (*b*) an injunction is sought ordering the defendant to do or refrain from doing anything within the jurisdiction[15] . . .,
>
> (*c*) the claim is brought to enforce, rescind, dissolve, annul or otherwise affect[16] a contract, or to recover damages or obtain other relief in respect of the breach of a contract being (in either case) a contract which—
>
> > (i) was made within the jurisdiction, or
> >
> > (ii) was made by or through an agent trading or residing within the jurisdiction on behalf of a principal trading or residing out of the jurisdiction, or
> >
> > (iii) is by its terms or by implication governed by English law . . .
>
> (*e*) the claim is brought in respect of a breach committed within the jurisdiction of a contract made within or out of the jurisdiction[17] . . .,
>
> (*m*) the claim is brought to enforce any judgment or arbitral award . . .'

Sub-rule *(c)*, in particular, is wide enough to cover claims for a declaration, an injunction, or damages where the arbitration agreement is governed by English law[18] or was made in England or through an agent in England.

Moreover, the Court always has jurisdiction to enforce an award, either under Order 73, rule 7(1A) or under Order ii, rule 1(1)(m), whenever it was made, whatever the nationality of the parties, and although the arbitration was governed in its entirety by foreign law.

4 Discretion of the English Court

(a) Claims as of right

Up to this point the discussion has simply addressed the question whether the English court can in principle assume jurisdiction over certain types of proceeding. As has already been explained, however, the Court nearly always, in the field of arbitration, either has a discretion whether to allow service out of the jurisdiction, or whether to grant a discretionary remedy.

There are only three cases where this is not so—

1 Where the conditions for a stay of proceedings under section 1 of the 1975 Act are satisfied, a stay follows as a matter of course[19].

---

[14] But, ex hypothesi, not present within the jurisdiction.

[15] Such as taking part in an arbitration within the jurisdiction.

[16] E.g. by making a declaration that it has come to an end: *BP Exploration (Libya) Ltd v Hunt* [1976] 1 Lloyd's Rep 471.

[17] We include this for completeness: but the only breach of an arbitration agreement likely to be committed is the commencement of proceedings here, for which the principal remedy is a stay.

[18] *Naviera Amazonica Peruana SA v Compania Internacional de Seguros del Peru* [1988] 1 Lloyd's Rep 116, 118–9.

[19] See Chapter 30, post.

2 Where the conditions for enforcing an award are satisfied, it will be enforced as a matter of course[20].

3 Since a claim for damages is not a discretionary remedy, a claim for damages for breach of the arbitration agreement can be brought as of right against a defendant sued within the jurisdiction, even though the arbitration agreement may be governed by a foreign law and provide for arbitration outside England[1].

In every other case the court has a discretion, and the exercise of the discretion will be strongly influenced against its jurisdiction being invoked or exercised if (a) the curial law is not English law, or (b) the seat of the arbitration is outside England. These two situations call for separate discussion.

(b) Foreign curial law

The choice of a foreign curial law does not, we submit, deprive the English court of jurisdiction[2]. It has never, so far as we are aware, been suggested that parties may validly contract out of the power to set aside or remit an award for misconduct[3]; and if an explicit agreement cannot accomplish this, it is hard to see how it could be achieved indirectly by the choice of a foreign curial law. Nevertheless the choice of a foreign curial law is a strong reason for the court refusing leave to serve proceedings abroad or to grant discretionary remedies.

It is indeed difficult to conceive of any circumstances in which the English Court would intervene in an arbitration abroad in matters governed by the curial law[4]. If the proper law of the arbitration agreement or of the reference were English law it is perhaps possible to envisage circumstances in which the English Court might allow service abroad for the purpose of giving effect to the agreement or its termination, but only if there were reasons why such remedies could not be obtained from the local court[5].

If, on the other hand, the reference is or has been held in England as the seat of the arbitration, the reluctance of the English court to intervene may be less strong, depending on the nature of the relief which is sought. Jurisdiction to set aside an award is assigned to the state in which an award is made, both by the

---

[20] See Chapter 28, post.

[1] This exception may seem anomalous, but it is unlikely to be of great practical importance. If it arises, the doctrine of *forum non conveniens* may come into play.

[2] *Miller v Whitworth Street Estates (Manchester) Ltd* [1970] AC 583 has sometimes been regarded as holding that the jurisdiction was ousted by a choice of curial law. We doubt whether this is the correct interpretation of the decision, in the light of *Bank Mellat v Helleniki Techniki SA* [1984] QB 291. See also *Gola Sports Ltd v General Sportcraft Co Ltd* [1982] Com LR51.

[3] *Tullis v Jacson* [1892] 3 Ch 441 is treated in the headnote to the report as having decided that parties can validly agree that fraud on the part of an arbitrator shall not be raised by them, but (a) the architect in that case had acted as a certifier, not an arbitrator, and (b) there was no application to remit or set aside the certificate, merely an attempt to treat it as a nullity on grounds of fraud.

[4] But Article V (1)(e) of the New York Convention (s. 5(e) of the 1975 Act) appears to envisage proceedings to set aside an award made under a curial law other than the law of the seat of the arbitration.

[5] The question whether leave should be granted in such a case was directly raised in *Black Clawson v Aschaffenburg* [1981] 2 Lloyd's Rep 446. This particular aspect of the discretion did not, however, arise for decision, since it was held that the arbitration agreement was not governed by English law, and that in any event the action for a declaration had no prospect of success.

New York Convention and the Geneva Convention[6]. Moreover the objections based on grounds of comity and practical convenience to intervening in an arbitration held abroad are less telling when the reference is conducted in England. Nevertheless there will be great practical difficulties in matching characteristically Anglo-Saxon remedies to a foreign procedure[7], and this will often lead to the conclusion that a particular remedy should not be granted[8]. Nevertheless there may be occasions where the remedy is sufficiently close to a procedure recognised by the curial law[9] that the English court could properly and conveniently lend its assistance to the reference.

Next, there is the question whether the English court would exercise, by means of appeal its jurisdiction to ensure that the award is correct in point of law. This is a problem which is most unlikely to arise in practice. In almost every case, a choice of foreign curial law will be accompanied by a choice of foreign substantive law: for it is hard to conceive of any reason why the parties should wish to have an arbitration in England under English substantive law, but to have it conducted in accordance with a foreign curial law. This being so, the question of an appeal will almost always solve itself, since foreign law is a question of fact before an English tribunal, and the English court has no jurisdiction to receive an appeal upon it. In the exceptional case where the substantive law is English, although the curial law is foreign, we believe that the court would treat the choice of curial law as a factor telling against the granting of leave to appeal[10].

(c) Foreign seat of arbitration

An express choice of a foreign seat of arbitration coupled with an express choice of English curial law is unusual but by no means unknown[11]. It may come about for one of two reasons. First because the substantive contract is governed by the law of a common law country, and the parties wish to have arbitrators familiar with the common law. This means that the tribunal will be most at ease with an adversarial system, and express provision is made for the conduct of the reference according to this system, even if for convenience the arbitration is held abroad. Or, second, the parties like the English system in general, but do not care for the appeal on a question of law and hope to avoid it by siting the hearings elsewhere.

In this situation the English court would be highly unlikely to assume

---

[6] Article V(1)(e) of the New York Convention (s. 5(e) of the 1975 Act), and Article 2(a) of the Geneva Convention (s. 37(2)(a) of the 1950 Act). See, however, the previous footnote.

[7] The procedural rules of one jurisdiction are peculiarly resistant to being exported to another; an English court could have no confidence that it had the correct 'feel' for the way in which the foreign court, seized of the matter, would have decided to handle it; and the exercise would be impossible if (as is very often the case) the foreign code assigned to a breach of the procedural rules a remedy unknown to English law, to be applied by an identified court in the foreign country.

[8] As in *Bank Mellat v Helleniki Techniki SA* [1984] QB 291, where, however, the remedy was refused mainly because of the international character of the proceedings: the curial law was in fact English.

[9] E.g. orders for the inspection or preservation of property.

[10] A simple choice of curial law would not in itself be sufficiently explicit to amount to an exclusion agreement under s. 3 of the 1979 Act: see Chapter 36, post.

[11] An implied choice of English curial law would be most improbable where the arbitration was to be held abroad.

jurisdiction to intervene in the reference or to set aside or remit the award[12]. Any attempt to exercise powers to appoint arbitrators or to give ancillary relief, such as orders for the inspection of property would in fact present formidable difficulties of enforcement. Moreover the prospect of two courts exercising supervisory powers over the same reference at the same time would appear to be unacceptable.

5 Interim relief in England in aid of a foreign arbitration

It is convenient to mention here the provisions of section 25(3) of the Civil Jurisdiction and Judgments Act 1982 which enables Orders in Council to be made extending the power of the Court to grant interim relief so as to make it exercisable in relation to arbitration proceedings. 'Interim relief' means interim relief of any kind which that court has power to grant in proceedings relating to matters within its jurisdiction in other than (a) a warrant for the arrest of property or (b) provision for obtaining evidence[13].

No Order in Council has yet been made for this purpose, and the principal source of powers to grant interim relief therefore is still the provisions of section 12(6) of the 1950 Act[14]. It has always been assumed that these powers are exercisable only in relation to an arbitration conducted in England, and we see no prospect of the court allowing them to be invoked in aid of a foreign arbitration, thus usurping the prerogative of extending interim relief to foreign arbitrations by means of an Order in Council.

---

[12] In *Naviera Amazonica Peruana SA v Compania Internacional de Seguros del Peru* [1988] 1 Lloyd's Rep 116, at 120 Kerr LJ went so far as to say that the Court has no jurisdiction over arbitrations held abroad, even under English curial law, because the jurisdiction is 'territorially limited'. If such a limit exists, it is limited to arbitrations, and does not appear to be a limit imposed on foreign courts in cases covered by Article V(1)(e) of the New York Convention, nor on the English court under Order 73, rule 7, both of which treat the curial law as carrying with it jurisdiction over an arbitration conducted outside the territory of the state exercising jurisdiction.

[13] S. 25(7).

[14] They are discussed in Chapter 23, below.

PART II

The agreement to arbitrate

CHAPTER 5

Introduction

An arbitration agreement may be analysed into two distinct obligations[1] which the courts will enforce –

1 One party, B, promises to the other party, A, that if a valid award is made in favour of A in relation to a dispute which falls within the scope of the agreement, B will perform the award.

2 B promises to A that if B has a claim which falls within the scope of the agreement, B will enforce that claim only by means of a reference to arbitration. These undertakings by B are matched by similar promises on the part of A.

The methods by which these obligations may be enforced are discussed later in the book[2]. In this part, we are concerned only with the following questions –

1 Has an agreement containing these obligations come into existence[3]?

2 Has a dispute or claim arisen which falls within the scope of the agreement[4]?

3 Are the claimant and defendant parties to the agreement[5]?

4 Is the dispute or claim one which the law recognises as a legitimate subject of an agreement to arbitrate[6]?

5 Do the parties to the agreement have the necessary capacity to enter into the agreement[7]?

These questions arise for consideration at various stages of an arbitration.

At the initial stage, the questions are relevant to two important practical matters. First, is the dispute or claim one which the claimant may refer to arbitration? Second, is it one which the claimant must refer to arbitration if the defendant so insists? Later, when the arbitrator enters on the reference, the questions are relevant when deciding whether the arbitrator has jurisdiction to decide the matters referred to him. Finally, after the arbitrator has published his award, the questions are relevant when deciding whether the award is binding on the parties.

When discussing these various questions it is convenient to consider separately two distinct types of arbitration agreement –

1 Agreements to refer future disputes to arbitration.

---

[1] In Chapter 32, post, p. 497, we consider the existence of a third implied obligation, namely a promise by each party to the other to cooperate in the conduct of the reference.

[2] Enforcement of the first obligation is discussed in Chapter 28. Enforcement of the second obligation is discussed in Chapter 30.

[3] See p. 105, post.

[4] This embraces two separate questions: (i) to what types of claim or dispute does the agreement apply, and (ii) has such a claim or dispute arisen? The first of these questions is discussed at pp. 108–121, post, and the second at pp. 122–131, post.

[5] See Chapter 8, post. The problems of joining co-defendants and third parties are considered in Chapter 9, post.

[6] See Chapter 10, post.

[7] See Chapter 11, post.

2 Agreements to refer existing disputes to arbitration (often called 'ad hoc agreements').

The first type of agreement is usually found in the form of an arbitration clause in the contract governing the substantive rights of the parties, and this feature gives rise to some difficult problems when the underlying contract is alleged to have come to an end, e.g. by virtue of the doctrines of discharge by breach or frustration, or to be affected by illegality, duress, etc. These problems are discussed in Chapter 6[8].

The second type of agreement does not share this feature; but it gives rise to its own special problems, which are discussed in Chapter 7[9].

The existence of an arbitration agreement does not afford a defence to an action brought in breach of it[10], nor does it deprive the Court of jurisdiction over the dispute. The Court retains a residual jurisdiction, superior to that of the arbitrator, which it may either assert or relinquish, depending on the circumstances. This is discussed in Chapter 12[11].

---

[8] Post, p. 105.

[9] Post, p. 132.

[10] Unless it is so worded as to provide that no right of action shall arise in the absence of a favourable award. Clauses in this form, called *Scott v Avery* clauses, are discussed in Chapter 13, post p. 161.

[11] Post, p. 154.

CHAPTER 6

Agreements to refer future disputes

A. EXISTENCE OF AGREEMENT

It is unusual to find an agreement to refer future disputes to arbitration completely isolated from any other contractual relationship. The agreement almost always forms part of, or is at least ancillary to, some underlying contract.

If the agreement takes this form, three questions must be considered when determining whether there is in existence a binding agreement to arbitrate[1] –

1 Did the underlying contract itself come into existence?

2 If so, does it incorporate an agreement to submit future disputes to arbitration?

3 If so, are the terms of that agreement sufficiently certain to be enforceable? These questions are discussed below.

1 Existence of underlying contract

Unless the underlying contract itself came into existence as a legally enforceable agreement it cannot contain an effective submission to arbitration. This principle is discussed in more detail later in this chapter[2].

2 Incorporation of agreement to arbitrate

As to the second question, it is well established that the parties need not set out the terms of their arbitration agreement in the contract itself. It is sufficient for the clause to be incorporated by reference either to a standard form of clause or to a set of trade terms which themselves include provisions requiring disputes to be submitted to arbitration[3]. Nor need the contract itself be contained in a single

---

[1] If the court is asked to stay proceedings on the ground that they are covered by an agreement to arbitrate, the question whether such an agreement exists should be decided by the Court at the outset: see p. 108, post.

[2] See p. 108, post.

[3] There are many examples in the reports relating to the rules of trade associations. Reference may also be made to *Wyndham Rather Ltd v Eagle Star* and *British Dominions Insurance Co Ltd* (1925) 21 Ll L Rep 214 (action on insurance slip, which was stated to be subject to proposal form, which in turn was subject to the usual conditions of the company policy, which contained an arbitration clause); *Beattie v E and F Beattie Ltd* [1938] Ch 708 (article of association of private company was not a written agreement to arbitrate within s. 4); *London Sack and Bag Co Ltd v Dixon and Lugton Ltd* [1943] 2 All E R 763; *Hickman v Kent and Romney Marsh Sheep-Breeders' Association* [1915] 1 Ch 881; *Excomm Ltd v Bamaodah, The St. Raphael* [1985] 1 Lloyd's Rep 403. It is not necessary to prove that the parties knew of the arbitration provisions thus incorporated: *Golodetz v Schrier* (1947) 80 Ll L Rep 647, explaining *McConnell and Reid v Smith* 1911 SC 635.

document; an agreement to arbitrate can be spelt out in an exchange of correspondence or telex messages[4] but the documents must be clear enough to show that the parties did indeed intend to incorporate an agreement to arbitrate[5]. Prima facie, a reference to the rules of a particular arbitral institution is a reference to the rules for the time being, not those in force at the time when the contract was made[6].

In principle an arbitration clause may be incorporated by a reference to a standard form of contract or the particular terms of another contract in which the clause is set out, even without express reference to the clause. But it must be clear that the parties intended the arbitration clause to apply[7].

3 Certainty

As regards the third question, it must be shown that the terms of the agreement to arbitrate are sufficiently certain to be enforceable. Allegations of uncertainty may arise in various ways.

(a) Inconsistent clauses

In the first place, it may happen that the contractual documents contain two or more apparently inconsistent provisions as to arbitration. In such a situation, the court will usually try to save the submission to arbitration[8], either by effecting a reconciliation between the clauses, or by construing one clause as applicable to the exclusion of the others[9]. Sometimes, however, the conflict will be so acute that the Court can make no sense of the arbitration provisions, read as a whole. In such a case, the underlying contract will not be void for uncertainty, but will be enforced as if it contained no provision for arbitration[10].

---

[4] See, for example, *Hattersley v Hatton* (1862) 3 F & F 116; *Morgan v William Harrison Ltd* [1907] 2 Ch 137; *Frank Fehr & Co v Kassam Jivraj & Co Ltd* (1949) 82 Ll L Rep 673, and see s. 7(1) of the 1975 Act.

[5] *Italian Delegation on Wheat Supplies v Certain Exporting Houses* (1925) 22 Ll L Rep 139; *Macleod Ross & Co Ltd v Compagnie d'Assurances Générales L'Helvetia* [1952] 1 Lloyd's Rep 12, [1952] 1 All ER 331 (certificate of insurance not incorporating foreign jurisdiction clause from policy). *The Elizabeth H* [1962] 1 Lloyd's Rep 172, as explained in *Modern Buildings Wales Ltd v Limmer and Trinidad Co Ltd* [1975] 2 Lloyds Rep 318.

[6] See p. 282, post.

[7] Where the arbitration clause is in terms which are prima facie inapt for the contract in question (e.g. where a clause covering disputes 'under this charterparty' is said to be incorporated into a bill of lading), the Court will not engage in the verbal manipulation necessary to make the clause fit the new context unless it is quite clear that this was what was intended: *T W Thomas & Co Ltd v Portsea Co Ltd* [1912] AC 1; *The Annefield* [1971] P 168, [1971] 2 WLR 320; *The Rena K* [1979] QB 377, [1978] 3 WLR 431; *Skips A/S Nordheim v Syrian Petroleum Co Ltd, The Varenna* [1983] 2 Lloyd's Rep 592; *Pine Top Insurance Co Ltd v Unione Italiana Anglo Saxon Reinsurance Co Ltd* [1987] 1 Lloyd's Rep 476.

[8] Cf. per Mocatta J in *Astro Vencedor Compania Naviera SA v Mabanaft GmbH* [1970] 2 Lloyd's Rep 267 at 271.

[9] See *Central Meat Products Co Ltd v JV McDaniel Ltd* [1952] 1 Lloyd's Rep 562.

[10] *Lovelock v Exportles* [1968] 1 Lloyds Rep 163. See also *Nicolene v Simmonds* [1953] 1 QB 543 at 550. These were cases where the contract had already been executed by the time the issue arose. The position might well be different, if the question were to be raised at a time when the bargain were still executory. See also *Gola Sports Ltd v General Sportcraft Co Ltd* [1982] Com LR 51.

(b) Abbreviated clauses

A similar question will arise, where the parties have agreed upon a term as to arbitration, but it is said that the term is too uncertain to be enforced. The courts will lean against frustrating the intention of the parties, and will try to give the clause a meaning. It is thus no objection that the clause is terse. Thus, 'Arbitration to be settled in London' is sufficiently clear to be enforced[11], and indeed it has been said that the single word 'Arbitration' will suffice[12].

(c) 'in the usual way'

One laconic form in common use[13] provides that disputes shall be decided by arbitration 'in the usual way'. The courts have invariably recognised this form as effective, in cases where it has come into question[14]. A provision in this form governs not only the mode of appointing the arbitrators, but also the conduct of the reference itself[15]. The 'usual way' does not mean 'in accordance with the Arbitration Acts'; it refers to the way in which disputes about the particular commodity or subject matter are usually dealt with in the trade.

In order to ascertain what is the usual practice, the Court will take into account any relevant standard trade terms[16], and will also receive evidence from persons with experience in the trade[17]. The evidence need not show that the practice is invariable, it need only be usual[18]. Some identifiable practice must, however, be proved. If it is not, the Court will simply fall back on the mode of conducting the arbitration prescribed by the Acts and by the common law[19].

4 Arbitration in absence of prior agreement

The preceding paragraphs set out the requirements which must be satisfied if

---

11 *Tritonia Shipping Inc v South Nelson Forest Products Corpn* [1966] 1 Lloyd's Rep 114; cf. *Transamerican Ocean Contractors Inc v Transchemical Rotterdam BV* [1978] 1 Lloyd's Rep 238.

12 Per Salmon LJ in *Hobbs Padgett & Co (Reinsurance) Ltd v JC Kirkland Ltd and Kirkland* [1969] 2 Lloyd's Rep 547 at 549. It was conceded that 'Arbitration Clause' would be an enforceable submission to arbitration.

13 This formula is of long standing: see *Wallis v Hirsch* (1856) 1 CBNS 316; *Hirsch v Im Thurn* (1858) 4 CBNS 569. It used to be commonplace. We believe that it is now much more rarely seen.

14 *Bright & Bros v Gibson & Co* (1916) 32 TLR 533; *Scrimaglio v Thornett and Fehr* (1923) 17 Ll L Rep 34, on appeal (1924) 18 Ll L Rep 148; *Naumann v Edward Nathan & Co Ltd* (1930) 36 Ll L Rep 268, on appeal 37 Ll L Rep 249; *Central Meat Products v McDaniel*, ante; *Roth Schmidt & Co v Nagase & Co Ltd* (1920) 2 Ll L Rep 36; *Palmer & Co Ltd v Pilot Trading Co Ltd* (1929) 33 Ll L Rep 42. See also *Hobbs Padgett v Kirkland*, ante, where the term was 'suitable arbitration clause', and *Hamlyn & Co v Talisker Distillery* [1894] AC 202 at 208.

15 *Naumann v Nathan*, supra. The contrary opinion expressed by Scrutton LJ in *Scrimaglio v Thornett and Fehr*, supra, is probably not of general application, but relates merely to the difficulty often experienced in proving what constitutes the practice.

16 *Central Meat Products v McDaniel*, ante, at 511–512; *African and Eastern (Malaya) Ltd v White, Palmer & Co Ltd* (1930) 36 Ll L Rep 113.

17 *Scrimaglio v Thornett and Fehr*, ante, and *Laertis Shipping Corpn v Exportadora Espanola de Cementos Portland SA, The Laertis* [1982] 1 Lloyd's Rep 613 (reference to two arbitrators and an umpire); *Naumann v Nathan*, ante (umpire given a free hand on evidence).

18 *Naumann v Nathan*, ante, per Scrutton LJ at 150.

19 It is submitted that the Court would take this course, in order to save the submission, rather than regard the clause as a nullity. See per Edmund Davies LJ in *Hobbs Padgett & Co (Reinsurance) Ltd v JC Kirkland Ltd and Kirkland*, ante, at 550.

the Court is to hold that the parties have bound themselves to submit their future disputes to arbitration. It may, however, be noted that even if the Court is driven to conclude that there was, at the outset, no binding agreement to arbitrate, either because there was no underlying contract at all, or because the arbitration provisions of the contract were defective, the arbitrator may yet be regarded as having jurisdiction, if the parties have ratified the contract or the arbitration provisions of the contract by seeking to enforce them – either by enforcing the contract itself, or by taking part in an arbitration[20].

B. SCOPE OF AGREEMENT

Whether in any particular case a dispute falls within an agreement to arbitrate depends primarily upon the wording of the agreement[1], and each reported case must be read in the light of the particular form of clause with which it was concerned. It is, however, possible to state certain general rules as to the types of dispute which are and are not capable of falling within an agreement to submit future disputes to arbitration[2].

1 Disputes as to the existence of the contract

The courts have been much exercised by the question whether an arbitrator, appointed by virtue of an arbitration clause in a contract, has jurisdiction to rule upon the existence of the contract. In this respect, a distinction must be drawn between two questions. First, did the contract ever come into existence at all? Second, if it did once exist, has something occurred to bring it to an end?

(a) Initial existence of the contract

On the first of these questions, it has in the past always been accepted in England that an arbitrator cannot make a binding award as to the initial existence of the contract, and that he cannot foreclose the question by making an award which takes it for granted[3]. For if in truth no contract was ever made, then the arbitration provisions of the supposed contract never bound the parties; and an arbitrator appointed under those provisions could have no authority to act. So, although an arbitrator, faced with a dispute about whether a contract ever came into existence or if it did, whether a party to the arbitration was a party to the

---

[20] Hence creating either an ad hoc submission (as to which see p. 133, post) or an estoppel (as to which see p. 579, post). See, for example, *Naumann v Nathan*, ante, and *Hobbs Padgett v Kirkland* at 548 and 550.

[1] *Heyman v Darwins Ltd* [1942] AC 356, per Lord Porter at 392.

[2] The discussion in the text is concerned with the most common form of arbitration agreement, namely an arbitration clause included in a contract, the remaining terms of which fix the substantive rights of the parties. There appears to be no limit (except as regards illegal transactions: see post, p. 113) to the types of dispute which may be referred under a separate agreement to arbitrate.

[3] See per Blackburn J in *Duke of Buccleuch v Metropolitan Board of Works* (1870) LR 5 Exch 221 at 222; on appeal (1872) LR 5 HL 418.

agreement[4], can and often should[5] consider and rule upon it, his ruling does not bind the parties, and may always be reopened by the Court[6]. Again, if the agreement is bad for want of consensus, or consideration[7], or for mistake, or for uncertainty[8], or if it is rendered unenforceable by the Statute of Frauds, the arbitration clause is ineffectual. Similarly, if the parties have agreed to annul the contract, not simply by bringing it to an end as regards future performance, but by treating it as if it had never existed, the elimination of the contractual relationship carries with it the elimination of the jurisdiction to arbitrate[9]. So also if the contract has been replaced by a completely fresh agreement[9], for example by a new agreement designed to act as a compromise of disputes arising under the original contract[10], unless of course the arbitration clause is incorporated by reference into the new contract.

The principles thus stated have been part of English law for many years, and remain so today. There are, however, many exponents of arbitration theory in other countries who would not accept them as sound. We see no purpose in adding to the voluminous literature on the topic of *competenz competenz*, since it is of quite modest practical importance. Nevertheless, the following observations may be made.

In the first place, although the general principle that an arbitration clause is to some degree a separate engagement from the substantive contract in which it is embedded is now accepted in England, as it is elsewhere, it is hard to see how in practice this can yield the result that the clause is good even if the remainder is a nullity, otherwise than in the most exceptional case. If the arbitration agreement is contained in article 17 of a contract composed of 20 articles, what kind of vitiating circumstance could it be which would cause articles 1 to 16 and 18 to 20 to be regarded as if the contract had never been signed, and yet leave article 17 to stand untouched amongst the ruins?

On the other hand, a critic could fairly respond that the intellectual purity of this stance has already been compromised by the recognition that a dispute as to the continued existence of a contract, acknowledged to have been valid *ab initio*, does fall within the scope of an appropriately-worded clause: see pp. 110–113, post. Why should it be assumed, as it must be assumed in order to make sense of the law, that when a party announces with the utmost finality that he does not intend to perform any part of his outstanding obligations, and when the other party exercises his right to treat this as a wrongful repudiation and

---

[4] As in *Tudor Marine Ltd v Tradax Export SA, The Virgo* [1976] 2 Lloyd's Rep 135, where the problem of jurisdiction was overcome by an ad hoc agreement; see also *Dalmia Dairy Industries Ltd v National Bank of Pakistan* [1978] 2 Lloyd's Rep 223 at 292.

[5] See Chapter 35, post, as to the procedure to be adopted when the arbitrator's jurisdiction is put in issue.

[6] *Heyman v Darwins Ltd*, ante, at 366, 371, 384, 398; *Produce Brokers Co Ltd v Olympia Oil and Cake Co Ltd* [1916] 1 AC 314 at 327; *Toller v Law Accident Insurance Society Ltd* (1936) 55 Ll L Rep 258.

[7] As in *Goldsack v Shore* [1950] 1 KB 708. If the argument on want of consideration in *SA Hersent v United Towing Co Ltd and White, The Tradesman* [1961] 2 Lloyd's Rep 183 had been sound, it would in our submission have made the agreement void, not voidable, as suggested by Karminski J.

[8] Which was one view of the facts in *Payne and Routh v Hugh Baird & Sons* (1921) 9 Ll L Rep 167.

[9] See *Heyman v Darwins Ltd*, ante, per Lord MacMillan at 371.

[10] *Kianta Osakeyhtio v Britain and Overseas Trading Co Ltd* [1954] 1 Lloyd's Rep 247; affg. the decision of Devlin J at [1953] 2 Lloyd's Rep 569. It is, of course, a matter for consideration in each case whether the new agreement causes the complete disappearance of the old contract: *Taylor v Warden Insurance Co Ltd* (1933) 45 Ll L Rep 218.

brings the contractual relationship to an end, each of them is adding the unspoken qualification, except of course as regards the arbitration clause?' Can the distinction between initial invalidity and subsequent dissolution, attractive as it is, be logically sustained?

This question underlies another problem, of more obvious practical importance, namely whether an arbitration clause can be devised which would allow the arbitrator to award upon the initial existence of the contract. This is an open question[11]. Certain well-known forms of arbitration contain provisions intended to achieve this result by providing that the arbitrator shall not cease to have jurisdiction by reason of a challenge to the validity of the contract, provided that he upholds the validity of the agreement to arbitrate, and that he shall continue to have jurisdiction to adjudicate on the merits even though the contract may be non-existent or void[12]. There seems to be no objection in principle to giving effect to such a clause to the extent that it seeks to confer jurisdiction to decide on the initial validity of the contract[13] giving effect to such a clause. If it purports to give jurisdiction to decide on the validity of the clause itself it does, however, appear to present insuperable logical difficulties.

(b) Continued existence of the contract

The proposition that an arbitrator cannot rule on the *initial* existence of the contract from which his jurisdiction derives has never been seriously open to doubt. More troublesome is the question whether the arbitrator can award upon the *continued* existence of the contract. If one of the parties contends that something has happened to bring the contract to an end, how can the arbitrator effectively rule in his favour? For such a ruling would entail that at the moment when the arbitrator was appointed to decide the dispute there was no longer an agreement in existence under which he was empowered to decide anything at all.

After some decades of uncertainty, the courts solved this problem by drawing a distinction between the arbitration clause and the remaining provisions of the contract. In the words of Lord MacMillan[14]:

---

[11] The passage in the text is founded on the opinions expressed in *Heyman v Darwins Ltd*, ante, by Lord Wright at 385 and Lord Porter at 393 and 397. Presumably their Lordships were speaking of separate or severable arbitration agreements, for otherwise the logic is a little hard to follow. Unless there is an agreement, there can scarcely be an agreement to arbitrate anything at all, however widely the clause is expressed.

[12] See Art 8(4) of the Rules of Arbitration of the International Chamber of Commerce; and *Deutsche Schachtbau- und Tiefbohr GmbH v Ras al Khaimah National Oil Co* [1987] 2 Lloyd's Rep 246 at 250. Article 14 of the Rules of the London Court of International Arbitration states even more explicitly that the arbitration clause is to be treated as an agreement independent of the contract of which it forms part. Similar provisions are to be found in the UNCITRAL Model Rules and Model Law.

[13] The *Prima Paint* case: 388 US 395 (1967), a decision of the US Supreme Ct under the Federal Arbitration Act; and P. Sanders, L'Autonomie de la Clause Compromissoire in *Hommage à Frédéric Eisemann* (1978).

[14] In *Heyman v Darwins*, ante, per Lord MacMillan at 373–374, 375, 377. It is submitted that this is the true ratio decidendi of *Heyman v Darwins*. Most of the discussion in subsequent cases has concerned the distinction between the original existence of the contract, and its continued existence: see for example *Mackender, Hill and White v Feldia AG* [1966] 2 Lloyd's Rep 449, [1967] 2 QB 590. This distinction is valid and important, but it is academic unless the arbitration clause is regarded as distinct from the remainder of the contract.

'. . . an arbitration clause in a contract . . . is quite distinct from the other clauses. The other clauses set out the obligations which the parties undertake towards each other . . . but the arbitration clause does not impose on one of the parties an obligation in favour of the other. It embodies the agreement of both parties that, if any dispute arises with regard to the obligations which the one party has undertaken to the other, such dispute shall be settled by a tribunal of their own constitution . . . What is commonly called repudiation or total breach of a contract . . . does not abrogate the contract, though it may relieve the injured party of the duty of further fulfilling the obligation which he has by the contract undertaken to the repudiating party. The contract is not put out of existence, though all further performance of the obligations undertaken by each party in favour of the other may cease. It survives for the purpose of measuring the claims arising out of the breach, and the arbitration clause survives for determining the mode of their settlement. The purposes of the contract have failed, but the arbitration clause is not one of the purposes of the contract'.

(i) **Repudiation.** It follows that if the issue is whether the conduct of one party amounts to a repudiation of the contract, and if so whether the other party has 'accepted' the repudiation and brought the contract to an end[15], the arbitrator has jurisdiction to answer in the affirmative and to award damages, even if this involves deciding that substantive obligations under the contract have ceased to exist[16]. So also if one of the parties complains that the conduct of the other amounts to a deviation[17]. The arbitration clause survives, although it may be that if it incorporates a provision barring claims which are not made within a specified time, the latter is annulled in the same manner as other exception clauses.

(ii) **Fundamental breach.** The position is, we submit, the same where the issue is one of fundamental breach, if indeed that doctrine still has any existence[18].

(iii) **Frustration.** A similar course of reasoning leads to the conclusion that an arbitrator has power to decide whether a contract has been discharged by

---

[15] It could not seriously be contended that an unaccepted repudiation deprives the arbitrator of jurisdiction, since it leaves the contract untouched: see per Scrutton LJ in *Golding v London and Edinburgh Insurance Co Ltd* (1932) 43 Ll L Rep 487 at 488; *Heyman v Darwins*, ante, at 361–362, 372–373, 381.

[16] *Heyman v Darwins*, ante, not following various dicta in *Johannesburg Municipal Council v D Stewart & Co* 1909 SC (HL) 53 at 54 and 56 and *Jureidini v National British and Irish Millers Insurance Co Ltd* [1915] AC 499 at 505. It does not necessarily follow from *Heyman v Darwins* that the decision in *Jureidini's* case was wrong. It may be justified on the ground of waiver, and also by the special terms of the clause, which was a *Scott v Avery* provision relating only to the quantification of loss. See *Stevens & Sons v Timber and General Mutual Accident Insurance Association Ltd* (1933) 102 LJ KB 337 at 342–343; *Woodall v Pearl Assurance Co Ltd* [1919] 1 KB 593 at 609; and *Heyman v Darwins*, *passim.* Certain statements of principle in *Stevens'* case and *Woodall's* case are no longer sustainable, since they were founded on the dicat in *Jureidini*.

[17] *Woolf v Collis Removal Service* [1948] 1 KB 11.

[18] The point was kept open in *Pinnock Bros v Lewis and Peat Ltd* [1923] 1 KB 690. See also *Photo Production Ltd v Securicor Transport Ltd* [1980] 1 All ER 556, per Lord Diplock at 567.

frustration[19], and to award consequential relief under the Law Reform (Frustrated Contracts) Act 1943[1]. For this purpose, it makes no difference whether the contract has been partly performed or is still executory[2].

(iv) Termination provisions; conditions precedent.   Again, the same reasoning applies where the contract comes to an end through the operation of some termination provision in the contract itself. Thus, for example, where an insurance policy provided that unless the insurers were given notice of any increase in the risk, 'the policy is void and no claim can be made', the parties continued to be bound by a clause which made the obtaining of an award a condition precedent to a right of recovery, even though the insurers claimed that appropriate notice had not been given[3]. Equally, an arbitration clause survives the failure of a condition precedent to the operation of the contract[4].

(v) Misrepresentation and non-disclosure.   Finally, the courts have adopted a similar approach in cases where one party seeks to avoid or rescind a contract on the ground of a misrepresentation or non-disclosure, whether fraudulent, negligent or innocent. Provided that the words of the clause are sufficiently wide, these are matters which can be referred to arbitration[5]. So also

---

[19] Strictly speaking, the point is still open for decision, since the dicta on frustration in *Heyman v Darwins*, ante, were obiter, and the dicta of Lord Summer in *Hirji Mulji v Cheong Yue SS Co Ltd* [1926] AC 497 have not yet been formally overruled. But the reasoning in *Hirji Mulji* cannot stand with *Heyman v Darwins*, particularly since frustration is a stronger case than repudiation, since it does not involve the problems of approbation and reprobation which exercised the courts in the repudiation cases. In *Kruse v Questier & Co* [1953] 1 Lloyd's Rep 310, [1953] 1 QB 669 Pilcher J applied the dicta in *Heyman v Darwins* and declined to follow *Hirji Mulji*. In *Government of Gibraltar v Kenney* [1956] 2 QB 410 it was conceded that the issue of frustration fell within the jurisdiction of the arbitrator; and it may be noted that all the 'Suez frustration cases' came before the courts on cases stated by arbitrators.

[1] *Government of Gibraltar v Kenney*, supra.

[2] *Kruse v Questier*, ante.

[3] *Woodall v Pearl Assurance*, ante; *Stevens v Timber and General* (where there was no express clause, but the case was treated as governed by *Woodall*); *Kruse v Questier*, ante, at 679 (clause permitting cancellation for prohibition of export); *Heyman v Darwins*, ante, per Lord MacMillan at 371; *Foresta Romana SA v Georges Mabro (Owners)* (1940) 66 Ll L Rep 139; *Freshwater v Western Australian Assurance Co* [1933] 1 KB 515.

[4] *De la Garde v Worsnop & Co* [1928] Ch 17. This is a strong decision. The terms in question read: 'The agreement is subject to the conditions following . . .'. It might perhaps have been said that the failure of the condition brought down the agreement ab initio, and with it the arbitration clause.

[5] *Stevens & Sons v Timber and General*, ante; *Golding v London & Edinburgh Insurance Co Ltd* (1932) 43 Ll L Rep 487 (where the policy had been reinstated on payment of an additional premium); *Mackender v Feldia AG*, ante; *Craig v National Indemnity Co*, Lloyd J, 25 July 1980, unreported. There are dicta of Lords Macmillan and Wright to the contrary effect in *Heyman v Darwins*, ante at 371 and 384. But they scarcely seem consistent with the general principle, or indeed with the reasoning of the speeches as a whole: they are not referred to in *Mackender v Feldia*. In *Pennsylvania Shipping Co v Compagnie Nationale de Navigation* (1936) 55 Ll L Rep 271, decided before *Heyman v Darwins*, it appears to have been assumed that the arbitrator would have no jurisdiction over a question of rescission for misrepresentation. The decision in *Munro v Bognor UDC* [1915] 3 KB 167 appears to turn on the fact that the plaintiff asserted that the misrepresentation rendered the contract not merely voidable, but void: as a proposition of law this was erroneous, but if it had been correct it would have deprived the arbitrator of jurisdiction: see *Ashville Investments Ltd v Elmer Contractors Ltd* [1988] 2 Lloyd's Rep 73, where this problematical case is explained. Its value as a precedent must now be very doubtful, although it may have been correctly decided on its special facts.

can a claim for damages in lieu of rescission[6] or for negligent mis-statement inducing the contract[7].

2 Illegality

The question has occasionally arisen whether an arbitrator has jurisdiction to entertain disputes under contracts which are alleged to be illegal. Two situations must be distinguished.

First, where the contract was ab initio illegal under English law, or under the proper law of the contract, or both. Here, the illegality strikes at the validity of the contract itself, and hence at the agreement to arbitrate[8]. The arbitrator appointed under an illegal contract of this nature has no jurisdiction to rule either on the issue of illegality itself, or on any other matter arising out of the contract.

Second, where the contract subsequently becomes illegal under English law or the proper law, or the law of the place of performance. If the illegality arises under English law the arbitrator must take note of the point and rule upon it. But he is not deprived of jurisdiction[9], unless the effect of the illegality is not merely to make performance of the contract unlawful but to render the whole contract void ab initio[10].

3 Mistake and duress

There appears to be no reported decision on the arbitrability of issues concerning other matters, such as mistake and duress, which bear upon the existence of a binding contract.

The application of the principles laid down in the cases on repudiation and frustration suggests that a distinction should be drawn between defects which go to the existence of an initial agreement, and those which simply make the agreement liable to be set aside. Certain forms of fundamental mistake render the contract void ab initio. Others merely make it voidable[11]. It appears, on the law as it stands at present, that most types of mistake merely make the contract voidable; and this is generally so for duress. Accordingly, it would appear that

---

6 This is explicitly recognised in s. 2(2) of the Misrepresentation Act 1967. The section also recognises that an arbitrator may be empowered to declare a contract subsisting despite a claim for rescission: it would be extraordinary if he could not also be empowered to allow the claim for rescission.

7 *Ashville Investments Ltd v Elmer Contractors Ltd*, supra. Whatever may be the ratio decidendi of *Monro v Bognor Regis UDC*, supra, it can no longer be regarded as authority for any contrary principle.

8 *Joe Lee Ltd v Lord Dalmery* [1927] 1 Ch 300.

9 *Heyman v Darwins Ltd* [1942] AC 356, per Viscount Simon LC at 366, and Lord Wright at 384; *Mackender v Feldia AG* [1966] 2 Lloyds Rep 449, per Diplock LJ at 456–457; *Smith, Coney and Barrett v Backer, Gray & Co* [1916] 2 Ch 86; *David Taylor & Son Ltd v Barnett* [1953] 1 WLR 562; *Prodexport State Co for Foreign Trade v ED and F Man Ltd* [1972] 2 Lloyd's Rep 375, [1973] 1 QB 389. A dictum of Lord Denning MR in *Mackender v Feldia* at 455 appears to contradict the first of the propositions in the text, but we respectfully submit that it is not in accord with the general line of authority.

10 *Dalmia Dairy Industries v National Bank of Pakistan* [1978] 2 Lloyd's Rep 223 at 285–293. Although this was a decision on the law of India, the Court of Appeal treated the proposition in the text as based on logic rather than authority.

11 For guidance on the difficult problems raised by fundamental mistakes of fact, reference should be made to works on the law of contracts.

in general, questions of mistake and duress do not affect the jurisdiction of the arbitrator[12].

4 Issues as to facts founding the jurisdiction

Just as an arbitrator cannot make a binding award as to the existence of a contract which, if it does exist, is the source of his authority to act, so also does he lack the power to make a binding decision as to the existence of the facts which are said to found his jurisdiction[13]. Thus, where a building contract provided that an arbitration should not take place until after completion of the works, it was held that the parties were not bound by a decision of the arbitrator that the works has been completed[14]. Similarly, if the jurisdiction of the tribunal depends upon the giving of a notice, the tribunal has no power to decide whether an appropriate notice has been given[15].

It is another aspect of the same principle that if the agreement to arbitrate provides that certain facts or events shall be conditions precedent to the right of recovery, the arbitrator cannot make a binding award unless all the conditions are fulfilled; and this is so even if he genuinely believes (and decides in his award) that the conditions are fulfilled, because he either misconstrues the submission or misunderstands the facts. Conversely, if an arbitrator, by incorrectly construing the submission, adds a condition precedent to those stated in the submission, and, because the new condition was not fulfilled, dismisses the claim, it may be that he is to be regarded as having acted without jurisdiction, since he has not decided the dispute submitted to him[16].

5 Rectification

There is no reason in principle why a claim for the rectification of a contract should not be referred to arbitration, if the words of the clause are sufficiently

---

[12] The statement in the text is founded on the general approach adopted by the House of Lords in *Heyman v Darwins*, ante. But there are dicta in that case which suggest that where the contract is said to be vitiated by duress or mistake, the arbitrator necessarily cannot have jurisdiction. See per Lords MacMillan and Wright at 371 and 384. Possibly duress and mistake may be said to negative a true consensus to arbitrate.

[13] *Produce Brokers Co Ltd v Olympia Oil and Cake Co Ltd* [1916] 1 AC 314 at 322, 324, 327 and 329; *Smith v Martin* [1925] 1 KB 745; *May v Mills* (1914) 30 TLR 287: the principle is clearly stated in this case although its application to the facts may be questionable; *Payne and Routh v Hugh Baird & Sons* (1921) 9 Ll L Rep 167; *Bankers and Shippers' Insurance Co of New York v Liverpool Marine and General Insurance Co Ltd* (1925) 21 Ll L Rep 86 at 92; *Cope v Cope* (1885) 52 LT 607. In the first two cases, an analogy was drawn with the rule that inferior courts have no power to determine their own jurisdiction. This should not perhaps be taken too far. Arbitration is consensual, and the parties may wish to give the arbitrator power to rule on questions of jurisdiction. A similar intention cannot be attributed to the legislature when fixing the jurisdiction of inferior courts. See *Anisminic Ltd v Foreign Compensation Commission* [1969] 2 AC 147; *Getreide-Import GmbH v Contimar SA Compania Industrial Comercial y Maritima* [1953] 1 WLR 793 at 807.

[14] *Smith v Martin*, supra.

[15] *Getreide v Contimar*, ante. (Notice of appeal to arbitration appeal committee: neither the original arbitrators nor the appeal committee had jurisdiction to determine the validity of the notice. No doubt the same principle applies to the notice of arbitration which initiates the reference.)

[16] This seems to be the best explanation of *Anisminic Ltd v Foreign Compensation Commission* [1969] 2 AC 147. Whether that difficult case has any application to the law of arbitration has yet to be decided.

wide[17]. Such a claim does not impeach the contract but merely seeks to ensure that it accurately reproduces the true agreement between the parties. It may, however, be noted that some forms of clause in common use are not sufficiently wide to embrace a claim for rectification. Thus, rectification is not a claim which 'arises in relation to these presents' – for 'these presents' means the contract in its existing form[18]. Nor does such a claim raise a dispute 'touching the construction of the agreement and the rights, duties and liabilities of the parties thereunder[19].

6 Disputes as to scope of submission

Where the question is whether a dispute which admittedly falls within the terms of an agreement to arbitrate has in fact been submitted to the arbitrator so as to invest him with jurisdiction to decide that particular dispute, there are in effect two areas of conflict between the parties. First, they differ as to the merits of the substantive dispute. Second, they differ as to the power of the arbitrator to decide the substantive dispute. There is, we submit, no reason in principle why the arbitrator should not be invested, by a submission in appropriate terms[20], with the power to adjudicate upon the second of these differences: for even if he decides that he ought not to entertain the substantive dispute, he is not thereby denying his own capacity to make any adjudication at all[1]. Thus, where the complaint concerns excess of jurisdiction[2], rather than complete absence of

---

[17] *Ashville Investments Ltd v Elmer Contractors Ltd* [1988] 2 Lloyd's Rep 73; *Overseas Union Insurance Ltd v AA Mutual International Insurance Co Ltd* [1988] 2 Lloyd's Rep 63.

[18] *Printing Machinery Co Ltd v Linotype and Machinery Ltd* [1912] 1 Ch 566.

[19] *Crane v Hegeman-Harris Co Inc* [1939] 4 All ER 68. The decision can be explained also on the grounds that it concerned a reference of existing disputes, and that the claim for rectification was not in existence at the time when the arbitration agreement was entered into.

[20] Most common forms of arbitration clause are not wide enough: see for example *Food Corpn of India v Achilles Halcoussis, The Petros Hadjikyriakos* [1988] 2 Lloyd's Rep 56 at 61.

[1] There are undoubtedly dicta which may be cited for the contrary view: e.g. those of Devlin J in the *Christopher Brown Case*, ante, and in *Kianta Osakeyhtio v Britain and Overseas Trading Co Ltd* [1953] 2 Lloyd's Rep 569 at 573 and also of Lord Parmoor in *A-G for Manitoba v Kelly* [1922] 1 AC 268. But these must, we submit, be regarded as dealing either with the situation in which the entire jurisdiction is in issue, or with one in which the submission is not widely enough expressed to give the arbitrator the jurisdiction to decide on his own right to exercise a particular procedural power. *Willesford v Watson* (1873) 8 Ch App 473; *Piercy v Young* (1879) 14 Ch D 200; *De Ricci v De Ricci* [1891] P 378 all indicate that if the submission is sufficiently wide, a dispute on the scope of the submission may be entertained by the arbitrators. (This is how *Willesford v Watson* was read in the two latter cases. Whether it is what the Court actually said is, despite the headnote, by no means clear.) The dicta in *Llanelly Rly and Dock Co v London and North-Western Rly Co* (1873) 8 Ch App 942 and *Hirji Mulji v Cheong Yue SS Co Ltd* [1926] AC 497 at 503, cannot now be relied on, in the light of *Heyman v Darwins*, ante.

[2] Excess of jurisdiction would commonly be understood as meaning the award of relief which lies outside the submission, or outside the powers of the arbitrator. It appears, however, from *Anisminic v Foreign Compensation Tribunal*, ante, that in the field of public law the award of nothing may amount to an excess of jurisdiction, if the party has an absolute right to the award of something once certain specified conditions are found to be satisfied. If the arbitrator mistakenly adds a condition, and consequently dismisses the claim, he is held to have acted without jurisdiction, and not merely to have made an error of law. Possibly this difficult doctrine depends upon a distinction between mistakes about the construction of the submission and mistakes about the construction of the agreement or instrument which creates the substantive rights of the parties.

jurisdiction, an arbitrator's decision is, if the submission is sufficiently wide, a valid and binding[3] determination of the issue[4].

7 Disputes as to the arbitrator's powers

There is, moreover, a distinction between disputes as to the jurisdiction of the arbitrator and disputes as to the way in which that jurisdiction should be exercised: i.e. disputes as to his powers. Thus, there may be a conflict as to the power of the arbitrator to grant a particular remedy, such as an injunction, a declaration, interest or costs, in a given set of circumstances; or as to his power to admit or reject evidence[5]. Disputes of this kind are matters upon which the arbitrator may make an effective ruling[6]. Drawing the line between jurisdiction and powers is far from easy, but the modern tendency of the Court is to regard matters relating to the conduct of the reference as being concerned with powers rather than jurisdiction[7].

8 Fraud

An issue of fraud is capable in principle of falling within the scope of an agreement to arbitrate[8]; whether or not it does so depends on the wording of the agreement[9].

The Court has, however, a jurisdiction to order that the arbitration agreement shall cease to have effect, and may also give leave to revoke the authority of the arbitrator, so far as may be necessary to enable an issue of fraud to be determined in the High Court[10].

---

[3] Subject to an appeal: see Chapter 36.

[4] The distinction between absence of jurisdiction and excess of jurisdiction may be criticised on the ground that the latter is merely a case where jurisdiction is absent in relation to a particular dispute. This criticism derives its force from a confusion of terminology. Where no process of arbitration has been called into being, the question is not so much one of want of jurisdiction, but of non-existence of the arbitration. A non-existent arbitration cannot lead to a valid award about *anything*; an existing arbitration may or may not, depending on the scope of the submission.

[5] The courts and the texts have often used 'jurisdiction' to denote what we have called 'powers'. In fact, this latter form is also insufficiently precise, as is shown by the examples given in the text, which are not really instances of the same concept. We have not mentioned in the text the further distinction between questions of jurisdiction and questions of substance, which raises problems of equal nicety. See also *Anisminic v Foreign Compensation Tribunal*, ante, and *Peralman v Keepers and Governors of Harrow School* [1979] QB 56.

[6] They are not necessarily matters upon which the arbitrator can make a *final* ruling. The powers of the arbitrator are usually regarded as matters of law, particularly where they depend upon the construction of express words in the arbitration agreement: see, by way of example, *Oakland Metal Co Ltd v D Benaim & Co* [1953] 2 Lloyd's Rep 192, [1953] 2 QB 261; *FF Hookway v Alfred Isaacs & Sons* [1954] 1 Lloyd's Rep 491; *Macleod Ross & Co v Cradock Manners Ltd* [1954] 1 Lloyd's Rep 258.

[7] *Bank Mellat v GAA Development and Construction Co* [1988] 2 Lloyd's Rep 44.

[8] This is assumed by s. 24(2) of the 1950 Act, and was stated by Lords Wright and Porter in *Heyman v Darwins Ltd* [1942] AC 356 at 378 and 392. (These dicta are, it is submitted, more in accord with principle than the contrary view expressed by Lord MacMillan, ibid., at 371.) See also *Trainor v Phoenix Fire Assurance* (1891) 65 LT 825; *Kenworthy v Queen Insurance Co* (1892) 8 TLR 211 (cases on '*Scott v Avery*' clause); and *May v Mills* (1914) 30 TLR 287.

[9] *Heyman v Darwins*, supra, at 378 and 392. See also p. 108, ante.

[10] S. 24(2) of the 1950 Act. See p. 50, post, and *Permavox Ltd v Royal Exchange Assurance* (1939) 64 Ll L Rep 145.

9 Claims in tort

If the agreement to arbitrate is drawn in sufficiently wide terms, it will give the arbitrator jurisdiction to decide a dispute arising from a claim in tort[11]. Most instances of claims in tort submitted to arbitration relate to 'contractual negligence': i.e. the breach of a duty of care arising from a contract. Most of the more common forms of arbitration clause are sufficiently wide to give the arbitrator jurisdiction over such claims[12].

In deciding whether a claim in tort lies within the arbitrator's jurisdiction, the enquiry takes place in two stages. The first is to identify the nature of the dispute, and the second is to decide whether the tortious claim has a sufficiently close connection with claims under the contract to bring it within the scope of the arbitration clause[13].

10 Variations of the contract

Where one contract operates by variation or replacement of another and only one of them contains an arbitration clause, it is a question of construction whether disputes under both contracts, or only under one, fall within the clause[14].

11 Particular forms of words

When faced with problems of jurisdiction, the courts have usually confined themselves to considering whether a particular type of issue falls within the compass of a particular form of words. In general, they have not embarked upon a general exposition of the scope of any particular form of words, particularly since one often finds more than one formula used in the same clause[15]; and when

---

[11] E.g. *Astro Vencedor Compania Naviera SA v Mabanaft GmbH* [1971] 1 Lloyd's Rep 502, [1971] 2 QB 588 (claim for wrongful arrest of ship was a 'dispute arising during the execution of this charterparty').

[12] See *Woolf v Collis Removal Service* [1948] 1 KB 11 ('any claims'); *Re Polemis and Furness, Withy & Co* [1921] 3 KB 560; and *Lonrho Ltd v Shell Petroleum Co Ltd* (1978) Times, 1 February, Brightman J; cf. *Radio Publicity (Universal) Ltd v Compagnie Luxembourgeoise de Radiodifusion* [1936] 2 All ER 721. A clause requiring the reference of claims arising 'under' the contract might be wide enough to cover contractual negligence, but not claims arising from breaches of a duty arising otherwise than *ex contractu*, such as for negligent misrepresentation. But words such as 'in connection with' are generally wide enough to cover tortious claims connected with the contract: *Ashville Investments Ltd v Elmer Contractors Ltd* [1988] 2 Lloyd's Rep 73, distinguishing *Monro v Bognor UDC*, ante.

[13] *Empresa Exportadora de Azucar v Industria Azucarera Nacional SA, The Playa Larga and Marble Islands* [1983] 2 Lloyd's Rep 171. The variety of clauses and the diversity of possible claims in tort makes it impossible to express the principles involved in anything other than broad generalities. The Court will, however, start from the prima facie assumption that the parties intended that related disputes arising in contract and tort should be decided by the same tribunal: see per Ackner Ltd at p. 183.

[14] *Hattersley v Hatton* (1862) 3 F & F 116; *Wade-Gery v Morrison* (1877) 37 LT 270; *Morgan v William Harrison Ltd* [1907] 2 Ch 137; *Taylor v Warden Insurance Co Ltd* (1933) 45 Ll L Rep 218; *Kingdom of Italy v Suzuki; Kianta Osakeyhtio v Britain and Overseas Trading Co Ltd* [1954] 1 Lloyd's Rep 247; *EB Aaby's Rederi A/S v Union of India, The Evje* [1974] 2 Lloyd's Rep 57, [1975] AC 797; *Faghirzadeh v Rudolf Woolf* (SA) (Pty) Ltd [1977] 1 Lloyd's Rep 630; *Compania Maritima Zorroza SA v Maritime Bulk Carriers Corpn, The Marques de Bolarque* [1980] 2 Lloyd's Rep 186.

[15] As in *Wade-Gery v Morrison* (1877) 37 LT 270, where Bacon V-C said that the clause was 'almost as full as the art of man could devise'. For other wide forms, see *Cope v Cope* (1885) 52 LT 607; *Freshwater v Western Australian Assurance Co Ltd* [1933] 1 KB 515.

comparisons have been drawn between the effects of various formulae, the results have not always been consistent. For these reasons any attempt to ascribe an immutable meaning to a particular form of words would be not only unprofitable but positively misleading. Each arbitration clause must be construed in the context of the contract as a whole, and the meaning of a particular formula may be broader or narrower depending on the nature of the transaction, the circumstances in which the arbitration clause came into existence, and the other provisions of the contract. A decision on a particular form of words in one contract is no sure guide to its meaning in another.

Nevertheless certain broad principles of construction may be said to be emerging from the more recent decisions[16]. First, the courts will make the prima facie assumption that the parties intended that all disputes relating to a particular transaction to be resolved by the same tribunal, and that by agreeing to arbitrate they have prima facie chosen arbitration as the appropriate tribunal. This consideration will be at its strongest in a situation where the same factual situation may give rise to different classifications of the parties' legal rights[17]. Second, it will be assumed, unless the words of the clause were clearly intended to limit the arbitrators' powers to invoke particular remedies, such as rescission or rectification, that the parties intended the arbitrator to have, to the extent allowed by law, at least those powers which are exercisable by the Court. Third, words of broad import, such as 'in connection with this contract' are to be given their natural meaning in the context in which they are found, and are not to be cut down by reference to earlier decisions giving a narrower meaning to the same or similar expressions in other contexts.

Provided that these broad principles are kept in mind, and particularly the third, we believe that there is no danger of misleading the reader, and indeed some benefit to be gained from the following brief discussion of some of the forms of words in common use.

(a) 'Claims'; 'differences'; 'disputes'

General words such as these confer the widest possible jurisdiction[18]. They must, however, be construed by reference to the subject matter of the contract in which they are included[19]. Thus, the inclusion in a mercantile contract of an arbitration clause in general terms would not endow the arbitrator with jurisdiction over disputes between the parties concerning, say, personal injuries

---

[16] The most recent cases are *The Playa Larga and Marble Islands*, supra; *Ashville Investments Ltd v Elmer Contractors Ltd*, supra; *Overseas Union Insurance Ltd v AA Mutual International Insurance Co Ltd* [1988] 2 Lloyd's Rep 63. But the principles, although not always explicitly invoked, may be said to underly most of the decisions in this field since at least the early 1970s.

[17] Thus, the same facts may give rise to claims under the contract or under a collateral contract, or to claims in contract or in tort.

[18] *Woolf v Collis Removal Service* [1948] 1 KB 11 at 18 ('claims'); *Re Hohenzollen Act fur Locomotivbahn and The City of London Contract Corpn* (1886) 54 LT 596 at 597 ('all disputes'); *F and G Sykes (Wessex) v Fine Fare Ltd* [1967] 1 Lloyd's Rep 53 ('differences').

[19] A decision in Chambers, giving a narrower interpretation to a clause of this type is cited in Russell at p. 96, but no details are available. In *Re Hohenzollern*, supra, at 597, Lord Esher MR read the word 'disputes' as meaning 'all disputes that may arise between the parties in consequence of this contract having been entered into'. This passage was cited in *Astro Vencedor Compania Naviera SA v Mabanaft GmbH* [1970] 2 Lloyd's Rep 267 at 269 (on appeal [1971] 1 Lloyd's Rep 502, [1971] 2 QB 588).

caused by one to the other, or over allegations of libel. Nor would a clause in a partnership agreement referring 'differences or disputes' to arbitration cover a quarrel about a horse race[20]. But it would, for example, if included in a contract of carriage, embrace claims for damage to the goods, even if framed in tort. It would also embrace all contractual remedies, apart from those which sought to impeach the initial existence of the contract, so that it would cover claims for damages arising from a repudiation or a deviation, claims for rectification, or avoidance on the ground of misrepresentation. It would, of course, include issues of law as well as fact[1].

(b) 'In connection with'; 'in relation to'

On the face of them, expressions of this sort would appear to be of considerable width and the current tendency is to enlarge rather than to diminish their scope where the context allows[2]. The courts have, however, in the past given them a surprisingly restricted interpretation. Thus, they have been held not to cover claims for damages based on the fraudulent inducement of the contract[3], or claims for payment on a quantum meruit in respect of work done under a contract which the claimant sought to declare void[4], or a claim for breach of an implied contract not to impede building works which were being carried out under the contract in question[5]. These earlier cases do not, however, decide that expressions of this type must always bear the same limited meaning. In the context of different transactions and differently worded contracts such expressions are capable of bearing, and prima facie do bear, a meaning which embraces any dispute other than one which is entirely unrelated to the transaction covered by the contract[6].

The words 'relating thereto', and 'relative to', have been treated as apt to cover cases where it is alleged that the contract has terminated through failure of a condition, or non-disclosure[7].

(c) 'In respect of'; 'with regard to'

It has been stated on high authority that these words cover disputes about whether there has been a breach by one side or the other, or whether circumstances have arisen which have discharged one or both parties from future performance[8]. 'In respect of this reinsurance' has been held to cover

---

[20] *Piercy v Young* (1879) 14 Ch D 200, per Jessel MR at 205.

[1] *Selby v Whitbread & Co* [1917] 1 KB 736 at 744 and see, for example, *Farr v Ministry of Transport* [1960] 1 WLR 956. The proposition could not now be doubted.

[2] See *A & B v C & D* [1982] 1 Lloyd's Rep 166, and *Ashville Investments Ltd v Elmer Contractors Ltd*, supra, in which the words 'in connection with' were held wide enough to cover claims for rectification and damages for innocent misrepresentation inducing the contract.

[3] *Monro v Bognor UDC* [1915] 3 KB 167; see the discussion of this case in notes 5 and 7 on pp. 112–113, ante.

[4] Ibid., per Pickford LJ at 170–171.

[5] *Lawson v Wallasey Local Board* (1883) 11 QBD 229.

[6] *Ashville Investments Ltd v Elmer Contractors Ltd*, supra; *Woolf v Collis Removal Services* [1948] 1 KB 11 at 18, per Asquith LJ.

[7] *De la Garde v Worsnop & Co* [1928] Ch 17; *Stevens & Sons v Timber and General Mutual Accident Insurance Association Ltd* (1933) 102 LJ KB 337.

[8] Per Viscount Simon LC in *Heyman v Darwins Ltd* [1942] AC 356 at 366.

claims based on an oral agreement said to amount to an implied term of the contract, or to a collateral contract, or to a common understanding founding a claim for rectification[9].

(d) 'Arising out of'

These words have been given a wide meaning. It has been said that they cover every dispute except a dispute as to whether there was ever a contract at all[10]. If the parties to a contract make provision in it as to their rights should certain events occur in the course of the contract, and a dispute arises between them as to their rights following the occurrence of those events, then that dispute as to their rights arises out of the contract[11]. The words embrace issues of frustration[12] and non-disclosure[13], construction[14], the existence of a custom, disputes as to any state of circumstances which, if proved, would be relevant on any issue as to the true meaning and effect of the contract[15], a dispute as to whether the contract has been varied or replaced by a fresh contract[16] and a claim for damages for breach of the arbitration agreement itself[17]. A disputed claim for general average arises 'out of' the charterparty under which the goods are carried, at any rate if the obligation arises from an express provision in the charterparty, rather than at common law[18]. And a claim by the owners of salved property against the salvor for negligence gives rise to a 'difference arising out of the Lloyds form of salvage agreement 'or the operations thereunder'[19]. By contrast, it has been held that a clause in this form does not give jurisdiction to arbitrators to decide whether notice of an appeal from the award of other arbitrators was given in the proper form, since the dispute arises from the award, and not from the original contract[20].

(e) 'Under'

Disputes arising 'under' a contract may have a narrower scope than those arising

---

[9] *Overseas Union Insurance Ltd v AA Mutual International Insurance Co Ltd* [1988] 2 Lloyd's Rep 63.

[10] Per Pilcher J in *HE Daniel Ltd v Carmel Exporters and Importers Ltd* [1953] 2 Lloyd's Rep 103, [1953] 2 QB 242 (question whether second claim barred by res judicata). See also *Government of Gibraltar v Kenney* [1956] 2 QB 410 at 421, and *Heyman v Darwins, ante.*

[11] Per Viscount Dilhorne in *The Evje* [1974] 2 Lloyd's Rep 57 at 65.

[12] *Kruse v Questier & Co* [1953] 1 Lloyd's Rep 310, [1953] 1 QB 669; *Government of Gibraltar v Kenney, ante.* See also *Gunter Henck v André & Cie SA* [1970] 1 Lloyd's Rep 235 at 240–241.

[13] *Stebbing v Liverpool and London and Globe Insurance Co Ltd* [1917] 2 KB 433.

[14] *Thorburn v Barnes* (1867) LR 2 CP 384.

[15] *Produce Brokers Co Ltd v Olympia Oil and Cake Co Ltd* [1916] 1 AC 314 at 327. In *Russian Oil Products Ltd v Caucasian Oil Co Ltd* (1928) 31 Ll L Rep 109, the Court rejected an argument that an umpire could not, under this form of wording, decide that a right prima facie given by the terms of a contract did not, in the particular circumstances exist.

[16] *Faghirzadeh v Rudolf Woolf SA (Pty) Ltd* [1977] 1 Lloyd's Rep 630.

[17] *Mantovani v Carapelli SpA* [1980] 1 Lloyd's Rep 375.

[18] *The Evje* [1974] 2 Lloyd's Rep 57, [1975] AC 797.

[19] *The Eschersheim* [1974] 2 Lloyd's Rep 188; affd. [1976] 1 Lloyd's Rep 81 at 88.

[20] *Getreide-Import GmbH v Contimar SA Compania Industrial Comercial y Maritima* [1953] 1 Lloyd's Rep 572, [1953] 1 WLR 793.

'out of' the contract[1]. They do, however, include issues of non-disclosure and supervening illegality[2], and also disputes arising from claims for general average[3].

(f) 'During the execution of'

The word 'execution' refers to the performance or purported performance of the contract, and is not used in its alternative legal meaning of 'making'. Disputes arising during the execution of a contract include those which arise from claims in tort, if there is a sufficiently close connection between the tort and the performance of the contract. Claims in general average are also covered[4].

12 Clauses of limited scope

Certain forms of arbitration agreement entrust the arbitrator with jurisdiction over liability but not over the amount of the claim, or vice versa. In the first category are clauses referring to the 'meaning and intention of the contract'[5]. The second type of clause is much more common. Clauses in this form are usually expressed in terms which make their purpose clear[6].

Again, some clauses provide that only certain categories of dispute shall be referable to arbitration[7] or they may provide that disputes of one type shall be referred to one particular arbitrator and other disputes to a different arbitrator[8].

13 Unilateral arbitration clauses

Commercial contracts occasionally give a unilateral right of arbitration. Sometimes they provide that claims by one party are to be the subject of arbitration, whereas claims by the other are not[9]. In other cases, one party has an option to call for arbitration, whilst the other party does not[10]. Such clauses are recognised by the Court as binding[11].

---

[1] Per Sellers J in *Government of Gibraltar v Keeney*, ante, at 421. See also *Heyman v Darwins*, ante, at 399 (contrast p. 383 and p. 394); *Nobel Bros Petroleum Production Co v Stewart & Co* (1890) 6 TLR 378. However, in *The Evje*, ante, Viscount Dilhorne and Lord Salmon, at 66 and 67 doubted this distinction.

[2] *Mackender, Hill and White v Feldia AG* [1966] 2 Lloyd's Rep 449, [1967] 2 QB 590.

[3] *Alma Shipping Corpn v Union of India, The Astraea*, [1971] 2 Lloyd's Rep 494; *The Evje*, ante.

[4] See *Astro Vencedor v Mabanaft* [1971] 1 Lloyd's Rep 502 (wrongful arrest); *Christopher Brown Ltd v Genossenschaft, Öesterriechischer* [1953] 2 Lloyd's Rep 373, [1954] 1 QB 8.

[5] *Richards v John Payne & Co* (1917) 86 LJ KB 937.

[6] There are many examples in the books of this type of clause. One case in which the wording was important was *Jureidini v National British and Irish Millers Insurance Co Ltd* [1915] AC 499; and see note 17, p. 111, ante.

[7] As in *Falkingham v Victorian Railways Comr* [1900] AC 452; *Ronassen & Son v Metsanomistajain Metsakeskus O/Y* (1931) 40 Ll L Rep 267 (clause covers disputes as to condition and quality of goods, but not injection).

[8] Engineering contracts not uncommonly distinguish in this way between technical and contractual disputes.

[9] *Woolf v Collis Removal Service* [1948] 1 KB 11 at 17.

[10] See, for example, *Barni v London General Insurance Co* (1933) 45 Ll L Rep 68; *Ronaasen & Son v Metsanomistajain Metsakeskus O/Y* (1931) 40 Ll L Rep 267.

[11] *Pittalis v Sherefettin* [1986] QB 868, [1986] 2 WLR 1003.

C. 'DISPUTES' AND 'DIFFERENCES'

1 Introduction

In the preceding sections we have disclosed the question whether various types of subject matter fall within various forms of agreement to arbitrate. There are two further questions which must be answered before it is known whether the matter is one which can, and must, be submitted to arbitration, namely –

1 whether it is necessary that there shall be a dispute in existence at the time when the arbitration is commenced; and

2 if so, whether in any given case there is a dispute at the material time.

If the question is whether the matter not only can, but must be referred to arbitration, the existence of a dispute becomes material in one further respect. Where the subject matter falls within the scope of a 'non-domestic' arbitration agreement', the obligation of the Court under section 1 of the 1975 Act to stay an action brought in respect of it does not apply where the Court is satisfied that there is not in fact any dispute between the parties with regard to the matter agreed to be referred. There is no equivalent qualification expressed in section 4(1) of the 1950 Act, which relates to 'domestic' arbitrations, but in practice the Court has always assumed it to be implicit.

The question whether a matter *can* be submitted to arbitration – i.e. whether a person can have jurisdiction to arbitrate upon it – depends upon the wording of the arbitration agreement.

2 Clauses requiring a 'dispute' or 'difference'

Arbitration clauses usually define the jurisdiction in terms of 'disputes' and 'differences'. Under clauses in this form, the existence of a dispute or difference is a condition precedent to the right to arbitrate. Two consequences flow from this:

(a) Undisputed claims

First, an action can properly be brought in the High Court in respect of an admitted claim, even though the contract contains an arbitration clause[12]. The claimant may apply for summary judgment, under RSC Ord. 14[13], and the defendant cannot either fend off judgment or obtain a stay simply by relying on the arbitration clause; for unless there is a dispute, there is nothing to be referred to arbitration. The same principle applies to a claim which is partly admitted: the claimant is entitled to judgment on the admitted portion, and a stay will be granted as to the remainder[14].

Where the defendant has not actively admitted the claim, but has so far failed to deny it, this does not mean that there is no 'dispute' then in existence, and the

---

[12] *London and North Western Rly Co v Jones* [1915] 2 KB 35; *London and North Western and Great-Western Joint Rly Companies v Billington* [1899] AC 79; *Cannan v Fowler* (1853) 14 CB 181.

[13] See pp. 492–496, post.

[14] *Bede Steam Shipping Co Ltd v Bunge y Born Ltd in SA* (1927) 27 Ll L Rep 410. This was a time-bar case, but the point is the same, since the event which had to be performed within the time was the calling into existence of a valid arbitration. See *The Evje* [1974] 2 Lloyd's Rep 57, [1975] AC 797.

claimant can prosecute his claim by arbitration, rather than by action[15]. However, if he really believes that the defendant is saying nothing because he has nothing to say, he can bring an action and apply for summary judgment.

(b) A genuine dispute

Theoretical problems of some difficulty may arise where the defendant does put forward an answer to the claim, but the claimant asserts that the answer does not raise a genuine dispute. Such an assertion may take two forms. First, where it is said that the defendant does not believe what he is saying, and is merely looking for an expedient to avoid or postpone payment. Second, where the defence is put forward with apparent good faith, but can nevertheless be seen to have no substance. Plainly, it may be difficult in certain instances to be sure into which of these categories a defence can properly be assigned.

When dealing with defences of this kind, three questions may arise –

1 Does the arbitrator have jurisdiction to entertain the claim, and to make a valid award in respect of it?

2 Must the Court grant a stay in respect of any action brought in respect of the claim, if the matter falls within section 1 of the 1975 Act, and may it grant a stay if it is within section 4(1) of the 1950 Act?

3 If an action is brought in respect of the claim, should the Court grant summary judgment for the amount claimed?

Whatever might be the position as regards a defence which is manifestly put forward in bad faith, there are strong logical arguments for the view that a bona fide if unsubstantial defence ought to be ruled upon by the arbitrator, not the Court. This is so especially where there is a non-domestic arbitration agreement, containing a valid agreement to exclude the power of appeal on questions of law. Here the parties are entitled by contract and statute to insist that their rights are decided by the arbitrator and nobody else. This entitlement plainly extends to cases where the defence is unsound in fact or law. A dispute which, it can be seen in retrospect, the plaintiff was always going to win is none the less a dispute. The practice whereby the Court pre-empts the sole jurisdiction of the arbitrator can therefore be justified only if it is legitimate to treat a dispute arising from a bad defence as ceasing to be a dispute at all when the defence is very bad indeed[16]. The correctness of this approach is not self-evident. Moreover, in all but the simplest of cases the Court will be required not merely to inspect the defence, but to enquire into it; a process which may, in matters of any complexity, take hours or even days. When carrying out the enquiry, the Court acts upon affidavits rather than oral evidence. The defendant might well object that this kind of trial in miniature by the Court is not something for which he bargained, when making an express contract to leave his rights to the sole adjudication of an arbitrator.

---

[15] See *Tradax Internacional SA v Cerrahogullari TAS, The M Eregli* [1981] 2 Lloyd's Rep 169 at 173; *Ellerine Bros (Pty) Ltd v Klinger* [1982] 1 WLR 1375; *First Steamship Co Ltd v CTS Commodity Transport Shipping Schiffahrtsgesellschaft mbH, The Ever Splendor* [1988] 1 Lloyd's Rep 245.

[16] The idea is often expressed by saying that the defendant has no 'genuine' defence. This may be said to involve an unjustified inference that a very weak defence is necessarily mala fide.

Whatever the logical merits of this view[17], the law is quite clearly established to the contrary[18]. Where the claimant contends that the defence has no real substance, the Court habitually brings on for hearing at the same time the application by the claimant for summary judgment, and the cross-application by the defendant for a stay, it being taken for granted that the success of one application determines the fate of the other[19].

One further point must be mentioned. The first of the questions listed above is whether the arbitrator has jurisdiction over a claim to which there is no defence. Since he has jurisdiction only where there is a dispute, the answer must be 'No', if the logic of the existing practice is carried through. For if there is not sufficient dispute to justify a stay, there can be no dispute empowering the arbitrator to enter upon a reference and make a valid award. This result makes commercial nonsense, and so far as we are aware, no court has ever suggested that it is correct. For practical reasons, the law simply proceeds on the hypothesis that in cases where the defence is very weak, both the Court and the arbitrator can properly assume jurisdiction over the claim.

Somewhat similar questions arise where the assertion is, not that there is no defence to the claim, but that the claim itself has no prospect of success. We suggest that the position as regards the jurisdiction of the arbitrator must be the same in the two situations. If, as we have suggested, the Court will accept that the arbitrator can make a valid award in favour of the claimant in the one case, then there seems no ground for denying that he can properly dismiss the claim in the other[20]. This would, however, be a very strong thing to do, and an arbitrator contemplating the possibility of a summary dismissal should consider very carefully, if there are foreign parties, whether problems in foreign courts concerning the recognition of the award in which the dismissal is embodied would not in the end make it wiser to bring the dispute to a full and speedy hearing.

---

[17] Support for the opinion that the question whether there should be a stay does not depend on the soundness of the defence could be found in *Russell v Pellegrini* (1856) 26 LJQB 75 and *Ramac Construction Co Ltd v JE Lesser (Properties) Ltd* [1975] 2 Lloyd's Rep 430. The former case is perhaps still just sustainable, on the basis of the language of the arbitration clause: see *A/S Gunnstein & Co K/S v Jensen, Krebs and Nielsen, The Alfa Nord* [1977] 2 Lloyd's Rep 434. The latter may perhaps be upheld, for the reasons stated in *Brightside Kilpatrick Engineering Services Ltd v Mitchell Construction (1973) Ltd* [1975] 2 Lloyd's Rep 493, although we venture to doubt this: the ratio decidendi of the *Lesser* case must, we think, be that a dispute arises as soon as the defendant refuses, on however insubstantial grounds, to accept the contentions of the claimant; see p. 433 of the report. We believe that it will be safer to assume that neither case is now good law.

[18] This proposition must now be treated as firmly and finally recognised by *Nova (Jersey) Knit Ltd v Kammgarn Spinnerei GmbH* [1977] 1 Lloyd's Rep 463, [1977] 1 WLR 713, and the *Gunnstein* case, supra.

[19] The formal criteria established for the grant of a stay and for the grant of summary judgment are not the same. The former requires a 'dispute'; the latter 'a question or issue in dispute *which ought to be tried*'. The distinction between a dispute and a worthwhile dispute has never, so far as we know, been observed and it is much too late now for anyone to suggest that the courts are mistaken in assuming that ss. 1 and 4(1), and Ord. 14 are opposite sides of the same coin. (For cases in which this assumption is made explicit, see *Association Bulk Carriers v Koch Shipping Inc, The Fuohsan Maru* [1978] 1 Lloyd's Rep 24 and *SL Sethia Liners Ltd v State Trading Corpn of India Ltd* [1986] 1 Lloyd's Rep 31).

[20] This must be right, for otherwise the arbitrator could not make the matter res judicata by dismissing the claim, or even make a valid award of costs in favour of the respondent, in respect of an obviously ill-founded claim.

(c) Disputes arising after appointment of arbitrator

A second consequence of the general rule that only disputes may be the subject of arbitration is that the arbitrator has no jurisdiction over disputes which were not in existence when he was appointed to act[1]. The appointment defines his jurisdiction at the same time as creating it, and cannot be taken to give him jurisdiction over something which does not at that time exist. A dispute may be created after the arbitration has commenced, either by the defendant for the first time raising a defence to the claim, or by the claimant introducing a new claim into an existing dispute. The first situation raises no practical problems. Initially, the arbitrator has in strict law no jurisdiction over the undisputed claim. But the conduct of the parties combines to give him jurisdiction: the claimant by bringing the claim before him, and the respondent by raising a defence to it in the arbitration. The arbitrator can therefore properly entertain both the claim and the defence. In the converse case, where the novelty lies in the claim, not in the defence, this solution is not available, and (unless the respondent consents) he must refuse to deal with the claim: for it is not something which falls within his jurisdiction, as defined by his appointment[2].

(d) Amendments

More difficult questions arise where a dispute concerning a particular subject matter has been referred to arbitration, and where subsequently one or other of the parties wishes to put forward his case in a new way[3]. It is plain, in general terms, that the arbitrator has no jurisdiction to entertain a dispute other than the one which has was appointed to decide; and this is reflected procedurally by saying that an arbitrator would have no power to allow amendment to the pleadings which would raise a new dispute. This principle can readily be applied to a case where the claimant has, for example, started an arbitration to recover damages for a particular breach of contract, and wishes to amend so as to claim further damages for a different breach of the same contract. In such a case, the arbitrator must say that he cannot deal with the new claim unless the parties agree to give him a special jurisdiction to do so, or unless a fresh notice of arbitration is given in respect of the new dispute, and he is again appointed arbitrator[4]. At the other end of the scale is the situation where the claimant merely wishes to attach a different legal label to the same damages and facts. Here the arbitrator is free to give leave to amend[5]. It is in the middle ground

---

[1] *London and North Western and Great Western Joint Rly Companies v Billington*, ante.
[2] This is the usual position. But in order to ascertain the jurisdiction, one must construe the appointment as well as the arbitration clause; and there seems no reason in principle why the appointment by the respondent should not expressly stipulate that the arbitrator should have power to decide future, as well as existing disputes.
[3] This problem has no connection with the High Court pleading rules about 'departures' in pleadings. A party may oppose an amendment on the grounds that it is not permitted by the Court's self-imposed rules. But once the amendment is allowed, it stands. An arbitrator, by contrast, achieves nothing by allowing amendment to raise a new dispute – apart from the possibility of a void award.
[4] For the problems which arise if it is alleged that the new claim is barred by lapse of time, see pp. 215–216, post.
[5] *Kawasaki Kisen Kaisha v Government of Ceylon* [1962] 1 Lloyd's Rep 424 at 429. Any other result would be unworkable, since very often the parties do not express their contentions in precise legal terminology before the arbitration is commenced.

that the problems arise. What should the arbitrator do if the claimant wishes to use the same facts to found a claim for a different measure of recovery; or if he wishes to recover the same damages by relying on a different breach of contract; or if the respondent desires to defend the claim on an entirely new ground? How can the arbitrator tell whether he is faced with a new dispute which he ought not to entertain?

(i) Amendments by respondent.   One may first consider the situation where it is the respondent who seeks leave to amend. For example, a buyer of goods rejects them on the ground that they were defective; an arbitration is commenced in which the seller claims damages for the failure to accept; the buyer subsequently discovers that he has an unanswerable defence on the ground that the goods were shipped out of time, and wishes to raise this in the arbitration. The seller could assert that the new plea should not be allowed, since the arbitrator was never entrusted with a dispute about late shipment; the buyer could reply that the original dispute was concerned with the issue whether he was entitled to reject the goods, and that the new plea is simply a variation on the same basic question. Logic does not point clearly to either solution, since the problem is essentially one of defining the word 'dispute'. Expediency does, however, suggest that the respondent should be allowed to amend – provided, of course, that the arbitrator considers that the circumstances make it fair for him to do so. Any other result would produce unjust results, because if the arbitrator will not entertain the defence there is no way in which the respondent can rely upon it at all, either in court or in arbitration.

(ii) Amendments by claimant.   This practical consideration does not apply with so much force where it is the claimant who wishes to amend; for if the arbitrator refuses leave, the only consequence is that the claimant is put to the trouble of starting a separate arbitration for the new claim. This makes it possible to argue that the arbitrator should adopt a broad commonsense view, giving effect to his own feeling about whether the arbitration, after the amendment, will in essence be concerned with the same dispute as before.

Whilst this approach has its attractions, we do not believe it to be sound. Commonsense is a good guide to the exercise of discretions, but not to questions of jurisdiction, which are concerned with the issue whether the arbitrator has the power, by publishing an award, to create an enforceable legal right. Something more solid than intuition ought to be the guide in such a case. It is, however, one matter to reject the broad approach, and another to propose one which is both clear and workable. Space does not permit a full discussion of the alternatives, but we would suggest that the best approach is to identify (if possible) the central issue upon which the granting or withholding of the remedy depends, and to permit all amendments except those which would replace that issue, or add another issue[6]. Thus, if a charterer were to cancel the charter on the ground of unseaworthiness and the shipowner were then to claim damages for wrongful repudiation, the claimant would properly be allowed to claim or

---

[6] This approach is consistent with *Mediterranean and Eastern Export Co Ltd v Fortress Fabrics (Manchester) Ltd* (1948) 81 Ll L Rep 401, and *Kawasaki Kisen Kaisha v Government of Ceylon* [1962] 1 Lloyd's Rep 424; and see *London and North Western and Great Western Joint Rly Companies v Billington* [1899] AC 79.

increase his claim, or to re-formulate it as a claim for money had and received, whilst the charterer could contend that he was justified in cancelling on the ground (say) that the ship did not have the warranted characteristics. In essence, the dispute revolves round the questions whether the charterer was justified in calcelling and, (if not), what were the legal consequences. The amendments would not alter this question but merely enlarge the number of factors which the arbitrator would have to take into account when answering it. But the shipowner could not amend to add a new claim for demurrage, for this is not what the parties were in dispute about when the matter was submitted to the arbitrator. This test may be adopted to deal with the case where the remedy depends, not upon the validity of an act, but on the existence of a state of affairs. For example, if a buyer claims an allowance because goods are of defective quality, he can amend to allege defects additional to those on which he originally relied; but he cannot add a new claim for non-compliance with sample[7].

(e) What is a 'dispute'?

Most disputes stem from claims. But the existence of a formulated claim is neither necessary nor sufficient to create a dispute. A claim is not necessary, for many disputes come into existence before payment is called for[8]. Very often, all that has been made explicit at the time when notice of arbitration is given, is a difference of opinion about the central issues: whether one party was entitled to cancel the contract, whether the goods were defective, and so on. The financial implications of the dispute may never be explored at all, until a statement of claim is served in the arbitration[9]. Moreover, it is becoming increasingly common for parties to arbitrate precisely in order to avoid the making of a claim[10]. There may be a genuine difference of opinion as to the future performance of a contract. For example, one party may be denying that any further performance is due, on the ground that the contract has been discharged by repudiation or frustration; or it may be common ground that the contract is subsisting, but the parties may be in dispute about whether a particular act would constitute a valid performance, or whether one party is entitled to give a particular order, or exercise an option in a particular way. If the parties stand their ground in such a situation, a time will come when it is too late for the right view to prevail; one party will be irremediably in the wrong; and serious financial loss is likely to ensue. A claim is then inevitable. All this can be prevented if the parties can mount an arbitration with sufficient speed to enable

---

[7] The idea of the 'central issue' as the test is open to the obvious criticism that it depends upon a correct identification of the central issue. *Panchaud Frères SA v Etablissements General Grain Co* [1970] 1 Lloyd's Rep 53 shows that opinions may differ on this. The Court of Appeal evidently considered that the quality and description of the goods was the central issue. Others might have shared Roskill J's view that the central issue was whether the buyers were justified in rejecting the goods.

[8] A dispute may even arise before the claimant has a fully constituted cause of action: *Romac Construction Co Ltd v JE Lesser (Properties) Ltd* [1975] 2 Lloyd's Rep 430. Cf. *Brightside Kilpatrick Engineering Services Ltd v Mitchell Construction (1973) Ltd* [1975] 2 Lloyd's Rep 493; *The American Sioux* [1980] 2 Lloyd's Rep 224.

[9] See per Viscount Dilhorne in *The Evje*, ante, at 65.

[10] See per Greer J in *JF Robertson & Co v AT James & Co* (1923) 16 Ll L Rep 34 at 36.

them to know the true position under the contract before the time for performance has finally expired[11].

On the other hand, even if a claim is not essential, there must be something in the nature of an assertion by one party: for a situation in which the parties neither agree nor disagree about the true position is not one in which there is a dispute. For example, if the parties agree that a reasonable person shall enquire into the matter and decide what is reasonable without the parties themselves putting forward any view, there is no dispute in existence between them. Just as a claim is not necessary to the creation of a dispute, neither is it sufficient in itself. If a debtor agrees that money is due, but simply fails to pay it, there is no dispute[12]; the creditor can and must proceed by action, rather than by arbitration. Equally, silence in the face of a claim does not raise a dispute, for it may simply indicate that the recipient is considering whether or not to deny the claim[13]. What is required is a rebuttal or denial of the claim[14].

(f) Disputes resolved before award

Where a dispute was at one time in existence, but has subsequently been resolved by agreement, the arbitrator's jurisdiction to award upon it depends upon the timing of the agreement. If it took place before the arbitrator was appointed, he has no jurisdiction, for this appointment relates only to current disputes. If it took place afterwards, the arbitrator will have jurisdiction, for it was not only his right but his duty to deal with all matters in dispute, and a matter does not cease to fall within his duty merely because the parties are agreed upon the outcome[15]. Where the debt has not merely been agreed, but has been paid, the position again depends upon the order of events. If payment was made before the commencement of the arbitration, there is no dispute, and hence no jurisdiction. If afterwards, the arbitrator does have jurisdiction, but his award must be for the respondent, since the debt has been discharged by payment[16].

(g) 'Differences'

Finally, there is the word 'differences'. There is authority for the view that this word has a wider scope than 'disputes'[17] although we know of no case where the

---

[11] Not infrequently the parties agree to carry on with the performance, on a 'without prejudice' basis, pending the reference to arbitration.

[12] See note 12, p. 122, ante.

[13] It will usually be possible to infer from the circumstances whether silence indicates a denial of liability.

[14] *The Evje* [1974] 2 Lloyd's Rep 57, per Lord Morris at 62.

[15] Of course, if the original debt has been discharged by an accord and satisfaction, the respondent will have a good defence in the arbitration.

[16] These points are more than academic, because they bear on the question of interest. See post, pp. 391–392.

[17] Per Danckwerks LJ in *F and G Sykes (Wessex) Ltd v Fine Fare Ltd* [1967] 1 Lloyd's Rep 53 at 60, stating that the word is 'particularly apt for a case where the parties have not agreed' and citing 'a failure to agree ... is a very different thing from a dispute', from the speech of Viscount Dunedin in *May and Butcher Ltd v R* [1934] 2 KB 17. We venture to doubt this. If the parties have tried to agree, and failed, have they not disagreed? Conversely, if the question of trying to agree has not yet arisen, how can they be said to have differed? Viscount Dunedin was concerned with the absence of the consensus necessary to make a contract, not with disagreement about the merits of a claim.

distinction has been decisive on an issue of jurisdiction. In practice, the words appear to have been used interchangeably. A dispute or difference is none the less so because the divergence of view as to law or fact has been indicated by phrases of courtesy rather than the language of violence[18].

3 Clauses requiring a 'claim'

Thus far, we have considered the situation in which the courts have regarded an existing dispute as essential to the commencement of an arbitration. The texts appear to treat the need for a dispute as if this were a rule of law. We suggest that it is not so, and that a dispute is treated as necessary simply because, in the great majority of cases, this is what the arbitration agreement says. Most arbitration clauses require the parties to submit certain types of dispute to arbitration. It necessarily follows from the wording of such a clause, that if there is no dispute there is nothing to submit. But some clauses are not so expressed. They require the parties to arbitrate in respect of all 'claims'. We can see no reason why these provisions should be be construed as meaning what they say – namely that arbitration is to be the exclusive means of enforcing all asserted rights of the stipulated types. Once a claim of that type has arisen, the claimant is obliged to submit it to arbitration, rather than the courts, irrespective of whether or not it has yet become the subject of a dispute[19]. The claimant's obligation to refer the matter to arbitration will not be enforceable by means of a mandatory stay under section 1 of the 1975 Act, which cannot be granted if there is no dispute, but the other remedies for breach of an agreement to arbitrate ought still, in principle, to be available[20].

4 Cross-claims in arbitration

It frequently happens in commercial transactions that the claims between the parties are not all in the same direction. The co-existence of asserted claims, set-offs and counter-claims may give rise to difficult theoretical and practical problems, upon which the reported cases give little guidance. The question may arise in several ways:

(a) The claimant has a claim which lies outside the arbitration clause. The respondent refuses to pay, on the ground that he has an arbitrable cross-claim of an equal or greater amount. Can the claimant be compelled to pursue his claim by arbitration, or may he start proceedings in Court?

(b) The claimant has a claim which prima facie falls within the arbitration clause, but which is not disputed except to the extent that the respondent asserts a cross-claim, which does fall within the clause, of an equal or greater amount. Can and must the claimant arbitrate in respect of his claim?

(c) The claimant has a disputed claim which falls within the arbitration

---

[18] Per McCardie J in *Selby v Whitbread & Co* [1917] 1 KB 736 at 745.

[19] This must surely be the case where the clause deals at the same time with arbitration and time-barring. If the clause requires all claims to be submitted to arbitration within a specified time, it would be absurd if a claimant who was ready and willing to start his arbitration in time should find his claim time-barred simply because his opponent had failed to dispute it.

[20] See post, pp. 459–462. The court could, we believe, properly grant a stay by virtue of its inherent jurisdiction, even if a stay under s. 1 is not available, just as it would if the agreement were to submit disputes to the exclusive jurisdiction of a foreign court.

clause. Can the respondent raise in the arbitration a cross-claim which lies outside the clause?

(d) The claimant has a disputed claim which falls within the arbitration clause. The respondent has a disputed cross-claim which also falls within the clause. Can the respondent insist on raising his cross-claim in the claimant's arbitration, or must he start a fresh arbitration?

The general law relating to cross-claims is difficult, quite apart from the problems introduced by the existence of an arbitration agreement. Space does not permit a full discussion but, in brief, the position is that there are four distinct ways in which a cross-claim is relied upon. First, where a ground of complaint operates to reduce a sum to which the claimant would otherwise be entitled, for example, where defective goods are delivered, the price is pro tanto reduced. The buyer could, if he wished, raise the complaint as a cross-claim; but he is entitled to treat it as true defence, and not merely a procedural response, to the claim. Second, one party has a statutory right to set off one debt against another debt. This right, which applies only to cross-debts and not to damages, is also available as a true defence. Third, one party has the right to set-off one cross-claim of any kind against another, provided that the connection between the two claims is sufficiently close to make it unfair to enforce one without taking the other into account. This is a procedural right, directed ultimately at enforcement, and does not operate by way of a true defence. Finally, there is the case where the cross-claim does not raise any kind of a set-off, but the tribunal finds it convenient to allow both claims to be decided in the course of the same proceedings.

(a) Claim outside clause: cross-claim within clause

In the situation giving rise to question (a), the sensible course will often be for the parties to agree that the respondent shall arbitrate on the cross-claim giving credit for the undisputed claim, and agreeing that if he loses, an award on the claim will follow. But in law the claimant cannot be compelled to take this course and, if he wishes, he may proceed to judgment in the High Court on his claim[1]. If the Court considers there is substance in the cross-claim, it will usually stay execution on the judgment (possibly on terms as to payment into Court) until the cross-claim has been arbitrated.

(b) Undisputed claim: cross-claim within clause

As regards the situation contemplated by question (b) – namely an arbitrable but undisputed claim, and a cross-claim which is arbitrable – the position should logically depend upon whether or not the cross-claim operates by way of true defence. If it does, the raising of the cross-claim brings into existence a dispute as to whether the claim is due, and provided that the point is taken before the proceedings are commenced, the position should be that both the claim and the

---

[1] *Nova (Jersey) Knit Ltd v Kammgarn Spinnerei GmbH* [1977] 1 Lloyd's Rep 463.

cross-claim are dealt with by the arbitrator. If the cross-claim does not operate by way of defence, the position is the same as under question (a) above[2].

(c) Claim within clause: cross-claim outside clause

The third question concerns the right to raise non-arbitrable cross-claims in the course of an arbitration on the claim. Here, the arbitrator should not entertain the cross-claim unless it provides a true defence, but should leave the respondent to pursue it in separate proceedings. Whether the Court will stay execution on the award, to take account of the cross-claim, depends on whether the latter is disputed and, no doubt, upon the Court's impression of its merits[3].

(d) Claim and cross-claim within clause

The fourth situation, in which both the claim and the cross-claim are arbitrable, is the one most commonly encountered in practice. The arbitrator should carefully consider whether the subject matter of the counter-claim was one of the matters submitted to him at the time of the appointment. If it is, then it is up to him whether to allow the matter to be raised by counter-claim, or made the subject of a separate arbitration. In practice, we have never known the second course to be followed. If, on the other hand, the cross-claim was not a dispute which was submitted to him, he should not entertain it unless it raises a pure defence, or unless the parties clearly agree that he is to have jurisdiction over it[4].

If the arbitrator does adjudicate upon the claim and cross-claim, he is not obliged to make them the subject of separate decisions in his award[5]: i.e. he can set-off against each other the sums awarded on claim and counter-claim. But he will often be wise to do so, if there is a risk that to award only a single figure may raise doubts as to whether he had dealt with all the issues. On some occasions, it may be unfair not to publish separate figures, for example if the claim is the subject of a guarantee, under which the claimant is entitled to recover the full amount of the claim without allowance for cross-claims.

---

[2] At any rate, if the arbitration clause is in the 'disputes' rather than the 'claims' form: see p. 129, ante. *Russell v Pellegrini* (1856) 6 E & B 1020 must (if it is indeed still good law) be considered as an example of a clause which was not limited to 'disputes'; *Nova (Jersey) Knit Ltd v Kammgarn Spinnerei*, supra; see also *Daunt v Lazard* (1858) 27 LJ Ex 399; *Seligmann v Le Boutillier* (1866) LR 1 CP 681; *Bede Steam Shipping Co Ltd v Bunge y Born Ltda SA* (1927) 27 Ll L Rep 410; *A/S Gunnstein v Jensen, Krebs and Nielsen, The Alfa Nord* [1977] 2 Lloyd's Rep 434.

[3] *ED and F Man v SA Tripolitaine des Usines de Raffinage de Sucre* [1970] 2 Lloyd's Rep 416; *Margulies Bros Ltd v Dafnis Thomaides & Co (UK) Ltd* [1958] 1 Lloyd's Rep 250.

[4] *Lambert and Krzysiak Ltd v British Commercial Overseas Co Ltd* (1923) 16 Ll L Rep 51, and *European Grain and Shipping Ltd v R Johnston* [1982] 1 Lloyd's Rep 414 provide good examples of the difficulties that can ensure from this type of situation.

[5] *Compagnie Financière pour le Commerce Extérieure SA v OY Vehna AB* [1963] 2 Lloyd's Rep 178. Unless, of course, one is a pure defence to the other.

CHAPTER 7

Agreements to refer existing disputes

A. TYPES OF AGREEMENT

In general, agreements to refer existing disputes to arbitration are governed by the same rules regarding their existence, construction and effect as agreements to refer future disputes, which have been discussed in the preceding chapter[1]. Agreements made after the dispute has arisen do, however, raise a number of questions requiring separate discussion. For this purpose they can be divided into two types: 1 express agreements, and 2 implied agreements. Whereas the former type will always result from a deliberate decision by both parties to the dispute to create or define the arbitrator's jurisdiction and powers to deal with the dispute, the latter will often arise through inadvertence or a mistake on the part of one or both parties. The two types of agreement are dealt with separately below.

1 Express agreements

Generally, an express agreement will be made because, although the parties are under no existing obligation to refer to arbitration a dispute which has arisen between them, they prefer to resolve the dispute by arbitration rather than in the courts. Sometimes, however, a fresh agreement may be desirable, or even necessary, although an agreement to arbitrate future disputes existed between the parties before the dispute arose. For instance, the prior agreement may not be wide enough to include all the matters which the parties wish to refer to arbitration; or it may be in terms which give rise to doubt as to its scope; or the parties may wish to vary the prior agreement by providing for a different method of appointment or different rules of procedure; or they may wish to enlarge or curtail the arbitrator's powers[2]. A common type of agreement combines a reference of the matter in dispute to a named arbitrator (or arbitrators) and an agreed timetable for matters such as pleadings and discovery of documents.

A fresh agreement is necessary where it is proposed to join additional parties to the reference, beyond those bound by the original arbitration agreement, either as co-claimants or as co-respondents or as third parties. This is of course only possible with the agreement of all concerned.

---

[1] Chapter 6, ante, p. 105. Two special features of agreements to refer future disputes are noted post, p. 134. These concern the courts' power to interfere where the arbitrator is or may not be impartial, or where the dispute involves an allegation of fraud.

[2] E.g. as to costs.

132

A fresh agreement is also necessary[3] where the arbitrator is to be given jurisdiction to decide a dispute as to the existence of the contract containing the original agreement[4] or as to facts on which his jurisdiction is founded[5].

But, apart from such special circumstances, it is unnecessary for the parties to enter into a fresh agreement to cover a dispute falling within the scope of an existing agreement to refer future disputes to arbitration. English arbitral procedure has no equivalent of the practice which prevails in other jurisdictions, whereby formal terms of reference, defining the arbitrator's jurisdiction and powers, must be agreed before the arbitration can get under way. The rules of some arbitral institutions do, it is true, contain express provision for procedures of this kind: but they have no place in the general system of English arbitral procedure. So that, whereas in other jurisdictions the terms of reference may be considered to be the source of the arbitrator's jurisdiction and powers, under the English practice it is the antecedent arbitration agreement which governs such matters. The reference of a particular dispute to arbitration pursuant to an existing arbitration agreement is not a consensual procedure, but is brought about by the claimant's unilateral action in invoking the procedures for beginning an arbitration: these are discussed in Part III.

Agreements to refer existing disputes to arbitration need not be made in writing in order to give the arbitrator jurisdiction. But if there is no 'written agreement' or 'agreement in writing' the Acts will not apply to the reference. This may give rise to great inconvenience[6], and the use of oral agreements should therefore be avoided. An agreement to refer an existing dispute to arbitration stands on its own, independent of the existence or continued existence of the substantive contract[7] to which the dispute relates[8]. In this it differs from an agreement to refer existing disputes to arbitration[9].

2 Implied agreements

Most agreements to refer existing disputes to arbitration are made expressly, and usually in writing rather than orally. But an agreement to arbitrate a dispute and to be bound by the arbitrator's award may be inferred from the conduct of the parties without any express agreement[10]. The most usual case of such an agreement is where an arbitration is already in progress under an existing express agreement and a fresh claim is brought before the arbitrator, which is outside the scope of the original agreement. If no objection is made to

---

3 Unless the original agreement is wide enough to cover the matters mentioned.
4 See pp. 108–110, ante.
5 See p. 114, ante.
6 See pp. 55–56, ante, where we suggest that an oral variation of a prior written agreement might itself be treated as a 'written agreement' to which the Acts would apply.
7 The agreement may, indeed, not relate to a claim in contract at all.
8 The argument to the contrary in *The Tradesman* [1961] 2 Lloyd's Rep 183 could, we submit, only have succeeded on the basis that the submission was not a fresh agreement to arbitrate superseding the earlier agreement, but merely an agreement as to procedure and as to the identity of the arbitrator.
9 See ante, pp. 108–113.
10 *Westminster Chemicals and Produce Ltd v Eichholz and Loeser* [1954] 1 Lloyd's Rep 99; *A/B Legis v V Berg & Sons Ltd* [1964] 1 Lloyd's Rep 203; *Luanda Exportadora SARL etc Lda v Wahbe Tamari & Sons Ltd and Jaffa Trading Co* [1967] 2 Lloyd's Rep 353; *The Tuyuti* [1984] 2 Lloyd's Rep 51 at 58.

the arbitrator's lack of jurisdiction to deal with the fresh claim[11], both parties will be bound by an award on the merits of the claim. The arbitrator's authority to make such an award derives from an agreement to be inferred from the conduct of the parties.

This situation should be distinguished from the case where the arbitration agreement is in terms wide enough to cover the fresh claim, but the claim is one which has not previously been referred to arbitration, or is one which the arbitrator has not been appointed to decide: this can arise where a reference to arbitration or an appointment of an arbitrator is in narrower terms than the original agreement to arbitrate. In this situation the party bringing the fresh claim before the arbitrator has a right to insist on it being referred to arbitration under the terms of the original agreement; no further agreement is necessary in order to give the arbitrator jurisdiction[12].

An implied agreement to arbitrate which is inferred from the conduct of the parties is not a 'written agreement' for the purposes of the Acts[13]. In order to avoid the inconvenience to which this gives rise[14], it would be better if such agreements were put into writing. Unfortunately it is sometimes not realised until later by one or even both of the parties that the fresh claim was not within the scope of the original agreement: one or both parties may have acted in the mistaken belief that the arbitrator had jurisdiction to deal with the claim. If the belief arises from a fundamental mistake of fact which is shared by both parties, or if it has been brought about by a misrepresentation, it vitiates any implied agreement which might otherwise have arisen. But generally the mistake will be merely a mistake of law as to the meaning of the original agreement; this affords no grounds for impeaching an award made under an implied agreement founded on the conduct of the parties[15].

B. SPECIAL FEATURES

Two features peculiar to agreements to refer existing disputes to arbitration should be noted.

First, where an application is made to the Court for leave to revoke the authority of the arbitrator or for an injunction to prevent the arbitration proceeding on the grounds that the arbitrator is or may not be impartial, the

---

[11] The procedure for making such an objection is discussed at p. 577, post.

[12] But it will be necessary to enlarge the scope of his appointment. This may cause problems if a relevant period of limitation has expired: see post, p. 215.

[13] *Altco Ltd v Sutherland* [1971] 2 Lloyd's Rep 515 at 519.

[14] See p. 51, ante.

[15] *Thames Iron Works and Shipbuilding Co Ltd v R* (1869) 10 B & S 33. This case was apparently not cited in *Altco Ltd v Sutherland* [1971] 2 Lloyd's Rep 515, where Donaldson J held that a mutual mistake as to the existence of a prior arbitration agreement prevented the formation of an implied ad hoc agreement. Unless the latter case can be treated as turning on a mistake of *fact* it appears to have been decided per incuriam. The earlier case is, we suggest, not only sounder in principle but produces a result which is more satisfactory in practice. In *Westminster Chemicals and Produce Ltd v Eichholz and Loeser* [1954] 1 Lloyd's Rep 99 at 109–110, Devlin J refers only to mistake of *fact*: A similar point was raised, but not decided, in *FW Berk & Co Ltd v Knowles and Foster* [1962] 1 Lloyd's Rep 430 (appeal from award mistakenly believed to be valid). See also *The Tradesman* [1961] 2 Lloyd's Rep 183 where the question of the validity of an ad hoc agreement which purported to be made under a prior agreement for which no consideration had been given was raised but not decided.

application may be refused, if the agreement is to refer an existing dispute, on the grounds that the applicant when he made the agreement knew or ought to have known that the arbitrator might not be impartial[16]. But this is not a ground for refusing the application if the dispute has arisen under an agreement to refer future disputes to arbitration[17].

Second, if a dispute arises involving the question whether a party to the arbitration agreement has been guilty of fraud, the Court has power to order that the agreement shall cease to have effect and to give leave to revoke the authority of the arbitrator, in order to enable the question to be tried by the Court[18]. But these powers are limited to the case where the agreement is to refer future disputes to arbitration[19]. There are no such powers in the case of agreements to refer existing disputes.

[16] The applicant may be said to have waived his objection to the partiality of the arbitrator: see Chapter 35, post, p. 579.
[17] Arbitration Act 1950, s. 24(1).
[18] See p. 501, post.
[19] Arbitration Act 1950, s. 24(2).

CHAPTER 8

Arbitration and third parties

Most arbitrations take place between persons who have from the outset been parties to the arbitration agreement, and to the substantive contract underlying that agreement. It occasionally happens, however, that the claim is made by or against someone who was not originally named as a party. In such circumstances, the questions whether the claim can be and must be the subject of arbitration may give rise to considerable difficulty. It is convenient to deal separately with the situations where the claimant was not, and the respondent was not, originally a party to the agreement.

A. CLAIMANT NOT NAMED AS A PARTY

Four situations may be distinguished.

1 The claimant was in reality always a party to the contract, although not named in it.

2 The claimant has succeeded by operation of law to the rights of the named party.

3 The claimant has become a party to the contract in substitution for the named party by virtue of a statutory or consensual novation.

4 The original party has assigned to the claimant either the underlying contract, together with the agreement to arbitrate which it incorporates, or the benefit of a claim which has already come into existence.

1 Agency: trusts

The first situation exists where the claimant is a person for whose benefit, or for whose account, the contract was made, e.g. the disclosed or undisclosed principal, where the named party was an agent; the beneficiary, where the named party was a trustee. Here, the position is reasonably straightforward. The claimant has throughout been a party to the contract and to the submission which it contains. He is therefore entitled to enforce the agreement to arbitrate by referring the dispute to arbitration in his own name[1]. Moreover, if he seeks to enforce his claim by an action, the defendant will be entitled to a stay, since the

---

[1] There are many instances where, in a High Court action, it will be necessary for the claimant to join the nominal party either as co-plaintiff or as co-defendant, so that he will be bound by the result of the proceedings, and the defendant will get a good discharge. There is no mechanism in arbitrations for joining the nominal party as an additional respondent, and the arbitrator ought not in our view to proceed to an award unless the nominal party consents to be named as an additional claimant. It is not unusual to see awards made in the name of an agent alone. We suggest that the principal ought also to be a party.

claimant is a person claiming 'through or under' the named party, within section 4(1) of the 1950 Act and section 1(1) of the 1975 Act[2].

2 Succession by operation of law

In the second situation, the claimant has succeeded by operation of law to the rights of the named party – for example where he is the personal representative of the named party[3], or where he is a trustee in bankruptcy who has adopted the contract and is seeking to enforce it[4]. Here again, the claimant can and must proceed by way of arbitration.

3 Novation

The third situation exists where, by virtue of a statutory or consensual novation, the claimant has replaced the person originally named as a party, who therefore has ceased to have any rights or duties under the contract. Such a situation may arise by statute[5], or by a novation, i.e. an agreement between the two original parties and the new party that the latter shall replace one of the original parties. Here, the new party can and must enforce the arbitration clause, for his position is the same as if he had been a party from the outset[6]. The original party cannot resort to arbitration, for he no longer has any status in the contractual relationship.

4 Assignment

The fourth situation is the one which most commonly arises. Here, the claimant is the assignee of the benefit of the contract – either by statute, or by a full legal assignment under section 136 of the Law of Property Act 1925[7] or by an equitable assignment. The decided cases on the rights of the parties in this

---

[2] The stay under s. 1 in favour of the first defendant in *Roussel-Uclaf v GD Searle & Co* [1978] 1 Lloyd's Rep 225 can perhaps be explained on the basis of agency: otherwise it is difficult to see how the first defendant could have taken any part in the arbitration.

[3] See s. 2(1) of the 1950 Act. See also Chapter 11.

[4] See s. 3(1) of the 1950 Act; *Piercy v Young* (1879) 14 Ch D 200. See also Chapter 11.

[5] For example, the Road Traffic Act 1930, and the Third Parties (Rights against Insurers) Act 1930. It may well be that s. 1 of the Bills of Lading Act 1855 also has this effect. The position of a person who becomes an additional party to a contract after its inception (for example, under the principle exemplified by *Brandt v Liverpool, Brazil and River Plate Steam Navigation Co Ltd* [1924] 1 KB 575) is no doubt the same as that of someone who becomes a party by novation: see *R and W Paul Ltd v National SS Co Ltd* (1937) 43 Com Cas 68 where the point was raised but not decided.

[6] *Smith v Pearl Assurance Co Ltd* (1939) 63 Ll L Rep 1, [1939] 1 All ER 95; *Dennehy v Bellamy* (1938) 60 Ll L Rep 269; *Freshwater v Western Australian Assurance Co Ltd* [1933] 1 KB 515; *Digby v General Accident Fire and Life Assurance Corpn Ltd* [1940] 2 KB 226 (statutory novations); *Pena Copper Mines Ltd v Rio Tinto Co Ltd* (1911) 105 LT 846; *Printing Machinery Co Ltd v Linotype and Machinery Ltd* [1912] 1 Ch 566; *Oakland Metal Co Ltd v D Benaim & Co Ltd* [1953] 2 Lloyd's Rep 192, [1953] 2 QB 261; *Socony Mobil Oil Co Ltd v West of England Ship Owners Mutual Insurance Association (London) Ltd, The Padre Island* [1984] 2 Lloyd's Rep 408.

[7] An assignment under s. 136 transfers 'all legal and other remedies', which we submit is wide enough to include the right to invoke an arbitration clause.

situation are not clear[8]. There would be much to be said for an argument that although the presence of the arbitration clause would not prevent the assignee from obtaining a valid right of claim, he would have to enforce his claim by action, rather than arbitration on the basis that the respondent agreed to arbitrate with the claimant, but not with some outsider[9]. It appears, however, that this is not the law, and that the position is as follows –

(i) The presence of an arbitration clause in a contract does not prevent the contract from being assigned.

(ii) The assignee can and must enforce his claim by arbitration, unless the clause is so worded as to make it clear that it binds only the original parties. This would be unusual. Section 16 of the 1950 Act provides that 'unless a contrary intention is expressed therein, every arbitration agreement shall, where such a provision is applicable to the reference, be deemed to contain a provision that the award to be made ... shall be final and binding on the parties and the persons claiming under them respectively'. Section 4 of the 1950 Act and section 1 of the 1975 Act both refer to persons claiming 'through or under' a party to the arbitration agreement. The ability of derivative parties covered by these expressions to invoke the arbitration agreement is not defeated by the fact that the arbitration agreement refers only to the immediate parties to the agreement[10].

(iii) Where there has been a legal assignment under the Law of Property Act 1925, the assignee may maintain an arbitration in his own name alone[11]. The assignor is allowed to arbitrate, but he will recover nothing[12]. Where the assignment is equitable, both the assignor and the assignee should join in the arbitration[13].

(iv) The mere fact that the claim is connected with the contract does not require the assignee to arbitrate. It is only if he is claiming to enforce the contract that he is bound by the clause[14].

---

[8] Although *Digby v General Accident etc. Corpn*, supra, is often cited in this context, is it not really a case on assignment. By virtue of the statute, the claimant was treated as if he was a party to the contract (see per Luxmoore LJ at 235). It was obviously sensible to treat him as party to the arbitration clause which formed part of the contract, particularly as it was in the *Scott v Avery* form. *Shayler v Woolf* [1946] Ch 320 is not a decision on the right of the assignee to sue, since the claimant was enforcing his rights by action. The ratio of *Cottage Club Estates Ltd v Woodside Estates Co (Amersham) Ltd* [1928] 2 KB 463, is not easy to reconcile with the other cases.

[9] The argument to the contrary rests on the basis that the respondent agreed to arbitrate rather than to litigate, and that his right to insist on arbitration should not be defeated by an assignment over which he has no control.

[10] *The Padre Island*, supra. With or without an arbitration clause, an assignment of rights under a contract nearly always requires some verbal adjustment to the terms of the contract. The fact that such adjustment is necessary does not ordinarily lead to the inference that the parties intended to exclude the possibility of enforcement by assignees.

[11] *Aspell v Seymour* [1929] WN 152; *Shayler v Woolf*, ante.

[12] *Cottage Club Estates Ltd v Woodside Estates Co (Amersham) Ltd*, ante.

[13] If the assignor will not agree to join as claimant, the Court will no doubt find some means of enabling the arbitration to proceed, either by ordering the assignor to execute a legal assignment, or by ordering him to allow his name to be used as claimant, against a proper indemnity as to the costs of the arbitration. It would no doubt be more convenient if the arbitrator could deal with these matters, but since the relief claimed by the assignee arises out of the assignment and not out of the contract, it is difficult to see how it could be within the jurisdiction of the arbitrator to grant it.

[14] *Bonnin v Neame* [1910] 1 Ch 732 where the plaintiff had a statutory right to an account, which was not directly derived from the partnership contract.

The position is the same where it is not the benefit of the whole contract which has been assigned, but merely a claim arising under it[15].

Thus far, we have discussed the position which exists where the arbitration clause is in the ordinary form. If the clause is of the *Scott v Avery* type, the claim must plainly be pursued by arbitration, since the original party could not, by assigning away his right, deprive the respondent of his right to rely on the contractual stipulation making an award a condition precedent to legal proceedings[16]. But who should be the parties to the arbitration? Should the assignee arbitrate in his own name, or should he cause the original party to arbitrate on his behalf? It appears that the former view is correct[17], unless the clause is so worded as to admit only of an arbitration between the original parties to the contract[18].

B. DEFENDANT NOT NAMED AS A PARTY

Three situations may be distinguished, where it is the defendant who was not named as a party in the contract.

1 The defendant was in reality always a party to the contract, although not named in it.

2 The defendant has succeeded by operation of law to the liabilities of the original party.

3 The defendant has incurred liabilities which are secondary to the primary liabilities contained in the contract.

The first two situations are similar to those discussed above, in relation to claimants. The principal or beneficiary can insist on arbitration, because he was in truth a party to the arbitration agreement[19]. The personal representative or trustee in a bankruptcy stands in the shoes of the original party[20].

The third situation is likely to occur most often in practice where the defendant has guaranteed the liability of a party to the contract. Here, the position depends upon whether the liability of the guarantor is expressed to be contingent upon the ascertainment of the liability under the primary contract, and also upon the terms of the arbitration clause in the primary contract.

In the simplest case, where the guarantee and the arbitration clause are in the ordinary form, the liability of the guarantor arises simultaneously with that of the principal debtor; the creditor need not arbitrate against the principal

---

[15] *Rumput (Panama) SA v Islamic Republic of Iran Shipping Lines, The Leage* [1984] 2 Lloyd's Rep 259; *Court Line Ltd v Akt Gøtaverken, The Halcyon the Great* [1984] 1 Lloyd's Rep 283 at 289.

[16] *Dennehy v Bellamy*, ante; *Freshwater v Western Australian Assurance Co Ltd*, ante; *Smith v Pearl Assurance Co Ltd* (1939) 63 Ll L Rep 1; see also the observation of Harman LJ in *Post Office v Norwich Union Fire Insurance Society* [1967] 1 Lloyd's Rep 216, [1967] 2 QB 363 that you cannot 'pick out the plums and leave the duff behind'.

[17] *Digby v General Accident*, ante; also *Dennehy v Bellamy*, ante, where this seems to have been taken for granted.

[18] If the assignor will not co-operate, the assignee will have to enlist the help of the Court to get the arbitration under way. The procedural mechanisms will not be easy to work out.

[19] See *Pyxis Special Shipping Co Ltd v Dritsas and Kaglis Bros Ltd, The Scaplake* [1978] 2 Lloyd's Rep 380, which raised the question whether the arbitrator had jurisdiction over the claim against the principal.

[20] See Chapter 11 for a fuller discussion.

debtor, but may proceed at once against the guarantor. If he does so, his claim will be brought in the High Court, for the guarantor is not a party to the arbitration clause, and is not a person 'claiming through or under' the principal debtor[1].

If, on the other hand, the arbitration clause is in the *Scott v Avery* form, the claimant must obtain an award against the principal debtor, before proceeding against the guarantor; for the obtaining of an award against the principal debtor is a condition precedent to the liability of the principal debtor, and the guarantor does not become liable until the principal debtor is liable.

Finally, if the guarantee expressly states that the obtaining of an award against the principal debtor is a condition precedent to the liability of the guarantor, then naturally the creditor must first arbitrate against the principal debtor and then bring an action against the guarantor[2].

---

[1] *Daunt v Lazard* (1858) 27 LJ Ex 399 (where the guarantor unsuccessfully sought to arbitrate by way of defence a cross-claim arising under the primary contract); *Re Kitchin, ex p Young* (1881) 17 Ch D 668; *Thermistocles Navegacion SA v Langton, The Queen Frederica* [1978] 2 Lloyd's Rep 164; *Bruns v Colocotronis, The Vasso* [1979] 2 Lloyd's Rep 412 at 418–419.

[2] As in *Compania Sudamericana de Fletes SA v African Continental Bank Ltd* [1973] 1 Lloyd's Rep 21.

CHAPTER 9

Multiple arbitrations

The type of arbitration with which this book is concerned is consensual in origin. It stems from an agreement to arbitrate: usually in the form of an arbitration clause included in a substantive contract. Since most contracts are bilateral, an arbitration agreement will usually take effect between two people, or between two groups of people[1]. It does not always happen, however, that when a dispute arises out of the subject matter of a contract, the parties to that contract are necessarily the only people involved. Other parties may have claims, or may be the recipients of claims, in respect of the same set of facts. Situations of this kind, where more than two parties are involved, may be divided into two categories:

A. Cases where one party to an arbitration agreement has two claims arising from the same set of facts: one against the other party to the agreement, and the other against someone who is not a party. This usually happens where the claimant has entered into separate contracts with two different people, the one subject to arbitration, and the other not. For example a building owner may have claims against his contractor and his architect; a shipowner may seek to recover contribution in general average under a charterparty and a bill of lading; a cargo owner may wish to proceed in respect of cargo damage both under a bill of lading and a sub-charter; and so on. However, the problem does not always arise where there are two contracts. Sometimes, the arbitrable claim arises in contract, where the other claim lies in tort. For example, the owner of goods may wish to proceed in contract against the carrier who has agreed to transport his goods, and in tort against the sub-contractor who has actually carried them.

B. Cases where a person against whom a claim is made under a contract containing an arbitration clause seeks recompense from someone else under another contract. Such chains of claim are common. For example, a building owner may give notice of arbitration against a contractor, who wishes to claim an indemnity from the sub-contractor who actually did the work. A claim by a purchaser may be passed along a string of intermediate buyers to the ultimate seller.

In the first of these situations, it is the claimant who faces the difficulty. His problem is to pursue two claims simultaneously, of which only one is susceptible to arbitration. In the second situation, the problem is that of the defendant. He must somehow combine his contingent claim against the third party, with the defence of the arbitration which is brought against him. We will consider these situations separately.

---

[1] Troublesome problems can arise when an arbitration clause is included in an agreement with more than two parties: see p. 178, post.

A. MULTIPLE DEFENDANTS

1 Nature of the problem

A claimant who has potential claims against two defendants, of which one is subject to an arbitration agreement and the other is not, must on the face of it bring two sets of proceedings: an arbitration, and an action in the High Court. This presents him with obvious difficulties. For the purpose of elaborating these difficulties, we will refer to the party to the arbitration agreement as 'the first defendant', and the other recipient of a claim as 'the second defendant'.

The first difficulty which faces the claimant is that the findings of fact made by one tribunal will not bind the other[2]. This leads to a risk of inconsistent fact-findings by the two tribunals. Experience shows that witnesses are unlikely to give exactly the same evidence twice; and the different tribunals may form different views on credibility and on the weight to be attached to particular points. If tribunals come to inconsistent conclusions of fact, the claimant may find that he has lost against both defendants, when he should have won against at least one of them.

Second, there is the risk that the two tribunals will arrive at different conclusions on the same or related questions of law. If the arbitration is held in England, a point of law may sometimes find its way to the High Court; and by the time it reaches there, the action may have been tried by a different judge. The risk is particularly acute if the arbitration is to take place abroad, and there is a real risk of inconsistent conclusions, especially if the arbitration takes place before the trial[3].

Third, the claimant may face difficulties of timing, if his claim against the second defendant is contingent upon the failure of his claim against the first. It is not uncommon to encounter claims expressed in the form: 'I say that the second defendant is liable, but if I am wrong in this, then you, the first defendant, must be liable'[4]. The claim against the first defendant cannot easily be pursued, whilst the claim against the second defendant is still pending.

Finally, the prosecution of claims in two separate proceedings is bound to be more expensive than fighting them both in the same action, and the claimant may be unable to recover against the defendant who is ultimately held liable the costs which he has wasted in pursuing his claim against the other defendant[5].

2 Solutions

In the face of these difficulties, the obvious tactic of the claimant must be to sue both defendants in the same action. But the first defendant has no incentive to concur in this procedure. The more difficulties he places in the way of the claimant, the more likely he is to obtain a favourable settlement of the dispute. Thus, in most cases he will apply for a stay of that part of the action which is brought against him. In the case of a 'non domestic' arbitration agreement, the

---

[2] Since the parties are different, the fact findings do not raise an issue estoppel.
[3] If the trial is held first, it would be a very headstrong arbitrator who insisted on expressing his own inconsistent view of the English law.
[4] See, for example, *The Pine Hill* [1958] 2 Lloyd's Rep 146.
[5] See post, p. 148.

stay will be granted automatically[6]. In the case of a 'domestic agreement, the court has a discretion, but the burden will rest upon the claimant to show why he should not be held to his agreement to arbitrate[7]. Towards the satisfaction of this burden, the claimant will point to the inconveniences listed above. It is clear from the authorities that these are indeed substantial matters to be weighed in the balance[8]. But they are not enough in themselves; some other factor must be present. Precisely what additional circumstances are sufficient to displace the burden cannot readily be stated, since the reported cases are few, and the matter is one for the discretion of the judge. It is, however, established that one feature is likely to be decisive if present, namely a degree of responsibility on the part of the first defendant for the fact that the claimant has made two contracts with different provisions for the settlement of disputes. Thus, for example, where a shipowner brought an action against a consignee of goods under the bill of lading, and against the charterer under a charterparty, of which the latter contained an arbitration clause and the former did not, the Court declined to stay an action against the charterer who had been joined as co-defendant, because the charterer himself had some responsibility for stipulating the form of bill of lading[9].

B. THIRD-PARTY SITUATIONS

1 Nature of the problem

One of the weakest features of English arbitral procedure[10] is its inability to deal with third-party situations: i.e. those in which a party against whom a claim is made seeks to recover from someone else an indemnity in respect of his liability. In such a situation, the defendant wishes above all to avoid fighting the same claim twice. He does not want to incur the costs of two actions, nor to run the risk that the two different tribunals will reach different conclusions on the facts or the law – for if they do he may find himself with a liability to the claimant which he cannot pass on to the third party. He also wishes to avoid the inconvenience of having to put forward diametrically opposed contentions in the two hearings. For if (for example) the claimant maintains that goods sold to him by the defendant were defective; the defendant will answer the claim by saying that they were sound; whereas if the defendant loses against the claimant, he will have to advance the opposite view in his own claim upon the third party. This is bound to place his witnesses in difficulty. Moreover, he will not wish to wait until he has been held liable to the claimant, before he prosecutes his claim against the third party.

The third-party procedure, which is available in a High Court action, satisfies

---

[6] See p. 462, post. The inconvenience to which this can give rise was pointed out by Mocatta J in *The Maria Gorthon* [1976] 2 Lloyd's Rep 720 at 722.

[7] See pp. 475–476, post.

[8] *The Pine Hill*, ante (claims under charter and bill of lading); *Taunton-Collins v Cromie* [1964] 1 WLR 633 (claims against builder and architect); *Bulk Oil (Zug) AG v Trans-Asiatic Oil SA* [1973] 1 Lloyd's Rep 129 (claims under two parallel contracts); *Green Star Shipping Co Ltd v London Assurance* (1928) 31 Ll L Rep 4 (claims against insurers under three separate policies).

[9] *The Pine Hill*, ante; see also *Bulk Oil (Zug) v Trans-Asiatic*, ante, at 137; and p. 477, post.

[10] English law is very far from being alone in this. In few jurisdictions has the problem been faced, and in fewer still (perhaps in none) has a satisfactory solution been achieved.

all these requirements. Subject to certain restrictions, the defendant can compel the third party to be joined in the proceedings initiated by the claimant, and can compel the claimant to allow the third party to take part in the action. Thereafter, the two sets of proceedings move forward together, at the same pace. The evidence and documents of all three parties form a pool of information upon which all three can draw. The same tribunal pronounces on both claims, and decisions of fact and law given in respect of one claim are binding on the parties to the other.

The position in an arbitration is quite different. It is easy to see why. The claimant and the defendant have agreed to submit their disputes to arbitration; and so perhaps have the defendant and the third party. But they have not submitted to the *same* arbitration. If the defendant seeks to join the third party to his arbitration with the claimant, the latter can reply with force that he agreed to arbitrate with the defendant, not with the defendant and third party. The claimant can point out that if the third party is brought in, it will increase the costs of the arbitration, and will compromise the privacy which is of the essence of arbitration. The third party's attitude will be much the same. He will say that a dispute between the claimant and the defendant under a different contract is no concern of his; and he will press the defendant to wait until he has concluded his differences with the claimant, before he starts to promote a dispute with the third party.

In such a situation, the defendant is in an unenviable position. He runs the risk of losing both arbitrations, if the tribunals arrive at inconsistent findings of fact and law[11]. Moreover, the defendant will find it difficult to proceed satisfactorily with his arbitration against the third party, whilst his dispute with the claimant is yet to be resolved[12].

2 Solutions

Viewed in the abstract, the sensible solution is for the parties to agree upon a tripartite arbitration before the same arbitrator, facilitated if necessary by an agreement to waive any inconsistencies in the two arbitration agreements. An orderly solution will not, however, necessarily appeal to all the parties. It is the defendant who is in difficulties, and the other parties may have no wish to accommodate him. What can be done if they elect to stand on their strict rights? There are three possibilities.

(a) Same arbitrator tries both claims

First, if the same arbitrator has been appointed in respect of two disputes he can,

---

[11] The suggestion is not fanciful. In *Focke & Co Ltd v Thomas Robinson, Sons & Co Ltd* (1935) 52 Ll L Rep 334, and *Focke & Co Ltd v Hecht & Co* (1938) 60 Ll L Rep 135, as the result of inconsistent findings, a seller was held liable to his buyer in one arbitration, and failed in the other arbitration against the person from whom he had bought the goods.

[12] The arbitrator in the third-party arbitration might be inclined, with a view to getting the proceedings moving, to allow the defendant to claim a declaration that if ultimately he is held liable to the claimant, he will be entitled to an indemnity from the third party. This may be a mistake. As the Court of Appeal pointed out in *Trans Trust SPRL v Danubian Trading Co Ltd* [1952] 2 QB 297 the third-party claim cannot be accurately decided until it is known precisely why the defendant has been held liable to the plaintiff.

in effect, order the matter to proceed in the same way as third-party proceedings in the High Court[13]. The solution is obviously sensible, but such an order would substantially infringe the contractual rights of the claimant and the third party and can only be made with the consent of all the parties[14]. Even where the arbitration agreement confers some kind of power to hold joint hearings, there may still be difficulties. Thus, the contracts may well call for different modes of arbitration. For example, a sole arbitrator in one case, and two arbitrators and an umpire in the other. Again, one contract may impose requirements as to the qualifications of the arbitrators ('the arbitrators to be commercial men'), which are absent in the other contract. Moreover, even where the modes of arbitration are in essence the same, it does not follow that the parties will appoint the same persons to act. In the first contract the parties may appoint P and Q as arbitrators, who may (upon disagreement) cause R to enter on the reference as umpire. Whereas in the second contract the parties may appoint Q and T as arbitrators, who may be able to make a joint award. The two disputes will thus come before quite different tribunals. No matter how carefully worded the arbitration agreement may be, difficulties of this kind are always likely to arise and cannot be overcome, unless the parties are prepared to cooperate[15].

(b) High Court tries both claims

A second possible solution is for the claimant to institute proceedings in the High Court, and for the defendant then to institute third-party proceedings. The difficulty is that this approach cannot be adopted unless the claimant takes the initiative: i.e. if he also, for some reason, does not wish to arbitrate. The defendant cannot take the initiative himself[16]. Moreover, even if the dispute between the claimant and the defendant is litigated in the High Court, it does

---

[13] In *Abu Dhabi Gas Liquefaction Co Ltd v Eastern Bechtel Corpn* [1982] 2 Lloyd's Rep 425 the Court tried to achieve this result by means of its power to appoint an arbitrator in the event of disagreement. But we are informed that the parties to the two arbitrations did not agree to joint proceedings and that the hearings took place separately.

[14] *Oxford Shipping Co Ltd v Nippon Yusen Kaisha, The Eastern Saga* [1984] 2 Lloyd's Rep 373. There has been much discussion in recent years of the possibility of legislation to enable the Court to order two or more arbitrations to be heard together before a common tribunal, or by the Court. Any solution depends in one way or another on altering the contractual right of at least one party to the tribunal of his choice. Such a solution is not only out of keeping with the current view that the parties should have complete autonomy over the constitution of the arbitral tribunal and the procedure which it is to follow, but would arguably be inconsistent with the international obligations of the United Kingdom under Article II of the New York Convention. If these objections can be overcome, the difficulties which remain, although formidable, are mainly of a technical rather than a theoretical kind.

[15] Or unless the Court can compel them to co-operate, under threat of taking a strong line if they do not. In *LE Cattan Ltd v A Michaelides & Co* [1958] 1 Lloyd's Rep 479, the dispute began as an action, with third- and fourth-party proceedings, but was then converted into a multiple arbitration: whether by consent or compulsion does not appear from the report. If a multiple arbitration does take place then the liability for the costs of all the parties should in the ordinary way be borne by the party at one end of the chain or the other who ultimately loses: ibid. The Court has power to make an order which will achieve this result under s. 51(1) of the Supreme Court Act 1981: *Aiden Shipping Co Ltd v Interbulk Ltd* [1986] AC 965, [1986] 2 WLR 1051. Section 18(1) of the Arbitration Act 1950, however, gives the arbitrator power only to make directions about 'the costs of the reference and award'.

[16] In theory, he could try to snatch jurisdiction by claiming declaratory relief against the plaintiff and the third party, but we do not believe that the Court would countenance this.

not follow that the same will apply to the third-party claim, since it will be open to the third party to apply for a stay of the third-party proceedings. If the arbitration agreement is 'non-domestic', the Court has no option but to grant a stay[17]. Whether a stay will be granted in a 'domestic' case is a matter for discretion[18], and no firm rules can be laid down, but it appears that the further down the chain of parties the action has passed without anyone applying for a stay, the less likely it is that a stay will be granted to a party still further down the chain[19].

(c) String contracts

Finally, the contract may expressly provide for a 'string' arbitration. The rules of several Commodity Trade Associations stipulate that where goods are sold and re-sold on terms which are identical, except as to date, price and names of parties, any dispute shall be settled between the first seller and the last buyer, the award being binding on the intermediate parties[20].

This procedure works satisfactorily, and saves considerable time and cost, if applied to suitable cases: for example, to straightforward disputes as to quality. But quite apart from theoretical problems which may arise, the string procedure can give rise to much trouble if employed without proper thought[1]. Space does not permit a full discussion of the difficulties which may arise, but the following may be mentioned.

(i) Existence of string.   First, the parties may be at odds about whether there is a string at all, within the meaning of the clause. Even if there is, it does not follow that because the written contracts are the same, the disputes are necessarily identical. For example, questions of collateral warranties, supervening illegality, prohibition of export or import and so on may arise between some of the parties, and not between others. In such a case, an arbitration between first seller and last buyer will be useless, since it will leave out the main points in issue; and it will plainly be unjust that the result of such an arbitration would bind all the intermediate parties, whose complaints and defences will never have been canvassed at all. In these and similar instances, where string arbitration clauses are applied to inappropriate cases, we believe that the Court would intervene and put the matter on a proper footing. We suggest that if any

---

[17] See pp. 462–466, post.

[18] See pp. 475–483, post.

[19] *Eastern Counties Farmers Ltd v J and J Cunningham Ltd* [1962] 1 Lloyd's Rep 261 (and see [1964] 1 Lloyd's Rep 81). But contrast *Bruce v Strong* [1951] 2 Lloyd's Rep 5, [1951] 2 KB 447, where the fourth-party proceedings were stayed. Perhaps the difference lies in the fact that the former case involved a difficult question of law whereas the latter did not.

[20] For an example, see *Burkett Sharpe & Co v Eastcheap Dried Fruit Co and Perera* [1961] 2 Lloyd's Rep 80 at 87. It appears that a string arbitration procedure may be implied from the custom of the trade even if it is not expressed in the contract: *Tricerri Ltd v Crosfields and Calthrop Ltd* [1958] 1 Lloyd's Rep 236 at 241.

[1] For example, if A, B and C are the members of a string, is there an arbitration agreement within the meaning of the Act? We think not, for the 'arbitration' contemplated must surely be an arbitration between the parties to the arbitration agreement: namely A and B, and B and C. If A began an action, we cannot see how B could obtain a stay under the Acts. But A and B have made a contractual promise to have their disputes resolved by an arbitration between A and C, and we believe that the Court might well enforce this promise by granting B a stay under the inherent jurisdiction: see p. 461, post.

question of a misapplication of a string clause should arise, the assistance of the Court should be invoked at the earliest possible stage[2]. Otherwise, if the matter goes to an award, there is almost certain to be an expensive and time-consuming dispute as to validity of the award and its effect on intermediate parties.

(ii) Failure to cooperate. Second, a string arbitration clause will not work unless all the parties cooperate. For example, the parties at the top of the chain may decide to litigate amongst themselves, instead of arbitrating. In such a case, the Court will, if it can, retain the action in the High Court, and will bring in the persons further down the chain by third- and fourth-party proceedings[3]. This solution will not, however, help where it is the parties at the bottom of the chain who refuse to cooperate. For example, if the first seller carries on business abroad and has no assets available for execution, he may not trouble himself to arbitrate, either with the last buyer or with anyone else. In such a case, a string arbitration makes no sense. Only the last buyer would be represented at the hearing, and it would plainly be unfair for an award made in such circumstances to be binding on intermediate parties[4]. Trade Associations sometimes tackle this difficulty by shortening the string, and making the penultimate buyer or seller the party to the arbitration and the award. But this is not what the clause says. The better course will be to have individual arbitrations along the chain, in which the parties will no doubt be content to appoint the same arbitrators. If this course runs into difficulties, either the parties or the arbitrators should devise a way of getting the Court to tell them what to do.

(iii) Status of award. Finally, it may be noted that a string arbitration will not usually produce an award which is immediately enforceable against anybody. For one thing, the status of the document published by the arbitrators as an award between each of the intermediate parties is unlikely to be clear enough to found an application for summary enforcement. And for another, there will be many instances where the arbitrators cannot make a money award. For instance, in a rejection case, the damages will depend upon the contract price of the goods, and since the price will vary from buyer to buyer, the damages awarded in respect of the intermediate disputes must necessarily be different. The most that the arbitrators can do is to declare the rejection good, and fix a price for invoicing back. Unless the court is prepared to give effect to the arithmetical consequences, a party who wishes to enforce the award will have to bring an action on the contract, relying on the award as giving rise to an estoppel on the issues of liability and quantum.

---

[2] Either by an action for a declaration that the string clause does not apply; or by an application for an injunction to restrain the string arbitration; or both, depending on the circumstances. It does, however, appear from the observations of Diplock J at first instance in *Burkett Sharp & Co v Eastcheap Dried Fruit Co and Perera* [1961] 2 Lloyd's Rep 80 at 88, that the question whether a string exists can be decided by the arbitrator. We submit that he cannot make a conclusive decision on this matter if it affects his jurisdiction – as it usually will.

[3] *Eastern Counties Farmers v Cunningham*, ante.

[4] In *Finzel, Berry & Co v Eastcheap Dried Fruit Co* [1962] 1 Lloyd's Rep 370, McNair J managed to give practical effect, in the context of a string arbitration, to a clause which entitled the trade association to appoint an arbitrator in default of appointment by one of the parties. His decision was upheld in the Court of Appeal (at [1962] 2 Lloyd's Rep 11).

C. COSTS IN MULTIPLE ARBITRATIONS

An arbitrator can only order costs to be paid as between parties to the arbitration over which he has jurisdiction. This has three consequences for multiple arbitrations –

1 If a claimant has sued two defendants in different proceedings, and has succeeded only against one, the arbitrator in one proceeding cannot order the unsuccessful defendant to pay to the successful defendant his costs of defending the claim against him in the other proceeding[5].

2 In a third-party situation, the arbitrator cannot order costs to be paid directly by the claimant to the third party or vice versa[6].

The fact that the arbitral tribunal has, by consent, consisted of the same individuals in both arbitrations and that the arbitrations have been heard together does not alter the position unless the parties have agreed that the proceedings should be amalgamated into a single arbitration[7].

3 The arbitrator has no jurisdiction to order an unsuccessful defendant in the arbitration before him to indemnify the claimant in that arbitration against his liability for the costs of a successful defendant in other proceedings[8]: nor to order an unsuccessful party in the arbitration before him to indemnify the other party against his liability for costs to the original claimant or third party in a chain of third-party proceedings[9]. Even when both arbitrations reach the High Court on appeal, the court has no power to consolidate the appeals, so that the defendant may recover from one party the costs he must pay to the other.

---

[5] I.e. he cannot make a 'Sanderson' order: see *Supreme Court Practice*, 62/2/39.

[6] *Wilhelmsen v Canadian Transport Co, The Takamine* [1980] 2 Lloyd's Rep 204 at 208.

[7] Ibid. See also *LE Cattan Ltd v A Michaelides & Co* [1958] 1 Lloyd's Rep 479; *Maritime Transport Overseas GmbH v Unitramp Salem Rederierna AB, The Antaios* [1981] 2 Lloyd's Rep 284.

[8] I.e. a 'Bullock' order: *Supreme Court Practice*, 62/2/39. See also n. 15, p. 145, ante.

[9] *The Antaios*, ante; and *Unimarine SA v Canadian Transport Co Ltd, The Catherine L* [1982] 1 Lloyd's Rep 484. In *Suzuki & Co Ltd v Burgett and Newsam* (1922) 10 Ll L Rep 223 at 227–229, the costs were awarded by way of damages, but this solution of the problem will only serve where the costs have been incurred as a direct and reasonably foreseeable consequence of an actionable wrong by the losing party.

CHAPTER 10

What matters may be arbitrated

A. GENERAL

In the preceding chapters we have considered the problems involved in the question whether a dispute or claim has arisen which falls within the scope of an arbitration agreement to which the claimant and defendant are parties. In this chapter we are concerned with the question whether, assuming such a dispute or claim to have arisen, the law recognises it as a fit subject for decision by arbitration.

This question may arise at different stages of the arbitration. At the outset, it may be relevant to the question whether the court will enforce the arbitration agreement by staying proceedings brought in breach of it or by the other means at its disposal. And at the conclusion of the arbitration it may be relevant to the question of whether the court will enforce the award[1].

In practice therefore, the question has not been whether a particular dispute is capable of settlement by arbitration, but whether it ought to be referred to arbitration or whether it has given rise to an enforceable award. No doubt for this reason, English law has never arrived at a general theory for distinguishing those disputes which may be settled by arbitration from those which may not. The general principle is, we submit, that any dispute or claim[2] concerning legal rights which can be the subject of an enforceable award, is capable of being settled by arbitration. This principle must be understood, however, subject to certain reservations.

First, certain types of dispute are resolved by methods which are not properly called arbitration. These are discussed in Chapter 2, ante.

Second, the types of remedies which the arbitrator can award are limited by considerations of public policy and by the fact that he is appointed by the parties and not by the state. For example, he cannot impose a fine or a term of imprisonment, commit a person for contempt or issue a writ of subpoena[2a]; nor can he make an award which is binding on third parties or affects the public at large, such as a judgment in rem against a ship, an assessment of the rateable value of land[3], a divorce decree, a winding-up order or a decision that an agreement is exempt from the competition rules of the EEC under Article 85(3) of the Treaty of Rome[4]. It would be wrong, however, to draw from this any

---

[1] The 1975 Act, which deals with both matters, applies only to agreements to refer matters 'capable of settlement by arbitration': s. 7(1). See also s. 5(3). Quite apart from this, the Court would not enforce an arbitration agreement or an award on a matter not capable of settlement by arbitration.

[2] We include 'claim' for the reasons discussed at p. 129, ante.

[2a] *Kursell v Timber Operators and Contractors Ltd* [1923] KB 202.

[3] *Thorp v Cole* (1835) 2 Cr M & R 367.

[4] This is exclusively within the province of the European Commission under Reg. 17 of 1962.

general rule that criminal, admiralty, family or company matters cannot be referred to arbitration: indeed, examples of each of these types of dispute being referred to arbitration are to be found in the reported cases[5]. Nor should one conclude that an arbitrator cannot effectively rule on a claim or defence raised under Articles 85 or 86 of the Treaty of Rome. Unless the nature of the question is such as to render the arbitration agreement itself void[6], or the European Commission has itself initiated proceedings on the question[7], the arbitrator can and should rule on it.

B. QUESTIONS OF ILLEGALITY

It has sometimes been stated that disputes arising out of an illegal contract cannot be referred to arbitration[8]. This is, we suggest, inaccurate. It is true that an arbitrator has in general no jurisdiction to decide a dispute under a contract which is void ab initio on grounds of illegality. But the reason for this is not that the dispute is incapable of settlement by arbitration, but that the illegality strikes at the validity of the arbitration agreement. Where the arbitration agreement itself is unaffected by illegality, the arbitrator can and must rule on any question of illegality[9]. It may be that if he makes an award which has the effect of enforcing an illegal contract or which offends against public policy, the Court will set it aside or refuse to enforce it[10], at any rate if the illegality or offence against public policy is apparent on the face of the award[11]. But if he makes an award giving effect, even wrongly, to a defence of illegality, the award is within his jurisdiction and a complete answer to a fresh claim on the same facts.

---

[5] The cases on criminal and matrimonial matters are collected in Russell (19th edn) pp. 28–31.

[6] See p. 113, ante.

[7] In which case the Commission has exclusive jurisdiction to examine the agreement.

[8] Halsbury's (4th edn) Vol. 2, para. 503; see also Russell (19th edn) p. 25.

[9] See p. 113, ante.

[10] *Aubert v Maze* (1801) 2 Bos & P 371; cf. *Prodexport State Co for Foreign Trade v ED and F Man Ltd* [1972] 2 Lloyd's Rep 375 at 382. It is a defence to enforcement of a foreign award under Part II of the 1950 Act that enforcement would be contrary to public policy or the law of England: s. 37(1). Similarly in the case of a Convention award under the 1975 Act: s. 5(3).

[11] *Prodexport v Man*, supra; *Birtley District Co-op Society Ltd v Windy Nook and District Industrial Co-op Society Ltd (No 2)* [1960] 2 QB 1. *Sed quaere*. If a point on illegality is raised, it is surely the duty of the court to look at all the facts, not just those stated in the award.

CHAPTER 11

Capacity of parties

A. CAPACITY GENERALLY

Capacity to make an arbitration agreement is generally co-extensive with capacity to make an ordinary contract[1]. In this chapter we discuss only those aspects of capacity which require special mention in the context of arbitration.

B. PARTICULAR CASES

1 The Crown

The Crown is a competent party to an arbitration agreement. Part I of the 1950 Act[2] and the 1979 Act[3] bind the Crown, but Part II of the 1950 Act and the 1975 Act[4] do not. An award against the Crown for the payment of money or costs may be enforced by the procedure for the satisfaction of orders against the Crown laid down by section 25 of the Crown Proceedings Act 1947[5].

2 State immunity[6]

A foreign or commonwealth state recognised by English law is a competent party to an arbitration agreement with a person who is not a state, and although such a state is as a general rule immune from the jurisdiction of the courts of the United Kingdom, the immunity does not apply to proceedings relating to an arbitration to which the state has agreed in writing to submit disputes[7]. The fact that a state is a party to an arbitration agreement does not prevent the court from exercising all the powers which would be available to it in the usual case of an arbitration between private persons.

There is, however, an important exception. The processes of execution and attachment are not available against the property of a state for the enforcement

---

[1] The rules governing capacity to contract lie outside the scope of this work. Reference should be made to the standard textbooks on the law of contract.

[2] S. 30, as amended by s. 8(2)(c) of the 1975 Act.

[3] S. 7(1)(c).

[4] Which deal with 'foreign' and 'convention' awards and the enforcement of non-domestic arbitration agreements.

[5] The award must first be converted into a judgment or order by means of an action at common law or under the summary procedure under s. 26 of the 1950 Act: see Chapter 28.

[6] The law relating to the recognition of states, state immunity and diplomatic privileges lies outside the scope of this work, and is summarised here only in so far as it relates to commercial arbitration.

[7] The general rule is stated in s. 1 of the State Immunity Act 1978, and the exception relating to arbitrations in s. 9.

of an arbitration award, unless that property is in use or intended for use for commercial purposes[8].

3 Trustees and personal representatives

Personal representatives and trustees may, if and as they think fit, submit to arbitration any debt, account, claim or thing whatever relating to the testator's or intestate's estate or to the trust[9].

4 Death

The death of a party does not discharge an arbitration agreement, either as respects the deceased or any other party: the agreement continues to be enforceable by or against the personal representative of the deceased[10]. The authority of an arbitrator is not revoked by the death of any party by whom he was appointed[11].

5 Bankruptcy

A bankrupt cannot submit to arbitration so as to bind his estate[12], but his trustee, with the permission of the creditors' committee or the court, may refer to arbitration any debts, claims or liabilities subsisting or supposed to subsist between the bankrupt and any person who may have incurred any liability to the bankrupt[13].

A bankruptcy order does not have the effect of discharging an existing arbitration agreement or of revoking the authority of an arbitrator appointed by the bankrupt[14]. But the arbitration agreement is not binding on, or enforceable by, his trustee[15], unless either –

1 the trustee adopts the contract containing the arbitration agreement[16];
or
2 on application by the trustee with the consent of the creditors' committee, or by any party to the agreement other than the bankrupt, the bankruptcy Court orders a matter to which the agreement applies to be referred to arbitration[17].

The making of a bankruptcy order does not operate as a stay of current arbitration proceedings, unless the Court has so ordered[18]. But after the making of a bankruptcy order, no creditor may commence an arbitration in respect of

---

8   State Immunity Act 1978, ss. 13(2)(b) and (4).
9   Trustee Act 1925, s. 15(f).
10   Arbitration Act 1950, s. 2(1). See also ante, p. 137.
11   Arbitration Act 1950, s. 2(2).
12   He may, however, bind himself: *Re Milnes and Robertson* (1854) 15 CB 451.
13   Insolvency Act 1986, s. 314(1) and Sch. 5, Part 1(6).
14   *Hemsworth v Brian* (1845) 1 CB 131.
15   *Marsh v Wood* (1829) 9 B & C 659; *Sturges v Lord Curzon* (1851) 7 Exch 17; *Pennel v Walker* (1856) 18 CB 651.
16   S. 3(1) of the 1950 Act.
17   S. 3(2) of the 1950 Act.
18   Under s. 285(1) of the Insolvency Act 1986.

any debt provable in bankruptcy unless with the leave of the Court and on such terms as the Court may impose[19].

6 Administrators and administrative receivers

An administrator or administrative receiver[20] has power to bring or defend arbitration proceedings in the name of and on behalf of the company and to refer to arbitration any question affecting the company[1].

7 Winding-up

The winding-up of a company does not discharge an arbitration agreement to which it is a party, nor revoke the authority of an arbitrator appointed by it, unless and until the agreement is disclaimed by the liquidator with the leave of the Court[2].

The liquidator may, with the sanction of the court or the committee for inspection in the case of a winding-up by the court, bring or defend arbitration proceedings in the name and on behalf of the company[3]. When a winding-up order has been made or a provisional liquidator appointed no arbitration may be proceeded with or commenced against the company except by leave of the court and subject to such terms as the court may impose[4].

---

[19] Insolvency Act 1986, s. 285(3)(b).
[20] Unless the debentures otherwise provide.
[1] Insolvency Act 1986, ss. 14, 42 and Sch. 1(5) and (6).
[2] Under s. 618 of the Companies Act 1985.
[3] Companies Act 1985, ss. 539(1)(a), 598(2), 610(1).
[4] Companies Act 1985, s. 525(2).

CHAPTER 12

The residual jurisdiction of the Court

1 Nature of the Court's residual jurisdiction

The law of arbitration is principally concerned with the relationship between the courts and those aspects of the arbitral process which concern the performance and enforcement of the agreement to arbitrate; with the questions whether the Court has jurisdiction to compel a party to arbitrate in accordance with the agreement and to honour the resulting award, whether it can intervene to remedy injustice resulting from defects in the conduct of the reference, and so on; and with the manner in which these and other powers should be exercised. The law of arbitration is thus mainly procedural in content. But it does also deal with certain substantive aspects of the arbitral process, in the sense that it creates and regulates the jurisdiction of the Court to intervene in the event of an erroneous decision by the arbitrator on some issue or issues arising in the dispute which is submitted to him pursuant to an agreement to arbitrate. This important topic, which is concerned, whatever precisely the terminology employed, with a jurisdiction essentially appellate in nature, is discussed in Chapters 36–37, post.

In this Chapter, however, we are concerned with a different question: namely, the extent to which the Court has an originating jurisdiction over the subject matter of the dispute. In other words, if the substantive contract contains an agreement to arbitrate, does the Court nevertheless have power itself to enter upon and decide the merits of a dispute arising under the contract?

(a) History of the jurisdiction

This question has a long and difficult history, which need not be discussed in detail here. Essentially, the problem arose from a conflict between three well-established principles.

First, where there was an agreement intended to create or affect legally recognisable rights, the parties could not by contract validly remove from the Court the jurisdiction to declare and enforce those rights, and confer it instead upon a private tribunal[1].

---

[1] Various reasons have been given for the rule that the parties cannot by contract 'oust the jurisdiction of the Court'. (This rule has at most a distant connection with the question whether parliament can by statute annul the supervisory jurisdiction of the Court over inferior non-consensual tribunals). One reason which has been suggested is a simple jurisdictional jealousy. Another is an argument based on repugnancy. If the parties have agreed that a contract shall create legal rights, a clause stipulating that those rights shall not be enforceable in court must be rejected as inconsistent with the main intent of the agreement. (This argument is criticised by Glanville Williams, (1944) 60 LQR at 73, on the ground that an agreement withdrawing disputes from the courts cannot ex hypothesi have been intended to create legally enforceable rights. We venture to express some reservations about this criticism, but the matter is now of only historical interest.) Whatever the true explanation of the rule, it was established by 1799 (*Thompson v Charnock* (1799) 8 Term Rep 139), and has been acted upon in several subsequent cases; most notably *Scott v Avery* (1856) 5 HL Cas 811.

Second, an agreement to refer disputes to arbitration was not contrary to public policy, but would be enforced by the courts, albeit in remedies more limited than those appropriate to ordinary contracts. Thus, for example, it was established at an early date that a breach of an arbitration agreement would be compensated in damages; and that an award could be pleaded as an answer to an action relating to the same issue. Equally, Parliament has, by a series of statutes, recognised the utility of private arbitration, and has enacted measures to improve its efficacy.

Third, the parties to an agreement are entitled to stipulate that it shall not create or affect any legal rights[2]. In the context of such an agreement, a stipulation excluding the jurisdiction of the courts is unobjectionable, although unnecessary: for in reality there is no jurisdiction to exclude.

(b) The modern rules

Ultimately, a rather precarious compromise was reached between these three propositions[3], on the following lines –

1 If, in the circumstances, a court would have territorial jurisdiction to determine a dispute arising in relation to a contract if that contract did not contain an arbitration clause[4], it retains that jurisdiction notwithstanding the inclusion of such a clause[5]. At the most, it furnishes a ground upon which the Court may, and in some circumstances must, stay the proceeding[6].

2 The presence of an arbitration clause in a contract does not furnish a

---

[2] The authorities for this proposition long antedate its conclusive statement in *Rose and Frank Co v JR Crompton & Bros Ltd* [1925] AC 445.

[3] The intellectual basis of these rules is difficult to explain with conviction. One possibility is that the Court was able to construe the arbitration clause as if it did not involve an intention to oust the jurisdiction, and hence could take effect, notwithstanding the rule as to ouster: or to put the idea in different words, as if the clause provided two alternative modes of deciding disputes, of which one (namely arbitration) could validly take effect, provided that the other (an action in court) was not involved. This interpretation hardly seems consistent with the main purpose of an arbitration agreement, which (as judges have often pointed out) is to withdraw disputes from the legalistic embrace of the courts, and submit them to what the parties anticipate will be the more practical and expeditious procedures of a private tribunal. Another explanation is suggested in the judgment of Fletcher Moulton LJ in *Doleman & Sons v Ossett Corpn* [1912] 3 KB 257, based on the procedural difficulties which were at one time involved (and to some extent still are) in enforcing an agreement to arbitrate – notably as regards the fact that a submission was formerly revocable at will at any time before award.

[4] We suggest that this is an important and necessary qualification, even if it is not supported by authority. The inherent and statutory jurisdiction of the court over arbitral procedures taking place in England, and its statutory appellate jurisdiction, arise because English arbitration law is the curial law of the arbitration. The position is different where the Court assumes primary jurisdiction over the merits of a dispute, in face of a valid or defunct arbitration clause. Here, the presence of an arbitration clause, ex hypothesi to be ignored, cannot confer on the Court a jurisdiction which it would not otherwise possess, either because of the defendant's presence within the jurisdiction, or because the case is one for service out of the jurisdiction pursuant to RSC Ord. 11, r. 1.

[5] *Doleman & Sons v Ossett Corpn* [1912] 3 KB 257; *Pinnock Bros v Lewis and Peat Ltd* [1923] 1 KB 690 at 696; *Thompson v Charnock*, ante; *Harris v Reynolds* (1845) 7 QB 71; *Lawson v Wallasey Local Board* (1883) 48 LT 507; *Heyman v Darwins Ltd* [1942] AC 356 at 373; *Roper v Lendon* (1859) 1 E & E 825; *Dawson v Fitzgerald* (1876) 1 Ex D 257; *Jager v Tolme and Runge and London Produce Clearing House Ltd* [1916] 1 KB 939; *The Purisima Concepcion* (1849) 13 Jur 545.

[6] See Chapter 30, post.

defence to an action on the contract[7], nor even an answer to a claim for summary judgment under RSC Ord. 14[8], except in the case where by one form of words or another, the obtaining of an award is made a condition precedent to the existence of a cause of action, or the right to enforce it[9].

3 Even the fact that an arbitration is already in progress at the time when the action is commenced does not furnish a defence to the action[10], provided that the arbitration has not proceeded as far as a valid award.

4 A contract, otherwise valid and enforceable, is regarded as effective to create or modify the legal rights of the parties, notwithstanding that it contains an arbitration clause.

5 Where the Court exercises its right, and in many instances its duty, to renounce jurisdiction over a dispute which falls within an agreement to arbitrate, this renunciation is only provisional. Until a valid award is published, the Court retains its underlying jurisdiction, which in certain circumstances it will be entitled to resume[11].

6 Where the Court renounces jurisdiction over a dispute by staying its own proceedings in favour of arbitration it does so only for the purpose of giving effect to the arbitration agreement. It retains jurisdiction for the purpose of making orders in aid of the process of arbitration[12].

2 Practical applications of the residual jurisdiction

The rules set out above are of practical importance in four situations.

(a) Proceedings brought in spite of arbitration agreement

First, the claimant institutes an action in the courts. Here, unless and until an application is made to stay the action[13], the jurisdiction of the courts takes effect in full; the action proceeds in precisely the same way as if there had been no arbitration agreement[14]; and, equally, the judgment of the Court is uncondition-

---

[7] See the cases cited in note 5, ante.

[8] The right course is for the respondent to make a cross-application to stay, supporting it by evidence that the claim is disputed, and that the dispute falls within the arbitration clause.

[9] By a *Scott v Avery* provision, of the type discussed in Chapter 13.

[10] *Harris v Reynolds*, ante; *Pena Copper Mines Ltd v Rio Tinto Co Ltd* (1911) 105 LT 846 at 851; *Doleman v Ossett*, ante, at 262, 267.

[11] *Hamlyn & Co v Talisker Distillery* [1894] AC 202 at 211; *Cameron v Cuddy* [1914] AC 651 at 656; *Neale v Richardson* [1938] 1 All ER 753 (a difficult case, because the plaintiff had made no attempt to procure the appointment of a replacement); *Fleming v JS Doig (Grimsby) Ltd* (1921) 38 RPC 57. It is assumed in s. 24(2) that if the power, there conferred, to order that the agreement shall cease to have effect in cases of fraud, is exercised, the court has jurisdiction to determine the issue.

[12] Such as arresting a ship or cargo: *The Tuyuti* [1984] QB 838; *The Silver Athens (No 2)* [1986] 2 Lloyd's Rep 583, or allowing an Admiralty action in rem to proceed to judgment if the award is not honoured: *The Rena K* [1978] 1 Lloyd's Rep 545.

[13] See Chapter 30, post.

[14] It is possible that the presence of an arbitration clause may have some procedural effect even in the absence of an application to stay. The courts have tended to take the view that the existence of an arbitration clause, like that of a foreign jurisdiction clause, is a matter which should be disclosed in the affidavit to lead an ex parte application for service out of the jurisdiction under Ord. 11, and that it weighs in the balance when deciding whether to grant such leave.

ally binding on the parties[15]. The situation is precisely the same if an arbitration is subsequently started by one or other of the parties. Until the Court decides to grant a stay, it is the action which is the medium for determining the dispute, since there cannot be two tribunals with co-existent powers to make binding decisions as to the rights of the parties. But the principle only applies to disputes as to the legal rights of the parties. It has no application to cases where the contract confers on the arbitrator the power to review the administrative or quasi-judicial decisions of others. Thus, where a building contract provides that the arbitrator shall have the power to open up, review and revise the certificates of the architect, the Court has no power to exercise this function so long as the machinery for obtaining a decision of the arbitrator is still available[16].

(b) Concurrent proceedings in Court and in arbitration

Second, the claimant begins an arbitration, and one or other of the parties subsequently institutes proceedings in Court. Until such time, if ever, as the Court decides to relinquish the dispute, any award made by the arbitrator is wholly ineffective, for otherwise there would be an unseemly race between the public and the private tribunals, in which the speediest would prevail[17]. It is not clear when the arbitration becomes ineffectual. The issue of a writ is not enough, nor is conduct on the part of a defendant which would forfeit his right to a stay, such as taking a step in the action[18]; and in the meantime the arbitration

---

[15] In *Scottish and Newcastle Breweries plc v Sir Richard Sutton's Settled Estates* (1985) 276 Estates Gazette 77 the jurisdiction was invoked by consent to settle certain preliminary questions of law on a construction summons, the remaining issues then being decided by the arbitrator. The same result could have been arrived at by an agreement withdrawing the preliminary issues from the scope of the reference. This unusual procedure appears to be a legitimate alternative to invoking the jurisdiction of the Court under s. 2 of the 1979 Act: see pp. 621–626, post.

[16] *Northern Regional Health Authority v Crouch Construction Co Ltd* [1984] QB 644, [1984] 2 WLR 676. See also *Oram (Builders) Ltd v Pemberton* (1984) 29 BLR 23; *Partington & Son (Builders) Ltd v Tameside Metropolitan Borough Council* (1985) 32 BLR 150; *Reed v Van der Vorm* (1985) 35 BLR 136. It is otherwise where the contractual machinery has broken down. Here the Court can substitute its own machinery, but upon a different principle from that under discussion: *Brodie v Cardiff Corpn* [1919] AC 337; *Cameron v Cuddy* [1914] AC 651; *Neale v Richardson* [1938] 1 All ER 753. It has yet to be decided whether the Court can substitute its own machinery where the contractual machinery is available, but has not been invoked, e.g. where the plaintiff has begun an action which the defendant has not applied to have stayed. The problem may not become apparent until substantial time and expense has been incurred in the action. Since the decision in the *Crouch* case it has become apparent that a solution lies in appointing an Official Referee as arbitrator (see pp. 272–273, post), but this threatens to place unacceptable strains on the administration of Official Referee's business. The answer would appear to lie in legislation to confer powers on the Court to exercise the administrative and quasi-judicial functions of arbitrators in such cases.

[17] *Doleman & Sons v Ossett Corpn* [1912] 3 KB 257 at 269. It is not, however, a contempt of court to maintain the arbitration, whilst the action is in being: ibid., at 262, per Vaughan-Williams LJ (who was dissenting but not on this particular point) – unless, perhaps the Court has already refused to grant a stay: ibid., at 273, per Farwell LJ. The principle has no application to proceedings in a foreign court: *World Pride Shipping Ltd v Daiichi Chuo Kisen Kaisha, The Golden Anne* [1984] 2 Lloyd's Rep 489.

[18] *Lloyd v Wright* [1983] QB 1065, [1983] 3 WLR 223. By the time the matter came before the Court of Appeal the Plaintiff had discontinued the action. It is not clear what would have happened otherwise because until the Court made some further order the Plaintiff could apparently pursue both the action and the arbitration. Presumably the Defendant could have applied for an injunction to restrain the Plaintiff from continuing with the arbitration (per Dunn LJ). It was too late for the Defendant to apply for a stay under the Court's statutory powers, but possibly he could have done so under the Court's inherent power. One way or another some means would have had to be found to put the Plaintiff to his election, or to make it for him if he declined to do so.

continues, although any resulting award will be nugatory unless the Court decides to relinquish the dispute. Nor is it clear what happens to the arbitration if it becomes ineffectual, or if it comes on while the Court remains seised of the dispute[19]. What is clear is that the mere commencement of proceedings does not bring the arbitration to an end, and until that happens the Court can make orders in the action which relate to the reference[20].

(c) Arbitration ineffective

The third instance, and the one which is most likely to be of practical importance in the future, exists where the contractual mode of resolving disputes has broken down, and where the Court must step in to fill the gap. The following situations may be envisaged –

1 The contractual mechanisms for establishing a tribunal have failed, and there are no statutory mechanisms for completing it, or none that operate effectively[1].

2 The Court has revoked the authority of the arbitrator (under section 1), or removed him for misconduct (section 23(1)) or delay (section 13(3)), and has made a consequential order under section 25(2)(b) that the arbitration agreement shall cease to have effect with respect to the dispute referred.

3 The arbitration agreement has been abandoned.[2]

4 The arbitration agreement has been frustrated[3].

5 (As alternatives to situations (3) or (4)) either – (a) the respondent has impeded the progress of the arbitration in a way which cannot be overcome by employing the default powers of the arbitrator or the Court, or (b) the arbitration has completely broken down in a way which cannot be repaired by the use of those powers.

6 The tribunal has been enjoined from proceeding with the reference, otherwise than on grounds for which the claimant is responsible, or in which he is implicated[4].

This list may require qualification in cases where the arbitration takes place under an agreement which is not a domestic arbitration agreement for the purposes of section 1 of the 1975 Act, because the Act requires the Court to grant a stay of any proceedings falling within the scope of such an agreement. No problem arises in relation to a domestic agreement, for here the stay is

---

[19] It is by no means clear how the arbitrator could make an award of costs or recover his fees. The solution may lie in applying the principles of restitution.

[20] Such as orders for discovery: *Lloyd v Wright*, supra; or to extend the time for commencing arbitration: *Tradax Internacional SA v Cerrahogullari TAS* [1981] 2 Lloyd's Rep 169.

[1] It was assumed by the Court of Appeal in *National Enterprises Ltd v Racal Communications Ltd* [1975] 1 Lloyd's Rep 225 at 228 that in such a situation the dispute would fall back on the Court. The position is less likely to arise in practice, now that s. 6(4) of the 1979 Act has filled the gap which that case revealed.

[2] This situation is discussed in Chapter 32, post. Logically the claimant should be free to bring an action in the High Court in spite of having abandoned his contractual right to make a claim by way of arbitration. In such a case, however, the Court would be able to prevent abuse by granting a stay, not under the defunct agreement to arbitrate but under the inherent jurisdiction of the court to stay abusive proceedings.

[3] See pp. 508–510, post.

[4] We add this qualification, because it is unlikely that the Court would allow the claimant to invoke the inherent jurisdiction if he had himself a responsibility for the circumstances which rendered the arbitration nugatory.

discretionary[5], and if the Court has reached the stage of deciding that its residual jurisdiction to entertain the merits of the dispute can properly be invoked, then it will inevitably refuse any application for a stay. The position is different where the agreement is of a non-domestic character, for in such a case the Court is compelled to grant a stay, unless the arbitration agreement is null, void, inoperative or incapable of being performed[6]. These words are likely to cover the great majority of the situations suggested in the list set out above, but they may perhaps not cover them all.

There remains the procedural mechanism for invoking the inherent jurisdiction. This has never been fully explained, but it would appear to involve the following steps –

1 turning the dispute into an action;
2 nullifying the agreement to arbitrate;
3 getting rid of any existing or future proceedings in the arbitration;
4 if the arbitration clause is in the *Scott v Avery* form[7], overcoming the difficulty created by the fact that the arbitration is a condition precedent to the right of action.

Stage 1 must presumably require the commencement of proceedings by the claimant by the issue and service of a writ[8]. The dispute cannot automatically become the subject of a pending action, simply because it is a by-product of a defunct English arbitration, even if the arbitration has become or has been declared defunct by a procedural application to the Court[9].

In many instances, stage 2 will not require any separate procedural step, since the residual jurisdiction will have become relevant precisely because the Court has done something which has brought the agreement to an end. The same can be said, in some cases, as regards stage 3. And in strict theory, neither stage is necessary for the effective exercise of the residual jurisdiction: for once the Court decides to avail itself of the jurisdiction, the promise to arbitrate and all subsequent proceedings become nugatory. Nevertheless, from a practical point of view it will often be prudent to obtain from the Court an order formalising the position, especially where it is contemplated that proceedings will be taken to enforce the judgment abroad: for otherwise the plaintiff may have difficulty in explaining to the enforcing court why he has started an action in a case which, on the face of it not only ought to have been, but in fact for a time was, the subject of an arbitration.

The problems of stage 4 are discussed at pp. 164–165, post.

(d) Award dishonoured

There would be much to be said in favour of allowing an action which has been stayed to be revived for the purpose of enforcing the award, if it is dishonoured. However, the general rule is that the original cause of action upon which the

---

[5] Under either s. 4(1) of the 1950 Act, or the inherent jurisdiction of the Court.
[6] See Chapter 30, post.
[7] See Chapter 13, post.
[8] Pursuant to leave granted under Ord. 11, r. 1, if the former respondent is out of the jurisdiction.
[9] Where the arbitration came into being as the result of a successful application to stay under the 1950 or the 1975 Acts, and if (as is usually the case) the order for a stay reserved liberty to apply, the dispute can be brought to the High Court by exercising the liberty, and reviving the action.

award is founded is superseded by a fresh cause of action on the award[10]. There are difficulties in converting the action on the original claim into an action on the award[11], and it would seem that fresh proceedings must be begun for the purpose of enforcing an award. There are however, exceptions to the general rule, the principal exception being Admiralty proceedings in rem[12]. Here the claimant has a choice; he can either bring an action on the award, or apply to have the stay lifted, relying on the award as giving rise to an issue estoppel[13].

---

[10] See pp. 409–413, post.
[11] The principal difficulty is that the proceedings would have been commenced before the cause of action on the award came into being.
[12] See pp. 410–411, post, where other possible exceptions are also considered.
[13] This may still be of value, even in cases to which s. 26 of the Civil Jurisdiction and Judgments Act 1982, applies: see pp. 339–341, post.

CHAPTER 13

Scott v Avery clauses

A. EFFECT OF SCOTT v AVERY CLAUSE

1 Postponement of access to Court

Some forms of arbitration clause do more than simply provide that disputes shall·be referred to arbitration. They also stipulate, in one form or another, that the award of an arbitrator is to be a condition precedent to the enforcement of any rights under the contract; so that a party has no cause of action in respect of a claim falling within the clause, unless and until a favourable award has been obtained[1].

Such a provision may take one of two forms[2] –

1 An express or implied[3] term of the contract that no action shall be brought until an arbitration has been conducted and an award made.

2 A provision that the only obligation of the defendant shall be to pay such sum as the arbitrator shall award[4].

The mere fact that the contract contains two covenants, one to perform an obligation, and the other to arbitrate, does not however entail that the obligation cannot be enforced by an action; for the two covenants are treated as independent. The court thus has jurisdiction to entertain the action, although in many cases it will enforce the separate covenant to arbitrate by granting a stay under section 4(1) of the 1950 Act or section 1 of the 1975 Act, and hence declining to exercise the jurisdiction[5].

Clauses of this type, which are commonly called 'Scott v Avery' clauses, after the name of a leading case[6] in which their efficacy was considered, have long been accepted as valid[7]. The practical effect of such a clause is that unless both parties consent to have the claim tried in the High Court, it must be referred to arbitration. It might well be thought that this amounts to an ouster of the jurisdiction, since in the absence of consent or waiver an action brought in defiance of the clause must inevitably fail. This is not, however, the position in

---

[1] Or unless the clause is anulled by the Court or the party has by his conduct forfeited the right to rely on it: see post, pp. 163–165.

[2] *Dawson v Fitzgerald* (1876) 1 Ex D 257 at 260.

[3] Such an implication is likely to be rare in the context of a commercial contract: see for example, *Hardwick Game Farm v Suffolk Agricultural and Poultry Producers' Association* [1964] 2 Lloyd's Rep 227 at 273 (at first instance).

[4] *Scott v Liverpool Corpn* (1858) 3 De G & J 334; *Braunstein v Accidental Death Insurance Co* (1861) 1 B & S 782; *Elliott v Royal Exchange Assurance Co* (1867) LR 2 Exch 237.

[5] See pp. 461–485, post.

[6] *Scott v Avery* (1856) 5 HL Cas 811.

[7] There would be little point in listing the numerous cases in which the efficacy of these clauses was considered. They include *Caledonian Insurance Co v Gilmour* [1893] AC 85; *Spurrier v La Cloche* [1902] AC 446; and *Heyman v Darwins Ltd* [1942] AC 356 at 377.

law. A *Scott v Avery* clause does not prevent the parties from bringing an action in the High Court. A writ issued in respect of a matter falling within the clause is not irregular, or a nullity; and if, for example, a defendant waives the right to insist on an award, the action proceeds in the normal way. The effect of the clause is not to invalidate the action, but to provide a defence; and since the effect of the condition precedent is to prevent any cause of action from arising until an award has been obtained, there is no ouster of the jurisdiction of the Court, since there is nothing to oust[8]. It has been said that such a clause 'postpones but does not annihilate the right of access to the Court'[9].

It is a question of construction in each case whether a particular claim falls within the ambit of a *Scott v Avery* clause[10]. For example, the clause may require disputes concerning claims under the contract to be arbitrated, leaving free for decision in the High Court the question whether the amount awarded should be reduced on the ground of some cross-claim[11]. Similarly, the ambit of the clause may be expressly limited, as frequently happens in contracts of insurance, where the provision requires the reference to arbitration of disputes as to quantum, whilst leaving open for decision in the High Court any questions concerning liability[12]. Again, *Scott v Avery* clauses are sometimes expressed so as to exclude from the ambit of the arbitration any issues in which allegations of fraud are involved[13].

Since *Scott v Avery* provisions are conditions precedent to the creation of liability, rather than exceptions to a liability which has accrued independently of the clause, they are not set aside by deviations, nor by repudiatory breaches of contract[14]. Equally, a repudiation of the contract does not vitiate a *Scott v Avery* clause[15].

A *Scott v Avery* clause in appropriate form is sufficient to bar, in the absence of an award, not only the right to sue for damages, but also a claim for ancillary

---

[8] Whether this reasoning will really bear examination may be questioned, but it is undoubtedly the law. A detailed critique can be found in Glanville Williams (1944) 60 LQR 69. A distinction is drawn in some of the earlier cases between agreements which make an award a condition precedent to an action, and those which provide that a cause of action, once existing, cannot be enforced in the courts. The former are valid; the latter not.

[9] *Freshwater v Western Australian Assurance Co Ltd* [1933] 1 KB 515, per Lord Hanworth MR at 523. As Maule J said in *Scott v Avery* (1853) 8 Exch 487 at 499 'There is no decision which prevents two persons from agreeing that a sum of money shall be payable on a contingency; but they cannot legally agree that when it is payable no action shall be maintained for it'. See also *Central Electricity Board v Halifax Corpn* [1963] AC 785 at 801, 806.

[10] See, for example, *Jager v Tolme and Runge and London Produce Clearing House Ltd* [1916] 1 KB 939.

[11] *Stokoe v Hall* (1864) 3 New Rep 566.

[12] See, for example, *Jureidini v National British and Irish Millers Insurance Co* [1915] AC 499. Also *Toronto Rly Co v National British and Irish Millers Insurance Co Ltd* (1914) 20 Com Cas 1, on the right of the claimant to obtain declaratory relief before the quantum is assessed.

[13] See *Stevens & Sons v Timber and General Mutual Accident Insurance Association Ltd* (1933) 45 Lloyd's Rep 43 at 44.

[14] So held for deviations in *Woolf v Collis Removal Service* [1948] 1 KB 11 (storage of goods in an inappropriate place). The same reasoning would seem to apply to repudiatory breaches of contract.

[15] See *Heyman v Darwins Ltd* [1942] AC 356 and the other cases cited at pp. 110–113 *ante*. *Heyman v Darwins* was not itself concerned with a *Scott v Avery* clause, but the reasoning is the same. The decision in *Jureidini v National*, ante, is explicable on the wording of the clause, or on the ground of waiver.

relief, such as an injunction[16]. Furthermore, where the contract itself expressly provides for remedies in the event of a breach then, if it contains a *Scott v Avery* clause, the obtaining of an award is a condition precedent to the exercise of the remedies[17].

A party who successfully pleads a *Scott v Avery* clause as a defence to an action cannot, when the matter has been remitted to arbitration and the claimant has succeeded in obtaining an award, afterwards object to the enforcement of the award on the ground that the arbitrator had no jurisdiction: for by enforcing the clause he has affirmed the jurisdiction of the arbitrator[18].

If a defendant succeeds in defeating an action, on the basis of a *Scott v Avery* clause, the plaintiff does not lose all his rights under the contract. He can still go to arbitration on the merits of the claim[19].

Where the contract contains a *Scott v Avery* clause, and the claimant obtains an award in his favour, his rights of suit thereafter are founded on the award and not on his original cause of action[20].

2 Loss of Scott v Avery rights

There are certainly two, and perhaps three, situations in which a party may be unable to rely on a *Scott v Avery* clause as a defence, even where there has been no award, or no reference at all, in respect of the matter in dispute.

(a) Annulment by Court

The first is where the Court exercises its statutory power to annul the clause. Here, a number of instances may be distinguished –

1 Where an arbitrator or umpire is removed under section 25(1) of the Act, and then by a consequential order under section 25(2) the arbitration agreement ceases to have effect, the Court may further order (under section 25(4)) that the *Scott v Avery* provision shall also cease to have effect.

2 Where the dispute involves a question of whether a party has been guilty of fraud, and the Court has ordered (under section 25(2)) that the arbitration agreement shall cease to have effect the Court may further order, under section 25(4), that the *Scott v Avery* clause shall cease to have effect[1].

3 Where the Court gives leave to revoke the authority of the arbitrator or

---

[16] There appears to be no decision in point, but the reasoning of the cases applies as much to final relief by way of injunction as to an award of damages. It is, however, possible that the position is different as regards provisional remedies such as an interlocutory injunction, since these do not require the Court to make any conclusive determination of the merits of the dispute.

[17] *Foster and Dicksee v Hastings Corpn* (1903) 87 LT 736; *Garrett v Salisbury and Dorset Junction Rly Co* (1866) LR 2 Eq 358; *Earl Harrowby v Leicester Corpn* (1915) 85 LJ Ch 150. It must in each case be a question of the construction of the clause.

[18] *South British Insurance Co v Gauci Bros & Co* [1928] AC 352.

[19] There is no issue estoppel, nor does the matter fall within the doctrine of *Conquer v Boot*, as to which see pp. 411–412, post. The survival of the right of claim was assumed in *South British v Gauci Bros & Co*, supra.

[20] *Woodall v Pearl Assurance Co Ltd* [1919] 1 KB 593, per Warrington LJ at 608. The statutory time limit for bringing proceedings on the original cause of action is unaffected by the *Scott v Avery* clause, but time begins to run afresh after publication of the award: see post, p. 418, post.

[1] It is submitted that the words 'under this section or any other enactment', in s. 25(4) can be stretched to cover an order made under a different section of the same Act. Any other reading produces absurd results.

removes him, under sections 13 or 23(1) there is no statutory power to revoke the *Scott v Avery* clause. Here, the requirement of arbitration as a condition precedent continues in being, and the reference goes ahead with a different tribunal.

4 Where the Court declares the arbitration agreement to be of no effect, before arbitrators have been appointed. It appears that in this situation there is no statutory power to nullify the *Scott v Avery* clause[2].

5 Where the Court declares, otherwise than by virtue of a statutory power, that the arbitration agreement is no longer binding. Here, there is no statutory jurisdiction to annul the *Scott v Avery* clause, since the declaration is not made (in the words of section 25(4)) 'under this section or any other enactment'.

(b) Conduct of defendant

The second situation where a *Scott v Avery* clause is not available as a defence exists where the conduct of the defendant disentitles him from relying on it. The reported cases disclose two distinct instances –

1 Where the defendant has waived reliance[3] on the clause, for example by defending the action without relying on the clause[4], or by himself instituting proceedings in breach of it.

2 Where the defendant has, by unduly influencing the arbitrator or hindering the progress of the reference, deprived the claimant of a proper opportunity to fulfil the condition precedent[5].

It seems to have been assumed in these cases that the failure of the originally contemplated mode of deciding the dispute left the matter free to fall on to the general residual jurisdiction of the Court. The possibility that the claimant should try again to fulfil the condition precedent, but this time with a more satisfactory tribunal, was not canvassed.

(c) Cesser of agreement to arbitrate

A third situation must also be considered, namely that which exists where the agreement to arbitrate has ceased to exist, otherwise than through the exercise of statutory powers. As we have already suggested, the Act does not empower the Court in such circumstances to annul the *Scott v Avery* clause. It is, however, possible that no such powers are needed. Where the provision makes an award a condition precedent to an action there is no great difficulty in holding that if the arbitration clause falls, then the condition precedent falls with it. This simple solution is not available where the condition precedent is introduced by making the obligee liable for 'such sum as the arbitrator shall award' – for if these words

---

[2] Because the power arises only where the High Court orders that the agreement shall cease to have effect: *Socony Mobil Oil Inc v West of England Ship Owners Mutual Insurance Association (London) Ltd (The Padre Island)* [1984] 2 Lloyd's Rep. 408. It seems that an order dismissing an application for a stay is not an order which invokes the jurisdiction to nullify a *Scott v Avery* clause: ibid., pp. 415–416.

[3] *Toronto Rly Co v National British and Irish Millers Insurance Co Ltd* (1914) 20 Com Cas 1.

[4] *Hardwick Game Farm v Suffolk Agricultural and Poultry Producers' Association* [1964] 2 Lloyd's Rep 227.

[5] *Hickman & Co v Roberts* [1913] AC 229; *Edwards v Aberayron Mutual Ship Insurance Society Ltd* (1876) 1 QBD 563; *Toronto Rly Co v National Insurance*, ante; *Woodall v Pearl Assurance Co Ltd* [1919] 1 KB 593, 607–608.

are treated as excised by the failure of the agreement to arbitrate, there is nothing left to create an obligation[6]. Perhaps the answer is to imply a term expressly conferring jurisdiction on the Court in the event of the arbitration agreement becoming, or being declared, ineffectual[7].

If this third method of avoiding a *Scott v Avery* provision does exist, then it may be envisaged as relevant in two situations. First, where the respondent's conduct is such as to be either a repudiatory breach of the arbitration agreement, or a renunciation of it. (This category might also be regarded as an instance of waiver, within the cases already cited.) Second, where, without any default on behalf of the respondent, the agreement to arbitrate is brought to an end by frustration[8].

A defendant does not lose his rights to rely on a *Scott v Avery* clause by contending that no contract ever came into existence – notwithstanding that this involves him in asserting that the clause never had any binding effect. If he fails to persuade the Court that there was never a contract, he can still rely on the failure of the condition precedent as another ground of defence[9]. Conversely, he can fight the case on the underlying merits and on the *Scott v Avery* clause at the same time, without being held to have waived the latter. But unless he can persuade the Court to try the merits and the *Scott v Avery* defence at the same time[10], he may be in peril on costs, since the *Scott v Avery* clause ought to be relied on at an earlier stage by way of application to stay[11].

B. PROCEDURE

A *Scott v Avery* clause performs two different functions. First, it creates an obligation to arbitrate: and as such, it gives the defendant to a High Court action the right to apply for a stay of the proceedings. Second, it creates a condition precedent to the plaintiff's right of action; and as such, it gives the defendant a substantive defence to the claim.

A defendant sued in breach of a *Scott v Avery* provision thus has a choice of remedies. In law, he is entitled to bide his time and rely on the *Scott v Avery* point at the trial. But the Court does not approve of this procedure, because it wastes the costs of the action. The right course is for him to apply for a stay. Upon the

---

[6] *Compania Panamena Europa Navagacion v Frederick v Leyland & Co* [1947] AC 428.
[7] Or to invoke the principle laid down by the cases referred to in n. 16 on p. 157, ante.
[8] See Chapter 35, post. Mere inactivity by the arbitrator would not be enough, unless prompted by the respondent, or unless serious enough to frustrate the contract. The claimant's remedy, in a less extreme case, is to remove the arbitrator under s. 13 of the Act, and start again with someone else. See *Neale v Richardson* [1938] 1 All ER 753.
[9] *Toller v Law Accident Insurance Society Ltd* (1936) 55 Ll L Rep 258. The situation is not the same as in respect to an ordinary arbitration clause where the applicant takes the point in an arbitration that the contract is void. There the defendant *simultaneously* asserts that there is no contract, and that the dispute should be arbitrated under the contract. But here, the points are taken in the alternative. The plaintiff is in obvious difficulties in such a case. If he arbitrates he will be met with the assertion that there is no contract and hence no jurisdiction to arbitrate; if he litigates, it will be said that he should have arbitrated. Unless the defendant is anxious to make the plaintiff waste costs, he will waive the *Scott v Avery* point in the action, or alternatively agree to an ad hoc submission on the existence of the contract.
[10] As in *Woodall v Pearl Assurance Co Ltd* [1919] 1 KB 593.
[11] See Chapter 30, p. 459, post.

hearing of the application, all questions of the applicability of the arbitration provisions can be dealt with, along with any issue as to whether the clause ought in the circumstances to be declared of no effect. If it is held that the clause does apply, then the action will be stayed and the matter can proceed to arbitration, no further costs being incurred in the action[12].

---

[12] *Golding v London and Edinburgh Insurance Co Ltd* (1932) 43 Ll L Rep 487; *Getreide-Import GmbH v Contimar SA Compania Industrial Commercial y-Maritima* [1953] 1 Lloyd's Rep 572, [1953] 1 WLR 793.

PART III

Beginning an arbitration

CHAPTER 14

Introduction

In Part II we have discussed the various types of agreement to arbitrate, and the species of claim which they embrace. We now turn to consider what steps a claimant should take, if he wishes to enforce by arbitration a claim which falls within the scope of a binding agreement to arbitrate.

It is common to use expressions such as 'a notice of arbitration' or 'the commencement of an arbitration' as if they had the same meaning for all purposes, in the context of all the various possible types of agreement to arbitrate. This is misleading, for when enquiring whether sufficient steps have been taken to set an arbitration in train, the answer may depend on the reason why the question is being asked. There are several different reasons why it may matter when the arbitration has begun. Of these, the following are probably the most important.

First, the question may be whether, at a given moment, there is any person or group of persons with jurisdiction to make an award, and power to give directions and make rulings in the course of the reference. For this purpose, what is being considered is whether the arbitration has reached the stage where there is a completely constituted arbitral tribunal.

Second, the problem may relate to the jurisdiction of the arbitrator. Thus, if there is a general reference of disputes the scope of the reference will be determined by the state of the disputes at the moment when the arbitration was begun. Disputes arising thereafter must be the subject of a separate arbitration, unless brought within the existing reference by consent.

Third, the purpose of the enquiry may be to ascertain whether the claimant has taken such steps as may be prescribed by statute or contract for the purpose of preventing his claim from being time barred.

Finally, it may be necessary to consider whether one party has taken sufficient steps towards setting the arbitration in motion to give him certain procedural advantages in the appointment of the tribunal: either as a preliminary to appointing his own nominee as sole arbitrator, or at least by way of preventing the other party from exercising his statutory right to make, or procure, a nomination in default.

It is plain that expressions such as 'the commencement of the arbitration' must have different meanings in these various contexts. For example, the giving of a notice to concur in the appointment of a sole arbitrator is sufficient to prevent time from running under the Limitation Act 1980; and it is also an essential first step towards the making of a default appointment under section 10(a) of the Arbitration Act. But the arbitration has not at this stage 'commenced' in any practical sense, since there is no person or group of persons charged with any authority to determine the matters in dispute.

Similarly, the use of expressions such as 'the appointment of an arbitrator'

169

without regard to the context may be a source of error. For example, it is often said that a conditional appointment of an arbitrator is invalid. This is no doubt correct, so far as concerns the third and fourth of the questions indicated above: i.e. the questions whether the appointment has been sufficient to stop time running under the Limitation Act, and to found an application for a default appointment. But it does not at all follow that a conditional appointment is completely nugatory, if the issue relates to the existence or extent of the arbitrator's authority. For a conditional appointment does confer some form of authority upon the arbitrator[1]; and indeed, once the condition is fulfilled the authority cannot be revoked without the leave of the Court. Again, it is stated that there can be no appointment of an arbitrator by one party without communication of the appointment to the other party. This is undoubtedly correct where the appointment is a step which has to be performed within a particular period of time, if the claim is not to be barred; and it is probably also correct when the issue is whether there has been a sufficient failure to appoint an arbitrator to justify the other party in operating the statutory mechanism for the making of a default appointment. But it does not at all follow that an appointment which has not yet been notified is of no legal effect. Such an appointment may be revocable at the will of the appointing party, and it may not confer on the arbitrator any immediate powers or duties. But it does create him, for the time being, the person chosen by the appointing party to act as arbitrator, and it is with reference to the terms of this appointment that any questions subsequently arising as to the scope of the arbitrator's jurisdiction will have to be solved.

In Chapter 15 we are concerned with the first and fourth of the questions listed above: namely, what steps must a party take to bring the arbitral tribunal into existence, and what can he do if his opponent fails to co-operate? The second question: namely, what disputes are referred to the arbitral tribunal when the arbitration was begun, has been discussed in Chapter 6. The third question: namely, what must a claimant do to prevent his claim from being time-barred, is discussed in Chapter 16.

---

[1] See n. 1, p. 182, post.

CHAPTER 15

Appointment of arbitrators and umpire

A. SUMMARY

There are several different types of arbitral tribunal, and many methods of bringing them into existence. We therefore begin by summarising the principal ways in which the following types of tribunal may be constituted –
1 a sole arbitrator;
2 a tribunal of two arbitrators[1], with an umpire in reserve;
3 a tribunal of three arbitrators;
4 a tribunal of more than three arbitrators[2]; and
5 an umpire.
We then proceed to deal with the various methods of appointment in more detail. Finally, we discuss the method of choosing an arbitrator.

1 A sole arbitrator

A dispute may be referred to a single arbitrator either because this is what the arbitration agreement expressly or impliedly provides, or because an intended reference to two arbitrators is impeded by the failure of one party to cooperate, or because there are features of the arbitration or of the tribunal which is conducting it which make it desirable to remit the case to the decision of a single person. The various methods of appointment are as follows:

(a) Appointment by agreement

The most usual basis for the appointment of a sole arbitrator is the agreement of the parties to the dispute. This will exist where –
1 the arbitrator is named in the arbitration agreement;
2 the agreement provides specifically for a reference to a sole arbitrator, and the parties agree (after a dispute has arisen) upon the choice of a person to act;
3 the agreement provides for a tribunal of more than one arbitrator but is varied by subsequent agreement;

---

[1] Statistics are not easy to come by, but the three-man tribunal is probably the most common to be appointed. It is probable that s. 6(2) of the 1979 Act has substantially reduced the number of two-man tribunals with an umpire, particularly in the field of maritime arbitration.

[2] It is unusual to have more than three arbitrators. The appellate tribunal of a two-tier arbitration system, such as is operated by a number of commodity Associations, is the only example encountered with any frequency in practice: see p. 190, post.

4 the agreement is silent as to the constitution of the tribunal, in which case it is construed as requiring a reference to a single arbitrator[3].

(b) Appointment by a third party

The agreement may provide for the arbitrator to be nominated by a third party or by the Court.

(c) Appointment by the Court in default of agreement

Where the arbitration agreement expressly or impliedly requires a reference to a sole arbitrator, but the parties cannot agree upon a choice, the Court has power to make the appointment[4].

(d) Appointment by the Court to fill a vacancy

If a sole arbitrator refuses to act, or is incapable of acting or dies, and the parties do not supply the vacancy, the Court may do so[5].

(e) Appointment in default of appointment of second arbitrator

Where the agreement provides for a reference to two arbitrators, one to be appointed by each party, and one party fails to make his appointment or to appoint a new arbitrator in place of one who has refused to act, or is incapable of acting, or has died, the other may appoint his own nominee as sole arbitrator. Such an appointment may be made either by virtue of the express terms of the arbitration agreement, or under powers conferred by the Act[6].

(f) Appointment by the Court upon revocation or removal

Where the authority of the tribunal is removed, or the tribunal is removed, the Court may appoint a sole arbitrator in its place – even if the tribunal as originally constituted had more than one member[7].

(g) Appointment of umpire as sole arbitrator

The High Court has power to order that an umpire shall enter on the reference as sole arbitrator, in place of the existing tribunal[8].

2 A tribunal of two arbitrators

It is a peculiarity of English arbitration procedure that an agreement to arbitrate is not always construed literally. This is so particularly where the agreement is for a reference to two or three arbitrators.

---

[3] S. 6 of the 1950 Act.
[4] S. 10 of the 1950 Act.
[5] S. 10(b) of the 1950 Act.
[6] S.7(b) of the 1950 Act.
[7] S. 25(2) of the 1950 Act.
[8] S. 8(3) of the 1950 Act.

If the parties agree for a tribunal of two arbitrators, such a tribunal is indeed the result; but unless the agreement otherwise provides (which in practice it rarely does) the two-man panel is reinforced by a secondary tribunal, consisting of an umpire appointed by the two arbitrators, who replaces the arbitrators if and when they disagree[9].

A reference to two arbitrators and an umpire never involves a tribunal consisting of three members. The dispute is decided either by the two arbitrators or by the umpire, depending upon whether or not the arbitrators have disagreed.

A two-man tribunal may be constituted, or re-constituted, as follows –

(a) Appointment by the parties

The most common method of appointing the two arbitrators is for one to be nominated by each party.

(b) Appointment by a third party

The agreement may validly provide for the nomination of the arbitrators by a third party; and for this purpose the High Court may act as the agreed nominating party.

(c) Appointment by a party to fill a vacancy

If an arbitrator refuses to act, or is incapable of acting, or dies, the party who appointed him may appoint a new arbitrator in his place[10].

(d) Appointment by the Court to fill a vacancy

If an arbitrator refuses to act, or is incapable of acting, or dies, and the party who appointed him does not make a fresh appointment to fill the vacancy, the High Court has power to make the necessary appointment. This is an alternative to the appointment of the surviving arbitrator as sole arbitrator (see above)[11].

(e) Appointment by the Court on removal of arbitrator

If the Court removes an arbitrator, it may appoint another to act in his place[12].

3 A tribunal of three arbitrators

An agreement for a reference to three arbitrators, however they are to be appointed, takes effect in accordance with its terms, and the award of any two of the arbitrators is binding[13]. Where the parties or the two arbitrators are at

---

[9] S. 8(1).
[10] S. 7(a) of the 1950 Act.
[11] S. 10(b) of the 1950 Act.
[12] S. 25(1) of the 1950 Act.
[13] S. 6(2) of the 1979 Act. Before the 1979 Act such an agreement took effect as an agreement for two arbitrators and an umpire, if the arbitrators were to be appointed by the parties and the third arbitrator by the two arbitrators so appointed.

liberty or required to appoint the third arbitrator and fail to do so, the Court has a power to appointment in default.

4 A tribunal of more than three arbitrators

In the comparatively rare cases where the tribunal exceeds three in number, the mode of appointment will almost invariably be prescribed by the contract. It is normally effected by the nomination of a third party – e.g. the Secretariat or governing body of a Trade Association selects the tribunal from a panel of persons willing and qualified to act as arbitrators.

5 An umpire

The modes of appointing an umpire are in many respects similar to those of appointing the arbitrators. He may be appointed by the arbitrators; by the parties; by a third party nominator; by the Court to fill a casual vacancy which the parties themselves have not filled; and by the Court as a replacement for an arbitrator who has been removed.

These various methods of appointment are discussed in more detail below.

B. DETAILED DISCUSSION

We now turn to deal with the various methods of appointment in more detail.

1 A sole arbitrator

An arbitration agreement calls for a reference to a single arbitrator, either if it contains an express stipulation to that effect, or if it is silent as to the mode of arbitration: for the 1950 Act lays down that unless a contrary intention is expressed, every arbitration agreement shall, if no other mode of reference is provided, be deemed to include a provision that the reference shall be to a single arbitrator[14].

As the 1950 Act itself makes plain, the parties may, if they wish, contract for a tribunal other than a sole arbitrator. Their intention need not be spelt out in detail in the arbitration agreement. It will be sufficient, for example, to incorporate by reference an arbitration provision from another document, or from another standard set of terms. There need not even be an explicit reference to any arbitration rules, provided the intention of the parties is made clear in the document. Thus an agreement to arbitrate in 'the usual way' will, if the usual method of arbitration is to have a tribunal of more than one arbitrator, be sufficient to exclude the statutory presumption[15]. But it must be possible to tell, either from the wording of the agreement itself, or from documents incorporated by reference into it, that the intention is to have more than one arbitrator. The wording of the statute leaves no room for an argument that if arbitrations in a particular trade are always submitted to (say) two arbitrators and an umpire,

---

[14] S. 6.

[15] *Naumann v Edward Nathan & Co Ltd* (1930) 37 Lloyd's Rep 249; *Laertis Shipping Corpn v Exportadora Espanola de Cementos Portland SA, The Laertis* [1982] 1 Lloyd's Rep 613, see p. 108, ante.

that mode of reference can (without more) be implied into any contract relating to that trade[16].

(a) Appointment by agreement

Where the arbitration clause is silent as to the method by which the sole arbitrator is to be selected, he must be appointed by agreement between the parties. There is no set formula for making such an appointment. All that is necessary is for the parties to reach agreement[17] on the choice of a person, and to obtain his consent to act[18]. Neither the agreement nor the appointment need be written, but if the arrangements are made orally it will be prudent to confirm them in writing. Otherwise, there may be misunderstandings, particularly as to the identity of the dispute submitted to the arbitrator. One convenient procedure, commonly employed, is for the claimant to submit to his opponent a name or list of names, as a suggestion for the choice of arbitrator. If the opponent agrees with the choice[19], one or both of them informally approaches the chosen person, to find out whether he is willing to act. If he is, they send him a joint written invitation to accept the reference, in response to which he sends a written acceptance. Whilst no particular formalities need be employed[20] the joint written invitation should be worded with care, since it will usually be one of the prime documents from which it can afterwards be ascertained what disputes have been submitted to the arbitrator, and hence what issues he has jurisdiction to decide[1].

The arbitrator should take the earliest opportunity of satisfying himself that his appointment accords with the provisions of the arbitration agreement. Otherwise, a waste of time and costs may may ensue if an objection is subsequently taken to his capacity to act[2]. Thus, if a person who is invited to act finds that the agreement provides for some tribunal other than a sole arbitrator; or that it calls for a method of appointment different from the one which has been adopted; or that it requires the arbitrator to have qualifications which he himself does not possess, then he should at once take the matter up with the persons who are seeking to appoint him. He should not accept the appointment,

---

[16] S. 6, which is a conflation of s. 2 of the 1889 Act with paragraph (b) of the First Schedule to that Act, reads rather curiously, for it contemplates two situations in which the presumption does not apply: (i) a contrary intention is expressed, (ii) no other mode of reference is provided. It might perhaps be argued that the contrast in the wording is intended to let in an implied exclusion of the Act, but 'provided' seems too strong for this. The view expressed in the text has the unsatisfactory corollary that a contract might by implication be subject to certain standard trading conditions, but with some of the arbitration provisions of such conditions left out. *Re Wilson & Son and Eastern Counties Navigation and Transport Co* [1892] 1 QB 81 and *Re Williams and Stepney* [1891] 2 QB 257 lay stress on the need for an express contrary provision; they do not really help on the meaning of s. 6.

[17] See also p. 191, post, for a discussion of the ways in which an agreed choice can be arrived at.

[18] Such a consent is essential. A person cannot validly be appointed without it. See post, p. 207.

[19] If they cannot agree, they will have to go to the Court, under s. 10: see p. 177, post.

[20] It has been stated that the original contract must be deposited with the arbitrator on his appointment. We suggest that this is not correct; although it is certainly good practice to give the arbitrator a copy of the contract when he is appointed.

[1] See pp. 203–204, post.

[2] As in *Rahcassi Shipping Co SA v Blue Star Line Ltd, The Bede* [1967] 2 Lloyd's Rep 261, [1969] 1 QB 173 where the arbitrators appointed an umpire who lacked the qualifications stipulated in the arbitration agreement. The result was a void award. See also post, p. 249.

or (if he has already accepted it) continue to act, unless he has received either a satisfactory explanation of any apparent discrepancies, or the explicit consent of the parties, or persons authorised to bind them, to the variation of the agreed arbitration procedure.

In order to enable the selected person to satisfy himself that he can properly agree to act as arbitrator, the written invitation should set out, or at least summarise, the terms of the arbitration agreement under which the appointment is being made; and if the parties have agreed in advance to alter the form of tribunal prescribed by the agreement in favour of appointing a sole arbitrator, this should be expressly stated in the letter of invitation.

The steps described above are those which are necessary, as a practical matter, to secure the appointment of a tribunal and hence get the arbitration under way. They are not the same as the steps which must be taken to 'commence' the arbitration so as to prevent the claim from being time-barred[3], or to initiate the procedure for the appointment of an arbitrator by the Court[4]. For these latter purposes, what is required is a notice to agree upon the appointment of an arbitrator. Such a notice need say no more than – 'I call upon you to concur in the appointment of an arbitrator', without naming any person who is suggested as a suitable subject for agreement[5]. Plainly, the performance of this formality will be of very little use in actually getting the arbitration under way.

(b) Appointment by third party

Arbitration agreements frequently provide that the arbitrator is to be nominated by a third party, such as the president of one of the various learned societies or a permanent arbitral institution. There is no doubt about the validity of such an agreement, but practical difficulties occasionally arise.

First, the person who is to make the appointment may refuse or neglect to do so. In this situation any party to the arbitration agreement may serve the person in question with a written notice to appoint an arbitrator, and if the appointment is not made within seven clear days[6] after service of the notice, the Court may, on the application of the party who served the notice, appoint an arbitrator with the same powers as if he had been appointed in accordance with the terms of the agreement. Before such a notice can be served, however, the person who is to make the appointment must either have refused to do so or have failed to do so within the time specified in the arbitration agreement or, if no time is specified, within a reasonable time[7].

Second, difficulties will arise if the third party nominates an arbitrator without first ascertaining that he is willing to act, and then discovers that he is

---

[3] S. 34(3) of the Limitation Act 1980. See p. 198, post.

[4] S. 10 of the 1950 Act. See p. 178, post.

[5] *Re Eyre and Leicester Corpn* [1892] 1 QB 136.

[6] I.e. seven days not counting the day on which the notice is served or the day of the application: see the notes to Ord. 3, r. 2 in the *Supreme Court Practice*.

[7] S. 10(2) of the 1950 Act, added by s. 6(4) of the 1979 Act. Previously the Court had no power to make such an appointment, with the consequence that the dispute fell back on the residual jurisdiction of the Court (see p. 154, ante): *National Enterprises Ltd v Racal Communications Ltd* [1975] 1 Lloyd's Rep 225, [1975] Ch 397.

not. In such a case, the Court has no power to fill the vacancy[8], and the right course is for the claimant to invite the nominating party to make a fresh nomination[9]. If this does not produce results, the claimant should start an action in the High Court, and use the deadlock as a ground for resisting a stay[10].

Finally, there are the difficulties which arise from the application of the Limitation Act 1980 to cases where the tribunal is to be nominated by a third party. The Act provides that an arbitration is to be commenced within the specified time limit, and lays down a series of formalities which amount to commencement for this purpose. None of these formalities can be applied to this particular method of appointment. The best view is probably that an arbitration is commenced, for the purposes of the Act, when the claimant calls on the defendant to submit the dispute to an arbitrator to be nominated[11].

It sometimes happens that the agreement describes a method of nomination which cannot be applied exactly to the circumstances of a particular case. In such a situation, the Court will adapt the literal wording of the clause so as to arrive at a procedure which will be effective[12].

Occasionally, an arbitration agreement will provide for a reference to a person nominated by the High Court. Such an agreement is valid, and, although there is no way of compelling the Court to make the nomination, in most instances the Court will be willing to assist[13]. This is, however, a form of agreement which should be avoided, since it necessarily involves the parties in the expense of an application to the Court.

(c) Appointment by the Court in default of agreement

Section 10 of the Act reads as follows –

> '10. In any of the following cases –
>> (a) where an arbitration agreement provides that the reference shall be to a single arbitrator, and all the parties do not, after differences have arisen, concur in the appointment of an arbitrator. . . .
>
> . . . .
>
> Any party may serve the other parties . . . with a written notice to . . . concur in appointing an arbitrator . . . and if the appointment is not made within seven clear days after the service of the notice, the High Court or a

---

[8] We submit that an arbitrator who has not yet agreed to act is not an 'appointed arbitrator' within s. 10(b) of the Act, and that his declining the appointment is not a refusal to act such as to bring into operation the Court's powers to appoint under that section.

[9] *Re Wilson & Son and Eastern Counties Navigation and Transport Co* [1892] 1 QB 81 (subsequently affirmed on another point).

[10] See pp. 464 and 473, post.

[11] On the basis that it is a notice requiring him to submit the dispute 'to a person designated in the agreement'. This is stretching the words of s. 34, but there must surely be some way of stopping time from running under the Statute.

[12] See *Finzel, Berry & Co v Eastcheap Dried Fruit Co* [1962] 2 Lloyd's Rep 11, where the contractual mechanism for appointment of an arbitrator provided for communication to be made through brokers. The Court of Appeal rejected this part of the contract as inapplicable, in a case where there was no broker. See also *Gola Sports Ltd v General Sportcraft Co Ltd* [1982] Com LR 51.

[13] As in *Medqv Lines SPA v Traelandsfos A/S* [1969] 2 Lloyd's Rep 225. The case was concerned with the appointment of second and third arbitrators, but the principle is the same.

judge thereof may, on application by the party who gave the notice, appoint an arbitrator ... who shall have the like powers to act in the reference and make an award as if he had been appointed by consent of all parties'.

This power of appointment, which yields to any contrary provision in the arbitration agreement[14], applies whenever the agreement either expressly stipulates for a reference to a single arbitrator, or makes no provision at all concerning the nature of the tribunal[15].

The power of appointment under the section does not come into existence until 'differences have arisen'. Thus, a claimant cannot proceed directly to a notice under section 10 the moment his claim has arisen. He must first bring a difference into existence: either by an explicit denial of the claim on the part of the defendant, or at least an evident failure to admit it[16].

The wording of the section indicates that the right to initiate the procedure under section 10 comes into existence as soon as a difference has arisen. The applicant need not show that he has first tried and failed to reach agreement with his opponent on the choice of arbitrator. He can proceed directly to the formal seven days' notice to concur in the appointment[17].

The first step in the initiation of the statutory procedure is the giving of a written notice to concur in appointing the arbitrator. This notice will also serve as the 'commencement' of the arbitration, so as to stop time running under the Limitation Act[18].

The notice under section 10 may be served by 'any party' on 'the other parties'. This venture into the plural is not easy to explain. Possibly it covers a truly multi-partite arbitration, where there are several parties to the agreement, each with different interests[19]. It is, however, more likely that the draftsman had in mind an arbitration in which there were only two 'sides', with one or both sides consisting of more than one person[20]. In such a case, if any one of the persons stands out against an agreed appointment, the statutory procedure can be brought into operation.

After the statutory notice to concur in an appointment has been served, the party must wait seven clear days before making his application to the Court. This period begins to run when the notice is actually served[1]. 'Seven clear days'

---

[14] So held by Donaldson J in *Medov Lines SPA v Traelandsfos*, supra, notwithstanding that s. 10 does not contain the words 'unless a contrary intention is expressed therein'. Contrast the mandatory effect given to s. 9(1) by Megaw J in *Marinos and Frangos Ltd v Dulien Steel Products Inc of Washington* [1961] 2 Lloyd's Rep 192. If a choice has to be made, we submit that the more rigorous approach of Megaw J is to be preferred.

[15] The word 'provides' in s. 10(a) includes a 'deemed' provision under s. 6: *Laertis Shipping Corpn v Exportadora Espanola de Cementos Portland SA, The Laertis* [1982] 1 Lloyd's Rep 613.

[16] See p. 127, ante.

[17] The words are 'do not ... concur in the appointment'. These denote simply an absence of concurrence, either because the parties have not tried to concur, or because they have tried and failed. See the comment on the rather different words of s. 7, at pp. 182–183, post.

[18] Presumably 'agree' in s. 34 of the Limitation Act 1980 has the same effect as 'concur' in s. 10 of the Arbitration Act.

[19] See p. 141, ante.

[20] For example, where one of the 'sides' consists of several joint contractors.

[1] The deeming provisions of s. 34(4)(b) and (c) of the Limitation Act 1980, do not apply to ss. 7 and 10 of the Arbitration Act, so that service for the purpose of stopping time from running, and service for the purpose of an appointment under the Act are not the same.

means seven days, not counting the day on which the notice is served or the day of the application[2].

The procedure laid down by section 10 is not really practical. A party can validly serve a notice which simply says – 'I call upon you to concur in the appointment of an arbitrator', without naming anybody in whose appointment the opposite party is asked to concur[3]. There is small prospect of a notice in this form producing agreement on an appointment within seven clear days; for the defendant's most likely response is – 'I will certainly concur, please suggest some names'. A favourable response of this sort would not be a concurrence 'in the appointment' of an arbitrator. No doubt, if the Court were faced with a situation such as this, it would consider whether the applicant had proceeded with undue haste to enforce his statutory rights; and in an appropriate case the Court might either exercise its discretion against making any appointment at all, or penalise the applicant in costs.

The power of the Court under section 10 is discretionary[4]. The Court is not obliged to make an appointment, even if the conditions laid down by section 10 have been fulfilled. The Court will, however, probably lean in favour of exercising its power[5], and an appointment would be withheld only if there were a very strong balance of convenience in having the matter dealt with in the High Court rather than by arbitration, or if the Court felt that the applicant had acted unreasonably in making the application.

It is a common practice for the party who makes the application under section 10 to suggest a list of possible appointees in his affidavit, having first satisfied himself that the persons named would be willing to act, if appointed.

(d) Appointment by the Court to fill a vacancy

It may occasionally happen that the office of sole arbitrator becomes vacant. The parties can, of course, fill the vacant position by the agreed appointment of a new sole arbitrator. But this will only be practicable if the parties agree that a vacancy exists, and if they agree on the identity of the person who is to assume the office.

If the parties cannot reach agreement on these lines, the Court has a limited power, under section 10(b) of the Act, to supply a casual vacancy. For the existence of this power, the following conditions must be fulfilled –

1 The arbitration agreement 'does not show that it was intended that the vacancy should not be supplied'. These words appear to exclude the power of the Court only in the very rare cases where it can be demonstrated[6], that the

---

[2] See notes to Ord. 3, r. 2 in the *Supreme Court Practice*.

[3] *Re Eyre and Leicester Corpn* [1892] 1 QB 136.

[4] *Re Bjornstad and Duse Shipping Co* [1924] 2 KB 673, explaining *Re Eyre and Leicester Corpn*, supra (applicant a foreigner resident abroad; condition imposed that applicant should give security for costs). See also the decision of Lyell J at first instance in *Tritonia Shipping Inc v South Nelson Forest Products Corpn* [1966] 1 Lloyd's Rep 114; *Miller, Gibb & Co v Smith and Tyler Ltd* [1916] 1 KB 419 at 420.

[5] It is submitted that the position is rather similar to that which exists upon an application to stay under s. 4(1). If the parties have contracted to submit their disputes to arbitration, the Court will in general tend to enforce the contract: thus, in *Davies, Middleton and Davies Ltd v Cardiff Corpn* (1964) 62 LGR 134, the parties had left a blank for the name of the arbitrator: held that the inclusion of an arbitration clause showed a clear intention to submit any differences to arbitration.

[6] The word 'show' may be wider than 'provides', elsewhere in the Act.

parties did not wish a casual vacancy to be filled at all – not merely that it should not be filled by the Court[7].

2 The case must be one in which the appointed[8] arbitrator 'refuses to act, or is incapable of acting or dies'. The problems to which these words give rise are discussed at pp. 533–534, post.

3 The parties have not themselves supplied the vacancy.

4 A notice to concur in the appointment of a replacement arbitrator has been served by one party on the other.

5 The party upon whom the notice has been served has failed to concur in the appointment of a new arbitrator.

6 The power to fill the vacancy is not specifically conferred by the arbitrator or some person or body other than the Court[9].

(e) Appointment in default of appointment of second arbitrator

In certain circumstances, an agreement to refer disputes to a tribunal of two arbitrators may result in a reference to a single arbitrator. This can happen where each of the parties is required by the agreement to nominate an arbitrator, and one party fails to make a nomination. If the appropriate conditions are fulfilled, the other party is entitled to have the dispute determined by his own appointee as sole arbitrator. This right may arise either by contract or by statute.

Not infrequently, the contract itself provides for what is to happen when one party fails to make the appropriate nomination. In such a case, it is the procedure prescribed by the agreement, not that set out in the Act, which must be complied with[10]; and the requirements of the contract must be strictly complied with if the appointment is to be valid[11]. When these formalities culminate in the appointment of a sole arbitrator, the appointment is not complete until it has been notified to the opposing party[12].

If the agreement contains no express provision regulating the procedure upon a default in the nomination of an arbitrator[13] the matter is regulated by section 7(b) of the Act, which reads as follows –

---

[7] This is what the Act says, although it may not be what was intended. The legislator may possibly have intended to exclude the case where the contract provides for the vacancy to be supplied by a third party; but the words are not apt.

[8] It is possible that an 'appointed' arbitrator may be one whom the parties have simply agreed to appoint and that a 'refusal' may arise from a mere refusal to accept the proffered office; the issue is not quite the same as the one which arises under s. 7 (see p. 186, post.). But we do not think that this is right.

[9] *Re Wilson & Son and Eastern Counties Navigation and Transport Co* [1892] 1 QB 81.

[10] 'Unless a contrary intention is expressed . . .': s. 7.

[11] *Vigers Bros Ltd v Montague L Meyer Ltd* (1938) 62 Ll L Rep 35 at 39.

[12] It does not matter by what channel the notification is conveyed to the other party: see per Lord Goddard CJ *in Kiril Mischeff Ltd v British Doughnut Co Ltd* [1954] 1 Lloyd's Rep 237. Singleton LJ, at 246, did not say that notice was unnecessary: merely that it did not have to be the appointing party who gave it.

[13] Such an agreement will not necessarily prescribe the appointment of a sole arbitrator; it may give a third party the right to nominate the second arbitrator, as in *Medov Lines SPA v Traelandsfos A/S* [1969] 2 Lloyd's Rep 225, where the third party was the Court itself.

'Where an arbitration agreement provides[14] that the reference shall be to two arbitrators, one to be appointed by each party, then, unless a contrary intention is expressed therein –

. . . .

(b) if, on such a reference, one party fails to appoint an arbitrator, either originally, or by way of substitution as aforesaid, for seven clear days after the other party, having appointed his arbitrator, has served the party making default with notice to make the appointment, the party who has appointed an arbitrator may appoint that arbitrator to act as sole arbitrator in the reference and his award shall be binding on both parties as if he had been appointed by consent:

Provided that the High Court or a judge thereof may set aside any appointment made in pursuance of this section'.

This section applies only where the arbitration agreement provides for a reference to two arbitrators, one to be appointed by each party. Such an agreement may take the following forms –

1 An explicit agreement that the tribunal shall consist solely of two arbitrators, and no one else. Such an agreement is very rare.

2 An agreement for a reference to two arbitrators, to which section 8(1) adds a requirement for the appointment of an umpire.

3 An agreement for a reference to three arbitrators, the third arbitrator being appointed by the two arbitrators named by the parties.

The section does not apply where the two arbitrators are to be appointed otherwise than by the parties, nor does it apply where the tribunal consists of three arbitrators, rather than two arbitrators and an umpire. A provision in the agreement that a majority decision of two out of the three arbitrators shall be binding does not bring the agreement within the section[15].

The procedure laid down by the Act operates in four stages –

1 The party who intends to avail himself of the section must first appoint his own arbitrator: i.e. he must entrust the office of arbitrator in respect of the dispute to a person who indicates his willingness to accept it[16].

2 The party proposing to avail himself of the section must serve on his opponent a notice calling upon him to appoint his arbitrator. There is no prescribed form for such a notice, but it should (we suggest) indicate to the opposite party that – (a) the sender has already appointed his own arbitrator, (b) if the recipient of the notice does not make an appointment within seven

---

[14] Whether expressly or by reference to a custom: *Laertis Shipping Corpn v Exportadora Espanola de Cementos Portland SA, The Laertis* [1982] 1 Lloyd's Rep 613.

[15] *Marinos and Frangos Ltd v Dulien Steel Products Inc of Washington,* ante. See also *Den of Airlie SS Co Ltd v Mitsui & Co Ltd and British Oil and Cake Mills Ltd* (1912) 17 Com Cas 116, which was decided at a time when there was no equivalent of s. 9(1), now amended by the 1979 Act.

[16] See *Tradax Export SA v Volkswagenwerk AG* [1970] 1 Lloyd's Rep 62, [1970] 1 QB 537. This was a time-bar case, but the requirement of willingness to act must apply to almost all cases where an 'appointment' is called for. Possibly the absence of a refusal to act would be enough, although plainly not in a time-bar case. It is, however, submitted that notification of the appointment is in theory (as it would be in other contexts) a part of the appointment itself; although in practice the notice under s. 7 will usually intimate the fact of the appointment.

clear days, the sender will appoint his own nominee as sole arbitrator. The notice must be actually served on the other party[17].

3 The party serving the notice must allow seven clear days[18] to elapse from the date of service. The party intending to employ section 7 should be careful not to abbreviate the prescribed interval of time.

4 The party who has served the notice must then appoint his own arbitrator to act as sole arbitrator. This appointment involves – (a) a firm indication to the arbitrator that he is henceforth to act as sole arbitrator, (b) an acknowledgment by the arbitrator that he is prepared so to act[19], (c) a notification to the other party that the person in question has been appointed to act as sole arbitrator.

Section 7 lays down strict requirements, which must be complied with, both as to the acts which are to be performed, and as to the order of their performance. Attempts to shorten the procedure by combining two or more stages merely results in an ineffectual appointment. Thus, for example, if the appointing party merely writes at stage two saying – 'If you do not appoint your arbitrator within seven clear days, my arbitrator Mr X will act as sole arbitrator', and then after seven days he simply proceeds to a hearing before X as sole arbitrator, any resulting award by X will be a nullity; for the third and fourth stages of the procedure will have been neglected. What is required by the section is a pause of seven days followed by a firm appointment[20]. A conditional appointment given in advance is not enough[1].

The Act does not make it clear when the power under section 7 first arises. The words 'the party making default'[2] might suggest that the party upon whom the notice has been served must in some way have been remiss in failing to make

---

[17] S. 7 of the Interpretation Act 1978 (which provides that proof that a letter has been properly addressed, prepaid and posted to the proper address of the person to be served and not returned to the Post Office affords prima facie evidence of due service in the ordinary course of post) does not apply, because s. 7 of the 1950 Act does not 'authorise or require' service by post. There must be evidence that the notice was received, not merely that it was sent. Substituted service would not appear to be an alternative: although the Court has apparently ordered a substituted service of a notice under s. 10 of the 1980 Act. (See note 65/4/1 in the *Supreme Court Practice* 1988.) It is not easy to see how this could have been done under Ord. 65, r. 4 which only applies to service under the Rules.

[18] See notes to Ord. 3, r. 2 in the *Supreme Court Practice.*

[19] This may be overcautious, but since appointment as arbitrator involves a consent to act, the same should logically be required for appointment as sole arbitrator, which involves an important change in function.

[20] *Rubin v W Smith & Co (Grimsby) Ltd* (1939) 64 Ll L Rep 7; *Drummond v Hamer* [1942] 1 KB 352; *Ministry of Food, Government of Bangladesh v Bengal Line Ltd* [1986] 2 Lloyd's Rep 167. If, however, the applicant correctly performs the four stages, there is no reason why he should not, at the time of his appointment of the sole arbitrator, indicate that he is still prepared to allow the other party to appoint a second arbitrator, for the appointment is not thereby made conditional: *Kyril Mischeff v British Doughnut Co,* ante.

[1] It is sometimes stated as a general proposition that a conditional appointment is a bad appointment. This is not, we submit, correct. There are good reasons why such an appointment will not suffice for the purposes of s. 7 and (probably) the Limitation Act. But there seems no reason why a conditional appointment should not be an effective way of investing the appointee with the office of arbitrator. If a party writes to his chosen arbitrator saying 'I am going to make one last attempt to settle the dispute, but if you do not hear from me by 1 January please act as my arbitrator', it would seem unduly technical to say that if the nominee agreed to act, and 1 January passed without further word, the nominee had no status to act as arbitrator. See the observations of Singleton LJ in *Kyril Mischeff v British Doughnut Co,* ante, at 254.

[2] The words cannot, as a matter of grammar, be read as a reference to a failure to appoint within the seven days.

the appointment – for example by being guilty of excessive delay. The better view, however, is that the power exists whenever a dispute has arisen, which falls within the arbitration agreement, and there is still one arbitrator remaining unappointed[3]. We suggest, however, that a party should not be too enthusiastic to avail himself of his rights under the section. It will be much better to wait and make sure, by at least one reminder, that the opposing party really is being obdurate in refusing or neglecting to appoint, before the second stage of the four-stage procedure is put in hand. Otherwise, if the Court feels that the appointing party has acted with unreasonable haste, it may set the appointment aside and make him pay the costs.

The power of the Court under section 7 applies not only to the failure by one party to appoint any arbitrator at all, but also to a failure to replace an arbitrator who has refused to act, or is incapable of acting, or dies. This means that where there is an agreement for two arbitrators, and there is a refusal, incapacity or death of one arbitrator, the party who appointed the other arbitrator has a choice of two procedures. He can apply to the Court under section 10 for the vacancy to be filled[4], the result being a renewed tribunal consisting of two arbitrators. Alternatively, without the assistance of the Court, he can appoint his own arbitrator to act as sole arbitrator. The second alternative is plainly cheaper and more advantageous for the appointing party, and it is the one which in practice is almost always employed[5].

The appointment of a sole arbitrator under section 7 is not necessarily final, since it may be set aside under the powers conferred by the proviso to the section. The exercise of this power does not entail that the person in question ceases to be an arbitrator at all; it is merely his appointment as *sole* arbitrator which is set aside. It follows that the powers which the Court would possess if he were removed from his office altogether, including in particular the power to appoint a substitute, do not arise when the Court exercises its discretion under the proviso[6].

The reported cases give little guidance as to the circumstances in which the discretion will be exercised, but the most likely occasions[7] will be those where there is manifest bias on the part of the person appointed as sole arbitrator, or excessive haste by the person making the appointment.

(f) Appointment by the Court upon revocation or removal

In addition to the powers described above, the Court has jurisdiction under section 25(2)(a) of the Act to appoint a sole arbitrator in two situations –

---

[3] We do not think that any weight can be given to the contrast in wording between s. 7(b) ('fails to') and s. 10(a) ('do not.')

[4] See p. 177, ante.

[5] The party will have no choice but to use s. 10 when the two arbitrators were appointed otherwise than by the parties themselves (notably, by a third-party nomination), for s. 7 does not apply to such a case.

[6] *Pace* Russell (19th edn) p. 529. The power is different in kind from those conferred by ss. 13(3) and 24. What is set aside is the appointment 'in pursuance of the section' – i.e. the appointment as sole arbitrator.

[7] See *Burkett, Sharp & Co v Eastcheap Dried Fruit Co and Perera*, ante. In that case, the power under the proviso did not need to be exercised, since the Court held that the appointment under s. 7 was invalid.

1 Where the authority of 'an arbitrator or arbitrators or an umpire' is revoked by the leave of the High Court. This revocation may occur under section 1 or section 24(1) of the Act: see p. 526, post.

2 Where 'a sole arbitrator or all the arbitrators or an umpire who has entered on the reference is removed by the High Court'. The removal may occur by virtue of sections 13(3) and 23(1); see pp. 529 et seq., post.

Although the section does not precisely say so, this power can plainly exist only where the Court decides to dispense with an entire tribunal (of however many composed) by means of revocation or removal.

The power conferred upon the Court by section 25(2)(a) gives it the opportunity of taking a middle course between simply replacing an arbitrator who has been removed, and cancelling the arbitration altogether. It is presumably intended to be used in the case where the Court considers that there is still some point in trying to have the matter decided by arbitration, but feels that it will be quicker and more satisfactory to proceed straight to the appointment of a sole arbitrator rather than force the parties to go again through the mechanism of setting up a multi-partite tribunal.

(g) Appointment of umpire as sole arbitrator

Where an umpire has been appointed, either by the arbitrators or by some other method, the Court has power, under section 8(3) of the Act, to order him to enter on the reference in lieu of the arbitrators and as if he were a sole arbitrator. This power is presumably intended to be exercised where the arbitration is proceeding badly, and the Court considers it desirable to get rid of the arbitrators and to speed matters up by proceeding with the umpire alone. The use of this procedure is very rare[8].

2 A tribunal of two arbitrators

(a) Appointment by the parties

Where the arbitration agreement provides for a reference to a tribunal of two arbitrators, one to be appointed[9] by each party, three steps must be taken before an arbitrator can be said to have been appointed[10] –

1 A communication by or on behalf of the appointor to the intended appointee authorising him to act in respect of the particular dispute.

2 An acceptance or agreement to act on the part of the intended appointee.

3 Notification of the appointment to the other party.

The appointment need not be made by the party himself. Very often it is

---

[8] It would appear that the objects of an application under s. 8(3) could equally well be achieved by a revocation under s. 1 followed by an appointment of the umpire as sole arbitrator under s. 25(2).

[9] Or named, or nominated: the precise wording of the agreement does not, we submit, make any difference.

[10] *Tradax Export SA v Volkswagenwerk AG* [1970] 1 Lloyd's Rep 62, [1970] 1 QB 537. This was a time-bar case, but the principle must be the same. The third requirement was not the subject of the dispute; but we submit that a person cannot have authority to act under a submission of this type unless the other party has notice that he has become a member of the tribunal: see *Thomas v Fredricks* (1847) 10 QB 775, and *Tew v Harris* (1847) 11 QB 7. In neither case did the contract actually use the word 'appoint'.

effected on his behalf by an agent, such as a solicitor or broker; and even where not expressly authorised the conduct of the party himself may amount to a ratification[11].

No particular form of words need be used for the communication to the appointee or the notification to the other side, but care should be taken in the wording of these documents, since their terms may have to be considered if there is any subsequent dispute as to the scope of the issues referred to the arbitrators.

When all these three requirements have been fulfilled, the person selected is invested with the office of arbitrator, and the appointing party has no power to change his mind and deprive him of his office[12]. The person appointed cannot, however, yet begin to exercise his powers as an arbitrator: for until his co-arbitrator is appointed, or he himself becomes sole arbitrator in default of such an appointment, the tribunal has not yet been constituted[13].

Whilst any of the three steps listed above remains to be performed, the appointment is incomplete, and the appointing party can withdraw from his choice of arbitrator[14].

Although the appointment of an arbitrator under this type of agreement is the act of each party alone, in which his opponent plays no part, the terms on which the two arbitrators are appointed are of importance to both parties: for if there is a discrepancy between the terms of the two appointments, real difficulties may arise as to the jurisdiction of the arbitrators[15]. This problem does not arise very often, since disputes are generally referred to arbitrators in such general terms that there is little scope for contradiction. It is, however, important that if one of the arbitrators is appointed with a specifically limited jurisdiction, he should consult with his co-arbitrator to make sure that their appointments are the same; and if it is found that they are not, then the arbitrators should not proceed with the reference until their jurisdiction has been clarified.

(b) Appointment by a third party

Agreements which stipulate for a third party to nominate both arbitrators are rarely encountered. Much more usual are the clauses which give the primary right of nomination to the parties, but which confer on a third party the power to make a nomination if one of the parties fails to do so. The nominating party may be either an independent third party or body, or the Court[16].

---

[11] As in *Loshak v Revillon Trading Co (London) Ltd* (1923) 14 Ll L Rep 425.

[12] S. 1 – except, of course, for one of the specific reasons stipulated in the Act. The point is discussed further at pp. 526 et seq., post.

[13] We know of no direct authority for this proposition, but it follows both from the undoubted general principle that in common law the tribunal must act unanimously, or (more simply) from the fact that the parties agreed to confer jurisdiction on a tribunal of two arbitrators: and half a tribunal is not a tribunal.

[14] 'Appointed' in s. 1 must, we submit, mean 'effectively appointed'.

[15] It is not clear whether the result of a difference between the appointments would be a tribunal with no proper existence at all, or a tribunal with jurisdiction limited to the disputes which both parties wished to have decided. Probably the latter. The party who wished for the wider issue might then seek a default appointment, under ss. 7 or 10, in respect of the remainder. The possibilities for confusion need no elaboration.

[16] See *Medov Lines SPA v Traelandsfos A/S* [1969] 2 Lloyd's Rep 225, where the Court nominated the second arbitrator as a default nomination, and the third arbitrator as a direct nomination: in each case under powers conferred by the agreement. Unless the parties cannot agree upon a suitable person to include in the agreement as the holder of the power to nominate, it is better not to confer the power on the Court, in view of the expense of making the application.

In general, the effect of a nomination by a third party or the Court is the same as if the arbitrator had been chosen by one of the parties but this is not necessarily so in every respect. As will appear from the discussion of the 'Arbitrator/Advocate' in Chapter 19, post, it is the practice in certain types of arbitration for the arbitrators, once they have disagreed and the umpire has entered upon the reference, to act as advocates in presenting the case to the umpire. When exercising this function, they have, as do other advocates, a certain limited authority to bind their principals. Thus, for example, they have the power to waive objections to acts of the umpire which might otherwise amount to misconduct; their knowledge of matters occurring during the reference is, in some degree, imputed to their principals. They may even, within limits, be able to enlarge the scope of the umpire's jurisdiction. Whatever the theoretical basis of this authority, it must in some way derive from the fact of the original appointment. This suggests that, as regards acts done by the arbitrator after the umpire has entered on the reference[17], there may be a difference between an arbitrator nominated by a party and an arbitrator nominated by someone else. In the former case, it is relatively easy to accept that the fact of the appointment constituted the arbitrator/advocate the agent of the party; much less so, in the latter case, where the party may have had no hand in the appointment at all. This particular problem has yet to be explored by the courts[18].

Where the nominating party fails or refuses to nominate an arbitrator, the court has a similar power of appointment as in the case of a sole arbitrator[19].

(c) Appointment by a party to fill a vacancy

Section 7(a) of the Act reads as follows –

'Where an arbitration agreement provides that the reference shall be to two arbitrators, one to be appointed by each party, then, unless a contrary intention is expressed therein –
(a) if either of the appointed arbitrators refuses to act, or is incapable of acting, or dies, the party who appointed him may appoint a new arbitrator in his place.

---

[17] As regards events occurring before the arbitrators disagree, it can make no difference how they were appointed. At this stage, they are acting in a judicial capacity, not as agents for the parties. At such a time, no question of ostensible authority (which is the important aspect of the status of an arbitrator/advocate) can arise: See *Rahcassi Shipping Co SA v Blue Star Line Ltd, The Bede* [1967] 2 Lloyd's Rep 261, [1969] 1 QB 173, in which the two arbitrators appointed an umpire who did not possess the qualifications required by the arbitration agreement. The appointment, and the subsequent award of the umpire, were held to be a nullity. The umpire was, in fact, appointed after the disagreement, but the arbitrators were at this stage plainly acting in a judicial capacity.

[18] The problem was touched upon, but not decided, in *Luanda Exportadora SARL v Wahbe Tamari & Sons etc Lda* [1967] 2 Lloyd's Rep 353 at 368. It is respectfully suggested that the passage there cited, from *Westminster Chemicals and Produce Ltd v Eichholz and Loeser* [1954] 1 Lloyd's Rep 99, was concerned with a rather different point. The matter might be relevant in relation to an application to have the arbitration brought to a halt on the ground of excessive delay; see pp. 503 et seq., post.

[19] See pp. 176–177, ante.

Provided that the High court or a judge thereof may set aside any appointment made in pursuance of this section'[20].

As its opening words make clear, the section applies only where the reference is to a tribunal of two arbitrators[1]. This includes, not only the case where the agreement expressly provides for such a tribunal, but also where the agreement has this effect by operation of law: i.e. where an agreement for a tribunal of three arbitrators is transformed by section 9(1) into an agreement for two arbitrators and an umpire: see p. 188, post. But the powers conferred by the section cannot be exercised where the agreement is for three arbitrators acting as such, or where the two arbitrators are to be appointed otherwise than by the parties themselves[2]. The meaning of the difficult words 'refuses to act, or is incapable of acting, or dies' is discussed elsewhere[3].

No formalities are prescribed for the making of an appointment under this section. In one form or another, the appointing party must –

1 communicate to the existing arbitrator (unless the power arises on his death) that he is no longer seized of the reference;

2 appoint a new arbitrator, by communicating to him the fact of his appointment and the circumstances of it, and receiving his agreement to act; and,

3 notifying the opposite party of the change in the tribunal.

By virtue of the proviso to the section, the High Court has power to set aside the appointment of an arbitrator to fill a vacancy.

(d) Appointment by the Court to fill a vacancy

If an appointed arbitrator 'refuses to act, or is incapable of acting or dies'[4] and the parties do not supply the vacancy[5], the Crown has power[6] under section 10(b) of the Act, upon the application of either party[7], to appoint another arbitrator in his stead. The procedure laid down by the statute involves the following steps –

---

[20] The section constitutes an erosion of the general principle that an arbitrator, once appointed, bears the independent mandate of both parties, having no special relationship with either. On the other hand, it makes good practical sense, for the vacancy must somehow be supplied. If it is supplied by contract, the tribunal will consist of one arbitrator nominated by the opposing party, one new arbitrator nominated by contract, and an umpire chosen by the arbitrators: a tribunal which is out of balance. The only alternative would be to have the vacancy supplied by the Court, in similar manner to the power conferred by s. 10(a) in the case of a sole arbitrator: but this would cause unnecessary expense and delay.

[1] *Marinos and Frangos v Dulien Steel Products* [1961] 2 Lloyd's Rep 192.

[2] See *Yeates v Caruth* [1895] 2 IR 146.

[3] See pp. 533–534, post.

[4] The meaning of these words is discussed at pp. 533–534, post.

[5] By agreement, or by the appointing party making further nomination under s. 7(a).

[6] If the arbitration agreement 'does not show that it was intended that the vacancy should not be supplied'. For a comment on this tortuous phrase, see p. 179, ante.

[7] The applicant will in practice always be the opponent of the party who originally made the appointment.

1 The applicant serves notice on his opponent to appoint an arbitrator, or to concur in the appointment of an arbitrator, whichever may be appropriate[8].

2 The applicant waits for seven clear days from the service of the notice : see p. 182, ante.

3 If the other party has failed to comply within the notice after seven clear days, application may be made to the Court.

The power of appointment vested in the Court by section 10(b) exists irrespective of whether the original arbitrator was appointed by one of the parties, or in some other way. In this respect, it differs from the power to fill a vacancy which the parties themselves possess under section 7(a).

(e) Appointment by the Court on removal of arbitrator

Where an arbitrator is removed by the High Court, the Court may on the application of any party to the arbitration agreement, appoint another arbitrator to act in his place[9].

The power does not exist where the Court intervenes, not by removing the arbitrator, but by revoking his authority. Here, the only powers available to the Court are to appoint a sole arbitrator[10], or to order that the arbitration agreement shall cease to have effect[11].

For a discussion of revocation and removal, see Chapter 32, post.

3 A tribunal of three arbitrators

Until the 1979 Act came into operation, a tribunal composed of three arbitrators was unusual in English procedure because of the stipulation in the 1950 Act that where the agreement provided for one arbitrator to be appointed by each party, and the third to be appointed by those two arbitrators, the reference was to a tribunal of two arbitrators and an umpire[12]. Now, in arbitrations to which the 1979 Act applies, such an agreement takes effect as a reference to three arbitrators, the award of any two being binding unless the agreement provides otherwise[13].

There are no special legal features attached to the nomination of the three arbitrators; but the panel must be completed by the appointment of the third arbitrator even if the two arbitrators agree, before any valid orders or awards can be made in the reference[14].

---

[8] The Act is not clear on this point. We submit that where the agreement requires each party to appoint an arbitrator, and the need for an application to the Court has arisen because one party will not use his power under s. 7(a) to fill the vacancy, the notice should call upon him to appoint a new arbitrator. In other cases, the appropriate form would appear to be a notice to concur in an appointment.

[9] S. 25(1).

[10] Which plainly will not be possible if the authority of only one out of several arbitrators is revoked.

[11] S. 25(2).

[12] S. 9(1) in its unamended form. See *British Metal Corpn Ltd v Ludlow Bros (1913) Ltd* [1938] 1 All ER 135.

[13] S. 6(2) of the 1979 Act.

[14] *Poliakoff v Brown Products Corpn Ltd* (1921) 8 Ll L Rep 501. The arbitration agreement may, however, authorise the two arbitrators to act on their own, as in *British Metal Corpn v Ludlow*, ante.

(a) Defaults in appointment

When considering the powers of the Court and the parties in relation to a default in the nomination of an arbitrator, under an agreement for a three-man tribunal, a distinction must be drawn between the third arbitrator, and the other two arbitrators.

As regards the first two arbitrators, if one party, having the power to appoint an arbitrator, refuses to do so, or does not do so within the time specified in the arbitration agreement or, if no time is specified, within a reasonable time, the other party may, having appointed his arbitrator, serve the party in default with a written notice to appoint an arbitrator and if the appointment is not made within seven clear days after the service of the notice, the Court has a power of appointment in default similar to that which exists in the case of a sole arbitrator[15]. If the power of appointment is vested in a third party, the Court has a similar power of appointment in default under section 10(2)[16].

As regards a default in the appointment of a third arbitrator, here again there is no power of appointment in an individual party. But the Court has power to appoint where the parties or the two arbitrators are at liberty or are required to appoint a third arbitrator and do not appoint him[17], or where the power of appointment is vested in a third party, who refuses or fails to make an appointment[16].

(b) Vacancies, revocation and removal

Where the third arbitrator 'refuses to act, or is incapable of acting, or dies' and the parties or the arbitrators do not supply the vacancy, a party may apply to the Court for an appointment under section 10(d). The various considerations applying to such an appointment are discussed at p. 180, ante.

The Court has also powers, where the authority of the third arbitrator is revoked[18] or where he is removed by the High Court[19], similar to those which exist in respect of the second arbitrator: see p. 188, ante.

4 A tribunal of more than three arbitrators

Tribunals of this type are almost always appointed by nomination in the manner prescribed by the contract. Disputes in relation to them are so rare that it is unnecessary to deal with them in detail.

The Court has no power to make an appointment in default of a nomination by the parties, but it has a power to make an appointment in default of nomination by a third party similar to that which exists in the case of a reference to a sole arbitrator[20]. Casual vacancies occurring after an appointment are usually filled by a further nomination, but the Court has power to appoint under

---

[15] Sub-s. 10(3) of the 1950 Act, inserted by the Administration of Justice Act 1985 to make good a gap in the Court's powers to which we drew attention in the first edition.
[16] See p. 176, ante. The Court has no such power, however, in arbitrations to which the 1979 Act does not apply.
[17] S. 10(c) of the 1950 Act, as amended by s. 6(3) of the 1979 Act.
[18] S. 25(2)(a).
[19] S. 25(1).
[20] See p. 176, ante.

section 10(b) if necessary[1]. The Court has powers of appointment on removal or revocation, similar to those described above in relation to the more usual types of tribunal[2].

5 An umpire

(a) Appointment by arbitrators

It is very unusual for an umpire to be appointed where the tribunal is composed of more than two arbitrators. It is also unusual for the umpire to be appointed otherwise than by the two arbitrators themselves. This is an appointment which they are obliged to make, even if the agreement makes no reference to an umpire[3]. The arbitrators may appoint the umpire at any time and must do so forthwith[4] if they cannot agree[5]. The arbitration agreement may require the arbitrators to appoint an umpire before disagreement; but failure to do so does not vitiate a joint award by them[6].

If the arbitration is of the informal type, conducted mainly or exclusively on documents, the arbitrators will often wish to see whether there is any possibility of an agreed award before making the appointment; for there is no practical value in spending time and trouble in appointing an umpire who is never going to enter on the reference[7].

There are, however, circumstances in which it will be better to have an umpire available from the outset. For example, if the dispute involves a substantial amount of oral evidence, it is very common for the umpire, as well as the arbitrators, to attend at the hearing, even though he has no powers or jurisdiction: for this avoids the necessity of a rehearing of the evidence in the event of the arbitrators being unable to agree. This procedure has the additional advantage of providing an unofficial chairman for the tribunal.

Lay arbitrators often find it helpful, when faced with a long hearing, in the course of which procedural problems will inevitably arise, to have a lawyer present as 'shadow' umpire, although in principle his role must be that of adviser only, since the power to make rulings remains with the arbitrators. The parties can, however, take the procedure a stage further by agreeing with the arbitrators that the umpire shall have the power to make all procedural rulings, or all such rulings of a particular type. This device has several advantages. It avoids the

---

[1] See p. 179, ante. The section includes the words 'the arbitration agreement does not show that it was intended that the vacancy should not be supplied': see p. 179, ante.

[2] See p. 188, ante.

[3] S. 8(1) is perhaps to be read distributively, so that the parties can contract out of the requirement to have an umpire at all, as well as the requirement for an immediate appointment. But in practice they never do.

[4] Which means 'as soon as reasonably possible'.

[5] S. 8(1) of the 1950 Act as amended by s. 6(1) of the 1979 Act. Presumably 'if they cannot agree "means" when a moment arrives when they have disagreed'.

[6] *Royal Commission on the Sugar Supply v Kwik-Hoo-Tong Trading Society* (1922) 11 Ll L Rep 163; *Termarea SRL v Rederi A/B Sally* [1979] 2 Lloyd's Rep 439.

[7] *The Myron v Tradax Export SA* [1969] 1 Lloyd's Rep 411 at 415. If the parties wished to have an umpire appointed before the arbitrators were willing to do so, they could either vary the arbitration agreement by giving themselves the power to appoint, and then making the appointment or by way of s. 10: *Taylor v Denny, Mott and Dickson Ltd* [1912] AC 666. It seems hardly likely that the arbitrators or the parties would wish to go ahead with the reference after such a bad start.

necessity of assembling the entire tribunal every time the parties need a ruling. It entrusts the day-to-day handling of the reference to the person who, by virtue of his experience, is best fitted to conduct it. Most important, it eliminates the possibility that the arbitrators, by disagreeing on some comparatively minor procedural issue, divest themselves of the reference; whereas the parties would prefer to have their expertise available for a decision on the substantive matters in dispute.

When the arbitrators decide to appoint an umpire, their first task is to agree upon a choice. The method of making the choice is discussed below. Once the choice has been made, the arbitrators proceed to make the appointment. No special formalities are required. In general, the procedure will be similar to the one employed for the appointment of a sole arbitrator[8] except that it is the arbitrators, rather than the parties, who make the appointment. Naturally, the arbitrators will keep the parties informed of what they are doing, and in cases of any delicacy it may be wise for an arbitrator to ask his 'appointor' for his views on the choice. But no individual party has a right to control the choice. It is however possible for the parties acting jointly to make the choice for themselves. The theory of such an appointment is that the parties first consent to vary the arbitration agreement by withdrawing the right of appointment from the arbitrators and conferring it on themselves; and then agree on the appointment. In practice the two stages are often combined.

(b) Powers of the Court

If the two arbitrators are at liberty to appoint, or have the duty to appoint, an umpire and do not appoint him, the Court has power to make an appointment under section 10(c). The Court also has power to apply a casual vacancy, under section 10(d). The procedures are the same as in respect of a third arbitrator[9].

In addition, the Court has powers upon revocation or removal similar to those which it has in respect of a third arbitrator[10], as well as powers in default of appointment by a third party similar to those which it has in respect of a sole arbitrator[11].

C. METHOD OF CHOOSING THE ARBITRATOR OR UMPIRE

The older texts deal in some detail with the method of choosing a person to act as arbitrator; and, in particular, with the question whether an arbitrator can properly be selected by chance. This topic is now of modest practical importance.

When the arbitrator is to be appointed by agreement between the parties, there is no ground of policy which prevents them from selecting his name at random. If they are prepared to take the risk, that is their own affair. So also where each side to the dispute is entitled to make his own appointment. Provided

---

[8] See pp. 175–176, ante.
[9] See p. 189, ante.
[10] See p. 189, ante.
[11] See pp. 176–177, ante.

the person nominated possesses the required qualifications, it is no concern of the other party or of the Court how his name was arrived at[12].

The position is not quite the same as regards an umpire who is to be appointed by the two arbitrators. Here, the agreement is so construed[13] as to require the arbitrators to apply their minds seriously to selecting by agreement a suitable person to act; the parties to the reference expect the concurring judgment of the two in the appointment of the third[14]. On the other hand, if the two arbitrators arrive at a list of persons all of whom they regard as suitable, but cannot reach agreement on which member of the list should be chosen, it is legitimate for them to make the choice by tossing a coin, or other random means: for here the arbitrators have together applied their minds to the choice of an appropriate appointee[15]. No doubt the same principle applies to the selection of an arbitrator or umpire by an independent nominating party. If he builds up a list of potential appointees by an act of conscious choice, he can properly make the selection from his list by some method involving the operation of chance[16].

The selection of an umpire or third arbitrator is of particular importance and delicacy in large international arbitrations, where there is a tendency for each party to appoint an arbitrator of his own nationality, thus encouraging the impression[17] that the third arbitrator will in practice decide the dispute by his vote. This tends to make the parties rather sensitive to the independence and capacity of the third arbitrator. One possible way to shorten this stage of the proceedings is to ask an independent body[18] for some names of people possessing recognised skill and experience in the field of international arbitration.

---

[12] *Re Shaw and Sims* (1851) 17 LTOS 160.

[13] Unless the parties by words or conduct agree to the contrary: *Re Tunno and Bird* (1833) 5 B & Ad 488; *Re Jamieson and Binns and Dean* (1836) 4 Ad & El 945; *Ford v Jones* (1832) 3 B & Ad 248.

[14] *Re Cassell* (1829) 9 B & C 624; *European and American SS Co Ltd v Crosskey* (1860) 8 CBNS 397; *Pescod v Pescod* (1887) 58 LT 76.

[15] *Morgan v Bolt* (1863) 1 New Rep 271; *Re Hopper* (1867) LR 2 QB 367.

[16] It is common to make the appointment by a rotating choice from a panel of potential appointees, which is a species of chance: see, as one of many examples, *Royal Commission on the Sugar Supply v Kwik-Hoo-Tong Trading Society* (1922) 11 Ll L Rep 163.

[17] Usually, it may be confidently stated, a mistaken impression.

[18] Such as the Secretariat of the International Chamber of Commerce. Obviously, if the arbitration is taking place under the auspices of a particular organisation, that organisation should be consulted in cases of difficulty.

CHAPTER 16

Lapse of time

A. INTRODUCTION

1 General

The party who permits time to elapse before seeking to enforce his rights by arbitration may be prejudiced in various ways. In the first place, the delay may form part of a course of conduct, the effect of which in law is to preclude the claimant from enforcing his rights; in this sense, delay may found a defence of estoppel or waiver. Again, the claimant's activity, or lack of it, in asserting his rights, may form part of the facts upon which the Court bases the exercise of its discretionary powers; so that if the claimant is guilty of delay, the Court may be induced to withhold from him a discretionary remedy of which he would otherwise have taken the benefit.

These various effects of delay are discussed elsewhere[1]. The present chapter is concerned with a different subject, namely those provisions of statutes and contracts which fix a specific time within which the claimant is to assert his rights, and which stipulate that failure to comply with this requirement is to deprive the claimant of his rights; i.e. we are here concerned with 'time-barring' provisions.

2 Lapse of time: jurisdiction and defence

A number of the problems raised by time-barring provisions arise in precisely the same way in an arbitration as they do in a High Court action. We shall not discuss these problems here, since they are dealt with in the standard works of reference. We shall concentrate on certain specific questions which arise in the context of arbitration. These sometimes prove to be surprisingly difficult, mainly because a plea of lapse of time in an arbitration may simultaneously raise two quite different issues.

First, there is the issue whether the time-bar constitutes a substantive defence to the claim: i.e. whether the effect of the lapse of time is that the respondent is entitled to an award in his favour.

Second, there is the issue of jurisdiction. The question here is not whether the arbitrator should dismiss the claim, but whether he should make any award on the claim at all.

Subject to one exception[2], time-barring clauses do not *directly* affect the jurisdiction of the arbitrator. In other words, he has power to adjudicate upon a claim even if it is barred by a lapse of time, although his adjudication will

---

[1] See p. 164, ante, and pp. 214 and 485, post.
[2] 'Remedy-barring' clauses: see p. 202, post.

necessarily be adverse to the claimant. But questions of jurisdiction may nevertheless become involved indirectly, particularly where the claimant seeks to expand or elaborate his claim after the stipulated time has elapsed, because an arbitrator cannot validly award upon *any* claim unless it has been referred to him, and the act which constitutes the reference is very often the same act as the one which has to be performed within the specified time if the claim is not to be time-barred. Thus, for example, if a claimant asks the arbitrator to consider and award upon a new claim which was not included in his original notice of arbitration, the arbitrator will have to ask himself two questions. First, whether he ought to pay any regard to the claim at all. For this purpose he will have to examine the documents which brought the arbitration into existence and constituted him the arbitrator in order to see whether the new claim falls within the scope of the original reference. If it does not, and if there has been no consent or waiver on the part of the respondent, the arbitrator must refuse to listen to the claim: for it is not a claim upon which he was ever appointed to act as arbitrator. Second, if he concludes that the claim is one which he has jurisdiction to decide, he must ask himself whether the existence of a time-bar makes it too late for the claimant to bring forward his new claim.

The relationship between these questions of jurisdiction and substance may be illustrated by the following examples, in each of which the contract is assumed to stipulate a twelve-month time limit for commencing arbitration.

1 After twelve months have passed, the claimant intimates a claim. The defendant says that the claim is already out of time, because no arbitration has been commenced. The dispute is referred to arbitration. Here, the arbitrator has jurisdiction to deal with the claim; but if he accepts the defendant's argument, he will make an award dismissing the claim.

2 The claimant intimates his claim to the defendant, and commences the arbitration within the twelve-month limit. Subsequently, and still within the prescribed time, he asks the arbitrator for leave to add another claim. In this situation, if the arbitrator decides that the claim is really new, and not merely a different way of putting the existing claim, he must refuse to entertain it, unless the respondent has given him jurisdiction to do so by waiver or consent. The arbitrator does not make an award dismissing the new claim. He simply declines to have anything to do with it[3].

3 The claimant gives notice of arbitration within the time limit in respect of a particular claim. Subsequently, after the twelve months have elapsed, the claimant asks for leave to add a new claim by way of amendment. Here, the arbitrator is faced with questions both of jurisdiction and of substance, and the fact that one question is answered in favour of a particular party does not necessarily mean that the other question will be answered in the same sense.

This inter-action of jurisdiction and substance is peculiar to the arbitral process. It does not arise in a High Court action, for the Court always has power to entertain a time-barred claim, or a new claim[4]. This difference between an action and an arbitration must constantly be kept in mind, and it is not safe to

---

[3] In order to avoid misunderstanding, the arbitrator might well intimate in his award that he has declined jurisdiction over the new claim. But this will not, strictly speaking, be an award in respect of the claim.

[4] Although its rules of procedure may prevent it from *exercising* its jurisdiction.

assume that High Court procedures relating to lapse of time can be applied without qualification to similar problems arising in arbitration.

There is one further respect in which proceedings in the High Court differ from those in an arbitration. The plaintiff in a High Court action is entitled to begin his proceedings completely out of the blue. He need not first intimate his claim to the defendant, or attempt to find out whether it is disputed. This is not so in an arbitration. In order to bring into existence a valid reference to arbitration, there must usually first be a dispute[5]: for unless there is a dispute, there is nothing in respect of which the arbitrator can be asked to adjudicate. This means that when the arbitrator is asking himself whether a particular claim has or has not been made the subject of arbitration within the limit of time fixed by statute or contract, he must begin by considering whether the claim had become the subject of a dispute within the time limit, for if there was no dispute it cannot have been the subject of a reference to arbitration.

We now turn to consider the various problems raised, in the context of arbitrations, by statutory and contractual time-barring provisions. Although there is substantial over-lapping, the two different types of time-bar raise rather different problems, and we will therefore consider them separately.

B. BARRING OF CLAIMS BY STATUTE

Where the respondent relies upon a statutory time limit as a defence to a claim in an arbitration, some or all of the following questions may arise –

1 Does the statute apply to claims in an arbitration?

2 When does the stipulated time begin to run under the statute?

3 In what circumstances is the stipulated time prolonged, so that failure to take the appropriate steps within the time limit does not bar the claim?

4 What steps must the claimant take within the prescribed time, to prevent his claim from being barred?

1 Statutory time limits in arbitration

Since the arbitrator is obliged to give effect to legal grounds of defence, he must dismiss any claim which has become time-barred by the expiry of a statutory period of limitation[6].

The most important statute which prescribes the time within which proceedings are to be brought is the Limitation Act 1980. This is specifically declared to apply to arbitrations as it does to actions in the High Court[7]. The period of time fixed by the statute for virtually every type of claim likely to be encountered in a commercial arbitration is six years.

There are, however, other statutes containing time limits, which may bear upon the subject matter of the dispute. Most of these impose limits shorter than six years.

---

[5] See pp. 122–129, ante.

[6] *Re Astley and Tyldesley Coal and Salt Co and Tyldesley Coal Co* (1889) 68 LJQB 252; *Board of Trade v Cayzer, Irvine & Co* [1927] AC 610 at 614.

[7] S. 34(1) of the Limitation Act 1980. Even before the legislation was altered so as to make it specifically applicable to arbitrations, it was applied to them by way of analogy: see the cases cited in *Chandris v Isbrandtsen-Moller Co Inc* (1950) 84 Ll L Rep 347, [1951] 1 KB 240.

Whether any of these statutes applies to a dispute which is referred to arbitration is a matter of construction of the statute in question. The Court is, however, likely to construe them as being so applicable, unless there are clear words to the contrary in the statute; for otherwise, the parties could by stipulating arbitration contract out of the statutory time limit[8]. Thus, the words 'unless suit is brought' in Article III, Rule 8 of the Hague Rules, are construed as meaning the pursuit of the appropriate remedy by the appropriate procedure, and hence as covering the commencement of an arbitration, where that is the contractual mode of determining disputes[9]. Where there is a conflict between a statute and a contractual time limit, it is a question of construction which prevails, but the most common result will be that the contract continues to be subject to arbitration, but with the statutory time limit substituted for the one which was stipulated in the contract[10].

2 The beginning of the limitation period

The moment at which the period limited for the enforcement of claims begins to run depends on the wording of the statute. In the case of the six-year period under the Limitation Act 1980, time begins to run when the cause of action sued upon is complete[11]. On the other hand, the twelve-month limitation period for cargo claims under the Carriage of Goods by Sea Act 1971 commences when the cargo has been delivered, or when it should have been delivered. Other statutes have different provisions. For the purpose of these various statutory provisions, there is no difference between arbitration and actions in the High Court.

There are, however, two points which should be mentioned. First, when an action is brought upon an award, the six-year period of limitation runs from the date when the implied promise to perform the award is broken and not from the moment when the claim arose, for the award itself gives rise to a new cause of action[12].

Second, where the contract contains a *Scott v Avery* clause, i.e. one which makes the obtaining of an award a condition precedent to the bringing of an action (see p. 161, ante), time does not run from the publication of the award, but from

---

[8] It is arguable that any statute which contains a time bar is an 'other limitation enactment', and hence is automatically applicable to arbitrations, by virtue of s. 34(1) of the Act of 1980. We suggest, however, that these words in s. 34(1) relate only to statutes exclusively, or at least mainly, concerned with limitation. The point was not taken in the Hague Rules cases, cited in note 9, post. Cf. the more general words 'any other enactment' in s. 39 of the Limitation Act 1980.

[9] The *Merak* [1964] 2 Lloyd's Rep 527, [1965] P 223, see especially per Davies LJ at 535; *Denny, Mott and Dickson v Lynn Shipping Co* [1963] 1 Lloyd's Rep 339; *Unicoopjapan and Mariheni Iida Co v Ion Shipping Co, The Ion* [1971] 1 Lloyd's Rep 541. These were all cases where the Rules were incorporated by contract, but the same principle must apply where they take effect by statute. See also *Coventry Sheppard & Co v Larrinaga SS Co Ltd* (1942) 73 Ll L Rep 256.

[10] See, for example, *The Ion*, supra. In that case there was a 'paramountcy' provision but the final result is likely to be the same in other instances, because it gives the maximum effect to the statute and to the intention of the parties.

[11] A cause of action has been defined as consisting of 'every fact which it would be necessary for the plaintiff to prove, if traversed, in order to support his right to the judgment of the Court': per Lord Esher in *Coburn v Colledge* [1897] 1 QB 702 at 706. See also *Chandris v Argo Insurance Co* [1963] 2 Lloyd's Rep 65; *Central Electricity Board v Halifax Corpn* [1963] AC 785.

[12] See post, p. 417.

the moment when it would have begun to run if no *Scott v Avery* clause had been present in the contract[13].

3 Prolongation of time

Various types of event may have the effect of enlarging the time prescribed by statute for the institution of proceedings, and hence of preserving a claim which would otherwise be time-barred.

First, there are the events which are declared by the statute itself to have this effect. One example is 'concealed fraud', within section 32 of the Limitation Act 1980. Special provisions of this kind raise no specific problems in relation to arbitration, and we do not deal with them here.

Second, the conduct of the defendant may be such as to preclude him, either by contract, waiver or estoppel, from alleging that the claim is time-barred. This principle is discussed at p. 208, post, in relation to contractual time limits.

Next, there is section 34(5) of the Limitation Act 1980, which deals with the case where an award is set aside or where, after the commencement of an arbitration, the Court orders that the aribtration shall cease to have effect[14]. The policy of the section is plain. If the award or the arbitration were set aside, the claimant might find that by the time the Court had dealt with the matter and had in effect caused the existing arbitration proceedings to disappear, it would be too late for him to start fresh proceedings without becoming time-barred[15]. Accordingly, the statute provides that the running of time is interrupted between the moment when the claimant commenced the original arbitration, and the moment when the Court makes the order setting the award or the arbitration aside. In effect, the claimant is left with such time for starting a fresh arbitration as remained to him when he gave his original notice to arbitrate. This provision does not apply to contractual time limits[16]; there may well also be statutory time limits to which it does not apply[17]. The section does not operate automatically, but merely gives the Court a discretion; so a claimant should remember to ask for an order prolonging the time, when a question of setting aside the award or the arbitration is before the Court.

Finally, it may be noted that the power under section 27 of the Arbitration Act to extend a time limit in cases of 'undue hardship' applies only where the

---

[13] S. 34(2) of the Limitation Act 1980. There is no contradiction between this rule and the one stated in the preceding paragraph. The one stipulates that if a claimant wishes to arbitrate under a contract containing a *Scott v Avery* clause, he must do so within a time measured in the normal way. The other states that if, having arbitrated successfully, he wishes to enforce the award, time begins to run against him afresh, after the award is published. The law on *Scott v Avery* clauses was different before the enactment of s. 34(2): *Board of Trade v Cayzer, Irvine & Co* [1927] AC 610.

[14] Pursuant to its powers under ss. 24(1) or 25 of the Arbitration Act 1950. The wording of s. 34(5) is curious. If the powers under the Arbitration Act are exercised, it is the agreement to arbitrate, not the arbitration itself, which ceases to have effect.

[15] The danger is not really very great, because even if the award or the agreement is set aside, the notice of arbitration will still survive, and it is this which prevents the claim from being barred.

[16] Although the claimant under a contractual time limit could no doubt obtain an extension for 'undue hardship', under s. 27, in analogous circumstances: see p. 210, post.

[17] The sub-section applies only to limits under the Act of 1980 or 'any other limitation enactment': see note 8, ante.

limit is imposed by contract, and does not give the Court a discretion to extend a limit fixed by statute[18].

4 The commencement of arbitration

In order to prevent a claim from being barred by lapse of time, a claimant must serve upon the defendant a notice complying with the following requirements[19] –

1 The notice must call upon the defendant to perform one of certain specified acts.

2 The notice must contain the proper particulars of the dispute in respect of which the arbitration is being commenced.

3 The notice must be served in the proper manner.

(a) Notice of arbitration : form

In order to stop time running under the statute[20], the claimant must serve on his opponent a notice in writing[1] complying with section 34(3) of the Limitation Act. Depending on the terms of the arbitration clause, the notice will call upon the defendant to do one of the following acts –

1 To appoint an arbitrator. This is the correct form where the arbitration agreement provides for a reference to two arbitrators, one to be appointed by each party.

2 To agree on the appointment of an arbitrator. This form is appropriate where the agreement provides for reference to a single arbitrator, or does not specify how many arbitrators are to conduct the reference[2].

3 To submit the dispute to any person named or designated in the agreement. This formula plainly applies only where somebody is named or designated[3].

It is desirable that the claimant should use the formula appropriate to the arbitration agreement in question. But failure to do so is not necessarily fatal. The Court does not adopt an unduly strict or technical approach to the requirements of a valid notice. It is sufficient if the notice contains a request for

---

[18] The wording of s. 27 seems clear. The section does, however, apply where a time limit contained in a statute is applied by contract: see p. 202, post.

[19] Requirements (1) and (3) are taken from s. 34(3) and (4) of the Act of 1980. These are also expressed to apply 'for the purposes of any other limitation enactment', and may not therefore apply directly to limitation provisions in non-limitation statutes: see note 8, ante, p. 196. But in any event, the Court is likely to apply them by analogy, whenever the words of the relevant statute permit: cf. *The Merak* [1964] 2 Lloyd's Rep 527, [1965] P 223.

[20] It is important to note than what is here written applies only to statutory time limits, since it is based on s. 34 of the Limitation Act 1980. What is required to stop time from running under a *contractual* time clause depends upon the wording of the clause, and may be quite different: see pp. 205–206, post.

[1] *Nea Agrex SA v Baltic Shipping Co Ltd* [1976] 2 Lloyd's Rep 47, [1976] QB 933.

[2] See s. 6, which stipulates that unless a contrary intention is expressed an arbitration agreement shall, if no other mode of reference is provided, be deemed to include a provision that the reference shall be to a single arbitrator.

[3] The word 'designated' is apt to cover 'the President for the time being of the Royal Institute of British Architects', but not if read literally 'a person to be appointed by the President for the time being of the R.I.B.A.'. The Court would no doubt stretch the sub-section to find a way of covering this formula.

the dispute to be referred to arbitration and calls on the respondent to take the appropriate steps even if it leaves open the possibility of an amicable settlement[4].

It is important to bear in mind that each of the forms of notice contemplated by section 34(3) is concerned with an appointment of an arbitrator by the defendant. A notice by the claimant that he himself has appointed an arbitrator is not a sufficient compliance with the statute,·and still less is a mere notice of claim. The latter might, depending on the terms of the contract, be sufficient to prevent the claim from becoming barred by a contractual limitation clause, but it would not be relevant to a statutory time limit.

(b) Notice of arbitration: particularity

It is plain that a notice under section 34(3) of the Limitation Act must contain at least some information about the dispute in respect of which the arbitrator is to be appointed[5]. A notice simply saying 'Please nominate your arbitrator', without stipulating the dispute in respect of which he is to act would clearly make no sense[6]. Precisely how much detail the notice should give is difficult to say. However, we submit that the position is as follows –

(i) A notice in the form 'Appoint your arbitrator in respect of all disputes existing between us in connection with [or whatever may be the words of the arbitration clause] the contract dated . . .' is valid, and satisfies the limitation statute in respect of all disputes existing at the time when the notice was given[7].

(ii) A notice specifically identifying a dispute takes effect only in respect of the claim which generates that dispute. Time continues to run in respect of all other claims.

(iii) A notice by the respondent appointing a second arbitrator or concurring in the appointment of a sole arbitrator will not stop time running against a counterclaim unless it is made clear to the claimant that the appointment is intended to apply to the counterclaim as well as to the claim[8].

(c) Notice of arbitration: service

The Limitation Act lays down four methods by which the notice to appoint an

---

[4] *Nea Agrex SA v Baltic Shipping Co Ltd* [1976] 2 Lloyd's Rep 47, [1976] QB 933 ('please advise your proposals in order to settle this matter, or name your arbitrators' held sufficient, although the agreement provided for a sole arbitrator). This case probably represents the limit of the Court's indulgence: see *Surrendra Overseas Ltd v Government of Sri Lanka* [1977] 1 Lloyd's Rep 653. Both cases leave open the question whether 'I require this dispute to be referred to arbitration' is sufficient.

[5] The nature of the dispute must be communicated to the other party, not just to the arbitrator: *Interbulk Ltd v Ponte dei Sospiri Shipping Co, The Standard Ardour* [1988] 2 Lloyd's Rep 159.

[6] It is not easy, as a pure matter of construction, to read 'the dispute' at the end of s. 34(3) into the earlier words of the sub-section. But the proposition in the text must, it is submitted, be right as a matter of common sense.

[7] The statement in the text contemplates that a notice under s. 34(3) may be much less specific than a notice of claim under a contractual limitation clause: see p. 205, post. We submit that this is consistent with the different policies of the different types of limitation provisions. The purpose of fixing a time for notice of claim is to give the defendant an early warning that a dispute is likely: the purpose of fixing a time for bringing proceedings is to ensure the early (or at any rate, not unduly late) determination of a dispute which has already arisen, and of which the defendant may be assumed already to have sufficient knowledge.

[8] *The Standard Ardour*, ante.

arbitrator may be served[9], but this does not exclude resort to other methods[10]. Service may be effected either –

1 by delivering the notice to the person on whom it is to be served[11]; or

2 by leaving it at the usual or last known place of abode[12] in England of that person; or

3 by sending it by post in a registered letter[13] addressed to the person at his usual or last known place of abode in England; or

4 by serving it in the manner, if any, stipulated by the arbitration agreement[14].

It will be noted that methods 2 and 3 can only be used in England, so that unless the agreement specifically provides otherwise, notices under section 34 addressed to persons resident abroad must be personally served.

Alternatively, service may be effected by letter, cable or telex: such service will take effect when the letter or cable arrives, or when the telex is transcribed, whether or not it is actually read[15].

As previously mentioned, the form and content of the notice under section 34 are not necessarily the same as those of a notice under a contractual time limit. The same applies to the method of service. What usually matters, in relation to a notice under a contractual time limit, is the moment at which the notice is received; unless the contract so provides, there is no scope for 'deemed' service, such as is contemplated in methods 2 and 3, ante.

C. LIMITATION OF TIME BY CONTRACT

1 General

It is common to find in mercantile contracts an express provision to the effect that certain formalities must be performed within a specified time, and that in default of due performance either the claim or the right to assert the claim in arbitration will be barred. A typical example of such a clause, which has

---

[9] S. 34(4).

[10] *NV Stoomv Maats De Maas v Nippon Yusen Kaisha, The Pendrecht* [1980] 2 Lloyd's Rep 56 at 64: and see *Nea Agrex SA v Baltic Shipping Co Ltd*, ante, at 55 and 58 where Goff LJ and Shaw LJ differed on this point. The powers of the High Court to order substituted service apply only to service under the RSC Ord. 65, r. 4.

[11] Notwithstanding the wording of the section, it is submitted that service on an agent of the defendant will be sufficient, provided he receives the notice within the scope of his actual or apparent authority: *Minerals and Metals Trading Corpn of India Ltd v Encounter Bay Shipping Co Ltd, The Samos Glory* [1986] 2 Lloyd's Rep 603. But this provision has no application to companies: *The Pendrecht*, supra.

[12] Presumably, in the case of an English corporation, this must be read as meaning its registered office. In the case of a foreign corporation, the reference must be to the corporation's place of business, whether or not registered under the Companies Act or to the person registered under s. 695 of the Companies Act 1985, if any.

[13] Or recorded delivery letter: Recorded Delivery Service Act 1962, s. 1(1). Unless the contrary is proved service is deemed to have been effected at the time at which the letter would be delivered in the ordinary course of post: Interpretation Act 1978, s. 7.

[14] It is not uncommon for arbitration agreements to provide for methods of serving notices of claim, etc.: many standard forms of commodity contracts contain such provisions. But reference to the method of serving notices under s. 34 is much less common.

[15] *The Pendrecht* and *The Samos Glory*, ante.

featured in several reported cases, is the 'Centrocon' arbitration clause, which reads as follows –

'. . . Any claim must be made in writing and claimants' arbitrator appointed within three months[16] of final discharge, and where this provision is not complied with the claim shall be deemed to be waived and absolutely barred . . .'[17].

Clauses of this type are variously expressed, both as to the nature of the formality to be performed, and as to the consequence of a failure to perform it. The effect of such a clause is ultimately a matter of construction[18]. There are, however, certain general principles which apply to all provisions of this type.

First, a contractual time-bar is accepted by the Court as intrinsically valid. It was at one time believed that clauses of this type, when coupled with arbitration provisions, involved an ouster of the jurisdiction of the Court. This view was repudiated by the House of Lords[19], and the courts have during the past five decades repeatedly recognised and enforced such clauses. Indeed, the courts now appear to regard a contractual time limit as a positively beneficial feature of a commercial contract. The objects of such a clause are, it has been stated – (i) to provide some limit to the uncertainties and expense of arbitration and litigation; (ii) to facilitate the obtaining of material evidence; and (iii) to facilitate the settling of accounts for each transaction as and when they fall due[20].

Second, there is no trace in the authorities of any notion that a short time limit offends against public policy. The three-month time limit fixed by the Centrocon clause has repeatedly been upheld[1]. Moreover, much shorter periods than this have been enforced without comment[2].

Third, clauses of this type must be construed strictly, and a claim will not be

---

[16] Now usually varied to nine months.

[17] As Mocatta J observed in *Agro Company of Canada Ltd v Richmond Shipping Ltd, The Simonburn* [1972] 2 Lloyd's Rep 355, this clause is 'extending its kingdom'. It is now widely used in contracts such as time charters, consecutive voyage charters, and bills of lading, for which it was not designed.

[18] Under the 'Centrocon' clause two acts must be performed within the time-limit: the making of a written claim and the appointment of the arbitrator. Omission of either act bars the claim: *Williams and Mordey v WH Muller & Co (London) Ltd* (1924) 18 Ll L Rep 50 at 52.

[19] *Atlantic Shipping and Trading Co Ltd v Louis Dreyfus & Co* (1922) 10 Ll L Rep 446, 707, [1922] 2 AC 250.

[20] Per Lord Denning MR in *Agro Company of Canada v Richmond Shipping Ltd, The Simonburn* [1973] 1 Lloyd's Rep 392 at 394, citing *The Himmerland* [1965] 2 Lloyd's Rep 353.

[1] *Atlantic Shipping v Dreyfus*, ante; *H Ford & Co v Compagnie Furness (France)* (1922) 12 Ll L Rep 281; *Williams and Mordey v WH Muller & Co (London) Ltd* (1924) 18 Ll L Rep 50; *Bede Steam Shipping Co Ltd v Bunge y Born Ltda SA* (1927) 27 Ll L Rep 410; *Luis de Ridder Ltda v Nivose Societa Di Navigazione* (1935) 53 Ll L Rep 21; *Bulgaris v La Plata Cereal Co SA* (1947) 80 Ll L Rep 455; *Jajasan Urusan Bahan Makanan v Compania de Navegacion Geamar Sociedade de Responsabilidad Ltda* [1953] 1 Lloyd's Rep 499 and 511; *G Sigalas & Sons v Man Mohan Singh & Co* [1958] 2 Lloyd's Rep 298; *SS Co of 1912 and SS Co Svendborg v Anglo-American Grain Co, The Leise Maersk* [1958] 2 Lloyd's Rep 341; *The Himmerland*, supra.; *Liberian Shipping Corpn v A King & Sons Ltd* [1967] 1 Lloyd's Rep 302; *Agro Company of Canada v Richmond Shipping*, supra.

[2] *Ayscough v Sheed, Thomson & Co Ltd* (1924) 19 Ll L Rep 104 (three days); *Mantoura & Sons v David* (1926) 32 Com Cas 1 (eight days); *Coventry Sheppard & Co v Larrinaga SS Co Ltd* (1942) 73 Ll L Rep 256 (ten days); *Smeaton Hanscomb v Sassoon I Setty Son & Co* [1953] 2 Lloyd's Rep 580, [1953] 1 WLR 1468 (fourteen days); *Alan v El Nasr Export and Import Co* [1971] 1 Lloyd's Rep 401 (seven, fourteen and thirty days); *A/B Legis v V Berg & Sons Ltd* [1964] 1 Lloyd's Rep 203 (fourteen days); *FE Hookway & Co Ltd v HW Hooper & Co* (1950) 84 Ll L Rep 335 and 443 (fourteen days); *Nestle Co v E Biggins & Co* [1958] 1 Lloyd's Rep 398 (fourteen days).

barred by lapse of time unless the provision clearly applies to the claim in question[3]. The Court will, however, be prepared to read a clause as a time-bar provision, even if no barring words are expressed, if this is necessary in order to give some meaning to the contract[4].

2 Barring the right and barring the remedy

In most cases failure to comply with the requirements of a statutory limit will destroy the claim[5], so that it is no longer capable of being enforced. It might reasonably be assumed that contractual time-barring clauses will have the same effect. This is not, however, necessarily so. The courts have drawn a distinction between two categories of clause.

First, there are the clauses which extinguish the claim, in the same way as a statutory time-bar. If the facts are such as to bring the clause into operation, and if the respondent takes the point, the claim is defeated. This does not mean that the claimant has no right to refer the claim to arbitration, or that the arbitrator has no jurisdiction to rule upon it[6]. The result is simply that when the arbitrator makes his award, it is to the effect that the claim fails.

Second, there are the clauses which bar the right to arbitration, but do not defeat the claim. Clauses of this type have precisely the opposite effect to those described in the preceding paragraph. The claim remains valid and capable of enforcement. The only effect of failure to comply with the time limit is that the enforcement cannot be effected by means of an arbitration. If the claimant wishes to assert his rights he must do so in the High Court; and if he tries to assert his rights in an arbitration, the arbitrator will have no jurisdiction to entertain the claim.

These two different types of time-barring provision may sometimes be combined in a single clause: failure to comply with the limits fixed by the clause destroys both the claim itself, and the arbitrator's right to adjudicate upon it.

In many instances, the distinction between these two species of clause gives rise to no difficulty, since it is common for the clause itself to state explicitly that failure to perform the required formality within the time limit will have the effect of barring the claim[7]. Thus, the clause may provide that in default of compliance 'the claim shall be deemed to be waived and absolutely barred'[8], or

---

[3] *Board of Trade v Steel Bros & Co Ltd* [1952] 1 Lloyd's Rep 87 (time limit on quality claims; claim for defective packaging not barred); *Alan v El Nasr*, supra (time limit for buyer's claims: seller's claim not barred); *Bunge SA v Deutsche Conti Handelsgesellschaft mbH (No 2)* [1980] 1 Lloyd's Rep 352; *Sabah Flour and Feedmills v Comfez Ltd* [1987] 2 Lloyd's Rep 647.

[4] See *Metalimex Foreign Trade Corpn v Eugenie Maritime Co Ltd* [1962] 1 Lloyd's Rep 378 at 385 ('Any claim arising under this Charterparty has to be made in writing within six months after final discharge' – construed as a barring clause).

[5] For a full discussion, see Dicey on the *Conflict of Laws* (11th edn) pp. 188 et seq.

[6] See *Smeaton Hanscomb v Sassoon I Setty*, ante, at 1427: and *Alan v El Nasr*, ante, at 420.

[7] A particularly clear example may be found in *Panchaud Frères SA v Etablissements General Grain Co* [1970] 1 Lloyd's Rep 53, where the clause made it plain that the arbitrators were to retain jurisdiction even if the claim was out of time.

[8] The 'Centrocon' clause. This has invariably been construed as a claim-barring clause – which is indeed what the clause says. The only possible exception is *Ford v Compagnie Furness*, ante. This case may have decided either that the Centrocon clause was a remedy-barring provision, or that a claim-barring clause affected the jurisdiction of the arbitrator. On neither view is the case consonant with the authorities as a whole.

that 'all claims shall be deemed to be waived'[9]. Rather less specific, but none the less sufficiently clear, are those clauses which stipulate that the formality to be performed within the time limit is the giving of a notice of claim, not (as in the case of some clauses[10]) the commencement of an arbitration. Here, there is no need to read the clause as having any effect on the party's right to arbitrate; if the clause stipulates that notice of claim must be given within a certain number of days, then the obvious interpretation is that if the notice is not so given, the claim is lost[11].

There remains an obstinate residue of clauses which do not provide such a clear indication as to their meaning. Concerning these, it is difficult to say more than that the Court will lean in favour of construing them as 'claim-barring' rather than 'remedy-barring'[12]. This is scarcely surprising. It is easy to see why the parties to a commercial contract should wish to bar a claim entirely, if it is not put forward promptly; but not at all easy to understand why, when they have troubled to stipulate that all claims shall be referred to arbitration, they should go on to provide that a stale claim should be litigated rather than arbitrated.

The distinction between claim-barring and remedy-barring clauses is highly technical, and may give rise to practical difficulties[13]. Most arbitrators understandably do not appreciate that the distinction exists[14], and even a careful arbitrator could make an award to the effect that the claimant is time-barred without clearly distinguishing between questions of defence and questions of jurisdiction. The problem may then arise whether the award operates as a bar to any further attempt to enforce the claim. The answer depends upon the terms of the contract, the precise nature of the issue which the parties left for the decision of the arbitrator, and the wording of the award. No general rule can be

---

9 See *Alma Shipping Corpn v Union of India, The Astraea* [1971] 2 Lloyd's Rep 494. It was assumed that the clause was a claim-barring provision: see p. 502.
10 See *Pinnock Bros v Lewis and Peat Ltd* [1923] 1 KB 690. The clause fixed time limits for 'notice of arbitration to be given and arbitrator nominated in writing'. The emphasis of the clause on the arbitration rather than on the claim probably lies at the heart of this rather difficult case. Perhaps *Young v Buckett* (1882) 51 LJ Ch 504 is to be explained in the same way.
11 See *Smeaton Hanscomb v Sassoon I Setty*, ante, at 1472.
12 The distinction between claim-barring and remedy-barring was discussed, touched upon or assumed in *Pinnock v Lewis and Peat*, ante; *Ayscough v Sheed*, ante; *Metalimex v Eugenie Maritime*, ante; *A/B Legis v Berg*, ante; *Government of Italy v Suzuki & Co* (1923) 15 Ll L Rep 219; affd. 17 Ll L Rep 251 (*Scott v Avery* clause) and *Hardwick Game Farm v Suffolk Agricultural and Poultry Producers' Association* [1964] 2 Lloyd's Rep 227 at 274. In only the last of these was there an unequivocal decision that the clause fell into the remedy-barring category. *Pinnock v Lewis and Peat* is usually cited as another example, but the ground of the decision was that the award, being addressed only to jurisdiction, was not a bar to an action: see per Viscount Cave in *Ayscough v Sheed*, ante, at 106. The view of Roche J as to the meaning of the clause was implicit rather than explicit. *Ford v Compagnie Furness* is discussed in note 8, ante. The view of Slessor LJ in *Pitchers Ltd v Plaza (Queensbury) Ltd* [1940] 1 All ER 151 that the *defendant* lost his right to arbitrate by not giving timely notice to arbitrate was obiter. In *Ayscough v Sheed*, ante, the House of Lords did not find it necessary to decide the point, although it is reasonably plain that their Lordships regarded the clause as a claim-barring provision. Apart from these cases, clauses imposing a limit of time have, so far as we can trace, invariably been decided or assumed to fall into the claim-barring category.
13 The distinction is a creature of the lawyers, not of the merchants. It must be very doubtful whether the draftsmen of the various clauses had the point in mind at all, still less intended to give effect to it. As the law stands at present, the distinction must be regarded as valid; but the point is open to review in the Court of Appeal, and it may yet be that the law will be simplified and improved.
14 Cf. *A/B Legis v V Berg & Sons Ltd* [1964] 1 Lloyd's Rep 203 at 217.

stated, but it is probable that if the arbitrator was asked to decide the whole question whether the claim should or should not be allowed to go on, and if on a fair reading of the award this is the point which he has decided, then the award is binding[15]. But if the clause goes only to jurisdiction, and if the award shows clearly that the arbitrator is merely declining jurisdiction, and not giving effect to a substantive defence, the award does not bar an action to assert the claim[16].

3 'Impossible' time limits

The question occasionally arises whether a limitation provision can operate to bar a claim in circumstances where it was not practicable for the claimant to comply with the specified formalities within the prescribed time.

Where the limitation clause provides that notice of claim shall be given within a stipulated time, the position is clear. The notice must be given, or the claim is lost. The fact that the claimant did not and could not know the facts which founded the claim does not affect the position, nor indeed does it matter that the claim did not even exist at the moment when the time expired. Thus, where a charterparty contained a three-month time limit, and the shipowner was sued by a third party after the limit had expired, the shipowner's claim against the charterer for an indemnity was held to be barred, notwithstanding that his cause of action from the indemnity had not arisen until after the time had run out[17].

The position as regards clauses which require, not the giving of a notice of claim, but the commencement of an arbitration, within a specified period is less clear. A valid notice of arbitration cannot usually be given unless there exists a dispute about which to arbitrate[18]; and there cannot, except in very special circumstances, be a dispute unless the claimant knows that he has a claim and intimates it[19], and the defendant in turn intimates his rejection of the claim. One possible view is that a clause of this type would not be construed as operative where no cause of action exists at the expiry of the limitation period; and possibly also when the claimant was unaware of the fact which gave rise to the claim[20]. Alternatively, it may be said that the clause means what it says, and that in such a case the claim is barred[1] unless the claimant can persuade the Court to grant an extension under the 'hardship' provisions of section 27[2].

---

[15] *Ayscough v Sheed*, ante; *A/B Legis v Berg*, supra. There is implicit in these decisions the view that the aribtrator can rule upon the nature of the clause. This in turn involves making a binding decision upon his own jurisdiction, which is not normally something which an arbitrator is empowered to do. An explanation is given in *Smeaton Hanscomb v Sassoon I Setty*, ante.

[16] *Pinnock v Lewis and Peat Ltd*, ante; and see *Alan v El Nasr*, ante.

[17] *The Himmerland*, ante. A similar point was left open in *Pinnock Bros v Lewis and Peat Ltd* [1923] 1 KB 690 at 695.

[18] See pp. 122 et seq., ante.

[19] Although there can be a dispute without a claim being *formulated*: see per Viscount Dilhorne in *The Evje* [1974] 2 Lloyd's Rep 57 at 74.

[20] See *Pinnock v Lewis and Peat Ltd*, ante, at 695–696; and *Hardwick Game Farm v Suffolk Agricultural and Poultry Producers's Association*, ante, at 273. Also *Bede Steam Shipping Co v Bunge y Born Ltda SA* (1927) 27 Ll L Rep 410: if no dispute, no time-bar.

[1] This more rigorous approach gains support from *The Evje*, ante, and *The Himmerland* [1965] 2 Lloyd's Rep 353.

[2] See per Lord Morris in *The Evje*, ante, at 63. It is reasonable to infer that Mocatta J would have granted an extension in *The Himmerland*, supra, if the claimants had acted more quickly.

4 Notice of claim

Broadly speaking, contractual limitation clauses are to two types: those which require a notice of claim to be given within the specified time, and those which require an arbitration to be commenced within that time. Not infrequently, the two types of provision are combined in a single clause.

Clauses of the first type operate without reference to the nature of the proceedings in which they are invoked as a defence. If the claim is barred, it is barred for a High Court action as much as for an arbitration, and there are no special rules governing the application of such a clause to arbitral proceedings. Nevertheless, since such provisions are often to be found in contracts which contain an arbitration clause, it is convenient to make certain comments upon them.

First, there must be an intimation that a claim is being made, not that a claim may be made in the future. Commercial men frequently state that they 'reserve their rights' to put forward a claim. This is not sufficiently clear[3]. The notice should be positive in its terms.

Moreover, the notice should give the recipient sufficient information as to the claim which he has to face[4]. We have previously suggested[5] that a notice to appoint arbitrators, sufficient to satisfy the requirements of a statutory limitation, may be expressed in general terms. This is not so, as regards the notice of claim under a contractual limitation clause, which must[6] –

'... be such a notice as will enable the party to whom it is given to take steps to meet the claim by preparing and obtaining appropriate evidence for that purpose'.

This need for particularity in the notice of claim requires the claimant to steer a difficult course. If too few details are given, he runs the risk of it being held that the notice is insufficient and that the claim or part of it is time-barred[7]. On the other hand, if the notice is too specific, the claimant may find himself handicapped in the future. It frequently happens that when the claimant comes to prepare his case for arbitration, he finds that he has a better way of putting his claim than the one which he originally adopted. If this happens after the specified time has elapsed, he may find that his original notice of claim is too

---

[3] See *A/S Rendal v Arcos Ltd* (1937) 58 Ll L Rep 287 at 293. See also *Bulgaris v La Plata Cereal Co SA* (1947) 80 Ll L Rep 455.

[4] Although the notice itself may not identify the claim, it will still be a good notice if it is clear from the context in which it is given that it is intended to refer to a particular dispute: *Court Line Ltd v Akt Gøtaverken, The Halcyon the Great* [1984] 1 Lloyd's Rep 283; *Bremer Handelgesellschaft mbH v Raffeisen Hauptgenossenschaft eG* [1982] 1 Lloyd's Rep 434.

[5] See p. 199, ante.

[6] *A/S Rendal v Arcos Ltd*, ante, at 292.

[7] There are few reported instances of claims failing for want of particularity in a notice (apart from the reversed decision of the Court of Appeal in *A/S Rendal v Arcos Ltd* (1936) 54 Ll L Rep 309: on appeal in HL (1937) 58 Ll L Rep 287). What the authorities do not discuss is the extent to which a defective notice may be cured by subsequent informal particularisation. We suggest that this can happen when further particulars are given before time expires, but not afterwards: see *Bunge SA v Schleswig-Holsteinische Landwirtschaftliche Hauptgenossenschaft Eingetr GmbH* [1978] 1 Lloyd's Rep 480, where the particulars missing from the notice had already been given in correspondence, and the notice was held good.

narrowly worded to cover his new contention, and that the latter is shut out by the operation of the time-bar[8].

Thus, for example, in a case where the purchasers of goods had rejected on the ground of defective quality, and had re-claimed the price, they subsequently wished to justify the rejection of the goods, and the claim for the return of the price, on the ground that the goods were shipped too late. This change of ground took place after the contractual time limit had expired. The Court of Appeal held that the buyers were not entitled to put forward this new basis of claim, as it constituted a new and different claim which had not been advanced in time[8].

It has been said that if the notice of claim as originally given by the claimant is insufficiently particularised, the claimant is nonetheless absolved from giving further details if the defendant repudiates the claim[9].

If the clause calls for a written notice of claim, an oral notice will not suffice, unless the defendant by his conduct waives the requirement of writing[10].

Where the clause requires a claim to be made within a specified time, the clause is complied with if notice of claim is given within the period, even though at that time no dispute has yet arisen[11].

The Limitation Act 1980 prescribes various methods by which the claimant may serve his notice of arbitration, in order to prevent the claim from being statute-barred: see p. 199, ante. These provisions do not apply to contractual time limits. If the contract itself provides how the notice is to be served, that method must be employed. Otherwise, the claimant must ensure that the notice is actually delivered, within the time limit, to the defendant or a person authorised by him to receive the notice[12].

5 Appointment of arbitrator

Some forms of limitation clause require that the claimant's arbitrator shall be

---

[8] *Panchaud Frères SA v Etablissements General Grain Co* [1970] 1 Lloyd's Rep 53. We cite this case in relation to notice of claim, because the Court of Appeal decided it in accordance with the principles enumerated in *A/S Rendal v Arcos*, supra. It may, however, be remembered that in *Panchaud* the clause was not concerned with a simple notice of claim but with the appointment of an arbitrator and notice of the 'claim for arbitration'. The two are not the same. If *Panchaud* is authority for the proposition that *no* notice of arbitration can be valid unless it contains the details called for by *A/S Rendal v Arcos* the decision is novel and far reaching, particularly since notices of arbitration virtually never give such details. And if *Panchaud* simply decides that a notice to save the time limit must be particularised, the rather odd result ensues that the notice may be good for the purposes of starting an arbitration, but not good to prevent the claim from being time-barred.

[9] *A/S Rendal v Arcos*, ante, per Lord Wright at 294. It is not entirely easy to see why this should be so, if the purpose of the details is to enable the defendant to prepare his defence. He will need them whether he immediately repudiates the claim or not. Presumably Lord Wright was referring to a repudiation before the expiry of the time limit: a subsequent repudiation would presumably be insufficient to revive a time-barred claim. A prudent defendant, faced with a possibly defective claim, will temporise.

[10] Failure to ask for a written notice may be enough: cf. *Lickiss v Milestone Motor Policies at Lloyds'* [1966] 2 Lloyd's Rep 1, [1966] 1 WLR 1334.

[11] *The Evje* [1974] 2 Lloyd's Rep 57, [1975] AC 797; *contra*, if the claim has not yet arisen: *Interbulk Ltd v Ponte dei Sospiri Shipping Co, The Standard Ardour* [1988] 2 Lloyd's Rep 159.

[12] *A/S Rendal v Arcos* (1937) 58 Ll L Rep 287; *Getreide-Import GmbH v Contimar SA Compania Industrial Comercial y Maritima* [1953] 1 Lloyd's Rep 572. As stated in *A/S Rendal v Arcos* it is also sufficient if the notice is delivered to a person who does not possess such authority provided in fact he transmits it to the defendant. It would seem that this method will not suffice unless the transmission occurred during the time limit.

'appointed' within a stipulated period. In order to comply with this requirement, three acts must take place –

1 The claimant must communicate with the intended arbitrator, authorising him to act in respect of the particular dispute.

2 The intended arbitrator must indicate to the claimant his willingness to act.

3 The fact of the appointment must be communicated to the defendant[13]. The arbitrator thus appointed must be one who possesses whatever qualifications are stipulated in the arbitration agreement[14].

It is unnecessary for the claimant to be named at the time of appointment so long as words are used which clearly identify the person by whom the appointment is made. Thus, an appointment by 'owners' is sufficient if it is clear from the context whether the registered owners or disponent owners are the appointors[15].

6 Relief from a time-bar

Failure by the claimant to comply with the contractual time limit does not necessarily entail that the claim is barred. The claimant may be relieved from the consequences of his delay in the following circumstances –

(a) Conduct on the part of the defendant which disentitles him from relying on the time limit. Such conduct may consist of –
  (i) a breach of the defendant's obligations under the contract; or
  (ii) acts evidencing an intention or election not to rely on the time bar, sufficient to constitute a waiver or estoppel.
(b) The operation of the Unfair Contract Terms Act 1977.
(c) The exercise of a discretion vested in the arbitrator or the Court to prolong the period of the time limit, and hence (in effect) to validate a claim which would otherwise be time-barred. Such a discretion is possessed –
  (i) by the arbitrator, if the contract expressly confers it upon him;
  (ii) by the Court, under section 27 of the Arbitration Act.
These various ways in which the claimant may escape from a plea of time-bar are discussed below.

(a) Conduct of defendant

(i) **Breach of contract.** A time-barring clause is a contractual provision which purports, in certain circumstances, to exclude the liability of a party for his own breach of contract. It is a general principle of the law of contract that there are limits to the efficacy of exemption clauses: and their application may be excluded on the ground of a deviation or on the footing that the clause, properly construed, is not wide enough to exclude liability for the breach in question[16]. There seems no reason why this principle should not also apply to contractual time-barring clauses, whether or not associated with agreements to

---

[13] *Tradax Export SA v Volkswagenwerk AG* [1970] 1 Lloyd's Rep 62, [1970] 1 QB 537; *Edm JM Mertens & Co PVBA v Veevoeder Import Export Vimex BV* [1979] 2 Lloyd's Rep 372 ('string' contracts).
[14] *The Evje* [1974] 2 Lloyd's Rep 57, per Lord Morris at 63.
[15] *Carras Shipping Co Ltd v Food Corpn of India The Delian Leto and The Delian Spirit* [1978] 2 Lloyd's Rep 433. Because of its potential for confusion, an appointment in this form should be avoided.
[16] *Photo Production Ltd v Securicor Transport Ltd* [1980] 1 Lloyd's Rep 545, [1980] AC 827.

arbitrate. The problem has on a few occasions been considered by the courts in the context of arbitrations, and it seems that the general principle has been applied[17]. The topic does not, however, involve any specific questions of arbitration procedure, and we therefore refer the reader for a further discussion to the standard works on contract, sale of goods and carriage.

(ii) Waiver and estoppel.   A defendant who would otherwise be entitled to rely on a time-limit may lose this defence if his conduct is such as to constitute a waiver or an estoppel. This difficult branch of the law is not specifically concerned with arbitration procedure[18], and we therefore do not deal with it in detail. Since, however, the question is occasionally raised in the course of an arbitration, it may be helpful to state the following propositions.

First, the conduct of the defendant is more likely to found a waiver or an estoppel if it occurs before, rather than after, the time limit has expired. If the defendant so behaves as to induce the claimant to believe that the defendant will not rely on the time limit, it may not be difficult to persuade the Court that the defendant cannot thereafter complain that the formalities were not completed in time. But if the claimant has already let the time run out, without the defendant having misled him in any way, it will be much less easy for the claimant to complain that the defendant's subsequent conduct in some way makes it unfair for him to raise the time bar[19].

Second, the continuation of negotiations between the parties whilst the limitation period is running does not in itself create any waiver or estoppel in favour of the claimant[20]. Nor does mere silence on the part of the defendant during this period suffice to destroy the defendant's right to rely on the time-bar. The defendant is entitled to lie low and watch the claim become time-barred. This being so, if the claimant wishes to negotiate, but sees the end of the limitation period approaching, he should either extract an explicit promise from the defendant to keep the time running during the negotiations, or comply with the necessary formalities before the time expires. However, although the currency of negotiations will not, without more, found a waiver or estoppel, it may be a ground upon which the Court will grant an extension under the 'undue hardship' provisions of section 27 of the Act: see p. 210, post. If the defendant acts in a way which is only consistent with the claim remaining in

---

[17] *Smeaton Hanscomb & Co v Sassoon I Setty Son & Co* [1953] 1 WLR 1468, per Devlin J at 1470 (fundamental breach and delivery of non-contractual goods); *Pinnock Bros v Lewis and Peat Ltd* [1923] 1 KB 690, per Roche J at 695 (non-contractual goods); also the cases cited in note 18, infra.

[18] Except as regards the problems raised by *H Ford & Co v Compagnie Furness (France)* (1922) 12 Ll L Rep 281, [1922] 2 KB 797 and *Atlantic Shipping and Trading Co Ltd v Louis Dreyfus & Co* (1922) 10 Ll L Rep 446 and 707, [1922] 2 AC 250 in relation to time-bars, and the jurisdiction of the arbitrator, where there is a breach of an *implied* warranty of seaworthiness.

[19] But see *Nippon Yusen Kaisha v Pacifica Navegacion SA, The Ion* [1980] 2 Lloyd's Rep 245, where the defendant's conduct induced the claimant to refrain from making an application under s. 27. The statement of Roskill J in *Alma Shipping Corpn v Union of India, The Astraea* [1971] 2 Lloyd's Rep 494 at 502 (where the conduct relied on took place after the time limit had expired), that nothing less would suffice than a new agreement supported by consideration, appears to put the matter rather more adversely to the claimant than some of the earlier cases.

[20] A clear example may be found in *Williams and Mordey v WH Muller & Co (London) Ltd* (1924) 18 Ll L Rep 50, where the claimants waited until a similar case had passed through the courts before beginning their arbitration.

existence[1], he may thereby waive the right to say that the claim has already been totally defeated by lapse of time. Thus, for example, if the contract expressly entitles the defendant to call upon the plaintiff to produce documents or evidence in support of his claim, and the defendant avails himself of this right, he may thereafter be prevented from saying that as a result of a time-bar there was no longer any claim to prove.

Where the clause is of the claim-barring type, the arbitrator has jurisdiction to decide whether it has been waived[2] although, since it is a matter of law, the Court will have the final word on the matter if the question comes before the Court by way of appeal.

(b) Unfair Contract Terms Act 1977

Sections 3 and 7 of the Unfair Contract Terms Act 1977 operate in certain circumstances to prevent a contractual term from excluding, restricting or altering liability for breach of contract, except in so far as the term satisfies the requirements of reasonableness[3]. The Act does not apply to 'an agreement in writing to submit present or future differences to arbitration[4]. But we consider that the Act does, in principle, apply to a term which provides that claims shall be barred unless arbitration is commenced within a specified period of time[5]: such a term is entirely distinct from the arbitration agreement to which it relates.

(c) Prolongation of time-limit

(i) **Prolongation by arbitrator.** Certain forms of contract expressly confer on the arbitrator or arbitral appeal tribunal[6] a discretion to extend the time limit[7], and hence to validate a claim which would otherwise have been time-barred[8]. If the existence of the discretion depends upon the existence of certain facts, then the findings of the arbitrator concerning those facts are final[9]; so also for all practical purposes is his decision on the way in which the discretion is to

---

[1] E.g. by agreeing to pay the claim: *Tradax Internacional SA v Cerrahogullari TAS, The M Eregli* [1981] 2 Lloyd's Rep 169 at 173.

[2] As in *Cerrito v North Eastern Timber Importers* [1952] 1 Lloyd's Rep 330.

[3] A full discussion of the 1977 Act and of the concept of 'reasonableness' lies outside the scope of this book. The reader is referred to the standard works on the law of contract, sale and hire-purchase.

[4] See s. 13(2) of the 1977 Act.

[5] There seems no doubt that it applies to contractual time-limits for the commencement of *actions*. It would be odd if arbitration were on a different footing.

[6] *Timmerman's Graan-en Maalhandel en Maalderij BV v Sachs* [1980] 1 Lloyd's Rep 194 (GAFTA Board of Appeal's discretion not fettered by the exercise of discretion at the first stage).

[7] In the absence of express provision the arbitrator has no power to extend the time limit: *Amalgamated Metal Corpn v Khoon Seng Co* [1977] 2 Lloyd's Rep 310.

[8] See *Agroexport Entreprise D'Etat pour le Commerce Exterieur v NV Goorden Import Cy SA* [1956] 1 Lloyd's Rep 319; *Panchaud Frères SA v Etablissements General Grain Co* [1969] 2 Lloyd's Rep 109; *Provimi Hellas AE v Warinco AG* [1978] 1 Lloyd's Rep 373; *Bunge SA v Kruse* [1979] 1 Lloyd's Rep 279; *Edm JM Mertens & Co PVBA v Veevoeder Import Export Vimex BV* [1979] 2 Lloyd's Rep 372; *Timmerman's v Sachs* [1980] 1 Lloyd's Rep 194. In the first of these cases, the clause did not in terms purport to confer a discretion, but this is no doubt what as intended.

[9] *Agroexport Entreprise D'Etat pour le Commerce Exterieur v NV Goorden Import Cy SA*, supra, at 323.

be exercised[10]. If, however, there is a question of law or construction on whether, in the particular circumstances of the case, the discretion actually exists, the question involves deciding whether the arbitrator had jurisdiction, which can only be decided by the Court[11].

The fact that the Court has refused an application for an extension of time under section 27[12] is not a bar to a further application to the arbitrator under such a clause: the two remedies are separate and cumulative[13]. It is doubtful whether the existence of a discretion vested in the arbitrator excludes or fetters the Court's jurisdiction to extend time under section 27[14].

(ii) Prolongation by the Court.   Section 27 of the Arbitration Act provides as follows –

> 'Where the terms of an agreement[15] to refer future disputes to arbitration provide that any claims to which the agreement applies shall be barred unless notice to appoint an arbitrator is given or an arbitrator is appointed or some other step to commence arbitration proceedings is taken within a time fixed by the agreement, and a dispute arises to which the agreement applies, the High Court, if it is of opinion that in the circumstances of the case undue hardship would otherwise be caused, and notwithstanding that the time so fixed has expired, may, on such terms, if any, as the justice of the case may require, but without prejudice to the provisions of any enactment limiting the time for the commencement of arbitration proceedings, extend the time for such period as it thinks proper'.

It will be observed that the section only applies in terms to those agreements which provide that in default of timely compliance with the specified formalities 'any claims to which the agreement applies shall be barred'. But relief under the section can be granted whether the effect of the clause is to bar the claim, or

---

[10] The Court has in principle power to review the exercise of any discretion by the arbitrator, even if it is described as an 'absolute discretion', either by way of appeal or by an application to set aside the award for misconduct. But it will only do so if the arbitrator has acted in bad faith or has taken account of a matter which could not conceivably be relevant: *Cook Industries Inc v BV Handelmaatschappij Jean Delvaux* [1985] 1 Lloyd's Rep 120, CA.

[11] *Compagnie Européenne de Cereals SA v Tradax Export SA* [1986] 2 Lloyd's Rep 301. In *Panchaud v General Grain*, ante, however, it was assumed that the question was one on which the arbitrator could state a case: see pp. 573–574, post.

[12] See below.

[13] *The Cunard Carrier, Eleranta and Martha* [1977] 2 Lloyd's Rep 261. It is difficult to see how the Court's refusal to extend time could give rise to a plea of res judicata if a fresh application were made to the arbitrators, unless the arbitrators' discretion is defined in the same terms as s. 27. Usually it is an unfettered discretion.

[14] *Etablissements Soules & Cie v International Trade Development Co* [1979] 2 Lloyd's Rep 122 at 138. With respect, we doubt whether it is correct, as Kerr J suggested in *The Cunard Carrier*, supra, that the Court might in its discretion decide to leave the matter to the arbitrators. The discretion is not delegable, but has to be exercised by the Court itself in accordance with the principles laid down by the cases. *Ets Soules*, supra, was followed, in preference to a later decision to the contrary of Parker J in *Timmerman's v Sachs* [1980] 1 Lloyd's Rep 194, by Leggatt J in *European Grain & Shipping Ltd v Dansk Landbrugs Grovvareslskab* [1986] 1 Lloyd's Rep 163, but not followed by Steyn J in *Comdel Commodities Ltd v Siporex Trade SA (No 2)* [1988] 2 Lloyd's Rep 590.

[15] Including terms incorporated by reference to another document: *Nea Agrex SA v Baltic Shipping Co Ltd* [1976] 2 Lloyd's Rep 47, [1976] QB 933.

merely to bar the right to have the claim decided in an arbitration[16]. Nor is the word 'claims' limited to causes of action: it applies to any claim to have an issue decided by arbitration[17].

The application of the section is also limited to those agreements where the formalities to be completed within the time limit consist either of the giving of notice to appoint an arbitrator, or the appointment of an arbitrator, or some other step to commence arbitration proceedings. The section has no application to limitation provisions under which the step to be taken is the giving of a notice of claim[18] otherwise than as part of the process of commencing arbitration[19].

Again, the wording of the section makes it plain that the only effect of an extension is to relieve the claimant from the consequence of non-compliance with a contractual time limit. The section will not protect him if the claim has become barred by statute. However, where a statutory time limit has been adopted by the parties as a term of the contract in circumstances where it would not otherwise have applied, the Court has power to give relief under the section[20].

The power conferred by section 27 may, as the section makes plain, be exercised either before or after the expiry of the time limit. In practice, the assistance of the Court is always invoked in respect of claims which have already become time-barred.

The propositions stated above are reasonably plain. Much less straightforward is the question when the discretion arises. The section requires the Court to form the opinion that 'undue hardship' will be caused if an extension is withheld. 'Hardship' is easy enough to comprehend: it might be said to exist whenever a claimant loses a valid claim[1] through failure to comply with a short time limit.

---

[16] *Consolidated Investment and Contracting Co v Saponaria Shipping Co Ltd, The Virgo* [1978] 2 Lloyd's Rep 167.

[17] E.g. the amount of a salvage award: *The American Sioux* [1980] 2 Lloyd's Rep 224.

[18] *Babanaft International SA v Avant Petroleum Inc* [1982] 1 WLR 871, overruling *Nestle Co v E Biggins & Co* [1958] 1 Lloyd's Rep 398. *Bulgaris v La Plata Cereal Co SA* (1947) 80 Ll L Rep 455 at 457, is presumably also overruled.

[19] *Tradax Export SA v Italcarbo Societa di Navigazione SpA (The Sandalion)* [1983] 1 Lloyd's Rep 514; *Jadrauska Slobodna Plovidba v Oleagine SA* [1984] 1 Lloyd's Rep 145; *Mariana Islands Steamship Corporation v Marimpex Mineraloelhandelsgesellschaft mbH & Co KG, The Medusa* [1986] 2 Lloyd's Rep 328; *Pittalis v Sherefettin* [1986] QB 868, [1986] 2 WLR 1003, CA. The question whether the giving of a notice of claim is an integral part of the process of commencing arbitration or merely a condition precedent to the commencement of an arbitration involves a question of construction which may lead to fine distinctions between clauses in different terms. The distinctions may be artificial, but this is perhaps no more than a reflection of the fact that for historical reasons the dispensing power conferred on the court by s. 27 relates only to arbitrations and not to contracts containing no arbitration clause. Perhaps the time has come for Parliament to extend s. 27 to all contracts, whether they provide for arbitration or not, or alternatively to repeal s. 27. The former course would require careful consideration by the legislature of the relationship between the extended section and Part II of the Limitation Act 1980, and also the policy considerations which bear upon the question whether a time limit should be 'disapplied'.

[20] *Nea Agrex SA v Baltic Shipping Co Ltd* [1976] 2 Lloyd's Rep 47, [1976] QB 933, where the Hague Rules time limit was incorporated in a charter to which the Hague Rules would not otherwise have applied. But s. 27 cannot be invoked in a case where the Hague (or Hague-Visky) Rules apply because they are given the force of law by statute: *Kenya Railways v Autares Co Pte Ltd* [1987] 1 Lloyd's Rep 424.

[1] If there is no claim, there is no hardship: *The Cunard Carrier* [1977] 2 Lloyd's Rep 261. See also *Sanko SS Co Ltd v Tradax Export SA* [1979] 2 Lloyd's Rep 273. But the Court cannot investigate the merits of the claim, beyond satisfying itself that it is not frivolous or doomed to failure: *Salenrederierna SA v Blue Star Line Ltd, The New York Star* [1982] 1 Lloyd's Rep 78.

But the word 'undue' plainly calls for something more than this. Precisely how much more is a matter upon which there have been two perceptible shifts in the attitude of the Court. When the power was first conferred, by the Act of 1934, the Court appears to have given a wide interpretation to the section[2]. There followed a period in which the courts adopted a much more severe interpretation of the section. It was said that the power should be exercised only in 'very restricted cases' or 'very special circumstances'[3]. This narrow interpretation deprived the section of most of its effect. For example, in two reported cases, extensions were refused where the claims were only two days and six days late[4]. This interpretation prevailed for some fifteen years, until in 1967 the Court of Appeal reviewed the matter, and reinstated the earlier and more liberal view of the section[5]. In the words of Lord Denning MR[6]:

> '"Undue" . . . simply means excessive. That is greater hardship than the circumstances warrant. Even though a claimant has been at fault himself, it is an undue hardship on him if the consequences are out of proportion to his fault'.

These alterations in the attitude of the Court mean that cases decided between 1950 and 1967 cannot be relied upon with confidence: and indeed some of them would probably nowadays have been decided differently.

The application of the principle, stated by Lord Denning in the passage quoted above, must depend upon the circumstances of each individual case, and an attempt to state rigid rules would be misleading. It may, however, be helpful to list some of the factors which the courts have regarded as favourable to an application under section 27[7] –

1 The existence of a misunderstanding about whether the time-bar exists or is being relied upon – the more particularly if the defendant has shared in[8] or contributed to[9] the mistake[10].

---

[2] See *Luis de Ridder Ltda SAC v Nivose Societa di Navigazione* (1935) 53 Ll L Rep 21; *Bulgaris v La Plata Cereal Co SA* (1947) 80 Ll L Rep 455.

[3] *G Sigalas & Sons v Man Mohan Singh & Co* [1958] 2 Lloyd's Rep 298; *SS Co of 1912 and SS Co Svendborg v Anglo-American Grain Co, The Leise Maersk* [1958] 2 Lloyd's Rep 341.

[4] *Sigalas v Man Mohan Singh*, supra, and *Jajasan Urusan Bahan Makanan v Compania de Navegacion Geamar etc* [1953] 1 Lloyd's Rep 499 and 511.

[5] In *Liberian Shipping Corpn v A King & Sons Ltd* [1967] 1 Lloyd's Rep 302, [1967] 2 QB 86.

[6] Ibid. at 307.

[7] The shorter list of relevant factors which is to be found in *Moscow V/O Exportkhleb v Helmville Ltd, The Jocelyne* [1977] 2 Lloyd's Rep 121, contains only those factors which were relevant to that particular case. It has, however, received the approval of the Court of Appeal in *Libra Shipping and Trading Corpn Ltd v Northern Sales Ltd, The Aspen Trader* [1981] 1 Lloyd's Rep 273, CA, and the latter case has proved its worth in practice as the leading authority on the factors relevant to the exercise of the Court's discretion.

[8] *Liberian v King*, ante, at 307.

[9] Ibid.; *SS Co of 1912 and SS Co Svendborg v Anglo-American Grain Co, The Leise Maersk* [1958] 2 Lloyd's Rep 341 at 344; *FE Hookway & Co v HW Hooper & Co* (1950) 84 Ll L Rep 335 and 443; *Rolimpex v Avra Shipping Co, The Angeliki* [1973] 2 Lloyd's Rep 226 at 228; *Intermare Transport GmbH v Naves Transoceanicas Armodora SA, The Aristokratis* [1976] 1 Lloyd's Rep 552. So far as *G Sigalas & Co v Man Mohan Singh & Co* [1958] 2 Lloyd's Rep 298 decides that a misunderstanding not caused or shared in by the respondent is fatal to an application under s. 27, it is probably no longer good law.

[10] Although the courts have yet to consider the point, their approach would no doubt be the same where a plaintiff, in the belief that a *Scott v Avery* clause was not being relied upon, had begun an action which was subsequently stayed.

2 The absence of fault on the part of the claimant in allowing the claim to become time-barred; or, at least, the existence of a modest degree of fault in comparison with the harm which he would suffer if the claim were time-barred[11].

3 The existence of an excusable mistake on the part of a claimant[12].

4 The fact that the possibility or necessity of a claim could not have been known to the claimant within the time limit; the more particularly if the claim did not even come into existence before the time expired[13], or is a claim for indemnity against a liability whose existence was unknown or shadowy throughout the limitation period[14].

5 The fact that the parties were in negotiation during the limitation period[15].

6 The substantial size of the sum which the claimant will lose if the claim is barred, particularly if the delay is short[16].

7 A reasonable, if mistaken, belief on the part of the claimant that a notice which he had previously given in time was sufficient to cover the claim in question[17].

8 The fact that a claimant has incurred liability to third parties, in respect of which he cannot obtain an indemnity if his claim against the respondent is time-barred[18].

9 The fact that a claim which is not time-barred depends upon the same facts as the one in respect of which the extension is sought[19].

---

11 *Hookway v Hooper*, ante; *Nestle v Biggins*, ante; *Eastern Counties Farmers v Cunningham* [1962] 1 Lloyd's Rep 261 at 263; and, indeed, many other cases. Absence of fault is a strong point in favour of the claimant; it is probable that since *Liberian v King* the presence of fault is no longer as strong an adverse factor as once it was; see the comments of Salmon LJ in *Liberian v King* or *Jajasan v Compania de Navigaceone Geamar* [1953] 1 Lloyd's Rep 499, 511; and *First Steamship Co Ltd v CTS Commodity Transport Shipping Schiffahrts GmbH, The Ever Splendor* [1988] 1 Lloyd's Rep 245, where, on rather unusual facts, an extension was granted although the claimant had deliberately delayed making his claim because of a belief that it would provoke a much larger but, as it happened, untenable counterclaim.

12 *Liberian v King*, supra, at 307. 'Excusable' probably means 'understandable'. The decision in *Sigalas v Man Mohan Singh*, ante, that simple forgetfulness is not enough must now be regarded as too favourable to the respondent: see *Libra Shipping and Trading Corpn Ltd v Northern Sales Ltd, The Aspen Trader* [1981] 1 Lloyd's Rep 273. On the other hand, ignorance of the claimant's legal rights under a commercial contract is apparently not excusable: *The Cunard Carrier* [1977] 2 Lloyd's Rep 261. Mistakes by his lawyer are presumably to be imputed to the claimant: see *Birkett v James* [1978] AC 297. So also are unreasonable delays by the claimant in instructing agents, lawyers and insurers, and by the agents in investigating the claim: *Irish Agricultural Wholesale Society Ltd v Partenreederei MS 'Eurotrader'* [1987] 1 Lloyd's Rep 418.

13 *Eastern Counties Farmers v Cunningham*, supra, at 263; *Etablissments Soules & Cie v International Trade Development Co* [1979] 2 Lloyd's Rep 122 at 138; possibly also *The Himmerland*, ante.

14 *The Cunard Carrier*, ante, at 267; *Atlantic Shipping Co SA v Tradax Internacional SA, The Bratislava* [1977] 2 Lloyd's Rep 269.

15 *Liberian v King*, ante; *International Tank and Pipe SAK v Kuwait Aviation Fuelling Co KSC* [1975] 1 Lloyd's Rep 8; *The Virgo*, ante. Facts may therefore found an application under s. 27 which would not sustain a plea of waiver or estoppel: see p. 208, ante.

16 *Liberian v King*, ante. See also *Nestle v Biggins*, ante; *H Kruidenier (London) Ltd v Egyptian Navigation Co, The El Amria (No 2)* [1980] 2 Lloyd's Rep 166; *The Aspen Trader*, ante. The fact that the applicant is wealthy is of little or no relevance: *Tote Bookmakers Ltd v Development and Property Holding Co Ltd* [1985] Ch 261, [1985] 2 WLR 603.

17 *Bulgaris v La Plata Cereal Co SA* (1947) 80 Ll L Rep 455; *SS Co of 1912 v Anglo-American Grain Co*, ante.

18 *Hookway v Hooper*, ante, per Denning LJ at 446; contract *Sanko SS Co Ltd v Tradax Export SA* [1979] 2 Lloyd's Rep 273.

19 *Bulgaris v La Plata Cereal Co SA*, as explained in *Liberian v King*, ante, at 310.

10 The fact that the claim is almost certain to succeed or is admitted[20].

It is not possible to build up from the cases a full list of factors which weigh against an application for an extension, but it is clear that the respondent will have a good prospect of resisting such an application if he can show that he would suffer real prejudice if the claim were revived – for example if the lapse of time has made it difficult for him to accumulate the evidence with which to conduct his defence[1] or to claim indemnity from a third party[2] or if a claim against a third party has in the meantime also become time-barred. The fact that the claimant is able to pursue his claim against another party will also tell against his application, particularly if he has allowed the alternative claim to become time-barred[3]. The fact that the arbitrator has declined to exercise a power vested in him under the contract to extend time will tell against the claimant's application[4]. And the Court will, of course, not grant an extension unless the claimant is able, by affidavit evidence, to give an explanation for the delay.

As the section makes clear, the grant of an extension is discretionary. Even if the Court forms the view that 'undue hardship' exists, it need not necessarily grant relief. The conduct of the claimant must be regarded. Thus, for example, if he starts an action in another jurisdiction whilst the application under section 27 is pending[5], the Court will not help him to save his claim in the arbitration; nor if he deliberately delays making his application in the expectation that the arbitrator will exercise a discretion to extend time in his favour[6]. But it is no bar to relief under section 27 that the claimant has issued proceedings for summary judgment on the footing that there is, apart from the time-bar, no defence to his claim[7].

The fact that the remedy is discretionary has one important consequence, namely that the Court will expect a claimant who wishes to apply for an extension of time, to bring his application before the Court with the minimum of delay[8]. Accordingly, if the defendant informs the claimant that he is taking a

---

[20] *The Al Faiha* [1981] 2 Lloyd's Rep 99 at 105; *The M Eregli* [1981] 2 Lloyd's Rep 169. Conversely, the fact that the claim will almost certainly fail will tell against the application. But the Court should not attempt to evaluate the merits of the dispute unless they are manifest: *National Mineral Development Corpn Ltd v Obestain Inc, The Sanix Ace* [1985] 1 Lloyd's Rep 246.

[1] *Moscow V/O Exportkhleb v Helmville Ltd The Jocelyne* [1977] 2 Lloyd's Rep 121; *Hookway v Hooper*, ante; *EB Aaby's Rederi A/S v Union of India, The Evje* [1972] 2 Lloyd's Rep 129.

[2] *Richmond Shipping Ltd v Agro Company of Canada Ltd The Simonburn (No 2)* [1973] 2 Lloyd's Rep 145. The absence of such prejudice was a material factor in *Intermare Transport GmbH v Naves Transoceanicas Armorada SA, The Aristokratis* [1976] 1 Lloyd's Rep 552; *The Virgo*, ante; *The Aspen Trader*, ante; *The New York Star*, ante and the *Ever Splendor*, ante. The question of prejudice is generally relevant to whether the hardship to the claimant would be 'undue': it is not a distinct enquiry, relevant only after undue hardship has been made out: *The Ever Splendor*.

[3] *The Cunard Carrier* [1977] 2 Lloyd's Rep 261.

[4] *European Grain and Shipping Ltd v Dansk Landbrugs Grovvareslskab* [1986] 1 Lloyd's Rep 163.

[5] See *Jajasan Urusan v Geamar*, ante, at 500.

[6] *Timmerman's v Sachs* [1980] 1 Lloyd's Rep 194; cf. *The El Amria*, ante.

[7] *Graham H Davies (UK) Ltd v Marc Rich & Co Ltd* [1985] 2 Lloyd's Rep 423.

[8] *The Himmerland* [1965] 2 Lloyd's Rep 353, following *Raymond and Reid v Granger* [1952] 2 All ER 152; *The Simonburn (No 2)* [1973] 2 Lloyd's Rep 145. In *Ets Soules & Cie v International Trade Development Co* [1979] 2 Lloyd's Rep 122 at 138, Goff J said that he would if necessary have allowed an application even as late as the hearing of the special case. But this can only have been because the arbitrators, by exercising a contractual power to extend time, had made an application under s. 27 unnecessary. Delay of this length will generally be fatal: see *Bunge SA v Schleswig-Holsteinische* [1978] 1 Lloyd's Rep 480 at 493.

time-bar point, the claimant should not linger over attempts to persuade the defendant to change his mind, but should at once issue his summons under section 27[9].

For the same reason, if the claimant disputes that the claim is time-barred he should start proceedings for a declaration that it is not, issue his summons under section 27 and have both matters brought on for hearing at the same time, in case his claim for a declaration fails[10].

Since an applicant who seeks an extension under section 27 is requesting the indulgence of the Court, he will usually be ordered to pay the costs of the application[11]; but sometimes, if the Court thinks that the attitude of the respondent has been unreasonable, the order may be 'costs in the arbitration' or 'applicant's costs in the arbitration'[12].

Although the powers of the Court under section 27 are discretionary, their exercise will be reviewed on appeal if the Judge applied an incorrect view of the law[13], or took into account some material factor which he ought not to have taken into account or failed to take into account some material factor which he ought to have taken into account[14].

D. NEW CLAIMS

If not infrequently happens that whilst an arbitration is in progress one or other party decides to broaden the issues by adding a new claim. As previously mentioned, an application to amend by adding a potentially time-barred claim involves questions both of jurisdiction and of substance.

The question of jurisdiction arises whenever a party to an arbitration seeks to add a claim which was not comprised in the original dispute. The question of substance arises when the respondent objects that the claim which forms the basis for the amendment has already become barred by lapse of time. If faced with this difficult situation, we suggest that the arbitrator should adopt the following procedure –

1 He should first consider whether he has any jurisdiction to admit the claim at all, quite apart from any questions of time limit.

2 If he decides that he has no jurisdiction, he should refuse leave to amend.

3 If he decides that he has jurisdiction he should then consider whether or not the claim is obviously time-barred.

4 If the claim is obviously time-barred, the arbitrator should refuse leave to

---

[9] *The Himmerland*, supra; *Bunge v Schleswig-Holsteinische* [1978] 1 Lloyd's Rep 480 at 493. Failure to act promptly is not necessarily fatal to the application but it is a factor of great importance: *Irish Agricultural Wholesale Society Ltd v Partenreederei MS 'Eurotrader'* [1987] 1 Lloyd's Rep 418.

[10] *The Simonburn (No 2)*, ante; *Intermare Transport GmbH v Naves Transoceanicas etc* [1976] 1 Lloyd's Rep 552.

[11] See, for example, *Bulgaris v La Plata Cereal Co SA*, ante; *Luis de Ridder Ltda v Nivose Societa di Navigazione* (1935) 53 Ll L Rep 21; *Liberian v King; The Simonburn (No 2)*, ante; *UN/FAO World Food Programme v Filia Enterprises SA* [1987] Com LR 58.

[12] *Nestle v Biggins*, ante; *SS Co of 1912 v Anglo American*, ante.

[13] *Liberian v King*, ante.

[14] *Cast Shipping Ltd v Tradax Export SA, The Hellas in Eternity* [1979] 2 Lloyd's Rep 280; *The Aspen Trader*, ante. The Court of Appeal will not interfere, however, merely on the ground that the judge has attached too much or too little weight to a material factor, unless the exercise of discretion was clearly wrong.

amend. Conversely, if it is obviously not time-barred, leave to amend should be granted.

5 If it is not clear whether or not the claim is time-barred he should adopt one of the following alternatives –

(i) At once hear full argument on the question whether the claim is time-barred, and give a final ruling on the matter, leaving the losing party to appeal to the High Court if he wishes.

(ii) Adjourn the application until the date fixed for the hearing of the arbitration, thus dealing with all the issues in the arbitration at the same time.

(iii) Adjourn the application while the parties have the matters decided by the High Court under section 2 of the 1979 Act, or (perhaps) on an application by the respondent to restrain the claimant from pursuing the claim.

Neither of the last mentioned alternatives is altogether convenient, and the arbitrator may be asked to adopt the simpler solution of granting leave to amend 'without prejudice to any question of time-bar'. This is a sensible procedure, but it is not permissible in a High Court action. We are not persuaded that the same considerations apply in an arbitration[15], but the arbitrator will probably be well advised to take the safe course by adopting one or other of alternatives (i) and (ii) above.

---

[15] S. 35 of the Limitation Act 1980 provides that any new claims (i.e. claims by way of set-off or counterclaim and any claims involving the addition or substitution of a new party) are deemed to have been commenced on the same date as the original action or third party proceedings. The Court has no power to allow new claims to be made after the expiry of any time limit under the Act, except claims by way of set off or counterclaim by a party who has not previously made any claim in the action, and in other limited cases. But this section has no application to arbitration: *Casillo Grani v Napier Shipping Co, The World Ares* [1984] 2 Lloyd's Rep 481 at 487; *Kenya Railways v Antares Co Pte Ltd* [1987] 1 Lloyd's Rep 424. It would be contrary to the consensual basis of arbitration for the Court to add or substitute new parties. Nor is there any scope for adding new causes of action, for the arbitrator's jurisdiction is confined to the dispute which has been referred to him.

PART IV

The Arbitrator

CHAPTER 17

The rights and duties of the arbitrator

A. THE RELATIONSHIP BETWEEN THE PARTIES AND THE ARBITRATOR

1 Why does it matter?

The books have little to say about the relationship between the arbitrator and the parties, so far as it concerns their mutual rights and obligations. This is not surprising. For centuries, lawyers and arbitrators were preoccupied by the absence of any effective means of compelling a party to arbitrate who had agreed to do so, and of compelling him to continue with an arbitration once begun. Until the fragility of the whole procedure[1] was finally remedied by the 1889 Act[2], there was little point in considering whether the acceptance of an appointment as arbitrator gave rise to legally enforceable duties on either side. Moreover, until quite recently, the problem was of modest practical importance. Traditionally, an appointment as arbitrator was regarded as having an honorary character: not so much that the arbitrator was expected to fulfil his duties without remuneration (although that was once the case) but that his appointment and agreement to act were at the same time a recognition of his standing and probity, and a recognition of the responsibilities owed by such persons to others engaged in the same trade. Such fees as were charged were usually paid without demur, as a lien on the award usually provided any necessary sanction. Even those cases where the arbitrator went unpaid were of no great matter, for even if arbitration was not necessarily a spare-time activity, the remuneration which resulted from it was not an essential part of the arbitrator's livelihood. Conversely, the question of enforcing remedies against an unsatisfactory arbitrator would rarely arise. If he acted unfairly, the award would be set aside. If he refused to sit at all, he could be removed. The problems of the arbitrator's conduct during a long drawn out reference did not need considering, precisely because references were designed to be brief.

The position has recently become rather different. It is still true that in the great majority of trade arbitrations the arbitrator consents to act because he regards it as a privilege and a duty to do so, and that although the remuneration of an arbitration tribunal comprising several members may be quite high, the fee of each arbitrator is in essence a recompense for time lost in the conduct of his principal business, rather than being an end in itself. Furthermore, the majority of references are still of short duration. What is new, however, is the

---

[1] Or, more accurately, of voluntary arbitration otherwise than pursuant to a rule of court.
[2] For an account of this problem, and its eventual solution, see Chapter 29.

emergence of a new type of arbitration, and a new type of arbitrator. Some disputes now being referred to arbitration involve great sums of money, and are so complex as to make heavy demands on the skill and experience of the tribunal. Those who have the qualities required to act as arbitrator in these disputes, and are willing to give up the necessary time, expect to be paid accordingly. The fees involved are on occasion very large. Moreover, even disputes of smaller size are often entrusted to persons who, whilst not necessarily engaging the whole of their time in the conduct of arbitration, nevertheless look to it for a substantial part of their livelihood. They are professional arbitrators, and cannot afford simply to write off their fees if the losing party refuses to pay.

Equally, arbitrators have come to appear different when seen from the viewpoint of the persons engaged in the dispute. Large sums of money may be at stake, not simply in regard to the dispute itself, but also in the cost of having it arbitrated. If the arbitrator proves unsatisfactory, it is not necessarily a consolation to know that if the worst comes to the worst he can be removed, or his award set aside. That would not rescue the costs already thrown away. Parties so situated may begin to wonder why, if they select and pay a professional arbitrator to conduct their dispute for them, he should not owe them a duty of diligence, if nothing more.

In these changed circumstances, one must envisage the possibility of legal proceedings between the arbitrator and the parties. In order to explore this territory, which is largely uncharted except as regards certain principles applying to the arbitrator's remuneration, it is necessary to consider the nature of the relationship between the arbitrator and the parties: and in particular, to ask whether, like the relationship between the parties themselves, it takes the shape of a contract.

2 Quasi-contract status or contract?

There are, we suggest, three ways in which the relationship between the parties and the arbitrator can be explained: in terms of restitutory or quasi-contractual rights; as a matter of status; or as a matter of contract.

(a) Quasi-contract

If the only problem were to account for the arbitrator's right to remuneration, the 'restitutory' remedies would provide by far the readiest solution. All that is required to found such a remedy is a request by one party that the other shall perform a service, in circumstances where it is contemplated that the service will be rewarded[3]. The request here is present in fact, in the express terms of the appointment so that there is no need for a request to be implied; and the right to remuneration is taken for granted, and indeed is not infrequently quantified by agreement before any services are performed.

(b) Status

This account of the arbitrator's right to remuneration is simple, but we are not convinced that it is sufficient. In the restitutory situation which we have

---

[3] Goff and Jones, *The Law of Restitution* (2nd edn), Chapter 1.

described, the person to whom the request is addressed stands in no fixed relation to the other party. He can please himself whether he complies; until he does so, the other can withdraw the request, and terminate the possibility of a relationship coming into existence. An arbitration does not look like this. A request to act as arbitrator, once accepted, cannot be withdrawn, except with the consent of the other party or through the intervention of the Court[4]. When the arbitrator enters on the reference, he is clothed with the power to affect the rights, not only of the appointing party but also of his opponent: and this power continues until the reference has run its course, and cannot be withdrawn short of this, otherwise than by consent or by order of the Court. Furthermore, it is a unique power, in the sense that no persons other than the arbitrator (or arbitrators) can validly be clothed with the same power. The substantive obligations of the parties become transmuted into a duty to honour an award made by the chosen tribunal, and no-one else. It is true, as we have pointed out, that the relationship between the parties and the arbitrator, considered as a person possessed of rights and duties, is not the same as that between the parties and the arbitrator, considered as a mandatary. Nevertheless, in practice the two relationships are closely linked, and the existence and substance of the latter does tend to suggest that there is more to the former than the contingent and intermittent unilateral obligation which is all that is implied in the restitutory explanation of the arbitrator's right to remuneration.

Thus, it seems legitimate to regard the office of arbitrator as involving some degree of permanent status: and this prompts the idea that status alone is all that is needed by way of theoretical underpinning for the mutual rights of the arbitrator and the parties. The Court would simply assert, essentially on grounds of public policy, that certain rights and duties are conferred on the arbitrator by the very fact of his having assumed that office[5].

(c) Contract

Finally, there is the more traditional approach, which is to assume a contract, and then round it out by implying terms. Certainly, the relationship does have some semblence of mutuality, and strict compliance with the doctrine of consideration is no longer essential to the existence of a contract, if the circumstances are such as to show that a legally enforceable contract is what the parties really intended[6]. Even so, if there is a contract between the arbitrator and the parties, it must be of a most unusual kind. Thus –

1 Although the arbitrator is appointed in the expectation that he will exercise skill, care and diligence in the conduct of the reference and the making of his award, and may be said to have a duty to do so, this duty is legally enforceable (to the limited extent that it is enforceable at all) in a quite different way from an ordinary contractual obligation. An action does not lie in respect of negligence in making an award or, presumably, in conducting the reference[7].

---

[4] Pursuant to s. 1 of the Act.
[5] As was the case, for example, of the relationship between bailor and bailee, or between consignor and common carrier, before their status became overlaid with contract. It would not, of course, follow that the relationship would be governed only by the positive law; there would be scope for consensual terms as well.
[6] *New Zealand Shipping Co v A M Satterthwaite & Co, The Eurymedon* [1974] 1 Lloyd's Rep 534, [1975] AC 154.
[7] Pp. 224–230, post.

Moreover, the Act already creates remedies for dealing with lack of diligence on the part of the arbitrator, and it is at least doubtful whether these leave any room for the orthodox contractual remedies in respect of serious breaches of contract, such as the right to treat the relationship as terminated and to sue for damages in respect of the loss of the bargain[8].

2 The most important of all the arbitrator's duties is that which requires him to act fairly. Whilst from a practical point of view the parties are the prime beneficiaries of this duty, it is not aimed at them personally, but is of a more general nature. The arbitrator must be fair, because this is what the interests of the state require. Even if the duty is in some degree personal, it is hard to see it as a contractual obligation.

3 Whilst the arbitrator has an enforceable right to be paid for a completed award, and is probably entitled to recover, at least in some instances, for the value of work done on a reference which stops short of a conclusion, it is unlikely that the parties impliedly engage to provide him with the opportunity to earn his remuneration[9].

4 The Act enables a party to remove the arbitrator from office against his will, with the assistance of the Court. Many of the occasions on which the Court will exercise its powers can, if desired, be categorised as instances of repudiatory breach of contract by the arbitrator. But this will not always be possible, and indeed an arbitrator may be parted from the reference without being in any way personally in default[10].

5 At common law the mandate of the arbitrator is revocable at will, and although this mandate is distinct from the arbitrator's status as arbitrator, nevertheless once the mandate is disappeared there is no practical significance in the status, and nothing left for the arbitrator to do. Even under the Act, revocation of the mandate can be permitted by the Court even where there is no personal default on the part of the arbitrator.

6 It is not altogether easy, though not impossible, to work out how a contract comes into existence between one party and the arbitrator appointed by the other.

In the past, the development of English commercial law has been carried out through the medium of the law of contract. The Court gives effect to its awareness of the practical needs to trade through the flexibility of the implied term and the concept of the reasonable businessman. These methods are still serving their purpose in the field of arbitration, as witness the use of the implied term as a ground for relief in the case of excessive delay by a party in pursuing the reference[11]. Thus far, the contractual way of dealing with problems in arbitration has been confined to the relationship between the parties, which undoubtedly is a contract, albeit of a rather special kind[12]. Similar methods could, if the Court chose, also be employed in the event of a dispute between a party and the arbitrator, for with a little ingenuity a contract between these two persons could undoubtedly be devised[13]. We suggest, however, that this would

---

[8] P. 231, post.

[9] See pp. 242–245, post.

[10] See pp. 526–529, post.

[11] *Bremer Vulcaan Schiffbau und Maschinenfabricken v South India Shipping Corpn* [1980] 1 Lloyd's Rep 255.

[12] See pp. 503–517, post.

[13] In *Compagnie Européenne de Cereales SA v Tradae Export SA* [1986] 2 Lloyd's Rep 301 at 306, Hobhouse J analysed acting without jurisdiction as a breach of contract which can be restrained by injunction: the arbitrator became party to the arbitration agreement by accepting

be a mistake. To proceed by finding a contract and then applying to it the ordinary principles of the law of contract will not produce a reliable answer unless a contract really exists to be found. Even in the extreme case of a massive reference, employing a professional arbitrator for a substantial remuneration, we doubt whether a businessman would, it he stopped to think, conceive that he was making a contract when appointing the arbitrator. Such an appointment is not like appointing an accountant, architect or lawyer. Indeed it is not like anything else at all. We hope that the courts will recognise this, and will not try to force the relationship between the arbitrator and party into an uncongenial theoretical framework, but will proceed directly to a consideration of what rights and duties ought, in the public interest, to be regarded as attaching to the status of arbitrator. Parliament has already done this on several occasions, with a view to making the system work more effectively, by attaching to some of the relationships created by an arbitrator special rules quite different from those which would follow from ordinary principles of contract; and the common law has also taken one step in that direction by conceding to the arbitrator a special immunity from suit in neligence. There seems no reason why the further development of the law should not proceed on equally pragmatic lines.

There is, however, need for caution. We have suggested that the appointment of an arbitrator is not like any other act. It might be said that an arbitrator does resemble someone else: namely, a judge. In one sense, this is obviously true. There are, however, important differences between the two. The jurisdiction of the judge over litigation as a whole, and over a particular dispute brought before him derives from the general law not from the consent of the parties. The procedure which he follows is prescribed by the Rules of Court, not by the express or implied terms of the arbitration agreement. His remuneration does not come from the parties, nor does the amount of it depend in any way upon the nature and extent of the services which he performs in relation to their dispute. Finally, he has coercive powers over the property and persons of the parties which derive from his position as officer of State, and are not (and cannot be) conferred on the arbitrator by consent. The analogy between arbitrator and judge is tempting, but if pressed too far can lead to false conclusions. It is better to tackle the problems of the arbitrator on their own merits.

Finally we must emphasise that whatever may be the rights and duties of the arbitrator, they are owed equally by and to both parties, even in those references where each of the two arbitrators is nominated by one of the parties. The right to nominate is part of the procedure for bringing the tribunal into existence. Once the arbitrator has accepted his office, all connection with his 'appointer' becomes a matter of history[14]. Thereafter, he stands squarely between the two parties, having no special affiliation to either[15].

---

appointment under it. The same result could, we submit, have been arrived at by analysing the arbitrator's powers and duties in terms of mandate, without the need to resort to an implied term not to act outside the terms of the agreement.

[14] We are speaking of the arbitrator's judicial function. In certain informal arbitrations, a party-appointed arbitrator may have an administrative function, as a channel of communication between his appointer and the tribunal. Moreover, where the arbitration agreement contemplates that he will act as arbitrator/advocate, a direct relationship with his appointer will spring up if and when the two arbitrators disagree. But this does not affect the principle, which is axiomatic, that in exercising a judicial function the party-appointed arbitrator is in no sense the delegate or representative of the person who appointed him.

[15] There is no direct authority for this proposition, if only because the entire topic is little discussed in the cases. But the proposition is well established, so far as the arbitrator's mandate is concerned.

B. OBLIGATIONS OF THE ARBITRATOR TO THE PARTIES

The majority of the reported cases on arbitration are concerned with establishing the way in which the arbitrator should conduct the reference: or, more accurately, with the way in which he should not conduct it. This body of authority makes it impossible to deny that the arbitrator is in some sense under a legal, as well as a moral, obligation to perform his duties in a proper and careful manner. All of the reported cases are, however, concerned with deciding, as between the parties to the dispute, whether the award has been procured in such a way that it ought to be recognised as giving one party enforceable rights against the other. When it is said that an arbitrator 'ought to' proceed in a certain way, this signifies merely that he must so proceed if he wishes his award to be effective. The cases contain no systematic discussion of the question whether the arbitrator is under a personal legal ability to the parties, in the sense that they have a remedy against him if he fails to perform his duties in the appropriate manner.

When accepting the burden of the reference, the arbitrator can be regarded as undertaking three principal duties – namely to take care, to proceed diligently, and to act impartially. The existence of a moral obligation to perform these duties is undeniable. The question is whether it is backed by legal sanctions.

1 Duty to take care

In Chapter 2 we discussed the problem of identifying those features of a process, intended to result in a decision binding between two or more parties, which make it appropriate to call the process and the person who makes the decision 'an arbitration' and 'an arbitrator', respectively. We are here concerned with a different problem. To what extent, if at all, is an arbitrator immune from suit in respect of loss resulting from failure to perform his duties with reasonable skill and care, and what are the criteria for distinguishing between those who are and those who are not entitled to this immunity? The problems are linked, but it is important to note that they are not the same, for it is at least possible that there are arbitrators who are not immune, and persons enjoying immunity who are not arbitrators.

Until quite recently, the topic of judicial immunity could fairly be regarded as settled. Two propositions were involved. First, it was incontrovertable that arbitrators were immune from suit, although no similar immunity was possessed by other professional men such as architects, accountants and engineers (grouped under the label of 'valuers') who also made important decisions intended to be binding on two or more parties. Second, persons who would ordinarily rank as valuers might on occasion perform functions so closely resembling those of an arbitrator as to partake for the occasion in the same immunity as an arbitrator. The existence of such a category of persons, often called 'quasi-arbitrators', was well-established, although it was not altogether easy to tell in practice whether or not a valuer should in any given instance be included within it. The second proposition was founded on several reported cases, binding on the Court of Appeal[16]. For the first, there was no direct authority. For centuries it was treated as axiomatic. It appeared repeatedly in the textbooks; it was taken as the unchallengeable starting point of the authorities which established the second proposition; and it was regarded as self-evident to such a degree that there appears to be no reported instance in which a disappointed party has ever even tried to recover damages from an arbitrator[17].

Two more recent decisions in the House of Lords, *Sutcliffe v Thackrah*[18] and *Arenson v Arenson and Casson, Beckman, Ruttey & Co*[19], have made it clear that this account of the law can no longer be relied upon as accurate.

Sutcliffe v Thackrah was concerned with the liability of architects who were employed by the plaintiffs as architects and quantity surveyors in connection with a building contract on the R.I.B.A. form. The defendants issued interim certificates in favour of the contractor which the plaintiff duly honoured. As the result of the defendants' negligence, the amount certified was too great. The plaintiff was unable to recover the excess from the contractor, who had become insolvent, and he therefore sued the defendants. The Official Referee held the defendants liable. The Court of Appeal, treating itself as bound by the decisions cited in note 16, ante, held that the defendants were entitled to immunity as quasi-arbitrators. The House of Lords restored the judgment of the Official Referee.

The argument in the House of Lords proceeded on a comparatively narrow front. It was conceded by the plaintiff[20] that the category of quasi-arbitrators existed, and that persons falling within it were immune from suit. The question was whether it was enough, in order to establish a claim for immunity, to show that the person concerned had to decide in a question arising between two or more parties in a manner which was fair to, and binding upon, all parties; or whether something more was required, and if so what it was. The House of Lords unanimously held that these requirements were not sufficient. There were many professional men whose decisions affected the rights of more than one party, who could not be regarded as immune. Nor was a duty to be fair enough in itself, for this too was a feature of many relationships not involving immunity[1]. A valuer could not be classed as a quasi-arbitrator, unless he exercised a judicial function. Such of the earlier cases as could not be explained on the ground that the particular circumstances in which the valuer was employed were such as to give him a judicial function should be overruled[2].

Thus far, there was no radical departure from the law as previously understood. Although the immunity of an arbitrator was not in issue, the existence of this immunity was emphatically re-stated[3]. Nor was the existence of

---

[16] Including *Pappa v Rose* (1871) LR 7 CP 32, (1872) LR 7 CP 525; *Tharsis Sulphur and Copper Co Ltd v Loftus* (1872) LR 8 CP 1; *Stevenson v Watson* (1879) 4 CPD 148; *Chambers v Goldthorpe* [1901] 1 KB 624; *Finnegan v Allen* [1943] KB 425.

[17] See *Tharsis Sulphur and Copper Co v Loftus*, per Bovill CJ and Brett J.

[18] [1974] 1 Lloyd's Rep 318, [1974] AC 727.

[19] [1976] 1 Lloyd's Rep 179, [1977] AC 405.

[20] [1974] AC at 731 E.

[1] See, especially, per Lord Dilhorne at 756 H.

[2] Notably, *Chambers v Goldthorpe*, ante.

[3] Per Lords Reid (with whom Lord Hodson agreed), Morris of Borth-y-Gest, Dilhorne and Salmon, at 735, 744, 754 and 758, respectively.

the category of quasi-arbitrators put in question, although its boundaries were more narrowly re-drawn. All that remained open for debate was how precisely it could be ascertained whether a person was exercising judicial function.

Three years later, the same topic was discussed again by the House, in *Arenson v Arenson*, this time with more radical consequences. The plaintiff had agreed to purchase shares in a company from a third party, at a 'fair price', which was defined as meaning the value of the shares as defined by the defendants 'whose valuation acting as experts and not as arbitrators shall be final and binding on both parties'. Here again, it was conceded that arbitrators are immune from suit[4], but on this occasion the rationale of the immunity was more closely examined: for in order to decide whether the defendants resembled more closely an arbitrator (who is immune) or the defendants in *Sutcliffe v Thackrah* (who were not) it was necessary to find a reason why any person acting as arbitrator should be free from the liability for want of skill and care to which all other professional men are exposed.

As a result of this fresh approach, the law can no longer be regarded as clear. We suggest that when the matter comes before the House for direct decision[5] any one of the following three propositions may be accepted as correct –

1 All arbitrators are entitled to immunity, as are some valuers, when performing a judicial function. The primary characteristic of such a function is that the person who performs it is required to adjudicate upon an existing formulated dispute. But there are other matters which help to show whether or not the person in question is acting judicially; in particular, whether he receives evidence and arguments from the parties. Weight must also be given to the terms of contract under, or in relation to which, he is appointed[6].

2 The line which divides those who are immune from those who are not does not run along the boundary between arbitrators and valuers. Some arbitrators are immune and others are not. So also with valuers. In each case, the criterion is whether the person is acting judicially, meaning for this purpose whether his role is to investigate the issues or to adjudge between two opposing cases presented in an adversarial manner[7].

3 Arbitrators are not immune from suit. There is no reason of public policy to exempt them from liability, nor any sound basis for distinguishing between arbitrators and valuers[8].

We do not think it useful to discuss these propositions in detail. The matter is essentially one of public policy. Existing precedents and texts do not compel any

---

[4] [1977] AC at 410–411.

[5] As it probably will, before very long. It seems likely that short of the House of Lords, the dicta in *Sutcliffe v Thackrah* will be treated as so powerfully persuasive as to compel a decision in favour of the orthodox view of the arbitrator's privileges.

[6] The speeches of Lord Morris of Borth-y-Gest and Viscount Dilhorne in *Sutcliffe v Thackrah* (at 745, 752 and 756) and Lords Simon and Wheatley in *Arenson v Arenson* (at 423 and 428) can be cited in favour of this view. It appears to have been taken for granted in *Palacath Ltd v Flanagan* [1985] 2 All ER 161.

[7] The principal support for this proposition lies in the speeches of Lord Salmon in the two cases under discussion. It may be that the text does not correctly state the essence of Lord Salmon's argument, and that in reality his Lordship was saying that all arbitrators *are* immune, but that not everyone who appears to be an arbitrator is in fact acting as such.

[8] See per Lords Kilbrandon and Fraser (at 431 and 442). *IRC v Hoogstraten* [1985] QB 1077, [1984] 3 WLR 933 is indicative of the Court's reluctance to extend immunity on grounds of public policy.

particular answer. When the matter comes before the House it will, we suggest, prove necessary to look, not only at the narrow question of the arbitrator's immunity, but also at the nature of the arbitral process and of the roles played by the various participants (including advocates[9]), and this in turn will require the whole problem to be set in a broad perspective of the relationship between private arbitrations and the State. Opinions on this broader question are so diverse, and the law of arbitration is at present undergoing such rapid and fundamental change, that it is impossible to predict what the status of the arbitral process will be when the matter of immunity falls to be argued. It would therefore be pointless to venture any firm prediction of what the outcome is likely to be. We would, however, offer the following comments.

In the first place, we suggest that the reasoning which underlies proposition 2 can fairly be summarised as follows: There is a close resemblance between judges and arbitrators; judges are immune from suit whilst carrying out a judicial process, and one would expect the same to apply to arbitrators; the essence of the judicial process in England is that it is adversarial not investigatory; thus a person engaged in a method of deciding a question which does not involve a consideration of rival evidence and contentions is not engaged in a judicial process, and is thus not entitled to judicial immunity; alternatively, he is not engaged in an arbitration at all, and hence cannot enjoy the arbitrator's immunity from suit. We venture to suggest that this chain of reasoning is open to attack in two respects. First, the analogy between judge and arbitrator is less exact than it appears[10], the principal difference being that the judge's relationship with the dispute does not depend on consent, nor is his remuneration derived from, or his duties owed directly to, the parties themselves rather than the State. Other officers of State, besides judges, are immune from personal liability in respect of acts done whilst performing their official functions[11], and it does not follow that a person engaged in performing what is essentially a private function should necessarily enjoy the same immunity; for different considerations of public policy apply to the two cases. Second, it cannot be stated without qualification that all processes generally recognised in England as judicial in nature are of an adversarial character. So far as concerns arbitrations, it has never previously been suggested that what would otherwise be an arbitration will lose its character as such if the parties dispense wholly or in part with argument and evidence, and leave the arbitrator to proceed by a direct inspection of the subject-matter in dispute[12]. To take away the supervisory powers of the Court over proceedings of this kind cannot, we think, be justified on grounds of policy. And if the answer is given that perhaps the proceedings do continue to be arbitrations, but the person making the decision loses his

---

[9] It would be strange if the barrister's limited immunity from claims in negligence were not the same as when he argues an identical dispute before the Court. It would be stranger still if he were immune, and the arbitrator not.

[10] See per Lord Kilbrandon in *Arenson v Arenson* at 431.

[11] In *Jones v Department of Employment* [1988] 2 WLR 493 it was considered material that there was a right of appeal against the adjudicators of the public employee whose decision was said to have been negligent.

[12] A substantial proportion of arbitrations in England arise from quality disputes, and these are very often decided on a 'touch-see' basis, without any formal proceedings at all see p. 280, post. Furthermore, it must be doubted whether the kind of two-man maritime arbitration conducted by arbitrator/advocates would rank as an arbitration up to the moment of disagreement, if proposition 2 is correct: yet the umpire *would* be an arbitrator, and hence entitled to immunity.

immunity, then we can only say that there seems no reason why this should be so. Furthermore, arbitration in England takes such a wide variety of shapes, not consisting simply of a fully formalised process at one extreme and something which could hardly be described as any kind of 'process' at the other, but also embracing all sorts of intermediate ways of conducting the dispute, that it would be hard to find any reliable way of distinguishing those procedures which do, and those which do not, confer immunity of those taking part[13].

Next, we refer to proposition 3. This derives its force from the circumstance that if (as the courts are bound by *Sutcliffe v Thackrah* to accept) a person who is employed to make a fair, careful and binding decision as between two parties who have not yet fallen into dispute is not entitled to immunity, there seems no logical reason why the position should be different as regards someone who takes on the task after a dispute has come into existence. Whilst that is true, the distinction has two merits. The first is simplicity. It is much more easy to operate than one which is based on a classification of the procedure which is actually employed in the conduct of the reference. Second, the distinction has already been part of the law of arbitration for nearly a century, since many of the statutory provisions governing the supervisory, appellate and enforcement jurisdictions of the High Court in relation to arbitration matters apply only to 'arbitration agreements': viz. 'agreements to submit present or future differences to arbitration'[14]. If the existence of a 'difference' is a distinguishing feature of those cases where the State will lend its support to the mechanisms whereby one person by consent makes decisions binding on others, then there is perhaps some logic in looking for the same feature when deciding whether that person is entitled to share in the immunity possessed of officers of State when exercising their judicial functions[15].

Finally, there is the question of public policy. As often happens, this points in more than one direction. Much stress was laid, in the two House of Lords cases, on the modern tendency to ensure that one person who has suffered loss through the fault of another is not left without legal remedy. A powerful case can be made for applying this principle to the careless arbitrator, the more so since one of the most cogent answers, namely that the aggrieved party can put at least some of the arbitrator's mistakes to right by having the award set aside for error, or by causing a case to be stated, or by attacking the award on the ground of misconduct, has been weakened by the limitation the right of recourse to the High Court brought about by the 1979 Act[16]. There is, however, a strong argument to the opposite effect. For many years, the English law has set out to encourage the process of commercial arbitration, and has done so because that is what commercial men want; and the law has recognised that it is what they want, notwithstanding that they consent to place themselves in the hands of a

---

[13] Moreover, there are many disputes in which the choice of procedure is not made, even by implication, until after the arbitrator has been appointed and the reference has got under way. It would be rather odd if the process changed its character, and the arbitrator gained or lost immunity, according to procedural decisions taken on grounds of convenience alone.

[14] S. 32.

[15] If it is held that a judge is immune from suit, but an arbitrator is not, an interesting question will arise about the immunity of a judge-arbitrator.

[16] It will be weakened further if current trends in arbitration law are maintained.

tribunal[17] whose mistakes are either incapable of correction, or capable of it only by a cumbersome and erratic procedure. The possibility of a mistake for which there is no legal redress is a price which commercial men have, down the years, been prepared to pay in the interests of what they regard as a more flexible and practical method of resolving their disputes, a method which also has the particular virtue of finality. Very recently, the legislature has hastened to act in accordance with what it conceived to be the wishes of commercial men, by abolishing the pervading supervisory jurisdiction of the Court over the legal content of the award, which had hitherto been regarded as a first principle of the law of arbitration: again in the interests of finality. In the face of this movement towards a dissociation of the substantive issues in arbitrations from the judicial system[18], there would be little consistency in creating, on grounds of public policy, a new jurisdiction which would involve the Court not only in re-trying the case on the facts (an enquiry upon which the courts have for centuries refused to engage) but also in deciding what a careful arbitrator would under all the circumstances have decided, and what loss this has caused to the person aggrieved[19]. This might be simple enough when, as in the two House of Lords cases, the matter in issue lay within a narrow compass. But many arbitrations are vastly more complex than this. Moreover, questions of law might be involved, and these would be questions which the legislature has recently decided should not be re-opened by the parties in the High Court. English arbitration law has set off in a new direction, and to introduce a new cause of action at the present stage would ensure that English arbitration had the worst of all worlds[20]. We believe that public policy speaks against the law taking this step[1].

In spite of this, there are three situations in which a party may be entitled to limited redress from an arbitrator who has acted carelessly.

1   The award may be set aside if the arbitrator admits a mistake. The setting aside of the award destroys both the award of fees which it contains and the

---

[17] It was often said that the parties must take the arbitrator for better or for worse. This was not realistic, since in many cases the party did not 'take' the arbitrator at all. With a two-man tribunal, one arbitrator would be thrust on him by his opponent; and in the choice of umpire neither had a say. What the party 'took' was the system, not the individual arbitrator.

[18] Although leaving the parties with the benefits of association with that system on matters of procedure and enforcement.

[19] The Court might even be required to consider to what extent the negligence of the person aggrieved had contributed to an award being made against him, or whether the arbitrator could claim contribution from the party in whose favour he was wrongly made an award. The undesirability of double litigation, which would involve this kind of inquiry, was given as one of the reasons for the immunity of barristers in *Saif Ali v Sydney Mitchell & Co* [1980] AC 198.

[20] It is worthy of note that arbitrators are specifically excluded from the operation of s. 13 of the Supply of Goods and Services Act 1982 (implied obligation of reasonable care and skill): see SI 1985/1.

[1] We have not referred to another consideration of policy which is frequently called up, namely that nobody would become an arbitrator if he were liable to be sued. There is less force in this than formerly, because so many more arbitrators regard arbitrations as an appreciable source of income. But arbitration is still in some real degree honorary, and arbitrators might feel reluctant to take a reference in the face of a possible suit, but for two practical solutions – 1 the potential liability can be insured against, no doubt at the price of inflating the arbitrator's fee, and 2 the arbitrator can make it clear that he will act only on terms that he accepts no liability. A somewhat similar practice appears to have been usual in the eighteenth century, and we cannot see that the proper dignity of the arbitral process would be in any way reduced if it became the practice again: see *Lingood v Croucher* (1742) 2 Atk 395.

right to remuneration, and hence enables the party to recover any sums which he has paid on taking up the award[2].

2 A series of glaring errors committed by the arbitrator in the course of the reference might perhaps be regarded as a reason for granting leave under section 1 of the Act to revoke the authority of the arbitrator since it might justify the inference that he is liable to make further mistakes during the remainder of the reference. The courts have repeatedly stated that parties who choose an arbitrator must take him for better or for worse. This robust view is entirely justified so far as concerns the effects of the mistake by the arbitrator on the relations between the two parties. If they agree to follow the arbitrator's decision, they must do so, whether it is mistaken or not. It does not follow that a party, who may not even have had a say in choosing the arbitrator, must resign himself to the possibility of still further errors in the future[3]. If the Court could be induced to revoke the authority on this ground[4], the right to further remuneration would be lost, and the parties could recover back any sums already paid[5].

3 There may just be room for an argument that even in cases where the consideration cannot be said to have totally failed, the mishandling of the reference may form a partial defence to an arbitrator's claim for fees, and a ground for recovering at least part of any that have been paid. Two distinct situations must be regarded –

(i) the arbitrator's mistakes have cost the parties money, and they seek to recompense themselves by reducing his fee[6];

(ii) the parties seek to reduce the arbitrator's fee by that amount which is attributable to the fact that his lack of care has caused him to spend more time on the reference than would otherwise have been necessary.

The Court might well find it possible to devise a contractual or 'restitutory' form of action which would enable the parties to gain this limited relief. But it must be confessed that if there are good reasons of policy for protecting the arbitrator from claims in damages, based on his negligence, there seems no logical reason for not applying the same immunity to complaints raised by way of defence. The arbitrator either is or is not under a legally enforceable obligation of care. There seems no room for a middle solution.

No doubt an arbitrator/advocate will be entitled to immunity from claims in negligence at all stages of his participation in the reference: before disagreement, because he is acting in a judicial capacity, and afterwards because he has the privileges of an advocate[7].

---

[2] See pp. 245–246, post. By no means all mistakes are the result of negligence. The limited right of redress referred to in the text therefore depends not on the existence of a mistake, but on whether the injured party can demonstrate negligence.

[3] Where there are two arbitrators, each party will usually have chosen only one; and it is possible that neither party has been consulted about the choice of an umpire.

[4] The revocation would probably best be explained, not on the ground of the mistakes as such, but on the basis that they show the arbitrator to be incompetent, and hence unfit to act.

[5] See pp. 245–246, post.

[6] Such a defence is usually available under contracts for services: see the discussion of *Mondel v Steel* in *Henriksens Rederi A/S v Rolimpex THZ, The Brede* [1973] 2 Lloyd's Rep 333, [1974] QB 233. If the arbitrator's right to fees is regarded as arising otherwise than *ex contractu*, the Court might feel it necessary to consider the territory opened up by *NV Bureau Wijsmuller v Tojo Maru (Owners), The Tojo Maru* [1971] 1 Lloyd's Rep 341, [1972] AC 242.

[7] There seems no reason why an arbitrator/advocate presenting a case to the umpire should be liable for failing to act with care if a barrister addressing the same argument would not. See the observations of Lords Wilberforce and Diplock on the immunity attaching to solicitors acting as advocates, at pp. 215 and 224 in *Saif Ali v Sydney Mitchell & Co* [1980] AC 198.

2 Duty to proceed diligently

The Act provides a limited remedy in the event of failure to proceed with reasonable dispatch: a dilatory arbitrator can be removed under section 13(3), and thereby deprived of his remuneration[8]. It may also be possible to treat prolonged delay as evidence of refusal to proceed, thus enabling a party to make a fresh appointment without the intervention of the Court, under the powers conferred by section 7(a). It will, however, be better to rely on section 13(3)[9].

These statutory sanctions fall short of a complete remedy. They may suffice when the delay occurs at the outset, since an arbitrator appointed by way of replacement may be able to make up the lost time. But delay at a later stage may result in serious financial loss. If evidence has been taken or arguments adduced, the parties will have to pay for the process to be repeated. An important witness may die or his recollection may be dimmed during the period of delay, so that the party who had intended to call him may find his case seriously weakened. The delay during the reference will postpone the moment at which the award is made, and at which the claimant can collect the sums to which he is entitled; the recovery of interest may not be an adequate remedy.

These and similar consequences prompt the idea of an action in damages against the arbitrator for failing to proceed with reasonable dispatch. Two commentators[10] suggest that the arbitrator is at least under an implied obligation to make an award, on the basis that this is the counterpart of the implied promise to pay a fee[11]. For our part we doubt whether the Court would be prepared to grant a remedy. If considerations of policy prohibit claims against the arbitrator for carrying out his duties carelessly the same considerations would suggest that he should not be under threat of liability in damages if he carries them out slowly[12].

Whatever may be the position as regards the arbitrator's liability in damages, it is clear that his obligation to proceed with reasonable dispatch will not be enforced by specific performance. Nothing would be less conducive to the proper administration of justice than the conduct of a reference by a reluctant arbitrator.

3 Duty to act impartially

There is no doubt that an arbitrator owes a duty to act impartially[13], and that this duty is to some degree legally enforceable. If the arbitrator has shown partiality in making his award, this is a ground for setting it aside. If the lack of fairness is displayed in the course of the reference itself, the arbitrator's connection with the reference can be severed, through the exercise of the Court's

---

[8] Failure of the two arbitrators to give notice of disagreement, after such disagreement has taken place, brings into play the powers under s. 13(3): ibid.

[9] See pp. 531 et seq., post. A party who contemplates the employment of the power under s. 13(3) should warn the arbitrator, and give him an opportunity to accelerate.

[10] Hogg, p. 89; Russell (19th edn.) p. 128.

[11] Whilst at first sight it appears that the arbitrator must be under at least some obligation as regards performance, if there is to be any consideration for his undoubted right to receive remuneration, this overlooks the possibility that the relationship takes the shape of a unilateral contract, under which the parties say – 'If you choose to perform, we will remunerate you'.

[12] See *Lewin v Holbrook* (1843) 11 M & W 110; *Crawshay v Collins* (1818) 1 Swan 40.

[13] See Chapter 18, post.

powers under sections 1, 23(1) and 24(1). In such a situation, the Court would have little difficulty in ensuring that the arbitrator receives no further remuneration, and is required to hand back whatever he has already been paid. Furthermore, if the party goes so far as to complain that the partiality results from corruption or improper collusion with his opponent, he should join the arbitrator as respondent to any application to set aside the award[14]. If the allegation is substantiated, the Court will hold the arbitrator liable for the costs of the application[15].

Much less clear is the question whether, and if so in what circumstances, the arbitrator can ever be made liable in damages for failure to act impartially. The problem has never been elaborately discussed. Such few judicial pronouncements as exist were made whilst the courts were discussing the arbitrator's immunity from liability for negligence. The courts have said that an arbitrator is not liable if he acts 'honestly', 'not in bad faith', 'without fraud'. They thus assume that arbitrators can be held liable in damages, in the event of serious want of impartiality, but give no guidance as to how far this liability extends.

We believe that where the award is procured by inducements or improper pressure, the injured party must have an action against the arbitrator and the colluding party jointly[16]. The claim need not be based on any implied term. A common law claim for conspiracy to defraud will suffice. The injured party might also succeed in obtaining an account and an order for payment of any sums improperly received by the arbitrator[17].

Any such action should be preceded by or coupled with an application to set aside the award. The injured party's damages will then be measured in terms of the costs and time thrown away in the abortive arbitration[18].

Not every case where the arbitrator has failed to act fairly involves personal dishonesty of this extreme variety. Nor need there necessarily be any collusion by the successful party. The arbitrator's personal likes, dislikes and prejudices may make him incapable of forming a balanced opinion. Again, he may lack the energy, determination or time to tackle the issues in a proper spirit, and may decide them in a random manner. Or he may, without any ill intent or want of zeal, conduct the arbitration in a way which is seriously unfair to one side. In all these cases, a party may suffer real financial hardship, for which removal of the arbitrator and a possible repayment of his fee is insufficient redress. We believe that the Court would regard this as a misfortune which the injured party must bear without recompense. Just as he must, on the law as it stands at present, take the risk that the arbitrator will prove to be careless, so also must he take the risk that the person appointed will be biased, lazy or unjudicial.

---

[14] Cf. *Weise v Wardle* (1874) LR 19 Eq 171; *Lendon v Keen* [1916] 1 KB 994. Apart from any other consideration, it is fair that a person accused of serious impropriety should have the chance to appear and to make his own case at the hearing, rather than merely to give evidence for the other party.

[15] *Lendon v Keen*, supra.

[16] We do not think that Lord Salmon was contemplating claims for conspiracy when, in *Sutcliffe v Thackrah*, ante, he assimilated the arbitrator's position to that of the 'absolute immunity from any form of civil action' enjoyed by witnesses, lawyers, judges and jurors in court proceedings.

[17] By analogy with similar claims against agents who have taken secret profits.

[18] If the respondent has honoured a money award, and finds that (after discovery of the impropriety) he cannot recover from his opponent, he may claim damages which include the amount of his payment. This may raise problems, since he will be required to prove that had there been no collusion the award would have been in his favour.

C. OBLIGATIONS OF THE PARTIES TO THE ARBITRATOR

When considering whether an arbitrator is entitled to payment for his services, three situations must be discussed –

1 The arbitrator completes the reference and publishes an award.

2 The reference comes to an end before he has published an award.

3 The arbitrator completes the reference and publishes an award, but the award is invalid or is subsequently set aside.

1 Remuneration for a completed reference

(a) Arbitrator

Where the parties have expressly agreed with the arbitrator that he shall be paid, he is entitled upon publication of an award to bring an action on the agreement for the amount of his remuneration[19]. If the amount has been agreed in advance, either as a single inclusive fee, or as a rate per hour or per day[20], the arbitrator may recover accordingly. If not, the arbitrator is entitled to a reasonable fee. Even if the parties and the arbitrator do not expressly agree amongst themselves for payment, it may be possible to imply a promise from the terms of the agreement between the parties.

Even when the parties have not made any specific provision for the arbitrator to be paid, an arbitrator appointed to decide a commercial dispute has a right to be paid a reasonable fee[1]. This is so whether the arbitrator is a lawyer or a layman[2].

(b) Umpire

There is no doubt that the implied right of remuneration extends to an umpire

---

[19] *Roberts v Eberhardt* (1857) 3 CBNS 482, 28 LJCP 74; *Re Coombs and Freshfield and Fernley* (1850) 4 Exch 839; *Hoggins v Gordon* (1842) 3 QB 466.

[20] In the past, it was not uncommon to include a stipulation that the arbitrator would be remunerated, for the purpose of rebutting the presumption that the appointment was honorary, without a fee being fixed. Nowadays, this is not often found. It has now become more common to agree on a rate rather than an inclusive fee, and also to stipulate that the rate should be applied to all hours or days worked, and not simply to the time spent at the hearing itself: see also p. 236, post.

[1] This must be so, whatever theory is adopted concerning the relationship between the arbitrator and the parties. (Ss. 18(1) and 19(1) of the Act assume the existence of the right, but do not create it.) There is nineteenth century authority for the view that the office of arbitrator is honorary: see, for example, *Burroughes v Clarke* (1831) 1 Dowl 48 and the cases discussed in *Crampton and Holt v Ridley & Co* (1887) 20 QBD 48. This is now out of date. Very occasionally, a commercial man might agree to settle a dispute on a friendly basis without any expectation of payment; but in arbitration under modern conditions of business, payment is looked for (see *MacIntyre Bros v Smith* 1913 50 Sc LR 261; *Murray v North British Rly Co* 1900 7 SLT 341) either because the arbitrator takes on the reference as part of his professional practice, or because he could not afford to take off time from his work on a purely gratuitous basis.

[2] At one time it was considered that the implied right of remuneration applied only to lay arbitrators: see Hogg, p. 90. We submit that the presumption in favour of payment is stronger, not weaker, in the case of a lawyer. A businessman might consent to settle a dispute between colleagues as a matter of fraternal courtesy. A lawyer would do so as part of his practice.

who has entered on the reference and made an award. The position is less straightforward where, as not infrequently happens, the umpire takes part in the proceedings as chairman, even though the arbitrators have not yet disagreed. Logically, it is not easy to see how the parties can be under an implied duty to pay him for his services, or how the arbitrators could tax his fees as part of the costs of the award when publishing their own joint award, for he does not participate in it. Yet we believe that the Court would be most reluctant to deprive the umpire of a reasonable fee in these circumstances[3]. One possibility would be to stretch the meaning of 'costs of the award', in section 18(1) of the Act. Another would be to draw an analogy with expenses incurred by the arbitrator in taking legal advice or in hiring premises or shorthand writers, on the ground that the fees of the umpire are a disbursement reasonably incurred to further the proper conduct of the reference. Perhaps the simplest solution is to hold that if the parties expressly request the umpire to sit before he has entered on the reference, or acquiesce in his doing so the law will impose an obligation to remunerate him, and will include in that obligation a duty to honour an award of his fees[4].

(c) Enforcement of the right to remuneration

The arbitrator or umpire may enforce his right to remuneration in two ways –
   (i) By exercising a lien on the award for the amount of the fee, withholding delivery of the award until the fee has been paid.
   (ii) By bringing an action.

(i) Lien.   It is convenient to deal first with the lien over the award, since this is nowadays the almost universal method for securing payment. The existence of the lien has long been recognised[5]. In many instances nowadays, particularly in the case of long arbitrations, the arbitrator makes sure of his fees, either by causing them to be secured by a deposit or otherwise, or by requiring payments on account. In instances where this does not happen, or where the arbitrator is at all apprehensive about his remuneration being forthcoming, it is not uncommon for the arbitrator to calculate the amount of his fees and expenses; to tax them in the award if he desires to do so[6]; and then to write to the parties informing them that the award is ready for collection upon payment of the sum so arrived at. Where the award contains (as it should) a direction as to who should pay the costs of the award, it is common to include a further direction that if the successful party has paid to take up the award, the other party shall forthwith reimburse him for any costs for which such other party is liable under the award. This enables the successful party to proceed to summary enforcement in respect of his outlays.
   The lien extends to the out-of-pocket expenses of the arbitrator, such as the

---

[3] In *Appleton v Norwich Union Fire Insurance Society Ltd* (1922) 13 Ll L Rep 345 it seems to have been assumed by the Divisional Court that the umpire's fee could properly be included in a joint award. The practice is very common, and we have never heard of an objection.

[4] This expedient can be reconciled with any of the theories of the relationship between the arbitrator and the parties discussed above.

[5] For example in *Re Coombs and Freshfield and Fernley* (1850) 4 Exch 839; *Roberts v Eberhardt* (1857) 3 CBNS 482, 28 LJCP 74. The lien is assumed by s. 19(1) of the Act.

[6] See p. 237, post.

cost of hiring a room, travelling expenses, and employing a shorthand writer or legal adviser[7], since these form part of the costs of the award. Where the award is made by an umpire, the lien extends to the fees of the arbitrators as well as those of the umpire himself[8].

The lien cannot be circumvented by serving the arbitrator with a subpoena duces tecum to produce the award in an action based upon it[9].

(ii) Action. The question of enforcing the right to remuneration by means of an action is likely to arise in practice only where the exercise of the lien has been frustrated by the failure of the parties to take up the award[10]. This situation can occasionally arise where it has become clear during the course of the hearing that the arbitrator is likely to make an award in favour of the respondent. In such a situation, neither party has an incentive to take up and pay for the award. The respondent does not need the award himself, in order to avoid payment of the sum claimed[11]; and the claimant does not want to pay for an award which he believes will be unfavourable. The arbitrator is therefore left in the vexing position of having a lien which neither party will pay to lift. He has then no alternative but to abandon his fees, or bring an action[12].

The parties are jointly liable for the fees of the arbitrator[13], and where the tribunal consists of more than one arbitrator, each party is liable for the fees of the whole tribunal, and not merely those of the arbitrator whom he has himself appointed[14].

(d) Fees of arbitrator/advocate

Where the tribunal consists of two arbitrators, with an umpire to act if they disagree, it is common for the arbitrators to continue with the reference, each acting no longer as a judge but as advocate for the party who originally appointed him (see Chapter 19). This is a service for which the arbitrator/advocate expects to be paid. The umpire can and should[14] tax the arbitrator's fees as an advocate in the award, but do they form part of the costs of the reference or of the award? Logically, the answer should be that the costs fall to be taxed as part of the costs of the reference, since they represent a part of the

---

[7] See *Government of Ceylon v Chandris* [1963] 1 Lloyd's Rep 214, [1963] 2 QB 327.

[8] This was assumed in *Government of Ceylon v Chandris*, supra.

[9] This is so in the case of an insurance broker's lien; see Arnould, *Marine Insurance* (15th edn.) §190, note 43.

[10] As in *Willis v Wakeley Bros* (1891) 7 TLR 604.

[11] The respondent will need the award if he wishes to recover from the claimant the costs of the reference. If the claimant is abroad, or if for some other reason he cannot be compelled to pay the costs, the respondent may well write them off, rather than spend more money in paying for the award.

[12] This may inhibit the course of the reference. In Court, the judge can occasionally perform a useful service for the parties by making it clear which way his mind is working. This may induce a settlement beneficial to both, or at least prevent the advocate from labouring a point where he has already won. The arbitrator will often find it prudent to be more reticent.

[13] *Crampton and Holt v Ridley & Co* (1887) 20 QBD 48, per AL Smith J at 54; *Brown v Llandovery Terra Cotta etc Co Ltd* (1909) 25 TLR 625. We suggest that the liability is not only joint, but joint and several.

[14] See pp. 237–239, post.

expense incurred by the party presenting his case to the umpire[15]. This is not, however, how they are treated in practice. Even if the umpire splits the arbitrator's fee into two parts, attributable respectively to his functions as judge and as advocate, the total amount is invariably brought into the figure for which the arbitrator exercises his lien on the award. This is sensible, since unless the whole of the arbitrator's fee is collected for him by the umpire, he may find that if he has 'lost' the arbitration, he will never be paid for acting as advocate. Nevertheless, whilst the practice undoubtedly makes it easier for foreign parties to provide themselves with advocates, we doubt whether it is strictly correct.

(e) The level of remuneration

It is not usually practicable for the arbitrator to fix his fee in advance. He should, however, endeavour to do so if the arbitration is likely to be prolonged, because this will prevent the parties from suffering an unpleasant surprise when they are asked to take up the award. It is usually better for the parties to negotiate an hourly or daily fee, rather than a lump sum. This eliminates the risk to the arbitrator that the reference will take longer than expected, and it also gives the parties a clearer idea of why they are being asked to pay what may well appear, under modern conditions, to be a substantial sum. In addition, it eliminates some of the problems which arise if the reference terminates without an award being made.

Some trade associations and other bodies prescribe a scale of fees for arbitrations held under their auspices, which is related solely or in part to the amount in dispute. This is unsatisfactory since it may result in the arbitrator being paid less for a long and difficult hearing than for one which is more straightforward, albeit involving a larger sum.

If the amount of the fee has been expressly agreed with either of the parties in advance and in writing, the agreement is conclusive as regards that party[16]. Where no fee has been agreed, the arbitrator is entitled to a reasonable remuneration. No rigid rules can be laid down for ascertaining the amount of such a fee[17]. Where the arbitration is relatively short, the arbitrator will probably be able to arrive at the correct figure without elaborate calculation. If, however, he lacks the necessary experience, or if the reference has been prolonged, it will probably be better for the arbitrator to begin by fixing a daily or hourly rate for the task, which will take into account the arbitrator's skill,

---

[15] *Ellison v Ackroyd* (1850) 1 LM & P 806, 20 LJQB 193 decided that the advocate's fee forms part of the costs of the award. The decision to the contrary effect in *Government of Ceylon v Chandris* [1963] 1 Lloyd's Rep 214, [1963] 2 QB 327 is preferable.

[16] The agreement should be in writing, if the arbitrator wishes to exclude the possibility of a taxation under s. 19(1) : see s. 19(2).

[17] The argument that parties who choose to appoint distinguished men cannot complain if they are expensive (see *Appleton v Norwich Union Fire Insurance Society Ltd* (1922) 13 Ll L Rep 345; *Llandrindod Wells Water Co v Hawksley* (1904) 20 TLR 241) ought not to be carried too far. It no doubt has its place in the situation where the parties have adopted a form of arbitration in which it is usual to appoint arbitrators of high standing, as in many trade associations: *SN Kurkjian (Commodity Brokers) Ltd v Marketing Exchange for Africa Ltd (No 2)* [1986] 2 Lloyd's Rep 618. But in other situations, where there are two arbitrators, each party will have chosen only one, and may not have been consulted on the choice of an umpire or third arbitrator. If a distinguished man agrees to arbitrate in a small matter, he cannot necessarily expect his usual fee.

qualifications and status[18], and then multiply this rate by the length of time involved[19].

This arithmetical approach provides a useful starting point[20], but it does not always yield the correct answer. Thus, for example, a short and difficult case involving a large sum might yield a small fee taxed on a time basis; and the arbitrator would, we believe, be justified in departing from a strict arithmetical basis to allow for the special responsibility and skill required. The arbitrator should therefore examine his calculated figure to see whether it needs adjustment to take account of other factors, such as –

(i) the complexity of the dispute and the difficulty or novelty of the questions involved;

(ii) the skill, specialised knowledge and responsibility required of the arbitrator;

(iii) the number and importance of the documents studied;

(iv) the place and circumstances in which the reference takes place;

(v) the importance of the dispute to the parties;

(vi) the value of the property involved, or the amount of the sum in issue[1].

If an umpire decides to tax and settle the fees of arbitrator/advocates, he should distinguish between that part of the fee which is referable to the judicial function before disagreement, and that part which is referable to the arbitrator's services as advocate. The purpose is to enable the Taxing Master, if the matter proceeds to taxation in the High Court, to distinguish between the part of the fees which constitute costs of the reference, and those which are costs of the award[2].

(f) Fixing a reasonable fee

Where the parties have not expressly agreed the fee to be paid, a reasonable fee must be ascertained in accordance with the principles indicated above. This may be done in the following ways –

(1) The arbitrator himself 'taxes or settles' the fee in the course of his award, pursuant to his powers under section 18(1) of the Act.

(2) The arbitrator does not tax the fees himself, but leaves them to be taxed in the High Court, under section 18(2) of the Act.

---

[18] A reasonable rate of remuneration is not the same thing as the going rate, although that is a relevant consideration if there is one. Nor does a reasonable rate depend upon the personal circumstances of the arbitrator, such as his remuneration from other sources, or upon the question whether he retains the fee or passes it on to his employer: *SN Kurkjian (Commodity Brokers) Ltd v Marketing Exchange for Afjica Ltd (No 2)* supra. This case illustrates not only the difficulty of arriving at a reasonable remuneration but also the fact that what may be appropriate for one type of arbitration (such as a tribunal drawn from senior members of a commodity association) is not necessarily appropriate for another (such as a tribunal consisting of professional maritime or construction arbitrators).

[19] The arbitrator's fees need not be limited to the frugal allowance usually made by Taxing Masters in a High Court taxation: *Appleton v Norwich Union*, supra. The same principle probably applies to the fees of the arbitrator/advocate when being taxed as between himself and parties, though not when taxed as between the parties themselves.

[20] And one which the arbitrator will be prudent to adopt in his own interests if the fee is large enough to raise any possibility of challenge.

[1] This list is based on the Supreme Court Taxing Rules.

[2] The duty of the umpire to separate the fees in this way was laid down in clear terms by Megaw J in *Government of Ceylon v Chandris*, ante, but many umpires still fail to comply.

(3) The party who takes up the award pays into Court the sum demanded by the arbitrator as a condition of releasing his lien, and then has the fees taxed in the High Court under section 19(2) of the Act.

The first method, namely taxation by the arbitrator himself, is the one most commonly used in practice. Section 18(1) empowers – but does not require – the arbitrator to tax to settle the amount of the costs of the award[3]. The word 'costs' has been held to include, not only the arbitrator's out-of-pocket expenses, but also his remuneration[4]. What is meant by the words 'or settle' is not clear[5].

When adopting this procedure, the arbitrator decides on the amount of the appropriate fee; states in the award that he taxes the fee at that amount; and orders by whom the fee is to be paid. The taxation must be expressed as such in the award itself. It is not enough simply to make a demand for fees as a condition for the release of the award[6]. Where the umpire publishes the award, he is empowered to tax the fees of the arbitrators, as well as his own fees.

The power conferred by section 19(1) extends only to references conducted pursuant to 'an arbitration agreement'. Accordingly, there is no power to tax the costs of the award under an oral submission.

The taxation of the arbitrators' fees by an umpire is a delicate matter. Any suggestion of over-charging generates strong emotions. Yet the umpire is not allowed simply to accept the figures put forward by the arbitrators. He must 'tax and settle' them: i.e. he must apply his own independent mind and judgment as to the fees demanded and the work done in order to be satisfied that they are fair and reasonable, bearing in mind the interests of the party who will have to pay them, as well as the legitimate interests of the arbitrator[7]. He need not go behind any agreement which has been made as to their amount but he must satisfy himself that the agreement has been made by someone with authority to bind the parties. The 'opposing' arbitrator does not have implied authority to this effect[7].

Taxation by the arbitrator or umpire of his own fees is equally delicate, since he is acting as judge in his own cause[8]. He must somehow arrive at a fee which not only is, but appears to be, fair to both himself and the parties[9].

The embarrassments and potential conflicts of interest which may arise where the fees are taxed in the award have led the courts to suggest[10] that it may be convenient for the tribunal to abstain from taxing the costs itself, leaving them

---

[3] The power may be excluded by an express provision in the arbitration agreement: s. 18(1). The power is never excluded in practice, except in cases where the agreement incorporates by reference a scale of fees.

[4] *Re Stephens, Smith & Co and Liverpool and London and Globe Insurance Co's Arbitration* (1892) 36 Sol Jo 464. This case was decided before the 1934 Act added the equivalent of s. 19(1), where the word 'fees' is used.

[5] They have always formed part of the statutory powers.

[6] *Re Prebble and Robinson* [1892] 2 QB 602.

[7] *Government of Ceylon v Chandris*, ante.

[8] Before the 1889 Act created a statutory power to tax the costs of the award, there was doubt as to whether the arbitrator had any jurisdiction to do so: contrast *Re Coombs and Freshfield and Fernley* (1850) 4 Exch 839; *Roberts v Eberhardt* (1857) 3 CBNS 482, 28 LJCP 74; *Fernley v Branson* (1851) 20 LJQB 178. Probably the better view is that there was such a jurisdiction. The position at common law is still relevant in the exceptional cases where the reference takes place otherwise than pursuant to an 'arbitration agreement'.

[9] The task was described by Donaldson J in *Rolimpex Centrala Handlu Zagranicznego v Haji E Dossa & Sons Ltd* [1971] 1 Lloyd's Rep 380 at 384 as being 'obviously as difficult as it is invidious'.

[10] In *Government of Ceylon v Chandris*, ante, and *Rolimpex v Haji E Dossa*, supra.

to be taxed in the High Court under section 18(2) or, in appropriate cases, under section 19(1). The attractions of this course are undeniable, but arbitrators should bear in mind that a taxation in the High Court involves delay and expense to the arbitrators themselves[11] as well as to the parties. The arbitrators may therefore think it best to omit a taxation only where[12] –

(i) the umpire feels that the sums claimed by the arbitrators may be on the high side, but either wishes to avoid the embarrassment of taxing them down, or has insufficient information on which to base as assessment;

(ii) the arbitrator considers that a fee which would fairly reflect his own skill and labours may seem to the parties unduly high having regard to (for example) the modest amount in dispute.

(g) Remedies where fees excessive

The remedies open to a party who considers that the fees claimed by the arbitrator are excessive depend upon whether or not the fees have been taxed in the award.

If the fees have not been taxed in the award, but are simply demanded by the arbitrator after the award has been delivered, the party can simply refuse to pay them, thus enforcing the arbitrator into a taxation under section 18(2). This situation very rarely arises, since the arbitrator will almost always exercise a lien by refusing to deliver the award except on payment of the fees demanded. In such a case, the complaining party may apply to the High Court under section 19(1) to pay the sums demanded into Court, against an Order that the arbitrator shall deliver the award to the payor[13]. The fees are then taxed by the Taxing Master. Such part as is reasonable is paid out to the arbitrator, and the balance is returned to the applicant. This procedure does not, however, apply if the fees have been fixed by a written agreement between the parties and the arbitrator.

The Court has not yet had occasion to deal with a case where the arbitrator does not tax the fees in the award, but takes a payment in advance on account of fees, and therefore has no need to exercise a lien. In such a case, there seems no obstacle to a taxation under section 18(2)[14], and no doubt the Court would find some quasi-contractual form of action enabling the parties to recover the excess.

Where the arbitrator has taxed and settled his fees, the position is different. Here there is no room to a taxation under section 18(1)[15]. The parties must therefore find some other way of persuading the Court to review the arbitrator's

---

[11] Since the arbitrators will no doubt wish to exercise their right to be presented on the taxation: see *Government of Ceylon v Chandris*, ante.

[12] Notwithstanding the observations of Donaldson J in *Rolimpex v Haji E Dossa*, ante, at 385, we doubt whether many awards omit a taxation.

[13] As an alternative, the complaining party may bring an action against the arbitrator for the return of the excess, on the ground that it was paid under duress: *Llandrindod Wells Water Co v Hawksley* (1904) 20 TLR 241; *Roberts v Eberhardt* (1857) 3 CBNS 482, 28 LJCP 74; *Fernley v Branson* (1851) 20 LJQB 178. The action is much less attractive than an application under s. 19.

[14] This was assumed to be so in *Rolimpex v Hadji E Dossa*, ante.

[15] This was assumed to be the case in *Rolimpex v Hadji E Dossa*, ante, and in the textbooks, presumably on the basis that by including a taxation in the award the arbitrator 'otherwise directs', for the purposes of s. 18(2).

taxation. One limited procedure for a direct review appears[16] to be created by section 19(1), in the case where the party pays money into Court to lift the arbitrator's lien: see above. Here, the Taxing Master carries out a fresh taxation and apportions to the arbitrator only such money as is reasonable. Unfortunately, this procedure is not available in cases where – (a) the arbitrator has taken payment in advance, and hence does not need to exercise a lien or (b) the party who complains of the excess is not the party who takes up the award[17].

If the situation is one in which a review under section 19 is not feasible, the complainant must find a way to nullify the taxation in the award, so that he can either resist a claim by the arbitrator or (if he has paid in advance) bring an action to recover the excess. For this purpose, he must attack the award itself, alleging that the charges are so excessive that the arbitrator commits misconduct by insisting upon them; and he must then induce the Court either to set the award aside, wholly or in part, or to remit the award to the arbitrator for reconsideration of the award relating to costs. There is no doubt that the Court has jurisdiction to make an order on these lines, since the discretion under section 18(1) is one which must be judicially exercised in good faith[18]. Thus, if the Court is satisfied from the size of the sum awarded, or from other evidence, that the arbitrator has either put his own interests before those of the parties, or has misconceived the basis on which he should carry out the taxation, there is misconduct which justifies the remission or setting aside of the award. Consideration of this issue is not the same as re-taxation under section 19. The Court does not substitute its own view for that of the arbitrator. In order to make good an allegation of misconduct, very clear evidence is required[19], and it is not enough to show that the amount demanded is more than the Court would have considered appropriate if it has been approaching the matter afresh.

The nature of the remedy granted will depend upon the degree of the misconduct which has occurred. If the facts are so extreme as to show that the arbitrator has acted dishonestly, the Court may conclude that he cannot be trusted to have decided any part of the dispute in a proper manner, and hence will set aside the entire award[20]. In less extreme cases, the Court will set aside the part of the award which related to costs, leaving the remainder to stand. Finally, where the Court simply forms the view that the abitrator may have mistaken the principles which he should apply, the award may be remitted for

---

[16] The language of s. 19(1), read literally, makes the procedure applicable to all cases where the lien is exercised, including those where the award contains a taxation. Donaldson J assumed this to be the correct reading in *Rolimpex v Hadji E Dossa*, ante. See also Hogg, p. 90. It may, however, be noted that ss. 18 and 19 were not a homogeneous piece of drafting. S. 19 was introduced by the 1934 Act, and it may be questioned whether the procedure under that section was intended to introduce an appeal from the otherwise conclusive taxation created by the 1889 Act. There seems no logic in having a right of appeal where the arbitrator exercises a lien, but not otherwise; and even then the appeal is available only to the party who has paid the fees.

[17] Donaldson J pointed out this gap in the procedure in *Rolimpex v Hadji E Dossa*, ante. The point is of some practical importance. The party who takes up the award is very often the party who believes that he has won, and that accordingly it will be his opponent who must ultimately bear the costs. A party in such a position has little incentive to incur the trouble and expense of proceeding under s. 19.

[18] *Appleton v Norwich Union*, ante, at 347.

[19] *British Metal Corpn Ltd v Ludlow Bros (1913) Ltd* (1938) 61 Ll L Rep 351 at 359.

[20] It appears to have been assumed in *Re Prebble and Robinson* [1892] 2 QB 602 at 604 and *Appleton v Norwich Union*, ante, that such an order could properly be made. Very strong facts would be required to justify putting the parties to the hardship of beginning the entire reference afresh.

reconsideration of the taxation[1]. This gives the arbitrator the choice between retaining the figure as originally taxed, substituting a new figure, of deleting the taxation altogether, and thus opening the way for a taxation in the High Court under section 18(2). Alternatively the award may be set aside so far as it comprises the offending taxation, so that the costs must be taxed in the High Court if the challenge to them is maintained[2].

If a party considers that the fee charged by the arbitrator is excessive, he should not immediately invoke the help of the Court. He should first invite the arbitrator to explain how the fee was calculated. He may find on reflection that the explanation is convincing. If he does not, then the explanation should be laid before the Court as part of his evidence on the application for relief. If the arbitrator declines to explain how his fee is calculated, or gives insufficient particulars, this may lead the Court to infer that the discretion has not been properly exercised[3].

If the party decides to carry his complaint to the High Court, he should serve notice of proceedings on the arbitrator. The latter is entitled to be heard on any taxation under section 19(1)[4], and even if he is not strictly entitled as of right to be present on an application to set aside or remit the award of costs, justice demands that he should be given an opportunity to appear and be represented in Court.

(h) Securing the arbitrator's fee

Most commercial arbitrators are busy men. Even if they are not amongst the small number of full-time arbitrators, they cannot afford to take time off from their business or profession to conduct a reference unless they are properly paid. Such people may suffer serious financial hardship, if a long reference stops short before reaching an award, or if the parties cannot or will not pay for the award once made. This has led arbitrators in recent years to look for means of securing their fees. This security may take the shape of a bank guarantee, a deposit with a neutral party (such as the trade association under whose auspices the arbitration is held), or a payment on account to the arbitrator himself.

No problems arise if the arbitrator realises from the outset that the reference is one which calls for security. He can with entire propriety make it a condition of accepting the burden of the reference that the parties shall provide him with adequate security. If they do not agree, he can refuse to act, and the parties can appoint someone else.

It is when the arbitration is already under way that problems may arise. The reference may develop into something on a larger scale than the arbitrator had been led to believe; there may be signs that the parties are contemplating the settlement of their disputes without providing for his fees; or he may begin to have doubts as to the readiness or ability of the parties to pay for any award which may be made. Where difficulties arise in this way, a distinction must be drawn between security for the reimbursement of the arbitrator's out-of-pocket

---

[1] As in *Government of Ceylon v Chandris*, ante.
[2] As in *SN Kurkjian (Commodity Brokers) v Marketing Exchange for Africa (No 2)* [1986] 2 Lloyd's Rep 618. A remission in this case might well have led to further embarrassment.
[3] See *Government of Ceylon v Chandris* [1963] 1 Lloyd's Rep 214, [1963] 2 QB 327.
[4] Ibid., sub-s. (4).

expenses, and security for the enforcement of his claim for fees. We believe that it can never be objectionable to demand security for expenses, and to enforce the demand by the only sanction at the arbitrator's disposal, namely a refusal to continue with the reference. When the arbitrator hires a room for the hearing, or employs a shorthand writer or legal adviser, he does so for the benefit of the parties, and they should be prepared to assure him that he will not be left to bear the cost. The position is different where the arbitrator wishes to ensure that he will be remunerated for the work which he has done. Whether he is justified in refusing to continue with the reference if a request for security is refused will depend on the circumstances of the case, and in particular on the stage which the arbitration has reached. If nothing has so far happened apart from routine interlocutory hearings, there is nothing morally or legally objectionable in the arbitrator refusing to act, since the proceedings can be transferred without difficulty to another arbitrator. If, on the other hand, the parties have already adduced evidence or argument, they will suffer hardship is they have to begin again with a new arbitrator. In such a situation, even if, as may well be the case, the parties have no legal ground of redress[5], the arbitrator ought not to take such a drastic step. Indeed, he may have only himself to blame for his difficulty. By the time the pleadings have closed and discovery has been completed, he should be able to form his own estimate of the likely duration of the hearing. If he concludes that the matter is so substantial that he does not wish to go ahead without security, he should say so then, and not as a time when it is too late to find someone else to act.

There is one further sanction which may be available to the arbitrator. The giving of reasons pursuant to the 1979 Act may involve him in a considerable extra expense, by way of employing shorthand writers at the hearing or legal advisers afterwards to help him with drafting the award. He may properly require security for the extra expenses to which he will be put, as a condition of consenting to give reasons[6]. He should, however, be careful not to claim an extravagant sum, or to use this sanction as a means for exacting security for his fees as a whole. Otherwise[6], he may find that his demand is treated as a refusal to give reasons, and is made the basis of an application to the Court under section 1 of the 1979 Act[7].

2 Remuneration for an uncompleted reference

Thus far, we have discussed the rights of the arbitrator to be paid for his services in completing the reference and publishing a valid award. We must now consider the very common situation in which the reference never proceeds to an award. The reported cases provide little guidance on this topic, and it is difficult to deduce the rules which should be applied from first principles, since the

---

[5] See p. 244, post.

[6] Even the making of a reasonable demand could be treated as a refusal, but the powers of the Court are discretionary, and in ordering reasons the Court would have power to impose a condition that the demand should be met.

[7] See *Rolimpex v Hadji E Dossa*, ante. The Court did not have occasion to consider whether, on the facts, there was anything excessive in the demand, but the case does not produce a useful illustration of the embarrassments which a party may suffer if met with a demand for security at a late stage of the reference.

theoretical basis of the relationship between the parties and the arbitrators is not clear.

(a) Arbitrator not involved in termination

The most straightforward situation is one in which no lump sum fee has been agreed, and the reference has come to an end for reasons which have nothing to do with the arbitrator. The plaintiffs may have agreed to compromise their dispute, so that there is no need to continue with the reference. Or perhaps the claimant has ceased to pursue his claim, because he can see that he is likely to lose, or that his opponent will not satisfy any award that may be made. We believe that the Court will have little difficultly in deciding that in such a case the arbitrator in entitled to be paid for the work which he has done: either on the basis of an implied promise, or a 'restitutory' claim, or on a right simply resulting from the arbitrator's status as such – depending upon what view is adopted of the relationship created by his appointment and agreement to act[8].

The position is not so clear where the parties have agreed a lump sum fee in advance. Since the fee must be taken to contemplate that the remuneration includes an element attributable to the reaching of a decision and the preparation of an award, the arbitrator can scarcely be entitled to recover it in full, if the reference has ended prematurely, for whatever reason[9]. Furthermore, if the relationship is correctly analysed in terms of a contract, the doctrine of entire contracts places an obstacle in the way of a recovery even of remuneration for such work as was actually done[10]. This objection does not apply if the right to remuneration is from the outset restitutionary in character (albeit quantified by prior agreement), or if it derives directly from the arbitrator's status as such: for in either event the way is open to the Court to hold that the arbitrator is entitled to such fee as is reasonable in the changed circumstances.

Apart from termination by the consent of the parties, the arbitrator's part in the reference may be brought to an end by the Court: either by revoking the authority of the arbitrator, or by removing him, or by ordering that the arbitration agreement shall cease to have effect[11]; or by enjoining the parties from proceeding further with the arbitration. In many cases the orders will be made because the arbitrator has been in some way at fault. But this will not always be so. For example the Court may simply decide that circumstances are such that it would be more satisfactory to proceed with a tribunal differently constituted, or that the dispute should be transferred to the Court, or that the dispute should no longer be pursued at all. If, in such a case the Court foresaw a real risk that the arbitrator might be left with no effective means of recovering payment for work already done, it would have power to make it a condition of granting relief that proper arrangements should be made to secure his position.

These are all cases in which the arbitrator seeks to be paid for work done before the reference came to an end. It is, however, possible that the arbitrator

---

[8] See pp. 220–223, ante.

[9] For the reasons discussed in the text to note 13 post, p. 245.

[10] *Cutter v Powell* (1795) 6 Term Rep 320. Perhaps the answer would be to treat the settlement of the dispute as an event frustrating the contract, leaving open a restitutionary claim. But even this runs into difficulties with *Cutter v Powell*. Conceivably, the Law Reform (Frustrated Contracts) Act 1943 could be invoked.

[11] There will not be many instances of these orders where the arbitrator is not is some way at fault.

will look for more than this. He may argue that but for the premature termination of the reference he would have been entitled to earn additional fees, and that the loss of fees is something for which he should be compensated. Such an argument may be isolated cases reflect a genuine hardship. The arbitrator may have been asked to set aside several weeks for the hearing. If the dispute is settled immediately beforehand, the arbitrator may not be able to fill the space with sufficiently remunerative work. The Court would no doubt feel sympathy in such a case, but it is unlikely to provide redress. A claim in damages would be hopeless, for even if the relationship could properly be explained in terms of contract, it would be absurd to contend that the parties committed a breach by failing to continue with the reference of a dispute which for practical purposes had ceased to exist: for example, because it was settled or because in the exercise of a statutory or common law jurisdiction the court had prevented it from being pursued. Nor is the proposition more attractive if the relationship is one of status, rather than contract. Public policy demands that the arbitrator should be paid for what he has done, but not that he should be paid for what he has not done. Indeeed, considerations of policy point the other way, for the Court would not wish to confer on the arbitrator a right to compensation, the existence of which might inhibit the freedom of the parties to settle the dispute as they think best, or to invoke the supervisory jurisdiction of the Court when circumstances so required. Much the better view, we suggest, is to treat the risk of a settlement as an occupational risk of arbitrating[12]. If a dispute is so large and the potential hardship to the arbitrator so great the risk appears unacceptable, there is nothing to prevent the arbitrator from stipulating as a condition for agreeing to accept the appointment that he shall be recompensed for keeping his time available.

(b) Arbitrator involved in termination but without fault

Sometimes an arbitrator's participation in a reference may terminate prematurely on grounds for which he is responsible, although not morally to blame. For example, he may die, or become incapable of acting, or resign with the consent of the parties. In such a case the question may arise whether he is entitled to payment for the work which he has done. The arbitrator could argue that if, as we have suggested, there is a right to payment in cases where the reference stops short as the result of an act by the parties, this must entail that the remuneration is regarded as a reward for work done, not for benefit conferred; and if this is so then the position must be the same whatever the reason for the curtailment of the reference. The arbitrator has, so it would be argued, a vested right to remuneration which is not lost if his participation in the reference comes to an end. We doubt whether the logic can be carried through in this way. Somebody has to suffer in this situation, and the distribution of the loss is a matter of policy. We suggest that it should fall on the arbitrator, on the ground that the loss of the fee due to reasons concerned with himself is a risk which the

---

[12] As it is for the lawyer.

arbitrator can reasonably be taken to have assumed, when he agreed to take on the reference[13].

(c) Termination through fault of the arbitrator

If we are right in the view expressed in the preceding paragraphs, there is no difficultly in concluding that the arbitrator forfeits his remuneration if his part in the arbitration comes to an end through removal or revocation of authority on the ground of his own fault[14].

3 Remuneration where the award is invalid

It sometimes happens that an arbitrator completes the reference and publishes a document which has the appearance of an award, and yet proves afterwards to have no legal effect. This can happen in three ways – (a) because the entire reference is from the outset a nullity; (b) because a valid reference is followed by an award which is a nullity or is set aside by the Court; and (c) because an award has to be remitted to the arbitrator for reconsideration.

(a) Reference a nullity

The reference may be a complete nullity from the outset if, for example, there is no binding agreement to arbitrate; or if the arbitrator lacks the necessary qualifications; or if the dispute referred lies outside the scope of the agreement to arbitrate. All the proceedings in a purported reference of this kind are no more than empty gestures. Is the arbitrator entitled to be paid for his part in them? Plainly, he cannot recover through the medium of his award, for that has no legal existence. Nor does he possess the right of recovery which, we have suggested, ordinarily stems from the relationship between the parties and himself, in his capacity as arbitrator: for no such relationship has ever come into existence. There may, however, be circumstances in which the arbitrator has a restitutory claim, based on the fact that the useless work was carried out at the request of the parties[15]. Such a remedy will not, however, always be available. For example if the arbitrator is not qualified to act, but the parties are unaware of this, it cannot be postulated that the request to act was made on the unspoken assumption that he would be paid for his work, whether he was qualified or not.

(b) Award a nullity

The position is not the same where the reference is valid, but where the

---

[13] But if he has in fact already paid on account, at the time of the termination, we cannot see the Court straining to find a way in which the parties can recover what has been paid – for by consenting to remuneration on this basis, they can be regarded as having taken on themselves the risk of premature termination.

[14] No inference can be drawn from the presence in the Act of one specific instance of forfeiture (s. 13(3): delay). The Act does not purport to contain a complete code. The case for refusing any remuneration in such a situation is made stronger by the absence of any convincing way in which the parties can recompense themselves by cross-claim or 'abatement' for the losses which they have suffered: see pp. 224–230, ante.

[15] Or one of them, where the arbitrator was appointed by one party.

arbitrator makes an award which either is void or is set aside by the Court. Here, the failure by the arbitrator to perform the service which lies at the heart of his right to be rewarded, namely the publication of an effective award, lies within his own sphere of influence, and the same result should be reached as in the case where the reference stops short of an award because of an event for which the arbitrator is responsible[16]. But the arbitrator's fee is not necessarily lost beyond recall, for even if the award is declared void or is set aside he may remain seized of the reference, and he may rescue his remuneration by putting right his mistake and making another, and this time valid, award.

(c) Award remitted

Finally, there is the question of the arbitrator's fee when the Court remits the award to him for reconsideration. Unlike a void award, or one which is set aside, the award remains intact, but it merely revised as may be necessary. The consideration for the fee therefore cannot be said to have failed. On the other hand, if the amount of work done by the arbitrator has been increased as a result of his own default – for example, if his misconduct has made it necessary to have a further hearing – we believe that the Court would devise some way of making sure that his extra work did not attract an extra fee.

---

[16] See p. 245, ante.

CHAPTER 18

Capacity, qualifications and impartiality of the arbitrator

A. CAPACITY AND QUALIFICATIONS

An arbitrator cannot be validly appointed unless he possesses the qualifications required by the common law and by the arbitration agreement. Consequently –

1 He must have the capacity which the law requires of every person who assumes the office of arbitrator.

2 He must possess all the qualifications, and none of the disqualifications, prescribed by the arbitration agreement.

3 He must be free from any such connection with the parties, or with the subject matter of the dispute, as would make him, or appear to make him, incapable of acting in an impartial manner.

Although these three requirements are commonly treated together, as aspects of the same problem, they are not all of the same character. The second is a true qualification. If this requirement is not satisfied, the person appointed is not in truth an arbitrator at all, and has no power to make a binding order or award. The first and third requirements are of a different kind. Failure to satisfy them does not make the appointment a nullity. It simply gives the Court power, if it thinks fit, to ensure that the arbitrator is no longer left in charge of the reference.

1 Capacity to arbitrate

Any natural person is capable in law of being the subject of a valid appointment as arbitrator, and of publishing a binding award. If the parties choose to have their disputes resolved by a person who is not equal to the task, they must abide by their choice. Extreme youth or age, mental or physical infirmity, do not deprive an arbitrator of the power to act, or render his award a nullity[1].

On the other hand, the person appointed as arbitrator must be a natural person. A limited company, possessing only corporate personality, cannot validly be appointed[2]. Nor can a group of people, such as a partnership firm, be nominated to act an an arbitrator[3].

---

[1] The law was not always stated thus. See the citations in Russell (19th edn.) p. 112 from the old texts; and also Kydd, who classed married women with villeins and serfs as persons who could not issue a valid award. We doubt whether the Court would now approach problems of incapacity in terms of formal validity, since this leaves the Court with no discretion. It is more likely to regard incapacity, if sufficiently serious, as grounds for using its discretionary powers to intervene in the reference.

[2] We can cite no authority for this proposition, but it must surely be corect. Arbitration agreements sometimes provide for a reference to a particular trade association. Where the association is an incorporated body, it is usual to read the agreement as if the reference were to persons nominated by the association from amongst its members.

[3] A group of people can, of course, be appointed to act as a complete tribunal, if that is what the

As previously stated, incapacity on the part of an arbitrator does not deprive him of jurisdiction; but it does not follow that a party is without remedy if the arbitrator proves completely unable to conduct the reference. The Court may, in appropriate cases, be able to order replacement under section 10 of the Act, removal under section 23, or may grant leave to revoke the authority of the arbitrator under section 1. Moreover, a party who finds that the reference is making no satisfactory headway because the arbitrator is incapable of carrying it further may have remedies by way of injunction or concurrent action[4].

2 Qualifications required by agreement

Commercial contracts frequently provide that the arbitrator shall possess certain stipulated qualifications. These may be expressed in a positive or a negative form. In some instances, the contract states positive qualifications: i.e. it stipulates those characteristics which the appointed arbitrator must possess. These may be expressed in precise terms: for example, the arbitrator may have to be a member of a specified trade association[5]. On other occasions, the qualifications are less specific: for example, the arbitrator may have to be chosen from persons engaged in a particular trade[6]. Sometimes again, the qualification is expressed in very general terms: for example the arbitrator is to be a 'merchant' or a 'commerical man'[7] or an 'indifferent person'[8]. Provided that the language in which the qualification is defined is sufficiently clear to enable the parties and the Court to tell whether or not a particular person is validly

---

agreement requires. A reference to the committee of a trade association has been assumed in several cases to be valid; but it should, we submit, be construed as referring to the committee as constituted at the moment of the appointment, not to the committee 'for the time being'. The constitution of the tribunal should remain the same throughout, for it is the duty of each arbitrator to adjudicate upon the whole of the dispute.

4 For a discussion of these and other remedies, see Chapter 31, post.

5 See, for example, *Jungheim, Hopkins & Co v Foukelmann* [1909] 2 KB 948. Often, the contract requires the arbitrator to be appointed from a panel of arbitrators maintained by a trade association: see *Oakland Metal Co Ltd v Benaim & Co Ltd* [1953] 2 Lloyd's Rep 192, [1953] 2 QB 261; *MacLeod Ross & Co Ltd v Cradock Manners & Co Ltd* [1954] 1 Lloyd's Rep 258 (the arbitrators were, but the umpire was not, required to be members of the panel).

6 See *Oakland Metal v Benaim*, supra; *The Myron v Tradax Export* [1969] 1 Lloyd's Rep 411. It is submitted that 'engaged' means 'currently engaged'. In *The Myron* at 415, Donaldson J stated that a person who is actively engaged throughout all available working hours in maritime arbitration is regarded in practice as being engaged in the shipping trade. Those who are engaged for only part of the time, such as the lawyers who regularly act as Baltic arbitrators, presumably do not qualify. See also *Royal Commission on Sugar Supply v Trading Society Kwik-Hoo-Tong* (1922) 11 Ll L Rep 163, where the arbitrator was to be a 'seller'.

7 The meaning of 'merchant' is not difficult to express. 'Commercial man' presents more problems. The general purpose of such a stipulation is plainly to ensure that the tribunal shall consist of men with a 'feel' for trade, rather than professional people, who are assumed to have a less informed and practical approach to business matters. But it is not easy to say where the line should be drawn. The curious may find eight possible interpretations of the expression stated in argument in *Rahcassi Shipping Co SA v Blue Star Line Ltd* [1967] 2 Lloyd's Rep 261 at 264. Roskill J declined to attempt a definition. In *Pando Compania Naviera SA v Filmo SAS* [1975] 1 Lloyd's Rep 560, [1975] QB 742, it was held that a full-time maritime arbitrator who had retired many years earlier from practice as a solicitor was a 'commercial man' under a charter party arbitration clause.

8 *Ewart & Son Ltd v Sun Insurance Office* (1925) 21 Ll L Rep 282 (assessors appointed as arbitrators in insurance dispute not disqualified by having previously acted for the respondents).

appointed, provisions of this nature are entirely legitimate and will be enforced by the courts.

The qualification may also be expressed in a negative form: characteristics are designated which the appointed arbitrator is not to possess. Sometimes the contract provides that no person shall act who has an interest in the goods or in the transaction[9]. Again, commercial contracts occasionally stipulate that the arbitrator 'shall not be a lawyer'[10].

Where the appointed arbitrator does not possess the required qualifications, his appointment is nugatory and any award which he may make is void. By their agreement to arbitrate, the parties contracted to honour an award made by a duly qualified arbitrator; but they promised nothing with regard to the award of anyone else[11]. Unlike the position where the complaint is of incapacity or bias, the Court has no discretion to uphold an appointment or award where the arbitrator lacks the qualifications stipulated in the contract. Subject to waiver, it has no choice but to treat the proceedings and the award as void[12].

It follows that the remedies available in a case of disqualification are different from those which are appropriate where incapacity or bias are alleged. Since the proceedings are totally void, the complaining party need not seek the active intervention of the Court, either during or after the reference. He may simply await the award, and then decline to pay, on the ground that it is not binding. It is, however, often difficult to adopt this policy without running the risk of waiver, and it will usually be more prudent, if disqualification comes to light before the award is made, for the complaining party to proceed at once in the High Court for a declaration that the arbitrator has no jurisdiction.

3 Interest and bias

There are statements in some of the older cases and works of reference which could, if read literally, be understood to mean that a person with an interest in the outcome of a dispute is disqualified from acting as arbitrator in respect of the dispute, in the sense that a purported appointment of him would be nugatory. This is not correct. Interest is just one example of a fact from which a reasonable person would often infer that there was a risk of the arbitrator

---

9 *Robinson, Fleming & Co v Warner, Barnes & Co* (1922) 10 Ll L Rep 331 (dispute as to whether there was a circle. If there was, the one member of the appeal committee had a minor pecuniary interest of the type prohibited by the contract). *F E Hookway & Co Ltd v Alfred Isaacs & Sons* [1954] 1 Lloyd's Rep 491; *Cook International Inc v BV Handelmaatschappij Jean Delvaux* [1985] 2 Lloyd's Rep 225 (an arbitrator does not have an 'interest in the transaction' merely because he is employed by a subsidiary of a creditor of one of the parties). A similar disqualification is implied at common law. But the effect is not the same. At common law the existence of an improper interest will empower the Court to exercise its powers of removal, etc.; whereas a *contractual* disqualification renders the proceedings entirely void.

10 See *Rahcassi Shipping Co v Blue Star Line*, ante. It is submitted that 'lawyer' means 'practising lawyer'. Rightly or wrongly, many businessmen feel that lawyers are altogether too pedantic and hidebound to approach a commerical dispute in a sensible way. What they wish to avoid is a legalistic attitude of mind; and this comes from the practice of the law, not from a legal qualification.

11 See the cases cited in notes 5 to 10, ante.

12 This can lead to absurd results. In *Rahcassi Shipping Co v Blue Star Line*, ante, a lawyer was chosen as umpire (by arbitrators who had no authority to vary the submission) precisely because the dispute was likely to involve legal issues. Yet the Court had no alternative but to hold that the entire proceedings, and the award, were void.

suffering from bias: i.e. from a predisposition to decide for or against one party, without proper regard to the true merits of the dispute. Interest will in appropriate cases justify the Court in revoking the appointment of the arbitrator, or refusing to stay an action brought in contravention of an agreement to submit the dispute to him for arbitration, or of setting aside any award which he has made. Nevertheless, unless something of this sort occurs, the appointment is effective, the reference is properly constituted, and the award is binding on the parties.

Since the general principles of law relating to bias apply in the same way to arbitrations as to other tribunals, and since instances which are sufficiently serious to bring about the intervention of the Court are very rare indeed, there is no need to deal with the subject in detail. The following comments are included in the hope that they may prove helpful in those instances where concern is felt as to the impartiality of the arbitrator. We shall deal first with bias in the strict sense, namely a predisposition to decide the dispute in a particular way, and later with the situation in which the arbitrator conducts the reference in a way which is said to be unduly favourable to one party.

(a) Antecedent bias

Bias may arise either from a relationship between the arbitrator and one of the parties, or from a relationship between the arbitrator and the subject matter of the dispute. The former is the instance which comes more readily to mind. It can take the shape of a favouritism of antipathy towards one of the parties which can actually be shown to exist. Actual bias of this kind is almost impossible to prove, in the absence of some incautious remark by the person nominated, either before or after the reference begins[13]. It is not, however, necessary to go as far as establishing actual bias[14], for the Court will in appropriate cases intervene if facts are proved which would lead a reasonable person, not knowing the arbitrator's true state of mind, to think it likely that there was bias[15]. Typical of

---

[13] As in *Parker v Burroughs* (1702) Colles 257, HL where the infamous Dr Titus Oates took his revenge on a family who had not invited him to preach at a funeral by procuring his appointment as arbitrator in a dispute about the will of the deceased and then declaring the will invalid. It is difficult to imagine any arbitrator in these times acting from such motives or expressing himself in the unguarded and colourful language which the reporter attributes to Dr Oates. See, however, *Re Catalina (Owners) and Norma MV (Owners)* (1938) 61 Ll L Rep 360, where the arbitrator was overheard to express strong preconceptions as to the inherent credibility of evidence given by persons belonging to certain ethnic groups.

[14] The underlying principle is expressed in Lord Hewart CJ's dictum in *R v Sussex Justices, ex p McCarthy* [1924] 1 KB 256 at 259 that it 'is of fundamental importance that justice should not only be done, but should manifestly and undoubtedly be seen to be done.' But the dictum should not be allowed to lead to 'the erroneous impression that it is more important that justice should appear to be done than that it should in fact be done': *R v Camborne Justices, ex p Pearce* [1955] 1 QB 41 at 52.

[15] See the discussion in *Metropolitan Properties Co (F G S) v Lannon* [1969] 1 QB 577, per Edmund Davies LJ at 606, and *R v Moore* [1969] 6 DLR (3d) 465. There is a long standing conflict of authorities in respect of other types of judicial or quasi-judicial tribunal, whether 'real likelihood' or 'reasonable suspicion' of bias is the correct test. The more recent decisions suggest that there is little, if any, difference between the two tests. The question is whether there exist grounds from which a reasonable person would think that there was a real likelihood that the arbitrator could not or would not fairly determine the issue on the basis of the evidence and arguments adduced before him: *Hagop Ardahalian v Unifert International SA, The Elissar* [1984] 2 Lloyd's Rep 84; *Hannam v Bradford City Council* [1970] 1 WLR 937; *R v Liverpool City Justices, ex p Topping* [1983] 1 WLR

such cases are those where the person nominated has a formal and continuous business relationship with one of the parties: for example, if he is an officer of an associated company, or of a managing company, of that party[16], or if he has a substantial shareholding in one of the parties[17], or becomes a member, even after appointment, of a body corporate which is one of the parties[18]. More troublesome are business relationships of an intermittent kind: for example, when the party is a good customer or a regular client[19] of the person nominated.

It is impossible to lay down any principle more precise than the test of what a reasonable man would think for ascertaining whether the relationship is close enough to be objectionable[20]. With the exercise of common sense, a situation

---

119; *Bremer Handelsgesellschaft mbH v Ets Soules et Cie* [1985] 2 Lloyd's Rep 199; *Tracomin SA v Gibbs Nathaniel (Canada) Ltd* [1985] 1 Lloyd's Rep 586; *Cook International Inc v BV Handelmaatschappij Jean Delvaux* [1985] 2 Lloyd's Rep 225. The reasonable man is to be put in the position of the complainant having all the complainants' knowledge and experience of the trade and the manner in which disputes are habitually resolved: *Bremer Handels-GmbH v Ets Soules et Cie*, supra. But he is not to be accredited with inside knowledge about the arbitrator's real characteristics: *Hannam v Bradford Corporation*, supra, as distinct from the arbitrator's public reputation (*The Elissar*, supra) unless the inside knowledge comes to light in time to allay the complainant's suspicions before the arbitrator adjudicates on the dispute: *Bremer Handelsgesellschaft mbH v Ets Soules et Cie* [1984] 1 Lloyd's Rep 160 (at first instance) Cf. *Tracomin SA v Gibbs Nathaniel (Canada) Ltd*, supra. Earlier cases on arbitration (for instance, *F F Ayriss & Co v Board of Industrial Relations* (1960) 23 DLR (2d) 584) should be read with this in mind.

16 *Burkett Sharp & Co v Eastcheap Dried Fruit Co and Perera* [1962] 1 Lloyd's Rep 267; *Veritas Shipping Corpn v Anglo-Canadian Cement Ltd* [1966] 1 Lloyd's Rep 76. In *Buchan v Melville* 1902 9 SLT 459 it was held that under the law of Scotland two contracting parties could validly agree to refer disputes arising under the contract to the advocate of one of the parties. We doubt whether an English court would now give effect to such a provision, or, if it were to do so, would hold that the proceedings in question would amount to an arbitration.

17 *Sellar v Highland Rly Co* 1919 SC (HL) 19 shows how careful the arbitrator must be to disclose a shareholding in such a case, even if it seems to him that it has no possible bearing on his impartiality. The House of Lords did not hear argument on the question whether the strict rules applying to the shareholdings of a judge (*Dimes v Grand Junction Canal* (1852) 3 HL Cas 759) are equally relevant to an arbitrator. It is arguable that they are not, but the arbitrator should not rely on it. See also *Re Elliott and the South Devon Rly Co* (1848) 2 De G & Sm 17.

18 *Edinburgh Magistrates v Lownie* 1903 5 F (Ct of Sess) 711. The connection had ceased by the time the award was made.

19 In *Bunten and Lancaster (Produce) Ltd v Kiril Mischeff Ltd* [1964] 1 Lloyd's Rep 386 the arbitrator retained a solicitor who was a member of the firm which frequently acted for one of the parties to draft an award. Held, that this was no ground to interfere. In *Bright v River Plate Construction Co Ltd* [1900] 2 Ch 835 the solicitors for one of the parties were held to be 'active and lucrative clients' of the arbitrator, who was a barrister. The arbitrator was named in the contract. Held, that this was no ground to restrain proceedings in the arbitration. (Barristers are nowadays very commonly appointed in such circumstances, and we have never heard the practice challenged.) See also *Addie & Sons v Henderson & Dimmack* 1879 17 SLR 15 and *Fetherstone v Cooper* (1803) 9 Ves 67, where similar conduct was held to be 'indelicate', but no ground for setting aside. But aliter where the arbitrator, or his firm, has himself an interest in the dispute in question: see *M'Dougall v Laird & Sons* (1894) 22 R 71. Here the Court will intervene as a matter of course: *Bremer Handelsgesellschaft mbH v Ets Soules et Cie* [1985] 2 Lloyd's Rep 199 at 202. See also *Re Hawke's Bay Electric-power Board and Napier Borough Council* [1930] NZLR 162.

20 *Morgan v Morgan* (1832) 2 LJ Ex 56 is a good example of the approach adopted by the Court. It was held that the award should not be set aside simply because the arbitrator was indebted to a party. The only effect would be to make the Court look more closely at the circumstances, to see whether the arbitrator had acted with propriety. See also *Morisons v Thomson's Trustees* 1880 18 SLR 97, where the arbitrator had unsuccessfully attempted to borrow money from one of the parties. In *Szilard v Szasz* [1955] 1 DLR 370 (arbitrator, umpire and appointer were joint purchasers of an apartment block) it was said (at 373–374) that it is the probability or the reasonable suspicion of biased appraisal and judgment, unintended though it may be, that defeats the adjudication at its threshold. In *Turnbul v Rural Municipality of Pipestone* (1915) 24 DLR 281, the fact that the arbitrator was the respondent's brother was held sufficient to disqualify him.

should never arise in which the arbitrator's personal impartiality is put in question. A person who is approached with a request to act, and knows that he has some kind of relationship with one of the parties, should remember that there is no keener sense of injustice than is felt by someone who has doubts about whether the arbitrator is doing his honest best. He should also bear in mind that the question is not just whether he really is impartial, but whether a reasonable outsider might consider that there is a risk that he is not. If the person nominated considered that a reasonable outsider might (not should) take this view, he should decline to act. If he considers that the case is on the borderline, he should disclose the circumstances which might give rise to suspicion: and he will very often find that no objection is taken to his appointment: candour is always the best way to prevent misunderstandings[1].

The other type of bias results from a connection, not between the arbitrator and a party, but between the arbitrator and the subject matter of the reference. In its crudest form, this exists where one party stands to gain if the arbitration is decided in a particular way – for example, if he is to receive a commission on the sum awarded. This is so extremely rare as not to merit discussion: the principles applicable are obvious[2]. The converse situation, where the arbitrator may suffer personal detriment if the arbitration is decided in a particular way, is also unusual[3]. More troublesome are the cases where the arbitrator has nothing personally to win or lose, but has already taken up a position in relation to some or all of the issues which casts doubt on his ability to assess them fairly. This can happen where, in advance of the reference, the arbitrator has already expressed himself on the very matter which is in dispute[4]. This is unusual. Rather less so is the situation where the arbitrator has decided the same issue of fact or law in the course of an arbitration between different parties[5]. Here, we suggest that there is no necessary obstacle to the appointment of the arbitrator: for he can be reminded that it is his duty to approach the issue afresh in the light of the evidence[6] and arguments addressed to him on each occasion. It is only if his conduct at the hearing discloses that his mind has been closed from the outset that the Court might, in extreme cases, be willing to interfere. Coming to the case with some preconceived ideas is not necessarily undesirable: indeed, it may

---

[1] Another variant is the situation where the nominee has advised, or otherwise identified himself with the interests of, someone involved in the dispute (for example, by advising someone who is not a party, or not yet a party, to the reference) in a way which creates a potential conflict of interest. It is sometimes very difficult to identify these conflicts in advance. If in doubt, the nominee should disclose the position.

[2] *Blanchard v Sun Fire Office* (1890) 6 TLR 365 concerned the scarcely credible situation where one of the arbitrators became an assignee of the claim.

[3] An example is *Kemp v Rose* (1858) 1 Giff 258, where an arbitrator/architect had promised the building owner that the cost would not exceed a stated amount.

[4] See *Re Elliott and South Devon Rly Co*, ante.

[5] This can occur, for example, where numerous arbitrations arise as the result of the same natural catastrophe or trade embargo affecting the performance of many individual contracts. See also *Re Haigh and London and North Western and Great Western Rly Companies* [1896] 1 QB 649 (an arbitrator had acted as witness for one party in another, but somewhat similar, matter after his appointment. Held, not a ground for setting aside the award), and *Ewart & Son Ltd v Sun Insurance Office* (1925) 21 Ll L Rep 282.

[6] The arbitrator may have difficulty in keeping out of his mind the evidence given at the previous hearing. We refer to this problem, under the heading of 'Arbitrator using his own knowledge' at pp. 360–361, post.

be a positive benefit. Very often an arbitrator is chosen precisely because his skill and expertise make it unnecessary to inform him by evidence of all the elements and details of the subject. Such an arbitrator is bound to have his own opinions on matters concerning the trade, and some of these may prove to be relevant to the arbitration. There is nothing wrong in this[7], provided that the arbitrator is willing to change his mind if the evidence and argument so require.

An objection to bias must be taken at the earliest opportunity, otherwise it will be waived[8]. There is, however, a special rule as regards agreements naming an arbitrator, and where the arbitrator has a relationship towards a party to the arbitration agreement which might render him incapable of impartiality. Even if the opponent knew or ought to have known of the interest at the time when the appointment was made, he is not automatically debarred from applying to the Court for relief on the ground that the arbitrator is not or may not be impartial[9].

Bias on the part of an arbitrator may have the effect of vitiating an award by an umpire after the arbitrators have disagreed[10]. But it must be shown that there was a real likelihood of the umpire's decision having been influenced by the arbitrator[11].

(b) Partiality in the conduct of the reference

Regrettably, it sometimes happens that the arbitrator conducts the reference in an unfair manner. In most cases this happens because an arbitrator, who is trying to do his honest best, misconceives what the interests of justice require. In such a situation, the aggrieved party can avail himself of the remedies for misconduct. These are discussed in Chapters 32 and 33. There are, however, occasions where the conduct of the arbitrator is so consistently unfair to one party that it founds or supports an inference that the arbitrator is incapable of maintaining an even balance between the parties: either because he was biassed from the outset, or because he has developed bias in the course of the reference. There is no point in discussing this topic at length. It is very little touched on in the reported cases, and is concerned with questions of degree and common sense, rather than matters of principle. There are, however, three aspects which may usefully be mentioned: (i) impartiality in making procedural decisions; (ii) impartiality of expression; (iii) personal contact between the arbitrator and the parties.

(i) Impartiality in making procedural decisions.

First, there is the question of impartiality in the taking of procedural decisions in the course of the reference. In a long arbitration, the tribunal may have to make numerous

---

[7] *Bremer Handels-GmbH v Ets Soules et Cie*, supra.

[8] We doubt whether it would now be held, as in *Re Elliott and South Devon Rly Co*, ante, that a person who objected to the arbitrator but continued with the reference, had waived the right to put forward his complaint before the Court.

[9] S. 24(1).

[10] *Blanchard v Sun Fire Office*, ante; *Sellar v Highland Rly Co*, ante.

[11] *Ghirardosi v Minister of Highways for British Columbia* (1964) 47 DLR (2d) 308. *A fortiori* where the effective decision is made by an appeal tribunal which has reheard the dispute and made its decision uninfluenced by the arbitrator whose impartiality is in question: *Cook International Inc v BV Handelmaatschappij Jean Delvaux* [1985] 2 Lloyd's Rep 225.

rulings on issues of procedure. In the nature of things, it will occasionally happen that the majority of the decisions will be in favour of one particular party. This may lead the opponent to feel such a sense of grievance as to suspect that the arbitrator is not approaching the matter impartially. This is of course illogical, since the arbitrator may be right in his decisions, or (even if wrong) may still be acting impartially. This is obvious, and we mention it only because arbitrators have sometimes seemed to become nervous in situations like this, and to run the risk of what is a real injustice, namely to redress an apparent imbalance by deciding points in favour of the aggrieved party contrary to the true merits of the issue. This temptation must be avoided at all costs[12], although the arbitrator may think it wise to take particular care, if he foresees such a situation developing, to demonstrate that he is approaching each procedural issue in a strictly judicial manner.

There is one particular instance of conduct during the reference which calls for particular mention. It occasionally happens that the reference becomes the subject of proceedings in the High Court: for example, to remove or reconstitute the tribunal; to restrain by injunction the further conduct of the reference; or to set aside or remit the award. It is often the right and on occasion the duty of the arbitrator to provide evidence for the Court as the circumstances which have given rise to the procedural dispute. This does not in itself disqualify him from the reference, even if the evidence strongly favours one of the parties, for the duty of impartiality cannot require the arbitrator to do otherwise than give his own version of the facts, and (where relevant) state his opinions upon them. He should, however, do his best to ensure that he does not give the appearance of having become partisan, so as to lead the Court to feel that the matter will best be dealt with by another arbitrator: a course which will put the parties to unnecessary expense[13].

(ii) **Impartiality of expression.**   Next, there is the question of partiality evinced by word, rather than by conduct. In the case of an umpire or sole arbitrator, it must be very rare indeed for the tribunal to say anything which would justify the Court in finding sufficient evidence of bias to justify the setting aside of the award, or the removal of the tribunal[14]. Of course the arbitrator must be careful not to say anything which might suggest that he has come to the case with preconceptions with no amount of evidence or argument will remove. On the other hand, if the arbitrator has come to provisional conclusions on an individual issue or issues there are occasions on which 'showing his hand' can

---

[12] We do not, of course, suggest that any responsible arbitrator would consciously decide to give a procedural consolation prize to a party who seemed to be doing rather poorly on interlocutory rulings. Unlike a trial in court, however, arbitration is a consensual procedure, as regards the choice of tribunal and of the method of resolving the dispute. There is sometimes an unrecognised pressure on arbitrators to ensure that parties who have made this choice do not go away dissatisfied. There is an element of humorous exaggeration in the adage that the decision most likely to be right is the one which leaves both parties dissatisfied; but neither is the contrary proposition true. The arbitrator's function is to decide the issue on its merits as he sees them. If, in doing so, he happens to please both sides, this is gratifying, but of only secondary importance.

[13] *G W Potts Ltd v MacPherson, Train & Co* (1927) 27 Ll L Rep 445; *Fratelli Schiavo de Gennaro v Richard J Hall Ltd* [1953] 2 Lloyd's Rep 169.

[14] *Re Catalina (Owners) and Norma M V (Owners)* (1938) 61 Ll L Rep 360 appears to be the only modern case.

produce tangible savings in time, and hence in expense[15], and the arbitrator should not be inhibited from doing so, in a proper case, by the fear that the Court might afterwards find evidence of bias. Moreover, although patience is an important attribute to any person acting judicially, there is no call for it to be limitless. Provided he displays courtesy and moderation, an arbitrator does not display bias by making it clear that he disapproves of the manner in which, or the length at which, a party is putting forward his case.

There is, however, one situation in which particular care is necessary: namely where the tribunal consists of two arbitrators, each appointed by one of the parties, together with an umpire and third arbitrator. Here, each arbitrator must avoid giving an appearance of excessive zeal on behalf of the party who nominated him[16].

(iii) Personal contacts with the parties. Finally, there is the question of personal contacts during the reference between the arbitrator and the parties. These are not a problem in litigation, nor as a rule in most formal arbitrations. The arbitrator appears at the beginning of the day, and leaves at the end. There is no occasion for personal contact between himself and the parties, and the performance of the procedural rituals itself ensures a proper detachment. A commercial arbitration is often quite different. Procedural niceties are abjured in the interests of speed and economy. Often, many of those involved in the reference are on close professional terms. Informality is the order of the day. This absence of a rigid procedural framework has many advantages, but it means that the arbitrator must form his own view of how to behave. Arbitrators who justifiably take for granted the probity of themselves and their colleagues sometimes forget that those who do not know either them or the system so well may not make the same assumptions. The arbitrator must therefore be alert to see that a friendly and informal way of conducting the reference does not lead an uninformed party to the mistaken conclusion that the arbitrator is not maintaining a truly judicial approach. It goes without saying that social contacts should take place in the presence of both parties[17]. Perhaps in exceptional

---

[15] See pp. 348–350, post.

[16] *Rolland v Cassidy* (1888) 13 App Cas 770 (where the excess of zeal was held not to be sufficient to vitiate the award); *The Myron (Owners) v Tradax Export SA* [1969] 1 Lloyd's Rep 411 at 415 and 417; *Re Enoch and Zaretzky, Bock & Co* [1910] 1 KB 327; *Oswald v Earl Grey* (1855) 24 LJQB 69.

[17] Some of the older cases appear to take a more tolerant view on this topic than we believe would be adopted today. Thus, in *Re Hopper* (1867) LR 2 QB 367, after the hearing, the umpire dined with the two arbitrators, and one of the parties and his attorney, at the residence of that party, an inn. 'Much wine was drunk'; frequent allusions were made to the arbitration, although evidently not in a serious spirit; the arbitrators at length retired to bed in the inn, insensible. Held, that although the arbitrators' conduct was a matter for criticism, it was not a ground for setting aside the award. On similar facts, a court today might well feel obliged to intervene, on the basis that the events of the evening gave the appearance of unfairness, even if in fact none existed. Other cases in which the acceptance of hospitality was held to be insufficient to justify the intervention of the Court were *Crossley v Clay* (1848) 5 CB 581; *Moseley v Simpson* (1873) LR 16 Eq 226; *Re Maunder* (1883) 49 LT 535. The practice of taking the midday meal with both parties is widespread, and harmless in itself. But it does place on the arbitrator a particular responsibility to dilute his affability with a strict impartiality of manner. The arbitrator should never have any social contact with a person involved in a pending reference, whether as party or otherwise, who may give evidence in circumstances where his credibility will be in issue. The judgment of the witness should be formed on the basis of his demeanour whilst giving evidence, not elsewhere.

circumstances, this rule may properly be broken[18]. If so, the arbitrator should take great care that the other party knows what is going to happen, so that he has an opportunity to object.

B. WAIVER AND ESTOPPEL

The difficult question whether a party is precluded by waiver or estoppel from relying on an objection to the proceedings or to the award is discussed at pp. 579–582, post. The following specific points may be made in relation to disqualification –

1 Where a party appoints someone as 'his own' arbitrator and thereafter continues with the arbitration, he impliedly represents to his opponent that the person appointed has the qualifications required by the contract. He cannot at a subsequent stage object to the award on the ground that the arbitrator was not in fact qualified[19].

2 Where a party knows that the person appointed by his opponent lacks the necessary qualifications, but nevertheless continues with the arbitration, he thereby waives his right to object, unless he makes a protest in such a way as to enable him to continue on a 'without prejudice' basis[20].

3 Where, however, the party if ignorant that his opponent's nominee is unqualified, he does not waive his objection by taking part in the reference[1].

4 An agent with the necessary authority may bind his principal to accept the appointment of an arbitrator who lacks the necessary qualifications[2].

5 Where an umpire is to be appointed by the two arbitrators, their authority[3] to make an appointment is defined by the arbitration agreement under which they themselves were appointed[4]. Neither before they disagree nor afterwards do they have ostensible authority to bind their appointing parties by choosing an umpire who lacks the necessary qualifications.

A party may apply for leave to revoke the authority of the arbitrator or for an injunction to restrain him from proceeding with the arbitration, on the

---

[18] Where the arbitrator and the parties are engaged in the same trade, meetings outside the context of the arbitration may be hard to avoid.

[19] *Oakland Metal Co Ltd v D Benaim & Co Ltd,* supra.

[20] The position may perhaps be different where the arbitration is expressly disqualified by the contract. It was held in *Robinson, Fleming & Co v Warner, Barnes & Co* (1922) 10 Ll L Rep 331, that a mere want of objection is insufficient: there must be positive acquiescence, amounting to variation of the contract. We doubt whether the judgment of Rigby Swift J is fully reported; want of objection is never in itself enough: its significance is that it constitutes evidence of acquiescence.

[1] *Jungheim, Hopkins & Co v Foukelmann* [1909] 2 KB 948.

[2] See *Backhouse v Taylor* (1851) 20 LJ QB 233 (representative present at choice of umpire by lot). See also *Rahcassi Shipping Co v Blue Star Line,* ante.

[3] See also *Palmer & Co Ltd v Pilot Trading Co Ltd* (1929) 33 Ll L Rep 42, where the arbitrators made the appointment on the printed form of a trade association, which incorporated rules providing for an appeal tribunal. Branson J held that this was not enough to vary the original submission, which had provided that the decision of the umpire would be final. It is, perhaps, slightly misleading to speak of 'authority', for this is the language of agency. What the arbitrators are doing, when they choose an umpire, is to exercise a power delegated to them through the medium of the arbitration agreement. They are not, when making the choice, agents of either party.

[4] *Rahcassi Shipping Co v Blue Star Line,* ante; and *Kawasaki Kisen Kaisha v Government of Ceylon* [1962] 1 Lloyd's Rep 424 at 429.

ground that he is not or may not be impartial, notwithstanding that at the time when he made the agreement he knew or ought to have known that the arbitrator, by reason of his relation towards any other party to the agreement or of his connection with the subject referred, might not be capable of impartiality[5].

---

[5] S. 24(1).

CHAPTER 19

The arbitrator advocate:
the umpire: disagreement

A. THE ARBITRATOR/ADVOCATE: GENERAL

From a practical point of view, the most striking feature of English commercial arbitration is that of the 'arbitrator/advocate'[1]. Where the arbitration agreement provides[2] that the reference shall be to two arbitrators, and then (in the event of a disagreement) to an umpire, under the orthodox law of arbitration the two arbitrators retain a fully judicial function until they have tried and failed to agree. Thereafter, they are functus officio, and have no right or duty to participate further in the reference. It is, however, not uncommonly found, in the field of shipping and commodity disputes that arbitrators are appointed with the intention, from the outset, that they shall not part company from the reference at the moment of disagreement, but shall remain in contact with the proceedings as the representatives and advocates of the parties, to present their evidence and arguments to the umpire[3]. The concept that the same man can properly fulfil, at successive moments, the incompatible roles of judge and advocate is offensive to theorists, and a source of surprise to those who have not previously encountered it. Moreover, it imposes considerable demands on the fairness and discretion of the arbitrators, the more so since the courts have not yet stated in precise terms the functions which they are required to perform at the two stages of the reference[4]. Nevertheless, the procedure works surprisingly well. There are few reported instances, out of all the many occasions in which it has been employed[5], in which it has been found that substantial injustice has ensued: and they have mostly been cases where the arbitrator has not kept clearly in mind which of his two functions he should have been fulfilling at the time in question. Moreover, experience has shown that the system gives the parties what they want, which is speed and saving in cost. The parties do not need lawyers; the foreigner does not need a local representative. Each simply sends his papers, his evidence and his arguments to the arbitrator whom he has appointed, and waits to hear if anything more is required. He need not attend the hearing (if there is one) nor appoint a lawyer to do so. Moreover, if the arbitrators disagree, the parties are not compelled to start the whole process

---

[1] The institution of the arbitrator/advocate may now be on the wane. Nothing in this chapter is intended to suggest that it is at all common or appropriate outside the field in which it has grown up.

[2] Expressly, or by way of the rule of construction contained in s. 8(1).

[3] And to the appeal tribunal if there is one – as in *Zwanenberg Ltd v McCallum & Sons* (1922) 13 Ll L Rep 350 at 351.

[4] This may be just as well, because it is likely that in this, as in other respects, the degree to which it is permissible to depart from the orthodox norms of procedure depends upon the meaning of the agreement to arbitrate, construed in the light of the practice in the particular trade.

[5] The number must run to tens of thousands.

over again in front of the umpire; they already have at hand, in the shape of the arbitrators, two persons who are in possession of the evidence and documents, who know what the dispute is about, and who can straight away present the whole matter to the umpire, with the minimum of delay and expense. Anomalous or not, the system has been found to work. It appears to have been commonplace at the beginning of the nineteenth century, and although it took some years for the law to catch up with the practice, it eventually became recognised by the courts as a permissible way of conducting commercial arbitrations. It is now so firmly established that there is no possibility of the practice being overturned on the grounds of general principle[6].

The arbitration agreement will very rarely state explicitly whether or not the arbitrators are to act as advocates. This will normally be an inference from the nature of the dispute[7], and the conduct of the parties. If the contract relates to the shipping or commodity trades or if the agreement provides that the arbitrators are to be 'commercial men', a tribunal of arbitrator/advocates can be assumed, in the absence of indication to the contrary. But if lawyers are chosen as arbitrators, or if the parties appoint legal representatives and set about the conduct of the reference in a formalistic way, then an orthodox procedure is likely to be what they intend. Naturally, if the arbitrator feels uncertain whether he is also intended to be an advocate, he should take the earliest opportunity to raise the matter with the parties.

For the purpose of discussion it is convenient to consider separately the status of the arbitrator/advocate before and after he has disagreed with his colleague, in comparison with the position of his counterpart in a conventional arbitration.

B. THE POSITION BEFORE DISAGREEMENT

In a conventional arbitration, each member of a two-man tribunal is in the same position as if he were a sole arbitrator. He must act judicially and without bias, and take care to show that he is in a position so to act[8]. His duties are owed

---

[6] Judicial acceptance was virtually complete by 1920. Dicta such as those of Swinfen-Eady MR in *Roff v British and French Chemical Manufacturing Co and Gibson* [1918] 2 KB 677 at 680, and of Lush J in *French Government v Tsurushima Maru* (1921) 7 Ll L Rep 244 represent the last traces of opposition. Some of the early instances of approval may be found in *Re Enoch and Zaretzky, Bock & Co's Arbitration* [1910] 1 KB 327 at 334; *Ritchie v W Jacks & Co* (1922) 10 Ll L Rep 519; *French Government v Tsurushima Maru* (1922) 8 Ll L Rep 403, 37 TLR 961; *Zwanenberg Ltd v McCallum & Sons* (1922) 13 Ll L Rep 350; *Russian Oil Products Ltd v Caucasian Oil Co Ltd* (1928) 31 Ll L Rep 109. The line of authority stretches through *Wessanen's Koninklijke Fabrieken NV v Isaac Modiano, Bro & Sons Ltd* [1960] 2 Lloyd's Rep 257 and *Rahcassi Shipping Co SA v Blue Star Line Ltd* [1967] 2 Lloyd's Rep 261, [1969] 1 QB 173, to the present day. There would be no point in attempting to cite all the authority for such a well-recognised principle.

[7] The inference cannot amount to a term that the reference *shall* proceed by the method of arbitrator/advocate, for otherwise a party could validly object if his opponent nominated someone who refused to act on such a basis; we do not think that the Court would countenance such an objection. The inference is, we suggest, permissive in nature. In the circumstances suggested in the text the arbitrators can properly adopt the arbitrator/advocate system in all its aspects without committing misconduct, unless one or both of the parties shows by words or conduct that a conventional arbitration is required. (For a discussion of the parties' right to revert to a full adversarial procedure, see p. 291, post.)

[8] *Veritas Shipping Corpn v Anglo-Canadian Cement Ltd* [1966] 1 Lloyd's Rep 76; *Gunter Henck v Andre & Cie SA* [1970] 1 Lloyd's Rep 235 at 246.

equally to both sides. It is not his function to represent the interests of the party who appointed him, to advise him, to argue his cause, or to act as his agent[9]. He has no authority to bind the party who appointed him, except by orders or awards. He must not communicate privately with either party, without the knowledge and consent of his co-arbitrator and of the other party. All documents and evidence which he receives must be disclosed to the other member of the tribunal.

The position of an arbitrator/advocate before disagreement is in principle the same. His duty is also to hold the balance fairly between the parties, attempting to find the just result, not the one which favours the party who appointed him. He is not, at this stage, the agent of either party[10]. Since, however, one of the chief practical advantages of the system is that it enables each arbitrator to function as a cheap and ready link between the party who appointed him, and the two-man tribunal, the way in which this primary duty is fulfilled is usually rather different. It has come to be seen that it is not essential to the just and efficient conduct of the dispute that everything said by one party to his arbitrator should be disclosed to the opponent and the other arbitrator. It is implied in this procedure that the parties waive the right to full disclosure, and leave it to the discretion of each arbitrator to edit and bring forward the material as he thinks fit[11]. In practice it follows that there is no adversary procedure, in the ordinary sense, with the parties addressing the tribunal. Indeed each member of the tribunal addresses the other, discussing with his colleagues the favourable aspects of his party's case. This involves no compromise of the arbitrator's impartiality, for he is not making a case, so much as testing and discussing it[12]. It also happens that an arbitrator will advise a party on the proper procedure to be followed or suggest to a party that certain information could usefully be obtained, even though the co-arbitrator has not yet commented on its absence. Here again, the arbitrator is neither acting as a lawyer does, when advising on the procedure which his client should adopt, or on the evidence which his client should produce in order to defeat the opponent, nor conducting a truly inquisitorial procedure, but is trying to ensure that parties take the proper steps to put before the tribunal all the evidence required to arrive at a just solution. It remains the duty of the parties to present their cases to the arbitrators and to work out how best to do so[13].

---

[9] *Myron (Owners) v Tradax Export SA* [1969] 1 Lloyd's Rep 411 at 415; *Ritchie v W Jacks & Co*, ante; *Oswald v Earl Grey* (1855) 24 LJQB 69.

[10] *Myron (Owners) v Tradax Export SA*, supra at 416; cf. *European Grain and Shipping Ltd v Johnston* [1982] 1 Lloyd's Rep 414 at 419.

[11] See *Wessanen's v Isaac Modiani*, ante; *Alpine Shipping Co v Vinbee (Manchester) Ltd* [1980] 1 Lloyd's Rep 400.

[12] The fact that the arbitrators are genuinely acting judicially, and not as mere instruments of those who appoint them, is demonstrated by the substantial proportion of awards which are made jointly by the two arbitrators.

[13] *Citland Ltd v Kanchan Oil Industries PVT Ltd* [1980] 2 Lloyd's Rep 274; *Thos P Gonzalez Corpn v Muller's Muhle, Muller GmbH & Co KG* [1978] 2 Lloyd's Rep 541; *Tracomin SA v Gibbs Nathaniel (Canada) Ltd* [1985] 1 Lloyd's Rep 586. This may appear to some a rather idealised sketch of the procedure. Of course, the edges do become blurred in practice, and sometimes arbitrators do not observe clearly enough the distinction between advocacy and judgment. Moreover, the fact that the arbitrator is permitted to communicate privately with the party who has appointed him makes it all the more important, as well as difficult, to avoid the appearance of partiality to the 'appointor' or 'principal': *Tracomin SA v Globe Nathaniel (Canada) Ltd*, supra. Nevertheless, it is a tribute to the seriousness and tact of most commercial arbitrators that, in the main, this difficult

The consequences of disagreement, which we have just summarised, are quite acceptable in the majority of arbitrations, but they can be inconvenient in a lengthy reference, where there will inevitably be ample scope for disagreement on procedural questions. The parties are unlikely to wish a single disagreement of this nature to sever the arbitrator's connection with the case, leaving the umpire in sole charge of the reference. This will be so particularly where the tribunal consists of two lay arbitrators with practical experience of the trade, and a lawyer as umpire, whose function is primarily to act as chairman and assist with questions of procedure and law. The parties hope that the arbitrators will remain seized of the reference throughout, and will ultimately make a joint award; a decision by the umpire on his own is not what the parties really intend. This being so, the parties may find it useful to make an express agreement, at the outset of the reference, whereby in the event of disagreement on any individual issue that issue shall be decided by the umpire, but the remaining issues remain within the jurisdiction of the two arbitrators. A similar agreement can usefully be made in the rather less common situation where the parties have agreed that the substantive issues in dispute shall be heard and decided successively, rather than by means of a single hearing and award.

Thus far, there is little anomalous in the position of an arbitrator/advocate before disagreement, and in recognising the practice, the Court does no more than acknowledge that in the right case the inquisitorial process may have practical advantages over the usual adversary methods. There are, however, some indications in the reported cases that the Court may be prepared to tolerate a more far-reaching departure from orthodoxy. The arbitrator has been described as a 'negotiating advocate'[14], the inference being that it is his task to strive for the best compromise result for the party who appointed him[15]. It is undeniable that many arbitrators do indeed act in this way. The legal implications of such a procedure are open to doubt. We suggest that a distinction should be drawn between two sorts of compromise. In the first, the arbitrators agree in general terms in the outcome of the dispute, but cannot agree as to the precise result – for example, they are not unanimous as to what constitutes the fair market price, a reasonable time, and so on. Here it is entirely legitimate for them to move towards the middle ground: the answer may not be exactly the one which either arbitrator would have given if sitting alone, but it is still one in which he genuinely concurs. There is nothing unjudicial about this. Quite different is the second type of compromise, where the arbitrators are divided, or do not even try to agree, on what the correct answer should be, but instead seek to arrive at a figure which represents an agreed view of the strengths and weaknesses of each side's case. The resulting figure cannot be logically justified as the correct award. It represents not a decision of the dispute, but a settlement of it. There is nothing harmful in such practice, and (provided the parties can be taken to have authorised the arbitrators to act as negotiators) the result is

---

procedure is operated in a true judicial spirit. An example of the difficulty which can be experienced in drawing the line is provided by *Estia Compania Navigacion SA v Deutsche Genussmittel GmbH, The Estia* [1981] 1 Lloyd's Rep 541.

[14] *Naumann v Edward Nathan & Co Ltd* (1930) 37 Ll L Rep 249; *Re Enoch and Zaretzky, Bock & Co* [1910] 1 KB 327.

[15] This is bluntly put by Scrutton J in *Naumann v Edward Nathan & Co Ltd*, supra, at 250. These dicta are almost certainly directed at the position of the arbitrators before disagreement, for it is at that stage that the negotiations take place, the umpire being called in if the negotiations fail.

binding in law. But the process is not arbitration, and the outcome is not an award[16].

C. DISAGREEMENT

Where the reference is in the hands of two arbitrators, it may be important to decide whether they have disagreed, for upon this may depend whether the umpire has power to enter upon the reference[17], and whether the arbitrators are functus officio, and may properly assume the status of arbitrator/advocates.

The courts have not yet defined precisely what constitutes a disagreement[18]. It is, however, clear that a disagreement may take place during the interlocutory stages of the reference, before the hearing itself begins[19]; that the disagreement may relate to procedure as well as the merits[20]; that it is sufficient for the parties to disagree on some, or even only one, of several issues which arise for consideration[1]; and that evident failure to agree is sufficient, even if there is no formal disagreement[2]. The matter may be tested this way: can the arbitration proceed if the arbitrators do not rule on the matter upon which they disagree? If the answer is 'No', then there is a sufficient disagreement to let in the umpire. Thus, for example, we consider that disagreements concerning pleadings, dates for hearings, adjournments, discovery, evidence and costs are all matters which are enough to make the arbitrators functus officio, and to give the umpire power to enter upon the reference[3].

The arbitrators should usually try to avoid a formal disagreement on procedural matters. The system of two arbitrators plus one umpire is chosen because the parties hope for an agreed award, and arbitrators should not lightly discard this function of considering the merits of the claim because of a difference on a matter of procedure. In practice, it is not unusual for the arbitrators to consult the umpire (if one is already appointed and sitting with them) as to his views on what orders should be made in the reference, and to follow his opinion. There is no harm in this, if the arbitrators do not obtrusively give the impression that the umpire has already taken over the conduct of the dispute.

Once the arbitrators have disagreed, and the umpire has entered upon the reference, he becomes seized of all the disputes in the case, and must deal in his

---

[16] For the position where the submission expressly confers on the arbitrators the power to decide in accordance with justice and equity, or in some other way authorises them to depart from the strict rule of law, see Chapter 4, ante.

[17] By virtue either of an express provision in the contract, or of s. 8(2) of the Act.

[18] The disagreement need not be expressed or arrived at in writing. But the umpire cannot enter on the reference until the arbitrators have given written notice to any party to the reference or to the umpire stating that they cannot agree: s. 8(2). The sub-section yields to a contrary express provision in the arbitration agreement.

[19] *Iossifoglu v Coumantaros* [1941] 1 KB 396.

[20] *Cudliff v Walters* (1839) 2 Mood & R 232; *Iossifoglu v Coumantaros*, supra.

[1] *Winteringham v Robertson* (1858) 27 LJ Ex 301; *Sinclair v Fraser* 1884 11 R 1139; *Lang v Brown* (1855) 25 LTOS 297; *Wicks v Cox* (1847) 11 Jur 542 (disagreement on costs alone); *Cerrito v North Eastern Timber Importers Ltd* [1952] 1 Lloyd's Rep 330.

[2] *Winteringham v Robertson*, supra; *Hill v Marshall* (1827) 5 LJOSCP 161.

[3] Logically, even a disagreement about the required appointment of an umpire under s. 8(1) of the Act would be sufficient to make the arbitrators functus officio. It seems that the correct course would then be for one party to serve on the other a notice to concur in appointing the umpire and, failing compliance, to apply to the Court under s. 10(c) of the Act.

award with all of them, even though there were some on which the arbitrators did not disagree[4].

The disagreement probably need not be expressed in writing[5].

D. THE POSITION AFTER DISAGREEMENT

After disagreement, the contrast between conventional arbitrations and those involving arbitrator/advocates becomes more sharply marked. In an ordinary arbitration the arbitrators cease upon disagreement to have any connection with the reference; they have no right to participate, and no power to make any binding order or award. The position of the arbitrator/advocate is entirely different. He is entitled, although apparently not bound[6], to maintain his participation in the reference. If he does so, his functions become the precise opposite of those which he performed before disagreement. Thus:

1 He is no longer required to be judicial. On the contrary, he must be partial; i.e. he should urge the case of his client[7] regardless of his views of its merits, and should advise his client on how best it should be presented.

2 The arbitrator/advocate becomes an agent of the client[8] so far as concerns the giving of notice and the imputing of knowledge. Disclosure to the arbitrator constitutes disclosure to the client.

3 The arbitrator/advocate is also an agent of the client[8] so as to bind him by agreements and waivers. He has power to consent on behalf of his client to procedures which would otherwise be objectionable[9]; and we believe that his ostensible authority would extend so far as to enable him to make a binding compromise of the dispute, even if the client had not actually authorised him to do so. What the arbitrator/advocate does not, however, have power to do is to bind his client (without actual authorisation)[10] to an enlargement of the umpire's jurisdiction. Thus he cannot consent to the inclusion in the reference of a claim which was not originally submitted to arbitration; and, a fortiori, he cannot validly agree that the umpire shall hear the dispute even though not possessing

---

[4] See the cases cited in note 1, ante; and *Orion Compania Espanola de Seguros v Belfort Moatschappij Voor Algemene Verzekgringeen* [1962] 2 Lloyd's Rep 257; *FW Berk & Co Ltd v Knowles and Foster* [1962] 1 Lloyd's Rep 430.

[5] See note 18, ante.

[6] *Veritas Shipping Corpn v Anglo-Canadian Cement Ltd* [1966] 1 Lloyd's Rep 76 at 77.

[7] We use the word 'client' designedly, because this accurately states the relationship, after disagreement, between the arbitrator/advocate and the party who appointed him, although it is a complete mis-statement of the position before disagreement. The word 'appointor' is often used in commercial arbitration.

[8] This may not be so where the arbitrator was appointed by a third party or the Court: see pp. 185 et seq., ante.

[9] *Biglin v Clarke* (1905) 49 Sol J 204; *French Government v Tsurushima Maru* (1922) 8 Ll L Rep 403 at 404; *Government of Ceylon v Chandris* [1963] 1 Lloyd's Rep 214, [1963] 2 QB 327; *Rahcassi Shipping Co SA v Blue Star Line Ltd* [1967] 2 Lloyd's Rep 261, [1969] 1 QB 173; *Kawasaki Kisen Kaisha v Government of Ceylon* [1962] 1 Lloyd's Rep 424; *Ritchie v W Jacks & Co*, ante, at 522; *Wessanen's v Modiano*, ante; *Hill Court Shipping Co SA v Compagnie Continentale (France) SA, The Yperagia* [1977] 1 Lloyd's Rep 29 at 36. For an early example, see *Hamilton v Bankin* (1850) 3 De G & Sm 782.

[10] Naturally, the arbitrator can validly agree to an increase in jurisdiction if he has the party's authorisation to do so. Such authorisation may be derived from the document in which the arbitrator himself is appointed, or from the subsequent conduct of the client: *Westminster Chemical and Produce Ltd v Eichholz and Loeser* [1954] 1 Lloyd's Rep 99 at 106.

the stipulated qualifications, or that the umpire shall award on a claim which lies outside the scope of the arbitration clause[11]. It follows that in all cases where the umpire is being asked by the arbitrators to do something which is prima facie outside his jurisdiction, he should call for evidence that they have the express authority of their clients, or at least of their clients' lawyers, to make the agreement.

4 The client must abide the consequences of tactical errors, misunderstandings and so on, of his arbitrator, just as if the advocate were a lawyer.

After the hearing is concluded, the arbitrator/advocate ceases to have any authority as agent for his client, except to act as a conduit for communication[12].

In the kind of reference in which the system of arbitrator/advocate is usually employed, the umpire is entitled to assume that the parties will be represented by the arbitrator/advocates and nobody else, unless the parties have expressed a desire to be otherwise represented[13]. If there are lawyers in the offing, the umpire should clarify who is to be regarded as the representative of the client, for otherwise muddles are likely to ensue[14].

---

[11] The distinction between procedure and jurisdiction is clearly deawn in *Rahcassi Shipping Co v Blue Star Line*, ante. The reasoning that the arbitrator derives his power on matters of jurisdiction from the submission and not from an agency relation with the party who appointed him seems much stronger in relation to agreements and waivers before the disagreement than those which occur afterwards.

[12] So held in *Re Fuerst Bros & Co Ltd and RS Stephenson* [1951] 1 Lloyd's Rep 429. Perhaps a more convincing basis for the decision would have been the fact that the communication was not made to the arbitrator in his capacity as such. See also *Kawasaki Kisen Kaisha v Government of Ceylon*, ante; *Bourgeois v Weddell & Co* [1924] 1 KB 539.

[13] *Wessanen's v Modiano*, ante, at 259.

[14] As in *Government of Ceylon v Chandris*, ante.

CHAPTER 20

Judicial arbitrators

A. JUDGE-ARBITRATOR

1 Appointment of a commercial judge as arbitrator or umpire

Section 4 of the Administration of Justice Act 1970 enables a judge of the Commercial Court in certain circumstances to accept appointment as sole arbitrator or as umpire[1].

Three conditions must be satisfied before he can accept such an appointment –

1 The appointment must be under an 'arbitration agreement' within the meaning of the 1950 Act[2].

2 The Lord Chief Justice must have informed the judge that, having regard to the state of business in the High Court and in the Crown Court, the judge can be made available to accept the appointment[3].

3 The dispute must appear to the judge to be of a commercial character[4].

Even when these conditions are satisfied, the judge has a discretion only to accept appointment as an arbitrator or umpire 'if in all the circumstances he thinks fit'. In practice, the judges of the Commercial Court will accept appointment only where the dispute involves a question of law of substantial importance or difficulty or which is for some other reason out of the ordinary run of commercial arbitrations[5]. The estimated length of the hearing is a material consideration, since judges cannot be spared for long periods away from their ordinary work unless the circumstances are exceptional. In practice, the system has not yet become widely employed. Only a handful of appointments are made each year. It is hoped that its use will become more widespread once the advantages become more generally known.

The fees payable for the services of a judge as arbitrator or umpire are taken

---

[1] But not as one of two or more arbitrators.

[2] See pp. 53 et seq., ante.

[3] This is by no means a mere formality.

[4] By analogy with Ord. 72, r. 1, which assigns 'commercial actions' to the Commercial Court, a dispute is presumably 'of a commercial character' if it arises out of the ordinary transactions of merchants and traders, e.g. if it relates to the construction of a mercantile document, the export or import of merchandise, affreightment, insurance, banking, mercantile agency and mercantile usage. This definition has in practice been liberally construed, and the same approach will no doubt apply to some extent to the system of judicial arbitration. It is not, however, intended that the spectrum of arbitrations under s. 4 should be as wide as the jurisdiction of the Commercial Court.

[5] *The Bamburi* [1982] 1 Lloyd's Rep 312 is a good example. The reference was heard on an agreed statement of facts to give authoritative guidance on a number of questions of marine insurance law arising out of the war between Iran and Iraq, which, it was said, affected some seventy vessels. *The Badegry* [1985] 1 Lloyd's Rep 395, on the other hand, was a case involving a point of law of limited application and which turned largely on its facts: the appointment might well not have been accepted under the present practice.

in the High Court in the same way as other court fees[6]. The amount is fixed from time to time by statutory instrument. The fees of arbitrators who have been appointed before the appointment of a judge-umpire are not subject to this constraint.

2 Judicial arbitration compared with other proceedings

The process of judicial arbitration occupies an intermediate position, between litigation and conventional arbitration.

Judicial arbitration differs from conventional arbitration principally in relation to the mechanisms of judicial control. Such appeals on questions of law as there may be, in the light of the 1979 Act[7], proceed directly to the Court of Appeal[8].

In a matter involving substantial issues of law, which would be likely to pass through the filtering mechanisms introduced by sections 1(4) and 1(7) of the 1979 Act, the parties may effect considerable savings of time and money by choosing judicial arbitration, and thus leaving out one link in the chain of appeals.

There is also a potential benefit resulting from the fact that judicial review of the reference on questions of procedure, through the remedies of misconduct and setting aside, is carried out by the Court of Appeal, not the High Court. In practice, this is likely to be less important, since even in conventional arbitrations questions of procedure, other than those relating to points of general principle, are rarely taken to the Court of Appeal. In addition, section 4(5) of the 1970 Act empowers the Court of Appeal to exercise in respect of a judicial arbitration any jurisdiction of the High Court exerciseable in relation to conventional arbitrations, otherwise than under the 1950 Act. This provision appears to be sufficiently wide to confer on the Court of Appeal the power, which would ordinarily be exercised by a judge of the High Court, to intervene in the reference by means of common law remedies such as injunctions and declaratory relief[9]. There are other differences, as regards the exercise of supervisory and ancillary powers, which we summarise in the Table, below.

Turning to the comparison between a judicial arbitration and a trial before a judge of the Commercial Court, it is often assumed that there is little difference between the two procedures, apart from the fact that the proceedings in judicial arbitrations take place in private[10], and the parties to such an arbitration have a limited right to choose their own judge. The differences are, however, more significant than this.

---

[6] S. 4(3) of the Administration of Justice Act 1970. They are paid to the Treasury, not to the judge.

[7] S. 3 of the 1979 Act (which deals with agreements excluding the right of appeal), read together with s. 4(5) of the Administration of Justice Act 1970, appears to apply to arbitrations before a judge-arbitrator or judge-umpire.

[8] Thus by-passing, it seems, the usual process of filtration under ss. 1(7) and 2(3) of the 1979 Act, which make it a condition of appeal to the Court of Appeal from 'a decision of the High Court' (which would not include a decision of a judge-arbitrator or judge-umpire) that it shall have been certified by the High Court that the question of law to which its decision relates either is one of general public importance or is one which for some other special reason should be considered by the Court of Appeal.

[9] See Chapter 32.

[10] An unsuccessful attempt was made, when the 1970 Act was before Parliament, to include a provision giving the Commercial Court power to sit in private.

In the first place, the procedures for appeal are quite different. An appeal may be brought as a matter of right from the decision of the commercial judge on an issue of fact. There is no appeal on the facts from his decision as judge-arbitrator. On questions of law there is an appeal as of right from the decision of the commercial judge except in respect of interlocutory matters. There is no such appeal in excluded arbitrations[11], and even in other types of judicial arbitration an appeal can only be brought with leave[12]. On questions of procedure, an interlocutory appeal may be made to the Court of Appeal whilst the action is still before the judge. If any such procedure exists in a judicial arbitration, its scope is very limited[13].

Another distinction relates to judicial control in procedural matters, otherwise than by way of interlocutory appeal. When the Court of Appeal hears an appeal against a judgment, based on an assertion that the trial was procedurally defective, it is the record of the trial which forms the basis for the review. An application to remit or set aside, or to exercise other forms of judicial control over a judge-arbitrator is an originating process, not necessarily governed by the same principles, or based on the same materials as an ordinary appeal: nor can it be assumed that the effect of the orders which the Court of Appeal can make will necessarily be the same in the two instances.

Finally, there are important distinctions between the procedures available to the tribunal under the two forms of procedure. In a judicial arbitration, the judge is free to adopt whatever procedure he considers appropriate, provided that it is consistent with the express or implied terms of the arbitration agreement. A judge is obliged to follow the procedures laid down by the Rules of the Supreme Court, unless the parties expressly dispense him from doing so. The procedural flexibility thus gained by giving the judge the functions of an arbitrator is, however, balanced by a diminution in his procedural powers. In his capacity as arbitrator, the judge has few coercive powers[14], and the powers to reinforce the arbitral process, which the High Court is currently developing in the field of conventional arbitration, are comparatively clumsy, and are made the more so in relation to judicial arbitrations, where the jurisdiction to exercise them rests with the Court of Appeal. Furthermore, there are certain procedures available in the High Court which cannot be employed in a judicial arbitration: for example, third-party proceedings, the compulsory hearing together of kindred disputes between different sets of parties, the bringing-together of cross-claims only some of which are covered by the arbitration agreement, and so on.

3 Allocation of procedural powers

The fact that the judge is partly a judge and partly an arbitrator has led to the distribution of procedural powers, which would in an ordinary arbitration be divided quite distinctly between the High Court and the arbitrator, being made

---

[11] Viz. cases where an agreement in writing to exclude the right of appeal has been validly made under s. 3(1) of the 1979 Act.

[12] There may also be a difference as to the materials brought before the Court of Appeal. In the case of an appeal from a trial, all the evidence and documents are available for review. We believe that this will not be the case, where an appeal is brought from a judge-arbitrator, and where his reasons form the basis of the appeal: see pp. 594 et seq., post.

[13] See pp. 620 et seq., post.

[14] S. 5(2) of the 1979 Act, which he can apply directly, by virtue of s. 5(3), is of only limited value.

in a rather complicated way between the Court of Appeal, the High Court, and the judge-arbitrator. The following summary may be of assistance.

Nature of power	Tribunal exercising power	Source of power
A. Enforcement of arbitration agreement		
(i) Ordering a stay of concurrent proceedings	High Court	1950 Act, s. 4 and 1975 Act, s. 1 (unaffected by 1970 Act)
(ii) Referring an interpleader issue to arbitration	High Court	1950 Act, s. 5 (unaffected by 1970 Act)
(iii) Enlarging the time for commencing an arbitration	High Court	1950 Act, s. 27 (unaffected by 1970 Act)
B. Constitution of tribunal		
(i) Filling casual vacancy	High Court (no power in party to fill vacancy)	1950 Act, s. 10; and 1970 Act, Sch. 3, para. 3
(ii) Revocation of authority of judge-arbitrator or judge-umpire	Court of Appeal	1950 Act, ss. 10(a) and 25, and 1970 Act, Sch. 3, paras. 2 and 11
Appointment to fill vacancy thereby created	Court of Appeal or High Court	
(iii) Revocation of authority of other members of tribunal and appointment to fill vacancy thereby created	High Court	1950 Act, ss. 10(a) and 25, and 1970 Act, Sch. 3, paras. 2 and 11
(iv) Removal of judge-arbitrator or judge-umpire for failure to proceed with reasonable despatch	None	1950 Act, s. 13(3), and 1970 Act, Sch. 3, para. 6
(v) Removal of judge-arbitrator or judge-umpire for misconduct	Court of Appeal	1950 Act, s. 23 and 1970 Act, Sch. 3, para. 9(i)
(vi) Judge-umpire entering on reference in place of arbitrators	Judge-umpire	1950 Act, s. 8(3) and 1970 Act, Sch. 3, para. 4
C. Interlocutory orders		
(i) Issuing subpoenas, ordering discovery, affidavit evidence, interim preservation, security for costs, injunctions, appointment of receivers, etc.	High Court or judge-arbitrator (or judge-umpire)[15]	1950 Act, s. 12(4), (5) and (6) and 1970 Act, Sch. 3, para. 5(1)

---

[15] It is presumably not contemplated that the alternative jurisdictions created in these and certain other instances shall be exercised twice in respect of the same procedural issues, as can happen in conventional arbitrations (see p. 296, post). Moreover, we do not consider that a party would be justified in making an application on a procedural matter in a judicial arbitration to another judge of the High Court, unless the arbitrator happened not be be available.

Nature of power	Tribunal exercising power	Source of power
(ii) Procedural orders which would be within the powers of the arbitrator in an ordinary arbitration	Judge-arbitrator (or judge-umpire)	1970 Act, Sch. 3, para. 5(2)
(iii) Enlargment of time for making award	Judge-arbitrator (or judge-umpire)	1970 Act, Sch. 3, para. 6
(iv) Transferring issues of fraud to the High Court	None	1950 Act, s. 24(2) and 1970 Act, Sch. 3, para. 10
(v) Common law ancillary relief such as *Mareva* injunctions	High Court	[We suggest that s. 4(5) of the 1970 Act does not apply.][16]
(vi) Continuation of reference in default of compliance with order	High Court or judge-arbitrator (or judge-umpire)	1979 Act, s. 5(3)

D. Supervision of the reference

(i) Remission and setting-aside of award	Court of Appeal	1950 Act, ss. 22 and 23, and 1970 Act, Sch. 3, para. 9(1)
(ii) Common law powers to intervene with injunction and declaratory relief	Court of Appeal	1970 Act, s. 4(5)[17].

E. Appeals

(i) Giving leave to appeal under the 1979 Act	Court of Appeal	1979 Act, s. 1(3) and (4), and 1979 Act, s. 4(5)
(ii) Hearing appeals under the 1979 Act	Court of Appeal	1979 Act, s. 1(2), and 1970 Act, s. 4(5)
(iii) Deciding preliminary points of law under the 1979 Act	Court of Appeal	1979 Act, s. 2, and 1970 Act s. 4(5)

[16] Because that section applies only to a jurisdiction 'in relation to arbitrators and umpires otherwise than under the Arbitration Act 1950', and not 'in relation to arbitrations. . .'.

[17] For a discussion of these powers, see Chapter 32. If we are right in the view that s. 4(5) does apply to these powers, the transfer of the supervisory function to the Court of Appeal is something of a novelty, since the originating jurisdiction of that Court in relation to injunctions has historically been limited to those which are designed to protect the interests of the parties pending the disposition of an appeal: see Halsbury's *Laws of England* (4th edn.) Vol. 10, para. 899. The idea of the Court of Appeal being able to grant a declaration, as an originating process, is even more unusual.

Nature of power	Tribunal exercising power	Source of power
F. Procedural orders subsequent to the award		
(i) Taxation of costs	High Court	1950 Act s. 18(2) (unaffected by 1970 Act)
(ii) Order to deliver award against payment into Court of fees	No power (but judge-umpire may withhold award until fees paid)	1970 Act, Sch. 3, para. 8
(iii) Summary enforcement of the award	High Court or judge-arbitrator (or judge-umpire)	1950 Act, s. 26 and 1970 Act, Sch. 3, para. 12[18].

It is to be noted that certain of the powers which arise in the case of an umpire apply only after he has entered on the reference and in some cases only after he has made an award, whereas others apply where he has been appointed and even before he has entered on the reference[19].

4 Suggested procedure for commencing judicial arbitrations

Although there is no settled procedure for launching a judicial arbitration, the following method has proved convenient. If a party forms the opinion that a judicial arbitration would be a suitable way of dealing with the dispute, he should first discuss the matter with his opponent, to see whether they can agree on the use of the procedure and, if possible, on the choice of judge whom they would like to appoint. If agreement results, it should be recorded in writing. If the agreement extends to the choice of judge-arbitrator, the parties should communicate with the Clerk to the Commercial Court, identifying the dispute, producing the agreement for judicial arbitration, naming the judge whom the parties wish to act, and summarising any relevant information such as the nature of the dispute, the estimated length of the hearing, the date when the parties expect to be ready, and the reasons why the parties desire a judicial arbitration. The Clerk will then investigate the availability[20] of the judge in question, and will enquire whether in principle the judge is willing to act. If he is, then further communications should be addressed direct to the judge's clerk. The parties' advisers will then be invited to discuss the matter in much more detail with the judge. If in due course the judge expresses himself willing to act,

---

[18] Para. 12 provides that leave may (not 'shall') be given by the judge-arbitrator.

[19] It is not possible to formulate a general rule for deciding which situation applies. It is necessary in each case to consider the precise words of the sub-section or paragraph in question.

[20] The availability of the judge will depend upon the state of the list in the Commercial Court. A judicial arbitrator is not intended to be a means of obtaining an earlier trial date than would be available for an action in the Commercial Court. But urgent matters can be dealt with urgently by judicial arbitration, just as they can in the Commercial Court.

the Judge in charge of the Commercial Court will seek the necessary consent of the Lord Chief Justice.

The procedure is similar if the parties have not agreed on a choice of judge amongst themselves; the Clerk to the Commercial Court will make informal enquiries as to which judges are available and willing to act. It is then for the parties to decide whether they accept any of these judges as their arbitrator.

Once a judge has been agreed upon, who has expressed himself willing to act, a formal written submission to arbitration should be presented to the judge. It should be discussed in draft with the judge, before being executed.

B. OFFICIAL REFEREE

1 History

The office of official referee[1] was created by section 83 of the Judicature Act 1873. It was established on the recommendation of the First Report of the Judicature Commissioners 1869, in order that there should be attached to the Supreme Court a body of permanent salaried officers to whom questions arising in a cause or matter might be referred for inquiry and report[2] or, in any cause or matter requiring a prolonged examination of documents or accounts or any scientific or local investigation which could not be conveniently made before a jury or conducted by the Court through its other ordinary offices[3], for trial on questions of fact or account[4].

The Act of 1873 considerably enlarged the power of the Court, under the Common Law Procedure Act 1854[5], to refer questions to an arbitrator appointed by the parties, to an officer of the Court, or a judge of the County Court, for report or trial: this was limited to matters of account. The Court's powers of controlling and reviewing the proceedings of official referees were, however, modelled on those contained in the Common Law Procedure Act, and included procedures, such as remission and the special case, which subsequently became part of the general law of arbitration. Indeed, from 1889 until 1925, inquiries and trials by referees were governed by sections 13 to 17 of the Arbitration Act 1889, under the general rubric 'References under Order of Court'.

This derivative jurisdiction of the official referees nowadays constitutes almost the whole of their business, although their proceedings no longer bear any resemblance to the process of arbitration[6]: They now have all the powers of a

---

[1] We use the expression of 'official referee' throughout this section, although the office of official referee has now been abolished. A reference in any enactment, rule of court or any other document is now to be construed as a reference to a circuit judge, deputy circuit judge or recorder nominated by the Lord Chancellor to deal with official referees' business: Supreme Court Act 1981, s. 68(1) and (7). An account of the practice in relation to official referees' business may be found in the notes to RSC, Ord 36 in the *Supreme Court Practice 1988*. For an account of the office until 1940, see Burrows, 'Official Referees' (1940) 56 LQR 504, and for a more up-to-date account, Atkin's Court Forms, Vol. 33, 'References'.

[2] Judicature Act 1873, s. 56.

[3] Such as the Master or Chief Clerk.

[4] Judicature Act 1873, s. 57. S. 9 of the Judicature Act 1884 extended the power to refer for trial so as to include the whole action, including question of costs.

[5] S. 10 of the Judicature Act 1873 enabled the Court to refer matters to an official referee under the Common Law Procedure Act 1854.

[6] The changes were effected by the Administration of Justice Acts of 1932 and 1956.

judge of the High Court, proceedings before them are conducted, as nearly as circumstances admit, in the like manner as proceedings before a judge and an appeal lies direct to the Court of Appeal on a point of law from a decision of an official referee[7].

We are not here concerned with this aspect of the business of the official referees but with the duty imposed on them by section 11 of the Arbitration Act 1950[8] to sit as arbitrators to decide any matter referred to them by agreement of the parties. It is important, however, when considering the powers and duties of official referees sitting as arbitrators, to remember that this function is historically quite distinct from the function of dealing with trials and inquiries under an order of the Court[9].

2 Official referee as arbitrator

Section 11 of the Arbitration Act 1950 reads as follows:

> 'Where an arbitration agreement provides that the reference shall be to an official referee, any official referee to whom application is made shall, subject to any order of the High Court or a judge thereof as to transfer or otherwise, hear and determine the matters agreed to be referred'.

The section imposes a duty on the official referee to whom the application is made under the section to accept the reference. He has no discretion in the matter, provided that the condition laid down by the section is satisfied, namely, that 'the arbitration agreement provides that the reference shall be to an official referee'. However, if this condition is not satisfied, the official referee has no power to accept the reference. In particular, the condition is not satisfied by an agreement to refer disputes to an arbitrator to be nominated by the parties or by a third party, even if an official referee is nominated under the agreement. In order to give effect to such a nomination for the purposes of the section it would be necessary to execute a fresh arbitration agreement providing that the dispute shall be referred to an official referee.

An application under the section is made to the referee to whom the reference has been allocated by the rota clerk to the senior official referee[10]. The business

---

[7] RSC Ord. 36, r. 4, and Ord. 58, r. 6.

[8] Re-enacting s. 3 of the Arbitration Act 1889, which itself re-enacted s. 11 of the Judicature Act 1884.

[9] The Arbitration Act 1889 marked the distinction between the two functions by dealing with one under the rubric 'References by Consent out of Court', which dealt with all consensual arbitrations, and the other under the rubric 'References under Order of Court', which dealt with references of court proceedings to official and special referees. The Judicature Act 1925 repealed and re-enacted separately the provisions of the 1889 Act concerning references under order of the Court, leaving the remainder of the 1889 Act untouched.

[10] RSC Ord. 36, r. 5(2) and (3). These rules, which are made under s. 68(6) of the Supreme Court Act 1981, appear to restrict the right given by s. 11 of the Arbitration Act 1950 to apply to any official referee. Parties who had a preference for a particular referee might wish to take the point that s. 25(4) gives no power to make rules for the distribution of arbitration business, on the grounds that arbitration business is not a case 'in which jurisdiction of the High Court may be exercised by an official referee' (see post, p. 274) and is therefore not 'official referees' business' for the purposes of s. 68 of the Supreme Court Act 1981. A similar point might be made in relation to Ord. 36, r. 7, which provides for orders for transfer of business between referees to be made by the Lord Chancellor or Lord Chief Justice or in some cases by an official referee himself, and which is in apparent conflict with s. 11, which confers power to make orders as to transfer on the High Court or a judge thereof and on no-one else.

is allocated by the rota clerk to the referees in rotation[11], and when it has been allocated to an official referee it must forthwith be entered with that referee's clerk[12].

It has sometimes been stated[13] that an official referee sitting as an arbitrator has 'the same jurisdiction, powers and duties (including the power of committal and discretion as to costs as a judge', and that the proceedings must 'as nearly as circumstances admit, be conducted in the like manner as the like proceedings before a judge'.

This proposition is based on Order 36, r. 4(1), the relevant parts of which are quoted in the preceding sentence. If it is correct, arbitrations before official referees have advantages over all other types of arbitration, including those before judge-arbitrators or judge-umpires. It would follow, for example, that the referee-arbitrator could grant interim and final injunctions, make default orders without the necessity of invoking the assistance of the High Court and possibly even join co-defendants and third parties[14], even if they were not parties to the arbitration agreement. Desirable as this might be, however, we doubt whether the proposition is correct. Order 36, r. 4(1) takes effect by virtue of section 68(1) of the Supreme Court Act 1981, which enables rules of court to be made 'as to the cases in which the jurisdiction of the High Court may be exercised' by official referees.

The jurisdiction and powers of the High Court in relation to arbitrations is either supervisory or auxiliary in character[15] and does not extend to the actual conduct of the arbitration itself. Clearer words than are to be found in section 68(1) or the rules made under it would be necessary in order to produce the radical[16] and probably unintended[17] result of conferring greater powers on a referee-arbitrator than on any other arbitrator, and greater powers than the legislature thought fit to confer on a judge-arbitrator or judge-umpire.

The right of appeal to the Court of Appeal from a decision of an official referee on a point of law or a question of fact relevant to a charge of fraud or breach of professional duty does not apply to an award of a referee-arbitrator[18]. The procedures for challenging such an award are the same as in the case of any other arbitrator[19].

---

[11] Ord. 36, r. 5(5).

[12] Ord. 36, r. 6(1).

[13] Russell (19th edn.) p. 238; 2 *Encyclopaedia Forms of Precedent* (4th edn.) 391.

[14] See Ord. 36, r. 4(2).

[15] The power of the Commercial judges to sit as arbitrators or umpires under the Administration of Justice Act 1970 is, we submit, personal to the Commercial judges, and not a power of the High Court or a judge of the High Court.

[16] If s. 68(1) were intended to deal with the functions of referees-arbitrators as well as their functions in dealing with trials and inquiries under an order of the Court, this would have been a complete departure from the previous legislative practice of treating the two functions separately: see note 9, ante, p. 272.

[17] The opening words of Ord. 36, r. 4(1) ('subject to any directions contained in the order referring any business to an official referee') indicate that the draftsman had only references under an order of the Court in mind.

[18] Although Ord. 58, r. 5(1), taken above, could be said to apply to awards, r. 5(2) makes it plain that the rule as a whole applies only to decisions on a reference under an order of court.

[19] See Chapters 33, 34 and 36.

3 Merits of arbitration by official referee

Until recently the power to refer disputes to arbitration before an official referee was seldom resorted to[20]. Seeing that the services of a circuit judge and his clerk, together with the use of a court room, are provided by the State for no more than the very modest fee payable on setting down the reference, regardless of the length or importance of the dispute, one might wonder why appointments were not more common. The explanation may lie in the fact that agreements to refer *future* disputes to an official referee are almost unheard of, and that if the parties are willing to agree, after a dispute has arisen, that it should be decided by an official referee, they will probably prefer to agree to dispense with arbitration altogether and go straight to the High Court, where the range of procedural powers is greater than in arbitration; the parties will still be able to apply, if they wish to do so, for the action to be referred to an official referee under an order of the Court. There may, however, be circumstances in which arbitration before an official referee has procedural advantages over an action in the High Court: for example –

1 The parties may wish the proceedings to be held informally and in private rather than in a court open to the press and public.

2 The parties may wish to take advantage of the power under section 3 of the Arbitration Act 1979 to exclude the right of appeal from the referee's award on a question of law[1].

3 An award may have advantages over a judgment when it comes to enforcement, e.g. under the terms of a guarantee, or in enforcement proceedings abroad.

4 The parties may wish to go straight to an official referee, without having first to make an application to the Court for an order referring the matter to him. This could well be an advantage in urgent cases, or where the dispute is of a kind which the Court would not ordinarily refer to an official referee.

5 An official referee sitting as an arbitrator has power to exercise non-judicial functions vested in the arbitrator under a contract, such as the power to open up and review architects' certificates, which he cannot exercise sitting as an official referee[2].

C. COUNTY COURT ARBITRATION

Claims falling within the jurisdiction of the County Courts may, and in certain circumstances must, be referred to arbitration before a County Court judge or registrar or an outside arbitrator[3]. In such cases the arbitrator's authority derives

---

[20] The decision in *Northern Regional Health Authority v Derek Crouch Construction Co Ltd* [1984] QB 644, [1984] 2 WLR 676 (see n. 2 below) brought about a rapid increase in the number of appointments.

[1] It should not be overlooked, however, that an agreement to exclude the right of appeal to the Court of Appeal can always be made in proceedings in the High Court.

[2] *Northern Regional Health Authority v Derek Crouch Construction Co Ltd*, supra. See p. 272, ante.

[3] County Courts Act 1984, s. 64; County Court Rules, Ord. 19.

from the order of the court and not from an arbitration agreement, and for that reason alone arbitrations in the County Courts fall outside the scope of this book. Moreover, such arbitrations are not subject to Part I of the 1950 Act or the 1979 Act, although the statutory rules of procedure laid down for them provide some interesting comparisons with the procedure with which this book is concerned[4].

---

[4] E.g. the power to remit: see *Meyer v Leanse* [1958] 2 QB 371, [1958] 3 All ER 213.

PART V

The conduct of the reference

CHAPTER 21

Procedural powers and duties

A. ABSENCE OF UNIFORM PROCEDURE

Every arbitrator has a degree of discretion as to the way in which he conducts the reference. When considering the manner in which the discretion should be exercised, two questions arise.

First, to what extent is the discretion circumscribed? What must the arbitrator do; and what must he refrain from doing? Here, we are concerned with the *duties* of the arbitrator. Failure to perform these duties amounts to what is technically, if unhappily, known as misconduct. Any serious instance of misconduct, if not acquiesced in by the parties, will render the award voidable[1], and may lead the Court to intervene in the reference[2].

Second, to what extent can the arbitrator impose his will on the parties, by compelling them to follow his directions as to the conduct of the reference? Here, it is the *powers* of the arbitrator which are in question. In addition, it must be enquired to what extent the help of the Court can be invoked if the powers of the arbitrator prove insufficient.

It is a distinctive feature of English arbitral procedure that it is impossible, except in the most general terms, to furnish answers to these questions which will hold good for all types of arbitration. There is no statutory code of procedure. The Arbitration Acts say little about the powers of the arbitrator, and nothing at all about his duties[3]. The principles must therefore be extracted from the reported cases. Since these almost always concern situations in which a party complains of an abuse of the arbitrator's powers or duties, the Court has naturally been more concerned to decide whether or not the arbitrator has done something wrong, rather than to attempt a general exposition of what is right. The law on the conduct of the reference is, in effect, the law of misconduct transformed from the negative into the affirmative, and it is difficult to make a reliable synthesis from this fragmentary material.

There is another reason why it is difficult to formulate specific rules of procedure. English arbitral law recgonises as legitimate a remarkably wide variety of procedures. At one extreme of the scale there are formal arbitrations, with pleadings, discovery of documents, oral evidence on oath, cross-examination, and arguments by counsel. These arbitrations often take as long as, and cost even more than, full-scale trials in the High Court.

---

[1] As to the effect of misconduct, see p. 550, post.

[2] See Chapter 32, post.

[3] We are here discussing the conduct of the reference. The Acts do have something to say about the arbitrator's powers and duties in relation to the making of the award.

At the other end of the scale there are proceedings of the most informal kind[4]. The arbitrators are commercial men. There are no pleadings, no discovery, no oral evidence and there is often no hearing at all. A reference of this nature bears little or no resemblance to a judicial process as commonly understood. Many commodity arbitrations are of this highly informal variety. A dispute arises as to the conformity of goods with sample, or as to the allowance which should be made for deficiencies in quality. After the umpire has entered on the reference, there is rarely a meeting between himself and the arbitrators, and more rarely still between himself and the parties. The umpire receives no evidence. As Scrutton LJ said:

> 'He performs the mystic operations of smelling, tasting, touching and handling ... and these tell him about the quality of the goods. There is never any further meeting; and there is never any intention of a further meeting; and he makes his award on his own judgment of the stuff submitted to him'[5].

Between the extremes of formality and informality there is ample scope for variations in procedure, and it is common to find references which involve witnesses and a hearing, but dispense with the interlocutory and evidentiary rigour of a full formal arbitration. Moreover, even at the informal end of the scale, many different types of procedure may be found[6].

It will readily be seen that conduct which would be a serious breach of duty by the arbitrator, if committed in the course of what was intended to be a formal arbitration, would be entirely acceptable in the context of an informal reference. Thus, any attempt to apply rigid rules of conduct, without regard to the nature of the proceedings, will inevitably lead to error.

B. ASCERTAINMENT OF THE PROCEDURE TO BE FOLLOWED

Since the Acts are silent, and the courts have been careful not to provide a list of rules which are to be applied by rote, irrespective of the circumstances, a newly-appointed arbitrator must look elsewhere for guidance on the way to conduct the reference. Since arbitration is a creature of agreement, one would expect to find the arbitrator's duties[7] defined in the arbitration agreement itself; and one would also expect the Court to enforce such an agreement, subject to such qualifications as are imposed by the overriding requirements of public policy.

---

[4] These are often called 'commercial' arbitrations. This term might be thought to echo the clear-cut distinction between commercial and non-commercial transactions, such as is found in certain continental codes of procedure, but which is unknown to English law. Moreover, many disputes which might well, in ordinary speech, be regarded as having a commercial origin are not conducted with the extreme informality described in the text. It therefore seems preferable to adopt a different terminology.

[5] *Naumann v Edward Nathan & Co Ltd* (1930) 37 Ll L Rep 249 at 260. See also *J Aron & Co Inc v Miall* (1928) 31 Ll L Rep 242 at 245.

[6] As Mocatta J pointed out in *Star International Hong Kong (UK) Ltd v Bergbau-Handel GmbH* [1966] 2 Lloyd's Rep 16 at 18.

[7] In this Chapter, we use the word 'duties' to denote rules which the arbitrator ought to follow, rather than the type of personal duty owed to one or both parties which, if broken, results in a liability in damages – a topic discussed in Chapter 17, ante.

This is indeed what is found, when the reported cases are examined. The process for ascertaining the duties of the arbitrator may be set out in formal terms as follows[8], although the arbitrator will rarely, if ever, be driven to making a deliberate step by step analysis of this nature –

1 Find out what the parties have expressly agreed about procedure, either in the underlying contract, or at the time when the dispute was submitted to arbitration, or on some subsequent occasion.

2 Ascertain whether, by their conduct during the reference, the parties have impliedly agreed that the particular aspect of procedure in question shall be dealt with in a particular way.

3 Reject any of the procedural rules thus agreed, insofar as they are inconsistent with public policy.

4 On any aspect of procedure which is not covered either by express agreement or by a specific agreement to be implied from conduct, enquire whether any term can be implied into the arbitration agreement from one or more of the following –

(a) The express terms of the arbitration agreement;
(b) The language of the arbitration agreement;
(c) The subject matter of the underlying contract, together with any relevant trade practice;
(d) The nature of the dispute;
(e) The identity of the tribunal;
(f) The requirements of natural justice.

We shall now discuss each step in this analysis.

1 Express agreement on procedure

The parties may expressly agree upon a procedure for the conduct of the reference either when they make the underlying contract, or when they submit the dispute to the arbitrator, or on a subsequent occasion. The effect of such an agreement depends upon when it is made.

If the parties have agreed upon a procedure before or at the time when the arbitrator is appointed, he is bound to follow it. If he does not care for the agreed method of conducting the reference, he should say so before, but not after, he accepts the appointment. Failure to comply with the agreement of the parties is misconduct, which may invalidate the award.

In practice, the underlying contract rarely sets out a full code of practice. Such a code, may, however, be incorporated by reference; for example, where the parties agree to arbitrate in accordance with the Rules of Arbitration of the International Chamber of Commerce, or where a commodity contract incorporates the conditions of sale of a trade association, which themselves refer to the association's rules of arbitration. Sometimes, the agreement simply provides that the arbitration shall be carried out 'in the usual way'[9].

---

[8] The judgment at first instance of Diplock J in *London Export Corpn Ltd v Jubilee Coffee Roasting Co Ltd* [1958] 1 Lloyd's Rep 197 (on appeal, [1958] 1 Lloyd's Rep 367) contains an illuminating discussion of this topic. Since the case arose from an allegation of misconduct, the learned judge was concerned with ascertaining what conduct was wrong, not what was right, and the discussion is centred on breach of duty, rather than on the duty itself. Nevertheless, it is believed that the analysis in the text is broadly in line with that of Diplock J.

[9] See p. 107, ante.

The agreement of procedural rules at the same time as the appointment of the arbitrator is most common where the parties have decided to appoint a lawyer as arbitrator, and where they are setting out from the start to have a formal arbitration. Agreement as to the times for exchanging pleadings, lists of documents and so on, saves the trouble and expense of consulting the arbitrator for preliminary directions. Another step which the parties may usefully take when submitting the dispute to the arbitrator is the inclusion of an express agreement as to the form in which evidence can be given at the hearing. Quite frequently, the parties feel that there are advantages in giving the arbitration the same general shape as a High Court action, but wish to avoid the evidential niceties which sometimes make an action unnecessarily expensive. In such a case, it is desirable for the parties to state in the agreement that the arbitrator will not be bound by the strict rules of evidence. This avoids the possibility of uncertainty and surprise at a later date, and frees the arbitrator from the duty to exclude written evidence and hearsay, which he might otherwise be required to do[10].

An agreement on procedure made by the parties after the arbitrator has agreed to act is on a rather different footing. Here, it cannot be said that compliance with the agreement is a condition of his appointment, and if the parties were to insist on a procedure which he found objectionable, he would be within his rights in declining to act. In practice, matters should never come to this pass. As a matter of prudence, as well as courtesy, the parties should seek the arbitrator's approval of the agreed procedure. The arbitrator may, and indeed should, make his views known if the parties propose a way of conducting the reference which he considers may lead to confusion, delay or expense. Nevertheless, if the parties decline to take his advice, he should yield. He is, after all, no more than the agreed instrument of the parties. If there is a conflict between the parties, an arbitrator who tries to please them both is likely to fall into error. But if they are in agreement, he should in the end do what they wish, for it is their money, and not his, which is being spent on the reference.

The spirit in which the Court or the arbitrator should approach the interpretation of an express agreement as to procedure depends upon the nature of the agreement, and the way it has come into existence. An agreement drawn up by lawyers should be strictly enforced, but one which has been prepared by commercial men, who may not be so practised in the use of technically exact language, may properly be given a broader interpretation[11].

Where the contract provides that disputes are to be decided in accordance with the rules of a particular tribunal this means, prima facie, that the rules for the time being are to apply, not the rules as they stood when the contract was made[12].

---

[10] See pp. 352–354, post.

[11] See, for example, *Finzel, Berry & Co v Eastcheap Dried Fruit Co* [1962] 2 Lloyd's Rep 11 at 14, where the Rules of a trade association were interpreted in a sense which might, perhaps, have been difficult to sustain if the agreement had been carefully negotiated between lawyers.

[12] *Perez v John Mercer & Sons* (1922) 10 Ll L Rep 584; *Offshore International SA v Banco Central SA and Hijos de J Barreras SA* [1976] 2 Lloyd's Rep 402; *Bunge SA v Kruse* [1979] 1 Lloyd's Rep 279; *Edm JM Mertens & Co PVBA v Veevoeder Import Export Vimex BV* [1979] 2 Lloyd's Rep 372. The particular context or words may, of course, yield a different interpretation.

2 Agreement implied from conduct

Even if the parties have not expressly provided for the way in which the dispute is to be conducted, it may be possible to infer an agreement on one or more aspects of the procedure, from the way in which the parties have already begun to conduct the reference. Thus, if they behave in a manner which shows that they take it for granted that there will be no oral hearing, the absence of a hearing will by implication become part of the agreed procedure[13].

3 Public policy

Where the parties have expressly agreed upon a procedure, the courts will in general recognise it as a proper, and indeed the only proper, means of conducting the reference. It is, however, possible to envisage contractual provisions of such an extreme nature that the Court would decline to enforce them. Recognition might be withheld by the courts in two different ways. First, the Court might conclude that the term was so alien to English concepts of the nature of an arbitration as to transform a process which the contract referred to as arbitration and which in other respects appeared to be one, into something fundamentally different. This would have the consequence that the Court would not exercise the powers to control and reinforce the reference and to enforce the resulting decision which it would possess in the case of a true arbitration[14]. Second, the Court might continue to recognise the process as an arbitration, but decline to give effect to the objectionable term[15]. The first alternative is outside the scope of this book. The second raises the difficult question of the extent to which considerations of public policy are material to the law of arbitration.

Until comparatively recently, it would have been possible to identify four classes of provision regarded by the Courts as contrary to public policy –

    1 Terms which affect the substantive content of the award, including[16] –

---

[13] See *Star International Hong Kong (UK) Ltd v Bergbau-Handel GmbH*, ante. Conduct of this type creates an implied agreement on the particular aspect of procedure with which it is concerned. Conduct may also be relevant for the light which it sheds on the general nature of the contemplated procedure: see pp. 286–287, post.

[14] The fact that the process is not an arbitration will not necessarily prevent the decision from being enforceable as a matter of contract. This will depend on the nature of the term which prevents the agreement under which the dispute is resolved from being an arbitration agreement.

[15] Since the number of recent instances (and only modern cases on this topic can now be relied upon) in which the courts have invoked public policy is so small, there is virtually no discussion of the extent to which objectionable terms can be severed from the remainder of the contract. The point was raised, but not decided, in *Perez v John Mercer & Sons* (1921) 7 Ll L Rep 1. Since it has now come to be clearly established that an arbitration clause is an undertaking collateral to the substantive contract in which it is contained, we suggest that the latter can in most if not all cases survive the striking-down of an objectionable term relating to arbitration. (We say 'most, if not all', because of the possibility that a term enabling the arbitrator to decide without reference to law would deprive the contract of any legal effect: see the discussion at pp. 83–85, ante.) We believe that the Court would also endeavour to sever an individual term regulating a particular aspect of the arbitral process from the remainder of the contractual provisions for arbitration.

[16] The instances given in the text are those which are likely to be most important in practice. It is possible to visualise other objectional terms relating to the substantive content of the award, or the mode of arriving at it: for example that in case of doubt the arbitrator shall decide by lot, or that the entire process of decision can be delegated by the arbitrator to someone else. Terms of this nature are, however, more likely to be relevant to the question whether the procedure is an arbitration at all, than to the validity of the term itself.

(i)   Those which entitle the arbitrator to decide otherwise than in accordance with the substantive law governing the underlying contract: for example those which require or empower him to decide ex aequo et bono.

(ii)   Those which require the arbitrator to enforce an illegal contract[17].

(iii) Certain terms which prescribe in advance what the terms of the award shall be[18].

2 Terms which purport to exclude or restrict the supervisory jurisdiction of the Court, including –

(i)   Those which exclude or restrict to an unacceptable degree the right of a party to appeal to the High Court on a question of law[19].

(ii)   Those which exclude or restrict to an unacceptable degree the right of a party to invoke the powers of the High Court to intervene if the reference has been conducted in an improper manner[20].

3 Terms which require the arbitrator to conduct the reference in an unacceptable manner, including –

(i)   Those which require the arbitrator to perform an illegal act in conducting the reference.

(ii)   Those which require or permit the arbitrator to conduct the reference in a manner inconsistent with the basic procedural requirements of English arbitration law.

4 Terms which purport to empower the arbitrator to carry out procedures or exercise powers which lie exclusively within the jurisdiction of the courts.

The case of illegality is dealt with at p. 113, and requires no separate discussion here. Category 1(i) is discussed in Chapter 4, at pp. 68–71. The remaining instances are discussed below.

One may first consider category 2(i), which concerns the power of the Court to intervene to correct errors of law. For many years, it was one of the very few axioms of English arbitration law that a term falling into this category would be disregarded by the courts, because it was contrary to public policy. The position is now quite different. So far as concerns agreements purporting to oust the right of appeal, the matter is now regulated by statute. The 1979 Act prescribes those situations in which the parties can, and those in which they cannot, validly exclude the right of appeal created by the Act. This new system of appeals is self contained, and there is no need for recourse to public policy[1].

The enforceability of a provision in category 2(ii), namely one which purports to exclude or restrict the right of the Court to intervene in cases of misconduct, is also a source of difficulty. One possible view is that such provisions are in principle valid, but that in certain instances their enforcement may be denied on the ground of public policy. In support of this view, it may be urged that misconduct is in almost every case no more than a procedural error,

---

[17] By which we mean a contract the making or performance of which is illegal by English law. Illegality by foreign law may be a defence to a claim under the contract, to which the arbitrator is bound to give effect when arriving at his decision; but this is a different matter.

[18] So far as we are aware, the only instance of this category is statutory in origin; s. 18(3) of the Act avoids any provision in an agreement for the arbitration of future disputes that a party or the parties shall in any event pay their own costs.

[19] E.g. *Macleod Ross & Co Ltd v Cradock Manners Ltd* [1954] 1 Lloyd's Rep 258 at 264.

[20] E.g. *E Rotheray & Sons Ltd v Carlo Bedarida & Co* [1961] 1 Lloyd's Rep 220.

[1]   Except perhaps in relation to an agreement which purports to exclude challenges to the arbitrator's decision on a question of law, otherwise than by the statutory appeal procedure: as to which, see Chapter 37, post.

unaccompanied by any shadow of conscious wrongdoing, and that all the offended party complains of in such a case is a failure by the arbitrator to perform the express or implied terms of the submission: so that there can be nothing objectionable in the parties' agreeing in advance that such non-compliance will not be relied upon as vitiating any resulting award. It may also be pointed out that the parties can agree in advance to permit a mode of proceeding which would otherwise amount to misconduct, and that they can condone misconduct by subsequent acts amounting to waiver. We are not impressed by these latter arguments. To consent in advance, of after the event, to a particular course of conduct which would otherwise be objectionable is not the same as an agreement which gives carte blanche to the arbitrator to proceed in whatever way he chooses even to the extent of departing from an express term of the agreement, as to the way in which the reference shall be conducted: for this is the practical consequence of an agreement excluding the right of an aggrieved party to complain to the court in the event of misconduct. Whether such an agreement is regarded as objectionable depends upon the view which the observer takes of the relationship between the arbitral process and the courts. To those who believe that the process is best left on its own, without even the most well-meaning interference by the judiciary in the most flagrant of cases, the question answers itself. A term excluding the right to complain of misconduct is no more than a demonstration by the parties that they have chosen arbitration for better or worse, and as such should be enforced not disregarded. This point of view was advanced with vigour during the discussion and debates preceding the passing of the 1979 Act, and we acknowledge the force of it. We do, however, suggest that the argument swims against the current of modern judicial thinking. Freedom of contract is no longer a self-evident virtue. Even in the commercial field, it has long since come to be fettered by domestic and international legislation. Furthermore, the courts have progressively been empowered, and have come to assume a power, even if not formally enabled by statute, to intervene in cases of flagrant unfairness in the procedures of subordinate and extra-legal bodies. This tendency recently came to the surface, in a rather unexpected manner, in the assertion by the Court of a general right to intervene where a reference to arbitrator, not yet carried as far as an award, shows signs of going badly wrong[2]. It seems rather unlikely, in the current climate of judicial opinion, that the courts will look kindly on the creation by contract of an autonomous para-judicial system free from control even in the case of the most flagrant abuse.

Next, there are terms falling within category 3(ii), namely those which purport to allow the arbitrator to conduct the reference in a manner which the law would otherwise regard as objectionable. In the nineteenth century, this category may well have been important; but the attitude of the courts has changed, and it is clear that many forms of procedural agreement which might once have been struck down will now be enforced: for example, agreements to permit the use of inadmissible evidence[3], or to exclude legal representation[4], or to allow one party to communicate with a member of the tribunal in the absence

---

[2] In *Japan Line Ltd v Aggeliki Charis Compania Maritima SA, and Davies and Potter, The Angelic Grace* [1980] 1 Lloyd's Rep 288 discussed at pp. 518 et seq., post.
[3] *Henry Bath & Son Ltd v Birgby Products* [1962] 1 Lloyd's Rep 389 at 399.
[4] Ibid. at 395.

of the other[5]. Almost certainly, however, the category still exists[6] for it must be possible to conceive of proceedings so repugnant to English ideas of justice that the Court would not recognise even express prior consent as justifying their use[7].

Finally, there are terms within category 4, namely those which purport to empower the arbitrator to carry out procedures or exercise powers, which are exclusively within the jurisdiction of the Court. The Court alone has power to enforce its orders by taking coercive action against the property or person of the individual or body against whom the order is made. The consent of the parties cannot empower the arbitrators to employ such measures of enforcement: a fortiori where the person or body concerned is not a party to the arbitration. Nor can the parties agree that the arbitrator shall have power to make an order of which the existence of such sanctions forms an essential part. Thus, for example, an arbitrator cannot issue a subpoena duces tecum requiring an individual to produce a document in Court, on pain of committal for contempt[8].

4 Implied agreement on procedure

If the parties have not by their words or conduct prescribed what procedure is to be followed, it is often possible to fill the gap by implying terms into the agreement to arbitrate. For this purpose, various factors must be weighed together[9].

(a) Express terms of agreement

First, regard must be had to the express terms of the arbitration agreement, to see what guidance they give, not only on particular aspects of the reference, but on the nature of the contemplated procedure as a whole. If, for example, the agreement provides for an exchange of pleadings, this is a strong hint that the other aspects of the procedure are intended to follow the same general lines as a High Court action. Similarly, even if the parties have expressly indicated that in general an informal arbitration is to take place, there may nevertheless be

---

[5] *Ritchie v Jacks & Co* (1922) 10 Ll L Rep 519 at 520–521. *London Export Corpn v Jubilee Coffee Roasting Co Ltd*, ante, at 202.

[6] The category certainly exists in relation to domestic tribunals. See, for example, *Lee v Showmen's Guild of Great Britain* [1952] 2 QB 329 at 342.

[7] It is, however, always necessary to bear in mind the distinction, to which we have already drawn attention, between terms which call for a procedure so exotic that it cannot be regarded as an arbitration, and hence does not call into play the judicial mechanisms of supervision and enforcement which are appropriate to an arbitration, and those terms which introduce an objectionable element into what is undoubtedly an arbitration.

[8] See for example *Kursell v Timber Operators and Contractors Ltd* [1923] 2 KB 202 at 206; *Re Unione Stearinerie Lanza and Weiner* [1917] 2 KB 558 at 562. Whether the particular term is to be regarded as void on the ground of public policy or whether it is simply ineffective on the ground that there is no means of enforcing it, is of only academic interest.

[9] Strictly speaking, conduct subsequent to the agreement cannot be used to construe, or imply terms into that agreement; it is no more than evidence of an implied variation. The courts have understandably ignored this technical point.

something in the agreement to suggest that the ordinary legal rules are not to be completely ignored[10].

(b) Language of agreement

Second, the language as well as the contents of the agreement to arbitrate may shed light on the contemplated procedure. The more legalistic the way in which the agreement is expressed the more easy it is to infer a consent to a formal arbitration[11].

(c) Subject matter of underlying contract

Next, the subject matter of the underlying contract often provides an indication of the desired procedure, especially if disputes relating to the trade in question are habitually conducted in a particular manner. Thus, informal arbitrations are very common in the shipping and commodity trades[12]. The term that the usual practice shall be followed is very readily implied. Nevertheless, it must be borne in mind that even a long-standing trade practice cannot prevail if it conflicts with the express terms of the arbitration agreement, or with the general tenor of the agreement[13]. Care must also be taken to have regard to the practice in the individual trade in question, for although shipping and commodity arbitrations share the general feature of informality, there are wide differences in the specific procedures adopted[14]. Moreover, certain types of dispute, such as those arising out of engineering and building contracts, are commonly conducted in a manner comparable to proceedings in the High Court; and an arbitrator seized of such a dispute could not properly apply an informal procedure of the type recognised in shipping and commodity arbitrations, without first warning, and obtaining the consent of, the parties.

(d) Nature of dispute

Another relevant factor is the nature of the dispute. The parties cannot be assumed to have contemplated that all potential disputes under the contract will necessarily be decided in the same way. It is easy to imply a term that quality

---

[10] As in *London Export Corpn v Jubilee Coffee Roasting Co Ltd*, ante, where an express provision insulating the umpire from any part in the selection of the appeal tribunal indicated that the latter was to be independant from the umpire, and hence made it possible to imply a customary term to the effect that the umpire could properly retire with the appeal tribunal when it was considering its award.

[11] See per Younger LJ in *Ritchie v Jacks*, ante, at 526.

[12] There are many instances in the reports. See, for example, *London Export Corpn v Jubilee Coffee Roasting Co*, ante; *Russian Oil Products Ltd v Caucasian Oil Co Ltd* (1928) 31 Ll L Rep 109; *French Government v Tsurushima Maru* (1921) 8 Ll L Rep 403; *Ritchie v Jacks*, ante; *Gunter Henck v Andre & Cie SA* [1970] 1 Lloyd's Rep 235; *Star International Hong Kong (UK) Ltd v Bergbau-Handel GmbH* [1966] 2 Lloyd's Rep 16; *The Myron (M/V) (Owners) v Tradax Export SA* [1969] 1 Lloyd's Rep 411, [1970] 1 QB 527.

[13] *London Export Corpn v Jubilee Coffee Roasting Co*, ante, in both courts. A distinction must be drawn between a customary mode of conducting proceedings and a long-established course of committing irregularities – ibid.

[14] *Star International Hong Kong (UK) Ltd v Bergbau-Handel*, ante, at 18.

disputes under commodity contracts shall be deciced by informal means[15], but more difficult to do so in relation to disputes under similar contracts raising complex issues of mixed fact and law.

(e) Identity of tribunal

The identity of the chosen arbitration tribunal may also shed light on the intention of the parties. If the arbitration clause provides that the arbitrators shall be 'commercial men and not lawyers', or 'merchants', or 'persons engaged in the shipping trade', the Court will readily infer that the parties wish the tribunal to exercise its own expertise, without receiving formal evidence or employing legalistic procedures. Conversely, the choice of a lawyer as arbitrator points towards a more formal type of proceeding[16].

(f) Natural justice

Finally regard must be had to the requirement of natural justice. The courts will not readily imply a mode of proceedings which would lead to unfair results[17].

5 Procedure in the absence of agreement

It will often happen that an application of the tests suggested in the preceding paragraphs yields no positive result: the parties cannot be said to have agreed anything about the procedure to be followed. It is not possible to extract from the reported cases any clear guidance on the shape which the reference should take in such a case. Two propositions can, however, be stated with reasonable confidence.

First, the procedure must be of an adversarial nature. That is to say, the function of the arbitrator is not to exercise his own initiative by carrying out an enquiry into the factual and legal issues, but instead to act as the passive recipient of evidence and argument presented by the parties, and to arrive at his decision by choosing between them[18].

---

[15] *French Government v Tsurushima Maru*, per Bankes LJ, at 404; *Ritchie v Jacks*, ante, per Lord Sterndale MR at 520.

[16] See, for example, *Mediterranean and Eastern Export Co Ltd v Fortress Fabrics (Manchester) Ltd* (1948) 81 Ll L Rep 401 at 403, and *London Export Corpn v Jubilee Coffee Roasting Co*, ante, at 202, on the contrast between legal and commercial arbitrators as regards the reception of expert evidence.

[17] It is perhaps preferable to speak of 'unfair' rather than 'contrary to natural justice'; the latter may, to a lawyer, have connotations which are sometimes too narrow, and sometimes too wide. See the judgment of Diplock J in *London Export Corpn v Jubilee Coffee Roasting Co*, ante; also *Wiseman v Borneman* [1971] AC 297 and *Norwest Holst Ltd v Secretary of State for Trade* [1978] Ch 201.

[18] This does not mean that an English arbitration can only be validly conducted by an adversarial process, nor can the judgments in *Bremer Vulkan Schiffbau und Maschinenfabrik v South India Shipping Corpn* [1980] 1 Lloyd's Rep 255 and [1981] 1 Lloyd's Rep 253 be understood in this sense, for the majority of commercial arbitrations (if not large-scale arbitrations) are to some degree inquisitorial in form. In a straightforward quality dispute the umpire inspects a sample or visits the warehouse or quay where the goods are stored. The parties do not usually tender evidence or argument but are content to rely on the umpire's expertise: although he must receive evidence and argument if they are tendered. In a shipping arbitration on the Baltic Exchange, the arbitrators look at the files, call for any necessary further documents, and discuss the matter between themselves. These are not adversarial procedures, and yet they have long been sanctioned by the courts. The reason is that the procedures are regarded as the result of an implied choice by the parties. The statement in the text relates to those instances where there is no chosen procedure.

Second, the arbitrator is not required to follow minutely the procedures of a High Court action, but can exercise a broad discretion, so long as he adopts a procedure which complies with the essential features of the English adversarial procedure. We suggest that the most important of these are as follows –

1 There must be a hearing at which the parties or their representatives have an opportunity to adduce evidence and address argument.

2 The arbitrator must not receive evidence or argument from one party in the absence of the other.

3 The arbitrator must act only upon evidence which would be admissible in a court of law.

4 Where there is more than one arbitrator, they must all act judicially throughout; they must not assume the roles of arbitrator-advocate, or representatives of the parties.

5 The arbitrator should not carry out his own investigations into the issues without the prior consent of the parties. If he obtains such consent, he must disclose the results of his investigation and give the parties an opportunity to comment, and to adduce their own evidence upon the issues.

6 He must, if called upon to do so, exercise a judicial discretion on whether to order discovery of documents, although it does not necessarily follow that he need order full discovery, or any discovery at all.

6 Attitude of the Court to informal arbitrations

It not infrequently happens that although the application of the tests described above yields no detailed guidance as to the procedures which the parties agreed to follow, it can still be inferred that they envisaged that it would be in some degree informal. In such a case, the courts permit the arbitrator to exercise a much wider discretion than would have been conceivable in the nineteenth century. Indeed, any case decided before, say, 1920 must be approached with great caution when deciding whether a commercial arbitrator has committed misconduct[19], for in more recent times the courts have repeatedly emphasised the desirability of upholding the decisions of commercial tribunals. The following extracts will serve as illustrations:

> '... Neither this Court nor any other Court should endeavour to put obstacles in [the parties'] way or attempt to fetter their discretion by fussy interference on technical points'[20].

> 'In my opinion we should impose no rules of practice on the conduct of the arbitrators or the umpire except such as are absolutely necessary to secure justice. They are entitled to have their own rules of practice as we have, unless they are manifestly contrary to natural justice'[1].

> 'The modern tendency is, in my opinion, more especially in commercial arbitrations, to endeavour to uphold awards of the skilled persons that the

---

[19] See the observations of McNair J in *Henry Bath & Son v Birgby Products*, ante, at 399.
[20] *Richard Clear & Co Ltd v Bloch* (1922) 13 Ll L Rep 462, per Bankes LJ at 463. The corollary of the Court's reluctance to interfere is the strong conviction that if commercial men choose to hold informal arbitrations they should respect the results, and not complain afterwards about the informality. As Scrutton LJ said in *Clear v Bloch*, '... let them take their beating when they get it'.
[1] Per Bray J at first instance in *French Government v Tsurushima Maru* (1921) 7 Ll L Rep 244 at 248.

parties themselves have selected to decide the questions at issue between them. If an arbitrator has acted within the terms of his submission and has not violated any rules of what is so often called natural justice, the Courts should be slow indeed to set aside his award'[2].

'The Court ought not to be too ready to find technical difficulties so as to defeat the very object of the parties in having their disputes decided by arbitration'[3].

There are, nevertheless, limits to the benevolence with which the courts will approach the arbitrations of commercial men. Several judgments express these limits in terms of 'natural justice'. This expression must be approached with caution, because it tends to suggest that there exists a package of procedural rules which must always be observed. This is not so, for the requirements of natural justice vary according to the circumstances. No immutable principles can be extracted from the reported cases. We believe, however, that an arbitrator is unlikely to be held at fault if he observes the following rules –

1 He should endeavour to act fairly between the parties, eliminating conscious, and so far as he can, unconscious bias.

2 He should not only be impartial in fact, but should act in such a way that the parties are confident of that fact.

3 He should pay careful attention to any evidence or arguments presented by the parties, and should be seen to be doing so.

4 He should keep the parties fully informed of what he is doing, and what he proposes to do[4].

The first three of these precepts are obvious, and there can be very few arbitrators who knowingly transgress them. Experience suggests, however, that the importance of the fourth[5] is not always appreciated. Many of the complaints adduced in misconduct proceedings involve, not so much the suggestion that the arbitrator has done something intrinsically unjust, but that he has done something different from what the complaining party had expected. The cutting of procedural corners is often beneficial, so long as everyone knows what is happening; for if a party does not like what is going to happen, he can make his objection known to the arbitrator, or if all else fails, to the Court, in order to prevent his interests from being prejudiced. But if the arbitrator adopts a short cut without giving proper warning, the parties will not know what has taken place until it is too late. A real risk as well as a feeling of injustice occurs if a party is taken by surprise. For example, his opponent adduces evidence or submissions of which he has not been warned, and therefore cannot take steps to meet. The arbitrator decides the dispute on the basis of a point of law which he has invented for himself, and which the losing party never had an opportunity to controvert. The arbitrator leads the parties to assume that there will be an

---

[2] Per Lord Goddard CJ in *Mediterranean and Eastern Export Co v Fortress Fabrics (Manchester) Ltd*, ante, at 404.

[3] Per Singleton LJ in *Kiril Mischeff Ltd v British Doughnut Co Ltd* [1954] 1 Lloyd's Rep 237 at 246. Similar expressions of opinion can be found in *Ocrotopulo & Sons v Ministry of Food* (1921) 9 Ll L Rep 274; *Henry Bath & Son Ltd v Birgby Products*, ante; *GW Potts Ltd v Macpherson, Train & Co* (1927) 27 Ll L Rep 445; *Re Hopper* (1867) LR 2 QB 367 at 375; and in several other cases.

[4] The first two rules are developed more fully in Chapter 18, and the last two in Chapter 22.

[5] Particularly if one of the parties is foreign: *Scrimaglio v Thornett and Fehr* (1923) 17 Ll L Rep 34; affd. (1924) 18 Ll L Rep 148, per Scrutton LJ.

oral hearing, and then decides the case on the documents. The arbitrator purports to apply a custom of the trade, whose existence had never been suggested to the parties. In many cases of this kind there is no objective injustice, in the sense that the answer to the dispute might well have been just the same even if the proper forms had been followed. This is not the point. What matters is that a party is left with the feeling that he has not received fair play. This feeling could be eliminated, and the already small number of applications to remit or set aside awards for misconduct could be reduced almost to nothing, if arbitral tribunals would take more care to keep the parties fully informed.

7 Alterations in procedure

An arbitrator occasionally comes to recognise, in the course of a reference, that the procedure which he is adopting is not the one best fitted to produce a just and convenient resolution of the dispute. The question will then arise whether he has a power to adopt a different procedure, without the consent of the parties. Plainly, he has none, if the original procedure is the one expressly laid down by the arbitration agreement, or by subsequent agreement between the parties. Logically, the answer should be the same where there is no express agreement as to procedure, but where a clear implication can be made from the nature of the transaction, the custom of the trade, the identity of the arbitrator and so on. This is undoubtedly the case, where the implied term posits a formal procedure. An arbitrator could never be justified in forcing an informal procedure on unwilling parties. Whether a change in the reverse direction is permissible is less clear. In theory, it would seem that it should be, for if the parties have impliedly chosen an informal arbitration, this is what they are entitled to expect[6]. There is, however, authority for the contrary view, that where the agreement for informal arbitration is implied rather than expressed, either party can always insist on reverting to a more formal process[7].

C. THE POWERS OF THE ARBITRATOR

Thus far, we have discussed the duties of the arbitrator: namely, those rules which prescribe what he must do if he is to avoid misconduct. We now turn to the question of his powers: namely, the means which he possesses to ensure that when he exercises his discretion in a particular way, the parties will comply with his directions. The concepts of powers and duties are often used interchangeably, as if they were the same. This is misleading. The duties define the minimum which the arbitrator himself must do; the powers define the maximum which he can compel the parties to do. In many instances, the

---

[6] This may have been the view of Lord Sterndale MR in *Ritchie v Jacks*, ante, at 522.

[7] See per Atkin LJ in *Ritchie v Jacks*, ante, at 524; per Bankes LJ in *French Government v Tsurushima Maru*, ante, at 404; per Donaldson J in *The Myron*, ante, at 415. The correct analysis may be that the implied agreement to an informal arbitration is itself impliedly qualified by a right to insist on a more formal procedure on giving notice. From a practical point of view there should be limits to this doctrine. Could a party to a straightforward quality dispute submitted to a trade arbitrator really insist on appearing by counsel and calling expert evidence? Penalising him in costs would be no answer. If he lost, he would have to pay all the costs anyway; and if he won, the arbitrator would need to be very sure of his ground to treat the extra costs as wasted.

arbitrator has powers which he is under no duty to exercise. For example, he *can* order discovery of documents, but it does not follow that he *must* do so. In truth, the powers of the arbitrator are co-extensive, not with his duties, but with his discretion.

It will be noted that Parliament has not sought, so far as concerns the conduct of the reference[8], to confer powers on the arbitrator in the abstract. The position of the arbitrator is therefore different from that of the High Court. In a given state of facts, the Judge always has the same powers, although he may have a discretion whether to exercise them. The powers of the arbitrator are not fixed in this way, but are dependent upon the express or implied agreement of the parties. Thus, although it is often convenient for the purposes of discussion to say that the arbitrator has power to make such and such an order, it is more accurate to express this as a power which he usually has, or which he will have in the absence of express agreement to the contrary.

1 Express powers

Subject to three limitations, the parties may confer upon the arbitrator whatever powers they wish.

The first limitation is that the parties cannot give the arbitrator powers, the exercise of which would be contrary to public policy[9].

Second, since the powers are created by the agreement of the parties, they cannot be exercised against persons who did not take part in that agreement. Thus, for example, the arbitrator has no power to order third parties to attend at the hearing, or to produce documents[10], or to allow another arbitration to which they are parties to be heard at the same time as the arbitration in question[11].

Third, there are certain powers which the Court reserves for itself, and which the parties cannot confer even by express agreement. These are powers of a kind 'which only a Judge can use'[12]. This exception appears to relate mainly to powers affecting the liberty of the subject, and it may be that it really goes no further than the second exception.

When making an agreement to confer powers upon an arbitrator, the parties should take care to qualify it by the words 'subject to any legal objection'[13], in case it should subsequently be argued that the parties have unintentionally taken away certain important rights: notably, the rights to treat certain evidence and documents as privileged.

2 Implied powers

Section 12(1) reads as follows –

'Unless a contrary intention is expressed therein, every arbitration

---

[8] The arbitrator does have general powers in relation to the making of awards.

[9] See p. 283, ante.

[10] *Kursell v Timber Operators and Contractors Ltd* [1923] 2 KB 202.

[11] See pp. 142–144, ante.

[12] *Kursell v Timber Operators and Contractors Ltd*, ante. This limitation appears to relate to powers conferred expressly, as well as by implication.

[13] These words are taken from s. 12(1) of the 1950 Act.

agreement shall . . . be deemed to contain a provision that the parties to the reference, and all persons claiming through them respectively, shall, subject to any legal objection, submit to be examined by the arbitrator or umpire, on oath or affirmation, in relation to the matters in dispute, and shall, subject as aforesaid, produce before the arbitrator or umpire all documents within their possession or power respectively which may be required or called for, and do all other things which during the proceedings on the reference the arbitrator or umpire may require'.

The sub-section falls into three parts.

(a) Power to take evidence on oath

The first part of section 12(1) deals with examination on oath or affirmation. This provision relates only to the evidence of the parties and those claiming through them; it says nothing about the evidence of other witnesses. Moreover, the sub-section can scarcely mean what it appears to say. Read literally, it would give the arbitrator the power to insist on a party giving evidence. A High Court Judge has no such power, and to confer it on an arbitrator would be wholly alien to the English adversary procedure under which it is the parties, not the tribunal, who decide what evidence is to be given[14]. We believe that the section would be read as entitling the arbitrator to say, not, 'You must give evidence before me on oath or affirmation' but 'If you choose to give evidence, it must be on oath or affirmation'. So construed, this part of section 12(1) is otiose, since the same power is conferred in more general terms by section 12(3).

(b) Powers relating to the production of documents

It is questionable whether the second part of section 12(1) confers a general power to order the disclosure and inspection of documents, as under an order for discovery in the High Court, or whether it is limited to the old Chancery procedure compelling the parties to produce identified individual documents. The latter view may well be correct[15], but the point is academic, since the third part of this sub-section undoubtedly confers power to make a full order for discovery[16].

(c) General statutory powers

The third part of section 12(1) is in broad terms. It empowers the arbitrator to do anything which he may require for determining facts or law in order that he may decide the reference[17], and imposes on the parties the widest possible duty of frank and loyal co-operation with the tribunal[18]. The sub-section is not,

---

[14] See p. 359, post, for a possible exception to this principle in the case where the arbitrator himself seeks expert advice.
[15] *Kursell v Timber Operators and Contractors Ltd*, ante.
[16] *Kursell v Timber Operators and Contractors Ltd*, ante; *Re Société les Affréteurs Réunis v Shipping Controller* (1921) 6 Ll L Rep 408, [1921] 3 KB 1.
[17] *Re Unione Stearinerie Lanza and Wiener* [1917] 2 KB 558.
[18] *Kursell v Timber Operators and Contractors*, ante.

however, all-embracing. It does not put the arbitrator in the same position as a judge[19].

He cannot, for example, deploy the personal remedies available to the judge for contempt of court or for non-compliance with his orders[20]. Nor may the arbitrator make orders which are merely ancillary to the reference, and are not concerned with the process of reaching a decision on fact or law – such as ordering the claimant to give security for costs[1].

(d) 'Subject to any legal objection'

These words apply to all three parts of section 12(1)[2]. They plainly enable a party to refuse compliance with an order which he could not be compelled to obey if made by the High Court, such as to disclose documents protected by Crown privilege[3], or legal professional privilege, or to answer incriminating questions. Whether the words 'any legal objection' go further than this is not clear. We suggest not[4].

3 Powers at common law

It is sometimes asserted that, independently of statute, the arbitrator has inherent procedural powers derived from the common law analogous to those possessed by a judge when trying an action in the High Court[5]. We suggest that this proposition is misconceived. The matter can best be approached historically.

In the past, the decision-making powers of the Court were divided between judge and jury. It was for the judge to rule on questions of law and procedure, whilst issues of fact were decided by the jury. Where the action involved technical matters or complex accounts a jury was not an ideal tribunal, and accordingly it became the practice for the parties to consent to this part of the dispute being referred by the Court to an independent person. The proceedings still retained their character as an action in court, but the decision-making power on questions of fact was transferred from the jury to the arbitrator. This had the advantage that the parties were on procedural matters still subject to the coercive powers of the Court, whilst there was a better prospect of obtaining an informed decision on the facts. The advantage was sufficiently great to prompt the idea that a somewhat similar division of powers could usefully be employed in the context of voluntary arbitrations, so it was provided by statute that a submission could be made a 'rule' or 'order' of Court. Thus, in the one case there was an action which had some of the characteristics of an arbitration;

---

19 *Re Unione Stearinerie Lanza and Wiener* [1917] 2 KB 558 at 561–562.
20 See p. 292, ante.
1 *Kursell v Timber Operators and Contractors Ltd*, ante; *Re Unione Stearinerie, Lanza and Wiener*, ante. It is not, perhaps entirely easy to extract this limitation from the words of s. 12(1) itself.
2 *Kursell v Timber Operators and Contractors Ltd*, ante.
3 *Re Société les Affréteurs Réunis v Shipping Controller*, ante.
4 But see *Re Unione Stearinerie, Lanza and Wiener*, ante, at 563, per Avory J.
5 This is one possible analysis of the ratio decidendi of *Chandris v Isbrandtsen-Moller Co Inc* (1950) 84 Ll L Rep 347, [1951] 1 KB 240 (in the Court of Appeal). For reasons which we explain in the text, we consider that the better analysis of the case is that it decided that there was an implied term of the submission that the arbitrator has power to award interest (see further, p. 391, post). The Court of Appeal's analysis of *Edwards v Great Western Rly Co* (1851) 11 CB 588 overlooks the fact, we submit, that the reference there was of an action under an order of the Court.

whereas in the other there was an arbitration which had some of the characteristics of an action. In the first, and perhaps also the second, case it was possible to regard the arbitrator as a substitute for the jury, so far as concerned the making of a decision on the issues of fact, and accordingly to hold that the powers of the arbitrator could be identified with those of the jury.

It is, however, plain that this reasoning does not apply to the type of voluntary arbitration with which this book is concerned. Under the old practice, the arbitration was an extension of the action in court, and the award of the arbitrator was treated as if it were the verdict of the jury: not because of any analogy between arbitrators and jury, but because the arbitrator was acting as a substitute for the jury[6].

This reasoning did not apply to the other functions of the arbitrator. The decision-making power on questions of law was retained by the judge. The Court remained in charge on procedural matters, but the arbitrator also had certain subordinate procedural powers of his own. These were additional to, not a substitute for, the powers of the Court; and they derived from consent, and not from any delegation by the Court[7]. So far as we are aware, it was never suggested, whilst this method of instituting a reference was still of practical importance, that the arbitrator enjoyed powers which were the same as those of the judge[8].

Still less can the assimilation of the fact-finding powers of an arbitrator to those of a jury for whom he was substituted under the old procedure be used to found any analogy between the procedural powers of the judge and of the arbitrator under a modern arbitration. In essence, a 'voluntary' arbitration is entirely independent of the Court. It is true that the Court has certain supervisory powers over the reference and the award, but these are exercised from outside the reference; the arbitrators' own powers are exercised within the framework of the reference, and are derived from an entirely different source from those of the judge. Nor indeed, in the more general sense, is there any true analogy between the position of a judge and that of an arbitrator[9]; and even if the parties wished to confer on their nominee the powers of the judge, there are important respects in which they would be unable to do so[10]. We therefore suggest that when the arbitration agreement is to be construed, in order to see whether expressly or by implication, it confers upon the arbitrator powers the same as, or similar to, those of a judge[11], the answer must be – 'No'[12].

---

[6] The judgment of the Full Court of the Supreme Court of Victoria in *Robert Salzer Construction v Barlin-Scott* (1982) VR 545 contains a learned, and we respectfully submit convincing, demonstration that this is the reason why, under the former procedure, the arbitrator had power to award interest on the sum due. See also *Government Insurance Office of New South Wales v Atkinson-Leighton Joint Venture* (1981) CLR 206.

[7] It was the practice to make an order of the Court that the reference should be 'on the usual terms': See Redman (5th edn) p. 233.

[8] The judges exercising the powers of Official Referees (as to whom, see pp. 271–274, ante) have powers very similar to those of a judge: but these are expressly conferred by RSC Ord. 36, and do not derive either by delegation from the High Court, or from any analogy drawn by the common law between a judge and a referee.

[9] For a summary of some of the distinctions, see p. 266, ante.

[10] See p. 292, ante.

[11] We do not, of course, suggest that the arbitrator can never exercise powers similar to those which the Court exercises in the course of an action. But where such powers exist, they derive from the general implied obligation to conduct the reference in a fair manner, and according to a

4 Supplementary powers of the Court

Under section 12(6) of the Act, the High Court has power to make certain procedural orders in a reference, by way of reinforcement of the arbitrator's own powers. The rather miscellaneous contents of this sub-section, which is mainly concerned with interim relief, are discussed in more detail below[13].

In certain respects, namely the ordering of discovery and interrogatories, the powers of the Court duplicate those of the arbitrator. When a party wishes to avail himself of these over-lapping powers, he should first have recourse to the arbitrator, and should not invoke the Court's power unless the arbitrator's order proves ineffectual[14].

Section 12(6) provides that in respect of the stipulated matters, the Court is to have the same powers 'as it has for the purpose of and in relation to an action or matter in the High Court'. Whilst the making of the order presents no special problems[15], it is not clear how any order which the Court does make can be enforced if the party disobeys it. Where a procedural order is made in the course of an action in the High Court, and the party fails to comply, the Court will usually enforce its will by exercising its inherent jurisdiction to stay or dismiss the action, to strike out the whole or parts of a pleading, or to penalise the offending party in costs. To exercise such powers in the course of an arbitration would seem to involve usurping the arbitrator's powers over the conduct of the reference[16]. Nevertheless it is well established that the Court may stay an arbitration in order to give effect to an order for security for costs[17], this being the method authorised by the Rules of Court for enforcing such an order during the course of the Court's own proceedings. There seems no reason in principle why similar powers should not be exercised by way of analogy in other cases[18]. Otherwise the Court is left only with its remedies against the property or person of the offending party, such as attachment and committal[19]. These seem too severe for any but a gross breach of a procedural order, and in any event are not of much value when the party concerned is outside the jurisdiction. There remain only the less specific remedies available in cases where a party is failing to cooperate in the conduct of the reference[20].

---

procedure which (in the absence of express or implied variation) is to have the 'adversarial' characteristics which we indicate in Chapter 22.

[12] The legislation would not have needed to introduce the very modest list of statutory implied powers, first encountered in Schedule 1 to the 1889 Act, if there has always existed a much wider set of common law implied powers derived from the supposed analogy between judge and arbitrator. *Bremer Vulkan Schiffbau und Maschinenfabrik v South India Shipping Corpn Ltd* [1981] 1 Lloyd's Rep 253 is now authority that no such term exists at common law.

[13] Post, pp. 323 et seq.

[14] Post, pp. 328–329.

[15] The application is made to a Master or to the commercial judge: Ord. 73, r. 3.

[16] The argument is less convincing where the Court is intervening to supplement a gap in the arbitrator's powers.

[17] See p. 337, post.

[18] The contrary view was expressed in the previous edition of this work. The view now expressed is prompted by the decision of the Court of Appeal in *Dorval Tankers Pty Ltd v Two Arrows Maritime and Port Services Ltd, The Argenpuma* [1984] 2 Lloyd's Rep 563.

[19] S. 5 of the 1979 Act has no application to orders made by the Court.

[20] See Chapter 32, post, p. 497.

D. DISPUTES ON PROCEDURE

Disputes occasionally arise in the course of a reference as to the power of the arbitrator to make a procedural order, or to impose conditions on such an order, or as to his duty to take or refrain from taking a particular step in the conduct of the reference. In the event of such a dispute, the aggrieved party, or the arbitrator himself, may wish to obtain the guidance of the Court. As the law appears to stand at present, there are two ways in which this may be achieved.

First, the parties or the arbitrator may avail themselves of the statutory procedures for obtaining a ruling from the Court on a preliminary point of law: for a dispute as to the extent of the arbitrator's powers and duties raises an issue of law[1]. Under the 1979 Act, the parties jointly, or one party with the consent of the arbitrator, can apply to the High Court for the determination of a question of law arising in the course of the reference[2]. This procedure is, however, of more limited application than the consultative case procedure under the former provisions of the 1950 Act, since – (a) the arbitrator cannot himself initiate the procedure; (b) the High Court has a discretion whether or not to determine the question[3]; and (c) where the parties have entered into a valid 'exclusion agreement', section 3(1)(c) excludes an application under section 2. It is important to note that the statutory procedure is available only to decide in principle whether the arbitrator does or does not have the power or duty to act (or refuse to act) in the manner which has given rise to the dispute. It cannot be used as a means of persuading the Court to instruct the arbitrator upon how, in the exercise of his discretion, a power or duty should be employed.

The alternative procedure employs mechanisms which are independent of the right of appeal under the Act. It has been held[4] that the Court has jurisdiction

---

[1] See for example, *Re Société les Affréteurs Réunis & Shipping Controller* [1921] 3 KB 1; *Kursell v Timber Operators and Contractors Ltd*, ante; *Panchaud Frères SA v Etablissements General Grain Co* [1969] 2 Lloyd's Rep 109; *Faure Fairclough Ltd v Premier Oil and Cabe Mills Ltd* [1968] 1 Lloyd's Rep 237. The existence and extent of a procedural power or duty will depend, according to the circumstances, upon – (i) the interpretation of the Acts; (ii) the principles established by decided cases, and (iii) the construction of the express or implied terms of the arbitration agreement and the submissions. All these are matters of law, although a ruling on a procedural matter may occasionally involve a decision on an issue of fact.

[2] S. 2(1).

[3] S. 2(1). For a discussion of the procedure under the 1979 Act, see pp. 620–626, post.

[4] In *The Angelic Grace*, ante. There is a theoretical problem here. Questions as to the powers and duties of the arbitrator are matters which fall within the scope of most, if not all, forms of arbitration clause: for the logic of the rule that there are certain types of disputes as to jurisdiction which the arbitrator can have no jurisdiction to decide does not apply to disputes as to powers and duties. In theory, the Court always has a concurrent jurisdiction over disputes which are the subject of a reference to arbitration, but so long as the reference remains in being this jurisdiction will not be exercised. Logically, therefore, there would be no answer to an application for a compulsory stay under s. 1(1) of the 1975 Act. This objection does not appear to have been relied upon in *The Angelic Grace*. The problem is particularly acute in relation to references which are subject to an 'exclusion agreement'. If we are right in the view that s. 2(1) of the 1979 Act cannot be used to ascertain the arbitrator's powers and duties, then it scarcely seems legitimate to use declaratory relief as a means of outflanking the agreement. (There is a kindred problem in relation to the ascertainment of the arbitrator's powers, as a by-product of misconduct proceedings after the making of an award.)

to entertain an action in which the Court is asked to declare whether or not the arbitrator has a particular right or duty. This may in some cases be quicker and cheaper than the procedure by way of a preliminary point of law, in that it does not require the arbitrator to produce any document required for an application under the 1979 Act[5]. It is also possible that the procedure by way of declaration may differ fundamentally from the preliminary point of law under the 1979 Act in that it can perhaps be used to call in issue before the Court the mode of exercise, as well as the existence and scope, of the arbitrator's powers and duty.

Whichever procedure is adopted, care should be taken not to ask the Court to answer a question of law which may prove academic. Thus, if there is a dispute as to the exercise of a power, and the Court holds that it does exist, but the arbitrator subsequently exercises his discretion in such a way as not to use the power, the proceedings in the High Court will have been wasted. The arbitrator should therefore be asked either to exercise the discretion (if he himself considers that he does not possess the power), or at least to give a firm indication of the way in which we would exercise it if the Court were to hold that the power did indeed exist.

---

[5] There may be other reasons why an action for a declaration is more suitable to the statutory procedure. In *The Angelic Grace*, ante, Waller LJ said that in the particular circumstance it was clearly preferable not to ask the arbitrator to state a special case, but it is not possible to tell from the report (which does not set out the circumstances in full) what factors the Lord Justice had in mind.

CHAPTER 22

A fair trial

A. INTRODUCTION

Unless the parties have agreed to the contrary, expressly or by implication, the arbitrator is required to adopt an 'adversary' rather than an 'inquisitorial' procedure. Under such a procedure it is not the function of the judge or arbitrator to seek out the truth by engaging in speculation, pursuing enquiries or calling for and examining witnesses. His task is to choose between two alternative versions of the truth, presented to him by the parties.

It is plain that a system of this nature cannot operate successfully unless the two alternative versions of the truth are fully presented and fully tested. This means, in effect, that three general principles must be observed –

1 Each party must have a full opportunity to present his own case to the tribunal.

2 Each party must be aware of his opponent's case, and must be given a full opportunity to test and rebut it.

3 The parties must be treated alike. Each must have the same opportunity to put forward his own case, and to test that of his opponent.

Judges have for so long regarded these rules an axiomatic to the proceedings which they themselves conduct, that when the courts concern themselves with the supervision of arbitrations it has naturally been taken for granted that the same principles should be applied. This is indeed logical when the reference takes the same shape as an action in the High Court. Problems may, however, arise when the Court seeks to apply the competing principle, that the parties to an arbitration should, so far as possible, be allowed to conduct the reference in whatever way they choose. Often, what they have chosen is either a full adversary procedure, or something resembling it. Sometimes, however, they prefer to adopt a different course. When the parties appoint an experienced merchant as arbitrator in a quality dispute, they do not expect him to behave as if he were a High Court Judge. Their wish is that he shall use skill and diligence in finding out the facts as quickly and cheaply as possible. In doing so he does not conduct an adversary process; an attempt to apply uncritically the rules which have been developed in relation to a High Court action would serve merely to confuse and irritate the commercial community, without improving the quality of arbitral justice.

It is therefore necessary – as the courts have come to realise during this century – to read any statement of general principle as to the way in which arbitrations should be conducted in the context of the particular type of reference which is under discussion. The inquiry begins in every case with the construction of the agreement to arbitrate. If the agreement expressly or impliedly provides for a formal procedure, or if the choice of such a procedure is presumed from the absence of any indication to the contrary[1], then it is correct to say, as did a nineteenth century judge 'The principles of universal justice require that the person who is to be prejudiced by the evidence ought to be present to hear it taken, to suggest cross-examination or himself to cross-examine, and to be able to find evidence, if he can, that shall meet and answer it; in short, to deal with it as in the ordinary course of legal proceedings'[2]. The same may be said for the statements, to be found in a number of nineteenth century cases, which deny the existence of any difference between mercantile and legal arbitrations[3]. Statements of this kind cannot, however, safely be applied in situations where it can be inferred from the agreement to arbitrate – whether 'mercantile' or 'legal' – that an informal procedure has been agreed. Many reported cases demonstrate that a failure to follow the form, or indeed the substance, of the High Court procedure is not necessarily misconduct[4].

In spite of this, the three principles stated above continue to exercise an influence on all forms of arbitration. The Court will always look first to the express terms of the agreement and, subject to any question of public policy[5], will enforce them. If, however, there is no express agreement, the Court must proceed by way of implication; and the more a particular procedure in in conflict with the substance of the three principles[6], the less likely the Court will be to find that the procedure has been agreed by implication.

In the following pages we endeavour to show how these principles have been reconciled in practice with the desire of commercial men to avoid excessively legalistic modes of procedure.

B. DISPENSING WITH A HEARING

Influenced by their own procedures, the courts have assumed that the most reliable way of giving effect to the principles indicated above is for the arbitrator to hold an oral hearing, attended by the parties, at which they put forward the whole of their evidence and arguments. The essential characteristics of such a hearing are discussed below[7]. The courts recognise that the parties may dispense with an oral hearing if they expressly[8] or impliedly agree to do so, and over the years the courts have shown themselves increasingly ready to recognise such an

---

[1] See p. 288, ante.
[2] Lord Cranworth in *Drew v Drew and Lebrun* (1855) 2 Macq 1 at 3.
[3] For example, *Harvey v Shelton* (1844) 7 Beav 455, per Lord Langdale MR and *Re Camillo Eitzen and Jewson & Sons* (1896) 40 Sol Jo 438. See pp. 289–290, ante, for dicta on the change in attitude of the courts during the present century.
[4] We refer to this point at p. 280, ante.
[5] See p. 283, ante.
[6] Although the Court will not necessarily be troubled if the difference lies not in the application of the principles, but of the means adopted for carrying them into practice.
[7] At pp. 302 et seq.
[8] *Oakland Metal Co Ltd v D Benaim & Co Ltd* [1953] 2 Lloyd's Rep 192 at 199; *Ritchie v W Jacks & Co* (1922) 10 Ll L Rep 519; *Russian Oil Products Ltd v Caucasian Oil Co Ltd* (1928) 31 Ll L Rep 109.

implication[9]. It still appears to be the law, however, that in the absence of any other indication an agreement for a full oral hearing will be presumed[10].

Where a full oral hearing is dispensed with the procedure may take various different forms. For instance, these may be a hearing of sorts at which the parties and their legal advisers do not attend. Such a hearing may consist either of a discussion between the two arbitrators, before they disagree, or of a meeting at which the arbitrators act as advocates in presenting the case to the umpire[11]. On other occasions, there may be no hearing at all. Either the arbitrator receives argument and evidence by correspondence or there may be even less in the way of a contested process, the parties simply giving the documents to the arbitrator or telling him where the goods are to be inspected. It can readily be seen that statements of principle which are apposite to formal arbitrations, make little sense when applied to references of this very informal kind.

The very informality of this type of reference can, however, give rise to misunderstandings between the parties and between the arbitrators and the parties, as to the procedure which is being followed. The arbitrator should take care to avoid such misunderstandings arising, by ensuring that the parties know exactly where they stand[12].

One further point may be mentioned. There is no doubt that the parties may by an express agreement irrevocably dispense with an oral hearing. It is less clear whether a final waiver of the right to a hearing can ever be the subject of an implied agreement. The better view appears to be that it may not, and that the waiver of a full hearing is always subject to the reservation of a right to insist on reverting to a procedure at which the parties can appear and take the evidence of the witnesses in person[13].

In the majority of cases, it will be obvious to all concerned with the reference what procedure is to be adopted. It is, however, the business of the arbitrator to make sure that both parties are fully aware of what is going to happen. If there is any scope for doubt, he should seek the explicit agreement of the parties to the procedure which he proposes to adopt. In particular, he should ensure that he does not by his conduct lead one or other party to suppose that there will be a hearing, and then proceed directly to an award on the documents alone.

---

[9] Experienced commercial judges have on several occasions drawn attention to the difference in the approach of courts to commercial arbitrations during (say) the past 60 years, by comparison with the approach displayed by the nineteenth century cases.

[10] *Altco Ltd v Sutherland* [1971] 2 Lloyd's Rep 515 at 518.

[11] For a discussion of 'arbitrator/advocates', see Chapter 19, ante.

[12] Failure to do so, although not amounting to misconduct, nearly resulted in a remission in *Sokratis Rokopoulos v Esperia SpA, The Aros* [1978] 1 Lloyd's Rep 456 (proceedings to award on documents without notice to the parties).

[13] *Ritchie v Jacks*, ante, per Lord Sterndale at 521; *AA Amram Ltd v Bremar Co Ltd* [1966] 1 Lloyd's Rep 494, per Megaw J at 499; *Star International Hong Kong (UK) Ltd v Bergbau-Handel GmbH* [1966] 2 Lloyd's Rep 16; *Henry Bath & Son Ltd v Birgby Products* [1962] 1 Lloyd's Rep 389, per McNair J at 398–399. These cases also show that, in the context of commercial arbitrations, a party who has not asked for an oral hearing cannot complain if he does not get one. In *The Myron (M/V) (Owners) v Tradax Export SA* [1969] 1 Lloyd's Rep 411 at 417, Donaldson J indicated that if an oral hearing is called for, the usual Court procedure will be followed. Might it not be possible to imply, in an ordinary mercantile arbitration, an agreement that even if a party insists on deviating from the more informal procedure, the arbitrator is not obliged to follow the formal judicial procedures in every particular?

C. THE HEARING: MINIMUM REQUIREMENTS

Where there is to be a full oral hearing, the following conditions must be observed –

1 Each party must have notice that the hearing is to take place.

2 Each party must have a reasonable opportunity to be present at the hearing, together with his advisers and witnesses.

3 Each party must have the opportunity to be present throughout the hearing.

4 Each party must have a reasonable opportunity to present evidence and argument in support of his own case.

5 Each party must have a reasonable opportunity to test his opponent's case by cross-examining his witnesses, presenting rebutting evidence and addressing oral argument.

6 The hearing must, unless the contrary is expressly agreed, be the occasion on which the parties present the whole of their evidence and argument.

1 Notice of hearing

As to the first requirement, it is obvious that a hearing cannot be properly conducted if one of the parties does not know that it is going to take place[14]. It must be very rare for an arbitrator deliberately to withhold from one party a notice which he has given to the other. Usually, this results from a misunderstanding or failure of communication. In extreme cases, one party may fail to realise even that an arbitration is in existence at all[15]. More commonly, he will know that there is an arbitration and that there is to be a hearing, but as the result of an error or misunderstanding, he will not be told when and where it is to take place[16]. Another possibility is that a party is led by the conduct of the arbitrator or his opponent to believe that the arbitration will proceed on documents alone[17] whereas in fact a hearing is subsequently held[18]. It is the business of the arbitrator to see that misunderstandings of this kind do not occur, for they amount to misconduct which will normally lead to the remission or setting aside of the award[19].

It is possible by express agreement to dispense with the requirement that both parties shall be notified of the hearing[20], although very clear words will be required to produce this result.

---

[14] *The Warwick* (1890) 15 PD 189; *Oswald v Earl Grey* (1855) 24 LJ QB 69, and many other cases.

[15] This seems to have been the situation contemplated in *Golodetz v Schrier* (1947) 80 Ll L Rep 647, per Lord Goddard LJ at 651.

[16] As in *Oakland v Benaim*, ante. The facts are rather obscurely reported. In *Oswald v Earl Grey*, ante, there was a hearing at which both parties attended, followed by a second hearing of which one party had no notice. See also *Chandmull Moolchand & Co v C Weis & Co Ltd* (1921) 9 Ll L Rep 412.

[17] Or by means of a meeting between arbitrators at which the parties are not expected to be present.

[18] This is the converse of the situation, mentioned above, where a party believes that there will be an oral hearing and then finds that the arbitrator has porceeded to an award on documents alone.

[19] So far as the observations of Lord Goddard LJ in *Golodetz v Schrier* suggest that misconduct of this kind might found a defence to an action on the award, as distinct from a ground for remission or setting-aside, it is submitted that they are not consistent with numerous decisions on the effect of misconduct, and on the decision on this specific point in *Thorburn v Barnes* (1867) LR 2 CP 384.

[20] *Oakland v Benaim*, ante, at 199; *Doleman & Sons v Ossett Corpn* [1912] 3 KB 257 at 271. This leads to an ex parte hearing, in the strict sense of the term: see p. 537, post.

A relinquishment of the right to receive notice of the hearing may also be implied from the conduct of the parties. The arbitrator should, however, be very cautious about this. For example, he should not take it for granted that he can dispense with notice, merely because one party has shown a disposition to ignore the arbitration altogether[1]. Even if the arbitrator is convinced that a party will not appear at the hearing, he should give him full notice of what is to occur.

2 Opportunity to attend

It is of no value to give a party notice of a hearing, if the arrangements are such that he has no reasonable opportunity to be present in person, with such legal advisers and witnesses as he wishes to bring with him. Thus, the arbitrator should ensure that the date for the hearing is not so close that the case cannot be properly prepared. Similarly, he should try to accommodate any party who is placed in difficulty by the absence abroad, illness or competing engagements of himself or of an important witness. But a party has no absolute right to insist on his convenience being consulted in every respect. The matter is within the discretion of the arbitrator, and the Court will intervene only in the cases of positive abuse[2]. In each case, the arbitrator must balance the legitimate interests of each party against the general purpose of arbitration, which is to provide a speedy method of resolving disputes[3].

Naturally, the arbitrator's duty goes no further than to ensure that a party has an opportunity to attend the hearing if he wishes. If a party, after being given proper notice, chooses not to appear, then the proceedings may properly continue in his absence[4].

The right to attend the hearing, and indeed the right to participate in the interlocutory stages of the reference, belongs only to the parties to the reference. But the right need not be exercised in person. It may, and in the case of corporations and other artificial persons, must be exercised through agents. Representation by lawyers is usual in the more elaborate commercial arbitrations[5], but it is quite legitimate for a party to appoint a person who is not a lawyer[6] to present his case. Such a person need not have any formal connection with the party he represents: he may, for example, be chosen simply because of his familiarity with the trade and its arbitration procedures.

It is, however, implicit in the nature of private arbitrations that the proceedings are confidential, and that strangers shall be excluded from the

---

[1] *Montrose Canned Foods Ltd v Eric Wells (Merchants) Ltd* [1965] 1 Lloyd's Rep 597.

[2] *Fetherstone v Cooper* (1803) 9 Ves 67; *Re Whitwham's Trustees etc. and Wrexham, Mold and Connah's Quay Rly Co* (1895) 39 Sol Jo 692; *Williams v Thomas* (1847) 8 LTOS 348; *Chandmull Moolchand v Weis*, ante; *Rushworth v Waddington* (1859) 1 LT 69; *Nares v Drury* (1864) 10 LT 305; *Ginder v Curtis* (1863) 14 CB NS 723. A party who wishes for an adjournment must apply for one, not wait until after the award is published and then complain: cf. *JH Rayner & Co v Fred Drughorn Ltd* (1924) 18 Ll L Rep 269.

[3] See the observations of Darling J in *British Oil and Cake Mills Ltd v Horace Battin & Co Ltd* (1922) 13 Ll L Rep 443.

[4] See p. 346, post.

[5] There is no absolute right to legal representation, however: see n 12 on p. 305, post.

[6] Or at any rate not an English lawyer. It is by no means unusual for foreign lawyers to appear in English arbitrations, particularly where the dispute is not subject to English law.

hearing[7]. A party's right to attend may not be exercised, except with the consent of all other parties, so as to allow persons to attend except for the purpose of conducting the reference or giving evidence.

3 Right to be present throughout the hearing

The arbitrator cannot properly exclude one party from a portion of the proceedings, without his consent[8]. This rule is, we suggest, subject to exception in the case where the behaviour of one party or his representatives is such as to make it impossible to conduct the arbitration in a fair and seemly manner unless one or all of them are excluded[9]. This is plainly a power which should be exercised only in the most exceptional circumstances. Any party who is sufficiently objectionable to make his removal seem necessary is unlikely to stop short of an application to set aside for misconduct any award which may ensue. The Court is likely to take the view, upon any proceedings to set aside the award, that the right to be present at the hearing is of such importance that the arbitrator can only be upheld in his decision to withhold it, upon the clearest of evidence. If there is any suspicion that the arbitrator may have acted over-hastily, the award will be set aside, with all the resulting waste of time and costs for the innocent party which that will entail. The arbitrator will be better advised to play safe. Patience and dignity will almost always carry him through[10].

4 Opportunity to present argument and evidence

It is the first principle of arbitration that each party shall have a reasonable opportunity to put forward his own case to the arbitrator[11]. This principle applies both to argument and to evidence.

(a) Argument

So far as concerns argument, each party must be given an opportunity to address

---

[7] *Oxford Shipping Co Ltd v Nippon Yusen Kaisha, The Eastern Saga* [1984] 2 Lloyd's Rep 373.

[8] When the arbitrator excludes *both* parties, and then continues with the business of the reference, there is in effect no hearing at all. As to the status of evidence received in the absence of both parties see p. 310, post.

[9] We do not base this proposition on *Hewlett v Laycock* (1827) 2 C & P 574, in view of the criticism addressed to that case in *Re Plews and Middleton* (1845) 6 QB 845, 14 LJ QB 139 and *Dobson v Groves* (1844) 6 QB 637, 14 LJ QB 17. There must, however, be some remedy in a situation where a party's behaviour passes all tolerable bounds, and an application to revoke the authority of the arbitrator which appears to be the only alternative is unlikely to be of practical value unless the party's objectionable conduct displays itself from the very start of the reference. As Turner LJ said in *Re Haigh, Haigh v Haigh* (1861) 3 De GF & J 157, 'I certainly do not mean to lay it down that an arbitrator is bound to submit to insults from those who attend him'.

[10] If the arbitrator does decide to exclude anyone from the hearing, he should take the best care that he can that the party who is affected by the exclusion is not prejudiced by it: per Turner LJ in *Re Haigh Haigh v Haigh*, supra, at 169.

[11] *Montrose Canned Foods v Eric Wells (Merchants)*, ante.

argument on the facts and on the law[12]. The arbitrator is not, however, expected to do more than is reasonable. The extent of his duty may in part be determined by the express terms of the submission[13]. Furthermore, even where his powers are not defined by express agreement, he has a general discretion in the conduct of the reference, and although he must be careful that he does not by constant interruption and interference prevent a party from presenting his case fairly, he is entitled, and indeed required, in the interests of economy and dispatch to try and focus the arguments on the material points, and to prevent the advocate from dealing with matters which are not relevant or in issue[14].

Arbitrations which proceed on documents and written submissions alone present a particular problem. In principle the process ought to be swifter and more economical than an arbitration which proceeds to an oral hearing. In practice the need to give each party a reasonable opportunity to present his own case and rebut that of his opponent tends to lead to proliferation of replies, rejoinders, surrebutters and the like. In these circumstances the arbitrator must balance the respondent's right to a reasonable time to meet the case against him against the injustice to the claimant which may result from unreasonable delay. The arbitrator is not obliged to allow every application to make further submissions, nor every application for further time, particularly if there is reason to believe that the respondent is simply playing for time[15].

It sometimes happens that after the hearing is concluded, but before the award is made, one of the parties asks to be allowed to address the arbitrator again either to raise a new point or to put a point which he has already made in a different way. It is within the arbitrator's discretion whether or not to allow such an application, but in general the arbitrator will be perfectly justified in refusing it unless there is some good reason why the point could not have been made at the proper time[16].

---

[12] See, for example, *Carey and Brown v Henderson and Liddell* (1920) 2 Ll L Rep 479; *Altco Ltd v Sutherland* [1971] 2 Lloyd's Rep 515 at 518; *Modern Engineering (Bristol) Ltd v C Miskin & Sons Ltd* [1981] 1 Lloyd's Rep 135. This does not mean that the party is necessarily entitled to present argument through the medium of lawyers. In *FE Hookway v Alfred Isaacs & Sons* [1954] 1 Lloyd's Rep 491, where the decision to exclude lawyers was arrived at by an incorrect process, Devlin J held that such a decision, properly arrived at would probably be unimpeachable. Moreover, we see no reason to doubt the validity of an agreement excluding or limiting legal representation in an ordinary commercial arbitration.

[13] For example, where the rules of a trade association required statements of case to be delivered within a certain time, the arbitrator would have been entitled to exclude from consideration any case served out of time: per McNair J obiter in *Henry Bath v Birgby Products*, ante, at 397. In general, arbitrators will be wise not to stand too strictly on rules of this nature.

[14] *Henry Bath v Birgby Products*, ante, at 398. In *Graig Shipping Co Ltd v International Paint and Compositions Co Ltd* (1944) 77 Ll L Rep 220, where an arbitration was by agreement conducted entirely on documents, it was held that there could come a point at which the arbitrator was entitled to call a halt to the exchange of documents, and make an award on the materials then before him, provided that he did not know one or other of the parties had a further point which they wished to bring to his notice. In spite of this, it will usually be better for the arbitrator to fix a final date for the delivery of documents, rather than simply make an award without warning.

[15] *Overseas Fortune Shipping Pte Ltd v Great Eastern Shipping Co Ltd* [1987] 1 Lloyd's Rep 270. If the arbitrator proposes to ignore an application for further time and to proceed directly to an award he should first tell the parties what he intends to do.

[16] *Yamashita Shinnihon SS Co Ltd v Elios SPA, The Lily Prima* [1976] 2 Lloyd's Rep 487.

(b) Evidence

The right of each party to put forward his case to the full extends to evidence as well as to argument. Within certain limits, the arbitrator must receive all evidence tendered by the parties. The shutting out of evidence which should have been admitted is misconduct[17], and may[18] result in the award being remitted or set aside.

There are undoubtedly limits to this rule. The parties do not have an unrestricted right to press upon the arbitrator whatever evidence they choose. Thus, the arbitrator need only receive such evidence as is relevant to issues which are in dispute[19]. Furthermore, the duty extends only to evidence which is admissible. In a formal arbitration, this means evidence which would be admissible in a court of law[20]. But if the arbitration agreement, properly construed, shows that the parties have expressly or impliedly agreed that evidence may be acted upon which would not be admissible in a court of law, then the arbitrator's positive duty to receive evidence will be correspondingly enlarged[1].

It is possible that the arbitrator may have a discretion to reject even such evidence as is relevant and admissible. The following situations may be material.

1 Where evidence is immaterial on the arbitrator's view of the law. Sometimes, evidence may be relevant or irrelevant, depending upon which opinion prevails as to a disputed question of law. If an arbitrator forms a clear and unshakable view of the law at an early stage, he may be justified, with a view to saving costs, in rejecting evidence which on that view would have no bearing on the result. In most cases, however, he will be unlikely to have such a firm view in mind at the stage when the evidence is being given[2], and in any event he would need to be sure, before he excluded the evidence, that the question of law would not be the subject of review by the courts.

2 Where the evidence would merely serve to reinforce a view of the facts which the arbitrator has already formed. Only in exceptional circumstances would the arbitrator be justified in rejecting evidence led by the claimant – for the respondent's evidence might lead the arbitrator to alter his provisional view, thus making it necessary for him to give leave to the claimant to call the additional evidence after the proper time.

---

[17] See *Lawton v Rodgers* (1844) 3 LTOS 40, 107; *Phipps v Ingram* (1835) 3 Dowl 669; *Paterson v Clayton* (1845) 6 LTOS 125, 132; *Rumbelow v Whalley* (1849) 13 LTOS 208; *Ritchie v Jacks*, ante, at 521; and the cases cited below.

[18] For the position where the evidence, if admitted, would not have affected the outcome of the dispute, see the discussion at pp. 552–553, post.

[19] See *Hookway v Isaacs*, ante, at 510; *Faure, Fairclough Ltd v Premier Oil and Cake Mills Ltd* [1968] 1 Lloyd's Rep 237. Where there are pleadings, these define the scope of the evidence which may be adduced. Plainly if an issue has ceased to be in dispute, the arbitrator should not allow time to be wasted by receiving evidence in relation to it. See also *Larchin v Ellis* (1863) 11 WR 281.

[20] See *Hookway v Isaacs*, ante, at 510.

[1] We do not know of any authority for this proposition, but it must surely be correct. For a discussion of the circumstances in which an arbitrator may act on technically inadmissible evidence, see pp. 352–354, post. In an arbitration of a semi-formal character, it sometimes happens that a tribunal takes a more strict view on admissibility than a party had expected. In such a case, it will often be right for the arbitrator to give the party an opportunity to present the evidence again in a more acceptable form, rather than shut it out altogether. See *Bunge & Co Ltd v Ross T Smyth & Co Ltd* (1926) 24 Ll L Rep 30.

[2] I.e. before the time for final speeches.

3 Where the evidence relates to a matter on which the arbitrator has expert knowledge. Whether the arbitrator has a discretion to exclude evidence in such circumstances is not clear[3].

The position may perhaps be different where the arbitration is of an informal nature, but in general the arbitrator will be better advised not to stand on his expert dignity and to admit all relevant and admissible evidence tendered to him even if he privately considers that he is better informed than the witness on the particular matter in question[4].

4 Where the volume of the evidence is disproportionate to the importance of the issue on which it is adduced. It may be that an arbitrator can properly exclude evidence, if a party sets about spending more time and money in establishing a particular fact than it is really worth. But if this power exists at all, it should be used sparingly. If an allegation of fact remains in issue, a party can scarcely be blamed for trying to establish his own version. The remedy for doing so with excessive zeal will normally lie in costs, rather than in excluding the evidence.

Where the circumstances are such that a party is entitled to tender oral evidence, he has the right to adduce it in the normal way, namely by asking questions of the witness. An arbitrator cannot insist on conducting the examination of the witness himself[5].

The parties may be express agreement exclude the right to tender certain types of evidence. Thus, for example, it is not uncommon for mercantile contracts to stipulate that the production of a particular document shall be conclusive evidence of a certain fact. In such a situation, the arbitrator not only may but must exclude all other evidence tending to establish or controvert that fact[6].

It appears, moreover, that the parties may validly exclude their right to adduce any evidence at all on some or all of the disputed issues[7] – as, for example, where they agree that the arbitrator shall reach his conclusion on the basis of his own knowledge or investigations. Such an agreement is unlikely to be a feature of a full oral hearing[8].

Although the obligation to receive evidence tendered by the parties involves

---

[3] Compare *Eads v Williams* (1854) 24 LJ Ch 531 at 533; *Faure, Fairclough Ltd v Premier Oil and Cake Mills Ltd, ante; Johnston v Cheape* (1817) 5 Dow 247. Cases such as *Mediterranean and Eastern Export Co Ltd v Fortress Fabrics (Manchester) Ltd* (1948) 81 Ll L Rep 401; *Jordeson & Co v Stora Kopparbergs Bergslags Aktiebolag* (1931) 41 Ll L Rep 201 and *Naumann v Edward Nathan & Co Ltd* (1930) 37 Ll L Rep 249 which are sometimes cited in this context are not really in point, for they were concerned with the question whether an arbitrator could properly found his decision on his own knowledge alone, without calling for further evidence – not whether he could decline such evidence, if tendered to him.

[4] Contrast *Hookway v Isaacs,* ante, at 510 with *Ritchie v Jacks,* ante, at 510 and *Myron v Tradax,* ante, at 417.

[5] *Faure, Fairclough Ltd v Premier Oil and Cake Mills Ltd,* ante.

[6] *Hookway v Isaacs,* ante, at 510. Such a clause will, however, be strictly construed: *WN Lindsay & Co Ltd v European Grain and Shipping Agency Ltd* [1963] 1 Lloyd's Rep 437.

[7] *Oakland v Benaim,* ante, at 199; *Ritchie v Jacks,* ante, at 521–522. Very clear and cogent evidence is required to show that the parties intended to give up their right to give evidence: see per Atkin LJ in *Ritchie v Jacks,* ante, at 524.

[8] As to an implied agreement to this effect, see p. 288, ante. Also *Hookway v Isaacs,* ante: a custom to exclude certain types of evidence is not readily established without proof that the custom has been challenged and subsequently acquiesced in. (Devlin J evidently regarded this as an important feature of the proof of custom: see his observations in *Stag Line Ltd v Board of Trade* (1950) 83 Ll L Rep 356.)

the arbitrator in a duty to pay proper attention to the evidence once received, he is not, of course, obliged to accept it as accurate[9]. Arriving at an opposite conclusion, even if mistaken, from the one indicated by the evidence is not a matter which vitiates the award[10].

It sometimes happens that a party is led to believe that a fact is not is issue, and thereupon elects not to lead evidence to prove it. If the arbitrator subsequently decides the issue of fact the opposite way, this is treated as a case where the party is deprived of his right to give evidence, and the award may be remitted or set aside[11].

5 Opportunity to controvert opponent's case

Each party must have a reasonable opportunity to challenge the case put forward by his opponent[12]. If this requirement is to be fulfilled, two conditions must be satisfied. First, each party must be able to find out what case he has to meet. Second, he must be enabled to test the opponent's case by cross-examining his witnesses and leading evidence in rebuttal, and to controvert his opponent's arguments on facts or law by making submissions in reply.

(a)   Hearing evidence in absence of party

The first of these conditions, namely that the party shall have notice of the case which he has to meet, is normally expressed, in the context of a full oral arbitration, as a rule prohibiting the arbitrator from receiving argument or evidence from one party in the absence of the other[13]. Such conduct is regarded by the courts as creating an unacceptable risk that the mind of the arbitrator may be improperly influenced by one party in a way which the other, if given notice, would have been able to prevent.

Although the courts have repeatedly stated the importance of this rule it does appear to admit of exceptions. In the first place, there is no reason to doubt that

---

[9] See *Lewis Emanuel & Son Ltd v Sammut* [1959] 2 Lloyd's Rep 629; *Faghirzadeh v Rudolf Wolff (SA) (Pty) Ltd* [1977] 1 Lloyd's Rep 630; *Fox v PG Wellfair Ltd* [1981] 2 Lloyd's Rep 514 at 528.

[10] There is perhaps a difference between positive and negative evidence. If party A calls evidence to prove a fact, and party B calls no evidence, a finding in favour of B could not be attacked, for the arbitrator might simply have disbelieved A's evidence. But if A calls evidence to deny a fact, and B calls no evidence, a finding that the fact has been proved may be open to attack, on the ground that the arbitrator has erred in law or that there was no evidence on which his finding could reasonably be based. But in those cases where there is no right of appeal on a question of law, there is nothing which can be done to correct the arbitrator's mistake.

[11] See *Peter Cassidy Seed Co v Osuustukkukauppa IL* [1954] 2 Lloyd's Rep 586. A similar result may be reached on the basis of the general discretion to remit or set aside in cases of injustice or misunderstanding: see p. 558, post.

[12] As to the position where the arbitrator puts forward a case of his own, on the facts or the law, see pp. 348–349, post.

[13] This was described by Bailhache J in *WH Ireland & Co v CT Bowring & Co Ltd* (1920) 2 Ll L Rep 220, as a 'sacred principle'. See *Government of Ceylon v Chandris* [1963] 1 Lloyd's Rep 214; *Re Fuerst Bros & Co and RS Stephenon* [1951] 1 Lloyd's Rep 429; *Walker v Frobisher* (1801) 6 Ves 70; *Royal Commission on Sugar Supply v Trading Society Kwik-Hoo-Tong* (1922) 11 Ll L Rep 163; *Re Brook, Delcomyn and Badart* (1864) 16 CB NS 403; *Oswald v Earl Grey* (1855) 24 LJ QB 69; *Re Hick* (1819) 8 Taunt 694; *Whittle v Holmes* (1857) 29 LTOS 122; *Bache v Billingham* [1894] 1 QB 107; *Re Gregson and Armstrong* (1894) 70 LT 106; *Dobson v Groves* (1844) 6 QB 637; *Drew v Drew and Lebrun* (1855) 2 Macq 1; *London Export Corpn Ltd v Jubilee Coffee Roasting Co Ltd* [1958] 1 Lloyd's Rep 197 at 202.

the right to hear the evidence of the opposition can be excluded by express agreement[14], provided the words of the agreement are sufficiently explicit. Equally, we suggest that the rule could be excluded by a really clear course of conduct. For example, if one party were to tender evidence in the absence of the other, he could hardly complain if he were himself treated in the same way[15]; and a clear warning of an intention to take evidence in the absence of one party, coupled with an absence of objection, would no doubt be treated as equivalent to consent or waiver.

The way in which the rule prohibiting the reception of evidence in the absence of one party is to be applied to informal arbitrations is not easy to state. On the one hand, the courts have on a number of occasions stated or assumed that the rule holds good for all forms of arbitration[16]. Yet the rule is infringed every day in cases where the arbitrators act first as judges and then, after disagreement, as advocates, and the courts have never regarded this as a ground for setting the award aside[17]. The position may, we suggest, be summarised as follows –

1 The rule applies prima facie to all types of arbitration, but it is in principle possible to modify it by an implied agreement resulting from trade practice. The more informal the contemplated procedure, the more easily such an agreement may be implied[18].

2 Where the agreed procedure is for a full oral hearing, no variation of the general rule will be implied, no matter what customary procedure may be alleged[19].

3 If the procedure is so informal that there is no hearing at all, and the arbitration is conducted solely on documents, or by means of a personal inspection by the arbitrator, the rule plainly cannot apply. Nevertheless, there still remains the obligation to ensure that each party knows what case he has to meet.

(b) Hearing argument in absence of party

Where there is an oral hearing, it is misconduct for the arbitrator to receive argument from one party in the absence of the other. The courts appear, however, to regard this as a less serious transgression than the one-sided

---

[14] Even the strongest dicta do not go so far as to suggest that such an agreement would be contrary to public policy.

[15] See, however, *W Ramsden & Co v Jacobs* [1922] 1 KB 640, which seems a strong decision, on the facts as briefly reported.

[16] See, for example, *WH Ireland & Co v CT Bowring & Co Ltd* (1920) 2 Ll L Rep 220 at 221. In several of the cases in which the principle was enunciated, the dispute was of a commercial character.

[17] In such cases the arbitrators habitually receive information, documents and contentions from the parties who have respectively appointed them, even at a time when they still retain a judicial capacity. See, for example, per Lord Sterndale MR in *Ritchie v Jacks*, ante, at 520.

[18] See the observations, in a rather different context, of Lord Sterndale MR in *Ritchie v Jacks*, ante, at 520.

[19] *Oswald v Earl Grey*, ante; *Re Brook, Delcomyn and Badart* (1864) 16 CB NS 403.

admission of evidence, and to treat it as something which does not necessarily vitiate the award[20].

(c) *Hearing evidence in the absence of both parties*

Most of the observations by the courts on the impropriety of receiving evidence in the absence of the parties have concerned situations in which one party has been present and the other absent. Rather different considerations apply where neither party is present, or has any part in tendering the evidence in question. In such a case, there is still a risk of surprise, but at least there is no longer the latent suspicion that the arbitrator may be the subject of improper pressure from one party. The Court has therefore tended to adopt a less rigorous attitude than in situations where only one party is placed at a disadvantage. In this respect, two distinct considerations arise. First, whether the parties have agreed to the arbitrator proceeding in their absence. Second, whether he has communicated the substance of the evidence to them, and given them an opportunity to deal with it.

An express agreement that the arbitrator shall make his own investigations, without communicating the results to the parties, is undoubtedly valid. It is equally clear that such an agreement may be implied from trade custom. For example, in quality disputes under contracts for the sale of goods, it is taken for granted that the umpire will inspect samples, and nobody anticipates that he will report his findings to the parties for comment, before he makes his award[1]. The arbitrator should, however, bear in mind that if his investigations reveal something which is entirely new, in the sense that it has not been brought out in the contentions of the parties, he should draw it to their attention and give them a chance to deal with it[2].

It is unlikely that any agreement for the arbitrator to receive evidence in the absence of both parties can be implied in formal or semi-formal arbitrations, if only for want of any usage to support it; still less, that any agreement that evidence so received can be acted upon without the parties being given an opportunity to address comments upon it.

If there is no express or implied agreement permitting the arbitrator to do so, it is wrong for him to receive evidence in the absence of the parties[3], for by doing so he assumes the role of investigator and subverts the adversary procedure. Nevertheless, it will not necessarily be fatal to the award if the arbitrator acts in this way, provided he subsequently tells the parties what he

---

[20] See the observations of Bailhache J in *Ireland v Bowring*, ante, at 221, and of Sankey J in *Niger Co Ltd v SA Spremitura Oil Vegetali* (1922) 12 Ll L Rep 497. This may be because the Court will be ready to assume that arguments presented informally are unlikely to carry much weight. The position is likely to be different if the argument is advanced orally, and particularly so if professional advocates are involved.

[1] See *Naumann v Edward Nathan & Co Ltd* (1930) 37 Ll L Rep 249, per Scrutton LJ at 250. That was a case where there was an express agreement, through the medium of the words 'in the usual way', but there is no doubt that the remarks of Scrutton LJ are equally apposite to cases where there is a settled trade practice.

[2] *Fox v PG Wellfair Ltd* [1981] 2 Lloyd's Rep 514 at 530. See p. 312, post for cases where points raised by the arbitrator take the parties by surprise.

[3] See *Youroveta Home and Foreign Trade Co Inc v Coopman* (1920) 3 Ll L Rep 242; *Re Enoch and Zaretzky, Bock & Co* [1910] 1 KB 327.

has done, and gives them a full opportunity to test the evidence by cross-examination and by calling rebutting evidence[4].

It is probable that even where an agreement to dispense with the presence of both parties and with subsequent communication can be implied, the agreement is always subject to the right of either party to require the arbitrator to revert to a more formal procedure[5].

(d) Communicating opponent's case

As previously stated, where the reference takes an informal shape, there will not necessarily be anything wrong in the arbitrator receiving evidence or argument from one party in the absence of the other. Commonsense would suggest that in such a case the interests of justice cannot properly be served without the substance of such evidence or argument being communicated to the absent party. Even this elementary safeguard may be dispensed with, if the parties expressly agree, or if their agreement can be inferred from a sufficiently unequivocal course of conduct[6], but in the absence of agreement some form of communication must take place.

Precisely how far the arbitrator need go in communicating to one party the case advanced by the other is not a matter upon which it is possible to generalise. The arbitrator must take into account the degree of formality which is being adopted[7], the degree to which the absent party is already aware of the general nature of the case which he has to meet, and the extent to which that party has displayed an interest in knowing the details of his opponent's case. Equally, the arbitrator must have regard to the form in which the evidence and submissions have been presented. If they are contained in voluminous documents, there will be no point in the arbitrator voluntarily copying them all; he need only tell the absent party what sort of evidence exists, and that he may inspect it if he wishes. Conversely, if the evidence consists of a single document, such as a survey report, it will be better to copy it than to attempt a precis. In every case, the arbitrator should bear in the forefront of his mind that it is his duty to ensure, so far as

---

4 *Thomas v Morris* (1867) 16 LT 398. Whether the subsequent communication prevents the arbitrator's acts from constituting misconduct, or whether it merely means that the Court will no longer consider it sufficiently objectionable to justify interference, is academic. The position appears to be different where only one party is absent. In such a case it seems that subsequent communication will not usually cure the misconduct: *Dobson v Groves* (1844) 6 QB 637; *Montrose Canned Foods Ltd v Eric Wells (Merchants) Ltd* [1965] 1 Lloyd's Rep 597 at 602 (where the communication was adventitious).

5 See per Scrutton LJ in *Naumann v Nathan*, ante, at 502.

6 As in *Ritchie v Jacks*, ante.

7 See the grounds upon which Donaldson J distinguished, in *Myron (M/V) Owners v Tradax Export SA* [1969] 1 Lloyd's Rep 411 at 417, the observations of Megaw J in *Montrose Canned Foods Ltd v Eric Wells (Merchants) Ltd* [1965] 1 Lloyd's Rep 597 and *Government of Ceylon v Chandris* [1963] 1 Lloyd's Rep 214, [1963] 2 QB 327. It is the duty of the arbitrator to see that each party has sufficient information in his possession to ascertain the opponent's case, but it is for the party to work out the implications for himself; the arbitrator cannot be expected to expound the dispute to the parties. See *Franz Haniel AG v Sabre Shipping Corpn* [1962] 1 Lloyd's Rep 531, distinguishing *Peter Cassidy Seed Co v Osuustukkukauppa IL* [1954] 2 Lloyd's Rep 586. A common source of misunderstanding is where one party is permitted to raise a new point in the course of the hearing. It is the duty of the arbitrator to make sure that the other party appreciates what has happened, and has a proper opportunity to deal with the point: *Gunter Henck v Andre & Cie* [1970] 1 Lloyd's Rep 235.

reasonably possible, that each of the parties to the dispute knows the case which has been put against him and has had an opportunity to put forward his own case[8].

6 Oral hearing exhaustive of evidence and argument

It is a feature of the English adversary system that the oral hearing is intended to be the occasion on which the whole of the evidence and argument is put forward, on which the tribunal arrives at its decision. Thus, the parties are entitled to proceed on the assumption that the arbitrator will receive no evidence or argument in advance of the hearing, otherwise than by express agreement – such, for example, as occurs where the evidence of a particular witness is for convenience taken out of turn, or where the parties by agreement deliver written statements of case instead of pleadings.

Again, the parties are entitled to assume that the award will be based solely on the evidence and argument deployed up to the moment when the hearing is concluded.

Any departure from this general approach is likely to give rise to injustice, and to a breach of one of the various principles discussed above. If the arbitrator decides the case on a point which he has invented for himself, he creates surprise and deprives the parties of their right to address full arguments on the base which they have to answer[9]. Similarly, if he receives evidence outside the course of the oral hearing, he breaks the rule that a party is entitled to know about and test the evidence led against him[10].

---

[8] *Montrose Canned Foods Ltd v Eric Wells (Merchants) Ltd*, supra, per Megaw J at 602.

[9] *Société Franco-Tunisienne D'Armement-Tunis v Government of Ceylon, The Massalia* [1959] 2 Lloyd's Rep 1; *Faghirzadeh v Rudolf Woolf (SA) (Pty) Ltd* [1977] 1 Lloyd's Rep 630; *Fox v Wellfair Ltd* [1981] 2 Lloyd's Rep 514; *Interbulk Ltd v Aiden Shipping Co Ltd, The Vimeira* [1984] 2 Lloyd's Rep 66. Cf. *Mabanaft GmbH v Concentino Shipping Co SA, The Achillet* [1984] 2 Lloyd's Rep 191.

[10] See pp. 308–309, ante. See *Eastcheap Dried Fruit Co v NV Gebroeders Catz Handelsvereeniging* [1962] 1 Lloyd's Rep 283. The decision in *Royal Commission on Sugar Supply v Kwik Hoo Tong Trading Society* (1922) 11 Ll L Rep 163, cited in that case, is not precisely in point, although the general principle is germane, because there does not appear to have been an oral hearing.

CHAPTER 23

The course of the reference: before the hearing

A. STAGES OF THE REFERENCE: SUMMARY

As we have already shown in Chapter 21, ante, English law accommodates a wide variety of arbitral procedures. There would be no point in setting out to describe the course of a typical reference to arbitration. Indeed, any such description would be misleading, for it might suggest that there is a set procedure which the arbitrator is obliged to follow, if he is not to commit misconduct. Precisely the reverse is true. Subject to a few general principles, the procedure is set by the express or implied terms of the arbitration agreement, and it is to those which the arbitrator must have regard.

Nevertheless, it is convenient to identify for the purposes of discussion a number of stages through which the arbitration may pass, between the moment when the tribunal in constituted and the date on which an enforceable award comes into existence. Few arbitrations will pass through all these stages; and even then, not necessarily in the stated order. In the most informal types of reference almost all of them will be omitted. The various stages are as follows[1] –

1 *Fixing the procedure.* The arbitrator and the parties satisfy themselves that there are no misunderstandings as to the general nature of the procedure to be adopted. The arbitrator also gives any detailed directions which are required.

2 *Defining the issues.* The parties, helped if necessary by the arbitrator, identify the issues of fact and law on which the arbitrator will be required to reach a decision when making his award.

3 *Production and preparation of the documents.* Relevant documents are disclosed and inspected by the parties, and are prepared for the hearing.

4 *Interim protection orders.* The arbitrator or the Court makes orders relating to any property which is either the subject matter of the dispute, or is the subject of an issue in the reference. The purpose of such orders may be to protect the property itself from harm; to preserve the rights of the parties until the dispute has been resolved; or to enable the parties to exploit the evidentiary value of the property to the full.

5 *Orders for security.* The arbitrator or the Court makes orders securing the right of the party who is ultimately successful to recover his costs of the arbitration; and securing the right of a successful claimant to be paid the amount of the award.

6 *Arranging the hearing.* If the arbitration is of a type which calls for an oral hearing, a date and place are appointed.

---

[1] The discussion in this Chapter is of the various stages of a reference which is taking its normal course. The powers of the Court to intervene in a reference which has gone wrong, and of the arbitrator to deal with procedural problems during the course of the reference, are dealt with in Part VII.

7 *Investigation of facts and law; the hearing.* If the arbitration is of a type which calls for an oral hearing, the parties and their representatives and witnesses appear before the arbitrator to present their case on the facts and the law. If the procedure does not involve a hearing, the same investigation takes place, but in an informal and abbreviated manner.

8 *The decision.* The arbitrator reaches his decision in the light of the evidence and arguments brought before him, and also in the light of any advice from third persons which it is permissible for him to obtain.

9 *The award.* The arbitrator embodies his decision in an award, which he then publishes.

10 *Appeal proceedings.* Where the contract so provides, an appellate arbitral tribunal reconsiders the decision of the arbitrator.

B. DETAILED DISCUSSION

1 Fixing the procedure

In most arbitrations, there is no doubt as to the general shape of the procedure which is to be followed. Very often, this is clear from the conduct of the parties themselves. Where they appoint a lawyer as arbitrator, and come to him armed with a submission which already provides for an exchange of pleadings and lists of documents, it is plain that a formal procedure is contemplated, and that any relaxation of formality will take place only at the suggestion of the parties. Conversely, in the great number of commercial arbitrations which are conducted by trade arbitrators, it is well understood from the start that there will be no pleadings, discovery of documents, oral evidence, or anything resembling a hearing. In such a case, there is no need for the arbitrator to call the parties together for the purpose of settling the procedures; it is taken for granted.

There is, however, a residue of arbitrations occupying the middle ground, where it is not possible to be sure, from the nature of the underlying contract, the terms of the arbitration agreement, and the conduct of the parties, precisely which variety of procedure is to be adopted. Here, there is a real possibility of injustice, not because the procedure which the arbitrator chooses to adopt is unfair in itself, but because one or other of the parties may not realise until too late that the arbitrator is working on different lines from those which he had anticipated.

Misunderstandings of this nature usually relate either to the presence or absence of an oral hearing, or to the form and content of the evidence for which the arbitrator is looking. Thus, a party may make elaborate preparations for an oral hearing, only to find that the award has already been published on the basis of documents alone. Conversely, he may assume that documentary evidence will be received as a matter of course, and then discover that his opponent objects to the evidence as inadmissible and calls for a form of strict proof which he is unable to provide.

At best, misunderstandings of this nature lead to adjournments and wasted costs; at worst, they may form the basis of applications to remit or set aside the award, and even greater expenditure of costs. It is the business of the arbitrator to see that such misunderstandings do not take place.

The best way to accomplish this is to bring the parties and their legal advisers together for a preliminary hearing, so that the ideas of the parties as to the conduct of the reference can be received, and any disagreements resolved by the arbitrator's order. Whether the arbitrator should himself call the preliminary meeting is a matter for his discretion. In general, if he knows that the parties are represented by lawyers, it will be better to leave them to take the initiative. Many arbitrators think it their duty to hurry along the proceedings, possibly feeling that it reflects upon their competence if something is not continually happening. This is an error of judgment, for progress may be made without it being apparent to the arbitrator. No arbitrator is at risk of being removed under section 13 of the Act, on the ground of inactivity, if neither party has asked him to be active[2]. The function of the arbitrator is to achieve a just result, and this is not necessarily accomplished by pressing the parties to go faster than they wish. Preparing a complex dispute for hearing may be a heavier task than it appears from the outside, and the parties themselves are usually the best judges of how quickly the matter should proceed.

The position will be different if the issues are comparatively simple, or if the parties are not legally represented, or if an informal procedure is contemplated. Here the arbitrator can legitimately force the pace by calling for the views of the parties – not necessarily in person, for an exchange of correspondence will often suffice.

Where the dispute is of a formal nature, the outcome of the preliminary hearing will usually be an explicit order by the arbitrator as to the next steps to be taken. If it is decided that pleadings are necessary, times should be prescribed within which they are to be delivered; if discovery is to be given, the method and timing should be laid down.

At the same time, the arbitrator may well think it prudent to ask the parties whether they contemplate any special agreement as to evidence. If they do – for example, if they agree that the arbitrator shall not be bound by the strict rules of evidence – their agreement should be formally recorded.

The arbitrator need not aim to map out the whole future of the arbitration in the course of a single preliminary hearing. An attempt to force a definite shape on the reference, or to make firm arrangements for the date and nature of the hearing, before the arbitrators and the parties have a clear idea of what the dispute is really about, will only lead to confusion and expense.

Later on, when pleadings have been exchanged, and perhaps discovery has been completed, the parties or the arbitrator may think it useful to convene a meeting at which to deal with the various procedural issues which tend to arise during the preparatory stages of the more formal type of arbitration. Here, the arbitrator can be asked to rule upon applications for further particulars of pleadings, or for additional discovery of documents; he can make orders for the exchange of experts' reports and witness statements, and he can fix the date for the hearing.

In complex disputes, benefits can result from convening, at a still later stage of the reference, what is sometimes called a 'pre-trial review'. There comes a time when all the activities taking place across the line which divides the two parties have come to an end: the pleadings are complete, particulars and interrogatories have been exchanged, documents have been disclosed, inspected and copied. There follows a period of apparent silence during which each party

---

[2] So held in *Succula Ltd v Harland and Wolff Ltd* [1980] 2 Lloyd's Rep 381.

is (or should be) engaged with his advisers in deciding upon and preparing the evidence which he will need to establish his own case and rebut that of his opponent. It is at this time that the arbitrator can usefully summon the parties for a full discussion as to the way in which the hearing should be conducted. The subject matter of the discussion will depend on the individual circumstances of the case. For example the parties can consider whether the issues in the case should be split amongst two or more separate hearings; whether there should be a limitation on the number of expert witnesses; whether there should be an exchange of experts' reports, and (if so) whether this should be a further exchange once there has been an opportunity to study the first round of reports; whether time can be saved by allowing the statements of factual witnesses to be put in evidence, subject to cross-examination. At the same time, the arbitrator may find himself in a position to form a view as to the shape of the dispute and to put pressure on the parties to abstain from contesting the more peripheral issues, for example by directing that the parties' legal advisers shall meet within a given period to attempt to reach agreement on minor issues and report to him on the outcome of the meeting. The opportunity can also be taken to extract from the parties a sensible estimate of the duration of the hearing (very important, when the arbitrators and lawyers have crowded professional lives) and on matters, such as the arrangement and pagination of documents, which although apparently mundane have a significant effect on the laboriousness of the hearing[3]. Moreover, if the case is not so complicated as to justify a discussion sufficiently prolonged and detailed to be dignified by the name of a pre-trial review, we suggest that the arbitrator can do a real service to the parties by bringing them and their respective lawyers together, and compelling them to think about the issues well in advance of the hearing, rather than at the last minute[4].

In cases where the reference is to a tribunal of two arbitrators, the question arises whether the umpire, if he has been appointed, should sit with the arbitrator at the preliminary hearing. Unless and until the arbitrators disagree, the umpire cannot enter upon the reference, and therefore can play no formal part in any decision on a disputed point of procedure. This being so, the parties may decide, in a case where the directions are straightforward, not to incur the expense of asking the umpire to sit. On the other hand, where the reference is likely to be complex, and where there is a real possibility of disagreement at an early stage, so that the umpire may have to conduct the substantive hearing

---

[3] This can be a useful opportunity for the arbitrator to make known his views on the policy to be adopted on the selection of documents for copying: see p. 326, post.

[4] Pre-trial reviews are not popular with busy lawyers, for they require much reading and thought to be performed months ahead of the hearing, and therefore give the appearance of requiring the same case to be prepared twice. It is for this reason that parties to High Court actions have very rarely availed themselves of the procedures recommended in Practice Direction [1962] 1 WLR 1216. The arbitrator has, however, two great advantages over the judge. First, the powers of the judge are circumscribed by the Rules of the Supreme Court, which give him no jurisdiction to call the parties together of his own volition. He can only act if one of the parties issues a summons or notice of motion. The powers of the arbitrator, by contrast, derive from the arbitration agreement, and we see no difficulty in finding an implied term empowering the arbitrator to convene a pre-trial review or similar meeting: and indeed the concluding words of s. 12(1) are probably sufficient in themselves to confer such a power. Second, the arbitrator can impose upon the parties whatever procedure he thinks fit, so long as it is consistent with the express or implied term of the arbitration agreement, and is not unfair.

himself, it will often be better for the umpire to sit with the arbitrators as an unofficial chairman, to offer whatever advice they may wish to invite from him. This means that he will not find himself, after a later disagreement, charged with the conduct of a hearing, the procedure for which has been fixed without reference to him, to lines of which he does not approve. It is, however, important that if the umpire does sit with the arbitrators, he should make it clear to the parties that he is acting in an advisory capacity only, and not as a voting member of the tribunal.

When discussing and ruling on matters of procedure, the arbitrators should bear in mind that if they find themselves at issue on a procedural point, this ranks as a disagreement for the purposes of section 8(2), just as much as a disagreement on an issue of fact and law[5], with the consequence that, unless the parties expressly agree to the contrary, the umpire must immediately replace them and take over the reference. This may not be at all what the parties desire. Very often, they hope and expect that the arbitrators will be able to agree on an award, the function of the umpire being to act as chairman and tribunal of last resort[6]. Each arbitrator must, of course, hold out for his own view when the tribunal at length comes to decide on its award on the substantive issues in the case, but he will do the parties no service if he insists on having his own way on every procedural point.

2 Defining the issues

(a) Reasons for defining the issues

In many arbitrations, the issues lie within a narrow compass, and it is plain from the outset what points the arbitrator must decide, and what case each party will have to meet. In other instances, the dispute opens up a wide field of issues, or potential issues; and in these cases it is desirable to carry out, in one form or another, a process whereby the issues are defined in writing. This process has two main functions.

First, it serves to inform the arbitrator of matters which he must decide when making his award. If he awards on issues which have not been left to him for decision, he commits misconduct and may also be acting in excess of jurisdiction[7]. It is equally misconduct if he fails to deal in his award with matters which he has been appointed to decide. A written statement of the issues should enable the arbitrator to avoid mistakes of this kind[8]. Moreover, it will help the arbitrator to conduct the reference in an orderly manner. Parties frequently

---

[5] See p. 262, ante.

[6] This approach is often adopted where the parties appoint commercial men as arbitrators, and the arbitrators choose a lawyer to act as umpire.

[7] See *Société Franco-Tunisienne D'Armement Tunis v Government of Ceylon, The Massalia* [1959] 2 Lloyd's Rep 1, where a shipowner claimed demurrage from the charterer. The arbitrator decided the case on a point of law which had not been argued, with the result that he not only dismissed the shipowner's claim for demurrage but also made an award of despatch-money in favour of the charterer. The award of despatch was set aside for want of jurisdiction, and the award on demurrage was remitted on the ground that the taking of a new point without notice constituted misconduct.

[8] This practice is not always successful, as witness *The Massalia*, supra, where the arbitrator/ advocates handed in written statements of case at the hearing. Even in that case, however, the statements did at least serve to identify the points which had been agreed.

shift their positions in the course of a reference. New arguments and assertions of fact are brought forward, and existing contentions fall into the background. If the issues are not defined in writing, this legitimate process may go so far as to convert the dispute into something entirely new. Unless the change is recognised in time, the party who has come prepared to meet one case may discover too late that he has been defeated by another. If the arbitrator is armed with documents which define the issues, he can make sure that the process of modification does not go too far.

Second, the clarification of issues is of value to the parties, since it enables each of them to know from the outset what case he has to meet. He can prepare himself with evidence on the contentious issues, and avoid wasting expense in preparing himself to deal with matters which are within the scope of the original submission to arbitration, but which are no longer live issues.

(b) Methods of defining the issues

The arbitrator is under no duty to order pleadings[9] or other written statements of case as a matter of course. In many cases, he would be wrong to do so. For example, in a commodity arbitration when the issue concerns the allowance to be made for an alleged deficiency in quality, it would be pointless to order pleadings. The parties know what the issue is; there is no question of surprise; and the arbitrator himself would not be helped by having the dispute elaborated in writing.

In other situations, the arbitrator or the parties may consider that clarification of the dispute will be of value. If so, the arbitrator will in broad terms have a choice between four different procedures –

(i) To order full pleadings, in the same manner as the High Court. These are written statements of the facts which the parties intend to prove in support of their respective contentions. They should contain only assertions of fact (at any rate in theory), and should not comprise arguments, evidence or propositions of law.

(ii) To order each party to deliver a full written statement of his case[10]. Such a statement would include arguments and evidence, as well as bare allegations of fact; it would annex copies of the relevant documents; and embrace the issues of law as well as of fact.

(iii) To order the delivery of brief informal letters setting out the parties' respective cases.

(iv) To find out what are the issues really in dispute by means of an oral discussion at a preliminary hearing, followed by the making of a written record of the issues as so determined.

The choice between these various ways of clarifying the issues depends upon the nature of the dispute, the qualifications of the tribunal, and the general nature of the procedure expressly or impliedly agreed by the parties.

---

[9] We are here using the word 'pleadings' in the technical English sense of documents which set out the facts which the parties intend to prove. We are not referring to oral 'plaidoiries', in the sense of speeches made to the Court by advocates.

[10] Resembling the 'briefs' submitted to the Court under certain forms of procedure in the United States.

(i) **Pleadings.** Pleadings are not the ideal way of isolating the essential issues in a dispute. An artfully drawn defence may conceal as much as it reveals. Even the most communicative of pleadings tells the reader little or nothing of the case which the party will advance on the issues of law, or of the evidence which he will adduce to prove his allegations of fact. Moreover, the use of pleadings tends to multiply the issues, because of the natural desire of the advocate to keep open all his arguments and options until the last possible moment, in the hope of some favourable turn of events. This means that a party who bases his preparation of the case on his opponent's pleadings may arm himself with evidence to meet a point which in the event is never seriously pressed.

For these reasons, and because pleadings are believed to imply a legalistic approach inappropriate to commercial arbitrations, many lay arbitrators prefer to avoid them. On the other hand, when properly used, pleadings can combine precision with economy of effort in a way which none of the alternative procedures can attain. Moreover, they have the great benefit of furnishing a ready-made procedure which all lawyers understand. If a lawyer is ordered to deliver Points of Claim or Points of Defence, he knows precisely what is expected, and there is much less risk of the confusion and misunderstandings which may attend other ways of clarifying the issues. Furthermore, where the arbitrator is a lawyer, he will usually feel more at ease if he has pleadings which he can use as a framework for the reference.

In the main, we suggest that an order for the delivery of pleadings should be reserved for cases where the issues are complex, where there is likely to be a full hearing with oral evidence, and where the parties are legally represented.

An order for pleadings should fix the times within which they are to be delivered. These should be realistic – unlike the times fixed by the rules of the Supreme Court for the delivery of pleadings in High Court actions. In an understandable effort to show the parties that they mean business, arbitrators sometimes fix unreasonably short times for pleadings and other interlocutory proceedings. This is harmful, because it means that costs have to be wasted on applications for extensions of time[11].

If the pleading is insufficiently informative, the arbitrator has power to order the delivery of Further and Better Particulars.

The arbitrator also has power to order the administration of interrogatories – viz. written questions addressed by one party to the other, intended to be answered on oath[12]. The Court has a similar power[13]. An order for interrogatories is a formal and inflexible device, which is only rarely appropriate for any form of arbitration, still less a commercial arbitration. If a party feels that the issues could profitably be narrowed by causing his opponent to commit himself in writing to allegations of fact which cannot be extracted by means of a request for particulars, the best course is for him to write a letter setting out his questions in clear and unlegalistic language, warning his opponent that the answers are

---

[11] On the powers of the arbitrator in the event of failure to comply with orders for the delivery of pleadings, see pp. 535–543, post.

[12] S. 12(1) and *Kursell v Timber Operators and Contractors Ltd* [1923] 2 KB 202.

[13] S. 12(6)(b). As to the relationship between the concurrent powers of the Court and the arbitrator, see p. 328, post.

intended to be treated as binding. An unreasonable refusal to respond may justify the arbitrator in penalising the opponent in costs[14].

Another method of narrowing the issues is a notice to admit facts, whereby one party formally asserts a fact or facts, and invites his opponent to agree that his assertions are true. An admission so made binds the party who makes the admission vis-à-vis the party who seeks it[15], although it does not bind him towards other parties or in other proceedings. If a party declines to admit assertions of fact which are ultimately proved to be true, the arbitrator has power to order that he shall pay the cost of proving them. This procedure, which could well be more widely adopted than it is at present, is mainly useful where either – (a) a party suspects that his opponent is denying his assertions more for the sake of routine or through a desire to be obstructive, than from any real conviction that they are untrue, or (b) the allegation of fact will be expensive to establish, and will not necessarily be decisive in the arbitration[16].

An arbitrator has power to allow the amendment of pleadings, although of course he is not bound to do so[17]. If the amendment is allowed, it is customary to make the order on terms that the amending party shall pay the costs 'of and occasioned by the amendment' in any event[18] and also on terms that the opponent shall have leave to make consequential amendments to his own pleading. The arbitrator should not be alert to reject applications to amend, even if they involve a radical change in the party's case. It is better, in the interests of justice, that the party should present his case correctly at the second attempt, rather than not at all. As was once observed – 'There is one panacea which heals every sore in litigation, and that is costs. I have very seldom, if ever, been unfortunate enough to come across an instance, where a person has made a mistake in his pleadings which has put the other side to such a disadvantage as that is cannot be cured by the application of that healing medicine'[19].

There is no reason in principle why amendments should not be allowed at any time up to the making of the award, if justice so requires. Nevertheless, the shorter the interval between the application to amend and the date fixed for the hearing, the less ready the arbitrator will be to allow the amendment, for the raising of a new point may impede the opponent's preparations for the hearing. If the arbitrator considers that it is right to allow the amendment, he may grant leave on terms that the opponent can, if he wishes, have an adjournment of the hearing, together with an order that the amending party shall pay the costs of the adjournment. The arbitrator should bear in mind that an adjournment may

---

14 See Scrutton on *Charterparties* (18th edn.) p. 477 on the sparing use of interrogatories in Commercial Court actions.
15 It is not absolutely binding. The arbitrator has power to permit the withdrawal of an admission.
16 If a fact is likely to be decisive there is little point in giving a notice to admit. The notice is unlikely to produce an affirmative answer, and if the person giving the notice proves the fact and thereby wins the arbitration, he will recover the cost of proof as part of the general order for costs resulting from his success.
17 *Re Crighton and Law Car, and General Insurance Corpn Ltd* [1910] 2 KB 738; *Edward Lloyd Ltd v Sturgeon Falls Pulp Co Ltd* (1901) 85 LT 162; *Exormisis Shipping SA v Oonsoo* [1975] 1 Lloyd's Rep 432; *Congimex SARL (Lisbon) v Continental Grain Export Corpn (New York)* [1979] 2 Lloyd's Rep 396.
18 Although there may be circumstances where such an order is not appropriate.
19 Per Bowen LJ in *Cropper v Smith* (1884) 26 Ch D 700 at 744.

cause hardship to the claimant, and he should look very carefully at any attempt by the respondent to introduce major amendments at a late stage[20].

When considering an application to amend a pleading, the arbitrator should also consider whether the amendment will – (a) raise a dispute which is not one of the disputes in respect of which he has appointed as arbitrator, or (b) raise a claim which is barred by lapse of time. If either of these questions does arise, the arbitrator should follow the procedure indicated at pp. 215–216, ante.

The question of an amendment is so much within the province of the arbitrator, as the person charged with the conduct of the reference, that the Court will only rarely be justified in preferring its own view to that of the arbitrator: so that, although there is certainly power to set aside or remit an award for misconduct on the ground of a wrongful grant or refusal of leave to amend[1], and possibly power to intervene in some other way in the course of the reference[2], there would need to be exceptional circumstances before such a power could properly be exercised.

(ii) Written statements of case. As an alternative to pleadings in a strict legal form, it is sometimes ordered[3] that the parties shall each deliver written statements of case, setting out their contentions on fact and law. Such documents should be more informative than pleadings, since they contain propositions of law with supporting arguments, and deal with the facts in a less elliptical way than many pleadings. The advantage of a full statement of case is that the arbitrator is enabled to familiarise himself with the case at a comparatively early stage, thus saving time at the hearing itself – a course which is not usually practicable where orthodox pleadings are delivered.

Where the dispute is of any complexity, a full statement of case is likely to be a long document, expensive and time-consuming to prepare. The use of such document is best confined to cases where the issues lie fairly readily to hand.

If the arbitrator decides to order the service of statements of case – which he will be unwise to do unless both parties consent – he should make it clear to

---

[20] See, for example, *Congimex v Continental Grain*, ante, where the respondent tried unsuccessfully to raise before the Board of Appeal a defence which had not been raised in the original arbitration, nor in the preliminary meeting before the Board of Appeal.

[1] As in *Exormisis Shipping SA v Oonsoo*, ante.

[2] See the discussion of *The Angelic Grace*, at pp. 518–523, post.

[3] The arbitration agreement sometimes provides that the parties shall deliver statements of case: see *Royal Commission on Sugar Supply v Kwik-Hoo-Tong Trading Society* (1922) 11 Ll L Rep 163, where the rules of a commodity association provided that the arbitrators should have the discretion whether to decide on written statements alone, or to call the parties before them and request the attendance of witnesses. Articles 3 to 6 of the Rule of Arbitration of the International Chamber of Commerce contain detailed provisions for written statements of case: see Appendix 4, post, pp. 751–752. The procedure is supplemented by the arbitrator drawing up terms of reference defining the issue to be determined and dealing with a number of other procedural matters: see Article 13. Lawyers familiar with the common law system of pleading tend to regard this two-stage procedure for defining the issues as unnecessary and cumbersome. It is certainly true that English arbitrations work perfectly well without it. But it would be wrong to underestimate the usefulness of the procedure, or its importance, in the complex type of case for which the Rules are mainly designed. Even in references following the English pattern it is usual for the arbitrator to set out the issues to be determined in the preliminary paragraphs of his award, and there is much to be said for a 'check list' of this kind being prepared at or before the hearing. All too often items which are (or seem to be) of minor importance are left to the closing stages of the hearing, when time may be short. The possibilities for misunderstanding, or for issues being overlooked, do not need to be stressed.

them what sort of documents he has in mind. Otherwise, it may be found that the opposing parties prepare their statements in such radically different ways that the two cannot easily be read together. For example, the arbitrator may find it helpful to tell the parties – (a) approximately how long the statements are intended to be, (b) whether they are supposed to be exhaustive expositions of the case, or merely summaries, and (c) whether the parties are to annex all or part of their documentary evidence.

(iii) Letters of claim and defence.   As another alternative to formal pleadings, commercial arbitrations are frequently conducted on the basis of an exchange of letters in which the parties set out informally their respective contentions. Sometimes this happens spontaneously, when each of the two arbitrators sends his file to the other, with an explanatory covering letter. On other occasions, the letters are exchanged by the parties' legal representatives. In the latter event, it is worthwhile for the arbitrator to ask whether the parties are advised by counsel, for if they are the exchange of letters tends to emerge as a kind of stunted pleadings, and it is usually more satisfactory to let the lawyers produce formal points of claim and points of defence in the way they know best.

(iv) Oral elucidation of issues.   It is sometimes suggested that the parties and the arbitrator should meet, in order to find out what the issues really are, and to see how far agreement can be reached on matters which the pleadings or statements of case have left formally in issue. Whether this procedure has any prospect of success depends on the nature of the reference.

If the arbitration is conducted in an informal manner, with the whole dispute being in effect in the hands of the two arbitrators with instructions to make what they can of it, the main issues often emerge naturally during the correspondence or discussions preliminary to the meeting at which the award is actually decided upon.

In more formal arbitrations, the procedure is less easy to operate. The arbitrator knows nothing of the dispute except what he can glean from the pleadings and what he is told by the representatives of the parties. On the basis of this limited information, he will not usually be in a position to apply any real pressure to the parties. It may be for this reason that the procedure is very little used in arbitrations[4]. The Boards of Appeal of some commodity associations do, however, operate a variant of the procedure when deciding whether to allow legal representation at the hearing and whether to state a case or give a reasoned award. Since legal representation is generally excluded at this preliminary hearing it is perhaps not surprising that it often fails to achieve its main objective, which is to identify the issues of law which arise for decision on the appeal.

3 Production and preparation of documents

An arbitration in which the parties lay before the arbitrator no documents at

---

[4] We refer at pp. 314–315, ante to the 'pre-trial' review. If a meeting of this kind is held, the issues will already have been formally established by the delivery of pleadings. But the meeting can sometimes produce an opportunity for the identification of those issues which are really 'live'.

all must be extremely rare. Even in the simplest quality arbitration, the arbitrator will usually have a copy of the contract note and the sampling certificates. In most cases, there will be the underlying contract; the correspondence or telex exchanges leading up to the dispute; the letters exchanged between the parties or their legal advisers after the dispute arose. All these are available to both sides, and can be produced without difficulty at the hearing if they are thought to be useful.

Equally, the parties may, if permitted by the form of procedure which is being adopted, produce documentary evidence, such as survey reports, called into existence after the dispute has arisen for the specific purpose of being used in the arbitration. The employment of documentary evidence is discussed at pp. 354 et seq., post.

We are here concerned with documents of a different kind, namely contemporary documents which come into the possession of one party, and are not at that time communicated to the other. This category comprises documents such as correspondence between one of the opposing parties and a third party, documents passing between various departments within the party's own organisation, confidential memoranda to the party from his agents, and so on. If the contents of these documents are favourable to the party who has possession of them, he will no doubt bring them forward at the hearing in the same way as the first two categories of document, mentioned above. But what if they are unfavourable? Can he nevertheless be compelled to disclose their existence, and produce them to the tribunal? We are here in the realm of discovery of documents, a uniquely Anglo-Saxon procedure.

There are two types of discovery[5], the difference between the two being more important in arbitrations than it is in a High Court action. First, there is general discovery of documents. Subject to certain exceptions, each party is obliged to disclose all documents material to the matters in dispute. There is no order specifying what documents are to be produced. It is the duty of each party to work out for himself which of the documents in his possession or power fall within the scope of his obligation of disclosure. Second, there is specific discovery, where a party is obliged to disclose identified documents, or documents falling into identified categories. In a High Court action, general discovery is the rule, and specific discovery is an ancillary procedure, which is only invoked if it is believed that a party has not fully complied with his obligations as to general discovery. As appears below, the position in an arbitration is different.

(a) The two types of discovery

A general order for discovery requires a party to produce a list of all documents which are or have been in his possession, custody or power[6].

The words 'relating to matters in question' have a wide scope. They are not limited to documents which are admissible in evidence, nor to those which prove or disprove any matters in question. Any document is disclosable which it is

---

[5] Strictly speaking, there are three types, if one includes the Chancery procedure of production, which may perhaps be the subject of s. 12(1): see p. 293, ante.

[6] The words 'possession, custody or power' are taken from RSC Ord. 24, r. 1. It will be noted that s. 12(1) omits the word 'custody', so that there may be a difference in scope between orders made under s. 12(1) and s. 12(6)(b). For a discussion of the meaning of these words, see the *Supreme Court Practice*, notes to Ord. 24, r. 2.

reasonable to suppose contains information which may enable a party either to advance his own case or to damage that of his adversary, or if it is a document which may fairly lead him to a train of enquiry which may have either of these two consequences[7].

In a High Court action, discovery of documents takes place automatically, after the exchange of pleadings, unless the Court makes an order to the contrary[8].

Discovery is given by listing every disclosable document, including those already possessed by the other side, and those which the disclosing party once had but no longer possesses – such as the top copies of outgoing correspondence. In the High Court, there is power to order that the party giving discovery shall verify on oath the accuracy of his list of documents. It is doubtful whether the arbitrator has this power[9], but it is clear that the High Court can, by virtue of its ancillary powers, require a party to verify on oath a list of documents delivered in an arbitration[10].

The procedure for specific discovery is available where a party has reason to believe that his opponent has not fully complied with his obligations as regards discovery – for example, where the disclosed documents refer to other documents which have not themselves been disclosed, or where it is obvious from the nature of the transaction that documents must have come into a party's possession or power, which are not included in the list[11]. The complaining party identifies the documents or classes of document which he alleges are missing, and his reasons for believing that they are relevant and that they must be, or have been, in the possession or power of the opponent[12]. If satisfied that the assertion is correct, the tribunal requires the opponent to make specific dislosure of the identified documents; if, in fact, no such documents exist, he must make a formal statement to this effect.

(b) Discovery in arbitrations

Discovery is an essential feature of the English adversary system[13]. Properly used, it is a powerful instrument of justice. In cases where all the information as to a particular event or fact lies in the hands of one party, discovery may provide the only means of ascertaining the truth.

---

[7] Per Esher MR in *Compagnie Financière et Commerciale Du Pacifique v Peruvian Guano Co* (1882) 11 QBD 55 at 62.

[8] The High Court procedure of automatic discovery was introduced after the enactment of the Arbitration Act. It is submitted that s. 12(6) does not have the effect of applying the new procedure to arbitration.

[9] He may possess it by virtue of s. 12(1).

[10] S. 12(6).

[11] For example the vessel's log-books, where the dispute concerns a maritime casualty; bills of lading and insurance certificates where it concerns a c.i.f. sale of goods; the site diary, where is concerns a large building contract. As an alternative to an order for specific discovery, the complaining party can apply for an order that his opponent shall serve a further and better list of documents. This creates a renewed general obligation of disclosure, as distinct from a limited and specific obligation: see the notes to Ord. 24, rr. 3 and 7, in the *Supreme Court Practice*.

[12] In the High Court, the application must be supported by an affidavit. There is no need to carry this requirement into the conduct of arbitrations, but the complaining party should make it clear in writing, before the hearing of his application, precisely what further discovery he requires, and what his reasons are for asserting that full discovery has not been given.

[13] It compensates for the tribunal's lack of inquisitorial powers.

On the other hand, if it is employed without discrimination, the procedure can have serious practical disadvantages. In complex cases, a full order for discovery may require the parties to list and produce large quantities of documents, all but a small fraction of which are of no interest or value to either party. If carried out thoroughly, the preparation of a list of documents involves the parties and their legal advisers in a great expenditure of time and money, much of which could be more usefully employed in preparing the evidence for the hearing.

Moreover, the making of an order for discovery takes it for granted that both sides will thoroughly comply with the order. If this assumption is falsified, and one party gives full discovery while the other does not, the former may be placed at a serious disadvantage. If injustice is to be avoided, the arbitrator must take care to see that the process is carried out fairly, if it is carried out at all. This means, in practice, that an order for discovery will often be useless unless the parties are represented by English solicitors. Many foreigners view with incredulity a system which requires them to produce (for example) documents passing within their own organisation, which were never intended for general distribution; and they point out with justice that the possibility of disclosure must serve to inhibit their freedom to express themselves frankly in writing. This can have the practical consequence that unless an experienced English lawyer is at hand, full discovery may be withheld. Furthermore, even a party who is determined to perform his obligations conscientiously by making a full disclosure of his documents may well be at a loss to know how far his obligations extend. Discovery is one of the most difficult aspects of English procedure, and although even an English lawyer may from time to time be daunted by the problems, at least his experience will give him a better chance than a layman of arriving at the correct solutions.

In these circumstances, the arbitrator should use discrimination in the employment of his power to order discovery. He should not feel that he is obliged to make any order for discovery at all, still less a full order. Conversely, he should not reject an application for discovery out of hand, simply because he regards it as legalistic and unfitted for the resolution of commercial disputes[14]. In particular, the arbitrator should remember that he need not necessarily employ the full extent of his powers. A restricted form of discovery may be appropriate to the particular dispute or procedure in question. Thus –

1 If the dispute turns on a few clearly defined issues, the arbitrator may be able to dispense with general discovery, and order specific discovery relating only to those issues[15].

2 Where the disclosable documents are numerous, there is no need for the parties to list them all individually. The arbitrator can order that the list shall identify bundles of documents and not the documents themselves, so that the list would contain items such as – 'File of correspondence with claimant's Genoa agents', 'Folder of repair invoices', and so on.

---

14 The principal considerations for and against making an order for discovery are summarised in *Sunderland SS P & I Association v Gatoil International Inc, The Lorenzo Halcoussi* [1988] 1 Lloyd's Rep 180 at 184.

15 This is what often happens in the most informal types of reference. There is no explicit order for discovery. The arbitrators, having familiarised themselves with the files supplied by the parties, are able to identify the further documents which they need, and simply write to the parties to get them.

3 Where the case falls into two or more clearly defined parts, and it is either certain or very probable that the hearing will be split into stages, the arbitrator may for the time being confine his order for discovery to the documents which are material to the first stage of the hearing.

4 Occasionally, where the documents are particularly numerous, and the arbitrator is confident that the parties can be relied on to make full disclosure, he may omit discovery altogether, and order the parties to proceed directly to inspection (see below). In other words, he simply directs that each party shall have all his relevant documents available at specified times and places, so that the other party can look at them, and take copies of those which are of interest to him.

No fixed rules can be laid down for the use of these and other modified forms of discovery. In each case, the procedure should be tailored to suit the circumstances.

(c) Inspection

Discovery of documents consists of the disclosure by the party of the existence (or former existence) of documents or classes of documents. In order to make the procedure useful, the opponent must have the opportunity to look at the documents themselves and to take copies. An order for discovery should therefore be associated with an order for inspection, for which a time-table should be laid down in the order for directions given by the arbitrator[16].

(d) Preparation of documents for the hearing

After discovery and inspection, the parties should put together an 'agreed' bundle or bundles, comprising all the documents which either or both of them consider should be before the arbitrator at the hearing[17]. This process of agreeing bundles can sometimes lead to misunderstandings, since it may involve one or both of two distinct processes –

1 The agreement of the documents 'as documents'. Each party admits that the documents in the bundle are what they purport to be. This means, for example, that a letter is admitted to have been written, and signed by the person whose apparent signature appears upon it, thus dispensing with the need to call the writer to prove the document.

2 Agreeing the documents 'as evidence of their contents'. Here, a party not only consents to the document being taken at its face value, but accepts that what is written in the document can be relied upon as evidence of the assertion of fact which it contains, even if it would not otherwise be admissible.

The difference between these two procedures may be illustrated by the example of an inspection certificate. If the certificate is agreed as a document,

---

[16] If there is no formal discovery, there need not necessarily be an order for inspection. In *James Laing, Son & Co (MC) Ltd v Eastcheap Dried Fruit Co* [1962] 1 Lloyd's Rep 285 at 290, McNair J held that, in the context of an informal arbitration, it was sufficient for the arbitrators to read out to the parties the documents which had been sent to the arbitrators, so that the parties could identify whether they had got them all or not. Except where there is unacceptable delay or obstruction, such as apparently existed in *Laing v Eastcheap*, the arbitrator will normally be safer to allow inspection to a party who is eager to have it.

[17] See p. 350, post.

the party making the agreement goes no further than admitting that a particular person or body did indeed issue the document. If the certificate is agreed as evidence of its contents, either party may use statements in the document as evidence that (for example) the goods were inspected on a certain day and found to be in a certain condition. The admission of the document does not, of course, amount to a concession that the goods were in that condition; merely that evidence of that fact exists, for whatever it may be worth.

There can be few arbitrations in which the parties cannot agree the disclosed documents as documents. If the tenor of the dispute is such that allegations of forgery or tampering with documents are a possibility, the dispute is one which may be better dealt with in the High Court: indeed, a party may be entitled to insist on transfer to the High Court under section 24(2)[18]. It does not, however, follow that the parties will necessarily want to agree to documents as evidence of their contents. If there is to be a full scale formal arbitration, with oral evidence and cross-examination, each party should therefore be careful that he does not, by agreeing the bundle of correspondence, let in some evidence that he would have preferred to exclude.

We have previously made reference to the fact that the bundle of documents should comprise all the documents which either or both of them consider should be before the arbitrator at the hearing. This states what the practice should be, not what it is. In the past, it used to be the task of the lawyers for each side to go through the disclosed documents, choosing those which could usefully be copied for inclusion in the agreed bundle. Nowadays, this rarely seems to happen. All the documents are copied and bundled, regardless of relevance. This is understandable. In a really big arbitration, the documents are numerous. Sorting through them is boring and time-consuming. A lawyer might well feel that his energies are better spent on more creative work, and that since documents can now be photocopied, rather than re-typed, it is cheaper as well as less trouble simply to copy them all (often in dozens of copies), leaving it to counsel and the arbitrators at the hearing to sift out those which are useful. We suggest that this is a short-sighted view. Recent experience has shown that the labour of conducting the hearing has been greatly increased, and hence the efficiency of the process has been materially reduced, by the need to man-handle large quantities of copy documents, most of them quite useless, and to keep track of the much smaller number which are really relevant; so much so, that it has now become the practice for each side to isolate a 'working bundle', containing the documents which are likely to be relied upon, and to ignore the 'agreed bundle' altogether. We suggest that arbitrators ought to recognise the inefficiency of this procedure, and take steps to see that it does not occur. If there is a 'pre-trial review', it will provide a good opportunity for the arbitrator to make clear his opposition to the deployment of large quantities of waste paper. In particularly bad cases, the arbitrator would be justified in penalising in costs a party whose lawyers have copied, not those documents which have in the event not proved to be useful (for this is hard to predict) but those which on any possible turn of events could not have been relevant.

Where the documents are in a foreign language, they must be translated, unless all the arbitrators are able to understand them. It should be possible for the parties to arrive at agreed translations, but in the absence of agreement the

---

[18] See pp. 501 et seq., post.

translations must be strictly proved by the evidence of expert translators[19]. Failure to follow this procedure will result in the remission or setting aside of the award, unless it can be shown unambiguously that the failure to follow the appropriate procedure has had no effect on the outcome of the dispute[20].

4 Interim protection orders

(a) Interim orders relating to property: general

From time to time, the interests of justice may require the making of orders in relation to goods or other property, pending the hearing and the award. Such orders fulfil two distinct functions –

1 They ensure that the property which is the subject of dispute does not come to harm, until the dispute has been resolved; and,

2 where the property, or an aspect of it, is an item of evidence in the reference, they ensure that the parties are able to exploit its evidentiary value to the full.

It would have been possible for the draftsman of the Act to prescribe the circumstances in which the Court and the arbitrator respectively would have the power to make orders of this nature. A different approach has, however, been adopted. As regards the Court, section 12(6) enumerates various types of order, and stipulates that the Court shall have the same power in respect of such orders, for the purpose of and in relation to a reference, as it has for the purpose of and in relation to an action or matter in the High Court. The Act does not, however, make any attempt to deal with the powers of the arbitrator in this respect, beyond stating that nothing in section 12(6) shall prejudice any powers which he may have.

This method of enactment entails that a party who wishes to avail himself of a particular form of interim relief may find that the power to grant it is vested in the arbitrator, or the Court, or neither. In order to ascertain whether the arbitrator has the power, he must construe the arbitration agreement, bearing in mind section 12(1), which creates an implication that, in the absence of express agreement to the contrary, the parties shall 'do all ... things which during the proceedings or reference the arbitrator or umpire may require'[1]. In order to ascertain whether the Court possesses the power in question, the party must first look through the list in section 12(6) to see whether the order which he seeks is one in respect of which the Court is given the same powers in respect of an arbitration as it would have if the matter were proceeding in the High Court. He must then go on to refer to the Rules of the Supreme Court, to find out whether, if the matter had been proceeding in the High Court, the Court would have had power to make the order in question[2].

This process will often disclose that both the Court and the arbitrator have power to make the order in question. In such a case, the proper course is to apply

---

[19] *E Rotheray & Sons Ltd v Carlo Bedarida & Co* [1961] 1 Lloyd's Rep 220.
[20] Ibid. at 224.
[1] See pp. 292–294, ante.
[2] Differences in wording between s. 12(6) and the Rules of the Supreme Court mean that the power of the High Court cannot in practice be invoked in every case falling within s. 12(6).

first to the arbitrator[3]. If the applicant obtains an order, and his opponent fails to comply with it, he can then apply for an order of the Court under section 12(6).

Furthermore, it is submitted that section 12(6) is available, not only to reinforce an order made by the arbitrator, but also by way of appeal[4] from a refusal to make an order[5].

The proper course for the party to pursue is less clear where there is a dispute about the power of the arbitrator to make any order at all on the application. One possible view is that it is more sensible in such a case to proceed straight to the Court. We suggest, however, that it would be better to put the matter to the arbitrator first, since his decision on the way which he will exercise his powers, assuming that he has any, is bound to carry weight with the Court.

(b) Safeguarding the subject matter of the dispute

The existence of a dispute may put at risk the property which forms the subject of the reference, or the rights of a party in respect of that property. Thus, the dispute may prevent perishable goods from being put to their intended use, or may impede the proper exploitation of a profit-earning article, such as a ship. If the disposition of the property has to wait until after the award has resolved the dispute, unnecessary hardship may be caused to the parties. Again, there may be a risk that if the property is left in the custody or control of one of the parties, pending the hearing, he may abuse his position in such a way that even if the other party ultimately succeeds in the arbitration, he will not obtain the full benefit of the award. In cases such as this, the Court (and in some instances the arbitrator) has power to intervene, for the purpose of maintaining the status quo until the award is made. The remedies available under the Act are as follows –

(i) The grant of an interlocutory injunction.

(ii) The appointment of a receiver.

(iii) The making of an order for the preservation, custody or sale of the property.

(iv) The securing of the amount in dispute.

(i) Interlocutory injunction to protect property. An interlocutory injunction is an order of the Court, normally negative in form, designed to protect the property or the rights of the parties from prejudice pending the resolution of the dispute. Circumstances in which an injunction may be ordered, and the conditions governing the exercise of the discretion, are so various as to

---

[3] The proviso to s. 12(6) shows that the powers of the Court and the arbitrator are cumulative, not alternative. Nothing in the Act expressly excludes the right of the party to apply direct to the Court, but it is the arbitrator, not the Court, who is in charge of the reference, and it is from him that the relief should in the first instance be sought.

[4] No guidance can be obtained from the decided cases on the way in which the Court reviews the decision of the arbitrator. In practice, the Court occasionally interferes even though the arbitrator has made no error in principle; but it does not do so unless a strong case of injustice is made. It was said in *Sunderland SS P & I Association v Gatoil International Inc, The Lorenzo Halcoussi* [1988] 1 Lloyd's Rep 180, at 183, to be a 'rather exceptional step' for the Court to order discovery when it has been refused by the arbitrator.

[5] The language of s. 12(6) is less apt to confer a power to revoke an order of the arbitrator, than to make an order which the arbitrator has himself refused to make.

be beyond the scope of this work. Reference should be made to the specialised texts on the subject.

An injunction is a powerful weapon, since it is backed by the powers of the Court of Equity to act in personam and these include, in the last resort, orders for the committal of a recalcitrant defendant, or that attachment of his property. In the context of an arbitration, an interlocutory injunction will usually fulfil one or other of two functions. First, to protect the property in issue from abuse by one of the parties: for example, to prohibit the removal of property from the United Kingdom, the object being to ensure that any order which the arbitrator may ultimately make as to the disposition of the property will not be rendered academic by the previous removal of the property. Second, to bring about a kind of interim specific performance of the contract. For example, if the issue is whether a charterparty has been validly terminated by the respondent, the Court may issue an injunction prohibiting the respondent from employing the vessel otherwise than in accordance with the charter: thus, in many cases, forcing him to keep the vessel in the service of the charterer pending the resolution of the dispute.

The Court has power to grant an interlocutory injunction in respect of matters which are the subject of an arbitration[6]. The making of an interlocutory injunction, or the pendency of an application for such an injunction, does not prevent the Court from granting a stay of any action which is brought in respect of the substantive dispute[7], the only purpose of the injunction being to maintain the status quo pending the award[8]. In general, the exercise of the discretion where there is a pending arbitration is likely to proceed on the same principles as in relation to an action in the High Court[9].

(ii) Appointment of receiver.   There are two types of receiver: those appointed by the Court, and those appointed out of Court. A receiver appointed by the Court is an officer of the Court, appointed to take possession of and deal impartially with the property or the fruits of the property, pending the outcome of proceedings, in circumstances where the Court considers that the property should not come into the possession of either party until the dispute has been resolved. By contrast, a receiver appointed out of Court acts as the agent of the party who appoints him, and not as a delegate of the Court. The appointment of a receiver out of Court is effected pursuant to a contract between the persons interested in the property – a common example being that of a receiver and

---

[6] S. 12(6)(h). The reference to 'interim' injunction must, it is submitted, include all forms of interlocutory injunction, and not merely those of strictly limited duration which are granted ex parte in an emergency.

[7] See p. 390, post.

[8] See *Foster and Dicksee v Hastings Corpn* (1903) 87 LT 736.

[9] This was not always so. Until *American Cyanamid Co v Ethicon* [1975] AC 396 it was widely believed that the Court would not grant an interlocutory injunction in the absence of at least a prima facie case for the grant of a final injunction at the trial. Since few arbitrations will result, whoever succeeds, in such an award, the scope for an interlocutory injunction seemed limited. It is now clear that an interlocutory injunction will be granted, as between the parties to a High Court action, wherever the justice of the case so requires. No doubt the same approach will be adopted in relation to arbitrations, subject to the reservation that the Court will take care not to become so involved in the underlying merits of the dispute as to trespass on the jurisdiction of the arbitrator.

manager appointed by the trustees to debenture stock pursuant to powers contained in the trust deed.

In theory, an arbitration agreement could, either directly or by way of a provision in the underlying substantive contract, confer on the arbitrator a power to order the appointment of a receiver out of Court. Such powers are however rarely, if ever, found, and it is therefore necessary to deal only with receivers appointed by the Court.

The appointment of a receiver by the Court may be necessary in two different situations. First, if the existence of the dispute impedes the commercial exploitation of the property, so that whatever the outcome of the dispute, both parties will be the losers. Second, if the property needs protection – either from risks which cannot be effectively countered because of the dispute, or from the possibility of improper interference by one of the parties[10].

The Court has power to order the appointment of a receiver in aid of arbitration proceedings in the same manner as if the dispute were the subject of a High Court action[11]. The fact that the Court has appointed a receiver is not in itself a ground for refusing an application to stay the proceedings under section 4 of the Act. The functions of the receiver are ancilliary to those of the arbitrator, and both can perform their functions fully without any risk of conflict[12].

In practice, the appointment of receivers in the context of an arbitration has been confined to partnership disputes. This seems a pity, since from a practical point of view a receiver may be a valuable alternative to the other, less flexible, forms of interim protective relief.

(iii) Detention, custody and preservation.   The Court has power to order the detention, custody and preservation of any property which is the subject of the reference[13]. These wide powers enable the Court to protect the subject matter from damage or deterioration, and also from being misappropriated by a party having custody or control of it.

Where goods[14] the subject of the reference are of a perishable nature or likely to deteriorate if kept, or if for any other reason it is desirable that they should be

---

10 For a full discussion of the circumstances in which the Court will appoint a reciever, see *Kerr on Receivers* (14th edn.).

11 S. 12(6)(h); *Compagnie du Sénégal v Woods & Co* (1883) 53 LJ Ch 166; *Pini v Roncoroni* [1892] 1 Ch 633; *Law v Garrett* (1878) 8 Ch D 26.

12 See *Compagnie du Sénégal v Woods*, supra; *Plews v Baker* (1973) LR 16 Eq 564. Russell (19th edn.) p. 327, suggests that the position may be different where the stay is ordered under the Arbitration Act 1975, since s. 28 does not apply to such orders. Our own view is that a receiver may be appointed concurrently with all forms of stay. The appointment is made, not as a term of the order, pursuant to s. 28, but as a distinct exercise of the Court's powers under s. 12.

13 S. 12(6)(e) and (g), read with Ord. 29, r. 2(1). The order may be made on such terms as the Court thinks just; ibid., r. 2(4).

14 The omission of words 'or other property' from s. 12(6)(e) creates an unwelcome lacuna in the powers of the Court. No doubt it was assumed that only goods could be perishable; but a power of sale for 'any other reason' could be useful in relation to 'other property' – for example, on a rapidly falling market. For the Court's power to order a sale in such a case, see *Coddington v Jacksonville, Pensacola and Mobile Rly Co* (1878) 39 LT 12 (bonds), and *Evans v Davies* [1893] 2 Ch 216 (shares).

sold forthwith the Court has power to order the sale[15]. The Court can then order the proceeds of sale to be paid into Court or otherwise secured[16].

(iv) Securing the sum in dispute.   Where the right of a party to a specific fund is in dispute in a reference, the Court has power to order the fund to be paid into Court or otherwise secured[17]. The forms of security most likely to be ordered are the provision of a bank guarantee or the payment of the fund into a bank account in the joint names of the parties or their advisers. It is probable that the Court alone, and not the arbitrator, has power to make such an order[18].

It will be noted that this power does not enable a party to recover sums on account of damages in advance of the hearing, even if liability is undisputed and it is clear that some monetary award will be made[19]. The power exists only where an identified fund is in dispute – as where, for example, it is alleged that the respondent is trustee for the claimant in respect of a specific sum of money.

(c) Protection of property for evidentiary purposes

As previously stated, interlocutory orders relating to goods or other property may be made for two distinct reasons. First, because the goods are assets which need to be protected until the rights of the parties have been determined. Second, because the goods have an evidentiary value which the parties must be allowed to exploit to the full. We are here concerned with the second of these aspects[20]. The topic is made needlessly complicated by the fact that the language of section 12(6)(g) of the Act, which defines the situations in which the Court can exercise interim powers in arbitrations analogous to those possessed in High Court actions, does not marry with the provisions in the Rules of the Supreme Court which deal with the powers of the High Court. Further difficulties are added by the existence of two parallel sets of rules, one of which applies only to Admiralty actions.[1]

In essence, however, the relief with which section 12(6)(g) is concerned may be divided into four categories –

    (i) Orders permitting examination by the arbitrator or his delegates;
    (ii) Orders permitting examination by the parties or their delegates;

---

[15] S. 12(6)(e) read with Ord. 29, r. 4(1). Paragraph (e) is narrower than r. 4(1), since it applies only to goods which are the subject matter of the reference, and does not cover goods as to which any question arises in the reference.

[16] On the basis that the proceeds become a part of the amount in dispute, within s. 12(6)(f).

[17] Under s. 12(6)(f), read with Ord. 29, r. 2(3). The order may be made on such terms as the Court thinks just: ibid., r. 2(4).

[18] This must certainly be so as regards an order for payment into Court, since the arbitrator cannot order the Court to receive the moneys.

[19] Even if an order for interim payment under Ord. 29, r. 12 falls within the words 'securing the amount in dispute', the power applies only to claims for personal injuries. As to the possibility of obtaining an interim award of the undisputed amount, see p. 000, post; and *Antco Shipping Ltd v Seabridge Shipping Ltd, The Furness Bridge* [1979] 2 Lloyd's Rep 267.

[20] Construed literally, s. 12(6)(e) is also apt to cover orders for evidentiary purposes. We believe, however, that paragraph (e) was intended to deal with orders whose function was to preserve the property as an asset, rather than as an item of evidence.

[1] RSC Ord. 75. We suggest that the Admiralty Rules can be invoked through the medium of s. 12(6) only where the dispute is one which, if it had been pursued by action rather than arbitration, would have fallen within the Admiralty jurisdiction of the High Court.

(iii) Orders designed to ensure that the property is made available for examination;

(iv) Orders for inspection etc. made before the reference has commenced.

(i) Examination by the arbitrator and his delegates. Unless the arbitration agreement otherwise provides[2], the arbitrator has power to inspect property in respect of which an issue arises in the arbitration. It is for him to decide whether or not to hold an inspection. He will naturally take into account matters such as the expense and delay which will ensue if the property to be inspected is at a distance. The arbitrator is under no obligation to exercise his powers merely because a party asks him to do so[3]. Personal inspection by the arbitrator constitutes evidence, but it is not exclusive evidence. Unless the arbitration agreement otherwise provides[4], the arbitrator must also receive any evidence which is tendered by the parties. However, having received it, he is still entitled to prefer his own judgment to that of the witnesses[5].

The arbitrator has a discretion as to the way in which the inspection is conducted[6]. Where the arbitration is of an informal nature, it will often be entirely satisfactory for the arbitrator to make a visit on his own to the place where the property is to be found[7]. On the other hand, where the arbitration has a more formal setting, it will be better for the arbitrator to attend in the company of the parties, so that they can point out to him any features which they wish him to observe. He should, of course, never carry out an inspection in the company of one party alone, unless he has the express prior consent of the other[8].

Where the arbitrator sits with an assessor, he may properly order that the assessor shall inspect the property and report his findings[9], which then become evidence in the case.

---

[2] An express exclusion of the power to inspect must be rare, but it is not inconceivable: for example, an agreement that the arbitration shall be conducted 'on documents alone'. Another example might be an agreement to arbitrate 'in London', when the property is situated abroad – see p. 344, post. An implied exclusion is difficult to visualise. Possibly the implication might be made where, by the custom of the trade, the arbitration is to be conducted in an economical or informal way – but this would probably be regarded as a case in which the arbitrator would possess the power to inspect, but would not usually be justified in exercising it.

[3] *Mundy v Black* (1861) 30 LJ CP 193.

[4] An implication to this effect may arise in cases where the whole point of the arbitration is that the arbitrator shall form his own conclusions on the basis of an inspection; for example, where a quality arbitration is conducted on an examination of samples.

[5] As Scrutton LJ pointed out in *J Aron & Co v Miall* (1928) 31 Ll L Rep 242 at 245, an experienced arbitrator may obtain more reliable results by exercising his own skill than by attempting to reconcile the conflicting views of the witnesses called by the parties.

[6] See *Heaven and Kesterton Ltd v Sven Widaeus A/B* [1958] 1 Lloyd's Rep 101.

[7] As happened, for example in *Heaven and Kesterton Ltd v Sven Widaeus A/B*, supra. See also the observations of Scrutton LJ in *Naumann v Edward Nathan & Co Ltd* (1930) 37 Ll L Rep 249 at 250.

[8] See pp. 308–309, ante.

[9] A number of reported Admiralty cases record the making of inspection by the Elder Bretheren of Trinity House, sitting as assessors: *The Duke of Buccleuch* (1889) 15 PD 86; *The Sound Fisher* (1937) 58 Ll L Rep 135; *Slieve Gallion v Cumberland Queen* (1921) 6 Ll L Rep 280; *Thomas Stone (Shipping) Ltd v Admiralty, The Albion* [1952] 1 Lloyd's Rep 38. Specific provision is made in RSC Ord. 75, r. 28, for inspection by assessors in Admiralty actions. There seems no reason why a practice recognised as appropriate in the High Court should be regarded as improper in an arbitration, although the arbitrator should be careful to remember that a 'view' is not always a substitute for oral evidence: see *London General Omnibus Co Ltd v Lavell* [1901] 1 Ch 135.

Even where no assessors are appointed, the arbitrator may properly order that the goods or samples of them shall be inspected by an independent expert[10]. He should, however, make sure that the parties have notice of what he is doing, and have an opportunity to call their own evidence if they wish to challenge the conclusion of the arbitrator's chosen expert[11].

In most of the situations with which we are here concerned, the Court has concurrent powers with the arbitrator to make orders for inspection, preservation, etc. A distinction must, however, be drawn between permissive and mandatory orders. The Court can order the parties to allow inspection by the arbitrator or his assessors; but there is no power in the Court to order the arbitrator to carry out an inspection against his wishes.

(ii) Examination by the parties and their delegates.   The arbitrator and the Court have concurrent powers to order that one party or his expert may inspect property in the possession of the other party[12], if the property is the subject matter of the reference, or of an issue in the reference[13].

It is doubtful whether the arbitrator has power to order the inspection of property which is not in the possession of a party to the reference[14]: his powers derive from the arbitration agreement, and cannot be employed against persons who are not parties to the agreement. By contrast, the Court does have the power to order inspection of property in the hands of third parties[15].

(iii) Orders facilitating examination.   The Court has power to make orders for the disposition of property, in order to ensure that the process of inspection can be carried out effectively. These orders relate to –

1 The detention, custody and preservation of the property[16];

2 The taking of samples and the trying of experiments[17];

3 The entry upon any land or building in the possession of any party to the reference[18].

---

[10] Cf. *Naumann v Nathan*, ante. There the arbitration was to be conducted 'in the usual way' (see 36 Ll L Rep 265), and the sending of samples to analysis was in accordance with the usual practice. See also the observations of Lord Macnaghten in *Colls v Home and Colonial Stores Ltd* [1904] AC 179 at 192.

[11] The status of an expert appointed by the arbitrator is quite different from that of a Court expert under various European systems of procedure. Under the English procedure the expert is not even primus inter pares: there is no question of his views being binding unless manifestly inconsistent with the true facts. Nor does English law recognise any procedure enabling the Court to appoint an impartial expert in a matter which will subsequently be referred to arbitration.

[12] The powers of the arbitrator arise by way of s. 12(1). The powers of the Court arise from a combination of s. 12(6)(g) and Ord. 29, r. 2.

[13] *The Vasso* [1983] 2 Lloyd's Rep 346, [1983] 1 WLR 838.

[14] The point was left open in *The Vasso*, supra.

[15] Under s. 12(6)(g) and RSC Ord. 29, r. 7A. The right applies to property which is either the subject matter of the reference, or is property as to which a question may arise in the reference: see ibid., r. 7A(3). The application is made by summons served on the person against whom the order is sought and on the other party to the reference: ibid., r. 7A(2). The order may be conditional on the giving of security for the costs of the person against whom it is made, or on other terms: ibid., r. 7A(5).

[16] S. 12(6)(e) and (g), read with Ord. 29, r. 2(1).

[17] S. 12(6)(g), read with Ord. 29, r. 3(1). Presumably the words 'for any of the purposes aforesaid', in para. (g), should be read as embracing 'inspection' as a purpose, notwithstanding the grammar of the paragraph.

[18] S. 12(6)(g), read with Ord. 29, rr. 2(2) and 3(2).

These powers have been widely construed. In particular, they have been taken to embrace the moving of the property from one place to another in order to facilitate inspection[19].

The arbitrator has, it is submitted, the same powers as the Court to make interim orders of this nature, for the purpose of facilitating inspection.

(iv) Orders for inspection before reference. It is probable, but not certain, that the Court has power to order the inspection of property at a time when the reference has not yet commenced – for example, in order to enable the complaining party to know whether there is sufficient substance in his claim to justify him in starting arbitration proceedings[20].

5 Order for security

(a) Security for costs

The defence of an arbitration can be an expensive business, even if the claim ultimately fails. The successful respondent will normally be awarded his costs, but this may not be a satisfactory recompense, for two reasons. First, if the costs of the defendant are subjected to taxation by the Taxing Master[1], it is unlikely that he will be fully indemnified for the moneys which he has been compelled to spend on his defence[2]. Second, there is no value in an order that the claimant shall pay the respondent's costs, if the respondent is unable to enforce it, either because the claimant has no money, or because he is outside the jurisdiction of the Court.

There is nothing to be done about the first of these disadvantages[3]. The second does, however, admit of a limited remedy, in the shape of an order that, as a condition of the arbitration being allowed to proceed, the claimant shall provide adequate security for any costs which may be awarded against him in the event of the claim being unsuccessful.

The arbitrator cannot himself make such an order[4], in the absence of express

---

[19] *SS New Orleans Co v London and Provincial Marine and General Insurance Co* [1909] 1 KB 943 (order for ship lying at Singapore to be brought to England for inspection). See also *Helmsville Ltd v Yorkshire Insurance Co Ltd, The Medina Princess* [1965] 1 Lloyd's Rep 361 at 395; *Chaplin v Puttick* [1898] 2 QB 160 (evidence being taken on commission, property sent abroad for identification by witnesses).

[20] Ord. 29, r. 7A(1). S. 12(6)(g) contains the words 'as to which any question may arise therein', and we doubt whether the immediately preceding words 'the reference' convey that paragraph (g) can only apply where a reference is already in existence. No doubt the power, if it exists, will be sparingly exercised.

[1] See p. 403, post.

[2] Recent changes in the basis of taxation in the High Court have resulted in more generous awards than under the earlier practice, but taxation still usually results in less than a full indemnity.

[3] At least the successful respondent in an English arbitration is in a better position than if the arbitration were conducted abroad, where in most jurisdictions he would be awarded either nothing, or a wholly insufficient sum, on account of his costs.

[4] The arbitrator may, perhaps, be able to achieve a similar practical result in a situation where the claimant is in procedural default, by consenting to be indulgent only on condition that the claimant provides security for costs. Experiments with this kind of 'order nisi' (which is discussed at p. 343, post) are perhaps best avoided in the field of security for costs, where a sufficient remedy can be obtained by an application to the courts.

agreement[5]. The Court does, however, have a power to order security for costs, by virtue of section 12(6)(a) of the Act, to the same extent as it would have in relation to an action in the High Court.

When considering the exercise of these powers, two questions arise. The first is whether the circumstances are such that the Court has a discretion to make an order for security[6]. There are several situations in which an order may be made, of which the two most likely to be of practical importance in an arbitration are –

(i) If a company is the claimant, and there is reason to believe that the company will be unable to pay the costs of the respondent if he is successful in his defence[7].

(ii) If the plaintiff is ordinarily resident abroad[8].

When considering whether the plaintiff is ordinarily resident abroad, it is the true facts which matter, and a provision such as is frequently found in the arbitration rules of trade associations, to the effect that the parties shall for the purposes of the arbitration be deemed to be resident in England, does not take away the power of the Court to make an order for security[9].

The second question is whether, if the circumstances are such as to give the Court a discretion to make an order for security for costs, it would be right for the discretion to be exercised. Various factors must be taken into account. Plainly, any express provision in the arbitration agreement is important[10]. The national character of the arbitration is also important[11], for example whether either of both of the parties is English, whether the arbitration rules are English or international in character, and whether England has been chosen as the seat of the arbitration with its arbitral rules specifically in mind, or whether it has been chosen, or designated by a third party, simply as a neutral venue[12]. Equally, it will be necessary to have regard to the type and complexity of the arbitration in question. An arbitration on documents will not normally attract

---

[5] It is clear from *Re Unione Stearinerie Lanza and Wiener* [1917] 2 KB 558 that an agreement may validly confer on the arbitrator power to make an order for security. See also *Mavani v Ralli Bros Ltd* [1973] 1 WLR 468 at 472 and *Bank Mellat v Helleniki Techniki SA* [1984] QB 291, [1983] 3 WLR 783. If the terms of the agreement are sufficiently wide, they may give the arbitrator power to make an order for security where no similar order could be made by the High Court. There seems no reason why, if he is given wide powers, the arbitrator should feel obliged to narrow them by limiting their use to cases where powers exist in the High Court.

[6] This power, unlike many of the powers created by the Act, cannot be ousted by agreement, since s. 12(6)(a) does not contain words such as 'unless a contrary intention is expressed': *Mavani v Ralli Bros*, supra. The terms of the arbitration agreement are, however, material to the question whether, in a particular case, the power should be exercised.

[7] By anology with the provisions of the Companies Act 1985, s. 726(1). See *Bank Mellat v Helleniki Techniki*, supra.

[8] RSC Ord. 23, r. 1(1)(a).

[9] *Mavani v Ralli Bros Ltd*, ante.

[10] *Mavani v Ralli Bros Ltd*, ante, at 474.

[11] *K/S A/S Bani and K/S A/S Havbulki v Korea Shipbuilding and Engineering Corpn* [1987] 2 Lloyd's Rep 445. An order for security will in principle be available in the traditional types of commercial arbitration held in London, e.g. those relating to maritime or commodity disputes.

[12] *Bank Mellat v Helliniki Techniki*, supra, in which it was held that security for costs will rarely, if ever, be ordered in an arbitration under the Rules of the ICC. Robert Goff LJ gave reasons which would have allowed an order to be made more readily on the ground that the claimant would be unable to pay the costs, than on the ground that he is resident abroad, but the reasoning of Kerr LJ, which is that of the majority, does not differentiate between the two cases.

an order for security unless[13] the documents and contentions are unusually elaborate. Again, the Court will have regard to the extent to which the claimant has assets available for execution within the jurisdiction, and to the likelihood of a successful respondent being able to enforce in the claimant's home country any award of costs which the arbitrator may make.

It is usually a term of an order for security that all further proceedings in the arbitration shall be stayed until the security has been provided[14].

There is no power to make an order that the respondent shall give security for the costs of the claimant, except to such extent as the respondent assumes the position of a claimant by putting forward a counter-claim[15]. There is, however, no reason in principle why, if the respondent applies to the Court or arbitrator for procedural relief or indulgence, it should not be made a condition of acceding to the application that the respondent shall provide security for the claimant's costs[16]. There will, however, be few cases in which it would be proper to impose such a condition.

The entirely different question whether the parties can be required to furnish security for the fees of the arbitrator is discussed at pp. 241 et seq., ante.

(b) Security for claims

Awards are usually honoured. But occasionally an unsuccessful respondent is reluctant to pay. If the respondent is resident abroad, and has no assets here, an order for summary enforcement is of little practical value, and enforcement of the award in the foreign country may be so problematical as to make the incurring of costs in an arbitration a very doubtful proposition. The prospect is slightly less depressing where the respondent is a foreigner, but is possessed of assets within the jurisdiction of the English court. Here, the danger is that by the time the reference is concluded, the respondent will have been prudent enough to take the assets elsewhere. There are two ways in which the claimant may seek to minimise this danger.

First, he may try to obtain an award, followed by an order for summary

---

[13] As in *Mavani v Ralli Bros Ltd*, ante.

[14] The Court does not have a general discretion to stay an arbitration, as distinct from restraining the parties by injunction from proceeding with it. The jurisdiction is created in this particular instance by a combination of s. 12(6)(a) and RSC Ord. 23, r. 2; *Dorval Tankers Pty Ltd v Two Arrows Maritime and Port Services Ltd, The Argenpuma* [1984] 2 Lloyd's Rep 563. The order is not a stay in the ordinary sense of the word, which is an order by a court bringing its own proceedings to a halt. The precise nature of the order has yet to be worked out. It most nearly resembles an injunction addressed to the claimant, and no doubt an injunction in aid of the stay could be ordered if it became necessary. It seems that the arbitration agreement and the authority of the arbitrators remains intact, but that the reference is, so to speak, comatose.

[15] See the Notes to Ord. 23, rr. 1–3, in the *Supreme Court Practice*; *Samuel J Cohl Co v Eastern Mediterranean Maritime Ltd, The Silver Fir* [1980] 1 Lloyd's Rep 371; and *Hitachi Shipbuilding and Engineering Co Ltd v Viafiel Companie Naviera SA* [1981] 2 Lloyd's Rep 498.

[16] See *Re Bjornstad and The Ouse Shipping Co Ltd* [1924] 2 KB 673, where the Court made it a condition of an order for the appointment of an arbitrator under what is now s. 10 of the Act, that the respondent should furnish security for the costs of the arbitration. In *Duff Development Co Ltd v Government of Kelantan* (1925) 41 TLR 375, an applicant for a special case was ordered to provide security for costs of the application, but not of the arbitration as a whole. See also *Japan Line Ltd v Aggeliki Charis Compania Maritima SA and Davies and Potter, The Angelic Grace* [1980] 1 Lloyd's Rep 288 where the Court held that an arbitrator could, as a term of making an interim award, legitimately require the respondent to secure the sum claimed in (and not merely the costs of) a separate dispute.

enforcement under section 26 of the 1950 Act, with sufficient speed to catch the assets before the respondent has had time to remove them. In general, the outlook for this procedure is not good. Even if the respondent elects to let the arbitration go by default, the arbitrator will have to give proper notice to the respondent of what is happening in the reference, and will then have to satisfy himself (whether or not he proceeds 'ex parte') that an award in favour of the claimant is justified. Afterwards, the claimant must issue his summons under Order 26, obtain leave under Order 73, rule 7 to serve it outside the jurisdiction, wait until the return date for the summons, obtain the order, and finally execute it. All this takes time, and unless the respondent is completely oblivious to the risk, the claimant may well find that his order for enforcement comes too late to be of any use.

The alternative approach is to find some way of ensuring that the respondent's assets do not leave the jurisdiction until the arbitration has been concluded. The claimant could attempt the following procedures –

(i) If the arbitration is concerned with rights to property, apply for an interim preservation order under section 12(6)(e), (f) or (g) of the Act.

(ii) If the arbitration is concerned with a claim against a ship, invoke the Admiralty jurisdiction in rem to arrest the ship, and then seek to keep the ship or any bail or guarantee provided to procure the release from arrest as security for a favourable award in the arbitration.

(iii) Apply for an injunction restraining the respondent from removing either the asset which is the subject of the arbitration, or the general assets of the respondent from the jurisdiction until the award is made.

(iv) Persuade the arbitrator that if the respondent wishes for a particular procedural benefit or indulgence, he should receive it only if he secures the claim.

In the following pages we consider these four courses of action in greater detail. It should be noted, however, that some forms of arbitration clause, particularly those of the *Scott v Avery* type, may have the effect of preventing the claimant from taking any steps to secure the amount in dispute, whether in England or abroad[17]. But the Court will be reluctant to give this effect to the clause, and will only do so where it is clear that it applies to all types of proceedings and not merely those which are directed solely to establishing questions of liability[18].

(i) Interim protection order.   Orders under section 12(6)(e), (f) or (g) can undoubtedly be made when the arbitration is concerned with rights to property or to a specifically identifiable fund[19]. But the section does not confer a power to arrest a ship, or keep a ship under arrest in the exercise of the jurisdiction in rem of the Admiralty Court, where the claim is simply for a debt or damages[20]. Nor does it confer on the High Court a power analogous to that

---

[17] E.g. *Mantovani v Carapelli SpA* [1980] 1 Lloyd's Rep 375 (clause prohibiting 'any action or other legal proceedings' extended to *saisie conservatoire* abroad).

[18] See the provisional views expressed in *Marazura Navegacion SA v Oceanus Mutual Underwriting Association (Bermuda) Ltd and John Laing (Management) Ltd* [1977] 1 Lloyd's Rep 283; and *Mike Trading and Transport Ltd v R Pagnan and Fratelli, The Lisboa* [1980] 2 Lloyd's Rep 546.

[19] See pp. 329–332, ante.

[20] *The Tuyuti* [1984] 2 Lloyd's Rep 51, [1984] QB 838, following *The Golden Trader* [1974] 1 Lloyd's Rep 378 at 384 and *The Rena K* [1978] 1 Lloyd's Rep 545 at 561.

exercised in proceedings under order 14, of giving leave to defend conditional on payment into court of a sum of money[1].

(ii) Arrest of ship. The second procedure raises difficult problems. Where the claim is of a type which falls within the Admiralty jurisdiction of the High Court, can the claimant arrest the vessel notwithstanding that the contract contains an arbitration clause? If he can, will he be permitted to treat the vessel, or any guarantee or bond supplied in order to obtain her release from arrest, as security for an award in the arbitration? When answering these questions it is necessary to distinguish between matters of jurisdiction and of discretion.

There can be no doubt that the Court has jurisdiction to arrest a vessel, notwithstanding that the claim falls within an agreement to arbitrate[2]. Such an agreement does not operate to annul the jurisdiction, but merely constitutes a ground upon which the Court can (or must, depending on the circumstances) temporarily yield up decision of the dispute to the arbitrator[3]. If the action is properly constituted, it must follow that the arrest, which forms an integral part of the action, is also valid.

As regards the question whether the vessel or any security provided to procure her release from arrest can be treated as security for an award in the arbitration, the matter is now put on a statutory footing by section 26 of the Civil Jurisdiction and Judgments Act 1982[4]. This provides as follows –

'(1) Where in England and Wales or Northern Ireland a court stays or dismisses Admiralty proceedings on the ground that the dispute in question should be submitted to arbitration[5] ..., the court may if in those proceedings property has been arrested or bail or other security has been given to prevent or obtain release from arrest –

(a) order that the property arrested be retained as security for the satisfaction of any award or judgment which –
  (i) is given in respect of the dispute in the arbitration ... in favour of which those proceedings are stayed or dismissed; and
  (ii) is enforceable in England or Wales or, as the case may be, in Northern Ireland; or
(b) order that the stay or dismissal of those proceedings be conditional on the provision of equivalent security for the satisfaction of any such award or judgment.

(2) Where a court makes an order under sub-section (1), it may attach such conditions to the order as it thinks fit, in particular conditions with respect to the institution of the relevant arbitration ... proceedings.'

The powers conferred by this section are discretionary. This gives rise to a

---

[1] *Gebr Van Weelde Scheepvaart Kantoor BV v Homeric Marine Services Ltd, The Agrabele* [1979] 2 Lloyd's Rep 117: *The Furness Bridge (No 2)* [1979] 2 Lloyd's Rep 267 at 272.
[2] *The Vasso* [1984] 1 Lloyd's Rep 235, 241–242.
[3] See Chapter 30, post.
[4] The full text is set out in Appendix I, p. 717, post. It came into force on 1 November 1984, but the power conferred by the section is not exercisable in relation to property arrested before that date, or in relation to bail or other security given before that date to prevent the arrest of property, or to obtain the release of property arrested before that date, or in substitution (whether directly or indirectly) for such security: Sch. 13, Part II, para. 6.
[5] Whether or not the arbitration has already commenced: *The Nordglimt* [1987] 2 Lloyd's Rep 470 at 484.

difficult and important question as to how the discretion should be exercised. Where property is arrested on a claim to which no arbitration clause applies, the court does not investigate the ability of the defendant to pay any resulting judgment if it goes against him, because the plaintiff has a right to a warrant of arrest in respect of any prima facie claim which is within the Admiralty in rem jurisdiction, regardless of whether the arrest is necessary to secure his claim[6]. But under the law as it stood before section 26 came into force, if the court stayed the proceedings because of the presence of an arbitration clause it had a discretion whether or not to retain the security in case it became necessary to lift the stay of proceedings so that judgment could be entered in terms of the award, and it would only do so if it could be shown that the defendant might well be unable to satisfy an award[7]. We submit that the latter practice is to be preferred[8], and that it is warranted by the terms of the Act. It is true that a successful defendant can usually recover the costs of providing security, either as part of the costs of the arbitration, or of the action in rem or, with more difficulty, as damages for wrongful arrest, but the need to provide counter-security for a bail bond or guarantee can reduce the defendant's available working capital and impair his ability to borrow for other purposes, even if he is well able to pay the claim against him. For this the successful defendant is unlikely to receive any compensation.

The function of a stay of proceedings is to give effect to the arbitration agreement, and the stay should not go beyond what is necessary for that purpose. Accordingly, if the stay is granted before the property is arrested or bail or other security is given it will not operate so as to prevent a warrant of arrest being issued or executed[9].

Where the court orders that the property arrested be retained as security for the satisfaction of any award, it is still presumably necessary to obtain an order of the court before execution can be levied, either in proceedings under section

---

[6] Historically, the purpose of the arrest may have been to compel the appearance of the defendant: for in former times a judgment in default was regarded as objectionable. But whatever its purpose, it developed as a matter of right, not of discretion.

[7] *The Tuyuti* [1984] 2 Lloyd's Rep 51, [1984] QB 838; *The Rena K* [1978] 1 Lloyd's Rep 545, [1979] QB 377. If this put the test somewhat more favourably to the plaintiff than the test for granting a *Mareva* injunction, there were good grounds for doing so. The plaintiff in an Admiralty action is prima facie entitled to the security of the res by virtue of his statutory lien and may be entitled to a maritime or possessory lien as well: the plaintiff claiming a Mareva injunction normally has no claim to rank as a secured creditor. It could indeed be said for this reason that the test was too favourable to the defendant.

[8] In support of the contrary opinion it might be said that to treat the plaintiff's right to retain the arrested property or security given in its place as depending on the defendant's ability to pay would erode the traditional relationship between the concept of the maritime lien and the right of the shipowner to limit his liability to the value of the ship. But while it may be true that the one was originally the quid pro quo for the other, the connection between the two is by now merely historical. The limitation figure bears little relationship to the true value of the ship, and the plaintiff has rights in personam against the defendant in addition to his rights against the res. There may still be many cases in which the res is the only effective security for the claim, but this is by no means always so. A more cogent argument is that the plaintiff in an Admiralty action in rem is prima facie a secured creditor (see note 7, supra) but this is, we submit, a ground for seeing that the discretion is exercised in such a way as to protect the plaintiff's secured position rather than for denying that the court has any discretion at all. It is submitted that the provisions of sub-s. (3), reproduced in Appendix I at p. 719, post, will enable effect to be given to the secured status and priority of the claimant.

[9] *The Silver Athens (No 2)* [1986] 2 Lloyd's Rep 583, applying *The Tuyuti*, supra, at 848.

26 of the 1950 Act or in a separate action to enforce the award[10]. This is not necessarily the case however where what is retained is 'equivalent security' under sub-section (2). It is not the original bail or other security which is retained, no doubt because the usual form of bail or security is apt to secure a judgment but not an award. Provided the court takes care to see that the equivalent security is in appropriate terms, there would seem to be no objection to enforcing it by an order in the proceedings which are stayed, should that become necessary.

Where the Court is required to stay the proceedings because they come within the mandatory provisions of section 1 of the 1975 Act, it has no power to impose conditions upon which the stay is ordered. It follows that in such a case the alternative form of order under sub-section (1)(b) is not available[11], nor the power to impose conditions under sub-section (2)[12]. Where the property is still capable of being arrested, the difficulty can readily be overcome by an order under sub-section (1) that the property arrested be retained as security for the satisfaction of the award: the court will decline to discharge the order unless and until the defendant volunteers security in terms which will have the equivalent effect to an order under sub-section (2). Where, on the other hand, bail or other security has already been given to prevent or obtain release from arrest, but in terms which are not apt to secure satisfaction of the award, the court will have to fall back on the powers available to it before the 1982 Act came into force, which entailed lifting the stay and allowing the action in rem to proceed to judgment, not on the award, but on the original cause of action, the award taking effect by way of issue estoppel[13].

(iii) Mareva injunction. We turn now to the third method of obtaining security, namely the grant of an injunction restraining the respondent from removing his assets from the jurisdiction of the English court, pending the hearing of the arbitration, and satisfaction of any resulting award[14]. Until recently, this procedure would have been thought impossible. Assets may be

---

[10] See Chapter 28. S. 26 of the 1982 Act refers to 'any judgment which is given in respect of the dispute', from which it is evident that the judgment need not necessarily be in the action which is stayed. An alternative procedure if the award is dishonoured is to apply for the stay to be lifted and to proceed on the original cause of action in rem, relying on the award as giving rise to an issue estoppel: *The Tuyuti*, and *The Rena K*, supra. See also p. 411, post.

[11] *The World Star* [1986] 2 Lloyd's Rep 274. It is doubtful whether this problem was foreseen by the draftsman, but it is difficult to see any escape from it. The essence of such a condition is that if it is not complied with the stay is removed and the action proceeds. But in cases falling within s. 1 of the 1975 Act the stay is mandatory, and the fact that the claimant may not be able to enforce his award is not a ground for holding that the arbitration agreement is 'null and void, inoperative or incapable of being performed': see pp. 464–465, post.

[12] This has not been expressly decided, but it would seem to follow from the reasoning expressed in the previous note, unless some way can be found of giving effect to a breach of the condition which has been imposed otherwise than by lifting the stay.

[13] *The Tuyuti* and *The Rena K*, supra.

[14] This remedy has nothing to do with the powers under s. 12(6) to protect the specific subject matter of the arbitration. It applies to all the assets of the respondent within the jurisdiction. Nor has it any connection with the jurisdiction exercised in the case of ships, although rather surprisingly not in other contexts, to restrain their employment otherwise than in accordance with a contract: *Empresa Cubana de Fletes v Lagonisis Shipping Co Ltd, The Georgios C* [1971] 1 Lloyd's Rep 7, [1971] 1 QB 488; *Associated Portland Cement Manufacturers Ltd v Teigland Shipping A/S, The Oakworth* [1975] 1 Lloyd's Rep 581. This is a method of obtaining specific enforcement, not of securing claims.

seized to satisfy judgment debts, by fieri facias if they are chattels, by garnishee proceedings if they take the form of debts owed to the judgment debtor. But it had been considered for decades that there was no method of securing a claim in advance of judgment, similar to the *saisie conservatoire* which forms an important part of the jurisdiction of a commercial tribunal in other countries.

Recently, the Court of Appeal has struck out into entirely new territory by granting injunctions to restrain the removal of assets from the jurisdiction in anticipation of judgment in pending proceedings[15]. Since we are only concerned here with the application of this new-found jurisdiction to arbitrations, an extended discussion of its scope and limitations would be out of place[16]. Its continued existence seems by now secure[17], and its boundaries fairly well defined. Its salient features are as follows –

1   The injunction generally takes the form of an order restraining the defendant from selling, disposing of or otherwise dealing with money or chattels or from removing them from the jurisdiction.

2   The plaintiff must show a good arguable case on the merits of his claim.

3   There must be grounds for believing that the defendant has assets within the jurisdiction, and that there is a risk of the assets being removed before the judgment is satisfied.

4   An injunction may be made ex parte where there are grounds for believing that if the defendant is given advance warning the assets will be removed.

5   The plaintiff must give an undertaking in damages, supported if necessary by a bond or security, in case the claim turns out to be unfounded.

6   The jurisdiction may be invoked whether or not the defendant is domiciled, resident or present within the jurisdiction[18].

7   The plaintiff does not acquire the position of a secured creditor as regards the assets frozen by the injunction[19].

8   The jurisdiction may be invoked to restrain the removal of a ship even in a case where the ship cannot be arrested[20].

The jurisdiction is available[1] to provide a claimant in an arbitration with security for the payment of any award which he may obtain. It may be invoked even before the arbitration has been commenced, but in such a case the Court will impose terms as to the commencement of the arbitration within a specified time. Moreover the jurisdiction is not excluded by the fact that the claim arises

---

[15]   *Nippon Yusen Kaisha v Karageorgis* [1975] 2 Lloyd's Rep 137 was the first in the growing line of cases. It was soon followed in *Mareva Compania Naviera SA v International Bulkcarriers SA* [1975] 2 Lloyd's Rep 509, after which this type of order became known as a 'Mareva injunction'.

[16]   A description of the current practice will be found in *Third Chandris Shipping Corpn v Unimarine SA, The Genie* [1979] 2 Lloyd's Rep 184, [1979] QB 645; *Z Ltd v A-Z and AA-LL* [1982] 1 Lloyd's Rep 240 (position of third parties); *Iraqui Ministry of Defence v Arcepey Shipping Co* [1980] 1 Lloyd's Rep 632 (release of funds or assets); *AJ Bekhor & Co Ltd v Bilton* [1981] 1 Lloyd's Rep 491 (discovery, interrogatories, cross-examination of defendant on affidavit); and in the notes to Ord. 29, r. 1 in the *Supreme Court Practice*.

[17]   In *Schorsch Meier GmbH v Hennin, The Siskina* [1975] 1 Lloyd's Rep 1, the House of Lords reserved the question of the correctness of the decisions establishing the jurisdiction, but was prepared to assume its existence: see also the Supreme Court Act 1981, s. 37(3).

[18]   Supreme Court Act 1981, s. 37(3).

[19]   *Cretanor Maritime Co Ltd v Irish Marine Management Ltd* [1978] 1 Lloyd's Rep 425.

[20]   *The Rena K*, ante, at 561–562; *Bank Mellat v Helleniki Techniki SA* [1984] QB 291, per Kerr LJ.

[1]   Under s. 37 of the Supreme Court Act 1981 or under s. 12(6)(h) of the 1950 Act; *The Rena K*, supra, at 561; *Mantovani v Carapelli SpA* [1980] 1 Lloyd's Rep 375 at 382.

under a 'non-domestic' arbitration agreement and must, if the defendant insists, be referred to arbitration[2].

The remedy is in principle available whenever the Court is seized of an action concerning the subject matter of the arbitration, whether or not the arbitration is to be held in England, since it may be used to obtain security for the eventual award. It will no doubt be granted more sparingly where the arbitration is to be held abroad. Where the defendant cannot be served with High Court proceedings, either in England or outside the jurisdiction under Order 11, there is at present no power to grant a Mareva injunction. Section 25(3)(c) of the Civil Jurisdiction and Judgments Act 1982 enables an Order in Council to be made extending the Court's power to grant interim relief in aid of foreign proceedings (including a Mareva injunction) to arbitration proceedings, but no Order has yet been made under the section[3].

(iv) Procedural 'orders nisi'.   Tribunals of limited jurisdiction have for many years contrived to make orders which lie beyond their powers by using a device which may be called the 'order *nisi*'. The essence of this strategem is for the tribunal to say, 'We have no power to order you to do X, but we do have power to do A (or refuse to do it), so that if you wish us to make (or refuse) an order to do A, you must agree to do X'. This versatile procedure can be used in many contexts, and we mention it here because it provides a means of obtaining security for the claim, where the arbitrator would not otherwise be entitled to order it[4].

6 Arranging the hearing

If the arbitration is of a type which calls for an oral hearing[5], a time and place must be appointed. This may be done at any stage of the reference, and in simple cases it may be convenient to do so as soon as the tribunal has been appointed. But in cases of any complexity it is usually better to wait until the issues have been defined and work on preparing the documents and evidence is well under way. By then the parties should be able to make a realistic estimate of how soon they will be ready and how long the hearing will last.

Arrangements for the hearing are very often made by telephone and then confirmed in writing. We suggest, however, that more use could be made than at present of the 'pre-trial conference' at which the parties attend before the arbitrator to fix a date for the hearing, explain how far their preparations have proceeded, apply for directions to tie up loose ends (e.g. orders for particulars, further discovery, exchange of experts' reports, etc.) and resolve any difficulties

---

[2] *The Rena K*, ante.
[3] See Appendix I, p. 718, post.
[4] This device was adopted in *Japan Line Ltd v Aggeliki Charis Compania Maritima SA and Davies and Potter, The Angelic Grace* [1980] 1 Lloyd's Rep 288, CA, where the arbitrators refused to make an interim award unless the respondents secured sums due in respect of disputes between the same parties under different contracts. The Court of Appeal held that this was an order which lay within the discretion of the arbitrators: and, with respect, this seems unassailable, for an arbitration can almost always proceed perfectly well without an interim award being made. But the arbitrators should be careful not to impose unreasonable conditions on the taking of important steps in the arbitration, for otherwise it may be held that the condition so impedes the progress of the reference that imposing it amounts to misconduct.
[5] See pp. 300–301, ante.

there may be about the availability of counsel, attendance of witnesses, and so on. A meeting of this kind can do much to focus the attention of the parties and their advisers on the matter in hand and to reduce the chances of a last-minute application for an adjournment of the hearing.

When fixing the date of the hearing and in dealing with an application for adjournment of the hearing, the arbitrator should bear in mind that both parties are entitled to reasonable notice of the hearing and to have a reasonable opportunity to be present at the hearing together with their advisers and witnesses. These requirements are discussed in more detail in Chapter 22[6].

Occasionally a busy arbitrator may find that the only time which he can make available for the hearing is so far ahead as to give rise to injustice to one or other of the parties, generally the claimant. An arbitrator who finds himself in this position should consider whether he should offer to surrender his appointment. Failure to do so may result in the embarrassment of an application to Court for his removal for failure to proceed with all reasonable despatch.

There is no objection in principle to fixing the hearing outside normal working hours or during weekends or public holidays, but there would have to be strong reasons for doing so if either party objected. Equally, there is no objection to sitting during the High Court vacations, although the arbitrator should try to avoid doing so if it means that either of the parties cannot be represented by the lawyer who has been handling his case.

The hearing need not take place on successive days; but prolonged adjournments can be wasteful and sometimes even productive of injustice, because of the tendency of evidence and argument to fade with the passage of time. If a split hearing cannot be avoided, the arbitrator would be well advised to try to deal fully with distinct issues at each session.

If the arbitration agreement stipulates that the hearing must be held in a particular place, the arbitrator has no power to sit elsewhere without the consent of the parties[7]. Express provisions of this kind are not uncommon[8]. But it may also be an implied term of any agreement of which the curial law[9] is English, that the arbitration shall not be held outside the jurisdiction of the High Court: to move the seat of such an arbitration outside the jurisdiction would be to run the risk of subjecting the parties and the arbitrator to the supervisory jurisdiction of a foreign court, which would not necessarily recognise the parties' choice of curial law. For this reason the arbitrator would be well advised in such a case not to sit abroad, even for the limited purpose of taking evidence, without the consent of both parties and agreement on the curial law which is to apply[10].

---

[6] See pp. 302–312, ante.

[7] Failure to sit at the agreed venue probably deprives the arbitrator of jurisdiction. At any rate the arbitrator should assume that this may be the case and act accordingly.

[8] E.g., 'arbitration in London' or 'in the City of London' or 'at the offices of the XYZ Association'.

[9] See p. 64, ante, for an explanation of this expression.

[10] If it is necessary for evidence to be taken abroad, this may be effected by means of an order by the Court, under s. 12(6)(d) of the 1950 Act, for the issue of a request for the examination of a witness out of the jurisdiction: see p. 351, post.

CHAPTER 24

The course of the reference:
the hearing and after

In the previous chapter we have described the stages of a reference up to the
stage where a time and place has been fixed for the hearing. In this chapter we
describe the ensuing stages of the reference, under the following headings –
    7 Investigation of facts and law: the hearing.
    8 The decision.
    9 The award.
    10 Appeal procedures[1].

7 Investigation of facts and law: the hearing

The discussion which follows is modelled on the type of hearing which takes
place when the arbitration agreement calls for an oral hearing at which the
usual adversarial procedure is to be followed. It is, however, a recurrent theme
of this work that English law recognises not just one, but many, types of
procedure: this has already been noted and discussed in Chapters 21 and 22.
There is, for example, no reason why the parties should not do away altogether
with the adversarial procedure and adopt in its place an inquisitorial procedure,
in which the initiative in bringing the arbitration to a conclusion, and the
investigation of the facts and law, is undertaken by the arbitrator, rather than
by the parties. As we have seen in Chapter 19, the function of the arbitrator/
advocate before disagreement bears some resemblance to that of an inquisitorial
tribunal. Nor is there any objection in principle to the parties dispensing with a
formal hearing altogether, as is often done in some types of commodity
arbitration.

Nevertheless, it would be impossible in a work of this kind to omit all
discussion of the procedure to be followed at a formal arbitration hearing of the
adversarial type, and we offer below a somewhat abbreviated discussion of the
various questions of procedure, evidence, and the like, which commonly arise in
the course of such a hearing.

(a) Failure to appear at the hearing

If the *respondent* fails to appear at the hearing, having been given reasonable
notice of the time and place fixed by the arbitrator, the hearing may proceed

---

[1] The numbering is taken from the summary of the stages of the reference at the beginning of
Chapter 23.

without him[2]. But it does not necessarily follow that there will automatically be an award against him for the full amount of the claim. The arbitrator must do two things before he can make an award adjudicating on the claim. First, he must be satisfied that the claimant has brought forward evidence sufficient to make out a prima facie case for the amount claimed. Second, he must take into consideration any evidence or submissions which the respondent has put before him on any previous occasion or in correspondence. Then, but only then, may the arbitrator proceed to make his award[3].

Failure of the *claimant* to appear after due notice must be very unusual, though it does occasionally occur. In the High Court, if the plaintiff fails to appear at the trial, the defendant is entitled to judgment as a matter of course. But the position in an arbitration is different. In the High Court the judge has no evidence before him on which he can adjudicate until it is put before him by one party or the other. An arbitrator, on the other hand, may well have had evidence and submissions put before him by the claimant prior to the hearing. He would, we consider, be obliged to consider such evidence and submissions even if the claimant failed to appear. And it they disclosed a prima facie claim which the respondent was unable to rebut, the arbitrator would not only have the power, but also the duty to make an award in favour of the claimant, even in his absence.

If *neither party* appears, and if the arbitrator already has before him written submissions and evidence there is no reason in principle why he should not decide the case then and there on the material before him. But he should not do so unless he is satisfied that each party knows what material the other has placed before the arbitrator and has had an opportunity to deal with it. If in doubt the arbitrator should simply make an order adjourning the hearing to a date to be fixed: adding, if he thinks fit, that his fees for the wasted hearing should be borne by the parties equally.

(b) Order of proceedings

(i) The usual order of proceedings.   The adversarial system of pleadings, both written and oral, works on the assumption that each party will read or hear his opponents' case and then have an opportunity to answer it. A basic tripartite pattern of proceedings follows naturally from this assumption. In the case of written pleadings the pattern is: 1 claim; 2 defence; 3 reply, whereas in the case of the oral proceedings at the hearing the pattern is as follows –

1 The claimant[4] opens by outlining the facts of his case and any legal submissions in support of it. He then leads his evidence, both written and oral, and after the evidence may make a further speech in support of his case.

---

[2] *Wood v Leake* (1806) 12 Ves 412; *Gladwin v Chilcote* (1841) 9 Dowl 550; *Scott v Van Sandau* (1844) 6 QB 237; *Golodetz v Schrier* (1947) 80 Ll L Rep 647; *Baroness Wenlock v River Dee Co* (1883) 53 LJ QB 208. If there is reason to think his absence is unintentional, the arbitrator would do well to adjourn the hearing for a short while in order to find out if there is a good reason why he has not appeared: *Tryer v Shaw* (1858) 27 LJ Ex 320. Cf. The *Myron (Owners) v Tradax Export SA* [1969] 1 Lloyd's Rep 411, [1970] 1 QB 527.

[3] A fuller discussion of the arbitrator's powers to proceed in the absence of the respondent will be found in Chapter 32, pp. 536–542, post.

[4] In this context the respondent may be treated as if he were the claimant, and vice versa; if the burden of all the issues in the proceedings lies on the respondent: cf. Ord. 35, r. 7(7).

2 The respondent then opens his case in the same way and then calls his evidence[5]. After the evidence, he may make a final speech closing his case.

3 The respondent then makes a speech in reply.

This pattern of procedure works well in the courts, where both judges and advocates are familiar with it and, generally speaking, it has also been found to be the best pattern of procedure for an oral hearing in an arbitration. There are, however, differences between a hearing in court and a hearing in arbitration, which make it necessary to adopt a somewhat more flexible approach to the order of proceedings in an arbitration than would be appropriate to a hearing in court. A number of these differences are discussed below.

(ii) Evidence and argument in rebuttal. In proceedings in court the general rule is that each party must call all his evidence at one time, and not wait to hear his opponent's case before deciding whether to call further evidence. This is a salutary rule, not only because it reduces the temptation for witnesses to tailor their evidence, but also because it prevents the proceedings becoming confused and disorderly. But it works well only on the assumption that each party knows the outlines of his opponent's case long enough before the hearing to be able to muster his evidence to meet it. In proceedings in court the exchange of pleadings normally ensures that this is the case: although even pleadings contain little if any legal argument and only the bare bones of the facts. In an arbitration the pleadings may be perfunctory or even dispensed with altogether. Moreover, marshalling all one's evidence at once requires a skill in anticipating the opponent's case which cannot be taken for granted when a party is presenting his own case, and it not always possessed even by professional advocates. So a more flexible approach to calling evidence in rebuttal is called for in arbitrations than might be allowed in proceedings in court.

It may be objected, when an application is made to call evidence in rebuttal, that the point to be rebutted ought to have been anticipated. But if there is merit in the objection, it is generally best reflected in a special order as to costs: the evidence should only be shut out if the party objecting has been prejudiced in some way that cannot be dealt with by an adjournment or by an order of costs, or both.

As far as concerns argument in rebuttal, the rule in court is that the defendant is allowed a further speech to deal with any fresh point of law or authority raised in the plaintiff's final speech.

(iii) Interventions and applications by the parties. Apart from cross-examination, each party generally waits until his opponent has closed his case before addressing the tribunal. But interventions may occasionally be justified. Some by their nature have to be made at once, such as objections to the admissibility of evidence. Others are made with the object (not always achieved) of saving time, e.g. by making admissions or attempting to clarify misunderstandings. But many interventions would be better left until a speech in reply, and

---

[5] If the respondent elects to call no evidence, he may claim the right to make the final speech, the claimant having the right to make a second speech after his evidence has been given: cf. Ord. 35, r. 7(3). But this order of speeches is inconvenient when issues of law of any difficulty are involved, and is often dispensed with in such cases in favour of the more usual order set out in the text.

some self-discipline is required of an advocate if his opponent is to be allowed to develop his case in an orderly fashion. Any lapses of discipline can be dealt with by a reminder that matters of comment should be left until the appropriate time.

Where an intervention is made which has to be ruled on at once, the same tripartite pattern of procedure should be adopted in miniature, i.e. the party intervening speaks first, his opponent second, and the party intervening has the right of reply. Much time can, however, often be saved by establishing at the outset exactly what ruling the arbitrator is being asked to make, and whether or not it is opposed. When the parties have made their submissions, the arbitrator should if possible rule on it at once and state clearly what his ruling is. Occasionally the arbitrator may be able to point the parties to an agreed solution, but he should not attempt to do so by declining to give a ruling or by delaying his decision. The ability to deal quickly and firmly with applications will enhance his reputation as an arbitrator quite as much as his ability to give a fair decision on the merits.

(iv) Interventions by the arbitrator.   Many arbitrators[6] take the view that an arbitrator's function is to listen to the evidence and argument and to intervene as little as possible, leaving the conduct of the case to the parties or their advocates. Broadly speaking, this view of the tribunal's function in the adversarial system is correct. Certainly, no intervention is to be preferred to too much[7]. But there are occasions when an arbitrator may intervene to advantage, and even some when it would be wrong for him to remain silent. We list below some of the more common examples –

1 The arbitrator ought to intervene when he is proposing to make a finding based on his own personal knowledge, so as to enable the party against whom the finding is to be made, to comment upon it[8].

2 The arbitrator should likewise intervene if he is minded to reach his decision on the basis of a view of the law or of the facts which has not been put forward by either party.

3 The arbitrator may intervene to put a question to a witness. If the question is put merely for the purpose of eliciting an answer to a question by one of the parties, it is best put straight away. So also if the arbitrator can see that the question may lead to a saving of time. But generally the arbitrator will do better to leave his questions until after the parties have put theirs, since an ill-timed question can occasionally do great harm to a carefully prepared line of examination or cross-examination[9]. The arbitrator should also bear in mind the natural tendency of a witness to agree with what he imagines to be the

---

6 Taking to heart Bacon's remark that 'an overspeaking judge is no well tuned cymbal': 'Of Judicature' in *Essays* (1625). The whole essay is still worth reading as a source of wisdom for arbitrators.
7 One of the dangers of excessive intervention is that the arbitrator 'so to speak descends into the arena and is liable to have his vision clouded by the dust of conflict': *Yuill v Yuill* [1945] P 15 at 20.
8 This is dealt with more fully at p. 360, post.
9 *Jones v National Coal Board* [1957] 2 QB 55, [1957] 2 WLR 760, in which it was said that a judge should only ask questions of witnesses when it is necessary to clear up any point that has been overlooked or left obscure.

implication behind a question put to him by the tribunal, and so try to put the question neutrally.

4 The arbitrator may intervene during a party's submissions with much greater freedom than during his evidence. The object of such intervention is not to engage in argument with the party or his advocate, but to ensure that his submissions have been properly understood and that any doubts which the arbitrator may have about their merits have been voiced at a time when they can be answered[10].

5 The arbitrator may intervene to prevent unseemly behaviour and procedural irregularities as well as to exclude irrelevancies and discourage repetition[11].

6 Where neither party is legally represented the arbitrator can and should play a more active part in ensuring that the parties' respective cases are properly brought out at the hearing. Where only one party is legally represented, it is the professional duty of the advocate for the other party to ensure that he does not take an unfair advantage of his greater skill and knowledge, and it is the function of the arbitrator to ensure that this duty is observed[12]. Most litigants in person are able to explain their own case, but many find it more difficult to expose the weakness of their opponent's case. Cross-examination in particular does not come easily to the unpractised. This does not mean, however, that the arbitrator should try to redress the balance by disallowing cross-examination by the professional advocate. Instead he should pick up the unrepresented parties' points and put them to the witness himself.

(v) 'Stopping counsel'. A particular form of intervention by the arbitrator which merits separate discussion is that of 'stopping counsel', which is used by arbitrators less than it might be. It involves indicating to a party's advocate that the arbitrator has accepted a particular submission and proposes to rule in his favour on it. Its chief function is to avoid the need for a claimant to take up time in his final speech on a point on which the arbitrator is in his favour[13]. But it may also be used during the claimant's or respondent's opening in order to indicate that further argument is unnecessary until the other party has been heard in reply: it should be used more sparingly in this situation, since it may turn out, on hearing the other party, that the point is less easy to decide than appeared at first sight.

The practice of stopping counsel is a useful one, but it should only be used when the arbitrator's decision is in a party's favour. It should not be used as a way of cutting short a long-winded argument when the arbitrator has decided *against* the party making the submission: to stop counsel in this situation and

---

[10] The object is 'to make sure by wise intervention that he follows the points that the advocates are making and can assess their worth': *Jones v National Coal Board*, supra, at 64.

[11] *Jones v National Coal Board*, supra, at 64.

[12] *Chilton v Saga Holidays plc* [1986] 1 All ER 841, CA. At the same time he must try to avoid the danger of seeming to take sides or of becoming too attached to a line of argument simply because he has thought of it himself.

[13] One reason why the technique of 'stopping counsel' is little used in arbitration may be the anxiety that, if the arbitrator indicates what his award will be, neither party will have any incentive to take up the award and pay the arbitrator's fees. But this need not deter an arbitrator from stopping counsel on an issue which does not decide the whole dispute. And the danger should not be exaggerated, since the winning party will generally wish to take up the award in order to enforce it, even if it is only for costs.

then to decide against his client might well amount to misconduct. The best course in this situation is for the arbitrator to summarise in his own words the submission which is being made so as to indicate that he has understood it, even if he does not necessarily agree with it: few advocates will go on repeating themselves once they are sure the point has been understood.

When the tribunal consists of more than one arbitrator, the decision to stop counsel must be a decision of the whole tribunal.

(vi) Reading the documents. If there is any documentary evidence in the case, it is usual for the claimant's advocate to refer to it before any oral evidence is called. This is generally preferable to reading individual documents as and when a witness refers to them. Often it proves necessary to read only some of the documents which have been prepared for the hearing: but the process of 'reading the bundles' can in some cases be very time-consuming. One way of shortening the process is to invite the arbitrator to read the documents before the hearing[14]. But it is difficult to read documents intelligently without some introduction to the case generally, and in all but the simplest cases, it will be preferable for the claimant to explain the issues in the case before the arbitrator retires to read the documents.

(c) Attendance of witnesses

If a witness within the United Kingdom refuses to attend and give evidence, the party who desires to call him is entitled to a High Court writ of subpoena ad testificandum to secure his attendance[15]. If a witness summoned by subpoena refuses without reasonable excuse to attend, or refuses to answer a question or questions, he is liable to be punished for contempt of court, provided that the writ has been served on him not less than four days[16] before the day on which his attendance before the arbitrator is required by the writ[17].

The High Court has power to order the examination of a witness on oath before an officer of the Court or any other person or to order the issue of a commission or request for the examination of a witness outside the jurisdiction[18]. In practice the taking of evidence on commission is obsolete[19]. The evidence is taken either by the court of the foreign country pursuant to letters of request or (in certain circumstances) by a special examiner appointed by the English Court or by the British Consul in the foreign country[20]. The appointment of an examiner is usually more convenient, since the foreign court will naturally tend to conduct the examination in accordance with its own rules of procedure, rather than those of the English Court.

---

[14] Some arbitrators do this as a matter of course, if the documents are sent to them. But the practice varies between different arbitrators and different types of tribunal, and it should not be taken for granted that an arbitrator will do so, particularly where the documents are numerous.

[15] S. 12(4) of the 1950 Act. No order of the Court is required: Ord. 38, r. 19(1); but the witness may apply to have the writ set aside: Ord. 38, r. 19(5).

[16] I.e. four working days: Ord. 3, r. 2(5).

[17] Ord. 38, r. 19(4). The Court may enlarge or abridge the period of four days.

[18] S. 12(6)(d) of the Act.

[19] See the *Supreme Court Practice*, note 39/1/1, where it is pointed out that the RSC no longer contain any reference to commissions.

[20] See Ord. 39, r. 2(1)(b) and (2) and the notes thereto in the *Supreme Court Practice*, for the practice concerning letters of request and appointment of examiners.

As an alternative in invoking the assistance of the High Court, the parties may simply agree that the arbitrator, or a deputy, shall take the evidence of a witness abroad. Before doing so, it would be prudent to check that there is no objection to this procedure under the local law.

In addition to attending to give evidence at the hearing, a person may be required to attend at the hearing to produce a material document. For this purpose the party desiring production makes use of a writ of subpoena duces tecum[1]. This procedure is quite different from discovery of documents[2]. The purpose of discovery is to obtain production of documents from one's opponent[3]. A subpoena duces tecum is a means of securing documents held by third parties.

The procedures of subpoena and letters of request are rarely used in commercial arbitrations. They are better not attempted without legal assistance.

(d) Evidence on oath

Subject to any express provision in the arbitration agreement, the arbitrator has a discretion whether or not to examine the witnesses on oath or affirmation[4]. It is not usual for an oath to be administered in commercial arbitrations, but if a party asks for the witnesses to be sworn, the arbitrator would be prudent to agree.

If the arbitrator administers an oath, he should do so in a proper form, since – (a) if the arbitrator is *required*[5] to administer an oath, he misconducts himself if he does not do so properly, and (b) the witness cannot be prosecuted for perjury unless he is lawfully sworn.

The proper forms for administering the oath to a witness are as follows[6] –

1 The usual form is for the person taking the oath to hold the New Testament, or, in the case of a Jew, the Old Testament, in his uplifted hand, and to say or repeat after the arbitrator: 'I swear by Almighty God that the evidence that I shall give shall be the truth, the whole truth, and nothing but the truth'.

2 In the case of a person who is neither a Christian nor a Jew the oath may be administered in such form and with such ceremonies as he declares to be binding, whether or not he has any religious belief, except that if it is not reasonably practicable without inconvenience or delay to administer an oath in the manner appropriate to his religious belief he may be required to affirm (see 4, post).

3 Any person who desires to take the oath in the Scottish manner, with uplifted hand but without either Testament, may do so in any part of the United Kingdom.

4 Any person who objects to being sworn may make his solemn affirmation instead of taking an oath. He does so by saying or repeating after the arbitrator:

---

[1] S. 12(4) of the Act.
[2] It is not to be used as a means of obtaining discovery from third parties, and unless the writ specifies and identifies the document or documents to be produced (as distinct from calling for production of documents in a particular category which may or may not exist) it is liable to be set aside as an abuse of the process of the court: *Sunderland Steamship P & I Association v Gatoil International Inc, The Lorenzo Halcoussi* [1988] 1 Lloyd's Rep 180.
[3] See pp. 322–326, ante.
[4] S. 12(2) of the Act.
[5] By express agreement in the submission or by the Court.
[6] The text is a summary of the relevant provisions of the Oaths Act 1978.

'I, – , do solemnly, sincerely and truly declare and affirm that the evidence that I shall give shall be the truth, the whole truth, and nothing but the truth'.

The oath to be administered to an interpreter is administered in the same manner, except that the words of the oath are: 'that I will well and faithfully interpret and true explanation make of all such matters and things as shall be required of me according to the best of my skill and understanding'.

(e) Refusal to answer questions

If the witness refuses without reasonable cause to answer a question, the arbitrator cannot compel him to answer, or punish him for his refusal, although he would be justified on taking the refusal into account, along with other aspects of the witness' demeanour, in forming a view as to his credibility.

If the party asking the question indicates that he proposes to invoke the assistance of the High Court in compelling the witness to answer[7], the arbitrator should not conclude the proceedings without giving the party time to make the application to the Court.

(f) Relaxation of strict rules of evidence

It is widely believed that an arbitrator, merely because he is an arbitrator, is empowered to act on evidence which would not be strictly admissible in a Court of Law. This is not so. Arbitrators are bound by the law of England, and the rules regarding admissibility of evidence are part of that law[8]. Thus, if an arbitrator admits evidence which is inadmissible, he commits an error of law which may be appealed against. Furthermore, if the arbitrator deliberately accepts evidence which is obviously inadmissible, he commits misconduct and the award will be set aside, at any rate if the evidence is important[9]. If, however, the misreception is due to an honest mistake, the Court will not interfere.

---

[7] The witness would in theory be liable to committal is he had been served with a subpoena, although the Court would be unlikely to use this remedy save in exceptional circumstances.

[8] *A-G v Davison* (1825) M'Cle & Y 160; *East and West India Dock Co v Kirk and Randall* (1887) 12 App Cas 738, HL; *Re Enoch and Zaretzky, Bock & Co* [1910] 1 KB 327, CA. There is authority for the contrary view in judgments of Lord Esher MR and possibly Lopes LJ in *Re Keighley Maxsted & Co and Bryan Durant & Co* [1893] 1 QB 405, CA, cited in *Wm Adolph & Co v Keene Co* (1921) 7 Ll L Rep 142. We submit that the statement of Farwell LJ in *Re Enoch* is to be preferred, and that the Court's unwillingness to interfere where the strict rules are not followed is better explained on the grounds of consent or waiver, than by a special rule relating to arbitrations.

[9] The statement in the text is an attempt to reconcile *Walford, Baker & Co v Macfie & Sons* (1915) 84 LJ KB 2221, 113 LT 180; *Wm Adolph & Co v Keene Co*, supra, and *Agroexport Enterprise d'Etat pour le Commerce Exterieur v NV Goorden Import Co SA* [1956] 1 Lloyd's Rep 319. In the report of *Walford* in the Law Journal, Lush and Atkin JJ are reported as saying that the reception of evidence which is 'absolutely' inadmissible goes to the root of the contract. But in the fuller report in the Law Times the reference is to evidence which is 'obviously' inadmissible, the result of acting upon which is to 'ignore' the real contract between the parties. This suggests that the judges had in mind a flagrant misreception of evidence. So explained, the case is just reconcilable with the statement in Russell (cited with approval in *Wm Adolph & Co v Keene Co* and the *Agroexport Case*) to the effect that 'in deciding as to admissibility of evidence tendered, the arbitrator must act honestly and judicially, and if while so acting he decides erroneously that evidence is or is not admissible, that is not in itself misconduct'. See also *A/S Laboremus v Steaua Francaise SA* (1923) 17 Ll L Rep 92.

This rule is, however, subject to qualifications which greatly reduce its practical importance.

First, the parties are at liberty to agree that the arbitrator need not follow the strict rules of evidence. Such an agreement sometimes forms an express term of the contract out of which the dispute has arisen[10]; alternatively it may be included in the subsequent reference to arbitration. It has never been doubted that such provisions are valid[11]. More important still, a relaxation of strict rules may often be *implied*. If a party agrees to a form of arbitration in which the strict rules are habitually disregarded, he has no complaint if the arbitration proceeds in the usual way[12].

Whether an agreement to relax the strict rules may be implied from the way in which the parties conduct the reference is less clear. We consider, however, that if conduct of one party leads the other to believe that the strict rules will not be insisted upon, in consequence of which the latter abstains from procuring formal evidence, the former will be estopped from changing his mind at the hearing and requiring formal proof. We doubt, however, whether an implied agreement or estoppel will operate in the other direction. Thus if the agreed submission expressly or impliedly relaxes the strict rules, the mere fact that the arbitration is conducted in a more formal way (e.g. with pleadings, discovery and legal representation) will not preclude the parties from adducing informal evidence.

Second, an objection to the admission of evidence may be waived[13]. The Court will be slow to uphold an objection after the publication of an award, if it was not made during the hearing.

Finally, the Court has shown itself reluctant to set aside or remit an award, unless convinced that the wrongly admitted evidence had a substantial bearing on the outcome of the case[14].

If the arbitration is completely formal, with solicitors and counsel, the hearing

---

[10] See for example *Henry Bath & Son Ltd v Birgby Products* [1962] 1 Lloyd's Rep 389; *Macpherson Train & Co Ltd v J Milhelm & Sons* [1955] 2 Lloyd's Rep 59, CA. But the usual form of agreement does not permit the parties to refer to 'without prejudice' discussions: *Finney Lock Seeds Ltd v George Mitchell (Chesterhall) Ltd* [1979] 2 Lloyd's Rep 301.

[11] At least so long as the arbitrator is still able to do justice: *FE Hookway & Co Ltd v Alfred Isaacs & Sons* [1954] 1 Lloyd's Rep 491 at 500. The technical rules of evidence form no part of the rules of natural justice. Any person exercising quasi-judicial functions must base his decision on evidence but this means no more than that it must be based on material which tends logically to show the existence or non-existence of facts relevant to the issue to be determined: *R v Deputy Industrial Injuries Comr, ex p Moore* [1965] 1 QB 456 at 488. An agreement that a disputed issue of fact should be decided otherwise than on such material, e.g. by spinning a coin or consulting a soothsayer, would not necessarily be a nullity, but would probably lead to the conclusion that the procedure was not intended to be on arbitration: see Chapter 2, ante.

[12] *Henry Bath & Son Ltd v Birgby Products*, supra. This is certainly the case if he does not complain until after the award is published, for his complaint will probably be defeated by waiver as well as implied consent. What happens if the complaint is made during the hearing has never, so far as we can trace, been decided. Logically, if it is an implied term that informal evidence will be received, the arbitrator errs if he shuts out such evidence, and we believe that the Court would support the arbitrator if he acted in accordance with the normal trade practice.

[13] *Macpherson Train & Co Ltd v J Milhelm & Sons* [1955] 1 Lloyd's Rep 597 at 600; affd. [1955] 2 Lloyd's Rep 59.

[14] See, for example, *Re M'Clean & Co and Marcus* (1890) 6 TLR 355; *Re Enoch and Zaretzky, Bock & Co* [1910] 1 KB 327 at 336; *Grand Trunk Rly Co of Canada v R* [1923] AC 150; *British Metal Corpn Ltd v Ludlow Bros (1913) Ltd* (1938) 61 Ll L Rep 351. See also p. 552, post, where many of the cases on this topic are cited.

proceeds on the same basis as in Court. If the arbitration is of the more informal type – as in quality disputes or maritime arbitrations 'on documents' – the usual practice will often be to ignore the rules of evidence altogether. But problems may arise in the middle ground[15]. Many arbitrations are conducted in a semi-formal way, which leaves the parties or their advisers uncertain whether to produce fully admissible evidence, and risk wasting costs; or to rely on informal evidence, and risk having it struck out. To avoid this uncertainty, it is prudent for the parties to make sure at the outset that they are at one about the type of arbitration they are going to conduct; and, if they agree that the strict rules are to be waived, to reduce this agreement to writing. Similarly, if the arbitrator is in doubt about whether the arbitration is of a type which is customarily conducted informally, he should ask the parties at the beginning of the hearing. If they disagree, he will probably be wise to insist on a more, rather than less, formal mode of procedure.

Since the admissibility of evidence is a question of law, it is matter upon which it is possible to invoke the decision of the High Court[16], and this power should normally be exercised, rather than leaving the aggrieved party to an application to set aside or remit[17]. If the dispute as to admissibility is of vital importance, it would be right to consult the Court during the reference, notwithstanding the delay which this might entail.

(g) Admissibility of evidence

Detailed discussion of the substantive rules of evidence would be beyond the scope of this book. Moreover, the Civil Evidence Act 1968[18], by greatly enlarging the categories of evidence which are admissible in civil proceedings, has correspondingly diminished the number of problems of admissibility of evidence which are likely to arise in arbitration, even when they are conducted in accordance with the strict rules of evidence. But there are certain comments on practical and procedural points which may usefully be made here.

(i) **Authenticity and admissibility of documents distinguished.** A

distinction must be drawn, when considering the status of a particular document upon which a party seeks to rely, between the following questions –

1 Is the document authentic? If the document is a letter, the arbitrator may have to decide whether it was written when it was dated or by the person who signed it: if it is an extract of a log book, whether it is a genuine extract: if it is a

---

[15] Even in cases where very informal arbitrations are customary, it may be necessary for the arbitrator to revert to a more formal procedure if the issues cannot be safely resolved merely by looking at a bundle of correspondence. In cases where there are serious issues as to credibility, or where the authenticity of documents is challenged, it may well be necessary for the arbitrator to insist on oral evidence, or at least sworn evidence in the form of affidavits. We have even known of cases where allegations of fraud have been decided on bundles of documents, and this cannot be right.

[16] *East and West India Dock Co v Kirk and Randall* (1887) 12 App Cas 738.

[17] *Agroexport Entreprise d'Etat pour le Commerce Exterieur v NV Goorden Import Co SA* [1956] 1 Lloyd's Rep 319. This may, however, be the only remedy where the parties have made a valid exclusion agreement under s. 3 of the 1979 Act.

[18] The provisions of this Act relating to hearsay evidence and the rules of court made under it, i.e. Ord. 38, Part III, apply to arbitrations other than those to which the strict rules of evidence do not apply: see s. 18(1).

translation, whether it is accurate: if it is a copy of a witness' statement, whether it was ever in fact made.

2 Are particular statements in the document admissible? Here the question is not whether the document is authentic but whether a statement of fact or opinion in the document is admissible as evidence of the fact or matter of opinion which the party seeks to establish.

Failure to distinguish between these questions can sometimes lead to misunderstanding. For example, making up an 'agreed bundle' merely entails that the parties do not dispute the authenticity of the documents: it does not involve any agreement as to their admissibility. Conversely, an agreement to relax the strict rules of evidence dispenses with the rules concerning admissibility: but it does not of itself dispense with the need to establish that the documents are authentic.

(ii) Hearsay evidence: statements in documents. It is not always possible or convenient for a party to prove a fact by calling a witness at the hearing to give direct oral evidence of it. It may be more convenient, or even sometimes necessary, for the party to establish the fact on which he relies by putting in evidence a statement made on some other occasion[19] by a person who had direct knowledge of it. In arbitrations conducted in accordance with the strict rules of evidence[20] such evidence is admissible if, but only if, the requirements of the Civil Evidence Act 1968 and the rules of court made under it[1] are complied with. These requirements may be summarised as follows[2] –

1 A party who desires to put such a statement in evidence must, within 21 days after the date for the hearing is fixed[3], or within such other period as the arbitrator may specify, serve on the other party notice of his desire to do so.

2 The notice must contain particulars of

(i)   the time, place and circumstances at or in which the statement was made;

(ii)   the person by whom, and the person to whom, the statement was made;

(iii)   the substance of the statement or, if material, the words used,

except that if the statement was made in a document, a copy or transcript of the document (or the relevant part) must be annexed to the notice and only such of the particulars under (i) and (ii) as are not apparent on the face of the document need be given.

3 If the party giving the notice alleges that the person who made the statement cannot or should not be called as a witness on the grounds that –

(i)   he is beyond the seas[4];

---

[19] E.g. in a report, or a letter, or in a statement to a solicitor.

[20] Civil Evidence Act, s. 18(1).

[1] I.e. Part III of Ord. 38, which is made directly applicable to such arbitrations by the Civil Evidence Act, s. 10(3).

[2] This is in effect a summary of Part III of Ord. 38 as it applies to out-of-court statements, with 'such modifications as may be appropriate': see Civil Evidence Act, s. 10(3) and (4).

[3] This is not wholly satisfactory as the equivalent of setting down or adjournment into court, but we cannot think of a better one.

[4] This reason can only be challenged on the grounds that the witness is *not* beyond the seas. No objection can be taken to the admissibility of his statement on the grounds that he can easily be brought to the hearing. But when assessing the weight to be given to the statement of a witness who could have been called without difficulty, the arbitrator is entitled to take into account the fact that the other party had been denied the opportunity to cross-examine him.

(ii) he is dead;

(iii) he is unfit by reason of his bodily or mental condition to attend as a witness;

(iv) despite the exercise of reasonable diligence it has not been possible to identify or find him; or that

(v) he cannot reasonably be expected to have any recollection of matters relevant to the accuracy or otherwise of the statement to which the notice relates,

the notice must contain a statement to that effect.

4 If the other party desires that the person who made the statement should be called as a witness he must serve a counternotice to that effect within 21 days and in addition, if it is alleged that the witness cannot or should not be called as a witness for any of the reasons in 3, ante, he must include in his counternotice a statment that the witness can or should be called and apply to the arbitrator for an order to that effect.

The arbitrator has, however, a discretion to dispense with or extend or abridge the time for the above requirements. In particular he has power to allow a statement to be given in evidence without calling the person who made it, even though none of the reasons set out in 3, ante, apply to the case. In exercising his discretion he should bear two things in mind. First, the procedural requirements are intended to prevent parties being taken by surprise at the hearing by applications to admit or exclude evidence, and that failure to comply with them should not result in the exclusion of admissible evidence or the failure of a valid objection to a witness not being called unless there has been some real prejudice to the other party. Second, the weight to be attached to a statement put in evidence without calling the person who made it is always a matter for the arbitrator.

Similar provisions to those of the Civil Evidence Act 1968 are laid down by the Civil Evidence Act 1972 with regard to statements of opinion, such as expert evidence.

Section 12(6)(c) of the 1950 Act empowers the High Court to order that evidence may be given by affidavit in an arbitration[5]. It will, however, be necessary to resort to this power only in the rare case where the arbitration is subject to the strict rules of evidence and the evidence cannot be given under the Civil Evidence Acts.

(iii) Expert evidence.   In arbitrations to which the strict rules of evidence apply the admissibility of expert evidence is governed by the Civil Evidence Act 1972 and the rules of court made under it[6]. The effect of these rules[7] is that, unless the arbitrator gives leave, no expert evidence may be given at the hearing unless the party seeking to adduce it has applied to the arbitrator to determine whether a direction should be given for the substance of the evidence to be disclosed to the other party in the form of a written report (with or without an order that the expert need not be called as a witness).

---

[5] See Ord. 38, r. 2. S. 12(6)(c) seems to assume that evidence in an arbitration cannot be given by affidavit, unless the arbitration agreement so provides. There is no provision enabling the Court to make an order in an arbitration corresponding to an order under Ord. 38, r. 3.

[6] S. 10 of the Civil Evidence Act 1968, as applied by s. 5(2) of the Civil Evidence Act 1972.

[7] See Part IV of Ord. 38.

The object of these provisions is to ensure that so far as possible each side is informed before the hearing of the substance of the opponent's expert's evidence, so that areas of agreement and disagreement can be identified and the expert witnesses can be given time to consider points in each other's reports which they might find it difficult to deal with at short notice at the hearing.

Although these rules do not apply automatically to an arbitration which is not being conducted in accordance with the strict rules of evidence we consider that an arbitrator in such an arbitration has power to make an order to the same effect, and he should certainly consider whether it is desirable to do so in any case involving issues of expert evidence.

(h) Privilege from proceedings for defamation

Although the point has not yet arisen directly for decision there is some authority to the effect that evidence and other statements made in arbitration proceedings may be covered by absolute privilege for the purpose of the law of defamation and are therefore not actionable even on proof of malice[8]. Whether or not this is so may however depend on the type of arbitration which is in question, and in particular whether the proceedings are sufficiently similar to those of a court of law to justify extending the scope of absolute privilege to them[9].

(i) Fresh evidence

It sometimes happens that a party comes into possession of fresh evidence at a late stage of the reference. If the party knows when the hearing is in progress that fuller evidence is going to become available, but has insufficient time to obtain it before the hearing is concluded, he should ask the arbitrator to adjourn until the evidence is available[10]. If the existence of the evidence comes to light after the close of the hearing, but before the award is made, the party should ask the arbitrator to withhold his award pending a further hearing at which the new evidence can be given.

The arbitrator has a discretion whether or not to adjourn the hearing or grant a further hearing. Before acceding to the application he should ask the party what the further evidence is likely to be so that he can judge whether it is likely to be material. If the arbitrator concludes that the new evidence is inadmissible, irrelevant or of no real weight, or if he decides that the application is made for the purpose of wasting time, he should reject it. If, however, there is any real possibility that the evidence will be of value he should give the party an opportunity to adduce it. For if he lets it in and it proves to be useless, he can

---

[8] *Tadd v Eastwood* [1985] IRLR 320; the point did not arise on appeal: [1985] ICR 132. The ratio of the decision was that the proceedings were not an arbitration, but a form of conciliation.

[9] This is perhaps somewhat illogical. If public policy warrants the extension of absolute privilege to arbitration at all, this must be on the grounds that those who take part in the administration of justice by a means recognised and sanctioned by law should be entirely uninfluenced by the possibility of proceedings for defamation. If so, it is difficult to see why absolute privilege should depend on whether the procedure does or does not resemble that of a court of law.

[10] *JH Rayner & Co v Fred Drughorn Ltd* (1924) 18 Ll L Rep 269. If the party does not ask for an adjournment, the fact that the evidence becomes available after the award is made is not a ground for remission. But the arbitrator need not wait indefinitely for such evidence: if it has not been obtained within a reasonable time he is entitled to make his decision without it: *British Oil & Cake Mills Ltd v Horace Battin & Co Ltd* (1922) 13 Ll L Rep 443.

always penalise the party in costs; whereas if he excludes reliable evidence the award may be remitted or even set aside[11].

If the new evidence does not come to light until after the publication of the award, the arbitrator has no power to take any action, and the remedy of the party seeking to rely on the evidence is to apply to the Court for an order that the award be remitted for a further hearing[12]. Such an order will not be granted unless the Court is satisfied that the party could not, by the exercise of reasonable diligence, have obtained the evidence in time to put it before the arbitrator, and that the evidence has at least some weight[13].

(j) Notes of proceedings

(i) Arbitrator's notes.   An arbitrator is not formally obliged to make notes of the evidence and submissions. Thus, if the hearing is very short, or if it is concerned solely with the repetition or elaboration of submissions already made in writing, the arbitrator may safely carry the whole proceedings in his head. On the other hand, it is usually desirable to take a note where there is any substantial amount of oral evidence, not only for the purpose of comparison and checking, but also because what is said (or not said) at an earlier stage may subsequently prove to be more important than had then been realised. Even in such a case, it would not in itself be misconduct to abstain from taking a note, but it is unlikely to increase the parties' confidence in the arbitrator, and might ultimately be relied upon as part of the evidence in an application, ostensibly on other grounds, to set the award aside or even to remove the arbitrator.

The arbitrator should always keep a record of any applications or objections by the parties and of his own ruling.

(ii) Shorthand note.   A shorthand note may save time and trouble in a long case, but it is expensive, and the arbitrator should not employ a shorthand writer unless the parties consent[14]. The arbitrator has no power to prevent a party from employing a shorthand writer[15].

It is plainly sensible that if anyone, whether arbitrator or party, has produced a shorthand note, then copies of the transcript should be made generally available, subject to proper arrangements for sharing the expense.

It sometimes happens that an arbitrator, who has arranged for a note to be taken, is asked by one of the parties to supply a transcript, so that the party may use it when preparing an application to set aside for misconduct. The arbitrator may legitimately enquire into the purpose of the request so that he may satisfy

---

[11] See *Rayner v Drughorn*, supra, at 271.
[12] *Re Keighley, Maxsted & Co and Bryan Durant & Co* [1893] 1 QB 405, CA.
[13] For a further discussion, see pp. 561–562, post.
[14] The consent may be implied from the custom of the trade. Many trade tribunals employ short-hand writers whenever a case is to be stated, and include the expense in the costs of the award. We believe that this often adds a quite unnecessary expense to the already considerable burdens of the parties. The tribunal ought not to procure a transcript simply as a matter of course but should consider whether it is really necessary. This is so particularly as regards a shorthand note of the arguments. If the tribunal sits with a legal adviser, he should be able to take a sufficient note of the argument.
[15] See *Re Haigh's Estate, Haigh v Haigh* (1861) 31 LJ Ch 420 at 424.

himself that it is genuine[16]. Subject to this, it is his duty to comply, so that the Court may have full and accurate information before it.

8 The decision

(a) Consulting third parties

The question often arises as to how far an arbitrator may, or indeed should, consult with third parties before arriving at his decision. The view might be taken that, as the parties have chosen the arbitrator to decide the dispute, he should consult with no-one else[17] before making his decision. This would, however, be too strict a view, for there is no doubt that an arbitrator may quite properly discuss the case with a friend or colleague[18]. There is also no doubt that in general an arbitrator may properly consult a third party for an expert opinion on an issue in the arbitration, so long as he exercises his own judgment in accepting or rejecting the opinion which he receives[19]. There are, however, dangers in doing so unless he is authorised to do so by the terms of the arbitration agreement[20] or has obtained the consent of the parties[1]. The main danger is that the impression may be given that he has not in fact exercised his own independent judgment[2]. Another is that if he omits to inform both parties of the opinion he has received and to allow them to comment on it, the award may be set aside for receiving evidence in the absence of one or both parties[3].

Quite apart from these dangers, if the parties have themselves led expert evidence and each has cross-examined the expert witness of the other, the arbitrator may be doing them a disservice by adding yet another expert opinion to those which have already been considered and commented upon. In such a case, if the arbitrator cannot reach a decision without expert advice, he would be well advised to obtain the agreement of the parties either that the expert should report privately to the arbitrator or that his conclusions should be binding as to the matters on which he has been consulted[4].

An arbitrator should be particularly careful before consulting a third party without the consent of the parties on a matter which requires an investigation of the facts, such as analysing samples, valuing property, or taking accounts. Although this may be permissible as regards facts which cannot be a matter of

---

[16] And to make sure that the note is not used as the basis for a concealed attack on the arbitrator's findings of fact or conclusion of law.

[17] Except of course his fellow arbitrators.

[18] *Dobson v Groves* (1844) 14 LJQB 17; *Ellison v Bray* (1864) 9 LT 730.

[19] *Anderson v Wallace* (1835) 3 CL & F 26; *Eastern Counties Rly Co v Eastern Union Rly Co* (1863) 3 DeG K & Sm 610; *Hopcraft v Hickman* (1824) 2 Sim & St 130; *Eads v Williams* (1854) 24 LJ Ch 531; *Ellison v Bray*, supra.

[20] As in *Naumann v Edward Nathan & Co Ltd* (1930) 37 Ll L Rep 249 ('arbitration in the usual way').

[1] The usage of a particular trade may make it unnecessary to obtain their express consent. For example, the appeal tribunals of many commodity associations sit with a legal adviser both at the hearing and during their deliberations afterwards.

[2] As in *Emery v Wase* (1803) 8 Ves 505 and *Johnson v Latham* (1850) 19 LJQB 329.

[3] As in *Re Eastern Counties Rly Co*, supra; *Royal Commission on the Sugar Supply v Kwik Hoo Tong Trading Society* (1922) 38 TLR 684; and *Dobson v Groves* (1844) 14 LJQB 17.

[4] Notwithstanding the dictum of Salter J in *Kursell v Timber Operators and Contractors Ltd* [1923] 2 KB 202 at 206, an agreement in the latter form would appear to be unobjectionable: see *Sharp v Nowell* (1848) 6 CB 253.

dispute[5] or investigations requiring no exercise of judgment, such as measuring the area of a piece of land[6], it is certainly not permissible where the third party has to decide on disputed facts or call for explanations from the parties themselves[7].

An arbitrator who is not legally qualified may retain a lawyer to draw up the award[8], and there is no objection to him taking advice on legal issues in the reference[9], so long as the decision remains his and not that of the lawyer[10]. It is, however, preferable that the parties' consent should first be obtained; and the arbitrator should take care to see that the facts laid before the lawyer for his advice are full and accurate.

(b) Delegating the working out of the award

An arbitrator may, by making an interim award, reserve to himself matters which are not dealt with in the award. But he cannot delegate the working out of the award to a third party, for example by directing that repairs shall be carried out to the satisfaction of a named surveyor, and an award which does this is a nullity unless the part which is delegated can be severed from the rest[11].

There are, however, a few exceptions to this rule. First, the arbitrator may leave the costs to be taxed in the High Court[12]. Second, the award will not be invalidated by a direction that the parties may apply to the Court for orders necessary to give effect to it[13]. Third, measurements and similar investigations requiring no exercise of judgment may be delegated to a third party[14].

(c) Arbitrator using own knowledge

As a matter of general principle, an arbitrator should not rely on his own knowledge of facts relating to the issues before him without telling the parties that he proposes to do so and giving them an opportunity to comment on it or call rebutting evidence[15].

There is, however, an important exception to the general principle where the

---

[5] This may be the explanation of *Eads v Williams* (1854) 24 LJ Ch 531. It is difficult otherwise to understand how an arbitrator entrusted with valuing a mine could properly have left it to his grandson to inspect it.

[6] *Thorp v Cole* (1835) 2 Cr M & R 367.

[7] *Re Haigh, Haigh v Haigh* (1861) 5 LT 507.

[8] *Behren v Bremer* (1854) 3 CLR 40; *Threlfall v Fanshawe* (1850) 19 LJQB 334; *Rolland v Cassidy* (1888) 13 App Cas 770 at 776–777.

[9] Unless the parties have specifically appointed a non-legal arbitrator: *Proctor v Williamson* (1860) 29 LJCP 157.

[10] *Baker v Cotterill* (1849) 18 LJQB 345; *Giacomo Costa fu Andrea v British Italian Trading Co Ltd* [1961] 2 Lloyd's Rep 392.

[11] *Tomlin v Fordwich Corpn* (1836) 5 A & El 147; *Re Tandy and Tandy* (1841) 9 Dowl 1044.

[12] S. 18(2) of the 1950 Act.

[13] *Lingood v Eade* (1742) 2 Atk 501.

[14] *Thorp v Cole* (1835) 2 Cr M & R 367. Cf. *Johnson v Latham* (1850) 19 LJQB 329. See also p. 342, post.

[15] *Grand Trunk Rly Co of Canada v R* [1923] AC 150; *Youroveta Home and Foreign Trade Co Inc v Coopman* (1920) 3 Ll L Rep 242; *Louis Dreyfus & Co v Produce Brokers' New Co (1924) Ltd* (1936) 54 Ll L Rep 60, 65; *Owen v Nicholl* [1948] 1 All ER 707. The suggestion by Tucker LJ in the last-named case, that the arbitrator cannot rely on his own knowledge at all, seems unnecessarily strict.

arbitrator has been chosen for his special experience or knowledge in a particular field, for here it is clear that the arbitrator not only may but ought to make use of his own experience and knowledge, and may do so without reference to the parties and without the benefit of evidence on the matter in hand[16]. This is not limited to matters of skill and experience, but in trade arbitrations extends to matters affecting the trade generally[17], such as the state of the market[18], or the effect of political events on commerce generally[19]. Moreover, an arbitrator appointed for his special experience or skill in valuing property or assessing the quality of goods may quite properly examine the property or goods in the absence of the parties and rely on his own examination[20]. There is always, however, the overriding consideration that neither party should be taken by surprise[1]; if the arbitrator is in any doubt as to whether the parties could reasonably expect him to be in possession of the knowledge which he is about to act upon or if he proposes to reject uncontroverted expert evidence[2], or to decide the case on a point which has not been canvassed during the reference[3], he should tell them what he proposes to do and invite their comments[4].

(d) Arbitrators acting together

Where the reference is to more than one arbitrator, all the arbitrators must act together[5], unless the arbitration agreement provides otherwise[6]. The parties are

[16] *Mediterranean and Eastern Export Co Ltd v Fortress Fabrics (Manchester) Ltd* (1948) 64 TLR 337; *Eads v Williams* (1854) 24 LJ Ch 531; *Wright v Howson* (1888) 4 TLR 386.

[17] The distinction has been drawn between general knowledge of the trade which a man in the arbitrator's position would be bound to acquire and special facts relating to a particular case: *Jordeson & Co v Stora Koppabergs Bergslags Akt* (1931) 41 Ll L Rep 201 at 204; *Fox v PG Wellfair Ltd* [1981] 2 Lloyd's Rep 514 at 529; *Navrom v Callitsis Ship Management SA, The Radauti* [1987] 2 Lloyd's Rep 276 at 284. The distinction is not always easy to apply, particularly when an arbitrator is appointed and hears evidence in numerous disputes arising out of the same incident, or where he is appointed to review rent or value property in an area which he knows well from his practice as a surveyor or from other arbitrations: *Top Shop Estates Ltd v Danino* (1984) 273 Estates Gazette 197.

[18] *Mediterranean & Eastern Export* case, ante.

[19] *British Oil & Cake Mills Ltd v Horace Battin & Co Ltd* (1922) 13 Ll L Rep 443, see also *Port Sudan Cotton Co v Govindaswamy Chettiar & Sons* [1977] 1 Lloyd's Rep 166 at 179.

[20] See for example, *Nauman v Edward Nathan & Co Ltd* (1930) 37 Ll L Rep 249 (quality); *Oswald v Earl Grey* (1855) 24 LJQB 69 (valuation); *Bottomley v Ambler* (1877) 38 LTNS 545 (valuation).

[1] As in *Thomas Borthwick (Glasgow) Ltd v Faure Fairclough Ltd* [1968] 1 Lloyd's Rep 16, where the arbitrators found a custom which had not been mentioned at the hearing. Cf. *Produce Brokers Co Ltd v Olympia Oil & Cake Co Ltd* [1916] 1 AC 314, 321; and *Mitsubishi International GmbH v Bremer Handelsgesellschaft mbH* [1981] 1 Lloyd's Rep 106.

[2] *Fox v P G Wellfair Ltd* [1981] 2 Lloyd's Rep 514.

[3] As in *Zermalt Holdings SA v Nu-Life Upholstery Repairs Ltd* (1985) 275 Estates Gazette 1134.

[4] *Top Shop Estates Ltd v Danino*, supra, is a good example of what can happen if he does not do so. The award was set aside because the arbitrator inspected the site himself, appointed a qualified assistant to carry out a pedestrian count and relied on knowledge gained in other arbitrations, all without giving the parties proper notice and an opportunity to comment before making an award under a rent review clause. We doubt whether any of these matters would have been grounds for objection, having regard to the nature of the arbitration, if he had told the parties what he was doing and allowed them to comment.

[5] *Re Plews and Middleton* (1845) 6 QB 845; *Lord v Lord* (1855) 5 E & B 404; *Re Beck and Jackson* (1857) 1 CBNS 695; *Mallozzi v Carapelli SpA* [1981] 1 Lloyd's Rep 552; *European Grain and Shipping Ltd v Johnston* [1982] 1 Lloyd's Rep 414.

[6] As in *British Metal Corpn Ltd v Ludlow Bros (1913) Ltd* [1938] 1 All ER 135, where the agreement provided that the two arbitrators need not appoint a third unless they deemed it necessary.

entitled to an impartial and fair consideration and resolution by the arbitrators, acting together, of all the issues in the case. This involves taking account of the views of a dissenting arbitrator even if it is clear that he will be in the minority. But so long as this governing principle is adhered to the arbitrators need not conduct the whole of their business in the physical presence of one another: arbitrators frequently have to communicate with one another by telephone, telex or letter, particularly so where they are drawn from different countries[7].

In the case of a reference to three arbitrators, section 9 of the 1950 Act[8] provides that, unless the contrary intention is expressed in the arbitration agreement, the award of any two of the arbitrators shall be binding. But this does not dispense with the need for all three arbitrators to participate in the reference, and this can give rise to problems.

The 1979 Act has abolished the rule, which prevailed since 1934[9], to the effect that where the arbitration clause provided for a tribunal of three arbitrators, the third being appointed by the two chosen by the parties, it should take effect as if it provided for the appointment of an umpire, not a third arbitrator. This special feature of English arbitration law caused some perplexity abroad, since in many countries a tribunal consisting of a sole arbitrator is much less common than that in England, and foreign parties to English arbitrations were disconcerted to find that if the arbitrators disagreed at an early stage, the reference was left in the hands of one man, without the sharing of ideas and responsibility amongst the tribunal which is regarded in many systems as an important part of the arbitral process. Accordingly, the law was changed in 1979[10] so as to bring the English practice into line with that prevailing elsewhere, and a clause stipulating for three arbitrators now takes effect according to its terms.

This innovation has led to practical results which perhaps were not foreseen. Even where the tribunal now consists of three members, parties in many City arbitrations still tend to follow the practice which has long prevailed[11] in regard to tribunals of two arbitrators with power to appoint an umpire, of sending their files to 'their own' arbitrators. It may well happen that an exchange of views between the two arbitrators, before they have reached the stage of choosing the third member, leads them to realise that they can agree on the terms of an award. Since the majority award of two arbitrators is binding[12], the views of the third arbitrator are for most[13] practical purposes irrelevant. Yet the two arbitrators are bound to appoint the third arbitrator, provide him with copies

---

[7] *Bank Mellat v GAA Development and Construction Co* [1988] 2 Lloyd's Rep 44, which contains a valuable discussion of the process of settling a majority award under the Rules of Arbitration of the International Chamber of Commerce, and of the part played by the ICC Court of Arbitration in scrutinizing the award.

[8] As amended by s. 6(2) of the 1979 Act.

[9] S. 4(1) of the 1934 Act, re-enacted by s. 9(1) of the 1950 Act. When recommending this change, together with a provision (reproduced as s. 8(1) of the 1950 Act) requiring the arbitrators to appoint the umpire immediately, the MacKinnon Committee evidently had in mind that the existing practice often involved a waste of costs. Unfortunately, this part of the Report is very compressed, and it is not possible to be sure precisely what abuses the Committee sought to remedy.

[10] S. 6(2) of the 1979 Act, effectively repealing s. 9(1) of the 1950 Act.

[11] See pp. 259–262, ante; and *European Grain and Shipping Ltd v Johnston*, ante.

[12] S. 6(2) of the 1979 Act, replacing s. 9(2) of the 1950 Act.

[13] One cannot say for *all* practical purposes, since there is always the possibility that the third arbitrator, once appointed, will prevail on one or both of the others to change his mind. But this calls for a high degree of zeal and tenacity.

of the documents, and deliberate with him[14], even though he is potentially out-voted before ever being appointed. In order to avoid what is seen in some quarters as an unnecessary expenditure of time and costs, a practice has begun to evolve whereby each arbitrator obtains the consent of his appointer to abstain from appointing a third arbitrator, in the event of their being able to agree an award. There is no technical objection to this practice, for the original agreement to have a three-man tribunal can effectively be varied by a subsequent agreement.

A three-man tribunal can sometimes turn out to be a cumbersome vehicle for making decisions on interlocutory matters, particularly if one or more of the arbitrators lives or travels abroad. Where the parties or the tribunal foresee that this may cause problems, it is not unusual for the parties, sometimes at the initiative of the tribunal, to agree either that the third arbitrator shall have power to rule on his own, or that the two arbitrators shall have power to rule without referring to the third. Again there is no technical objection to such a variation of the original agreement, but is prudent to specify what are and what are not interlocutory matters, and to provide that if there is a dispute about this it must be decided by the full tribunal.

9 The award

Once the arbitrator has made his decision, he embodies it in a formal written award ready to be published to the parties. The precise form that the award should take, and the matters that it should and should not contain, are topics which require more extended discussion than can conveniently be contained in this chapter. A full discussion will be found in Chapters 25 and 26 under the headings 'Types of award' and 'Form and contents of a valid award'.

10 Appeal procedures

Where an arbitration is constituted under the auspices of a trade association which provides regular facilities for arbitrations, it is not uncommon to find that the rules of the association establish a system of appeal to a further arbitral tribunal from the decision of the original arbitrators or umpire. Such rules sometimes stipulate that the original award shall not be reversed or varied unless a stated majority, greater than a simple majority, of the appeal tribunal are in favour of so doing. Sometimes the rules provide that the appeal shall be on questions of fact alone[15].

---

[14] Although the award itself may properly reflect the views of only two members, all three must participate in the reference. As Cresswell J observed in *Re Beck and Jackson* (1857) 1 CBNS 695 (citing Russell): '... the parties are entitled to have recourse to the arguments, experience and judgment of each arbitrator at every stage of the proceedings brought to bear on the minds of his fellow judges so that by conference they shall mutually assist each other in arriving together at a just conclusion'. See also *Eardley v Steer* (1835) 4 Dowl 423.

[15] Provisions of this latter type are unusual, and it is not necessary to discuss in detail the difficult questions of procedure to which they may give rise. We suggest, however, that the strong Court of Appeal in *African and Eastern (Malaya) Ltd v White, Palmer & Co Ltd* (1930) 36 Ll L Rep 113 erred in stating that under this form of appeal procedure the appeal tribunal cannot be asked to state a case. The tribunal may not have jurisdiction to *change* the view of the law adopted at first instance, even if that view of the law appears from the first award (which it usually will not). But it must still *form* a view on the law, in order to direct itself on the right view of the facts; and there seems no reason why the Court should not be invited to say that the tribunal's view of the law is wrong.

Very often, the issues take on a different shape when the matter is before the appeal tribunal than when the original tribunal was seized of the matter. Second thoughts may have caused a party to recognise the weaknesses of one submission, and to conceive that his case can be more cogently advanced another way. This frequently happens if lawyers become involved for the first time at the stage of an appeal. In such a situation, the appeal tribunal should ensure that the opponent realises the shift in emphasis[16].

A multiple-tier appeal system provides for a series of successive arbitrations[17], not for a single arbitration conducted in stages[18]. The provisions of the appeal rules constitute a supplementary submission to arbitration, which is to be invoked in the circumstances laid down in the rules. If a party does not comply with the requirements of the rules, he is not entitled to ask the appeal tribunal to make an award, for the other party has only agreed to a supplementary arbitration on the conditions set out in the rules[19]. The question whether the conditions have been complied with is for the Court, not for the original arbitrators nor the appeal tribunal[20], unless the rules expressly so stipulate[1]. Nor[2] does the appeal tribunal have power to dispense with compliance with the conditions on which its jurisdiction depends[3].

When the appeal tribunal has made an award, whether confirming, reversing or varying the decision of the original arbitrators, it is the award of the appeal tribunal which defines the rights of the parties. Any action must be brought upon that award[4]; time runs from the publication of that award[4]; and if the Court decides to intervene, for misconduct or other reasons, it is the award of the appeal tribunal, and not that of the arbitrators, which is the subject of the order[5]. The Court has no jurisdiction – or indeed reason – to set aside or remit

---

[16] Otherwise there will be the risk of the kind of mishap which occurred in *Gunter Henck v André & Cie SA* [1970] 1 Lloyd's Rep 235.

[17] This is the effect of almost all the appeal provisions in common use. Nevertheless, as McNair J recognised in *Giacomo Costa Fu Andrea v British Italian Trading Co Ltd* [1961] 2 Lloyd's Rep 392, the matter depends on the interpretation of the agreement. It may be that under certain forms, the revising authority is to be regarded as fulfilling an administrative function, and not as conducting a second arbitration.

[18] *Getreide-Import GmbH v Contimar SA Compania Industrial Commercial y Maritime* [1953] 1 Lloyd's Rep 572; *Andrea v British Italian Trading Co Ltd* [1962] 1 Lloyd's Rep 151 at 156. There is a contrast with the position where the matter goes before two arbitrators and an umpire. In such a case there is a single arbitration in two stages, and only one valid award can ensue.

[19] *Getreide-Import GmbH v Contimar*, supra, at 584; *Amalgamated Metal Corpn Ltd v Khoon Seng Co* [1977] 2 Lloyd's Rep 310.

[20] *Getreide-Import v Contimar*, ante. The original arbitrators have no jurisdiction, (a) because they are functi officio, and (b) because their jurisdiction is limited to disputes arising under the contract, and a dispute concerning the right to appeal does not so arise. (Sed quaere, as to the latter reason.) The appeal tribunal cannot decide the matter, as the performance of the conditions affects the jurisdiction of the tribunal, upon which the tribunal has no jurisdiction to decide.

[1] As they sometimes do: see *Provimi Hellas AE v Warinco AG* [1978] 1 Lloyd's Rep 373; *Ets Soules & Cie v International Trade Development Co Ltd* [1979] 2 Lloyd's Rep 122. Such rules in effect empower the arbitrators to decide on their own jurisdiction.

[2] Unless the rules expressly so provide: *Provimi Hellas v Warinco*, supra.

[3] *Amalgamated Metal v Khoon Seng*, ante.

[4] Per McNair J in *Giacomo Costa fu Andrea v British Italian Trading Co Ltd* [1961] 2 Lloyd's Rep 392 at 405.

[5] Per McNair J and Diplock LJ in *Andrea v British Italian*, supra. Contrast *Cantzlaar and Schalkwijk & Co v Basler Spiers & Co's Handelsmaatschappij* (1921) 8 Ll L Rep 430.

the award of the original arbitrators[6], and the misconduct of those arbitrators is no longer material[7]. If the award of the appellate tribunal is set aside, this has the effect of reinstating the award of the original arbitrators[8].

It may occasionally happen that the original award which is the subject of the appeal is not merely erroneous or subject to vitiating misconduct, but is a complete nullity. In such a case, the result may be that the award of the appeal tribunal is also a nullity. Whether or not this is so depends upon the reason why the underlying award is invalid, and upon the circumstances of the appeal. Thus, if the original award is bad for want of jurisdiction, the same must apply to the award of the appeal tribunal[9]. Again, an award of an appeal tribunal upholding the original award may be void, on the ground that the submission to the tribunal was made under the fundamental mistake that the original award was valid[10].

The status of the original award pending an appeal depends upon the interpretation of the rules governing the appeal procedure[11]. In the absence of express stipulation, three things are clear. First, the original award is immediately effective, notwithstanding the existence of the appeal procedure. Second, the original arbitrators become functi officio as soon as they have published their award[12]. Third, the appellate award, once made, completely replaces the original award of the arbitrators[13]. What is less plain is how the award stands pending a notice of appeal. We believe that the Court would imply a term in the arbitration agreement whereby the successful party is precluded from enforcing the award once notice of appeal has been given[14]; and even in the absence of notice, the Court might well exercise its inherent jurisdiction to stay or adjourn proceedings founded on an award if satisfied that the losing party had a genuine intention to appeal.

---

[6] It is sometimes preferable to make a clean sweep and begin again. But unless the original arbitrators were also guilty of misconduct, there is no jurisdiction to take this course, otherwise than by consent (as happened in *Robinson, Fleming & Co v Warner, Barnes & Co* (1922) 10 Ll L Rep 331.)

[7] *Andrea v British Italian*, ante. It is perhaps unwise to assume that the principle applies without exception. It is possible to imagine cases where the original misconduct continues so as to infect the subsequent appeal proceedings.

[8] *London Export Corpn Ltd v Jubilee Coffee Roasting Co Ltd* [1958] 1 Lloyd's Rep 197 at 204 and 367 at 378.

[9] Unless an ad hoc submission can be inferred from conduct.

[10] *FW Berk & Co Ltd v Knowles and Foster* [1962] 1 Lloyd's Rep 430 at 435. This will not often be so. The submission to the arbitral tribunal will usually be constituted by the original agreement to arbitrate; at this time, no underlying award exists, and there is no mutual mistake. Another possible ground for arguing that the appellate award is a nullity is that an award which confirms a null award must itself be null. This is not convincing.

[11] See, for example, *MacLeod Ross & Co Ltd v Cradock Manners Ltd* [1954] 1 Lloyd's Rep 258, where the rules provided that the original award was to be final and binding unless notice of appeal was lodged within a specified time, and where there were provisions relative to the status of the award pending the decision of the appeal arbitrators.

[12] *Getreide-Import v Contimar SA*, ante, at 585; *Andrea v British Italian*, ante, at 156.

[13] *Andrea v British Italian*, ante, at 156 and 161. This results not, we suggest, from any merger of one award in the other, but simply because it is a term of the arbitration agreement that the one award shall replace the other.

[14] At any rate if the appeal is prosecuted with reasonable diligence.

Unless the arbitration agreement otherwise provides[15], a party who complains that the original award is invalid or defective (as distinct from merely erroneous), or that the arbitrators were guilty of misconduct, is not necessarily obliged to avail himself of the appeal procedure, in order to remedy his grievance[16]. He can proceed directly to the High Court, and the Court will then have a discretion whether to grant him any relief, or to remit him to the appellate procedure. Cases in which the Court is likely to exercise its powers include – (i) those where there would be undue delay if the matter went to appeal[17]; (ii) those where, by contrast, the conduct of the original arbitration has been so completely unsatisfactory that it would be more fair to start completely afresh[18]; and (iii) those where the defects in the award could be cured by the original arbitrators, without the need for an appeal.

Unless the arbitration agreement otherwise provides a party may ask the original arbitrators to invoke the decision of the Court on a question of law, notwithstanding the existence of an appeal procedure[19]. It does not, however, follow that he will be wise to take such a course, or that the Court would lend its assistance if the arbitrator refused to cooperate. Unless the point of law is short, and the facts are straightforward[20], invoking the decision of the Court is not an enterprise which should be embarked upon without a full hearing and, in most instances, legal representation. Where there is a two-tier system of arbitration, the stage at first instance is usually conducted in an informal manner, and would indeed lose most of its point if it were not. In practice, an elaborate investigation of evidence and documents, and the receipt of legal argument, is almost always reserved for the appellate stage; and it is on this occasion that it will usually be appropriate to invoke the decision of the Court. One possible exception is where it is desired to decide one point of law in advance of the main bulk of the reference. The first stage of the arbitration could conveniently be used as a vehicle for obtaining the decision of the Court on the point of law, leaving the evidence and the bulk of the argument to the appellate stage. We do not, however, know of any instance where this course has been adopted.

The fact that an appeal procedure exists is not in itself a bar to an application

---

[15] Megaw J plainly contemplated in *Montrose Canned Foods Ltd v Eric Wells (Merchants) Ltd* [1965] 1 Lloyd's Rep 597 that such a provision could be effective. There seems no reason why it should be regarded as contrary to public policy to provide an alternative consensual remedy to the remedies exercised by the Court under s. 23 of the Act. It may, however, be noted that the remedies are not the same. Where the Court intervenes, it is concerned with the conduct of the reference, and its decision does not bear upon the merits of the dispute. On an appeal, the position is different. The appellant is concerned to argue, not that the arbitrators arrived at their decision by unsatisfactory means, but that the decision itself is wrong.

[16] *Montrose Canned Foods Ltd v Eric Wells (Merchants) Ltd*, supra. The contrary was argued, but not decided in *AA Amram Ltd v Bremar Co Ltd* [1966] 1 Lloyd's Rep 494.

[17] As in *Montrose Canned Foods Ltd v Eric Wells (Merchants) Ltd*, ante.

[18] This situation might exist where the appeal rules provide, as they often do, that an award will not be varied unless a substantial majority of the appeal tribunal so decide. A party might not be able to shake off the effects of an unfair award to a sufficient degree to overcome this initial disadvantage. (The dicta of Diplock LJ in *Andrea v British Italian*, ante, do not, we suggest, lead to a different conclusion.)

[19] *Re Fischel & Co and Mann and Cook* [1919] 2 KB 431. The wording of ss. 1 and 2 of the 1979 Act and of s. 21 of the 1950 Act leave no doubt of this. It is not possible to imply a term postponing the right to involve the decision of the Court until the appellate stage.

[20] As in *Loders and Nucoline Ltd v Bank of New Zealand* (1929) 33 Ll L Rep 70, where Wright J approved the arbitrators' conduct in stating a case on a pure point of law without the umpire or appeal tribunal ever being involved.

to set aside or remit the original award, e.g. for misconduct. But it is a factor which the Court will take into account: and it will generally leave the complainant to pursue his remedy by way of appeal if the appeal tribunal is able to deal fully with the grounds of his complaint[1].

Where an appeal tribunal makes an award for the purposes of obtaining the decision of the Court on a point of law, it should not cut corners by incorporating by reference the contents of the original arbitrators' award. It should set out all the facts and questions in full[2].

---

[1] *Thos P Gonzalez Corpn v Mullers Muhle, Muller GmbH & Co* [1978] 2 Lloyd's Rep 541.
[2] *Steels and Busks Ltd v Bleecker Bik & Co Ltd* [1956] 1 Lloyd's Rep 228.

PART VI

The award

CHAPTER 25

Types of award

The law affords the arbitrator a considerable variety of forms from which to choose the type of award best suited to the circumstances of the case. The choice is not always easy, and failure to distinguish between the different types of award may occasionally lead to unintended procedural difficulties[1]. The wide variety of powers available to the arbitrator may sometimes prove an embarrassment, for the choice of the wrong form of award may cause the parties considerable inconvenience and expense. The arbitrator should therefore think carefully what form will suit his purpose best[2], and then make sure that the document which he issues is really what he intends it to be. Making the right choice depends on the answer to two questions:

A. Should the award be interim or final? In other words should it decide only one or some of the issues in the case, or should it dispose of all of them?

B. Should the award be in such a form as to enable a question of law to be brought before the Court for decision?

A. INTERIM OR FINAL?

In all but the simplest cases, the resolution of a dispute will involve a decision on more than one issue of fact or law. For example, a claim for damages for wrongful rejection of goods may involve an issue as to liability as well as quantum: and the issue of liability may itself involve separate issues as to the nature of the buyer's obligations as a matter of law, and whether those obligations have been broken as a matter of fact. A decision on any one of these issues may determine the outcome of the whole case without the need for a decision on the other issues. Thus, in the example just given, a decision in the buyer's favour on the issue of liability would make in unnecessary to decide any issue of damages.

Occasionally it may be possible to achieve a saving of time and expense by breaking down a dispute in this way into separate issues and making an interim award on one issue before embarking on an investigation of the rest.

There is no doubt that an arbitrator generally[3] has power to order a preliminary issue to be tried and to give effect to his decision by publishing

---

[1] As in *Fidelitas Shipping Co Ltd v V/O Exportchleb* [1965] 1 Lloyd's Rep 223, [1966] 1 QB 630.

[2] Although he should give weight to the suggestions of the parties, he should make his own decision on the most convenient course: the choice of a form different from that suggested by one party is not in itself misconduct: *Mitrovitch Bros & Co v Hickson & Partners Ltd* (1923) 14 Ll L Rep 164.

[3] Except in the rare case where the statutory power to make an interim award is expressly excluded by a term in the arbitration agreement: see s. 14 of the 1950 Act. The power to make an interim award may also be excluded by the terms of the submission to arbitration: *Minerals and Metals Trading Corpn of India Ltd v Encounter Bay Shipping Co Ltd, The Samos Glory (No 2)* [1988] 1 Lloyd's Rep 51.

either an interim award[4] or, if the decision disposes of the whole dispute, a final award.

But before embarking on the trial of a preliminary issue the arbitrator should give careful thought as to whether it is advisable to do so. For although it may seem attractive at the outset to deal with some parts of the dispute before others, in practice this tends to increase rather than reduce the duration and cost of the reference. This is particularly likely to be the case where there is a possibility of a point of law being brought before the Court for decision. But there are other reasons why a preliminary issue may turn out to be of less benefit than seemed at first sight. One reason is that the issue, if it is to produce any saving at all, has to be formulated at a fairly early stage of the reference, at a time when the dispute may not have acquired its final shape. Another is that an issue which seems at first to afford a short answer to a dispute may turn out on examination not to do so[5].

The arbitrator should in general adhere to the same practice as the courts[6], and reserve interim awards on preliminary points of law for cases where the decision of the preliminary issue in one way will dispose of the case altogether[7]. There are, of course, exceptions to the rule. It sometimes happens that the dispute largely turns on a few major issues, and then even if a decision on these would not in any event formally dispose of the whole case, nevertheless it would enable the parties to know enough about their position to have a fair chance of reaching a settlement. In such a case, if the arbitrator were satisfied that the parties really knew what they were doing, he would be justified in taking the main issues first: but such a case would be exceptional.

Joint arbitrators should be particularly hesitant about making an award which is not final. They may agree on the preliminary issue, but if they later disagree on another issue, the dispute must be decided by the umpire, who may take a view of the case which means that the preliminary issue is not decisive of the dispute whichever way it is resolved, or possibly even irrelevant.

B. AWARDS GIVING RECOURSE TO THE COURT ON A QUESTION OF LAW

The other question which has to be considered when deciding on the type of award to be employed is whether it ought to be in such a form as to enable a question of law to be brought before the Court for decision, and if so what form it should take.

---

[4] S. 14 of the 1950 Act.
[5] See for example, *Compagnie D'Armement Maritime SA v Compagnie Tunisienne De Navigation SA* [1971] AC 572, which went to the House of Lords on a preliminary issue to establish that the proper law of a contract was French law: the arbitrators later found as a fact that French law did not differ materially from English law.
[6] See for example *Windsor Refrigerator Co Ltd v Branch Nominees Ltd* [1961] Ch 88; *Yeoman Credit Ltd v Latter* [1961] 1 WLR 828; *Sumner v William Henderson & Sons Ltd* [1963] 1 Lloyd's Rep 537.
[7] We are not speaking here of interim awards in respect of sums which are clearly due, subject only to a cross-claim: see p. 494, post; nor of interim awards in respect of separate heads of claim. Interim awards in such cases are a valuable remedy in the arbitrator's repertoire.

1 Introduction

Sections 1 and 2 of the Arbitration Act 1979 provide for two different procedures by which a question of law may be brought before the Court. These procedures are discussed in detail in Chapter 35. For present purposes the following summary will suffice to introduce the discussion of how the arbitrator should choose and draft the appropriate type of award.

1 Section 1 provides for an appeal on a question of law arising out of an award, either with the consent of all parties or, where the parties have not validly excluded the jurisdiction of the Court by agreement, with the leave of the Court. If the award does not or does not sufficiently set out the reasons for the award, the Court has power to order the reasons to be given in sufficient detail to enable it to consider the question of law should an appeal be brought. But further reasons may not be ordered by the Court unless either (a) one of the parties gave notice before the award was made that a reasoned award would be required or (b) there is some special reason why such a notice was not given.

2 Section 2 provides for the determination by the Court of a question of law arising in the course of the reference, either with the consent of the arbitrator or umpire, or with the consent of all the parties.

The scheme of the Act therefore requires the arbitrator to consider first whether he has a duty to make a reasoned award. If he concludes that he has a duty to do so, he must next decide what reasons are necessary to comply with the Act. If he decides that he has no duty to make a reasoned award, he may nevertheless consider that he should volunteer one, or consent to an application under section 2. Finally, if he decides to do none of these things, he should still consider whether to give reasons in a separate document which does not form part of the award.

2 The duty to make a reasoned award

(a) Scope of the duty

The power to call for reasons under the 1979 Act is introduced simply as a vehicle for the prosecution of an appeal. There is no duty to give reasons, and no power in the Court to order reasons for the purpose of determining a preliminary question of law under section 2. In many instances, therefore, neither the parties nor the Court can compel the arbitrator to make a reasoned award, if he chooses not to do so[8]. Thus, he need not furnish reasons if –

1 The award is the subject of a valid exclusion agreement under section 3(1)[9].

---

[8] This is not to say that he should not give any reasons. We are here concerned with the duty to make a reasoned award, ie an award in which the reasons are set out or incorporated in such a way as to make them part of the award, not with reasons which do not form part of the award. Even in the simplest type of arbitration each party, and particularly the losing party, is entitled to a rational explanation for the decision.

[9] This is a curious result. A desire to exclude judicial supervision has nothing to do with the exclusion of a right to be given reasons. Much of the motive power for the change in procedure came from those 'transnational' corporations whose disputes were conceived as standing above and outside the ordinary rules of domestic justice. It is precisely such disputes that will be of sufficient complexity to call for reasoned awards. Perhaps a sanction will lie in the fact that the arbitrators will know that reasons are expected of them, and that they cannot look to appointments in the future if the expectations are disappointed. It may be noted that the parties can apply by consent for an order for further reasons, even if there is an exclusion agreement, but this right applies only to reasons which are needed for the prosecution of an appeal: s. 1(5)(a).

2 The dispute is solely concerned with an issue or issues of fact.

3 The arbitrator has decided the issues of fact in such a way that the questions of law raised by the dispute have become academic.

4 Neither party had given notice, before the award was made, that a reasoned award would be required (unless there was 'some special reason' for not giving such a notice, in which case the Court has power to order that reasons shall be given)[10].

There is one qualification. The submission may expressly provide that the arbitrator shall make a reasoned award. Clearly, this agreement cannot be specifically enforced, in the sense that the Court will require the arbitrator to comply. On the other hand, if the arbitrator consents to act on terms that he will furnish reasons, he is in breach of his own relationship with the parties, and has also failed to comply with his mandate. This is a default for which the law should be able to find some remedy[11], even if only in the shape of a refusal to permit the arbitrator to retain his fee[12].

(b) Request for reasons

Where a party contemplates that he may wish to appeal, if the award is adverse, he will usually[13] give notice pursuant to section 1(6)(a) that a reasoned award will be required: for otherwise he may be out of court, if the arbitrator gives no reasons at all[14].

Such a request should always be accompanied by a formulation of the question of law upon which the party desires to appeal. Otherwise, the arbitrator may waste time by preparing findings which are not needed, and may also omit findings which are needed, so that the award has to be sent back under section 1(5)[15]. An insistence on the accurate formulation of the question whilst the matter is still before the arbitrator is a discipline which the parties and the arbitrator have to impose upon themselves. To pin down the applicant at the

---

[10] S. 1(6)(b).

[11] Cases decided in the first half of the nineteenth century, whilst the Court was developing the procedure which was later to obtain statutory recognition in the shape of the appeal by way of special case, suggest that a failure to give reasons in breach of the submission would rank as misconduct, sufficient to permit the setting-aside of the award. A modern court might hesitate to go so far. A party who has lost the arbitration without knowing why certainly has a grievance, but not sufficient to justify the Court in taking away from his opponent, who is not to blame, the benefit of the favourable award, and compelling him to start afresh. The alternative remedy of remission will not help, if the arbitrator continues to be recalcitrant.

[12] In strict theory, it is not easy to find a route to this conclusion, either through a contractual analysis of the mandate or by means of ss. 1, 13(3) or 23(1), which does not imperil the validity of the award itself. Moreover the consideration for a reference conducted to the stage of an award, albeit without the giving of reasons, can scarcely be said to have totally failed.

[13] We add this qualification because, just as under the old system, the party has to make a tactical decision on whether to ask for reasons. The preparation of a well-drafted reasoned award involves a good deal of work, which the arbitrator will not always greet with enthusiasm; and some arbitrators mistakenly regard the intimation of an appeal as a slight on their competence, or as a breach of the understanding in the trade that awards ought to be treated as binding. The party may hesitate to ask for reasons, if he believes that he will win the arbitration.

[14] Unless there was some special reason why he has not given such a notice: s. 1(6)(b).

[15] Another reason why the arbitrator should insist on the question being formulated is that if he gives reasons at large, he opens up the possibility that the losing party may, upon scrutiny of the award, find scope for arguing the law on a basis which had never been contemplated whilst the reference was in progress.

earliest opportunity to the question on which he wishes to appeal is an essential function of the arbitrator if there is not to be a discrepancy between the contents of his reasons and the information which the Court will need in order to determine the appeal.

We suggest that the request may properly be in a contingent form[16]. Thus the arbitrator may be asked to give reasons only if his decision is adverse to the party making the request[17], or to give reasons on point B only if he decides point A in a particular way.

(c) Costs of giving reasons

It will be noted that the new system involves a potential waste of effort which was not present under the former practice. If the arbitrator acceded to a request to state a special case, he knew that it was virtually certain to be set down for argument, and heard by the Court. This is not so, under the new system, since there is the possibility that the Court will refuse leave to appeal, thus leaving the reasons without any useful purpose. Common sense would suggest that in such an event the unsuccessful applicant ought to pay the wasted costs. The High Court does not, however, have any direct jurisdiction over the costs of the reference[18], and it may be that the arbitrator should deal separately in his award with the costs of preparing the reasons, and make alternative awards, to follow the success or failure of the application and any ultimate appeal[19].

(d) Requests for findings of fact

A practice which attracted particular criticism when the 1979 Act was in contemplation, was that whereby the legal advisers of the parties would submit to the arbitrator lists of findings which they wished to see included in the award. This had indeed reached proportions which could verge on the absurd. Nevertheless, it had its origin, not in the legislation, but in features of an appeal to one tribunal on facts found by another which cannot be legislated out of existence by a change in terminology.

Where the dispute concerns a single question of law, capable of being answered only by a clear-cut positive or negative, and turning on relatively few facts, the furnishing of reasons raises no serious problems. In most instances where an appeal is in contemplation the hearing will be conducted by lawyers

---

[16] The Act refers to a notice that a reasoned award 'would be required', not 'might be required', but the Court is likely to strain the language to achieve a sensible result.

[17] This is likely to provide a similar request from his opponent. The result may be that there is a mutual consent to the appeal, so that leave to appeal is no longer required: see s. 1(3)(a). Much will depend upon the precise wording of the requests, and the Court may well lean against an interpretation which takes aways its choice of the appeals which it will entertain: see *Bulk Oil (Zug) AG v Sun International Ltd* [1983] 1 Lloyd's Rep 655 at 659 (Bingham J) and [1983] 2 Lloyd's Rep 587 at 589, CA.

[18] The Court does have power to vary the award, when determining the substantive appeal, and this power embraces the award of costs: see p. 617, below. There is no similar power on the hearing of the application for leave.

[19] In many instances this will not be necessary for, if the arbitration is concerned with a single issue, failure on the appeal will leave the applicant with the responsibility for all the costs. If, however, the arbitration is more complex, it will be possible for the applicant to fail in the High Court and still save some of the costs of the reference.

who will conclude the proceedings with oral submissions on the evidence and the law. Each will emphasise those aspects of the evidence which are germane to the contention of law which he advances, and an arbitrator who keeps a careful note of the argument should have no great difficulty in identifying those matters of disputed or undisputed fact upon which the Court will need findings if it is to answer the question of law.

The task of the arbitrator at once becomes more difficult if the question admits of an intermediate answer, or if the answer depends upon a chain of contingencies as to how the facts are found. Here each advocate is likely to concentrate on the facts which are relevant to the solution most favourable to his client, and the arbitrator may not be able to obtain, from a consideration of the arguments alone, a complete picture of the findings which will be required to enable the Court to arrive at a final resolution of the dispute, whatever view of the law it may express. Furthermore, the arguments before the arbitrator may well take a different shape from that which they assume on the appeal, since the advocates cannot know in advance how the arbitrator will decide the essential primary facts. The arbitrator will therefore have to consider for himself how the case is likely to proceed in court, once the shape of the dispute has been finally determined by his findings on those essential facts. To a great extent it will be obvious what findings will be required, but a forecasting of everything that may turn out to be relevant, after a prolonged and detailed scrutiny in the High Court, is a difficult matter, even for an experienced professional arbitrator, and there is always the risk that however much care is taken, gaps will be left in the findings. In such an event, the Court will be forced either to decide the case on incomplete material, with a consequent risk of injustice, or to remit the award so that the arbitrator can fill the gaps, thereby wasting time and money, and requiring the arbitrator to address himself again to a matter which he may already have forgotten.

Broadly speaking, there are two ways to tackle this problem. The first, which prevailed under the old system, was for the Court to discourage applications to remit for further findings, leaving the loss to lie where it fell if a party could not point to findings in the award sufficient to enable him to succeed on the question of law. The Court would, however, intervene if it could be shown that the arbitrator had been asked to make the relevant findings, but had failed to do so. This practice encouraged the submission of written lists of draft findings, for two reasons. First, because this made it less likely that the arbitrator would omit a necessary finding through oversight, or failure to recognise its relevance. Second, because it enabled the party to convince the Court that the finding had been requested: a matter on which there could be a genuine difference of recollection, if oral submissions alone had been made to the arbitrator.

The alternative is for the Court to be more liberal in the grant of remission, so that the parties can safely leave it to the arbitrator to decide for himself what facts are likely to be required as the basis for an appeal. We suggest that this is the better approach, and that the Court should regard the interests of speed and simplicity in the making of the award as sufficient to outweigh the risk of delays by avoidable remissions[20], consistently with the shift of judicial policy as to the

---

[20] In two respects, the risk is less than before. First, because the need to obtain leave to appeal, administered in the manner prescribed by *The Nema* has reduced the number of appeals, and hence the number of occasions on which further findings may be required. There remains,

balance between the roles of the court and the arbitrator in relation to issues of law[1].

(e) Reasons for part of the award

Since the purpose of the reasons contemplated by the 1979 Act is not to inform the parties of the grounds upon which they have won and lost, but to place the Court in a position to decide an appeal, the arbitrator is not obliged[2] to give reasons for –

1 his findings of fact;

2 his decision on any issue which is not to be the subject of an appeal.

It is not unusual, where a dispute involves several issues, for the parties to desire an appeal on only one or some of them. In such a case, the arbitrator will be better advised simply to state his decision, without reasons, on those issues which are not intended to be the subject of an appeal. Otherwise, he may inadvertently leave the way open for an appeal by a party who, finding that he has lost, may think better of his original wish for a final determination[3].

3 What reasons should be given?

The 1979 Act calls for the arbitrator to state his reasons, not his reasoning. The practice should in general be as follows[4] –

1 The award should set out all the facts necessary for a decision by the Court on the question of law.

2 The award should not set out the evidence from which the arbitrator has deduced his findings of fact. These findings are not open to review, so that a statement of the evidence will serve no useful purpose. On the contrary, it may cause confusion, since the Court may not be sure how much of the evidence has been accepted by the arbitrator.

---

however, the possibility of a remission before leave is granted, so as to give the Court sufficient information to know whether leave should be granted. Second, because the Court has a new, and very useful power under s. 1(2)(b), when deciding the substantive appeal, to remit the award to the arbitrator in order that he shall give effect to the Court's opinion on the question of law. It is therefore no longer necessary for the Court to answer the question Yes or No, and hence to remit the award if the award contains insufficient reasons to permit such an answer with a consequential extra hearing in court. Instead the Court can simply give an opinion on the question based on alternative hypotheses of fact, and send it back to the arbitrator to find the extra facts, apply the opinion to them, and award accordingly.

[1] This approach is clearly displayed in the judgment of Donaldson LJ in *Bremer Handelsgesellschaft mbH v Westzucker GmbH (No 2)* [1981] 2 Lloyd's Rep 130. A number of subsequent decisions seem to indicate a return to the stricter approach, but should, we suggest, be limited to cases where the arbitrator's decision is said to be one which no reasonable arbitrator could reach, or to involve a finding of fact made without evidence to support it: *Athens Cape Naviera SA v Deutsche Dampfschiffahrtsgesellschaft 'Hansa' AG, The Barenbels* [1985] 1 Lloyd's Rep 528; *Mafracht v Parnes Shipping Co SA, The Apollonius* [1986] 2 Lloyd's Rep 405; *Universal Petroleum Co Ltd v Handels und Transport GmbH* [1987] 1 Lloyd's Rep 517, [1987] 1 WLR 1178.

[2] Unless an agreement to give reasons is part of his mandate: see p. 373, ante.

[3] This was the practice under the old system, and there seems two reasons why it should be modified in the light of the 1979 Act. It may be possible for the arbitrator to state his reasons for the decisions which were not notified to him as the likely subject of an appeal, in a manner which prevents them from ranking as 'Reasons', for the purposes of s. 1: see p. 596, post.

[4] See especially *Bremer v Westzucker*, ante, and *JH Rayner (Mincing Lane) Ltd v Shaher Trading Co* [1982] 1 Lloyd's Rep 632.

3 The arbitrator should explain briefly how he arrived at his own decision on the question of law. In particular, if his chain of reasoning includes a conclusion of mixed fact and law – for example that the contract was frustrated on a particular date, or that a notice was given within a reasonable time, the arbitrator should state his conclusion in the award, for then it will carry considerable weight on the hearing of the application for leave to appeal.

4 Where a party has argued for a finding of fact with which the arbitrator does not agree, the award should state explicitly that the allegation has not been proved. Otherwise there may be a suggestion that the matter has been accidentally overlooked.

5 If the arbitrator's conclusion is supported by more than one reason he should set out each of his reasons, and not just one. Unless this is done, there is a risk that, if the Court is minded to give leave to appeal on the one reason which he has given, the award may have to be remitted for further reasons on the point which he has not decided[5].

Under the system which prevailed before the 1979 Act, the special case always set out the question or questions of law to be decided by the Court, the answers to which determined the choice between the various alternative awards. There is no such requirement in relation to a reasoned award under the 1979 Act. Nevertheless, if the reasons are given pursuant to a notice under section 1(6), and if (as ought to happen) the notice identifies the questions of law upon which it is desired to appeal, or if they have been identified in oral argument, they ought to be reproduced in the award.

Awards in the form of a special case, under the old system, used frequently to contain a summary of the contentions advanced by the parties. Although there was nothing in the Act, or in the authorities, which made this mandatory, it was a useful practice because it helped to avoid argument about whether a point of law which it was desired to argue in the High Court had been raised before the arbitrator[6]. Equally, the new legislation is silent on the matter. We believe that on occasion it will be helpful for the arbitrator to summarise the arguments. This should not, however, be allowed to become a source of delay, or cause a lay arbitrator to seek legal assistance when he would otherwise have felt equal to expressing the award in his own words.

Before the 1979 Act, the practice had developed of drafting a special case according to a rigid structure, divided into sections headed 'Contentions', 'Findings', 'Recitals' and so on, all expressed in formal language. The preparation of such a case was felt by some arbitrators to be a daunting task which they should not attempt without help. There is nothing in the 1979 Act which explicitly calls for a more relaxed approach. Nevertheless, a new spirit has entered the law of arbitration since the 1979 Act came into force, and there is no doubt that the Court can be relied upon not to look askance at an award in everyday language[7]. Indeed, if the reasons are expressed in the shape of a chronological narrative, rather than as a series of groups of findings related to

---

[5] If this situation arises, the Court will admit evidence that there was another ground on which the arbitrator's decision might have been based, but this will be unlikely to avoid a remission unless it is clear that it could only have been decided in favour of the successful party: *Universal Petroleum Co Ltd v Handels und Transport GmbH* [1987] 1 Lloyd's Rep 517, [1987] 1 WLR 1178.

[6] And also because it helped to put the findings in context, and to explain apparent ambiguities.

[7] See especially per Donaldson LJ in *Bremer v Westzucker*, ante.

individual issues, the task of the Court will be much simplified, particularly on the hearing of the application for leave to appeal.

It must, however, be borne in mind that although the shape and mode of expression of a reasoned award under the new system may be different, the content of a reasoned award will not differ substantially from that of a special case. For example, although the award may no longer have a separate section headed 'Recitals', the material which was formerly grouped under this title ought nevertheless to be set out. Thus, the award ought to give particulars of the contract from which the dispute arose; of the arbitration agreement; of the arising of a dispute which fell within the agreement; of the manner in which the arbitrators were appointed, or (if the award is made by an umpire) of the fact that the arbitrators have disagreed and the umpire has entered on the reference; of the proceedings in the reference, whether they were written or oral, whether oral evidence was given, and so on. If the award may have to be enforced abroad, the inclusion of some at least of these particulars may be essential. Even if not, they ought to be included in order to foreclose disputes about jurisdiction, and to give the Court an immediate picture of the type of dispute in respect of which leave to appeal is being sought[8].

Again, although they may be differently expressed or arranged, the findings of fact which were previously required for an award in the form of a special case must all be included in a reasoned award under the new system. Moreover, although the arbitrator is encouraged to avoid legal jargon, clarity of expression is still essential.

4 Reasons given voluntarily

There is nothing in the Act to prevent the arbitrator from giving reasons of his own accord, even if not asked or ordered to do so and even if no appeal is in contemplation. Nor is there any ground upon which it could be said that an appeal does not lie from an award accompanied by voluntary reasons, even if the question of an appeal has never been mentioned until after the award is published[9]. There is, however, power to refuse leave to appeal, and failure to ask for reasons is an important factor in inducing the Court to refuse leave to appeal, particularly if the omission was deliberate.[10]

In practice, however, the risk that volunteering reasons may lead to an appeal has led to the continuation[11] of the old system, whereby reasons given voluntarily are kept off the face of the award, by formulae such as – 'These reasons do not

---

[8] So, for example, if the reference is conducted hastily, with a view to a quick award, the arbitrator should place the fact on record. So also with any other aspects of the arbitration, which the Court may wish to consider, when deciding whether to grant leave to appeal. The inclusion of introductory material is more, not less, important under the new and less rigid system, for the general shape of the reference may have a powerful influence on the exercise of the much wider jurisdiction to withhold leave to appeal.

[9] The Act could easily have retained the old practice, whereby the making of a request to the arbitrator in advance of the award was treated as a condition precedent to the ordering of a special case and hence to the exercise by the court of its power to hear an appeal; and indeed s. 1(6)(b) imposes just such a condition on the power to order reasons where none are given.

[10] See p. 607, post. A fortiori if the application for leave to appeal involves an application for further reasons under s. 1(5).

[11] With the approval of the Court: *Warde v Feedex International Inc* [1984] 1 Lloyd's Rep 310 at 315.

form part of my award, and may not be referred to in legal proceedings without my consent[12].

Occasionally circumstances may arise in which the arbitrator may think it appropriate to volunteer a reasoned award, without being requested to do so, in order to facilitate, or even to encourage an application for leave to appeal. In this situation he would be well advised to warn the parties that he proposes to do so, and he would need to be confident that there were good reasons for doing so if both parties requested him not to make a reasoned award. He should explain in the award why he has chosen to give reasons, otherwise the fact that no request for a reasoned award was made will tell against a party applying for leave to appeal[13].

5 Preliminary question of law

Where a party wishes to have a point of law decided as a preliminary issue he may, instead of asking for a reasoned interim award, apply directly to the Court under section 2 of the 1979 Act for the question of law to be determined. The Court has, however, no jurisdiction to entertain such an application without the consent either of the arbitrator or of all the parties, and even then has a discretion whether or not to entertain the application[14]. It is to be noted that the arbitrator does not initiate the application; he merely consents to it or not as the case may be. Moreover, his consent only becomes necessary when one of the parties opposes the application.

The arbitrator should not generally consent to an application which one of the parties intends to oppose, unless he considers that the decision on the point of law at that stage of the reference will save time or expense, or in some other way lead to the just and efficient resolution of the case[15]. Even when he is minded to consent, he would do well to consider and to suggest that the parties consider, whether the purpose might not be better served by an interim reasoned award[16]. The problem about a preliminary issue is that the Court cannot and will not decide a question of law without an underlying basis of fact. Since a preliminary issue involves no finding of fact which is binding on the parties or, for that matter, the arbitrator[17], the Court must either be asked to assume facts or simply be informed of the factual issues without any indication of the likely outcome. The more elaborate the facts the more artificial this approach, and a preliminary issue on a complicated dispute has a considerable potential for going wrong.

If the arbitrator consents to the use of the procedure he should produce a document very similar to a consultative case, but given some other name[18]. The form of this will depend upon the circumstances. It should however state all the

---

12 Formulae of this kind are effective to ensure that the Court cannot examine the reasons for the purpose of seeing whether they contain an error of law: *Mutual Shipping Corp v Bayshore Shipping Co, The Montan* [1985], 1 Lloyd's Rep 189, [1985] 1 WLR 625.

13 The arbitrator's explanation will be taken into account by the Court, but will not be decisive: see *Aden Refinery Co Ltd v Ugland Management Co Ltd* [1986] 2 Lloyd's Rep 336, [1987] QB 650 (reasons given voluntarily to resolve conflicting decisions among maritime arbitrators).

14 See further, pp. 620–626, post.

15 See p. 371, ante.

16 Particularly if the question concerns his procedural powers, rather than the merits of the dispute: see p 574, post.

17 *Fidelitas Shipping Co Ltd v V/O Exportchleb* [1965] 1 Lloyd's Rep 223, [1966] 1 QB 630.

18 Such as 'Request for a determination by the Court of a question of law'.

facts necessary for the decision, making it plain whether these are – (a) found by the arbitrator, (b) admitted by the parties, (c) assumed for the purposes of the application. The question of law should be clearly and specifically set out. The arbitrator may also think it helpful to include a summary of the contentions advanced before him – if indeed any have been advanced, which will not always be the case.

6 Reasons given outside the award

If the arbitrator decides that he is not under a duty to make a reasoned award, and that he should neither volunteer one nor consent to the determination of a preliminary question of law, he should nevertheless give his reasons for his award in a document which is separate from the award and expressed to be so. Whether he is under a legal obligation to do so, in the absence of express provision in the arbitration agreement to that effect, is debatable[19]. In some fields of arbitration the practice of giving reasons in a separate document is so universal that it may be said to have become an implied term of the arbitration agreement. In other fields this may be less clear.

Nevertheless an arbitrator ought always to explain, however briefly, the reasons for his decision even if he is not obliged in law to do so. Few things give greater dissatisfaction than losing an arbitration without being told why. Moreover, experience suggests that the process of expressing reasons in writing leads to better decisions than those which are based simply on 'feel'. Nothing exposes unsound reasoning more effectively than committing it to paper.

---

[19] See p. 373, ante, for a discussion of how law such as obligation might be enforced.

CHAPTER 26

Form and contents of award

The objects of an award are to inform the parties of the arbitrator's decision and to enable the successful party to enforce the award through the courts if the unsuccessful party fails to honour it. In this chapter we consider, under the headings 'Formal requirements' and 'Substantive requirements', how the award should be written in order to achieve these objects.

A. FORMAL REQUIREMENTS

Unless the arbitration agreement requires the award to be in a particular form, there are no formal requirements for a valid award under English law[1]. But in practice it is desirable that a number of simple formalities should be observed, since they may ease the task of enforcing the award through the courts[2] if that becomes necessary. The following points deserve mention:

1 Writing and signature

The award will normally be in writing and signed by the arbitrator, arbitrators or umpire, as the case may be. It is common, but not obligatory, for the signatures to be attested by a witness, who also signs. Where the award is made by more than one arbitrator, the arbitrators should execute it in the presence of each other, otherwise the award is invalid[3]. But if this is not done, the Court will remit the award for it to be properly executed[4]. In practice we believe that the rule is often ignored. It presents great practical problems, particularly with arbitrators in different countries, and seems to serve no useful purpose other than to ensure that the award is made by the arbitrators acting together. Given the ease of communications by modern methods it is very much open to doubt whether the rule is still good law[5].

2 Parties

The parties should be named and not merely referred to as, for example, 'the owners' or 'the buyers', unless the persons referred to by these expressions have

---

[1] Even an award by word of mouth will be enforced (see *Roberts v Watkins* (1863) 32 LJCP 291); but it must be communicated to the parties: *Thompson v Miller* (1867) 15 WR 353.

[2] Particularly foreign courts, where the formal requirements of a valid award may be stricter than in England.

[3] *Wade v Dowling* (1854) 4 E & B 44.

[4] *Anning v Hartley* (1858) 27 LJ Ex 145.

[5] *Bank Mellat v GAA Development and Construction Co* [1988] 2 Lloyd's Rep 44, and pp. 361–362, ante.

already been identified in the award[6]. Where the parties appear or have contracted through intermediaries, it is the parties themselves who should be named and not the intermediaries.

3 Recitals

Awards often contain recitals, in which the arbitrator sets out the nature of the dispute and the circumstances in which he has come to be adjudicating upon it. From the point of view of the English court, these recitals add nothing[7]; and indeed they may be a source of confusion and dispute, if they are inaccurate[8]. The most that can be said for them is that they may serve to persuade a foreign court that the award is prima facie within the arbitrator's jurisdiction. We suggest, however, that they should be kept short, and an arbitrator would not be wrong to omit them altogether[9].

4 Date

Except when the arbitration agreement contains an express time limit for the making of the award, or in the case of an award remitted under section 22 of the 1950 Act or under section 1 of the 1979 Act[10], an arbitrator or umpire has power to make an award at any time; so his jurisdiction is not affected by the date on which the award is made[11]. But it is still usual for awards to be dated, and in the case of an award for the payment of a sum of money it is desirable for the award to be dated so as to fix the time from which interest on the award is to run under section 20 of the Act[12].

5 Publication

Arbitration awards are not public documents and do not require registration or any other form of publication to the world at large[13]. Nor, unless the arbitration agreement requires it[14], is publication to the parties necessary to the validity of an award. But for obvious reasons, the arbitrator invariably writes to the parties

---

6 *Gabela v Aris (Owners)* (1927) 29 Ll L Rep 289.

7 Thus, an award is not invalid for excess of jurisdiction merely because it recites the submission too narrowly: *Thames Iron Works and Shipbuilding Co Ltd v R* (1869) 20 LT 318, or fails to recite that the arbitrators disagreed before the umpire entered on the reference: *Sprigens v Nash* (1816) 5 M & S 193. Conversely, an arbitrator cannot, by reciting the submission too widely, give himself a jurisdiction which he does not really possess: *Price v Popkin* (1839) 10 Ad & El 139. See also *Harlow v Read* (1845) 1 CB 733; *Paull v Paull* (1833) 2 Cr & M 235; *Re Addison and Spittle* (1848) 18 LJQB 151; *White v Sharp* (1844) 12 M & W 712.

8 As in *TA Ruf & Co v Pauwels* [1919] 1 KB 660, where there was an apparent contradiction between a recital and the substantive award.

9 See per Parke B in *Baker v Hunter* (1847) 16 M & W 672 at 674.

10 When an arbitrator must make his award within three months after the date of the order remitting the award, unless the order otherwise directs.

11 S. 13(1) of the Act. In the two cases mentioned, the Court has power to enlarge the time for making an award, whether that time has expired or not: see s. 13(2).

12 See post, p. 389.

13 Unless this is required by the arbitration agreement.

14 'Publication' and 'delivery' are now so rarely required by the arbitration agreement that the old cases on these topics are now considered obsolete.

informing them that he has made his award, and indicating that it is available for collection, on payment of the costs of the award.

6 Stamp

An award does not attract stamp duty[15].

B. SUBSTANTIVE REQUIREMENTS

The Court will not enforce an award unless it is –
1 cogent;
2 complete;
3 certain;
4 final;
5 enforceable.
These expressions are not self-explanatory, and they are discussed in some detail in the following pages[16].

1 Cogency

Although it is not necessary for the arbitrator to use technical expressions when drafting his award[17], it is essential that the document contains an adjudication on the matter in dispute, and not merely an expression of expectation, hope or opinion[18]. By far the best course is for the arbitrator to express money awards in the form of an order that one party shall pay the specified sum to the other, and to express declaratory awards in the form of a bald statement of the position as the arbitrator considers it to be. Thus, the award should say 'I award that the buyer is entitled to reject the goods', not 'I consider that the seller ought to accept the return of the goods'.

2 Completeness

A final award should contain an adjudication on all the disputes submitted to the arbitrator. An award which disposes of some of those disputes and leaves others of them undecided, or leaves it in doubt as to any of them whether they were meant to be and have been decided or not, cannot be maintained[19].

It is not, however, necessary for the award to deal separately with all the

---

[15] Finance Act 1949, s. 35, Sch 8.
[16] See post, pp. 384–388.
[17] *Matson v Trower* (1824) Ry & M 17; *Lock v Vulliamy* (1833) 5 B & Ad 600. See also *Andrea v British Italian Trading Co Ltd* [1962] 1 Lloyd's Rep 151 at 161 generally on the approach of the Court to non-technical awards. We think that the Court would nowadays go to some lengths to avoid declaring an award invalid merely because on a strict reading it is not entirely cogent.
[18] *Lock v Vulliamy*, supra: suggestion in an award (otherwise in favour of the respondent) that a sum should be paid 'to meet the circumstances of the case in liberal manner', held unenforceable. *Smith v Hartley* (1851) 20 LJCP 169 is sometimes cited as authority for the view that an award in the form of a request is valid. We doubt this. The case turned on the construction of the pleading, not of the award.
[19] *Wakefield v Llanelly Rly and Dock Co* (1865) 3 De GJ & Sm 11, per Turner LJ: *Re O'Conor and Whitlaw's Arbitration* (1919) 88 LJKB 1242.

matters in dispute. It is sufficient if it can be demonstrated that the arbitrator has taken into consideration all the matters submitted to his judgment in arriving at his conclusion[20]. Thus, for example, it is permissible for the arbitrator to make a single lump sum award in respect of a series of claims[20] unless, of course, the submission expressly or impliedly requires separate awards[1]. The arbitrator may, however, feel that the parties would prefer him to deal separately with the various items of claim, so that they can see who has succeeded on each of them, and he would not be wrong to do so. Where there are claims and cross-claims, it may be sufficient to award simply a balance of account without dealing specifically with the cross-claims[2]. But it will be safer to make an explicit award on the cross-claims. The question whether an award deals with all the matters in dispute must, of course, depend upon the extent of the questions which were submitted to the arbitrator; so that an award which would be valid and complete under one form of submission would be incomplete in the context of another[3]. Thus, for example, if a buyer has rejected goods on the ground of alleged defects, and claims damages for non-delivery and in the alternative damages for defective delivery, with a cross-claim by the seller for the price, an arbitrator to whom the whole dispute has been submitted must not only decide whether the rejection is justified, but must also award on the monetary claims[4]. But if the only matter referred is whether the rejection was justified, then a money award would be bad for excess of jurisdiction[5].

The arbitrator need not decide every issue falling within the strict wording of the submission, if by the time that he comes to deal with the matter some of the issues are no longer left to him for decision[6].

Under section 14 of the 1950 Act, the arbitrator has power to make a valid interim award dealing with only part of the dispute. If the arbitrator decides to exercise this power, he should frame the award in such a way as to make it clear what it is intended to be, so that the parties or the Court do not mistake his interim award for an incomplete, and hence invalid, final award[7]. Thus, the arbitrator could head the award 'Interim Award' and recite in the award that it is intended to be of an interim nature.

Since the validity of an apparently incomplete award may depend upon exactly what was submitted to the arbitrator, the Court will admit evidence as to the scope of the submission[8]. It seems that in the absence of contrary evidence, it will be presumed that the award is complete, and this presumption will be

---

[20] *Aitcheson v Cargey* (1824) 2 Bing 199, per Best CJ at 204; *Wrightson v Bywater* (1838) 3 M & W 199; *Wynne v Edwards* (1844) 12 M & W 708; *Whitworth v Hulse* (1866) LR 1 Exch 251.

[1] As in cases such as *Ellis v Desilva* (1881) 6 QBD 521.

[2] *Whitworth v Hulse*, ante; *Jewell v Christie* (1867) LR 2 CP 296 and *Compagnie Financière pour le Commerce Extérieur SA v Oy Vehna AB* [1963] 2 Lloyd's Rep 178.

[3] See, for example, *Hindley & Co v Crosby Trading Co* (1923) 15 Ll L Rep 177; *JF Robertson & Co v AT James & Co* (1923) 16 Ll L Rep 34, affd 17 Ll L Rep 102, *Lambert and Krzysiak Ltd v British Commercial Overseas Co Ltd* (1923) 16 Ll L Rep 51, *Wrightson v Bywater*, ante.

[4] See *Heyworth v Hutchinson* (1867) LR 2 QB 447.

[5] *Sinidino, Ralli & Co v Kitchen & Co* (1883) Cab & El 217; *Lambert and Krzysiak Ltd v British Commercial Overseas Co Ltd*, ante, at 178.

[6] *Rees v Waters* (1847) 16 M & W 263; *Hawksworth v Brammall* (1840) 5 My & Cr 281; *Abraham and Westminster Improvements Co* (1849) 14 LTOS 203.

[7] Cf. *Heaven and Kesterton v Etablissements Francois Albiac & Cie* [1956] 2 Lloyd's Rep 316.

[8] See *Obaseki Bros v Reif & Son* [1952] 2 Lloyd's Rep 364; *Day v Bonnin* (1836) 3 Bing NC 219; *Duke of Beaufort v Welch* (1839) 10 Ad & El 527; and the cases cited ante.

reinforced if the arbitrator expressly states in his award that he has taken into account all matters submitted to him[9].

The Court will normally remit to an arbitrator an award which is defective on the ground of incompleteness. In some of the older cases the Court set the award aside: but these were decided before there was power to remit, and it is plainly more convenient that the award should be put right by the person who is already seized of the issues[10].

3 Certainty

It must be possible to ascertain from the award precisely what decision the arbitrator has reached in relation to the matters in dispute. An award which is uncertain is invalid[11]. When applying this principle, regard must be paid to the scope of the submission, and it is possible that an award which, to an outsider, might appear uncertain, is nevertheless clear enough to the parties to be a valid adjudication[12].

An award which contains inconsistent adjudications is bad for uncertainty[13].

If all the materials for identifying the precise adjudication are present on the face of the award, it will be valid, even though the arbitrator has not himself made the adjudication in the award[14]. Thus, for example, if he awards that damages are to be paid at a stated rate on a stated quantity of goods, the award is good even though the arbitrator does not set out the result of the calculation in his award. But if the damages are to be based on a quantity which is not

9   *Aitcheson v Cargey*, ante; *Jewell v Christie*, ante; *Day v Bonnin*, supra; *Re Brown and Croydon Canal Co* (1839) 9 Ad & El 522.

10   *Lambert and Krzysiak Ltd v British Commercial Overseas Co Ltd* (1923) 16 Ll L Rep 51; *Panchaud Frères SA v Pagnan and Fratelli* [1974] 1 Lloyd's Rep 394.

11   *Re Marshall and Dresser* (1843) 3 QB 878; *Smith v Hartley* (1851) 20 LJCP 169; *Re Tribe and Upperton* (1835) 3 Ad & El 295; *Simpson v IRC* [1914] 2 KB 842; *Hopcraft v Hickman* (1824) 2 Sim & St 130; *Margulies Bros Ltd v Dafnis Thomaides & Co (UK) Ltd* [1958] 1 Lloyd's Rep 250 at 253; *River Plate Products Netherlands BV v Etablissement Coargrain* [1982] 1 Lloyd's Rep 628.

12   *Waddle v Downman* (1844) 12 M & W 562 (award that the defendant should pay 'such sum as the same amounts to according to the present price of pig-iron.': this was explained by Cresswell J in *Gordon v Whitehouse* (1856) 18 CB 747 at 755–756 as one example of the maxim id certum, but we think that it was really a case on a construction of the submission: see the observation of Williams J in *Gordon v Whitehouse*); *Plummer v Lee* (1837) 2 M & W 495 (award of interest from 'the date of the last settlement': good, because the parties were not in dispute about what the date was); *Round v Hatton* (1842) 10 M & W 660; *Wrightson v Bywater* (1838) 3 M & W 199; *Wohlenberg v Lageman* (1815) 6 Taunt 251 (award that the plaintiff and the defendant should pay a debt in proportion to their shares in a ship, but not stating what the shares were; good, because the shares were not in dispute); *Nickels v Hancock* (1855) 7 De GM & G 300 (award that certain deed should be set aside 'if and in so far as' the arbitrator had jurisdiction: bad). See also *Hewitt v Hewitt* (1841) 1 QB 110; *Fabrica Lombarda Di Acido Tartarico v Fuerst Bros Ltd* (1921) 8 Ll L Rep 57.

13   Semble, *Seccombe v Babb* (1840) 6 M & W 129; *Williams v Moulsdale* (1840) 7 M & W 134; *Grenfell v Edgecombe* (1845) 7 QB 661; *Duke of Beaufort v Welch* (1839) 10 Ad & El 527; *Ames v Milward* (1818) 8 Taunt 637.

14   We doubt whether this principle extends beyond the case of 'mere arithmetic' contemplated in *Higgins v Willes* (1828) 3 Man & Ry KB 382 and *Margulies v Thomaides*, ante, at 253. Most of the cases usually cited in support of the proposition were really concerned with the construction of the submission: see note 12.

stated, or if the arbitrator merely directs the losing party to pay damages, without saying how much is to be paid[15] the award will usually[16] be bad[17].

The Court will refuse to enforce an award which is uncertain. In addition, it will either set the award aside or remit it, depending upon the degree and nature of the uncertainty[18]. Where one part of the award is valid, and the remainder is uncertain, it may be possible to enforce the valid parts, whilst setting aside or remitting the remainder[19].

4 Finality

The arbitrator should dispose of all the issues himself, and should not leave some of them to be decided by a third party: for if he does, the award is not final, and is invalid[20]. There is a possible exception to this principle, where the decision reserved is of a 'ministerial' rather than a judicial character. If this distinction still exists, it is of a very limited application, and the arbitrator should not rely upon it, but should decide all the issues himself[1]. Not only should the arbitrator avoid the delegation of issues to third parties, but he should also take care not to reserve matters for his own future decision, for his award will be bad for want of finality[2]: unless, of course, he wishes to issue an interim award, in which case he should make it clear what the award is intended to do[3].

5 Enforceability

If the terms of the submission are such as to call for a money award, the award should be in such a form as to be enforceable by action or under section 26 of the 1950 Act [4]. Thus, if the award deals with liability but not quantum, or with

---

[15] *Montrose Canned Foods Ltd v Eric Wells (Merchants) Ltd* [1965] 1 Lloyd's Rep 597.

[16] Except in the type of case where the submission does not require a complete adjudication: see note 12, ante.

[17] For the remedy in such a case see pp. 556–557, post.

[18] As mentioned above, we think it likely that a court would nowadays remit an award, rather than set it aside, where the defect consists of incompleteness. No doubt the same approach would be adopted in a case of uncertainty, where the uncertainty arises from the fact that the arbitrator has failed to include in his award all the data for the quantification of the sum awarded – e.g. where he awards a rate of damages per ton of goods without stating the tonnage. In such a case the uncertainty really differs little from mere incompleteness (see ante) and the award will no doubt be sent back for completion. But if the award were so contradictory as to be unintelligible, the Court would be more likely to order a completely fresh start.

[19] Semble, *Miller v de Burgh* (1850) 4 Exch 809. But this is not so if the valid part is inextricably linked to the part which is invalid.

[20] *Tomlin v Fordwich Corpn* (1836) 5 Ad & El 147; *Johnson v Latham* (1850) 19 LJQB 329; *Re Goddard & Mansfield* (1850) 19 LJQB 305; *Dresser v Finnis* (1855) 25 LTOS 81.

[1] Apart from a few isolated instances (e.g. *Thorp v Cole* (1835) 2 Cr M & R 367, and dicta that it is permissible to order that the form of conveyances shall be settled by counsel: but see *Re Tandy and Tandy* (1814) 9 Dowl 1044), the only application of this rule has been to the taxation of costs. This is now dealt with by the 1950 Act.

[2] Or completeness: the two points are almost indistinguishable.

[3] *Stockport Metropolitan Borough Council v O'Reilly* [1978] 1 Lloyd's Rep 595.

[4] *Margulies Bros v Dafnis Thomaides & Co (UK) Ltd* [1958] 1 Lloyd's Rep 250; *Oricon Waren-Handelsgesellschaft mbH v Intergraan NV* [1967] 2 Lloyd's Rep 82 at 98. The statement in the text relates, as do the cases cited, to money awards. But it goes further than this. The arbitrator has power under s. 15 to order specific performance, and such an order should also be made in an enforceable form: see p. 389, post.

quantum but not liability[5]; or if it purports to award a sum of money without saying what the sum is or giving sufficient detail to enable the sum to be calculated from the materials on the face of the award, it will be sent back to the arbitrator. It should, however, be noted that an award which is unenforceable is not necessarily invalid, in the sense of being completely ineffective. Thus, for example –

1 If the submission expressly or impliedly permits the arbitrator to make a declaratory order, an award of a declaration is valid even though it cannot be enforced under section 26. Thus, for example, if the question referred to arbitration is whether goods should be 'invoiced back' to the seller at a particular price, an order to this effect is valid, even though it cannot be turned directly into a money judgment. But if the question is whether the buyer (or seller) is entitled to recover a particular sum, the arbitrator should make a money award, and should not simply order invoicing back[6].

2 Even if an award is not enforceable, it may still amount to an adjudication on the merits, and may thus make everything, except the precise amount due to the successful party, res judicata between the parties[7].

3 The fact that an award is not enforceable under section 26 'in the same manner as a judgment or order to the like effect', does not prevent the award from giving rise to enforceable legal obligations, breach of which entitles the claimant to a remedy in damages[8].

C. REASONS

The questions of whether an award must contain reasons and if so in what form, and whether, if reasons are not compulsory, they should nevertheless be given, either in the award or in some other document is discussed in Chapter 25[9].

D. RELIEF AND REMEDIES

The forms of relief and remedies available to the arbitrator when making his award[10] are largely the same as those available in the High Court, although it must be remembered that the power of executing awards by committal, writ of fieri facias, sequestration, etc. lies with the Court and not with the arbitrator. The following forms of relief and remedies are discussed below –

1 Awards for the payment of money.

---

[5] *Re Willesden Local Board and Wright* [1896] 2 QB 412 at 417.

[6] *Oricon v Intergraan*, ante, at 98. There are several reported examples of awards for invoicing back, where no objection was taken. We suggest that the rule concerning enforceability is really no more than an illustration of the rules that awards must be cogent, certain, and dispose of all the matters referred.

[7] See pp. 409–414, post.

[8] *Dalmia Cement Ltd v National Bank of Pakistan* [1974] 2 Lloyd's Rep 98, [1975] QB 9; *Dalmia Dairy Industries Ltd v National Bank of Pakistan* [1978] 2 Lloyd's Rep 223. The award could not be enforced as a judgment because it provided for payment of money in India, but the claimant recovered the equivalent of the sum awarded as damages.

[9] See pp. 373 et seq., ante.

[10] The various types of interlocutory relief available during the course of the reference are discussed ante at pp. 322–343.

2 Specific performance.
3 Injunctions.
4 Declaratory relief.
5 Indemnity.
6 Interest.
7 Dissolution of partnership.
The question of costs is dealt with separately in section E at p. 394.

1 Awards for the payment of money

An award that A shall pay B a sum of money, whether as debt or damages, is probably the most common type of award. Unless the award otherwise directs, such an award carries interest from the date of the award[11]. The rate is the same as for a judgment debt[12] and this rate cannot be altered, although the arbitrator has power to order that the award shall not carry interest[13].

An arbitrator has power to order payment of a sum in foreign currency[14] and it is no longer necessary for such an award to be converted into sterling for the purpose of enforcement as a judgment[15].

2 Specific performance

Section 15 of the Act provides that 'unless a contrary intention is expressed therein, every arbitration agreement shall, where such a provision is applicable to the reference, be deemed to contain a provision that the arbitrator or umpire shall have the same power as the High Court[16] to order specific performance of any contract other than a contract relating to land or any interest in land'.

The power conferred by this section does not, however, give the award the same force as an order of the High Court: it is still necessary to bring an action on the award or to apply for an order under section 26 of the Act for leave to enforce the award in the same manner as a judgment or order, before an award of specific performance can be enforced by sequestration or committal.

Since the award must be in a form capable of enforcement as a judgment, an award which requires a person to do an act must specify the time within which the act is to be done, unless the order is for the payment of money, possession of land, or delivery of goods[17].

---

[11] S. 20 of the Act.

[12] See s. 17 of the Judgments Act 1838 and s. 44 of the Administration of Justice Act 1970. The rate which applies is the rate under the Order in Council under the Judgment Act at the date of the award, regardless of any later Order in Council altering the rate, and the Court has no power to alter the rate: *Rocco Giuseppe & Figli v Tradax Export SA* [1983] 2 Lloyd's Rep 434, [1984] 1 WLR 742.

[13] *Timber Shipping Co SA v London and Overseas Freighters Ltd* [1971] 1 Lloyd's Rep 523.

[14] *Jugoslavenska Oceanska Plovidba v Castle Investment Co Inc* [1973] 2 Lloyd's Rep 1, [1974] QB 292; *Services Europe Atlantique Sud (SEAS) v Stockholms Rederiaktiebolag Svea, The Folias* [1979] 1 Lloyd's Rep 1, [1979] AC 685. The power may, however, be excluded by the terms of the submission: *The Teh Hu* [1969] 2 Lloyd's Rep 365, [1970] P 106. The question of which currency is appropriate in any given case forms part of the substantive law and lies outside the scope of this book.

[15] *Miliangos v George Frank (Textiles) Ltd* [1976] 1 Lloyd's Rep 201, [1976] AC 443. It is only at the stage of execution that any question of conversion arises.

[16] As to which, see Fry, *Specific Performance.*

[17] RSC Ord. 42, r. 2.

3 Injunction

There would seem to be no reason in principle why an arbitrator should not be given power to make an award in the form of an interim or final injunction[18]. But the essence of relief by way of injunction is that it should be available quickly, and such an award cannot be enforced by way of committal until the appropriate steps have been taken to have it enforced as a judgment[19]. The better course for a party seeking an injunction is therefore to begin an action on his claim in the High Court and to apply for an interim injunction[20]. If the defendant to the action applies for a stay[1] and is successful, the Court has power under section 12 of the Act to grant an interim injunction pending the outcome of the arbitration[2].

4 Declaratory relief

An arbitrator has power to make an award declaring what the rights of the parties are, and in some cases the arbitrator's power may be limited by the terms of the submission to making such an award. Thus, if an arbitrator is appointed to decide 'whether the buyer was entitled to reject the goods', he may award 'that the buyer was not entitled to reject the goods' but cannot go on to award damages for wrongful rejection.

The power to make a declaratory award is of great value where a dispute has arisen about the meaning of a contract or a lease[3] which still has some time to run, and where the dispute can be expected to recur in the future. But the arbitrator should beware of being lured into deciding hypothetical questions on an assumed basis of fact, remembering that he only has jurisdiction to decide bona fide disputes and that his award may simply give rise to further disagreement if the assumed facts later turn out to be wrong[4].

5 Indemnity

An arbitrator has power to declare that one party is entitled to be indemnified by the other against liability or expenditure incurred by him. This form of award is of particular value where the liability has not been established or the expenditure has not been incurred or cannot be properly assessed at the date of the award. But if the arbitrator is to retain power to decide disputes as to the scope of the indemnity and to make further money awards of any amount found due under the indemnity, he should make it clear that his award is an interim award[5].

---

[18] *Birtley and District Co-operative Society v Windy Nook and District Industrial Co-operative Society (No 2)* [1960] 2 QB 1, [1959] 2 WLR 415. The proviso to s. 12 of the Act seems to contemplate that an arbitrator may be given power to make an award in the form of an interim injunction. But it is doubtful whether the power to make awards in the form of injunctions is to be implied in the usual forms of arbitration agreement: see *Chandris v Isbrandtsen-Moller* [1951] 1 KB 240 at 262, per Tucker LJ.
[19] See Chapter 28, post.
[20] *Foster and Dicksee v Hastings Corpn* (1903) 87 LT 736.
[1] Under s. 4 of the Act or under s. 1 of the 1975 Act.
[2] See pp. 329–330, ante.
[3] Rent review arbitrations usually result in nothing more than a declaration.
[4] See the notes to Ord. 15, r. 16 in the *Supreme Court Practice* ('The White Book').
[5] The reasons for this are discussed in Chapter 25, ante.

6 Interest

The power of an arbitrator to award interest is to a large extent governed by statute, under section 19A of the Arbitration Act 1950[6]. There may, however, be occasions when the statutory powers are inadequate to compensate the claimant for his real loss from being out of pocket, and in such cases it may be necessary to resort to powers which exist independently of section 19A.

(a) Section 19A of the Act of 1950

The statutory power to award interest is conferred by sub-section (1) of section 19A of the 1950 Act, which is in the following terms –

'Unless a contrary agreement is expressed therein, every arbitration agreement shall, where such a provision is applicable to the reference[7], be deemed to contain a provision that the arbitrator or umpire may, if he thinks fit, award simple interest at such rate as he thinks fit –

(a) on any sum which is the subject of the reference but which is paid before the award, for such period ending not later than the date of payment as he thinks fit; and
(b) on any sum which he awards, for such period ending not later than the date of the award as he thinks fit.'

The statutory power may be excluded by express agreement, but clear words are necessary to achieve this result. Probably nothing short of an express reference to the statutory power will suffice: anything less will be assumed to exclude only a right to interest under the contract[8].

The power to award interest applies not only to a sum in respect of which the arbitrator has made an award, but also to a sum which is paid before the award. But in the latter case the sum must be 'the subject of the reference': the effect of this is that there is no statutory power to award interest on any sum which has been paid before the reference has begun[9]. This presents a creditor with a problem. If he is offered payment of a sum of money after the time when it should have been paid, but without interest, he will lose the ability to recover

---

[6] Inserted by the Administration of Justice Act 1982, s. 15(6) and Sch. 1, Part IV. The section has retrospective effect: *Food Corpn of India v Marastro Compania Naviera SA, The Trade Fortitude* [1986] 2 Lloyd's Rep 209, [1987] 1 WLR 134.

[7] The purpose of introducing this qualification is unclear. It appears to envisage the case where the reference involves a claim for a sum of money (for otherwise the section has no application at all) but the power to award interest is nevertheless inapplicable. It is difficult to imagine when such a case could arise, although there might well be cases when it would be inappropriate to exercise the power.

[8] *Socony Mobil Oil Co Inc v West of England Ship Owners Mutual Insurance Association Ltd, The Padre Island (No 2)* [1987] 2 Lloyd's Rep 529.

[9] The enactment of section 19A resulted from Report No 88 of the Law Commission (Cmnd. 729), which stated that the inability to recover interest on sums paid before proceedings were commenced was one of its major criticisms of the law which then governed an award of interest, s. 1 of the Law Reform (Miscellaneous Provisions) Act 1934. The Law Commission recommended the replacement of the discretion to award interest by a statutory right to interest, with minor exceptions, on all monetary obligations including damages. This solution was not adopted by the legislature, but the debates in Parliament yield no explanation, beyond the fact that there was a strong difference of opinion among the various bodies whom the Government had consulted about the proposal.

interest under section 19A if he accepts it: it will probably not assist him if he reserves his right to claim interest[10], for the section requires that the principal sum, not the interest on it, shall be the subject of the reference[11]. If the debtor has not appropriated the sum, the creditor may consider appropriating the payment first to interest and then to the principal sum which he claims: but it is by no means clear that a creditor has the right to appropriate payment to interest which is not due until the arbitrator has exercised his discretion to award it. Another possibility is to decline to accept the payment unless interest is paid on it, and to refer the claim for principal and interest to arbitration. This will give the arbitrator jurisdiction to award interest, and the creditor will not be at risk of paying the costs on the grounds that the debtor has tendered payment[12]. But it may be unattractive on commercial grounds to turn down an offer of immediate payment: and in any event the transfer of money may be complete before any decision can be taken to intercept it. If none of the previous expedients can be adopted, the claimant will have to fall back on a claim outside the terms of the statute, in one of the ways discussed below.

The rate of interest is a matter within the discretion of the arbitrator. In principle the discretion ought not to be exercised with the object of penalising the losing party, but only for the purpose of compensating the claimant for not having had the benefit of the money between the date when it ought to have been paid and the date of the award or earlier payment[13]. There is, however, an important limitation on the arbitrator's statutory power to compensate the claimant, which is that the award must be of simple interest, not compound. Where the claimant has had to finance the loss of the money due to him by borrowing in the market, he will usually himself be charged compound interest or have been obliged to make further borrowings to pay the interest on the amount he has borrowed. It is difficult to see how an award of simple interest can be made to compensate the claimant for his loss in this type of case, unless the rate of simple interest is increased so as to yield the same money sum that an award of compound interest at the market rate would have yielded: but this is implicitly ruled out by the fact that the section refers expressly to simple interest[14].

Where the sum on which interest is claimed has been paid between the commencement of the reference and the date of the award, the arbitrator may only award interest up to the date of payment. There is no power under section 19A to award further interest on the interest unpaid at the date of payment.

---

[10] See, however, *Edmunds v Lloyd Italico* [1986] 1 Lloyd's Rep 326, [1986] 1 WLR 492.

[11] There may, moreover, be a theoretical objection, quite apart from the provisions of s. 19A, to the arbitrator assuming jurisdiction over a claim for interest on money paid before he was appointed, since, unless the claim for interest can be treated as a distinct subject matter of arbitration falling within the terms of the arbitration clause, it is difficult to see how he could ever be seised of it.

[12] Tender of the sum due after the time for payment does not support a plea of tender: *Dixon v Clark* (1848) 5 CB 365. A fortiori where it is unaccompanied by an offer to pay interest.

[13] *Kemp v Tolland* [1956] 2 Lloyd's Rep 681 at 691. A detailed discussion of the principles involved is to be found in McGregor on *Damages*.

[14] Arbitrators who are conscious of the difficulty may try to get round it by erring on the side of generosity in the rate of simple interest which they award. To do so explicitly would, however, invite a challenge to the award, and where the sum has been outstanding for a long time the increase may have to be so great, if it is to reproduce exactly an award of compound interest, that this may in itself invite challenge.

(b) Interest apart from statute

Sub-section 19A(2) of the 1950 Act provides that the statutory power to award interest conferred by the section is without prejudice to any other power of an arbitrator or umpire to award interest. Four other powers to award interest call for consideration.

1 Interest may be recovered at common law as special damages for the late payment of money. The general rule, that interest is not recoverable as general damages[15], is now so well established as to be beyond challenge[16]. It rests upon the legal presumption that in the usual course of events a person does not suffer any loss by reason of the late payment of money: accordingly a claimant is not entitled to recover interest as damages for late payment merely by alleging and proving that the money was paid late. The presumption is, however, rebuttable[17] by proof that the loss was within the reasonable contemplation of the parties and in fact resulted from the late payment of the sum claimed[18]. On proof of these matters the claimant has a legal right to interest as damages: it is not simply a matter for the arbitrator's discretion. Moreover, the right to interest as damages is not circumscribed by any of the limitations imposed by section 19A of the 1950 Act on the arbitrator's discretion to award interest. Among the consequences of this, two may in particular be noted.

First, the award of damages may be for compound interest, if that represents the true measure of the claimant's loss.

Second, the claim for interest as damages for late payment is an independent legal right which is capable of being referred to arbitration even though the principal sum claimed has already been paid, provided the arbitration clause is in terms which are apt to cover such a claim.

2 Interest is recoverable as of right if there is an express or implied term of the contract or arbitration agreement to that effect.

3 Equity has power to award compound interest where profits resulting from a breach of fiduciary duty have been used for business purposes[19].

4 An arbitrator has power to award simple interest on any claim for a sum

---

[15] I.e. loss which is presumed to result to the plaintiff in the ordinary course of events, in contrast to special damages, which must be specifically pleaded and proven as having been foreseeable and as having in fact resulted from the defendant's wrongdoing.

[16] It has the authority of two decisions of the House of Lords: *London, Chatham and Dover Railway Co v South Eastern Railway Co* [1893] AC 429 and *President of India v La Pintada Navigacion Co SA, La Pintada* [1984] 2 Lloyd's Rep 9, [1985] AC 104. Cf. *Cook v Fowler* (1874) LR 7 HL 27. The rule is limited to claims in respect of interest: *President of India v Lips Maritime Corpn, The Lips* [1987] 2 Lloyd's Rep 311.

[17] Probably without much difficulty in most commercial arbitrations, provided the claimant remembers to take the necessary procedural steps to plead and prove the claim for interest as a claim for special damages. See, for example, *Department of the Environment for Northern Ireland v Farrans (Construction) Ltd* (1981) 19 BLR 1.

[18] *Wadsworth v Lydall* [1981] 1 WLR 598; *La Pintada*, supra, as explained in *International Minerals and Chemical Corpn v Karl O Helm AG* [1986] 1 Lloyd's Rep 81, *Knibb and Knibb v National Coal Board* [1986] 3 WLR 895, [1987] QB 906, and *The Lips*, supra, in the Court of Appeal [1987] 1 Lloyd's Rep 131 (not overruled on this point by the House of Lords). If Lord Brandon's reference in *La Pintada* to the distinction between general and special damages were misunderstood as referring to the distinction between the first and second rules in *Hadley v Baxendale*, and not to the distinction drawn above, this would lead to the absurd conclusion that loss of interest would not be recoverable as damages where it was obviously foreseeable within the first rule, but only when the loss was foreseeable because of special circumstances bringing it within the second rule.

[19] *O'Sullivan v Management Agency and Music Ltd* [1985] QB 428, [1984] 3 WLR 448.

in respect of which he makes an award, if the claim is one which falls within the Admiralty jurisdiction of the High Court[20].

(c) Power to review the exercise of a discretion as to interest

Although the power to award interest under section 19A is discretionary, it ought ordinarily to be awarded; if the arbitrator decides not to award interest he should give his reasons for doing so in the award. It is prima facie misconduct to award a sum of money without awarding interest for delay in payment and unless the award contains a sufficient explanation for not awarding interest it will be remitted for the question of interest to be reconsidered[1]. If the failure to award interest is an oversight, the arbitrator has power to add an award of interest under the 'slip rule'[2]. Where the award does contain such an explanation or where the arbitrator volunteers an explanation the Court will not remit the award merely because it disagrees with the way the arbitrator has exercised his discretion, but only if it is clear that the arbitrator has misdirected himself as to the principles on which the discretion ought to be exercised[3]. But it is wrong in principle not to award interest on a successful claim merely on the grounds that there has been delay in bringing the claim to a hearing[4] or that there has been no evidence as to the rate at which interest ought to be given, or as to the period for which it ought to run[5].

7 Dissolution of partnership

Under an appropriately worded arbitration clause, the arbitrator has power to order the dissolution of a partnership[6].

E. COSTS

1 The arbitrator's discretion as to costs

Unless the arbitration agreement otherwise provides[7], the costs of the award and

---

[20]   *Tehno-Impex v Gebr van Weelde Schepvaartkontoor BV* [1981] 1 Lloyd's Rep 587, read subject to the dicta of Lord Brandon in *La Pintada*, supra. This power is now largely, if not entirely superseded by s. 19A.

[1]   *Panchaud Frères SA v Pagnan and Fratelli* [1974] 1 Lloyd's Rep 394. *PJ Van Der Zijden Wildhandel NV v Tucker and Cross Ltd* [1976] 1 Lloyd's Rep 341; *Thos P Gonzalez Corpn v FR Waring (International) (Pty) Ltd* [1976] 1 Lloyd's Rep 494 at 505; *Warinco AG v Andre & Cie SA* [1979] 2 Lloyd's Rep 298. Unless the parties consent, the Court has no power to make it own award of interest: *Wildhandel NV v Tucker and Cross*, ibid., 343.

[2]   *Pancommerce SA v Veecheema BV* [1983] 2 Lloyd's Rep 304. The 'slip rule' (section 17 of the 1950 Act) is discussed at pp. 405–407, post.

[3]   *Cargill Inc v Marpro Ltd* [1983] 2 Lloyd's Rep 570. The same approach is adopted when reviewing the arbitrator's decision on costs: see post, p. 398 et seq.

[4]   *Panchaud v Pagnan*, ante. Unreasonable delay on the part of the claimant may justify a special order as to interest, *Cayill Inc v Narpro Ltd*, supra.

[5]   *Wildhandel NV v Tucker and Cross*, ante.

[6]   *Walmsley v White* (1892) 40 WR 675; *Phoenix v Pope* [1974] 1 WLR 719.

[7]   As in *Mansfield v Robinson* [1928] 2 KB 353, where the parties agreed that the successful party should have costs on the High Court Scale.

of the reference are within the discretion of the arbitrator, who may direct by and to whom and in what manner these costs or any part of them shall be paid[8].

The arbitrator's discretion in respect of costs does not extend to the costs of argument on an appeal to the High Court. These are within the disposition of the Court, and ought not to be dealt with in the award[9].

Although the Act gives the arbitrator a full discretion as to costs, his exercise of the discretion is limited to this extent, that he must apply the same principles when deciding upon his award of costs as are applied in the High Court[10]. This means that the discretion must be exercised judicially: the arbitrator must confine his attention strictly to facts connected with or leading up to the litigation which have been proved before him or which he has himself observed during the progress of the case, and must not take into account conduct unconnected with the cause of action or (of course) prejudice of race or religion, or sympathy with the unsuccessful party[11].

The practice of the High Court is that 'costs follow the event': i.e. that in the ordinary way, the successful party should receive his costs[12]. The arbitrator must apply the same principle[13]. Thus if, without giving good reasons, the arbitrator awards that the costs shall be borne in the same way whether questions in a special case are answered in favour of one party or the other, 'that shows sufficiently ... that he is excluding from his mind in arriving at his order what ought to be the most important consideration affecting it' and he is guilty of

---

[8] S. 18(1). The words 'by and to whom' are very wide. It is, however, difficult to see how the arbitrator could ever order costs to be paid to persons other than the parties or the arbitrator, or paid by persons other than the parties (cf. *Forbes-Smith v Forbes-Smith and Chadwick* [1901] P 258 at 271). The power to award 'in what manner' the costs are to be paid no doubt includes a power to award that interlocutory costs shall be paid immediately; that costs shall be paid by instalments; and that they shall be set off against any other sums awarded to be paid by the party in whose favour the award of costs is to be made.

[9] *Higham v Havant and Waterloo UDC* [1951] 2 TLR 87 at 90; *Arnhold Karberg & Co v Blythe, Green, Jourdain & Co* [1915] 2 KB 379 at 393. These are decisions on the costs of arguing a special case, but the position would appear to be the same with regard to appeals under the 1979 Act.

[10] See *Lloyd Del Pacifico v Board of Trade* (1930) 35 Com Cas 325; *Stotesbury v Turner* [1943] KB 370; *Matheson & Co Ltd v A Tabah & Sons* [1963] 2 Lloyd's Rep 270 at 273.

[11] See the cases cited in note 20, ante, and also *Perry v Stopher* [1959] 1 WLR 415; *Smeaton Hanscomb & Co v Sassoon I Setty, Son & Co (No 2)* [1953] 2 Lloyd's Rep 585, [1953] 1 WLR 1481; *Heaven and Kesterton v Sven Widaeus AB* [1958] 1 Lloyd's Rep 101, [1958] 1 WLR 248; *Messers Ltd v Heidner & Co* [1961] 1 Lloyd's Rep 107 at 115; *Heaven and Kesterton v Establissements Francois Albiac & Cie* [1956] 2 Lloyd's Rep 316 at 322; *Dineen v Walpole* [1969] 1 Lloyd's Rep 261. The discretion must be exercised afresh in each case and not by applying an invariable rule of practice: *James Allen (Liverpool) Ltd v London Export Corpn Ltd* [1981] 2 Lloyd's Rep 632.

[12] *Donald Campbell & Co v Pollak* [1927] AC 732. Where there is a claim and counterclaim on which each party has succeeded wholly or in part, the most usual form of order is that 'the claimant shall have the costs of the claim and the respondent shall have the costs of the counterclaim'. But if the counterclaim is in substance only a defence to the claim, it is generally preferable to order that one or other or neither party should be awarded some or all or some proportion of the total costs of the reference: *Tramountana Armadora SA v Atlantic Shipping Co SA* [1978] 1 Lloyd's Rep 391 at 399.

[13] See the cases cited in notes 7 and 8, ante, and *Lewis v Haverfordwest RDC* [1953] 1 WLR 1486; *Portland SS Co Ltd v Charlton Steam Shipping Co* (1925) 23 Ll L Rep 268 at 271. It follows that the practice which is sometimes followed in commercial arbitrations of leaving each party to pay his own costs, possibly on the ground that any other order appears too 'litigious', is not correct (see *Lewis v Haverfordwest*, ante) – unless the special circumstances of the case justify such an order, or unless the parties have made an agreement to that effect *after* the dispute has arisen: see note 11, post, p. 398.

technical misconduct so that that part of the award may be set aside[14]. This rule is not, however, inflexible; and if the special circumstances of the case so demand, the arbitrator may deprive the successful party of the whole or part of his own costs[15]. A successful claimant may, in exceptional circumstances, even be ordered to pay the whole of the respondents' costs – for instance, if the claimant recovers less than was tendered by the respondent[16]. But the arbitrator should not depart from the rule that costs follow the event without substantial reasons, and he should always bear in mind the duty to act judicially, by excluding from his mind any matter not strictly connected with the arbitration. If he is minded to depart from the rule he should give the parties an opportunity to address him on costs before he makes his award: but failure to do so will not invalidate his award if the parties ought to have contemplated a special award as to costs[17].

The following examples from reported cases on arbitrations illustrate the way in which the rule that costs follow the event has been applied[18].

(a) Matters justifying a departure from the general rule[19]

Gross exaggeration of the claim[20].

Unsatisfactory conduct by a party in the course of the arbitration or unreasonable or obstructive conduct which has protracted the proceedings or increased the costs by the other party[1].

---

[14] *Smeaton Hanscomb*, ante, per Devlin J at 1484. See also *Faghirzadeh v Rudolf Wolff (SA) Pty Ltd* [1977] 1 Lloyd's Rep 630.

[15] Unless the arbitrator knows what costs have been incurred, it is better not to make use of an award of a lump sum as a means of depriving the successful party of part of his costs: *P Rosen & Co Ltd v Dowley and Selby* [1943] 2 All ER 172 at 175.

[16] Cf. *Childs v Blacker* [1954] 1 WLR 809. But a successful respondent should never be made to pay the whole of the claimants' costs: although there may be cases where it is proper to order him to bear his own: see the cases cited in Halsbury's *Laws of England* (3rd edn.) Vol. 30, p. 422(q) and *Lloyd Del Pacifico v Board of Trade* (1930) 37 Ll L Rep 103 at 107. (A successful respondent may, however, properly be ordered to pay the costs of a particular issue on which he has failed: see note 2, p. 397, post.)

[17] *Blue Horizon Shipping Co SA v ED and F Man Ltd, The Aghios Nicolaos* [1980] 1 Lloyd's Rep 17.

[18] These are examples taken from arbitration cases. There are many other decisions arising out of actions in the High Court. These are equally relevant, since the principles are the same. Useful digests may be found in the *Supreme Court Practice* para. 62/2/9, and in Halsbury's *Laws of England* (3rd edn.) Vol. 30, pp. 421 et seq.

[19] In *Messers Ltd v Heidner & Co* [1960] 1 Lloyd's Rep 500, ante, at 502, Pearson J referred without disapproval to a provision in the arbitration clause requiring the arbitrators to take certain matters into account when deciding as to costs. See also *Heaven and Kesterton v Sven Widaeus A/B* [1958] 1 WLR 248 at 256.

[20] *Re Fearon and Flinn* (1869) LR 5 CP 34; *Matheson v Tabah*, ante, at 273; *Perry v Stopher* [1959] 1 WLR 415 at 425; *Dineen v Walpole* [1969] 1 Lloyd's Rep 261; *Tramountana Armadora SA v Atlantic Shipping Co SAV* [1978] 1 Lloyd's Rep 391 at 398. But the mere fact that the successful party has not recovered all that he claimed does not compel the arbitrator to disallow some or all of his costs. In the words of McNair J in *Demolition and Construction Co Ltd v Kent River Board* [1963] 2 Lloyd's Rep 7 at 15: 'I know of no principle of law in relation to costs which compels an arbitrator or a judge in his award or judgment to reflect the measure of success which one party or the other has achieved'. Only in wholly exceptional circumstances would exaggeration of the claim justify an order that the claimant should pay the respondent's costs: *Tramountana v Atlantic*, ibid.

[1] *Matheson v Tabah*, ante, at 273; *Unimarine SA v Canadian Transport Co Ltd, The Catherine L* [1982] 1 Lloyd's Rep 484. No doubt this would include a party who had not made proper discovery or complied fully with the orders of the arbitrator. The arbitrator should endeavour to make the penalty proportionate to the time and money wasted by the unsatisfactory conduct, rather than to use the discretion over costs as a means of fining a recalcitrant party.

Failure by the successful party on an issue or issues on which a large amount of time was spent[2].

An offer[3] by one party before or during the reference to compromise the dispute, which the other party has unreasonably failed to accept. Where the dispute involved a simple money claim the respondent is usually entitled to his costs if, but only if, the amount of the offer was for a sum equal to or greater than the amount awarded, and the respondent was ready and able to pay it in cash[4]. In more complex cases the question to be considered, we submit, is whether the claimant acted unreasonably in continuing with the reference, which will usually be the case unless the award is in some material respect an improvement on what the claimant would have obtained by accepting the offer. Where such an offer has been made the general rule is that the respondent is entitled to the costs incurred by him after the date of the offer, and departure from this general rule without good reason will result in the award being remitted[5].

Extravagance in the conduct of the hearing, e.g. the employment of an excessive number of counsel or expert witnesses[6].

(b) Matters not justifying a departure from the general rule

A feeling on the part of the arbitrator that the conduct of the successful party before the commencement of the reference was immoral[7].

---

[2] *Heaven and Kesterton v Widaeus*, ante; *Matheson v Tabah*, ante; *Lewis Emanuel & Son Ltd v Sammut* [1959] 2 Lloyd's Rep 629 at 635; *Perry v Stopher* [1959] 1 WLR 415; *Centrala Morska Importowo Eksportowa (known as Centromor) v Companhia Nacional De Navegacao SARL* [1975] 2 Lloyd's Rep 69; *Blue Horizon Shipping Co SA v ED and F Man, The Aghios Nicolaos* [1980] 1 Lloyd's Rep 17; *Ismail v Polish Ocean Lines, The Chiechocinek (No 2)* [1980] 1 Lloyd's Rep 97. In the High Court a party who has given his opponent notice to admit a material fact and who succeeds in proving the fact at the hearing, usually recovers the costs of such proof, irrespective of whether he has succeeded in the action as a whole. An arbitrator has, we suggest, a similar power which he should not be slow to exercise, as notices to admit are a useful way of simplifying disputes. It is not uncommon for a judge or arbitrator, who has resolved to award the costs of a particular issue, to reflect this in the award of a 'fractional' order as to cost. For example, if the claimant has won the arbitration, but has failed on a major missue, the order might be that the respondent shall pay the claimant two-thirds of his costs. See the observations of Pearson J in *Emanuel v Sammutt*, supra, at 635, and *Matheson v Tabah*, ante, at 273.

[3] The offer may be made 'without prejudice', in which case it should not be mentioned to the arbitrator until after he has made his award on the merits. But if it is to be referred to as affecting the arbitrator's discretion on costs, it must contain an express reservation of the right to do so: *Cutts v Head* [1984] Ch 290, [1984] 2 WLR 349. A 'without prejudice' letter in this form is sometimes called a *Calderbank* letter, after the decision in *Calderbank v Calderbank* [1976] Fam 93, [1975] 3 WLR 586.

[4] *Lewis v Haverfordwest RDC* [1953] 1 WLR 1486 at 1488; *Demolition and Construction v Kent River Board*, ante; *Matheson v Tabah*, ante. The usual practice is for the offer to be handed to the arbitrator in a sealed envelope, to be opened by him after he has made his decision on the merits but before he comes to consider the question of costs. An alternative method is to ask the arbitrator to make his award without dealing with the question of costs, and to have a further hearing on the question of costs under s. 18(4) of the Act when the open offer may be shown to the arbitrator: *Huron Liberian Co v Rheinoel GmbH* [1985] 2 Lloyd's Rep 58. Such offers should include an amount in respect of interest, but not costs: *Tramountana v Atlantic*, supra. There is, however, no rigid formula to be followed when drafting an offer, particularly when the dispute involves claims on either side: *Archital Luxfer Ltd v Henry Boot Construction Ltd* [1981] 1 Lloyd's Rep 642.

[5] *The Ios I* [1987] 1 Lloyd's Rep 321; but refusal to accept an offer generally only justifies an order awarding the respondent the costs incurred after the date of the offer: *Tramountana Armadora SA v Atlantic Shipping Co SA* [1978] 1 Lloyd's Rep 391. The fact that the offer has been withdrawn or has lapsed because the claimant rejected it or made a counter-offer may justify a departure from the general rule stated in the text: *Huron Liberian Co v Rheinoel GmbH*, supra.

The small size of the claim[8].

Insistence by the successful party on the stating of a case[9].

Taking a technical point of which the arbitrator disapproves[10].

Where the reference takes place under an agreement for arbitration (such as an arbitration clause in a contract) made before a dispute has arisen, any term in the agreement to the effect that either or both parties shall in any event pay the whole or part of their own costs is void[11]. But where the arbitration agreement is made *after* the dispute has arisen, such an agreement is enforceable[11].

2 Judicial control over the award of costs

If the Court considers that the arbitrator has not applied the correct principles as to costs, it will remit the award for reconsideration[12], although if the arbitrator cannot be shown to have erred in principle, the Court will not interfere merely because it would not have arrived at the same conclusion[13]. In theory, the order of the arbitrator as to costs is subject to review by the High Court, to the same extent as the order of a judge may be reviewed by the Court of Appeal[14]. In practice, however, the position differs in two respects.

First, the Court of Appeal has power to substitute its own order as to costs for that of the trial judge. This the High Court cannot do in relation to the order of an arbitrator. It can only remit the award for reconsideration[15], unless the parties empower it by consent to direct how the costs of the award should be borne[16].

Second, and more important, arbitration awards, unlike judgments of the

---

[6]   Semble, P *Rosen & Co Ltd v Dowley and Selby* [1943] 2 All ER 172.

[7]   *Lloyd Del Pacifico v Board of Trade* (1930) 35 Com Cas 325 at 332, 334. Contrast the position as regards unsatisfactory conduct during the arbitration: see note 1, p. 396, ante.

[8]   *Messers Ltd v Heidner & Co* [1961] 1 Lloyd's Rep 107 at 116.

[9]   *Messers Ltd v Heidner & Co* [1960] 1 Lloyd's Rep 500, and *Messers Ltd v Heidner* [1961] 1 Lloyd's Rep 107. The principle would apply equally to insistence on a reasoned award.

[10] See *Messers v Heidner (No 2)*, supra. The decision in *Maritime Insurance Co Ltd v Assecuranz-Union Von 1865* (1935) 52 Ll L Rep 16 at 20, is to the opposite effect, but we believe that this reflected the extreme disfavour with which the courts regarded insurers who took points on the Stamp Acts, and does not exemplify any general principle.

[11] S. 18(3). Quaere, whether the sub-section invalidates such as agreement as to costs if it is not a term of the arbitration agreement itself, as in *Fitsimmons v Lord Mostyn* [1904] AC 46.

[12] The source of the Court's power to interfere is not altogether clear. One possibility is that an arbitrator who errs in principle thereby exceeds his jurisdiction. This it not wholly convincing – see the cases cited in *Smeaton Hanscomb & Co Ltd v Sassoon I Setty, Son & Co (No 2)* [1953] 2 All ER 1588 at 1589 – and the more commonly accepted view is that the jurisdiction is founded on misconduct: *Dineen v Walpole* [1969] 1 Lloyd's Rep 261.

[13] *Blue Horizon Shipping Co SA v ED and F Man, The Aghios Nicolaos* [1980] 1 Lloyd's Rep 17; *Eleifthernia Niki Compania Naviera SA v Eastern Mediterranean Marine Ltd, The Eleftheria Niki* [1980] 2 Lloyd's Rep 252.

[14] *Anglo-Saxon Petroleum Co Ltd v Adamastos Shipping Co Ltd* [1957] 1 Lloyd's Rep 73 and 91; *Smeaton Hanscomb & Co Ltd v Sassoon I Setty*, supra, at 1590. Cf. *Gray v Lord Ashburton* [1917] AC 26; *Bradshaw v Air Council* [1926] Ch 329; *P Rosen & Co Ltd v Dowley and Selby* [1943] 2 All ER 172.

[15] *Anglo-Saxon Petroleum v Adamastos Shipping Co*, supra, at 93. However, the Court can, and not infrequently does, send the award back with a strong intimation about the course which the arbitrator should take; as in *Heaven and Kesterton v Etablissements Francois Albiac et Cie* [1956] 2 Lloyd's Rep 316.

[16] As in *Messers Ltd v Heidner & Co (No 2)* [1961] 1 Lloyd's Rep 107 at 116; and *Dineen v Walpole* [1969] 1 Lloyd's Rep 261.

High Court, often do not contain reasons. The question therefore arises whether the arbitrator ought to give, or can be made to give, the reasons for his award of costs. Where the award is in the form of a reasoned award under the 1979 Act, the answer is – 'Yes'; for the object of such an award is to bring the dispute before the Court, which ought to be given sufficient materials to decide whether there was a proper exercise of the discretion[17]. If the arbitrator gives no reasons, or insufficient reasons to enable the Court to form a view, the Court will remit the award so that the arbitrator can supply them[18].

Where the award is final, the Court will not compel the arbitrator to give reasons[19] (although the arbitrator ought generally to do so in order to save the parties the trouble and expense of trying to find what his reasons were[20]). Instead it treats an award depriving a successful party of all or part of the costs without stating any reason as prima facie evidence of misconduct, and on an application to set aside or remit the award of costs on the grounds of such misconduct evidence is admissible as to the grounds or lack of grounds for the exercise of discretion by the arbitrator[1]. But although the prima facie presumption of misconduct is sufficient to let in such evidence, the burden remains on the party alleging misconduct to show that there were no grounds on which the arbitrator could have exercised his discretion as he did: an application to set aside the award will fail if there were grounds on which the arbitrator might properly have exercised his discretion[2]. Moreover, there is no presumption of misconduct where the award itself discloses grounds on which the arbitrator might properly have exercised his discretion, for example, the fact that the claim was grossly exaggerated[3].

If either party suspects that the arbitrator may intend an award of costs which

---

[17] *Smeaton Hanscomb & Co Ltd v Sassoon I Setty, Son & Co (No 2)* [1953] 2 All ER 1588 at 1591; cf. *Pepys v London Transport Executive* [1975] 1 WLR 234.

[18] *Heaven and Kesterton v Etablissement Francois Albiac et Cie* [1956] 2 Lloyd's Rep 316 at 322–323; *Messers Ltd v Heidner* [1960] 1 Lloyd's Rep 500.

[19] *Perry v Stopher* [1959] 1 WLR 415; *Heaven and Kesterton v Sven Widaeus*, ante; *Matheson & Co v A Tabah & Sons* [1963] 2 Lloyd's Rep 270 at 273; *Dineen v Walpole* [1969] 1 Lloyd's Rep 261 at 265, per Davis LJ; *L Figueiredo Navegacas SA v Reederei Richard Schroeder KG, The Erich Schroeder* [1974] 1 Lloyd's Rep 192 at 193; *Centromor v Companhia Nacional* [1975] 2 Lloyd's Rep 69. But if the arbitrator volunteers his reasons, e.g. in an affidavit, the Court will examine them: *Matheson v Tabah*, ibid., at 275. The arbitrator should be served with the notice of notion challenging the award, so as to enable him, if he thinks fit, to make an affidavit for the assistance of the Court: *Ismail v Polish Ocean Lines, The Ciechocinek (No 2)* [1980] 1 Lloyd's Rep 97. If the arbitrator indicates he would like to reconsider the costs, the Court will remit the award to him so that he may do so: *Anglo-Saxon v Adamastos*, ante, at 91.

[20] *Centromor v Companhia Nacional*, supra, at 71.

[1] *Dineen v Walpole*, ante; *The Eric Schroeder*, ante; *Centromor v Companhia Nacional*, ante. On this point *Matheson v Tabah*, ante, would seem to be no longer good law.

[2] *The Eric Schroder*, ante; *Warinco AG v Andre & Cie SA* [1979] 2 Lloyd's Rep 298; *Wilhelmsen v Canadian Transport Co, The Takamine* [1980] 2 Lloyd's Rep 204. If the Court is in doubt whether there were such grounds, it may remit the award for the costs to be reconsidered: *Centromor v Companhia Nacional*, ante; *Patroclos Shipping Co v Société Secopa* [1980] 1 Lloyd's Rep 405. Where the arbitrator has given reasons which are insufficient, the Court *must* remit the award: it cannot uphold the award on grounds which the arbitrator might have, but has not given: *Leif Hoegh and Co A/S v Maritime Mineral Carriers Ltd, The Marques de Bolarque* [1982] 1 Lloyd's Rep 68.

[3] This would appear to be the explanation of the decision in *Perry v Stopher* [1959] 1 WLR 415: see *Dineen v Walpole*, ante, at 265, per Davies LJ. Very occasionally the award may go beyond prima facie evidence of misconduct and actually reveal in its face that the arbitrator cannot have exercised his discretion properly: see for example, *Cattan v A Michaelides & Co* [1958] 1 Lloyd's Rep 479.

would involve an error of law he may ask for a reasoned award upon the matter[4] but such prescience may be difficult to achieve in practice.

If the award is not in the form of a reasoned award the Court will not interfere with the arbitrator's exercise of his discretion if it was well exercised on the view he took of the law. This is so even if it knows (for example from an affidavit he has put in his reply) that his view of the law was wrong. The Court must, in reviewing the exercise of the discretion, put itself in the arbitrator's position with all the errors he might have made[5].

3 Costs of award and costs of reference

It is the usual practice for the arbitrator to separate the costs of the award from the costs of reference. The costs of the award consist of the fees of the arbitrator or arbitrators and of the umpire[6] (if any), together with any expenses which they have incurred. The costs of the reference are the costs, other than the costs of the award, incurred by the party in whose favour the order as to costs is made[7]. They include the costs of negotiating and settling the terms of the submission[8].

Thus, for example, the costs of hiring a room for the hearing, the cost of providing a transcript of the proceedings for the use of the tribunal, the fees of any technical or legal assessors employed by the arbitrators, and the fees of a lawyer employed to assist in the preparation of the award, should all be dealt with as part of the costs of the award. On the other hand, the costs incurred by a party in the preparation and presentation of his case are part of the costs of the reference.

4 Costs in reasoned award

A reasoned award should deal with all the costs of the award and of the reference. The arbitrator should not leave the Court to deal with the costs of the arbitration, over which the Court has no jurisdiction[9]. On the determination of an appeal from a reasoned award, the Court has power to confirm, vary, or set aside the award[10], including any award of costs, but this does not give the Court jurisdiction to make an order for costs when the arbitrator has omitted to do so.

---

4   See *Demolition and Construction Co Ltd v Kent River Board*, ante (special case).

5   *Heaven and Kesterton Ltd v Sven Widaeus A/B* [1958] 1 Lloyd's Rep 101.

6   The fees of the umpire and arbitrators should be awarded as separate amounts for the purposes of taxation: *Re Gilbert and Wright* (1904) 20 TLR 164.

7   See per Megaw J in *Government of Ceylon v Chandris* [1963] 2 QB 327 at 333. There is no difference between the costs of the award or the costs of the reference, as regards the arbitrator's duty to act judicially and the Court's power to review: see *Smeaton Hanscomb & Co Ltd v Sassoon I Setty, Son & Co (No 2)* [1953] 2 All ER 1588 at 1590.

8   *Re Autothreptic Steam Boiler Co Ltd and Townsend, Hook & Co* (1888) 21 QBD 182.

9   So held in relation to costs in a special case. See *Re Knight and Tabernacle Permanent Building Society* [1892] 2 QB 613; *Lloyd del Pacifico v Board of Trade* (1930) 37 Ll L Rep 103 at 105; *Salamis Shipping (Panama) SA v Edm van Meerbeeck & Co SA* [1970] 2 Lloyd's Rep 405 at 408. In *May and Hassell Ltd v Vsesojuznoje Objedinenije Exportles (No 2)* (1941) 69 Ll L Rep 103 at 109 the Court appears to have accepted an invitation by the arbitrator to deal with the costs of the award, but it cannot be assumed that the Court will do so again. Indeed it is difficult to see how it could do so if it refused leave to appeal, since it would have insufficient material before it upon which to exercise a discretion as to costs.

10   Arbitration Act 1979, s. 1(2)(a); *Cargill Inc v Marpro Ltd* [1983] 2 Lloyd's Rep 570 at 578.

5 Costs of interim award and consultative case

The arbitrator can make orders as to costs in an interim award. But he need not do so, and can leave the costs to be dealt with in his final award[11]. Since a preliminary question under section 2 of the 1979 Act is not embodied in an award, it is difficult to see how it can contain an effective order as to costs, and the safer course will be to leave the costs to the final award.

6 No order for costs in award

Section 18(4) of the 1950 Act provides that if an award does not make provision with respect to the costs of the reference, any party to the reference may within fourteen days of the publication of the award or such further time as the Court may direct, apply to the arbitrator for an order directing by and to whom the costs are to be paid. The arbitrator must then, after hearing any party who may desire to be heard, amend his award to deal with the costs[12]. The provision was no doubt intended to deal principally with the case where the arbitrator has simply overlooked the question of costs. But it is also of practical value in cases where it is convenient to defer argument on costs until after the award has been published, for example where there are a number of different disputes or issues to be decided, or where one party wishes to draw the arbitrator's attention to the terms of a 'sealed offer'[13]. In order to avoid misunderstanding the arbitrator should state in his award that he has not provided for the costs of the reference so as to enable the parties to address him on costs under section 18(4), and remind the parties that they must do so within fourteen days of the publication of the award.

Apart from section 18(4), if the award does not deal with the costs of the award or of the reference, it is incomplete, and the Court will send the award back so that the arbitrator can deal with them[14].

7 Interlocutory costs

When costs have been incurred in interlocutory proceedings[15] these must be dealt with in the award. It is very common, especially in the less formal type of arbitration, simply to treat these as part of the costs of the reference: so that whoever wins the arbitration receives all the costs, irrespective of what happened during the interlocutory hearing. This will frequently be the correct course, but it need not always be so. Sometimes costs are wasted because one of the parties

---

[11] If the point of law on which the interim award is stated is one which, if answered in a particular way, will dispose of the whole dispute, it may be better to deal with the costs in the award, to save the need for a further hearing and final award on costs alone.

[12] It is not clear why this section does not also deal with the costs of the award. One possible explanation is that the costs of the award largely consist of the fees payable to the arbitrator, and it might be said that if the arbitrator does not care to deal with them, there is no reason why the parties should compel him to do so. But this is not right, because the successful party may have to pay the costs of the award to take up the award, and will need an order to recover them from the other party.

[13] See p. 397, ante.

[14] Even though s. 18(1) merely says that the arbitrator 'may' give directions about costs: see *Re Becker, Shillan & Co and Barry Bros* [1921] 1 KB 391. This principle applies equally to an arbitration on documents alone, without an oral hearing: *Mavani v Ralli Bros Ltd* [1973] 1 WLR 468 at 475.

[15] On interlocutory proceedings, see p. 317 et seq., ante.

behaves unreasonably during the interlocutory stages. In such a case, it is right that this party should bear the expense, even if he ultimately wins the arbitration. Thus, for example, if a party wrongfully refuses to give particulars or discovery, with the result that his opponent has to make an application to the arbitrator, it may be right to make him pay the costs of the application. An arbitrator, having the same powers as the Court, is entitled to make such an order. He is not, however, bound to do so. The matter is within his discretion (which he should exercise by considering whether the party who has lost on the interlocutory hearing acted unreasonably in making or resisting the application).

Since a considerable time may elapse between the hearing of an interlocutory application and the hearing of the arbitration itself, during which time memories may grow dim, it is desirable for the arbitrator to avoid omissions and arguments by making a written order for costs every time he issues directions. The terms of the order, which will form part of the directions, will vary according to the circumstances. The three forms which will most usually be employed are –

1 'The costs of this application shall be costs in the reference'. Under this order, the costs 'follow the event' of the main arbitration.

2 'The costs of the application shall be the claimant's (or respondent's, as the case may be) in any event'. Under this form, the claimant or the respondent gets his costs of the application, even if he loses the arbitration.

3 'The costs of the application shall be the claimant's (or the respondent's, as the case may be) costs in the arbitration'. Under this form of order the claimant or the respondent gets his costs of the application if he wins the arbitration, but is not liable for his opponent's costs of the application if he loses the arbitration.

If orders have been made awarding interlocutory costs to one party, and the arbitrator ultimately decides the arbitration in favour of the other, he should remember to exclude these interlocutory costs from any award of the costs of the reference which he may make in favour of the winning party. Any party who has previously obtained an award of interlocutory costs should remind the arbitrator of this fact at the hearing, to make sure that he does not forget them in his award.

Where interlocutory costs are awarded, they will not normally be taxed and paid until after the reference has ended. It is, however, open to an arbitrator to order on the hearing of an interlocutory application, not only that the losing party shall bear the costs, but also that they shall be 'taxed and paid immediately'. Such an order enables the party who has succeeded on the application to obtain his costs at once, without waiting until the end of the reference. This very extreme form of order should only be employed in exceptional circumstances, where the arbitrator considers that the losing party's conduct has been so bad that his opponent is entitled to be indemnified at once.

8 Scale of costs

The arbitrator has power to award costs to be paid 'as between solicitor and client'[16]. This is not, as one might suppose, a method of assessing the costs to be paid by one of the parties to his solicitor, but a more generous scale of costs as

---

[16] S. 18(1) of the 1950 Act. This presumably must now be taken to mean as between solicitor and client on the 'common fund basis' and not as between solicitor and client: see Ord. 62, r. 28 and the note to sub-r. (4) in the White Book, and cf. r. 29.

between the parties themselves than would ordinarily be allowed. An order for costs to be taxed on this basis will generally only be appropriate where the arbitrator considers that the party ordered to pay the costs has in some way acted improperly.

9 Taxation of costs

The arbitrator has power to tax or settle the amount of the costs of the reference and award[17], in order to avoid the need for taxation in the High Court. As regards the costs of the reference, it is generally preferable to leave taxation to be dealt with in the High Court. No special order is needed, since the Act provides that any costs directed by an award to be paid shall, unless the award otherwise directs, be taxable in the High Court[18].

The arbitrator may obtain the services of a lawyer to assist him, if he decides to tax the costs himself[19].

The costs of the award[20] are usually settled by the arbitrator and may be taxed in the award itself[1]. In most cases the arbitrator will exercise a lien on the award to compel payment, and in such a case the party taking up the award may obtain an order of the Court under section 19(1) of the Act, that the arbitrator shall deliver his award on payment into court of the costs of the award. The costs are then taxed by the taxing officer of the Court. But this procedure gives no remedy to an unsuccessful party who has not taken up and paid for the award in the first instance, nor in any case where the arbitrator does not exercise a lien for his fees[2]. Many arbitrators therefore prefer not to tax the costs of the award, but instead to inform the parties by letter that the award is available on payment of a specified sum. Either party may then apply for a taxation of the costs of the award under section 18(2) of the Act[3].

---

[17] S. 28(1).

[18] S. 18(2). The words 'unless the award otherwise directs' presumably are intended to cover the cases (a) where the arbitrator himself taxes the costs in the award itself, or (b) where the arbitrator reserves to himself the power to tax the costs in the event of dispute. The sub-section would not appear to give the arbitrator power to direct taxation by a third party other than the taxing officer of the High Court.

[19] *Rowcliffe v Devon and Somerset Rly Co* (1873) 21 WR 433. In the first edition we suggested that he could also take the advice of a costs clerk and this practice, which can lead to a more rapid and economical taxation than in the High Court, is now not unusual.

[20] As to what are 'costs of the award' see ante, p. 400.

[1] Taxation of the tribunal's own fees is a delicate matter: see pp. 235–242. But taxation of other costs of the award, such as the fees of a legal adviser, may also give rise to embarrassment. The arbitrator must first inform himself of the object and principles of taxation and then obtain a sufficient statement of the charges claimed to enable him to apply those principles: *SN Kurkjian (Commodity Brokers) Ltd v Market Exchange for Africa Ltd (No 2)* [1986] 2 Lloyd's Rep 618. An arbitrator who has doubts about his ability to carry out this process properly and without embarrassment will do better to leave taxation to the Court.

[2] E.g. because the fees have been paid or secured in advance.

[3] *Rolimpex Centrala Handlu Zagranicznego v Haji E Dossa & Sons* [1971] 1 Lloyd's Rep 380 at 384–385.

CHAPTER 27

The effect of a valid award

A. GENERAL

The making of a valid award has a number of important effects, both on the powers of the arbitrator and on the parties to the arbitration. Generally speaking, however, third parties are not affected by an award, although, as will be explained, there may be exceptions to this rule.

Before discussing in detail the effects of the award, we should emphasise that in this chapter we are dealing only with a valid award, not with one that is void[1] or has been set aside or remitted on grounds making the award voidable, such as misconduct. An award which is merely voidable rather than void[2] has, however, all the effects of a valid award unless and until the appropriate steps have been taken to have it set aside or remitted[3]. Moreover, where proceedings have been brought in breach of an agreement to arbitrate and the defendant has either failed to ask for, or been refused, a stay of the proceedings, a subsequent award has no effect on the rights of the parties[4] unless the plaintiff has taken part in the arbitration[5].

B. THE EFFECT OF A VALID AWARD ON THE ARBITRATOR

1 'Functus officio'

When an arbitrator makes a valid award[6] his authority as an arbitrator comes to an end and with it his powers and duties in the reference: he is then said to be functus officio[7]. This at least is the general rule, although it needs qualification in two respects[8]:

---

[1] For example, because the arbitrator has purported to make an award on matters outside his jurisdiction, see pp. 108–131, ante: or because the award does not satisfy the necessary formal or substantive requirements: see pp. 382–388, ante.

[2] For the distinction between void and voidable awards, see Chapter 33, post.

[3] *FJ Bloemen Pty Ltd v Gold Coast City Council* [1973] AC 115, [1972] 3 WLR 43. The effect of setting aside or remission of an award that is otherwise valid is discussed at pp. 565–567, post.

[4] *Doleman & Sons v Ossett Corpn* [1912] 3 KB 257: see ante, pp. 156–157.

[5] Ibid., per Farwell LJ at 273.

[6] If the award is defective, e.g. because it is uncertain, it seems that the arbitrator has power to cure the defect, and for that purpose is not functus officio: *Montrose Canned Foods Ltd v Eric Wells (Merchants) Ltd* [1965] 1 Lloyd's Rep 597.

[7] The expression functus officio is also used in a different context in connection with arbitrators who have disagreed: see p. 258, ante.

[8] Whether his authority ends when the award is executed or when he notifies the parties that he has made it or when it is delivered to the party who takes it up would appear to depend on whether these various steps are necessary for the validity of the award, and this in turn depends on the construction of the submission: *Brooke v Mitchell* (1840) 9 LJ Ex 269.

First, if the award is merely an interim award, the arbitrator still has authority to deal with the matters left over, although he is functus officio as regards matters dealt with in the award[9].

Second, if the award is remitted to the arbitrator by the Court for reconsideration he has authority to deal with the matters on which the award has been remitted and to make a fresh award[9].

Apart from these two cases, however, nothing which the arbitrator does after he has made his award can have any effect on the rights of the parties to the reference. For instance, if, after making his award he issues a document setting out the reasons for his decision, it forms no part of his award and cannot be used to support an application to challenge the award, even if it contains an error of law[10].

In practice, the most important consequence of the arbitrator becoming functus officio after making his award is that he has no power to alter the award without the consent of the parties[11]. If he does so his altered award is a nullity[12]. At common law this rule was applied with great strictness: the arbitrator could not remedy either clerical errors nor even obvious slips of the pen[13]. In many cases the parties could (and still can) apply to the Court[14] to have the award remitted to the arbitrator on the grounds of an admitted mistake[15], but this procedure involved some time and expense. To remedy to some extent the inconvenience which this caused, the arbitrator has now been given by sections 17 and 18(4) of the Arbitration Act 1950 certain powers to correct errors and deal with costs[16]. These are discussed below[17]. But it will be seen that the statutory powers still leave limited scope for amending the award. In particular, there is no way in which the arbitrator can alter the substance of what he has decided, either on the basis of fresh argument or evidence, or simply because he has changed his mind, or indeed for any other reason, without the agreement of the parties. Nor, without such agreement, is there any means by which the arbitrator can explain the meaning of his award.

2 Section 17 ('the slip rule')

This section reads as follows –

---

[9] *Fidelitas Shipping Co Ltd v V/O Exportchleb* [1965] 1 Lloyd's Rep 223 at 231.
[10] *Aktiebolaget Legis v Berg & Sons Ltd* [1964] 1 Lloyd's Rep 203 at 213–214. We are not here referring to further reasons given pursuant to an order of the Court under s. 1(5) of the 1979 Act, or for the purpose of enabling the award to be treated as a reasoned award for the purposes of an appeal: see p. 374, note 15.
[11] In principle the parties should be able, by agreement, to revive the authority of the arbitrator so as to enable him to alter his award. See *IRC v Hunter* [1914] 3 KB 423 at 428.
[12] The validity of the award in its original form is not affected by the alteration: *Henfree v Bromley* (1805) 6 East 309.
[13] See for example, *Ward v Dean* (1832) 3 B & Ad 234 where the arbitrator in awarding costs wrote 'defendant' by mistake for 'plaintiff', and *Mordue v Palmer* (1870) 6 Ch App 22, where the arbitrator's clerk omitted some words when copying the draft award. Both cases would now fall within the 'slip rule': see post, pp. 405–407.
[14] Under s. 8 of the Common Law Procedure Act 1854 or its successors: *Mordue v Palmer*, ante.
[15] This remedy is discussed at pp. 558–561, post. The Court itself has no power to amend the award: *Hall v Alderson* (1825) 2 Bing 476.
[16] These provisions re-enact, respectively, s. 7(c) of the Arbitration Act 1889, and s. 12(2) of the Arbitration Act 1934.
[17] See pp. 405–407, post.

'Unless a contrary intention is expressed in the arbitration agreement[18] the arbitrator or umpire shall have power to correct in an award any clerical mistake or error arising from any accidental slip or omission'[19].

It might be thought that the word 'clerical' applies to 'error' as well as 'mistake'. But this is not so. The section enables the arbitrator to correct two categories of lapse –

(1) clerical mistakes; and

(2) errors arising from any accidental slip or omission[20].

A 'clerical' mistake refers to any mechanical or administrative mistake in drawing up the award, whether it be a slip of pen by the arbitrator himself or a mistake by his clerk or secretary in drawing up the award. But the second category encompasses a wider class of errors, limited only by the requirement that they must result from 'any accidental slip or omission'. These words are wide enough to embrace an accidental slip or omission by someone besides the arbitrator, such as one of the parties or his solicitor or counsel[1]. They enable the arbitrator to make an award on a claim which he has inadvertently overlooked, such as an award of interest[2], or to correct errors of accounting and arithmetic, such as attributing a credit item to the wrong party[3]. But the section does not give the arbitrator licence to give effect to second thoughts on matters on which he has made a conscious act of judgment[4]. The arbitrator may consider that he was in error in reaching a particular conclusion of fact or in accepting a particular proposition of law, but errors of judgment cannot be corrected under the section[5].

The arbitrator or umpire will usually exercise his powers under the section at the request of one or possibly both of the parties: but there would appear to be no objection to his making the correction without such a request. Whichever course is followed, all concerned should be informed in writing of what is happening and the reasons for it[6].

Before making a correction in his award, the arbitrator or umpire should

---

[18] It must rarely, if ever, happen in practice that the power under this section is excluded by the arbitration agreement.

[19] RSC Ord. 20, r. 11 (the modern version of the original 'slip rule') is in very similar terms to s. 17 of the Act. The Court, unlike an arbitrator, has an inherent power to vary its own judgments and orders, and the cases concerning Ord. 20, r. 11 do not always clearly distinguish between the inherent power and the statutory power. Provided that this is borne in mind, the cases on the Court's power of correction may be resorted to for assistance on the scope of the arbitrator's power under s. 17: *Mutual Shipping Corpn v Bayshore Shipping Co, The Montan* [1985] 1 Lloyd's Rep 189 at 194–5, where the history of the Court's powers is set out.

[20] *The Montan*, supra.

[1] Per Robert Goff LJ in *The Montan*, supra, at 195, and the cases there cited.

[2] *Pancommerce SA v Veecheema BV* [1983] 2 Lloyd's Rep 304.

[3] *The Montan*, supra.

[4] This is to be contrasted with an error resulting from a 'mental lapse': the expression is taken from the judgment of Sir Roger Ormrod in *The Montan*, supra, at 198.

[5] *R v Cripps, ex p Muldoon* [1984] QB 686, [1984] 3 WLR 53; *The Montan*, supra. In the previous edition of this book it was asserted, on the authority of *Sutherland & Co v Hannevig Bros Ltd* [1921] 1 KB 336, that the section does not give the arbitrator power to alter or add to the words which he has chosen to express his meaning merely because they do not on their true construction bear the meaning which they intended. This must now be doubtful in view of the decision in *Adam & Harvey Ltd v International Supplies Co Ltd* [1966] 1 Lloyd's Rep 571, [1967] 1 WLR 445: see *The Montan*, supra at 196–197, per Robert Goff LJ. Cf. *Pedler v Hardy* (1902) 18 TLR 591, and *Benabu & Co v Produce Brokers Co* (1921) 7 Ll L Rep 45.

[6] *IRC v Hunter* [1914] 3 KB 423.

satisfy himself that he has power to do so under section 17. If he makes the correction and his power to do so is challenged, the steps to be taken by the aggrieved party depend on whether the arbitrator or umpire has authority to decide whether the correction is within his powers. We submit that this question concerns the arbitrator's or umpire's powers and not his jurisdiction and that he does have authority to decide the question[7]. The proper way to challenge the correction would therefore be to ask the arbitrator or umpire, before he makes the correction, to issue a reasoned award on the question whether he has power to make it[8].

Even in a case falling within the section, the arbitrator or umpire has a discretion whether or not to make a correction and there may be occasions where justice requires that the correction should not be made. For instance, if the aggrieved party delays in making his request for the correction, the other party may be prejudiced by the delay, particularly if he has acted on the original award. Unless this can be dealt with by putting the applicant on terms[9], it may be better to refuse the request for correction and to leave the applicant to apply to the Court, if he can, for the award to be remitted.

If the mistake is one which is not within the 'slip rule' and the arbitrator admits his mistake, the proper course is to apply to the Court for the award to be remitted[10]: and this may be the more convenient course if it is doubtful whether the 'slip rule' applies and the arbitrator's power to correct his own mistake is challenged[11].

3 Sub-section 18(4)

This sub-section reads as follows –

> 'If no provision is made by an award with respect to the costs of the reference, any party to the reference may, within fourteen days of the publication of the award or such further time as the High Court or a judge thereof may direct[12], apply to the arbitrator for an order directing by and to whom those costs shall be paid, and thereupon the arbitrator shall, after hearing any party who may desire to be heard, amend his award by

---

[7] The distinction between questions of jurisdiction and questions of powers is discussed at pp. 114–116, ante.

[8] We submit that, although otherwise functus officio, the arbitrator or umpire retains sufficient authority to make a reasoned award on questions arising under s. 17. If, contrary to our view, the arbitrator or umpire has no authority to determine the extent of his own powers under s. 17, the remedy of the aggrieved party is not to ask for a reasoned award but either (a) to bring an action for a declaration that the amended award is a nullity or (b) to wait until the other party tries to enforce the amended award and to raise the defence that the amendment was made without jurisdiction, or possibly (c) to apply to set aside the amended award. The last course has been followed in a number of the reported cases since the enactment of the 'slip rule', in spite of the theoretical difficulties inherent in the idea of setting aside something that is a nullity (see p. 554, post). But in none of these cases was any objection taken to the form of the proceedings, and the point under discussion does not seem to have been considered.

[9] See s. 28.

[10] See pp. 558–561, post: and *Fuga AG v Bunge AG* [1975] 2 Lloyd's Rep 192.

[11] *The Montan*, supra.

[12] The words from 'within fourteen days' to 'may direct' do not apply in the case of a judge-arbitrator: Administration of Justice Act 1970, Sch. 3, para. 7(1).

adding thereto such directions as he may think proper with respect to the payment of the costs of the reference'.

Although the question of costs in general is dealt with elsewhere[13] it is convenient to discuss this sub-section when considering the powers of an arbitrator after he has made his award.

Before 1934, the parties' only remedy if an arbitrator failed to deal with the costs of the reference in his award was to go to the Court to get it remitted. Sub-section 18(4)[14] now provides a simpler remedy. But it is limited to cases where the arbitrator has failed to make any provision at all dealing with the costs of the reference[15]. An application under the sub-section is not appropriate where the point which is being made is that the arbitrator's award of costs has been made on some wrong basis[16].

The sub-section is not in terms limited to submissions where the arbitrator has a discretion to award costs[17], but we submit that the sub-section is not intended to enlarge the arbitrator's powers but merely extends the time within which these powers can be exercised.

There are a number of limitations on the power conferred by the sub-section. First, it can only be exercised if an application is made by one of the parties; the arbitrator cannot add an award of costs of his own motion. If he wishes to do so he should write to both parties saying that he has omitted to deal with the question of costs and inviting them, if they wish to do so, to make an application to him under the sub-section. Second, the sub-section, for no obvious reason, extends the time for directing by whom and to whom the costs shall be paid, but not for taxing or settling the costs. Third, the sub-section in terms only extends the time for an *arbitrator* to give directions as to costs, not an *umpire*[18].

An application under the sub-section must be made within fourteen days of the publication of the award, which in this context presumably means fourteen days from the date on which notice is given to the parties that the award has been made. But provided the application is made in time, the sub-section does not limit the time within which the arbitrator must make his directions as to costs. An application to the Court for an extension of time under the sub-section is made in the Commercial Court to the Commercial Judge in chambers, otherwise to a master[19].

There is nothing in the sub-section to prevent the arbitrator on an application under the sub-section from awarding that each party shall bear his own costs: but he must amend his award to say so expressly.

---

[13] See pp. 394–403, ante.

[14] The sub-section re-enacts s. 12(2) of the Arbitration Act 1934.

[15] So it would not apply where the arbitrator has expressly directed that each party shall bear its own costs.

[16] The proper way to make such an application, if it can be made at all, is discussed at pp. 398–400, ante.

[17] See p. 394, ante.

[18] Although the Act elsewhere uses the expression 'the arbitrator or umpire' when this is meant, we submit that on a beneficial reading of s. 18(4) 'arbitrator' should be taken to include 'umpire'.

[19] RSC Ord. 73, r. 3(1); and Ord. 72, r. 2(3).

C. THE EFFECT OF A VALID AWARD ON THE PARTIES

1 Introduction

A valid award[20] confers on the successful claimant a new right of action, in substitution for the right on which his claim was founded. Every submission to arbitration contains an implied promise by each party to abide by the award of the arbitrator, and to perform his award. It is on this promise that the claimant proceeds, when he takes action to enforce the award[1].

In addition to this positive effect, of conferring a new right of action on the successful claimant, a valid award has two negative consequences[2].

First, the successful claimant is precluded by the award from bringing the same claim again in a fresh arbitration or action[3].

Second, both parties are precluded by the award from contradicting the decision of the arbitrator on a question of law or fact decided by his award[4].

Similar principles apply to claims or defences which were within the arbitrator's jurisdiction but which, whether deliberately or by inadvertence, were not brought to his attention during the reference[5].

A party to an arbitration who wishes to take the point that a claim made against him is being brought for the second time, or that an issue in the arbitration has already been decided in earlier proceedings, should raise the point in the arbitration and if necessary ask for a reasoned award if he wishes to challenge the arbitrator's decision on the point. Otherwise, if the arbitrator decides against him, he will be unable to argue the point in the High Court[6].

2 The award as a bar to further proceedings

The question whether an award operates as a bar to further proceedings depends on whether the arbitrator has made an award of damages, or for the payment of a debt, or has merely made a declaration as to the rights of the parties. Moreover, the position may be different depending on whether the further proceedings are in personam or in rem.

---

[20] See our introductory remarks at p. 404, ante.

[1] *Bremer Oeltransport GmbH v Drewry* [1933] 1 KB 753. The nature of an action 'on the award' is discussed further at pp. 417–418, post.

[2] There is a valuable discussion of the distinction between the two aspects of the doctrine of res judicata in Spencer Bower and Turner on *Res Judicata* (2nd edn.) pp. 355 et seq.

[3] See post, p. 410.

[4] See post, p. 413.

[5] See note 14, p. 413.

[6] *IIE Daniels Ltd v Carmel Exporters and Importers Ltd* [1953] 2 QB 242. Contrast *Glasgow and South-Western Rly Co v Boyd and Forrest* 1918 SC (HL) 14 where the House of Lords held that an injunction ought to be granted to restrain arbitration proceedings on a matter which was *res judicata*. The decision is probably to be explained on the ground that there could be no dispute as to the plea of *res judicata* and that if there was no dispute the arbitrator had no jurisdiction: it was on this ground that an injunction was granted in *Cie Europeenne de Cereals SA v Tradax Export SA* [1986] 2 Lloyd's Rep 301.

(a) Award of damages

Where the arbitrator has awarded the payment of damages for breach of contract, the new right of action created by the award supersedes the original right of action, and the claimant cannot properly bring a further arbitration or action in personam in respect of the same breach, even if the damages payable under the award have not been paid[7]. The claimant's remedy is enforcement of the award, not an action for the original breach of contract.

The precise theoretical basis for this principle is not clear. It must be doubtful whether the doctrine of merger in its strict sense applies to English arbitration awards[8]. A contract debt merges in a judgment because the judgment is a 'higher security'. An award would appear to be a security of the same degree as the original contract[9]. Indeed where the original contract is under seal and the award is not, the award would appear to be a lesser security[10]. A possible view is that an award based on a consensual submission is an accord and satisfaction[11]. It is, however, an accord and satisfaction of a special kind, since the satisfaction is almost always wholly executory: yet it has long been the law that an award is a bar to a fresh action even though it has not been satisfied[12]. The best explanation, we submit, is that the rule is a practical application of the maxim 'nemo debet vexari bis pro unam et eadem causa', the observance of which is essential to the orderly administration of justice.

(b) Award of debt

The position may be different where the arbitrator has awarded, not damages for breach of contract, but the payment of a debt[13]. It seems that the award creates no new right, and that the claimant can still bring an action for the original debt. He will, however, be unable to contradict the arbitrator's decision as to the amount due to him[14].

(c) Declaration

Where the award does not order the payment of any sum, but simply declares the existence of a right to be paid or its amount, the party in whose favour the declaration is made is free to bring fresh proceedings to enforce the right[15], relying on the declaration as res judicata.

---

[7] *Gascoyne v Edwards* (1826) 1 Y & J 19.
[8] As distinct from judgments enforcing awards: *Gabela v Aris (Owners)* (1927) 29 Ll L Rep 289; *The Rena K* [1978] 1 Lloyd's Rep 545 at 560.
[9] See per Pilcher J in *HE Daniels Ltd v Carmel Exporters and Importers Ltd* [1953] 2 QB 242 at 255.
[10] See *Blake's Case* (1606) 6 Co Rep 43b.
[11] See per Lord Goddard CJ in *Daniels v Carmel Exporters and Importers Ltd*, ante, at 244, and *FJ Bloemen Pty Ltd v Gold Coast City Council* [1973] AC 115.
[12] *Purslow v Baily* (1705) 2 Ld Raym 1039.
[13] *Allen v Milner* (1831) 2 Cr & J 47, as explained in *Commings v Heard* (1869) LR 4 QB 669. See also *Richard Adler v Soutos (Hellas) Maritime Corpn, The Argo Hellas* [1954] 1 Lloyd's Rep 296. It is not easy to find a rational basis for the distinction.
[14] *Commings v Heard*, supra. This is an example of the application of the principles discussed post, at p. 413.
[15] *FJ Bloemen Pty Ltd v Gold Coast City Council* [1973] AC 115 at 126; *Whitehead v Tattersall* (1834) 1 Ad & El 491 is an example of such proceedings.

(d) Action in rem

The rule that an award of damages is a bar to further proceedings needs modification in the case of an Admiralty action in rem. A cause of action in rem, being of a different character from a cause of action in personam, remains available to the claimant so long as an award on the cause of action in personam remains unsatisfied[16].

(e) The rule in Conquer v Boot

The most obvious application of the principle that an award of damages supersedes the original cause of action is where the claimant brings, in the second arbitration, a claim which is identical as to facts, legal formulation, and remedies, to the one which he brought in the first. This is unlikely to happen often. More common will be the case where the claimant finds that he has suffered more damage than he claimed in the first arbitration, and starts a further arbitration to recover his further loss. This is not generally permissible, since the principle requires that damages resulting from one and the same cause of action, including anticipated future damages, must be assessed once and for all in one proceeding[17]: this aspect of the general principle is known as 'the rule in *Conquer v Boot*'[18]. Claimants sometimes try to escape from this rule by dressing up their new claim as a fresh cause of action[19]. In such a case, the second arbitrator must decide whether the new claim is really just the old claim in disguise, or whether it does indeed amount to a new and distinct cause of action. Discussion of the principles which the arbitrator should apply when considering this difficult point is beyond the scope of this book[20].

Claimants should bear in mind that the rule may form a trap for the unwary, and indeed for the wary as well. Whilst a claimant might well be expected to put forward at the same time all his claims for known accrued damage, the rule may work unjustly where the damage has not yet materialised at the time of the first award or its existence is unknown[1]. It appears that the parties can contract

---

[16] *The Rena K* [1978] 1 Lloyd's Rep 545 at 560. The plaintiff in the action in rem can proceed to judgment on the basis of the award, without having to prove his claim all over again, the award giving rise to an issue estoppel: *The Tuyuti* [1984] 2 Lloyd's Rep 51, [1984] QB 838; and see post, p. 413.

[17] *Brunsden v Humphrey* (1884) 14 QBD 141; *Darley Main Colliery Co v Mitchell* (1886) 11 App Cas 127 at 132; *Speak v Taylor* (1894) 10 TLR 224; *Conquer v Boot* [1928] 2 KB 336; *EE and Brian Smith (1928) Ltd v Wheatsheaf Mills Ltd* (1939) 63 Ll L Rep 237, [1939] 2 KB 302 at 311.

[18] From the case of that name cited in the previous note.

[19] To which the rule does not apply: *Telfair Shipping Corpn v Inersea Carriers SA, The Caroline P* [1983] 2 Lloyd's Rep 351. But a separate cause of action may still be barred under the principles referred to at pp. 412–413, post.

[20] The topic is treated in detail in *Spencer Bower and Turner*, op. cit., pp. 372 et seq. The cases of *Clegg v Dearden* (1848) 12 QB 576 and *Smalley v Blackburn Rly Co* (1857) 2 H & N 158 may be taken as illustrating the difficulties of the arbitrator's task.

[1] The rule does not apply, however, to a claim whose existence has been fraudulently concealed from the claimant: *Charter v Trevelyan* (1844) 11 Cl & Fin 714; and equity may intervene to prevent the rule being used as a means of unjust enrichment: e.g. *Spencer v Spencer* (1828) 2 Y & J 249.

out of the rule either expressly[2] or by implication, e.g. from the arbitral practice in a particular trade[3]. Otherwise, where the damage has not yet materialised, the claimant should ask the arbitrator to make an interim award on the quantified damage, expressly reserving in his award the possibility of a further award on the future damage[4].

(f) The rule in Henderson v Henderson[5]

The doctrine of res judicata in its narrower sense applies only to matters directly decided by the award or necessarily involved in the decision[6]. Res judicata in this sense confers substantive rights on the party who is entitled to invoke it[7]. There is, however, a wider sense in which the doctrine may be appealed to, so that it becomes an abuse of process to raise in subsequent proceedings matters which could and should have been raised in earlier proceedings. Used in this sense, res judicata gives rise to procedural remedies which are a matter of discretion and not a matter of right. A party will not be permitted to raise an issue which was so clearly part of the subject matter of the earlier reference and so clearly could have been raised that it would be an abuse of process to allow the issue to be raised in fresh proceedings. In special circumstances justice may require that the rule should not be invoked, but it will almost always be necessary to show that the issue could not have been raised in the earlier proceeding by the exercise of reasonable diligence. Negligence, inadvertence or accident are not enough. Parties to proceedings should take care to bring forward the whole of their case and not keep parts of it back or allow part of it to go by default; otherwise it will be too late for them, after the arbitrator has made his award, to raise fresh claims or defences which ought to have been put forward earlier[8].

There is, however, one respect in which this aspect of the doctrine of res judicata is of narrower application to arbitrations than to court proceedings. The arbitrator's jurisdiction is limited to issues falling within the scope of the

---

[2] This appears to be one reason for the decision in *The Sylph* (1867) LR 2 A & E 24, that the award of damages in personam did not bar a fresh action in rem against the ship. The decision may also turn on the difference in character between actions in rem and in personam: see *The Cella* (1888) 13 PD 82, per Sir James Hannen at 85; and *The Rena K* [1978] 1 Lloyd's Rep 545, per Brandon J at 560.

[3] *EE and Brian Smith (1928) Ltd v Wheatsheaf Mills Ltd* (1939) 63 Ll L Rep 237, [1939] 2 KB 302. Contrast *HE Daniel Ltd v Carmel Exporters and Importers Ltd* [1953] 2 Lloyd's Rep 103, [1953] 2 QB 242, in which *EE and Brian Smith (1928) Ltd v Wheatsheaf Mills Ltd* does not appear to have been cited and where Pilcher J was unable on the evidence to find an express or implied contract excluding the rule, with *Purser & Co (Hillingdon) Ltd v Jackson* [1977] QB 166.

[4] *Trans Trust SPRL v Danubian Trading Co Ltd* [1952] 1 Lloyd's Rep 348, [1952] 2 QB 297 indicates that, notwithstanding the rule under discussion, this is a permissible procedure – at any rate where the reserved claim is for an indemnity.

[5] (1843) 3 Hare 100.

[6] See p. 413, post.

[7] The fact that this type of res judicata gives rise to substantive rights does not preclude the exercise of procedural remedies, such as striking out a claim which is clearly res judicata: *Dallal v Bank Mellat* [1986] QB 441, [1986] 2 WLR 745; or possibly an injunction restraining the claimant from referring the matter to arbitration: see p. 409, ante, n. 6.

[8] *Smith v Johnson* (1812) 15 East 213; *Trimingham v Trimingham* (1835) 4 Nev & MKB 786; *Dunn v Murray* (1829) 9 B & C 780; *Henderson v Henderson*, supra; *Fidelitas Shipping v V/O Exportchleb* [1965] 1 Lloyd's Rep 223, [1966] 1 QB 630; *Yat Tung Investment Co Ltd v Dao Heng Bank Ltd* [1975] AC 581; *Siporex Trade SA v Comdel Commodities Ltd* [1986] 2 Lloyd's Rep 428.

arbitration agreement, and may be further limited by the terms of his appointment for the particular reference with which he is concerned. The doctrine of res judicata, in either its broad or its narrow sense, has no application to issues falling outside the terms of the arbitration agreement[9]; and it is doubtful whether the rule in *Henderson v Henderson* applies to issues which are outside the scope of the matters referred to the arbitrator even though they fall within the terms of the arbitration agreement[10]. On the other hand, a claim which does fall within the scope of the reference is deemed to be abandoned if it is not repeated in the claimant's pleading, and although the arbitrator has a discretion to allow it to be revived by amendment during the reference, the abandonment becomes irrevocable once the arbitrator has made his award[11].

3 The award as conclusive of issues of fact and law

Just as an award prevents a party from raising a second time a claim on which he has succeeded, so also the award prevents him f. om disputing a second time an issue on which he has failed[12]. The losing party cannot be permitted to try again, just because he believes that on the second occasion he may have a more sympathetic tribunal, more convincing witnesses, or a better advocate. There must be an end to disputes.

So much is obvious. What is less obvious is that the award precludes the parties not only from reopening the whole of the dispute over which the arbitrator had jurisdiction, but also from reopening in a later dispute individual issues of law or fact which are necessarily[13] decided by the award[14]. This may cause difficulty where a party to arbitration decides to make an admission or to concede a point which he may need to reopen in future proceedings against the same opponent: his best course may be to make it clear that the admission or

---

[9] *Ravee v Farmer* (1791) 4 Term Rep 146; *Gueret v Audouy* (1893) 62 LJQB 633; *Crane v Hegemann-Harris Co Inc* [1939] 4 All ER 68; *Telfair Shipping Corpn v Inersea Carriers SA, The Caroline P* [1983] 2 Lloyd's Rep 351; *Excomm Ltd v Guan Guan Shipping (Pte) Ltd, The Golden Bear* [1987] 1 Lloyd's Rep 330.

[10] A claimant may, it seems, refer different claims to separate arbitrations even if they arise under the same contract: *Brunsden v Humphrey* (1884) 14 QBD 141, and Spencer Bower and Turner, op. cit., pp. 378 et seq. Or deal with questions of liability and quantum in two successive references: *Compagnie Grainiere SA v Fritz Kopp AG* [1978] 1 Lloyd's Rep 511; *Siporex Trade SA v Comdel Commodities Ltd*, supra. But it is not easy to see why the rule in *Henderson v Henderson* should not apply in principle in such cases, and it would be unwise for a claimant to assume that it does not. Sometimes the arbitration agreement incorporates rules which require all claims arising out of the same transaction to be put forward at one time, thus putting the matter beyond doubt.

[11] *The Golden Bear*, supra.

[12] *Whitehead v Tattersall* (1834) 1 Ad & El 491; *Roland v Hall* (1835) 1 Hodg 111: *Ayscough v Sheed Thompson & Co* (1924) 30 Com Cas 23; *Aktiebolaget Legis v V Berg & Sons Ltd* [1964] 1 Lloyd's Rep 203.

[13] The arbitrator is generally taken to have decided all the issues raised before him although not specifically dealt with in his award: *Middlemiss and Gould (a firm) v Hartlepool Corpn* [1972] 1 WLR 1643 (and see pp. 411–412, ante). Contrast *Newall v Elliot* (1863) 1 H & C 797.

[14] *Gueret v Audouy* (1893) 62 LJQB 633. This principle undoubtedly applies to awards: *Fidelitas Shipping Co v V/O Exportchleb* [1965] 1 Lloyd's Rep 223 at 231, per Diplock LJ. But its application to particular cases is often extremely difficult: see for example *Carl-Zeiss Stiftung v Rayner and Keeler Ltd (No 2)* [1967] 1 AC 853, where the *Fidelitas* case is discussed. A detailed analysis of the principles involved is beyond the scope of this book; readers should refer to Spencer Bower and Turner, op. cit., pp. 146 et seq.

concession is being made for the purpose of the present arbitration alone, and to ask the arbitrator to recite this fact in his award.

4 Transfer of title

Although an award is binding on the parties as regards questions of title decided by it, it cannot of itself operate as a conveyance of land[15] nor, unless assented to, can it transfer the property in goods[16].

D. THE EFFECT OF AN AWARD ON THIRD PARTIES

Generally speaking an award has no effect whatever on those who were not parties to the arbitration, and neither confers rights nor imposes obligations upon them[17]. However, this general statement is subject to a number of qualifications:

First, section 16 of the Arbitration Act 1950 provides that 'unless a contrary agreement is expressed therein, every arbitration agreement shall, where such a provision is applicable to the reference, be deemed to contain a provision that the award to be made by the arbitrator or umpire shall be final and binding on the parties and the persons claiming under them respectively[18]. The extent to which this obscure and difficult section affects third parties is discussed elsewhere[19].

Second, third parties who, because they have an interest in the subject matter of the reference, attend the hearing, run the risk of being found to have assented to or acquiesced in the reference and so being bound by the award[20]. Even if they do not attend the hearing, if they have notice of it and their rights may be affected by it, they may be bound by the result if they allow the reference to proceed[1]. If in doubt, those who find themselves in this position should take steps to make it clear that they do not agree to be bound by the result of the arbitration.

---

[15] *Doe d Morris v Rosser* (1802) 3 East 15; *Henry v Kirwan* (1859) 9 ICLR 459. See also *Johnson v Wilson* (1740) Willes 248 (partition of tenancy in common) and *Thorpe v Eyre* (1834) 1 Ad & El 926 (termination of tenancy). Cf. *Trusloe v Yewre* (1591) Cro Eliz 223.

[16] At any rate, it cannot do so if it merely directs that the goods shall be delivered up on payment of a sum of money, and delivery does not take place: *Hunter v Rice* (1812) 15 East 100.

[17] *Tunbridge Wells Local Board v Akroyd* (1880) 5 Ex D 199; *R v Cotton* (1813) 3 Camp 444; *Thompson v Noel* (1738) 1 Atk 60; *Re Kitchin, ex p Young* (1881) 17 Ch D 668; *Hill v Levey* (1858) 3 H & N 702; *Wenman v Mackenzie* (1855) 5 E & B 447.

[18] Quite apart from the section, it has been said that an award is binding on everyone who, by claiming through or under the parties to the reference, is privy to the reference; per Lord Blackburn in *Martin v Boulanger* (1883) 8 App Cas 296 at 302.

[19] See Chapter 8.

[20] *Dod v Herring, ex p Herring* (1830) 1 Russ & M 153; *Taylor v Parry* (1840) 1 Man & G 604.

[1] *Govett v Richmond* (1834) 7 Sim 1; *Thomas v Atherton* (1877) 10 Ch D 185. The first of these cases, if it was rightly decided (see *Martin v London, Chatham and Dover Rly Co* (1866) 1 Ch App 501) seems to turn on some form of laches or acquiescence or possibly on privity of interest. The second may perhaps be explained on the basis of ratification. We submit that the principle, if any, to be deduced from these cases should not be extended, since it offends against the principle that a man should not be bound by proceedings to which he is not a party and in which he has no opportunity to put his case.

Third, an award against a person who is jointly liable with someone who is not a party to the reference, or whose liability is alternative to the liability of the third party, may have the effect of discharging the third party's liability, even if the award is unsatisfied[2].

Fourth, a third party may agree to be bound by the outcome of an arbitration[3].

E. AWARDS OF FOREIGN ARBITRATORS

So far we have been discussing the effect of a valid award in the context of an English arbitration. The award of a foreign arbitrator requires separate consideration.

The rule that an award extinguishes the cause of action on which it is based should in principle apply also to an award of a foreign arbitrator. There was formerly an anomalous rule that foreign judgments, unlike English judgments, did not extinguish the causes of action on which they were based. But since this rule was abrogated by section 34 of the Civil Jurisdiction and Judgments Act 1982, we can no longer see any reason for treating foreign awards any differently in this respect from English awards[4].

A valid award[5] of a foreign arbitrator which is final and conclusive on the merits[6] is at common law conclusive of issues and fact and law in the same way as an award of an English arbitrator[7]. Moreover a 'Convention award' as defined in the Arbitration Act 1975[8] is by statute to be 'treated as binding for all purposes on the persons as between whom it was made, and may accordingly be relied on by any of those persons by way of defence, set off or otherwise in any legal proceedings in the United Kingdom'. Part II of the Arbitration Act 1950 contains an identical provision in relation to a 'foreign award' as defined in that Act[9]. Both statutes would appear to apply to awards dismissing a claim as well as to awards in favour of the claimant[10].

---

[2] For a fuller discussion of this topic, the reader is referred to Glanville Williams, *Joint Obligations* §43, and Bowstead, *Agency* (14th edn) Arts. 86 and 118 (election between principal and agent).

[3] Such an agreement does not necessarily carry with it an implied undertaking to pay the costs of the reference if the award is unfavourable: *Jackson & Co Ltd v Henderson Craig & Co Ltd* (1916) 115 LT 36.

[4] Provided of course that the award is recognised and enforceable in England.

[5] The tests of validity in relation to foreign awards is discussed post, pp. 421–427 in relation to the enforcement of awards. The tests vary in minor details depending on whether the award is a 'foreign award' or a 'Convention award' or is neither a 'foreign award' nor a 'Convention award'.

[6] Not on some purely procedural point, such as a time-bar which bars the remedy without extinguishing the cause of action; *Black-Clawson v Papierwerke Waldhof-Aschaffenburg AG* [1975] 2 Lloyd's Rep 11, [1975] AC 591. The distinction between the two types of time-bar is discussed, in relation to contractual periods of limitation, at pp. 202–204, ante.

[7] The common law is as stated in the text in relation to foreign judgments: *Carl Zeiss Stiftung v Rayner and Keeler Ltd (No 2)* [1967] 1 AC 853; Dicey and Morris, *Conflict of Laws* (9th edn.) pp. 1018–1022.

[8] See s. 3(2) of the 1975 Act.

[9] See s. 36(2) of the 1950 Act.

[10] Cf. *Black Clawson Ltd v Papierwerke Waldhof-Aschaffenburg AG*, ante, per Viscount Dilhorne at 619, Lord Diplock at 635, Lord Simon at 652 (a decision on a similar provision in s. 8 of the Foreign Judgments (Reciprocal Enforcement) Act 1933).

CHAPTER 28

Enforcement of the award

A. INTRODUCTION

An arbitrator's award, unlike an order or judgment of a court, does not immediately entitle the successful party to levy execution against the assets of the unsuccessful party or to apply to have him committed for contempt. It is first necessary to convert the award into a judgment or order of the court. Only then can the successful party levy execution[1]. In this chapter we discuss first the various ways in which the successful party can invoke the assistance of the English court[2] in order to obtain a judgment or order on which he can levy execution[3]. Second, we discuss the conditions which have to be satisfied before a judgment or order can be obtained on an award which has been made in a foreign arbitration[4]. Finally, we discuss the disciplinary action which may be taken by trade associations for non-compliance with awards[5].

B. OBTAINING A JUDGMENT OR ORDER

There are two ways[6] in which a judgment or court order can be obtained on an award –
1 By the so-called 'action on the award';[7]
2 By an application under section 26 of the Arbitration Act 1950[8].

---

[1] It is beyond the scope of this book to discuss the various forms which execution can take, such as seizure and sale of goods under a writ of *fieri facias*, garnishment of debts, charging orders, receiverships, commital, sequestration of assets, etc. The reader should consult the *Supreme Court Practice*, and the standard works on bankruptcy and winding up.

[2] The enforcement of awards abroad is beyond the scope of this book. Many countries are parties to the 1927 Geneva Convention on the Execution of Foreign Arbitral Awards or to the 1958 New York Convention on the Recognition of Foreign Arbitral Awards, or (as in the case of the United Kingdom) to both.

[3] See pp. 416–421, post.

[4] See pp. 421–427, post.

[5] See p. 427, post.

[6] Where the submission is in the form of a bond, an action may be brought on the bond: but arbitration bonds are now virtually obsolete. The remedies of attachment and rules under the Judgments Act 1838 are no longer available as a result of the repeal of the provision in section 1 of the 1889 Act whereby a submission, unless a contrary intention was expressed therein, had the same effect as if it had been made an order of the court: see pp. 445–446, post.

[7] Post, pp. 417–418.

[8] Post, pp. 418–419.

416

1 Action on the award

Parties to an arbitration agreement impliedly promise to perform a valid award[9]. If the award is not performed the successful claimant can proceed by action in the ordinary courts for breach of this implied promise and obtain a judgment giving effect to the award. The court may give judgment for the amount of the award[10], or damages for failure to perform the award[11]. It may also, in appropriate cases, decree specific performance of the award[12], grant an injunction preventing the losing party from disobeying the award[13], or make a declaration that the award is valid, or as to its construction and effect[14].

The action is commonly described as an 'action on the award', and indeed it has been suggested that an action may lie on an implied promise contained in the award itself without the necessity of pleading an arbitration agreement[15]. We submit that the better view is that the plaintiff must plead and prove both the arbitration agreement and the award: both are essential elements of his cause of action[16]. It has sometimes been necessary to decide whether the action is 'grounded upon a contract'[17] or is brought 'to enforce a contract'[18]. These problems of classification necessarily give greater weight to one or other element of the cause of action, depending on the circumstances, but they should not be allowed to obscure the fact that both elements must be present before the plaintiff can sue[19].

---

[9] *Purslow v Baily* (1704) 2 Ld Raym 1039; *Bremer Oeltransport GmbH v Drewry* [1933] 1 KB 753; *Bloemen v Gold Coast City Council* [1973] AC 115.

[10] The Court has power to order specific performance of an obligation to pay a sum of money: *Beswick v Beswick* [1968] AC 58. But an action on an award is probably a simple action for the recovery of a debt: *Coastal States Trading (UK) Ltd v Mebro Mineraloelhandels GmbH* [1986] 1 Lloyd's Rep 465 at 467.

[11] *Birtley District Cooperative Society v Windy Nook and District Industrial Cooperative Society (No 2)* [1960] 2 QB 1; *Dalmia Dairy Industries Ltd v National Bank of Pakistan* [1978] 2 Lloyd's Rep 223 at 273.

[12] The circumstances in which the equitable remedies of specific performance and injunctions will be granted in an action on an award lie outside the scope of this book. Examples of the application of the equitable remedies to awards will be found in Hogg, at pp. 160–161 and Fry, *Specific Performance* (6th edn.) pp. 723–726.

[13] *Birtley District Cooperative Society v Windy Nook and District Industrial Cooperative Society (No 2)* [1960] 2 QB 1; *Blackett v Bates* (1865) 1 Ch App 117.

[14] *Birtley District Cooperative Society v Windy Nook and District Industrial Cooperative Society (No 2)* [1960] 2 QB 1; *Selby v Whitbread & Co* [1917] 1 KB 736; *Merrifield, Ziegler & Co v Liverpool Cotton Association Ltd* (1911) 105 LT 97.

[15] Slesser LJ in *Bremer Oeltransport GmbH v Drewry*, ante, at 758–765, discussed the problem at length and eventually left it undecided.

[16] *Ferrer and Rollason v Owen* (1827) 7 B & C 427.

[17] So as to bring it within the six-year period under the old Statute of Limitations: see *Hodsden v Harridge* (1671) 2 Wms Saund 61, in which Twysden J held that it was not 'grounded upon a contract': cf. *Turner v Midland Rly Co* [1911] 1 KB 832.

[18] So as to bring it within Ord. 11 of the Rules of the Supreme Court, thus giving the Court jurisdiction to allow the writ by which the action is begun is to be served abroad: see *Bremer Oeltransport GmbH v Drewry*, ante, where the CA held that the action was to enforce the arbitration agreement. Order 11 has now been amended to deal specifically with actions to enforce an award: see Chapter 4, ante, at p 89.

[19] However, objections to the admissibility in evidence, or to the legality of the contract out of which the dispute arises, will not be fatal to the cause of action in cases where the promise to perform the award can be treated as having an existence independent of the original contract: see *Whiteman v Newey* (1912) 28 TLR 240 (gaming contract) and *Norske Atlas Insurance Co Ltd v London General Insurance Co Ltd* (1927) 43 TLR 541 (contract insufficiently stamped as a policy but not as a submission).

Thus, for the purposes of the Limitation Act 1980, it is necessary to classify an action on an award either as 'an action to enforce an award, where the submission is not by an instrument under seal', for which the limitation period is six years[20], or as 'an action upon a specialty', for which the limitation period is twelve years[1]. Time begins to run from the date on which the implied promise to perform the award is broken, not from the date of the arbitration agreement nor from the date of the award[2].

In addition to pleading and proving the arbitration agreement and the award, the plaintiff must establish that the dispute was within the terms of the submission, and that the arbitrator was duly appointed[3]. It will be a good defence to an action to enforce an award that the award is void for failure to comply with some formal or substantive requirement[4], or that it was made in excess of jurisdiction or that it has been set aside or remitted[5], or that the authority of the arbitrator was validly revoked before he made his award[6], but not that the award ought to be set aside or remitted on grounds not rendering the award void but merely voidable[7].

An action on an award made under an arbitration clause in charterparty or bill of lading is a 'claim arising out of any agreement relating to the carriage of goods in a ship or to the use or hire of a ship', and can be brought as an Admiralty action in rem[8].

2 Application under section 26 of 1950 Act

Section 26[9] combines two remedies from earlier Arbitration Acts –

(i) *An order* giving leave to enforce an award in the same manner as a judgment or order to the same effect. This remedy was introduced by section 12 of the 1889 Act.

(ii) *A judgment* in terms of the award. This remedy was added by section 10 of the 1934 Act. It is only available in conjunction with the earlier remedy[10].

Normally an order giving leave to enforce the award in the same manner as a judgment is sufficient to give the successful party the benefit of the court's

---

[20] Limitation Act 1980, s. 7.

[1] Ibid., s. 8. An action on an award made under a submission by deed would presumably be within the section. But cf. *Smith v Trowsdale* (1854) 3 E & B 83, in which it was held that such an action is not, properly speaking, on the deed of submission, and so can be discharged by an accord and satisfaction not under seal.

[2] *Agromet Motoimport Ltd v Maulden Engineering Co (Beds) Ltd* [1985] 1 WLR 762.

[3] *Christopher Brown Ltd v Genossenschaft Oesterreichischer Waldbesitzer etc* [1953] 2 Lloyd's Rep 373, [1954] 1 QB 8; *Kianta Osakeyhito v Britain and Overseas Trading Co* [1953] 2 Lloyd's Rep 569; affd, [1954] 1 Lloyd's Rep 247, 250–251.

[4] See pp. 382–388, ante.

[5] See pp. 547–568 and 576–578, post.

[6] See pp. 526–529, post.

[7] See pp. 546–547, post.

[8] *The St Anna* [1983] 1 Lloyd's Rep 637.

[9] The section only applies to awards on written arbitration agreements; see s. 32.

[10] This is clear from the wording of s. 26. But we submit that the application for a judgment need not be made at the same time at the application for leave to enforce the award in the same manner as a judgment: See *China Steam Navigation Co Ltd v Van Laun* (1905) 22 TLR 26 for the position before the 1934 Act.

powers of execution[11]. But it may sometimes be of advantage to have a formal judgment, for instance, where a judgment is necessary in order to enforce the award abroad, or in order to serve a bankruptcy notice[12].

The requirements which have to be satisfied and the defences which are available on an application under section 26 are the same as those for an action on the award. The section does not affect any question of substance; it merely provides a quicker and cheaper remedy than an action on the award[13].

But because the application under section 26 is a summary form of procedure intended to dispense with the full formalities of a trial, such as pleadings, discovery of documents and oral evidence, it is not suitable where an objection is taken to the award which cannot properly be disposed of without a trial. It used to be said that section 26 could only be invoked in 'reasonably clear cases'[14]. But this did not prevent the Court from deciding summarily questions of law which did not involve issues of fact, and the Court would probably now only refuse the application where the objection cannot properly be disposed of without a trial[15]. If the application under section 26 is refused, the plaintiff is left to enforce the award, if he can, by action. In such a case the Court has power, in order to save the time and expense of commencing fresh proceedings, to order that the proceedings should continue as if begun by writ and to give directions for the further conduct of the action[16].

An application under section 26 is not appropriate if the award deals with only one of several issues necessary to give the claimant a complete cause of action, for instance if the arbitrator has decided questions of quantum but not of liability. In such a case the claimant must proceed by action and rely on the award as an estoppel on the issues which it decides[17]. Nor can the award be enforced under section 26 if it is not in a form in which it can be entered as a judgment, although it may be possible for it to be remitted to the arbitrator so that it can be put into a suitable form for entry as a judgment[18]. If it cannot be remitted for this purpose, it may still be possible to bring an action on the award claiming damages for failure to honour the award[19].

---

[11] Including, in appropriate cases, those forms of execution whose coercive effect is indirect, such as committal and sequestration; see *Bailey v Plant* [1901] 1 KB 31.

[12] See *Re A Bankruptcy Notice* [1907] 1 KB 478; and *Re A Bankruptcy Petition, ex p Caucasian Trading Corpn Ltd* [1896] 1 QB 368.

[13] *Coastal States Trading (UK) Ltd v Mebro Mineraloelhandelsgesellschaft mbH* [1986] 1 Lloyd's Rep 465.

[14] *Re Boks & Co and Peters Rushton & Co Ltd* [1919] KB 491, per Scrutton LJ at 497; *Grech v Board of Trade* (1923) 130 LT 15; *Frank Fehr & Co v Kassam Jivraj & Co Ltd* (1949) 82 Ll L Rep 673; *Sarandis v P Wigham-Richardson & Co Ltd* (1950) 84 Ll L Rep 188; *Union Nationale des Cooperatives Agricoles de Céréales v Robert Catterall & Co* [1959] 2 QB 44 at 52.

[15] *Middlemiss and Gould (a firm) v Hartlepool Corpn* [1972] 1 WLR 1643: see also *Hall and Wodehouse Ltd v Panorama Hotel Properties Ltd* [1974] 2 Lloyd's Rep 413. A more cautious approach may be taken to the summary enforcement of foreign awards: see *Dalmia Cement Ltd v National Bank of Pakistan* [1974] 2 Lloyd's Rep 98, [1975] QB 9. The Court would no doubt adjourn the application if there was in being a pending application to set aside or remit the award.

[16] Ord. 28, r. 8.

[17] *Re Walker and Beckenham Kent District Local Board* (1884) 50 LT 207; *Re Willesden Local Board and Wright* [1896] 2 QB 412.

[18] *Margulies Bros Ltd v Dafnis Thomaides & Co Ltd* [1958] 1 Lloyd's Rep 205.

[19] See *Dalmia Cement Ltd v National Bank of Pakistan* [1975] QB 9 at 13. The award could not be enforced summarily because it directed payment or a sum of money 'in India' and an English court would not give a judgment in such terms; see p. 24. Cf. *Bank Mellat v GAA Development and Construction Co* [1988] 2 Lloyd's Rep 44 at 54–55.

3 Practice

An order or judgment enforcing an award may include the costs awarded by the arbitrator and the arbitrator's fees even though they have not been taxed or agreed[20]. A sum directed to be paid by an award carries interest as from the date of the award and at the same rate as a judgment debt[1]. The arbitrator has power to direct that the award shall not carry interest, but not to alter the rate[2].

Section 26 requires judgment to be entered 'in terms of the award'. This makes it impossible to include the costs of the application in the judgment: but the order giving leave to enter judgment will normally make provision for the costs of the application as well as for the costs of signing judgment, and this order can itself be enforced as if it were a judgment. Interest on the award, under section 20 is not usually expressly provided for in the award but, even if it is not, judgment 'in terms of the award' may include interest on the award, because section 20 is in effect a term of the award implied by statute[3].

Leave may be given under section 26 to enforce an award in a foreign currency[4], and judgment may be given on an award in a foreign currency either under section 26 or in an action on an award[5]. The amount will be converted into sterling at the rate of exchange on the date when the court authorises execution[6].

Where part of the award has been paid, an order or judgment may be made under section 26 in respect of the amount remaining unpaid[7]. The existence of a cross-claim in other proceedings may be grounds for ordering a stay of execution[8].

An application to the High Court[9] under section 26 may be made before the Commercial[10] Judge in chambers in commercial cases[11], otherwise it is made before a master. The application may be made by originating summons[12] or ex parte on affidavit alone[13]: but the master or judge hearing an ex parte application may direct an originating summons to be issued[13], and will no doubt do so where the right to enforce the award as a judgment is not clearly made out[14]. A summons under section 26 may, with the leave of the Court, be served

---

[20] *Holdsworth v Wilson* (1863) 32 LJQB 289; *Lewis v Rossiter* (1875) 44 LJ Ex 136; *Metropolitan District Rly Co v Sharpe* (1880) 5 App Cas 425.

[1] Arbitration Act 1950, s. 20. The rate is laid down from time to time by Statutory Instruments made under s. 44 of the Administration of Justice Act 1970 and is generally below commercial rates.

[2] *London and Overseas Freighters v Timber Shipping Co SA* [1971] 1 Lloyd's Rep 523, [1972] AC 1.

[3] *Continental Grain Co v Bremer Handelsgesellschaft mbH (No 2)* [1984] 2 Lloyd's Rep 121.

[4] *Jugoslavenska Oceanska Plovidba v Castle Investment Co Inc* [1973] 2 Lloyd's Rep 1, [1974] QB 292.

[5] *Miliangos v George Frank (Textiles) Ltd* [1976] 1 Lloyd's Rep 201, [1976] AC 443.

[6] In this respect we submit that the rule in *Miliangos* supersedes the rule in *Jugoslavenska.*

[7] *Continental Grain Co v Bremer Handelsgesellschaft mbH (No 2)*, supra.

[8] *ED and F Man v SA Tripolitaine des Usines de Raffinage dé Sucre* [1970] 2 Lloyd's Rep 416; *Margulies Bros Ltd v Dafnis Thomaidis (UK) Ltd* [1958] 1 Lloyd's Rep 250, [1958] 1 WLR 398; *Agromet Motoimport Ltd v Maulden Engineering Co (Beds) Ltd* [1958] 1 WLR 762.

[9] If the amount sought to be recovered does not exceed the current limit on the jurisdiction of the county courts, the application may be made to the county court: s. 26(2).

[10] See Ord. 72, and Ord. 73, r. 6.

[11] Ord. 73, r. 3(1).

[12] Ord. 5, r. 3.

[13] Ord. 73, r. 10(1) and (2).

[14] The affidavit in support of an ex parte order must make full and frank disclosure of all material matters: *Excomm Ltd v Bamaodah, The St Raphael* [1985] 1 Lloyd's Rep 403, CA.

out of the jurisdiction whether or not the arbitration is governed by English law[15].

The application must be supported by an affidavit[16] –

(i) exhibiting the arbitration agreement, and the original award, or in either case, a copy thereof[17];

(ii) stating the name and the usual or last known place of abode or business[18] of the applicant ('the creditor') and the person against whom it is sought to enforce the award ('the debtor');

(iii) stating either that the award has not been complied with or the extent to which it has not been complied with at the date of the application[19].

An ex parte[20] order giving leave to enforce an award under section 26 must be drawn up and served by the creditor on the debtor by delivering a copy to him personally or by sending a copy to him at his usual or last known place of abode or business[20] or in such other manner as the Court shall direct[1]. The order may be served out of the jurisdiction without leave[2]. Within fourteen days after service of the order, or if the order is to be served out of the jurisdiction, within such other period as the Court may fix, the debtor may apply to set aside the order and the award may not be enforced until after the expiration of that period, or, if the debtor applies within that period to set aside the order, until after the application is finally disposed of[3].

A writ by which an action on an award is begun may, with the leave of the court, be served out of the jurisdiction[4].

C. ENFORCING AWARDS OF FOREIGN ARBITRATORS[5]

The procedures for enforcing awards made by foreign arbitrators are the same as those for enforcing awards of English arbitrators, i.e. an action on the award or an application under section 26 of the Arbitration Act 1950[6]. The conditions which have to be satisfied before an award of a foreign arbitrator will be enforced depend on whether the award is being enforced –

---

[15] Ord. 73, r. 7(1A).

[16] Failure to comply with these requirements does not automatically render the proceedings a nullity: the Court has a discretion to allow the irregularities to be cured, although the plaintiff will usually be ordered to do so at his own expense: *Agromet Motoimport Ltd v Maulden Engineering Co (Beds) Ltd* [1985] 1 WLR 762.

[17] For the documents to be exhibited in the case of awards of foreign arbitrators, see s. 38 of the 1950 Act and s. 4 of the 1975 Act, and pp. 425 and 427, post.

[18] Or in the case of a body corporate, its registered or principal address: Ord. 73, r. 10(8).

[19] Ord. 73, r. 10(3). The deponent should testify than in his belief the case is a proper one for enforcement by the summary procedure.

[20] The provisions of Ord. 73, r. 10(4) to (6) are in terms wide enough to apply to an order made inter partes but are plainly not intended to do so.

[1] Ord. 73, r. 10(4).

[2] Ord. 73, r. 10(5). Service is in accordance with Ord. 11, rr. 5, 6 and 8.

[3] Ord. 73, r. 10(6).

[4] Ord. 11, r. 1(1)(m).

[5] A more detailed discussion of this complex subject will be found in Dicey and Morris, *Conflict of Laws* (UK edn.) Chapter 16.

[6] Awards made by the International Centre for the Settlement of Investment Disputes are enforced by a special procedure under the Arbitration (International Investment Disputes) Act 1966.

(1) at common law by action or under section 26 of the Arbitration Act 1950;

(2) under the Arbitration Act 1975, and a 'Convention award'; or

(3) under Part II of the Arbitration Act 1950, as a 'foreign award'.

The expressions 'Convention award' and 'foreign award' are defined in the legislation in such a way that an award may be either one or the other (or neither) but can never be both. The reason for this is that the 1975 Act gives effect to the New York Convention on the Recognition of Foreign Arbitral Awards; this is intended in due course to supersede the provisions of Part II of the 1950 Act, which is based on the earlier Geneva Convention on the Execution of Foreign Arbitral Awards. We discuss the various regimes of enforcement in more detail below[7]. Before doing so, it is convenient to discuss the problems which may arise where a foreign court has given judgment on the award[8] or where the award has 'become enforceable in the same manner as a judgment'.

If judgment has been entered abroad on the award of a foreign arbitrator, the judgment can be enforced in England in the same manner as any judgment of a foreign court[9]. Provision has also been made in by Statute[10] for the registration and enforcement of awards made in certain Commonwealth countries[11] which have 'become enforceable in the same manner as a judgment given by a court in that place'[12]. The meaning of this expression is unclear; but probably what is intended is a case where the Commonwealth Court has made an order comparable to an order under section 26 of the English Arbitration Act 1950, giving leave for the award to be enforced in the same manner as a judgment or order to the same effect[13].

The Carriage of Goods by Road Act contains a similar provision for enforcing by registration under Part I of the Foreign Judgments (Reciprocal Enforcement) Act 1933 an award on a claim falling within the 1956 Geneva Convention on the International Carriage of Goods by Road, which has been made in a country which is a party to the Convention and has 'become enforceable' in that country[14].

Where the award or the judgment on the award is enforceable by registration under Part I of the Foreign Judgment (Reciprocal Enforcement) Act 1933, no proceedings other than proceedings by way of registration can be brought for the recovery of a sum payable under it[15]. If in such a case the award in question is a 'Convention award' as defined in the Arbitration Act 1975 or a 'foreign award' as defined in Part II of the Arbitration Act 1950, it would appear that the enforcement procedures under the two latter Acts are unavailable. This result may not have been comtemplated by Parliament, but it has the merit of

---

[7] See pp. 423–427, post.

[8] E.g. by way of exequatur.

[9] The various ways of enforcing foreign judgments are discussed in detail in Halsbury, (4th edn.) Vol. 8, paras. 715 et seq; and in Dicey and Morris, *Conflict of Laws* (11th edn.) Chapter 16. See also Ord. 73, r. 8.

[10] Administration of Justice Act 1920, Part II; Foreign Judgments (Reciprocal Enforcement) Act 1933, Part I: Administration of Justice Act 1956, s. 51.

[11] I.e. those countries to which Part II of the Administration of Justice Act 1920 has been extended.

[12] Administration of Justice Act 1920, s. 12(1) and Administration of Justice Act 1956, s. 51(a).

[13] Cf. *Union Nationale des Cooperatives Agricoles de Céréales v Robert Catterall & Co* [1959] 1 Lloyd's Rep 111, [1959] 2 QB 44.

[14] Carriage of Goods by Road Act 1965, ss. 4(1), 7(1).

[15] S. 6.

avoiding two different regimes of enforcement being in force simultaneously for what is in substance only one cause of action.

Apart from such cases, however, it would appear that the fact that judgment has been entered on the award in a foreign court does not, unless the judgment has been satisfied, prevent the award being enforced in England. The reason is that a foreign judgment, unlike an English judgment, does not extinguish the cause of action on which it is based.[16] This rule is, however, anomalous and it leads to the rather odd result that two regimes of enforcement with somewhat different requirements may be in existence simultaneously when judgment has been entered abroad on a 'Convention award' or a 'foreign award' – one to enforce the judgment and the other to enforce the award.

1 Enforcement at common law by action or under section 26

An award of a foreign arbitrator may be enforced at common law by action or under section 26[17] of the Arbitration Act 1950, whether or not it is a 'Convention award' as defined in the Arbitration Act 1975[18] or a 'foreign award' as defined in Part II of the Arbitration Act 1950[19].

The facts which have to be established by the claimant and the defences which may be raised are the same as in the case of an award of an English arbitrator[20], except that many of the questions which arise will be governed by foreign rather than English law.

Thus, the validity and effect of the arbitration agreement will be determined according to the proper law of the agreement[1]: this will include any question as to whether the dispute falls within the scope of the agreement. In this connection 'the proper law' of the agreement must be understood to mean the substantive rules of the proper law of the agreement and not rules which are merely procedural in character. Thus, an English court will not enforce an award, which, by the proper law of the arbitration agreement, was made without jurisdiction, even though by that law (or indeed by the curial law) the time for challenging the award has expired[2]. Any question as to whether the arbitration has been conducted in accordance with the proper procedure will be determined by the curial law of the arbitration[3].

In order to be enforced by action or under section 26 an award of a foreign arbitrator must be 'final' in the English sense of the word[4], although this may involve considering the effect of the award under the proper law of the arbitration agreement and under the curial law[5]. But 'finality' must be distinguished from 'enforceability' and an award may be 'final' even though (as

---

[16] *Re Henderson, Nouvion v Freeman* (1887) 37 Ch D 244 at 250. See also *Oppenheim & Co v Mahomed Haneef* [1922] 1 AC 482.

[17] To be enforceable under s. 26 the award must be made on an arbitration agreement in writing: see s. 32.

[18] See s. 6, and *Dalmia Cement Ltd v National Bank of Pakistan* [1974] 2 Lloyd's Rep 98, [1975] QB 9.

[19] See s. 40(a) and *Dalmia Cement*, supra.

[20] See p. 418, ante.

[1] *Hamlyn & Co v Talisker Distillery* [1894] AC 202; and see p. 62, ante.

[2] *Kianta v Britain and Overseas Trading* [1954] 1 Lloyd's Rep 247.

[3] The question of what is the curial law is discussed at pp. 64–68, ante.

[4] See p. 387, ante for a discussion of the requirement of finality in English law.

[5] The Court does not recognise orders affecting the finality of the award made by foreign courts unless they are competent to make such orders.

in some countries, including England) it is not enforceable by execution without the intervention of a court of law[6], or the time for enforcing the award has expired[7].

2 Enforcement of 'Convention awards'

The Arbitration Act 1975[8] gives effect in the United Kingdom to the 1958 New York Convention on the Recognition of Foreign Arbitral Awards[9]. It provides for the enforcement in England of 'Convention awards' either by action or 'in the same manner as the award of an arbitrator is enforceable by virtue of section 26 of the Arbitration Act 1950'[10].

A 'Convention award' is defined as 'an award made in pursuance of an arbitration agreement in the territory of a State, other than the United Kingdom, which is a party to the New York Convention'[11], and an 'arbitration agreement' is defined as 'an agreement in writing (including an agreement contained in an exchange of letters or telegrams) to submit to arbitration present or future differences capable of settlement by arbitration'[12].

By section 5(1) 'Enforcement of a convention award shall not be refused' except upon proof of certain specified defences. So although enforcement may be by action, the ingredients of the cause of action and the defences which may be set up are those laid down by the Act and not those laid down by the common law. But the Court may still refuse to enforce the award summarily under section 26 in cases where the objection to enforcement cannot be disposed of without a trial. This would not amount to a refusal to enforce the award, merely to a refusal to enforce it in a particular way[13].

The only defences permitted by the Act are the following –

1 That a party to the arbitration agreement was (under the law applicable to him) under some incapacity.

2 That the arbitration agreement was not valid under the law to which the parties subjected it or, failing any indication thereon, under the law of the country where the award was made[14].

3 That the person against whom the award was invoked was not given

---

[6] *Union Nationale des Cooperatives Agricoles de Céréales v Robert Catterall & Co* [1959] 1 Lloyd's Rep 111, [1959] 2 QB 44, CA. Although the decision turned on the meaning of ss. 37(1) (d) and 39 in Part II of the 1950 Act, the reasoning is, we submit, equally applicable to enforcement otherwise than under Part II. The earlier decision of Eve J to the contrary in *Merrifield, Ziegler & Co v Liverpool Cotton Association Ltd* (1911) 105 LT 97 must now be read as turning on its special facts: see *Dalmia Dairy Industries Ltd v National Bank of Pakistan* [1978] 2 Lloyd's Rep 223, 249–250.

[7] *Dalmia Dairy Industries Ltd v National Bank of Pakistan*, supra.

[8] See Appendix 1, p. 705, post.

[9] The convention is reprinted in Appendix 2, post. It is also reprinted with a commentary, as an appendix to the Fifth Report of the International Law Committee, 1961, Cmnd. 1515.

[10] S. 3(1).

[11] The states which are parties to the Convention are listed in Appendix 1, post, pp. 707–708. An award is a 'Convention award' if the state in question is a party to the Convention at the time of the proceedings for enforcement of the award, whether or not the state in question was a party to the Convention at the date of the award or at the date of the arbitration agreement: *Minister of Public Works of the Government of Kuwait v Sir Frederick Snow & Partners* [1983] 1 Lloyd's Rep 596.

[12] S. 7(1).

[13] Cf. *Dalmia Cement Ltd v National Bank of Pakistan* [1974] 2 Lloyd's Rep 98, [1975] QB 9, a decision on Part II of the 1950 Act.

[14] See pp. 62–63, ante.

proper notice of the appointment of the arbitrator or of the arbitration proceedings or was otherwise unable to present his case.

4 That the award deals with a difference not contemplated by or not falling within the terms of the submission to arbitration or contains decisions on matters beyond the scope of the submission to arbitration[15].

5 That the composition of the arbitral authority or the arbitral procedure was not in accordance with the agreement of the parties or, failing such agreement, with the law of the country where the arbitration took place[16].

6 That the award has not yet become binding on the parties, or has been set aside or suspended by a competent authority of the country in which, or under the law of which, it was made[17].

7 That the award is in respect of a matter which by the law of England[18] is not capable of settlement by arbitration, or if it would be contrary to public policy to enforce the award[19].

The burden of establishing that any of these grounds for withholding enforcement exist lies on the person seeking to resist enforcement[20].

The party seeking to enforce a convention award must produce –

1 The duly authenticated original award or a duly certified copy of it.

2 The original arbitration agreement or a duly certified copy of it.

3 Where the award or agreement is in a foreign language a translation of it certified by an official or sworn translator or by a diplomatic or consular agent[1].

The references to documents being 'duly authenticated' or 'duly certified' are unfamiliar in an English context, but probably add nothing to the ordinary rules of evidence concerning proof of documents: the most convenient method of proof will generally be by exhibiting the document to an affidavit deposing to its authenticity, accuracy as a copy, or truth as a translation, as the case may be[2].

3 Enforcement of 'foreign awards'

Part II of the Arbitration Act 1950, which re-enacts the Arbitration (Foreign Awards) Act 1930, gives effect in the United Kingdom to the 1927 Geneva Convention on the Execution of Foreign Arbitral Awards[3]. It provides for the enforcement in England of 'foreign awards' either by action of 'in the same

---

[15] If the award contains decisions on matters not submitted to arbitration it may be enforced to the extent that it contains decisions on matters submitted to arbitration which can be separated from those on matters which were not so submitted: s. 5(4).

[16] See pp. 64–68, ante.

[17] Where an application for the setting aside or suspension of the award has been made to such a competent authority, the proceedings to enforce the award may be adjourned; but the defendant may be required to give security: s. 5(5).

[18] The words 'by the law of England' do not appear in the Act, but are clearly to be implied: see Article V(2) of the Convention.

[19] Defences 1 to 6 are taken from s. 5(2), and defence 7 from s. 5(3).

[20] *Deutsche Schachtbau und Tiefbohrgesellschaft mbH v Ras al Khaimah National Oil Co* [1987] 2 Lloyd's Rep 246 at 251.

[1] S. 4. The procedure for summary enforcement is the same as under s. 26 of the 1950 Act (see pp. 420–421, ante) except that the documents to be exhibited to the affidavit are those set out in the text: Ord. 73, r. 10(3) (a) (ii).

[2] Cf. Ord. 73, r. 10(3).

[3] The Convention is set out in the Second Schedule to the 1950 Act: See Appendix 1, Part 1, p. 675, post.

manner as the award of an arbitrator is enforceable by virtue of section 26 of this Act'[4].

A 'foreign award' is an award other than a 'Convention award'[5] made (a) in pursuance of an agreement to which the 1923 Protocol on Arbitration Clauses applies[6], (b) between a person subject to the jurisdiction of a power which is a party to the Convention and a person subject to the jurisdiction of some other such power, (c) in the territory to which the Convention applies[7], and (d) on an arbitration agreement which is not governed by the law of England[8].

In order that a 'foreign award' may be enforceable under Part II of the 1950 Act it must have –

1 been made in pursuance of an agreement which was valid by the law by which it was governed[9];

2 been made by the tribunal provided for in the agreement or constituted in manner agreed upon by the parties;

3 been made in conformity with the law governing the arbitration procedure[10];

4 become final in the country in which it was made[11];

5 been in respect of a matter which may lawfully be referred to arbitration under the law of England[12];

and the enforcement thereof must not be contrary to public policy or the law of England[13].

Moreover, a 'foreign award' is not enforceable if the court dealing with the case is satisfied that –

6 the award has been annulled in the country in which it was made; or

7 the party against whom it is sought to enforce the award was not given notice of the arbitration proceedings in sufficient time to enable him to present his case, or was under some legal incapacity and was not properly represented; or

8 the award does not deal with all the questions referred[14] or contains decisions on matters beyond the scope of the agreement for arbitration[15].

If a party seeking to resist enforcement proves that there is any ground (other than the non-existence of conditions 1 to 5 the existence of conditions 6 to 8) entitling him to contest the validity of the award, the court may either refuse

---

[4] S. 36(1).

[5] Arbitration Act 1975, s. 2. A 'Convention award' must therefore be enforced under the 1975 Act, and not as a 'foreign award' under Part II of the 1950 Act.

[6] The Protocol is set out in the First Schedule to the 1950 Act: see Appendix 1, pp. 674–675, post.

[7] S. 35(1). Orders in Council have been made declaring the parties to the Convention and the territories to which the Convention applies: see Appendix 1, pp. 669–671, post.

[8] S. 40(b).

[9] Which must be determined in accordance with the ordinary rules for determining the proper law of the agreement.

[10] See pp. 64–68, ante.

[11] See the discussion of *Union Nationale des Cooperatives Agricoles de Céréales v Robert Catterall & Co* [1959] 1 Lloyd's Rep 111, [1959] 2 QB 44, ante.

[12] See Chapter 10, ante.

[13] S. 37(1).

[14] In such a case the court may, instead of refusing enforcement, either postpone enforcement or order enforcement subject to the giving of such security (e.g. in respect of a cross-claim) by the person seeking enforcement as the court may think fit: s. 37(2), proviso.

[15] S. 37(2). See *Kianta Osakeyhito v Britain and Overseas Trading Co Ltd* [1954] 1 Lloyd's Rep 247.

enforcement or adjourn the hearing for such period as appears to the court to be reasonably sufficient to enable that party to take the necessary steps to have the award annulled by the competent tribunal[16].

A party seeking to enforce a foreign award must produce –

(i) The original award or a copy thereof duly authenticated in manner required by the law of the country in which it was made;

(ii) evidence proving that the award has become final;

(iii) such evidence as may be necessary to prove that the award is a foreign award and that conditions 1, 2 and 3, ante, are satisfied[17].

If any of the required documents is in a foreign language the party seeking enforcement must also produce a translation certified as correct by a diplomatic or consular agent of the country which that party belongs, or certified as correct in such other manner as may be sufficient according to the law of England[18].

If the application is made under section 26 of the 1950 Act[19] the requirements of Order 73, rule 10 must also be complied with[20].

D. DISCIPLINARY ACTION BY TRADE ASSOCIATIONS

Enforcement of awards made under the arbitration rules of trade associations can sometimes be indirectly enforced by invoking the disciplinary powers of the association itself.[1] The nature and extent of the association's powers will be determined by the constitution and rules of the association[2], subject to the general principles of the common law concerning restraint of trade and the requirements of natural justice. Care should be taken when circularising the names of defaulters that the circular is not defamatory, particularly if the defaulter has a cross-claim or some other excuse (whether or not sufficient in law) for refusing to honour the award.

---

[16] S. 37(3).
[17] S. 38(1).
[18] E.g. by an affidavit of a suitably qualified translator.
[19] S. 38(2).
[20] See pp. 420–421, ante.
[1] Detailed discussion of this topic lies outside the scope of this book.
[2] See, for example *Merrifield, Ziegler & Co v Liverpool Cotton Association Ltd* (1911) 105 LT 97.

PART VII

Problems and remedies

CHAPTER 29

Judicial control: a historical survey

A. INTRODUCTION

In the late 1970's, after several decades of consolidation, the English law of arbitration suddenly sprung vigorously to life. Within the space of eighteen months, the coming into force of the Arbitration Act 1979 and the successive decisions of the Court of Appeal and the House of Lords in the *Bremer Vulkan* case[1] not only made important changes in the law, but also compelled a reappraisal of the traditional balance between the supervisory powers of the High Court and the freedom of the arbitral process. So far as they go, the rules created or newly declared by the legislature and the highest tribunal are fixed. But the new regime does not set out to provide a complete definition of the relation between the Court and the arbitral process. Plainly, those responsible for these recent developments did not intend to overturn the existing system, but rather to reinforce it procedurally, and to expose the fundamental principles of it with greater clarity. Nevertheless formidable problems have already arisen, and will undoubtedly continue to arise during the next few years, in accommodating these fresh ideas within a well-established framework of arbitration law. We suggest that reliable solutions cannot be achieved without an understanding, not only of the statutes and reported cases, as they stood at the beginning of the last quarter of the twentieth century, but of the steps by which, and the reasons for which, the law has come into its present state.

The narrative which follows is an attempt to provide a perspective of the successive developments, by statute, the common law and equity which have led to the present-day supervisory jurisdiction of the High Court over the arbitral process. We do not make extensive reference to the reported cases[2], since these are not of immediate practical importance, although certain lines of authority are discussed elsewhere in the book[3]. It is, however, hoped that this summary will provide, in an accessible form, a sufficient general framework for a historical appreciation of this difficult branch of the law.

---

[1] *Bremer Vulkan Schiffbau und Maschinenf v South India Shipping Corpn Ltd* [1980] 1 Lloyd's Rep 255; revsd. [1981] 1 Lloyd's Rep 253, [1981] AC 909.

[2] Excellent accounts of the law as it stood on various dates can be found in Kyd (1791), Caldwell (1817), Watson (3rd edn., 1846), Russell (1st edn., 1849), Redman (1872) and Hogg (1936). There are succinct and useful accounts of the history of various branches of arbitration law in the Working Paper on Arbitration by the Law Reform Commission of New South Wales (1973). Unfortunately, these works are not readily available. For the practitioner, the most convenient means of access to the older cases is provided by the annotated reports of *Vynior's Case* (1610) 8 Co Rep 80 and *Veale v Warner* (1669) 1 Saund 323 at 326. In particular, the successive notes to the latter case by Edmund Saunders himself, Serjeant Williams, Patteson J and Edmund Vaughan Williams, as set out in 85 ER 468, are a masterpiece of compression.

[3] Especially in relation to equitable control: see pp. 519–521, post.

Although the development of the law has been continuous, it is more easy to assimilate if considered in sections. For this purpose, we have divided the account by reference to three great legislative landmarks: the Statute of 1698 (9 & 10 Will III c. 15); the Common Law Procedure Act 1854; and the Arbitration Act 1979.

It is not proposed to trace the development of all the powers claimed by, or conferred on, the High Court, but to concentrate on those which appear the most important, namely: (i) the power of the Court to enforce compliance with agreements to arbitrate; (ii) the power to intervene where the arbitrator has conducted the reference in an unfair manner; and (iii) the power to supervise the legal content of the award by correcting errors of law.

We must first, however, describe the different methods of arbitration which were in existence during the whole of the eighteenth and much of the nineteenth centuries.

B. THREE METHODS OF PRIVATE ARBITRATION

For centuries, the only form of private arbitration known to English law was a voluntary submission out of court. Superficially similar to the form of consensual reference in general use today, the process was subject to some degree of intervention by courts of law and equity. The relationship between the courts and arbitrations was, however, far from satisfactory. The process was neither free from judicial intervention, often of a highly technical nature, nor subject to a continuous or methodical supervision. Furthermore, the Court persistently declined to lend its coercive powers to enforce compliance with the agreement to arbitrate[4].

These weaknesses led to the development during the sixteenth century of an entirely different system. Instead of being subject to intermittent supervision from outside, the arbitration took place within the structure of the legal process itself. Where an action was pending in a court of common law or equity, the parties could by consent obtain an order referring some or all of the issues in suit[5] to the decision of an arbitrator, who was in effect substituted for the jury as the tribunal of fact[6]. This procedure had great advantages, by comparison with a voluntary submission out of court. The parties were free to choose a tribunal better suited than a jury for dealing with technical issues or complex matters of account. But the action remained in being. Although the Court delegated part of its functions to the arbitrator, it retained the remainder. No statutory powers

---

[4] It was the practice to secure the performance of the submission by a mutual penal bond, the obligation to honour the bond being subject to discharge if the party honoured the award. See note 9, p. 434, post. In practice, this arrangement was vulnerable to the revocation of the arbitrator's authority: see p. 434, post.

[5] And, in later years, additional issues not embraced by the original action.

[6] The procedure took various forms. The reference could be made directly the subject of a rule by one of the three courts of common law, or by a court of equity. Or the order could be made by a judge in chambers, or by a judge sitting at the nisi prius, and afterwards made a rule of court. If the reference was ordered at nisi prius, the jury could be disseized of the matter by withdrawing one juror; or a verdict could be taken by consent for the sum claimed, with power to the arbitrator to vary the amount. The order for reference usually contained elaborate terms, regulating discovery, the taking of evidence on oath, the stay of the pending action, an undertaking by the parties not to invoke equitable remedies, and so on.

were needed to enable the Court to intervene in case of error or misconduct; it possessed these powers inherently, because the arbitrator's mandate from the Court was limited to the conduct of the reference in a proper manner. When supervising the reference, the Court was doing no more than regulate an offshoot of its own process. Moreover, by about 1670 the courts had been persuaded to treat the order referring the cause as an undertaking given by the parties to the Court that they would abide by the terms of the order and would honour any resulting award. If broken, this undertaking attracted the penalties appropriate to a contempt of court, in particular the liability of the offender to attachment of his goods and in extreme cases, of his person.

This innovation proved a success[7]. The procedure was, however, available only in the context of a pending suit, and even then only by consent. Accordingly, in 1698 the gap was partially[8] filled by legislation. The preamble to the Statute 9 & 10 Will III c. 15 read:

'Whereas it hath been found by experience, that references made by rule of court have contributed much to the ease of the subject, in the determination of controversies, because the parties become thereby obliged to submit to the award of the arbitrators, under the penalty of imprisonment for their contempt, in case they refuse submission: now for promoting trade, and rendering the award of arbitrators more effectual in all cases for the final determination of controversies referred to them by merchants and traders, or others, concerning matters of account of trade, or other matters, be it enacted. . . .'

The Statute went on to provide that parties who wished to submit a dispute to arbitration could agree that their submission to arbitration should be made a rule of any court of record of their choice. Upon production of such an agreement, the Court would by summary process make the submission a rule. Failure to comply with the submission would render the offender liable to process for contempt of court. The Statute also contained provisions, to which we shall later refer, empowering the court to intervene in the case of misconduct by the arbitrator.

It followed that in the years after the enactment of the 1698 Act, there were three quite different systems of arbitration in existence at the same time, namely –

1 A reference in a pending cause. The submission to arbitration came after, not before, the involvement of the Court in the dispute. The process of judicial intervention derived from the inherent jurisdiction of the Court to regulate its own process.

2 A reference under the 1698 Act. Here the submission was consensual, and preceded the involvement of the Court. The effect of an order making the submission a rule of court was not to turn the arbitration into an action, but to attach to the submission certain characteristics which were similar to those possessed by a reference in a pending cause. The Court did not, therefore, have any general inherent jurisdiction to intervene in the reference. Its powers were created and defined by the Act.

---

[7] Although Kyd, at p. 155, quotes an unnamed judge as saying of references at nisi prius that he never knew any good to arise from them.

[8] See p. 436, post.

3 Voluntary submissions out of court, not falling within the Act. These consisted of –

(i) Submissions which could not be made a rule: for example an oral submission, or a submission which did not expressly provide that it might be made a rule.

(ii) Submissions which did contain such a provision, but which had not in fact been made a rule.

Here, the arbitration proceeded independently of the courts, and the powers of judicial intervention were more narrow than in the case where the submission was a rule of court, although not wholly non-existent.

This regime remained in force for more than 150 years. It is essential when reading old cases on arbitration to understand the distinction between the three procedures, and in particular the different sources from which the courts drew their power to intervene in the reference. Authorities on these former procedures may be misleading when used to ascertain the powers which the courts possess today.

C. THE POSITION BEFORE THE ACT OF 1698

1 Enforcement

We have already referred to the fact that the form of arbitration in use at the beginning of the seventeenth century was a voluntary submission out of court, secured by a penal bond[9]. This procedure was, subject to a potentially fatal weakness[10], namely that the arbitrator's authority was conceived to be a mandate revocable at the will of either party, at any time before award. This meant that a party could frustrate the reference simply by withdrawing the authority of the arbitrator. The revocation was treated as a breach of contract, for which damages would lie[11], and an action could also be brought on the bond. But these did not always permit a complete remedy. A revocation did not attract the penalties appropriate to a contempt of court, since the submission was a private contract; and the position was not improved by an insertion in the submission of an agreement not to revoke it, since the mandate was regarded as being intrinsically revocable. The existence of an agreement to arbitrate did not constitute a defence to an action at law; nor would equity decree specific performance of the agreement to arbitrate. Furthermore, the Court would not grant a stay of proceedings brought in breach of an agreement to arbitrate. So there were neither positive nor negative means of enforcing the submission.

It was this weakness that led to the popularity of a reference in a pending suit; and actions were started simply in order that they could be made the subject of a reference. We have already mentioned the improvements which this innovation brought about. But the system was still vulnerable to the risk that

---

[9] Which, in typical form, obliged each party to 'stand to, abide, observe, perform, fulfill and keep the rule, order, judgment, arbitrament, sentence and final determination' of the arbitrator, on pain of forfeiting the penal sum.

[10] Exposed in *Vynior's Case* (1610) 8 Co Rep 80, but almost certainly recognised before that time. Coke calls up a Year Book case from the reign of Edward IV.

[11] *Newgate v Degelder* (1666) 2 Keb 10, 20, 24.

the submission would be revoked by one party before the other had applied for a rule.

2 Judicial intervention in the reference

Judicial control over a voluntary reference out of Court was clumsy and unsystematic. Misconduct by the arbitrator was never recognised as a defence to an action on the award or on the penal bond[12]. Nor was there ever a jurisdiction in a court of common law to set aside an award for misconduct[13]. The only available remedy was a bill in equity. The jurisdiction to intervene in a voluntary reference is very old; but the rules as to the situations in which it would be exercised had not yet become systematised, during the period under discussion.

With the coming into use of the new procedure, whereby a reference would be ordered in the course of a pending suit, the relationship between arbitration and the courts was entirely changed. As we have said, the Court exercised its jurisdiction from within, not outside, the reference. No statute was needed to give the Court power to interfere in such a case; the power came from the fact that the arbitration was an offshoot of the original action. As Gibbs LCJ said in a much later case[14] –

'Where a cause is referred to arbitration, the court still reserves a superintendary authority over the award, and in such a case it proceeds on this authority'[15].

This jurisdiction was exercised in a miscellany of situations, all of them characterised by what would now be called misconduct of the arbitration.

3 Mistake of law

There are traces in the authorities of a jurisdiction exercised at this early stage to interfere with an award which could be shown on its face, or by extrinsic evidence, to have been founded on a mistake by the arbitrator.

---

[12] Sergeant Williams, in his note 3 to *Veale v Warner* (1681) 1 Saund 323 at 327a, said that 'there seems no case or dictum, where a plea of this sort has been said to be pleadable, nor a precedent of such a plea to be found in any of the books of entries'. As the commentator points out, if such a plea had been available, Saunders would have raised it in *Veale v Warner*, and would not have 'had recourse to that unworthy trick for which he was so justly censured' (viz. tempting the plaintiff into a technical error).

[13] Russell (1st edn.) p. 614; Watson 263–264; *Ansell v Evans* (1796) 7 Term Rep 1; *Rogers v Dallimore* (1815) 1 Marsh 471 at 472. There are other authorities to the like effect. The point is important, because in recent times there have been statements that the Court has an inherent jurisdiction at common law to interfere in the reference. This is not so. See Chapter 32, post.

[14] *Rogers v Dallimore* (1815) 1 Marsh 471. The dictum is reported in different words in 6 Taunt 114, but the idea is the same. The principle was taken for granted in several other cases.

[15] And accordingly the Court had jurisdiction even if the reference was not made a rule under the Act of 1698: so that the time limits for moving to set the award aside prescribed by that Act did not apply.

D. 1698 TO 1854

1 Enforcement of the agreement to arbitrate

We need not repeat what has already been said about the improvement introduced by the Act of 1698 in the enforceability of voluntary submissions out of court. There remained, however, a number of weaknesses. In particular, the Act had no application in those cases where the submission did not expressly provide that it might be made a rule of court. Nor did it enable a rule to be made before the tribunal had been constituted, so that a party could permanently obstruct the reference by declining to appoint an arbitrator[16]. Furthermore, an application for a rule involved expense, and for the sake of economy the reference very often proceeded without a rule being made, even if the submission conferred a liability to apply for one. If either party revoked the authority of the arbitrator during the period before a rule was applied for, the reference was brought to an end. And even a revocation after the making of a rule was effective, although liable to be treated as a contempt of court. This latter weakness was remedied by section 39 of the Civil Procedure Act of 1833[17], which stipulated that where an arbitrator had been appointed pursuant to an order, made either in a pending suit or by virtue of the 1698 Act, the power and authority of the arbitrator should not be revocable[18] by a party to the reference without the leave of the court which had made the rule. This provision is the origin of section 1 of 1950 Act[19].

Some progress was also made by consensual means to improve the enforceability of agreements to arbitrate. At common law, the existence of a pending arbitration was no bar to an action in court relating to the same subject matter[20]. It did, however, become a very common practice to include in the order made for a reference in a pending suit, that all proceedings in the action should be stayed for the purposes of the arbitration.

2 Judicial intervention in the reference

When the new procedure was introduced in 1698, whereby the parties to a voluntary submission out of court could if the submission so provided make the submission a rule of court, it would have been possible to argue that the making of a rule brought into existence a sufficiently close connection between the court and the reference to enable the court to exercise an inherent right of control, similar to that which existed in respect of references which had originally sprung from a rule in a pending suit[1]. In fact, however, the question of judicial

---

[16] See *Re Smith and Service and Nelson & Sons* (1890) 25 QBD 545.

[17] 3 & 4 Will IV, c. 42.

[18] The agreement to refer disputes to arbitration (which in the text we have referred to as 'the submission') was never revocable at common law, at any time in the history of the law of arbitration.

[19] The use of s. 1 in very recent years as a method by which the Court can interfere in the reference differs markedly from the original purpose of the legislation, which was to inhibit the revocation of the arbitrator's authority, not to encourage it.

[20] The idea of an inherent jurisdiction to restrain actions brought in breach of a contract to arbitrate, which was current for some years but is now discredited, so far as concerns agreements to arbitrate in England (see p. 460, post), was a much later invention.

[1] p. 434, ante.

supervision was specifically dealt with in the 1698 Act, by a provision which empowered the Court in which the rule had been made to set aside the award on proof that it was 'procured by corruption or other undue means'. The Act also forbade the use of equitable remedies in respect of submissions falling within the Act.

From these provisions sprang two long-standing controversies.

First, which (if any) were the differences between the various types of arbitration as to the circumstances in which the Court was empowered to intervene? The 1698 Act referred only to 'corruption or other undue means'. At first, these words were strictly construed, but by the last quarter of the eighteenth century it had come to be accepted that any ground could be relied upon to set aside an award in a reference made under the statute, which could have been relied upon if the reference had sprung from a pending cause. Equally, the rather imprecise boundaries of the equitable power to intervene had settled down to give broadly the same jurisdiction[2] as was exerciseable by the common law courts in respect of references under the Act or in a pending suit[3].

Second, there was the question of the extent to which the equitable jurisdiction survived the new Act. Eventually[4], it was held that the exclusion of this jurisdiction applied only to those cases where (a) the submission had actually been made a rule of court by virtue of the Act, or (b) the submission contained an agreement that it could be made a rule, even if no rule had in fact been sought. The jurisdiction continued to be available, however, in those cases where the reference was made in a pending cause[5], or where it was made out of court without any express agreement that a rule could be applied for.

The position may therefore be summarised as follows –

(i) Submissions by rule of court in a pending action.

Here, the common law courts had a jurisdiction which was inherent, and did not come from the Act, to set aside the award for misconduct. The Courts of Equity had a concurrent inherent jurisdiction, exerciseable on broadly similar lines. In addition, the court out of which the rule had issued would withhold the remedy of attachment if it was shown that the proceedings were tainted with misconduct.

(ii) Submissions out of court made a rule of court under the 1698 Act.

Here, the common law courts had a jurisdiction to set aside for misconduct which was exclusively statutory in origin. The court could in addition refuse the remedy of attachment even if no application had been made to set aside[6]. There

---

[2] In a note to *Brown v Brown* (1683) 1 Vern 157 (3rd edn.), 23 ER 785 there is a full collection of cases, which the commentator writing in 1827 summarises as indicating that there is jurisdiction to intervene where there is a fraud, partiality, want of due notice, or wilful misbehaviour in the arbitrator or parties. See also Russell (3rd edn.) p. 672 and Watson p. 390.

[3] Although the remedies were available in broadly similar situations, the procedures by which they were sought were quite different. Where the reference was in a pending suit, the application was by motion; under the Act, there was a summary procedure; in equity, it was by means of a bill.

[4] In *Nichols v Roe* (1834) 3 My & K 431. The long history of this controversy is summarised in Russell pp. 667–672.

[5] *Lonsdale v Littledale* (1794) 2 Ves 451. See also Russell (1st edn.) p. 666.

[6] *Hutchins v Hutchins* (1738) Andr 297; *Pedley v Goddard* (1796) 7 Term Rep 73.

was no inherent jurisdiction in such a case[7]. The equitable courts had no power to intervene[8].

(iii) Submissions out of court, not made a rule of court under the Act.   Here the common law had no inherent or statutory power to intervene. A bill in Equity was the sole remedy.

Thus far, we have referred to the statutory and inherent jurisdictions of the Court to set aside the award. What the court did not have during the period under review was any power to remit the award for reconsideration or correction. The statutes were silent on the point, and there was not (and never has been) any inherent power to remit at common law[9]. Once the arbitrator has made his award he has discharged the office which the parties agreed to confer on him, and the Court has no power at common law to revive this office unless both of the parties agree. This gap in the jurisdiction of the Court led to great inconvenience, for it meant that in cases where the defect was too serious to be regarded as de minimis, the Court had no choice but to set aside the award in its entirety, even though the more just course would have been to remit it to the arbitrator so that he could correct the mistake[10].

During the first half of the nineteenth century it became the practice to remedy this gap in the jurisdiction of the Court by including in those submissions to arbitration which were made a rule of court an express provision[11] that in the event of either of the parties disputing the validity of the award, or moving to set it aside, the Court should have power to remit the matters referred, or any of them, to the reconsideration of the arbitrator. The wording of this clause made it plain that the purpose was to mitigate the rigour of the existing law by giving the Court an alternative remedy in cases where it would otherwise have set the award aside; and the courts did not as a rule interpret the clause as conferring a general discretion to remit on grounds other than those which would have sustained an application to set aside[12].

There were, however, two respects in which the grounds for remission pursuant to the clause extended beyond those upon which an award could be set aside. First, the Court hesitantly allowed remission where the arbitrator had admitted the mistake and invited the Court to send the award back for the purpose of correction. Second, the Court assumed the power to remit where

---

[7] *Rogers v Dallimore* (1815) 1 Marsh 471 at 472, per Gibbs CJ arguendo.

[8] Except in those cases where it was the Court of Equity which had itself made the submission a rule of court.

[9] *Simpson v IRC* [1914] 2 KB 842; *Ex p Cuerton* (1826) 7 Dow & Ry KB 774; *Re Keighley, Maxted & Co and Durant & Co* [1893] 1 QB 405 at 409; *Meyer v Leanse* [1958] 2 QB 371; *Potato Marketing Board v Merricks* [1958] 2 QB 316. It was taken for granted in *Hodgkinson v Fernie* (1857) 3 CBNS 189 that there was no power to remit at common law.

[10] There are instances in the older cases where the courts contrived to find devices which achieved the same practical results as remission. There was never any doubt, however, about the absence of a general power to remit at common law.

[11] Sometimes called 'Mr. Richards' Clause', after its inventor. Several versions can be found in the reported cases.

[12] An illustration of the purpose which the clause was intended to fulfil may be found in *Howett v Clements* (1845) 1 CB 128, where an arbitrator mistakenly referred to the claimant as James Charles Howett instead of Joseph Charles Howett, and the award was remitted so that he could correct the mistake.

fresh evidence had been discovered since the award which, in the opinion of the arbitrator, would have influenced his decision[13].

3 Mistake of law

After a great deal of conflict and uncertainty, the law had by the middle of the nineteenth century become settled that an award could not in general be impeached either at law or in equity on the ground that the arbitrator had committed an error of fact or law[14]. To this general principle there were two exceptions.

The first was that the Court would set aside[15] an award, if the arbitrator admitted that he had acted under a mistake of law or fact.

The second, and more important, exception was that an award might be set aside if it was apparent from the award itself, or from documents incorporated in the award, that the conclusion of the arbitrator involved a material error of law[16].

Although this jurisdiction attracted much censure in later years, it made available to those parties (always more numerous than the critics have been willing to recognise) who wished for it, a consensual means of appealing to the court from the arbitrator's decision of law. Although in its origin, the jurisdiction was exercised by one party against the opposition of the other, a practice developed whereby the parties to a reference would jointly ask the arbitrator to state his award so that there appeared on the face of it all the facts necessary to enable the court to set the award aside if an error of law could be detected[17]. Later, it became customary to insert in the submission a term requiring the arbitrator to state his reasons on the face, and it even became recognised that a failure by the arbitrator to comply with such a term could amount to misconduct[18].

Later still, the practice was refined so as to facilitate the disposal of the matter after the court had given its decision. Having stated the facts, the award would

---

[13] *Burnard v Wainwright* (1850) 19 LJ QB 423. For a discussion of these two grounds for remission, see pp. 558–562, post.

[14] The references to the admissibility of extrinsic evidence to justify a setting aside in the case of 'gross error', in cases such as *Knox v Symmonds* (1791) 1 Ves 369 must, we think, be taken as referring to admitted error: see *Anderson v Darcy* (1812) 18 Ves 447.

[15] Or remit, if the submission expressly so permitted: see note 11, p. 438, ante.

[16] *Kent v Elstob* (1802) 3 East 18. Various suggestions have been made as to the rationale of this rule. It has been said that a submission to arbitration involves an agreement that the arbitrator shall decide in accordance with the law, so that a decision founded on an erroneous principle is not binding on the parties. Another explanation was that an arbitrator is under an obligation to decide according to the law, and that if he fails to do so, he commits misconduct. On this view, the jurisdiction to set aside for error on the face of the award was not an anomalous exception to the general rule, but was merely an instance of the old common law power to set aside for misconduct. Another possibility was that the Court had an inherent power to review all 'speaking' awards of inferior tribunals. Another theory was that an error on the face of the award is simply an example of patent substantive invalidity, which has always been regarded as a ground for setting aside. Finally, an award containing an error of law on the face might be regarded as a primitive example of an award in the form of a special case; for by setting out in the award his process of legal reasoning, the arbitrator may be regarded as having invited the Court to decide whether it is correct. What is quite clear is that the jurisdiction was inherent, and not dependent on any statute: *Re Jones and Carter's Arbitration* [1922] 2 Ch 599.

[17] For example, *Re Webb* (1818) 8 Taunt 443; *Anderson v Fuller* (1838) 4 M & W 470.

[18] For example, *Sherry v Oke* (1835) 3 Dowl 349.

contain a decision reflecting the arbitrator's decision or the issues of law. But it would also include an alternative decision which was to take effect if the court was of a different opinion on the law. By 1840 it had come to be recognised that there was a power to make an award in this form, even without an express provision in the order of reference[19]. At about the same time, the nomenclature began to assume a modern form. The arbitrator was to have power to state 'points' or 'matters of law' for the opinion of the Court; to 'report specifically to the Court'; to 'reserve' or 'raise' any point of law for the decision of the Court[20].

We thus see that as long ago as the first half of the nineteenth century, parties had already begun to employ by consent a procedure not entirely different from the award in the form of a special case.

E. 1854 TO 1889

1 The move towards reform[1]

During the early years of the nineteenth century there was a rising tide of dissatisfaction with the whole system of procedure in civil actions. This led to the formation of two Commissions[2] which between the years 1829 and 1853 produced a series of reports embracing the whole field of civil procedure. Since one of the matters discussed by the Commissions was the improvement of the existing methods for trying issues of fact, it was natural that consideration should be given to the establishment of new means whereby complex disputes arising in the course of an action could be referred to arbitration. It was equally natural that if the powers of the court were to be used to compel the arbitration of such issues, there would be consideration of the degree to which, and the manner in which, the court should ensure that the matters referred were properly tried. But there was no attempt at a general review of the law of arbitration. The Commissions were concerned with litigation, not with voluntary arbitration. Thus, although the Common Law Procedure Act 1854, which followed upon 25 years of debate, is often treated as the foundation of the modern law of arbitration, it must be recognised that it was not an Arbitration Act, and that the important alterations which it made were the by-products of reforms aimed at the administration of justice in court, and that they left the formal structure of arbitration law substantially unchanged.

---

[19] The procedure was originally sanctioned by holding that if the arbitrator's view was right, the (ex hypothesi) erroneous alternative award would be rejected as surplusage. There were rather more problems if the Court considered that the alternative award was right. The primary award could be set aside for error on the face. Upholding the alternative was more difficult: see, for example, *Barton v Ransom* (1838) 3 M & W 322; *Re Wright and Cromford Canal Co* (1841) 1 QB 98. There was also a procedure, akin to the consultative case, which was in use until 1979, whereby the arbitrator made no decision himself, but simply found the facts and left the decision to the Court. The validity of this procedure was controversial: see *Anderson v Fuller*, ante; *Jephson v Howkins* (1841) 2 Man & G 366; *Grocers Co v Donne* (1836) 3 Bing NC 34.

[20] *Sherry v Oke*, ante; *Jephson v Howkins*, ante; *Wood v Hotham* (1839) 5 M & W 674; *Scott v Van Sandau* (1844) 6 QB 237; *Richards v Easto* (1846) 15 M & W 244.

[1] We are indebted to Mr Mark Hapgood, LLB, Barrister, for much valuable information on the early history of the special case.

[2] The members were known as the 'Early' and the 'Late' Commissioners. All were of the highest excellence.

One of the proposals made by the Early Commissioners[3] was designed to deal with the problems of trying questions of account before a jury. It often happened that the judges would point out the undesirability of leaving such question to the jury, and suggest that they should be transferred by consent to a referee[4]. The parties might well be reluctant to agree, having incurred the expense of a trial, and being anxious for an immediate decision; and the judge had no power to compel them. The Commissioners therefore proposed that on questions of account only, the judges should have power to order a reference without the consent of the parties, and that this could be done upon an application by either party, after issue joined and before the trial. It was, however, considered that where the reference was compulsory the court should have wider powers of control over the reference than in relation to the three modes of private arbitration then current. It was accordingly proposed that the Court should have the right to intervene, not only in the event of misconduct, but also on the ground of any mistake, in point of law, whether appearing on the face of the award or not, or of gross error on a question of fact.

In addition, an entirely separate proposal, having no connection with arbitration, was put forward[5], whereby the parties to an action should have a power to state a case for the opinion of the court on agreed facts without pleadings.

The first-mentioned proposal met with strong opposition from those[6] who believed that arbitration was an inefficient method of resolving disputes, and it was withdrawn when the bill which became the Act of 1833[7] was before Parliament. But the idea of a special case stated within the confines of the action survived, as section 25 of the Act.

It appears from the first report[8] of the Late Commissioners that the procedure of a special case in an action was widely used, and certain improvements to it were recommended[9]. Meanwhile, the special case had already become an established practice in several fields. As we have seen, it had been in use for several decades, in form if not name, as a feature of references to arbitration by rule of court. Provision was also made for the stating of a case by statutes regulating other subordinate tribunals.

It is therefore not surprising that the concept of a special case as a procedure in a voluntary arbitration should have been brought forward for consideration. In 1853 Lord Brougham presented[10] his Arbitration Law Amendment Bill[11]. This was primarily aimed at securing enforcement of the reference to arbitration. The promoter had considered, but rejected, the idea (proposed by the Early Commissioners) of a compulsory reference to arbitration without the consent of the parties, on questions of account. There were, however, provisions of interest relating to references made pursuant to a rule of court: namely that the

---

[3] In the second report of 26 February 1838, Commons Papers 1830 XI p. 547.

[4] The expressions 'referee' and 'arbitrator' were often used interchangeably, at this time.

[5] In the Parliamentary Bill. It was not, so far as we can trace, a recommendation of the Commissioners themselves.

[6] Notably Lord Eldon. Hansard, House of Lords 1833, Vol. 16, 1067.

[7] 3 & 4 Will 4 c. 42.

[8] Commons Papers 1851 page 567.

[9] Enacted in s. 46 of the Common Law Procedure Act 1852.

[10] The speech of Lord Brougham introducing the Bill gives a very unflattering picture of arbitrations as currently practised: Hansard, House of Lords 1853, Vol. 129, 839.

[11] This had been drafted in consultation with 'City gentlemen' and Francis Russell.

arbitrator should be at liberty to state a case[12], and that the court should have power to remit the award to the arbitrator, even if the order for reference contained no express provision empowering either of these procedures[13].

This Bill never became law, being withdrawn by its promoter, almost certainly because of the imminence of the debate which led to the Common Law Procedure Act 1854[14]. This great piece of legislation which covered the whole field of current procedure, otherwise, than in courts of equity, brought about several important changes in the law of arbitration, which may be summarised as follows –

1 A system of compulsory references on matters of account was introduced, such as had originally been proposed by the Early Commissioners[15].

2 The arbitrator was empowered to state a case in compulsory references, and those references which had been or could be made a rule of court.

3 Every submission could now be made a rule of court, except those which expressly provided to the contrary.

4 The Court was empowered to remit an award to the consideration of the arbitrator.

5 The Court was empowered to stay proceedings brought in breach of an agreement to arbitrate.

6 Several new powers were conferred relating to the filling of vacancies, the appointment of an umpire, and the time limit for making an award.

We now refer to some of these changes in more detail.

2 Enforcement of the agreement to arbitrate

The enforcement of an agreement to refer was taken two stages further by the Act of 1854.

First, the procedure for making the submission a rule of court was made more readily available by section 17, which provided that any written submission could be made a rule, on the application of either party, unless the submission contained words purporting that the parties intended that it should not be made a rule[16]. There still remained the position, however, that if no application was made, pursuant to this section, a voluntary reference did not attract any of the coercive powers of the court by way of attachment and otherwise, such as existed with a reference pursuant to a rule in a pending cause, or a voluntary submission made a rule under the statute[17].

---

[12] Including a consultative case, stated in the course of the reference.

[13] As it commonly did: see p. 438, ante.

[14] This had its origin in the work of the Late Commissioners, supplemented by a Lords Select Committee consisting of Lords Cranwall, Lyndhurst, Brougham, Overstone, Truro and St Leonards.

[15] There was strong opposition from Lord St Leonards, chiefly on the ground that arbitration was dilatory and inefficient: Hansard, House of Lords 1854, Vol. 133, 787. This provision, contained in s. 3 of the Act, is the origin of the modern system of referees: see Chapter 20, ante.

[16] It might be expected that few submissions would contain an express exclusion of the right to apply for a rule. As Russell (3rd edn., 1864) pointed out at p. 63, such a provision was disadvantageous. The submission could be revoked; the court exercised no supervision over the reference; and there was no means of summary enforcement. The fact that Russell thought the matter worth mentioning may suggest that there were parties who felt (just as some persons feel to-day) that they would prefer to keep their disputes away from the courts altogether.

[17] *Harris v Reynolds* (1845) 7 QB 71; *Livingstone v Ralli* (1855) 24 LJQB 269.

The Act also made it more difficult for a party to a written submission to bring legal proceedings in breach of his agreement to arbitrate. There was no serious problem in relation to arbitrations which sprang from a reference in a pending suit, since it had already become the practice to include a covenant to stay the action, as part of the order to refer; and this the court would enforce by virtue of its right to control its own proceedings. But a mere voluntary submission did not operate as an absolute bar to an action, even if the reference was already in progress[18], and the Court had no inherent power to stay such proceedings, even if the submission contained a covenant not to sue[19]. This gap was almost completely[20] filled by section 11 of the 1854 Act, which conferred on the Court a discretion to stay an action brought in breach of an agreement to refer existing or future differences to arbitration, in terms very similar to those of the Arbitration Act 1950[1].

3 Judicial intervention in the reference

We have previously[2] summarised the position as regards judicial intervention in the three prevailing types of reference. The 1854 Act introduced another procedure, the compulsory reference to which both parties did not consent. This was subject to the same powers of intervention as a reference pursuant to a rule of court[3].

Of more immediate relevance are the changes effected by the enlargement of the power to make a submission a rule of court, and the introduction of the new statutory power to remit[4]. The result was as follows –

(i) Submissions by rule of court in a pending action. There was an inherent power to set aside, and a statutory power to remit.

(ii) Submissions out of court which had already been made a rule under the 1698 Act. These were now likely to be more numerous, and there was a new power to remit. The jurisdiction to set aside was also statutory.

(iii) Voluntary submissions out of court, not made a rule of court. The position here was the same as before. Only equity had jurisdiction to intervene.

4 Mistake of law

The principal innovation of the 1854 Act in this field was, as we have seen, to give statutory force to the existing practice, whereby an arbitrator was empowered to state a special case for the opinion of the court on a question of law[5]. The following features of this procedure may be noted –

1 The procedure applied only to – (a) compulsory references, and (b)

---

[18] It still does not operate as a bar, and the residual jurisdiction of the Court still subsists, even where the circumstances of the Court are such as to call for a compulsory stay under the 1975 Act.

[19] The inconvenience could to some extent be mitigated by the device upheld in *Scott v Avery* (1856) 5 HL Cas 811, whereby the obtaining of an award was by contract made a condition precedent to a right of suit.

[20] Not entirely filled, because the power to stay did not apply to oral submissions: nor indeed does any statutory power to stay exist at the present time where the submission is not in writing.

[1] See Chapter 30, post.

[2] At pp. 432–434, ante.

[3] S. 7.

[4] S. 8.

[5] S. 5.

references by consent where the submission was made a rule of court, and (c) references by consent where the submission might in accordance with its terms be made a reference. There was no power to state a case in a voluntary reference not complying with these requirements.

2 The arbitrator was empowered to state a case. The court had no power to order him to do so.

3 The arbitrator could only state an award in the form of a special case. There was no power to state a consultative case, in the course of the reference, before an award was made.

4 The power to state a case could be excluded by an express term of the submission[6].

In addition to the newly created *statutory* right to invoke the power of the court to enquire into the legal content of the award, there still remained the *inherent* power of the court to supervise the award through the medium of setting aside the award for error on the face. This jurisdiction, which survived the Act of 1854[7], existed independently of any election by the arbitrator to state a case. If there was an error on the face of the award, the Court had an inherent jurisdiction to intervene, quite independent of section 5[8].

F. 1889 TO 1979

1 The Acts of 1889, 1934 and 1950

During the years immediately preceding the enactment of the Arbitration Act 1889 there took place the only serious attempt to codify the English law of arbitration. Lord Bramwell[9] devoted several years to the task, and produced a draft bill, of some 140 clauses, which set out to embody the whole of the law, as contained in reported cases as well as statutes. The enterprise proved too ambitious, and after more than one attempt to secure its passage, the Bill was withdrawn, to make way for the much less elaborate and controversial Bill which became the 1889 Act[10].

The latter Act took effect, partly as a consolidation of existing law, and partly as innovatory legislation, based to some extent on existing practice. It repealed the Act of 1698, and those parts of the Acts of 1835 and 1854 which related to arbitration. In their place it established a simple regime for voluntary arbitration, instead of the three systems which were previously in force. It repeated several parts of the 1854 Act relating to the establishment of the tribunal and other administrative matters, and created a group of statutory

---

[6] Thus, whereas it was permissible for the parties to contract in to a power or duty (according to the terms of the submission) they could now *contract out* of the power to state a case.

[7] Insufficient of the deliberations which preceded the 1854 Act have survived for it to be possible now to ascertain why it was decided to allow the former jurisdiction to set aside for error on the face to survive, once proceedings by way of special case had received statutory backing.

[8] The position as it stands today provides a curious echo of the direct power of review for mistake of law which existed after the 1854 Act; see pp. 456–458, post.

[9] Assisted, amongst others, by Sir Montague Chalmers, Mr Russell, and Sir Courtney Sebert. Space does not permit discussion of this very interesting document.

[10] In a debate on the Arbitration Bill of 1934, Lord Askwith said that the 1889 Act (which he described as 'skeletal') resulted from committees and inquiries over a series of years.

implied terms[11], which reproduced, with a few alterations, the language of those submissions which can be found in the precedent books of the mid-nineteenth century[12].

Apart from important provisions relating to the special case, the Act of 1934[13] made no changes in the formal structure of the relationship between the courts and the arbitral procedure. It was concerned principally with the filling of gaps in the existing legislation, in order to make the process more efficient.

The Act of 1950 was designed as a consolidating statute, and was therefore intended to make no substantial alterations in the law of arbitration: although, as we shall see, it did make one important change, probably by accident[14]. The Acts of 1889 and 1934 were repealed, and their substance reproduced in the new Act, not with complete success. The incorporation of the implied terms, formerly scheduled in the 1889 Act, into the body of the text, without significant alterations in the language, has created uncertainty as to those terms which are mandatory, and those which are not[15]. Problems on the interpretation of the Act may call for recourse to the earlier statutes[16].

2 Enforcement of the agreement to arbitrate

The Acts of 1889, 1934 and 1950 made four important improvements in the enforceability of the agreement to arbitrate.

First, the procedure for making the submission a rule of court became obsolete. Section 1 of the Act of 1889 provided that a submission[17] should have the same effect for all purposes as if it had been made a rule. This meant that a party had available all the remedies appropriate for a contempt of court, without the need to apply for a rule[18]. In fact, applications for an attachment seem to have become unnecessary, since the 1889 Act had[19] created a less cumbersome procedure for summary enforcement[20]. The 1934 Act made no changes in this part of the law, but the 1950 Act completed the process of eliminating the procedures which had existed for 250 years. By repealing section 1 of the 1889 Act[1], which had replaced all the relevant parts of the prior legislation, the law was restored to the situation in which it had been before the Act of 1698. Thus, it is still in theory possible to make an order by consent in a pending cause referring an issue or issues to arbitration; but there is no longer any provision deeming this to have been done, or any means of compelling such a rule to be

---

[11] In the first Schedule.

[12] E.g. Kay & Elphinstone's *Compendium of Precedents in Conveyancing* (2nd edn, 1883), pp. 148–151.

[13] This Act followed many, but by no means all, of the recommendations of the Mackinnon Committee, which had reported in 1927. The promoters of the Bill did not adopt the recommendation that the existing legislation should be repealed.

[14] See pp. 519–521, post.

[15] There was also a controversy, only recently resolved by *Imperial Metal Industries (Kynoch) Ltd v Amalgamated Union of Engineering Workers* [1979] 1 All ER 847 as to whether the Act applied otherwise than to references taking place otherwise than pursuant to an 'arbitration agreement': i.e. a written agreement to submit present or future differences to arbitration.

[16] As in *Imperial Metal Industries (Kynoch) Ltd v AUEW*, supra.

[17] I.e. a written agreement to submit present or future disputes to arbitration.

[18] The procedure of applying for a rule remained available, but fell into disuse.

[19] By s. 12.

[20] Hogg (writing in 1936) described the procedure for attachment as 'nearly, but not quite, obsolete'.

[1] Through s. 44(3).

made. The major implications of this change in the law are discussed, post. For the present it is sufficient to say that the remedies of attachment for contempt are no longer available in practice for non-compliance with an agreement to arbitrate, or for failing to honour an award[2].

Second, the 1889 Act provided that a submission should be irrevocable without leave of the Court. A submission was now defined as 'a written agreement to submit present or future disputes to arbitration, whether an arbitrator is named therein or not'[3]. The concluding words had the effect of ensuring that the restrictions on revocations no longer applied only to pending references, but now to all arbitration agreements.

Third, the legislation progressively restricted the power of one party to obstruct an arbitration by refusing to appoint an arbitrator. The Court or the opposing party, or both, were given power to fill a vacancy resulting from failure to appoint, in most situations likely to occur in practice[4].

Finally, there were provisions relating to the inhibition of proceedings brought in breach of an agreement to arbitrate. The 1889 Act substantially reproduced the terms of the 1854 Act, which conferred on the Court a discretion to stay such proceedings. This provision was carried into the 1950 Act[5] which, as interpreted by a long course of judicial decisions, imposed on the plaintiff the burden of showing why the agreement to arbitrate should not be enforced. An important innovation was, however, the mandatory stay of actions in respect of certain 'non-domestic' disputes, originally introduced by the Arbitration Clauses (Protocol) Act 1924 and now superseded by the Arbitration Act 1975[6].

3 Judicial intervention in the reference

As we have seen, the power of the Court to set aside an award was either statutory or inherent, depending on the nature of the reference.

By section 11(2) of the 1889 Act, the statutory power to set aside was extended

---

[2] Orders are, of course, constantly being made by the courts, pursuant to the power to order a stay of proceedings in breach of an agreement to arbitrate: see post, pp. 462–483. In practice these usually result in the dispute being dealt with by means of arbitration. But the Court does not *order* a reference: it merely prohibits the claimant from pursuing his claim in any other way. The parties can by consent obtain an order for a reference in a pending suit, but such orders are very rare indeed, and we doubt whether it occurs to the parties that the effect of making such an order is to expose them to a potential liability for contempt of court.

[3] S. 27. This definition created serious technical problems. A reference to arbitration involves two distinct relationships; the contract between the parties to abide by the decision of the arbitrator, and the mandate conferred on the arbitrator to make a binding decision (properly called the submission). The legislation had been intended to cure the defect that the mandate was revocable at will. The contract between the parties had never been capable of revocation. The transfer of the word 'submission' from the former to the latter sense, meant that for the first time the Court was given power to annul the contract inter partes. This seems to have been recognised as a mistake and in the 1934 Act the definition quoted in the text was altered so that it described an 'arbitration agreement' not a 'submission'. The result was a serious terminological confusion, since the 1889 and 1934 Acts were both in force at the same time: see Hogg, p. 21. The distinction was restored by the 1950 Act, s. 1 of which gives jurisdiction to revoke 'the authority of an arbitrator or umpire', whilst s. 25(1) gives a limited power to 'order that the arbitration agreement shall cease to have effect with respect to the dispute referred'.

[4] Ss. 5 and 6 of the 1889 Act.

[5] S. 4(1).

[6] See pp. 462–466, post.

to all types of reference, except those arising from an oral agreement[7]. Moreover, the wide interpretation which had been given to the words 'corruptions or other undue means' in the Act of 1698, was now recognised by the use of the general expression '. . . if the arbitrator has misconducted himself'. In 1934 the words '. . . or the reference' were added[8]. This expanded definition was carried into section 23(2) with the substitution of 'proceedings' for 'reference'.

The statutory power to remit was maintained in the 1889 Act, and the subsequent legislation, in terms which contained no qualification on the power of the Court. There was imposed, however, by a course of judicial interpretation, a limitation on the exercise of the power which has only recently begun to disappear.

As regards the inherent powers of the Court, section 1 of the 1889 Act provided that all submissions should, unless a contrary intention was expressed therein, take effect as if they had been made an order of court. The effect was thus to bring virtually all references under the direct and continuous supervision of the Court, which would exercise powers by virtue of its own inherent right of control, quite distinct from the statutory powers to intervene by setting aside and remission. This last step in the progressive assimilation of voluntary arbitration to a process carried on under the aegis of the Court was for some reason abruptly reversed by the 1950 Act.

Section 44(3) of this Act repealed the 1889 Act in its entirety, including that part of it which provided that submissions should have the same effect as if made by rule of court. Since the 1889 Act had itself repealed the earlier legislation, there was no longer any statutory provision linking the process of arbitration to the procedures of the Court. True, it was still possible in theory to have a submission made a rule of court, just as it had been before 1698. But this procedure had for so long been unnecessary that it had fallen completely into disuse. Thus, whereas before 1950 all voluntary references to arbitration pursuant to written submissions had attracted the High Court's inherent powers of enforcement and supervision, thereafter no submissions had this effect[9].

In the great majority of cases, this alteration in the law had not the least significance. The Court's powers to compel observance of the agreement to arbitrate, and compliance with the award, were quite sufficient, without the need to have recourse to the more severe measures appropriate to a contempt of court. So far as concerned supervision of the reference, there were statutory powers to set aside the award for 'misconduct', and to remit the award under a general discretion, amply sufficient to deal with the complaints most likely to be encountered in practice. But there were certain powers which, at least on a traditional view, were derived solely from the court's inherent jurisdiction over references regarded as dependent upon its own procedures, and which were not dependent on the statutory jurisdiction to set aside for misconduct. These consisted of the powers to set aside for admitted mistake, error on the face of the

---

[7] We add this qualification in deference to *Imperial Metal Industries (Kynoch) Ltd v AUEW*, ante. There were, however, no express limitations on the power to set aside.

[8] Following the recommendation of the Mackinnon Committee, which acknowledged the sensitivity of the arbitrators to the implications of the word 'misconduct'.

[9] Since the 1950 Act was a consolidating statute, it was not debated in Parliament. We have not been able to trace any public discussion of its provisions. It is, perhaps, legitimate to surmise that the important change in the law wrought by s. 44(3) was not intended.

award, and excess of jurisdiction. The sweeping-away of these powers seems to have passed unnoticed.

4 Mistake of law

At the outset of the period under review, there existed two distinct methods of controlling the legal content of the award.

First, there was the jurisdiction to set aside an award for error of law on the face. This had for a substantial period been an unpopular procedure. It operated in an erratic manner, since everything depended on the chance of whether the arbitrator had included sufficient documents 'on the face' of the award to give the applicant facts enough to suggest that the decision must imply an error of law. It had become highly technical, so far as concerned the rules prescribing what was and was not 'on the face'. And it was crude in operation, since the result of a successful application to set aside was that the entire arbitration had to begin again; whereas with a properly drawn award in the form of a special case the court could, upon disagreeing with the arbitrator, substitute the award which it considered correct. For decades the jurisdiction had attracted judicial protests. But no step was taken to eliminate it in any of the arbitration statutes, nor did the Court grasp the opportunity to hold that it had been abolished in 1950 by the repeal of the 1889 Act.

During the same period, the mechanism of the special case became more highly developed. Under the 1854 Act the arbitrator was given power, in the absence of a contrary intention expressed in the submission, to state the whole or part[10] of his award in the form of a special case. This power, which was permissive but not obligatory[11], was preserved by the 1889 Act. The Act did, however, add a new power[12], namely to state what would until very recently have been called a consultative case: that is to say, a case stated in a pending reference, outside the confines of an award. The novelty here lay not only in the form of the award, but also in the jurisdiction of the Court, since the section prescribed not only that the arbitrator 'may' state such a case, but that he 'shall, if so directed by the court' state a case[13].

The 1934 Act took the matter a logical step further[14], by reducing the two forms of case to the same footing. In the result there was an implied discretionary power to state both a consultative case and an award in the form of a special case, and a duty to do so if directed by the Court. The parties were no longer free to 'contract out' of the supervisory jurisdiction of the Court[15].

---

[10] I.e. to make that very useful form of award which was final as to some issues (including perhaps some issues of law) and subject to the opinion of the court on others.

[11] Although if the submission required the arbitrator to state his reasons on the face of the award, it was still regarded as misconduct for him not to do so: see Russell (7th edn., 1891) p. 320.

[12] Under s. 19.

[13] The idea of a duty to state a case, enforceable by the Court, was no novelty; since (as we have indicated) an arbitrator could validly be obliged by contract to set out his reason on the face. But the remedy here was to set the award aside, if the arbitrator did not do so. What was new was that the Court would compel the arbitrator to comply.

[14] By s. 9, reproduced in s. 21 of the 1950 Act.

[15] In *Czarnikow v Roth, Schmidt & Co* [1922] 2 KB 478, the Court of Appeal held that a clause purporting to prohibit the parties from applying to the arbitrator or the Court for a special case was contrary to public policy and invalid as purporting to oust the jurisdiction of the Court.

G. 1979 AND AFTER

1 The beginning of 1979

One may now take stock of the law and practice relating to judicial control, as it stood at the beginning of 1979.

(a) *Judicial control over procedure*

So far as concerned the control of procedure in the reference, the powers of the Court were limited almost exclusively to those capable of being exercised after the conclusion of the arbitration, and were directed either at the award or at the steps taken to enforce it. Primarily, the Court exercised its powers through the statutory jurisdiction to set aside and remit, although relief by way of injunction or declaration was available, and sometimes proved useful[16]. The old inherent jurisdiction to set aside had fallen away, with the severing of the formal link between the courts and the reference, and the equitable power to intervene had been lost from view. Intervention in the course of the reference, before award, took place only in exceptional circumstances[17].

Although the statutory powers had come to be regarded as sufficiently wide to permit setting aside or remission of the award, on account of virtually any kind of procedural mishap, the Court explicitly set out to create, during the 1920s, a policy of non-intervention in the field of commercial arbitration, so far as concerned matters of procedure. Emphasis was placed on the consensual nature of a reference. By contracting to have their disputes resolved by arbitration, the parties were taken to have given their implied consent to the adoption of whatever procedure was usual in the trade. Repeatedly the courts expressed the opinion that if the parties chose to arbitrate, they could not afterwards complain when the arbitrator conducted the arbitration in a manner which seemed unduly peremptory or lax; if the parties had wanted the rigour and precision of a full judicial enquiry, they should not have consented to arbitrate. True, there were occasions where the Court was willing to intervene, if the procedures had created positive unfairness; but these were few. In the main, the Court would tolerate to a remarkable extent a departure from the ordinary norms[18].

(b) *Judicial control over errors of law*

By contrast with this permissive attitude in the field of procedure, the courts insisted on the retention of a power to intervene in the event of an error of law by the arbitrator, if the mechanisms for invoking the power had been set in motion at the proper time. The finality of the award was indeed respected, in matters of law as well as fact. No extrinsic evidence could be adduced to prove a mistake, however egregious. On the other hand, the Court would not allow the parties to deprive themselves of the right to invoke the supervisory jurisdiction over the Court by way of special case. The parties thus had a choice.

---

[16] See pp. 518–523, 525–526, 568–569, post.
[17] See pp. 518–526, post.
[18] For example the institution of the 'arbitrator/advocate': see Chapter 19.

They could let the matter proceed to an award without asking for a special case. If they took this course, the award was final, however wrong it might be – save only for the inroads, much regretted, made by the existence of the jurisdiction to set the award aside for error on the face. If on the other hand, they wished to ask the arbitrator to state a case, they could not by a prior contract deprive themselves of the right to do so[19]. The formal basis of the rule was the centuries-old principle that the courts had a jurisdiction over all civil disputes within the Kingdom, which the parties could not oust by private contract[20]. The motives of policy were quite clear. If access to the Court, could be excluded, there would be no means of preventing arbitrators from quite deliberately choosing to decide a question of law in a way different from the way in which the courts would have decided it; and if this happened systematically, as it would tend to do with the confines of a single trade, where the contents of awards would become known and discussed, there would develop a series of individual systems of commercial law, differing not only from the law of England, but also from each other. The result would be that a party who contracted to have his rights regulated by English law would find, when it came to a dispute, that he was being given something different. The courts regarded the existence of the bodies of parallel bodies of law as something which could not be tolerated.

Another risk was that an arbitrator who was not subject to judicial control would not apply English law or even a system of pseudo-law built up by precedent from awards within a particular trade, but no law at all[1]. The arbitrator would simply give effect to his own individual ideas of what seemed fair in the circumstances. This was not in itself objectionable, if it was what the parties wanted. But if they had contracted to have their disputes decided according to English substantive law by a process known as arbitration, they were entitled to have them so decided; and a Court could not properly lend its powers of enforcement to an award arrived at in some other way. Since an arbitrator who was proposing to base his award on personal notions of equity would be unlikely to disclose his reasoning on the face of the award, the power of either party, and if necessary the Court, to require him to state a case was regarded as an essential safeguard[2].

---

[19] *Czarnikow v Roth, Schmidt & Co* [1922] 2 KB 478 was decided when the exercise of the arbitrator's power to state an award in the form of a special case could not be compelled by the Court.

[20] It is plain from the judgment in *Czarnikow v Roth, Schmidt & Co*, supra, that the decision was founded on this principle, and not as any rule of public policy specifically directed to the special case.

[1] Rather surprisingly, this does not appear to have been the main preoccupation of the judges. There are few traces in the authorities of hostility towards decisions which never even purported to be made in accordance with the law: see pp. 68–71, ante. What troubled the courts was the possibility that powerful trade associations would force persons to contract in accordance with forms containing their arbitration rules if they contracted at all, and would thereby compel them to accept decisions according to systems of pseudo-law, rather than English law, as the contracts elsewhere provided.

[2] The writers have personal experience of instances where arbitrators who disapproved of particular rules of law established by judicial decision, which the arbitrators regarded as ill-conceived and commercially unsound, would have ignored the rules and decided according to their own ideas of fairness, if not restrained by an intimation that a special case would be called for.

(c) Summary

We thus see a consistent development during the nineteenth and twentieth centuries towards a two-fold view of the arbitral process, which gave English arbitration law its quite distinctive flavour. First, the law moved toward a permissive attitude on procedural questions. Only in cases of real injustice would the court intervene after an award was made. Intervention whilst the reference was still in progress was virtually unknown in practice, even if permitted in theory[3]. Second, successive Acts of Parliament had first given legislative force to a procedure by way of special case which was originally consensual in origin, adopted because the parties to an individual reference thought that it would be useful, and had then progressively strengthened it and widened its field of application. Thus, there were concurrent trends away from judicial intervention in the reference, and towards judicial control over the legal content of the award.

2 Developments in 1979

(a) Judicial policy

In the course of a single year this long course of development was totally reversed. During 1979 two decisions in the Court of Appeal employed the remedy of an injunction to intervene in a pending reference in a manner different from anything previously seen[4]. These decisions seemed to mark the end of the permissive attitude towards the arbitral process. This new trend was however short-lived. Eighteen months later the House of Lords held that there was no general power at common law to intervene; the jurisdiction of the Court being limited to those cases where it was specifically conferred by statute. There still remains a power, the practical implications of which have yet to be fully worked out, to restrain further proceedings in the reference, where an arbitration

---

[3] See *Exormisis Shipping SA v Oonsoo etc* [1975] 1 Lloyd's Rep 432, discussed at p. 523, post. The power under s. 1 of the 1950 Act, and its predecessors, to revoke the authority of the arbitrators during the reference was very sparingly employed. This is not surprising. The purpose of the legislation was originally to *inhibit* the revocation of the authority by the parties (see p. 436, ante), and although it came to be worded in such a way as to *permit* revocation by the Court, the language was rightly not understood as an encouragement by the legislature to meddle in a pending reference.

[4] *Japan Line Ltd v Aggeliki Charis Compania Maritima SA, The Angelic Grace* [1980] 1 Lloyd's Rep 288; and *Bremer Vulkan Schiffbau und Maschinenf v South India Shipping Corpn Ltd* [1980] 1 Lloyd's Rep 255. The second of these decisions was much discussed. The first went largely unnoticed, because of delays in reporting, but it was the more important. The *Bremer Vulkan* case was concerned with the special question whether the Court had power to halt an arbitration which had been so delayed as to inhibit a fair trial: *The Angelic Grace* appeared to assert a new jurisdiction to prevent an arbitrator from acting in a way which the Court regarded as unjust. In a really bad case of injustice, a Court already possessing the power to prevent the arbitrator from doing wrong, might find it a small step to assume a power to make him do right. This would inevitably have led to a host of applications for orders that the arbitrator should permit adjournments, refuse amendments, hear evidence and so on. We suggest that this would have been a retrograde step. In principle, it would have been misconceived, for the parties contract to have the arbitration conducted by the arbitrator and not the Court; and it would have been inefficient to allow the arbitrator and the judge to control the proceedings in tandem, since in all but the simplest of cases the judge could not be put into sufficient possession of the history of the matter to give him a proper feel for the procedural shape of the dispute.

agreement has been brought to a premature end[5]. This is not however an interference in the reference, but merely a recognition that proceedings under the former contract to arbitrate no longer have any meaning[6].

(b) Origins of the 1979 Act

At almost exactly the same time as this fundamental, but temporary, change in the Court's attitude towards procedures in the reference, there occurred an equally fundamental, but this time almost certainly permanent, contraction of judicial control over the legal content of the reference. As we have shown, in the case of certain types of reference, the parties had originally been able to 'contract in' to the power and (if the submission specifically so provided) duty of the arbitrator to state a special case on a question of law for the decision of the Court. The first statutory provision enabled them to contract out of this power. Then the procedure was extended to all types of reference: then the arbitrator was made subject to a duty, if asked to state a consultative case; then finally this duty was extended to an award in the form of a special case. This last step in the strengthening of judicial control took place in 1934. Every statutory extension of the power had been accompanied by consultation amongst the merchants as well as the lawyers, and there were few traces during 150 years of development that there was widespread discontent about the supervisory jurisdiction which the Court was being enabled to exercise.

It was not until the 1950s that controversy about the role of the special case first came to the surface, when a number of judges in the commercial court drew attention to the clumsiness of the system, when employed in arbitrations involving complex and interlinked questions of fact and law. There was, however, no suggestion that judicial control over the reference was undesirable; merely that the methods were not suitable for certain types of arbitration, in respect of which (so these judges considered) the parties would be wiser to take their disputes directly to the commercial court, where fact and law could be dealt with together[7]. These views were controversial[8]. Some efforts were made to introduce a more widespread use of clauses conferring jurisdiction on the commercial court, but these never really took root. Instead the balance was tipped decisively in favour of arbitration as opposed to litigation, by the fortuitous coming together during the 1970s, of several different strands of

---

[5] By frustration, wrongful repudiation, or express or implied consent. See pp. 503–517, post.

[6] This period did see a strengthening of the coercive powers available to a party in the event of a failure by his opponent properly to honour the arbitration agreement. This took the shape of the jurisdiction of the Court conferred by s. 5 of the 1979 Act, to empower the arbitrator, in the event of failure by a party to comply with an order of the arbitrator, to proceed in default in the same manner as a judge might continue if the matter were the subject of litigation not arbitration. This jurisdiction is discussed at p. 539, post. This jurisdiction is not, however, an example of judicial interference in the reference. The effect is simply to enlarge the powers of the arbitrator.

[7] Rather similar opinions had on occasions been expressed in the 1920s, by members of the Court of Appeal. But they appear to have made little practical impact.

[8] Echoes of the controversy may be detected in the report of the arguments in *Universal Cargo Carriers Corpn v Citati* [1957] 1 Lloyd's Rep 174 at 183 et seq.

opinion[9]. It came to be widely accepted that some kind of change was essential, but there was no unanimity about what change, and for what reasons. One simply-expressed opinion was that the special case ought to be abolished altogether.

Amongst the reasons advanced by different persons or groups were the following –

1 Merchants insert arbitration clauses in their contracts because they regard arbitration as a more efficient way than litigation of dealing with trade disputes. Allowing lawyers to interfere in the arbitral process serves only to ensure that the parties get the worst of all worlds. Ideally, the courts should be kept entirely away from the process; but if this is asking too much, then at least they should leave the award alone[10].

2 Disputes are becoming increasingly complex, as society itself becomes more complex. The special case may have been a satisfactory way of dealing with short points of law or simple facts, but it is a slow and erratic procedure in disputes of the type which occupy much of the Court's attention today. Arbitrators are now skilled and reliable; they do not need to be kept in order by the Court; the system is out of date, and it should be discarded.

3 Many large disputes now concern companies which are 'supra-national' or 'trans-national' in that they owe no allegiance to any single system of national law. If they choose to have their disputes decided by arbitration, they should not be compelled to submit themselves to the supervision of any system of national courts. From a procedural point of view, they should be treated as extra-territorial. If other organisations prefer to remain within a given system of national law, they should equally be free to do so. The possibility of recourse on questions of law need not be wholly excluded, but the parties should be empowered to contract out of it[11].

4 The trading agencies of sovereign states are becoming increasingly involved in the type of large-scale transaction which leads to massive arbitrations. Rightly

---

[9] Two events had a marked influence on the climate of opinion in the mid-1970s. The first was the occurrence of an unprecedented number of individual disputes arising out of the same events (the impact of an embargo on the exportation of American soyabean meal) many of which led to the stating of a special case. The result was to swamp the arbitrators, and to a lesser degree the courts. The resulting delay provided plentiful ammunition for the opponents of judicial control, and also to apprehension amongst those concerned with the well-being of English arbitration that parties would in future decide to take their disputes elsewhere. The second factor was the rapid increase in number of very large 'supra-national disputes', of a magnitude virtually unknown even a decade before. Questions were asked about the desirability and practicability of submitting these disputes to judicial control.

[10] This is a more widespread point of view than is generally appreciated, although it is rare to find it publicly expressed. Intellectually, it is hard to sustain. Most parties are glad to have the courts lend a hand, if the need arises. It is unreasonable to expect the courts to lend their powers of enforcement to the awards resulting from a reference to arbitration, if they are to have no word at all in how the arbitration in conducted. Those who emphasise the consensual and extra-legal nature of the arbitral process would scarcely wish to have the law revert to what it was in 1650, before the courts began to play an effective part in the reinforcement of that process. The real problem is, as it has always been, to strike a realistic balance between meddling and indifference.

[11] This is not the most extreme way of putting the case in respect of 'trans-national' disputes. Some participants in the debate would have been glad to see a right to contract out of all the local court's right of control. Whether this would also have involved the right to contract out of the court's power to reinforce the agreement to arbitrate (for example by staying proceedings brought in breach of an agreement to arbitrate and by granting summary enforcement of the award) was an open question.

or wrongly, such agencies regard it as inappropriate that disputes which they had agreed to refer to arbitration should afterwards to subjected to public scrutiny by the courts[12].

5 The machinery of the special case was being used as an instrument of delay by debtors who were unwilling to honour awards which were properly made against them. Delay was always a source of injustice, but the hardship to the claimant was particularly great in a time of inflation, high interest rates and restrictions on the availability of cash.

6 Foreigners do not like the idea of the courts involving themselves in the merits of arbitrations, and this tends to drive them away from England to other jurisdictions, where the courts adopt a more passive role.

The opponents of radical change did not deny that the procedures for judicial control needed to be overhauled. This could, it was argued, be achieved[13] without dismantling the system, or allowing a right to contract out which right would fatally weaken it. The system should be retained not only because it ensured that arbitral decisions followed the law, but also because it gave the Court access to a wide variety of disputes, which enabled the courts to develop a detailed and up-to-date law of commerce, on a scale not achieved by any other system of law.

These differing points of view were systematically discussed[14] during the late 1970s. A consensus proved impossible to reach. Nevertheless there was agreement[15] to this extent, that it would do no harm, and could be expected to do some good, if some freedom was conferred to contract out of the mandatory special case.

The benefits anticipated from the new system were two-fold.

First, the English procedure would no longer drive away the large arbitrations between trans-national corporations and those involving state trading enterprises. This was taken to be a benefit, probably on the basis of a feeling, never clearly articulated but undoubtedly present, that it would simply be desirable in itself; and partly on the more specific grounds that the presence of large international arbitrations would add prestige to the City of London, and that

---

12 Such agencies have not hitherto shown any reluctance to invoke the public procedures of appeal, if they have lost the arbitration. The idea of a state trading agency being in any way above the law, so far as concerns foreign courts, is hard to reconcile with modern ideas of sovereign immunity.

13 There were two reasons why the system involved delays. First, the stating of a special case was a time-consuming business. Second, because the parties had to wait for the case to come on for argument in the High Court and quite often wait again for a hearing in the Court of Appeal. These delays cannot be wholly eliminated if any right of judicial review is to be retained. There was, it was believed, scope for reduction in the delays. Some way could have been found to give the case stated a priority of hearing. But whether it would have been justified to prefer the rights of participants in arbitration to other types of litigant was obviously debatable: and even so, some elements of delay would have remained. This could only be eliminated by abolishing judicial review altogether.

14 Particular mention may be made of reports by – the Commercial Court Committee; an ad hoc committee convened by Mr Mark Littman QC, with powerful representation from corporate lawyers on the east coast of the United States; and Lord Diplock's Alexander Lecture to the Institute of Arbitrators.

15 At least amongst the majority of the more influential speakers. As Viscount Hailsham observed, in relation to the discussion in the House of Lords, this was a 'debate between grandees'. (Hansard, House of Lords, 5th Series, Vol. 397, col. 459 and 1199: references hereafter are to the Volume and column numbers of this series).

the influx of such arbitrations would create a valuable invisible export, of benefit to the country's balance of payments[16]. In addition, it was sensible to give the participants in a consensual process the type of procedure which they wanted[17].

Second, there would be a more efficient method for dealing with those cases where a right of appeal to the High Court on questions of law was to be retained.

Looking at matters from the other side, there were safeguards which would ensure that the new system did no harm. In the first place, the right to contract out in advance of proceedings would be confined principally to those who were capable of looking after their own interests, and who could be assumed to have given thought to the question whether they really wished to cede their right of recourse to the High Court. These would be the parties to the large specially negotiated (or 'one-off') international contracts. Persons in a less favoured position would still have a right of appeal: these would include parties to 'contrats d'adhésion', whose terms had to be accepted if the party wanted to contract at all, and those who were in an inferior bargaining position. The rights of persons in these categories would be protected by denying them the possibility of contracting out, except in cases where it could be shown (perhaps by a system of registering exclusion agreements) that the parties had genuinely addressed their minds to, and consented to, the loss of their right to appeal.

In the second place, the disappearance from the High Court of appeals in the case of 'one-off' contracts would not damage the development and authority of the common law. There would be no risk of creating systems of pseudo-law, since each contract would raise problems peculiar to itself, and a decision upon it would not set a precedent for others. Nor would the courts be deprived of the opportunity to enrich the common law by decisions on general principles made in the course of arbitration appeals; for those types of dispute which had in the past been the most fruitful source of such decisions would continue to be subject to appeal[18].

Whilst this solution to the problem commanded substantial support, it did not win the day, for there were technical and tactical considerations which worked against it. On the technical side, it proved impossible to devise a workable definition of the 'one-off' contract, or a practicable system for registering exclusion agreements. Tactically, the movement towards a change in the law was much influenced by an accident of political history which made it possible to find sufficient parliamentary time for the enactment of a new arbitration bill, provided that it was not controversial. This could be achieved only if some common ground could be reached between those who wanted to see all judicial

---

[16] This was a constant theme of the debates: see Hansard 392/95; 392/96; 392/90; 392/100; 392/104–105; 392/107; 392/111; 392/113; 397/443. Since the Act of 1979 must be the first legal procedural reform ever introduced with the explicit aim of attracting business to the United Kingdom, it is rather surprising that not even a rough estimate was made of the likely gain of foreign exchange. The only figure mentioned in the debates was £500,000,000 per annum, based on an expenditure of £100,000 per arbitration in each of 5,000 arbitrations (Debates 392/99). The latter figure is, the writers venture to submit, in error by a factor of about 100. There are already more than 5,000 arbitrations conducted annually in England but the number of very large arbitrations which would be likely to come to England because of the new legislation must be very much smaller.

[17] Attention was concentrated on the 'customers' of the system who participated in large international arbitrations: see Commercial Court Committee, § 53.

[18] For an exposition of this general approach to the restriction of the right of appeal, see in particular Lord Diplock, op. cit.

control (and not just control over errors of law) eliminated in relation to large international disputes, and those who were anxious lest a desire to attract a small number of very specialised arbitrations to England would lead to the loss of procedures which worked well enough (and could be made to work much better) in relation to the much greater number of more mundane disputes[19]. Ground had to be yielded by both sides if some modification of the entrenched right of appeal, which was generally if not universally regarded as desirable, was to have a chance of becoming law.

The result was what has been called a 'pragmatic compromise'[20] of an interim nature and with no claims to logical rigour[1]. The general shape of the Act followed the main lines of the recommendations put forward by the Commercial Court Committee[2].

The Act does not exclude the right of recourse to the High Court on questions of law. It merely enables the parties, in certain circumstances, to make for themselves a binding agreement to exclude such recourse. The parties may in every case enter into an agreement after the commencement of the arbitration. But an exclusion agreement made in advance of the arbitration is invalid if it relates to a 'domestic' arbitration agreement[3] or to one of three categories of disputes – viz., broadly speaking, those arising from maritime, insurance or commodity transactions. There is power in the Secretary of State to order[4] that these categories shall be narrowed, but not that they shall be enlarged. The original proposal has thus been reversed. Instead of taking 'one off' contracts out of the power to order a special case, leaving all other references subject to the existing regime, there is now a liberty to contract out in all cases, except those which are specially identified[5].

As well as creating a category of arbitration in which the parties can, if they wish, exclude the right of recourse to the High Court on questions of law, the 1979 Act has established a new procedure for those arbitrations where the right is retained. It has abolished not only the special case procedure but also the

---

[19] It is the view of the writers that the extent to which the special case was employed in practice, and hence its deleterious effect on the speedy resolution of disputes, was much less than generally believed. Statistics in the field are very hard to come by. On the basis of enquiries, we would estimate a figure of 10,000 as being the right order of magnitude for the number of references instituted annually. Of these, the great majority would involve no question of law. The number of disputes which actually reached the High Court was between 20 and 30 per annum. The real impact of the special case on arbitration was in the restraining influence which it exercised on arbitrators who might otherwise be inclined to decide contrary to law.

[20] C.S. Staughton QC (1979) NLJ 920.

[1] The bill was not opposed in the Lords, except by those who thought it did not go far enough, but who withdrew their amendments in order not to prejudice the enactment of those features with which they did agree. Nobody spoke to the effect that it went too far. There was no debate at all in the Commons, for want of time.

[2] The subject of appeals under the 1979 Act is discussed in detail in Chapter 36, post.

[3] I.e. one pursuant to which the arbitration is to take place in the United Kingdom, between United Kingdom nationals or residents, or corporations with their central management in or control in the United Kingdom.

[4] Subject to a negative resolution of Parliament.

[5] The domestic arbitrations were seen as those in which imparity of bargain is most likely to be a factor. The maritime, insurance and commodity arbitrations were visualised as being most open to the risk of creating pseudo-laws, and also as providing the most fertile ground for judicial development of commercial law.

jurisdiction to set aside an award for error of law[6] or fact on the face of the award, and has instituted in their place a procedure by way of 'appeal'[7]. The hearing in the High Court takes place on the basis of a reasoned award, which not only states the facts, but also summarises the reasons why the arbitrator has arrived at his conclusion of law[8]. Before the hearing of the appeal takes place, a preliminary application must first be made to the Court for leave to appeal. This requirement gave rise almost at once to a controversy as to whether it was intended merely to continue the former practice, whereby the Courts had ordered arbitrators to state a case on *any* question of law which was real, substantial and fairly arguable[9], or whether some more stringent form of filtering process was intended. It has now been authoritatively decided that the legislative intended the latter result[10].

The 1979 Act also answered, but only partially, the criticisms which were frequently made of the English practice of making awards which gave no reasons for the decision[11]. The dissatisfaction arose partly from the fact that in certain foreign countries 'unmotivated' awards could not be enforced, and partly from the frustration felt by persons who had spent time and money in the arbitration of their disputes, and yet could never find out why they had won or lost, or why the sum awarded was different from the amount claimed; the most straightforward solution was to stipulate that all awards should contain reasons, but this met strong opposition from certain groups of arbitrators[12]. Instead, the Act produced a compromise, on the following lines[13] –

1 Where an award is the subject of an appeal on a question of law, it must contain sufficient reasons to enable the Court to determine the question. The Court will not usually order the arbitrator to give reasons unless he was asked to do so before the award was made[14].

2 In the absence of an appeal, the arbitrator need not give reasons for the legal aspect of his decision.

---

[6] As we have previously suggested, it may be that the jurisdiction had already disappeared, in consequence of the 1950 Act.

[7] Except in those cases where the right is validly excluded.

[8] See pp. 373 et seq., ante.

[9] For a fuller discussion, see Appendix 3 in the first edition.

[10] *BTP Tioxide Ltd v Pioneer Shipping Ltd, The Nema* [1981] 2 Lloyd's Rep 239. The House of Lords arrived at Parliament's intention by the process of construing the Act.

[11] The excuse often given was that a reasoned award would leave the way open to an attempt to set aside the award, for error on the face, thus destroying the speed and finality which the parties had intended to achieve by choosing arbitration as their forum. But this was never a ground to abstain from giving reasons for the factual part of the decision. Moreover, the problem could always be solved by adopting the well-recognised practice of stating the reasons in a separate document, explicitly declared not to form part of the award.

[12] Amongst the grounds advanced were that lay arbitrators inexperienced in detailed exposition on paper might be unwilling to act if they had to give reasons, with a resultant loss of persons who might be best qualified to handle the dispute; also that awards with reasons would take longer to prepare, and would be more expensive.

[13] Reasons are discussed in more detail at pp. 373–381, ante, 596–600, post.

[14] In its original form, the Bill contained no provision penalising a party who had not asked for reasons before the publication of the award. The change was made because the arbitrators feared that if they were not ordered to give reasons until a later stage, they might have forgotten about the case. Whilst there is force in this point, the amendment is in some respects to be regretted, because it restores the former practice whereby parties would ask for a case to safeguard against the possibility of having lost, and would then find that time and expense had been wasted, as in fact they had won.

3 The arbitrator need not give reasons for his decisions on issues of fact. It follows that in those cases which turn exclusively on issues of fact, or which result from a reference in relation to which the right of appeal has been validly excluded, or where there is a right of appeal in theory, but where the Court has refused leave to appeal, the parties may still receive an award which gives no reasons at all. Even where an appeal is on foot, the award can properly consist of a bare series of findings of fact, without any statement of how they were arrived at[15].

---

[15] This is a particularly odd result, because much of the pressure to create categories of dispute in which an appeal is not possible was related to large 'one-off' international arbitrations: and these are the types of dispute in which the parties would be most likely to look for a fully reasoned award. Perhaps the practical answer is that the arbitrator would know that if he gave an award without reasons in an important case, the fact would become known in the comparatively small world of large international arbitrations, and he would be unlikely to receive any appointment again.

CHAPTER 30

Court proceedings wrongly brought

A. PROCEEDINGS IN BREACH OF AGREEMENT TO ARBITRATE

An arbitration clause contains an agreement, which the courts will recognise and enforce, that claims falling within the scope of the clause will be enforced only by means of a reference to arbitration. It is, however, of a different nature from the other provisions of the contract: not merely because the rights which it creates are procedural rather than substantive, but in other respects as well. Three important points of difference may be noted.

First, the arbitration agreement has a life of its own, separate from that of the underlying substantive contract. The obligation to arbitrate may remain in existence for the purpose of determining the accrued rights of the parties, even when the underlying contract has come to an end[1]. Conversely, the obligations created by the agreement may terminate, whilst the underlying contract continues in being[2].

Second, the Court has in certain cases a discretion whether to give effect to the agreement to arbitrate and need not do so if it thinks it better to do otherwise.

Third, the remedies for a breach of the obligation to arbitrate are different from those available where there is a breach of the underlying contract. The classic remedies for the breach of a substantive obligation, such as to deliver goods or to convey land, are damages, specific performance, and an injunction. For breach of an arbitration agreement, damages may in theory be awarded, but will not normally be a useful remedy; an injunction is rarely granted, and specific performance is not available at all[3]. Instead, the Court enforces the agreement by negative means. By staying an action brought in breach of the arbitration agreement and by refusing to enforce a foreign judgment made in defiance of an arbitration agreement it compels the claimant to proceed by way of arbitration, or lose his claim altogether. The reasons why the remedies take this particular form are discussed below, under the following headings –

1 An injunction to restrain the proceedings.

2 Damages for breach of the agreement to arbitrate.

---

[1] See pp. 108–111, ante.

[2] If the Court exercises its statutory power to order that the arbitration agreement shall cease to have effect (see p. 498, post), and possibly if the arbitration agreement comes to an end through the operation of the doctrine of frustration, or by repudiation or abandonment (see pp. 506 et seq., post). If the arbitration agreement is wholly separate from the underlying contract — e.g. if there is an ad hoc submission of an existing dispute — it may be void or voidable even if the underlying contract is entirely valid.

[3] *Street v Rigby* (1802) 6 Ves 815; *The Purimisa Concepcion* (1849) 13 Jur 545; *Gourlay v Duke of Somerset* (1815) 19 Ves 429; *Agar v Macklew* (1825) 4 LJOS Ch 16; *Pena Copper Mines v Rio Tinto Co* (1911) 105 LT 846 at 851; *Re Smith and Service* (1890) 25 QBD 548, per Lord Esher MR and Bowen LJ.

3 A stay under the inherent jurisdiction of the Court.

4 A compulsory stay under section 1 of the 1975 Act, which applies only to non-domestic arbitration agreements.

5 A discretionary stay under section 4(1) of the 1950 Act which applies only to domestic arbitration agreements[4].

6 Interpleader proceedings.

7 Foreign judgments given contrary to an agreement to arbitrate.

1 Injunction to restrain proceedings

The textbooks state[5] that an injunction will not be granted to restrain a party from bringing proceedings in the English courts in breach of an agreement to submit disputes to arbitration[6]. Different principles apply where the action is brought abroad. In such a case, the English Court can provide no alternative remedy in the shape of a stay, nor does any principle of English public policy arise, as regards ousting the jurisdiction of the foreign court. Accordingly, there seems no reason in principle why the Court should not grant an injunction restraining the parties from proceeding in breach of their agreement to arbitrate[7]. The Court will, no doubt, be cautious in granting the remedy, given that it might be regarded as an unacceptable infringement of the prerogatives of the foreign court[8]; and it is in any event unlikely to be granted unless the claimant is or has assets within the jurisdiction, and hence amenable to coercion if he acts in defiance of the order, or has at least submitted to the jurisdiction[9].

Where the case falls within the New York Convention, and possibly in other cases as well, we suggest that the right course is for the aggrieved party to exhaust his local remedies by seeking a stay or kindred relief from the local courts, before asking the English Court to intervene. It is only in cases where something has plainly gone badly wrong in the local courts that the English Court should grant the extreme remedy of an injunction.

An injunction is unlikely to be granted where the defendant has taken active steps to defend the foreign proceedings. The Court is likely to consider that the balance of convenience is in favour of allowing the foreign proceedings to continue[10].

---

[4] The meaning of 'non-domestic' and 'domestic' is discussed at pp. 466–467, post.

[5] For example Hogg, p. 68.

[6] We know of no instance where an injunction has been sought. No doubt the reason is that since the Judicature Acts, a stay, rather than an injunction, is the appropriate means of restraining objectionable proceedings. (See, however, a different reason given by Fletcher Moulton LJ in *Pena Copper Mines Ltd v Rio Tinto Co Ltd* (1911) 105 LT 846.)

[7] *Pena Copper Mines Ltd v Rio Tinto Co Ltd* (1911) 105 LT 846. (The contract contained a *Scott v Avery* clause.)

[8] *World Pride Shipping Ltd v Daiichi Chuo KK, The Golden Anne* [1984] 2 Lloyd's Rep 489.

[9] *Mike Trading and Transport Ltd v Pagnan and Fratelli, The Lisboa* [1980] 2 Lloyd's Rep 546. In the *Pena Copper* case there was a very clear submission to the jurisdiction of the English courts, quite apart from the arbitration clause. Moreover the contract was expressly governed by English law, and there was a *Scott v Avery* clause. An analogy may exist with *Royal Exchange Assurance Co v Compania Naviera Santi SA, The Tropaioforos (No 2)* [1962] 2 Lloyds Rep 410, where an assured sued a representative underwriter in the English Court, agreeing with the remainder of the underwriters to be bound by the result of the action. Having failed in the action, he then sued other underwriters abroad. The Court granted an injunction restraining the plaintiff from pursuing the proceedings.

[10] *Gorthon Invest AB v Ford Motor Co Ltd, The Maria Gorthon* [1976] 2 Lloyd's Rep 720.

2 Damages

If a party commits a breach of his agreement to arbitrate by impeding the progress of the arbitration, the injured party has a cause of action, and may recover whatever damages he can prove[11]. There is no reason in principle why the same considerations should not apply where the breach consists of the institution of legal proceedings, rather than an arbitration, to enforce a disputed claim. It is hard to visualise a situation in which the complainant could ever recover substantial damages for such a breach, where the offending action is brought in England[12]. The same will not, however, necessarily be the case where the action is brought abroad. There may be no provisions for staying the proceedings in the foreign jurisdiction or the Court there may decline to exercise whatever powers may exist. Equally, the foreign court may have no power, or wish, to compensate the defendant for the costs which he has incurred in the foreign action. Again, the foreign court may have ordered the arrest of the defendant's property, thus causing him financial loss through the detention and the cost of providing security[13]. In cases such as these, there seems no reason why the defendant should not recover any losses which he has suffered, over and above any expenditure to which he would have been put if the agreement to arbitrate had been honoured[14].

Whether the arbitrator would have jurisdiction to entertain such a claim, or whether it is one which can only be brought by an action, will depend upon the wording of the arbitration clause. Under most forms in common use, we suggest that the arbitrator would have jurisdiction[15].

3 Stay under the inherent jurisdiction

As matter of its own affairs, the Court has an inherent power to stay any action which it considers should not be allowed to continue[16]. This power is independent of any specific powers conferred by statute. We submit that this power could, in an appropriate case, be employed to deal with an action brought in breach of an agreement to arbitrate. It is frequently invoked where the action in England constitutes a breach of an agreement to submit disputes to the exclusive

---

[11] See p. 524, post.

[12] If he obtains a stay, he will receive his costs of the stayed action. In theory, he might recover the difference between the taxed costs and the costs actually thrown away; but there is no trace in the books of any such claim ever having been made.

[13] As in *Mantovani v Carapelli SpA* [1980] 1 Lloyd's Rep 375, where the arbitration clause was of the *Scott v Avery* type.

[14] An interesting question would arise if the foreign court proceeded to give judgment against the defendant. If he were able to persuade the English Court that if the matter had gone to arbitration he would have been bound to win (for example, if the foreign court took the wrong view on a question of English law), could he recover an indemnity for any sums which he had been compelled to pay, as damages for breach of the arbitration agreement? The English courts are in the main reluctant to reopen the merits of foreign judgments, even where questions of English law are involved, but possibly the position might be different in cases where the plaintiff was wrong ever to invoke the jurisdiction of the foreign court.

[15] *Mantovani v Carapelli SpA*, ante ('dispute arising out of or under this contract').

[16] On the grounds that the action is frivolous, vexatious, oppressive or an abuse of the process of the Court.

jurisdiction of a foreign court, and there is no difference in principle between such an agreement and one which requires the submission to be to an arbitrator[17].

Recourse to this procedure in the case of arbitration is rare[18]. It may, however, be of value in cases where a remedy under section 1 of the 1975 Act or section 4(1) of the 1950 Act is not available, either because there is no written 'arbitration agreement', or because for some other reason the Court lacks jurisdiction under the Acts[19]. The principles upon which the inherent discretion to stay will be exercised are not well established, although it is probable that they correspond in a broad sense with those discussed below in relation to section 4(1). It is submitted, however, that those restrictions on the powers of the Court specifically created by section 4(1)[20] do not preclude the application of the inherent jurisdiction although they may affect the way in which the jurisdiction is exercised as a matter of discretion[1].

4 Compulsory stay: non-domestic arbitration

In certain circumstances section 1 of the 1975 Act entitles a party against whom proceedings are brought in an English court in breach of an arbitration agreement which is not a domestic arbitration agreement[2] to insist on the proceedings being stayed. No question of discretion can arise under this section. The stay is mandatory[3], and the Court has no power to impose terms as a condition of an order for a stay under the section[4].

The existence of an arbitration clause which would, if invoked, inevitably result in the proceedings being stayed, is no bar to an ex parte application for leave to serve proceedings out of the jurisdiction under Order 11, for the defendant may choose not to rely on the clause. But if the defendant seeks to set aside the order made ex parte and does rely on the clause, the Court will set aside the proceedings, even without a formal application under section 1[5].

Two groups of conditions are prescribed by the section: those which must be

---

[17] Until comparatively recently, it was believed that a foreign jurisdiction clause was an arbitration clause, and fell to be dealt with under s. 4 of the 1950 Act: see *The Fehmarn* [1957] 2 Lloyd's Rep 551, applying the observations of MacKinnon LJ in *Racecourse Betting Control Board v Secretary for Air* [1944] Ch 114 at 126.

[18] *Roussel-Uclaf v GD Searle & Co* [1978] 1 Lloyd's Rep 225 appears to be the only reported example.

[19] It might, for example, be useful in the case of 'string contracts': see pp. 146–147, ante.

[20] For example, the requirement that the defendant shall not have taken a step in the action.

[1] *Etri Frans Ltd v NMB (UK) Ltd* [1987] 2 Lloyd's Rep 565.

[2] For the meaning of 'domestic arbitration agreement' see p. 466, post.

[3] *Nova (Jersey) Knit Ltd v Kammgarn Spinnerei GmbH* [1977] 1 Lloyd's Rep 463; *Associated Bulk Carriers Ltd v Koch Shipping Inc, The Fuohsan Maru* [1978] 1 Lloyd's Rep 24; *Roussel-Uclaf v GD Searle & Co* [1978] 1 Lloyd's Rep 225 ('not' is obviously missing in the right hand column of p. 228). The absence of a discretion to refuse a stay has from time to time been regretted, particularly where the dispute involves persons who are not parties to the arbitration agreement and who must therefore sue or be sued by proceedings in court, thus giving rise to two sets of proceedings concerning the same dispute.

[4] *The Rena K* [1978] 1 Lloyd's Rep 545 at 557; *The World Star* [1986] 2 Lloyd's Rep 274. The Court may, however, in certain circumstances refuse to release a vessel from arrest although the action is stayed; and a stay is no obstacle to a Mareva injunction: see pp. 329 and 341, ante.

[5] *A and B v C and D* [1982] 1 Lloyd's Rep 166. This was a case where the defendant's claim for a stay would have been irresistable. In a less clear case, or where the stay would have been granted, if at all, under s. 4 which gives the Court a discretion, the Court would be likely to insist on the application for a stay being brought on formally and supported by affidavit evidence.

satisfied if the defendant is to be granted a stay, and those which, if satisfied, destroy the defendant's prima facie claim for a stay.

(a) Prerequisites of a compulsory stay

If the Court is to have the power, and the duty, to grant a stay under section 1 of the 1975 Act, the following conditions must be satisfied –

(i) There must be in existence an arbitration agreement to which section 1 of the 1975 Act applies, i.e. an arbitration agreement in writing which is not a domestic arbitration agreement[6].

(ii) The proceedings in respect of which a stay is sought must be legal proceedings in any court.

(iii) The proceedings must be in respect of any matter agreed to be referred.

(iv) The proceedings must be brought by a party to the arbitration agreement, or by a person claiming through or under such a person.

(v) The applicant must be a party to the arbitration agreement or a person claiming through or under such a person.

(vi) The applicant must be a party to the legal proceedings.

(vii) The application must be made after appearance[7], but before delivering any pleadings or taking any other steps in the proceedings.

Conditions (ii) to (vii) also apply in the case of a discretionary stay under section 4(1) of the 1950 Act and are discussed in relation to that section[8]. It will be noted that section 1 of the 1975 Act, unlike section 4(1) of the 1950 Act, does not contain any explicit requirement that the applicant shall be ready and willing to do all things necessary to the proper conduct of the arbitration. But an applicant may lose the right to a stay if he has shown he is not 'ready and willing' by taking a step in the proceedings[9], or by causing the agreement to become inoperative or incapable of being performed[10]; or if by his conduct he has forfeited the right to arbitrate[11].

The first of the conditions listed above (namely the existence of an arbitration agreement to which section 1 of the 1975 Act applies) can be broken down into four separate requirements. First, there must be not merely a purported agreement to arbitrate, but an actual binding agreement[12]. Second, the agreement must be 'an agreement in writing (including an agreement contained in an exchange of letters or telegrams) to submit to arbitration present or future differences'[13]. Third, the differences to which the agreement relates must be 'capable of settlement by arbitration'[14]. This topic has been discussed in a

---

[6] For the meaning of an arbitration agreement in writing, see p. 54, ante and for the meaning of 'domestic arbitration agreement' see p. 466, post.

[7] The Act refers to 'appearance' but this must now be read as 'acknowledgment of service': RSC Ord. 12, r. 10.

[8] Post, pp. 469–473.

[9] Post, pp. 472–473.

[10] Post, pp. 464–465.

[11] Post, pp. 485–486.

[12] The problems to which this gives rise also exist under s. 4(1) of the 1950 Act and are discussed at pp. 467–469, post. As to the burden of proof, see p. 464, post.

[13] S. 7(1) of the 1975 Act. Compare the definition of 'arbitration agreement' in s. 32 of the 1950 Act, discussed at pp. 54–56, ante. The words in brackets are probably already implicit in s. 32.

[14] S. 7(1) of the 1975 Act.

previous Chapter[15]. Fourth, the arbitration agreement must not be a 'domestic arbitration': if it is, an application may be made under the Court's inherent jurisdiction or under section 4(1) of the 1950 Act. The meaning of 'domestic arbitration agreement' is discussed later[16] in relation to section 4(1) of the 1950 Act.

(b) Circumstances precluding compulsory stay

Even if the jurisdiction requirements summarised above are shown to exist, there are still circumstances in which the Court must[17] refuse an order, namely:

(i) if the Court is satisfied that the arbitration agreement is null and void or inoperative or incapable of being performed;

(ii) if the Court is satisfied that there is not in fact any dispute between the parties with regard to the matter agreed to be referred.

The burden of proof in each of these respects is on the person resisting the stay.

(i) 'Null and void, inoperative, or incapable of being performed'.
The words 'null and void' would appear to include not only the case where a purported arbitration agreement has never come into existence, e.g. because there was no concluded offer and acceptance, but also the case where an arbitration agreement has come into existence but has become void ab initio, e.g. by rescission on the grounds of misrepresentation. In such cases there is no 'arbitration agreement' to which section 1 of the 1975 Act applies. This raises the question whether it is for the applicant to prove the existence of such an agreement, so as to establish one of the necessary conditions for the exercise of the Court's power to stay the proceedings, or for the plaintiff to disprove the existence of such an agreement. It is for the applicant to prove the existence of a purported agreement, and that the burden then shifts to the plaintiff to show that the purported agreement is in fact null and void[18].

The expression 'inoperative' has no accepted meaning in English law, but it would seem apt to describe an agreement which, although not void ab initio, has for some reason ceased to have effect for the future. Three situations can be envisaged in which an arbitration agreement might be said to be 'inoperative'. First, where the English Court has ordered that the arbitration agreement shall cease to have effect[19], or a foreign court has made a similar order which the English Court will recognise. Second, as is discussed in Chapter 32[20], there may be circumstances in which an arbitration agreement might become 'inoperative' by virtue of the common law doctrines of frustration, discharge by breach, etc. Third, the agreement may have ceased to operate by reason of some further agreement between the parties[1]. But the fact that issues in the arbitration

---

[15] Chapter 10, ante, p. 149.

[16] Post, p. 466.

[17] The section contemplates the exercise of judgment but not of discretion.

[18] *Overseas Union Insurance Ltd v AA Mutual International Insurance Co Ltd* [1988] 2 Lloyd's Rep 63, 70.

[19] See pp. 498–503, post.

[20] See pp. 503–517, post.

[1] As was unsuccessfully argued in *H Kruidenier (London) Ltd v Egyptian Navigation Co, The El Amria (No 2)* [1980] 2 Lloyd's Rep 166.

overlap issues in proceedings between parties who are not bound by the arbitration agreement does not make the agreement 'inoperative'[2].

'Incapable of being performed' connotes something more than mere difficulty or inconvenience or delay in performing the arbitration. There must be some obstacle which cannot be overcome even if the parties are ready, able and willing to perform the agreement[3]: for example, where the mechanism for constituting the tribunal breaks down in a way which the Court has no ability to repair, or where a sole arbitrator named in the agreement cannot or will not act. The fact that the claim is time-barred does not in itself render the arbitration incapable of being performed[4]: the arbitration can proceed, although it will inevitably result in the claim being dismissed. Where the effect of the time limit is not to bar the claim but merely to bar the right to arbitrate[5] the position is, however, less clear. It might be argued in such a case that the arbitration agreement was not 'incapable of being performed', but merely 'incapable of being invoked'. But we consider that this argument is unsound, and that the plaintiff should be permitted to pursue his claim by action, as was presumably the intention of the parties in agreeing to a time bar which barred the right to arbitration without extinguishing the claim.

The fact that the applicant has not the means to honour an award if the claim against him is successful does not in itself render the arbitration agreement 'incapable of being performed'[6].

(ii) 'Not in fact any dispute'.
The Court has no jurisdiction to order a stay where it is satisfied that 'there is not in fact any dispute between the parties with respect to the matters agreed to be referred'[7]. The words 'in fact' mean 'really' or 'in truth', rather than 'as to the facts': but of what must the Court be satisfied? It cannot be merely that the dispute falls within the scope of the reference, for this is already a prerequisite of jurisdiction by virtue of the words 'in respect of a matter agreed to be referred', where they appear earlier in the section. It seems therefore that the section is excluded if the plaintiff can show that his claim has

---

[2] *Lonrho Ltd v Shell Petroleum Co Ltd* (1978) Times, 1 February. This is not a situation in which the Court should exercise its powers under s. 1 and s. 25(2)(b) so as to render the arbitration agreement 'inoperative': *City Centre Properties (ITC Pensions) Ltd v Matthew Hall & Co Ltd* [1969] 1 WLR 772.

[3] *Paczy v Haendler and Natermann GmbH* [1981] 1 Lloyd's Rep 302.

[4] It was conceded in *The Merak* [1964] 2 Lloyd's Rep 283 at 295 that this does not mean that the arbitration has become inoperative or cannot proceed' within the meaning of s. 4(2) of the 1950 Act (now repealed).

[5] Such time limits are rare: see pp. 202–204, ante.

[6] *The Tuyuti* [1984] QB 838; *The Rena K* [1978] 1 Lloyd's Rep 545, [1979] QB 377. It would follow from the reasoning of Brandon J that if the applicant has the means to honour the award but it would be impossible to enforce such an award against him (e.g. because his assets are in a country where the award would not be recognised), the agreement is nevertheless not 'incapable of being performed'.

[7] These words do not appear in the New York Convention. They owe their origin to the report of the Mackinnon Committee (Cmd. 2817), which had noted complaints that s. 1(1) of the Arbitration Clauses (Protocol) Act 1924, a precursor of s. 1 of the 1975 Act, was being abused. The words were added by s. 8 of the Arbitration (Foreign Awards) Act 1930.

never been denied[8], and also, if he can demonstrate that the defendant has no defence, and that there is accordingly no genuine dispute[9].

(c) Removing the stay

The stay of proceedings does not permanently deprive the Court of jurisdiction over the dispute[10]. The Court's jurisdiction may be resumed in two circumstances. First, if the proceedings take the form of an Admiralty action in rem, the proceedings remain available for the purpose of enforcing an award in the plaintiff's favour, and the stay will be lifted to enable this to be done[11]. Second, the arbitration agreement may become 'null and void, inoperative or incapable of being performed' after the stay has been granted. In these circumstances we submit that the Court may, and if asked to do so, must lift the stay and take the matter into its own hands again[12].

(d) Extent of proceedings stayed: interim relief

The function of a stay under section 1 is to give effect to the arbitration agreement, and the proceedings will only be stayed to the extent necessary for that purpose. The proceedings will be allowed to continue for the purpose of adjudicating on matters falling outside the terms of the agreement to arbitrate, or to enable the plaintiff to obtain interim relief in aid of his claim which does not involve the court adjudicating on the merits of the claim, for example by the arrest of a ship as security for the claim[13].

5 Discretionary stay: domestic arbitration

The Court has a general discretion under section 4(1) of the 1950 Act to stay proceedings brought in breach of a 'domestic arbitration agreement'[14]. This expression means an arbitration agreement which does not provide[15], expressly or by implication, for arbitration in a State other than the United Kingdom and to which neither (1) an individual who is a national of, or habitually resident in, any State other than the United Kingdom nor (2) a body corporate

---

[8] So that at the moment when the application is made, there is no dispute between the parties, and nothing in respect of which an arbitrator can validly be appointed. This appears to reverse the burden of proof by comparison with s. 4(1), where it is for the person who seeks a stay to show that there is something about which to arbitrate.

[9] *A/S Gunnstein & Co K/S v Jensen, Krebs and Neilsen, The Alfa Nord* [1977] 2 Lloyd's Rep 434; *Eagle Star Insurance Co Ltd v Yuval Insurance Co Ltd* [1978] 1 Lloyd's Rep 357, per Goff LJ at 362. This topic is more fully discussed at pp. 123–124, ante.

[10] See pp. 155–156, ante.

[11] *The Rena K* [1978] 1 Lloyd's Rep 545, [1979] QB 377. See also p. 338, ante.

[12] *Paczy v Haendler*, ante, at 307. This was undoubtedly the case under s. 4(2) of the 1950 Act: *The Golden Trader* [1974] 1 Lloyd's Rep 378, [1975] QB 348. The French text of the Protocol made this plain. S. 1 of the 1975 Act does not deal with the point explicitly, but it would, we submit, be wrong for the Court to maintain a stay in the face of circumstances which, if they had existed when the order was applied for, would have deprived the Court of jurisdiction to grant it.

[13] *The Tuyuti* [1984] QB 838.

[14] The section does not apply to an agreement which is not a 'domestic arbitration agreement' see s. 1(2) of the 1975 Act.

[15] Presumably this is a question for the proper law of the arbitration agreement. See Chapter 4, ante, pp. 62–63.

which is incorporated in, or whose central management and control is exercised in, any State other than the United Kingdom, is a party at the time the proceedings are commenced[16]. It is to be noted that an agreement may be concluded in England, governed by English law, provide for arbitration in England, relate to disputes arising out of a purely English transaction, and yet not be a 'domestic arbitration agreement'. It is the character of the parties to the agreement which alone determines whether it is a 'domestic' agreement or not.

The requirements of section 4(1) of the 1950 Act may be summarised as follows –

(a) The person applying for the stay must prove the existence of an arbitration agreement, viz. a written agreement[17] to submit present or future differences to arbitration.

(b) The applicant must prove that the proceedings in respect of which a stay is sought are of a type to which section 4(1) applies, namely that –

(i) they are legal proceedings commenced in a Court;

(ii) they are brought in respect of any matters agreed to be referred;

(iii) they are brought by a party to the arbitration agreement or by a person claiming through or under such a person[18].

(c) The applicant must prove that the application is made in an appropriate manner, namely that –

(i) the applicant is a party to the arbitration agreement or a person claiming through or under such a person;

(ii) the applicant is a party to the legal proceedings;

(iii) the application is made after the applicant has entered an appearance[19] but before he has delivered any pleadings or taken any other steps in the proceedings.

(d) The Court must be satisfied that –

(i) the applicant was and is ready and willing to do all things necessary to the proper conduct of the arbitration;

(ii) there is no sufficient reason why the dispute should not be referred to arbitration.

(e) If the above requirements are satisfied, the applicant has a prima facie right to stay, and the Court will grant one unless the person resisting the application persuades the Court that there are good reasons why one should not be granted.

The burden of proof shifts whilst the Court goes through the process of ascertaining whether the requirements are satisfied. Logically, it should remain on the applicant throughout stages (a) to (d), shifting to the plaintiff at stage (e). It appears, however, that the burden is also on the plaintiff in respect of requirement (d)(i)[20].

The various requirements are discussed in turn below.

---

[16] S. 1(4) of the 1975 Act.

[17] For the meaning of 'written agreement', see p. 54, ante.

[18] Hereafter for convenience referred to as the plaintiff. Occasionally, he may be someone else, as for example where the application is made in third-party proceedings.

[19] The Act refers to 'appearance' but this must now be read as 'acknowledgment of service': RSC Ord. 12, r. 10.

[20] See p. 473, post.

(a) Arbitration agreement

An applicant who relies on section 4(1) must prove the existence of an 'arbitration agreement', namely a written agreement to submit present or future disputes to arbitration[1]. A party to an oral agreement is not entitled to relief under section 4(1)[2], although he may perhaps have the prospect of a stay under the inherent jurisdiction of the Court to intervene in cases where an action constitutes an abuse of the process of the Court[3].

An agreement to submit disputes to arbitration abroad is capable of being an 'arbitration agreement' for the purpose of section 4(1)[4].

The need to prove the existence of an arbitration agreement gives rise to problems where the agreement is alleged to have consisted of a term in an underlying substantive contract, and where one or other party has put in issue the existence or enforceability of that underlying contract. Similar problems arise where the arbitration agreement is said to spring from the underlying contract, and the question is whether the arbitration agreement was ever incorporated in that contract.

Where the issue concerns the initial, or continued, existence of the underlying contract, the following propositions are clear[5] –

(i) The applicant cannot at the same time assert that no underlying contract ever came into existence, and yet at the same time rely on section 4(1). Denial of the underlying contract, and hence of the arbitration agreement is inconsistent with proof that the Court has jurisdiction under section 4(1)[6].

(ii) An applicant is not precluded from claiming relief under section 4(1) merely because he or his opponent is asserting that the underlying contract has ceased to exist – by frustration, repudiation, avoidance for misrepresentation or non-disclosure, or for some other reason. An arbitration clause is an agreement distinct from the underlying contract in which it is embodied, and if expressed in appropriate terms may continue to govern disputes between the parties even if that contract has ceased to bind.

A more difficult question arises where it is the plaintiff, not the applicant, who asserts either that the arbitration agreement was not incorporated in the underlying contract, or if it was, that the underlying contract not only has ceased to bind, but never came into existence at all, e.g. because there was no concluded offer and acceptance or the bargain was vitiated by mistake[7]. Here, there is no inconsistency in the applicant's case, for he is maintaining that the contract should be enforced according to all its terms, including those of the arbitration clause. There is thus no logical objection to the grant of a stay, and

---

[1] S. 32. See p. 54, ante. The incidence of the burden of proof is probably different under s. 1 of the 1975 Act: see ante, p. 464.

[2] See, for example, *Fleming v JS Doig (Grimsby) Ltd* (1921) 38 RPC 57.

[3] See pp. 461–462, ante.

[4] The Court may, however, think it appropriate to refuse a stay if the foreign arbitrator would be called on to decide difficult questions of English law: see *Temperley Steam Shipping Co v Smyth & Co* [1905] 2 KB 791.

[5] For a more detailed discussion, see pp. 108–113, ante.

[6] *Republic of Liberia v Gulf Oceanic Inc* [1985], 1 Lloyd's Rep 539. But see *Metal Scrap Trade Corp Ltd v Kate Shipping Co Ltd* [1988] 1 WLR 767 (under appeal).

[7] Such an assertion will usually be made where the plaintiff wishes to claim in tort, and to deny the existence of a contract, so as to avoid the effect of contractual exceptions. In such a situation it may also be necessary to look carefully at the question whether the arbitration clause, if it binds at all, is wide enough to cover this particular dispute.

indeed it would be wrong for the Court to refuse one as a matter of course, for this would mean that the plaintiff would deny the applicant his contractual rights to arbitrate merely by making an unfounded assertion as to the non-existence of the contract. On the other hand, it must be borne in mind that an arbitrator has no power to make a binding award, or to state a case, on a matter which affects his own jurisdiction[8]. This means that if it subsequently proves, on a full investigation, that there has indeed never been a contract or that the contract did not incorporate the arbitration clause, the arbitration will simply have been a waste of time, and proceedings in Court will be inevitable.

In these circumstances, the right course will be for the Court to decide the issue at the time when the application is made for a stay. If necessary oral evidence on the matter must be adduced[9].

(b) (i) Legal proceedings commenced in any court

The remedy under section 4(1) is available only in respect of legal proceedings commenced in any Court. It extends to proceedings in the County Court[10], but not to claims advanced before administrative or other quasi-judicial tribunals[11].

Legal proceedings include proceedings which are instituted otherwise than by way of writ, such as those launched by originating summons or third-party notice or by the delivery of a counter-claim[12].

It is unnecessary to discuss questions which might in theory arise as to the stage at which proceedings are 'commenced' — for example, whether this word embraces situations in which a writ has been issued but not served, or where the proceedings are instituted ex parte[13]. In practice, any premature attempt to obtain a stay will be ruled out by the requirement that the application must be made after acknowledgment of service.

Since the remedy of a stay is only available in respect of legal proceedings, it cannot be used so as to prevent a defendant raising by way of defence to an action an issue falling within the arbitration agreement[14].

---

[8] See *Modern Buildings Wales Ltd v Limmer and Trinidad Co Ltd* [1975] 2 Lloyd's Rep 318. The contrary appears to have been assumed in *SA Hersent v United Towing Co Ltd and White, The Tradesman* [1961] 2 Lloyd's Rep 183, but the distinction between disputes as to the initial existence of the contract and disputes as to its continued existence does not seem to have been brought to the attention of the Court.

[9] *Morgan Guarantee Trust Co v Hadjantonakis* [1988] 1 Lloyd's Rep 381, following *Modern Buildings Wales Ltd v Limmer and Trinidad Co Ltd* [1975] 2 Lloyd's Rep 318, in turn explaining *The Elizabeth H* [1962] 1 Lloyd's Rep 172. *SA Hersent v United Towing Co Ltd and White, The Tradesman* [1961] 2 Lloyd's Rep 183 must now be regarded as wrong.

[10] The definition of 'Court' in the 1889 Act left room for doubt as to the position in the County Court, although it was ultimately held that such a Court could grant a stay: *Morriston Tinplate Co v Brooker Dore & Co* [1908] 1 KB 403; *Austin and Whiteley Ltd v S Bowley & Son* (1913) 108 LT 921; *Parker Gaines & Co Ltd v Turpin* [1918] 1 KB 358. The position under the 1950 Act is clear.

[11] See Chapter 2, ante.

[12] *Chappell v North* [1891] 2 QB 252.

[13] See *Anglo-Newfoundland Development Co Ltd v R* [1920] 2 KB 214, where the granting of the Attorney-General's fiat was held not to constitute the commencement of proceedings.

[14] *Bulk Oil (Zug) AG v Trans-Asiatic Oil Ltd SA* [1973] 1 Lloyd's Rep 129 at 135.

(b) (ii) Matters agreed to be referred

The burden is on the applicant to show that the matters in respect of which a stay is sought fall within the scope of the arbitration agreement.

Generally, this will involve the interpretation of the arbitration agreement, a topic discussed in Chapter 6. There are, however, two matters which should be mentioned here.

First, the question whether the claim falls within the scope of the agreement depends upon the way in which it is actually formulated, and not upon whether there is another way in which it could or should be framed. If the claim indicated in the writ or other pleading[15] lies outside the scope of the agreement, no stay will be granted. It will not avail the applicant to point out that the claim as put forward is misconceived in law or ill-founded in fact, and that if it were reformulated in the only tenable way it would fall within the agreement. The consequence of the plaintiff pressing ahead with the wrong cause of action will no doubt be that the claim falls, and that he is barred by the adverse judgment from subsequently putting forward another claim on the correct basis. But this does not mean that the applicant can force the plaintiff to replead his case in such a manner as to enable the applicant to obtain a stay[16].

Second, the question may sometimes arise whether the application of the arbitration agreement should be judged by reference to the nature of the claim alone, or to the whole of the dispute arising between the parties, including issues raised by way of defence. The problem may be illustrated by reference to the case of goods entrusted to the defendant for carriage or safe custody, under a contract containing a narrow form of arbitration clause[17]. If the goods are misdelivered, the plaintiff may in certain circumstances have a cause of action in conversion, entirely independent of any right to claim for breach of contract. An action of this nature cannot be said to arise out of the contract, yet the defendant may have defences which do so arise, in the scope of an assertion that his liability is excluded or limited by the express terms of the contract. Thus, if the Court must have regard to the nature of the claim, then the matter lies outside the scope of the agreement; whereas the contrary will be the case if it is the nature of the dispute which is crucial.

There appears to be no reported discussion of this problem. In some instances, the wording of the clause will provide a ready solution. Thus, if it stipulates for arbitration in respect of '*all claims* arising under the contract' then it must be taken at its face value, and only contractual claims will be the subject of a stay. If the clause provides for the arbitration of '*all disputes* arising under the contract' the answer will be less straightforward. It is suggested, however, that in such a case the Court must consider what passed between the parties before the commencement of the proceedings, together with any evidence filed on the application for a stay, in order to ascertain whether there is a genuine dispute as

---

[15] Or, we suggest, in correspondence.

[16] *Monro v Bognor UDC* [1915] 3 KB 167. The classification of the claim and the interpretation of the agreement may raise closely connected issues; as in *J Braconnot et Cie v Compagnie des Messageries Maritimes, The Sindh* [1975] 1 Lloyd's Rep 372, where the agreement was governed by French law which was applied to determine the issue whether a claim pleaded in tort in an English writ fell within the words 'all disputes caused by the interpretation or the execution of the present Bill of Lading'.

[17] For example, one which extends only to matters 'arising under the contract'.

to the effect of the contract, and should grant a stay irrespective of the nature of the claim, if satisfied that such a dispute exists[18].

(b) (iii) The plaintiff as a party to the agreement

The applicant must show that the person whose claim he seeks to stay is either a party to the arbitration agreement or a person claiming through or under such a party. But he need not show that the claimant was a party to the arbitration agreement when he commenced legal proceedings, nor even that the arbitration agreement was in existence at that time. A stay may be granted in respect of an arbitration agreement made after the commencement of proceedings[19].

It occasionally happens that the plaintiff is not himself a party to the arbitration agreement on which the application is founded. Two situations may be recognised:

(i) the plaintiff has acquired the rights, which the action is brought to enforce, from someone who is a party to an arbitration agreement with the defendant[20];

(ii) the plaintiff is bringing the action on behalf of someone else, who is a party to an arbitration agreement with the defendant.

These situations are discussed in Chapter 8, ante.

(c) (i) and (ii) The identity of the applicant

Section 4(1) imposes two requirements as to the identity of the applicant. First, he must be 'any . . . party to the agreement, or any person claiming through or under him'. Second, he must be 'any party to those legal proceedings'. Neither of these requirements is happily worded.

The first requirement dates from the 1854 Act. Since the person who makes the application will be receiving, not asserting, a claim it is not easy to see how he can be said to be 'claiming under' the party to the arbitration agreement. On the first occasion when the expression is used in the subsection, the words 'claiming under' plainly relate to the substantive right which is being asserted. Apparently, on this second occasion, they refer to the assertion of the right to arbitrate – or perhaps the section assumes that the substantive contract and the arbitration agreement form a single entity, so that the words refer to any person who asserts a derivative right to this entity[1].

The second requirement can scarcely be interpreted in its literal sense, since this would mean that a person could claim a stay even though not a party to the

---

[18] See, however, *J Braconnot et Cie v Compagnie des Messageries Maritimes*, ante, where it was assumed that it was the claim, not the dispute, which required to be classified; but the point did not arise for decision. The extent to which the Court should concern itself with validity or genuineness of the claim is questionable. By parity of reasoning with *Monro v Bognor UDC*, ante, it would seem that defences must be taken at their face value; subject only to this, that if the defence is plainly hopeless, the Court would be entitled to hold that there was no genuine dispute, and hence nothing which could be referred to arbitration: see p. 123 et seq., ante.

[19] *The Tuyuti* [1984] QB 838, a decision on s. 1 of the 1975 Act, assisted by recourse to the text of the New York Convention, to which the section gives effect. Robert Goff LJ was inclined to accept a similar construction of s. 4 of the 1950 Act, for reasons which we respectfully submit are convincing.

[20] As in *Aspell v Seymour* [1929] WN 152.

[1] Such as a trustee in bankruptcy: see *Piercy v Young* (1879) 14 Ch D 200. See generally, Chapter 8.

arbitration agreement[2]. No doubt the purpose is simply to make clear that not all the parties to the arbitration agreement need join in the application to stay[3]. The applicant must be a party against whom the legal proceedings have been brought rather than a party intervening on his own application[4].

(c) (iii) 'Step in the proceedings'

The application for a stay must be made after appearance[5], but before the applicant has delivered any pleadings or has taken any other step in the proceedings. The taking of a step nullifies the jurisdiction of the Court to grant a stay[6]; it is not simply a matter which is to be weighed when the Court exercises its discretion.

The reported cases are difficult to reconcile, and they give no clear guidance on the nature of a step in the proceedings. It appears, however, that two requirements must be satisfied. First, the conduct of the applicant must be such as to demonstrate an election to abandon his right to stay, in favour of allowing the action to proceed[7]. Second, the act in question must have the effect of invoking the jurisdiction of the Court[8]. An extra-judicial proceeding in the action, such as obtaining by correspondence a consent to the enlargement of time for delivery of pleadings, is not sufficient[9].

The circumstances which accompany an act may be looked at to see whether the act amounts to an election to give up the right to a stay. Thus, an application to the Court which might otherwise amount to a step in the proceedings is deprived of this characteristic if the applicant makes it clear – by stating that his application is without prejudice to a subsequent request for a stay, or by simultaneously taking out a summons to stay – that he intends to insist on a reference to arbitration[10].

An act carried out as a preliminary to proceedings is not a step in

---

[2] See, however, the curious case *Roussel-Uclaf v GD Searle & Co* [1978] 1 Lloyd's Rep 225.

[3] This was in any event the law, before the 1889 Act adopted the present words: see *Willesford v Watson* (1873) 8 Ch App 473 (joint lessees of mine: no objection that only two of them applied for a stay).

[4] *Etri Fans Ltd v NMB UK Ltd* [1987] 2 Lloyd's Rep 565.

[5] The Act refers to 'appearance' but this must now be read as 'acknowledgment of service': RSC Ord. 12, r. 10.

[6] *Chappel v North* [1891] 2 QB 252.

[7] *Eagle Star Insurance Co v Yuval Insurance Co* [1978] 1 Lloyd's Rep 357; *Metropolitan Tunnel and Public Words v London Electric Rly Co* [1926] Ch 371, per Lord Hanworth MR at 374; *Ives and Barker v Willans* [1894] 2 Ch 478 at 484, 490, 494; *Ford's Hotel Co Ltd v Bartlett* [1896] AC 1 at 6; *Austin and Whiteley Ltd v S Bowley & Son* (1913) 108 LT 921. Treating a step in the action as evidence of election not to proceed by means of arbitration does not accord well with the decision in *Parker, Gaines & Co Ltd v Turpin* [1918] 1 KB 358 that an act taken in ignorance of the agreement to arbitrate is none the less a step for the purposes of s. 4(1).

[8] This does not mean that the defendant must himself have made a substantive application to the court: it is sufficient if he concurs in an application made by the plaintiff: *Turner & Goudy v McConnell* [1985] 1 WLR 898.

[9] *Ives and Barker v Willans*, supra, per Lindley LJ at 484; *Lane v Herman* [1939] 3 All ER 353; *Ford's Hotel Co Ltd v Bartlett*, supra, per Lord Shand at 6; *Chappell v North*, ante; *Brighton Marine Palace and Pier Ltd v Woodhouse* [1893] 2 Ch 486; *Zalinoff v Hammond* [1898] 2 Ch 92.

[10] *Metropolitan Tunnel and Public Works v London Electric Rly Co*, ante; *London Sack and Bag Co Ltd v Dixon and Lugton Ltd* [1943] 2 All ER 763; *Pitchers Ltd v Plaza (Queensbury) Ltd* [1940] 1 All ER 151; *Richardson v Le Maître* [1903] 2 Ch 222 at 225 (no request for an adjournment); *Brighton Marine Palace and Pier Ltd v Woodhouse*, supra (as regards the second request for further time).

proceedings[11]. Moreover, a defendant does not necessarily take a step himself if he invites the plaintiff to take a step: for example, where he calls for the delivery of a statement of claim so that he can find out the nature of the allegations made against him[12].

The making of an application for interim relief, such as an injunction or the appointment of a receiver[13], designed to maintain the status quo pending the award is not a step in the action, since it is not inconsistent with a desire to have the substantive dispute decided by arbitration.

The following decisions on the status of particular acts may be noted –

1 Requiring the delivery of a statement of claim is a step if made by means of an application to the Court, but not if made by letter[14].

2 Obtaining an Order for discovery[15] or interrogatories[16] is a step.

3 Issuing a summons for further and better particulars is a step[17].

4 Appearing on a summons for directions and acquiescing in the Orders made thereon is probably a step[18].

5 Filing an affidavit asking for leave to defend application for summary judgment under Order[14] is a step unless at the same time an application is made for a stay[19].

6 Resisting an application for an interlocutory injunction by putting in evidence and appearing in Court[20] is not a step.

(d) (i) 'Ready and willing'

The applicant must show that he is ready and willing to do all things necessary to the proper conduct of the arbitration[1]. This requirement relates both to the time when the proceedings were commenced and to the time when the Court is called on to exercise its discretion. Evidence that the applicant is ready and willing must be furnished by affidavit[2].

---

[11] *Anglo-Newfoundland Development Co v R* [1920] 2 KB 214 (obtaining fiat of Attorney General). Plainly, the same principle would apply to (say) a letter before action in respect of a counterclaim.

[12] *Ives and Barker v Willans*, ante. The defendant may not always be sure, until the claim is spelt out in the statement of claim, whether the issues raised in the action fall within the agreement to arbitrate. If the defendant decides to ask, in such a case, for particularisation of the claim, he will be well advised to make it clear that he does so without prejudice to a possible application to stay.

[13] *Compagnie du Sénégal v Woods & Co* (1883) 53 LJ Ch 166 at 169.

[14] See note 12, p. 473, ante, and *County Theatres and Hotels Ltd v Knowles* [1902] 1 KB 480; *Adams v Catley* (1892) 66 LT 687; *Steven v Buncle* [1902] WN 44. Applying to strike out a claim for want of particulars is not necessarily a step in the action: *Eagle Star Insurance Co v Yuval Insurance Co*, ante.

[15] *Parker, Gaines & Co Ltd v Turpin*, ante.

[16] *Chappell v North*, ante.

[17] *Chappell v North*, ante: but see *Parker, Gaines & Co Ltd v Turpin*, ante.

[18] *Parker, Gaines & Co Ltd v Turpin*, ante; *County Theatres and Hotels Ltd v Knowles*, ante; *Richardson v Le Maître*, ante; *Ochs v Ochs Bros* [1909] 2 Ch 121; *Cohen v Arthur* (1912) 56 Sol Jo 344; contrast *Metropolitan Tunnel and Public Works v London Electric Rly Co*, ante.

[19] *Pitchers Ltd v Plaza (Queensbury) Ltd* [1940] 1 All ER 151; *Rumput (Panama) SA v Islamic Republic of Iran Shipping Lines, The Leage* [1984] 2 Lloyd's Rep 259; *Turner & Gouly v McConnell*, ante.

[20] *Roussel-Uclaf v GD Searle & Co* [1978] 1 Lloyd's Rep 225.

[1] This is probably a reflection of the same principle as the rule that a stay will not be granted if the applicant has taken a step in the proceedings. The applicant must unequivocally elect to have the dispute decided by arbitration. See *Adams v Catley* (1892) 66 LT 687.

[2] *Piercy v Young* (1879) 14 Ch D 200 at 209. The position is radically different from that which exists under s. 1 of the 1975 Act, where it is for the party resisting the stay to prove that the arbitration and null and void, inoperative, or incapable of being performed.

In order to satisfy this requirement, the applicant must show that he does not intend simply to use the arbitration as a means for postponing or preventing the resolution of the dispute. Manifestly, an applicant who intends to block the progress of the arbitration by refusing to appoint an arbitrator in circumstances where the Court has no residual jurisdiction to appoint one on his behalf, cannot obtain a stay[3]. The same result will apply in cases where the delay by the applicant is so great as to justify the inference that he does not really wish the arbitration to be effective[4].

The applicant must show, not only that he genuinely wishes to have the dispute resolved at all, but also that he wishes it to be decided by arbitration rather than some other means. Thus, for example, if he has brought a cross-action in respect of the same dispute in the courts of another jurisdiction, the English Court may take the view that his intention is not so much to have the dispute arbitrated, as to avoid an adjudication by the English Court. The fact that the applicant has in the past indicated a preference for some other form of tribunal does not, however, debar him from obtaining a stay if the Court is satisfied that he is now genuinely willing to arbitrate[5].

Willingness to allow a dispute to go to arbitration does not require the applicant to abandon his right to allege that he will have a perfect defence to the claim once the arbitration is instituted. Thus, he can maintain that he is ready and willing to do everything necessary for the proper conduct of the arbitration, notwithstanding his intention to rely on the fact that the contractual time limit for instituting the arbitration has already expired[6]. An arbitration can still be properly conducted even if the claim is doomed.

In practice, the plaintiff will usually find it difficult to rebut the commonform statement in the defendant's affidavit that he is ready and willing to arbitrate. At an early stage there is little that the defendant is obliged to do in the arbitration, beyond showing a willingness to appoint an arbitrator so that there is no great opportunity for the plaintiff to show that the defendant is in default of his obligations. Unwillingness to arbitrate usually manifests itself, if at all, when the interlocutory stages of the arbitration are under way. This is too late to prevent the Order for a stay being made, but in an extreme case it will justify the Court in exercising its residual jurisdiction over the dispute by lifting the stay and taking the dispute into its own hands: see pp. 158–159, ante.

---

[3] See *Manchester Ship Canal Co Ltd v Pearson & Son Ltd* [1900] 2 QB 606.

[4] Mere delay is not sufficient: *Hodson v Railway Passengers' Assurance Co* [1904] 2 KB 833 at 841; it is the inference to be drawn from the delay which matters. But quite apart from its relevance to the issue of 'ready and willing', delay is material to the exercise of the Court's discretion. *Bell v Sun Fire Insurance Office* (1927) 29 Ll L Rep 236 is perhaps best explained as a case where the defendants were at the material time refusing to appoint an arbitrator at all, rather than as a decision that expedition is an essential element in readiness and willingness.

[5] *Foresta Romana SA v 'Georges Mabro' (Owners)* (1940) 66 Ll L Rep 139. For a discussion of whether the dismissal of a plaintiff employee by the defendant is equivalent to a refusal by the defendant to arbitrate on the matters which are alleged to have justified the dismissal, see *Davis v Starr* (1889) 41 Ch D 242; *Renshaw v Queen Anne Residential Mansions and Hotel Co Ltd* [1897] 1 QB 662; *Parry v Liverpool Malt Co* [1900] 1 QB 339.

[6] *W Bruce Ltd v Strong* [1951] 2 KB 447. It was significant that the arbitration clause was in the *Scott v Avery* form. To refuse a stay would have deprived the defendant of a conclusive defence to the action. The position might perhaps have been different if the clause had been in a different form. See p. 481, post. See also *Eastern Counties Farmers Ltd v J and J Cunningham Ltd* [1962] 1 Lloyd's Rep 261.

(d) (ii) 'No sufficient reason'

Section 4 of the Act provides that the Court '. . . if satisfied that there is no sufficient reason why the matter should not be referred in accordance with the agreement . . . may make an Order staying the proceedings'. It is plain that these words call for an enquiry in two stages. The first is concerned with the existence of a jurisdiction to grant a stay; the second with the question whether, as a matter of discretion, the jurisdiction should be exercised.

The existence of these two elements in section 4[7] has occasionally been noticed by the courts[8], but never discussed in detail. In particular, no court has drawn attention to the fact that if the section is construed literally, the burden of proof at the two stages of the enquiry is different. Where a statute requires the Court to be satisfied that there is no sufficient reason why something should not be done, the burden of satisfying the Court must rest on the person who wishes that thing to be done — in the present case the applicant for the stay. At the second stage, where the discretion is left at large, it was open to the courts to decide (as they undoubtedly have decided) that the burden lies on the person who opposes the enforcement of the arbitration agreement. In recent years, no weight has been given to this verbal distinction. The presumption in favour of granting a stay, which in recent years has been almost overwhelming, has swamped any meticulous consideration of the question whether the discretion to grant a stay has been shown to exist at all[9].

In the end, this question is probably academic. It is hard to conceive of a judge who, having once decided that there were sufficient reasons why a case should not be referred to arbitration, would nevertheless exercise his discretion in favour of so referring it; and harder still to conceive that if there were no sufficient reasons for refusing a stay, a judge would hold that the presumption in favour of the stay had been rebutted. Nevertheless, recognition that the distinction exists may serve to temper the warmth which the courts display to the enforcement of agreements to arbitrate.

(e) The discretion

(i) General. If the applicant can show that the conditions referred to at pp. 466–467, ante, are satisfied, the Court has a discretion to grant a stay. From the outset, the courts have approached the exercise of this discretion on the footing that in general those who make a contract to arbitrate should be compelled to do so[10]. 'A bargain is a bargain, and the parties ought to abide by it, unless a

---

[7] Apart from slight alterations in wording, the shape of the section has been the same since the Act of 1854. The section has sometimes been said to involve a double discretion. This is not strictly accurate; the first stage of the enquiry does not involve a discretion.

[8] *Taunton-Collins v Cromie* [1964] 1 WLR 633; *Robert W Blackwell & Co Ltd v Derby Corpn* (1909) 75 JP 129.

[9] Recognition that the words of the section place the initial burden on the applicant may perhaps be found in the curious case of *G Freeman & Sons v Chester RDC* [1911] 1 KB 783. The passage beginning at the foot of the first column on p. 135 of *Bulk Oil Zug (AG) v Trans-Atlantic Oil Ltd SA* [1973] 1 Lloyd's Rep 129 is almost certainly mis-transcribed.

[10] As Lord Moulton said in *Bristol Corpn v John Aird & Co* [1913] AC 241 at 256–257, the introduction of the stay by the 1854 Act enabled submissions to arbitration to be made the subject of indirect decrees of specific performance.

clear reason applies for their not doing so'[11]. The burden is on the plaintiff to persuade the Court that it is proper to refuse a stay[12]. Originally, there was only a prima facie presumption in favour of a stay[13]. Later decisions by courts of high authority have put the matter much more emphatically. There is now a very pronounced bias in favour of enforcing the arbitration agreement[14]. A strong cause for refusing a stay must be shown[15]. Whether this is what was intended by the draftsmen of the 1854 Act may be questioned. The heavy burden of proof entails that there are now very few cases in which the Court can be persuaded to refuse a stay. The result is that disputes are sent to arbitration which are wholly unsuitable for such a procedure, particularly where the dispute involves elaborate issues of mixed fact and law. It may be doubted whether the 1854 Act, the purpose of which was to remedy the abuses arising from the difficulty of enforcing arbitration agreements was ever intended to go to the opposite extreme by enabling a virtually automatic enforcement under the guise of a discretion[16].

(ii) Factors material to the discretion. It is impossible to define, and undesirable to attempt to define, with any precision the circumstances which will induce the Court to refuse a stay[17]. Moreover, factors which may be insufficient in themselves may yet be sufficient to justify the refusal of a stay when operating cumulatively. Nevertheless, it may be helpful to indicate some of the grounds to which the courts have attributed greater or lesser weight in the exercise of the discretion.

(a) Delay. Delay is material to the exercise of the discretion in two respects. First, because a party who wishes to claim a stay must do so promptly[18]. Second,

---

[11] Per Martin B in *Wickham v Harding* (1859) 28 LJ Ex 215.

[12] This proposition has been stated or assumed in almost every reported case on s. 4 and its predecessors. Full citation is unnecessary but reference may be made to *Heyman v Darwins Ltd* [1942] AC 356 and *Bristol Corpn v John Aird & Co* [1913] AC 241.

[13] *Willesford v Watson* (1873) 8 Ch App 473 at 486; *Law v Garrett* (1878) 8 Ch D 26 at 37; *Lyon v Johnson* (1889) 40 Ch D 579.

[14] See, for example, *Bristol Corpn v John Aird & Co*, ante, at 259; *Smith, Coney and Barrett v Becker, Gray & Co* [1916] 2 Ch 86; *Metropolitan Tunnel and Public Works Ltd v London Electric Rly Co* [1926] Ch 371 at 390; *Halifax Overseas Freighters v Rasno Export, Technoprominport and Polskie Linie Oceaniczne PPW, The Pine Hill* [1958] 2 Lloyd's Rep 146 at 151.

[15] *The Eleftheria* [1969] 1 Lloyd's Rep 237, [1970] P 94 (a case on a foreign jurisdiction clause) cited and followed in *Bulk Oil (Zug) AG v Trans-Asiatic Oil Ltd SA*, ante.

[16] It is curious that the courts should have become progressively more willing to enforce agreements to arbitration come what may, at a time when ideas of the sanctity of contract are steadily losing ground. Possibly it is too late to right this particular battle, since the 1975 Act with its provisions for automatic enforcement is likely to influence judicial attitudes towards s. 4(1). But it is still possible to hope that the courts may yet be persuaded to withdraw towards the test of 'solid grounds' proposed by Davies LJ in *Ford v Clarksons Holidays Ltd* [1971] 1 WLR 1412 at 1417 which provides a realistic and workable criterion.

[17] Per Lord Moulton in *Bristol Corpn v John Aird & Co* [1913] AC 241 at 260. See also per Lord Denning MR in *Fakes v Taylor Woodrow Construction Ltd* [1973] QB 436; per Scrutton LJ in *Czarnikow v Roth, Schmidt & Co* [1922] 2 KB 478. A list of some material factors, in relation to the enforcement of foreign jurisdiction clauses was given by Brandon J in *The Eleftheria* [1970] P 94 at 99, and was adopted in the context of s. 4 by Kerr J in *Bulk Oil (Zug) AG v Trans-Asiatic Oil Ltd SA* [1973] 1 Lloyd's Rep 129 at 136.

[18] *Doleman & Sons v Ossett Corpn* [1912] 3 KB 257, per Fletcher-Moulton LJ at 268; *Minifie v Railway Passengers Assurance Co* (1881) 44 LT 552 at 554; *Pitchers Ltd v Plaza (Queensbury) Ltd* [1940] 1 All ER 151. See also *Permavox Ltd v Royal Exchange Assurance* (1939) 64 Ll L Rep 145. Delay will be particularly significant if the plaintiff has in the meantime expended money and effort in pursuing the action. Delay may also be evidence of waiver, as in *The Elizabeth H* [1962] 1 Lloyd's Rep 172.

because if the dispute is one which requires to be resolved quickly, this may induce the Court to take the dispute into its own hands, particularly if there is reason to believe that the respondent might impede the progress of the arbitration[19]. The circumstance that if an action is stayed, an arbitration will be out of time is not in itself a ground for refusing a stay[20]. Conversely, the possibility that the refusal of a stay will deprive the defendant of a doubtful defence of a time-bar in the arbitration is not conclusive in favour of granting a stay[1].

(b) Issues of law. The weight to be attached to the consideration that the matters in dispute include questions of law has been much discussed. The reported cases are not in accord. The current position is probably that the presence of an issue or issues of law is not in itself a decisive ground for refusing a stay[2], unless perhaps they are the only issues in dispute[3], but that it is a matter to be weighed with other considerations in the exercise of the discretion[4]. The logic of this distinction may not be compelling, but it makes practical sense.

The parties must be taken to have foreseen, when they agreed to have their disputes resolved by arbitration, that the disputes might involve questions of law as well as of fact; and a skilled arbitration tribunal might be just as successful in resolving a dispute involving both types of issue as a Judge of the High Court[5]. Nevertheless, it is precisely in the case where complex issues of law and fact are closely interlocked that the English law of arbitration has been seen at its least successful[6]. If the parties are not prepared to entrust the whole of the dispute to the final decision of the arbitrator (and very frequently they are not) they may be better advised not to insist on a stay, but to proceed directly to the High Court.

(c) Multiplicity of proceedings. Where the grant of a stay would involve one or all of the parties in the delay and extra expense involved in having the same issues

---

[19] See *Gilbert-Ash (Northern) Ltd v Northern Engineering (Bristol) Ltd* [1973] 3 WLR 421 at 452; *Barnes v Youngs* [1898] 1 Ch 414. Sometimes, the Court will take the view that the arbitration is likely to proceed more quickly than an action: see *The Tradesman* [1961] 2 Lloyd's Rep 183.

[20] *W Bruce Ltd v Strong* [1915] 2 KB 447; *The Jemrix* [1981] 2 Lloyd's Rep 544; cf. *The Eschersheim* [1976] 1 Lloyd's Rep 81.

[1] *The Eschersheim* [1974] 2 Lloyd's Rep 188; affd. [1976] 1 Lloyd's Rep 81, CA.

[2] *Randegger v Holmes* (1866) LR 1 CP 679; *Valle-Jones v Liverpool and London and Globe Insurance Co Ltd* (1933) 46 Ll L Rep 313; *Hyams v Docker* [1969] 1 Lloyd's Rep 341; *Green Star Shipping Co v London Assurance* (1928) 31 Ll L Rep 4; *Lock v Army, Navy and General Assurance Association Ltd* (1915) 31 TLR 297; *Rowe Bros & Co Ltd v Crossley Bros Ltd* (1912) 108 LT 11; *Re Phoenix Timber Co Ltd's Application* [1958] 1 Lloyd's Rep 305, [1958] 2 QB 1 (stay refused in respect of a dispute 'eminently suitable' for trial in Court). If *Re Carlisle, Clegg & Clegg* (1890) 44 Ch D 200; *Clough v County Live Stock Insurance Association Ltd* (1916) 85 LJ KB 1185; and *Navarino Salvors Ltd v Navarino Recovery Ltd* (1925) 23 Ll L Rep 36 are to be understood in the opposite sense, they do not accord with the main line of authority.

[3] *Rowe Bros & Co Ltd v Crossley Bros Ltd*, supra, at 14; *Bristol Corpn v John Aird & Co*, ante, at 262; *De La Garde v Worsnop & Co* [1928] Ch 17 at 22; *Heyman v Darwins Ltd* [1942] AC 356 at 391.

[4] *Bonnin v Neame* [1910] 1 Ch 732; *Green Star Shipping Co v London Assurance* (1928) 31 Ll L Rep 4; *Halifax Overseas Freighters Ltd v Rasno Export etc* [1958] 2 Lloyd's Rep 146; *Eastern Counties Farmers Ltd v J and J Cunningham Ltd* [1962] 1 Lloyd's Rep 261; *Foresta Romana SA v Georges Mabro (Owners)* (1940) 66 Ll L Rep 139. If the clause stipulates for arbitration abroad, the Court might be reluctant to stay the action if the dispute involves question of English law: see *Temperley Steam Shipping Co v Smyth & Co* [1905] 2 KB 791.

[5] As Hamilton LJ observed in *Rowe Bros & Co Ltd v Crossley Bros Ltd* (1912) 108 LT 11 at 17: 'it is quite as difficult to make the lawyer understand the engine so as to make the engineer understand the law'.

[6] *The Eschersheim* [1976] 1 Lloyd's Rep 81 at 90.

debated in more than one jurisdiction, this is a strong ground – albeit not a decisive ground[7] – for refusing a stay. Three situations may be distinguished –

(i) Part of the relief claimed lies outside the powers of the arbitrator[8], or does not fall within the scope of the agreement to arbitrate[9]; so that whether or not the stay is granted, some part of the proceedings must be retained in the High Court. Here, so long as there is a real prospect of the relief being granted, the Court may take the view that it is better to retain the whole dispute.

(ii) Proceedings between the same parties, in relation to the same or related issues, are already in progress in the High Court or in another jurisdiction. In practice, this situation will usually arise where the proceedings have been instituted by the defendant, in which case it may well be held that he has failed to prove that he is ready and willing to arbitrate, or that he has waived his right to insist on the agreement to arbitrate[10].

(iii) One of the parties to the arbitration agreement is or will be involved with other parties in High Court proceedings in respect of the same or related issues[11].

(d) Allegations of impropriety. Where the parties have agreed that future disputes shall be referred to arbitration, and a dispute has arisen which involves the question whether a party has been guilty of fraud, the Court may so far as necessary to enable the issue of fraud to be determined, refuse to stay an action

---

[7] *Bulk Oil (Zug) v Trans-Asiatic Oil Ltd SA* [1973] 1 Lloyd's Rep 129 provides a striking illustration of the fact that multiplicity alone is not necessarily enough to justify the refusal of a stay. Kerr J plainly considered that the most sensible course would be to have all the disputes determined by the same tribunal (see p. 171), but nevertheless granted a stay. The learned judge attached weight to the consideration that the plaintiffs had themselves created the risk of multiplicity and hence of inconsistent decisions by entering into two contracts with the defendants, with related subject matter but different jurisdiction clauses.

[8] Contrast *Willesford v Watson* (1873) 8 Ch App 473; *Law v Garrett* (1877) 8 Ch D 26; *Kirchner & Co v Gruban* [1909] 1 Ch 413, with *Compagnie du Sénégal v Woods & Co* (1883) 53 LJ Ch 166; *Wade-Gery v Morrison* (1877) 37 LT 270; *Brighton Marine Palace and Pier Ltd v Woodhouse* [1893] 2 Ch 486. See also *Young v Buckett* (1882) 51 LJ Ch 504, through which lapse of time the right to refer most of the disputes to arbitration had been lost. Where the issues involve a claim for rectification there is a strong case for refusing a stay. It would be absurd to have the meaning of a written agreement determined by the arbitrator, and then to litigate the question whether the document really reflected the true contract between the parties. See, for example, *Printing Machinery Co Ltd v Linotype and Machinery Ltd* [1912] 1 Ch 566; *James Murchie & Co Ltd v Fuerst Bros Ltd* (1922) 10 Ll L Rep 515.

[9] If the matters outside the scope of the submission are trifling, this will not be a ground for refusing a stay: *Ives and Barker v Willans* [1894] 2 Ch 478. Contrast *Turnock v Sartoris* (1889) 43 Ch D 150. See also *Wheatley v Westminster Brymbo Coal and Coke Co Ltd* (1865) 11 LT 728; *Rowe Bros & Co Ltd v Crossley Bros Ltd* (1912) 108 LT 11; *Young v Buckett* (1882) 51 LJ Ch 504; *Brazendale & Co Ltd v Saint Frères SA* [1970] 2 Lloyd's Rep 34. Particular reference may be made to the importance attached by Hamilton LJ in *Rowe v Crossley*, supra, at 17, to the question whether the matter outside the arbitration clause raises substantially the same facts and rights as would fall to be determined within the arbitration clause.

[10] As to the risk of inconsistent decisions, see note 7, ante, *Brazendale & Co Ltd v Saint Frères SA*, supra, and *The Jemrix* [1981] 2 Lloyd's Rep 544.

[11] *Navarino Salvors Ltd v Navarino Recovery Ltd* (1925) 23 Ll L Rep 36; *Halifax Overseas Freighters v Rasno Export, etc* [1958] 2 Lloyd's Rep 146; *Taunton-Collins v Cromie* [1964] 1 WLR 633. See also *The Eschersheim* [1974] 2 Lloyd's Rep 188; affd. [1976] 1 Lloyd's Rep 8, CA; and *City Centre Properties (ITC Pensions) Ltd v Matthew Hall & Co Ltd* [1969] 1 WLR 772 (application to revoke the authority of the arbitrator).

brought on the agreement[12]. In order to make this provision effective, the Court has power in such a case to order that a *Scott v Avery* provision shall cease to have effect as regards the dispute[13].

Quite apart from these statutory powers[14], it has always been clear that the existence of an allegation of fraud is sufficient ground for refusing a stay : partly because it is only fair that a party against whom a serious charge is made should have the opportunity of an investigation in open court, and partly because of a feeling that the judge is better capable of dealing with such an issue than an arbitrator[15]. The principle applies whether the allegation is made by the defendant or by the plaintiff. If made by the defendant, it applies almost as a matter of course. If made by the plaintiff there must be circumstances beyond the mere allegation of fraud, for example, if there is a special public interest in the charge or if it is undesirable that the particular arbitrator should decide it. In either case, however, there must be substance in the charge[16]; neither party will be allowed to make use of a wild allegation of impropriety to avoid a reference to arbitration.

Although there can be little doubt on the cases that the discretion of the Court to refuse a stay is not limited to the instances of fraud in the strict legal sense of the word, it is not clear precisely how far the discretion extends. It probably covers all cases of dishonesty, deliberate misrepresentation or other morally wrongful conduct[17] of the parties or those in whose shoes they stand[18]. Allegations of a serious dereliction of professional duty of such a nature as to damage the plaintiff's reputation might suffice, but not a mere assertion that the plaintiff's servants have been negligent[19].

---

[12] S. 24(2) and (3) of the Act, see post, pp. 499, 501–503. The mechanism established by the sub-sections is that the former empowers the Court in questions of fraud to order that the arbitration agreement shall cease to have effect, and the latter enables the Court to refuse a stay. Sub-s. (2) is presumably intended to enable the Court to take over pending arbitrations where an allegation of fraud is made in the course of the arbitration; sub-s. (3) deals with situations where the arbitration has not yet commenced. See *Permavox Ltd v Royal Exchange Assurance* (1939) 64 Ll L Rep 145.

[13] S. 25(4). In *Permavox Ltd v Royal Exchange Assurance*, supra, Greaves LJ revoked the entire submission with a view to enabling the dispute to be heard in the High Court. It is submitted that this would not be technically correct, in view of the words 'so far as may be necessary', unless fraud were the only – and not merely the principal – issue in dispute. The point is academic, except where the submission may contain a *Scott v Avery* clause, since the Court could always decline a stay on such parts of the stay as did not fall strictly within the powers under s. 24(2).

[14] Since *Wallis v Hirsch* (1856) 1 CBNS 316. This was decided shortly after the statutory power to stay was created.

[15] As Willes J pointed out in *Wallis v Hirsch*, supra – 'Brokers would naturally shrink from a charge of fraud made against a person in the market'.

[16] *Wallis v Hirsch*, ante (distinguished in *Hirsch v Im Thurn* (1858) 4 CBNS 569); *Russell v Russell* (1880) 14 Ch D 471; *Barnes v Youngs* [1898] 1 Ch 414 (approved on this point in *Green v Howell* [1910] 1 Ch 495); *Minifie v Rly Passengers Assurance Co* (1881) 44 LT 552; *Camilla Cotton Oil Co v Granadex SA and Tracomin SA* [1976] 2 Lloyd's Rep 10; *Cunningham–Reid v Buchanan–Jardine* [1988] 1 WLR 678.

[17] *Vawdrey v Simpson* [1896] 1 Ch 166 – 'changes which are too serious to be tried by an arbitrator'. *Radford v Hair* [1971] Ch 758 – 'actual dishonesty'. An allegation involving the use of the word 'fraud' is not essential to the exercise of the power: ibid. at 764.

[18] For example, a beneficiary where the action is brought by the trustee, or a deceased when the plaintiff is a personal representative: see *Minifie v Rly Passengers Assurance Co* (1881) 44 LT 552.

[19] *Charles Osenton & Co v Johnston* [1942] AC 130. See, however, per Pennycuick VC in *Radford v Hair*, ante, at 962–963.

(e) Identity of arbitrator. Where an arbitrator has already been appointed by the time of the application to stay, the Court will have regard to his identity and characteristics, in order to satisfy itself that he will be able to conduct the arbitration in a proper and impartial way. For this purpose, the Court must consider whether there is anything in the personal conduct of the arbitrator, or the position in which his actions have placed him, which makes him an unfit person to be a judge in the matter[20]. When considering the weight to be attached to this factor, a distinction must be drawn[1] between cases where the arbitrator is specifically identified in the submission; those where he is nominated by an outsider; and those where he is nominated by one of the parties to the dispute.

Cases in the first category give rise to little difficulty where the lack of impartiality manifests itself after the submission has been made. The Court is unlikely to regard the discovery of bias as a ground for refusing a stay, for this would destroy what might otherwise be a perfectly unobjectionable agreement to arbitrate[2]. Instead, the Court will take steps to see that the arbitration takes place in a satisfactory manner – either by giving leave under section 1 of the Act to revoke the appointment of the nominated arbitrator, or by making it a condition of the grant of a stay that the applicant consents to the appointment of a different arbitrator.

More serious problems can arise when it is obvious from the outset that the arbitrator may be placed in a position where duty and interest conflict. In the past, this situation has arisen on several occasions in the context of an agreement for the execution of building and engineering works, where it was at one time common to stipulate that the arbitrator should be a specified employee or agent of one party, or (even more anomalously) that the arbitrator should be one of the parties himself. An arbitrator in such a position might well have to combine the functions of judge, litigant and witness, a task which required heroic feats of impartiality[3].

A substantial body of learning grew up in which the courts attempted to mitigate the more obviously undesirable consequences of this conflict of interest[4], whilst at the same time maintaining the principle, then generally accepted, that a person who made a bargain with his eyes open should not afterwards be allowed to complain that it had undesirable consequences[5]. It is unnecessary to analyse the decisions on this topic[6], since it is now unusual to find a party or

---

[20] Per Lord Moulton in *Bristol Corpn v John Aird & Co* [1913] AC 241 at 258.

[1] As was observed in *Eckersley v Mersey Docks and Harbour Board* [1894] 2 QB 667.

[2] We doubt whether in this respect *Bonnin v Neame* [1910] 1 Ch 732, which was in any event an unusual case, would now be followed.

[3] The Court did not expect the arbitrator to display 'the icy impartiality of a Rhadamanthus': *Jackson v Barry Rly Co* [1893] 1 Ch 238 at 248, per Bowen LJ.

[4] A striking example may be found in *Pickthall v Merthyr Tydvil Local Board* (1886) 2 TLR 805, where the clerk of a local board, who was named in the contract as arbitrator, instructed counsel in relation to the dispute, on behalf of his employers. See *Hickman & Co v Roberts* [1913] AC 229 for a statement of the high standard of impartiality required of the architect or engineer in such circumstances.

[5] A reasoned exposition of the latter principle is contained in the speech of Lord Moulton in *Bristol Corpn v John Aird & Co*, ante.

[6] See *Pickthall v Merthyr Tydvil Local Board*, ante; *Nuttall v Manchester Corpn* (1892) 8 TLR 513; *Ives and Barker v Willans* [1894] 2 Ch 478; *Eckersley v Mersey Docks and Harbour Board*, ante; *The City of Calcutta* (1898) 79 LT 517; *Robert W Blackwell & Co Ltd v Derby Corpn* (1909) 75 JP 129; *Bonnin v Neame* [1910] 1 Ch 732; *Freeman & Sons v Chester RDC* [1911] 1 KB 783; *Bristol Corpn v John Aird & Co*, ante.

employee acting as arbitrator in cases where his decision is not open to review by an independent third party. Moreover, the Court now has power[7] to revoke the authority of an arbitrator named or designated in the arbitration agreement on the ground that he is not or may not be impartial; and it is no ground for refusing the application that the party knew, or ought to have known, that the arbitrator by reason of his relation towards any other party to the agreement or of his connection with the subject referred, might not be capable of impartiality.

As regards the situation where the arbitrator is appointed, not directly by the submission itself, but by the nomination of a third party pursuant to the submission, we doubt whether the Court would regard a want of impartiality as a ground for refusing a stay, but would instead find a method of ensuring that the arbitration continued with a more suitable arbitrator. The same conclusion applies to a nomination made by one of the parties, without the concurrence of the other.

(f) Scott v Avery clause. The presence of a *Scott v Avery* clause in the submission, making the publication of an award a condition precedent to any right of action under the contract, will normally lead to the automatic grant of a stay, even if the plaintiff will be out of time for beginning an arbitration[8], for it would be pointless to allow the action to continue in circumstances where is would at once be defeated by a plea that the condition precedent had not been fulfilled[9].

There are, however, circumstances in which a stay will be denied notwithstanding the presence of a *Scott v Avery* clause. Thus, there will be no stay if –

(i) the pre-conditions for the exercise of the jurisdiction to stay are not satisfied[10];

(ii) the Court exercises its power under section 25(4) of the Act to order that the *Scott v Avery* clause shall cease to have effect as regards the dispute[11];

(iii) the conduct of the defendant is such as to amount to a waiver of the right to rely on the *Scott v Avery* provision, or otherwise to disentitle him from doing so[12];

(iv) there is a dispute as to the jurisdiction of the arbitrator; the Court would not stay an action designed to test the question of jurisdication by means of a claim for a declaration[13].

(g) Expense. For all its advantages of informality and expertise, an arbitration can be a more costly proceeding than a High Court action. Unlike the Court,

---

[7] S. 24(1). The power was introduced by the 1934 Act, as the result of representations made to the MacKinnon Committee.

[8] *W Bruce Ltd v Strong* [1951] 2 KB 447. The proper course is for the plaintiff to apply for an extension of time under s. 27 of the 1950 Act: see ante, p. 210, or in an appropriate case, for an order that the *Scott v Avery* clause shall cease to have effect as regards the dispute: see p. 163, ante.

[9] See *Smith Coney and Barrett v Becker, Gray & Co* [1916] 2 Ch 86, per Phillimore LJ; *Smith v Pearl Assurance Co Ltd* (1939) 63 Ll L Rep 1; *Bruce v Strong*, supra; *Dennehy v Bellamy* (1938) 60 Ll L Rep 269.

[10] For example, if the applicant cannot prove that he is ready and willing to arbitrate, as in *Bell v Sun Fire Insurance Office* (1927) 29 Ll L Rep 236. It will not usually be wise for the plaintiff to take this point, for unless he can establish waiver, he will be faced with a defence based on the *Scott v Avery* clause.

[11] See p. 163, ante.

[12] See p. 164, ante. It does not follow that the applicant automatically loses his right to a stay; merely that he no longer has the benefit of the strong presumption created by the *Scott v Avery* clause.

[13] *Getreide-Import-Gesellschaft mbH v Contimar SA Compania Industrial Commercial y Maritima* [1953] 1 Lloyd's Rep 572.

the arbitrators require payment for their services, and a hearing by a tribunal of arbitrators is not the cheapest way of resolving a small dispute. Moreover, where issues of law are involved, it may in the long run prove more expensive to have a hearing before the arbitrators, followed by the argument of the questions of law on appeal, than to have the entire dispute decided at a single hearing in the High Court. It is, however, clear that additional expense is not a decisive factor, if indeed it is a factor at all, in the refusal to grant a stay[14]. The fact that the person resisting a stay is too poor to sustain the extra expense of an arbitration, or cannot obtain legal aid for the purpose, is equally immaterial[15], except perhaps in the case where there is evidence that the wrongful conduct of the defendant is itself responsible for the plaintiff's poor financial position[16].

(h) Exclusion of legal representation. We submit that if the agreement purports to exclude the right of the parties to legal representation at the hearing, this will be a factor weighing against the grant of a stay, if the dispute raises issues of principle[17].

(iii) The terms of the stay.   Under section 4(1), the Court has a discretion as to the terms on which a stay is granted. For example, a stay may be granted on condition that the applicant agrees – (i) to give security for costs[18]; (ii) to permit a change in the composition of the tribunal; (iii) to consent to an appeal on a question of law arising out of the award or to allow the arbitrator to state his award in the form of a special case; (iv) to proceed with dispatch, or according to a specified timetable; (v) to abandon a particular claim or argument.

The Court need not necessarily order a stay of the entire action. It has power to order that some of the issues will be referred to arbitration, whilst the action remains alive as regards the remainder[19]. In particular, the issues of fact may be severed in this way from issues of law[20]. This is a perilous procedure which should not be used unless the questions of law can be clearly stated and answered in the abstract. Otherwise it will be found that a decision has to be postponed until the arbitrator has found the facts with consequent waste of time and money. It is usually better to avoid short cuts, and let the whole matter go to the arbitrator in the first instance, returning to the Court on case stated, if need be.

The grant or refusal of a stay does not necessarily amount to a final choice of the tribunal which is to determine the issues in the dispute. By virtue of its residual jurisdiction, the Court has power to take a dispute back into its hands,

---

[14] *Ford v Clarksons Holidays Ltd* [1971] 1 WLR 1412. See, however, *Denton v Legge* (1895) 72 LT 626; *Halifax Overseas Freighters v Rasno Export etc* [1958] 2 Lloyd's Rep 146 at 152, where saving of expense was regarded as a material factor.

[15] *Smith v Pearl Assurance Co Ltd* (1939) 63 Ll L Rep 1; *Ford v Clarksons Holidays Ltd* [1971] 1 WLR 1412; *Goodman v Winchester & Alton Rly plc* [1985] 1 WLR 141.

[16] *Fakes v Taylor Woodrow Construction Ltd* [1973] QB 436, [1973] 2 WLR 161.

[17] *Perez v John Mercer & Sons* (1921) 7 Ll L Rep 1, per Bankes LJ at 2.

[18] Cf. *Re Bjornstadt and Ouse Shipping Co Ltd* [1924] 2 KB 673 (a case on security as a condition for the appointment of an arbitrator).

[19] The splitting-up of issues in this way is inevitable if a stay is granted in respect of an action where part of the relief claimed is outside the jurisdiction of the arbitrator; see p. 478, ante, and *Radio Publicity (Universal) Ltd v Compagnie Luxembourgeoise de Radiofusion and Wireless Publicity Ltd* [1936] 2 All ER 721.

[20] See, for example, *Hyams v Docker* [1969] 1 Lloyd's Rep 341; *Re Carlisle, Clegg v Clegg* (1890) 44 Ch D 200; *Temperley Steam Shipping Co v Smyth & Co* [1905] 2 KB 791.

where the conduct of the arbitration has run into difficulties[1]. It also has power to modify the terms of any stay which it has granted[2].

Conversely, the Court may retain the dispute provisionally, withholding the immediate dismissal of the application for a stay, in case it should appear, after the questions of law have been decided by the Court, that there are issues which would be suitable for reference to arbitration[3].

The order should always contain a liberty to apply[4]. It provides a convenient means of enabling the Court to take the dispute back into its own hands, if the arbitration completely breaks down or if a condition incorporated in the order is not complied with. Similarly, it enables the Court to vary the terms on which the stay was originally granted. The liberty also enables the Court to grant ancillary relief, such as an injunction, which the arbitrator has no power to award[5].

6 Interpleader proceedings

Where relief by way of interpleader is granted and it appears to the High Court that the claims in question are matters to which an arbitration agreement, to which the claimants are parties, applies, the High Court has power under section 5 of the 1950 Act to direct that the issues between the claimants shall be determined in accordance with the agreement. Construed literally, section 5 would give the Court an unlimited discretion, but it has been held[5] that the discretion should be exercised in a similar way to the discretion under section 4(1) of the 1950 Act[6]. It appears that the Court may make an order of its own motion, without an application to that effect by either party[7].

7 Foreign judgments given contrary to an agreement to arbitrate

(a) Section 32 of the Civil Jurisdiction and Judgment Act 1982

The majority of foreign states[8] recognises and enforces agreements to arbitrate. But not all of them do so in all cases, and the application of local rules, including conflicts of law rules, may lead to a decision that the arbitration agreement should be disregarded as being null and void, or unenforceable, or for other reasons.

---

[1] See p. 158, ante. Presumably, this is what would have happened in the curious case of *Digby v General Accident Fire and Life Assurance Corpn Ltd* (1940) 67 Ll L Rep 205, [1940] 2 KB 226 if the defendants had made good their contention that the dispute was not arbitrable.

[2] This power was conferred by the 1854 Act. It does not appear in the current legislation but there can be little doubt that it still exists, by virtue of the residual jurisdiction of the Court over an action which has been stayed.

[3] *Printing Machinery Co Ltd v Linotype and Machinery Ltd* [1912] 1 Ch 566; *Re Carlisle, Clegg v Clegg* (1890) 44 Ch D 200.

[4] It has been the practice for many years to include a liberty to apply. See *Compagnie du Sénégal v Woods Co* (1883) 53 LJ Ch 166.

[5] *Re Phoenix Timber Co Ltd's Application* [1958] 1 Lloyd's Rep 305, [1958] 2 QB 1.

[6] S. 5 omits the references in s. 4(1) to 'no sufficient reason' and 'ready and willing'. These are, strictly speaking, not germane to the way in which the discretion is exercised, but to the existence of any discretion at all.

[7] Unlike s. 4(1), s. 5 contains no reference to an application by a party to the proceedings.

[8] Including all of those who are parties to the New York Convention or the General Protocol: see post pp. 707 and 669.

The resulting judgment could in principle be enforced in England if the foreign court was regarded as having jurisdiction over the defendant in accordance with the ordinary rules for the recognition and enforcement of foreign judgment. In order to guard against the possibility that a valid arbitration agreement might by this means be circumvented by the claimant, it is enacted by section 32 of the Civil Jurisdiction and Judgments Act 1982 that a judgment given by a court of an overseas country[9] shall not be recognised or enforced in the United Kingdom if the bringing of those proceedings was to be settled otherwise than by proceedings in the courts of that country. However, in order to resist enforcement or recognition of the judgment the person against whom the judgment was given must also establish that:

(a) the proceedings in the overseas court were not brought by him;
(b) the proceedings were not brought with his agreement;
(c) he did not counterclaim in the proceedings or otherwise submit to the jurisdiction of the overseas court[10].

Section 32 does not apply, however, where the arbitration agreement was illegal, void or unenforceable or incapable of being performed[11] for reasons not attributable to the fault of the party bringing the proceedings in which the judgment was given, and in deciding on these matters a court in the United Kingdom is not bound by any decision of the overseas court, but must approach them afresh, applying its own law, including its own conflicts of laws rules[12].

The section applies to judgments of an overseas court whether given before or after the section came into force[13].

(b) Validity of section 32 under the European Judgments Conventions

Section 32 does not affect the recognition or enforcement of judgments under a number of treaties to which effect has been given in the United Kingdom[14]. In particular it does not apply to a 'judgment which is required to be recognised or enforced' in the United Kingdom under the 1968 Judgments Convention. This provision intentionally leaves open the question whether a judgment of the court of a Contracting State in proceedings brought contrary to an arbitration agreement is one which is required to be recognised or enforced under the 1968 Convention, having regard to the fact that the Convention is expressed not to apply to arbitration[15]. At the time of the negotiations for the Accession Convention the United Kingdom expressed the view that the consequence of this was to remove altogether from the ambit of the Convention all disputes which the parties had agreed should be settled by arbitration. The original Contracting States held a narrower view, namely that the exclusion of

---

[9] Ie any country or territory outside the United Kingdom: section 50 of the CJJA 1982.

[10] CJJA 1982, s. 32(1)(b) and (c). Applying for a stay of the proceedings does not amount to a submission to the jurisdiction: CJJA, s. 33(1) (b); *Tracomin SA v Sudan Oil Seeds Co Ltd* [1983] 1 Lloyd's Rep 560.

[11] It is not clear why this formula was used in preference to that adopted by s. 1. of the 1975 Act ('null and void, inoperative or incapable of being performed'), and it seems unlikely that the words were intended to carry a different meaning. The formula in s. 32 corresponds more closely to conventional English terminology: perhaps this is why it was chosen.

[12] CJJA, s. 32(3).

[13] *Tracomin SA v Sudan Oil Seeds Co Ltd*, supra.

[14] CJJA Act, s. 32(4). It is unnecessary to set them out here.

[15] Article I(4).

arbitration from the scope of the convention was limited to proceedings relating to the arbitration itself, such as proceedings to appoint or remove arbitrators or to set aside or to enforce an award. The differences of view were not resolved by an amendment to the Convention. Instead it was agreed that the new Contracting States could deal with the question of interpretation of the Convention in the legislation giving effect to it[16]. The question remains open for decision by the European Court.

B. LOSS OF THE RIGHT TO ARBITRATE

We have already given a specific example of a situation where the conduct of the defendant disentitles him from relying on an agreement to arbitrate – namely, where he has already taken a step in the action in respect of which he seeks a stay. It is, however, probable that this is no more than an instance of a more general principle that a party to an arbitration may so conduct himself as to lose his rights, either by agreement, estoppel or waiver.

The fact that there are very few clear examples in the reported cases[17] concerning loss of the right to arbitrate by estoppel or waiver is no doubt accounted for by the varieties of opportunity which there are in section 4(1) of the 1950 Act for the plaintiff to resist the stay. He may assert that the defendant's conduct amounts to a step in the action, or that he has thereby shown himself not to be 'ready and willing to do all things necessary to the proper conduct of the arbitration', or that his conduct is such that the Court ought not to exercise its discretion in favour of granting a stay.

In future, the question of estoppel or waiver is likely to become more important. Since the enactment of the 1975 Act, many types of arbitration agreement which would have fallen within section 4(1) are now to be regarded as non-domestic agreements, within section 1(1) of the 1975 Act. The question of 'ready and willing' is no longer material, and the language of the section is mandatory. If the requisite conditions are satisfied, the Court 'shall' make an order staying the action: there is no room for the exercise of a discretion.

In spite of this change in the law, there must still be cases where the right to arbitrate under even a non-domestic agreement may be forfeited by the person who relies upon it. For example, if the parties have agreed that, notwithstanding an arbitration clause, a particular dispute shall be decided by the Commercial Court, they will undoubtedly be held to their bargain: either because the arbitration agreement has become 'inoperative' within the wording of section 1(1) of the 1975 Act or on the simpler ground that the defendant would be in breach of contract if he tried to assert his former right to arbitrate. Similarly, if the defendant were to tell the plaintiff that he did not propose to insist on an arbitration, and the plaintiff in consequence wasted his time and costs in starting an action, or if the defendant took steps to defend the action, there would be

---

[16] Report of Prof P Schlosser on the Accession Convention, OJ 1979 No C59, paras 61–65. See CJJA 1982, s. 3(3)(b).

[17] An unusual example is to be found in *Government of Swaziland Central Transport Administration v Leila Maritime Co Ltd, The Leila* [1985] 2 Lloyd's Rep 172.

good grounds for saying that the defendant was estopped from thereafter invoking his rights under the arbitration agreement[18].

There remains the situation where the conduct of the defendant is related, not to the claim in respect of which he seeks a stay, but to some other claim of his own which also falls within the agreement to arbitrate. For example, the respondent may have started his own action in respect of the contract in some foreign jurisdiction, in order to gain a procedural advantage, such as an order for *saisie conservatoire* which he could not obtain through the medium of arbitration. Does he thereby forfeit his right to require the claimant to submit his own claim to arbitration?[19] The answer must depend upon the degree of connection between claim and cross-claim, the nature of the foreign proceedings, and the lengths to which they are pursued. If the cross-claim is no more than a different reflection of the same dispute[20], and if the proceedings abroad are being actively prosecuted, the Court may well treat the right to insist on arbitration as waived, or at least make the respondent choose between abandoning the foreign proceedings, and giving up the right to arbitrate the claim. If, however, the purpose of the foreign action is merely to obtain a procedural advantage, without inviting the foreign Court to pass upon the merits of the claim – as may well be the case where *saisie conservatoire* is obtained – there seems no reason to treat the arbitration agreement as waived, so long as the foreign action is taken no further than is necessary to maintain procedural benefit[1]. Again, if claim and cross-claim are wholly distinct, apart from the fact that they arise under the same contract, a waiver of the right to insist on the arbitration of the claim is unlikely to be inferred, although if the facts are extreme the Court may, perhaps, be prepared to treat the entire arbitration agreement as repudiated[2].

---

[18] In *The Elizabeth H* [1962] 1 Lloyd's Rep 172, Hewson J was inclined to treat a situation of this kind as involving a variation of the agreement to arbitrate rather than a waiver. The precise route by which the conclusion is reached is not of great importance.

[19] It cannot be taken for granted that conduct of this type shows the respondent to be unwilling to arbitrate, within s. 4(1). He may be very willing to arbitrate the claim, whilst pursuing his own cross-claim by different means.

[20] For example if the dispute concerns the termination of a contract, and each party if claiming damages for repudiation.

[1] There is nothing inconsistent between an agreement that disputes shall be decided by arbitration, and the institution of proceedings which will not involve any decision on the dispute.

[2] See post, p. 506.

CHAPTER 31

Hopeless claims and defences

A. THE ABUSES

It happens more often than it should that a party puts forward a claim or a defence which has no substance.

The hardship suffered by a person whose justified claim is answered by a spurious defence is obvious, and has become even more conspicuous in recent years. Money is now difficult and expensive to borrow. Trading conditions are so adverse that reasonably prompt payment of debts is essential if a merchant or manufacturer is to stay in business. It is no consolation to a claimant to be told that when he receives judgment or an award he will also be awarded interest in respect of the period of default. What he needs is cash now, not later. Debtors know this, and may by raising spurious defences be able to settle the claim at an unfair discount.

The hardship on a defendant who is subjected to a spurious claim is less obvious, but none the less real. An award of costs enables the successful party to recoup only part of his expenditure in fighting the arbitration, and makes no recompense at all for the loss suffered by a respondent who has to spend the energy and time of himself and his employees, which ought to be devoted to running his business. Moreover, the known existence of a claim, however tenuous, may impair the credit of the respondent, and may have to be the subject of provision in his published accounts. Most serious of all, the claimant may have succeeded in freezing the respondent's assets by a Mareva injunction[1]. If these assets include balances on bank accounts, the results may be that cheques are dishonoured, and the respondent's commercial reputation is irretrievably damaged. In practice, the respondent will often be forced to provide a bank guarantee, in order to restore his liquidity. This is not easy to arrange; it is expensive; and it entails the use of other assets as counter-security[2]. If granted in respect of a claim which is in fact without foundation, the Mareva injunction can force the respondent to offer terms of settlement which do not reflect the justice of the case[3].

The courts have not so far attempted a systematic review of these problems. We discuss below the ways in which this type of abuse may in certain circumstances be remedied.

---

[1] See pp. 341–343, ante.

[2] As a matter of course, the claimant is required to give a cross-undertaking on damages, which not infrequently is secured. But this is no real recompense for a respondent whose goods have been wrongfully enjoined.

[3] Mareva injunctions ought not to be granted in support of invalid claims. Nevertheless, these are very difficult for the judge to detect at the stage of ex parte applications; and not at all easy even when the defendant comes in with affidavits to discharge the injunction.

B. RELEVANT PRINCIPLES

It is convenient to begin by stating, without discussion, certain principles which may prove to be relevant.

1 The arbitrator has jurisdiction over a claim to which there is no defence[4].

2 The arbitrator has jurisdiction over a claim to which there is a complete defence[5].

3 The Court has jurisdiction over all claims within its territorial jurisdiction as defined by RSC Ord. 11, r. 1, even if the claim or dispute falls within an arbitration agreement[6].

4 The Court has the power, but is not obliged, to stay proceedings brought in breach of a 'domestic' arbitration agreement. It may, as a condition of granting a stay, require the defendant to bring into Court, the whole or part of the sum claimed[7].

5 The Court must stay proceedings brought in breach of an effective 'non-domestic' arbitration agreement falling within the 1975 Act unless it is satisfied that there is not in fact any dispute between the parties with regard to the matter agreed to be referred, and has no power to impose any condition in respect of such a stay[8].

6 The Court has power to grant summary judgment under RSC Ord. 14 where the defendant raises no question or issue which ought to be tried. As a condition of granting leave to defend, the Court has power to require the defendant to bring into Court the whole or part of the sum claimed.

7 The Court has power to strike out a claim in an action if it is manifestly bad in law, and also (in the clearest of cases) where it is demonstrably bad on the facts[9].

C. HOPELESS CLAIMS

Two situations must be distinguished. The first, which is very rare, exists when the claimant not only appreciates, but will if pressed be prepared to acknowledge, that his claim is ill-founded in law. In effect, he asserts that his claim has commercial and moral merit; that if the law gives him no remedy, there is a defect in the law; and that a commercial arbitrator ought to award him something in recognition of the true merits.

Here, we believe that there is scope for interference by the Court[10]. There is

---

[4] See pp. 122–125, ante.

[5] See p. 124, ante.

[6] For the residual jurisdiction of the Court, see Chapter 12, ante.

[7] See p. 482, ante.

[8] See p. 485, ante.

[9] This is a compressed and over-simplified summary of some very difficult law. The cases are conveniently set out in the Supreme Court Practice, Notes 18/19/3 and 19/19/10A. A recent case in this line is *Liff v Peasley* [1980] 1 WLR 781 (decided partly but not entirely, on the basis of Ord. 15, r. 6). This procedure, which involves a kind of Ord. 14 in reverse, deserves closer study than is practicable here.

[10] For the duty of the arbitrator to decide in accordance with the law, see pp. 68–71, ante. The case where the claim is admittedly bad is not the same as where the arbitrator is deliberately setting out to decide inconsistently with the law, and the remedies are likely to be different; see further, pp. 640–648, post.

undoubtedly jurisdiction to interfere by way of injunction to prevent the respondent from being harassed by a claim which can never lead to a valid award, for example in cases where the claim is brought in respect of an alleged arbitration agreement which does not really exist, or which has ceased to exist. So also, where the dispute lies outside the scope of the arbitration agreement[11]. By parity of reasoning, the Court should be prepared to intervene where the claimant and the respondent are at one as to the absence of legal merits, so that it can be said that there is no real dispute[12].

The respondent might also seek to protect himself by recourse to the arbitrator. He cannot ask the arbitrator to rule that there is no dispute, since this would be a matter affecting his own jurisdiction. An alternative would be to invite the arbitrator summarily to dismiss the claim. It would appear safer, however, to leave the matter to the Court.

More difficult problems arise where the claim is demonstrably, but not admittedly, unsound. Here, one must distinguish between defects of law and of fact.

1 Defects in law

(a) Intervention by the Court

Where it is said that the claim is bad in law, the following avenues of intervention must be considered –

1 direct interference by striking out the claim and terminating the reference;

2 a summary decision of the claim, by means of a declaration that it is not entitled to succeed, coupled with an injunction to restrain further proceedings in the reference;

3 a decision that there is no dispute and that accordingly the arbitrator has no jurisdiction over the matter coupled with an injunction to restrain further proceedings[13].

Direct interference, on the lines of possibility 1 can no longer be regarded as a serious course of action. It is now clearly established that the Court has no inherent power of supervision of a pending reference conducted pursuant to a valid and substituting arbitration agreement. The fact that it may be unfair to

---

[11] For these various situations, see pp. 571–573, post.

[12] Perhaps this was what happened in *Sissons v Oates* (1894) 10 TLR 392, the report of which does not clearly disclose the basis of the decision. In strict theory, the analogy is not sound. The line of decisions which culminated in *Bremer Vulkan* demonstrates the existence of a jurisdiction to restrain a reference, so as to protect the respondent from being harassed by proceedings which cannot lead to an effective award. This situation exists where the arbitrator never had jurisdiction over the claim, and where a jurisdiction which once existed has disappeared as the result of repudiation or frustration of the agreement to be bound by an award. The position is different where the reference stems from an unsound claim. Once it is conceded – as we believe it must be: see p. 124, ante – that an arbitrator has jurisdiction over such a claim, it follows that both the reference and the award are effective. The Court might, however, be prepared to overlook this distinction in the interests of justice.

[13] By analogy with the procedure which the House of Lords held in *Bremer Vulkan*, to be appropriate when the agreement to arbitrate had disappeared, as the result of frustration or repudiation.

subject the respondent to proceedings in respect of a hopeless claim does not justify the Court in granting an injunction[14].

Possibility 3 must, we believe, also be discarded[15]. There is no true analogy with the practice relating to insubstantive defences, whereby the Court declines to stay the action, asserts its own jurisdiction, and gives summary judgment on the claim. When availing itself of these remedies, the Court does not need to assert that an arbitrator, if appointed, would have no jurisdiction; but merely that the Court also has jurisdiction which it ought to exercise, and not cede to an arbitrator. The two tribunals thus have concurrent jurisdictions. The position is quite different where the claimant himself has already chosen to avail himself of the agreement to arbitrate. Here, it would not be a question of the Court deciding to retain for itself a jurisdiction which had been legitimately invoked, but of taking away from an arbitrator a jurisdiction of which he was properly seized[16].

It is hard to see any theoretical ground upon whicht the Court could intervene to terminate the reference. Nor, indeed, do we believe that there would be sound practical reasons for doing so. The parties have contracted to abide by the final decision of the arbitrator on matters of law. This contract must be taken to have envisaged the exercise of the rights of appeal conferred by the 1979 Act, except where validly excluded; but not that the mechanism for such an appeal should be short-circuited by a peremptory assertion of jurisdiction by the Court. This objection is even stronger in cases where the parties have made a valid exclusion agreement, within section 4 of the 1979 Act. Here, the Court ought, in conformity with the spirit of the Act, to leave matters of law entirely to the arbitrator; and this includes the question whether the claim is without legal foundation.

The same objection applies to alternative 2. Here the fact that the claim is without foundation leads not merely to a procedural remedy, but to a direct and final substantive remedy[17]. The Court does not simply take steps to ensure that the arbitrator does not decide in favour of the claimant; it actually decides on its own account in favour of the respondent. The Court may have formal jurisdiction to grant relief in this way; but it is in our view a jurisdiction which the Court ought to exercise sparingly, if at all[18].

---

[14] In the *Bremer Vulkan* case the House of Lords held that even though there had been such delay in the conduct of the arbitration as to expose the respondent to risk of injustice the Court had no direct power to intervene by enjoining the continuation of the reference (although it did have power to intervene by declaring the reference to have been terminated by repudiation or frustration). It must follow that there is no power to grant an injunction where the unfairness takes the shape of harassment by an ill-founded claim.

[15] See, however, the suggestion by Evans J in *Overseas Union Insurance Ltd v AA Mutual International Insurance Co Ltd* [1988] 2 Lloyd's Rep 63 at 71, that the Court might refuse a stay if satisfied that the obligation on which the claim was based was unenforceable.

[16] As we have suggested at p. 124, ante, it would for practical reasons be impossible to deny that the arbitrator has jurisdiction over a hopeless claim.

[17] But see *AE Farr Ltd v Ministry of Transport* [1960] 1 WLR 956 at 967.

[18] *Glasgow and South Western Rly Co v Boyd and Forrest* 1918 SC (HL) 14 may be an example of this type of relief: but the precise juridical basis on which the injunction was granted is not easy to explain. *Compagnie Européenne de Cereals SA v Tradax Export SA* [1986] 2 Lloyd's Rep 301, may be another example: but it is perhaps best treated as a case of an injunction to restrain the claimant from arbitrating a dispute over which the arbitrator had no jurisdiction. *Allied Marine Transport Ltd v Vale do Rio Doce Navegaçao SA* [1983] 2 Lloyd's Rep 411, 413.

(b) Powers of the arbitrator

Turning to the powers of the arbitrator, there are two ways in which he might be invited to cut short a reference founded on a hopeless claim.

First, it could be argued that the arbitrator has power, analogous to that of the High Court, to dismiss such a claim summarily, as being an abuse of the arbitral process. Any direct inference from the powers of a High Court judge would be unsound, because those powers derive from the Rules of the Supreme Court, and the inherent jurisdiction of the Court to control its own proceedings. The powers of the arbitrator, by contrast, are solely the creation of the agreement to refer. Nevertheless, we believe that until quite recently, it would have been distinctly arguable that the arbitration agreement impliedly authorised the arbitrator to adopt summary procedures, not contrary to natural justice, in order to achieve a fair resolution of the matter referred; and since the High Court. asserts a power to dismiss abusive actions, the adoption of a similar procedure by the arbitrator could scarcely be regarded as inherently unjust. This view can, however, no longer be sustained. The fact that the continued conduct of the reference exposes the respondent to the risk of unfair prejudice does not justify the arbitrator in bringing the reference to a premature end[19].

The fact that the arbitrator cannot safely cut short the reference, before it ever reaches a substantive hearing, does not, however, inhibit the respondent from employing the second of the suggested procedures, namely the acceleration of a substantive hearing on the issue of law. If pleadings have been delivered, the arbitrator can properly appoint a hearing, in advance of any investigation of the facts, to consider whether on the facts alleged and admitted in the pleadings, the cause of action alleged has no foundation in law, or whether even is there is an arguable prima facie cause of action, the claimant's right of recovery is excluded by an uncontrovertable defence, for example that the claim is barred by lapse of time.

Where there are no formal pleadings, the procedure is less readily employed. It may perhaps emerge from the documents made available to the arbitrator that the claimant is asserting a claim which cannot be supported in law. In cases where the position is less clear, the arbitrator may be able to bring the legal issues into focus by ordering the delivery of pleadings, or by calling for an explicit formulation of the parties' contentions by oral or written statements of case. The arbitrator should, however, remember that all this takes time, and that it may take more time still if the claimant has an opportunity to call for an appeal under the 1979 Act. The arbitrator must therefore consider whether, given the degree of investigation of the facts which will have to take place if the claim is allowed to proceed, it is in the interests of justice to investigate the respondent's assertions that the claim ought to be nipped in the bud: bearing in mind of course that although it is unfair to allow a respondent to be harassed by a hopeless claim, it is equally unfair to a claimant who does in reality have a

---

[19] So held, in the context of undue delay, in the *Bremer Vulkan* case, following *Crawford v Prowting* [1973] QB 1 and applying, by analogy, *Re Unione Stearinerie Lanza and Wiener* [1917] 2 KB 558. It could perhaps be argued that the analogy is not exact, because the dismissal of a claim does involve some kind of adjudication, whereas the grant of a stay does not. The theory was at one time proposed that the mandate to decide the dispute embraced a mandate to decide that it was no longer capable of fair decision. This argument does not appear to have been advanced in the cases cited.

valid claim that he should be delayed in the collection of sums due to him by a preliminary investigation of the legal soundness of his cause of action.

2 Defects in fact

The position is rather more clear-cut where the respondent asserts that the claim is ill-founded on the facts. The considerations to which we have already referred, in relation to a possible intervention by the Court, apply with especial force to such a case. The arbitrator is sole master of the facts, and the Court should not interfere.

The arbitrator himself should not agree too readily to an appeal by the respondent that the reference should be halted in its tracks. The adoption of summary remedies, or of informal procedures in references to which they are not appropriate, will merely encourage applications to remit or set-aside for misconduct, with all the delay which this involves. It is much better for the arbitrator who suspects that a claim is spurious to keep up the momentum of the proceedings, with a view to a prompt hearing; and to ensure that the claim is clearly formulated and particularised, so that whatever weaknesses it may possess are brought into the open. The arbitrator may well find that the apparently slow and cumbersome procedure of formal proceedings and full discovery of documents will, provided that reasonable time limits are fixed and insisted upon, lead to a quicker and safer result than more dramatic efforts to cut the proceedings short.

D. HOPELESS DEFENCES[20]

The law has more resources where the allegation is that the defendant has no answer to the claim. Here, the claimant has a choice between two remedies.

One alternative is to bring an action in the High Court, and set out to demonstrate by means of affidavit evidence that there is no arguable defence to the claim and that there is therefore not in fact any dispute with regard to the claim[1]. If this can be shown, the Court will not stay the proceedings, but will give summary judgment under RSC Ord. 14[2].

Where the claim falls within the scope of a 'non-domestic' arbitration agreement, so that the application for a stay is brought under section 4(1) of the 1950 Act, the Court has power to impose conditions on the grant of a stay. Since there is also power under Order 14, r. 4(3) to impose conditions on the grant of leave to defend the action, it is legitimate for the Court, in a case where it considers that the defence cannot be described as wholly unarguable but is nevertheless shadowy or unsubstantial, to abstain from granting summary judgment only on condition that the defendant shows his good faith by bringing into Court security for the claim. This procedure cannot, however, be employed in the case of a non-domestic agreement within the 1979 Act, for the grant of an

---

[20] For brevity, we use this expression to include those cases where the defence takes the shape of a cross-claim raised by set-off. Such a defence can be hopeless either because the cross-claim is bad, or because even if it is valid, it does not take effect as a set-off.

[1] See pp. 123–124, ante.

[2] See p. 488, ante.

unconditional stay is mandatory, once the Court is satisfied that there is a dispute falling within the scope of the agreement: and a defence which is dubious, but not demonstrably unarguable, does give rise to a dispute[3].

If the claimant puts forward two or more claims, of which one or some raise a genuine dispute, and the others do not, the Court can give judgment for those in respect of which liability is clear, whilst sending the remainder to arbitration. The position is the same where there is a single claim, and it is admitted or established that part of the claim is clearly due. Judgment may be given for that part, and a stay granted in respect of the balance. Where the most that can be said is that some amount is undoubtedly due, but it cannot clearly be established what is the minimum sum which the claimant will recover, the Court has power to make an order for an interim payment under Order 29, r. 11, leaving the dispute as to the true amount due to be decided in the arbitration[4].

The claimant's alternative course is to ignore the Court, and proceed directly to arbitration, in the hope of obtaining a speedy award for at least part of the sum claimed. One possibility would be to invite the arbitrator to adopt a summary procedure analogous to Order 14. We believe that the arbitrator would be unwise to accede to such a request. He is appointed to decide the dispute; not to decide that there is nothing to decide. Moreover he is empowered to adopt only those procedures which are fairly implicit in the agreement to arbitrate. There are, we suggest, real grounds for doubting whether, even in a case where an informal procedure is contemplated, the agreement can be said to embrace a procedure as informal as that provided by Order 14. The arbitrator will have done the claimant no favour if he publishes a summary award which, after lengthy recourse to the courts, is ultimately set aside for misconduct. Moreover, if the respondent is resident abroad, the claimant may have to obtain a decree for the execution of the award in a foreign court; and the summary procedures of Order 14 are not regarded by all such courts as being in conformity with the local ideas of public policy and natural justice.

Another possibility would be to invite the arbitrator to make an order for interim payment, relying on implied powers similar to those exercised by the Court under Order 29. However, for reasons suggested elsewhere[5], it is open to doubt whether any such implication is legitimate[6]. Moreover, the procedure under Order 29 cannot be carried unaltered into an arbitration, since it contemplates orders for payment into Court, which cannot be made by an arbitrator, and, more significantly, requires that an order for payment into Court shall not be disclosed to the trial judge, a requirement which cannot be met in an arbitration, for obvious reasons.

It does not, however, follow that the arbitrator can do nothing to accelerate

---

[3] It makes no difference that the issue is one of law rather than fact. Unless the defence is so clearly bad in law that it does not give rise to a bona fide dispute, the 1979 Act requires the Court to stay the action. Moreover, if there is a bona fide dispute about any issue of fact or law the Court will stay the whole proceedings in respect of that claim, even though one ground of defence is clearly bad in law: *SL Sethia Liners Ltd v State Trading Corporation of India Ltd* [1986] 1 Lloyd's Rep 31.

[4] *Texaco Ltd v Eurogulf Shipping Co Ltd* [1987] 2 Lloyd's Rep 541. As a condition of making such an order the Court will require an undertaking from the plaintiff to refund any overpayment with interest, or else order payment into court.

[5] See pp. 294–296, ante.

[6] Unless perhaps it is within the implied powers of the arbitrator under s. 12(1) of the 1950 Act which imposes implied obligations on the power 'to do all other things which during the proceedings on the reference of the arbitrator or umpire may require'.

the moment of payment, in cases where the defence is of doubtful quality: for there may be scope for him to bring in the whole or part of the dispute to an early hearing. There is an important difference between the summary disposal of a matter and a speedy trial. The former involves no more than an investigation into the question whether there is anything real to try. The latter is a full determination of the issues albeit on a time-scale shorter than would usually be appropriate; and it can, under some if not all forms of arbitration agreement, be regarded as a proper fulfilment of the mandate conferred on the arbitrator by the agreement.

This is not to say, of course, that an arbitrator will always be right to hasten the hearing just because the claimant seems to have a very strong case. Proper time must be allowed for preparation, otherwise there may be procedural confusion, and time will be wasted, not saved. Moreover, if the respondent is given grounds to complain that he has had no proper opportunity to prepare his case, he will apply in the High Court to set aside or remit the award for misconduct, and even if he fails the enforcement of the award is likely to be delayed.

In practice, it seems likely that accelerated proceedings can most usefully be employed in cases where it is clear that the respondent is liable for something, but it is not clear how much. Here, there is scope for a procedure involving the following elements –

1 A hearing on liability.

2 A hearing on the question whether there is any sum which is undoubtedly due.

3 A hearing on the liability of the respondent for the balance of the claim.

The first two stages can very often be conducted at the same time and followed, if the result is favourable to the claimant, by an interim award of the sum found to be indisputably due[7]. The claim for the balance can then be reserved for a subsequent hearing, preceded if necessary by more formal interlocutory steps such as an exchange of pleadings and discovery of documents.

An arrangement of this nature may be particularly useful in cases where the defence takes the shape of a cross-claim, raised by way of set-off against a claim which is not in itself disputed. Here, it is quite often possible to see without difficulty that even if the cross-claim is well-founded, the amount recoverable by the respondent cannot exceed a particular sum, which is less than the amount due to the claimants. The arbitrator may then make an interim award in favour of the plaintiff for the difference between the claim and the maximum recovery under the cross-claim[8], and the claimant can proceed to enforcement of this award at once, leaving the remainder of the claim and cross-claim to be dealt with subsequently by a final award.

There are thus two quite distinct procedures whereby the claimant can seek a quick remedy in respect of a very strong claim: either to start an action, or to proceed directly to arbitration. Which will offer the better prospects will depend

---

[7] *Antco Shipping Ltd v Seabridge Shipping Ltd, The Furness Bridge (No 2)* [1979] 2 Lloyd's Rep 267 at 269; and see *SL Sethia Liners Ltd v Naviagro Maritime Corpn, The Kostas Melas* [1981] 1 Lloyd's Rep 18; *Tradax Internacional SA v Cerrahogullari TAS, The M Eregli* [1981] 2 Lloyd's Rep 169. If the arbitral agreement expressly or impliedly incorporates the arbitration rules of a trade association, it may be found that they lay down a rigid procedure, from which as a matter of contract the parties cannot depart.

[8] *SL Sethia Liners Ltd v Naviagro Maritime Corpn, The Kostas Melas* [1981] 1 Lloyd's Rep 18.

very much on the circumstances, but the claimant should bear the following considerations in mind –

1 In a case where the defendant is likely to refuse all cooperation, there is a better prospect of avoiding delay in the earlier stages of the proceedings where the claimant chooses arbitration rather than the Court, and this is so particularly where the defendant resides or carries on business abroad. Notice of the writ must be served in the foreign country; a considerable time elapses before the defendant is required to file the acknowledgment of service and notice of intention to defend; the Order 14 summons must also be served, together with the affidavit in support; the defendant must be given adequate time to file an affidavit to support his applications for leave to defend and for a stay; and the plaintiff may himself wish to adduce further affidavit evidence. All this takes time, and it is likely to be a matter of weeks before the applications are ready for hearing. In an arbitration, the only formality required by the law consists of the proper constitution of the tribunal. This need not take long, even if the defendant will not cooperate, since a failure by him to appoint his arbitrator may be remedied by a seven-day notice under section 7(b)[9]. Thereafter, the procedure lies in the hands of the tribunal, who may well be able to insist on a less formal, or more abbreviated, procedure than is permissible under Order 14.

2 The speed with which the claim is actually determined depends not only on the pace at which the preliminaries are conducted, but also on the availability of the tribunal. The ability of the Court to give a reasonably early date depends on the state of the Court's business, which may vary in a rapid and unpredictable manner. Since commercial arbitrators may, if persuaded that it is necessary, be prepared to sit on days and at times when the Court is not available, there can be occasions when an arbitration will yield much more speedy returns than proceedings under Order 14. The claimant may therefore find it prudent to verify both the present state of the Court's list, and the availability of the arbitrator whom he would propose to appoint. He should also bear in mind that if the respondent does appoint an arbitrator, he cannot be relied upon to choose one who is able or willing to act at short notice.

3 If the claimant proceeds under Order 14 and fails, and his action is stayed, he must begin completely again in an arbitration, whereas if he starts an arbitration straight away and is unable to pursuade the tribunal to grant speedy relief, at least some of the time will have been usefully employed in constituting the tribunal, and acquainting the arbitrators with the subject matter in dispute.

4 As previously stated, the Court has power, in the case of a domestic arbitration agreement, to require the defendant to bring into Court the amount of the claim, as a condition of abstaining from giving summary judgment against the defendant.

5 In order to resist summary judgment under Order 14, the defendant has to produce an affidavit, in which he or his solicitor deposes to the nature and validity of his defence. The existence of such an affidavit may afterwards give the claimant a valuable procedural advantage, even if the application for summary judgment does not succeed. Even if the arbitrator orders formal pleadings, this may not be of great help. Under the English system, an artful pleader may draw the points of defence in such a manner as to give away little

---

[9] There is, however, no mechanism for dealing with a failure to agree on a single arbitrator other than an application to the Court under s. 10 of the 1950 Act.

of the respondent's case; and furthermore, the pleading is not on oath, so that the respondent cannot effectively be cross-examined upon any discrepancies between the assertions which it contains, and those which he advances at the hearing. The claimant should, however, remember that the Court now receives numerous applications for summary judgment at the suit of persons who swear, but do not necessarily believe, that there is no defence to the claim. It is the duty of the Court, if faced with a spurious application, not simply to give unconditional leave to defend, but to dismiss the application; and to dismiss it with costs, which the Court may properly order to be paid at once. The Court ought to ensure that the institution of Order 14 proceedings in a case to which they are not apposite, on the off-chance of obtaining a procedural advantage, will prove to be an expensive mistake. Moreover, the claimant ought to bear in mind that his own affidavits in support of the application commit him on oath to a formulation of his case which may afterwards prove embarrassing, if the Court orders the matter to be referred to arbitration.

CHAPTER 32

Remedies available during the reference

A. INTRODUCTION

Even with the best of goodwill on all sides, things will occasionally go wrong in the course of an arbitration. If this happens, the party whose interests have suffered has a choice as to his course of action. He may wait until the award is published, meanwhile reserving his rights, and then use his complaint as a ground for declining to honour the award, or as the basis for an application to have the award remitted or set aside. Alternatively, he may at once invite the Court to intervene and put the matter right. The first alternative course of action is discussed in Chapter 33; we are here concerned with the second.

We shall begin by setting out the remedies which are available to the Court and to the tribunal, and will then consider the circumstances in which these remedies can properly be exercised.

B. THE REPERTORY: SUMMARY

The remedies which may be employed during a pending reference[1] are as follows –

1 Remedies possessed by the Court

(a) Directed towards the agreement to arbitrate

(i) An order that the arbitration agreement 'shall cease to have effect', pursuant to sections 24(2) or 25(2)(b).

(ii) A declaration at common law that the arbitration agreement is no longer binding, coupled with an injunction to restrain the further conduct of the reference.

(iii) Revocation of a *Scott v Avery* clause, pursuant to section 25(4).

(iv) Refusal to stay an action brought in spite of the agreement to arbitrate.

(b) Directed towards the parties

(i) An injunction to restrain the further conduct of the reference.

---

[1] All orders made in the exercise of these powers, with the exception of the one identified as (c)(vi) in the list overleaf are interlocutory in character, for the purposes of an appeal from the High Court to the Court of Appeal: RSC Ord. 59, r. 1A (7)(b).

(ii) An award of damages.

(iii) A declaration as to the status of the agreement to arbitrate, or as to the jurisdiction of the arbitrator.

(c) Directed towards the arbitrator

(i) An order granting leave to revoke the authority of the arbitrator, pursuant to section 1, or section 24(2).

(ii) Removal of the arbitrator, pursuant to section 23(1), or section 13(3).

(iii) Appointment of a new arbitrator or arbitrators or umpire, pursuant to section 25(1) or 25(2).

(iv) An injunction to restrain the arbitrator from taking any further step in the reference.

(v) (Possibly) a declaration at common law that the contract between the arbitrator and the parties has come to an end.

(vi) An order for the determination of a preliminary question of law, as to the powers of the arbitrator, pursuant to section 2(1) of the 1979 Act.

(d) Directed towards a future award

A declaration that any award which may result from the reference will be void or otherwise ineffectual.

2 Remedies possessed by the arbitrator

The arbitrator has certain powers where a party fails to perform his procedural obligations.

C. THE REPERTORY: DETAILED DISCUSSION

1 Remedies possessed by the Court

(a) Directed towards the agreement to arbitrate

(i) Revocation of the agreement to arbitrate. The Court has two distinct powers to order that an arbitration agreement shall cease to have effect: a general power and a specific power[2]. The general power arises under section 25(2)(b) of the Act, which reads as follows –

---

[2] Some texts and the Singapore Arbitration Act, s. 3, appear to assimilate an order that the arbitration agreement shall cease to have effect to an order revoking the authority of the arbitrator. We submit that this confuses two quite different remedies. See per Bowen LJ in *Re Smith and Service and Nelson & Sons* (1890) 25 QBD 545 at 553. Originally, the legislation made the 'submission' irrevocable, subject to a power in the Court to grant leave to revoke: s. 1 of the 1889 Act. 'Submission' meant an agreement to refer disputes to arbitration: see s. 27 of the 1889 Act. Subsequently, the 1934 Act added a power to declare that the 'arbitration agreement' should cease to have effect, the former definition of 'submission' being transferred to 'arbitration agreement': ss. 3, 14 and 21. But s. 1 was left unaffected, the word 'submission' still being employed. Finally, in 1950 the powers relating to revocation of the submission were replaced by powers to revoke the authority of the arbitrator: ss. 1, 24(2) and 25(2). Whether these alterations in terminology were intended to alter the repertoire of remedies may be questioned, but there can, it is submitted, be no doubt that revocation of the agreement and revocation of the authority are two different powers: as, indeed, is made plain by the concluding words of s. 24(2). For a discussion of the change in terminology, up to the stage of the 1934 Act, see Hogg, pp. 21 et seq.

'(2) Where the authority of an arbitrator or arbitrators or umpire is revoked by leave of the High Court, or a sole arbitrator or all the arbitrators or an umpire who has entered on the reference is or are removed by the High Court, the High Court may, on the application of either party to the arbitration agreement . . .

(b) order that the arbitration agreement shall cease to have effect with regard to the dispute referred'.

The specific power arises under section 24(2), which reads as follows –

'(2) Where an agreement between any parties provides that disputes which may arise in the future between them shall be referred to arbitration, and a dispute which so arises involves the question whether any such party has been guilty of fraud, the High Court shall, so far as may be necessary to enable that question to be determined by the High Court, have power to order that the agreement shall cease to have effect and power to give leave to revoke the authority of any arbitrator or umpire appointed by or by virtue of the agreement'.

The latter power is not available where the parties have made an exclusion agreement under section 3(1) of the 1979 Act[3].

The powers conferred by the two sections operate in different circumstances. Section 24(2) deals with a specific situation, namely where the dispute involves an issue of fraud. In this situation, an order that the arbitration agreement shall cease to have effect is one of the primary remedies. Under section 25(2)(b), on the other hand, the statute does not prescribe any specific situation in which the remedy is to be employed; but it is a secondary remedy, which is available only if other remedies[4] are also granted.

It will be noted that the power to revoke an agreement exists only in the two special situations prescribed by the Act. There is no power to revoke at common law, and no general statutory power of revocation. This is a pity, because many of the expedients into which the Court was forced in the *Bremer Vulkan*[5] line of cases would have been unnecessary, if the Court had been able to strike down the arbitration directly, rather than by means of declaratory relief.

The general power: section 25(2)(b).   In theory, section 25(2)(b) gives the Court an unlimited power to order that the agreement shall cease to have effect: for it is available whenever the authority of an arbitrator is revoked, and the jurisdiction conferred by section 1 of the Act to order revocation is not subject

---

[3] The legislative policy underlying this special exemption is not easy to follow. The Debates suggest that it is contrary to the dignity of state enterprises, and contrary to the inclination of multinational corporations, that they should be drawn into the High Court to suffer an inquiry on the question whether they have committed fraud. Leaving aside the question whether such bodies merit special treatment, there seems no practical need for it, since it is only the party against whom fraud is alleged who can apply for the matter to be transferred to the High Court: *Camilla Cotton Oil Co v Granadex SA and Tracomin SA* [1976] 2 Lloyd's Rep 10: and see note 19, post, p. 502.

[4] There is, however, a gap in the legislation. The parties may make an ad hoc submission, and subsequently find that the dispute involves issues of fraud. S. 24(2) does not apply to this situation; and the Court would be unlikely to fill the gap by using the introduction of fraud as a ground for revoking the authority of the arbitrator, and hence bringing into play the general power under s. 25(2).

[5] *Bremer Vulkan Schiffbau und Maschinenfabrik v South India Shipping Corpn* [1981] 1 Lloyd's Rep 253, [1981] AC 909, discussed at pp. 504–506, post.

to any specific limitation[6]. The remedy is, however, likely to be reserved for cases where the arbitration has gone irreparably wrong[7].

It will be noted that section 25(2)(b) draws a distinction between revocation and removal, in that the order that the agreement shall cease to have effect cannot be made if the authority of any member of the tribunal is revoked, but only if the whole of the tribunal is removed[8].

Unlike the special power under section 24(2), the general power under section 25(2) can be exercised only when an arbitration has already been commenced: it cannot be used to stifle the arbitration in advance[9].

Section 25(2) enables the Court to order that the arbitration agreement shall cease to have effect with respect to 'the dispute referred'. These latter words must mean 'the dispute or disputes referred to the arbitrator or arbitrators who are removed or whose authority is removed'. It follows that an order under section 25(2), unlike a similar order under section 24(2), does not involve the splitting of the arbitration into parts. If any order is made at all, the whole arbitration comes to an end.

Since the effect of an order under sections 24(1) or 25(2) is to terminate the reference, not the cause of action upon which the reference was founded, the claimant must in principle be entitled to re-assert his rights by means of an action in Court, unless they have become time-barred[10]. Such an action would, however, be open to the possibility of a stay under section 4 of the 1950 Act, or section 1 of the 1975 Act. This problem is only partially dealt with by the Act.

Section 24(3) of the Act provides where an order is made under section 24 that an arbitration agreement shall cease to have effect, the High Court may refuse to stay an action brought in breach of the agreement. No similar consequential power is conferred in respect of an order made under section 25[11].

It is difficult to see any reason for this contrast between the two sections. Possibly the draftsman had in mind that section 24(2) will mainly be used before an arbitration is commenced, whereas section 25, dependent as it is upon the removal or revocation of authority of an existing arbitrator, can only be brought into effect afterwards. This is not convincing, however. The powers under section 24(2) may be needed when an issue of fraud emerges in the course of an arbitration. And whichever section is used, the Court must be given a discretion to refuse a stay, otherwise the claimant will be left with no remedy at all. It is submitted that no significance can be attached to the contrast between the two sections, and that whatever the foundation for the order that the agreement

---

[6] The policy underlying s. 25(2)(b) is difficult to fathom. The shape of the secion indicates that revocation and removal are regarded as the primary remedies. Yet the consequential remedy of an order that the agreement shall cease to have effect is more far-reaching, since it strikes at the arbitrability of the dispute, and not merely at the tribunal. Moreover, once the remedy is exercised, removal and revocation are unnecessary, since the jurisdiction of the tribunal must fall with the agreement.

[7] As, for example, in *Pratt v Swanmore Builders Ltd and Baker* [1980] 2 Lloyd's Rep 504.

[8] The reason for this distinction is obscure.

[9] Because there can be no revocation or removal where the tribunal does not yet exist.

[10] We believe that the Court would not use its statutory power to revoke the arbitration agreement in a case where an action would be time-barred, unless it decided to use s. 1 as a mechanism for getting rid of the arbitration and the claim at the same time, because of some gross breach on the part of the claimant.

[11] See p. 502, post.

shall cease to have effect, the disputes in respect of which the order is made may be litigated in the High Court[12].

A problem arises in respect of arbitration agreements falling within section 1 of the 1975 Act. There is no doubt that, in general, the Court has no choice but to order a stay of an action brought in breach of such an agreement[13]. The effect of such an order is that the dispute must be referred to arbitration: but if the arbitration agreement ceases to have effect the dispute *cannot* be referred to arbitration. It is submitted that the Court would resolve the conflict by holding that the supervisory powers of the Court under sections 24 and 25, which were created to deal with a situation not contemplated by the arbitration agreement – namely something having gone badly wrong with the conduct of the reference – override its general duty under section 1 to give effect to the agreement[14].

The specific power: section 24(2). A number of points arise on the wording of section 24(2) –

(a) 'an agreement'. There is a contrast here with the expression 'arbitration agreement' used elsewhere in the Act. Section 24(2) applies to all agreements to arbitrate, whether or not falling within the definition in section 32: in particular, to oral arbitration agreements.

(b) 'which may arise in the future between them'. Plainly, if the parties choose to make an ad hoc agreement for the reference of an existing dispute involving allegations of fraud, there is no reason why one of them should thereafter be entitled to transfer the dispute to the High Court[15].

(c) 'guilty of fraud'. The meaning of these words is not clear. One possible view is that they are intended to confer a right of trial in the High Court whenever the personal character of a party is put in issue, thus producing the result that the discretion under section 24(2) to remove the issues from the arbitration is exercised on similar lines to the discretion to refuse a stay in cases where personal imputations are made[16]. This interpretation produces a satisfactorily neat result; but it is not what the section says. 'Fraud' is a technical term with a precise legal meaning: namely the knowing or reckless making of a misstatement. It is far from embracing all forms of personal misconduct[17]. Section 24(2) confers an extensive power to set aside an agreement deliberately made. It should be construed strictly and the words used should be given their technical legal meaning[18]. So construed, the powers under the section will not be available where the allegation is merely one of negligent misrepresentation, or where the

---

[12] Quite apart from s. 4(1), it might be said that s. 24(3) is otiose: for if the agreement has 'no effect' in relation to particular issues, it is hard to see how that agreement could found an order that those issues should be remitted to arbitration.

[13] As to which, see p. 462, ante.

[14] The Court could justify this conclusion by holding that where an order is made under ss. 24(2) or 25(2)(b) the agreement has become 'null and void' or 'inoperative'.

[15] See p. 499, ante.

[16] See p. 478, ante.

[17] For which a word such as 'dishonesty' would have been much more apt.

[18] If the view expressed in the text is correct, a party who foresees an allegation of misconduct short of fraud will be well advised to issue his writ before his opponent has an opportunity to commence the arbitration: he can then use the allegation as a ground for resisting a stay. There might even be a case for a person against whom such an allegation is made claiming negative declaratory relief, so as to give the judge an opportunity to keep the case in the High Court.

party is charged with conduct which is illegal or reprehensible, but not in a technical sense fraudulent. Whatever exactly the section means, there must be a concrete and specific issue of fraud sufficient to make out a prima facie case; a vague and undefined imputation is not enough[19].

Where the charge of fraud is made against the person who wishes the action transferred to the High Court, the powers under section 24 will be used almost as a matter of course. Where, however the person against whom the charge of fraud is made does not wish the matter to be tried in the High Court, the fact that the charge has been made will not in itself justify an order under section 24, or a decision under section 24 not to stay the action[20].

(d) 'shall have power'. The powers of the Court override any contrary provision in the arbitration agreement[1]. They are discretionary, and the Court can, if it thinks fit, leave an issue of fraud with the arbitrator[2]. In theory the Court may make an order under the section of its own motion, without being invited to do so by either party[3], although in practice it is hard to see how the Court could become seized of the matter, without an application.

(e) 'so far as may be necessary'. It is not merely the issue of fraud itself which is removed from the scope of the arbitration agreement. The Court can nullify the agreement to a sufficient extent to enable the issue to be fully tried. Thus if the Court would be inhibited in reaching a decision on the question of fraud if it could not also investigate other matters, not themselves directly embracing any charge of fraud, the latter may properly be made the subject of an order under section 25(2). But the order must be 'necessary' to enable the question of fraud to be determined: it is not sufficient if the Court merely considers it sensible or convenient for all the issues to be tried together.

(f) 'shall cease to have effect'. The making of an order under section 24(2) does not entirely abrogate the arbitration agreement. It leaves the agreement undisturbed as regards: (a) disputes already the subject of the arbitration which are not concerned with the question of fraud, and (b) disputes which have not yet come into existence or have not yet been referred to arbitration.

So far as concerns those disputes which fall within the scope of the order, either party is free to bring them before the Court by writ: and section 24(3) ensures that the action will not be stayed.

It will be noted that the power under section 24(3) to refuse the stay of an action is unlimited in its terms. Once *any* order is made under section 24(3), the Court may refuse to stay an action brought in breach of the arbitration agreement.

It follows that if a party foresees an allegation of fraud, he should apply under section 24(2) before an arbitration is commenced, and at the same time issue a writ claiming the whole of the relief which he seeks. He can then use his order

---

[19] See *Camilla Cotton Oil Co v Granadex SA and Tracomin SA* [1976] 2 Lloyd's Rep 10; *Cunningham-Reid v Buchanan-Jardine* [1988] 1 WLR 678. These were cases about a stay, but the principle must apply a fortiori to an application under s. 24.

[20] *Cunningham-Reid v Buchanan-Jardine*, supra. In the latter case s. 24 cannot be invoked unless there are grounds additional to the charge of fraud, e.g. if there is a special public interest arising from the charge of fraud, or if it is undesirable that a particular arbitrator should try the issue of fraud.

[1] The section does not contain the words '. . . unless a contrary intention is expressed therein . . .'.

[2] It will rarely take this course, unless there has been some form of waiver or acquiescence by the party applying for the order: e.g. by pleading fraud in the arbitration.

[3] The words 'on the application of either party to the arbitration agreement' are absent: contrast s. 25(1) and (2).

under section 24(2) as a vehicle for resisting a stay of the action, and hence keeping the whole matter in the High Court[4].

Theoretically, there is no reason why the arbitrator should not continue to deal with the remaining issues in the reference, whilst the High Court action is still pending. But it will rarely be wise for him to do so, unless the issues which he is left to try are totally independent of those transferred to the High Court; otherwise he may find that some of the same facts are being considered by two tribunals at once. Moreover, he will be much better advised to adjourn the arbitration if any of the outstanding issues involves questions of credibility. If one of the parties is to be held guilty of fraud, this is a fact which the arbitrator will want to know before he makes up his mind as to whom to believe.

(ii) Termination at common law. An arbitration agreement is a mutual undertaking by the parties to submit their disputes to arbitration, and to abide by the award of an arbitrator validly appointed in accordance with the agreement. As such, it possesses all the attributes of a legally enforceable contract. This fact has long been recognised, although it has also been accepted that in certain respects the contract to arbitrate has special attributes: notably, that it is not directly[5] susceptible of specific enforcement. The contractual character of a submission to arbitration dominated the eighteenth and nineteenth century approach to the mandate and powers of the arbitrator. Apart from certain piecemeal statutory reinforcements, these were conceived primarily as deriving from implied terms of the reference[6].

The contractual approach to arbitration was further explored in the twentieth century when, after one or two hesitations, it was accepted that the agreement to arbitrate constituted a separate contract, distinct from the contract which created the substantive rights of the parties. The latter were primary rights. The purpose of the arbitration agreement was to enable the parties to enforce the secondary rights arising from non-performance of the substantive contract.[7] This difference in character between the two groups of contractual relationships meant that although a commercial agreement containing an arbitration clause might look like a single indivisible agreement, in fact it embodied two contracts, which were as distinct as if they had been expressed in separate documents. It followed that the termination of the primary substantive agreement did not necessarily entail the termination of the secondary agreement to arbitrate: and indeed this was a practical necessity, since the rights and remedies arising from a wrongful termination of the substantive contract might be precisely those which a party most wished to enforce through the medium of the agreement to arbitrate[8].

---

[4] He might indeed employ the same device after the arbitration is commenced. He could seek to transfer part of the arbitration to the High Court under s. 24(2), and then issue a writ covering the same ground as the arbitration, using s. 24(3) to resist a stay, the remainder of the arbitration being left in limbo. We doubt whether the Court would accede to this use of s. 24(3).

[5] The agreement may be enforced indirectly, by obtaining a stay in respect of any Court proceedings brought in breach of the agreement. Moreover, the agreement is also enforceable, in the sense that once the reference has been commenced, it cannot be brought to an end by the simple election of either party: see pp. 526–529, post.

[6] See the First Schedule to the 1889 Act, and the whole of the common law relating to the revocability of the arbitrator's mandate.

[7] See *Moschi v Lep Air Services Ltd* [1973] AC 331 at 350.

[8] See *Heyman v Darwins Ltd* [1942] AC 356, and the cases there discussed.

The practical importance of this distinction lay in the fact that a party who asserted that an agreement, once valid, had been brought to a premature end by (say) frustration or a wrongful repudiation, could nevertheless insist on the ascertainment of his resulting rights by means of arbitration, through the medium of a stay of any court proceedings brought in defiance of the agreement to arbitrate.

There the matter rested for about 30 years. The idea then came into circulation that the contractual approach to arbitration could be taken further. If the secondary agreement to arbitrate was capable of surviving the primary substantive agreement of which it performed an apparent part, why should it not also be capable of predeceasing it? And if the agreement partook of the general attributes of a legally enforceable contract, why should not such premature termination occur as a result, for example, of a repudiation of the agreement by the wrongful refusal of one party to perform the whole or part of the obligations which he undertook when he agreed to submit his disputes to arbitration? Equally, why should not the secondary agreement be capable of discharge by supervening impossibility of performance, or by frustration?

(a) The Bremer Vulkan case.   These ideas ultimately bore fruit in the *Bremer Vulkan*[9] case, one of the most important decisions in the history of English arbitration.

The point which arose for direct decision was of comparatively limited scope. If the claimant in an arbitration delayed the pursuit of his claim to such a degree that a fair hearing of the dispute was no longer possible, did the arbitrator or the Court have a power to bring the reference to an end, by exercising a jurisdiction similar to that available to the High Court when dismissing an action for want of prosecution?

From a practical point of view it seemed that this question should receive an affirmative answer. It was unacceptable that a party should have no remedy at all in such a case. One possibility would be to hold that the arbitrator has a power to dismiss a claim in the event of excessive delay. The Court of Appeal and House of Lords rejected this solution[10]. Another was to treat the situation as one in which the Court should give leave under section 1 to revoke the authority of the arbitrator and then go on to exercise the consequential power under section 25(2) to order that the arbitration agreement should cease to have effect. We do not know whether this straightforward answer was ever suggested; at all events, there is no mention of it in the judgments or speeches[11].

There was, however, another form of judicial intervention, not by statute, but under powers asserted at common law, namely an injunction to restrain the future conduct of the reference. This procedure found favour in the Court of Appeal, but was rejected by the majority of the House of Lords. The very

---

[9] *Bremer Vulkan Schiffbau und Maschinenfabrik v South India Shipping Corpn* [1981] 1 Lloyd's Rep 253, [1981] AC 909.

[10] See p. 491, ante.

[11] Revocation of the arbitrator's authority would have left intact the continuous agreement to arbitrate. It would, however, have effectively put an end to the individual reference. Revocation of the agreement to arbitrate would have ensured that the claimant could not validly call another reference into existence by giving a fresh notice of arbitration. An attempt to pursue the claim in the High Court could have been frustrated by the grant of a stay under the inherent jurisdiction; see p. 461, ante.

important repercussions on the English law of arbitration are discussed at pp. 518–523, post.

Finally, there was the idea of the severable contract to arbitrate. If a term could be found, requiring the claimant to pursue the arbitration with despatch, then a grave breach of the term would be a repudiation, entitling the respondent to bring the arbitration agreement to an end. The Court would then be able to grant an injunction, to protect the respondent from being harassed by proceedings which would no longer have any contractual foundation. The relief so granted would not take the shape of an intervention in the pending reference, but would be of an essentially declaratory nature, recognising that, quite apart from any order of the Court, the arbitration agreement had come to a premature end. The possibility of such a solution was accepted in principle by the Court of Appeal and the House of Lords, although in the event the majority in the House held that whatever term as to the pursuit of the reference could be implied by statute or at common law, it was not wide enough to justify the grant of the relief claimed on the particular facts of the case. The speeches delivered in the House of Lords must now be regarded as containing the statements of principle from which any further discussion of the contractual analysis must begin[12].

The most immediate problem is this. If there is a frustration or repudiation, resulting from events which impinge on an individual reference, what happens to the mechanism for resolving future disputes, regarded as a whole? There are no conceptual difficulties in holding that the severable arbitration agreement can survive, even if the substantive contract has come to an end; the secondary rights stemming from a breach of the latter remain in existence, to be remedied through the mechanism of the arbitration agreement. But the converse situation is not so easy to resolve. If the substantive contract is of long duration, there may be disputes which have not yet arisen at the time when the reference is enjoined; and even if the substantive contract has already come to an end, in the ordinary course of time, when the individual reference is made the subject of attack, there may be pending disputes which are not the subject of that reference. Is the effect of the repudiation or frustration that these future, or other, disputes must be dealt with in Court rather than by arbitration?

The answer appears to be a qualified – 'No'. If the arbitration agreement were to be regarded as a single indivisible contract, creating not only the duty to refer disputes to arbitration, but also the obligation to conduct each individual reference in a proper manner, it must follow that repudiatory conduct in relation to one reference would put an end to the entire arrangement for the resolution of disputes under the substantive contract: for there cannot be a repudiation or frustration of part of an indivisible contract. The House of Lords rejected this view of the agreement to arbitrate, preferring instead to envisage a contractual structure operating at two levels[13]. At one level, there is the continuous agreement to submit future disputes to arbitration. This does not itself regulate the conduct of the arbitrations to which disputes are referred, but merely contains the seeds of the rules which will govern such references, if and

---

[12] See the subsequent decisions of the House of Lords in *Paal Wilson & Co A/S v Partenreederei Hannah Blumenthal, The Hannah Blumenthal* [1983] 1 AC 854, and *Food Corpn of India v Antclizo Shipping Corpn, The Antclizo* [1988] 2 Lloyd's Rep 130, CA.

[13] We are not here speaking of an ad hoc reference to arbitration. The analysis of such a reference in terms of the orthodox law of contract presents fewer problems.

when they take place. At the second level is a new contract, or series of contracts, which are called into existence upon the occurrence of two events, viz. (a) the happening of a dispute or claim[14] which falls within the scope of the agreement, and (b) the exercise by one party of the right to call for arbitration in respect of that particular dispute or claim[15].

The relationship created by an arbitration clause in a substantive agreement may therefore be seen as being nearly, if not quite, a mutual conditional option[16].

Against this background, one must now turn to consider in what circumstances the secondary contract to arbitrate will come to an end. The *Bremer Vulkan* case, and the subsequent decisions[17] in which the theory of the contractual analysis has been addressed, suggest that the problem should be approached by reference to the traditional doctrines of the law of contract. If this is so, then one may expect to find a termination resulting from an event in one of the following categories –

(i) 'Repudiation'. This term is loosely employed to embrace –
(a) a verbal renunciation of the obligation to arbitrate;
(b) conduct by which a party 'evinces an intention no longer to be bound by the contract';
(c) the inability of one party to perform his part of the bargain[18];
(d) a breach of the agreement to arbitrate, sufficiently serious to go to the root of the contract.

(ii) Supervening impossibility of performance, or the occurrence of events which destroy the foundation of the contract to arbitrate.

(iii) Supervening illegality of performance.

(iv) An express or implied agreement to discharge the arbitration agreement.

(vi) A representation by one party communicated to and relied upon by the other party that the arbitration agreement is at an end.

(vii) (Perhaps) abandonment of the agreement by one party.

(b) Repudiation. Little time need be taken over an explicit verbal renunciation. This is likely to be rare in practice. In theory, however, there can be no doubt that if the orthodox doctrines are applied, a party who states that he no longer wishes his disputes to be submitted to arbitration gives his opponent

---

[14] If the clause is in the 'claim' form: see p. 129, ante.

[15] The two-stage concept of the contractual relations in an arbitration is made explicit only in the speech of Lord Diplock. But it must be taken to underlie the reasoning of all the Law Lords and Lords Justice who adopted the contractual approach in the *Bremer Vulkan* case and in *André et Compagnie SA Marine Transocean Ltd, The Splendid Sun* [1981] 2 Lloyd's Rep 29, [1981] QB 694.

[16] The precise classification of the relationship is a matter of some nicety. It is not a simple 'if' contract, because the occurrence of the condition (viz. the happening of an arbitral dispute) does not call up the new set of obligations: one or other party must go on to initiate the arbitration. It is not a unilateral contract, of the kind discussed in *New Zealand Shipping Co Ltd v AM Satterthwaite & Co Ltd Corpn* [1975] AC 154, for the offers to arbitrate are bilateral. A conditional mutual option nearly fits, but not quite; for the parties do not have a complete freedom of choice, once the condition precedent has been fulfilled. Neither party can compel the other to pursue a dispute; but if it is pursued, the claimant can be made to arbitrate, rather than litigate. (Even this is not really accurate enough: unless the case falls within the 1975 Act, the claimant cannot always be made to arbitrate.)

[17] Notably The *Splendid Sun*, ante; *The Hannah Blumenthal*, ante; *Allied Marine Transport Ltd v Vale do Rio Doce Navegaçao SA, The Leonidas D* [1985] 2 Lloyd's Rep 18, [1985] 1 WLR 925.

[18] See *Universal Cargo Carriers Corpn v Pedro Citati (No 2)* [1958] 2 Lloyd's Rep 17, [1958] 2 QB 254.

the option to choose whether or not he will maintain the agreement in existence. If he wishes, he can accept the statement as a wrongful renunciation of the contract to arbitrate, and bring the individual reference to an end. Furthermore, if the renunciation is so expressed as to apply not only to the second-tier contract to refer the individual dispute, but also to the continuous contract to refer future disputes, then the latter may also be treated as ended. A party cannot sensibly be looked upon as having an obligation to go on giving notices of arbitration, if his opponent has made it clear in advance that he does not intend to play his proper part in any reference which may ensue. The aggrieved party may, however, choose to take a different course, and keep the reference in existence, in the hope that he will obtain an 'ex parte' award in his favour[19].

The opportunity to treat the arbitration agreement as terminated may also arise as a result of an intimation, not by words but by conduct, that the party no longer intends to be bound by his obligation to arbitrate[20]. This is most likely to occur in a case where one party behaves in relation to a particular reference in such a way as to show that he has lost interest in the whole idea of arbitration, so as to justify the inference that the obligations under the continuous agreement, and not merely the individual agreement to refer, have been finally renounced. This mode of renunciation may, however, also apply where the issue is whether the individual agreement to refer has been brought to an end[1]. In each case, the act relied upon as a repudiation must unequivocally show an intention not to pursue[2] the arbitration.

If the orthodox doctrines of the law of contract can be carried intact into this special field, another possibility of termination ought to exist where one of the parties, although willing to perform his obligations under the arbitration

---

[19] In this, as in other instances of repudiation by the respondent, the claimant may be faced with a difficult tactical choice. A default award is never very attractive, where it has to be enforced abroad; and it may take some time to obtain. The claimant may therefore do better to avoid the arbitration agreement and proceed for a default or summary judgment in the High Court. But here he may run into delay if the respondent relies on s. 1 of the 1975 Act, even if in the end such an argument could be defeated: see pp. 464–465, ante. Moreover, a judgment under Ord. 14 may be even more troublesome to enforce abroad than a default award, especially where there is an arbitration agreement in the background.

[20] At first sight, it seems rather strange that this mode of repudiation was not discussed in the *Bremer Vulkan* case, where attention was concentrated entirely on the question whether there was an actual breach of contract sufficiently serious to amount to a breach of condition. One possible reason is that, on the facts, the claimant was not showing any intention to abandon his rights, or to renounce his obligations: see per Eveleigh LJ in *The Splendid Sun*, ante, at 55F. Another is that the conduct of the plaintiff tended to show that he had lost interest in pursuing the claim at all, rather than in pursuing it by arbitration: so that there was not unequivocally a renunciation of the agreement to arbitrate as distinct from a breach of the obligation to arbitrate properly. Be that as it may, the judgment of Eveleigh LJ is support for the proposition that the arbitration agreement can be discharged by an accepted renunciation.

[1] There here seems to be a valid analogy with the law relating to instalment contracts for the sale of goods, such as *Mersey Steel and Iron Co v Naylor, Benzon & Co* (1884) 9 App Cas 434, and *Maple Flock Co Ltd v Universal Furniture Products (Wembley) Ltd* [1934] 1 KB 148; and these are indeed called-up in passages cited by Eveleigh LJ.

[2] Thus, in *Rederi Kommanditselskaabet Merc-Scandia IV v Couniniotis SA, The Mercanaut* [1980] 2 Lloyd's Rep 183, the issuing of a protective writ of abroad, by a claimant who was not sure whether to sue under a bill of lading or a charter, was held not to be a repudiation of the charter party agreement to arbitrate. See also *World Pride Shipping Ltd v Daiichi Chuo KK, The Golden Anne* [1984] 2 Lloyd's Rep 489. Nor is it ipso facto a repudiation of the arbitration agreement for the claimant to bring an action in England in respect of his claim: *Lloyd v Wright* [1973] 3 WLR 223.

agreement, is wholly and finally disabled from doing so[3]. Thus, for example, if one party could show that his opponent would be unable, because of regulations applied by the law of his own country, to produce those documents which ought to be produced on discovery, when the appropriate moment arose in the future, then if full discovery lay sufficiently close to the heart of the case, he could contend that he was no longer obliged to submit to arbitration: for the arbitration agreement contemplates a full mutual performance of the obligations which it creates, and if a party should find out in advance that his opponent will not be able to perform, there is no reason for him to wait (spending money on costs in the meantime) until a default in performance actually takes place[4].

Finally, so far as concerns repudiation, there is the possibility of an actual breach by one party going to the root of the contract to arbitrate. The terms with which the parties are to comply may be found in the express provisions of the arbitration agreement; the terms incorporated therein by reference, the terms to be implied at statute or by common law; and the orders made by the arbitrator, provided that these are consistent with the express or implied terms of the arbitration agreement[5].

One particular aspect of repudiatory breach concerns the effect of inordinate delay on the part of the claimant of such a degree that a fair trial of the dispute is no longer possible. It was held in the *Bremer Vulkan* case that in a situation where the arbitration agreement contained no express provision requiring the claimant to pursue the reference with despatch, where the claimant was not in breach of any order made by the arbitrator and where the respondent has himself done nothing to accelerate the procedure, there is no implied term of the agreement which would allow the delay to be treated as a repudiatory breach by the claimant.

(c) Frustration.   Next, there must be mentioned the possibility that the contract will be discharged by the occurrence of supervening external events. Here, it is necessary to distinguish between: (a) events which make it impossible for the parties to submit their disputes in accordance with the agreed procedure to a tribunal constituted in accordance with the arbitration agreement, and (b) those which destroy the foundation of the agreement to arbitrate.

Cases of discharge by supervening impossibility, in the strict sense, are likely

---

[3]   There seems no reason why the principle of *Universal Cargo Carriers Corpn v Citati*, ante, should not be applicable to the dissolution of an agreement to arbitrate. This would not, it may be noted, be a case of supervening impossibility of performance, which discharges *both* parties, without breach.

[4]   We have referred to inability to give discovery only for the purposes of illustration. In fact, it would only be in the context of a very long arbitration, with a very clear case for saying that discovery would at the same time be crucial but impossible, that a party would be justified in alleging a repudiation, rather than trying for some form of default relief under s. 5 of the 1979 Act. After all, the result of establishing a repudiation would simply be to get rid of the contract to arbitrate, leaving open the possibility of the claim being pursued by litigation. A more attractive result would be a default award in favour of the aggrieved party.

[5]   We add this qualification with due deference to the opinion expressed in *Bremer Vulkan* at 985. The arbitrator cannot, we suggest, be sufficiently master of the procedure to impose on the parties a way of conducting the case which is inconsistent with the implied terms of the agreement: for his mandate is limited by that agreement. See p. 286, ante. We do not regard this view as inconsistent with s. 12(1). The words 'Unless a contrary intention is expressed therein . . .' mean that the parties can withdraw from the arbitrator some of the procedural powers which he would otherwise have possessed, not that he can require the parties to do something which is not what the parties agreed.

to be rare[6]. Problems associated with the constitution of the tribunal can almost always be solved. Death, incapacity and total inactivity on the part of the arbitrator[7] can be remedied by his replacement under section 10(b) or (d). Delay on his part can result on his removal and replacement under sections 13(3) and 25(2)(a)[8]. So far as we can see, the only causes which could lead to discharge by impossibility are: (a) events preventing both parties from presenting their case, or having it presented for them, in England; or (b) events making it legally or physically impossible for the dispute to be determined in accordance with the procedures stipulated in the contract[9].

The question whether an arbitration agreement can be 'frustrated' by events falling short of an actual physical impossibility was considered by the House of Lords in *The Hannah Blumenthal* case[10], in which an unsuccessful attempt was made to persuade the House to depart from its earlier decision in the *Bremer Vulkan* case. Underlying the discussion in the *Bremer Vulkan* case was the idea that the agreement to arbitrate presupposes the need to ensure a 'fair' disposition of the dispute. This seemed to lead to the conclusion that if something happens which does not in itself prevent the chosen procedure from being followed before the chosen tribunal in the chosen place, but which nevertheless prevents the procedure from being followed 'fairly', the contract to arbitrate is automatically discharged. For example, all the essential documents in a case are destroyed by fire; samples or inspection reports are lost in the post. When this happens, does the arbitration agreement come to an end? If it does, the result is not that the dispute ceases to be capable of resolution, but merely that it can no longer be resolved by arbitration. The claimant can issue a writ, if his claim is not time-barred, and the Court will have to do the best it can with the available material, assisted if necessary by rules relating to the burden of proof. The outcome will be that the dispute is decided in a manner which is ex hypothesi 'unfair'. Furthermore, there may be misfortunes affecting one side alone which put the reference irrevocably out of balance. For example, if the case of one party hinges on the oral evidence of a witness, who dies before the hearing, can it really be said that the death discharges the arbitration agreement?

The fact that the argument could be carried to these absurd limits suggested that there was something wrong with the analysis, and in *The Hannah Blumenthal* the House of Lords identified the flaw as lying in the assumption that the parties contract on the footing that there will necessarily be a just resolution of their

---

[6] There is no doubt, however, that an arbitration agreement can in theory, like any other contract, be discharged by frustration: *The Hannah Blumenthal*, ante.

[7] This power exists, we suggest, where the aribtrator is identified by name in the arbitration agreement: for he is an 'appointed' arbitrator. The occurrence of a vacancy would frustrate the contract only in the very rare circumstance that the agreement expressly provided that the named person and no other should act as arbitrator.

[8] The problem of the inactive arbitrator arose in *Estia Compania Navigacion SA v Deutsche Genussmittel GmbH, The Estia* [1981] 1 Lloyd's Rep 541. This case was decided before the *Bremer Vulkan* case reached the House of Lords, at a time when it was still thought that the respondent was entitled to 'let sleeping dogs lie'. The possibility that not only the claimant but also the respondent should have urged on the arbitrator, and if necessary had him replaced by the Court, was not taken into account. It may, however, be noted that in *The Splendid Sun*, ante, where the arbitrator appointed by party Y died during a long period of inactivity by party X, Lord Denning MR stated that he could not see why Y should have been expected to appoint anyone in his place.

[9] For example, if the contract stipulates that the award shall be based on the examination of a sample, and the sample is accidentally destroyed.

[10] See p. 505, ante.

disputes. The parties contract on the footing that there will be a satisfactory trial of the dispute in the sense that the arbitrator will conduct the proceedings in a way which is, and is seen to be, as impartial, careful and diligent as the circumstances permit: and the circumstances include the state of the evidence which the parties are able to bring forward. They do not contract on the footing that the arbitration will automatically come to an end if the passage of time makes it more difficult to establish the facts.

There is, moreover, a further reason why the contract to arbitrate can never be discharged by inordinate delay by the parties in the conduct of the reference. Since the decision in the *Bremer Vulkan* case, delay in the conduct of the reference by one party must always also be the fault of the other, since it is his obligation to apply to the arbitrator for the necessary procedural directions in order to keep the reference moving. Accordingly mere inactivity on the part of one or both of the parties can never result in the contract to arbitrate being discharged by the doctrine of frustration, because the doctrine cannot be invoked by a party whose own default has brought about the change of circumstances which he claims has led to the contract being frustrated[11].

(d) Supervening illegality.   We now turn to the possibility of a termination by supervening illegality. This need not be discussed at length. It is hard to imagine events sufficient to render unenforceable the agreement to submit disputes to arbitration, which do not also have the effect of making the claim incapable of enforcement by any means: so that the status of the arbitration as a contract severable from the substantive agreement is of no great significance.

(e) Termination by consent.   Another possibility is that the agreement to arbitrate is brought to an end by express or implied consent. There is no problem as regards express consent. The possibility of termination by an implied agreement is less straightforward. Nevertheless, the fact that performance of a contract has been allowed to fall into desuetude for a long period may justify the inference that the parties have mutually treated the contract as abandoned. This principle is equally applicable to the case of a contract to arbitrate[12]. Whether or not the parties have impliedly agreed to abandon the contract to arbitrate depends on the application of the ordinary principles governing the formation of contracts. This is by no means straightforward. The difficulty lies not so much in stating these principles as in applying them to the facts of individual cases, particularly where the only outward sign of each party's intentions has been total inactivity over a long period of time. Nevertheless we venture to state the following propositions –

---

[11]   *The Hannah Blumenthal*, ante. The case of delay on the part of the arbitrator does not present the same difficulty, but even so, such delay is unlikely to lead to the frustration of the contract to arbitrate, for the reason given in the preceding paragraph.

[12]   This is the basis of the reasoning adopted by Eveleigh and Fox LJJ in *The Splendid Sun* and approved by the House of Lords in *The Hannah Blumenthal*. There is a narrow but real distinction between this mode of termination and an accepted repudiation. 'I have decided to drop my claim, and therefore cannot trouble to go on with the arbitration' attracts the response 'So be it, let us treat the arbitration, and the agreement to arbitrate, as extinct'. Where the party says 'I do not care what I ought to do, but I can tell you that I am not going to perform my obligations under my agreement to arbitrate', the form of the response is 'You have no right to do that, and I will treat your wrongful act as bringing the agreement to an end'. The latter exchange involves a breach, with a potential liability in damages; the other does not.

1 A contract to abandon the reference can in principle be inferred from the conduct of the parties.

2 To entitle one party (A) to rely on such a contract, he must show that the other party (O) so conducted himself as to entitle A to assume that O was offering to enter into an agreement to abandon the reference. A will not be entitled to make this assumption unless the conduct of O leads unequivocally to this conclusion. In particular A will not be entitled to assume from the mere fact that O has taken no step in the reference for a long time that O is offering to abandon the reference, because inactivity on its own is equally consistent with O having forgotten the existence of the reference or having negligently failed to proceed with despatch[13].

3 A must further show that he did in fact assume that O was offering to enter into an agreement to abandon the reference[14], and that by his conduct, communicated to O, he accepted O's offer. Here again, mere inaction on the part of A will not constitute acceptance, since he too may have been inactive through forgetfulness or neglect.

4 It is uncertain whether A must show that O assumed that A intended to accept O's offer[15].

5 Sufficient consideration for the contract of abandonment is to be found in the mutual promises of the parties to abandon their right to proceed to an

---

[13] *The Leonidas D*, ante, at p. 27. The decision of the Court of Appeal seems to leave no room for a presumption of any kind that conduct, particularly in a commercial context, is conscious and deliberate. There must be evidence of an intention to abandon the reference going beyond mere inactivity. It is not possible to state precisely what evidence will be sufficient, since every case will turn on its own facts. There are, however, a number of reported cases where the Court has found a contract of abandonment on very little more than evidence of inactivity on either side: see, for example *The Splendid Sun*, ante, approved by the House of Lords in *The Hannah Blumenthal*; *Excomm Ltd v Guan Guan Shipping Ltd, The Golden Bear* [1987] 1 Lloyd's Rep 330. But cf. *The Leonidas D*, supra; *MSC Mediterranean Shipping Co SA v BRE-Metro Ltd* [1985] 2 Lloyd's Rep 239; *Cie Française d'Importation et de Distribution SA v Deutsche Continental Handelsgesellschaft* [1985] 2 Lloyd's Rep 592; *Gebr van Weelde Scheepvaartkantor BV v Compania Naviera Sea Orient SA, The Agrabele* [1987] 2 Lloyd's Rep 223; *Food Corpn of India v Antclizo Shipping Corpn, The Antclizo* [1988] 2 Lloyd's Rep 130, CA; *Tankrederei Ahrenkiel GmbH v Frahuil SA, The Multitank Holsatia* [1988] 2 Lloyd's Rep 486.

[14] This part of the proposition is derived from the judgment of the Court of Appeal in *The Leonidas D*, ante at p. 27, explaining apparently conflicting dicta on the point in the speeches of some of their Lordships in *The Hannah Blumenthal*. See also *The Agrabele*, ante at p. 235, per Neill LJ. But the better view, we submit, is that A's state of mind is immaterial unless O's conduct, viewed objectively, amounted to an offer which he did not in fact intend to make: see per Nicholls LJ in *Food Corpn of India v Antclizo Shipping Corpn* [1987] 2 Lloyd's Rep 130, at 145–146; *The Multitank Holsatia*, supra. In such a case it would be unjust to hold O bound by the outward appearance of his conduct if A did not in fact believe that O intended to make a contract: see *Hartog v Colin & Shields* [1939] 3 All ER 566. (The fact that Lord Diplock had resort to the concept of injurious reliance in discussing this topic in *The Hannah Blumenthal* indicates that he had only in mind the situation where O's outward conduct did not correspond to what he intended: the concept has no part to play where the two things do correspond.) If O *does* intend to make a contract, and A so conducts himself as to lead O reasonably to assume that A has accepted his offer, the existence of a contract should not, it is submitted, depend on whether A believed that O intended to make a contract or whether A himself intended to do so. The point is of some practical importance, since by the time a respondent to an arbitration needs to invoke the doctrine of abandonment by consent, the point may well have been reached that he has ceased to give any thought whatever to the reference: see *The Golden Bear*, ante, at 341.

[15] Bingham LJ, in *The Antclizo*, ante, at 138, said that the point was unclear. Neill LJ in *The Agrabele*, ante, at 235, assumed that this further requirement would be consistent with the rule that acceptance of an offer must be communicated. For the reasons given in the previous note, we submit that O's state of mind is only relevant if A has unintentionally acted in such a way that, viewed objectively, he has accepted O's offer.

award, even though in the case of the respondent this might amount to an award of nothing more than costs and the dismissal of the claim[16].

6 Prima facie, if O's conduct is such as to amount to an offer to abandon the reference, it will also carry with it an implied offer to abandon the claim[17]. But this is not necessarily the case, if there are circumstances from which it is to be inferred that O has merely offered to abandon the reference, while reserving the right to bring a fresh arbitration on the claim[18]. In practice, however, this is unlikely to arise otherwise than as the result of an express agreement.

(f) Estoppel.   In principle a similar result to a termination by mutual consent can be brought about by a representation by one party, communicated to and acted upon by the other, that the arbitration agreement is at an end[19]. A representation to this effect may be express or implied, but it must be unequivocal[20] and is unlikely to be inferred from mere inactivity. Nor is mere inactivity likely to be enough to amount to reliance on the representation sufficient to give rise to an estoppel, unless it has resulted in some material disadvantage to the representee[1].

The consequences of such an estoppel being established have not been fully worked out. It does not in truth put an end to the arbitration agreement, but merely prevents one party from asserting its existence. The other party may, if he chooses, forego the benefit of the estoppel and continue with the reference. Or he may issue proceedings claiming a declaration that the agreement is terminated (to which he will be entitled by virtue of the estoppel) and an injunction on restraining further proceedings in the reference.

(g) Abandonment.   Finally, it is necessary to mention the suggestion that an arbitration agreement can be terminated by abandonment on the part of the claimant. We suggest that a distinction must be drawn between abandonment of the claim and abandonment of the agreement to arbitrate. 'I do not any longer wish to pursue my claim against the respondent' is not the same as 'I refuse to perform my obligation to submit the claim to arbitration': The claimant can of course effectively give up his right to recover what he originally claimed: and such an abandonment may be inferred from conduct as well as words. It does not, however, dispose of the contract to arbitrate. The respondent is entitled to have the matter formalised by an award; such an award cannot be

---

[16] *The Leonidas D*, ante, at 23.

[17] Ibid. If so, and the offer is accepted, the respondent will be able to counter any attempt to revive the claim by pleading the agreement to abandon by way of defence. Whether in addition he will be able to resist any attempt to start a fresh arbitration on the same claim will turn on whether the contract of abandonment amounts not only to an agreement to abandon the particular reference, but also the continuing agreement to arbitrate. If it does, the claimant must proceed by action rather than by arbitration. In the end, however, the outcome will be the same, since either the court or a newly constituted arbitral tribunal will give effect to the agreement to abandon the claim by dismissing it.

[18] See per Mustill J in *The Leonidas D* [1983] 2 Lloyd's Rep 411, at 414–415, where it is also said that if the claim is abandoned the reference is automatically abandoned, since there is no longer any dispute in existence: but this is not necessarily so, since there may still be a dispute as to costs.

[19] *The Hannah Blumenthal, The Antclizo*, and *The Leonidas D*, ante, all recognise the possibility of an estoppel of this kind.

[20] *Woodhouse AC Israel Cocoa Ltd SA v Nigerian Produce Marketing Co Ltd* [1972] AC 741.

[1] See the cases referred to in note 19, supra, and *The Multitank Holsatia*, supra.

made if the agreement is terminated; and the right to the award, and to the maintenance of the arbitration agreement until the award is made, is a right which cannot be taken away by any unilateral act on the part of the claimant[2]. Nor can the respondent be deprived of his right to pursue a cross-claim in the arbitration[3]. It may, however, be the case that the conduct of the claimant which evinces an intention to give up the claim, also evinces a willingness to give up the agreement to arbitrate; and the respondent may by his conduct accept this as an offer to terminate the arbitration agreement, so far as it concerns the particular claim which has brought into existence the individual agreement to refer[3]. Such a course of events will not, however, operate as a termination of the continuous agreement to refer future disputes.

(h) Affirmation of the arbitration agreement.   We now turn to one of the more difficult aspects of the contractual approach to arbitration, namely the impact of affirmation, waiver and estoppel on an assertion that the agreement to refer has come to an end. Plainly, the injured party cannot at the same time take a step which is consistent only with the continued obligation of his opponent to pursue the reference, and with the continual mandate of the arbitrator to give directions, and at the same time insist that the agreement and the mandate are no longer extant. In particular, it may happen that one party takes steps to force his opponent into compliance with his procedural obligations under the agreement to arbitrate; and then having failed to gain satisfaction, uses his opponent's default as the basis for terminating the agreement. It is impossible to offer a useful general discussion of the problems which will then arise, for so much depends on the course of events in the individual reference. It will, however, be noted that a solution may often depend on the mode of discharge chosen by the aggrieved party as the basis of his argument that the contract has been terminated. Imagine, for example, that there has been a continuous course of total or nearly total inactivity on the part of the claimant, punctuated by attempts on the part of the respondent to get the arbitration going, by applying to the arbitrator for peremptory directions. It would seem that in such a case –

(i) The respondent cannot argue that a discharge took place by consent at any time up to and including the moment when he applied to the arbitrator. Such an application is consistent only with the continued existence of the submission.

(ii) The same conclusion must apply to the argument that the agreement has been terminated by renunciation. An unaccepted renunciation has no effect on the continued existence of a contract.

(iii) The party in default can put himself right by resuming a proper

---

[2] See *Anangel Peace v Bacchus International Commerce Corpn, The Anangel Peace* [1981] 1 Lloyd's Rep 452 at 454.

[3] See per Eveleigh LJ in *The Splendid Sun* at 52B. It is conceivable that by bringing an action on the claim the claimant might be held to have abandoned his right to proceed by arbitration, under the doctrine which requires a person to elect between inconsistent remedies: see *Lloyd v Wright* [1983] QB 1065, [1983] 3 WLR 223, where, however, the claimant discontinued the action before the election to proceed by action became irrevocable. It does not appear to have been argued that the defendant's participation in the action was sufficient to found an estoppel, no doubt because if the plaintiff's conduct was not, as the Court of Appeal held, a sufficiently clear renunciation of the arbitration agreement to amount to a repudiation, it was not sufficiently clear to give rise to an estoppel by representation.

UPPER3 276669$32C   02-15-89 09-09-29 Commercial Arbitration Unit 276669$32A

performance before his opponent takes some step, by notice of termination or the issuing of a writ, to declare the contract at an end.

(iv) Past events are not, however, necessarily irrelevant. If, after the innocent party's attempt to put the arbitration in motion, the wrongdoer again lapses into inactivity, or makes only a feeble attempt at compliance with the arbitrator's orders, it will be permissible to set his most recent failure in the context of his past conduct, to see whether it can be inferred that there is, looking at the matter overall – (a) an evinced intention to abandon the claim; or (b) an evinced intention not to perform the arbitration agreement; or (c) an actual repudiatory breach.

(i) Effect of termination.   Next, it is necessary to consider the effect of a termination on the subsequent rights of the parties. If it is the claimant who elects to bring the agreement to an end, on the ground of a breach by the respondent, what disappears is the obligation to put forward the claim by arbitration. The claim itself survives, and the claimant can reassert it by proceedings in Court, if it has not become time-barred[4].

At first sight, section 1 of the 1975 Act may appear to stand in the way of a fresh action. We believe, however, that the Court will find itself able to hold that the arbitration agreement has become 'inoperative', by reading the words 'the arbitration agreement' as referring not to the continuous agreement to submit future disputes, but the individual agreement called into existence in relation to the claim.

If, on the other hand, it is the respondent who elects to terminate the agreement, a more difficult problem may arise. All the cases in which the severable arbitration agreement have been discussed have arisen from cases of delay by the claimant: and it seems to have been assumed that by getting rid of the arbitration the Court had finally disposed of the dispute. In most cases, this assumption would be justified. Usually, the claim would be so old that a fresh action would be time-barred. Again, the events which found the termination may be such as to justify the inference that the claim itself, and not just the contractual mode of adjudicating upon it, has been abandoned[5].

Nevertheless, there is likely to remain a residue of cases in which the claimant is left with a live cause of action after the arbitration agreement has become extinct. He may in such a case attempt to reassert his claim by proceeding in court. Such a proceeding would have all the appearance of an abuse. Having originally chosen to arbitrate, and lost his right to do so through his own fault or abandonment, it would not be right to allow him to choose another tribunal, and start again. We believe that the Court would stay any action brought in such circumstances, under its inherent jurisdiction[6].

Another problem concerns the recoupment of the costs expended by the

---

[4] We suggest that the original notice of arbitration would not be sufficient to prevent time from running for the purposes of the action: see p. 198, ante. The risk of a time-bar is one of several matters which will make it necessary for the aggrieved party to think carefully before electing to terminate the arbitration agreement. He may be better served by aiming to obtain some form of accelerated relief from the arbitrator, since this will make the substantive issues res judicata, which a 'dismissal' of the reference will not.

[5] This is the prima facie inference: see ante, p. 512.

[6] There would, we suggest, be nothing abusive in the claimant instituting new proceedings if the agreement had been frustrated without fault on his part.

aggrieved party in pursuing the abortive arbitration. He cannot recover these directly, by means of an award, since the termination of the agreement brings down the arbitrator's mandate to make a binding adjudication. But there seems no reason why he should not recover his expenditure by action, as damages for breach of the agreement to arbitrate[7] – that is, if he can find a breach, as distinct from a consensual termination or a frustration[8].

The termination of the agreement to arbitrate may also face the arbitrator with some difficulties. In the ordinary way, he will look to recover his fees and disbursements through the medium of his award. But he no longer has a mandate to make an award in his own favour, once the arbitration agreement has gone. In such a case, he must look to the arguments which we discussed, in more general terms, at pp. 242 et seq., ante.

(j) **Procedure.** Finally, we must mention two questions of procedure. First, is it necessary for a party who contemplates treating the contract as repudiated by his opponent's default, but who has in the past gone ahead with the reference notwithstanding such default, to give a notice calling upon his opponent to resume a proper performance of the agreement to arbitrate? If the ordinary principles of contract law are to be applied, the answer ought to be – 'Yes'[9], in every case where the allegation that the arbitration agreement has come to an end is founded on a repudiatory breach, rather that a consensual termination or frustration. It must, however, be acknowledged that no such requirement was referred to in the *Bremer Vulkan* and *Splendid Sun* cases[10].

Second, there is the question how the aggrieved party should exercise his right to treat the contract as terminated. There are several possibilities. First, he can simply do nothing at all, and hope that the claim will never be heard of again. This has the advantage of not stimulating the claimant into life. On the other hand, the respondent runs the risk that his opponent will wake up, and by taking some step in the arbitration put a serious, if not fatal, obstacle in the way of a contention that the agreement has been terminated by a repudiatory breach. Alternatively, the aggrieved party may give a notice in writing to his opponent, intimating that he is treating the arbitration agreement as terminated, and then

---

[7] We suggest that the damages would not be limited to the costs which the party would have recovered if he had persevered with the arbitration, and received a favourable award. What he has wasted is the whole of his expenditure, not just his taxable costs; and the loss includes even those costs which he himself has been ordered to bear by some interlocutory order made by the arbitrator before the termination of the reference.

[8] The fact that damages will attach to one mode of termination, but not to others, may make it necessary, where large amounts have been spent on costs in the aborted reference, for the aggrieved party to think very carefully how he formulates his argument that the reference has come to an end. In particular, he may wish to consider s. 1(3) of the Law Reform (Frustrated Contracts) Act 1943.

[9] In accordance with the principles of equitable estoppel, displayed in *Charles Rickards Ltd v Oppenhaim* [1950] 1 KB 616.

[10] Although it was, we understand, referred to in argument. The point is not covered by the decision that the respondent is not permitted to 'let sleeping dogs lie'. What he is required to do is to set the scene for a breach by obtaining a procedural direction from the arbitrator. Until he does this, there is no breach. The question of a *Charles Rickards Ltd v Oppenhaim* notice arises only after breach.

simply sit back to await developments[11]. This will serve to freeze the position. If the agreement has indeed gone, then nothing that the opponent does thereafter will serve to revive it. Next, the aggrieved party may seek to have his rights formally ascertained, by following up his written notice by issuing a writ, claiming a declaration that the agreement has been validly terminated, together with an injunction to restrain the future conduct of the reference. Finally, the aggrieved party may proceed directly to an action, without giving an intermediate notice of termination; but if he does so, he should make it clear (if he intends to allege a wrongful repudiation) that the writ is to serve as the 'acceptance' of the repudiation.

(k) The problem of delay. The large and growing number of cases, beginning with *Bremer Vulkan*, in which the courts have explored the possibilities of the arbitration agreement being terminated under the ordinary principles relating to the discharge of contractual obligations, have all come about because of the problem of inordinate and inexcusable delay on the part of the claimant. In the High Court such delay, even if it does not involve disobedience of a specific order of the Court, may in appropriate circumstances lead to dismissal of the claim 'for want of prosecution'[12]. The lack of any similar power either in the arbitrator or in the Court to deal with the corresponding problem in an arbitration[13] has led to widespread dissatisfaction amongst those concerned for the well-being of commercial arbitration. Two attempts to persuade the House

---

[11] The difficulty is to give a notice in such a way that it does not shut out an alternative argument that the agreement has passed away by consent. The mere fact that the claimant wakes up and takes a procedural step does not in itself rule out a finding that the agreement has been terminated by implied assent; for the inactivity of the two parties may have gone on for so long that by the time the claimant resorts to action it is too late.

[12] The principles are discussed in the notes to Order 25, r. 1 of the current *Supreme Court Practice.*

[13] This was not always the case. Before 1934, arbitrators were required to make their award 'within three months after entering on the reference, or after having been called upon to act by notice in writing from any party to the submission, or on or before any later day to which the arbitrators, by any writing signed by them, may from time to time enlarge the time for making the award.' (See Arbitration Act 1889, s. 2 and First Schedule, para. (c), re-enacting provisions in the Common Law Procedure Act 1854, s. 15.) The court had power to enlarge the time: Arbitration Act 1889, s. 9, consolidating provisions formerly in Civil Procedure Act 1833, s. 39 and Common Law Procedure Act 1854, s. 15. But it would not do so where the submission conferred power on the arbitrator to enlarge the time and the time had been intentionally allowed to expire: *Doe d Jones v Powell* (1839) 7 Dowl 539. Nor where there had been prolonged delay in proceeding with the reference: *Lambert v Hutchinson* (1841) 2 Man & G 858; *Doe d Mays v Cannell* (1853) 22 LJ QB 321. There appears to be no authority on whether the claimant could bring a fresh arbitration before a different arbitrator, or proceed by action. But presumably (1) neither course was possible if the claim was statute barred, (2) an action was liable to be met by a claim for a stay, and an application for the appointment of new arbitrators might be refused.

Section 6 of the Arbitration Act 1934 (now s.13(1) of the 1950 Act) abolished the statutory time limit, save where the award was remitted. But it is still possible for the arbitration agreement to contain a contractual time limit, which the Court has power to enlarge under s. 13(2) of the 1950 Act, and in such a case, admittedly unusual (see, however, *Court Line Ltd v Akt Götaverken* [1984] 1 Lloyd's Rep 283 at 290), it may be necessary to resort to the earlier cases to see how the discretion ought to be exercised. (Section 6 of the Act of 1934 was enacted on the recommendation of the Mackinnon Committee (1927), with the object of *preventing* delay: para. 5. The principal cause of delay at the time appears to have been delay by the arbitrator, sometimes instigated by his appointor. The three-month time limit was of no practical value in preventing delay from this source, because it could be, and frequently was, extended by the arbitrator as a matter of course.

of Lords to reverse its decision in *Bremer Vulkan* have failed[14]. The contractual solutions to the problem have been demonstrated to be cumbersome and artificial – cumbersome because they involve adducing oral evidence, sometimes for many days of court time, of events stretching back many years of which no one can be expected to have any clear recollection; and artificial, because the contractual analysis has little to do with what ought to be the real question, namely, whether a fair trial of the dispute is still possible. Moreover the number of arbitrations begun but not proceeded with is in some fields of commerce the majority by a considerable margin[15].

In these circumstances the case for legislation providing an improved solution to the problem of delay is compelling[16]. A recommendation has been made by the Departmental Advisory Committee on Arbitration to the Ministers responsible for the law of arbitration that a power to dismiss for want of prosecution should be vested in the arbitrator, and it is to be hoped that such legislation will be introduced during the currency of the present edition of this work. However, there is at present no draft bill to give effect to the recommendation, and it would therefore be premature to discuss here how any such legislation might operate in practice.

(iii) Annulment of Scott v Avery clause.   Where the arbitration agreement contains a *Scott v Avery* provision[17], an order that the agreement shall cease to have effect as regards a particular dispute may carry with it an order that the *Scott v Avery* provision shall also cease to have effect as regards that dispute[18]. This ancillary power of the Court arises whether the agreement is revoked under section 24(2) or under section 25(2)[19]. However, the order may have to be differently drawn, depending on which section is involved. An order under section 25(2) will usually, if not always, mean the end of the arbitration, so that the *Scott v Avery* provision will have to be annulled in full, if the claimant is not to be left without a remedy. But under section 24(2) the arbitration agreement is only revoked so far as may be necessary to enable the question of fraud to be tried by the Court. This may leave part of the arbitration still in being. In order to avoid complications, it may be simpler in such a case, rather than making a limited order under section 25(4), to send the case back to the arbitrator, after the issue fraud has been decided by the Court, to enable him to make a final award in conformity with the decision of the Court.

The fact that the plaintiff is claiming by virtue of a statutory novation under the Third Parties (Rights against Insurers) Act 1930, or similar legislation, is

---

[14] First in *The Hannah Blumenthal* and secondly in *The Antclizo*, ante.

[15] See *The Golden Bear*, ante, at p. 337.

[16] Judicial support for an improved solution and criticism of the status quo is to be found, inter alia, in the judgments of the Court of Appeal and the speeches in the House of Lords in *The Antclizo*, ante.

[17] See Chapter 13, ante.

[18] S. 25(1) of the 1950 Act.

[19] The words 'or any other enactment' in s. 25(4) are wide enough to cover s. 24. The power was exercised in *Permavox Ltd v Royal Exchange Assurance* (1939) 64 Ll L Rep 145, where an issue of fraud came to light on service of the points of defence in the arbitration. The brief report makes no reference to the equivalent in the 1934 Act of s. 25(4), but merely states that the Court made an order under the equivalent of s. 24(2) that the arbitration agreement should cease to have effect. This would not have been enough, unless the *Scott v Avery* provision was also annulled.

not in itself a sufficient ground for making an order that a *Scott v Avery* provision shall cease to have effect[20].

(iv) Refusal to stay action.   In the preceding paragraphs we have discussed the power of the Court to intervene actively in the agreed mode of resolving the disputes by revoking the agreement to arbitrate. As an alternative the Court may give a more passive form of relief by leaving the agreement in existence, but declining to enforce it. If a party breaks the agreement by commencing High Court proceedings in respect of a dispute falling within its scope, the Court has a general discretion[1] to refuse to stay the action, thus effectively abrogating the agreement[2]. This remedy is less sparingly granted than an order declaring that the agreement shall cease to have effect[3]. For a further discussion of the power to refuse a stay, see pp. 478–483, ante. For the specific power under section 24(3) to refuse a stay in cases of fraud, see p. 501, ante.

(b) Remedies directed towards the parties

(i) Injunction to restrain further proceedings.   Between 1979 and 1981 there was nearly, but not quite, a revolution in the relationship between the Courts and the participants in a validly constituted reference. In *Japan Line v Aggeliki Charis Compania SA and Davies and Potter, The Angelic Grace*[4] and in *Bremer Vulkan Schiffbau und Maschinenfabrik v South India Shipping Corpn*[5] the Court of Appeal asserted a general supervisory jurisdiction over a pending reference, based not upon statute but upon the inherent powers of the Court. On appeal, in the latter case, the House of Lords rejected this doctrine, by a majority of one vote.

In order to appreciate the significance of these decisions, it is necessary to set them in the context of the law on judicial supervision, as it stood when *The Angelic Grace* came to be argued. It could then be said that there were in the offing five potential sources of a power to intervene in a pending reference –

1 a jurisdiction by way of prerogative order, the reference being treated as the proceeding of a subordinate tribunal;

2 a jurisdiction under statute;

3 a general inherent common law power of intervention, capable of being enlarged so as to bear on pending references as well as awards;

---

20 *Dennehy v Bellamy* (1938) 60 Ll L Rep 269. Notwithstanding a decision by Slade J, and a dictum of Somervell LJ to the contrary in *W Bruce Ltd v Strong* [1951] 2 Lloyd's Rep 5, [1951] 2 KB 447 (where it was said that a *Scott v Avery* provision could be annulled so as to relieve the plaintiff from a time-bar) it seems clear that the Court has no power to make an order annulling such a provision otherwise than in the situations covered by s. 25(4) of the 1950 Act.

1 Except in cases falling within s. 1 of the 1975 Act where (if the agreement is to be attacked at all) the party will have to seek an order that the agreement shall cease to have effect; see p. 464, ante.

2 Unless an injunction is granted, there is nothing to prevent the arbitrator from proceeding with the reference, but any order or award which he makes will be nugatory, since as soon as the Court elects not to stay the action, the arbitrator becomes functus officio: see per Fletcher Moulton LJ in *Doleman & Sons v Ossett Corpn* [1912] 3 KB 257 at 269.

3 In *City Centre Properties (ITC Pensions) Ltd v Matthew Hall & Co Ltd* [1969] 1 WLR 772, Harman LJ stated that a stronger case was needed to justify an order under s. 1 giving leave to revoke the authority of the arbitrator, than under s. 4 refusing a stay. The same must be true, a fortiori, of an order that the agreement shall cease to have effect, since this is an even more drastic remedy.

4 [1980] 1 Lloyd's Rep 288.

5 [1980] 1 Lloyd's Rep 255, [1981] AC 909.

4 an inherent equitable power to intervene;

5 a power to intervene by way of injunction.

The first route, which would have provided an easy solution to the problems of jurisdiction, and would have given the courts instant access to a large body of reported authority in which the courts have worked out the theory and practice of judicial control over tribunals lying outside the structure of the courts of law, had already been closed[6]. The reason assigned was that the inherent power of the superior courts of record to control the actions of tribunals having legal authority to determine questions affecting the rights of the subject, by means of the prerogative orders (now re-named judicial review), has never applied to bodies whose authority derives from the consent of those whose rights are affected, rather than being imposed on such persons from outside. Any possibility of re-opening this particular avenue has now been put out of reach by the House of Lords in the *Bremer Vulkan* case[7].

As regards the second line of attack, the Court undoubtedly has wide supervisory powers by statute, over the conduct of the reference; although, as we shall suggest, these have traditionally been exercised in a very sparing way. In practice, the jurisdiction is most commonly exercised against the award, by means of orders to set aside and remit under sections 22 and 23. The Court does, however, also have statutory powers to intervene whilst the reference is still in progress. Thus, it can give leave to revoke the authority of the arbitrator, under section 1. Again, it may remove the arbitrator for misconduct, under section 23(1), and can either replace him under section 25(2)(a), or order that the agreement to refer shall cease to have effect, under section 25(2)(b).

The next possibility, that of a general inherent power to intervene at common law, is discussed in detail in Chapter 29, ante. It is sufficient for present purposes to summarise the history as follows. With the exception of a jurisdiction in equity, to which we refer below, the Court had originally no general power of supervision over a voluntary reference. There were, however, cases where the reference took place pursuant to an order (or 'rule') of the Court, made in the course of a pending action; and in these instances the Court did assert a right of control, since the reference was regarded as an off-shoot from its own proceedings, over which it had ex facio an inherent jurisdiction. Later, this procedure was enlarged so that a voluntary submission to arbitration could be made a rule of court, even in the absence of a pending action; and later still a reference was deemed to have the same effect as if it had been the subject of a rule of court, even if no rule had been obtained. All such references were subject to the inherent supervisory jurisdiction of the Court, by an extension of the reasoning which had been applied to references in a pending action. There was superimposed upon this inherent power a statutory power to set aside the award, in certain defined circumstances.

The procedure by rule of court ultimately fell into disuse, when it became possible to obtain the advantages which it provided, by other and simpler means. Finally, the 1950 Act abolished the presumption whereby voluntary submissions, not containing a stipulation to the contrary, were deemed to be made pursuant to a rule of court; and this struck away the foundations of the

---

[6] By the Divisional Court in *R v National Joint Council for the Craft of Dental Technicians (Disputes Committee), ex p Neate* [1953] 1 QB 704, [1953] 2 WLR 342.

[7] See per Lord Diplock, at 148, following *Ex p. Neate*, ante.

inherent jurisdiction to intervene at common law. At the time when *The Angelic Grace* was argued, it could be said with some confidence that, apart from the limited remedies in equity and by way of injunction to which we shall refer, there was no inherent jurisdiction of the Court to supervise a reference or an award.

The same conclusion applied, a fortiori, to any possibility of intervening, by way of relief aimed, not towards an award said to have resulted from an unsatisfactory reference already concluded, but towards the parties or the arbitrator, at a time when the reference is still in progress. Apart from the decisions on injunctive relief, there appears to be no instance where the Court had ever intervened, otherwise than under a statutory power, before an award had been made.

By way of exception, there did exist in more distant times an equitable jurisdiction to set aside an award, in cases of fraud, partiality of the arbitrators, and what would now be loosely regarded as misconduct. This jurisdiction, invoked by means of a bill in equity, dated back at least to the beginning of the eighteenth century[8], and it was still alive by the middle of the nineteenth[9]. It had, however, ceased by then to be of great practical importance, because after a long course of judicial controversy[10], it had been settled that the jurisdiction would not be exercised where the submission had been made a rule of court. Since this category of cases came to form the majority, the equitable jurisdiction correspondingly diminished; and since the statutory remedies of remission and setting aside were just as effective as those conferred by equity, and were not encumbered by considerations such as laches, the power to set aside in equity seems to have vanished almost entirely from sight[11].

There was, however, a very important theoretical change in 1950, when the repeal[12] of section 1 of the 1889 Act struck down the whole of the existing structure, enabling voluntary references to be treated as if they were made pursuant to rules of court. This change in the law, which was important in more than one respect, and which may have been unintentional, seems to have passed unnoticed. It did, however, provide a possible source of authority for an extension of the Court's powers into the realm of a pending reference; although it must be acknowledged that the old cases seem to have been concerned with the award, rather than with a reference still in progress.

Finally, it was possible to argue that the aggrieved party.could seek relief by way of injunction. Jurisdiction to grant such relief undoubtedly existed. It was used on occasion to restrain an arbitrator from acting, where he could not be

---

[8] *Brown v Brown* (1683) 1 Vern 157 (see the note in 23 ER 785, where there is a full collection of subsequent cases); *Harris v Mitchell* (1704) 2 Vern 485 (umpire chosen by lot); *Burton v Knight* (1705) 2 Vern 514 (partiality); *Lonsdale v Littledale* (1794) 2 Ves 451.

[9] Watson, pp. 287 et seq.; Russell (1st edn.) pp. 666 et seq.

[10] Ending in *Nichols v Roe* (1834) 3 My & K 431. The dispute is described in Russell (1st edn.) pp. 667–672.

[11] By as early as the end of the eighteenth century it had become the practice, where the parties gained the procedural advantages of a rule of court, to exclude the rival jurisdiction in equity by means of an express provision in the rule that the parties should bring no bill in equity: see *Lonsdale v Littledale, ante.*

[12] By s. 44(3) of the 1950 Act. The 1889 Act had itself repealed the Act of William III.

relied upon to be impartial[13], but this practice had become obsolete by the 1970s, since the 1950 Act and its predecessors offered better statutory methods for dealing with an unsatisfactory arbitration. There were a few other cases, which were hard to reconcile. Perhaps these established that the Court would not intervene, where the complaint was that the reference was wholly ineffectual, because the arbitration agreement was invalid or the dispute lay outside its terms[14]; or perhaps the cases, truly understood, did not found a jurisdiction where the dispute was said to lie outside the submission, or where it was alleged that there was no dispute at all[15]. In truth, it would have been difficult to discern any clear principle underlying these isolated decisions[16], until the matter was put into perspective by the speeches in the House of Lords.

Against this background, one may turn to the *Bremer Vulkan* case. The question for immediate decision was whether any form of relief was available where the claimant had delayed so long in the pursuant of the reference that a fair trial of the issues was no longer possible; and, in particular, whether there was a power to dismiss an arbitration for want of prosecution similar to the procedure existing in relation to actions in the High Court.

One possible solution was that the arbitrator himself had an implied power to dismiss for want of prosecution. This idea was rejected by all the judges[17], and need no longer be taken into account. All that the arbitrator can do is to fix a date for the hearing, and if necessary proceed in default, using any powers which may have been conferred on him under section 5 of the 1979 Act[18].

Also rejected were propositions that the Court had jurisdiction by way of

---

[13] *Beddow v Beddow* (1878) 9 Ch D 89; *Jackson v Barry Rly Co* [1893] 1 Ch 238; *Malmesbury Rly Co v Budd* (1876) 2 Ch D 113; *Farrar v Cooper* (1890) 44 Ch D 323. See also *Pescod v Pescod* (1887) 58 LT 76 (umpire chosen by lot). This line of authority was explained in the *Bremer Vulkan* case, ante, on the ground that the reference to a biased arbitrator was a breach of the obligation to refer. But what if he only became biased after the appointment was made? The reasoning presumably does not apply to the case of a sole arbitrator, chosen jointly by the parties. Perhaps in such a case no injunction would lie. It is sometimes said that s. 24(1) confers a power to grant an injunction. This is not strictly correct; it only recognises, by implication, the existence of such a power.

[14] Because if the arbitration was nugatory, the award would be void, and hence the respondent had nothing to lose by allowing the reference to go ahead. The reasoning is not attractive. *The Ithaka* (1939) 64 Ll L Rep 259 is an example of a case where the court declined to intervene, not on this ground, but simply by reference to the balance of convenience, which seems a much sounder approach.

[15] In the *Bremer Vulkan* case, it is said that there would be no injunction in such an instance, because the question whether there is a dispute (or perhaps, whether there is a dispute within the agreement to refer) is a matter to be decided by the arbitrator. Thus not at first sight easy to reconcile with the principle that an arbitrator has in general no power to make a binding decision on a matter which goes to his own jurisdiction. See Chapter 34, post.

[16] The cases include *North London Rly Co v Great Northern Rly Co* (1883) 11 QBD 30; *Wood v Lillies* (1892) 61 LJ Ch 158; *Sissons v Oates* (1894) 10 TLR 392; *M'Harg v Universal Stock Exchange Ltd* [1895] 2 QB 81; *Kitts v Moore* [1895] 1 QB 253; *The Ithaka* (1939) 64 Ll L Rep 141 at 259; *Compagnie Nouvelle France Navigation SA v Compagnie Navale Afrique du Nord, The Oranie and the Tunisie* [1966] 1 Lloyd's Rep 477; *Frota Nacional de Petroleiros v Skibsaktieselskapet Thorsholm* [1957] 1 Lloyd's Rep 1.

[17] Following *Crawford v AEA Prowting* [1973] QB 1, [1972] 2 WLR 749. During the 1960s the idea was current that, although an arbitrator's mandate was to make decisions, this included an authority to decide that the dispute was no longer susceptible of a fair decision on the merits. It is impossible to tell from the reports whether this was argued in *Crawford v AEA Prowting Ltd* or the *Bremer Vulkan* case, but there is plainly no prospect of reviving it now.

[18] See pp. 539–543, post.

judicial review, and an inherent supervisory power at common law[19]. The position was thus restored to what it had been before *The Angelic Grace*. The old line of equitable cases seems to have escaped attention. Perhaps they may yet have a part to play.

This left the remedy by way of injunction. In the event, the majority ruled against the grant of relief, but acknowledged that an injunction may in certain circumstances properly be granted, in the context of a pending reference. But when? This has still to be worked out. It does, however, seem that the following propositions can be stated with confidence –

1 An injunction will be granted if, but only if, it is required in order to enforce or protect a legal or equitable right.

2 Such a right can exist where the circumstances are such that the contract to arbitrate either has ended, or is susceptible of being ended by the election of one party.

3 No right of the respondent is infringed if the claimant delays in the pursuit of the reference, without the respondent taking sufficient steps to make him proceed at a proper pace.

These propositions are not enough to solve all the problems which may arise. For this purpose it will be necessary to identify the theoretical foundation of the *Bremer Vulkan* case. One further step may, we suggest, be taken in reasonable safety.

4 The securing of a fair trial is a right which may be protected by an injunction; but only if the absence of fairness will result from the infraction of a legal right[20]. In other words, the loss of a fair trial may be the test of a repudiatory breach, but it does not constitute a repudiatory breach. As a corollary of this proposition, one may go on to add another:

5 Mere harassment by unfair or futile proceedings does not found a remedy; the party must be harassed by the infringement of a legal or equitable right[1].

These propositions are all concerned with the position which exists where one

---

[19] The idea that the absence of an inherent supervisory power to correct errors in a pending reference is a lacuna in the law was firmly rejected in *K/S A/S Bill Biakh v Hyundai Corpn* [1988] 1 Lloyd's Rep 187 at 189, where it is observed that a power to correct during the course of a reference, procedural rulings of an arbitrator within his jurisdiction is unknown in advanced abitration systems, including our own.

[20] The proposition is advanced in these terms for the following reasons. The minority considered that there was a legal right – being the same right as had been protected in *Beddow v Beddow*, ante, and discussed in *North London Rly Co v Great Northern Rly Co*, ante – to be free from harassment by an unfair process. This was not just an implied condition precedent to an obligation to proceed. It would be a breach of the arbitration agreement, if one party acted so as to prejudice the other's right. The majority, on the other hand, held that there was no right as such to a fair trial, or an obligation on either party alone to act so as to produce one, but only a duty to act in accordance with the arbitrator's directions. The need for a fair trial cannot, however, be wholly irrelevant: for the majority expressly held that an injunction to inhibit the actions of an unfair *arbitrator* was legitimate. It can hardly be an immaterial circumstance – once a breach is established – that the breach produces an unfair *reference*, if the appointment of an unfair *tribunal* is itself a breach.

[1] This is rather important, and not at all obvious. The majority did not say that the right was to escape harassment by a reference which was a nullity, or otherwise futile: for this would not have fitted in with the earlier cases. Instead, it was held that the right under protection was the liberty of a promisee to treat a repudiatory breach as a ground for terminating the agreement: see page 981A of the report. (It might have been argued that the promisee does not need an injunction to protect his right to 'accept' the repudiatory conduct, for nobody can stop him doing so. What he does need is protection of the rights which he derives from *having* accepted the repudiation: namely to treat himself as free from the burden of further proceedings in the reference. But this argument has not prevailed.)

of the parties can be treated as having been in breach. But what happens where the termination of the reference flows from circumstances which do not involve a breach, such as frustration or discharge by express or implied consent? It has been generally assumed that an injunction is an appropriate remedy in such a case, and indeed an injunction was granted in *The Splendid Sun*[2] after it had been held that the arbitration had been discharged on one or both of these grounds. There are, however, problems in reconciling this decision with the majority of the reasoning in the *Bremer Vulkan* case. The question may need to be explored further in the future[3].

There remains one important question. The brief life of the general supervisory jurisdiction has ended, but the injunction lives on. Does it still have a part to play in a reference?[4] We believe that its function will be strictly limited. If something has gone wrong with the tribunal, the Act provides better remedies than bringing the reference to a complete and permanent halt. If the fault lies with a party, it will almost always consist of a failure to do right, not the commission of a wrong. The peremptory powers of the arbitrator, reinforced if necessary by an order under section 5 of the 1979 Act, will usually if not always provide an adequate remedy. If the complaint is that the arbitrator is conducting the reference in an unfair way, if all else fails he can be replaced. In less serious or obvious cases, the more practical course, in the long run, will be to let the reference take its course, and then, if it proves that the complaining party has lost the arbitration, and has done so in circumstances amounting to real and causative injustice, to set aside or remit the award[5].

---

[2] *André et Compagnie SA v Marine Transocean Ltd, The Splendid Sun* [1981] 2 Lloyd's Rep 29, [1981] QB 694.

[3] This topic is considered further in relation to questions of jurisdiction at pp. 571–572, post.

[4] We are not here speaking of an injunction which is used to support, rather than intervene in, the reference. For example a Mareva injunction, or an interim injunction under s. 12(6)(h) or under the general equitable jurisdiction (as in *Foster and Dicksee v Hastings Corpn* (1903) 87 LT 736), or to restrain proceedings abroad in breach of a *Scott v Avery* clause (as in *Pena Copper Mines Ltd v Rio Tinto Co Ltd* (1911) 105 LT 846). In such cases, the injunction can play a useful role, free from any constraints imposed by the *Bremer Vulkan* case.

[5] We are very conscious of the reasons, powerfully expressed in the speeches of the minority in the *Bremer Vulkan* case, why it can be regarded as unsatisfactory that the Court should be obliged to wait helpless in face of an apparent injustice; and absurd that it should wait to intervene until the parties and the tribunal have spent time and money on carrying the reference through to an award. Nevertheless, with due respect to the contrary opinion, we believe that the Court was right to deny itself a free power of intervention, and that the decision in *Exormisis Shipping SA v Oonsoo etc* [1975] 1 Lloyd's Rep 432, was perfectly correct, and perfectly consistent with the decision of the same judge at a later stage of the same dispute, reported at [1975] 2 Lloyd's Rep 402. What the parties have contracted for is a process conducted by the arbitrator, not a judge. However hard he tries, the latter must inevitably find it difficult to subordinate his own procedural judgment to that of the arbitrator, even though he knows that the latter is likely to have a better 'feeling' for the way in which the individual reference is going than he can himself possess. The only direct relief which the judge can give is negative in form: so that he must halt the reference entirely, if he is to give any relief at all. This may lead him to make an order which is implicitly if not explicitly an order nisi: i.e. an order that if the party does not do X, the reference will be halted. The risk that the courts would in this way gradually be led to meddle in the day to day conduct of references would no doubt be perceived and resisted. But it would remain, as would the possibility for parties to hold up the reference during applications to the Court for interlocutory intervention. This would not promote the well-being of the consensual process of arbitration, and the possibility of wasting time and money in the occasional case by waiting until the reference has ended and the award has been made is one which, in the long view, it is better to accept.

(ii) Damages. Since it is now clearly established that the agrement to arbitrate has the attributes of a legally enforceable contract, there is no reason in principle why a breach of this contract should not be capable of being remedied by an award of damages[6]. In practice, such awards are virtually, if not completely, unknown, simply because it is only in the most unusual case that the aggrieved party will be able to prove any financial loss. The following situations may be considered.

First, where a claimant enforces his claim by instituting an action, instead of referring it to arbitration in accordance with the agreement. Here, the primary remedy is a stay of the action, not damages[7]. If a stay is granted, the defendant can recoup the monies which he has spent in enforcing the arbitration agreement, through an award of costs in the action. If, in the exercise of its discretion, the Court refuses a stay, the defendant may be aggrieved that the claimant has failed to honour his agreement to arbitrate, but the grievance is unlikely to be accompanied by any measurable financial loss. It is, however, possible that substantial damages could be proved if the breach consisted of the wrongful institution of an action abroad[8].

Rather different considerations apply where the complaint is not that the claimant has prosecuted his claim in the wrong way, but that having chosen correctly to refer it to arbitration, he has not performed the procedural obligations which this entailed. Awards of damages for such a breach may be rare, but there is no reason in principle why an award should not be made, once a financial loss is proved[9]. For this purpose, a distinction must be drawn between cases where the breach is of a repudiatory character and leads to the termination of the reference, and those which are either of a less serious nature, or are not relied upon by the aggrieved party as a means of bringing the arbitration agreement to an end.

We have already suggested[10] that if the arbitration agreement has been terminated as the result of wrongful repudiation by a party of his procedural obligations in the reference, the wasted costs of the arbitration may be recovered as damages.

It is much less easy to see a place for an award of damages if the reference is allowed to continue, for the arbitrator has a discretion to make an award of costs if the aggrieved party has had to spend money in bringing the offender up to the mark. It is true that this is unlikely to provide a full measure of recoupment for the party's expenditures; but neither does an award of costs in an action. We think it most unlikely that the Court would construe the arbitration agreement as conferring a full right of indemnity for any deviation, even in good faith,

---

[6] See *Doleman & Sons v Ossett Corpn* [1912] 3 KB 257 at 268, per Fletcher-Moulton LJ; *Pena Copper Mines Ltd v Rio Tinto Co Ltd* (1911) 105 LT 846 at 851; *Bankers and Shippers Insurance Co of New York v Liverpool Marine and General Insurance Co Ltd* (1925) 21 Ll L Rep 86 at 92; also *Livingstone v Ralli* (1885) 5 E & B 132; *Brunsdon v Staines Local Board* (1884) Cab & El 272; *Warburton v Storr* (1825) 4 B & C 103; *Thomas v Fredricks* (1847) 10 QB 775. The observations of Lord MacMillan in *Heyman v Darwins Ltd* [1942] AC 356, 374 are not conclusive against a claim for damages in a proper case.

[7] *Heyman v Darwins Ltd* [1942] AC 356 at 373; *Doleman & Sons v Ossett Corpn* [1912] 3 KB 257 at 268.

[8] See further, p. 461, ante.

[9] The possibility of an award of damages for breach of the contractual obligations resulting from the exercise of the option to refer a particular dispute to arbitration was expressly recognised in the *Bremer Vulkan* case, at 982D.

[10] See ante.

from what the arbitrator may regard as a complete compliance with the party's obligations in the reference.

A party cannot be held liable simply because the arbitrator whom he has nominated is responsible for the breakdown of the arbitration, for the arbitrator is not his agent[11].

(iii) Declaratory relief. The Court has frequently exercised a jurisdiction to grant declaratory relief in the context of a pending arbitration[12].

This form of relief can be particularly useful in two situations. The first exists where it is said that a purported reference is in fact a nullity: on the ground that the arbitration agreement is void, or that the dispute lies outside its scope, or that the arbitrator was improperly appointed or does not possess the required qualifications. In none of these instances can the arbitrator himself give any remedy. The party can, of course, continue with the reference until an award is made, and then if it is adverse resist enforcement on the ground that it is void for want of jurisdiction. This is not, however, usually a convenient method. The person who attacks the jurisdiction may find himself in considerable difficulty on the question of waiver, if he plays any part in the reference at all, and he will have to spend money on costs which he may have some difficulty in recovering. It is much better for all concerned, if there is going to be a challenge to the jurisdiction, for the aggrieved party to proceed by pre-emptive action, in the shape of an originating summons. There are many recent instances of this being done[13]. If the decision is to the effect that there is no jurisdiction, it is most unlikely that the claimant will persist in his claim, since even if he obtains an award it will be known in advance to have no validity. This being so, the fact that there may be some question as to the power of the Court to grant an injunction in cases where the jurisdiction of the arbitrator is in doubt[14] is of no great practical importance.

The procedure by way of declaratory relief may also be useful where a problem arises during the reference as to the power of the arbitrator to make or refuse a particular procedural order[15]. Questions of principle concerning the procedural powers of the arbitrator are ultimately dependent on the interpretation of the agreement to arbitrate. This is a question upon which the

---

[11] See *Cooper v Shuttleworth* (1856) 25 LJ Ex 114. Unless and until he becomes an arbitrator/advocate, when different considerations may apply.

[12] The source of this jurisdiction is not entirely clear, in particular in a case where the party against whom the declaration is sought is resident abroad. It does not stem from the residual jurisdiction of the Court, discussed in Chapter 12, ante, for that relates to the substantive issues in the dispute. It cannot be an aspect of a general supervisory jurisdiction, for the *Bremer Vulkan* case shows that there is no such jurisdiction. Perhaps it is best explained as a mode of interpreting and enforcing the arbitration agreement. Since this is an agreement to be performed in England, and (in virtually every case) governed by the law of England, the Court would have extra-territorial jurisdiction under Ord. 11, r. 1(1)(f). We have never heard of any challenge to the general propriety of declaratory relief.

[13] One sometimes sees an application to remove an arbitrator, or to revoke his authority, consequent upon an allegation that he is acting without jurisdiction. This is illogical where the allegation is that the whole of the reference is a nullity, since there is nobody to remove, and nothing to revoke.

[14] See pp. 571–572, post.

[15] Some support for this is to be found in *K/S A/S Bill Biakh v Hyundai Corpn* [1988] 1 Lloyd's Rep 187 at 190 where, however, the point at issue was not the existence of the power but how it should be exercised. This is not a proper question for declaratory relief.

opinion of the Court can properly be taken, even if there is in existence a valid exclusion agreement under the 1979 Act[16].

Finally, we must mention a suggestion which is sometimes made, to the effect that the Court can properly be asked to declare that as a result of misconduct which has already happened in the course of the reference, any award which may result will be void for misconduct. We believe this idea to be totally misconceived. From a practical point of view, it is plainly unsound, since it will not be possible to know until the award is published whether the aggrieved party may not in fact have won the arbitration, and whether the supposed misconduct has had any influence on the outcome of the dispute. But more important, a procedure of this kind would be a covert assertion of a jurisdiction to meddle in the reference, of a kind which the House of Lords decisively repudiated in the *Bremer Vulkan* case.

(c) *Remedies directed towards the arbitrator*

(i) **Revocation of authority of arbitrator.**   Section 1 of the Act provides as follows –

'1. The authority of an arbitrator or umpire appointed by virtue of an arbitration agreement shall, unless a contrary intention is expressed in the agreement, be irrevocable except by leave of the High Court or a judge thereof'.

Two special features of the relief under section 1 are immediately apparent from the language of the section.

First, the primary purpose of the section is to impose a constraint, not to give a new remedy. The purpose is to improve the enforceability of the arbitration agreement by taking away the unrestricted power of a party at common law to frustrate the reference by revoking the mandate of the arbitration[17].

Second, the constraint applies only to arbitrators appointed pursuant to an 'arbitration agreement'[18]. Thus, an appointment pursuant to an oral arbitration agreement can still be revoked at will.

So far as concerns the position of the arbitrator, the practical result of an order under section 1 will be much the same as an order removing him under sections 13(3) or 23(1). But the two remedies differ both as to the circumstances in which they are available, and as to their effect on the future conduct of the dispute[19]. The following distinctions may be noted –

1 Section 1 enables the Court to give a party leave to revoke an appointment. When the order is made, the party is at liberty to issue a notice of revocation; until he does so, the arbitrator retains his authority. An order for removal, on

---

[16] The contrary view can be based on the proposition that s. 2 of the 1979 Act contains the only mechanism for raising questions of law in the course of a reference and that when these have been excluded by an agreement under s. 3(1)(c), there is no means at all of obtaining the view of the Court, until after the award has been published. We believe that this conclusion can be avoided by reading 'any question of law arising in the course of the reference' as referring only to questions of law under the substantive contract. We certainly hope that the Court will find a way of holding that the statute has not inadvertently taken away this useful jurisdiction.

[17] For the history of this topic, see Chapter 29, ante.

[18] See pp. 54–56, ante.

[19] Pace Russell (19th edn.) p. 150.

the other hand, takes effect immediately. One remedy is exercised by the party, the other by the Court.

2 Since the purpose of an order under section 1 is to enable a party to revoke the authority which he has conferred, it is available for use only against an arbitrator upon whom the party had himself conferred authority to act. Thus if A appoints X as arbitrator and B appoints Y, an order under section 1 will enable A to revoke the authority of X, but not that of Y[20]. We submit, however, that the power is available to either party, where the tribunal consists of a sole arbitrator[1], or where the arbitrator was appointed by an independent nominator[2].

3 The facts which bring the powers of the Court into operation are not the same for the two remedies. The Court has a general discretion under section 1 to give leave to revoke the authority of the arbitrator. There is a specific discretion under section 24(2), where the dispute involves an issue of fraud; and the Act also assumes, but does not state, that there is a discretion where the arbitrator is not or may not be impartial[3]. By contrast, the power to remove is limited to cases of misconduct or delay[4].

4 Where the Court gives leave to revoke the authority of an arbitrator, it has a consequential power under section 24(3) to refuse to stay an action brought in breach of the arbitration agreement. This express power does not exist where the arbitrator is merely removed[5].

5 The steps which can be taken to reconstitute the tribunal after the authority of an arbitrator has been revoked are not the same as those which follow upon a removal: see p. 533, post.

The granting of leave to revoke the authority of an arbitrator is an extreme

---

[20] The text is based on the statement of Denning LJ in *Frota Nacional de Petroleiros v Skibsaktieselskapet Thorsholm* [1957] 1 Lloyd's Rep 1. With due respect, however, we wonder whether the use of the word 'authority' in s. 1 (where it really means 'submission': pace Farwell LJ in *Den of Airlie SS Co Ltd v Mitsui & Co Ltd and British Oil and Cake Mills Ltd* (1912) 17 Com Cas 116 at 131) has not proved misleading. X is in no true sense the arbitrator 'of' A, just because A was the party who caused him to become an arbitrator. He has a mandate to bind A and B by an award in which he participates, and all his duties are owed to A and B alike. We suggest that it would be consonant with principle for the mandate jointly conferred on X and Y to be revoked (with the leave of the Court) as regards either or both of them by A, or B, or both of them. It may be noted that in *Burkett Sharp & Co v Eastcheap Dried Fruit Co and Perera* [1962] 1 Lloyd's Rep 267 at 276, Pearson LJ treated s. 1 as creating a remedy which could be used in cases not covered by s. 7(a): which appears to assume that s. 1 applies to any arbitrator, no matter by whom appointed. (A discussion of the relationship between A and B and X in the context of the resignation of an arbitrator, may be found in *Succula Ltd and Pomona Shipping Co Ltd v Harland and Wolff* [1980] 2 Lloyd's Rep 381.)

[1] Even where he has been appointed sole arbitrator in default of a nomination by one party: *Fraser v Ehrensperger* (1883) 12 QBD 310 at 317 (decided before leave of the Court was required).

[2] The power to confer the authority being delegated by the party to the nominator. See *Pratt v Swanmore Builders Ltd and Baker* [1980] 2 Lloyd's Rep 504 at 512.

[3] S. 24(1). This sub-section provides that want of impartiality is a ground for granting leave to revoke, even if the party knew or ought to have known, when he made the agreement, that the arbitrator, by reason of his relation towards any other party or of his connection with the subject matter referred, might not be capable of impartiality.

[4] Ss. 23(1) and 13(3).

[5] If the Court goes on to exercise its consequential power under s. 25(1) to revoke the agreement to arbitrate, it may be that the condition for the grant of a stay will no longer exist: see p. 467, ante.

remedy, which is used sparingly, and only in unusual cases[6], because it deprives the other party of his contractual rights[7].

Little guidance is given by the authorities on the specific circumstances in which the Court will exercise the general discretion conferred by section1[8]. It is submitted, however, that the remedy will be appropriate in the following cases[9] –

1 Serious and irreparable misconduct on the part of the arbitrator[10].

2 Actual or potential bias on the part of the arbitrator[11].

3 Deficiencies in the capability or performance of the arbitrator for which the Act provides no other remedy[12].

4 Situations in which justice demands[13] that the arbitration proceedings

---

[6] *City Centre Properties (ITC Pensions) Ltd v Matthew Hall & Co* [1969] 1 WLR 772 at 778; *Den of Airlie SS Co Ltd v Mitsui & Co Ltd and British Oil and Cake Mills Ltd* (1912) 17 Com Cas 116; *Scott v Van Sandau* (1841) 1 QB 102 at 110. See also *Succula Ltd and Pomona Shipping Co Ltd v Harland and Wolff Ltd* [1980] 2 Lloyd's Rep 381 and *Stockport Metropolitan Borough Council v O'Reilly* [1983] 2 Lloyd's Rep 70, at 78–9.

[7] *City Centre Properties (ITC Pensions) Ltd v Matthew Hall & Co*, supra, per Harman LJ at 780–781; *World Pride Shipping Ltd v Daiichi Chuo KK, The Golden Anne* [1984] 2 Lloyd's Rep 489. In *Den of Airlie SS Co Ltd v Mitsui*, supra, at 131 Farwell LJ said that there must always be something in the nature of a personal disqualification which renders it improper for that particular arbitrator to act. We are not sure, however, that the Court would today be inclined to limit this useful residual remedy to such a narrow field. In the *City Centre* case, Harman LJ referred to misconduct and the like. The jurisdiction is not simply a mirror of that which exists under s. 4. Even stronger facts are needed to justify interference in a pending arbitration than to induce the Court to leave in existence a pending action: see the contrasting decisions in the *City Centre* case and *Taunton-Collins v Cromie* [1964] 1 WLR 633.

[8] The older case should be read in the context of the other remedies which were then available. For example, in *East and West India Dock Co v Kirk and Randall* (1887) 12 App Cas 738, the House of Lords asserted a jurisdiction to revoke the authority of an arbitrator who was going wrong in law during the reference. But there was then no power to order the arbitrator to state a consultative case. We do not believe that the Court would make an order in such circumstances nowadays.

[9] This passage was cited with approval in *The Golden Anne*, supra. But cf. *Property Investments Holdings Ltd v Byfield Building Services* (1985) 31 BLR 47. Russell would add to the list those cases where the arbitrator exceeds or refuses the jurisdiction which has been given to him by the parties: see 20th edn., p. 154. The proposition certainly gains support from the cases cited, but we doubt whether leave to revoke is the appropriate remedy for excess of jurisdiction, quite apart from the fact that the excess in question concerned the admission or rejection of evidence, a matter which would not nowadays be regarded as a matter of jurisdiction. The grant of a declaration or an injunction would be a more suitable remedy, if the Court were inclined to intervene before the stage of an award was reached.

[10] See *City Centre Properties (ITC Pensions) Ltd v Matthew Hall & Co* [1969] 1 WLR 772 at 779, 780, per Lord Denning MR. We have added the words 'serious and irreparable' because there are many types of error by the arbitrator which would amount to misconduct, but would not justify the Court in exercising its power under s. 1. If at all possible, the Court would prefer to see the arbitrator correct his mistake, rather than force the parties to start again with a fresh arbitrator.

[11] This is assumed by s. 24(1). Russell would add (19th edn., p. 165) 'disqualification of the arbitrator'. We doubt whether this is right. Under s. 1 the Court gives the party leave to revoke the authority which he has conferred on the arbitrator. If he has chosen to confer it on someone who is disqualified, it is hard to see why he should afterwards be allowed to use the disqualification as a ground for changing his mind.

[12] See per Pearson LJ in *Burkett Sharp & Co v Eastcheap Dried Fruit Co and Perera* [1962] 1 Lloyd's Rep 267 at 276 on the possibility of using s. 1 in cases where there is not a sufficient 'refusal' to act to bring s. 7(a) into operation. We believe that in practice there will be very few cases in which ss. 7(a), 10(b), 13(3) and 23(1) do not provide an adequate remedy.

[13] Justice rarely will so demand, given the waste of time and money which will be the almost inevitable consequence of an order under s. 1. Nor is it sufficient merely to show that the balance of convenience lies in favour of revoking the arbitrator's authority: *The Golden Anne*, supra.

should be temporarily halted or permanently brought to an end, and no other method of doing so is available to the Court[14].

It is possible that in coming years the Court will recognise the potential of section 1, particularly in conjunction with section 25(2), as a medium for imposing its will on the arbitrator's conduct of the reference[15]. If so, it is to be hoped that the process will not be carried too far. The purpose of section 1 and its predecessors was to protect the interests of parties who had contracted for the resolution of their disputes by an arbitrator from having the arbitrator's mandate promiscuously revoked. The aim of the Court should be to ensure that the contract is honoured, and should not produce a situation in which the dispute is decided by someone other than an arbitrator chosen in accordance with the contractual mechanism, merely because it is dissatisfied with the way in which the procedure in the reference is being handled.

The consequences of an order granting leave to revoke the authority of an arbitrator will depend upon whether the Court also exercises its power to issue a concurrent order that the arbitration agreement shall cease to have effect[16]. If it does, the whole tribunal is automatically divested of any authority to adjudicate upon the dispute. If it does not, the arbitration continues, but there is a vacancy in the tribunal. How is the vacancy to be filled? The position appears to be as follows. If the authority of the whole tribunal is revoked, then the vacancy is filled by the High Court. The new tribunal must consist of a sole arbitrator, no matter how many persons were originally appointed[17]. If, however, the revocation applies to an individual arbitrator, the party who originally conferred the authority, and who now has leave to revoke it, has the power to make a fresh appointment[18]. If he fails to do so, the various default powers of the opposing party and the Court, under sections 7 and 10, may be employed to fill the vacancy[19].

(ii) Removal of arbitrator. The Court has jurisdiction to remove an arbitrator in two specific situations.

(a) Removal for misconduct. First, the Court has jurisdiction to remove an arbitrator where he has 'misconducted himself or the proceedings': section

---

[14] Such a case would exist if the Court decided that the only just course was to get rid of the arbitration altogether, and have the matter litigated in the High Court. An order for removal would be of no use for this purpose and an injunction might not be enough. The Court could solve the problem by using its general discretion under s. 1 to make an order for leave to revoke, and then use that order as a vehicle for an order that the agreement should cease to have effect, under s. 25(2)(b) as in *Stockport Metropolitan Borough Council v O'Reilly*, ante. It is uncertain, however, whether s. 1 provides a solution to the problem of inordinate delay on the part of the claimant: *The Anclizo*, supra; cf. *The Multitank Holsatia*, supra.

[15] Particularly since it could give a positive direction as to the conduct of the reference by making an 'order nisi': i.e. by decreeing that the authority could be revoked unless the arbitrator took the steps which the Court desired.

[16] S. 25(2)(b).

[17] S. 25(2)(a). This power must be limited to cases where the authority of the whole tribunal is revoked. The Court plainly cannot appoint a sole arbitrator if one or more of the original arbitrators still has authority to act. Why the legislature did not give a power of replacement similar to that which exists under s. 25(1) in the case of removal is difficult to comprehend.

[18] The Act does not say so, but the power must be inherent in the nature of the remedy.

[19] See Chapter 15, ante. Ss. 7(a) and 10(a) and (c) may require some stretching for this purpose; but there must be some method of filling the vacancy.

23(1). This provision is cast in wide terms[20]. It undoubtedly covers all instances of what would ordinarily be understood as misconduct in the course of the reference: see pp. 550–553, post. But it also embraces situations in which, although the arbitrator has not necessarily acted unfairly, he has allowed himself to get into a position where unfairness might reasonably be suspected or foreseen[1]. The arbitrator must not only show no bias, but must also appear to be in a position to act judicially and without any bias[2].

The fact that the Court is given a wide power to remove the arbitrator in cases of misconduct does not mean that the power will be freely exercised. An arbitrator may commit errors – even serious errors – in the course of the reference, and yet remain perfectly able to carry the arbitration to a successful conclusion once his mistakes have been pointed out. Justice requires that in such a case the arbitrator should be left in office, rather than that the parties should suffer the delay and expense of beginning the arbitration afresh[3]. The remedy is therefore likely to be confined to those cases where the arbitration simply cannot be allowed to continue with the particular arbitrator in office – either because he has shown actual or potential bias[4] or because his conduct has given serious grounds for destroying the confidence of one or both parties in his ability to conduct the dispute judicially[5] or competently[6].

(b) Removal for delay. In addition to the power to remove for misconduct under section 23(1), the Court has jurisdiction to remove an arbitrator or umpire who

---

[20] The latter part of the phrase was added by the 1934 Act in order to allay the long-standing resentment of arbitrators about the use of the word 'misconduct'. The idea was that an arbitrator could be accused of misconducting the proceedings, rather than himself, without any imputation on his integrity. Whether the amendment had any substantial effect is questionable.
[1] *SS Catalina (Owners) v MV Norma (Owners)* (1938) 61 Ll L Rep 360; *Veritas Shipping Corpn v Anglo-Canadian Cement Ltd* [1966] 1 Lloyd's Rep 76; *Burkett Sharp & Co v Eastcheap Dried Fruit Co and Perera* [1961] 2 Lloyd's Rep 80. In each of these cases, a person possessing close links with one party accepted an appointment as arbitrator. See pp. 249–256, ante.
[2] *Veritas Shipping Corpn v Anglo-Canadian Cement Ltd,* supra, per McNair J at 77.
[3] See *Schofield v Allen* (1904) 48 Sol Jo 176; *Miller's Timber Trust Co Ltd v Plywood Factory Julius Potempa Ltd* (1939) 63 Ll L Rep 184.
[4] See note 1, ante. The bias need not necessarily be ill-conceived. For example, a perfectly fair and competent arbitrator might take such exception to the way in which one party was conducting its case that he could no longer approach the issues in a full judicial spirit. The Court would no doubt require strong evidence before holding that any such event had occurred. See *Lewis Emanual & Son Ltd v Sammut* [1959] 2 Lloyd's Rep 629.
[5] As in *Re Enoch and Zaretzky, Bock & Co* [1910] 1 KB 327; and in *Modern Engineering (Bristol) Ltd v C Miskin & Son Ltd* [1981] 1 Lloyd's Rep 135 (a strong case: the arbitrator had already embarked on the formal hearing). In *Spurrier v La Cloche* [1902] AC 446 the Privy Council reversed a decision of a Jersey Court removing an arbitrator on the ground that he had acted unreasonably in refusing to agree upon an umpire resident in Jersey to decide an arbitration relating to facts arising in Jersey. The test, as in all cases of potential bias, is an objective one: see pp. 250–253.
[6] We do not know of any case where incompetence, with nothing more, has been the basis of an order for removal. *Pratt v Swanmore Builders Ltd and Baker* [1980] 2 Lloyd's Rep 504 comes fairly close, but there were other respects, besides an incapacity to conduct the reference competently, which led to the grant of relief. There must, however, come a point at which the arbitrator has shown himself so incapable of dealing with the matter that the only safe course is to exclude him from any further responsibility: although it may be that revocation is a more appropriate remedy than removal, given the wider terms of s. 1. We believe that the Court would be very slow indeed to remove for incompetence any arbitrator who was jointly appointed. If the parties select someone who is not equal to the task, they have nobody but themselves to blame.

'fails to use all reasonable dispatch in entering on and proceeding with the reference and making an award': section 13(3)[7].

This section largely speaks for itself. What is reasonable dispatch depends upon the type of arbitration, and the size and complexity of the dispute[8]. It is submitted that the question of reasonableness should be determined by reference to the nature of the arbitration and the interests of the parties, not the individual circumstances of the arbitrator. Thus, if the arbitrator were delayed in proceeding by illness or unexpected absence abroad, he would be open to removal, even though not personally at fault. Conversely, fault is not sufficient to amount to a failure to use all reasonable dispatch: an arbitrator may be incompetent or guilty of misconduct and yet not be guilty of such delay as will being section 13(3) into play[9].

In recent years two factors have combined to produce a situation in which the jurisdiction under section 13(3) may become more important than in the past. First, the rapid growth in the numbers of commercial arbitrations taking place in London has led to the establishment of a group of professional arbitrators, who devote all or most of their time to conducting references. Many of these are very busy. Second, the frequency of very long arbitrations has increased beyond all recognition. The result is that the arbitrator may have insufficient time to give continuous attention to the reference, with the result that the hearing extends over months or even years; and indeed, it may be a substantial time before the arbitrator is even in a position to start the hearing.

Where both parties are aggrieved by the arbitrator's inability to make real progress, the matter can often be dealt with by a joint suggestion to the arbitrator that he should ask to be relieved from his office. It does, however, sometimes happen that only one party if sufficiently exasperated to wish to be rid of the arbitrator. In such a case, the Court will be faced with a delicate decision, in which the following factors will have to be weighed –

1 The extent to which time and costs have been spent on the reference, which will be wasted if it has to begin again before a new tribunal. Time is usually most important to the claimant; but the respondent may also be vitally interested, especially if Mareva relief has been obtained. Wasted costs are important to both parties, particularly since there will not usually be any means by which they can be recouped.

2 The extent of the information given to the arbitrator at the time when he was invited to act, as to the likely weight and duration of the reference.

3 The extent to which the weight and duration of the reference have surpassed expectations.

4 Any warnings which the arbitrator gave as to possible restrictions on his

---

[7] This provision was introduced in 1934 to replace the previous law that an arbitrator should make his award within three months, unless the time was enlarged by the Court or by the arbitrator himself: 1889 Act, s. 2 and Sch. 1. The change was made partly because the period of three months was in practice a dead letter, and partly because it had become common for respondents to cause their arbitrators to delay the proceedings deliberately: MacKinnon Report, para. 5.

[8] In *Lewis Emanual & Son Ltd v Sammut*, ante, a delay of four months after what appears to have been a short hearing was described by Pearson J as 'very considerable'. Successful applications to remove on the ground of delay are very rare. Courtesy, if not the Statute, demands that the arbitrator be given warning that the party is considering an application to remove. Most arbitrators will readily take the hint.

[9] *Pratt v Swanmore Builders Ltd and Baker* [1980] 2 Lloyd's Rep 504 at 512.

full availability, and any information which the parties had, or should have had, as to his general state of availability[10].

5 The identity of the party by whom the arbitrator was nominated, if the tribunal consists of two arbitrators, one chosen by each party, plus a third arbitrator or umpire[11].

Whatever the precise circumstances, an arbitrator cannot be removed on the ground of delay simply because he has done nothing; for he may never have been asked to do anything. Delay must mean culpable delay[12].

The section specifically provides[13] that where an arbitrator is removed on the ground of delay, he shall not be entitled to receive any remuneration in respect of his services[14].

In any case where an application is made to remove an arbitrator, the arbitrator should be notified of the application, and given the opportuinity to place before the Court any comments which he may wish to make on the grounds of application. This is particularly important where there is reason to believe that the application may not be strenuously resisted; since otherwise the Court may be presented with a one-sided version of events, and may in all good faith embody this version in a judgment, the publication of which could do serious harm to the arbitrator's personal and professional standing[15].

The removal of an arbitrator leaves a vacancy in the tribunal. The method of supplying the vacancy is rather more straightforward than in the case of revocation: see p. 527, ante. The power is exercised by the Court on the application of either party. If the entire tribunal is removed, the Court may replace it with a sole arbitrator[16], or order that the arbitration agreement shall cease to have effect with respect to the dispute referred[17]. If the removal relates to only one or some of the arbitrators, or an umpire who has not yet entered on the reference, the Court may replace the person or persons so removed[18].

---

[10] An arbitrator ought not to take on more work than he can properly handle; but at the same time, if a party chooses a notoriously overworked arbitrator for a heavy arbitration, he can scarcely complain if his nominee gives it less attention than someone less successful, or more selective.

[11] Once appointed, an arbitrator becomes the mandatory of both parties, owing equal duties to each. Nevertheless, when considering the removal of an arbitrator for delay, and perhaps for other reasons as well, the Court cannot ignore the fact that whereas one party had the opportunity to consider in advance whether the arbitrator was a suitable choice, the other had no say in the matter.

[12] For it is penalised by loss of fees. See *Succula Ltd and Pomona Shipping Co Ltd v Harland and Wolff Ltd* [1980] 2 Lloyd's Rep 381 at 384.

[13] For the general position as regards remuneration and costs where the court intervenes in the course of the reference, see pp. 242–246, ante.

[14] Rather surprisingly, the Act confers no discretion. An arbitrator might do sterling work in the early stages of an arbitration, and it seems hard that a subsequent onset of delay should deprive him of all right to payment. This is a potent reason why, if the Court decides that the arbitration ought to go on before a different tribunal, or ought not to go at all, it should hesitate before using the powers available under s. 13, rather than some other route. A party who wants to get rid of an arbitrator who has performed useful services, before falling into delay, may find it expedient to make an offer to pay him a reasonable sum, even if not obliged to do so.

[15] A similar view was expressed in *Succula Ltd and Pomona Shipping Co Ltd v Harland and Wolff Ltd* [1980] 2 Lloyd's Rep 381 at 384. Another reason for serving the application on the arbitrator is to enable him to be joined as a defendant: *Pratt v Swanmore Builders Ltd and Baker* [1980] 2 Lloyd's Rep 504 at 506.

[16] S. 25(2)(a).

[17] S. 25(2)(b).

[18] S. 25(1).

Where the umpire has already entered upon the reference at the time when he is removed, the statutory power of the Court to make a fresh appointment does not apply, and the appointment must be made by the two arbitrators[19].

Where an arbitrator has been removed and replaced, the arbitration must in theory begin completely afresh before the reconstituted tribunal, for an arbitrator has a duty to deal with the whole dispute in all of its aspects[20]. It should, however, be posssible with reasonable good will from the parties, to salvage some part of the interlocutory proceedings, such as pleadings and discovery. Sometimes, the parties will allow the new arbitrator to take over the reference at the point where his predecessor left off, by reading the transcript of any evidence which has been given. But where there is no transcript, or where credibility of the witnesses is in issue, there is no option but to begin the hearing again. Where the dispute is complex this is a powerful argument against the exercise of any discretion to change the composition of the tribunal.

(iii) Replacement of arbitrator.   If an arbitrator 'refuses to act, or is incapable of acting, or dies', the following powers arise[1] –

1 If the arbitration agreement provides that the reference shall be to two arbitrators, one to be appointed by each party, the arbitrator who appointed him may himself appoint a new arbitrator in his place without the intervention of the Court: section 7(a). Alternatively either party may invite the Court to fill the vacancy: section 10(b).

2 If the reference is to a sole arbitrator, either party may invite the Court to fill the vacancy: section 10(b).

3 Where the person concerned is an umpire or third arbitrator, either party may invite the Court to fill the vacancy: section 10(d).

Where it is asserted that the arbitrator is 'incapable of acting' the availability of these remedies will depend upon the extent to which his functions are impaired. The words probably refer to the physical or mental capacity of the arbitrator, and not to other matters such as unavailability for business reasons or the loss of a qualification to act, which make it impossible for him to continue with the reference[2]. Nor do the words cover the case of an arbitrator who is willing to act, but lacks the skill to conduct the reference properly. The physical or mental incapacity need not be life-long, but they must be such as to put the arbitrator out of action altogether so far as the particular reference is concerned[3].

The words 'refuses to act' mean a refusal to act as arbitrator at all, not a refusal to act in a particular manner in the course of an arbitration. A mere

---

[19] As happened in *Re Enoch and Zaretzky, Bock & Co* [1910] 1 KB 327. There was at the time no statutory power equivalent to s. 25(1). It is not clear why the 1934 Act gave the Court power only where the umpire had not entered on the reference.

[20] Removal of an arbitrator does not, however, nullify an interim award previously made by him on a separate, severable dispute: *Fox v PG Wellfair Ltd* [1981] 2 Lloyd's Rep 514 at 520. It is doubtful whether the same is true for interlocutory orders or an interim award on a preliminary issue in the dispute which is to be decided by the incoming arbitrator

[1] Since the appointment of the arbitrator has its origin in the contract to arbitrate, even if the actual choice was not made by agreement, he can always be removed from office by a further agreement between the parties, without recourse to the statutory procedures.

[2] The word is 'incapable', not 'unable'.

[3] See *Burkett Sharp & Co v Eastcheap Dried Fruit Co and Perera* [1962] 1 Lloyd's Rep 267 at 276, and *Succula Ltd v Harland and Wolff Ltd*, supra, at 388.

hesitation about whether he should continue to act, or to act in a particular way is not enough[4].

In cases where the refusal or incapacity is of a more temporary or qualified nature, or where the arbitrator does not refuse to act, but simply fails to do so, the complaining party must fall back on other remedies. If the conduct of the arbitrator is wrongful or mistaken, the Court may well be able to find a sufficient degree of technical misconduct to justify a removal under section 23(1). And if the arbitrator is free from blame, the delay which results from his inability or unwillingness to proceed will, if sufficiently prolonged, justify an application to remove under section 13(3)[5].

(iv) Injunction.   The possibility of the Court granting an injunction restraining the arbitrator from taking any further step in the reference has already been discussed in connection with the grant of an injunction against the parties[6].

(v) Declaration as to status of the arbitrator.   So much attention has been given to the contractual analysis of the relationship between the two parties to a contract to refer, that it has tended to be overlooked that there is also a relationship, having some of the qualities of a contract, between each party and the arbitrator. Although the precise nature of the relationship is a matter of controversy[7], this seems no reason in principle why it should not be regarded as one which is susceptible of termination in the same manner as the agreement between the two parties. We cannot at present see why any party should wish to allege that his contract with the arbitrator has been determined by repudiatory breach of contract on the part of the latter, since there are ample statutory means of getting rid of an unsatisfactory tribunal[8]. Just conceivably, there may be cases in which the arbitrator himself would find the conduct of one or other of the parties so unsatisfactory that he would wish to rid himself of his mandate, and possibly to claim damages as well: and in such a case, there is the theoretical possibility that he could contend that his mandate has been wrongfully repudiated. We believe, however, that in all but the most exceptional circumstances his duty would be to consider the interests of the party not in

---

[4] *Burkett Sharp & Co v Eastcheap Dried Fruit Co and Perera* [1961] 2 Lloyd's Rep 80 at 88, per Diplock J and [1962] 1 Lloyd's Rep 267 at 276, per Pearson LJ. It apparently makes no difference under ss. 7 and 10 whether the refusal to act in the specified manner was justified or unjustified: although this will no doubt be relevant to any application to remove for misconduct. See also *Neale v Richardson* [1938] 1 All ER 753 (unwillingness to act otherwise than through a deputy: held refusal), and *Re Hawley, Bridgewood and Goodwin and North Staffordshire Rly Co* (1848) 2 De G & Sm 33. The language of s. 10 shows that the power exists only where what has happened is sufficiently serious to amount to a 'vacancy'. It was suggested in *Succula Ltd and Pomona Shipping Co v Harland and Wolff Ltd,* supra, that the powers should be used so as to fill a vacancy, not to create one.

[5] The narrow meaning attributed to ss. 7(a) and 10(b) and (d) may occasionally cause inconvenience. For example, if the arbitrator suffers a serious illness but is unwilling to retire, the parties must waste time waiting for an unreasonable delay to occur, before they can remove him, since the wording of s. 13 seems to leave no scope for removal on the ground of 'anticipatory delay'. In such a case, it would be worth applying under s. 1, for leave to revoke the arbitrator's authority.

[6] See pp. 518–523, ante.

[7] See pp. 220–223, ante.

[8] Unless, perhaps, the party is looking for some way of obtaining damages in respect of extra costs resulting from the unacceptable conduct of the arbitrator.

default, and to use his own peremptory powers to force the arbitration to a conclusion. If all else failed, he could simply refuse to go on, and leave it to the parties to take whatever steps they thought fit to remove him from his unwelcome office.

(vi) Preliminary question on arbitrator's powers.   In the past, there was a useful procedure whereby the arbitrator could state on his own initiative a consultative case for the opinion of the Court, on the extent of his own powers. This procedure is now rapidly falling into obsolescence, as the appeal procedures under the 1979 Act replace the former powers to state a special or consultative case. Consistently with the view which we have previously expressed, in relation to the right to declaratory relief[9], it seems that in a case where a valid exclusion agreement has been made the arbitrator no longer has any means of asking for the help of the Court. In such circumstances, it seems that the most he can do is to invite one of the parties to seek declaratory relief[9].

(d) Declaration as to status of future award

The Court would have formal jurisdiction to issue a declaration that any award made in the future will be void or voidable, on the ground of some jurisdictional or procedural objection. We believe that such a power would never in practice be exercised.

As regards questions of jurisdiction, it would be quite sufficient for the Court to declare that (depending on circumstances) the agreement to refer is void, or the dispute lies outside the scope of the agreement, or the arbitrator has not been validly appointed, or whatever else is the particular objection raised. There is no need to go on and say anything about a putative award, the status of which will be obvious from the nature of the declaration concerning the current state of the reference.

As regards procedural objections, we have already suggested that the Court should not assume under the guise of declaratory relief, a power to pronounce upon the future effect of what may at the present time appear to be an instance of misconduct.

2 Remedies of the arbitrator: default proceedings

General

In one sense, a discussion of the remedies available to the arbitrator is out of place in this Chapter, which is concerned with intervention in a pending reference; the arbitrator is himself part of the mechanism of the reference, and can hardly be able to intervene in it. Nevertheless, there are circumstances in which the Court and the arbitrator may have alternative powers to put right something which has gone wrong, and on occasion these powers reinforce one another. We do not deal here with the supportive powers of the Court under section 12(6), but rather with the jurisdiction to take the reference out of its ordinary course, by bringing it to a premature end. Essentially, there are two situations –

---

[9] See p. 525, ante.

(i) A party does nothing at all or, having at first done something, comes to a complete halt.

(ii) A party complies with his procedural obligations, but does so very slowly or very poorly.

(i) Total default.   In the first situation, the powers derived from the common law analysis of the arbitration agreement, the statutory powers of the Court and the arbitrator under the 1979 Act, and the powers implicit in the mandate given to the arbitrator, can all be found to converge. One must distinguish here between the cases where the offending party has, and has not, been ordered to take a procedural step; and in the latter case a distinction must be drawn between situations where the arbitrator has, and has not, been called upon by the other party to make a procedural order.

One may take the last case first, for this is the situation dealt with by the *Bremer Vulkan* case. The parties have a mutual obligation to press forward the reference; if one flags, the other must urge him on. If the latter does nothing, the arbitration becomes immobile. There may be the opportunity to say that the agreement to refer has disappeared by implied consent. But the offending party has done nothing wrong; neither the Court nor the arbitrator have occasion to apply sanctions.

Next, there is the case where the arbitrator has been asked to hasten the reference, but has not done so. Here the remedies must be aimed primarily at the arbitrator himself: if he will not respond he must be replaced, by one or other of the available methods.

Finally, there is the case of the party who remains totally inert in face of a procedural direction validly made. Here, the aggrieved party has a choice. He can treat his opponent's conduct as a wrongful repudiation, in the way which we have already discussed. This may be good tactics if he is the respondent, but probably not so good if he is the claimant. Furthermore, he may take this step without first applying for an order under section 5 of the 1979 Act, which does not define the obligations of the parties, but merely provides a remedy which is alternative to those derived from the character of the arbitration agreement as an enforceable contract.

Alternatively, the aggrieved party can keep the reference alive, and press the arbitrator to use his 'default powers'. This expression has tended to obscure the distinction between procedures which are quite different in character.

1 A true default procedure is one whereby the tribunal moves directly to an award against the defaulting party, with no intervening procedural steps, and without any hearing.

2 The term is, however, also used to denote the making of an order to the effect that a party is debarred from reliance at the hearing on any part of his case in respect of which he has committed a procedural default. So that, for example, if he has failed to give particulars or discovery in respect of an allegation which he has pleaded, he cannot rely upon the allegation when the dispute comes on for hearing.

3 Again, the term may refer to the practice whereby, if a party is falling short of his procedural obligations, the arbitrator will dispense with all pre-trial stages of the hearing, and fix a prompt date for the hearing.

4 Finally, it may refer to what is often called an 'ex parte' hearing[10]: namely a hearing which takes place in the absence of one party.

Arbitrator's powers at common law. Before the passing of the 1979 Act, the choice between these four forms of default procedure was an anxious matter for the arbitrator. On the one hand, he would feel himself under pressure to bring the reference to a reasonably prompt conclusion, since one of the reasons why parties choose arbitration is that they conceive it to be speedier than litigation. Against this a good arbitrator would have in mind that a hasty award against a respondent residing abroad would be of no use if the Court, through the medium of which the claimant sought execution, regarded a default procedure as so stunted as to offend against the rules of natural justice. Nor would the arbitrator do either party any favour if the result of excessive zeal were to leave the award exposed to being set aside for misconduct.

It is impossible to state in general terms how a balance between these opposing considerations was commonly struck in practice, for everything turned on the circumstances of the individual case. Nevertheless, we can say with confidence that very few experienced arbitrators would have thought of employing a default power of type (1), in other words proceeding directly from a default in (say) discovery of documents to an award against the defaulting party. On the other hand, an order of type (2), depriving a party of the right to rely at the hearing on an allegation not backed by proper particulars or discovery, has always been regarded an unobjectionable. This procedure can play a valuable role, and it is a pity that arbitrators are reluctant to make use of it[11].

The third type of procedure is one in which the arbitrator in effect gives up the attempt to secure a full performance of the procedural routine, but instead fixes an early date for a hearing, making it clear that he will not receive submissions from either party of which proper notice has not been given. This procedure can take many forms, and it needs to be used with care. Nevertheless, it is perfectly acceptable in principle[12].

Finally, there is the 'ex parte' award. This is made where one side appears and participates in the hearing, and the other does not. It is frequently, and properly, employed in cases where it is plain to the arbitrator that one party has not only failed to take part in the reference during the earlier stages, but has no intention of doing so in the future. Here, provided that the arbitrator is meticulous in giving the offending party written notice of what he is about to do, and sufficient time to mend his ways, the arbitrator can properly go to a trial without the need to carry out the full regime of preliminary meetings, pleadings, particulars, discovery and so on.

Precisely what should happen at the hearing is not so easily stated. The

---

[10] The expression is widely used in this sense. Nevertheless it is a misnomer. Proceedings ex parte are those which are launched by one party without notifying the other, and with the intention that the hearing will take place in his absence. This is not at all the same as a hearing at which only one party is present, because the other, although aware that it will be held, has chosen not to attend. We find it hard to conceive how an arbitrator could ever properly hold an ex parte hearing in the strict sense. S. 5 of the 1979 Act has nothing to say about this.

[11] The propriety of such an order was impliedly, if not specifically, recognised in the *Bremer Vulkan* case at 156.

[12] A procedure somewhat on these lines was upheld in *Congimex SARL (Lisbon) v Continental Grain Export Corpn (New York)* [1979] 2 Lloyd's Rep 346, a case cited with approval by the majority in the *Bremer Vulkan* case.

arbitrator will have to balance the need to save time and money, with a degree of caution about short cuts which may subsequently lead to trouble. In general, we suggest that he will be well advised to bear in mind the burden of proof. If it is the claimant who fails to appear at the hearing, it will usually be safe to dismiss his claim out of hand, on the basis that he has failed even to begin to make it good. If, however, it is the respondent who is absent, the arbitrator will have to move more carefully. He cannot properly make an award, unless the claimant has proved his case[13]. How this should be done, will depend entirely upon the nature of the reference. We would, however, suggest that –

1 The degree of formality required if the respondent fails to appear will depend in part upon the form which the proceedings would have taken if he had taken part. If it would have been an arbitration of the type conducted by arbitrator/advocates on bundles of documents, without any hearing, then plainly the tribunal has no need to call for anything in the way of 'evidence'; and can simply proceed to an award on the basis of what is found in the available documents. If, on the other hand, it is clear from the terms of the arbitration agreement or from the nature of the transaction that if all had gone well a full oral hearing would have taken place at which the strict rules of evidence would have applied, then the arbitrator must observe some degree of formality. We are, however, inclined to believe that it will be sufficient for him to require that the evidence for the claimant should be put on affidavit, and that he need not insist on it being given in person on oath[14].

2 The arbitrator must properly address himself to the question whether the claimant's evidence proves his case. This requires him not only to make sure that the evidence bears out the claimant's assertion, but also that it has the appearance of being true, and is internally consistent. Further than this, he need not, and indeed should not, go. It is not this function to search out the truth, but to choose between two versions presented to him; and if only one version is presented, he does not thereby become an advocate for the other side[15].

3 It occasionally happens that the respondent has got as far as indicating a defence, before giving up. Here, the arbitrator's proper course depends on the nature of the defence. If it is of such a nature as to impeach the arbitrator's right to proceed at all[16], the arbitrator ought to call on the claimant to satisfy him that it is ill-founded. We believe the same to be the case where the defence appears to the arbitrator to be sound: for after all, it is his duty to apply the law,

---

[13] Of course, the pleadings may contain admissions by the respondent which involve him in accepting the burden of proof. The fact that the claimant does not appear will not mean that an award can automatically be made against him on a counterclaim, for here he is in the position of a respondent.

[14] The proposition is stated in this half-hearted way, because it presents some theoretical difficulties: for if the law imposes a requirement that evidence in an arbitration shall be on oath, in the absence of consent of waiver, it is not altogether easy to explain how it can be dispensed with if the respondent is not there to consent or waive. Perhaps the answer lies in a qualification of the implied term as to the form of the evidence, so that it requires the evidence to be given in person only if the arbitration is fought. Or perhaps a waiver could be inferred from the failure to appear. For a discussion of evidence generally, see pp. 351–358, ante.

[15] See *Fox v PG Wellfair Ltd* [1981] 2 Lloyd's Rep 514. This is not to say that an arbitration is always a purely adversarial procedure: see pp. 48 and 345, ante. If it can be inferred that the reference is to be essentially of an investigatory nature, then the problem of evidence on a default will scarcely arise. The text is aimed at the more orthodox procedures.

[16] For example, if it is addressed to jurisdiction or illegality.

and he should not make an award which he does not honestly believe to be right. But if the defence is one which might be well-founded and might not, the arbitrator can reasonably say that it is for the preson who asserts a proposition to make it good. The same approach is justified, where the defence raises an issue of fact, in respect of which the respondent has the burden of proof. If the respondent does come forward to support his case, the arbitrator can ignore it.

Arbitrator's powers under section 5 of the 1979 Act. Thus far, we have considered the powers of the arbitrator at common law. The position has been complicated by section 5 of the 1979 Act, which reads as follows –

'5(1) If any party to a reference under an arbitration agreement fails within the time specified in the order or, if no time is so specified, within a reasonable time to comply with an order made by the arbitrator or umpire in the course of the reference, then, on the application of the arbitrator or umpire or of any party to the reference, the High Court may make an order extending the powers of the arbitrator or umpire as mentioned in subsection (2) below.

(2) If an order is made by the High Court under this section, the arbitrator or umpire shall have power, to the extent and subject to any conditions specified in that order, to continue with the reference in default of appearance or of any other act by one of the parties in like manner as a judge of the High Court might continue with proceedings in that court where a party fails to comply with an order of that court or a requirement of rules of court'.

This is a difficult piece of legislation. It has been widely assumed that the purpose was to remedy what was seen as a gap in the arbitrator's powers, by enabling him to make a 'default' award or to dismiss a claim peremptorily, or to proceed 'ex parte'. If this is so, the wording of the section seems less than apt.

Sub-section (1) gives rise to few problems. 'Failure to comply' presumably means 'failure properly to comply', so that total non-complicance is not a pre-requisite of an order – although presumably the Court will not make an order unless the failure is serious enough to create such an injustice towards the aggrieved party as to justify the use of an abbreviated procedure. The power to impose a condition on the order is valuable, for it will enable the Court to make sure that the arbitrator does not employ more drastic remedies than are justified by the gravity of the default.

Sub-section (2) is less easy to interpret. Its general scheme is to say, first, what the arbitrator is enabled to do and, second, how he may do it.

What the arbitrator is enabled to do, is to 'proceed with the reference'. This expression is wide enough to permit the fulfilment of the arbitrator's mandate by accelerated means: i.e. to enable him to bring the reference to a full conclusion by publishing an award allowing or dismissing the claim, and thereby making the dispute res judicata between the parties, even where the procedure employed is of such a summary nature that the award might otherwise have been voidable for misconduct. The expression does not, however, seem at all appropriate to describe the happening of something which brings the reference to a halt, permanently or until some condition is satisfied: for the wording suggests that the idea is to put the arbitrator in a position to press the contractual mode of determining disputes to its intended conclusion, fortified by his new powers. It must, however, be acknowledged that this interpretation of section 5 deprives it in a substantial degree of its intended purpose, for it means that there is no power in an arbitrator to dismiss a claim out of hand, on the ground of procedural defaults by the claimant: and this power, on the authority of the House of Lords in the *Bremer Vulkan* case, section 5 undoubtedly confers[17]. So it must be taken that the words 'shall have power to continue with the reference', are wide enough to embrace a power to discontinue the reference.

What does this involve? First, the arbitrator is to 'continue with the reference in default of appearance'. This expression has been the subject of adverse comment. It is pointed out that 'default of appearance ' is[18] a technical term, denoting a failure to appear in an action: that is, to perform the act whereby a person served with proceedings formally acknowledges the jurisdiction of the Court, and intimates his intention to defend the suit. This sense of the term is meaningless in the context of an arbitration. The nearest equivalent is the appointment of, or joining in the appointment of, an arbitrator. Obviously, this was not what the legislature had in mind, for section 5 contemplates a default occurring during a reference, and there is no reference until the tribunal has been appointed. So the phrase must mean something else. It seems most likely that the intention was to use appearance in the sense of physically putting in an appearance, so that 'in default of appearance' means 'if one of the parties does not appear at the hearing'[19]. This fits in neatly enough with 'or any other act by one of the parties', which can now be understood as referring to procedural acts other than those carried out at the hearing itself.

This being so, the first part of sub-section (2) can be taken to empower the arbitrator to proceed with the arbitration even if one of the parties does not participate at all, or participates only intermittently.

The second part defines how this power is to be exercised. It would seem at first sight that it does so by drawing an analogy with the powers of the Court. Unfortunately, the analogy does not work at all well, because proceedings in litigation and arbitration are fundamentally different in character. In a High Court action, a succession of procedural steps are laid down by the Rules of Court which must be followed, and promptly followed, if one or other party is not to find himself in default; and upon the occurrence of such a default, the Court has punitive powers, most of which are themselves laid down by the Rules. In an arbitration, there are no rules, except for those which are expressed in the arbitration agreement, or some specific procedural agreement between the parties. Apart from this, the parties have only to comply with valid directions given by the arbitrator. Unless he orders them to do something, they need not do it; and what he does order may bear no resemblance to the procedural steps which must be taken as a matter of course in an action. One may take as example the very first step, namely the delivery of a statement of claim. This is something which every plaintiff must do within fourteen days, unless he has obtained an

---

[17] See pp. 156E/9, 168F. There are dicta to the same effect in the speeches of Lords Brandon and Roskill in *The Hannah Blumeuthal*, ante.

[18] Or more accurately, was at the time when the 1979 Act was passed. The terminology is now different: see RSC Ord. 12.

[19] By this we mean 'If one of the parties chooses not to appear at the hearing'. The occurrence of an antecedent procedural default cannot have been intended to confer a power to press forward with the hearing, regardless of whether the offending party has an opportunity to attend ot not. The section is concerned with 'default' in appearance.

order dispensing with pleadings or enlarging the time for delivery. If he does not comply, he is in default, and RSC Ord. 19 empowers the Court to dismiss the claim out of hand, without any investigation of the merits. In an arbitration, by contrast, the claimant is not obliged to deliver a statement of claim unless he is ordered to do so; and in the majority of arbitrations no such order will be made. The same is the case as regards orders for 'defence', 'discovery', 'inspection' and so on, which have no counterpart in the ordinary run of arbitrations. Conversely, the arbitrator may order a procedural step in the reference which is not like anything found in the High Court. For example, it is not uncommon to find that the arbitrator orders the parties to exchange full statements of their cases, summarising their evidence, and arguments on fact and law, and annexing the documents on which they rely. These documents are not pleadings, and the production of documents is not discovery. Does it follow that in the event of non-compliance, the aggrieved party cannot obtain an extension order under section 5? Surely this cannot have been intended.

Since an attempt at a direct analogy with proceedings in Court breaks down, and since the second part of section 5(2) must mean something, it appears that the intention must have been to give the same *sort* of powers, upon default in compliance with one of his orders, as the Court would have if one of its own rules was disobeyed. If this is right, then the following would appear to be the general scheme[20] –

1 A major failure by the claimant to comply with procedural directions – summary dismissal of claim.

2 A major failure by the respondent – an immediate award for the amount claimed, if the sum is liquidated: if not, at interim award on liability in favour of the claimant, followed by a hearing on damages[1].

3 A failure by either party relating to a severable part of the dispute – an order disentitling the party from relying on that part of his case in respect of which he has made default.

4 Failure by either party to appear at the hearing – a proceeding conducted in his absence, in the manner suggested above.

Two comments may be made upon the structure thus suggested. The first is that section 5 appears to confer on the arbitrator few powers which he does not already possess at common law[2]. This is largely true, but the section does give two useful measures of reassurance. First, to the arbitrator, who is likely to be safe from allegations of misconduct, if he proceeds under cover of an extension order. Second, to the aggrieved party, who may wish to rely on a 'default' or 'ex parte' award in a foreign country, and can if challenged point to an express prior authorisation by the Court.

Second, there is an apparent discontinuity between the events which create the power in the Court to make an extension order, and the powers which can be exercised once an order has been made. Any procedural default opens the

---

[20] The arbitrator is not of course obliged to use these powers to the full, and often would be wrong to do so.

[1] By analogy with RSC Ord. 19, r. 3.

[2] It has been said that s. 5 now enables the arbitrator to strike out a claim for want of prosecution. But it does not. This power is exercised in the High Court when the plaintiff has done nothing for a long time, even if not ordered to do so. There is, as the *Bremer Vulkan* case shows, no such power in an arbitration at common law. Nor is there under s. 5, for the Court has no power to make an extension order, unless the arbitrator has made an order which has been disobeyed.

way to the exercise of all the remedies conferred by section 5(2). Thus, for example, a failure to provide particulars of a pleading could lead to an order empowering the arbitrator to proceed in the absence of one party, even if, at the time when the order was made, there was not the least reason to suppose that either party would be absent from the hearing. In practice, it seems very unlikely that the Court would allow the section to be operated in this haphazard way. We believe that what would happen is as follows –

1 The Court would make an order delineating the powers of the arbitrator in respect of the default which had already occurred.

2 If the Court found solid grounds for thinking that the offending party would go on to make defaults at later stages, it would make a conditional order, giving the arbitrator powers to be exercised if, but only if, such defaults should take place.

(ii) **Partial default.** We now turn from the case of total default to the situation in which a party complies slowly, or imperfectly, with the direct orders of the arbitrator. Here the practical problems are much more difficult, although the underlying theory is the same. Essentially the difficulty is this. The aggrieved party has a choice between two general lines of approach. First, he may attempt to cut through the thicket of delay and inefficiency by means of a summary disposal of the reference. This will necessitate –

1 Arguing that the agreement to refer has been repudiated or discharged by consent. This remedy is useless to a claimant in a case where the reference is making some, albeit halting, progress, for the only result will be that he has to start the entire dispute again, in the High Court. A declaration that the reference has terminated will be at least a major tactical victory for a respondent, if not always the end of the war; but it will be very hard to obtain in a case where the claimant is making some intermittent progress; or

2 Obtaining relief under section 5. This involves three steps: (i) applying to the arbitrator for the necessary procedural order, and waiting for time to expire; (ii) applying to the Court for an extension order, and satisfying the Court that matters are serious enough to make one necessary; (iii) returning to the arbitrator for an order giving effect to his new powers. This all takes time, and success is not assured. Moreover, unless the offender is resolved not to trouble with the arbitration any longer, it is likely that the intimation of the process will galvanize him into life, and lead to the repair of the default during one of the intervals between the three stages of the process. Although it is too early to be sure, we suspect that there will be few instances of the exercise of powers conferred by an extension order, in cases where the offender intends to participate in the reference; or

3 Persuading the arbitrator to use his default power at common law. The problem here is that these powers will rarely be available where the complaint is that performance is slow or unsatisfactory, rather than non-existent.

In these circumstances, it seems that the aggrieved party will in most cases be constrained to go ahead with the reference: and the further it has progressed, the less his incentive to attempt anything drastic. He must therefore try to urge matters forward; and this means that he must be able to suggest to the arbitrator a course of action which will bring about an improvement, without involving a serious risk of misconduct. Of these, by far the most effective is an order precluding the offender from setting up at the hearing any case of which he has not given adequate notice[3], or in respect of which he has made default in giving particulars or discovery[4].

An alternative often suggested is to fix an early date for the hearing. This is, of course, a sensible procedure where the offending party is totally in default, and appears to have given up entirely. But it may produce more injustice than it cures, if imprudently used. For example, the respondent may be slow to give proper discovery. Quite often, the claimant may do best to ignore this, and to press forward with the reference. The arbitrator may also be justified in taking the same course; for the power to order discovery is discretionary, and a meticulous insistence on full compliance may do more harm than good. There are, however, certain cases where the claimant needs the respondent's discovery in order to complete his case, and it does him no favour to deprive him of the chance to obtain it. An accelerated reference may give the impression of efficiency, but it is of little use if the hearing ultimately takes place on the basis of inadequate material.

D. SITUATIONS AND REMEDIES: SUMMARY

As will have been observed, English law provides no coherent system for dealing with problems which arise during the reference. Some of the remedies overlap and there are situations for which there is no convenient remedy. We set out below, in a very compressed form, the remedies which usually ought to be considered, in the cases most likely to arise in practice. The material on which the summary is based may be found in the earlier parts of this Chapter, and in Chapters 12, 30 and 34. The choice between the remedies will depend very much on the circumstances of the individual case.

Total breakdown of arbitration

An order that the arbitration agreement shall cease to have effect, plus (if it is the claimant who is complaining) a writ claiming the same substantive relief in the High Court (if there is territorial jurisdiction) resisting a stay.

Alternatively, a notice treating the agreement to refer as frustrated, plus an originating summons for a declaration that the agreement is at an end, plus (if it is the respondent who is complaining) an injunction to restrain the further conduct of the reference, or plus (if it is the claimant who is complaining) a writ claiming the same substantive relief in the High Court.

Prolonged inactivity by the claimant

A formal order from the arbitrator giving peremptory directions, then in the event of non-compliance, an order under section 5(2) of the 1979 Act, followed by an 'ex parte' award dismissing the claim.

---

[3] As in *Congimex SARL (Lisbon) v Continental Grain Export Corpn (New York)* [1979] 2 Lloyd's Rep 346, cited with approval in the *Bremer Vulkan* case.
[4] This works well enough where the offender is putting forward a positive case. If his case is simply a denial, it is a stronger thing to shut him out from even this, for the result may effectively be a default award, with the hearing a bare formality.

Alternatively, abstain from any application to the arbitrator; allow time to pass, and then give notice treating the agreement as terminated or apply for leave to revoke under s. 1, followed by a writ claiming (a) a declaration and (b) an injunction.

Prolonged inactivity by the respondent

A formal order from the arbitrator giving peremptory directions, then in the event of non-compliance an order under section 5(2) of the 1979 Act, followed by an 'ex parte' award for the amount claimed, or an interim award on liability followed by a further hearing on damages. Alternatively, give notice treating the agreement as terminated or apply for leave to revoke under section 1, followed by a writ claiming (a) a declaration that the agreement is terminated, (b) the substantive relief originally claimed in the arbitration, and (c) damages for breach of the arbitration agreement. Resist a stay of the action in respect of the substantive relief. If necessary, apply for orders under section 25(2)(b) annulling the arbitration agreement, under section 25(4) annulling a *Scott v Avery* clause, and under section 34(5)(b) of the Limitation Act 1980 extending the time for commencing proceedings (see p. 197, ante).

Refusal by either party to comply with procedural obligations

A peremptory order from the arbitrator and then proceed as under 'Prolonged inactivity' above.

Prolonged inactivity by the arbitrator

First, a warning to the arbitrator. In the event of no improvement, removal under section 13(3) plus an order forfeiting the arbitrator's fees, plus (a) (if the order applies to the entire tribunal, an order that the arbitration agreement shall cease to have effect, plus an order nullifying any *Scott v Avery* provision; or (b) the appointment of a new arbitrator. If alternative (a) is adopted, issue a writ for the substantive relief originally claimed in the arbitration. Consider an action for damages against the arbitrator.

Serious mishandling of the reference

Removal under section 23(1) plus (a) an order that the arbitration agreement shall cease to have effect, or (b) appointment of a new arbitrator.

Alternatively, an order giving leave to revoke the appointment, plus alternatives (a) or (b).

If alternative (a) is chosen, issue a writ for the substantive relief originally claimed in the arbitration.

Lack of impartiality

Application for leave to revoke the appointment.

Alternatively, if the lack of impartiality has been manifested by actual misconduct, removal under section 23(2).

Plus, in either event, alternatives (a) or (b), as above.

Alternatively, if it is the respondent who complains, an injunction to restrain the claimant and the arbitrator from proceeding with the reference.

Refusal to act, incapacity or death of the arbitrator

Replacement by a new arbitrator under sections 7(a), or 10(b) or (d).

Jurisdictional problems

If concerned with the existence or continued validity of the arbitration agreement, the validity of the notice to arbitrate or the qualifications of the arbitrator, issue an originating summons for a declaration. Alternatively, wait until after the award and then set aside the award or raise the objection as a ground for resisting enforcement.

Alternatively, in some of these instances, if it is the respondent who complains, (possibly) an injunction to restrain the arbitrator from continuing to act.

If concerned with the application of the arbitration agreement to the particular dispute in question, issue a writ for a declaration, or alternatively wait until after the award, and then set aside in part, or resist execution of the part of the award.

Problems as to the arbitrator's powers

If there is no exclusion agreement under the 1979 Act, issue an originating summons for a declaration, or (possibly) raise a question of law under section 2 of the Act.

If there is an exclusion agreement, issue an originating summons for a declaration.

CHAPTER 33

Remedies available after the reference

The remedies which exist after the award has been published are less sparingly exercised than those available whilst the reference is still in progress. There are two categories: passive remedies and active remedies.

A. PASSIVE REMEDIES

A party avails himself of a passive remedy when he does not himself take any initiative to attack the award, but simply waits until his opponent seeks to enforce the award by action or summary process, and then relies upon his matter of complaint as a ground why the Court should refuse enforcement. A remedy of this kind is available in two situations –

1 where the award is so defective in form or substance that it is incapable of enforcement[1];

2 where the whole or part of the award is ineffective on the ground that the relief granted lies outside the jurisdiction of the arbitrator[2].

It is important to note that these are the only instances where a passive remedy is available, and, in particular, that a party cannot resist the enforcement of an award on the ground that the conclusions expressed in the award were wrong in law or fact, or that it was arrived at by an unfair or unsatisfactory procedure. Mistakes of law or fact on the part of the arbitrator may occasionally be a ground for interference by a court[3], but the interference is by way of motion to set aside or remit, and never by way of a substantive defence to proceedings to enforce the award. Similarly, it has been clear for centuries that it is no defence to such proceedings that the decision was the result of bias, misconduct or misunderstanding. These are grounds for a motion to set aside or remit, not for a defence[4]; they do not put in question the jurisdiction of the

---

[1] See pp. 382–388 ante.

[2] See pp. 108–110 ante.

[3] Where there is an admitted mistake coupled with a request by the arbitrator for remission: see pp. 558–559, post; or (possibly) in the circumstances discussed in Chapter 37.

[4] See the principles stated by Serjeant Williams in *Veale v Warner* (1669) 1 Saund 323 at 326, note 3. In more recent times the same proposition has repeatedly been emphasised: see, for example, *Thorburn v Barnes* (1867) LR 2 CP 384; *Lord v Lord* (1855) 5 E & B 404; *Bache v Billingham* [1894] 1 QB 107; *L Oppenheim & Co v Mahomed Haneef* [1922] 1 AC 482; *Scrimaglio v Thornett and Fehr* (1924) 131 LT 174; *White, Tomkins and Courage v Compagnie Lyonnaise de Madagascar* (1921) 7 Ll L Rep 134; *Niger Co Ltd v SA Spremitura Oli Vegetali* (1922) 12 Ll L Rep 497; *Birtley District Co-operative Society Ltd v Windy Nook and District Industrial Co-operative Society* [1959] 1 WLR 142.

arbitrator[5]. Misconduct makes an award voidable, not void[6]. Thus, where an unsuccessful respondent finds that his opponent is proceeding to summary enforcement of the award, either section 26 or RSC Ord. 14, it is of no use for him to produce an affidavit or serve a defence setting out his complaint. He must launch a motion to set aside or remit the award, and either see that is is brought on at the same time as the application for summary relief, or at least ensure that the Court which is being called upon to enforce the award is informed of the existence of the motion[7].

B. ACTIVE REMEDIES

In practice, it is uncommon for a party who has a complaint about the conduct of the reference to content himself with a passive remedy. The party will usually be unwilling to leave the status of the award in doubt until such time as his opponent chooses to enforce it. Moreover, even when the complaint does constitute a true defence to the action, there will often be other matters upon which the party wishes to rely, which can only be raised by way of motion to set aside or remit; and since the motion must be launched within a specified time[8], it will not be safe for the party to wait until his opponent sues on the award. It is therefore usual to find that challenges to an award are maintained by means of one or more of the following procedures –

1 A motion to set aside or remit the award
2 A declaration that the award is invalid
3 An injunction to restrain the enforcement of the award.

These procedures are discussed in detail, below.

1 Setting aside and remission

Where a losing party complains that the reference has not been conducted in a fair and proper manner, it is almost invariable for him to claim in the alternative that the award should be set aside in whole or in part, or that it should be remitted to the arbitrator for further consideration; and even if setting aside alone is claimed, the Court will always consider of its own accord whether the remission would not be a more appropriate remedy. This has given rise to the notion that the two remedies are merely different versions of the same general power of supervision, remission being treated as a milder version of setting aside, useful as a means of patching up unsatisfactory references, and awards in situations where the defect is not so serious as to justify the delay and expense which inevitably attend the setting aside of the award. This idea is mistaken. We have already shown, in Chapter 29, that the two remedies have a quite different jurisdictional history. Furthermore, the grounds upon which remission

---

[5] *Scrimaglio v Thornett and Fehr*, supra; *Termarea SRL v Rederiaktiebolaget Sally* [1979] 2 Lloyd's Rep 439 at 442.
[6] *Bache v Billingham*, ante.
[7] In this event, an application for summary enforcement would no doubt be adjourned, although the Court could, if it thought fit, order the defendant to give security for the amount of the award. See also s. 5(5) of the 1975 Act.
[8] See Ord. 73, r. 5, in Appendix 1, at pp. 721–722, post.

can be ordered do not necessarily coincide exactly with those which found an application to set aside.

In summary the position is as follows:

(a) Setting aside

(i) The Court has a statutory jurisdiction under section 23(1) of the 1950 Act to set aside an award where the arbitrator has misconducted himself or the proceedings, or where the award has been improperly procured.

(ii) The Court had for many years[9] an inherent jurisdiction to set aside an award which –

1 was subject to an error of law on the face of the award; or
2 was wholly or part in excess of jurisdiction; or
3 was subject to a patent substantive defect.

The jurisdiction to set aside for error on the face was abolished by section 1(1) of the 1979 Act. It is at least possible that this jurisdiction had already disappeared, together with the other two instances of the inherent jurisdiction, as the result of the repeal by the 1950 Act of section 1 of the 1889 Act[10].

(b) Remission

(i) The Court has a statutory jurisdiction under section 22(1) of the 1950 Act to remit the matters referred, or any of them, to the reconsideration of the arbitrator. This discretion is unlimited in terms, but it may be subject to restrictions imposed by judicial decision[11].

(ii) The Court has no inherent jurisdiction to remit either the award or the matters which were the subject of the reference.

2 The jurisdiction to remit

Originally, the power to remit derived from a special provision in the submission, devised during the first half of the nineteenth century. The success of this procedure led to the creation, by section 8 of the 1854 Act, of a statutory power to remit. The provision, and its successors in the 1889 and 1950 Acts, contained no express limitations on the discretion of the Court to remit, and for a time it was maintained that the discretion was completely at large. However, within a very few years it had been made plain that this view was incorrect. The courts were evidently oppressed by the possibility of numerous attempts to reopen the merits of the dispute under the guise of an application to remit. It was therefore firmly stated that the purpose of section 8 was simply to give statutory effect to the remission clause, and that remission would not be ordered except in cases where, but for the existence of the new power, the Court would have set the award aside[12]. It subsequently became apparent that the latter part of this proposition was too narrowly expressed, since there were cases – for example,

---

[9] See Chapter 29, ante.
[10] See pp. 446–448, ante.
[11] See pp. 550–562, post.
[12] *Mills v Bowyers' Society* (1856) 3 K & J 66; *Hodgkinson v Fernie* (1857) 3 CBNS 189; *Hogge v Burgess* (1858) 3 H & N 293.

admitted mistake and the discovery of fresh evidence – which probably did not found an application to set aside, but did enable the Court to remit under the remission clause. In due course, these were acknowledged as grounds upon which the Court could exercise the statutory power of remission[13], but the general principle remained unchallenged, and in 1898[14] the Court of Appeal was able to accept as correct the proposition that there were only four grounds upon which a matter could be remitted to the arbitrator for reconsideration, namely –

1 where the award was bad on the face of it[15];

2 where there was misconduct on the part of the arbitrator[16];

3 where there had been an admitted mistake and the arbitrator himself had asked that the matter be remitted;

4 where additional evidence had been discovered after the making of the award.

Since this list was endorsed by the courts, certain additional or more specific categories have been recognised.

First, where the arbitrator puts forward a question of law for the decision of the Court by stating an award in the form of a special case, but fails to set out in the award sufficient facts to enable the question to be decided, the Court will remit the case for further findings[17].

Second, the Court has enlarged the category of awards which are defective on their face by including those awards in the form of a special case which are not clearly enough expressed to enable the Court to arrive at a conclusion on the question of law[18].

A rather similar jurisdiction may exist in respect of awards which are the subject of an appeal under section 1 of the 1979 Act, and which do not contain sufficient reasons to enable the Court to decide the question of law. There is, however, a statutory power under section 1(5) to order the giving of sufficient reasons, and it will in general be sufficient to rely on this, without having recourse to any jurisdiction arising from section 22(1) of the 1950 Act[19].

Third, in recent years it has been held that an award may be remitted if there

---

[13] *Dinn v Blake* (1875) LR 10 CP 388 (admitted mistake); *Re Keighley, Maxsted & Co and Bryan Durant & Co* [1893] 1 QB 405 (fresh evidence).

[14] *Re Montgomery Jones & Co and Liebenthal & Co* (1898) 78 LT 406. The 1889 Act had retained the wording of the 1854 Act, apart from the deletion of 'at any time' and 're-determination'. It was not suggested that these amendments altered the effect of the legislation.

[15] Error on the face almost always led to setting-aside, rather than remission.

[16] In *Margulies Bros Ltd v Dafnis Thomaides & Co (UK) Ltd* [1958] 1 Lloyds Rep 250 at 252 Diplock J expressed the view that the inclusion of misconduct in the list involved an extension of the jurisdiction which had hitherto been exercised on the grounds of fraud and corruption.

[17] We have not been able to trace when the jurisdiction was first exercised. Certainly, it was well-recognised by 1920. Whether this involved an extension of the discretion to remit is of only academic interest. An arbitrator who fails to state a case in the appropriate manner may be regarded as having committed a highly technical form of misconduct: cf. *Margulies Bros Ltd v Dafnis Thomaides & Co Ltd*, supra, where it was regarded as misconduct not to put the award in an enforceable form. Another view is that the power was derived from s. 21(1) of the 1950 Act, which gave the Court power to order an arbitrator to state a special case. This might be said to embrace an order to restate a case in the proper form. At all events, the power has been so frequently exercised in recent times that its existence cannot now be doubted.

[18] This jurisdiction, which is now virtually obsolete, is discussed in more detail at p. 557, post.

[19] It may, however, be noted that the power under s. 1(5) may be exercised only on the application of a party or parties to the reference, whereas that under s. 22(1) may be exercised by the judge of his own motion. For the question of reasons generally, see pp. 373–381, ante, 596–600, post.

has been a misunderstanding leading to injustice, even though the arbitrator has not committed misconduct[20]. These decisions undoubtedly go beyond the list set out above[1]. Whether they are sustainable on the law as it now stands depends upon whether the list is exclusive, or whether the Court has a general discretion to remit whenever justice so demands, the list furnishing no more than illustrations and guidance as to the way in which the Court will intervene. This question is at present controversial: there is strong authority for each view[2]. The weight of the existing authority is in favour of the more restricted view[3]. The matter is, however, open in the House of Lords, and the power to remit is so useful that the opportunity might well be taken to restore to section 22(1) the full literal effect of its words.

3 Grounds for setting aside or remitting

Having referred to certain problems material to the jurisdiction to remit, we now turn to various individual grounds upon which the Court will, in appropriate circumstances, have a discretion to set aside or remit the award.

(a) Misconduct

Little would be gained by attempting a complete definition of the behaviour which constitutes 'misconduct'[4]. No matter what customary procedure may be alleged the law has always approached the question pragmatically. It might perhaps be possible to deduce from the reported cases a few categories of behaviour which always are, or never are, regarded as amounting to misconduct, but the practical value of such an undertaking would be small. The great

---

[20] *Peter Cassidy Seed Co Ltd v Osuustukkukauppa IL* [1954] 2 Lloyd's Rep 586; *Franz Haniel AG v Sabre Shipping Corpn*, supra; *Aktiebolaget Legis v V Berg & Sons Ltd* [1964] 1 Lloyd's Rep 203; *Compagnie Financière pour le Commerce Extérieur SA v O Y Vehna AB* [1963] 2 Lloyd's Rep 178; *Exormisis Shipping SA v Oonsoo, The Aristedes Xilas* [1975] 2 Lloyd's Rep 402; *GKN Centrax Gears Ltd v Matbro Ltd* [1976] 2 Lloyd's Rep 555 at 581–582; *Sokratis Rokopoulos v Esperia SpA, The Aros* [1978] 1 Lloyd's Rep 456; *Bulk Oil (Zug) AG v Sun International Ltd (No 2)* [1984] 1 Lloyd's Rep 531.

[1] In the *Peter Cassidy* case it does not appear whether any authority was cited.

[2] For the narrower view may be cited *Mills v Bowyers' Society* (1856) 3 K & J 66; *Hodgkinson v Fernie* (1857) 3 CBNS 189; *Dinn v Blake* (1875) LR 10 CP 388; *Re Keighley, Maxsted & Co and Bryan Durant & Co* [1893] 1 QB 405; *Re Montgomery, Jones & Co and Liebenthal & Co's Arbitration* (1898) 78 LT 406; *Champsey Bhara & Co v Jivraj Balloo Spinning and Weaving Co Ltd* [1923] AC 480; *Stone v Licences and General Insurance Co Ltd* (1941) 71 Ll L Rep 256; *Atlantic Lines & Navigation Co Inc v Italmare SpA, The Apollon* [1985] 1 Lloyd's Rep 597 at 600. The contrary line of authority begins with the dictum of Moulton LJ in *Re Baxters and Midlands Rly Co* (1906) 22 TLR 616; and includes *Ben Line Steamers Ltd v Compagnie Optorg of Saigon* (1937) 57 Ll L Rep 194 at 196; *Lambert and Krzysiak Ltd v British Commercial Overseas Co Ltd* (1923) 16 Ll L Rep 51; *Universal Cargo Carriers Corpn v Pedro Citati* [1957] 2 Lloyd's Rep 191; *Margulies Bros Ltd v Dafnis Thomaides & Co (UK) Ltd*, ante; *Franz Haniel AG v Sabre Shipping Corpn*, ante; *Aktiebolaget Legis V Berg & Sons* [1964] 1 Lloyd's Rep 203; *Granvias Oceanical Armadora SA v Jibsen Trading Co, The Kavo Peiratis* [1977] 2 Lloyd's Rep 344 at 353. Almost all the judicial pronouncements on the subject are obiter.

[3] Even if the wider view of the jurisdiction is correct, the references to the interests of justice, which can be found in some of the cases, plainly cannot be given a literal effect. Many people would say that justice required an erroneous award to be put right. This has never been the law. The reference to justice must be taken in the context of the principle that if the parties choose a tribunal, they must abide by its decision.

[4] Many different formulations may be found in the cases. One of the most helpful is that of Atkin J in *Williams v Wallis and Cox* [1914] 2 KB 478 at 485 – 'such a mishandling of the arbitration as is likely to amount to some substantial miscarriage of justice'.

majority of cases lie in the middle ground where the question of misconduct or no misconduct depends on the nature of the submission, and the circumstances of the case. The task of formulating a general definition is made the more difficult by the fact that various types of conduct which have prompted the Court to remit or set aside an award can equally well be categorised as misconduct or as separate grounds giving the Court jurisdiction to intervene. For example, excess of jurisdiction and defects in the form of the award are probably best regarded as separate grounds for invoking the jurisdiction of the Court, but there is substantial authority for the view that they also amount to misconduct.

It is, however, possible to say that –

1 Failure to conduct the reference in the manner expressly or impliedly prescribed by the submission will (unless both parties consent) always amount to misconduct, although not necessarily to misconduct which will lead the Court to intervene.

2 Whatever the provisions of the submission, it is misconduct to behave in a way regarded by the courts as contrary to public policy.

3 Unless the submission expressly or impliedly permits, or unless the parties consent, it is misconduct to behave in a way which is, or gives the appearance of being, unfair[5].

4 For this purpose, fairness does not necessarily involve conducting the proceedings in the same way as an action in Court; regard must be had to the identity of the parties, and of the chosen arbitrator, and to the nature of the subject matter.

5 There are, however, certain minimum requirements – notably the hearing of both sides, and abstention from receiving evidence or argument in the absence of one party – which are regarded as essential to the fair conduct of the reference.

These propositions are developed in more detail in Chapter 22, ante.

Although, from the point of view of logic, the word 'misconduct' is entirely appropriate to describe the conduct of proceedings otherwise than in the way required by law, the choice of language has proved to be unfortunate[6], especially since the 1889 Act referred only to the arbitrator having misconducted himself. Arbitrators, who would have felt regret, but no more, on being informed by the Court that they had conducted the reference in a way which did not comply with their legal obligations, were understandably resentful of the implication that the work which they had carried out in good faith involved personal misconduct. The courts have been sensitive to this resentment, and have constantly taken pains to point out to arbitrators that allegations of misconduct

---

5 It is possible to regard this principle simply as the reflection of an implied term in the submission that the arbitrator will act fairly: see *Faure, Fairclough Ltd v Premier Oil and Cake Mills Ltd* [1968] 1 Lloyd's Rep 237 at 240. The illuminating judgment of Diplock LJ in *London Export Corpn Ltd v Jubilee Coffee Roasting Co Ltd* [1958] 1 Lloyd's Rep 197 proceeds on the basis that the question of natural justice is to be regarded as arising at the second stage of the enquiry, after the Court has decided whether the conduct in question is prohibited by the express or implied terms of the submission.

6 In retrospect it is a pity that the legislature did not retain the phrase 'undue means', which had long been understood to connote an infringement of natural justice: see, for example, *Re Plews and Middleton* (1845) 6 QB 845.

do not necessarily mean what they appear to say[7]. Two unsatisfactory results have ensued.

First, the legislature has endeavoured to make the language of the statute less abrasive by adding the words 'or the proceedings' to the words 'has misconducted himself'[8]. this has naturally caused speculation as to the difference between the two forms of words. The distinction is of no practical importance, for the available remedies are the same, and it is hard to imagine a way in which the arbitrator could misconduct himself, without at the same time misconducting the proceedings.

Second, there has been a tendency to invent a category of 'technical misconduct' which is contrasted with misconduct of a more personal nature. This contrast does not reflect any true legal distinction, and only serves to mislead, since it may suggest that technical misconduct attracts the lesser remedy of remission, whilst setting aside is reserved for cases which put in question the probity of the arbitrator. No such rigid distinction exists. Naturally, the particular remedy which is chosen will depend upon the nature of the misconduct, and the Court may be more ready to set aside than to remit, if the misconduct is concerned with the probity and impartiality of the arbitrator, rather than with a misconception on his part as to the way in which the proceedings should have been conducted. This does not, however, have any connection with the words added by the 1934 Act. All allegations of misconduct assert that the arbitrator has acted in breach of duty; and most involve the contention that the arbitrator has failed to act fairly, or at least to appear to act fairly. There is nothing 'technical' in such a breach of duty[9].

The question has occasionally arisen, where the arbitrator has infringed the principles discussed in the preceding paragraphs, whether the Court will entertain an argument that the award should stand because the outcome of the dispute would have been the same even if the proper procedure had been followed. The law is not altogether clear[10]. We suggest, however, that a

---

[7] *Re Fuerst Bros & Co Ltd and RS Stephenson* [1951] 1 Lloyd's Rep 429 at 431, is one of several instances. The practice of reassuring the arbitrator can go almost too far: as witness the statement in *Gunter Henck v André & Cie SA* [1970] 1 Lloyd's Rep 235 at 242, that the assertion of misconduct was an essential preliminary to an application to set aside (and hence was a form of words which did not necessarily have pejorative overtones). This is not so: the applicant could have contended himself with saying that the tribunal had misconducted the proceedings.

[8] The words were added by s. 15 of the Arbitration Act 1934 on the recommendation of the MacKinnon Committee. In para. 67 of its 1978 report on arbitration (Cmnd 7284) the Commercial Court Committee recommended that some term should be substituted which reflects the idea of irregularity rather than misconduct. The recommendation has not been adopted.

[9] This point was forcefully made by Donaldson J in *Thomas Borthwick (Glasgow) Ltd v Faure Fairclough Ltd* [1968] 1 Lloyd's Rep 16 at 29.

[10] Among the numerous cases where the question has been considered, one may cite *Walker v Frobisher* (1801) 6 Ves 70; *Dobson v Groves* (1844) 6 QB 637; *Re Morphett* (1845) 14 LJQB 259; *Mills v Bowyers' Society* (1856) 3 K & J 66; *Thorburn v Barnes* (1867) LR 2 CP 384; *Re Brien and Brien* [1910] 2 IR 84, per Boyd J at 89; *WH Ireland & Co v CT Bowring & Co Ltd* (1920) 2 Ll L Rep 220; *Watson & Co v Produce Brokers' Co* (1921) 8 Ll L Rep 364, on appeal (1922) 10 Ll L Rep 709; *Ritchie v W Jacks & Co* (1922) 10 Ll L Rep 519; *Royal Commission on Sugar Supply v Kwik Hoo Tong Trading Society* (1922) 11 Ll L Rep 163; *Niger Co Ltd v SA Spremitura Oli Vegetali* (1922) 12 Ll L Rep 497; *Black v John Williams* 1924 SC 497; *W Ramsden & Co v Jacobs* [1922] 1 KB 640; *Jordeson & Co v Stora Kopparbergs Bergslags AB* (1931) 41 Ll L Rep 201; *Hookway & Co Ltd v Isaacs & Sons* [1954] 1 Lloyd's Rep 491; *Eastcheap Dried Fruit Co v NV Gebroeders Catz' Handelsvereeniging* [1962] 1 Lloyd's Rep 283; *Sokratis Rokopoulos v Esperia SpA, The Aros* [1978] 1 Lloyd's Rep 456; *Peter Cremer GmbH & Co v Sugat Food Industries Ltd, The Rimon* [1981] 2 Lloyd's Rep 640; *Overseas Fortune Shipping Pte Ltd v Great Eastern Shipping Co* [1987] 1 Lloyd's Rep 270 and the cases in note 14 on p. 353, ante.

distinction must be drawn between cases where the misconduct *could* not have had any effect on the result, and those where it is merely asserted that in fact it *did* not have any effect.

The former category comprises cases such as those where the arbitrator has received a letter from one party, but it is shown that he never read it or never comprehended it; or if he wrongly failed to give notice of a meeting, but nothing happened at the meeting; or where he wrongly admitted evidence on a particular issue in the absence of one party, but then decided the issue in favour of that party. In this type of case, the Court will not usually interfere, except perhaps in situations where the misconduct is so flagrant that the Court feels a need to uphold the principle, even though no actual injustice has ensued.

The Court is much less ready to accept an argument that although the misconduct might have affected the result, in fact it did not do so[11]. Except perhaps in cases where the evidence or argument wrongly received is trivial, the only way to demonstrate this fact is for the arbitrator to say so himself. The Courts have been understandably reluctant to act on such evidence; partly because the evidence might unconsciously be coloured by the desire of the arbitrator to see his award upheld, and partly because a person who complains of misconduct cannot lightly be deprived of his rights on the word of the person whose conduct is impugned.

Whenever an application is made to the Court to set aside or remit an award on grounds of misconduct, 'technical' or otherwise, the notice of motion should be served on the arbitrator or umpire concerned. He may then either (a) take an active part in the proceedings or (b) file an affidavit for the assistance of the court[12] or (c) take no action[13].

(b) Error on the face of the award

Section 1(1) of the 1979 Act abolished the Court's jurisdiction to set aside or remit an award on the grounds of errors of law or fact on the face of the award. The jurisdiction may still exist in relation to arbitrations to which the 1979 Act does not apply, but in view of the fact that this ground of interference is virtually obsolete, we omit any detailed discussion of it. Even before 1979, the jurisdiction was in practice rarely exercised or even invoked: arbitrators could, and did, shield their awards from attack by ensuring that the process of legal reasoning by which they had reached a decision was not referred to in the award but in a

---

[11] Generally speaking, where there has been a breach of natural justice, the Court does not speculate what would have been the result if the principles of fairness had been applied: *Interbulk Ltd v Aiden Shipping Ltd, The Vimeira* [1984] 2 Lloyd's Rep 66.

[12] Although the arbitrator may volunteer his reasons for his award or his conduct of the reference he cannot be compelled to do so, and the evidence is inadmissible on the question whether the award ought to be remitted or set aside: *Top Shop Estates Ltd v Danino* (1984) 273 Estates Gazette 197; *Duke of Buccleugh v Metropolitan Board of Works* (1872) LR 5 HL 418.

[13] *Port Sudan Cotton Co v Govindaswamy Chettiar & Sons* [1977] 1 Lloyd's Rep 166. If the allegation of misconduct fails, the arbitrator or umpire will be entitled to an order for costs if he appears, and (presumably) the costs of any affidavit filed by him. If the allegation succeeds, costs will not be awarded against the arbitration or umpire save in exceptional circumstances, e.g. fraud, or where the arbitrator or umpire has been the protagonist in the proceedings. In exceptional circumstances the court may allow the application to proceed although the arbitrator has not been served: *Bank Mellat v GAA Development and Construction Co* [1988] 2 Lloyd's Rep 44.

separate document issued to the parties on the express understanding that it was not to be referred to in proceedings to impeach the award.

(c) Excess of jurisdiction

An award will be entirely void if the parties never made a binding arbitration agreement; if the matters in dispute fell outside the scope of the agreement; if the arbitrator was not validly appointed, or lacked the necessary qualifications; or if the whole of the relief granted lay outside the powers of the arbitrator. The award will be partially void if the relief granted related to a matter which was not referred, or if for some other reason it was outside the jurisdiction of the arbitrator. In all these situations, the primary active remedy is for the Court to declare that the award is void, in whole or in part. Alternatively, the complaining party may wait until the time comes for enforcement of the award, and then rely on the want of jurisdiction as a defence.

It is, however, clearly established that the Court may, as an alternative to granting declaratory relief, set aside or remit the award. This is illogical. Want of jurisdiction makes an award void, not merely voidable; and the Court cannot set aside something which has no legal existence[14]. Nevertheless, there is no doubt that the jurisdiction has been asserted[15]. Whether the making of an award in excess of jurisdiction amounts of misconduct[16], or is a separate ground for relief, is not clear; the cases tend to suggest that the latter view is correct.

It is not always easy to distinguish between instances where there is a want of jurisdiction, and those where there is error of law or fact[17]. A particular difficulty arises where the contract prescribes the remedy which must be granted in the event of a breach. In such a case if the arbitrator, having found a breach, mistakenly proceeds to award a remedy other than the one prescribed by the contract, is this outside his jurisdiction, so as to render the award void, or is it simply a mistake of law which, like a mistake as to the primary rights and obligations under the contract, does not amount to an excess of jurisdiction? It seems that the latter is the correct view, and that there is no distinction to be drawn in this connection between a mistake as to primary rights and obligations

---

[14] *Prodexport State Co for Foreign Trade v ED and F Man Ltd* [1972] 2 Lloyd's Rep 375, per Mocatta J at 382. *Finzel, Berry & Co v Eastcheap Dried Fruit Co* [1962] 1 Lloyd's Rep 370 (at first instance); *Oil Products Trading Co Ltd v Société Anonyme Société de Gestion D'Entreprises Coloniales* (1934) 150 LT 475. See also *Anisminic Ltd v Foreign Compensation Commission* [1969] 2 AC 147; *May v Mills* (1914) 30 TLR 287.

[15] *Bowes v Fernie* (1838) 4 My & Cr 150; *Atkinson v Jones* (1843) 1 Dow & L 225; *Re Green & Co and Balfour, Williamson & Co* (1890) 63 LT 325; *L Freeman & Sons v National Benefit Assusrance Co* (1922) 13 Ll L Rep 270; *Fountain Manufacturing Co (Bury) Ltd v Fish & Co* (1921) 8 Ll L Rep 363; *Société Franco-Tunisienne d'Armement-Tunis v Government of Ceylon, The Massalia* [1959] 2 Lloyd's Rep 1; *Nilo Heime Akt v G Merel & Co Ltd* [1959] 2 Lloyd's Rep 292; *Graig Shipping Co Ltd v International Paint and Compositions Co Ltd* (1944) 77 Lloyd's Rep 220; *Howards (Colney) Ltd v George Aylwin & Son* [1958] 2 Lloyd's Rep 556; *Kawasaki Kisen Kaisha Ltd v Government of Ceylon* [1962] 1 Lloyd's Rep 424, where Devlin J evidently took it for granted that the choice of remedies was a matter of form alone; *Altco Ltd v Sutherland* [1971] 2 Lloyd's Rep 515. *Ayscough v Sheed Thomson & Co Ltd* (1924) 19 Ll L Rep 104.

[16] As McNair J indicated in *Kawasaki Kisen Kaisha Ltd v Government of Ceylon*, supra (a case where there was excess, not absence, of jurisdiction), there can scarcely be misconduct where there is no agreement to arbitrate, and no valid appointment; for the arbitrator has never conducted the arbitration at all.

[17] See pp. 558–561, post.

and a mistake as to the remedies prescribed by the contract[18]. If, however, he applies the correct remedy, but does so in an incorrect way – for example by miscalculating the damages which the submission empowers him to award – then there is no excess of jurisdiction[19]. An error, however gross, in the exercise of his powers does not take an arbitrator outside his jurisdiction and this is so whether his decision is on a matter of substance or procedure[20].

Where the award is made entirely without jurisdiction, in the sense that there has never been an effective arbitration at all, the appropriate remedy is to set the award aside. On the other hand, where there has been a valid arbitration, but the arbitrator has merely given relief which is outside his powers, the Court has a choice. Often, remission will be chosen, because it is cheaper to return to the same arbitrator than to begin the entire proceedings again. Where the award is defective only in part, and the good can be severed from the bad, the better course[1] is to set aside the defective part rather than remit[2]. Where severance is not possible, an order for remission should be made, with directions to the arbitrator to make a proper award[3].

When deciding whether there had been an excess of jurisdiction, the Court is not limited to the matters which appear on the face of the award. The scope of the disputes submitted to arbitration may be proved by extrinsic evidence[4]. Where the allegation is made that there was no authority to make an award, there is no presumption in favour of the validity of the award, and the person relying upon it must show that it is valid. Where the dispute is merely whether the arbitrator has acted in excess of an admitted jurisdiction, it is for the party asserting the invalidity to prove it[5]. The decision of the arbitrator as to the extent of his own jurisdiction has no binding effect[6].

---

[18] See *Bank Mellat v GAA Development and Construction Co* [1988] 2 Lloyd's Rep 44, 53–4, in which, however, the question of remedies appears to have been expressly referred to the arbitrator. In this connection, the cases of *Roth, Schmidt & Co v D Nagase & Co Ltd* (1920) 2 Ll L Rep 36, and *African and Eastern (Malaya) Ltd v White, Palmer & Co Ltd* (1930) 36 Ll L Rep 113 require careful study. They cannot, we suggest, be read as deciding that even if the contract in question had, on its true construction, excluded the remedy in question (rejection of defective goods), the arbitrators would have acted within their jurisdiction in awarding it. See also *Re Dare Valley Rly Co* (1868) LR 6 Eq 429, a case which would scarcely be decided in the same way today.

[19] See *James Laing, Son & Co (M/C) Ltd v Eastcheap Dried Fruit Co* [1961] 2 Lloyd's Rep 277.

[20] To allow such an error to entrain the remedies for excess of jurisdiction 'would be driving a juggernaut through the philosophy of the 1979 Act': per Steyn J in *K/S A/S Bill Biakh v Hyundai Corpn* [1988] 1 Lloyd's Rep 187 at 190.

[1] Because it is the cheaper course.

[2] See *The Massalia*, ante; *Nils Heime Akt v G Merel & Co*, ante; *Fountain Manufacturing Co (Bury) Ltd v Fish & Co*, ante; *Ronaasen & Son v Metsanomistajain Metsakeskus O/Y* (1931) 40 Ll L Rep 267. In *Howards (Colney) Ltd v George Aylwin & Son*, ante, the award was remitted for the arbitrator to delete the surplusage. Read literally, s. 23 does not permit a partial setting aside, unlike s. 22, which plainly contemplates a partial remission. If the power to set aside for want of jurisdiction arises at common law, and does not derive from s. 23, there is no problem. The point is not discussed in the cases.

[3] In *Nils Heime Akt v G Merel & Co*, supra, an unseverable award was set aside, but the possibility of remission does not appear to have been argued.

[4] *Christopher Brown Ltd v Genossenschaft Oesterreichischer etc* [1954] 1 QB 8 at 10. See also *Fountain v Fish*, ante; *James Laing, Son & Co v Eastcheap Dried Fruit Co* [1961] 1 Lloyd's Rep 142 (at first instance); *W J Alan & Co Ltd v El Nasr Export and Import Co* [1971] 1 Lloyd's Rep 401 at 411.

[5] *Falkingham v Victorian Rlys Comrs* [1900] AC 452 at 463; *Christopher Brown Ltd v Genossenschaft Oesterreichischer*, supra. See also *Kianta Osakeyhtio v Britain and Overseas Trading Co Ltd* [1954] 1 Lloyd's Rep 247.

[6] *Christopher Brown Ltd v Genossenschaft Oesterreichischcer*, ante; *Golodetz v Schrier* (1947) 80 Ll L Rep 647 at 650; *Luanda Exportadora SARL etc v Wahhe Tamari & Sons and Jaffa Trading Co* [1967] 2 Lloyd's Rep 353 at 365. See also *Anisminic Ltd v Foreign Compensation Commission* [1969] 2 AC 147.

(d) Patent defects in the award

The Court has jurisdiction to set aside or remit an award if it fails to comply with the requirements imposed by the submission or the common law, and if this failure is apparent on the face of the award. Under this heading may be grouped the following requirements –

1 The award must be cogent – i.e. it must contain a decision, and not merely a request or an expression of opinion.

2 The award must be complete[7], in that it contains an adjudication upon all the issues submitted to arbitration[8].

3 The award must be certain. It must be possible to ascertain from the award what decision the arbitrator has reached on the issues[9]; and where the award is in the form of a special case, it must be possible to ascertain the findings of the arbitrator on all the issues of fact relevant to the issues of law.

4 The award must be final. It must contain a decision by the arbitrator himself on all the matters to be decided, without any delegation to third parties.

5 Unless the submission otherwise provides, expressly or by implication, the award must be in a form which enables the Court to proceed to direct enforcement under section 26 of the Act.

These requirements are discussed in Chapter 26. We mention here only a few matters relevant to the choice of the remedy which the Court will employ if the requirements are not complied with.

In the first place, the Court nowadays adopts a benevolent approach to the construction of awards, particularly those of lay arbitrators. If a sympathetic reading entails that the award is not defective, it will be read in that sense even though the correct technical language is not used[10].

Moreover, the discretion to set aside or remit the award is discretionary. If the defect is trivial, the Court is entitled to disregard it altogether[11].

If the award contains a defect which is sufficiently substantial to require the intervention of the Court, the modern practice is to prefer remission to setting aside, if this is at all possible. An award which is uncertain will be remitted[12] so

---

[7] Strictly speaking, incompleteness is out of place in this list, since it often cannot be determined without extrinsic evidence.

[8] Unless the arbitrator has purported to exercise his statutory power to state an interim award. If the Court could save the award by construing it as an interim award, it would no doubt do so.

[9] As distinct from the process of reasoning leading to the decision: uncertainty of reasoning is not a ground for setting aside or remission: *Moran v Lloyds* [1983] 1 Lloyd's Rep 472.

[10] See pp. 569–570, post

[11] *Cia Argentina de Pesca v Eagle Oil and Shipping Co Ltd* (1939) 65 Ll L Rep 168 at 172. This use of the de minimis rule was important before 1854, when the Court had no choice but to set aside the award if it interfered at all. The need to employ the technique is now much less, since trivial defects can be corrected by remission or by the use of the slip rule (see pp. 405–407, *ante*). The older cases, in which the de minimis principle was strained to the utmost, should be approached with caution.

[12] *Oleificio Zucchi SpA v Northern Sales Ltd* [1965] 2 Lloyd's Rep 496 at 522; *Oakland Metal Co Ltd v D Benaim & Co Ltd* [1953] 2 Lloyd's Rep 192 at 202; *Arcos Ltd v London and Northern Trading Co Ltd* (1933) 45 Ll L Rep 297 (uncertain whether award intended to have a particular meaning; if it was there was error on the face; award remitted with instructions as to the law); *Margulies Bros Ltd v Dafnis Thomaides & Co (UK) Ltd* [1958] 1 Lloyd's Rep 250; *Cremer v Samanta and Samanta* [1968] 1 Lloyd's Rep 156. (The two last cited cases could equally be regarded as instances of lack of finality; *Montrose Canned Foods Ltd v Eric Wells (Merchants) Ltd* [1965] 1 Lloyd's Rep 597 (failure to quantify damages); *Sunbeam Shipping Co Ltd v President of India, The Atlantic Sunbeam* [1973] 1 Lloyd's Rep 482; *Mallozzi v Carapelli SpA* [1975] 1 Lloyd's Rep 229 (court uncertain whether finding of mixed fact and law based on correct principle of law.)

that the arbitrator can make it certain, unless it is so confused and incomprehensible as to suggest that the arbitrator is incapable of performing his function, and that the best course will be to start the entire reference again[13]. If the award fails to deal with all the issues[14], the matter will be remitted so that the arbitrator can fill the gaps[15]. If it is doubtful whether the arbitrator has in fact decided all the issues, extrinsic evidence will be admitted to resolve the doubt, including evidence from the arbitrator himself[16]. Alternatively, the Court can send the matter back to the arbitrator, for him either to clarify the award or to arrive at a decision, depending upon whether he had or had not already decided the apparently outstanding issues[17].

The example of remission to cure a patent defect which was formerly most commonly encountered in practice was that which occurred where a court hearing argument on a special case considered either that there were insufficient findings in the award, or that the findings were insufficiently clear[18], to enable it to decide the question of law set down for argument. In such a case, the Court had jurisdiction to remit the matter so that the arbitrator could supply the necessary additional findings[19].

The jurisdiction to remit for the purpose of eliciting findings to enable the Court to decide a question of law is in principle available where the question is brought before the Court under the 1979 Act. But in practice the Court looks to the express power conferred by section 1(5) of that Act as the source of the jurisdiction, rather than the more general provisions of the 1950 Act[20].

---

[13] See *West Export (Ch Abram) v Baird & Co Ltd* (1933) 46 Ll L Rep 132 (confusion and uncertainty equated with error on the face); *J Pattison & Co Ltd v Allied National Corpn Ltd* [1953] 1 Lloyd's Rep 520.

[14] They must have been live issues at the time of the reference. See *Kleinjan and Holst v Bremer Handelsgesellschaft mbH Hamburg* [1972] 2 Lloyd's Rep 11 where the Court refused to remit an award so that the arbitrator could deal with interest, when it was not proved that he had ever been asked to do so. See also *Rees v Waters* (1847) 16 M & W 263.

[15] *Re Arbitration between Becker Shillan & Co and Barry Bros* [1921] 1 KB 391 (costs); *Lambert and Krzysiak Ltd v British Commercial Overseas Co Ltd* (1923) 16 Ll L Rep 51; *Orion Compania Espanola de Seguros v Belfort Maatschappij Voor Algemene Verzekgringeen* [1962] 2 Lloyd's Rep 257 (possibility that umpire has not reached his own decision on an issue on which the arbitrators had agreed). Before the 1854 Act, the Court would have had no alternative but to set the award aside: *Re Tribe and Upperton* (1835) 3 Ad & El 295; *Samuel v Cooper* (1835) 2 Ad & El 752. The attitude of the courts was not as technical as it might appear. If a group of issues was submitted to arbitration, there might be injustice to one party if the arbitrator made an award against him on one issue whilst leaving the others undecided.

[16] *Obaseki Bros v Reif and Son Ltd* [1952] 2 Lloyd's Rep 364; *Poliakoff v Stromwall* (1921) 8 Ll L Rep 388 and 442 (matter sent back to arbitrator to state whether he had considered a particular issue). See also *Blackford & Sons (Calne) Ltd v Christchurch Corpn* [1962] 1 Lloyd's Rep 349 (interim award; extrinsic evidence to ascertain what issues were treated as preliminary).

[17] *Orion Compania Espanola de Seguros v Belfort Maats Chappij Voor Algemene Verzekgringeen*, ante.

[18] *Polemis v Furness, Withy & Co Ltd* (1921) 6 Ll L Rep 223; *Compania Primera de Navigacion Ltda v Compania Arrendataria del Monopolio de Petroleos SA* (1939) 65 Ll L Rep 7.

[19] The first edition of this work contained at pp. 500–502 an extended discussion of the jurisdiction, which we have omitted from the present edition in view of the fact that the abolition by the 1979 Act of the special case procedure has rendered the jurisdiction virtually obsolete.

[20] See pp. 596–600, post.

(e) Misunderstandings[21]

The Court has in recent years asserted a jurisdiction to remit awards in the interest of justice, even in the absence of misconduct by the arbitrator, where as the result of a misunderstanding one of the parties has failed to deploy his case in an effective manner[1]. The source of this jurisdiction is not clear[2], and the wisdom of the practice is not perhaps beyond controversy. It is always tempting for the Court to intervene in cases where it feels that the arbitrator has gone wrong, and that one of the parties has suffered an injustice. Yet the cases show that this temptation has consistently and stoutly been resisted[3]. The most obvious injustice a party can suffer is for an arbitrator to arrive at the wrong conclusions on fact or law. The courts have always been insistent that a mistake of this kind gives no reason for the Court to intervene, and it is strange that the position should be different where the mistake is that of the party himself. On any view, the jurisdiction will not be exercised if the misunderstanding arises from the failure by the party who seeks remission to use the information which was in his possession[4].

(f) Mistakes by the arbitrator

Mistakes by the arbitrator in the conclusions of law[5] or fact[6] implicit or explicit

---

21 The whole of this paragraph was cited with approval by Leggatt J in *Compagnie Nationale Algérienne de Navigation v Hecate Shipping Co* [1985] 2 Lloyd's Rep 588 at 591.

1 *Peter Cassidy Seed Co Ltd v Osuustukkukauppa IL* [1954] 2 Lloyd's Rep 586 (it does not appear from the report whether any authorities were cited); *Compagnie Financière pour le Commerce Extérieur SA v OY Vehna AB* [1963] 2 Lloyd's Rep 178; *Centrala Morska Importowo Eksportowa (known as Centromor) v Companhia Nacional de Navegacao SARL* [1975] 2 Lloyd's Rep 69; *The Aristides Xilas* [1975] 2 Lloyd's Rep 402; *Hill Court Shipping Co SA v Compagnie Continentale (France) SA v The Yperagia* [1977] 1 Lloyd's Rep 29; *Ismail v Polish Ocean Lines* [1977] 2 Lloyd's Rep 134; *Sokratis Rokopoulos v Esperia SpA, The Aros* [1978] 1 Lloyd's Rep 456. In *Fuga AG v Bunge AG* [1975] 2 Lloyd's Rep 192, the injustice was used as a ground for remitting an award where the arbitrators had mistakenly awarded the wrong amount. It is submitted that this was contrary to the rule that mistake is not in itself a ground for remission. The same result could, without violence to principle, have been reached by treating the case as one of admitted mistake: see p. 559, post. *F W Berk & Co Ltd v Knowles and Foster* [1962] 1 Lloyd's Rep 430 and *Bunge & Co Ltd v Ross T Smyth & Co Ltd* (1926) 24 Ll L Rep 30 may have been early examples of the jurisdiction, although the Court did not in fact remit. See also *Franz Haniel AG v Sabre Shipping Corpn* [1962] 1 Lloyd's Rep 531 at 538 and *Aktiebolaget Legis v V Berg & Sons Ltd* [1964] 1 Lloyd's Rep 203, where the existence of the power to remit in such cases was taken for granted. The jurisdiction will not be exercised unless the applicant can show that what went wrong either has caused him injustice, or at least may well have done so: *The Aros*, ante; *Mabanaft GmbH v Consentino Shipping Co SA, The Achillet* [1984] 2 Lloyd's Rep 191, 194; *Mafracht v Parnes Shipping Co SA, The Appolonius* [1986] 2 Lloyd's Rep 405 at 412; and see p. 552, note 10, ante.

2 See p. 550, ante.

3 See for example, *GKN Centrax Gears Ltd v Matbro Ltd* [1976] 2 Lloyd's Rep 555. The courts have, of course, referred on many occasions to the interests of justice when deciding how to exercise the jurisdiction to remit or set aside; but in such cases the requirements of justice control the exercise of the discretion, rather than create it.

4 See *Franz Haniel v Sabre*, ante; *Compagnie Nationale Algérienne de Navigation v Hecate Shipping Co* [1985] 2 Lloyd's Rep 588. Of course, the Court will intervene if one party deliberately deceives the other.

5 A mistake of law, or inconsistency of reasons, may in certain circumstances be the subject of an appeal, but applications under ss. 22 and 23 will not be permitted to circumvent the restrictions imposed by the 1979 Act on appeals on questions of law: *Moran v Lloyds* [1983] 1 Lloyd's Rep 472.

6 Procedural mistakes do, by contrast, found a remedy. Almost all instances of misconduct arise from honest but misguided attempts by the arbitrator to conduct the reference in the way he thinks best. The courts have never attempted to reconcile their repeated assertions that the decisions of the arbitrator are taken for better or for worse, with their assumption of the right to interfere where the arbitrator makes a wrong decision on a procedural matter.

in a final award or in an interlocutory ruling[7] do not in general form a ground for remission or setting aside[8]. To this general principle there are the following exceptions –

(i) In arbitrations to which the 1979 Act does not apply, error of law, apparent on the face of the award.

(ii) A mistake admitted by the arbitrator.

(iii) (Possibly) a deliberate ignoring or perversion of the applicable principles of law.

The first of these exceptions is now of limited practical importance and is not discussed in this work, for the reasons already mentioned.

As to the second, there seems no doubt that where the arbitrator admits a mistake and asks for an opportunity to correct it, the Court has jurisdiction to remit[9]. This jurisdiction is distinct from the power of the arbitrator to correct a 'clerical mistake or error arising from any accidental slip or omission', under section 17, without the intervention of the Court[10]. The limits of the jurisdiction are less clear. As a general rule[11] there must be a clear admission of the mistake by the arbitrator and it will carry more weight if the admission is made to the

---

[7] *K/S A/S Bill Biakh v Hyundai Corporation* [1988] 1 Lloyd's Rep 187.

[8] This principle is so well established that there would be no point in setting out all the authorities. Amongst these are the following: *Hagger v Baker* (1845) 14 M & W 9; *Hodgkinson v Fernie* (1857) 3 CBNS 189; *Phillips v Evans* (1843) 13 LJ Ex 80; *Hogge v Burgess* (1858) 3 H & N 293; *Dinn v Blake* (1875) LR 10 CP 388; *AG for Manitoba v Kelly* [1922] 1 AC 268 at 281; *Charles Weis & Co Ltd v Peters, Rushton & Co Ltd* (1922) 10 Ll L Rep 312 (a strong case, since Atkin LJ plainly thought that the arbitrators were wrong); *Gillespie Bros & Co v Thompson Bros & Co* (1922) 13 Ll L Rep 519; *Russian Oil Products Ltd v Caucasian Oil Co Ltd* (1928) 31 Ll L Rep 109; *Temple SS Co Ltd v VO Sovfracht* (1943) 76 Ll L Rep 35; *Nello Simoni v A/S M/S Straum* (1949) 83 Ll L Rep 157 at 161; *MacPherson Train & Co Ltd v J Milhem & Sons* [1955] 2 Lloyd's Rep 59; *RS Hartley Ltd v Provincial Insurance Co Ltd* [1957] 1 Lloyd's Rep 121; *Tersons Ltd v Stevenage Development Corpn* [1963] 2 Lloyd's Rep 333; *Oleificio Zucchi SpA v Northern Sales Ltd* [1965] 2 Lloyd's Rep 496; *Prodexport State Co for Foreign Trade v E D and F Man Ltd* [1972] 2 Lloyd's Rep 375 at 380–381; *Moran v Lloyd's*, supra; *Bulk Oil (Zug) AG v Sun International Ltd (No 2)* [1984] 1 Lloyd's Rep 531. The statement of principle in *Gabela v Vergottis & Co* (1926) 26 Ll L Rep 238 must be misreported, unless mistake was intended to connote admitted mistake.

[9] Cases of admitted mistake before the 1854 Act, such as *Re Hall and Hinds* (1841) 2 Man & G 847 and *Hutchinson v Shepperton* (1849) 13 QB 955 should be read with caution. It was precisely to avoid the serious consequences of an order to set aside that the statutory power to remit was introduced.

[10] See p. 405, ante. Recent decisions have tended to assimilate the jurisdiction to remit for admitted mistake to the cases in which the arbitrator has power to correct errors under s. 17. This has been done by extending the boundaries of the arbitrator's jurisdiction rather than by narrowing the boundaries of the court's jurisdiction, and there may still be cases in which the Court alone can enable a mistake to be put right. But in most cases the first resort should be to the arbitrator, leaving an application to remit to cases falling outside s. 17, or where the arbitrator's powers are in doubt: see *The Montan*, infra.

[11] In the previous edition it was stated that there was no doubt that an admission of the mistake by the arbitrator was essential. We express the rule in this edition in more guarded terms in deference to the dicta in *The Montan*, infra. But there are good reasons both on grounds of authority and convenience for stating the rule as an invariable one, as was decided by Webster J in *Atlantic Lines & Navigation Co Inc v Italmare SpA, The Apollon* [1985] 1 Lloyd's Rep 597.

Court on affidavit, rather than informally to one of the parties[12], and if the arbitrator also asks the Court for the opportunity to put the mistake right[13].

The cases give no clear guidance on the types of mistake which may found an application for remission. The power embraces clerical errors, in which the arbitrator means one thing but accidently writes something else. But it goes beyond this[14]. The arbitrator may correct his award so as to add something which he left out as the result of a mistake[15] – e.g. by adding an order for costs[16], or bringing into the calculation of the sum finally awarded a payment on account which he had forgotten[17]. Whether the arbitrator can also be given the opportunity to alter a decision which he has already made is less clear[18]. The exercise of the Court's discretion involves balancing the interests of justice against the need for finality in litigation, and particularly in arbitration. Justice requires that accidental errors and omissions should not be allowed to result in a miscarriage of justice. But finality requires that the award should not be remitted simply because the arbitrator has had second thoughts about the way in which he has exercised his judgment on issues of fact or law[19].

It sometimes happens that a party asserts, not only that the arbitrator's decision on the facts is wrong, but that it could not possibly be right, since there is no evidence to support it; or that the arbitrator has exercised a discretion in a way which is wholly wrong in principle[20]. Such an attack fails, for the same reasons as other challenges to the arbitrator's decision. To arrive at a wrong conclusion of fact or to exercise a discretion on a wrong principle is at most an error of law, and does not found an application for relief except by those

---

[12] *Mutual Shipping Corpn v Bayshore Shipping Co, The Montan* [1985] 1 Lloyd's Rep 189. The earlier cases illustrate the general principles governing the Court's discretion, rather than establishing hard and fast rules. They include *Phillips v Evans* (1843) 12 M & W 309; *Mills v Bowyers' Society* (1856) 3 K & J 66; *Flynn v Robertson* (1869) LR 4 CP 324; *Hogge v Burgess* (1858) 3 H & N 293; *Dinn v Blake* (1875) LR 10 CP 388. See also *Re Keighley, Maxsted & Co and Durant & Co* [1893] 1 QB 405; *Re Baxters and Midland Rly Co* (1906) 95 LT 20; *The Mello* (1948) 81 Ll L Rep 230; *Anglo-Saxon Petroleum Co Ltd v Adamastos Shipping Co Ltd* [1957] 1 Lloyd's Rep 79 at 91. *Re Whiteley and Roberts* [1891] 1 Ch 558 defies explanation.

[13] *Dinn v Blake*, supra; *Re Keighley, Maxsted & Co and Durant & Co*, supra. In *Anglo-Saxon Petroleum Co v Adamastos Shipping Co*, supra, Devlin J said that a request was always something to bear in mind when exercising the discretion.

[14] Several of the cases were decided after the 1889 Act introduced the 'slip rule'.

[15] It is possible that the cases on accidental omission are best treated as examples of awards which contain incomplete adjudications.

[16] *Re Baxters and Midland Rly Co*, ante; *Caswell v Groucutt* (1862) 31 LJ Ex 361. The power vested in the arbitrator by s. 18(4) of the 1950 Act, to amend his award so as to add an order for costs, does not depend on mistake.

[17] *Flynn v Robertson*, ante. The three judges gave differing explanations of the jurisdiction to remit.

[18] *Re Baxters and Midland Rly Co*, ante, suggests that there is no jurisdiction to alter the award, but this is not consistent with *The Mello*, ante, or with the observations of Devlin J in *Anglo-Saxon Petroleum Co Ltd v Adamastos Shipping Co Ltd*, ante.

[19] *Mutual Shipping Corpn v Bayshore Shipping Co, The Montan* [1985] 1 Lloyd's Rep 189. A case could be argued for allowing the arbitrator to give effect to second thoughts, at least if the application for remission were made promptly. But we believe this would be a mistake, because it would tend to expose the arbitrator to undesirable pressure from the disappointed party to persuade him to change his mind. Arbitrators who have to take difficult decisions should not be encouraged to think that the Court will give them a second chance. Still less should an arbitrator be allowed to feel that he can or should reopen the reference because the losing party has induced in him a sense of doubt about the correctness of his decision.

[20] *The Vasso* [1983] 2 Lloyd's Rep 346 at 350.

mechanisms which are available for appeals on questions of law[1]. For the same reasons, an award will not be remitted on the grounds that the arbitrator has arrived at a decision which can only be explained by assuming that he has made some mistake in his reasoning[2].

If a party suspects that the tribunal is about to make a finding against him for which there is no evidence, he should ask the tribunal to give a reasoned award raising the question for an appeal under the 1979 Act[3] whether there is any evidence to support the finding[4].

It is conceivable that where the state of the evidence is such as to show, not merely that no reasonable arbitrator would reach a particular conclusion of fact upon the basis of it, but also that there is no evidence at all to sustain the finding, the award can be attacked – either on the ground that the arbitrator has acted unjudicially[5], or on the ground that by deciding that contrary to the obvious facts he has taken the parties by surprise[6], and hence been guilty of misconduct.

(g) Fresh evidence

The Court has jurisdiction to order remission where the losing party has discovered, after the publication of the award, fresh evidence which might have affected the decision of the arbitrator if it had been adduced at the hearing[7]. Two conditions must be satisfied before there will be remission on the ground[8].

1 The evidence must be of weight. It must be such as would probably have a substantial effect, or an important influence on the result of the case having

---

[1] See particularly *Gillespie Bros & Co v Thompson Bros & Co* (1922) 13 Ll L Rep 519 at 524–525; per Atkin LJ *Tersons Ltd v Stevenage Development Corpn* [1963] 2 Lloyd's Rep 333 at 359, 360, per Willmer LJ. Also *Oleificio Zucchi SpA v Northern Sales Ltd* [1965] 2 Lloyd's Rep 496; *Nello Simoni v A/S M/S Straum* (1949) 83 Ll L Rep 157; *Pagnan and Fratelli v Corbisa Industrial Agropacuaria Ltda* [1970] 2 Lloyd's Rep 14; *GKN Centrax Gears Ltd v Matbro Ltd* [1976] 2 Lloyd's Rep 555; *Bulk Oil (Zug) AG v Sun International Ltd (No 2)*, supra.

[2] *Food Corpn of India v Marastro Cia Naviera SA, The Trade Fortitude* [1986] 2 Lloyd's Rep 209.

[3] There is nothing that he can do, when there is a valid agreement to exclude the right of appeal pursuant to s. 3 of the 1979 Act: except perhaps in a case where the arbitrator is deliberately distorting the effect of the evidence: see Chapter 37, post.

[4] But see p. 373, ante.

[5] Some support for such an argument can be found in *Temple SS Co Ltd v V/O Sovfracht* (1943) 76 Ll L Rep 35 at 36–37, per Scott LJ (but see the judgment of du Parcq LJ); *Evanghelinos v Leslie and Anderson* (1920) 4 Ll L Rep 17; *Jordeson & Co v Stora Kopparbergs Bergslags Aktiebolag* (1931) 41 Ll L Rep 201.

[6] See p. 558, ante.

[7] *Re Keighley, Maxsted & Co and Durant & Co* [1893] 1 QB 405; following *Re Burnand and Wainwright* (1850) 19 LJ QB 423 (a case under the remission clause, before the 1854 Act), *Sprague v Allen & Sons* (1899) 15 TLR 150, and the cases cited post. *EM Dower & Co v Corrie, MacColl & Son Ltd* (1925) 22 Ll L Rep 256; *NV Arnold Otto Meyer v Andre Aune* (1939) 64 Ll L Rep 121 (dispute as to date of shipment; the contract provided that the bill of lading was to be considered as proof of date of shipment in the absence of conclusive evidence to the contrary; application to remit so that the buyers could produce the ship's manifest, refused, as this would not be conclusive evidence).

[8] Most formulations of the test assume that these are conditions precedent to the exercise of the jurisdiction rather than factors affecting the exercise of the discretion. But presumably it is also relevant to the discretion whether the conditions are clearly made out, or have been satisfied only by a narrow margin.

regard inter alia, to its apparent credibility[9]. Where the arbitrator is not bound by the strict rules of evidence, it need not be evidence which would be admissible in Court[10]. A statement by the arbitrator that the evidence would have affected his mind is important, but not essential[11]. In considering whether this condition is satisfied, the Court will have regard to any other evidence, whether given at the hearing, or adduced at the application to remit, which is relevant to the cogency and credibility of the evidence on which the application is founded[12].

2 The evidence must not have been available to the party at the time of the hearing. This requirement is unfulfilled if the party – (a) had the evidence in his possession but failed to use it, (b) realised its existence but failed to take reasonable steps to obtain it (including an application for an adjournment, if necessary)[13], or (c) failed through lack of reasonable foresight to realise the actual or potential existence of the evidence[14].

Even if these two conditions are satisfied the Court still retains a discretion whether or not to order remission. English procedure attaches great importance to the principle that the proper moment to adduce evidence and argument is at the hearing and that once the hearing is concluded the tribunal should proceed to a final decision. Once an award is made the need for finality is the predominant consideration, which will only be overcome if the Court is satisfied that in the particular circumstances the need for an accurate decision should prevail over the need for a final decision, and that this can be allowed to take place without injustice[15].

If the award is remitted to the arbitrator to hear fresh evidence on one point, the arbitrator is under no duty nor entitled to hear fresh evidence at that stage on any other point[16].

4 Looking at confidential reasons

Unless asked to provide a speaking award an arbitrator will usually give his

---

[9] It is not easy to state with precision the test for deciding whether the evidence is sufficiently cogent to warrant remission. We have adopted the formulation approved by Hirst J in *Aiden Shipping Ltd v Interbulk Ltd, The Vimeira (No 2)* [1985] 2 Lloyd's Rep 377 at 400, after a review of all the earlier cases.

[10] *National Petroleum Co v Athelviscount (Owners)* (1934) 48 Ll L Rep 164 at 168.

[11] *Re Burnand and Wainwright*, supra; *Re Keighley, Maxsted & Co and Durant & Co*, supra. The later cases do not mention this requirement. It may be wise not to seek a statement from the arbitrator in case it should make him appear partial, and hence prevent remission to him: cf. *Fratelli Schiavo di Gennaro v Richard J Hall Ltd* [1953] 2 Lloyd's Rep 169. Even if such a statement is proffered, the Court is entitled to disregard it: *The Vimeira*, supra, at 407–9. In the last resort it is for the Court and not the arbitrator to assess whether the evidence is of sufficient weight to justify remission.

[12] *The Vimeira*, supra, at 409 and passim.

[13] As to (a) and (b) see *Shedden v Patrick* (1869) LR 1 Sc & Div 470, cited in *Compagnie Nationale Algérienne de Navigation v Hecate Shipping Co* [1985] 2 Lloyd's Rep 588, at 591.

[14] *Re Burnand and Wainwright*, ante; *Re Keighley, Maxsted & Co and Durant & Co*, ante; *J H Rayner & Co v Fred Drughorn Ltd* (1924) 18 Ll L Rep 269; *EM Dower & Co v Corrie, MacColl & Sons Ltd*, ante; *National Petroleum Co v Athelviscount (Owners)*, ante; *Ben Line Steamers Ltd v Compagnie Optorg of Saigon* (1936) 56 Ll L Rep 83; *Meyer v Aune*, ante; *Whitehall Shipping Co Ltd v Kompass Schiffahrtskontor GmbH, The Staninless Patriot* [1979] 1 Lloyd's Rep 589; *Nicoban Shipping Co v Alam Maritime Ltd, The Evdokia* [1980] 2 Lloyd's Rep 107; *The Vimeira*, supra.

[15] Thus, delay in making the application, and the likelihood of prejudice to the party who has an award in his favour, will both tell against the application: *The Vimeira*, supra.

[16] *Re Huntley* (1853) 1 E & B 787; *The Vimeira*, supra, at pp. 410–411.

reasons in a separate document from the award itself. Where this is done it is common practice, particularly in maritime arbitrations, for the arbitrator to stipulate that the reasons are not to be referred to in any proceedings in connection with the award. The main object of doing so is to prevent the reasons forming the basis of an appeal[17]. However, it was at one time widely assumed that such a stipulation was effective to prevent the Court from looking at the reasons on an application to set aside or remit the award. This assumption has now been held to be erroneous[18]. However wide the terms of the stipulation may be, they cannot oust the jurisdiction of the Court to remit or set aside an award where justice requires it to intervene[19]. Accordingly, the Court may look at such reasons despite the undertaking of confidentiality[20]. This is so whatever the grounds on which the Court's jurisdiction is invoked: it is not limited to cases of fraud or misconduct. But the Court retains a discretion whether or not to look at confidential reasons and in many cases will decline to do so[1].

5 Choice of setting aside or remission

In most cases, the Court will have a discretion whether to order the setting aside of the award or to remit some or all of the matters in issue. This discretion must be exercised with regard to all the circumstances of the case[2]. Where appropriate, the Court will admit evidence to help it in the choice of remedy[3]. As with all matters of discretion, complete consistency of decision cannot be expected, and indeed it is undesirable to attempt a close definition of the factors which influence the choice. The following comments may, however, be made.

Plainly, the nature of the arbitrator's default will be an important consideration. A serious error or miscarriage of justice will lead to setting-aside[4]. Conversely, where further findings are required[5], it will almost always be sensible to send a case back to the arbitrator who is already seized of the evidence; so also where the error is due to inadvertence[6].

Where the case lies between these extremes the courts will tend, if possible, to

---

[17] See pp. 596–600, post.
[18] *Mutual Shipping Corpn v Bayshore Shipping Co, The Montan* [1985] 1 Lloyd's Rep 189.
[19] This is clearly the basis of the Master of the Rolls' decision in *The Montan* at 192, less clearly that of Sir Roger Ormerod at 198: Robert Goff LJ expressed no opinion on the point.
[20] The precise theoretical basis for the undertaking is a matter of some debate: see *The Montan*, supra at 198, and at first instance: [1984] 1 Lloyd's Rep 389 at 392–393. Nevertheless there is no doubt that it is effective for other purposes, such as excluding examination of the reasons for the purpose of an appeal on a question of law.
[1] *The Montan*, supra, at 198. The Court will no doubt weigh the requirements of justice against the need for finality, and it will be relevant to consider whether the parties specifically asked for an award in this form or simply tacitly accepted an award in common form.
[2] *Odlum v Vancouver City* (1915) 85 LJ PC 95 at 98.
[3] *Kiril Mischeff Ltd v Constant, Smith & Co* (1950) 83 Ll L Rep 496, [1950] 2 KB 616 (evidence admitted to show whether error on the face, or omission of finding). *Arcos Ltd v London and Northern Trading Co Ltd* (1933) 45 Ll L Rep 297 appears to be another example.
[4] So ordinarily (although not always) did error on the face, see *Cassir, Moore & Co Ltd v Eastcheap Dried Fruit Co* [1962] 1 Lloyd's Rep 400 (delaying tactics).
[5] See the cases cited at p. 557, ante.
[6] *Royal Commission on Sugar Supply v Kwik-Hoo-Tong Trading Society* (1922) 11 Ll L Rep 163.

avoid the additional expense of setting aside[7], by remitting the award[8] if confident that the arbitrator can be relied upon to conduct the renewed reference in a fair manner[9]. But there will be no remission if a further hearing would be pointless, e.g. where the arbitrator is bound to find for the respondent or to decide that he has no jurisdiction to decide the matter[10], or where there is a risk that the arbitrator might show a disposition to favour one party[11].

Sometimes, where the award is bad in part, but the Court cannot remedy the defect by partial setting-aside, because the award is not severable, it will grant remission so that the arbitrator can make a further award, leaving out of account the objectionable part[12].

There are several reported instances where the Court has granted both remedies at once, in respect of the whole of the award: i.e. where it has ordered setting-aside of the award and the remission of the matters in issue[13]. This scarcely seems necessary, if we are right in the view that remission automatically annuls that part of the award which relates to the matters remitted[14]. One possible practical application may be to procure the re-hearing of the arbitration by a differently constituted tribunal[15]. In addition to this, the Court undoubtedly has power to set aside part of the award, and remit the remainder[16].

---

[7] There are cases where remission will not save money, and where the Court will accordingly be more ready to set aside: see *Eastcheap Dried Fruit Co v NV Gebroeders Catz Handelsvereeniging* [1962] 1 Lloyd's Rep 283.

[8] See, for example, *Kiril Mischeff Ltd v Constant, Smith & Co*, ante; *Lambert and Krzysiak Ltd v British Commercial Overseas Co Ltd* (1923) 16 Ll L Rep 51; *Orion Compania Espanola de Seguros v Belfort Maatschappij Voor Algemene Verzekgringeen* [1962] 2 Lloyd's Rep 257; *Mediterranean and Eastern Export Co Ltd v Fortress Fabrics (Manchester), Ltd* (1948) 81 Ll L Rep 401.

[9] See, for example, *FE Hookway & Co Ltd v Alfred Isaacs & Sons* [1954] 1 Lloyd's Rep 491; *Youroveta Home and Foreign Trade Co Inc v Coopman* (1920) 3 Ll L Rep 242; *Faure, Fairclough Ltd v Premier Oil and Cake Mills Ltd* [1968] 1 Lloyd's Rep 237. The test is not whether the party complaining of the arbitrator's conduct has lost confidence in him but whether that would be the reaction of a reasonable person: *Hagop Ardahalian v Unifert International SA, The Elissar* [1984] 2 Lloyd's Rep 84. See also p. 250, ante.

[10] *Altco Ltd v Sutherland* [1971] 2 Lloyd's Rep 515 (want of jurisdiction); *David Taylor & Son Ltd v Barnett* [1953] 1 Lloyd's Rep 181 (illegality).

[11] *E Rotheray & Sons Ltd v Carlo Bedarida & Co* [1961] 1 Lloyd's Rep 220; *Miller's Timber Trust Co Ltd v Plywood Factory Julius Potempa Ltd* (1939) 63 Lloyd's Rep 184; *Re Fischel & Co and Mann and Cook* [1919] 2 KB 431. The fact that the attitude of one party may have provoked the tribunal into showing a degree of irritation, or even hostility, is not in itself a sufficient ground for choosing to set aside rather than remit: see *F E Hookway & Co Ltd v Alfred Isaacs & Sons* [1954] 1 Lloyd's Rep 491 at 515.

[12] As in *Société Franco-Tunisienne d'Armement-Tunis v Government of Ceylon, The Massalia* [1959] 1 Lloyd's Rep 244 (at first instance).

[13] *Carey and Browne v Henderson and Liddell* (1920) 2 Ll L Rep 479. Examples include *Royal Commission on Sugar Supply v Kwik-Hoo-Tong Trading Society*, ante; *L Freeman & Sons v National Benefit Assurance Co* (1922) 13 Ll L Rep 270; *Arcos Ltd v London and Northern Trading Co Ltd* (1933) 45 Ll L Rep 297; *F E Hookway & Co Ltd v Alfred Isaacs & Sons* [1954] 1 Lloyd's Rep 491; *London Export Corpn Ltd v Jubilee Coffee Roasting Co Ltd* [1958] 1 Lloyd's Rep 197 (at first instance); *Lombard Australia Ltd v NRMA Insurance Ltd* [1969] 1 Lloyd's Rep 575.

[14] See p. 565, post. This proposition was apparently doubted by Greer J in *Mitrovitch Bros & Co v Hickson & Partners Ltd* (1923) 14 Ll L Rep 164, at any rate as regards remission for the purpose of altering the award. The judgment may not be accurately reported.

[15] As in *Henry Rooke, Sons & Co v Piper and May* (1927) 28 Ll L Rep 49; *London Export Corpn v Jubilee Coffee Roasting Co*, ante.

[16] *Nilo Heime Akt v G Merel & Co Ltd* [1959] 2 Lloyd's Rep 292; *The Massalia*, ante.

6 The effect of setting aside and remission

There are many reported cases in which the Court has ordered setting-aside or remission, but few in which the opportunity has been taken to explore the consequences of the remedy, once granted.

As regards setting-aside, it is clear that the effect of an order is to deprive the award of all legal effect, so that the position is the same as if the award had never been made[17]. It is much less clear what happens to the arbitration after the award has been set aside. Logically, the consequence should be that the arbitration reverts to the position in which it stood immediately before the arbitrator published his award; i.e. that he is not yet functus officio and remains seized of the reference. We have not been able to find any reported cases in which this result (which has the same practical effect as remission) has been contemplated, and it would be entirely inconsistent with the assumption in the more recent cases that setting-aside should in the main be reserved for instances where the conduct of the arbitrator has made it undesirable to entrust him with the further conduct of the reference[18].

Another possible view is that the setting-aside of the award frustrates the entire arbitral process, and that the dispute falls back on the inherent jurisdiction of the Court[19]. This proposition is not theoretically sound[20]. No doubt the same dispute cannot be arbitrated twice, so that the arbitral process is spent once the arbitral has become functus officio. This does not, however, touch the question of setting-aside, which entails the arbitrators have never validly completed the reference. If the parties have agreed to submit their dispute to arbitration, and no effective award has yet ensued, the arbitration agreement remains in force.

It appears that so far as the courts have given any consideration to the consequences of setting aside, they have assumed that the Order not only annuls the award, but also desseizes the arbitrator of the reference, so that the whole of the arbitral process has to be recommenced[1]. The dispute is, however, still susceptible of arbitration, albeit with a freshly constituted tribunal[2]. Logically,

---

[17] Presumably the avoidance is retrospective, so that (say) an order for summary enforcement would fall with the award.

[18] In *Stockport Metropolitan Borough Council v O'Reilly* [1983] 2 Lloyd's Rep 70 at p. 80, Neill J assumed that the arbitrator could not resume his jurisdiction over the matters dealt with in the award after it was set aside unless the court remitted them to him for his reconsideration under s. 22.

[19] *Kemp v Rose* (1858) 1 Giff 258 might be cited as authority for this view. Also the perplexing case of *J Pattison & Co Ltd v Allied National Corpn Ltd* [1953] 1 Lloyd's Rep 520. The parties are, of course, at liberty to agree that the action shall proceed in Court, as they did in *E Rotheray & Sons v Carlo Bedarida & Co*, ante.

[20] Nor would it work in practice, particularly in cases where the submission is in the *Scott v Avery* form, as in *Czarnikow v Roth, Schmidt & Co* [1922] 2 KB 478.

[1] This is implicit in the cases where the awards of appellate tribunals have been set aside. The courts have assumed that the order revives the award of the original arbitrator, so that the matter is open for a further appeal. See *Hookway v Isaacs*, ante; *Henry Rooke, Sons & Co v Piper and May* (1927) 28 Ll L Rep 49; *London Export Corpn v Jubilee Coffee Roasting Co*, ante. It does not appear to have been argued that the original award ceased to have its effect as soon as the appeal award was published, so that when the latter was set aside, there was no award left in existence. See also *Eastcheap Dried Fruit Co v NV Gebroeders Catz Handelsvereeniging* [1962] 1 Lloyd's Rep 283; *Orion Compania Espanola de Seguros v Belfort Maatschappij voor Algemene Verzekgringeen* [1962] 2 Lloyd's Rep 257; *Czarnikow v Roth, Schmidt & Co*, ante.

[2] This must be the result which the courts have intended to produce. The mechanisms are not clear. The setting-aside of the award does not automatically result in the removal of the arbitrator: contrast sub-ss. (1) and (2) of s. 23. The point is of no real practical importance. If the Court decides to order setting-aside because it considers that the dispute can be more satisfactorily

the new tribunal should be chosen by the mechanisms which led to the choice of the former arbitrators. A new umpire should be chosen by the arbitrators. A new sole arbitrator should be chosen by agreement between the parties, or by the Court under section 10(a). A new appeal tribunal should be chosen from the appeal panel of the trade association: and so on[3].

Where the award is severable, and part is set aside, the valid part remains as an effective adjudication. The remainder disappears[4].

The courts have worked out the effect of a remission rather more fully[5]. It appears that where the order embraces all the matters referred, the arbitrator resumes all his authority over the dispute, and the original award completely falls away. When the remission applies to only some of the matters referred[6], the arbitrator no longer has power to vary his award in respect of those matters which the Court has left untouched[7]. He must, as a matter of form, make a fresh award covering the whole of the matters originally submitted to him; but as regards those not remitted he must simply repeat his original decision. Until this new award is published, there is no binding adjudication on any of the matters referred[8]: so that, apparently, the successful party could not proceed to enforcement even on the parts of the original award which were irreproachable[9].

---

decided by a different arbitrator, an order for removal or revocation of authority (with appropriate penalties as to costs) would be granted as of course, if asked for, together with an order, if necessary, under s. 34(5) of the Limitation Act 1980 extending the time for commencing proceedings before the new tribunal. If, on the other hand, the Court decides to order setting-aside in order to enable the dispute to be decided by the Court, it will in addition make an order under s. 25(2)(b) revoking the arbitration agreement, and, if necessary, under s. 34(5) of the Limitation Act 1980 so as to extend the time for commencing proceedings before the court: *Stockport Municipal Borough Council v O'Reilly*, ante.

3 In *Fratelli Schiavo di Gennaro v Richard J Hall Ltd* [1953] 2 Lloyd's Rep 169, the Court appears to have assumed a jurisdiction to appoint the new umpire itself, as part of the order to set aside. This can scarcely be right, unless this step was taken by consent.

4 See per Wright J in *Lloyd del Pacificio v Board of Trade* (1930) 37 Ll L Rep 103 at 110. It is not clear what happens to the severed part of the dispute, in cases where the award is bad for reasons other than excess of jurisdiction. Presumably it cannot be left unresolved; yet it will often be inconvenient to arbitrate a small part of the dispute once again from scratch. Unless the misconduct is gross, it will be better to remit, rather than set aside in part.

5 If not in a manner which satisfies all the problems. When the text of the UNCITRAL Model Law was under consideration the United Kingdom delegation pressed (successfully in the result) for the inclusion in Article 34 of a provision establishing a procedure short of setting aside, akin to the English remedy of remission. Members of other delegations, although willing enough to recognise the practical utility of such a remedy, were perplexed to know how an arbitral tribunal, once *functus officio* would ever resume its powers and duties, otherwise than with the consent of the parties.

6 Partial remission is authorised by the words 'or any of them' in s. 22(1). There are numerous reported examples. Where partial remission is not possible, the Court may nevertheless make it a condition that the party applying for remission shall pay to the other party so much of the sum awarded as cannot be affected by the remission: *Congimex SARL (Lisbon) v Continental Grain Export Corpn (New York)* [1979] 2 Lloyd's Rep 346 at 356–357.

7 *The Vimeira*, ante, at 410. Disputes as to the scope of the remission are decided on application to the court which ordered it: ibid.

8 *Johnson v Latham* (1851) 20 LJQB 236; *Re Stringer and Riley Bros* [1901] 1 KB 105.

9 See, however, *Shield Properties & Investments Ltd v Anglo Overseas Transport Co Ltd* (1986) 279 Estates Gazette 1088, in which it was suggested that the award is binding unless and until it is superseded by a new award on remission, but that in the meantime the Court might refuse to enforce it. (The reference to an injunction is presumably to be read as meaning a stay of the proceedings to enforce the award). If this view is correct it ought to be possible to enforce parts of the original award which were (a) severable and (b) not the subject of the order for remission.

Section 22(1) of the Act empowers the Court to remit the 'matters referred or any of them' to the reconsideration of the arbitrator: so that it is the issues, not the award itself, which form the subject of the remission. Yet the wording of section 22(2) contemplates that an award may be remitted[10]. The terminology has been the subject of occasional comment by the Court[11], but no practical significance has ever been attached to it. The language of sub-section (1) is probably the more accurate. When remission is ordered, the award disappears, and the arbitrator is empowered to reconsider the matters in issue.

The Court has several times ordered remission to different arbitrators from those who made the original award. Whether in strict law it has power to do so is questionable. The words 'remit' and 'reconsideration' imply the sending back of the matters in issue: not dispatching them to someone who has never previously considered them[12].

Where an award is remitted, the arbitrator or umpire must make his award within three months from the date of the order, unless the order otherwise directs[13]. An order for remission may be made on terms that the party challenging the award shall give security for costs[14].

Where an award made by a majority of two out of three arbitrators is remitted, it seems that it should be remitted to the whole panel of three and not just to the two who have agreed[15].

7 Procedure for setting aside and remission

An application to remit an award under section 22 or to set aside an award under section 23(2) of the 1950 Act must be made by originating motion to a single judge in Court[16]. In the case of arbitrations under the 1979 Act, the motion is heard by a Commercial judge unless any such judge otherwise directs[17].

The time within which the application must be launched and the steps necessary to comply with the time limit depend on whether the arbitration was or was not conducted under the provisions of the 1979 Act[18] –

1 If the arbitration was conducted under the 1979 Act, the application must be made[19] and the notice of motion served within 21 days after the award has been made and published to the parties[20].

---

10 This apparent inconsistency dates from the 1889 Act.
11 For example, in *Millers Timber Trust v Potempka*, ante, at 188.
12 See *Richard Clear & Co Ltd v Bloch* (1922) 13 Ll L Rep 462; *Re Fuerst Bros & Co Ltd and RS Stephenson* [1951] 1 Lloyd's Rep 429; *Peterson v Ayre* (1854) 14 CB 665. The 1889 Act omitted the word 'said' from the expression 'the reconsideration . . . of the said arbitrator' in the 1854 Act. Under 'Mr Richards' clause' (see p. 438, ante) the consensual power to remit could plainly only refer to the original arbitrator.
13 S. 22(2) of the 1950 Act.
14 *Hill Court Shipping Co SA v Compagnie Continentale (France) SA, The Yperagia* [1977] 1 Lloyd's Rep 29.
15 *Richard Clear & Co Ltd v Bloch* (1922) 13 Ll L Rep 462.
16 Ord. 73, r. 2.
17 Ord. 73, r. 6(1). But this does not prevent the powers of a Commercial judge being exercised by any judge of the High Court, as was done in *Pratt v Swanmore Builders Ltd and Baker* [1980] 2 Lloyd's Rep 504.
18 See Ord. 73, r. 5(1) and the note thereto at pp. 721–722, post.
19 Making the application involves no more than procuring the issue of the notice of motion in the Central Office: *Fox v PG Wellfair Ltd* [1981] 2 Lloyd's Rep 514 at 516. The motion need not be *heard* within the time limited for making the application. See also *Re Gallop and Central Queensland Meat Export Co* (1890) 25 QBD 230.
20 'Publication' in this context takes place when the parties have notice that the award has been made and is available to the parties, whether or not they have notice of its contents: *Bulk Transport Corpn v Sissy SS Co Ltd, The Archipelagos* [1979] 2 Lloyd's Rep 289.

2 If the arbitration was not conducted under the 1979 Act, it is sufficient if the application is made[1] within six weeks after the award has been made and published to the parties[20]. The notice of motion need not be served within that period.

In either case the applicant must serve together with the notice of motion a copy of every affidavit intended to be used in support of the application, and the notice of motion must state the grounds on which the application is made[2].

The Court has a general discretion to extend the period within which the application must be made and the notice of motion served. In exercising this discretion the Court will have regard to the following factors[3] –

1 The desirability of adhering to time limits prescribed by Rules of Court.

2 The likelihood of prejudice to the party opposing the application if the time is extended.

3 The length of the delay by the applicant.

4 Whether the applicant has been guilty of unreasonable or culpable delay.

5 Whether the applicant has a good arguable case on the merits.

This list is probably not exhaustive, and does not lay down a rigid test: the final criterion is whether the interests of justice require that the time should be enlarged, and the weight to be given to each factor will depend on the circumstances of the case[4].

An order made on an application to set aside or remit an award otherwise than an order made under section 1(2) of the 1979 Act is interlocutory for the purposes of an appeal to the Court of Appeal[5].

8 Declaration of invalidity of award

A party who wishes to take active steps to impeach an award on the grounds that it is a nullity, may, as an alternative to applying to set aside the award, commence proceedings for a declaration that the award is invalid[6].

This remedy will generally be invoked when the objection to the award is that the arbitrator had no jurisdiction to make it. But it may also be used to attack an award which does not satisfy the requirements of a valid award laid down by the common law or by the arbitration agreement[7]. It may also be a useful medium for bringing before the Court the question whether the arbitrator

---

[1] See note 19, ante, p. 567.
[2] Ord. 73, r. 5.
[3] See *Sokratis Rokopoulos v Esperia SpA, The Aros* [1978] 1 Lloyd's Rep 456; *The Archipelagos*, ante; *Ismail v Polish Ocean Lines* [1977] 2 Lloyd's Rep 134; *Compania Maritima Zorroza SA v Maritime Bulk Carriers Corpn, The Marques de Bolarque* [1980] 2 Lloyd's Rep 186; *Industria de Oleos Pacaembu SA v NV Bunge* [1982] 1 Lloyd's Rep 490.
[4] *Citland Ltd v Kanchan Oil Industries PVT Ltd* [1980] 2 Lloyd's Rep 274.
[5] *Moran v Lloyd's* [1983] 1 Lloyd's Rep 472. The position is now regulated by RSC Ord. 59, r. 1A(7) (b)(ii).
[6] *Oil Products Trading Co Ltd v Société Anonyme Société de Gestion d'Entreprises Coloniales* (1934) 150 LT 475; *Luanda Exportadora SARL v Wahbe Tamari & Sons Ltd* [1967] 2 Lloyd's Rep 353; *Oakland Metal Co Ltd v D Benaim & Co Ltd* [1953] 2 Lloyd's Rep 192, [1953] 2 QB 261; *Jungheim, Hopkins & Co v Foukelmann* [1909] 2 KB 948; *Rahcassi Shipping Co SA v Blue Star Line Ltd, The Bede* [1967] 2 Lloyd's Rep 261, [1969] 1 QB 173; *Burkett Sharp & Co v Eastcheap Dried Fruit Co and Perera* [1962] 1 Lloyd's Rep 267.
[7] See pp. 382–388, ante.

has in fact adjudicated upon a particular dispute and, if so, what is the meaning and effect of his award[8].

Proceedings for a declaration may be begun by a writ or by originating summons or, where the grounds for the declaration are that the award was made without jurisdiction[9], by originating motion to a single judge in Court.

An action for a declaration can be begun any time within six years from the date of the award. For this reason it might be thought to be a means of rescuing a party from the consequences of having failed to apply for the award to be set aside within the time laid down by the rules of court[10]. But we submit that this is only the case where the grounds of the application are that the award is void. If the grounds are merely that the award is voidable[11], e.g. for misconduct, the award is good until set aside or remitted by the Court: if it is too late for this to be done, an action for a declaration that the award is a nullity or liable to be set aside or remitted, will fail.

9 Injunction to restrain enforcement of award

An injunction cannot be granted to restrain proceedings brought in England to enforce an award[12]. A party who wishes to prevent an award being enforced in such proceedings must do so by way of defence, supported where appropriate by an application to set aside or remit the award or a counterclaim for a declaration that the award is invalid, or by applying for a stay of execution pending the determination of a cross-claim.

However, an injunction may be granted where the claimant is attempting to enforce an award by other means, e.g. in proceedings outside England or by 'posting' the losing party as a defaulter[13]. But even in such cases the Court is unlikely to grant either a final or an interim injunction unless substantive proceedings are on foot to attack the validity of the award. Moreover it is unlikely to restrain foreign enforcement proceedings by injunction unless the claimant is within the jurisdiction and, in a case falling within the New York Convention[14], has exhausted his local remedies for impeaching the award.

C. THE BENEVOLENT INTERPRETATION OF AWARDS

Just as the courts have shown themselves increasingly willing to accommodate procedural discrepancies when there is no resulting injustice[15], so also have they

---

[8] As in *Aktiebolaget Legis v V Berg & Sons Ltd* [1964] 1 Lloyd's Rep 203.

[9] But not otherwise: see Ord. 73, r. 2(3). The object of this rule is to enable a claim for a declaration to be made in the same proceedings as an application to remit or set aside the award. But the judge may refuse to make a declaration in proceedings begun by motion, e.g. if the validity of the award cannot be investigated without pleadings or discovery.

[10] See p. 567, ante.

[11] See pp. 456–457, ante for the distinction between void and voidable awards.

[12] This has been the case since 1873: see now s. 49 of the Supreme Court Act 1981.

[13] *Burkett Sharp & Co v Eastcheap Dried Fruit Co and Perera* [1962] 1 Lloyd's Rep 267 is authority for the existence of the power to grant an injunction, but it is not clear why it was applied for or granted in that case.

[14] To which the United Kingdom has given effect by the 1975 Act.

[15] See pp. 279–280, ante.

adopted a more benevolent attitude to the interpretation of arbitral awards and particularly to those made by commercial men[16].

Thus, an award will be construed liberally and in accordance with the dictates of commonsense, and as far as possible in accordance with the real intention of the arbitrator[17]. The Court will not go out of its way to find uncertainty or error in the award merely because the arbitrator has not expressed his conclusions in the correct legal language[18]. Furthermore, not only will the Court not be astute to look for defects, but in case of uncertainty it will so far as possible construe the award in such a way as to make it valid rather than invalid. Thus, if it is alleged that an award is subject to error on the face, but the award contains insufficient facts to enable the Court to tell whether the arbitrator's conclusion of law was justified or not, it will assume that any justifying facts which could exist did exist, even though the arbitrator has not found them[19]. This process cannot, however, be carried too far. The Court is not concerned with fanciful hypotheses in order to support awards. It must have regard to probabilities, and not to flights of fancy[20].

---

[16] 'As a matter of general approach, the courts strive to uphold arbitration awards. They do not approach them with a meticulous legal eye endeavouring to pick holes, inconsistencies and faults in awards and with the objective of upsetting or frustrating the process of arbitration. Far from it. The approach is to read an arbitration award in a reasonable and commercial way, expecting, as is usually the case, that there will be no substantial fault that can be found with it': per Bingham J in *Zermalt Holdings SA v Nu-Life Upholstery Repair Ltd* (1985) 275 Estates Gazette 1134.

[17] *Larrinaga & Co v Société Franco-Americaine des Phosphates de Medulla Paris* (1922) 10 Ll L Rep 254 at 262, quoting Russell.

[18] *Aktiebolaget Legis v V Berg & Sons Ltd* [1964] 1 Lloyd's Rep 203 at 214; *Luanda Exportadora SARL v Wahbe Tamari & Sons Ltd* [1967] 2 Lloyd's Rep 353 at 357; *Cia Argentina de Pesca v Eagle Oil and Shipping Co Ltd* (1939) 65 Ll L Rep 168; *Panchaud Frères SA v Etablissements General Grain Co* [1969] 2 Lloyd's Rep 109; *Oakland Metal Co Ltd v D Benaim & Co Ltd* [1953] 2 Lloyd's Rep 192, [1953] 2 QB 261; *Selby v Whitbread & Co* [1917] 1 KB 736 at 744. The principle is sometimes expressed by saying that the Court should not examine awards with a fine toothcomb (or, perhaps, a fine-toothed comb).

[19] *Christopher Brown Ltd v Genossenschaft Oesterreichischer etc* [1954] 1 QB 8, [1953] 2 Lloyd's Rep 373; *James Clark (Brush Materials) Ltd v Carters (Merchants) Ltd* [1944] 1 KB 566; *Andrea v British Italian Trading Co Ltd* [1962] 1 Lloyd's Rep 151 at 161; *Aktiebolaget Legis v V Berg & Sons*, supra; *British Dyewood Co Ltd v Fuerst Bros & Co Ltd* (1933) 46 Ll L Rep 249; *Stockport Metropolitan Borough Council v O'Reilly* [1978] 1 Lloyd's Rep 595. See also *Kiril Mischeff Ltd v Constant, Smith & Co* (1950) 83 Ll L Rep 496, [1950] 2 KB 616, where Devlin J remitted an award, apparently bad on its face, so that the arbitrator could consider whether to make a finding which would save it; *Howards (Colney) Ltd v George Aylwin & Son* [1958] 2 Lloyd's Rep 556, where Diplock J ignored an erroneous and unnecessary direction in the award, in order to save remission. In *Agro-Export Entreprise d'Etat pour le Commerce Extérieur v NV Goorden Import Cy SA* [1956] 1 Lloyd's Rep 319, the contract contained a time limit, with a discretion in the tribunal to extend the time in special circumstances. The Court proceeded on the assumption that the special circumstances had been found to exist, even though this was not specifically stated in the award.

[20] *Gunter Henck v André & Cie SA* [1970] 1 Lloyd's Rep 235 at 239, per Mocatta J. See also *Ross T Smyth & Co Ltd v WN Lindsay Ltd* [1953] 2 Lloyd's Rep 378.

CHAPTER 34

Questions of jurisdiction

Where an issue is raised in the course of the reference as to the jurisdiction of the arbitrator to conduct the arbitration at all, the problem may be tackled in a number of ways, none wholly convenient. The following alternatives are open –

A. In a clear case, the party who alleges the excess of jurisdiction may seek to restrain the proceedings by an injunction.

B. The party may start an action in the High Court for a declaration that the arbitrator does not possess the jurisdiction which is being asserted.

C. In certain circumstances, the arbitrator may, of his own motion or at the initiative of a party, invite the High Court to decide whether he possesses the disputed jurisdiction.

D. The arbitrator can, and should, conduct his own enquiries into the extent of his jurisdiction, although such enquiries will not as a rule have any binding force.

E. The complaining party can make his objection known, and then bide his time until the award has been made, afterwards either attacking the award by a declaratory action or a motion to set aside the award, or by resisting enforcement of the award on the basis that there was an excess of jurisdiction.

A. INJUNCTION TO RESTRAIN ARBITRATION

If the complaining party is very sure of his ground he can apply to the High Court for an injunction restraining his opponent from proceeding with the arbitration. The existence and limits of the jurisdiction to grant such an injunction are not yet entirely clear[1]. The current position is probably as follows –

1 The Court has jurisdiction[2] to restrain the parties and the arbitrator from proceeding with the reference.

---

[1] *North London Rly Co v Great Northern Rly Co* (1883) 11 QBD 30; *Den of Airlie SS Co Ltd v Mitsui & Co Ltd and British Oil and Cake Mills Ltd* (1912) 17 Com Cas 116; *Government of Gibraltar v Kenny* [1956] 2 QB 410; *Compagnie Nouvelle France Navigation SA v Compagnie Navale Afrique du Nord, The Oranie and the Tunisie* [1966] 1 Lloyd's Rep 477; *Beddow v Beddow* (1878) 9 Ch D 89; *Wood v Lillies* (1892) 61 LJ Ch 158; *Farrar v Cooper* (1890) 44 Ch D 323; *Sissons v Oates* (1894) 10 TLR 392; *Kitts v Moore* [1895] 1 QB 253; *Smith, Coney and Barrett v Becker, Gray & Co* [1916] 2 Ch 86; *Malmesbury Rly Co v Budd* (1876) 2 Ch D 113; *Jackson v Barry Rly Co* [1893] 1 Ch 238; *McHarg v Universal Stock Exchange Ltd* [1895] 2 QB 81. See also pp. 518–523, ante.

[2] The existence of the jurisdiction is scarcely open to doubt. Yet its theoretical basis is uncertain. It is well established that an injunction will only be granted in aid of some legal or equitable right. But what right is infringed by the institution or maintenance of an arbitration which can only result in an award which is a nullity? It has been said that to invite an arbitrator to exceed his powers is a breach of the arbitration agreement, or an attempt to induce the arbitrator to break the agreement: *Cie Européenne de Céréales SA v Tradax Export SA* [1986] 2 Lloyd's Rep 301. But in the case where there is no arbitration agreement at all, a different basis for the injunction must be found. Perhaps the solution lies in resort to the Court's inherent power to restrain the usurpation of its own jurisdiction by other purported tribunals.

2 An injunction will not as a rule be granted unless there are clear grounds for holding that the submission to arbitration is invalid, or is open to attack on the basis of fraud or some other equitable ground[3].

3 Even in such cases, an injunction is unlikely to be granted unless proceedings are in existence in the High Court or abroad, or are about to be launched in which the jurisdiction of the arbitrator is challenged[4].

4 The later the stage of the reference at which the injunction is sought, the less likely it is that relief will be granted.

In practice, we doubt whether a final injunction will ever be an appropriate remedy. Moreover, although on occasions an interlocutory injunction may be useful[5], a situation should never be allowed to arise in which it is necessary to press for relief. If the party tells the arbitrator that he is about to apply for declaratory relief, the arbitrator should suspend the reference until the Court has arrived at a decision[6]. If he feels that this will involves undue delay, there is no reason why he should not say so, in which case the Court will no doubt take his remarks into account when fixing a date for the hearing of the declaratory action.

B. DECLARATORY RELIEF

Although it is always open to a party to wait until after the award before taking any steps to challenge the jurisdiction, there may be practical reasons why he would prefer to get the matter cleared up at an early stage of the reference. For example, he may be oppressed by the difficulties of keeping open his objection whilst still playing a part in the hearing[7]. Moreover, he may not wish to have an award made against him, even with the possibility of having it subsequently declared bad; either because this would give an unscrupulous opponent the chance to obtain enforcement abroad, or because even the temporary existence of an award could be damaging to his commercial standing and credit.

In such circumstances, the appropriate course is for the complaining party to issue a writ or originating summons, claiming a declaration that the arbitrator has no jurisdiction or power to act in the way proposed[8]. There is no doubt that

---

[3] In *Sissons v Oates*, supra, an injunction was granted where the claimant had no arguable claim, and there was hence no real dispute to submit to arbitration. See also *Allied Marine Transport Ltd v Vale do Rio Doce Navegaçao SA* [1983] 2 Lloyd's Rep 411, and *Compagnie Européenne de Céréales SA v Tradax Export SA*, supra.

[4] Even this may not lead to the grant of an injunction if the balance of convenience is in favour of allowing the arbitration to proceed: *Industrie Chimiche Italia Centrale v Alexander G Tsavliris & Son Maritime Co, The Choko Star* [1987] 1 Lloyd's Rep 508 (no injunction to restrain Lloyd's salvage arbitration although cargo-owners had commenced action in which they claimed they were not bound by the master's signature of Lloyd's open form).

[5] Eg, if the complaining party has started proceedings for a declaration that the arbitrator is acting in excess of jurisdiction, but fears that in the meantime his opponent will obtain an award, and enforce it against assets abroad: *Compagnie Européenne de Céréales SA v Tradax Export SA*, supra.

[6] Otherwise the parties will spend money on proceedings which may prove to be nugatory.

[7] See p. 577, post.

[8] There may be circumstances where the claimant, rather than the respondent, would wish to ask for a declaration as to jurisdiction, for example, if the respondent had indicated an objection to the jurisdiction which he was unwilling to put to the test until after the award.

the Court has jurisdiction to grant such a declaration[9]. But the relief is discretionary, and will not be granted automatically[10]. The Court will take into account, when deciding to allow the claim to proceed to trial –

1 The stage which the arbitration has reached when the objection is taken.

2 The time during which the arbitration will remain at a standstill whilst the question of jurisdiction is decided.

3 The degree to which, if the objection is upheld, it will dispose of the reference, and the amount of time and costs which will thereby be saved.

4 The degree to which it will be necessary to investigate facts – and in particular, facts which are in issue in the arbitration itself – in order to decide the question of jurisdiction.

5 The extent to which the respondent runs the risk of hardship if the question of jurisdiction is postponed until after the award is made.

Thus if a short question of construction will decide whether the agreement ever existed at all, or if the arbitrator was ever validly appointed, the Court will be likely to entertain the claim; the more so, if the arbitration promises to be long and expensive. But if the answer to the question of jurisdiction will delay the reference, without substantially shortening the hearing, the Court will probably think it better to leave the question over until it is seen whether, ultimately, the arbitrator grants the relief to which objection is taken. In such a case, the Court will no doubt find a way of making it clear that the respondent can participate in the hearing without waiving his objection, and may also urge (although it cannot compel) the parties to make an ad hoc submission empowering the arbitrator to decide upon the question of jurisdiction[11].

It is desirable that any challenge to the jurisdiction should be resolved as early as possible. A bona fide application, made promptly, for a declaration that the arbitrator has no jurisdiction, will not expose the applicant to the risk of a counterclaim on the substance of the dispute if the challenge fails[12].

C. ARBITRATOR INVOKING THE DECISION OF THE COURT

It is often said that an arbitrator cannot invoke the decision of the Court on questions concerning his own jurisdiction. This proposition is expressed too broadly. The power of the arbitrator to invoke the decision of the Court depends upon his jurisdiction to decide the issue in question[13]. If the essence of the issue is whether any valid arbitration could ever be, or is now, taking place between the parties or whether the person who purports to act as arbitrator has been validly appointed as such, the proposition is no doubt correct. If the arbitrator has no jurisdiction to deal with the dispute, he will have no jurisdiction to bring

---

[9] Even though the courts do not, as a general rule, welcome claims for negative declaratory relief.

[10] Two questions arise. First, should the Court, given the facts proved and the view which it takes of the law, grant a declaration as claimed? Second, are the circumstances such that a claim for declaration ought to be entertained at all? The first question arises at the trial. The second, which is the one discussed in the text, should be raised at an earlier stage, either on the summons for directions, or by an application to strike out or stay under the inherent jurisdiction.

[11] See p. 133, ante.

[12] *Metal Scrap Trade Corpn Ltd v Kate Shipping Co Ltd, The Gladys* [1988] 2 Lloyd's Rep 221, CA. A fuller discussion of this case must await the outcome of the appeal to the House of Lords.

[13] It appears that in *May v Mills* (1914) 30 TLR 287 a consultative case was stated on whether the arbitrator had jurisdiction to decide upon the issue whether the agreement was tainted by fraud. But the claim seems to have been for damages, not rescission.

it before the Court[14]. If he has no jurisdiction over the dispute, he is not an 'arbitrator or umpire' in respect of that dispute: and the statutory powers[15] to bring questions before the Court for decision apply only to an 'arbitrator' or 'umpire'[16].

If, however, the issue as to jurisdiction is one which the arbitrator does have power to decide then there is no reason why he should not have power to invoke the decision of the Court upon it[17]. Since the question whether, in particular circumstances, an arbitrator has power to invoke the decision of the Court on his own jurisdiction may well be controversial, it will not usually be right to involve the parties in the cost of what may be an abortive proceeding unless they both agree. If only one party wishes the matter to be decided by the law, it will probably be better to leave him to start proceedings for declaratory relief[18].

Even if the submission is not wide enough to cover the question of jurisdiction, it is always open to the parties to make a fresh submission, giving the arbitrator power to invoke the decision of the Court on the disputed question[19].

D. ARBITRATOR INVESTIGATING HIS OWN JURISDICTION

An arbitrator is under no legal duty to raise questions of jurisdiction on his own initiative. Unlike objections on the ground of illegality, which the arbitrator is bound to investigate irrespective of what the parties desire, jurisdiction involves no considerations of public policy[20]. On the other hand, common sense demands that any obvious objection to the jurisdiction should be dealt with at an early stage, in order to spare both the arbitrator[1] and the parties the waste of time and

---

[14] *Windsor RDC v Otterway and Try* [1954] 1 WLR 1494, per Devlin LJ. The statement of Farwell LJ to the contrary in *Den of Airlie SS Co Ltd v Mitsui & Co Ltd and British Oil and Cake Mills Ltd* (1912) 17 Com Cas 116 at 132 is (at best) too broad.

[15] I.e. ss. 1 and 2 of the 1979 Act.

[16] A possible escape from this logical difficulty would be to bring the matter before the Court as a question of law arising in the course of the reference, and to invite the Court to decide whether it has jurisdiction to decide the question. In order to decide whether it has jurisdiction, the Court must decide whether the arbitratror or umpire has jurisdiction to invoke the decision of the Court. The answer to whether the Court has jurisdiction will generally decide the question whether the arbitrator has jurisdiction.

[17] See, for example, *Re Crighton and Law Car and General Insurance Corpn Ltd* [1910] 2 KB 738, where the arbitrator stated a case on his power to allow or disallow an amendment. Also *Ayscough v Sheed Thomson & Co* (1924) 19 Ll L Rep 104; *May and Hassell Ltd v Vsesojuznoje Objedinenije Exportles (No 2)* (1941) 69 Ll L Rep 102. It may be that the dispute in that case was not in fact concerned with jurisdiction, but the Court treated it as such and nevertheless ordered a case to be stated. The same comment may be made on the observations of Pilcher J in *HE Daniels Ltd v Carmel Exporters and Importers Ltd* [1953] 2 QB 242 at 256. (Question whether second arbitration was barred by full award, treated as one of jurisdiction. Perhaps it was in reality a defence.) Reference may also be made to *Government of Italy v Suzuki & Co* (1923) 17 Lloyd's Rep 251, and to *Macleod Ross & Co Ltd v Cradock Manners Ltd* [1954] 1 Lloyd's Rep 258 at 264.

[18] None of the procedures under the 1979 Act for invoking the decision of the Court on a question relating to the powers of an arbitrator are particularly well adapted to the purpose: see pp. 620–626, post.

[19] *Digby v General Accident Fire and Life Assurance Corpn Ltd* [1940] 2 KB 226 is an example.

[20] *FW Berk & Co v Knowles and Foster* [1962] 1 Lloyd's Rep 430 at 435, per Megaw J. (The dictum concerned the duty of the Court, but the same principle must apply to the arbitrator.)

[1] Because he may well have no right to be paid for conducting a null reference: see p. 244, ante.

money involved in conducting a reference which ultimately proves to be a nullity. Thus, before accepting an invitation to act, or at the latest before making any substantial progress with the reference, the arbitrator should study the arbitration agreement to see whether, for example, it prescribes any qualification or disqualifications which might affect the validity of his appointment[2]. Similarly, when the details of the claim are first brought to his attention, by the points of claim or other written formulation, he should see whether they include anything which, on the face of it, appears to fall outside the scope of the reference: such as a claim which came into existence after the commencement of the arbitration, or one which has no connection with the subject matter of the agreement to arbitrate. Points of this nature should be raised with the parties and their representatives[3], and an explicit assurance obtained that no objection is being taken. This will serve two purposes. First, it enables the merits of any objection to be investigated straight away, rather than after costs have been spent on the reference. Second, it may prevent future disputes as to jurisdiction, by bringing into existence a waiver or an ad hoc submission.

The arbitrator should take care, however, not to carry his enquiries into his jurisdiction too far. He should confine himself to the more obvious objections. Anything of a more recondite nature should be left for the parties to raise.

If a question is raised on the jurisdiction of the arbitrator, either by a party or by the arbitrator himself, and if the objection is pressed, the arbitrator should see whether the parties will themselves take steps to obtain a final ruling on the question of jurisdiction – by seeking declaratory relief, or by empowering him to decide the matter himself, or to state a case upon it.

If the parties remain inactive, the arbitrator can choose between two procedures –

1 to decide the question of jurisdiction himself, subsequently continuing or abandoning the arbitration according to what he decides; or

2 to set the question of jurisdiction on one side, leaving the parties to raise it in Court, either before or after the award has been published[4].

Which course the arbitrator should adopt will depend on the circumstances. If the objection is straightforward, he may consider it better to rule at once, always bearing in mind that if either party is dissatisfied the matter can be reopened by the Court. On the other hand, if the question of jurisdiction is difficult, or if the hearing on the merits is unlikely to be expensive, so that even a null award will not involve a great waste of costs, the arbitrator may think it better to proceed with the reference, warning the claimant that he goes ahead at his peril.

It not infrequently happens that a party who objects root and branch to the jurisdiction of the arbitrator declines to take any part in the proceedings at all,

---

[2] So also, if there is any fact which might lay him open to a suggestion of partiality, he should disclose it: *Re Haigh and London and North Western and Great Western Rly Companies* [1896] 1 QB 649.

[3] Where the person in question is an umpire, the representatives of the parties may well be the two arbitrators. Clearance from them will be of no use unless they have actual authority from the parties to waive the objection: *Rahcassi Shipping Co SA v Blue Star Line, The Bede* [1967] 2 Lloyd's Rep 261, [1969] 1 QB 173. *Kawasaki, Kisen Kaisha Ltd v Government of Ceylon* [1962] 1 Lloyd's Rep 424. The umpire can, however, reasonably assume that the arbitrators will have sufficient sense to seek instructions from the parties on any point which he may raise.

[4] *Christopher Brown v Genossenschaft Oesterreichischer*, ante, at 376; *Luanda Exportadora SARL v Wahbe Tamari & Sons* [1967] 2 Lloyd's Rep 353 at 364; *Golodetz v Schrier* (1947) 80 Ll L Rep 647 at 650.

even to the extent of refusing to attend a hearing on the issue of jurisdiction. Here, the proper course is for the arbitrator to consider whether, on the information brought before him, he appears to have jurisdiction over the dispute. If it is said that he has no qualifications to act, then he must study the terms of the arbitration agreement. If it is alleged that there is no contract, he must call on the plaintiff to furnish proof of the contract. If questions of construction appear to arise, he must call on the claimant to argue the matter. But he is not obliged to investigate the matter in depth, or to conduct an elaborate cross-examination of the claimant. If the defendant does not choose to hear and challenge the claimant's case, there is no reason why the arbitrator should do so on his behalf. Naturally, if it is plain that there is no jurisdiction, the arbitrator should not proceed, for the production of an award which is obviously bad for want of jurisdiction does no good to anyone. But in any other cases, the arbitrator can properly go ahead with the reference, warning the claimant that when he seeks to enforce the award he may be met with the answer that it is a nullity[5].

E. OBJECTIONS AFTER PUBLICATION OF THE AWARD

Rather than bringing his objection before the Court whilst the reference is in progress, the respondent will often prefer to postpone the issue until after the award has been published. If he believes that he has a strong defence on the merits, it will be better for the respondent to fight the arbitration and endeavour to win it, rather than to make a pre-emptive application to the Court. This will almost always be the right choice when the objection is merely to part of the relief claimed, rather than to the arbitrator's jurisdiction to hear the dispute at all.

If the respondent takes this course, and finds that the award is against him, he can take the initiative by launching proceedings in Court to attack the award, in the shape of an action for a declaration that he is not bound by the award[6] or part of it or a motion to set aside the award in whole or in part[7], or to remit it

---

[5] *Golodetz v Schrier*, supra, at 650.

[6] As in *Kaukomarkkinat O/Y v Elbe Transport-Union GmbH, The Kelo* [1985] 2 Lloyd's Rep 85.

[7] See pp. 554–555, ante. In *Cook International Inc v BV Handelsmaatschappij Jean Delvaux* [1985] 2 Lloyd's Rep 225 it is said that an award made without jurisdiction is effective until set aside or declared invalid. It is by no means clear in what sense such an award is 'effective', since the judge also held that such an award is void. It is possible that what the judge had in mind was that the lack of jurisdiction could not be raised as a defence unless proceedings had first been taken to set aside the award or to obtain a declaration that it was invalid. If, as was also held in this case, the time limit for bringing proceedings for a declaration is the same as for an application to set aside, this would be a novel and important point, since it has always been assumed that lack of jurisdiction may be taken as a defence at any time and without launching any active proceedings to impeach the award. It is, we submit, wrong in principle that a person against whom an award has been made without jurisdiction should be required to take the initiative in order to render it ineffective. Moreover, we venture to doubt the correctness of the decision that the time limit laid down by RSC Ord. 73, r. 5(1) for applications to set aside an award applies to proceedings for a declaration that the award is void. The Rule applies to 'an application to set aside an award', i.e. an order changing the status of the award. But a declaration does not change the status of an award: it merely declares what its status is.

for the deletion of any objectionable part[8]. At the same time, he can, if the circumstances are appropriate, apply for an injunction to restrain the enforcement of the award until the question of jurisdiction has been decided.

Alternatively[9], he can simply refuse to honour the award, taking his objections to jurisdiction as a defence when the successful claimant launches enforcement proceedings. The choice between the active and the passive approach will largely be dictated by commercial considerations. Many businessmen would not care for the idea of appearing to default on an award, particularly if their credit would suffer, or if they risked being 'posted' by their trade association. The damage done by a default may be much reduced if the losing party is able to say that proceedings to challenge the award are already under way. On the other hand, the active approach involves the expenditure of costs, which the respondent may be unable to recover from a foreign claimant, even if he wins; and he may think it more economical to lie low, in case his opponent does not even try to enforce the award[10].

Whichever the course the respondent decides to adopt, he will be faced with two practical problems. The first, and more serious, is that of maintaining his objection to the jurisdiction, whilst continuing to take part in the reference. There is no great difficulty where the objection relates only to part of the relief claimed, for there is no inconsistency between acknowledging the arbitrator's right to hear the dispute, whilst challenging his power to decide it in a particular way. But where the essence of the objection is that there has never been a valid agreement to arbitrate, or that the dispute lies outside the agreement, or that the arbitrator was not properly appointed, the respondent cannot logically fight the arbitration whilst asserting that it has no legal existence. The claimant can complain that the respondent should not be allowed to take part in the hearing, if he is subsequently going to allege that the hearing is nugatory, for this will increase the costs which the claimant will waste if the objection to jurisdiction is upheld[11]. Although the merits of this argument are undeniable[12], we believe

---

[8] The remission is not strictly necessary, since the parts which are declared by the judgment to be bad for want of jurisdiction have no legal effect. Nevertheless, it is sometimes a useful remedy, particularly if there is a risk of enforcement abroad: for it means that instead of having to construe the award in the light of the judgment the document ultimately published by the arbitrator is one which contains a valid adjudication, and nothing else. *Re Green & Co and Balfour, Williamson & Co* (1890) 63 LT 325; *Société Franco-Tunisienne d'Armement-Tunis v Government of Ceylon* [1959] 2 Lloyd's Rep 1; *Nilo Heime Akt v G Merel & Co Ltd* [1959] 2 Lloyd's Rep 292. (There are a number of reported cases, of which *Kawasaki Kisen Kaisha v Government of Ceylon*, ante, is an example, in which orders were made setting aside awards for excess or absence of jurisdiction. It is submitted that these orders were not in accordance with principle; although no doubt in practice the choice of remedy made no difference.)

[9] If he takes active steps to challenge the award and fails, he cannot, when the claimant seeks to enforce the award, resist enforcement on any ground which he either did or could have relied on in the proceedings to challenge the award: *Hall and Wodehouse Ltd v Panorama Hotel Properties Ltd* [1974] 2 Lloyd's Rep 413.

[10] If there is a possibility of enforcement abroad, the respondent should make sure that his objections to jurisdiction are valid in the foreign country before he gives up the chance to attack the award in England.

[11] In practice the arbitrator will usually allow the respondent to take part: *Westminster Chemicals and Produce Ltd v Eichholz and Loeser* [1954] 1 Lloyd's Rep 99 at 105.

[12] In the related field of objections to the jurisdiction of foreign courts, the argument appears to have been accepted. In *Henry v Geoprosco International Ltd* [1975] 2 Lloyd's Rep 148, [1976] QB 726 the Court of Appeal held that a conditional appearance under protest in a foreign court amounts to a submission to its jurisdiction if not sustained by the foreign court. But it was recognised that a party could safely take part in an arbitration under protest without thereby submitting to the arbitrator's jurisdiction: see p. 747. The suggested explanation for the distinction was that the jurisdiction of a foreign court is compulsory, whereas an arbitrator's jurisdiction is wholly consensual.

that it reflects too rigid an approach. If a party to a commercial dispute has a genuine defence to the claim, and also has a genuine reason for saying that the arbitrator is not the correct tribunal to rule upon it, he should be allowed to take both points, in whatever order is more convenient – which in practice will often mean that the issue on jurisdiction is postponed until after the award – and should not be forced into a position where he must either take pre-emptive action or lose his right to challenge the jurisdiction. Provided the respondent has made a clear protest, and has emphasised that his continued participation in the reference is without prejudice to his case on jurisdiction[13], we believe that a court should, in the interests of common sense, hold that there has been no waiver[14]. If the claimant feels that he is likely to suffer harm, because the costs of the reference will be enlarged (see ante) he can foreclose the question of jurisdiction by launching his own action for a declaration that the arbitrator does indeed have jurisdiction. If the claimant does not take this step, we believe the respondent should be entitled to take part in the hearing and, if the award is in his favour, to waive his objection to the jurisdiction of the arbitrator and rely on the award as a bar to further proceedings against him for the same claim[15].

The second practical difficulty relates to the respondent's costs of the arbitration. If he fights the arbitration and wins it, he will plainly abandon his objection to the jurisdiction and recover his costs through the award. If, on the other hand, he loses the arbitration, but subsequently establishes that the award is a nullity, for want of jurisdiction, there seems no way in which he can obtain reimbursement for the costs of the hearing. Ex hypothesi, the arbitrator has no jurisdiction to award them; and the Court has no powers in respect of the costs of the arbitration, as distinct from the costs of the proceedings in which the award is declared a nullity. There is no real injustice in this, for if the respondent could have elected to rely only on his challenge to the jurisdiction, he could have saved the costs of the hearing; and if he has chosen in addition to rely on a defence which has proved to be without foundation, there is no reason why he should not pay for it.

---

13 *Westminster Chemicals and Produce Ltd v Eichholz and Loeser* [1954] 1 Lloyd's Rep 99, 105; *Cia Maritima Zorroza SA v Sesostris SA, The Marques de Bolarque* [1984] 1 Lloyd's Rep 652. An explicit objection is, of course, essential. Otherwise, by taking part in the reference the respondent will be held either to have waived his objection, or to have made an ad hoc submission. It will be prudent to make the objection in writing: partly in order to avoid misunderstanding, and partly so that if the respondent is ultimately faced with proceedings for summary enforcement, he can show the Court that his objection is genuine, and not a mere afterthought, devised in order to postpone the moment of payment. The objection must be taken at the earliest opportunity if waiver is to be avoided: *Westminster Chemicals and Produce Ltd v Eichholz and Loeser,* supra.

14 For cases in which the Court has so held, see *Westminster Chemicals v Eichholz and Loeser,* supra; *Ringland v Lowndes* (1864) 33 LJCP 337; *Davies v Price,* ante; *Sheonath v Ramnath* (1865) 35 LJPC 1; *Ronaasen & Son v Metsanomistajain Metsakeskus O/Y* (1931) 40 Ll L Rep 267; *Dalmia Dairy Industries Ltd v National Bank of Pakistan* [1978] 2 Lloyd's Rep 223 at 233, 280. See also *Hamlyn v Betteley* (1880) 6 QBD 63 at 65; *Henry v Geoprosco International,* ante, at 747–748.

15 We do not believe that he would be estopped from changing his attitude in this way. The difficulty of a respondent, who has all along challenged the jurisdiction, relying on an award in his favour as a bar to a later action on the same claim (noted by Pollock CB arguendo in *Davies v Price* (1864) 34 LJQB 8) should not, we consider, lead the Court to the conclusion that the later action should be allowed to proceed, with the possibility of the Court reaching a different decision from the arbitrator.

CHAPTER 35

Waiver

A. WAIVER GENERALLY

In previous chapters we have described how irregularities in the course of an arbitration may give a party the right to seek the intervention of the court, either during the reference or after the award has been made[1]. In this Chapter we consider the various ways in which a party objecting to an irregularity may lose this right. Although we have adopted the expression 'waiver' to cover the subject under discussion, it is in reality a somewhat diffuse topic embracing a number of different, but related, principles such as waiver, estoppel, acquiescence, election, ratification, etc. The precise limits and interrelationships of these principles have still not been fully explored by the courts, and there has been a tendency, particularly in the earlier cases, to use expressions such as 'waiver' or 'acquiescence' to cover the application of all these principles without attempting to differentiate between them.

The subject of waiver in relation to arbitration has, however, greatly diminished in importance as a result of the greater readiness of the courts in recent times to recognise and sanction informal modes of procedure in arbitrations[2]. Practices which would have been regarded as irregular in the last century, such as communicating with a member of the tribunal in the absence of the other, are now recognised as ordinary occurrences in certain types of arbitration. As a result, where a nineteenth century court would have resorted to the doctrine of waiver or some similar principle to justify a refusal to upset an award made after an informal procedure, the court would nowadays tend to treat participation in the reference without objection as evidence, not of waiver, but of an implied agreement to depart from a more formal method of conducting the arbitration[3].

B. WHAT MAY BE WAIVED

There is probably no limit to the types of irregularity which can be waived[4]. The following may be taken as illustrative of the types of irregularity which may be waived, as well as of the ways in which waiver may take place[5] –

---

[1] See Chapters 32 and 33, ante.
[2] See Chapter 21, ante.
[3] See ante, p. 283.
[4] *Moseley v Simpson* (1873) LR 16 Eq 226 at 236; *Wessanen's Koninklijke Fabrieken NV v Isaac Modiano, Brother & Sons Ltd* [1960] 2 Lloyd's Rep 257.
[5] Discussion of the substantive requirements of waiver, estoppel, etc. lies outside the scope of this book. The reader is referred to the standard textbooks on the subject, particularly Spenser Bower, *Estoppel by Representation*.

1 Partiality on the part of the arbitrator[6].
2 Arbitrators acting as advocates before disagreement[7].
3 Failing to examine witnesses on oath[8].
4 Choosing an umpire by lot[9].
5 Proceeding without hearing evidence or argument[10].
6 Failure by the umpire to rehear the evidence[11].
7 Taking evidence in the absence of one party[12].
8 Reading counsel's opinion on the merits of party's case[13].

However, it may be that a distinction must be drawn between mere irregularities of procedure and matters affecting the jurisdiction of the arbitrator. Irregularities of procedure can be waived; but it has been said that the jurisdiction of the arbitrator must always depend on an agreement by the parties[14] to abide by his award[15].

There are, however, a number of apparent exceptions to this general statement of principle[16], of which the following may be noted:

1 Where there is already an arbitration agreement in existence, the doctrine of estoppel may operate so as to prevent a party from asserting that a requirement essential to the jurisdiction of the arbitrator has not been satisfied[17]. Thus a party who appoints an unqualified arbitrator cannot afterwards complain that the arbitrator had no authority[18].

2 A party who asserts that he has appointed an arbitrator cannot afterwards

---

[6] *Re Elliot and South Devon Rly Co* (1848) 2 De G & Sm 17; *Drew v Drew and Leburn* 1855 2 Macq 1; *Re Clout and Metropolitan and District Rly Companies* (1882) 46 LT 141. But knowledge that an arbitrator may not be capable of impartiality when agreeing to refer *future* disputes to arbitration is not a ground for refusing an application for leave to revoke the arbitrator's authority or for an injunction to restrain further proceedings in the arbitration: see s. 24(1) of the Act.

[7] *Biglin v Clark* (1905) 49 Sol Jo 204.

[8] *Ridoat v Pye* (1797) 1 Bos & P 91; *Allen v Francis* (1845) 9 Jur 691; *Drew v Drew and Leburn* 1855 2 Macq 1; cf. *Wakefield v Llanelly Rly and Dock Co* (1864) 34 Beav 245; *Faure, Fairclough Ltd v Premier Oil and Cake Mills Ltd* [1968] 1 Lloyd's Rep 237.

[9] *Re Tunno and Bird* (1833) 5 B & Ad 488; *Backhouse v Taylor* (1851) 20 LJQB 233. See also ante, pp. 191–192.

[10] *Ritchie v W Jacks & Co* (1922) 10 Ll L Rep 519. This case may also be explained as an example of an implied agreement for an informal procedure.

[11] *Re Salkeld and Slater and Harrison* (1840) 12 Ad & El 767; *Re Tunno and Bird* (1833) 5 B & Ad 488; cf. *Re Jenkins and Leggo* (1841) 11 LJQB 71.

[12] *Kingwell v Elliot* (1839) 7 Dowl 423; *Bignall v Gale* (1841) 10 LJCP 169; *Hamilton v Bankin* (1850) 3 De G & Sm 782; *Thomas v Morris* (1867) 16 LT 398; *Ashwin v Société Maritime et Commerciale du Pacifique* (1922) 13 Ll L Rep 164; *Wessanen's Koninklijke Fabrieken NV v Isaac Modiano, Brother & Sons Ltd* [1960] 2 Lloyd's Rep 257; *Government of Ceylon v Chandris* [1963] 1 Lloyd's Rep 214; cf. *Dobson v Groves* (1844) 14 LJQB 17; *W Ramsden & Co Ltd v Jacobs* [1922] 1 KB 640.

[13] *Wessanen's Koninklijke Fabrieken NV v Isaac Modiano, Brother & Sons Ltd*, supra.

[14] The agreement may be implied from the conduct of the parties in continuing with the reference: see pp. 133–134, ante.

[15] See *Robinson, Fleming & Co v Warner, Barnes & Co* (1922) 10 Ll L Rep 331 (arbitrator unqualified); *Ringland v Lowndes* (1864) 33 LJ CP 337 (award made out of time). Treating a third arbitrator as an umpire may fall in the same category: see *Moseley v Simpson* (1873) LR 16 Eq 226; *Re Marsh* (1847) 16 LJQB 330; *Peterson v Ayre* (1854) 14 CB 665; *Matson v Trower* (1824) Ry & M 17.

[16] It may be questioned whether the principle itself can any longer be said to be correct, given the breadth of the modern law of estoppel, and in particular the recognition that in certain circumstances an estoppel may form the basis of a cause of action: see in particular *Amalgamated Investment & Property Co Ltd v Texas Commerce International* [1982] QB 84.

[17] *Tyerman v Smith* (1856) 6 E & B 719; see also *Palmer v Metropolitan Rly Co* (1862) 31 LJQB 259.

[18] *Jungheim Hopkins & Co v Foukelmann* [1909] 2 KB 948; *Oakland Metal Co Ltd v D Benaim & Co Ltd* [1953] 2 QB 261. See also ante, pp. 256–257.

be heard to say that he has not, if the other party has acted in reliance upon that assertion[19].

3 A party who relies on an arbitration agreement to have an action stayed and the claim referred to arbitration cannot later assert that the claim is outside the scope of the agreement[20].

4 A party who takes a benefit under an award, by seeking to enforce it through the Courts or otherwise, cannot later assert that it was made without authority[1].

5 The arbitration agreement need not be between parties of full capacity, if the party against whom the award is to be enforced agreed to arbitrate with knowledge of the other party's incapacity[2].

6 Where the existence of an agreement to arbitrate is not in question, a party who invokes the arbitration agreement in respect of a particular dispute is precluded from later asserting that the dispute was not within the scope of the agreement[3].

Moreover, where the defect, although affecting the arbitrator's jurisdiction, is procedural in character, the courts have been less strict in insisting on a fresh agreement to cure the defect. This is particularly true of cases where the arbitrator has made his award out of time[4].

C. DEALING WITH IRREGULARITIES

Waiver can, of course, occur as a result of an express statement by one party that he will not rely on an irregularity in later proceedings to challenge the award: and where both parties wish to cure an irregularity which has come to light, particularly if it goes beyond a mere irregularity of procedure and affects the tribunal's jurisdiction, they will be well advised to do so by an agreement in writing.

But generally the problem is not how to bring about the waiver of an

---

[19] *Legumbres SACIFIA v Central de Cooperativas de Productores do Rio Grande do Sul Ltda* [1986] 1 Lloyd's Rep 401; similarly where one party has admitted in his pleading that he was a party to the contract containing the arbitration clause: *Sea Calm Shipping Co SA v Chantiers Navals de l'Esterel, The Uhenbels* [1986] 2 Lloyd's Rep 294.

[20] *Macaura v Northern Assurance Co Ltd* [1925] AC 619; *South British Insurance Co Ltd v Gauci Bros & Co (Egypt)* [1928] AC 352.

[1] *Gapp v Elwes* (1852) 20 LTOS 100; *European Grain and Shipping Ltd v Johnston* [1982] 1 Lloyd's Rep 414. In *Cook International Inc v BV Handelmaatschappij Jean Delvaux* [1985] 2 Lloyd's Rep 225 it was held that by taking up and arguing a special case a party lost the right to challenge the jurisdiction of the arbitral tribunal. No doubt the same would apply to an appeal under the 1979 Act. This places a party who wishes to challenge an award as made without jurisdiction or to appeal from it if his challenge fails, in a difficult position, since he must comply with the time limits for each application, and may be too late to appeal if he waits until the jurisdiction point is decided. Presumably he can safeguard his position by making it plain that the appeal proceedings are without prejudice to his application to challenge the validity of the award.

[2] *Wrightson v Bywater* (1838) 3 M & W 199; *Jones v Powell* (1838) 6 Dowl 483; *Re Warner* (1844) 2 Dow & L 148. *Re Wyld, ex p Wyld* (1860) 30 LJ Bcy 10 can perhaps be explained in this way.

[3] *A and B v C and D* [1982] 1 Lloyd's Rep 166 at 172–173.

[4] See *R v Hill* (1819) 7 Price 636; *Leggett v Finlay* (1829) 6 Bing 255; *Burley v Stephens* (1836) 1 M & W 156; *Hallett v Hallett* (1839) 7 Dowl 389; *Hawksworth v Brammall* (1839) 5 My & Cr 281; *Bennett v Watson* (1860) 29 LJ Ex 357; *Caledonian Rly Co v Lockhart* (1860) 3 Macq 808. In *Lord v Lee* (1868) LR 3 QB 404, Blackburn J expressly decided the case on the basis of ratification, not on the grounds of a new submission. Cf. *Ringland v Lowndes*, ante.

irregularity but how to avoid it. Many of the cases in which it has been held that a party has waived an irregularity have arisen because the party has continued to take part in the arbitration after the irregularity has come to light.

In order to avoid further participation in the reference giving rise to waiver by conduct, the party complaining of the irregularity should state his objection at once and make it clear that he is not abandoning his right to insist on the objection at a later stage. This gives all concerned an opportunity to rectify the irregularity, if that is possible; and provided the objection is stated clearly and in time there should be no danger of the Court later holding that it has been waived[5]. It is true that in cases of serious irregularity the party complaining may be able to seek the intervention of the Court at once without waiting for the tribunal to make its award[6]. But this is a drastic step to take and we believe that the court would be reluctant to hold that a party who has chosen not to disrupt the reference by applying for the immediate intervention of the Court had thereby lost the right to insist on his objection at a later stage[7].

It should, however, be remembered that an irregularity in procedure, as distinct from acting without jurisdiction, makes an award voidable and not void[8]: the party complaining of an irregularity should therefore move to have the award set aside or remitted within the time laid down by the Rules of Court[9] and not simply wait to raise the objection as a ground for resisting enforcement of the award, for by then it will be too late.

A further consequence of the fact that irregularities make an award voidable and not void are that a party who affirms an award whether expressly[10] or by conduct[11], after it has been published, cannot later seek to avoid it on the grounds of irregularity in the course of the arbitration. Merely taking up the award and paying the arbitrator's fees, however, is not an affirmation of the award nor a waiver of irregularities during the reference[12].

---

[5] The procedure for dealing with objections to the *jurisdiction* of the tribunal, as distinct from irregularities, is discussed in Chapter 34.

[6] See Chapter 32.

[7] But if the intervention of the court *is* to be invoked during the reference the application should be made promptly, for continued participation in the reference may be grounds for refusing discretionary relief, such as an injunction to restrain further proceedings in the reference: *Compagnie Nouvelle France Navigation SA v Compagnie Newale Afrique du Nord, The Oranie and The Tunisie* [1966] 1 Lloyd's Rep 477.

[8] See pp. 456–457, ante.

[9] See Ord. 73, r. 5: Appendix 1, pp. 721–722, post.

[10] As in *AA Amram Ltd v Bremar Co Ltd* [1966] 1 Lloyd's Rep 494, where the successful party incurred costs in proceedings to enforce an award in reliance on a letter from the losing party accepting the arbitrator's decision. See also *Aiden Shipping Co Ltd v Interbulk Ltd, The Vimeira* [1985] 2 Lloyd's Rep 377 (waiver of right to remission by obtaining order for enforcement).

[11] As in *Dexters Ltd v Hill Crest Oil Co (Bradford) Ltd* [1926] 1 KB 348, where the party complaining had already received payment under the award. But cf. *Lissenden v CAV Bosch Ltd* [1940] AC 412. See also *Parrott v Shellard* (1868) 16 WR 928; *Kennard v Harris* (1824) 2 B & C 801; *Goodman v Sayers* (1820) 2 Jac & W 249 (settlement of action to enforce award); *Gapp v Elwes* (1852) 20 LTOS 100; cf. *Bartle v Musgrave* (1841) 1 Dowl N S 325 *Hayward v Phillips* (1837) 6 Ad & El 119.

[12] *Rokopoulos v Esperia SpA, The Aros* [1978] 1 Lloyd's Rep 456.

CHAPTER 36

Appeals

A. INTRODUCTION

We have already described, in Chapter 29, the stages by which the courts came to assume a limited jurisdiction to remedy errors of law on the part of the arbitrator. Two distinct procedures were involved. First, the jurisdiction to set aside an award for error of law on the face, derived from the inherent power of the Court to supervise references to arbitration which were, through a historical accident, treated as an off-shoot of proceedings in the High Court. Second, the power, and eventually the duty, of the arbitrator to state a special case on a question of law arising on an award. This power was first conferred because the parties desired it; and the duty was later imposed because, for at least a century, the legislature conceived that the interests of the commercial community were best served by the existence of some restraint on the power of the arbitrator, accidentally or by design, to bind the parties by an award which did not give effect to the true legal rights created by their contract.

The Arbitration Act 1979 reversed the development of this process, previously thought to be beneficial. Certain disputes were placed beyond the jurisdiction of the courts to exercise judicial review on questions of law[1]. In respect of others, a new power was given to the courts to refuse audience to those appeals whose prosecution was thought to be contrary to the legislative policy of the new Act. Even in respect of those appeals which were allowed to proceed, the principles by which they are determined are such that a successful challenge to the decision of an arbitrator is much less common than in the past.

The purpose of the present Chapter is to set out, within the limitations imposed by a line of judicial authority, the effect of the 1979 Act. It is necessary to begin by summarising the procedures for judicial supervision as they existed under the 1950 Act. At the present time, there are few arbitrations still in progress to which the procedures of the 1950 Act must be applied. However, some knowledge of the former system is necessary to a proper understanding of the law as it now stands, if only because of the contrasts drawn by judicial comment between the features of the two procedures. Since, however, the procedure by way of case stated is almost wholly obsolete, we shall include only a brief outline. The reader who requires more details of the procedures under the 1950 Act is referred to Appendix 3 of the first edition of this work. In this Chapter we call the procedure under the 1950 Act 'the old system'; and the procedure under the 1979 Act 'the new system'.

---

[1] Except perhaps by the methods discussed in Chapter 37, post.

1 The old system

The system may be summarised as follows.

If a party so required, the arbitrator was obliged to state a case on a question of law. If he refused, the Court would order him to do so. But the Court had first to be satisfied that the dispute involved a genuine question of law, not a question of fact dressed up to resemble a question of law. There had also to be a question which was open to serious argument, of importance to the resolution of the dispute, raised bona fide and without an ulterior motive such as a desire to cause delay[2].

The parties could not validly contract to deprive the arbitrator of the power to state a case, or to take away jurisdiction of the court to order him to do so[3].

The issues of law to be argued in the High Court were defined by the question of law set out in the special case. Where the question was expressed in wide terms, as came to be the practice in recent times, the parties were free to raise every issue of law comprised within that question, even if it had not been brought forward on the hearing of the arbitration. In this regard, the proceeding in the High Court was not so much an appeal as an independent hearing on issues of law, based on the findings set out in the award.

These principles were carried into practice as follows. A party who wished the arbitrator to state a case was obliged to do so as soon as possible, and in any event before the award was made. After that it was too late. He was obliged to formulate with precision what question of law he considered appropriate for decision by the Court. If the arbitrator then decided to state a case, he could not at once proceed to a final award, but was obliged to give the party time to apply to the High Court for an order requiring the arbitrator to comply with the request.

If the arbitrator agreed or was willing to state a case, he set out in his award the facts which he considered to be relevant to the question of law. Very often, the parties would supply him with lists of findings which they considered should be included in the award. The arbitrator was to include in the award only his findings of fact, not the evidence on which they were based.

The special case invariably contained at least two alternative awards. The first was the outcome of the arbitrator's own decision on the question of law, as applied to the facts which he had found. The special case would stipulate that the primary award was to become effective unless the case was set down for argument within a specified period, usually six weeks. The alternative award or awards were included to allow for the contingency that the court would take a different view from that of the arbitrator, so that instead of simply setting aside the arbitrator's decision so that the matter had to be returned to him, the Court could create an immediately enforceable obligation by adopting the alternative award.

Upon the hearing of the special case, the Court was confined to the facts set out in the award. There was no question of extrinsic evidence being adduced to amplify or explain what was contained in the special case.

In parallel to the procedure thus described there existed the jurisdiction to set

---

[2] *Halfdan Greig A/S v Sterling Coal and Navigation Corpn, The Lysland* [1973] 1 Lloyd's Rep 296, [1973] QB 843. In practice this meant that there was virtually a right of appeal in a genuine case.

[3] This rule came to be regarded as a reflection of the arbitrator's duty to decide the dispute in accordance with the law: see Chapter 29, *ante*.

aside an award for an error of law appearing on its face: a procedure entirely distinct in its practical application from that of the case stated[4]. If it could be seen from the facts set out in the award, or appearing from documents incorporated by reference into the award, that the decision of the arbitrator was wrong in law, the award would be set aside.

This jurisdiction was never popular. It was clumsy. Since the award was not intended by the arbitrator to be the subject of judicial review (for if it had been, he would have stated it in the form of a special case), it did not contain alternative awards, so that if the Court disagreed with the arbitrator it had no choice but to set the award aside, with the result that the arbitration had to begin again.

The procedure was also capricious. Everything depended on whether the arbitrator had stated enough facts in his award, or had incorporated enough documents, to make the error detectable. Since an arbitrator was not obliged, under English law, to give reasons for his award, it was often a matter of chance whether the arbitrator had been incautious enough to say something from which a question of law could be extracted. Equally, the rules which described whether a particular document was or was not to be treated as 'on the face' tended to operate in a most erratic way.

Finally, the risk that the losing party would attempt to attack an award which was intended to be final caused many arbitrators either to give no reasons at all for their award or to give them in a document so drafted as not to be 'on the face' of the award. The former practice was objectionable, and the latter gave rise to problems of enforcement in countries where an 'unmotivated' award was regarded as contrary to public policy.

2 The new system

The new system applies to all arbitrations commenced after 31 August 1979. The parties may also apply it by consent to arbitrations already in existence on that date. The main features of the system are as follows –

1 The procedures by way of special and consultative case are abolished, as is the jurisdiction to set aside or remit[5] an award on an arbitration agreement[6] for error of law on the face[7]. The 1979 Act also declares that there is no jurisdiction

---

[4] For references to the rise and fall of this procedure, see Chapter 29, ante. As we there suggest, the two procedures, although apparently so dissimilar, did have a common origin.

[5] So far as we are aware, the Court never asserted a jurisdiction to remit an award for error on the face, although it did have such a jurisdiction where an error not on the face was admitted by the arbitrator.

[6] These words appear to mean that whatever jurisdiction there was to set aside for error on the face of an award not on an 'arbitration agreement' (e.g. an award pursuant to an oral submission) still remains in being. If, however, we have correctly stated the historical origins of the jurisdiction in Chapter 29, ante, we think it very unlikely that the Court ever had a power of this nature.

[7] S. 1(1). (Unless otherwise stated, all references in this Chapter are to the 1979 Act). For the reasons stated in Chapter 29, ante, it may well be that the jurisdiction to set aside for error on the face had already been abolished by the 1950 Act. For the question whether the jurisdiction has been revived by the 1979 Act under another name, see p. 593, post.

to set aside or remit an award on an arbitration agreement for error of fact on the face[8].

2 These procedures are replaced by a qualified right of appeal on a question of law arising out of an award made on an arbitration agreement[9]. The Court also has jurisdiction to determine any question of law arising in the course of the reference[10], i.e. before an award is made.

3 In principle, the new system applies to all arbitrations conducted pursuant to written arbitration agreements[11], but the parties have the right, in certain circumstances, to exclude the right of recourse to the High Court on questions of law[12], by means of a written 'exclusion agreement'[13].

4 A valid exclusion agreement takes effect, not only to oust the right of appeal, but also the jurisdictions (a) to determine a question of law arising in the course of the reference, and (b) to transfer[14] into the High Court a dispute involving an issue of fraud[15].

5 The validity of an exclusion agreement depends upon (a) the nature of the arbitration, (b) the nationality of the parties, (c) the nature of the substantive contract which is the subject of the reference, and (d) the stage at which the exclusion agreement is made.

6 An exclusion agreement has no effect in relation to a statutory arbitration[16].

7 An exclusion agreement concerning 'a domestic arbitration agreement'[17] is valid only if it is entered into after the commencement of the arbitration[18].

8 An exclusion agreement concerning a non-domestic arbitration agreement is valid whether made before or after the commencement of the arbitration, unless it relates to disputes concerning a maritime, insurance or commodity transaction[19]. Even in respect of such disputes, an exclusion agreement is valid if entered into after the commencement of the arbitration, *or* if it relates to a

---

[8] S. 1(1). This provision is hard to fathom. Perhaps the best view is that it is purely declaratory, and is aimed at foreign parties who have not taken advice from English lawyers. If it is to be construed as changing the law, the results may be unfortunate. If the expression 'set aside . . . on the ground of errors of fact . . . on the face of the award' is read literally, no change was required since, so far as we are aware, it was never held that any such jurisdiction existed: unless, conceivably, it was intended to deal with the problems raised by *Edwards v Bairstow* [1956] AC 14, which are discussed at pp. 592 et seq., post. The only other jurisdiction which probably did exist was a power to interfere if the award contained a patent inconsistency between its findings. There appears to be no clear authority to support this power, but we believe that the court must be able to interfere (at least by remission) if findings x and non-x are included in the same award. It would be a pity if s. 1(1) were to be construed as ruling this out. The power to remit for the correction of mistakes admitted by the arbitrator cannot have been the target of the section, since such mistakes are only rarely apparent on the face; and in any case, there seems no reason why the legislature should have wished to annul this old-established and useful jurisdiction.
[9] S. 1(2).
[10] S. 2(1).
[11] There is thus no right of appeal from an award based on an oral submission. For some reason, this qualification does not apply to the obtaining of a High Court decision on a question of law arising in the course of a reference.
[12] S. 3(1).
[13] For a discussion of this term, see pp. 631–637, post.
[14] Under the powers conferred by s. 24(2) of the 1950 Act. See pp. 498–503, ante.
[15] S. 3(1)(c) and 3(3).
[16] S. 3(5). For the meaning of 'statutory arbitration' see s. 31(1) of the 1950 Act.
[17] For an explanation of this term, see pp. 631–632, post.
[18] S. 3(6).
[19] For a more accurate description of the types of contract which are singled out for special treatment, see pp. 632–634, post.

contract which is expressed to be governed by a law other than the law of England and Wales.

9   There is still no general obligation on the arbitrator to give reasons for his award. The Court does, however, have jurisdiction, in a case where no valid exclusion agreement is in force, to order the arbitrator to state his reasons in sufficient detail to enable the Court to consider a question of law arising on an appeal[20].

10   Even where there is no valid exclusion agreement, there no longer exists an automatic right of appeal to the High Court on a question of law. Appeals may be brought only with the consent of all parties, or with the leave of the Court[1]. There is one formal constraint on the grant of leave to appeal, namely that the determination of the question of law could substantially affect 'the right of one or more parties to the arbitration agreement'. Additional practical limitations have been placed by judicial decision on the circumstances in which, even if this formal requirement is fulfilled, the Court will exercise its discretion to grant leave to appeal[2].

11   No appeal lies to the Court of Appeal from a decision of the High Court on an appeal from an award, or from a decision of the High Court on a preliminary point of law, unless (a) the High Court or the Court of Appeal gives leave, and (b) it is certified by the High Court that the question of law to which its decision relates either is one of general public importance or is one which for some other special reason should be considered by the Court of Appeal[3].

B. THE NATURE OF APPEAL

Four questions of principle arise in connection with the right of appeal to the High Court from the award of an arbitrator.

1   First, to what extent does the Court have the right to decide which appeals it has a duty to decide, and according to what principles should the right be exercised?

2   Second, what types of issue are subject to review?

3   Third, according to what principles should the Court exercise its power to review an award?

4   Fourth, is a finding of fact made without evidence reviewable as an error of law?

1   Extent of duty to hear appeals: The Nema[4]

The new system presents a very different picture from the special case procedure under the old system. In respect of some awards (viz. those encompassed by a valid exclusion agreement) there is no right of appeal at all, even on a question of law which is crucial to the dispute. Where a right of appeal still exists in principle, the procedure is not the same. The Court now controls the access to

---

[20] S. 1(5).
[1] S. 1(3).
[2] S. 1(4).
[3] Ss. 1(7) and 2(3).
[4] *Pioneer Shipping Ltd v BTP Tioxide Ltd, The Nema* [1981] 2 Lloyd's Rep 239, [1982] AC 724.

the appellate jurisdiction in all cases, and not (as in the past) only in those where the arbitrator has refused to cooperate. The award in the form of a special case, and the power to set aside the award for error on the face have gone, to be replaced by a right of 'appeal', conducted on the basis of a reasoned award.

It had been widely assumed, before the enactment of the legislation, and for over a year thereafter, that in those instances where a right of appeal was preserved, both the appeal itself, and the selection of cases deemed to be fit for appeal, were to be conducted on the same general principles, mutatis mutandis, as under the former regime. This view was decisively repudiated, by the decisions and dicta of the House of Lords in *The Nema*.

So far as concerns the extent and nature of the right of review, the effect of *The Nema* must be considered in the light of two previous cases.

Tsakiroglou & Co v Noblee Thorl GmbH[5] concerned a c.i.f. contract for goods which, in the ordinary way, would have been carried to the port of destination on a voyage through the Suez Canal. After the contract was made, but before shipment, the Canal was closed, with the result that the goods would have to be shipped via the Cape of Good Hope. The question was whether the contract of sale was frustrated, by virtue of the extra cost and time involved in the prolonged transit. The arbitrators held that it was not. In their award the arbitrators stated that – 'So far as it is a question of fact we find and as far as it is a question of law we hold: . . . (vi) the performance of the contract by shipping the goods on a vessel routed via the Cape of Good Hope was not commercially or fundamentally different from its being performed by shipping the goods on vessels routed via the Suez Canal'. At first instance, the judge held that this was a finding of fact which concluded the matter in favour of the charterers, and therefore upheld the award. The Court of Appeal and the House of Lords reviewed the decision of the arbitrators, concluded that it was right, and therefore affirmed the award. The reasoning was, however, different from that of the judge at first instance, for the finding of the arbitrators was not treated as one of fact, or at least as the type of finding of fact which was incapable of review[6]. There was some divergence between the speeches as to the way in which the finding should be categorised[7], but this may well have been a matter of terminology rather than concept. Four members of the House emphasised that the finding nevertheless carried great weight[8].

Edwards (Inspector of Taxes) v Bairstow[9] arose from a special case stated by the General Commissioner of Income Tax. The question was whether profits arising from a transaction were liable to tax as being profits arising from an 'adventure . . . in the nature of trade'. The Commissioners held that they were not. Appeals to the High Court and thence to the Court of Appeal were dismissed, on the ground that the question was one of fact, upon which the decision of the Commissioners could not be upset unless it was perverse. In the House of Lords, however, the appeal was allowed. Much of the discussion concerned the question

---

[5] [1961] 1 Lloyd's Rep 329, [1962] AC 93.
[6] Per Viscount Simonds at 116; Lord Reid at 124; Lord Hodson at 129–130; Lord Guest at 134.
[7] It was described as 'evidential only', Viscount Simonds at 116; 'a question of law', Lord Reid at 119; 'a question of mixed fact and law', Lord Reid at 123; 'a finding in law', Lord Hodson at 134.
[8] The finding was stated to be 'of great value' Viscount Simonds at 116; 'of the utmost relevance', Lord Radcliffe at 123; one which 'almost completely determined' the dispute; one which would 'go virtually the whole way towards determining the legal result', Lord Radcliffe at 124.
[9] [1956] AC 14.

whether (as the courts in Scotland had held) the issue was one of mixed fact and law, or whether (as it had been decided in England) it was one of fact alone. The House of Lords was, however, unanimous on the view that, whichever approach was correct, the appellants were entitled to succeed. Space does not permit full citation of the valuable statements of principle contained in the speeches. The following are amongst the most important:

'For it is universally conceded that, though it is a pure finding of fact, it may be set aside on the grounds which have been stated in various ways but are I think fairly summarised by saying that the Court should [allow the appeal] if it appears that the Commissioners have acted without any evidence or upon a view of the facts which could not reasonably be entertained . . .'[10].

'When the Commissioners, having found the so-called primary facts . . . proceed to their finding in the supplemental case that "the transaction, the subject-matter of this case, was not an adventure in the nature of trade", this is a finding which is in truth no more than an inference from the facts already found. It could aptly be preceded by the word "therefore". Is it, then, an inference of fact? My Lords, it appears to me that the authority is over-whelmingly for saying that it is'[11].

'But it cannot, and has not been, questioned, that an inference, though regarded as a mere inference of fact, yet can be challenged as a matter of law on the grounds that I have already mentioned, and this is I think the safest way to leave it'[12].

'When the case comes before the court it is its duty to examine the determination having regard to its knowledge of the relevant law. If the case contains anything *ex facie* which is bad law and which bears upon the determination, it is, obviously, erroneous in point of law. But, without any misconception appearing *ex facie*, it may be that the facts found are such that no person acting judicially and properly instructed as to the relevant law could have come to the determination under appeal. In those circumstances, too, the court must intervene. It has no option but to assume that there has been some misconception of the law and that this has been responsible for the determination. So there, too, there has been error in point of law. I do not think that it much matters whether this state of affairs is described as one in which there is no evidence to support the determination or as one in which the evidence is inconsistent with and contradictory of the determination, or as one in which the true and only reasonable conclusion contradicts the determination'[13].

In the light of these cases, one may turn to *The Nema*. The contract in question was a charterparty, and the question was whether the vessel was still obliged to proceed in accordance with the charterers' orders, or whether (as the owners contended) the contract had been frustrated by a prolonged strike. The parties arranged an immediate arbitration in order to resolve the dispute. The

---

[10] Per Viscount Simonds at 29.
[11] Per Viscount Simonds at 30.
[12] Per Viscount Simonds at 32.
[13] Per Lord Radcliffe at 36.

arbitration published a reasoned award holding in favour of the owners that the contract was frustrated. The charterers sought and obtained leave to appeal; the owners appealed to the Court of Appeal against the order granting leave, but their appeal was dismissed. The substantive appeal was then argued in the High Court. The judge allowed the appeal, and held that the contract was not frustrated. On appeal, the Court of Appeal restored the decision of the arbitrator. Against this decision, a further appeal was brought to the House of Lords.

Two questions arose for direct decision by the House. First, according to what principles should a court, seized of an appeal under the 1979 Act, decide whether or not to allow the appeal? Second, in the instance case, should the award of the arbitrator be upheld?

In addition, much attention was devoted in the first of the two leading speeches, to the principles upon which the High Court should proceed when deciding whether to grant leave to appeal. This matter did not arise at all on the appeal, since the grant of leave had been affirmed by the Court of Appeal, as a decision against which there had been no further appeal. The House did, however, take the opportunity of providing guidance as to the way in which applications for leave should be dealt with in future, and although the statements of principle are obiter, they have been, and will continue to be, taken as the starting point of all further discussion on the matter.

We consider later in this Chapter[14] the implications of *The Nema* and subsequent cases on the practice of granting leave to appeal. It is, however, essential to note at the present stage that the guidelines laid down in relation to the grant of leave have no bearing on the decision of the substantive appeal, once leave has been granted[15]. At the stage of an application for leave, the matter is one of discretion. The appeal itself involves no discretion; the principles for deciding appeals must be directly applied. The distinction is clearly marked in the speeches of the House, but it is one which may easily be overlooked.

The principles now to be applied in determining appeals under the 1979 Act were stated in each of the two leading speeches. After pointing out that the power to require the arbitrator to state a special case under the 1950 Act was not expressly limited to questions of law, and that this limitation arose by implication[16], whereas there was an express provision to this effect in the 1979 Act, Lord Diplock continued:

'... ever since the decision of this House 25 years ago in *Edwards v Bairstow*, [the words] have been understood (at least where the tribunal from which such an appeal lies is not itself a court of law) as bearing the precise meaning as to the function of the court to which an appeal on a question of law is brought that is stated in the classic passage to be found in the speech of Lord Radcliffe ...

[then followed part of the passage quoted above].

---

[14]   At pp. 602–613, post.

[15]   We do not of course, suggest that the converse proposition is true. The principles for deciding appeals are relevant to the grant of leave, for one of the matters which the judge will take into account when exercising his discretion is whether, if leave were granted, the application of these principles would be likely to lead to the success of the appeal.

[16]   The words 'any question of law' were, however, used in s. 21(1)(a), in relation to a consultative case.

'Or, as Lord Denning MR summarised it in dealing with the question of frustration in the instant case: to justify interference with the arbitrator's award it must be shown (i) that the arbitrator misdirected himself in law or (ii) the decision was such that no reasonable arbitrator could reach'.

Lord Roskill said:

'My Lords, In *Edwards v Bairstow* Lord Radcliffe made it plain that the court should only interfere with the conclusion of the special commissioners if it were shown either that they had erred in law or that they had reached a conclusion on the facts which they had found which no reasonable person, applying the relevant law, could have reached. My Lords, when it is shown on the face of a reasoned award that the appointed tribunal has applied the right test, the court should in my view only interfere if on the facts found as applied to that right legal test, no reasonable person could have reached that conclusion. It ought not to interfere merely because the court thinks that upon those facts and applying that test, it would not or might not itself have reached the same conclusion, for to do that would be for the court to usurp what is the sole function of the tribunal of fact'.

2 Types of reviewable issues

The classification of issues affected by the power to review, turning as it does on the distinction between issues of fact and law, poses a problem as troublesome in the law of arbitration as in other fields of judicial control. Moreover, the relevant principles have now been restated[17] in terms which make it unwise to rely on any of the earlier cases[18].

It is convenient to discuss the principles involved by reference to four examples.

(a) The arbitrator decides on the true construction of the contract, in the light of any relevant statute or rule of law, that upon the happening of a particular event a party was obliged to give notice thereof to the other party, in such a manner that it reached him in a reasonable time.

(b) The arbitrator decides, in the light of the oral evidence, that the event has happened, and that the party posted a notice thereof to the other party.

(c) There is no direct evidence as to the time when the notice was received, but the arbitrator infers from all the facts of which there was direct evidence, or from matters within his own knowledge properly taken into account, that it was received ten days after the happening of the event.

(d) The arbitrator decides that ten days was a reasonable time.

(a) Conclusions of law

A decision of type '(a)' raises a question of law. Upon this, the Court has a full power of review which it will exercise if either (a) it can be seen from what the arbitrator has said in his award, or any reasons given subsequently, that he has

---

[17] In *BTP Tioxide Ltd v Pioneer Shipping Ltd, The Nema* [1981] 2 Lloyd's Rep 239, [1982] AC 724, discussed below.
[18] Appendix 5 of the first edition of this work contained a list and brief description of some of the earlier cases.

arrived at his conclusion through a mistaken understanding of the law, or (b) irrespective of what he has said, a mistake of law can be inferred by reading his conclusion in the light of the facts which he has found. Only two points need to be made.

1 First, there is nothing in the Act or in *The Nema* which make the power of review a matter of discretion if the Court has given leave to appeal. If the award proceeds on a wrong basis of law, the court must put it right.

2 Second, it is immaterial whether the court can see at once that the decision is erroneous in law, or whether this opinion is arrived at only after a lengthy and finely-balanced investigation of complex principles. The legal basis of the decision is either right or wrong. If the latter, it must be corrected, however near to the line the point may be[19]. In this respect, *The Nema* has not demonstrated any change in the principle of judicial review.

(b) 'Primary' findings of fact and (c) 'Secondary' findings of fact

A decision of type '(b)', often called a 'pure' finding of fact, or a finding of 'primary' fact[20], or of type (b), often called a 'secondary' finding of fact or an inference of fact, is in principle not subject to review. A mistake of fact by the arbitrator, unless admitted by him, is not a ground either of appeal, or of an application to set aside or remit the award[1]. To this general principle there may be one exception, or apparent exception, namely that the question whether there was any evidence to support a particular finding of fact made by the arbitrator is regarded as a question of law[1].

The view has, however, been expressed that *The Nema* has, against all expectations, widened the power of the Court to interfere with the decision of arbitrators: the argument being that the House of Lords has introduced the whole of the principles of review described in *Edwards v Bairstow* into the law of arbitration, and that this includes a power to correct any award in respect of which the arbitrators have, in making a particular finding of fact 'acted without any evidence or upon a view of the facts which could not reasonably be entertained'. (Viscount Simonds, in the passage quoted above.) Thus, so it is argued, the House of Lords have opened a breach in the fundamental principle that the arbitrator's findings of fact are inviolable.

If this were indeed a correct interpretation of *The Nema*, the result would be a startling repudiation of the legislative policy underlying the 1979 Act; for although it could be strongly argued that no narrowing of the basis of judicial review could legitimately be inferred in those instances where a right of appeal was entrenched, or where the parties had not availed themselves of the liberty to make an exclusion agreement, the possibility that the grounds for attacking an award had been widened would act as a further deterrent to those foreign

---

[19] The presence of the word 'obviously' in the passage quoted from *Edwards v Bairstow*, supra, has led to some misapprehension. Lord Radcliffe was not suggesting that the Court could interfere only if the decision was obviously wrong. The word denotes the obviousness of Lord Radcliffe's proposition, not the obviousness of the error.

[20] The whole topic of the distinction between fact and law is bedevilled by ambiguous terminology, not always consistently applied.

[1] There may be one exception, or apparent exception, to this principle, namely that the question whether there was *any* evidence to support a particular finding of fact is capable of amounting to a question of law: see p. 596, post.

interests who disliked the power of review on questions of law. We believe, however, that this is not the correct interpretation of the speeches in *The Nema*, for two reasons.

1 First, if any distinction could be drawn between the doctrines of *Edwards v Bairstow* as a whole, and those set out in the passage from Lord Radcliffe's speech quoted by Lord Diplock, it would in our submission be held on a reading of the language which we have quoted from the two leading speeches, that the House of Lords had intended to adopt only the principles explicitly stated in the quoted passage[2].

2 Second, we suggest that the discussion in *Edwards v Bairstow* was not concerned with the relationship between the 'raw' evidence and the tribunal's findings of primary fact: or, at least, was not discussing it in a manner which can be applied directly to the law of arbitration. When considering an allegation of perversity against the verdict of a jury, or other tribunal which gives no reasons for its decisions, the reviewing court has no alternative but to look at the raw evidence, for there is nothing else at which to look. But *Edwards v Bairstow* was concerned with a different situation. There the decision was not one of pure fact; it fell into category (d). Nor was it a decision unsupported by reasons, for the matter was before the court in the form of a special case, which contained findings of primary fact, as well as a conclusion based on the commissioners' assessment of the word 'trade' in the light of those findings. Thus, in the context of *Edwards v Bairstow*, the 'evidence' consisted of the findings set out in the special case. So also with an arbitration. The principle of *Edwards v Bairstow* should be applied, so as to treat the findings of fact in the arbitrator's reasons for his award as the 'evidence', with which the conclusion is brought face to face[3].

For this reason, we consider that the interpretation given to the 1979 Act by the speeches in *The Nema* has not altered the principles of review in connection with decisions on issues of primary and secondary fact.

(d) Mixed conclusions of fact and law

The real practical problems arise from category '(d)' which concerns the stage of the decision-making process at which the arbitrator puts together the facts and the law, to arrive at a conclusion.

Three situations can be distinguished –

1 The arbitrator finds facts A, B and C. The application of legal principle P would lead inevitably to a decision X, without the need for any further exercise of judgment on the part of the arbitrator.

2 The arbitrator finds facts A, B and C. The application of principle P would not lead inevitably to decision X. A careful arbitrator, acting judicially in the light of an accurate understanding of the law, might come to decision X or Y. In the event, the arbitrator arrived at decision Y.

---

[2] It would have been a surprising step to incorporate the whole of the common law relating to judicial review of the decisions of subordinate tribunals for error of law bodily into the law of arbitration, for the jurisdiction asserted by the courts over such tribunals is being progressively extended by devices quite foreign to the law of arbitration, and quite contrary in spirit to the legislative policy of the 1979 Act: see de Smith, Judicial Review of Administrative Action.

[3] This is, we believe, in accord with the opinion expressed by Upjohn LJ in *Tersons v Stevenage Development Corpn*, supra, at 54.

3 The situation is the same as in example (2), but the arbitrator arrives at decision Z.

Example (1) presents no problem. If the arbitrator has indeed arrived at the logically inevitable decision – viz. decision X – the Court will not intervene; for if he has made a mistake at all, it concerns the finding of facts A, B and C, and this is not open to review. If, however, the arbitrator has arrived at a decision other than X, then the Court can intervene, basing its jurisdiction on the assumption that the arbitrator's illogical answer must have flowed from a misunderstanding of the legal principle.

Example (2) produces a different result. In principle the Court will not intervene. The judge will say – 'Well, I would not myself have regarded ten days as a reasonable time, but I can see that others might, and I will therefore allow the arbitrator's own opinion to stand'.

Example (3) is also reasonably clear in principle. The Court will approach it in the same way as example (1), by assuming that the preference of Z and X or Y stemmed from a covert misunderstanding of the true legal principles.

We do not consider that *The Nema* has brought about any change in the principles upon which decisions in category (d) should be reviewed. The House did not decide that such decisions are immune from appeal. If this had been the intention, the House would have explained that the approach in *Tsakiroglou v Noblee Thorl* was not appropriate to appeals under the new Act, and would have proceeded directly to the inevitable conclusion that the appeal must fail[4]. Instead, there is no suggestion that the type of analysis found in *Tsakiroglou* should now be discarded; and the speech of Lord Roskill, with which the other members concurred, discussed in detail the question whether the decision of the arbitrator was correct. The tenor of the speeches is entirely consistent with the application of the methods applied before the 1979 Act came into force[5].

3 Nature of the review

As to the remaining question, namely the nature of the review undertaken on questions of law, there is no doubt. Once satisfied that the decision is one in respect of which there is power to intervene, the Court will simply measure the decision against the facts, and if its own judgment differs from that of the arbitrator, the latter will yield. There is no question of exercising a discretion. The Court decides whether the arbitrator was right or wrong, and gives judgment accordingly, although weight is attached to the findings of arbitrators experienced in the trade in question[6].

4 What are reasons?

We now consider briefly the problem of identifying the material to which the

---

[4] Equally, the House would have stated that leave should never be given to appeal against a decision in category (d), since the appeal would be bound to fail. Instead, the full discussion of the 'guidelines' for the grant of leave is quite irreconcilable with any such views.

[5] *Finelvet AG v Vinava Shipping Co Ltd, The Chrysalis* [1983] 1 Lloyd's Rep 503; *Atisa SA v Aztec AG* [1983] 2 Lloyd's Rep 579 at 585.

[6] See *The Nema*, ante, at 116 at 123, 124 (frustration); *André & Cie v Cook Industries Inc* [1986] 2 Lloyd's Rep 200 at 204 (construction of commercial correspondence); cf. *Gill & Duffus SA v Soc. pour l'Exportation des Sucres SA* [1986] 1 Lloyd's Rep 322, 325.

Court may have regard when considering an appeal. Section 1(6)(a) refers to 'a reasoned award', an expression suggesting that the reasons must form part of the structure of the award itself. We believe that the Court would not read the section so narrowly, and would hold that an award will 'set out the reasons for the award' if they are contained in a document which is so expressed, or delivered in such a manner, as to justify the inference that for the purposes of any ultimate appeal the formal award and the document were intended to be read together[7]. This would happen if the award referred to the document; or vice versa, in such terms as to show that the two amounted to a single award; or if they were physically attached to one another; or if they were delivered contemporaneously without any indication that the reasons were not to be read as part of the award[8]. In most cases, however, there will be no practical reason why the arbitrator should not incorporate the reasons in the body of the award, and this is what he ought to do, in order to avoid the possibility of argument.

Rather less straightforward in theory is the situation where the arbitrator delivers his reasons after the publication of the award, because of the rule that once an arbitrator has published his award he is functus officio[9]. If the effect of the rule is that the arbitrator has no power to defer giving reasons for his award until after publication, considerable inconvenience may result in cases where the parties are anxious to have a quick decision without waiting for the arbitrator to formulate his reasons in writing[10]. We suggest, however, that the rule does not go this far, and that it merely prevents the arbitrator from varying his award after it has been published[11]. It is clear that an arbitrator has power to issue reasons after publication of the award, if ordered to do so by the Court under section 1(5): and it would be entirely consistent with the policy of the 1979 Act to hold that he has power to do so without an order. But until the point has been settled it will be safer for the arbitrator to obtain the express agreement of the parties if he proposes to defer giving reasons until after publication of the award.

---

[7] Under the old system the courts evinced a marked reluctance to look at documents which were referred to, but not physically embodied or reproduced in the award, for the purpose of challenging an award on the grounds of error on the face: see, for example *Andrea v British Italian Trading Co Ltd* [1962] 1 Lloyd's Rep 151, [1963] 1 QB 201; and; *A/B Legis v V Berg & Sons Ltd* [1964] 1 Lloyd's Rep 203. Under the new system, however, there is no reason of policy why the court should not read any document which the arbitrator intended should be read in the event of an appeal, including any document referred to in the reasons, even if not physically incorporated in them.

[8] In *Pearl Marin Shipping A/B v Pietro Cingolani SAS* [1982] 1 Lloyd's Rep 17 the Court of Appeal held that where reasons for award were delivered in the same envelope as the award itself, without any covering letter, but also without any express statement that they were not to form part of the award, they were 'on the face of the award' for the purposes of the old system. We suggest that this conclusion will apply, a fortiori, to appeals under the new Act. Contrast *SL Sethia Liners Ltd v Naviagro Maritime Corpn, The Kostas Melas* [1981] 1 Lloyd's Rep 18 at 29–30, in which the court declined to treat as 'reasons' a document prepared for the purpose of rebutting an allegation of misconduct.

[9] *A/B Legis v V Berg & Sons Ltd*, ante.

[10] Because the logical consequences of the rule would be that the reasons would have been given by a person who was no longer an arbitrator. The problem could only be overcome by an application under s. 1(5): but, in the absence of some special reason, such an application could not be made where the 'arbitrator' had given reasons voluntarily.

[11] See p. 405, ante.

5 Finding of fact made without evidence

There remains one question to be considered: namely, whether it is still permissible, as it was under the old system[12], to invoke the processes of appeal in a case where it is said that a finding of primary or secondary fact was arrived at without any evidence. If the analysis set out above is correct, we suggest that this jurisdiction should no longer be recognised. But, in any event, the courts will be likely to stifle such appeals at the stage of the application for leave, on the ground that they are out of accord both with the general principle that the arbitrator is master of the facts, and with the specific commercial aims of the new system[13].

C. REASONS

1 Introduction

The system of appeals under section 1 of the 1979 Act depends on there being before the Court a document containing the arbitrator's decision on the point of law and the facts and legal reasoning which underly the decision. Such a document is referred to in the Act as a 'reasoned award'[14]. If there is no such document, or if the Court considers that the reasons are stated in insufficient detail to enable it to consider the question of law, the Court has, subject to certain conditions being satisfied, power to remit the award to the arbitrator to give reasons or further reasons.

The material parts of section 1 read as follows –

'(5) Subject to subsection (6) below, if an award is made and, on an application made by any of the parties to the references, –
(a) with the consent of all the other parties to the reference, or
(b) subject to section 3 below, with the leave of the court,
it appears to the High Court that the award does not or does not sufficiently set out the reasons for the award, the court may order the arbitrator or umpire concerned to state the reasons for his award in sufficient detail to

---

[12] The practice of treating this as a question of law which could be made the subject of a special case gained impetus, if it was not actually engendered, by a dictum of Devlin J in *Nello Simoni v A/S M/ S Straum* (1949) 83 Ll L Rep 157 at 161. Although the existence of the jurisdiction was from time to time used as a means of applying pressure to the arbitrator whilst the reference was still in progress, we are not aware of any case in which it was successfully invoked in the High Court and its use was strongly discouraged: *Granvias Oceanicas Armadora SA v Jibsen Trading Co, The Kavo Peiratis* [1977] 2 Lloyd's Rep 344 at 352 (special order as to costs); *GKN Centrax Gear Ltd v Matbro Ltd* [1976] 2 Lloyd's Rep 555 at 584; *Zim Israel Navigation Co Ltd v Effy Shipping Corpn, The Effy* [1972] 1 Lloyd's Rep 18. The jurisprudential basis of the asserted right to interfere with primary and secondary findings of fact was never fully explored. The nearest approach was in *Tersons v Stevenage Development Corpn* [1963] 2 Lloyd's Rep 333, [1965] 1 QB 37, but this was concerned with a finding in category (d). It may be noted that Pearson LJ, at 56, asserted that findings of primary fact should not normally be made the subject of a special case. (We believe that the Lord Justice used this expression to include what we have called 'secondary findings of fact', and that he used the word 'secondary' to denote findings in category (d)).

[13] See, for example, *Mondial Trading Co GmbH v Gill and Duffus Zuckerhandelsgesellschaft mbH* [1980] 2 Lloyd's Rep 376; *Universal Petroleum Co Ltd v Handels-und Transport GmbH* [1987] 1 WLR 1178.

[14] S. 1(6)(a).

enable the court, should an appeal be brought under this section, to consider any question of law arising out of the award.

(6) In any case where an award is made without any reason being given, the High Court shall not make an order under subsection (5) above unless it is satisfied –

(a) that before the award was made one of the parties to the reference gave notice to the arbitrator or umpire concerned that a reasoned award would be required; or

(b) that there is some special reason why such a notice was not given'.

The circumstances in which an arbitrator has a duty to make a reasoned award, and what such an award should contain, are discussed in Chapter 25. We are here concerned with the consequences of the arbitrator failing to comply with his duty, whether by failing to make a reasoned award at all, or by failing to give sufficient reasons.

2 Court's power to order reasons

(a) Jurisdiction

The Court has jurisdiction to order the arbitrator to state his reasons in either of two cases –

1 Where the arbitrator has not set out any reason for his award.

2 Where he has not sufficiently set out the reasons for his award.

In case (1) the Court must first also be satisfied either (a) that one of the parties gave notice to him before the award was made that a reasoned award would be required, or (b) that there is 'some special reason' why such a notice was not given. This expression no doubt encompasses a case where the party was led to believe that his opponent had given notice; or where the arbitrator had indicated an intention to make a reasoned award; or where, because of a misunderstanding, the applicant has acted in the genuine belief that a reasoned award would be given[15]; or where a notice has gone astray by accident[16].

Where neither of these conditions is satisfied, the Court has no jurisdiction unless the arbitrator has at least set out to give some reasons. For this purpose it is not sufficient for the applicant to show simply that the arbitrator has set out some of the relevant facts nor even that he has given some explanation for his award, for even the simplest non-speaking award requires some narrative and explanatory material. The arbitrator should not feel that in including such material he is giving a hostage to fortune. The Court will be slow to conclude that an arbitrator intended to make a reasoned award when he has not been requested to do so, and it will not order further reasons in the absence of a prior request or special reasons excusing such a request unless it is satisfied that the

---

[15] *Warde v Feedex International Inc* [1984] 1 Lloyd's Rep 310.

[16] *Hayn Roman & Co SA v Cominter (UK) Ltd* [1982] 1 Lloyd's Rep 295. The application should be made promptly: per Goff J at 296; and in any event within 21 days of the publication of the award: RSC Ord. 73, r. 5(1)(c).

arbitrator consciously set out to create an appealable award, but has failed to go far enough in his reasons to achieve this result[17].

(b) Discretion

Even where the Court has power to order further reasons it retains a discretion whether or not to do so. Since the only purpose of ordering the arbitrator to give reasons or further reasons is to enable the Court, should it give leave to appeal, to consider any question of law arising out of the award, the overriding consideration is whether the Court would in any event be likely to give leave to appeal if full reasons were ordered. No order for further reasons will be made unless there is a real prospect of leave to appeal being granted[18]. Nor will the Court order further reasons where they are material only to a point which was not argued before the arbitrator[19].

In many cases it will be apparent from the award itself whether the reasons are sufficient to enable the question of law to be considered on appeal. In other cases, however, the inadequacy of the reasons may only be demonstrable by evidence as to what evidence and arguments were adduced at the arbitration. The extent to which such evidence is admissible, if at all, raises some difficult problems. Three situations need to be considered.

1 The arbitrator makes a finding of fact for which there is said to be no evidence or reaches a conclusion of mixed fact and law which is said to be a conclusion which no reasonable arbitrator could have reached. In this situation evidence about the factual material on which the arbitrator bases his award is inadmissible, unless the arbitrator has been specifically requested at the arbitration to state the reasons for his conclusions on the issue[20].

2 The arbitrator fails altogether to deal with a submission made to him at the arbitration. Here the Court will admit evidence about what arguments were addressed to him, for the purpose of seeing whether he has dealt with them adequately or at all in his award[1].

---

[17] *Trave Schiffahrtsgesellschaft mbH v Ninemia Maritime Corp, The Niedersachsen* [1986] 1 Lloyd's Rep 393. The fact that the arbitrator had given privileged reasons was a strong indication that he had not intended a reasoned award.

[18] *Universal Petroleum Co Ltd v Handels und Transport GmbH* [1987] 1 WLR 1178; *Warde v Feedex International Inc* [1984] 1 Lloyd's Rep 310. It is impracticable and entirely contrary to the spirit of the new legislation to require arbitrators to make findings on every detailed point canvassed before them': per Bingham J in *Bulk Oil (Zug) AG v Sun International Ltd (No 2)* [1984] 1 Lloyd's Rep 531 at 551.

[19] *Schiffahrtsagentur Hamburg Middle East Line GmbH v Virtue Shipping Corpn, The Oinoussian Virtue* [1981] 1 Lloyd's Rep 533, 539; *Bremer Handelsgesellschaft mbH v Westzucker GmbH (No 2)* [1981] 2 Lloyd's Rep 130.

[20] It is implicit in the judgment of Kerr LJ in *Universal Petroleum v Handels und Transport GmbH*, supra, that evidence of such a request is admissible, since he expressly refers to the possibility of further reasons when the necessary foundation for such a challenge has been laid. Moreover, without at least some evidence of what evidence or argument was adduced, it is difficult to see how the Court could tell whether or not the arbitrator has complied with the request. Challenges of this kind are, however, firmly discouraged by the courts: see p. 596.

[1] *Kansa General Insurance Co Ltd v Bishopsgate Insurance plc* [1988] 1 Lloyd's Rep 503. As Hirst J points out, if such evidence were inadmissible, the result would be that the more inadequate the arbitrator's reasons the more difficult it would be to obtain an order for further reasons. Remission under s. 22 of the 1950 Act might afford an alternative remedy, but it seems preferable to remain within the statutory framework of the 1979 Act where remission is sought in aid of an appeal under that Act. See also *Vermala Shipping Enterprises Ltd v Minerals and Metals Trading Corpn of India Ltd* [1982] 1 Lloyd's Rep 469.

3 The arbitrator fails altogether to make a finding of fact on a matter which could materially affect the prospects of an appeal. Unless the Court can be told that there was evidence of the fact, which may indeed have been admitted, real injustice may be suffered by the losing party. Deliberate or improper suppression of facts may well found an application for remission under section 22 of the 1950 Act[2]. But such a case, if it were ever to arise, would be extremely difficult to prove. In practice the omission of facts is more likely to be the result of inadvertence. In such a case, provided the arbitrator has been requested[3] to make a finding of the particular fact, it seems that evidence may be given of the fact of the request and of any evidence to support the finding which was requested[4]. But it remains the duty of each party to draw the arbitrator's attention to facts which he maintains are relevant to the legal issues in the reference, and if he fails to do so he cannot later complain that the award does not contain the necessary findings to enable him to launch an appeal.

Although the Court has jurisdiction to order further reasons where the arbitrator has given reasons spontaneously and not pursuant to a request by either of the parties, the fact that no request has been made tells heavily against sending the award back to the arbitrator[5].

The Court has jurisdiction to impose a condition on an order for further reasons that the amount of the award be brought into court, wholly or in part[6].

3 Remission under section 22

In general, the Court will remit under section 1(5), rather than under the general power conferred by section 22 of the 1950 Act, when the purpose is to obtain additional findings[7]. There are, however, circumstances in which the general power will be useful: for example if there has been a change in the law since the appeal was argued[8], or if the Court considers it necessary to remit of its own motion[9]. Apart from the statutory provisions, however, an arbitrator cannot be ordered to give evidence as to his reasons[10].

---

[2] Or perhaps under s. 1(5) itself: *Mafracht v Parnes Shipping Co SA, The Apollonius* [1986] 2 Lloyd's Rep 405, 415–416.

[3] We do not suggest that the request should be in writing: this would bring about a return to the much-criticised practice under the old system of submitting detailed written requests for findings of fact to the arbitrator before he made his award: see p. 375, ante. All that is necessary, we submit, is that the arbitrator should have been put on notice that the fact was said to be relevant to a live issue of law. In some cases, particularly where the fact is not in issue and is obviously relevant, very little will be needed to satisfy the Court that the arbitrator was on notice that a finding was necessary.

[4] There are dicta in *Universal Petroleum Co Ltd v Handels und Transportgesellschaft mbH*, and *The Apollonius*, supra, which indicate a stricter approach, but we suggest that these should be understood as referring to the specific types of challenge which were in issue in that case, namely an assertion that a finding of fact had been made without evidence, or that a mixed conclusion of fact and law was perverse.

[5] *The Niedersachsen*, supra.

[6] *Warde v Feedex International Inc* [1984] 1 Lloyd's Rep 310, 316.

[7] *Schiffahrtsagentur Hamburg Middle East Line GmbH v Virtue Shipping Corpn, The Oinoussian Virtue* [1981] 1 Lloyd's Rep 533 at 539; *JH Rayner (Mincing Lane) Ltd v Shaher Trading Co* [1982] 1 Lloyd's Rep 632; *Bulk Oil (Zug) AG v Sun International Ltd (No 2)* [1984] 1 Lloyd's Rep 531.

[8] *Bremer Handelsgesellschaft mbH v Westzucker GmbH (No 2)* [1981] 2 Lloyd's Rep 130.

[9] This is permissible under s. 22. S. 1(5) of the 1979 Act gives jurisdiction to remit only on the application of one of the parties to the reference.

[10] *Duke of Buccleugh v Metropolitan Board of Works* (1872) LR 5 HL 418.

There is a curious feature of section 1(5) which seems to add an unnecessary extra stage to the procedure. The order for additional reasons is made pursuant to an application, which itself is made (a) with the consent of all parties, or (b) with the leave of the Court. It therefore appears that the party must apply for leave to apply for additional reasons. In practice the Court will usually allow time to be saved by bringing both applications on at the same time, together with the application for leave to appeal[11].

It is unlikely that the Court will order further reasons, where they are material only to a point which was not argued before the arbitrators[12].

4 Inferences of fact

A question which arose frequently under the old system, and is likely to recur under the new, is whether the Court has power to avoid a remission for further reasons by drawing inferences of fact. On the hearing of a special case it was well established that the Court had power to draw inferences of fact, and that this power was derived from the Rule of the Supreme Court[13]. There is, however, no comparable Rule enabling inferences to be drawn on an appeal under the new system[14], and it is doubtful whether a court which is not seized of an appeal on the facts has an inherent power to draw inferences[15], however clear it may be that only one inference could possibly be drawn. If this is indeed the case, the only way in which a missing fact can be brought before the Court is by remitting the award for further reasons, either under section 1(5) of the 1979 Act or under section 22 of the 1950 Act[16].

In practice, however, this problem may not often arise. Even under the old system the Court would not draw inferences of fact unless they flowed inevitably from the other facts found[17]. If the inference is indeed inevitable the parties are likely to agree that it should be drawn in order to avoid the expense and delay of a remission: and a party who insists on a remission and has the fact found against him may find himself liable to pay the costs of the remission.

D. LEAVE TO APPEAL

1 Introduction

The 1979 Act, as interpreted in subsequent decided cases, has radically changed the mechanisms for judicial review on questions of law. Formerly, the Court was for all practical purposes obliged to determine a question of law raised by an award in the form of a special case. A discretion existed only where the arbitrator had been asked to state a case, but had refused to do so. Under the new system, there are two discretions. First, to order reasons to be given where the arbitrator

---

[11] *Bulk Oil (Zug) AG v Sun International Ltd (No 2)*, supra at 540–541; *Warde v Feedex International Inc* [1984] 1 Lloyd's Rep 310 at 311.

[12] See p. 609, post.

[13] Ord. 56, r. 11; formerly Ord. 34, r. 1: see *Universal Cargo Carrier's Corpn v Citati (No 2)* [1958] 2 Lloyd's Rep 17, [1958] 2 QB 254 and cf. Ord. 59, r. 10(3).

[14] Unless Ord. 55, r. 7(3) applies to such appeals: see pp. 636–637, post.

[15] See the cases in the notes to Ord. 59, r. 10(3) in the *Supreme Court Practice*.

[16] Unless the parties agree the missing fact.

[17] *Sunbeam Shipping Co Ltd v The President of India, The Atlantic Sunbeam* [1973] 1 Lloyd's Rep 482.

has failed to comply with a request for a reasoned award. Second, to refuse leave for any appeal to be brought at all in a case where one of the parties to the reference withholds his consent to an appeal. The first discretion has some resemblance to the former power to order a special case[18]. The second is entirely new. Its presence means that appeals are fewer, even in those cases where there is no valid exclusion agreement. On the other hand, appeals take longer to prosecute.

When an application is made for leave to appeal, the Court must consider two distinct questions. First, it must decide whether –

'... having regard to all the circumstances, the determination of the question of law could substantially affect the rights of one or more parties to the arbitration agreement'[19].

If this requirement is not satisfied, the Court has no jurisdiction to entertain the appeal.

Second, there is the general discretion conferred by the provision in section 1(3)(b) that an appeal may be brought 'with the leave of the court'.

There are no major conceptual difficulties in relation to the first stage of the enquiry. The word 'could', as distinct from 'will', was no doubt chosen to deal with the case where the application for leave is brought before the arbitrator's findings of fact are known, so that it is impossible to predict whether or not the decision will ultimately affect the parties' rights. The word 'substantially' is a fertile source of ambiguity. In this particular context, we believe that it does not mean 'more than de minimis', but denotes an effect on the rights of the parties which is of major importance, in the context of the dispute as a whole[20].

The real difficulty has been to appreciate the basis on which the general discretion should be exercised under section 1(3)(b). Both before and after the enactment of the new system, there was speculation as to the way in which the courts would interpret their novel powers. One view was that since the right of appeal had been expressly preserved for those cases where the parties were not permitted, or had not chosen, to exclude by consent the supervisory jurisdiction of the Court, this jurisdiction would continue to be exercised on the same lines as before. This opinion was decisively repudiated by the House of Lords in *BTP Tioxide v Pioneer Shipping Co, The Nema*[1] in a series of propositions, described as 'guidelines'. Although technically these were obiter dicta, they were immediately accepted[2] as authoritative statements of principle, which should form the starting-point of any subsequent discussion.

---

[18] The resemblance is superficial, because reasons will not be ordered unless either leave to appeal has already been given, or there is at least a reasonable prospect that leave will be given, once the findings of fact are known.

[19] S. 1(4).

[20] The importance of the issue has thus far been treated as relevant to the exercise of the discretion, rather than a formal condition precedent to jurisdiction: see, for example *International Sea Tankers Inc v Hemisphere Shipping Co, The Wenjiang* [1982] 1 Lloyd's Rep 128, and *Retla SS Co v Gryphon Shipping Co SA, The Evimeria* [1982] 1 Lloyd's Rep 55.

[1] [1981] 2 Lloyd's Rep 239, [1981] 3 WLR 292.

[2] Notably, in *Italmare Shipping Co v Ocean Tanker Co Inc, The Rio Sun* [1981] 2 Lloyd's Rep 489 and *International Sea Tankers v Hemisphere Shipping Co, The Wenjiang, ante.*

2 The Nema guidelines: a new philosophy

After *The Nema*, difficulty was experienced in adapting the guidelines to the circumstances of individual applications for leave, and a formidable body of authority rapidly sprang up[3] culminating in a further decision of the House of Lords in *The Antaios*[4], which resolved most of the points of difficulty which had arisen in practice, and permitted the jurisdiction to be exercised in a more settled, efficient and predictable manner. Points of principle do still arise for decision on occasion, but in the main it is now possible to regard the two decisions in *The Nema* and *The Antaios* as the principal cases, and the only ones which need to be considered in straightforward situations.

It is convenient at this stage to set out the material passages from the speech of Lord Diplock, in which the other members of the House concurred[5]:

'Where, as in the instant case, a question of law involved is the construction of a 'one-off' clause the application of which to the particular facts of the case is an issue in the arbitration, leave should not normally be given unless it is apparent to the judge upon a mere perusal of the reasoned award itself without the benefit of adversarial argument, that the meaning ascribed to the clause by the arbitrator is obviously wrong. But if on such perusal it appears to the judge that it is possible that argument might persuade him, despite first impression to the contrary, that the arbitrator might be right, he should not grant leave; the parties should be left to accept, for better or for worse, the decision of the tribunal that they had chosen to decide the matter in the first instance. The instant case was clearly one in which there was more than one possible view as to the meaning of the 'one-off' clause as it affected the issue of divisibility. It took two days' argument by counsel before the learned judge to satisfy him that the arbitrator was wrong on this and upon the interdependent question of frustration, four days' argument before the Court of Appeal to convince them that the judge was wrong and the arbitrator right and over three days' argument in trying to persuade this House to the contrary, even though it was not found necessary to call upon the respondent to address us on the merits. Even apart from the reasons special to this case mentioned at the outset, which led Moccata J and Donaldson J to conclude that it was a case in which no court would grant leave to appeal from the arbitrator's award, it is in my view typical of the sort of case in which leave to appeal on a question of construction ought not to be granted.

For reasons already sufficiently discussed, rather less strict criteria are in my view appropriate where questions of construction of contracts in standard terms are concerned. That there should be as high a degree of

---

[3] *The Rio Sun*, ante; *BVS and The Khuzestan Water and Power Authority v Kerman Shipping Co, The Kerman* [1982] 1 Lloyd's Rep 62; *Retla SS Co v Gryphon Shipping Co, The Evimeria*, ante; *Marrealeza Compania Naviera SA v Tradax Export SA, The Nichols A* [1982] 1 Lloyd's Rep 52; *Astro Valiente Compania Naviera SA v Government of Pakistan, The Emmanuel Colocotronis* [1982] 1 Lloyd's Rep 297; *National Rumour Co SA v Lloyd's Libra Navigacio SA* [1982] 1 Lloyd's Rep 472, *The Wenjiang*, ante; *Tor Line AB v Alltrans Group of Canada Ltd, The TFL Prosperity* [1982] 1 Lloyd's Rep 617; *Phoenix Shipping Corpn v Apex Shipping Corpn, The Apex* [1982] 1 Lloyd's Rep 476; *Bulk Oil (Zug) AG v Sun International Ltd* [1983] 2 Lloyd's Rep 587.

[4] *Antaios Compania Naviera SA v Salen Rederna AB* [1985] AC 191.

[5] The speech of Lord Roskill was concerned almost entirely with the merits of the substantive appeal.

legal certainty as it is practicable to obtain as to how such terms apply upon the occurrence of events of a kind that it is not unlikely may reproduce themselves in similar transactions between other parties engaged in the same trade, is a public interest that is recognised by the Act, particularly in section 4. So, if the decision of the question of construction in the circumstances of the particular case would add significantly to the clarity and certainty of English commercial law it would be proper to give leave in a case sufficiently substantial to escape the ban imposed by the first part of section 1(4) bearing in mind always that a superabundance of citable judicial decisions arising out of slightly different facts is calculated to hinder rather than to promote clarity in settled principles of commercial law. But leave should not be given even in such a case, unless the judge considered that a strong prima facie case had been made out that the arbitrator had been wrong in his construction; and when the events to which the standard clause fell to be applied in the particular arbitration were themselves 'one-off' events, stricter criteria should be applied on the same lines as those that I have suggested as appropriate to 'one-off' clauses . . .

In deciding how to exercise his discretion whether to give leave to appeal under section 1(2) what the judge should normally ask himself in this type of arbitration[6], particularly where the events relied upon are 'one-off' events, is not whether he agrees with the decision reached by the arbitrator, but: does it appear upon perusal of the award either that the arbitrator mis-directed himself in law or that his decision was such that no reasonable arbitrator could reach? While this should, in my view, be the normal practice, there may be cases where the events relied upon as amounting to frustration are not 'one-off' events affecting only the transaction between the particular parties to the arbitration, but events of a general character that affect similar transactions between many other persons engaged in the same kind of commercial activity, the closing of the Suez Canal, the United States soya bean embargo, the war between Iraq and Iran, are instances within the last two decades that spring to mind. Where such is the case it is in the interests of legal certainty that there should be some uniformity in the decision of arbitrators as to the effect, frustrating or otherwise, of such an event upon similar transactions, in order that other traders may be sufficiently certain where they stand as to be able to close their own transactions without recourse to arbitration. In such a case, unless there were prospects of an appeal being brought by consent of all the parties as a test case under section 1(3)(a) it might be a proper exercise of the judge's discretion to give leave to appeal in order to express a conclusion as to the frustrating effect of the event that would afford guidance binding upon the arbitrators in other arbitrations arising out of the same event, if the judge thought that in the particular case in which leave to appeal was sought the conclusion reached by the arbitrator, although not deserving to be stigmatised as one which no reasonable person could have reached was, in the judge's view, not right. But such was far from being the instant case.'

These, and other passages in the judgments delivered in *The Nema*, reinforced

---

[6] We believe that the observations relating to 'this type of arbitration' relate to all arbitrations where the decision is one of mixed fact and law, made by a lay tribunal.

by similar observations by the House of the Lords in *The Antaios*, disclose a new philosophy of arbitration, which may be summarised as follows.

First, even in those cases where Parliament has preserved the jurisdiction to entertain appeals, it is no longer axiomatic that the courts should be alert to protect parties against decisions made contrary to that system of law which they have expressly or impliedly selected as applicable to their disputes. Nor is there any longer a paramount public interest in protecting the community from the growth in particular trades or practices whereby the rights of the parties are determined according to rules peculiar to those trades, and differing from the general law of the land. Instead, the Court will proceed on the assumption that the parties to an arbitration agreement are content to take the risk that the arbitrator will make mistakes of law, just as they have always been understood as willing to take the risk that he will make mistakes of fact. There is now a presumption in favour of the chosen tribunal, not the chosen law.

Second, there are limits to this presumption. The parties are not assumed, in general, to have submitted themselves unequivocally to honour an award which can be shown to be founded upon a manifest error of law.

Third, the strength of the presumption will vary from case to case.

Fourth, there is one consideration of public policy which on occasion will take priority over the wishes of the parties: namely, the need to retain arbitration appeals as a means of providing the raw material for decisions by the Court on matters of general legal import[7]. Arbitration appeals help to ensure that – (a) English law will maintain an up to date repertory of rules, sufficient to deal with the complexities of modern commerce, and (b) the courts can furnish authoritative guidance to arbitrators on the principles by which they should apply their own practical knowledge to individual commercial disputes, enabling them to decide these disputes in a consistent and orderly fashion.

Fifth, the Court regards delay as a prime source of prejudice, both to the efficacy of the arbitration system as a whole, and to the rights of the successful claimant in particular[8]. In the interests of eliminating the delay resulting from an unmeritorious appeal the Court will very often regard it as acceptable to run some risk of lending its own powers of enforcement to an award which the individual judge may consider to be wrong[9].

3 The Nema guidelines in practice

Since *The Nema* was decided, the courts have put into practice the principles laid down by the House of Lords. At first, the tendency was naturally to assume that this could best be achieved by directly applying the language of the

---

[7] This consideration of public policy recurs at the stage of an appeal to the Court of Appeal: see p. 627, post; ss. 1(7) and 2(3) and per Lord Diplock in *The Nema* at 246.

[8] This aspect received particular emphasis in the speech of Lord Roskill in *The Antaios*, ante, with which Lords Keith, Scarman and Brandon agreed.

[9] This principle cannot be carried too far. Speed is often an important attribute of arbitration, but this is not always so. It is well recognised that arbitration will not necessarily be the quickest way of resolving a dispute; whether this is so will depend on the nature and complexity of the dispute. Considerations such as procedural flexibility, privacy, and the right to nominate the tribunal may be given more weight in the individual case than any possible advantage in terms of speed; and at least some parties are willing to risk what promises to be a long reference made longer still by an appeal, so as to ensure that the benefits gained by sending the matter to arbitration are not lost because the arbitrator has made an uncorrected error of law.

guidelines to the circumstances of the individual case. This led to problems: attempts to focus on the precise language in which the new philosophy was expressed led to qualifications and refinements which tended to obscure the fact that the guidelines were intended to show the direction in which the new jurisdiction should move and to lay down broad principles rather than rigid and detailed rules for the solution of every problem[10]. A growing body of jurisprudence threatened to turn the simplest application for leave to appeal into an exercise in textual analysis of the speeches in *The Nema* and the judgments in the cases in which it had itself been analysed and discussed. All this came to an end with the decision in *The Antaios*, in which the House of Lords took the opportunity to restate the guidelines laid down in *The Nema*. At the same time it pointed the way to a simpler and quicker procedure for applications, which at once curtailed the expanding jurisprudence, save in the exceptional case where the guidelines needed reconsideration to take account of changing practices and unforeseen circumstances, and enabled applications which previously had lasted for hours or even days, to be disposed of within minutes.

The procedural changes which came about as the result of *The Antaios* are dealt with later[11]. Here we are concerned with the impact of *The Nema*, reinforced by *The Antaios*, on the court's approach to the question of whether leave to appeal should be granted. In the great majority of cases a sufficiently general picture of the spirit in which the 1979 Act should be applied has emerged from the two principal cases[12] to dispense the Court from the need for minute verbal analysis. Instead, the Court approaches the matter by reference to principles of a more general nature, such as those which we have endeavoured to summarise, and simply asks whether, in the light of these principles, it can be said that the interests of justice to the individual parties, and the need to promote the health of the common law, and to preserve the integrity of the arbitral process, require that the question of law should be argued again and decided in the High Court.

Accordingly, it is rarely necessary in practice to attempt a more precise formulation of the principles governing the grant of leave to appeal. We suggest, however, that the following propositions can be justified –

1 The strength of the presumption in favour of the award is not constant, but depends upon several factors.

2 As a general rule, the most important factor will be the utility of the decision on the question of law as a means either to clarify and develop a general principle of law likely to provide the solution to many different individual problems, or of supplying the answer to a specific question which is liable to recur frequently in practice.

3 Thus, the presumption will usually be at its strongest in the case of a 'one-off' contract, namely a contract which has been specially drafted by the parties for an individual transaction in terms which are unlikely to be reproduced in subsequent contracts, or a 'one-off' situation, namely a set of facts which is unlikely to recur. These expressions provide concise and useful descriptions of the instances where leave to appeal will not ordinarily be given, but they should not be used uncritically. A dispute under a 'one-off' contract may raise an

---

[10] *Aden Refinery Ltd v Ugland Management Ltd* [1987] QB 650.

[11] See pp. 609–611, post.

[12] *The Nema* and *The Antaios*, ante.

important question of principle, and it is only where the question not only arises under such a contract but concerns the meaning of its unique form of words, that the presumption is at its strongest. Again, the set of facts may be most unlikely to recur in precisely the same form, and yet may exemplify a type of situation on which authoritative legal guidance would be valuable. What really matters is whether the question raises a 'one-off' *point*. Conversely, the mere fact that a general principle is involved in the dispute does not necessarily make the case apt for appeal: for if a decision depends on the application of a well established principle to an individual set of facts, an appeal will do nothing to clarify or refine that principle so as to make it more readily apply to other situations arising in the future[13].

4 At the other extreme is the situation where the same point not only may occur, but has already occurred in relation to a series of current disputes[14]. Here, even if the relevant contracts and circumstances are not precisely similar, a decision by the Court will greatly reduce the risk that different arbitrators will arrive at different conclusions on the same issues, causing confusion and injustice, and discrediting the arbitral process[15].

5 Also at this end of the scale are to be found disputes which depend uoon the interpretation of contracts or clauses in general use in a particular trade[16].

6 The guidelines do not set out to describe the strength of the presumption where the dispute is of an intermediate character. All one can say is that the presumption will become steadily weaker, the less unique the point of law raised by the appeal[17].

7 At the 'one-off' end of the scale, the presumption is very strong, although it is never incapable of being rebutted. Various expressions have been used to

---

[13] This was the position in *The Nema.*

[14] Identifying a point which has already recurred presents little difficulty. It may be less easy to predict whether a point will recur in the *future*. But the effort must be made, since failure to identify a recurrent problem may result in the unhappy situation where the court may on one occasion refuse leave to appeal from the decision of Mr A, on the grounds that it raised a one-off point and is 'not obviously wrong', but in later years, when the point recurs before Mr B give leave to appeal and go on to decide that the decision of Mr A, contrary to appearances, was indeed wrong. An even less happy situation could perhaps be envisaged in which the court might on different occasions refuse leave to appeal from conflicting decisions of Mr C and Mr D on the grounds that neither was 'obviously wrong'.

[15] Conflicting decisions of arbitrators or judges at first instance on a recurrent point of law can and ordinarily should be resolved by using the appellate process to obtain an authoritative ruling: *Aden Refinery Co Ltd v Ugland Management Co Ltd* [1987] QB 650. But the process should not be used to resolve conflicting dicta: *The Antaios*, supra, at 204; *CA Venezolana de Navegacion v Bank Line Ltd, The Roachbank* [1988] 2 Lloyd's Rep 337. And when mixed questions of fact and law are involved, the possibility of conflicting decisions on the same or similar facts is the price that may have to be paid in the interests of finality: *Finelvet AG v Vinara Shipping Co Ltd, The Chrysalis* [1983] 1 Lloyd's Rep 503, 508.

[16] It is necessary to bear in mind that the need to enhance the common law is not the only proper motive for granting leave to appeal. For this purpose, what matters is whether the *point* is of general importance, and in this context the question is not whether an individual clause is in common use, but whether the dispute is of a type which can be seen to arise not infrequently on a clause of a particular type. See, for example, *The Apex*, ante.

[17] Rent review arbitrations provide a good example. A rent review clause is unlikely to be in a standard form, but it may well give rise to questions of law of wider general importance; moreover the arbitrator's decision may be decisive of questions material to future reviews under the same lease. Where both factors are present the court can properly give leave to appeal on less than a strong prima facie case that the arbitrator's decision was wrong: *Lucas Industries plc v Welsh Development Agency* [1986] Ch 500.

denote the degree to which the judge's provisional view on the question should differ from that reflected in the award, before leave to appeal should be given. Thus, it is said that the award must be 'obviously wrong on mere perusal'; that it must be 'clearly wrong'; that the judge 'would need a good deal of convincing that the arbitrator was right'. Leave would however be given if the judge received the decision with 'very considerable surprise'. It is not, however, always enough to show 'very considerable doubt'. On the other hand, the bare word 'wrong' has also been employed. No doubt other expressions can and will be used in the future. We suggest that it is unprofitable and indeed misleading to attempt a reconciliation. These turns of phrase reflect the reaction of the court to a particular award, in relation to a particular question of law, and they show that the principles for the exercise of the discretion are not confined to rigid categories.

8 Towards the other end of the scale, leave will be more readily given, but at least a real possibility of error by the arbitrator must still be apparent. In most cases, the applicant will have to establish a strong prima facie case that the arbitrator was wrong, and also demonstrate that a decision will add significantly to the clarity and certainty of the law[18]. In exceptional cases, however, where the point is of great general importance, it may well be enough to show that the arbitrator may have been wrong, or that the point is capable of serious argument[19].

9 The fact that the appeal raises a question of Community law does not put it into a separate category giving an automatic right of appeal. The guidelines must still be applied in the ordinary way. But in considering the likelihood of an appeal succeeding the Court must have regard to its duty to ensure the observance of Community law, if necessary by making a reference under Art 177 of the Treaty of Rome[20], and should bear in mind the advantage enjoyed by the Court of Justice over national courts when deciding questions of Community law, and the possibility that its own view of the law may be wrong[1].

10 Other factors may have a powerful influence on the exercise of the discretion: more powerful, on occasion, than the judge's estimate of the general utility of a decision. Thus, if the way in which the reference was brought into existence and conducted was such as to suggest that both parties wished for a speedy resolution of the dispute, or if the parties deliberately abstained from asking for a reasoned award[2], it is less likely that leave will be given: indeed, in the case of a quick reference on a 'one-off' point, the interests of finality will prevail even if the judge thinks it clear that the arbitrator is wrong, unless there are some other exceptional factors to be taken into account[3]. Conversely, if the arbitrator is asked to make a reasoned award, this will be some evidence that the desire for speed and finality was not paramount[4].

---

[18] These requirements are cumulative, not alternative: *The Nichos A*, ante, at 53; *The Kerman*, ante, at 66.

[19] *The Rio Sun*; *The Kerman*, ante, at 67.

[20] *Nordsee v Reederei Mond* 102/81 [1982] ECR 1095.

[1] *Bulk Oil (Zug) AG v Sun International Ltd* [1983] 2 Lloyd's Rep 587.

[2] *Trave Schiffahrtsgesellschaft mbH & Co KG v Ninemia Maritime Corporation, The Niedersachsen* [1986] 1 Lloyd's Rep 393.

[3] *The Nema*, ante, at 296–297; *National Rumour v Lloyd's*, ante.

[4] *The Rio Sun*, ante. This cannot be a conclusive factor, even if the requirement is made by both sides, for they may wish to have reasons so as to know how the arbitrator has arrived at his award, and not for the purposes of an appeal.

11 Again, the identity of the arbitrator may have an influence on the exercise of the discretion. Where a layman is chosen for his experience and knowledge of the commercial background and usages of the trade, this is some indication that the parties wished for finality rather than review by the Court[5]. Similarly, the selection of a lawyer to decide upon a purely legal issue requiring no special commercial experience may point the same way[6]. The weight, if any, to be attributed to this factor will depend upon the nature of the issue.

12 The extent to which the appeal relates only to one of a number of severable issues will also be a ground for exercising the discretion against the grant of leave[7], quite apart from its relevance to the formal requirement that the determination of the question could substantially affect the rights of the parties[8].

Since *The Nema* did not purport to lay down exclusive criteria for the grant of leave to appeal, other factors will on occasion have to be taken into account. Thus, the presumption against an appeal may be weaker if, notwithstanding that the subject matter lies outside the special categories established by section 4, the parties have not taken the opportunity to make an exclusion agreement. Another relevant consideration may be the identity of the applicant for leave. One of the most important aims of the 1979 Act was to restrict the opportunity for the losing party to postpone payment by launching a unmeritorious appeal. The injustice resulting from delay bears much harder on a successful claimant than a successful respondent, and it may be that the Court would take note of the fact that if a claimant is seeking leave to appeal against the dismissal of his claim, the respondent is not being kept out of his money meanwhile[9].

---

[5] *The Nema*, ante, at 297. We suggest that this criterion should be applied with caution, and that weight should be given to it only if the Court is satisfied that this really was the reason for choice. This cannot be inferred simply from the selection of an arbitrator who is not a lawyer in active practice. The choice may have been made because the nominee is respected for his balanced and practical acquaintance with the matter in dispute. Commercial arbitrations often raise issues of fact, or of mixed fact and law at some remove from the immediate subject matter of the contract from which the reference has sprung. For example, shipping or commodity transactions may on occasion give rise to issues concerned with banking or insurance. A person with practical experience in the trade which concerns itself with such contracts will not necessarily be better equipped than a lawyer to deal with all the issues thus arising. Indeed on occasion a lawyer, although without any direct experience at all, may yet have gained a knowledge from years spent in handling a wide variety of commercial disputes, of how numerous different aspects of commercial life actually work in practice, which will make him better able to decide the matter than a practical man with a more direct, but less broad, range of experience. The same may well be true of the professional arbitrator, who is neither a practising lawyer nor a 'lay' arbitrator, in the ordinary sense of the term. The problem was clearly stated by Goff J in *The Oinoussian Virtue* in a passage which was not criticised in *The Nema*. If weight is to be given to the identity of the arbitrator, at the stage of the application for leave, or on the hearing of the substantive appeal, on the ground that the parties have applied the principle of 'horses for courses', the Court must be sure that it is correctly appraised of the individual arbitrator's expertise: a fact which may be difficult, and indeed invidious.

[6] *The Kerman*, ante, at 67.

[7] See *The Evimera*, ante. The issue involved $20,000. The total sum in dispute was $164,000.

[8] For example, the appeal may raise a point of general public importance but in such a way that the point only becomes relevant if the appellant succeeds on some other 'one-off' point.

[9] This could not, of course, be a conclusive factor. It was assumed, when the 1979 legislation was being promoted, that finality as well as speed was a motive for choosing arbitration, and a respondent can legitimately feel that he is entitled to be rid of the claim, once he has obtained a favourable award.

4 Leave to appeal on a new point of law

It might have been expected that one consequence of the new system, as analysed in *The Nema*, would have been that appeals would never be allowed for the purpose of arguing a point of law which was not canvassed before the arbitrator. It is clear, however, that the Court has jurisdiction to entertain such an appeal: section 1 of the 1979 Act confers jurisdiction to hear an appeal 'on any question of law arising out of an award', not 'on any question of law determined by the award'. What was for some time unclear was how *The Nema* guidelines would be applied in such a case, particularly if an appeal on the new point of law required remission for further reasons[10].

The practice has now become more settled, and the following guidelines apply where it is sought to argue a new point of law[11].

1 The fact that the point was not argued before the arbitrator is not an absolute bar to an appeal. It has to be borne in mind that it is not always possible during the course of argument at a hearing to forecast how the facts will be found and how one should argue the law in relation to them.

2 The fact that the point was not argued must, however, be taken into account in the exercise of the discretion to give or to refuse leave to appeal.

3 Where the failure to argue the point below has had the result that all the necessary facts are not found[12], this will be a powerful factor against granting leave.

4 Even in such a case it may in very special circumstances be right to remit the award for further facts to be found with a view to granting leave, but this would probably be very unusual.

5 If all the necessary facts have been found, the judge should give such weight as he thinks fit to the failure to argue the point before the arbitrator. In particular, he should have regard, on the one hand, to whether the new point is similar to points that were argued, perhaps a variant of one of those points or a different way of putting it, or, on the other hand, whether it is a totally new and different point.

5 Application for leave to appeal

In the first few years of its existence the new jurisdiction gave rise to difficulties of practice as well as principle. Most of the common problems have now been resolved by judicial decision, by practice directions issued by the judges, or by amendments to the Rules of the Supreme Court. The practice is as follows –

1 Applications for leave to appeal are made to a judge in chambers, and are heard by a Commercial Judge, unless any such judge otherwise directs[13]. The practice is for applications relating to disputes which would qualify as

---

[10] Among the earlier decisions are *Schiffahrtsagentur Hamburg Middle East Line GmbH v Virtue Shipping Corpn, The Oinoussian Virtue* [1981] 1 Lloyd's Rep 533 (decided before *The Nema*); and *Bremer Handelsgesellschaft mbH v Westzucker GmbH (No 2)* [1981] 2 Lloyd's Rep 130. See also *Socony Mobil Oil Co Inc v West of England Ship Owners Mutual Insurance Association Ltd, The Padre Island (No 2)* [1987] 2 Lloyd's Rep 529; and *Indian Oil Corpn Ltd v Greenstone Shipping SA (Panama), The Ypatianna* [1988] QB 345.

[11] They are paraphrased from the decision of the Court of Appeal in *Petraco (Bermuda) Ltd v Petromed International SA* [1988] 2 Lloyd's Rep 357.

[12] A fortiori, we submit, if they were not even investigated.

[13] Ord. 73, rr. 3(2)(a) and 6(1).

'commercial actions'[14] if they were brought before the court to be retained by the Commercial Judge. Other types of dispute may be referred elsewhere: for example, rent review arbitrations are usually dealt with by a Chancery judge, and construction arbitrations by the official Referees.

2 The application is made by originating summons[15] which must be served within 21 days after the award is made and published to the parties[16]. The time for serving the notice of originating motion by which the appeal is initiated, if leave is given, and for entering the appeal, is the same[17]. It is therefore usual to serve both the originating summons and the notice of originating motion and to enter the appeal at the same time.

3 The notice of originating motion and the originating summons must each state the grounds of the appeal or application, and where the appeal or application is founded on evidence by affidavit, or is made with the consent of the arbitrator or of the other parties, a copy of every affidavit intended to be used or of every consent giving in writing must be served at the same time[18].

4 The grounds of appeal must specify the relevant parts of the award and reasons, and a copy of the award or reasons, or the relevant parts of them, must be lodged with the court and served with the notice of originating motion[19].

5 On an application for leave to appeal, any affidavit verifying the facts in support of a contention that the question of law concerns a term of a contract or an event which is not a one-off term or event must be lodged with the court and served with the notice of motion[20]. Any affidavit in reply must be lodged with the court and served not less than two clear days before the hearing of the application[1].

6 If the respondent to the application for leave to appeal desires to contend that the award should be upheld on grounds not expressed or not fully expressed in the award and reasons must lodge with the court and serve on the applicant not less than two days before the hearing of the application a 'respondent's notice' specifying the grounds of his contention[2].

7 The notice of motion and respondent's notice, if any, should contain specific reference to any authority relied on, and a copy should be provided of any

---

[14] I.e. 'any cause arising out of the ordinary transactions of merchants': see Ord. 72, r. 1(2), which gives a number of examples.

[15] Ord. 73, r. 3(3). If an action is pending, however, the application must be made by summons in the action.

[16] Ord. 73, r. 5(2). But if reasons material to the appeal are given after publication of the award, time runs from the date on which reasons are given.

[17] Ibid.

[18] Ord. 73, r. 5(5).

[19] Ord. 73, r. 5(6).

[20] Order 73, r. 5(7). The Rules do not say that such facts may only be proved by affidavit, but we suggest that the Court would be justified in declining to accept proof in any other way, e.g. by a statement by counsel, unless they were not in dispute.

[1] Order 73, r. 5(8).

[2] Order 73, r. 5(9). The rule does not cover the case where the respondent is dissatisfied with reasons which *are* expressed in the award. If the real nature of his complaint is that he is dissatisfied with the result of the arbitration as expressed in the award itself, he should not serve a respondent's notice, but launch his own substantive appeal and application for leave to appeal, abiding by the relevant time limits. If on the other hand, his complaint is as to part of the arbitrator's reasons which has not affected the result, but might do so if the appeal were to succeed, he should serve a respondent's notice, even though the Rules may not strictly require that he should do so: *President of India v Taygetos Shipping Co SA, The Agenor* [1985] 1 Lloyd's Rep 155; *Heinrich Hanno & Co BV v Fairlight Shipping Co Ltd, The Kostas K* [1985] 1 Lloyd's Rep 231.

authority not contained in the Law Reports, the Weekly Law reports, the All England Law reports, Lloyd's Law Reports or the English Reports[3].

8 The hearing of the application takes place inter partes, and usually takes no more than 10 or 15 minutes, the judge having previously read the papers lodged with the court. The hearing is not intended as an opportunity to rehearse the arguments in support of the substantive appeal, but to debate whether or not the application falls within the *Nema* guidelines. No reasons are given for the judge's decision to give or to refuse leave to appeal[4], except in the very unusual case where the judge considers that the existing guidelines laid down by appellate courts call for amplification, elucidation or adaptation to changing practices: in such a case, but only in such a case, the judge should give reasons for his decision and give leave to appeal to the Court of Appeal[5].

9 It is the duty of the appellant to prosecute his application for leave to appeal and, if leave is granted, the appeal itself with proper despatch. Failure to do so may lead to the application or the appeal being struck out[6].

6 Citation of awards

We have mentioned the problem which may arise in the case where the arbitrator has not set out his reasoning, as distinct from his 'reasons'. One special aspect of this problem exists where the arbitrator has adopted the reasoning of a different tribunal engaged upon a different reference. The 1979 Act has undoubtedly increased the incidence of reasoned awards, even in those cases where there is an exclusion agreement, or where the arbitrator has not been asked to give reasons. Occasionally, these awards are reported in trade publications. Others pass into limited circulation amongst lawyers practising in this field. The result has been the initiation of a body of arbitral precedent existing parallel to, or in the interstices of, the judicial precedents which create the common law. More frequently than before, decisions given in one reference are cited in subsequent arbitrations. On a smaller scale, this has always happened. What would, however, have been very unusual[7], until recently, would be the citation in court of an arbitrator's decision in relation to a dispute which is not itself the subject of any appeal. Perhaps the practice will now change. The judgments and speeches delivered in *The Nema* attach great weight to the views of trade arbitrators, particularly on questions of construction. This being so, it is hard to see why in logic the court should not properly be asked to pay regard to the views of other arbitrators, not concerned with the dispute currently under appeal, who happen to have made awards on the matter which

---

[3] *Practice Direction* [1985] 2 Lloyd's Rep 300.

[4] The practice is based on observations in the speech of Lord Diplock in *The Antaios*, ante. Lord Diplock stated that in exceptional circumstances the application might be dismissed without a hearing if the judge is of opinion, on reading the papers, that it could not possibly succeed. But the rules now appear to contemplate that an oral hearing will always take place.

[5] *The Antaios*, ante; *Patraco (Bermuda) Ltd v Petromed International SA* [1988] 1 WLR 896.

[6] *Leon Corporation v Atlantic Lines and Navigation Co Inc, The Leon* [1985] 2 Lloyd's Rep 470. See also *Mebro Oil SA v Gatoil International Inc* [1985] 2 Lloyd's Rep 235. The convenience of counsel is no ground for delaying the fixing of a date for the hearing: *The Leon*, supra; *Rheinoel GmbH v Huron Liberian Co, The Concordia C* [1985] 2 Lloyd's Rep 55.

[7] There are a few cases in which senior legal arbitrators have embarked upon a general review of the law on a particular topic of general importance, where the awards have passed into general circulation, and have on very rare occasions been cited in argument in the High Court.

have come into the hands of the parties to the application. Notwithstanding the logic of this solution, it is important to note the risks which it may entail. The practice of using privately-owned sets of awards gives an unfair advantage to those parties who are represented by lawyers whose practice is such as to give access to them[8], and if this objection is answered by the publication of regular reports of awards, on the American model, not only would the privacy of the arbitral process be imperilled, but there will also be a risk of individual systems of 'para-law' springing up in competition with the common law. That this was not the intent of the promoters of the 1979 Act is made clear by the stress repeatedly laid in the cases which have expounded it on the importance of the appeal as a method of clarifying and elaborating the common law. This is not at all to belittle the role of lay tribunals in the development of commercial law. There is, however, a significant difference between the way in which an arbitrator arrives at his conclusion, and the procedures applied at the time when City of London special juries performed their important functions. The special jury operated in the immediate context of a trial, under the control of a judge who knew what matters were laid before the jury, and who could maintain a careful distinction between questions of fact and law. The judge, on receipt of the jury's special verdicts, would know exactly how they fitted into the pattern of the case as a whole, and could ensure that they provided reliable guidance on matters which lay outside the province of pure law. The position is altogether different when the court is faced with an arbitral award made in a dispute other than the one which is the subject of appeal. Unless the counsel or solicitors presenting the argument happen to have been involved in the previous reference, the judge may have no means of knowing what type of reference was involved; whether the proceedings involved oral argument, or only a submission on documents; whether evidence was called; what arguments were adduced; whether relevant reported cases were drawn to the attention of the arbitrators; and, in some cases, whether the arbitrators had any personal practical acquaintance with the matters in dispute. Decisions in other cases, shorn of their context, may be misleading unless used with caution.

7 Citation of decisions on leave to appeal

A practice which showed signs of developing as a result of *The Nema* guidelines, was that of reporting decisions of the Commercial Judge refusing leave to appeal as if they carried some kind of authority for the proposition appealed from. This was perhaps not surprising. The judgments were at that time[9] given in open court and transcripts could be obtained: and if, as was intended, the *Nema* guidelines reduced the number of cases on points of commercial law which come before the courts for decision, such judgments might have become a valuable, and in some cases possibly the only, source of judge-made law on topics of general interest in a particular trade. Moreover, if the practice of citing awards had become more prevalent, there would be a natural tendency to claim that an

---

[8] As used to be the case in the early days of the common law, before the existence of systematic law reports.

[9] But no longer: see p. 616, post.

award which had been the object of an unsuccessful application for leave to appeal carries greater authority than one which has gone unchallenged[10].

The practice of reporting such decisions ceased after *The Antaios*, when judges no longer gave reasons for their decisions on applications for leave to appeal[11]. This was no bad thing. It is one thing to rely on a decision that the award of Mr A is 'plainly right' as authority for the proposition which he has decided, although the value of even a decision as definite as this must be read in the light of the fact that it will almost certainly have been made after less than full argument. But it is quite another thing to rely on a decision that the award of Mr B is 'not obviously wrong'. Such a decision is of little or no value as an authority and although a number of such decisions were reported before *The Antaios*, few, if any, of the reports were of the slightest value[12].

8 Enforcement of award pending appeal

It had been hoped that one of the anticipated benefits of the new system would be that, instead of obtaining an award in the form of a special case, which could not be enforced until after the court had affirmed the arbitrator's decision on the question of law, the claimant would now receive an award which was expressed to be final and could therefore be enforced immediately, without waiting for the outcome of any proceedings to challenge it by way of appeal.

It is undoubtedly the case that an award under the new system will always be in a form in which, although it may be the subject of an appeal, it is in principle capable of immediate enforcement. Whether it will be so in practice will depend on the attitude which the Court adopts to proceedings to enforce an award in the situation where the respondent has either applied for, or been granted, leave to appeal. It appears that the Court will be faced with a choice[13] between two broad lines of approach.

1 The first would be for the court to abjure any inquiry into the merits of the proposed appeal, and to exercise its undoubted discretion to stay or adjourn the enforcement proceedings solely for the purpose of ensuring that, if the appeal succeeds, the respondent will not find that he cannot recover back what he has been compelled to pay to the claimant. The court would, in other words, follow the practice governing an application for a stay of execution pending an appeal from the High Court to the Court of Appeal[14]. The rule here is that, unless the judge or the Court of Appeal otherwise directs, an appeal does not operate as a stay of execution or of proceedings under the judge's decision. The court acts on a presumption in favour of immediate execution and, save in exceptional circumstances, will only order a stay of execution on evidence being given by affidavit that if the judgment and costs were paid there would be no reasonable

---

[10] Although an equally powerful claim might be made for the award which has gone unchallenged, on the grounds that if the losing party accepted it, it must have been right.

[11] This was one of the intended results of the change in practice: see per Lord Diplock in *The Antaios*, ante, at p. 206.

[12] A regrettable tendency is emerging for the judgments of the single Lord Justice giving or refusing leave to appeal to the Court of Appeal to be reported. It is difficult to imagine how such a decision could ever have any value as a precedent.

[13] Although we are only concerned here with enforcement in England, a similar choice will no doubt face a foreign court, if it is sought to enforce the award under the New York Convention (see Article VI) or the Geneva Convention (see Article 3).

[14] See Ord. 59, r. 13(1) and the notes thereto in the *Supreme Court Practice*.

probability of recovering them if the appeal succeeded. Even in such a case, a stay is not generally granted unconditionally, but only on condition that the amount of the judgment is paid into court[15]: and the plaintiff can generally avoid a stay being granted by offering satisfactory security for repayment. If the appeal succeeds, the plaintiff is ordered to repay any proceeds of execution, with interest[16].

2 The alternative approach would be for the Court to attempt to form a provisional view as to the likely outcome of the appeal and to act on this view by adjourning or staying the enforcement proceedings wherever the respondent had made out an 'arguable' case, or perhaps a 'good arguable' or even a 'very strong' case that the appeal was likely to succeed. The Court would, in other words, apply the kind of test which was adopted under the old system when the question arose whether the arbitrator could properly make it a condition of stating a case that the respondent should give security for the claim[17].

The Court's instinct is likely to be to prefer the first of these two approaches, as being more in conformity with the underlying philosophy of the Act. But it may in practice prove difficult for the Court to refrain altogether from considering the respondent's likely prospects of success. An application for summary enforcement of an award may be made ex parte[18]; but if the claimant is aware, as he generally will be, that the respondent intends to appeal, he will be obliged to disclose this fact to the Court, which will almost certainly refuse to proceed ex parte, and will direct a summons to be issued. This all takes time, and the result is likely to be that in the great majority of cases the application to enforce the award[19] will come on for hearing either at the same time as, or after, the respondent's application for leave to appeal. If the judge gives leave to appeal, he will have done so after forming a provisional view of the merits of the appeal, and, in the case of a 'one-off' point, a provisional view which will be strongly favourable to the respondent[20]. In such circumstances it is difficult to envisage that the court would nevertheless allow the claimant to enforce the award, or, for that matter, order the respondent to bring the amount of the award into court. It can still be said, however, that the new system is likely to have brought about a climate in which the presumption is in favour of granting immediate enforcement unless the respondent shows cause why it should not be granted[1].

---

[15] The effect of payment into court is to make the plaintiff a secured creditor in any subsequent bankruptcy or winding-up: *Re Gordon, ex p Navalchand* [1897] 2 QB 516.

[16] *Rodger v Comptoir d'Escompte de Paris* (1871) LR 3 PC 465.

[17] See p. 613, ante.

[18] Ord. 73, r. 10(1). An order made ex parte may be set aside on application by the respondent within fourteen days after service of the order (if the order is to be served out of the jurisdiction) or within such other period as the court may fix, and may not be enforced until after the expiration of that period or, if the respondent applies within that period to set aside the order, until after the application is finally disposed of.

[19] Or, if the Court has proceeded ex parte, the respondent's application to set aside the order for enforcement.

[20] See pp. 604–608, ante.

[1] This would undoubtedly represent an improvement on the old system, which we described in the first edition at pp. 567–568.

9 Conditions on leave to appeal

Section 1(4) of the Act provides that the Court may make any leave to appeal which it gives, under section 1(3)(b), conditional upon the applicant complying with such conditions as it considers appropriate. It would be undesirable, if it indeed were possible, to attempt to enumerate the types of condition which the Court could properly attach to an order granting leave to appeal, or the circumstances in which it would be proper to impose conditions. The following, however, are amongst the types of condition which are likely to be encountered.

(a) Security for costs

The court has power under section 1(4) to order the appellant to give security for the costs of the respondent to the appeal, and will ordinarily do so where (i) the appellant is ordinarily resident out of the jurisdiction, unless he has property within the jurisdiction which will be available to meet the respondent's costs if the appeal is dismissed[2], or (ii) the appellant is a limited company and there is reason to believe that it will be unable to pay the respondent's costs if the appeal is dismissed[3].

(b) Security for the amount of the award

The court has power under section 1(4) to order the appellant to pay into court or otherwise secure the amount of the award, and it has already been decided that it is appropriate to make such an order when the Court infers that the appeal is being pursued for the purpose of delay, or where the appellant's argument is flimsy[4]. A case could, however, be made out for imposing a condition that the amount of the award should be brought into court as a matter of course in any case where, if the claimant had issued a summons for summary enforcement of the award[5], the Court would either have ordered enforcement or would have stayed the enforcement proceedings conditionally upon the respondent paying the amount of the award into court[6].

(c) Limiting the scope of the appeal

The Court also has power under section 1(4) to limit the grounds on which the appeal may be argued, or to limit the scope of the appeal to certain parts of the award[7]. But this power will generally be limited to cases where the award deals

---

[2] *Mondial Trading Co GmbH v Gill and Duffus Zuckerhandelsgesellschaft mbH* [1980] 2 Lloyd's Rep 376 at 380; *Schiffahrtsagentur Hamburg Middle East Line GmbH v Virtue Shipping Corpn, The Oinoussian Virtue* [1981] 1 Lloyd's Rep 533 at 539.

[3] The statement in the text is based on the practice of the Court of Appeal: see Ord. 59, r. 10(5) and Ord. 23, and the notes thereto in the *Supreme Court Practice*. The circumstances in which security will be ordered are not limited to those set out in the text.

[4] *Mondial v Gill and Duffus*, ante, decided before the decision of the House of Lords in *The Nema*. Since that decision, a conclusion by the court that the appeal is being pursued for the purposes of delay, or that the argument is flimsy, is more likely to result in an appeal being refused altogether than leave being granted subject to conditions. See also *The Apex*, ante, at p. 480.

[5] He may actually have done so.

[6] This topic is discussed more fully at pp. 613–614, ante.

[7] This power is no doubt also inherent in the Court's general power to grant or refuse leave to appeal.

with separate disputes, some of which justify leave while others do not: or where a particular point of law which justifies leave to appeal has no bearing on another point which does not. If the disputes or points of law are interrelated the court will generally give leave in relation to all of them even if one of the points would not on its own have merited an appeal[8].

(d) Costs

The usual order for costs, if leave is granted, is that the costs of the application for leave to appeal shall be costs in the appeal[9].

E. ORDERS ON APPEAL

Under the 1950 Act, the outcome of a hearing on the argument of a special case was a judgment delivered orally in open court, in which the judge would give his decision on the question of law and set out his reasons for reaching that decision. The actual decision would be simply in the form of an answer to the question stated in the special case. This would then be embodied in a formal declaratory order of the Court setting out the question and the answer to it, but without referring to the judge's reasons. The award and the order could then be read together as a final adjudication on the dispute which had given rise to the question of law[10].

Under the new system, the outcome of an appeal still results in an oral judgment, delivered in open court, in which the judge gives a reasoned decision on the question of law raised by the appeal. But there the similarity with the procedure under the old system comes to an end. Under the new system, the Court does not dispose of the appeal simply by issuing a declaratory order answering a question of law, since no question will formally have been asked of it. Instead, section 1(2) of the 1979 Act enables the Court to choose from a variety of different types of order in order to give effect to its determination of the question of law. The range of possible orders is as follows –

1   An order confirming the award.

2   An order varying the award.

3   An order setting aside the award.

4   An order remitting the award to the reconsideration of the arbitrator or umpire together with the Court's opinion on the question of law which was the subject of the appeal.

These different types of order are discussed below.

---

[8]   *Kodros Shipping Corpn v Empresa Cubana de Fletes, The Evia (No 2)* [1981] 2 Lloyd's Rep 613 at 631, per Goff J; *Heinrich Hanno & Co BV v Fairlight Shipping Co, The Kostas K* [1985] 1 Lloyd's Rep 231, at 236–237. Similar considerations apply to a cross appeal on interrelated issues: *International Sea Tankers Inc v Hemisphere Shipping Co Ltd, The Wenjiang* [1981] 2 Lloyd's Rep 308 at 315.

[9]   *The Oinoussian Virtue*, ante at 540.

[10]   This, at any rate, was the position where the special case followed the usual pattern and contained alternative awards conditioned to take effect on the Court's answering the question of law one way or the other. In other cases, it was sometimes necessary, depending on how the court answered the question of law, for the award to be remitted to the arbitrator so that he could give effect to the Court's decision.

1 Confirming the award

An order confirming the award will obviously be the appropriate order where an appeal has been wholly unsuccessful. What is less obvious is whether the court has power to confirm part of an award when the appeal has been only partially successful, as may happen if the award deals with two separate disputes raising appeals on two distinct points of law. On a strict reading of section 1(2) it could perhaps be argued that the court has no power to confirm part of an award while varying, setting aside or remitting other parts of it. But this would be an inconvenient result, which the Court would strive to avoid, and it could do so without violence to the words of section 1(2) either by reading 'the award' as including any severable part of an award, and by treating the various types of order, although expressed as alternatives, as capable of being used cumulatively or in conjunction with one another; or by treating the power to 'vary' an award as including a power to confirm an award in part.

An order confirming an award is not of course an order enabling the award to be enforced as if it were a judgment or order of the Court[11]. An order to this effect can only be obtained by commencing an action on the award, or, in an appropriate case, by summary proceedings under section 26 of the 1950 Act. However, in a case where summary proceedings *are* appropriate, there is no reason why the application should not be brought on at the same time as the hearing of the appeal.

2 Varying the award

An order varying the award will not necessarily result as a matter of course from a successful appeal. We suggest that such an order will only be appropriate where the variation (including any variation of the award on costs) follows inevitably from the Court's determination of the question of law. Where this is not the case, it is not for the Court to speculate as to what the arbitrator's decision would or might have been; the proper course is to remit the award for reconsideration, together with the Court's opinion on the question of law[12].

The mechanism for variation is somewhat obscure. Section 1(8) provides that –

> 'Where the award of an arbitrator or umpire is varied on appeal, the award as varied shall have effect . . . as if it were the award of the arbitrator or umpire'.

This appears to assume that the arbitrator or umpire does not himself alter the actual document containing the award[13]: but if he does not do so, who does? The Rules of the Supreme Court do not provide any machinery which would fit the purpose: and this seems to lead to the conclusion that the award itself

---

[11] Under the old system, there was some divergency between various foreign systems of law as to whether a decision of the High Court on a special case was enforceable as a judgment or an award. From the English point of view an award which has been confirmed (or, we suggest, varied) remains an award and does not become a judgment. Whether the same view will be taken abroad remains to be seen.

[12] *River Plate Products Netherlands BV v Etablissement Coargrain* [1982] 1 Lloyd's Rep 628.

[13] If this view is wrong, the provisions of s. 39 of the Supreme Court Act 1981 may presumably be invoked in the extremely unlikely event of the arbitrator or umpire refusing to vary the document.

continues to exist in its unaltered state but must be read subject to the order by which it is 'varied'. If the award had to be the subject of enforcement proceedings abroad this could raise a difficult question as to whether the proceedings were for the enforcement of an award or a judgment[14]. Where there is any possibility of enforcement abroad, it may therefore be preferable to remit the award so that it can be physically altered by the arbitrator himself rather than simply to order that the award 'is varied'[15].

3 Setting aside

It is not easy to envisage circumstances in which the Court would on an appeal (as distinct from a motion to set aside on grounds such as misconduct) set aside a final award without at the same time remitting it to the arbitrator in order to make a fresh award: for otherwise the arbitration would never reach a conclusion. The position may be different where the appeal arises on an interim award, because the Court may decide that it was inappropriate for the arbitrator to make any award at that stage of the reference; but even then there would be likely to be questions of costs to be dealt with on remission.

The power to set aside an award may, however, be valuable when used in conjunction with the power to remit under section 1(2), since it will put beyond question what is already implicit in an order to remit, namely, that the award which is remitted is no longer an effective adjudication on the dispute – a matter which might not be obvious to a foreign lawyer or foreign court seeking to establish the status of a remitted award.

4 Remission[16]

An order remitting the award to the reconsideration of the arbitrator or umpire will be appropriate whenever the Court allows an appeal on a question of law on grounds which require the arbitrator to exercise his judgment afresh, whether on questions of law or fact. The award is remitted together with the Court's 'opinion' on the question of law which was the subject of the appeal. This expression has had a long and complex history and it is unfortunate that it has once again been revived in the context of the new legislation.

The doubts which once existed as to the effect of an 'opinion' of the Court arose from the provisions of section 19 of the Judicature Act 1873 which conferred on the newly constituted Court of Appeal jurisdiction to hear and determine appeals from 'any judgment or order' of the High Court. Questions very soon arose as to whether an 'opinion' or 'decision' or 'determination' of the High Court, under the various procedures for reviewing decisions of arbitrators and other tribunals then in existence, amounted to a 'judgment or order'. After

---

[14] In most jurisdictions, as in England, the procedures for enforcing an award are quite different from those for enforcing a judgment. Moreover, some countries recognise foreign awards, but not judgments, and vice versa.

[15] If a judgment is needed for the purposes of enforcement abroad, it will be necessary to institute fresh proceedings in England in order to obtain an English judgment on the award.

[16] We are concerned here with remission after the Court has determined the appeal, not with remission for further reasons for the purpose of advancing an appeal. The latter topic is discussed at pp. 596–599, ante.

an initial period of uncertainty the position was settled by the courts as follows –

1 The 'opinion' of the Court on an award in the form of a special case was an order of the High Court which could be the subject of an appeal to the Court of Appeal[17].

2 The 'opinion of the Court' on a consultative case was not an order of the High Court, and[18] could not be made the subject of an appeal to the Court of Appeal[19].

A further distinction between the two types of procedure was that the 'opinion' of the Court on an award in the form of special case was res judicata, whereas an 'opinion' on a consultative case was not. An arbitrator who had sought and obtained a consultative opinion was still seized of the whole dispute, entrusted with the duty of making his own award on the question of law, and vested with the jurisdiction to do so. Failure to heed the opinion of the Court did not invalidate the award; it merely made it liable to be set aside on grounds of misconduct or error on the face[20].

The Arbitration Act 1934 changed the position as it stood at that time by creating a statutory right of appeal from a consultative case, subject to the leave of the High Court or of the Court of Appeal. At the same time it abandoned the expression 'opinion' in favour of 'decision', both for special and consultative cases, but without thereby affecting the principle that a decision on an award in the form of a special case was res judicata but a decision on a consultative case was not[1].

The 1979 Act has revived the expression 'opinion', but its use is now confined to the context of an order remitting an award for reconsideration on the outcome of an appeal. Elsewhere the expressions 'determination of an appeal', 'determination of a question of law', 'consider a question of law' and 'decision on an appeal', are used in the context of an appeal under section 1 of the Act[2]. 'Determination' and 'decision' are also used in the context of a preliminary point of law under section 2, in which context it has been authoritatively stated that they do not connote a procedure which results in the question of law becoming res judicata[3]. It is for this reason that section 2(3) provides that a decision of the High Court on a preliminary point of law 'shall be deemed to be a judgment of the court within the meaning of section 16 of the Supreme Court Act 1981 (appeals to the Court of Appeal)'. There is, however, no similar provision in section 1, presumably because the legislature considered that a decision of the High Court under that section *is* an order of the High Court[4] and does not need to be deemed so by enactment. The use of the word 'opinion' in section 1(2)(b) is, however, curious. At first blush, it would appear that a distinction is intended

---

[17] *Re Bidder and North Staffordshire Rly Co* (1878) 4 QBD 412, decided on the wording of s. 5 of the Common Law Procedure Act 1854, which was re-enacted in s. 7(b) of the Arbitration Act 1889.

[18] Until s. 9 of the Arbitration Act 1934 gave a statutory right of appeal, with the leave of the High Court or the Court of Appeal.

[19] *Re Knight and Tabernacle Permanent Building Society* [1892] 2 QB 613.

[20] *British Westinghouse Electric and Manufacturing Co Ltd v Underground Electric Railways Co of London Ltd* [1912] AC 673; *Re Knight and Tabernacle*, ante.

[1] *Fidelitas Shipping Co Ltd v V/O Exportchleb* [1965] 1 Lloyd's Rep 223, [1966] 1 QB 630.

[2] See ss. 1(2); 1(4); 1(5); 1(7).

[3] *Babanaft International Co SA v Avant Petroleum Inc, The Oltenia* [1982] 1 Lloyd's Rep 448 per Donaldson LJ.

[4] On the basis of the decision in *Bidder v North Staffordshire Rly Co*, ante.

between an 'opinion' on the one hand and a 'decision' or 'determination' on the other: on this view the latter two expressions would connote res judicata, whereas 'opinion' would not. But this seems unlikely, because the corollary of this would be that an 'opinion' under section 1(2)(b) would not be an order of the High Court and therefore could not be made the subject of an appeal to the Court of Appeal, even with leave. Section 1(7), however, is apparently drafted on the assumption that such an appeal is possible: and there seems no good reason why the legislature should have wished to exclude an appeal from such an opinion. It seems, therefore, that the expression 'opinion' has no special significance, and is used merely as an alternative to 'decision'[5].

F. PRELIMINARY QUESTIONS OF LAW

Under the 1979 Act, as under the old system, it is possible (in the absence of an exclusion agreement) to bring before the High Court a question of law arising in the course of the reference. There are two procedures –

First, there is an interim award by the arbitrator, made the subject of appeal to the High Court under section 1(2)[6].

Second, there is a determination of a question of law, under section 2(1).

There are important differences between the two procedures. Thus: the procedure under section 2(1) applies to disputes covered by oral as well as written arbitration agreements[7]; the persons who can initiate the procedure are not the same; it takes place without there being any need for an award or decision by the arbitrator; there is no provision for a document similar to the 'reasons' called for by section 1; the conditions precedent to the existence of a jurisdiction to determine the question of law are radically different; and whereas a decision under section 1(2) results in the question of law becoming res judicata, a decision under section 2(1) does not[8].

It is not easy to say why the legislature should have thought it necessary to establish two such different procedures aimed at essentially the same result. In practice, it seems likely that the procedure under section 1 will be most useful where an issue can be separated completely from the remainder of the dispute; where the facts can satisfactorily be investigated and decided without advance knowledge of the answer to the question of law; and where the decision of the Court has at least a reasonable prospect of concluding the dispute in favour of one party or the other. Thus, an interim award followed by an appeal may usefully be employed where (for example) the question of liability can be wholly detached from matters of quantum, or for a decision on whether a claim was barred by lapse of time.

---

[5] Another explanation for the use of the expression may be that when remitting the award the judge may not be seized of sufficient facts to 'decide' the question of law, and may therefore be unable to do more than express an opinion.

[6] Read with s. 7(1) of the 1979 Act, and s. 14 of the 1950 Act.

[7] Because s. 2(1) refers only to 'a reference', and makes no mention of an 'arbitration agreement'.

[8] *The Oltenia*, ante. This has the consequence, as under the old system, that a decision on a preliminary point of law can in theory be called in question by means of an appeal from the final award. In practice, as is pointed out in the decision just cited, the differing mechanisms for appeals under the Act will almost always prevent this occurring. But it is unfortunate that this unsatisfactory feature of the old system has been perpetuated under the new.

The procedure under section 1 may also present a more workable solution to the problem faced by an arbitrator who wishes to have a decision of the Court on the extent of his procedural powers, but against the wishes of the parties: the procedure under section 2 is not well adapted to this situation[9].

The procedure under section 2 is perhaps better adapted for use in a case where the question of law dominates the whole arbitration, not just a part of it, so that the arbitrator and the parties cannot sensibly approach the investigation of the facts without knowing, in the light of the answer to the question, what facts are really material.

1 Interim award

Turning now to the way in which the procedures are to be operated, the interim award followed by an appeal calls for no special discussion; the position is the same, mutatis mutandis, as if the award were final and not interim.

2 Determination of question of law under section 2

The procedure under section 2 raises more problems. The procedure is more complicated than the old system, and inspection of the 1979 Act suggests that the process will take place in the following five stages.

(a) First stage: the decision to invoke section 2

By virtue of section 2(1) a party who wishes to invoke the procedure must obtain the consent either of arbitrator (or the umpire), or of all the other parties. Conversely, if it is the arbitrator who wishes to have the question decided by the Court, he must obtain the consent of at least one party, who will make the application on his behalf. Four comments may be made on this stage of the procedure.

First, the arbitrator no longer has the power to seek the guidance of the Court of his own volition, against the wishes of the parties[10].

Second, a party who wishes to use the procedure must persuade either his opponent or the arbitrator to concur. This is in contrast to the position regarding an appeal from an interim award, where it makes no difference to the jurisdiction of the Court whether or not the arbitrator agrees, and where one party can (if the Court grants leave) bring an appeal even if his opponent disagrees[11].

Third, there is no longer any power in the Court to order the hearing of a preliminary question at the instance of one party, against the wishes of the other party and the arbitrator[10].

Fourth, the sub-section requires only the consent of 'an arbitrator who has entered on the reference'. The 1950 and 1979 Acts otherwise refer to 'the arbitrator'. This can readily enough be understood as meaning 'the tribunal', so as to encompass the case where there are two or more arbitrators. This solution

---

[9] For the reasons given in *The Vasso* [1983] 2 Lloyd's Rep 346.
[10] Contrast s. 21(1)(a) of the 1950 Act.
[11] S. 1(4).

does not seem open, where the reference is to 'an' arbitrator[12], and it would appear that the consent of any one arbitrator will suffice, even if the majority disagree with him.

(b) Second stage: the application

The Act says nothing about the form in which the application is to be made. Order 73, rule 2(1)(c) stipulates that it shall be by originating motion to a single judge. This means a Commercial Judge, unless such a judge otherwise directs[13].

There remains, however, the problem of how the question of law is to be brought before the Court. There was no difficulty under the old system. The arbitrator stated a consultative case which, if properly drawn, provided the Court with all the necessary material for deciding the question. Nor is there any difficulty where an appeal is brought under section 1, since here the arbitrator's reasons will serve the same purpose. But the position is different under section 2. The consultative case has been abolished by section 1(1), and has not been replaced by section 2; nor will there necessarily be reasons, since the arbitrator may not yet have reached a decision by the time the matter comes before the Court.

It seems that two procedures may be envisaged.

First, if the arbitrator consents to the procedure, it will be his responsibility to see that the material necessary to decide the question of law is placed before the Court[14]. This will require reinforcement by an affidavit from the applicant containing the material necessary to satisfy the Court that the conditions of jurisdiction under section 2(2) are satisfied, and that the case is appropriate for the exercise of the Court's discretion.

Second, if the arbitrator does not consent to the procedure or fails to carry out his responsibility to bring the necessary material before the Court, the applicant will have to bring forward the material himself, through the medium of an affidavit. The main purpose is to show the Court: (i) what is the question of law; (ii) what facts the parties are asserting (if suitable, by reference to the pleadings if there are any); (iii) what facts are common ground; (iv) what facts are to be assumed for the purpose of the determination. The affidavit should then go on to set out the material relevant to jurisdiction and the exercise of the discretion, as suggested above. Care should be taken not to encumber the affidavit with contentious material on the merits. The Court will be concerned with the merits when and if the question of law is brought forward for argument, not on the application for leave[15].

(c) Third stage: the decision to entertain the application

The third stage of the procedure under section 2 involves a decision by the Court whether or not to entertain the application. Here a distinction must be

---

[12] Possibly 'an' was used in place of 'the' to avoid awkwardness with the words immediately following. But there would have been other ways of dealing with this. The Interpretation Act does not provide a solution, nor does the common law rule that in making an award all the arbitrators must act together.

[13] Ord. 73, r. 6(1).

[14] See p. 380, ante.

[15] But see pp. 623–625, post.

drawn between (a) an application made with the consent of an arbitrator or umpire and (b) an application made with the consent of all the parties other than the applicant.

(i) Application by consent of arbitrator or umpire. In the case where the application is made with the consent of an arbitrator or an umpire, but all the other parties do not consent[16] section 2(2) lays down two conditions precedent to the existence of a jurisdiction in the High Court. The sub-section does not say that if the conditions are satisfied the Court shall have jurisdiction to decide the question of law, but that it shall have jurisdiction to entertain an application under section 2(1). This indicates, more clearly that in the case of an appeal under section 1, that the Court has a general discretion whether or not to decide the question. Thus, the Court begins by deciding whether, in accordance with section 2(2), it has jurisdiction, and then goes on to consider under section 2(1) whether or not to decide the question of law.

The first condition prescribed by section 2(2) is that the court shall be satisfied that –

'(a) the determination of the application might produce savings in costs to the parties'.

Although a saving in costs[17] is obviously an important factor to be considered when considering whether it would be proper to decide the question, it is rather surprising that this has been singled out as a formal prerequisite to jurisdiction.

The word 'might' is important. The sub-section does not require the Court to be sure that there will be a saving, or even that one is probable[18]. Nor need the Court be satisfied that there might be a saving however the question is decided; so that if a decision in favour of A might save costs, although a decision in favour of B definitely would not, this is enough to confer jurisdiction[19].

The second condition is that the Court shall be satisfied that –

'(b) the question of law is one in respect of which leave to appeal would be likely to be given under section 1(3)(b) above'.

Presumably, this condition requires the Court to consider whether leave would have been given if the reference had proceeded to a final award, and leave had been sought to appeal against this award[20]. If this is so, there are real problems. The Court will have a double discretion. First, the discretion which would have been exercised if an event had happened which ex hypothesi will never happen – a discretion which would, if it had happened, have been decided

---

[16] *Gebr. Broere BV v Saras Chimica SpA* [1982] 2 Lloyd's Rep 436.
[17] Presumably sub-s. (2)(a) refers to the costs of the arbitration, not the costs of the arbitration plus those of the hearing in the High Court.
[18] Contrast the words 'would be likely to' in s. 2(2)(b).
[19] This seems to have been the basis on which the Court assumed jurisdiction in *The Vasso* [1983] 2 Lloyd's Rep 346, despite the doubts expressed by Lloyd J.
[20] It cannot mean that there is an additional formal constraint on jurisdiction equivalent to that existing in respect of a final award; partly because if this is what was meant, the legislature would have said so, and partly because the condition of jurisdiction under s. 1(4) is inevitably satisfied if s. 2(2)(b) is satisfied.

in the light of all the circumstances then known to exist[1]. Moreover, the Court is to decide, not simply whether the decision might have gone in favour of allowing an appeal, but whether the Court 'would be likely to have given' leave. This will face the Court with a difficult task.

Then the Court will have to go on to exercise its discretion again, this time in the light of the situation as it actually exists when the application is made.

There is another, even less tractable, problem. Sub-section 2(2) requires the Court to forecast what would happen if the arbitration were to go ahead and culminate in an appeal against a final award. But the procedure under section 2 is not designed to deal solely with appeals against an interim decision of the arbitrator; for these will in the main be brought under section 1, read in the light of section 7(1)(a): see above.

An important function of the jurisdiction under section 2 will be to deal with cases where the arbitrator has not yet made any decision, at the time when the application is made. Plainly, criteria relating to the grant of leave to appeal cannot be transferred bodily to a situation where there is nothing against which to appeal. The problem is well illustrated by the guidelines in *The Nema*. These require the Court to consider whether the decision of the arbitrator appears to be right: a criterion which cannot be applied if no such decision exists.

We do not know of any satisfactory solution to this problem. The following appear to be the only possibilities –

(i) The procedure under section 2 is not available where the arbitrator has made no decision. This cannot be right. A separate procedure for interim appeals is expressly created by sections 1 and 7(1)(a). Section 2 does not speak of an appeal, but of a determination, which must cover the case where the Court, not the arbitrator, makes the first decision on the question of law.

(ii) Sub-section 2(b) does not apply where the arbitrator has made no decision. There is no warrant for this. The Act is quite explicit, and unlimited in its terms.

(iii) Section 2(2) applies, but without the *Nema* guidelines. There are theoretical and practical objections to this solution. It is unsatisfying in principle, because it requires the Court to carry out an enquiry different from the one which the Act prescribes: namely to consider what the position would be on a final appeal[2]. In practice, the Court will find it hard to decide how an application for leave to appeal would have fared if the law had been the opposite of what was laid down by the House of Lords. Nevertheless, in the absence of anything better, we believe that this is the solution to which the Court would be driven.

This problem has another aspect. Since an application to which the jurisdictional conditions imposed by section 2(2) comes before the Court with the support of the arbitrator or the umpire, the Court will know that a

---

[1] On an application for leave to appeal in respect of one point of law, against a final award, the Court will be able to look at the individual point in the context of everything else that has been decided on law or fact in respect of the dispute. These factors are unknown at the time of the application under s. 2, and the Court can scarcely be expected to speculate upon them.

[2] The objection cannot be answered by saying that the *Nema* guidelines were not intended to apply to preliminary questions. Certainly they were not, but this is not the point. What s. 2 calls for, if read literally, is for the guidelines to be used to determine the hypothetical application for final leave to appeal. For very similar reasons, the problem cannot be evaded by saying that the *Nema* did no more than lay down guidelines, which the Court need not apply if inappropriate: for they would be appropriate, in the context of the exercise to be performed under s. 2(2)(b), since this presumes the existence of something against which to appeal.

determination of the question is regarded as desirable by a majority[3] of the persons most directly concerned with the dispute and the course of the reference. The Court may therefore be expected to approach the application sympathetically, even if not in the event finding it to be well-conceived.

The position is quite different under section 1. Here, the application is likely to be opposed. Moreover, the courts have laid down that a cautious, if not inimical, approach should be adopted, in order to prevent the immediate enforcement of an award from being delayed by an insubstantial appeal. No such consideration exists in the case of an application under section 2.

(ii) Applications with the consent of all the parties. In the case of an application brought with the consent of all the parties other than the applicant himself, the Court's jurisdiction is unfettered by the conditions imposed by section 2(2), no doubt because the legislature considered that the parties could be trusted to make their own decision as to whether it was in their best interests to seek the determination of a preliminary question of law.

Even where the application is made with the consent of all the parties, however, the Court still has a discretion whether or not to exercise its jurisdiction under section 2; this is a matter which arises at the fourth stage of the application: see below.

(d) Fourth stage: the discretion

Even where the Court has jurisdiction to entertain an application under section 2, either because the conditions laid down by section 2(2) are satisfied, or because the application is brought with the consent of all the parties, the Court must still consider as a matter of discretion, whether the jurisdiction should be exercised[4]. Generally speaking it will be exercised, since the filtering process imposed by the requirement that the applicant must either show that the conditions in section 2(2) are satisfied or obtain the consent of all the other parties will eliminate most of the unsuitable applications. But this is by no means a foregone conclusion. Where section 2(2) applies, an application must be made to the Court for a date for the hearing of the main argument, and no date will be fixed unless the Court is satisfied of the matters set out in the section[5]. In every case the Court will examine the application, if need be of its own motion, to see that the procedure is not being abused, to satisfy itself that the question of law has been formulated in such a way that it can be satisfactorily answered and is not misconceived, and to ensure that the Court has before it all the findings or assumptions of fact which are needed in order to answer the question.

We have already drawn attention, in Chapter 25, to the caution which should be adopted when considering when and how to raise a preliminary question of law for decision by the Court, particularly if the decision is to be made on the basis of assumed facts. If the chosen procedure is an application under section 2, the questions should be short and to the point. The more complicated and

---

[3] Subject to the point on 'an' arbitrator, mentioned in note 12 at p. 622, ante.
[4] *Babanaft International Co SA v Avant Petroleum Inc, The Oltenia* [1982] 1 Lloyd's Rep 448.
[5] *Gebr. Broere BV v Saras Chimica SpA* [1982] 2 Lloyd's Rep 436; *The Vasso* [1983] 2 Lloyd's Rep 346, 348–349.

contingent[6] the questions, the more likely the Court is to complain about being set an 'examination paper', and refuse to hear the matter at all[7].

(e) Fifth stage: the decision

The courts have not yet had occasion to explain the basis on which the courts are to carry out the determination of a preliminary question. In those cases, however, where the arbitrator has not made a decision, there seems no reason why the Court should approach the matter on the footing of any presumption adverse to the applicant. One thing does seem to be clear, that the principles laid down in the *Nema* and other cases have no logical relation to section 2. This produces the curious result that the Court may well give a different answer to the same question of law on the same facts depending on whether it is brought forward as a preliminary point under section 2, or as part of a final appeal under section 1. There is nothing in the prior discussions or Debates, or in the judgment and speeches in the *Nema*, to suggest that this is what the new system was intended to achieve.

The powers of the Court to confirm, vary, set aside or remit under section 1 do not apply to the procedure under section 2, since the latter is not an 'appeal'. The 'determination' by the Court will take the form of a declaratory judgment.

By virtue of section 2(3) an appeal lies to the Court of Appeal against a determination by the High Court. There is, however, the same filtering mechanism as exists in relation to final appeals[8].

G. LEAVE TO APPEAL TO THE COURT OF APPEAL

The 1979 Act (as amended by the Supreme Court Act 1981) has introduced a number of new constraints on appeals to the Court of Appeal. These are, in outline, as follows –

(a) As regards appeal on matters of law, as distinct from procedural appeals, the requirement that leave to appeal must be obtained from either the High Court or the Court of Appeal is now extended to cover not only the consultative jurisdiction of the High Court, as under the old system, but also its appellate jurisdiction. In addition, no appeal lies to the Court of Appeal without the certificate of the High Court that the question of law either is one of general public importance or is one which for some other special reason should be considered by the Court of Appeal.

---

[6] It would be possible to say that the Court can never be asked a contingent question, because s. 2(1) applies only to questions of law 'arising' in the course of the reference. There is warrant for this view in *Aktiebolaget Gotaverken v Westminster Corpn of Monrovia* [1971] 2 Lloyd's Rep 505 at 511. We suggest, however, that this cannot be carried too far, for this would mean that the Court could never be asked a question on the basis of assumed facts. This would take away a most useful jurisdiction – for example to decide whether a pleading disclosed a cause of action. A question can surely 'arise' in a reference if it has been raised and if it is potentially relevant, even if there is a possibility that when all the facts and the rest of the law have been decided it will prove not to be relevant after all. We suggest that the best protection against abuse is a firm exercise of the discretion.

[7] *Aktiebolaget Gotaverken v Westminster Corpn of Monrovia*, supra, provides an excellent example of how the procedure should not be used.

[8] See pp. 627–630, post.

(b) As regards appeals on procedural matters[9] under the 1979 Act, the position since the enactment of the Supreme Court Act 1981 is that no appeal lies to the Court of Appeal without the leave of the High Court, whose decision is final.

1 Appeals on questions of law

The restrictions imposed by the 1979 Act on appeals to the Court of Appeal are an important feature of the new system. In part, they were intended to impose a check on abuses of the appellate system: but the main abuse complained of, namely delay, could nearly always be dealt with, even under the old system, by refusing a stay of execution on the award, or by granting a stay only on terms that security should be provided for the amount of the award and the claimants' costs. A more powerful reason for the new restrictions on appeals was the desire to avoid overburdening the appellate courts with numerous appeals as of right from decisions of arbitrators, particularly in the commodity trades, raising points of law of little or no general importance, even to the trade in question; often highly technical; and generally on findings of fact of considerable complexity. In the five years or so preceding the 1979 Act this had become something of a problem, and it was believed that the problem was likely to persist and needed to be dealt with.

In the result the 1979 Act imposed two separate conditions, both of which have to be satisfied before the Court of Appeal can exercise its appellate jurisdiction over appeals from a decision of the High Court under section 1 (appeals) or under section 2 (preliminary points of law). They are as follows –

(a) The party who desires to appeal must apply for and obtain a certificate of the High Court that the question of law to which its decision relates either is one of general public importance or is one which for some other reason should be considered by the Court of Appeal[10].

(b) He must also apply for and obtain the leave of either the High Court or the Court of Appeal for the prosecution of the appeal[11].

These conditions are cumulative, no alternative. The party seeking to appeal may obtain a certificate but fail to obtain leave to appeal[12]: or he may obtain leave to appeal but fail to obtain a certificate: in either case he is barred from recourse to the Court of Appeal.

(a) The certificate

Section 1(7)(b) of the Act lays down two grounds on which the High Court may grant a certificate. The first is that the question of law to which its decision relates is one of general public importance. Since the decision of the House of

---

[9] See pp. 630–631, post, for an explanation of the term 'procedural matters'.
[10] Ss. 1(7)(b) and 2(3)(b).
[11] Ss 1(7)(a) and 2(3)(a).
[12] It is sometimes argued that if the judge certifies that the question of law is of general public importance leave to appeal should follow automatically. But this is misconceived. The importance of the question is a factor in deciding whether to give leave, but it is not decisive, and leave will not usually be given if the law is clearly laid down by the judge and there is no real likelihood of the appeal succeeding: *Marc Rich & Co Ltd v Tourlotti Compania Navievra SA, The Kalliopi A* [1987] 2 Lloyd's Rep 268.

Lords in *The Nema* it has become apparent that the categorisation of a question as being of general public importance is one that has to be made not only at the stage of leave to appeal to the Court of Appeal but also, at least on a provisional basis, on the initial application for leave to appeal from the arbitrator to the High Court, or for the hearing of a preliminary point of law[13]. A number of cases have already been reported in which the question of a certificate has arisen[14], but the earlier of these decisions now have to be read in the light of the stringent test, laid down by Lord Diplock in *The Nema*, as to what is and is not a 'one-off' question. The test to be applied may, we suggest, be summarised in the following propositions –

1 The most important characteristics of a question of general public importance are (a) that it has recurred or is likely to recur with a fair degree of frequency and (b) that it raises a point of legal principle of general application.

2 A question is not of general public importance if it arises out of the construction or application of a 'one-off' clause.

3 Even a question arising out of a standard clause is not of general public importance unless it turns on the application of the clause to 'events of a kind that it is not unlikely may reproduce themselves in similar transactions between other parties engaged in the same trade'[15].

4 The expression 'public' is used in contrast to 'private' and does not connote the public at large. A question may be of general public importance although its impact is limited to persons engaged in a particular trade or other sector of the public[16]: but not if its importance is limited to the parties to a particular private transaction, even though they may, as a class, include more persons than the parties to the actual arbitration from which the question has arisen[17].

5 A mixed question of fact and law will rarely, if ever, give rise to a question of general public importance[18].

In some cases the judge may be able to form a view simply on the basis of his own experience as to whether a question is of general public importance. But this will not always be so: sometimes the importance of a point will only be apparent to those who practice regularly in a particular field of legal activity. In the past the practice has been, where an application for leave to appeal has been put forward on the grounds that the point at issue has aroused general interest, for counsel simply to inform the judge, on instructions, of the reasons why the point is of general importance. This will no doubt continue to be sufficient in cases where the importance of the question is obvious or notorious: but in other cases, particularly where the application for a certificate is opposed, it may be found more convenient to bring the relevant facts before the Court in a more formal manner, by incorporating them in an affidavit.

---

[13] See the discussion at pp. 602–608, ante.

[14] The cases include *BTP Tioxide Ltd v Pioneer Shipping Ltd, and Armada Marine SA, The Nema* [1980] 2 Lloyd's Rep 83 at 93–94, per Goff J; [1981] 2 Lloyd's Rep 239 at 246, per Lord Diplock; *Maritime Transport Overseas GmbH v Unitramp Salen Rederierna A/B, The Antaios* [1981] 2 Lloyd's Rep 284 at 300; *Schiffahrtsagentur Hamburg Middle East Line GmbH v Virtue Shipping Corpn, The Oinoussian Virtue (No 2)* [1981] 2 Lloyd's Rep 300 at 308; *Italmare Shipping Co v Ocean Tanker Co Inc, The Rio Sun* [1982] 1 Lloyd's Rep 404 at 409; *Babanaft International Co SA v Avant Petroleum Inc, The Oltenia* [1982] Com LR 104.

[15] Per Lord Diplock in *The Nema*, ante, at 246.

[16] Per Goff J in *The Nema*, ante, at 93–94; and per Lord Diplock at 246.

[17] *The Oltenia*, ante.

[18] *The Nema*, in the House of Lords.

The second ground on which a certificate may be granted is that 'for some other reason' the question 'should be considered by the Court of Appeal'. This is a catch-all provision from which it is difficult to extract any single guiding principle: indeed it is probably undesirable even to attempt to do so. The philosophy underlying the 1979 Act, as expounded in *The Nema*, plainly requires that 'some other reason' should be an important reason and sufficient to oust the prima facie presumption in favour of finality: beyond that, however, one can only say that the discretion must be exercised according to the facts of each case. It is unlikely that any one factor will be decisive. So, for example, the mere size of the sum in issue would not be a sufficient reason[19]: nor, we suggest, the mere fact that the judge has overruled the arbitrator's decision[20], or has done so only with considerable hesitation. But the cumulative effect of these and other factors could on occasion justify a certificate being granted on this ground. It has to be borne in mind that in the great majority of cases where no point of general public importance is involved the judge will not have granted leave to appeal to the High Court unless there was a very strong probability of the award being reversed. In practice this is likely to mean that most 'one-off' cases which reach the stage of a hearing on the merits will result in the arbitrator's decision being reversed and a certificate of general public importance being refused. In the long term this is likely to give rise to a risk that the reputation of the arbitral and appellate process will be harmed, unless from time to time the occasional 'one-off' case finds its way to the Court of Appeal so that it can be ruled upon with the authority which that Court commands.

The decision of the High Court to refuse to grant a certificate is not open to challenge by way of appeal, because it is not 'a judgment or order' of the High Court for the purposes of section 16 of the Supreme Court Act 1981, which defines the appellate jurisdiction of the Court of Appeal[1].

The certificate is the certificate of the High Court and can therefore be given by any judge of the High Court; but, save in special circumstances, the application should be made to the judge who has heard the appeal.

(b) Leave to appeal

The second condition which must be satisfied before the Court of Appeal has jurisdiction to hear an appeal on the question of law, is that leave to appeal shall have been given either by the Court of Appeal or the High Court. The criteria to be applied in deciding whether to give leave are the same whether the application is made to the Court of Appeal or the High Court[2], and may be summarised as follows –

---

[19] See *The Oltenia*, ante.

[20] However respected the arbitrator: *Damon Compania Naviera v EAL Europe Africka Line GmbH, The Nicki R* [1984] 2 Lloyd's Rep 186, 190; *Pera Shipping Corporation v Petroship SA, The Pera* [1985] 2 Lloyd's Rep 103 at 105, 108. Differing from another judge may, however, be a sufficient reason: *Vargas Pena Apazteguia y Cia SAIC v Peter Cremer GmbH* [1987] 1 Lloyd's Rep 394 at 400.

[1] *National Westminster Bank Plc v Arthur Young McClelland Moores & Co* [1985] 1 WLR 1123; *Cie Europeenne des Petroles v Vitol BV* [1988] 1 Lloyd's Rep 577.

[2] The application should be made to the High Court in the first instance, and only if it fails, to the Court of Appeal. The jurisdiction of the Court of Appeal to give leave is an originating jurisdiction, not by way of appeal. Accordingly, a decision by the High Court to refuse *or to give* leave cannot be the subject of an appeal, although a refusal does not bar a subsequent application for leave to the Court of Appeal.

1 The test to be applied is similar to that laid down in *The Nema* when considering whether to grant leave to appeal to the High Court from the arbitrator[3].

2 But, although it is similar, the test is not the same, because the cause of uniformity of arbitral decision may already have been sufficiently served by a decision of a High Court judge which will bind all arbitrators[4].

3 The fact that the parties have consented to the question of law being decided by the High Court has no bearing on the question of whether there should be a further appeal to the Court of Appeal, unless there is also consent to this further stage in the proceedings.

4 Leave to appeal will be less readily granted in relation to a preliminary question of law under section 2 than in relation to an appeal under section 1, unless the determination of the preliminary question is capable of effectively determining the whole dispute between the parties.

2 Appeals on procedural matters

The Court of Appeal has jurisdiction to hear appeals from the High Court on the following procedural matters under the Act –

1 The grant or refusal of leave to appeal to the High Court under section 1(3)(b).

2 The grant or refusal of leave for an application to order the arbitrator to give reasons under section 1(5)(b).

3 The making or withholding of an order for the arbitrator to give reasons under section 1(5).

4 The decision to entertain or not to entertain an application for the determination of a preliminary question of law under section 2(1)(a), i.e. an application made with the consent of an arbitrator or umpire but not of all the parties.

5 The decision to entertain or not to entertain an application for the determination of a preliminary question of law under section 2(1)(b), i.e. an application made with the consent of all the parties.

In cases 1 to 4 an appeal may only be brought with leave of the High Court[5]: if the High Court refuses leave, the Court of Appeal does not, unlike the position where the appeal goes to the merits of a question of law, have power to entertain a fresh application for leave[6]. In case 5, however, it appears that an appeal lies[7]

---

[3] *CA Venezolana de Navegacion v Bank Line Ltd, The Roachbank* [1988] 2 Lloyd's Rep 337. Presumably under s. 1, in assessing the likelihood of the judge being reversed on appeal, some account may be taken of the fact that he was not the first to have given a decision on the question of law raised by the appeal: so that weight may properly be given to the decision of the arbitrator.

[4] *The Oltenia*, ante, per Donaldson LJ. Contra, if there is a divergence of opinion between judges of first instance; or if the grounds of the judge's decision are unclear: *Arab Maritime Petroleum Transport Co v Luxor Trading Corpn* [1987] 1 Lloyd's Rep 124.

[5] See, as to cases 1 and 2, s. 1(6A), and as to cases 3 and 4, s. 2(2A). These provisions were introduced into the Act by the Supreme Court Act 1981 in order to eliminate a source of procedural delay which had not been perceived by the legislature at the time of the passing of the 1979 Act.

[6] Nor an appeal from the refusal to give leave to appeal: *Aden Refinery Ltd v Ugland Management Co Ltd* [1987] QB 650.

[7] Under s. 16(1) of the Supreme Court Act 1981. Such an appeal is not excluded by s. 18(g) of the 1981 Act.

to the Court of Appeal with the leave either of the High Court or of the Court of Appeal itself[8].

Whether the application for leave to appeal is made to the High Court or, in case 5, to the Court of Appeal, it will only be granted in the rare instance where some genuine point of principle is involved, on which it is desirable that there should be a decision of the Court of Appeal rather than a decision of the judge[9].

H. EXCLUSION AGREEMENTS

As previously stated, the effect of an exclusion agreement depends upon whether or not the arbitration agreement is a 'domestic arbitration agreement'.

Where the arbitration agreement is a 'domestic' agreement, the exclusion agreement is valid only if it is made after the commencement of the arbitration.

Where the arbitration agreement is not 'domestic' it is effective whenever made, unless it falls into the 'special category', in which case it is effective either if it is made after the commencement of the arbitration, or it is expressed[10] to be governed by a law other than the law of England and Wales.

1 Domestic and non-domestic agreements

Section 3(7) defines a domestic agreement as –

'... an arbitration agreement which does not provide, expressly or by implication, for arbitration in a State other than the United Kingdom and to which neither –
(a) an individual who is a national of, or habitually resident in, any State other than the United Kingdom, nor
(b) a body corporate which is incorporated in, or whose central management or control is exercised in, any State other than the United Kingdom,
is a party at the time the arbitration agreement is entered into'.

If the negatives are eliminated from the first part of the sub-section it follows[11] that a domestic agreement is one which does provide expressly or by implication for arbitration in the United Kingdom[12]. Two points may be noted. First, the

---

[8] This appears to follow from the omission, from s. 2(2A), of any reference to s. 2(1)(b).

[9] *BVS SA v Kerman Shipping Co SA, The Kerman* [1982] 1 Lloyd's Rep 62 at 68; *The Antaios*, ante.

[10] The limitation of the validity of prior exclusion agreements concerning special category contracts to those which are *expressly* governed by a foreign law is rather surprising. If the prime justification for creating the special category is to further the growth of judicially-developed commercial law – as comment before and after the enactment of the legislation would suggest – it might have been expected that exclusion agreements would also be effective where the contract is impliedly governed by a foreign law. Perhaps the legislature had in mind that contracts whose proper law was really foreign would still be adjudicated in accordance with English law, by virtue of the evidentiary presumption that foreign law is the same as English law: but this would apply even where there was an express choice of foreign law.

[11] Perhaps the negatives cannot be eliminated. Can there be an arbitration agreement in which there is no express or implied choice of forum?

[12] It is not clear why 'the United Kingdom' was referred to here, in contrast to England and Wales. An agreement requiring arbitration in Scotland is not really 'domestic' – since Scotland has an entirely distinct system of arbitration to which the 1979 Act does not apply: s. 8(4).

definition contemplates an implied choice of forum. This is in contrast with section 4(1)(ii), where one might expect, but does not find, a reference to an implied choice of proper law. This may be a source of uncertainty, which is regrettable, since the parties ought to be able to know from the outset whether or not their exclusion agreement will be effective[13].

Second, the section does not expressly cater for the case, not uncommonly met in practice, where the parties decide to conduct the reference somewhere other than the place stipulated in the clause. We believe that, for the purposes of section 3(7), this would be an instance where the agreement provides (through a consensual variation) for arbitration at the new forum. If this is so, the parties will need to take care that a change made for administrative convenience does not invalidate their exclusion agreement.

The position is the opposite as regards the second element of the definition. An individual party may change his residence, or a corporate party may change the location of its central management, between the making of the arbitration agreement[14], and the commencement of the reference. This does not, however, bear upon the efficacy of the exclusion agreement.

2 'Special category' disputes

The power to exclude, in advance, an appeal to the High Court does not apply to certain types of disputes, namely –

    (a) a question or claim falling within the Admiralty jurisdiction of the High Court, or
    (b) a dispute arising out of a contract of insurance, or
    (c) a dispute arising out of a commodity contract' (section 4(1)).

The discussions and debates leading up to the enactment of the new system tended to speak in rather general terms of 'maritime disputes'. We believe that this expression was generally understood as referring to disputes concerning salvage and towage, and to the kind of dispute which was the subject of a typical 'Baltic arbitration': viz. one which related to a charterparty, or a bill of lading or (perhaps) to a contract for the building or sale of a ship. The Act defines the categories in much wider terms; but the matter is, perhaps, of quite modest practical importance, since most of the disputes falling within the Admiralty jurisdiction, apart from those at which the 1979 Act was aimed, would rarely, if ever, be the subject of arbitration. It would be beyond the scope of this work to embark on a complete survey of the Admiralty Jurisdiction of the High Court. The jurisdiction is presently defined by section 20 of the Supreme Court Act 1981.

A distinction may be noted between the expressions 'a question or claim' and 'a dispute'. This is of some theoretical interest, but we do not at present see how it can have any practical significance. There is, however, another distinction

---

[13] An implied choice might arise through the inclusion of a term that the arbitration shall be conducted according to the rules of a body located in a particular country.

[14] There is an important difference between the definitions of 'domestic arbitration agreement' in the 1975 and 1979 Acts. Under the former, the question whether the individual or body is foreign depends upon the position at the date when the proceedings are commenced: i.e. the proceedings which it is sought to stay. Under the 1979 Act, it is the date of the arbitration agreement which matters.

between the treatment of maritime disputes on the one hand, and insurance and commodity disputes on the other, which is of real importance. The former are defined by reference to the nature of the dispute, the latter by reference to the type of contract from which the dispute arises[15]. In the result, even the most mundane of questions may be made the subject of appeal (at least in principle) provided that it arises from an insurance or commodity contract.

A commodity contract is denied in section 4(2)(a) as a contract 'for the sale of goods regularly dealt with on a commodity market or exchange in England or Wales which is specified for the purposes of this section by an order made by the Secretary of State'. The order currently in force is set out in Appendix 1 at p. 715, post.

The Act provides, by section 4(3), that the Secretary of State may abolish or modify the special category of disputes, by a statutory instrument, subject to annulment by a resolution of either House of Parliament. It was originally contemplated[16] that this power would be used so as to validate exclusion agreements made before the commencement of the reference, in those cases where the agreement was separate from the arbitration agreement itself, and was registered with the High Court[17]. The power is, of course, expressed in much wider terms, and may yet be used to abolish the special category of disputes altogether.

We have already referred to the fact that the existence of a 'special category' of disputes is relevant only to the parties' power to exclude in advance the right of appeal. It has no bearing on a waiver of that right made after the commencement of the arbitration[18].

There is, however, another instance in which an exclusion agreement will be valid, even in relation to a special category dispute: namely if the award or question relates to a contract which is expressed to be governed by a law other than the law of England and Wales[19]. This is an odd provision. It does not apply to agreements which are by implication subject to a foreign law: contrast section 3(7). Moreover, there was no need to exclude an appeal on foreign law[20], when

---

[15] It may also be noted that the expression 'arising out of' may well be wider than other terms (such as 'arising in connection with') commonly employed in arbitration clauses: see p. 120, ante.

[16] See the Report of the Commercial Court Committee Cmnd. 7284, para. 50. The idea was that the act of registration of an agreement deliberately made, and separate from the main contract, would show a conscious choice to eliminate the right of appeal which could not necessarily be inferred from an exclusion clause in a standard form of contract.

[17] The notion of a system of registration which was much discussed during the years leading up to the enactment of the new system, appears for the moment to have disappeared from view.

[18] It will be noted that the material date is when the arbitration is commenced, not the date when the dispute arises. This is of some practical importance, since parties to a dispute do occasionally make ad hoc arrangements for a reference before the reference is formally called into being; so that if those arrangements include an agreement to exclude the right of appeal, the parties must be sure to restate the agreement, once the reference is under way.

[19] S. 4(1)(ii). The law of Scotland is therefore a foreign law for the purpose. This provides an easy method of exploiting the 'Bermuda gap': the parties contract for their disputes to be governed by the law of Scotland. Since on most matters of maritime law and insurance, and many aspects of international sales, the laws of Scotland and England are the same, the parties obtain the advantage of a law which they know, and an arbitration by an experienced tribunal in London, without the possibility of an appeal.

[20] Cmnd. 7284, para. 52(a) contemplated that the parties to a contract governed by foreign law should be able to contract into a right of appeal on a question concerning that law. There is no trace of this idea in the Act.

issues of foreign law are questions of fact for the arbitrator, and accordingly are not susceptible of appeal[1].

3 The terms of an exclusion agreement

Some uncertainty has arisen as to the correct way in which to express an exclusion agreement. The 1979 Act has two provisions which appear to bear on the matter. These are –

> '3(1) Subject to the following provisions of this section and section 4 below –
> (a) the High Court shall not, under section 1(3)(b) above, grant leave to appeal with respect to a question of law arising out of an award, and
> (b) the High Court shall not, under section 1(5)(b) above, grant leave to make an application with respect to an award, and
> (c) no application may be made under section 2(1)(a) above with respect to a question of law,
> if the parties to the reference in question have entered into an agreement in writing (in this section referred to as an 'exclusion agreement') which excludes the right of appeal under section 1 above in relation to that award, or, in a case falling within paragraph (c) above, in relation to an award to which the determination of the question of law is material'.
> '3(4) Except as provided by subsection (1) above, sections 1 and 2 above shall have effect notwithstanding anything in any agreement purporting –
> (a) to prohibit or restrict access to the High Court; or
> (b) to restrict the jurisdiction of the court; or
> (c) to prohibit or restrict the making of a reasoned award'.

The problem is to decide whether the exclusion agreement should explicitly exclude all four of the supervisory powers listed in sections 3(1) and 3(13) – namely the powers to entertain an appeal, to order the arbitrator to state further reasons for his award, to entertain a preliminary question of law, and to transfer to the High Court a dispute involving an issue of fraud – or whether it is enough simply to exclude the right of appeal. We suggest that the latter is the correct

---

[1] The reasons assigned in the Debate (Hansard, H.L., Vol. 397, at 1226) were as follows: (i) some foreign lawyers consider that foreign law is a question of law in the English court; (ii) there is a problem of renvoi. With due respect, these scarcely seem convincing. It is unusual and hardly desirable to enact legislation on the footing that principles of English law, well understood by English lawyers, are less well understood elsewhere, especially since the legislation was designed to attract to English arbitration precisely the type of large corporation which could well afford to take the best English legal advice. Not do we see how a question of renvoi could arise where there is an express contractual choice of a foreign law. There is, however, one additional point which may be mentioned. If a contract governed by a foreign law becomes the subject of dispute before an English tribunal, there is an evidentiary presumption that foreign law is the same as English law, unless proved by expert evidence to be different. In practice, this presumption has the result that may disputes, nominally governed by a foreign law, are argued and decided on the basis of English law alone. S. 4(1)(ii) might therefore serve a purpose in making it clear that there is no right of appeal in such a case. No such motive is, however, referred to in the preliminary works, and in any event it is hard to see why the sub-section should be limited to cases where the choice of law is express.

view[2]. There would also seem, on reading sub-section (1) alone, to be no reason why any particular form of words should be employed for this purpose. Consistently with the general practice of the courts to give effect to the commercial policy underlying the 1979 Act, it would be quite permissible to take a clause generally purporting to oust the supervisory jurisdiction of the courts, treat it as ineffective in relation to those jurisdictions which cannot be ousted (e.g. to set aside the award for misconduct) and give effect to the remainder as an exclusion agreement. It may, however, be said that this proposition cannot be reconciled with sub-section 4, on the ground that the sub-section would be superfluous if a general ouster would suffice. This objection is not altogether convincing, for the purpose of the sub-section is apparently to ensure that only a valid exclusion agreement (i.e. one which qualifies under section 3(6) or section 4 will suffice to oust the general right of appeal.

It must, however, be acknowledged that there is some room for uncertainty as to what exactly the Act contemplates by way of exclusion agreement, and we believe that the safest course will be to use a form of words which expressly excludes all four supervisory powers[3].

This leads to the next question. All rights of appeal in respect of what? Here the Act is clear. According to section 3(2) the exclusion may relate to a particular award; to awards under a particular reference; or to any other description of awards, whether arising out of the same reference or not.

If the exclusion agreement is made after the commencement of the arbitration – as it will be, if the arbitration agreement is 'domestic', or the dispute relates to a 'special category' of transaction – then the agreement will normally relate to all awards made in the course of the reference, to cater for the possibility that the arbitrator will make an interim award. If the exclusion agreement is made beforehand, as part of an arbitration agreement, it can be expressed to exclude all appeals arising out of any reference pursuant to the arbitration agreement.

The exclusion agreement must be in writing but it need not be set out in the arbitration agreement itself. It may be incorporated by reference to another document[4]. The agreement need not be signed, and the document need not actually constitute the agreement, so that a document recording an oral exclusion agreement is sufficient[5].

An exclusion agreement may be waived by a further agreement or under the doctrine of promissory estoppel, but only by a clear promise or representation to that effect: a request for a reasoned award is not enough[6].

---

[2] Because the last two lines of s. 3(1) speak of an exclusion relating to an award, not to a question. In other words, once there is an exclusion relating to an award, all the other exclusions take effect automatically.

[3] See *Supreme Court Practice 1988* Vol. 2, para. 5885.

[4] Such as the Rules of Arbitration of the International Chamber of Commerce, Article 24 of which contains a waiver by the parties 'of their right to any form of appeal insofar as such waiver can validly be made': *Arab African Energy Corpn Ltd v Olieprodukten Nederland BV* [1983] 2 Lloyd's Rep 419; *Marine Contractors Inc v Shell Petroleum Development Co of Nigeria Ltd* [1984] 2 Lloyd's Rep 77.

[5] See the cases cited in the preceding note, and the authorities on the statutory definitions of 'arbitration agreement' at pp. 54–56, ante.

[6] *Marine Contractors Inc v Shell Petroleum Development Co of Nigeria Ltd*, supra.

I. RSC ORDER 55

Finally, we should mention a puzzling aspect of the new system: namely its relationship with the procedures laid down by RSC Order 55. This Order applies to:

'... every appeal which by or under any enactment lies to the High Court from any court, tribunal or person'.

(Order 55, r. 1(1)). The Order does not apply to appeals by way of case stated, which are governed by Order 56.

On the face of it, this Order is expressed so as to govern appeals under the 1979 Act, for although the arbitrator is not a 'tribunal'[7], there seems no reason to doubt that he is a person[8].

To read the Order as applicable in full to appeals under the 1979 Act would have far-reaching results, since it would bring into the law of arbitration the following procedures –

1 The notice of motion must state the grounds of appeal, and (subject to an amendment made with leave not less than seven days before the day appointed for the hearing of the appeal) the appellant cannot rely on any other grounds, without the leave of the court[9].

2 The notice of appeal must be served within 28 days of the decision, and the arbitrator must be among those served with the notice[10].

3 Subject to a contrary direction by the Court, the appeal cannot be heard sooner than 21 days after the service of the notice of motion[11].

4 The appellant is obliged to supply to the Court a signed copy of a note taken at the proceedings[12].

5 The Court has power to receive further evidence on findings of fact, by oral examination, affidavit or deposition[13].

6 The Court has power to order security for the costs of the appeal[14].

7 The Court shall not be bound to allow the appeal on the ground of misdirection, unless in the opinion of the Court substantial wrong or miscarriage has been thereby occasioned[15].

8 The appeal is by way of rehearing[16].

9 The Court has power to draw inferences of fact[17].

It is, we suggest, quite plain that the legislature never intended Order 55 to apply to appeals under the 1979 Act. So far as we can trace, it was never mentioned in any of the discussions and Debates preceding the Act, nor was it

---

[7] Because the arbitrators are given jurisdiction by a private contract, not by any enactment: see Ord. 55, r. 1(5).

[8] This word cannot be limited to a person whose jurisdiction is derived from the enactment which at the same time confers the right of appeal, for such a person already qualifies as a 'tribunal', under r. 1(5).

[9] R. 3(2); r. 6(1) and (3).

[10] R. 4(1)(b) and 4(2).

[11] R. 5.

[12] R. 7(4).

[13] R. 7(2).

[14] R. 7(6).

[15] R. 7(7).

[16] R. 3(1).

[17] R. 7(3).

referred to in *The Nema*[18] and the other cases in which the nature of the appeal has been pronounced upon. Nevertheless the Order is there, and the courts will either have to apply it or find some way of holding that despite its language it has no relevance to the new system.

To a considerable extent, the Court will be able to hold that the consequences listed above do not ensue, for the rules of Order 55 have effect:

'. . . subject to any provision made in relation to that appeal by any other provision of these rules or by or under any enactment'[19].

Thus, items (4) and (5) in the list will not be applicable, since these are inconsistent with a right of appeal expressly confined to a question of law[20]. Equally, it should be possible to dispose of items (1), (2) and (3) on the ground that they are inconsistent with the system laid down by the Act in terms which do not impose these restrictions on the exercise of the jurisdiction. Item (6) is unimportant, since the Court already has a power to require the provision of security for the costs of an appeal, by virtue of its general power under section 1(4) to impose conditions on the grant of leave.

Items (7) and (8)[1], however, cannot be so easily disposed of, for they raise difficult and important problems. It is quite clear that whatever the precise nature of the appeal[2], it has not been understood by the courts as a 'rehearing'. Moreover, although on one interpretation of the speeches in *The Nema* the Court is subject to constraint on the free exercise of the power of review[3], it has never yet been suggested that they correspond with those summarised in item (7). Yet we cannot see anything in the language of the Act, speaking as it does of 'an appeal' which is inconsistent with the application of this part of Order 55.

From a practical point of view the most ready solution to this problem would be to bring about an amendment of Order 55, r. 1 so as to exclude arbitration from its scope. For the time being, the courts appear to be ignoring Order 55 altogether.

---

[18] *BTP Tioxide Ltd v Pioneer Shipping Ltd and Armada Marine SA, The Nema* [1981] 2 Lloyd's Rep 239.
[19] R. 1(4).
[20] See *Green v Minister of Housing and Local Government* [1967] 2 QB 606, [1967] 2 WLR 192.
[1] And, to a lesser extent, item (9).
[2] A topic discussed at pp. 587–596, ante.
[3] See p. 593, ante.

CHAPTER 37

Recourse against unappealable errors of law

A. JUDICIAL CONTROL OTHERWISE THAN BY APPEAL

It seems likely that before very long the Court will have to tackle a problem which until 1979 was hidden by the availability of procedures for exercising judicial control over the legal content of the award. The problem concerns the extent to which the Court can and should withhold its powers of enforcement or intervene in cases where the award discloses an open and fundamental disaccord between the principles to which the arbitrator has given effect, and those to which the parties bound themselves when they entered into the contract. The problem may arise in several ways. For present purposes, it is sufficient to give two illustrations.

First, imagine a contract expressly governed by English law containing an exclusion agreement under section 3(1) of the 1979 Act, under which a dispute is referred to arbitration in England. Imagine also that the award of the arbitrator contains a passage on the following lines:

> 'I am well aware that if I apply the firmly established rules of the English law to the facts which I have found, I will be compelled to decide in favour of the respondent. I have always thought that the law on this topic is unfair nonsense. This is very clearly demonstrated by the present case. In my view, the only just course is to divide the loss equally between the two parties, and I shall give effect to my opinion by awarding the claimant 50 per cent of his claim'[1].

Under the former practice, a case such as this would present no problems. If an award had ever been published in such a transparent form, it could at once have been set aside for error on the face. Moreover, if the course of the hearing had shown which way the wind was blowing, the respondent could have called on the arbitrator to state his award in the form of a special case, and in practice this would have forced him to make an award properly in conformity with the

---

[1] This is a highly coloured example, and few arbitrators would be so candid or so incautious. Nevertheless, decisions arrived at more or less overtly on these lines are more common than is generally acknowledged, and the authors have come across instances in practice where arbitrators would have divided the loss between the parties, contrary to legal principle, if they had not been inhibited by the threat of a request for a special case. Many arbitrators see nothing wrong in this, for they take the view that the parties choose arbitration because it is regarded as substituting fairness for technicality. There is some force in this view, where the dispute involves numerous small items, some of which may raise controversial questions of law. An arbitrator who insists on ploughing every legal furrow, at no matter what cost to the parties, would not in many quarters be regarded as a better arbitrator then one who apportions the items on a rule-of-thumb basis, even if in a way which an official referee would not feel free to adopt.

law[2]. The 1979 Act has now closed both these roads. The award is apparently impregnable. If the claimant applies for summary enforcement under section 26, there is no orthodox means of escape. Is the Court really obliged to lend its coercive powers, so as to compel a result which is not one which the parties contracted to obtain, through the medium of a document which openly defies the law?

The second problem raises many of the same theoretical issues. Imagine that a particular event has affected the performance of numerous contracts between different parties, all in the same standard form, and that this has led to a series of distinct arbitrations, raising identical questions of law on identical facts. Some of these are in the hands of Mr X as umpire. He considers that the contracts should be interpreted in favour of the claimant. Other disputes are entrusted to Mr Y, who takes the opposite view. Both are men of integrity and repute, whose views carry great weight in the trade; and their conflicting opinions on this particular issue have become well known. The result is confusion. The claimants in the arbitrations will win or lose according to the chance of whether X or Y is appointed as umpire; disputes which have not yet reached a conclusion cannot be settled, because the outcome will depend upon who is chosen as umpire; if a similar problem arises again, the parties to the dispute will not know how to act, because they cannot tell what the outcome will be if the case comes to an arbitration. If it happens to be the case that one of the arbitrators is quite clearly mistaken, and that there is really no doubt about the law which ought to be applied, is there anything which the courts can do to put right this unsatisfactory state of affairs[3]?

It must be said at once that the answer to the second question is – No. The occurrence of conflicting decisions on issues of law by tribunals which are immune from appeal is nothing new[4] and the legislature must be assumed to have foreseen it, when the 1979 Act was under consideration, and to have regarded it as a risk worth taking, in order to secure what was seen as the benefit of release from judicial review. We discuss in the following parts of the Chapter the various routes by which an aggrieved party might try to bring his dispute before the Court. The practical answer to all of them is that in a context where the legislature has abolished the existing methods of control, and replaced them with one which is susceptible of exclusion by consent, it is hardly conceivable that the Court will allow itself to develop a new common law method of appeal, the operation of which cannot be excluded by the will of the parties.

---

[2] If there had been signs that the implied threat was not proving effective, the party could have brought the matter formally to a head by asking for a consultative case.

[3] The parties to one of the disputes could waive the exclusion agreement, and allow the matter to be determined by the Court. But this would not help if one of the arbitrators in the other disputes respectfully but firmly stuck to his guns.

[4] *Pearlman v Keepers and Governors of Harrow School* [1979] QB 56, [1978] 3 WLR 736, is a very striking example. All over the country, county court judges had been deciding whether the installation of central heating was an improvement, the cost of which should be taken into account when ascertaining the rateable value of the premises, for the purposes of the Leasehold Reform Act 1967. Some thought that it was; others that it was not. The result was a series of inconsistent decisions, which were not subject to appeal, since this was expressly excluded by s. 107 of the County Courts Act 1959. The position of the lessee therefore depended upon which county court jurisdiction happened to encompass his premises. The controversy surrounding the divided opinion in the Court of Appeal as to the possibility of relief by way of certiorari was in full spate at the time when the 1979 Act was under consideration by Parliament, and cannot have been overlooked.

Furthermore, the Court would rightly be very cautious about the use of any procedure, which might leave the way open to widespread applications for some kind of extra-appellate review, on the basis of extrinsic evidence that the arbitrator had erred in law.

The solution to the first problem is not, however, so obvious. Here, it may be said that the parties cannot pick and choose. If they wish their disputes to be conducted entirely outside the framework of the law, then they are free to do so. But if they wish to have the support of the law in the reinforcement of the reference, and the putting into effect of an award, then this must be related to a course of decision which at least attempts to conform with the law, rather than overtly contradict it.

B. POSSIBLE METHODS OF RECOURSE

Any inquiry into these and similar problems should begin by addressing the question whether an award ought in principle to conform with English law in the absence of some express provision to the contrary. The question itself raises certain conceptual problems, which are discussed in Chapter 4[5]. For present purposes, we propose to make two assumptions. First, that for the reasons just stated an arbitrator who decides otherwise than in accordance with the law does something which is contrary to his mandate. Second, in the interest of finality, the courts will not permit an enquiry into the question whether the arbitrator has unintentionally departed from his duty to apply the law. Starting from these assumptions, we shall examine those arguments on the basis of which the Court might have held, but in fact has not held, that a simple error of law entitles the Court to intervene; and will then enquire whether the fact that the error is deliberate makes any difference to the outcome.

For the purpose of discussion, it is convenient to borrow the term 'manifest disregard' from judgments delivered in the United States, in order to denote a departure from the law which is both open and deliberate.

We suggest that when a case of manifest disregard comes before the English courts, those who seek to argue against the award are likely to consider, if not necessarily advance, the following arguments –

1 The award is void or voidable for want of jurisdiction.

2 The Court has power to remit, so as to enable the arbitrator to apply the law correctly.

3 The Court has an inherent equitable jurisdiction to remedy the injustice resulting from a deliberate failure to apply the law.

4 By his wilful refusal to execute the mandate conferred upon him, the arbitrator has repudiated the contractual relationship. The aggrieved party can rely upon this as a ground for terminating the mandate, and hence deprive the arbitrator of the power to make an effective award.

5 The Court has power during the reference to remove an arbitrator or allow his authority to be revoked, if it can be shown that he is going wrong in law.

6 Although judicial review (in the technical sense) does not apply to the proceedings of arbitrators, the case of manifest disregard gives the courts an exceptional power to intervene.

---

[5] Pp. 68–71, ante.

7 A deliberate disregard by the arbitrator of the terms of his mandate amounts to misconduct, permitting the removal of the arbitrator and the setting aside of the award.

1 Jurisdiction

The first possibility would be to argue that the award is void or voidable for want of jurisdiction. We use 'jurisdiction', because it is constantly employed in this context. It is, however, potentially misleading. The jurisdiction of an arbitrator is of a quite different character from that of a Court or other tribunal exercising non-consensual powers over the rights of citizens. The area within which the latter can properly operate is delineated either by the constraints which the Court imposes on itself in the exercise of its sovereign authority, or (if the tribunal is not a superior court of record) by the legislative act which called it into existence. The role of an arbitrator is, by contrast, entirely defined by the arbitration agreement. In order to ascertain the extent of the questions which the arbitrator is empowered to investigate, the principles which he is to apply when deciding upon them, and the procedures which he is to adopt in the course of his investigation, recourse must be had solely to the express and implied terms of the private contract between the parties[6]. In this respect, arbitration is a specialised branch of the law of agency, not of public administrative law. It is quite unsafe to assume that because in given circumstances an administrative or other tribunal would be regarded as having acted in excess of jurisdiction, the award of an arbitrator could in similar circumstances properly be treated as void.

There is another reason why the word 'jurisdiction' must be used with caution. Namely, that questions of jurisdiction are of several quite distinct types. Those which are important here relate to –

1 The capacity of the tribunal to concern itself with the particular dispute in issue.

2 The degree to which the validity of the decision is dependent on the requirements of substantive law.

3 The relationship between the validity of a decision and the nature of the procedure by which it is arrived at.

If it were possible to make a fresh start with the law of arbitration, an argument of considerable logical force could be constructed, to the effect that an award made in deliberate disregard of the governing law is void for want of jurisdiction in either or both of the first two of these possible meanings.

In the first place, it could be argued that an arbitrator who is appointed in respect of a dispute arising under a contract expressly or impliedly governed by English law is authorised by the parties to pronounce upon the issues in accordance with that law, and in no other way. Any decision which proceeds on a different basis lies outside the scope of the arbitrator's mandate to bind the parties. The award is accordingly void for want of jurisdiction, since the arbitrator has done something which the parties never authorised him to do[7].

---

[6] Apart from the very exceptional cases where restraints are imposed by public policy. There are, of course, limits to the powers which the parties can confer on the arbitrator, but these simply reflect the fact that there are limits to what can be done by a private contract.

[7] The jurisdictional approach has been adopted in foreign jurisdictions.

Second, it would be possible to draw support from a line of authority culminating in three important decisions[8] which approach the question whether a tribunal can effectively decide contrary to law by using the word 'jurisdiction' in the first of the three senses indicated above. Whilst a reconciliation of these decisions is a matter for a treatise on administrative law, there is no doubt that in relation to certain kinds of tribunal the law has recognised a distinction between errors of law which go to jurisdiction and those which do not; and that there is a difference between a tribunal which has arrived at a decision by asking itself the wrong question, and one which has correctly identified the question, but has supplied the wrong answer in terms of law. Following up this line of authority, it could be said that an arbitrator empowered to decide the rights of the parties under a contract governed by English law, who asks himself, not what English law has to say about those rights, but what the rights ought to be if assessed in accordance with his own ideas of an extra-legal concept of justice, is either asking himself the wrong question[9], or not really asking a question at all.

We do not believe that the first way of putting the argument has any perceptible chance of being accepted by the courts[10]. Once it is asserted that a decision contrary to the law which the arbitrator is authorised to apply makes the award bad for want of jurisdiction, this conclusion must follow in every case where the arbitrator can be shown to have gone wrong in law, whether or not the deviation was intentional. For this purpose, it would be permissible to lead extrinsic evidence to demonstrate the mistake, since such evidence is always admissible on a plea directed to the jurisdiction. Such a conclusion would be contrary to centuries of established law[11]. The courts have never clearly explained why an error of law should not make an award bad for want of jurisdiction, or why extrinsic evidence of error is inadmissible. But this is the express or implied basis of countless decisions, no doubt founded on the premise that some degree of finality is essential to the arbitral process. It is inconceivable that, in order to solve the rare problem of manifest disregard, the courts would now give effect to a course of reasoning which, however sound in point of logic, would open the way to a whole new field of judicial intervention.

The second argument is much less open to objection on this ground. It does, however, present serious difficulties from both a theoretical and a practical point of view. So far as we are aware, none of the very few cases which have looked at

---

[8] *Anisminic Ltd v Foreign Compensation Commission* [1969] 2 AC 147, [1969] 2 WLR 163; *Pearlman v Keepers and Governors of Harrow School* [1979] QB 56, [1978] 3 WLR 736; *South East Asia Fire Brick Sdn Bhd v Non-Metallic Mineral Products Manufacturing Employees Union* [1981] AC 363, [1980] 3 WLR 318.

[9] Perhaps *Bunge & Co v Dewar and Webb* (1921) 8 Ll L Rep 436 is an example of the tribunal asking itself the wrong question.

[10] *K/S A/S Bill Biakh v Hyundai Corpn* [1988] 1 Lloyd's Rep 187 and *Bank Mellat v GAA Development and Construction Co* [1988] 2 Lloyd's Rep 44, 52–3 both explicitly reject the analysis based on jurisdiction.

[11] This is one of the demonstrations that error on the face does not go to jurisdiction; for want of jurisdiction can in general be demonstrated by evidence. (It is not easy to see why arbitration awards should be regarded as being in a special category simply because their jurisdiction is consensual in origin: for, after all, *Lee v Showmen's Guild of Great Britain* [1952] 2 QB 329 is an example of such a jurisdiction being subjected to judicial review.) It is disappointing that the decisions on the question whether error of law goes to jurisdiction should not have been brought up in the context of the same question where other inferior tribunals were concerned, and vice versa. The common law system of creating new law does not work efficiently unless the tribunal is furnished with all the relevant decisions. The isolated status of the law of arbitration is a conspicuous instance of a failure of the common law, in matters of fundamental theory.

the question of a conscious failure to apply the law have approached the matter in terms of jurisdiction. Nor has there been any point of contact between the lines of authority which discuss the problem of decisions which are wrong in law, in the fields of arbitration and other types of subordinate tribunal. It is most unfortunate that, even in very recent times, the reported cases in one field appear never to have been cited to the Court when questions in the other field were in issue. Opposition to the suggested argument would undoubtedly lay great weight on the fact that the regime of judicial review does not apply to the decisions of arbitrators, and this will be said to reflect a recognition that arbitration is a mode of procedure which is entirely sui generis. Furthermore, although the Court would no doubt be most careful to confine the grant of leave to those cases in which the arbitrator had not addressed himself at all to the legal issues in the case, this would not deter the parties from attempting to prove an absence of jurisdiction where none in fact existed. In tune with the current trend of legislative and judicial thinking, the Court might well take the view that it should renounce the possibility of intervention even in the case of deliberate mistake, in the general interest of finality and speed.

It is impossible to predict what result the Court will reach, when it is ultimately presented with this problem. The pragmatic nature of decisions in the field of arbitration suggests that the answer may well depend upon the circumstances of the individual case. It is only if the Court conceives the decision of the arbitrator to be capricious, and the result to be at variance with the Court's own assessment of the underlying commercial merits, that there is any real prospect of a remedy being afforded.

Finally, mention must be made of the third meaning of the word 'jurisdiction'. There is undoubtedly authority in the line of cases relating to other types of subordinate tribunal that procedural errors may render a decision void; and want of jurisdiction is often cited as the reason. It is, however, quite clear in the field of arbitration that misconduct makes an award voidable not void. Why there should be this difference between the two situations is not clear. Nevertheless it exists. If a deliberate failure to decide in accordance with the law does amount to misconduct – a topic to which we return later – the remedy is to set aside an award, not to have it declared a nullity.

2 Remission

From time to time during the last 150 years the suggestion has been made that the Court, recognising that the arbitrator has gone wrong in law, could remit the award to him with instructions to put the matter right. This argument was firmly repelled in 1857[12], only three years after the Common Law Procedure Act had created a statutory power to remit, in replacement of the previous contractual power. A similar argument failed in 1875[13], and 1898[14]. Thereafter little was heard of this idea, until it made an unexpected re-appearance in

---

[12] In *Hodgkinson v Fernie* (1857) 3 CBNS 189.
[13] *Dinn v Blake* (1875) LR 10 CP 388.
[14] *Re Montgomery, Jones & Co and Liebenthal & Co's Arbitration* (1898) 78 LT 406.

1981[15]. The circumstances were then very special, and it seems unlikely that remission will prove to be a practical solution even to the most extreme cases of manifest disregard.

3 Intervention in equity

We have already referred[16] to an old line of cases which might have been used as the basis for a contemporary reassertion of an inherent right of judicial control. It could perhaps be suggested that these provide the basis for a remedy in the event of manifest disregard. We doubt, however, whether much could be expected of this. The authorities have a very old-fashioned ring and the remedy was never available unless there was an error on the face[17].

4 Renunciation of mandate

In Chapter 32 we have discussed how the courts have sought to develop new remedies through the application of orthodox contractual doctrines to the special type of contract created by the agreement to arbitrate. This might prompt the idea that the same technique can be brought to bear on the contract or contracts between the arbitrator and the two parties. If the reference can be terminated, and the arbitrator thereby indirectly deprived of jurisdiction, when a serious breach by one party of his contractual obligations is accepted by the other as a wrongful repudiation, cannot a similar analysis be employed when the arbitrator disregards his obligation to decide the dispute according to law?

We doubt whether this approach would prove fruitful. In the first place, when the arbitrator publishes an award, he thereby effects a valid discharge of his mandate[18] so that unless the misconduct is discovered, and treated as a wrongful repudiation whilst the reference is still in being, it will be too late for the injured party to deploy a contractual remedy.

Second, if the arbitrator has evinced an intention to decide contrary to law, whilst still conducting the reference, and if the aggrieved party has acted quickly enough to treat this as a repudiation which brings the arbitration to an end before the award is made, the effect will be to revoke the authority of the arbitrator. But this is a remedy which, by virtue of section 1, can only be

---

[15] In *Elizabeth v Motor Insurers Bureau* [1981] RTR 405, CA. The case is of some importance in the present context, because one of the grounds was that the decision of the arbitrator was not susceptible of appeal. Another feature was relied upon in the leading judgment, namely that the reference was conducted upon documents alone. Yet this can be said of many arbitrations. Perhaps there were special features, which do not emerge from the report. No authorities were referred to in the judgments.

[16] At pp. 519–521, ante.

[17] *Brown v Brown* (1683) 1 Vern 157, and notes at 23 ER 785; *Dick v Milligan* (1792) 2 Ves 23; *Knox v Symmonds* (1791) 1 Ves 369; *Ching v Ching* (1801) 6 Ves 282.

[18] This assumes that the wrongful departure from the law does not make the arbitration void or voidable. It is only on this assumption that it is worth considering the more roundabout forms of relief.

exercised with the leave of the Court[19]. If the injured party can only use his contractual remedy in conjunction with an application under section 1, he might just as well employ section 1 as a means of direct judicial interference, without troubling with the contract. Either a divergence from the law is a ground for granting leave under section 1, or it is not. The contractual analysis adds nothing.

5 Removal of the arbitrator

During the latter part of the nineteenth century a series of cases[20] recognised that it was a proper use of the powers under the predecessor of section 1 to allow the authority of the arbitrator to be revoked if it could be shown, whilst the reference was pending, that the arbitrator was about to go wrong in law. This was, however, always regarded as an anomalous jurisdiction, which ran counter to the general policy of making awards inviolable except for error on the face[1], and it was exercised largely because in the absence of any power at that time to compel the statement of a special case, it was the only available means of keeping the arbitrator on the right legal lines. In essence, the procedure was used as a precursor of the consultative case.

It could now be argued that since, in cases where there is a valid exclusion agreement, the 1979 Act has taken away from the Court the right to intervene by way of appeal either during or after the reference, even where the arbitrator has quite obviously mistaken the law, the old jurisdiction has resumed its former usefulness, and ought once again to be employed, rather than allow the Court to remain a helpless spectator in circumstances where the arbitrator is proposing to bind the parties to a decision which is contrary to their will.

We do not see any prospect that this argument would succeed. By abolishing[2] the jurisdiction to set aside for error on the face the legislature has demonstrated in the clearest terms that whenever there is an exclusion agreement the Court must remain passive in the face of an actual or threatened departure from the law, however evident. The interests of finality have[3] been preferred to those of complete substantive justice. To permit a revival of the powers formally exercised under section 1 would run directly counter to this explicit legislative policy.

---

[19] Originally, the arbitrator's mandate was revocable at will, and it was in order to frustrate the abuses to which this led that the predecessor of s. 1 was first enacted. It could be said, therefore, that s. 1 has no application where the mandate is revoked for cause. The wording of the section is, however, wide enough to cover this kind of revocation, and we believe that the courts would construe it in this sense, to avoid the risk that dissatisfaction with the arbitrator's performance will enable the parties to use contractual modes of intervention which escape judicial control.

[20] Including *Re Hart v Duke* (1862) 32 LJ QB 55; *Robinson & Co v Davies & Co* (1879) 5 QBD 26; *East and West India Dock Co v Kirk and Randall* (1887) 12 App Cas 738; *Re Arbitration between Lord Gerard and London and North Western Rly Co* [1894] 2 QB 915; affd. [1895] 1 QB 459.

[1] See p. 439 and pp. 558–561, ante.

[2] Or subsequently recognising that the 1950 Act had already achieved the abolition: see pp. 446–448, ante.

[3] Not by any means for the first time in the history of the law of arbitration.

6 Judicial review

As we have already stated, it appears to be well established law that direct intervention through the medium of what used to be known as the prerogative orders, and is now called judicial review, is not available as a means of controlling arbitral proceedings, however gross the abuse[4].

7 Misconduct

At first sight it appears that there would be no ground for the Court to hold that a decision contrary to law could ever amount to misconduct, founding an application to set the award aside. It has been clear for at least 200 years[5] that it is not misconduct for an arbitrator to make a mistake of law or fact[6]. It makes no difference that the error is obvious, in the absence of a jurisdiction to set aside for error on the face. Nor does it matter if the error is gross; the Court has never allowed itself to be drawn into admitting extrinsic evidence of error, merely because of an allegation that the error is more serious than usual.

There is, however, another way of approaching the matter. Instead of concentrating on the erroneous nature of the law applied by the arbitrator, the Court might be persuaded to enquire why the error took place. Once the motives of the arbitrator became open to question, there would be the possibility of treating a studied decision by the arbitrator to disregard his obligation to apply the law as an instance of bad faith, and this would make an attack on the award much easier to mount. Perhaps English law will develop a doctrine similar to that of 'manifest disregard' which is tentatively believed to exist in the law of the United States[7].

Three questions arise here. First, would the Court have jurisdiction to intervene, if the conduct of the arbitrator could be characterised as male fides? There can be no doubt as to an affirmative answer. The precise judicial mechanism is open to doubt. Perhaps the doctrine could be borrowed from administrative law, so as to hold that the award is void. But it would be more in

---

[4] *R v National Joint Council for the Craft of Dental Technicians, ex p Neate* [1953] 1 QB 704, [1953] 2 WLR 342; *R v Industrial Court, ex p ASSET* [1965] 1 QB 377. It may, however, be noted that although the reason assigned for excluding arbitrations from the purview of judicial review is that the procedure has no application to bodies whose power to determine the rights of the parties derives from a private contract, in *Lee v Showman's Guild of Great Britain* [1952] 2 QB 329 the court did assert a right of supervision over the legal content of a decision made by a tribunal established by contract. The means appear to have been a development of the jurisdictional approach, rather than judicial review, as such.

[5] Except perhaps so far as misconduct was one of the explanations for the exceptional jurisdiction to set aside for error on the face; see p. 439, ante.

[6] The authorities are so numerous and unchallenged that it would be pointless to set them out. The following may particularly be mentioned: *Dinn v Blake* (1875) LR 10 CP 388; *Phillips v Evans* (1843) 12 M & W 309; *Hodgkinson v Fernie* (1857) 3 CBNS 189; *A-G for Manitoba v Kelly* [1922] 1 AC 268; *Gillespie Bros & Co v Thompson Bros & Co* (1922) 13 Ll L Rep 519; *British Westinghouse Electric and Manufacturing Co Ltd v Underground Electric Rlys Co of London Ltd* [1912] AC 673; *Tersons Ltd v Stevenage Development Corpn* [1963] 2 Lloyd's Rep 333, [1965] 1 QB 37; *Oleificio Zucchi SPA v Northern Sales* [1965] 2 Lloyd's Rep 496.

[7] The topic was discussed in Appendix 4 of the first edition, at a time when it seemed that the English courts would fairly soon have to consider the development of a parallel doctrine in England. The subject has proved to be less topical than we expected and for the present we omit any discussion of the United States law on this subject.

---

conformity with the general approach of the law of arbitration to treat the award as voidable[8].

Second, would there be room for the Court to treat a studied disregard of the mandate as bad faith, if for reasons of policy it was desired to adopt this line of reasoning? There is a real difference between an unintentional and a deliberate departure from the law. The former concerns the substance of the award, and the latter the process by which it is arrived at. A number of scattered dicta support the view that deliberate departure from the law is in a category of its own[9].

Finally, there is the question whether the Court would in practice be willing to treat a conscious disregard of the law as an example of the type of bad faith which founds an application to set aside. No doubt it will be urged, in support of the view that the Court should not take this step, that the legislature and the courts have in recent years been solicitous to give the parties to arbitration agreements what they want, and that what they want is a speedy process coupled with the elimination of opportunities for delay; and it will be said that it would be contrary to current policy to reintroduce even a small part of the judicial control which the legislature has been at pains to take away. It will be said that it is an offensive misuse of language to characterise as bad faith a decision by the arbitrator not to apply a law which seems to him out of touch with commercial reality. It will also be said that from a practical point of view a distinction between accidental and deliberate mistake will often be impossible to draw.

These are impressive arguments, but we believe them to be misconceived. The proponents of an entirely liberated system of arbitration overlook the essential fact that commerce is concerned with transactions, not with disputes, and that a reasonable degree of certainty lies at the heart of the ordinary conduct of business. Where a contract is governed by English law, the promisor ought to perform the promises expressed or implied by the contract, in the sense given to them by English law; for this forms the consideration given for the reciprocal performance undertaken by the promisee. Unless the bargain proceeds on the assumption that the promisee can insist on a full performance of the promise, understood in accordance with the governing law, he will receive less than value for his price, and the commercial structure of the bargain will be distorted. So also, if the matter comes to a dispute. Just as disputed bargains form only a tiny proportion of those which are entered into, so also do concluded arbitrations amount to a small minority of those which are begun. Business

---

[8] There is a fundamental difference here between administrative and arbitration law which is very difficult to explain. Of course, the tribunals derive their jurisdiction from different sources, but it is hard to see why in one case a decision arrived at by an unacceptable procedure has no effect at all, whereas in the other it is binding unless steps are taken to set it aside.

[9] *Bank Mellat v GAA Development and Construction Co* [1988] 2 Lloyd's Rep 44 at 52, 54; *South East Asia Fire Bricks Sdn Bhd v Non-Metallic Mineral Products Manufacturing Employees Union* [1980] 2 All ER 689 at 693 citing *Kannan v Menteri Buruh Dan Tenaga Rakyat* [1974] 1 MLJ 90 at 92; *Colonial Bank of Australasia v Willan* (1874) LR 5 PC 417 at 422; *R v Murray, ex p Proctor* (1949) 77 CLR 387; *David Taylor & Son Ltd v Barnett* [1953] 1 Lloyd's Rep 181 (the context was illegality, which raises special problems, but a clear distinction was drawn between cases where the arbitrator did and did not know of the facts constituting the illegality; the dicta at pp. 184, 185, 186 and 188 are expressed in very general terms); *Chace v Westmore* (1811) 13 East 357; *Sharman v Bell* (1816) 5 M & S 504 at 505 and 506; *Ching v Ching* (1801) 6 Ves 282. Reference may also be made to the cases where an arbitrator has admitted evidence which was obviously inadmissible: see p. 352, ante, note 9.

people need to be able to settle their disputes by assessing the likely outcome of the arbitration. This they can only do if they are confident that the arbitrator will at least try to apply an objectively ascertainable system of law. They must, of course, recognise the possibility that the arbitrator will make a mistake, but this is not fatal to the settlement. The parties can accommodate error, but not chance. Moreover, when one comes to regard the arbitrator himself, it is seen that he is appointed to ascertain the rights of the parties. These are the rights which, for good consideration, they have chosen to confer on each other. It is not a proper discharge of his trust to give them, not the rights for which they bargained, but a reformulated set of rights of his own choosing. It is no answer to say that the arbitrator acts with the best of intentions. If he deliberately transgresses his mandate, he is knowingly doing something which he should not do. An award made in such circumstances should not stand, and if the likelihood that such an award will be made is detected whilst the reference is still in progress, the arbitrator should not be allowed to continue in his office.

Nor in our submission is it an answer to say that the distinction between deliberate transgression and an honest error is unworkable. It has been long established in the English law, and judges are well capable of giving effect to it. Certainly, the utmost caution will need to be used, if allegations of manifest disregard are not to be used as an expedient for delay. Relief is likely to be granted on the most sparing basis, if it is ever granted at all. But the maintenance of a right to intervene, in the rare cases where the arbitrator knowingly steps outside his proper function, is in our submission an essential safeguard, now that the more traditional methods of control have been so greatly attenuated.

8 Methods of recourse against a decision under an equity clause

Two distinct problems arise in relation to the exercise of judicial control over an arbitration conducted pursuant to an equity clause[10].

First, is there a right of appeal to the Court under the 1979 Act? If the clause is so construed as to give the arbitrator a complete liberty to deviate from the law, the answer must surely be that there is no right of appeal: for the right exists only in relation to a question of law, and no such question can arise where the arbitrator can please himself whether or not he applies the law. Nor indeed would the Court be able to receive such an appeal. Logically, if the arbitrator is free to disregard the law, then any Court exercising an appellate jurisdiction ought to be in the same position[11]. Deliberately to decide otherwise than in accordance with the law is not a permissible activity for a judge[12].

The position is rather less straightforward if the clause is interpreted as giving the arbitrator only a limited right to deviate from the rules of law and the

---

[10] The subject of equity clauses is discussed in Chapter 4, ante, pp. 74–86.

[11] The problem is solved in some jurisdictions by an express statutory provision that where the arbitrator sits as amiable compositeur, so also does the Court which hears the appeal.

[12] Constraints of space prevent a full discussion of the statement in the text. Judges do of course try cases where the law is not strictly enforced in every respect – e.g. where one party declines to rely on a time-bar. But there must come a point at which a divergence of the law becomes inconsistent with the judicial oath, even if the parties consent. Perhaps the judge could be regarded as sitting extra cursum curiae, as happened on occasion in the nineteenth century; see, for example *Bustros v White* (1876) 1 QBD 423; *Bickett v Morris* (1866) LR 1 Sc & Div 47; *White v Duke of Buccleuch* (1886) LR 1 Sc & Div 70. But a judge cannot be acting in this capacity if he is purporting to hear an appeal on a question of law.

provisions of the contract. Here, the dispute could be regarded as capable of raising a question of law, since there is some substratum of law in the contract which the arbitrator is bound to enforce. If his award indicates that he has in fact applied the law, without making use of his liberty, is there any scope for an appeal? At first sight, an affirmative answer might seem sensible. There would, however, be some formidable practical problems. In particular, there will be a discordance between the two stages of the procedure. If the arbitrator has chosen not to exercise the freedom which the parties conferred upon him, the choice forms one of the reasons for his decision. The judge on the other hand has no choice, even if he (unlike the arbitrator) would like to make use of it. Such a result would be in accordance neither with common sense nor with the intention of the parties. In practice, we suspect that the Court would dispose of this and similar difficulties by refusing leave to appeal in any case involving an equity clause.

The second question is whether the Court could and would intervene if it appeared that the arbitrator had misunderstood the scope of the liberty confirmed by the clause. Common sense suggests that a remedy should be available in such a case, but it is not altogether easy to see how it could be invoked. If we are right in the views just expressed, an appeal would not be possible. Declaratory relief does not seem appropriate, since the objection would not go to the jurisdiction of the arbitrator. Perhaps the Court would cut through the problem by assuming that the arbitrator was guilty of technical misconduct[13].

---

[13] Whether this solution will stand up to examination depends upon whether English law recognises a doctrine of 'manifest disregard'.

Appendices

Legislation affecting arbitration

Arbitration Act 1950
Arbitration (International Investment Disputes) Act 1966
Administration of Justice Act 1970, s. 4 and Sch. 3
Arbitration Act 1975
Arbitration Act 1979
 'Arbitration Act 1979 (Commencement) Order 1979
 Arbitration (Commodity Contracts) Order 1979
Limitation Act 1980, s. 34
Supreme Court Act 1981, s. 18
Civil Jurisdiction and Judgments Act 1982, ss. 25, 26, 32 and 33
Rules of Supreme Court, Ord. 73; Ord. 59, rule 1A

INTRODUCTORY NOTE

This Appendix contains the most important of the current Statutes, Statutory Instruments, and Rules of Court affecting arbitration. It should, however, be noted that the Arbitration Act 1979 and the Rules of Court made in conjunction with the Act[1], including the repeals and amendments of earlier legislation which it effected, apply only in the following cases[2] –

1 An arbitration commenced[3] on or after 1 August 1979 is wholly subject to the 1979 legislation.

2 An arbitration commenced[3] before 1 August 1979 is subject to the 1979 legislation if, but only if, the parties to the reference have agreed in writing that the Arbitration Act 1979 should apply to that arbitration. In such a case the 1979 legislation applies from 1 August 1979 or the date of the agreement, whichever is the later.

In every other case, the legislation which applies to the arbitration is that in force immediately before 1 August 1979.

The legislation (including the Rules of Court) is printed, post, with the repeals and amendments brought about by the Arbitration Act 1979 and the new Rules of Court made in conjunction with the Act. The law in force immediately before 1 August 1979 will be found in the notes to each section or rule repealed or amended by the 1979 legislation.

---

[1] *The Marques de Bolarque* [1980] 2 Lloyd's Rep 186.

[2] Arbitration Act 1979 (Commencement) Order 1979 (S.I. 1979 No. 750): see p. 714, post.

[3] The provision of s. 29 (2) and (3) of the Arbitration Act 1950 will determine when an arbitration has been commenced for the purposes of the Commencement Order: see. s. 7(2) of the Arbitration Act 1979, in which 'for the purposes of this Act' may be taken to include 'for the purposes of any Statutory Instrument made under this Act'. See also *Peter Cremer GmbH & Co v Sugat Food Industries Ltd, The Rimon* [1981] 2 Lloyd's Rep 640.

Arbitration Act 1950
(14 Geo. 6. c. 27)

Arrangement of sections

the Assembly of the League of Nations held on the twenty-fourth day of September, nineteen hundred and twenty-three.
Second Schedule.
Convention on the Execution of Foreign Arbitral Awards signed at Geneva on behalf of His Majesty on the twenty-sixth day of September, nineteen hundred and twenty-seven.

An Act to consolidate the Arbitration Acts 1889 to 1934.

Part 1

GENERAL PROVISIONS AS TO ARBITRATION

Effect of arbitration agreements, &c.

1 Authority of arbitrators and umpires to be irrevocable The authority of an arbitrator or umpire appointed by or by virtue of an arbitration agreement shall, unless a contrary intention is expressed in the agreement, be irrevocable except by leave of the High Court or a judge thereof.

Note: This section has its origins in s. 1 of the Arbitration Act 1889 and s. 39 of the Civil Procedure Act 1833.

2 Death of party (a) An arbitration agreement shall not be discharged by the death of any party thereto, either as respects the deceased or any other party, but shall in such an event be enforceable by or against the personal representative of the deceased.

(2) The authority of an arbitrator shall not be revoked by the death of any party by whom he was appointed.

(3) Nothing in this section shall be taken to affect the operation of any enactment or rule of law by virtue of which any right of action is extinguished by the death of a person.

Note: This section re-enacts s. 1 of the Arbitration Act 1934.

3 Bankruptcy (1) Where it is provided by a term in a contract to which a bankrupt is a party that any differences arising thereout or in connection therewith shall be referred to arbitration, the said term shall, if the trustee in bankruptcy adopts the contract, be enforceable by or against him so far as relates to any such differences.

(2) Where a person who has been adjudged bankrupt had, before the commencement of the bankruptcy, become a party to an arbitration agreement, and any matter to which the agreement applies requires to be determined in connection with or for the purposes of the bankruptcy proceedings, then, if the case is one to which subsection (1) of this section does not apply, any other party to the agreement or, with the consent of the committee of inspection, the trustee in bankruptcy, may apply to the court having jurisdiction in the bankruptcy proceedings for an order directing that the matter in question shall be referred to arbitration in accordance with the agreement, and that court may, if it is of

opinion that, having regard to all the circumstances of the case, the matter ought to be determined by arbitration, make an order accordingly.

Note: This section re-enacts s. 2 of the Arbitration Act 1934.

4 Staying court proceedings where there is submission to arbitration (1) If any party to an arbitration agreement, or any person claiming through or under him, commences any legal proceedings in any court against any other party to the agreement, or any person claiming through or under him, in respect of any matter agreed to be referred, any party to those legal proceedings may at any time after appearance, and before delivering any pleadings or taking any other steps in the proceedings, apply to that court to stay the proceedings, and that court or a judge thereof, if satisfied that there is no sufficient reason why the matter should not be referred in accordance with the agreement, and that the applicant was, at the time when the proceedings were commenced, and still remains, ready and willing to do all things necessary to the proper conduct of the arbitration, may make an order staying the proceedings.

[(2) Notwithstanding anything in this Part of this Act, if any party to a submission to arbitration made in pursuance of an agreement to which the protocol set out in the First Schedule to this Act applies, or any person claiming through or under him, commences any legal proceedings in any court against any other party to the submission, or any person claiming through or under him, in respect of any matter agreed to be referred, any party to those legal proceedings may at any time after appearance, and before delivering any pleadings or taking any other steps in the proceedings, apply to that court to stay the proceedings, and that court or a judge thereof, unless satisfied that the agreement or arbitration has become inoperative or cannot proceed or that there is not in fact any dispute between the parties with regard to the matter agreed to be referred, shall make an order staying the proceedings.]

Note: The words in square brackets were repealed by s. 8(2)(a) of the Arbitration Act 1975. Sub-s. (1) substantially re-enacts s. 4 of the Arbitration Act 1889 which had its origins in s. 11 of the Common Law Procedure Act 1854. Sub-s. (2) re-enacted s. 1 of Arbitration Clauses (Protocol) Act 1924 as amended by s. 8 of the Arbitration (Foreign Awards) Act 1930.

5 Reference of interpleader issues to arbitration Where relief by way of interpleader is granted and it appears to the High Court that the claims in question are matters to which an arbitration agreement, to which the claimants are parties, applies, the High Court may direct the issue between the claimants to be determined in accordance with the agreement.

Note: This section re-enacts sub-s. 8(2) of the Arbitration Act 1934.

Arbitrators and umpires

6 When reference is to a single arbitrator Unless a contrary intention is expressed therein, every arbitration agreement shall, if no other mode of reference is provided, be deemed to include a provision that the reference shall be to a single arbitrator.

Note: This section re-enacts para. (a) of Sch. 1 of the Arbitration Act 1889.

7 Power of parties in certain cases to supply vacancy   Where an arbitration agreement provides that the reference shall be to two arbitrators, one to be appointed by each party then, unless a contrary intention is expressed therein –

(a) if either of the appointed arbitrators refuses to act, or is incapable of acting, or dies, the party who appointed him may appoint a new arbitrator in his place;

(b) if, on such a reference, one party fails to appoint an arbitrator, either originally, or by way of substitution as aforesaid, for seven clear days after the other party having appointed his arbitrator, has served the party making default with notice to make the appointment, the party who has appointed an arbitrator may appoint that arbitrator to act as sole arbitrator in the reference and his award shall be binding on both parties as if he had been appointed by consent:

Provided that the High Court or a judge thereof may set aside any appointment made in pursuance of this section.

Note: This section re-enacts s. 6 of the Arbitration Act 1889, which re-enacted s. 13 of the Common Law Procedure Act 1854.

8 Umpires   (1) Unless a contrary intention is expressed therein, every arbitration agreement shall, where the reference is to two arbitrators, be deemed to include a provision that the two arbitrators may appoint an umpire at any time after they are themselves appointed, and shall do so forthwith if they cannot agree.

(2) Unless a contrary intention is expressed therein, every arbitration agreement shall, where such a provision is applicable to the reference, be deemed to include a provision that if the arbitrators have delivered to any party to the arbitration agreement, or to the umpire, a notice in writing stating that they cannot agree, the umpire may forthwith enter on the reference in lieu of the arbitrators.

(3) At any time after the appointment of an umpire, however appointed, the High Court may, on the application of any party to the reference and notwithstanding anything to the contrary in the arbitration agreement, order that the umpire shall enter upon the reference in lieu of the arbitrators and as if he were a sole arbitrator.

Note: Sub-s. (1) reads as printed above in consequence of the amendment brought about by s. 6(1) of the Arbitration Act 1979. In relation to arbitrations to which the Arbitration Act 1979 does not apply (see Introductory note to this Appendix), sub-s. (1) applies in its unamended form, as follows –

'Unless a contrary intention is expressed therein, every arbitration agreement shall, where the reference is to two arbitrators be deemed to include a provision that the two arbitrators shall appoint an umpire at any time after they are themselves appointed'.

The amendments were affected by s. 6(1) of the Arbitration Act 1979. Sub-s (1) re-enacts para. (b) of Sch. 1 to the Arbitration Act 1889 (as amended by s. 5(1) of the Arbitration Act 1934) which itself originated in s. 14 of the Common Law Procedure Act 1854. Sub-s. (2) re-enacts para. (d) of Sch. 1 to the Arbitration Act 1889 (as amended by s. 21 and Sch. 3 to the Arbitration Act 1934). Sub-s. (3) re-enacts s. 5(2) of the Arbitration Act 1934.

9 Majority award of three arbitrators   Unless the contrary intention is expressed in the arbitration agreement, in any case where there is a reference to three arbitrators, the award of any two of the arbitrators shall be binding.

Note: This section reads as printed above in consequence of the amendment brought about by s. 6(2) of the Arbitration Act 1979. In relation to arbitrations to which the Arbitration Act 1979 does not apply (see Introductory note to this Appendix), the section applies in its unamended form which reads as follows:

'9 (1) Where an arbitration agreement provides that the reference shall be to three arbitrators, one to be appointed by each party and the third to be appointed by the two appointed by the parties, the agreement shall have effect as if it provided for the appointment of an umpire, and not for the appointment of a third arbitrator, by the two arbitrators appointed by the parties.

(2) Where an arbitration agreement provides that the reference shall be to three arbitrators to be appointed otherwise than as mentioned in subsection (1) of this section, the award of any two of the arbitrators shall be binding'.

In its unamended form, it re-enacted s. 4 of the Arbitration Act 1934.

10 Power of court in certain cases to appoint an arbitrator or umpire

(1) In any of the following cases –
  (a) where an arbitration agreement provides that the reference shall be to a single arbitrator, and all the parties do not, after differences have arisen, concur in the appointment of an arbitrator;
  (b) if an appointed arbitrator refuses to act, or is incapable of acting, or dies, and the arbitration agreement does not show that it was intended that the vacancy should not be supplied and the parties do not supply the vacancy;
  (c) where the parties or two arbitrators are required or are at liberty to appoint an umpire or third arbitrator and do not appoint him;
  (d) where an appointed umpire or third arbitrator refuses to act, or is incapable of acting, or dies, and the arbitration agreement does not show that it was intended that the vacancy should not be supplied, and the parties or arbitrators do not supply the vacancy;
any party may serve the other parties or the arbitrators, as the case may be, with a written notice to appoint or, as the case may be, concur in appointing, an arbitrator, umpire or third arbitrator, and if the appointment is not made within seven clear days after the service of the notice, the High Court or a judge thereof may, on application by the party who gave the notice, appoint an arbitrator, umpire or third arbitrator who shall have the like powers to act in the reference and make an award as if he had been appointed by consent of all parties.

(2) In any case where –
  (a) an arbitration agreement provides for the appointment of an arbitrator or umpire by a person who is neither one of the parties nor an existing arbitrator (whether the provision applies directly or in default of agreement by the parties or otherwise), and
  (b) that person refuses to make the appointment or does not make it within the time specified in the agreement or, if no time is so specified, within a reasonable time
any party to the agreement may serve the person in question with a written

notice to appoint an arbitrator or umpire and, if the appointment is not made within seven clear days after the service of the notice, the High Court or a judge thereof may, on the application of the party who gave the notice, appoint an arbitrator or umpire who shall have the like powers to act in the reference and make an award as if he had been appointed in accordance with the terms of the agreement.

(3) In any case where –

(a) an arbitration agreement provides that the reference shall be to three arbitrators, one to be appointed by each party and the third to be appointed by the two appointed by the parties or in some other manner specified in the agreement; and

(b) one of the parties 'the party in default' refuses to appoint an arbitrator or does not do so within the time specified in the agreement or, if no time is specified, within a reasonable time,

the other party to the agreement, having appointed his arbitrator, may serve the party in default with a written notice to appoint an arbitrator and, if the appointment is not made within seven clear days after the service of the notice, the High Court or a judge thereof may, on the application of the party who gave the notice, appoint an arbitrator on behalf of the party in default who shall have the like powers to act in the reference and make an award (and, if the case so requires, the like duty in relation to the appointment of a third arbitrator) as if he had been appointed in accordance with the terms of the agreement.

(4) Except in a case where the arbitration agreement shows that it was intended that the vacancy should not be supplied, paragraph (b) of each of subsections (2) and (3) shall be construed as extending to any such refusal or failure by a person as is there mentioned arising in connection with the replacement of an arbitrator who was appointed by that person (or, in default of being so appointed, was appointed under that subsection) but who refuses to act, or is incapable of acting or has died.

Note: This section reads as printed above in consequence of the amendment to sub-s. (1) by s. 6(3) of the Arbitration Act 1979, the addition of sub-s. (2) by s. 6(4) of the Arbitration Act 1979 and the addition of sub-s. (3) by s. 58 of the Administration of Justice Act 1985. In relation to arbitrations to which the Arbitration Act 1979 does not apply (see Introductory Note to this Appendix) the section reads as if the words 'required or are' were omitted from para. (c) of sub-s. (1), and sub-s. (2) were omitted altogether.

Sub-s. (1) in its unamended form re-enacted s. 5 of the Arbitration Act 1889 (as amended by s. 5 of the Arbitration Act 1934), which itself re-enacted s. 12 of the Common Law Procedure Act 1854.

Sub-s. (3) applies to an arbitration agreement whether it was entered into before or after the date on which it was inserted in s. 9: see the Administration of Justice Act 1985, s. 69(5) and Sch. 9, para 15.

11 Reference to official referee   Where an arbitration agreement provides that the reference shall be to an official referee, any official referee to whom application is made shall, subject to any order of the High Court or a judge thereof as to transfer or otherwise, hear and determine the matters agreed to be referred.

Note: This section re-enacts s. 3 of the Arbitration Act 1889, which itself re-enacted s. 11 of the Supreme Court of Judicature Act 1884.

Conduct of proceedings, witnesses, &c.

12 Conduct of proceedings, witnesses, &c. (1) Unless a contrary intention is expressed therein, every arbitration agreement shall, where such a provision is applicable to the reference, be deemed to contain a provision that the parties to the reference, and all persons claiming through them respectively, shall, subject to any legal objection, submit to be examined by the arbitrator or umpire, on oath or affirmation, in relation to the matters in dispute, and shall, subject as aforesaid, produce before the arbitrator or umpire all documents within their possession or power respectively which may be required or called for, and do all other things which during the proceedings on the reference the arbitrator or umpire may require.

(2) Unless a contrary intention is expressed therein, every arbitration agreement shall, where such a provision is applicable to the reference, be deemed to contain a provision that the witnesses on the reference shall, if the arbitrator or umpire thinks fit, be examined on oath or affirmation.

(3) An arbitrator or umpire shall, unless a contrary intention is expressed in the arbitration agreement, have power to administer oaths to, or take the affirmations of, the parties to and witnesses on a reference under the agreement.

(4) Any party to a reference under an arbitration agreement may sue out a writ of subpoena ad testificandum or a writ of subpoena duces tecum, but no person shall be compelled under any such writ to produce any document which he could not be compelled to produce on the trial of an action, and the High Court or a judge thereof may order that a writ of subpoena ad testificandum or of subpoena duces tecum shall issue to compel the attendance before an arbitrator or umpire of a witness wherever he may be within the United Kingdom.

(5) The High Court or a judge thereof may also order that a writ of habeas corpus ad testificandum shall issue to bring up a prisoner for examination before an arbitrator or umpire.

(6) The High Court shall have, for the purpose of and in relation to a reference, the same power of making orders in respect of –

(a) security for costs;
(b) discovery of documents and interrogatories;
(c) the giving of evidence by affidavit;
(d) examination on oath of any witness before an officer of the High Court or any other person, and the issue of a commission or request for the examination of a witness out of the jurisdiction;
(e) the preservation, interim custody or sale of any goods which are the subject matter of the reference;
(f) securing the amount in dispute in the reference;
(g) the detention, preservation or inspection of any property or thing which is the subject of the reference or as to which any question may arise therein, and authorising for any of the purposes aforesaid any persons to enter upon or into any land or building in the possession of any party to the reference, or authorising any samples to be taken or any observation to be made or experiment to be tried which may be necessary or expedient for the purpose of obtaining full information or evidence; and
(h) interim injunctions or the appointment of a receiver;

as it has for the purpose of and in relation to an action or matter in the High Court:

Provided that nothing in this subsection shall be taken to prejudice any power which may be vested in an arbitrator or umpire of making orders with respect to any of the matters aforesaid.

Note: Sub-s. (1) re-enacts para. (f) and sub-s. (2) re-enacts para. (g) of Sch. 1 to the Arbitration Act 1889. Sub-s. (3) re-enacts s. 7(a) of the Arbitration Act 1889, which originated in s. 41 of the Civil Procedure Act 1833. Sub-ss. (4) and (5) re-enact ss. 8 and 18 of the Arbitration Act 1884, which originated in s. 40 of the Civil Procedure Act 1833. Sub-s (6) re-enacts s. 8(1) of and Sch. 1 to the Arbitration Act 1934.

Provisions as to awards

13 Time for making award　(1) Subject to the provisions of subsection (2) of section twenty-two of this Act, and anything to the contrary in the arbitration agreement, an arbitrator or umpire shall have power to make an award at any time.

(2) The time, if any, limited for making an award, whether under this Act or otherwise, may from time to time be enlarged by order of the High Court or a judge thereof, whether that time has expired or not.

(3) The High Court may, on the application of any party to a reference, remove an arbitrator or umpire who fails to use all reasonable dispatch in entering on and proceeding with the reference and making an award, and an arbitrator or umpire who is removed by the High Court under this subsection shall not be entitled to receive any remuneration in respect of his services.

For the purposes of this subsection, the expression 'proceeding with a reference' includes, in a case where two arbitrators are unable to agree, giving notice of that fact to the parties and to the umpire.

Note: Sub-ss. (1) and (3) re-enact s. 6 of the Arbitration Act 1934. Sub-s. (2) re-enacts s. 9 of the Arbitration Act 1889 which originated in s. 39 of the Civil Procedure Act 1833. The law before 1934 was different: see paras. (c) and (e) of Sch. 1 to the Arbitration Act 1889, ante; and s. 15 of the Common Law Procedure Act 1854.

14 Interim awards　Unless a contrary intention is expressed therein, every arbitration agreement shall, where such a provision is applicable to the reference, be deemed to contain a provision that the arbitrator or umpire may, if he thinks fit, make an interim award, and any reference in this Part of this Act to an award includes a reference to an interim award.

Note: This section re-enacts para. (k) of Sch. 1 to the Arbitration Act 1889 (as inserted by s. 7 of the Arbitration Act 1934) and s. 21(3) of the Arbitration Act 1934.

15 Specific performance　Unless a contrary intention is expressed therein, every arbitration agreement shall, where such a provision is applicable to the reference, be deemed to contain a provision that the arbitrator or umpire shall have the same power as the High Court to order specific performance of any contract other than a contract relating to land or any interest in land.

Note: This section re-enacts para. (j) of Sch. 1 to the Arbitration Act 1889 (as inserted by s. 7 of the Arbitration Act 1934).

16 Awards to be final   Unless a contrary intention is expressed therein, every arbitration agreement shall, where such a provision is applicable to the reference, be deemed to contain a provision that the award to be made by the arbitrator or umpire shall be final and binding on the parties and the persons claiming under them respectively.

Note: This section re-enacts para. (h) of Sch. 1 to the Arbitration Act 1889.

17 Power to correct slips   Unless a contrary intention is expressed in the arbitration agreement, the arbitrator or umpire shall have power to correct in an award any clerical mistake or error arising from any accidental slip or omission.

Note: This section re-enacts s. 7(c) of the Arbitration Act 1889.

Costs, fees and interest

18 Costs   (1) Unless a contrary intention is expressed therein, every arbitration agreement shall be deemed to include a provision that the costs of the reference and award shall be in the discretion of the arbitrator or umpire, who may direct to and by whom and in what manner those costs or any part thereof shall be paid, and may tax or settle the amount of costs to be so paid or any part thereof, and may award costs to be paid as between solicitor and client.

(2) Any costs directed by an award to be paid shall, unless the award otherwise directs, be taxable in the High Court.

(3) Any provision in an arbitration agreement to the effect that the parties or any party thereto shall in any event pay their or his own costs of the reference or award or any part thereof shall be void, and this Part of this Act shall, in the case of an arbitration agreement containing any such provision, have effect as if that provision were not contained therein:

Provided that nothing in this subsection shall invalidate such a provision when it is a part of an agreement to submit to arbitration a dispute which has arisen before the making of that agreement.

(4) If no provision is made by an award with respect to the costs of the reference, any party to the reference may, within fourteen days of the publication of the award or such further time as the High Court or a judge thereof may direct, apply to the arbitrator for an order directing by and to whom those costs shall be paid, and thereupon the arbitrator shall, after hearing any party who may desire to be heard, amend his award by adding thereto such directions as he may think proper with respect to the payment of the costs of the reference.

(5) Section sixty-nine of the Solicitors Act 1932 (which empowers a court before which any proceeding is being heard or is pending to charge property recovered or preserved in the proceeding with the payment of solicitors' costs) shall apply as if an arbitration were a proceeding in the High Court, and the High Court may make declarations and orders accordingly.

Note: Sub-s. (1) re-enacts para. (i) of Sch. 1 to the Arbitration Act 1889. Sub-s. (2) does not directly re-enact any previous enactment, but is presumably derived from s. 1 of the Arbitration Act 1889; formerly, the Court's power to tax the costs awarded by the arbitrator depended on the submission being made an order of the Court. Sub-ss (3) and (4) re-enacts s. 12 of the Arbitration Act 1934. Sub-s (5) re-enacts s. 17 of the Arbitration Act 1934.

19 Taxation of arbitrator's or umpire's fees   (1) If in any case an arbitrator or umpire refuses to deliver his award except on payment of the fees demanded by him, the High Court may, on an application for the purpose, order that the arbitrator or umpire shall deliver the award to the applicant on payment into court by the applicant of the fees demanded, and further that the fees demanded shall be taxed by the taxing officer and that out of the money paid into court there shall be paid out to the arbitrator or umpire by way of fees such sum as may be found reasonable on taxation and that the balance of the money, if any, shall be paid out to the applicant.

(2) An application for the purposes of this section may be made by any party to the reference unless the fees demanded have been fixed by a written agreement between him and the arbitrator or umpire.

(3) A taxation of fees under this section may be reviewed in the same manner as a taxation of costs.

(4) The arbitrator or umpire shall be entitled to appear and be heard on any taxation or review of taxation under this section.

Note: This section re-enacts s.13 of the Arbitration Act 1934.

20 Interest on awards   A sum directed to be paid by an award shall, unless the award otherwise directs, carry interest as from the date of the award and at the same rate as a judgment debt.

Note: This section re-enacts s. 11 of the Arbitration Act 1934.

Special cases, remission and setting aside of awards, &c.

21 Statement of case   [Repealed.]

Note: The repeal of this section was brought about by s. 8(3)(b) of the Arbitration Act 1979. In relation to arbitrations to which the Arbitration Act 1979 does not apply (see the Introductory Note to this Appendix), the section applies in its unrepealed form, as follows:

'(1) An arbitrator or umpire may, and shall if so directed by the High Court, state –
(a) any question of law arising in the course of the reference; or
(b) an award or any part of an award,
in the form of a special case for the decision of the High Court.

(2) A special case with respect to an interim award or with respect to a question of law arising in the course of a reference may be stated, or may be directed by the High Court to be stated, notwithstanding that proceedings under the reference are still pending.

(3) A decision of the High Court under this section shall be deemed to be a judgment of the Court within the meaning of section twenty-seven of the Supreme Court of Judicature (Consolidation) Act 1925 (which relates to the jurisdiction of the Court of Appeal to hear and determine appeals from any judgment of the High Court), but no appeal shall lie from the decision of the High Court on any case stated under paragraph (a) of subsection (1) of this section without the leave of the High Court or of the Court of Appeal'.

In this form the section re-enacted s. 9 of the Arbitration Act 1934 and s. 19 of the Arbitration Act 1889. For the earlier legislative history of the special case, see. s. 5 of the Common Law Procedure Act 1854 and s. 7(b) of the Arbitration Act 1889.

22 Power to remit award   (1) In all cases of reference to arbitration the High Court or a judge thereof may from time to time remit the matters referred, or any of them, to the reconsideration of the arbitrator or umpire.

(2) Where an award is remitted, the arbitrator or umpire shall, unless the order otherwise directs, make his award within three months after the date of the order.

Note: This section re-enacts s. 10 of the Arbitration Act 1889, which itself originated in s. 8 of the Common Law Procedure Act 1854.

23 Removal of arbitrator and setting aside of award   (1) Where an arbitrator or umpire has misconducted himself or the proceedings, the High Court may remove him.

(2) Where an arbitrator or umpire has misconducted himself or the proceedings, or an arbitration or award has been improperly procured, the High Court may set the award aside.

(3) Where an application is made to set aside an award, the High Court may order that any money made payable by the award shall be brought into court or otherwise secured pending the determination of the application.

Note: Sub-ss. (1) and (2) re-enact s. 11 of the Arbitration Act 1889, as amended by s. 15 of the Arbitration Act 1934. These provisions originate in the Arbitration Act 1698.

24 Power of court to give relief where arbitrator is not impartial or the dispute involves question of fraud   (1) Where an agreement between any parties provides that disputes which may arise in the future between them shall be referred to an arbitrator named or designated in the agreement, and after a dispute has arisen any party applies, on the ground that the arbitrator so named or designated is not or may not be impartial, for leave to revoke the authority of the arbitrator or for an injunction to restrain any other party or the arbitrator from proceeding with the arbitration, it shall not be a ground for refusing the application that the said party at the time when he made the agreement knew, or ought to have known, that the arbitrator, by reason of his relation towards any other party to the agreement or of his connection with the subject referred, might not be capable of impartiality.

(2) Where an agreement between any parties provides that disputes which may arise in the future between them shall be referred to arbitration, and a dispute which so arises involves the question whether any such party has been guilty of fraud, the High Court shall, so far as may be necessary to enable that question to be determined by the High Court, have power to order that the agreement shall cease to have effect and power to give leave to revoke the authority of any arbitrator or umpire appointed by or by virtue of the agreement.

(3) In any case where by virtue of this section the High Court has power to order that an arbitration agreement shall cease to have effect or to give leave to revoke the authority of an arbitrator or umpire, the High Court may refuse to stay any action brought in breach of the agreement.

Note: This section re-enacts s. 14 of the Arbitration Act 1934.

25 Power of court where arbitrator is removed or authority of arbitrator is revoked (1) Where an arbitrator (not being a sole arbitrator), or two or more arbitrators (not being all the arbitrators) or an umpire who has not entered on the reference is or are removed by the High Court or the Court of Appeal, the High Court may, on the application of any party to the arbitration agreement, appoint a person or persons to act as arbitrator or arbitrators or umpire in place of the person or persons so removed.

(2) Where the authority of an arbitrator or arbitrators or umpire is revoked by leave of the High Court or the Court of Appeal, or a sole arbitrator or all the arbitrators or an umpire who has entered on the reference is or are removed by the High Court or the Court of Appeal, the High Court may, on the application of any party to the arbitration agreement, either –

(a) appoint a person to act as sole arbitrator in place of the person or persons removed; or

(b) order that the arbitration agreement shall cease to have effect with respect to the dispute referred.

(3) A person appointed under this section by the High Court or the Court of Appeal, as an arbitrator or umpire, shall have the like power to act in the reference and to make an award as if he had been appointed in accordance with the terms of the arbitration agreement.

(4) Where it is provided (whether by means of a provision in the arbitration agreement or otherwise) that an award under an arbitration agreement shall be a condition precedent to the bringing of an action with respect to any matter to which the agreement applies, the High Court or the Court of Appeal, if it orders (whether under this section or under any other enactment) that the agreement shall cease to have effect as regards any particular dispute, may further order that the provision making an award a condition precedent to the bringing of an action shall also cease to have effect as regards that dispute.

Note: This section re-enacts s. 3 of the Arbitration Act 1934. The references to the Court of Appeal were added by para. 11 of Sch. 3 to the Administration of Justice Act 1970 (see p. 704, post).

Enforcement of award

26 Enforcement of award (1) An award on an arbitration agreement may, by leave of the High Court or a judge thereof, be enforced in the same manner as a judgment or order to the same effect, and where leave is so given, judgment may be entered in terms of the award.

(2) If –

(a) the amount sought to be recovered does not exceed the current limit on jurisdiction in s. 40 of the County Courts Act 1959, and

(b) a county court so orders,

it shall be recoverable (by execution issued from the county court or otherwise) as if payable under an order of that court and shall not be enforceable under subsection (1) above.

(3) An application to the High Court under this section shall preclude an application to a county court, and an application to a county court under this section shall preclude an application to the High Court.

Note: Sub-s. (1) re-enacts s. 12 of the Arbitration Act 1889 and s. 10 of the Arbitration Act 1934. Sub-ss. (2) and (3) were added by the Administration of Justice Act 1977, s. 18(2).

Miscellaneous

27 Power of court to extend time for commencing arbitration proceedings Where the terms of an agreement to refer future disputes to arbitration provide that any claims to which the agreement applies shall be barred unless notice to appoint an arbitrator is given or an arbitrator is appointed or some other step to commence arbitration proceedings is taken within a time fixed by the agreement, and a dispute arises to which the agreement applies, the High Court, if it is of opinion that in the circumstances of the case undue hardship would otherwise be caused, and notwithstanding that the time so fixed has expired, may, on such terms, if any, as the justice of the case may require, but without prejudice to the provisions of any enactment limiting the time for the commencement of arbitration proceedings, extend the time for such period as it thinks proper.

Note: This section re-enacts s. 16(6) of the Arbitration Act 1934.

28 Terms as to costs, &c. Any order made under this Part of this Act may be made on such terms as to costs or otherwise as the authority making the order thinks just:

[Provided that this section shall not apply to any order made under subsection (2) of section four of this Act.]

Note: This section re-enacts s. 20 of the Arbitration Act 1889. The words in square brackets were repealed by s. 8(2)(b) nf the Arbitration Act 1975.

29 Extension of s. 496 of the Merchant Shipping Act 1894 (1) In subsection (3) of section four hundred and ninety-six of the Merchant Shipping Act 1894 (which requires a sum deposited with a wharfinger by an owner of goods to be repaid unless legal proceedings are instituted by the shipowner), the expression 'legal proceedings' shall be deemed to include arbitration.

(2) For the purposes of the said section four hundred and ninety-six, as amended by this section, an arbitration shall be deemed to be commenced when one party to the arbitration agreement serves on the other party or parties a notice requiring him or them to appoint or concur in appointing an arbitrator, or, where the arbitration agreement provides that the reference shall be to a person named or designated in the agreement, requiring him or them to submit the dispute to the person so named or designated.

(3) Any such notice as is mentioned in subsection (2) of this section may be served either –
(a) by delivering it to the person on whom it is to be served; or
(b) by leaving it at the usual or last known place of abode in England of that person; or
(c) by sending it by post in a registered letter addressed to that person at his usual or last known place of abode in England;
as well as in any other manner provided in the arbitration agreement; where a notice is sent by post in manner prescribed by paragraph (c) of this subsection,

service thereof shall, unless the contrary is proved, be deemed to have been effected at the time at which the letter would have been delivered in the ordinary course of post.

Note: This section re-enacts sub-ss. 16(3) – (5) of the Arbitration Act 1934.

30 Crown to be bound   This Part of this Act [(except the provisions of subsection (2) of section four thereof)] shall apply to any arbitration to which His Majesty, either in right of the Crown or of the Duchy of Lancaster or otherwise, or the Duke of Cornwall, is a party.

Note: This section re-enacts s. 23 of the Arbitration Act 1889. The words in square brackets were repealed by s. 8(2)(c) of the Arbitration Act 1975.

31 Application of Part I to statutory arbitrations   (1) Subject to the provisions of section thirty-three of this Act, this Part of this Act, except the provisions thereof specified in subsection (2) of this section, shall apply to every arbitration under any other Act (whether passed before or after the commencement of this Act) as if the arbitration were pursuant to an arbitration agreement and as if that other Act were an arbitration agreement, except in so far as this Act is inconsistent with that other Act or with any rules or procedure authorised or recognised thereby.

(2) The provisions referred to in subsection (1) of this section are subsection (1) of section two, section three, [subsection (2) of section four,] section five, subsection (3) of section eighteen and sections twenty-four, twenty-five, twenty-seven and twenty-nine.

Note: This section re-enacts s. 24 of the Arbitration Act 1889 and s. 20 of Sch. 2 to the Arbitration Act 1934. The words in square brackets were repealed by s. 8(2)(d) of the Arbitration Act 1975.

32 Meaning of 'arbitration agreement'   In this Part of this Act, unless the context otherwise requires, the expression 'arbitration agreement' means a written agreement to submit present or future differences to arbitration, whether an arbitrator is named therein or not.

Note: This section re-enacts s. 21(2) of the Arbitration Act 1934. Contrast the terminology of s. 27 of the Arbitration Act 1889.

33 Operation of Part I   This Part of this Act shall not affect any arbitration commenced (within the meaning of subsection (2) of section twenty-nine of this Act) before the commencement of this Act, but shall apply to an arbitration so commenced after the commencement of this Act under an agreement made before the commencement of this Act.

34 Extent of Part I   [Subsection (2) of section four of this Act shall –
   (a) extend to Scotland, with the omission of the words 'Notwithstanding anything in this Part of this Act' and with the substitution, for references to staying proceedings, of references to sisting proceedings; and
   (b) extend to Northern Ireland, with the omission of the words 'Notwithstanding anything in this Part of this Act';

but,] save as aforesaid, none of the provisions of this Part of this Act shall extend to Scotland or Northern Ireland.

Note: This section re-enacts s. 28 of the Arbitration Act 1889, s. 1(2) of the Arbitration Clauses (Protocol) Act 1924, and s. 21(5) of the Arbitration Act 1934. The words in square brackets were repealed by s. 8(2)(e) of the Arbitration Act 1975.

Part II

ENFORCEMENT OF CERTAIN FOREIGN AWARDS

Note: Part II re-enacts Part I of the Arbitration (Foreign Awards) Act 1930.

35 Awards to which Part II applies (1) This Part of this Act applies to any award made after the twenty-eighth day of July, nineteen hundred and twenty-four –

(a) in pursuance of an agreement for arbitration to which the protocol set out in the First Schedule to this Act applies; and

(b) between persons of whom one is subject to the jurisdiction of some one of such Powers as His Majesty, being satisfied that reciprocal provisions have been made, may by Order in Council declare to be parties to the convention set out in the Second Schedule to this Act, and of whom the other is subject to the jurisdiction of some other of the Powers aforesaid; and

(c) in one of such territories as His Majesty, being satisfied that reciprocal provisions have been made, may by Order in Council declare to be territories to which the said convention applies;

and an award to which this Part of this Act applies is in this Part of this Act referred to as 'a foreign award'.

(2) His Majesty may by a subsequent Order in Council vary or revoke any Order previously made under this section.

(3) Any Order in Council under section one of the Arbitration (Foreign Awards) Act 1930, which is in force at the commencement of this Act shall have effect as if it had been made under this section.

Note:

1 The following states become Contracting States for the purposes of the protocol in the First Schedule:

Albania (T.S. 56/1925 Cmd. 2577).
Austria (T.S. 29/1928 Cmd. 3266).
Bahamas (T.S. 43/1931 Cmd. 4015).
Belgium (T.S. 56/1925 Cmd. 2577).
Brazil (T.S. 38/1932 Cmd. 4249).
British Guiana (T.S. 32/1926 Cmd. 2804).
British Honduras (T.S. 32/1926 Cmd. 2804).
Burma (excluding Karenni States) (T.S. 75/1938 Cmd. 5930).
Ceylon (T.S. 75/1926 Cmd. 2804).
Czechoslovakia (T.S. 43/1931 Cmd. 4015).
Danzig (T.S. 75/1938 Cmd. 5930).
Denmark (T.S. 56/1925 Cmd. 2577).
Estonia (T.S. 33/1929 Cmd. 3491).
Falkland Islands and Dependencies (T.S. 32/1926 Cmd. 2804 & T.S. 39/1934 Cmd. 4809).
Finland (T.S. 56/1925 Cmd. 2577).
France (T.S. 29/1928 Cmd. 3266).
Gambia (Colony and Protectorate) (T.S. 32/1926 Cmd. 2804 & T.S. 39/1934 Cmd. 4809).
Germany (T.S. 56/1925 Cmd. 2577).
Gibraltar (T.S. 32/1926 Cmd. 2804).
Gold Coast (including Ashanti, Northern Territories and Togoland under British Mandate) (T.S. 32/1926 Cmd. 2804 & T.S. 43/1931 Cmd. 4015).
Greece (T.S. 32/1926 Cmd. 2804).
India (T.S. 56/1937 Cmd. 5654).

Iraq (T.S. 32/1926 Cmd. 2804).

Italy (T.S. 56/1925 Cmd. 2577).

Jamaica (including Turks and Caicos Islands and the Cayman Islands) (T.S. 32/1926 Cmd. 2804 & T.S. 43/1931 Cmd. 4015).

Japan (including Chosen, Taiwan, Karafuto, leased territory of Kwangtung and Japanese Mandated Territories) (T.S. 28/1928 Cmd. 3266 & T.S. 33/1929 Cmd. 3491).

Kenya (Colony & Protectorate) (T.S. 32/1926 Cmd. 2804 & T.S. 39/1934 Cmd. 4809).

Leeward Islands (T.S. 32/1926 Cmd. 2804).

Luxemburg (T.S. 52/1930 Cmd. 3816).

Malta (T.S. 32/1926 Cmd. 2804).

Mauritius (T.S. 32/1926 Cmd. 2804).

Monaco (T.S. 29/1927 Cmd. 3022).

Netherlands (including Netherlands Indies, Surinam and Curaçao) (T.S. 56/1925 Cmd. 2577; T.S. 75/1938 Cmd. 5930 & T.S. 31/1940 Cmd. 6253).

Newfoundland (T.S. 56/1925 Cmd. 2577).

New Zealand (T.S. 32/1926 Cmd. 2804).

Northern Rhodesia (T.S. 32/1926 Cmd. 2804).

Norway (T.S. 29/1927 Cmd. 3022).

Palestine (excluding Trans-Jordan) (T.S. 32/1926 Cmd. 2804 & T.S. 39/1934 Cmd. 4809).

Poland (T.S. 43/1931 Cmd. 4015).

Portugal (T.S. 52/1930 Cmd. 3816).

Roumania (T.S. 56/1925 Cmd. 2577).

St. Helena (T.S. 32/1926 Cmd. 2804).

Siam (T.S. 52/1930 Cmd. 3816).

Southern Rhodesia (T.S. 56/1925 Cmd. 2577).

Spain (T.S. 32/1926 Cmd. 2804).

Sweden (T.S. 33/1929 Cmd. 3491).

Switzerland (T.S. 29/1928 Cmd. 3266).

Tanganyika Territory (T.S. 32/1926 Cmd. 2804).

Trans-Jordan (T.S. 39/1934 Cmd. 4809).

Uganda (T.S. 33/1929 Cmd. 3491).

United Kingdom of Great Britain and Northern Ireland (T.S. 4/1925 Cmd. 2312).

Windward Islands (Granada, St. Lucia, St. Vincent) (T.S. 32/1926 Cmd. 2804).

Zanzibar (T.S. 32/1926 Cmd. 2804).

2 Orders in Council made under the Act of 1930 are still in force for the following territories whose sovereigns are parties to the convention in the Second Schedule:

Antigua (S.R. & O. 1933 No. 42).

Bahamas (S.R. & O. 1931 No. 669).

Belgium (S.R. & O. 1930 No. 674). with Congo and Ruanda-Urundi (S.R. & O. 1930 No. 1096).

British Guiana (S.R. & O. 1931 No. 669).

British Honduras (S.R. & O. 1931 No. 669).

Burma (S.R. & O. 1939 No. 152).

Danzig (S.R. & O. 1938 No. 1360).

Denmark (S.R. & O. 1930 No. 674).

Dominica (S.R. & O. 1933 No. 42).

Estonia (S.R. & O. 1930 No. 674).

Falkland Is. (S.R. & O. 1931 No. 669).

France (S.R. & O. 1931 No. 669).

Germany (S.R. & O. 1930 No. 1096).

Gibraltar (S.R. & O. 1931 No. 669).

Gold Coast ((*a*) Colony; (*b*) Ashanti; (*c*) Northern Territories; (*d*) Togoland under British Mandate) (S.R. & O. 1931 No. 669).

Italy (S.R. & O. 1931 No. 166).

Jamaica (including Turks and Caicos Islands and Cayman Islands) (S.R. & O. 1931 No. 669).

Kenya (S.R. & O. 1931 No. 669).

Leeward Islands (S.R. & O. 1933 No. 42).

Luxemburg (S.R. & O. 1930 No. 1096).

Malta (S.R. & O. 1935 No. 133).

Mauritius (S.R. & O. 1931 No. 898).

Newfoundland (S.R. & O. 1931 No. 166).

New Zealand (with Western Samoa) (S.R. & O. 1930 No. 674).

Northern Rhodesia (S.R. & O. 1931 No. 898).

Palestine (excluding Trans-Jordan) (S.R. & O. 1931 No. 669).

Portugal (S.R. & O. 1931 No. 166).

Roumania (S.R. & O. 1931 No. 898).

Siam (S.R. & O. 1931 No. 898).

Spain (S.R. & O. 1930 No. 674).

Sweden (S.R. & O. 1930 No. 674).

Switzerland (S.R. & O. 1930 No. 1096).

Tanganyika Territory (S.R. & O. 1931 No. 669).

Uganda Protectorate (S.R. & O. 1931 No. 669).

United Kingdom (S.R. & O. 1930 No. 674).

Windward Islands (S.R. & O. 1931 No. 669).

Zanzibar (S.R. & O. 1939 No. 669).

3 Orders in Council under the 1950 Act have been made in respect of the following territories whose sovereigns are parties to the convention in the Second Schedule (see S. I. 1978 No. 186, and (for Grenada) S. I. 1979. No. 304):

The United Kingdom of Great Britain and Northern Ireland

Belize

British Virgin Islands

Cayman Islands

Falkland Islands and Dependencies

Gibraltar

Hong Kong

Montserrat

Turks and Caicos Islands

West Indies, Associated States (Antigua, Dominica, St. Lucia, St. Vincent, St. Christopher, Nevis and Anguilla)

Austria

Belgium

Czechoslovakia

Denmark

Finland

France	Mauritius
Federal Republic of Germany	Netherlands (including the Netherland Antilles)
German Democratic Republic	New Zealand
Greece	Pakistan
Grenada	Portugal
India	Romania
The Republic of Ireland	Spain
Israel	Sweden
Italy	Switzerland
Japan	United Republic of Tanzania
Kenya	Thailand
Luxembourg	Yugoslavia

4 For the position where there has been a change of sovereignty since the relevant Order in Council, see *Dalmia Cement v National Bank of Pakistan* [1974] 2 Lloyd's Rep 98, [1975] QB 9 (decided before S.I. 1978 No. 186 was made in relation to Pakistan).

36 Effect of foreign awards   (1) A foreign award shall, subject to the provisions of this Part of this Act, be enforceable in England either by action or in the same manner as the award of an arbitrator is enforceable by virtue of section twenty-six of this Act.

(2) Any foreign award which would be enforceable under this Part of this Act shall be treated as binding for all purposes on the persons as between whom it was made, and may accordingly be relied on by any of those persons by way of defence, set off or otherwise in any legal proceedings in England, and any references in this Part of this Act to enforcing a foreign award shall be construed as including references to relying on an award.

37 Conditions for enforcement of foreign awards   (1) In order that a foreign award may be enforceable under this Part of this Act it must have —
 (a) been made in pursuance of an agreement for arbitration which was valid under the law by which it was governed;
 (b) been made by the tribunal provided for in the agreement or constituted in manner agreed upon by the parties;
 (c) been made in conformity with the law governing the arbitration procedure;
 (d) become final in the country in which it vas made;
 (e) been in respect of a matter which may lawfully be referred to arbitration under the law of England;
and the enforcement thereof must not be contrary to the public policy or the law of England.

(2) Subject to the provisions of this subsection, a foreign award shall not be enforceable under this Part of this Act if the court dealing with the case is satisfied that –
 (a) the award has been annulled in the country in which it was made; or
 (b) the party against whom it is sought to enforce the award was not given notice of the arbitration proceedings in sufficient time to enable him to present his case, or was under some legal incapacity and was not properly represented; or
 (c) the award does not deal with all the questions referred or contains decisions on matters beyond the scope of the agreement for arbitration.

Provided that, if the award does not deal with all the questions referred, the court may, if it thinks fit, either postpone the enforcement of the award or order its enforcement subject to the giving of such security by the person seeking to enforce it as the court may think fit.

(3) If a party seeking to resist the enforcement of a foreign award proves that there is any ground other than the non-existence of the conditions specified in paragraphs (a), (b) and (c) of subsection (1) of this section, or the existence of the conditions specified in paragraphs (b) and (c) of subsection (2) of this section, entitling him to contest the validity of the award, the court may, if it thinks fit, either refuse to enforce the award or adjourn the hearing until after the expiration of such period as appears to the court to be reasonably sufficient to enable that party to take the necessary steps to have the award annulled by the competent tribunal.

38 Evidence　(1) The party seeking to enforce a foreign award must produce –
- (a) the original award or a copy thereof duly authenticated in manner required by the law of the country in which it was made; and
- (b) evidence proving that the award has become final; and
- (c) such evidence as may be necessary to prove that the award is a foreign award and that the conditions mentioned in paragraphs (a), (b) and (c) of subsection (1) of the last foregoing section are satisfied.

(2) In any case where any document required to be produced under subsection (1) of this section is in a foreign language, it shall be the duty of the party seeking to enforce the award to produce a translation certified as correct by a diplomatic or consular agent of the country to which that party belongs, or certified as correct in such other manner as may be sufficient according to the law of England.

(3) Subject to the provisions of this section, rules of court may be made under section [84 of the Supreme Court Act 1981], with respect to the evidence which must be furnished by a party seeking to enforce an award under this Part of this Act.

Note:　The words in square brackets were substituted by the Supreme Court Act 1981, Sch. 5.

39 Meaning of 'final award'　For the purposes of this Part of this Act, an award shall not be deemed final if any proceedings for the purpose of contesting the validity of the award are pending in the country in which it was made.

40 Saving for other rights, &c.　Nothing in this Part of this Act shall –
- (a) prejudice any rights which any person would have had of enforcing in England any award or of availing himself in England of any award if neither this Part of this Act nor Part I of the Arbitration (Foreign Awards) Act 1930, had been enacted; or
- (b) apply to any award made on an arbitration agreement governed by the law of England.

41 Application of Part II to Scotland　(1) The following provisions of this section shall have effect for the purpose of the application of this Part of this Act to Scotland.

(2) For the references to England there shall be substituted references to Scotland.

(3) For subsection (1) of section thirty-six there shall be substituted the following subsection: –

'(1) A foreign award shall, subject to the provisions of this Part of this Act, be enforceable by action, or, if the agreement for arbitration contains consent to the registration of the award in the Books of Council and Session for execution and the award is so registered, it shall, subject as aforesaid, be enforceable by summary diligence'.

(4) For subsection (3) of section thirty-eight there shall be substituted the following subsection: –

'(3) The Court of Session shall, subject to the provision of this section, have power, exercisable by statutory instrument, to make provision by Act of Sederunt with respect to the evidence which must be furnished by a party seeking to enforce in Scotland an award under this Part of this Act'.

Note: This section is printed as amended by the Statutory Instruments Act 1946 and the Law Reform Miscellaneous Provisions (Scotland) Act 1966.

42 Application of Part II to Northern Ireland (1) The following provisions of this section shall have effect for the purpose of the application of this Part of this Act to Northern Ireland.

(2) For the references to England there shall be substituted references to Northern Ireland.

(3) For subsection (1) of section thirty-six there shall be substituted the following subsection: –

'(1) A foreign award shall, subject to the provisions of this Part of this Act, be enforceable either by action or in the same manner as the award of an arbitrator under the provisions of the Common Law Procedure Amendment Act (Ireland) 1856 was enforceable at the date of the passing of the Arbitration (Foreign Awards) Act 1930'.

[(4) For the reference, in subsection (3) of section thirty-eight, to section ninety-nine of the Supreme Court of Judicature (Consolidation) Act 1925, there shall be substituted a reference to section sixty-one of the Supreme Court of Judicature (Ireland) Act 1877, as amended by any subsequent enactment.]

Note: The words in square brackets, as amended by Sch. 1 to the Northern Ireland Act 1962, were repealed by s. 122(2) of and Sch. 7 to the Judicature (Northern Ireland) Act 1978.

[43 Saving for pending proceedings Any proceedings instituted under Part I of the Arbitration (Foreign Awards) Act 1930 which are uncompleted at the commencement of this Act may be carried on and completed under this Part of this Act as if they had been instituted thereunder.]

Note: This section was repealed by the Statute Law (Revision) Act 1978.

Part III

GENERAL

44 Short title, commencement and repeal   (1) This Act may be cited as the Arbitration Act 1950.

(2) This Act shall come into operation on the first day of September, nineteen hundred and fifty.

(3) The Arbitration Act 1889, the Arbitration Clauses (Protocol) Act 1924, and the Arbitration Act 1934 are hereby repealed except in relation to arbitrations commenced (within the meaning of subsection (2) of section twenty-nine of this Act) before the commencement of this Act, and the Arbitration (Foreign Awards) Act 1930 is hereby repealed; and any reference in any Act or other document to any enactment hereby repealed shall be construed as including a reference to the corresponding provision of this Act.

SCHEDULES

FIRST SCHEDULE

Protocol on Arbitration Clauses signed on behalf of His Majesty at a Meeting of the Assembly of the League of Nations held on the twenty-fourth day of September, nineteen hundred and twenty-three

The undersigned, being duly authorised, declare that they accept, on behalf of the countries which they represent, the following provisions: —

1 Each of the Contracting States recognises the validity of an agreement whether relating to existing or future differences between parties, subject respectively to the jurisdiction of different Contracting States by which the parties to a contract agree to submit to arbitration all or any differences that may arise in connection with such contract relating to commercial matters or to any other matter capable of settlement by arbitration, whether or not the arbitration is to take place in a country to whose jurisdiction none of the parties is subject.

Each Contracting State reserves the right to limit the obligation mentioned above to contracts which are considered as commercial under its national law. Any Contracting State which avails itself of this right will notify the Secretary-General of the League of Nations, in order that the other Contracting States may be so informed.

2 The arbitral procedure, including the constitution of the arbitral tribunal, shall be governed by the will of the parties and by the law of the country in whose territory the arbitration takes place.

The Contracting States agree to facilitate all steps in the procedure which require to be taken in their own territories, in accordance with the provisions of their law governing arbitral procedure applicable to existing differences.

3 Each Contracting State undertakes to ensure the execution by its authorities and in accordance with the provisions of its national laws of arbitral awards made in its own territory under the preceding articles.

4 The tribunals of the Contracting Parties, on being seized of a dispute

regarding a contract made between persons to whom Article 1 applies and including an arbitration agreement whether referring to present or future differences which is valid in virtue of the said article and capable of being carried into effect, shall refer the parties on the application of either of them to the decision of the arbitrators.

Such reference shall not prejudice the competence of the judicial tribunals in case the agreement or the arbitration cannot proceed or becomes inoperative.

5 The present Protocol, which shall remain open for signature by all States, shall be ratified. The ratifications shall be deposited as soon as possible with the Secretary-General of the League of Nations, who shall notify such deposit to all the signatory States.

6 The present Protocol shall come into force as soon as two ratifications have been deposited. Thereafter it will take effect, in the case of each Contracting State, one month after the notification by the Secretary-General of the deposit of its ratification.

7 The present Protocol may be denounced by any Contracting State on giving one year's notice. Denunciation shall be effected by a notification addressed to the Secretary-General of the League, who will immediately transmit copies of such notification to all the other signatory States and inform them of the date of which it was received. The denunciation shall take effect one year after the date on which it was notified to the Secretary-General, and shall operate only in respect of the notifying State.

8 The Contracting States may declare that their acceptance of the present Protocol does not include any or all of the under-mentioned territories: that is to say, their colonies, overseas possessions or territories, protectorates or the territories over which they exercise a mandate.

The said States may subsequently adhere separately on behalf of any territory thus excluded. The Secretary-General of the League of Nations shall be informed as soon as possible of such adhesions. He shall notify such adhesions to all signatory States. They will take effect one month after the notification by the Secretary-General to all signatory States.

The Contracting States may also denounce the Protocol separately on behalf of any of the territories referred to above. Article 7 applies to such denunciation.

SECOND SCHEDULE   Section 35

Convention on the Execution of Foreign Arbitral Awards signed at Geneva on behalf of His Majesty on the twenty-sixth day of September, nineteen hundred and twenty-seven

Article 1

In the territories of any High Contracting Party to which the present Convention applies, an arbitral award made in pursuance of an agreement, whether relating to existing or future differences (herein-after called 'a submission to arbitration') covered by the Protocol on Arbitration Clauses, opened at Geneva on September 24th 1923, shall be recognised as binding and shall be enforced in accordance with the rules of the procedure of the territory where the award is relied upon, provided that the said award has been made in a territory of one of the High Contracting Parties to which the present Convention applies and between persons who are subject to the jurisdiction of one of the High Contracting Parties.

To obtain such recognition or enforcement, it shall, further, be necessary: –

(a) That the award has been made in pursuance of a submission to arbitration which is valid under the law applicable thereto;

(b) That the subject-matter of the award is capable of settlement by arbitration under the law of the country in which the award is sought to be relied upon;

(c) That the award has been made by the Arbitral Tribunal provided for in the submission to arbitration or constituted in the manner agreed upon by the parties and in conformity with the law governing the arbitration procedure;

(d) That the award has become final in the country in which it has been made, in the sense that it will not be considered as such if it is open to *opposition, appel* or *pourvoi en cassation* (in the countries where such forms of procedure exist) or if it is proved that any proceedings for the purpose of contesting the validity of the award are pending;

(e) That the recognition or enforcement of the award is not contrary to the public policy or to the principles of the law of the country in which it is sought to be relied upon.

Article 2

Even if the conditions laid down in Article 1 hereof are fulfilled, recognition and enforcement of the award shall be refused if the Court is satisfied: –

(a) That the award has been annulled in the country in which it was made;

(b) That the party against whom it is sought to use the award was not given notice of the arbitration proceedings in sufficient time to enable him to present his case; or that being under a legal incapacity, he was not properly represented;

(c) That the award does not deal with the differences contemplated by or falling within the terms of the submission to arbitration or that it contains decisions on matters beyond the scope of the submission to arbitration.

If the award has not covered all the questions submitted to the arbitral tribunal, the competent authority of the country where recognition or enforcement of the award is sought can, if it think fit, postpone such recognition or enforcement or grant it subject to such guarantee as that authority may decide.

Article 3

If the party against whom the award has been made proves that under the law governing the arbitration procedure, there is a ground, other than the grounds referred to in Article 1 (a) and (c), and Article 2 (b) and (c), entitling him to contest the validity of the award in a Court of Law, the Court may, if it thinks fit, either refuse recognition or enforcement of the award or adjourn the consideration thereof, giving such party a reasonable time within which to have the award annulled by the competent tribunal.

Article 4

The party relying upon an award or claiming its enforcement must supply, in particular: –

(1) The original award or a copy thereof duly authenticated, according to the requirements of the law of the country in which it was made;

(2) Documentary or other evidence to prove that the award has become final, in the sense defined in Article 1(d), in the country in which it was made;

(3) When necessary, documentary or other evidence to prove that the conditions laid down in Article 1, paragraph 1 and paragraph 2(a) and (c), have been fulfilled.

A translation of the award and of the other documents mentioned in this Article into the official language of the country where the award is sought to be relied upon may be demanded. Such translation must be certified correct by a diplomatic or consular agent of the country to which the party who seeks to rely upon the award belongs or by a sworn translator of the country where the award is sought to be relied upon.

Article 5

The provisions of the above Articles shall not deprive any interested party of the right of availing himself of an arbitral award in the manner and to the extent allowed by the law or the treaties of the country where such award is sought to be relied upon.

Article 6

The present Convention applies only to arbitral awards made after the coming into force of the Protocol on Arbitration Clauses, opened at Geneva on September 24th 1923.

Article 7

The present Convention, which will remain open to the signature of all the signatories of the Protocol of 1923 on Arbitration Clauses, shall be ratified.

It may be ratified only on behalf of those Members of the League of Nations and non-Member States on whose behalf the Protocol of 1923 shall have been ratified.

Ratifications shall be deposited as soon as possible with the Secretary-General of the League of Nations, who will notify such deposit to all the signatories.

Article 8

The present Convention shall come into force three months after it shall have been ratified on behalf of two High Contracting Parties. Thereafter, it shall take effect, in the case of each High Contracting Party, three months after the deposit of the ratification on its behalf with the Secretary-General of the League of Nations.

Article 9

The present Convention may be denounced on behalf of any Member of the League or non-Member State. Denunciation shall be notified in writing to the Secretary-General of the League of Nations, who will immediately send a copy thereof, certified to be in conformity with the notification, to all the other Contracting Parties, at the same time informing them of the date on which he received it.

The denunciation shall come into force only in respect of the High Contracting Party which shall have notified it and one year after such notification shall have reached the Secretary-General of the League of Nations.

The denunciation of the Protocol on Arbitration Clauses shall entail, ipso facto, the denunciation of the present Convention.

Article 10

The present Convention does not apply to the Colonies, Protectorates or territories under suzerainty or mandate of any High Contracting Party unless they are specially mentioned.

The application of this Convention to one or more of such Colonies, Protectorates or territories to which the Protocol on Arbitration Clauses, opened at Geneva at September 24th 1923, applies, can be effected at any time by means of a declaration addressed to the Secretary-General of the League of Nations by one of the High Contracting Parties.

Such declaration shall take effect three months after the deposit thereof.

The High Contracting Parties can at any time denounce the Convention for all or any of the Colonies, Protectorates or territories referred to above. Article 9 hereof applies to such denunciation.

Article 11

A certified copy of the present Convention shall be transmitted by the Secretary-General of the League of Nations to every Member of the League of Nations and to every non-Member State which signs the same.

Arbitration (International Investment Disputes) Act 1966
(1966 c. 41)

Arrangement of sections

An Act to implement an international Convention on the settlement of investment disputes between States and nationals of other States
[13 December 1966]

ENFORCEMENT OF CONVENTION AWARDS

1 Registration of Convention awards   (1) This section has effect as respects awards rendered pursuant to the Convention on the settlement of investment disputes between States and nationals of other States which was opened for signature in Washington on 18th March 1965.

That Convention is in this Act called 'the Convention', and its text is set out in the Schedule to this Act.

(2) A person seeking recognition or enforcement of such an award shall be entitled to have the award registered in the High Court subject to proof of the prescribed matters and to the other provisions of this Act.

(3) ...

(4) In addition to the pecuniary obligations imposed by the award, the award shall be registered for the reasonable costs of and incidental to registration.

(5) If at the date of the application for registration the pecuniary obligations

imposed by the award have been partly satisfied, the award shall be registered only in respect of the balance, and accordingly if those obligations have then been wholly satisfied, the award shall not be registered.

(6) The power to make rules of court under section [84 of the Supreme Court Act 1981] shall include power –

    (a) to prescribe the procedure for applying for registration under this section, and to require an applicant to give prior notice of his intention to other parties,

    (b) to prescribe the matters to be proved on the application and the manner of proof, and in particular to require the applicant to furnish a copy of the award certified pursuant to the Convention,

    (c) to provide for the service of notice of registration of the award by the applicant on other parties,

and in this and the next following section 'prescribed' means prescribed by rules of court.

(7) For the purposes of this and the next following section –

    (a) 'award' shall include any decision interpreting, revising or annulling an award, being a decision pursuant to the Convention, and any decision as to costs which under the Convention is to form part of the award,

    (b) an award shall be deemed to have been rendered pursuant to the Convention on the date on which certified copies of the award were pursuant to the Convention dispatched to the parties.

(8) This and the next following section shall bind the Crown (but not so as to make an award enforceable against the Crown in a manner in which a judgment would not be enforceable against the Crown).

Note: Sub-s. (3) was repealed by the Administration of Justice Act 1977, ss. 4(1), (2), (4), 32(4), Sch. 5, Pt. I, except in relation to awards registered before 29 August 1977.
The words in square brackets in sub-s. (6) were substituted by the Supreme Court Act 1981, s. 152(1), Sch. 5.

2 Effect of registration   (1) Subject to the provisions of this Act, an award registered under section 1 above shall, as respects the pecuniary obligations which it imposes, be of the same force and effect for the purposes of execution as if it had been a judgment of the High Court given when the award was rendered pursuant to the Convention and entered on the date of registration under this Act, and, so far as relates to such pecuniary obligations –

    (a) proceedings may be taken on the award,

    (b) the sum for which the award is registered shall carry interest,

    (c) the High Court shall have the same control over the execution of the award,

as if the award had been such a judgment of the High Court.

(2) Rules of court under section [84 of the Supreme Court Act 1981] may contain provisions requiring the court on proof of the prescribed matters to stay execution of any award registered under this Act so as to take account of cases where enforcement of the award has been stayed (whether provisionally or otherwise) pursuant to the Convention, and may provide for the provisional stay of execution of the award where an application is made pursuant to the Convention which, if granted, might result in a stay of enforcement of the award.

Note: The words in square brackets in sub-s. (2) were substituted by the Supreme Court Act 1981, s. 152(1), Sch. 5.

RSC Ord 73, r 9(6), has been made by virtue of sub-s (2) above.

PROCEDURAL PROVISIONS

3 Application of Arbitration Act 1950 and other enactments   (1) The Lord Chancellor may by order direct that any of the provision contained in –

(a) section 12 of the Arbitration Act 1950 (attendance of witnesses, production of documents, etc) or any corresponding enactments forming part of the law of Northern Ireland, . . .

(b) . . .

shall apply to such proceedings pursuant to the Convention as are specified in the order, with or without any modifications or exceptions specified in the order.

(2) Subject to subsection (1) above, neither the Arbitration Act 1950 nor the Arbitration Act (Northern Ireland) 1937 shall apply to proceedings pursuant to the Convention, but this subsection shall not be taken as affecting section 4 (1) of the Arbitration Act 1950 (stay of court proceedings where there is submission to arbitration) or section 4 of the said Act of Northern Ireland.

(3) An order made under this section –

(a) may be varied or revoked by a subsequent order so made, and

(b) shall be contained in a statutory instrument.

Note: The words omitted from sub-s. (1) were repealed by the Evidence (Proceedings in Other Jurisdictions) Act 1975, s. 8(2), Sch. 2.

IMMUNITIES AND PRIVILEGES

4 Status, immunities and privileges conferred by the Convention (1) In Section 6 of Chapter I of the Convention (which governs the status, immunities and privileges of the International Centre for Settlements of Investment Disputes established by the Convention, of members of its Council and Secretariat and of persons concerned with conciliation or arbitration under the Convention) Articles 18 to 20, Article 21 (a) (with Article 22 as it applies Article 21 (a)), Article 23 (1) and Article 24 shall have the force of law.

(2) Nothing in Article 24 (1) of the Convention as given the force of law by this section shall be construed as –

(a) entitling the said Centre to import goods free of customs duty without any restriction on their subsequent sale in the country to which they were imported, or

(b) conferring on that Centre any exemption from duties or taxes which form part of the price of goods sold, or

(c) conferring on that Centre any exemption from duties or taxes which are no more than charges for services rendered.

(3) For the purposes of Article 20 and Article 21 (a) of the Convention as given the force of law by this section, a statement to the effect that the said Centre has waived an immunity in the circumstances specified in the statement,

being a statement certified by the Secretary-General of the said Centre (or by the person acting as Secretary-General), shall be conclusive evidence.

SUPPLEMENTAL

5 Government contribution to expenses under the Convention   The Treasury may discharge any obligations of Her Majesty's Government in the United Kingdom arising under Article 17 of the Convention (which obliges the Contracting States to meet any deficit of the International Centre for Settlement of Investment Disputes established under the Convention), and any sums required for that purpose shall be met out of money provided by Parliament.

6 Application to British possessions, etc   (1) Her Majesty may by Order in Council direct that the provisions of this Act shall extend, with such exceptions, adaptations and modifications as may be specified in the Order, to –
  (a) the Isle of Man,
  (b) any of the Channel Islands,
  (c) any colony, or any country or place outside Her Majesty's dominions in which for the time being Her Majesty has jurisdiction, or any territory consisting partly of one or more colonies and partly of one or more such countries or places.
  (2) An Order in Council under this section –
  (a) may contain such transitional and other supplemental provisions as appear to Her Majesty to be expedient;
  (b) may be varied or revoked by a subsequent Order in Council under this section.

Note: The Arbitration (International Investment Disputes) Act 1966 (Application to Colonies etc) Order 1967, S.I. 1967 No. 159, as amended by S.I. 1967 No. 249 extends this Act, with certain exceptions, adaptations and modifications, to the following territories (many of which have subsequently become independent Commonwealth countries): Antigua, Bahamas, Bermuda, British Honduras, British Solomon Islands Protectorate, Cayman Islands, Dominica, Falkland Islands, Fiji, Gibraltar, Gilbert and Ellice Islands Colony, Grenada, Hong Kong, Mauritius, Montserrat, St Christopher, Nevis and Anguilla, St Helena, St Lucia, St Vincent, Seychelles, Swaziland, Turks and Caicos Islands and Virgin Islands; the Arbitration (International Investment Disputes) Act 1966 (Application to Tonga) Order 1967, S.I. 1967 No. 585 extends this Act to Tonga (now an independent Commonwealth country); the Arbitration (International Investment Disputes) (Guernsey) Order 1968, S.I. 1968 No. 1199 extends this Act to Guernsey, the Arbitration (International Investment Disputes) (Jersey) Order 1979, S.I. 1979 No. 572 extends this Act to Jersey.

7 Application to Scotland   In the application of this Act to Scotland –
  (a) for any reference to the High Court there shall be substituted a reference to the Court of Session;
  (b) the Court of Session shall have power by Act of Sederunt to make rules for the purposes specified in section 1 (6) and section 2 (2) of this Act;
  (c) registration under section 1 of this Act shall be effected by registering in the Books of Council and Session, or in such manner as the Court of Session may by Act of Sederunt prescribe;
  (d) for any reference to the entering of a judgment there shall be substituted a reference to the signing of the interlocutor embodying the judgment;

(e) for section 3 of this Act there shall be substituted the following section:

'**3. Proceedings in Scotland**   (1) The Secretary of State may by order make provision, in relation to such proceedings pursuant to the Convention as are specified in the order, being proceedings taking place in Scotland, for the attendance of witnesses, the taking of evidence and the production of documents.

(2) The Secretary of State may by order direct that the Foreign Tribunals Evidence Act 1856 (which relates to the taking of evidence in the United Kingdom for the purpose of proceedings before a foreign tribunal) shall apply to such proceedings pursuant to the Convention as are specified in the order, with or without any modifications or exceptions specified in the order.

(3) An order made under this section –
   (a) may be varied or revoked by a subsequent order so made, and
   (b) shall be contained in a statutory instrument.';

and in any reference in this Act, or in the Convention as given the force of law in Scotland by this Act, to the staying of execution or enforcement of an award registered under this Act the expression 'stay' shall be construed as meaning sist.

8 Application to Northern Ireland   In the application of this Act to Northern Ireland –
   (a) references to the High Court shall, unless the context otherwise requires, be construed as references to the High Court in Northern Ireland,
   (b) for the references to section 99 of the Supreme Court of Judicature (Consolidation) Act 1925 there shall be substituted references to [section 55 of the Judicature (Northern Ireland) Act 1978].

Note: The words in square brackets in para. (b) were substituted by the Judicature (Northern Ireland) Act 1978, s. 122(1), Sch. 5, Pt. II.

9 Short title and commencement   (1) This Act may be cited as the Arbitration (International Investment Disputes) Act 1966.

(2) This Act shall come into force on such day as Her Majesty may by Order in Council certify to be the day on which the Convention comes into force as regards the United Kingdom.

Note: The Arbitration (International Investment Disputes) Act 1966 (Commencement) Order 1966, SI 1966/1597 certified that the Convention came into force as regards the United Kingdom on 18 January 1967.

SCHEDULE   Section 1

TEXT OF CONVENTION

Convention on the settlement of investment disputes between states and nationals of other states

Preamble

The Contracting States
Considering the need for international co-operation for economic development, and the role of private international investment therein;

Bearing in mind the possibility that from time to time disputes may arise in connection with such investment between Contracting States and nationals of other Contracting States;

Recognizing that while such disputes would usually be subject to national legal processes, international methods of settlement may be appropriate in certain cases;

Attaching particular importance to the availability of facilities for international conciliation or arbitration to which Contracting States and nationals of other Contracting States may submit such disputes if they so desire;

Desiring to establish such facilities under the auspices of the International Bank for Reconstruction and Development;

Recognizing that mutual consent by the parties to submit such disputes to conciliation or to arbitration through such facilities constitutes a binding agreement which requires in particular that due consideration be given to any recommendation of conciliators, and that any arbitral award be complied with; and

Declaring that no Contracting State shall by the mere fact of its ratification acceptance or approval of this Convention and without its consent be deemed to be under any obligation to submit any particular dispute to conciliation or arbitration.

Have agreed as follows:

CHAPTER I   INTERNATIONAL CENTRE FOR SETTLEMENT OF INVESTMENT DISPUTES

Section 1   Establishment and Organization

Article 1

(1) There is hereby established the International Centre for Settlement of Investment Disputes (hereinafter called the Centre).

(2) The purpose of the Centre shall be to provide facilities for conciliation and arbitration of investment disputes between Contracting States and nationals of other Contracting States in accordance with the provisions of this Convention.

Article 2

The seat of the Centre shall be at the principal office of the International Bank for Reconstruction and Development (hereinafter called the Bank). The seat may be moved to another place by decision of the Administrative Council adopted by a majority of two-thirds of its members.

Article 3

The Centre shall have an Administrative Council and a Secretariat and shall maintain a Panel of Conciliators and a Panel of Arbitrators.

Section 2   The Administrative Council

Article 4

(1) The Administrative Council shall be composed of one representative of each Contracting State. An alternate may act as representative in case of his principal's absence from a meeting or inability to act.

(2) In the absence of a contrary designation, each governor and alternate governor of the Bank appointed by a Contracting State shall be *ex officio* its representative and its alternate respectively.

Article 5

The President of the Bank shall be *ex officio* Chairman of the Administrative Council (hereinafter called the Chairman) but shall have no vote. During his absence or inability to act and during any vacancy in the office of President of the Bank, the person for the time being acting as President shall act as Chairman of the Administrative Council.

Article 6

(1) Without prejudice to the powers and functions vested in it by other provisions of this Convention, the Administrative Council shall
  (a) adopt the administrative and financial regulations of the Centre;
  (b) adopt the rules of procedure for the institution of conciliation and arbitration proceedings;
  (c) adopt the rules of procedure for conciliation and arbitration proceedings (hereinafter called the Conciliation Rules and the Arbitration Rules);
  (d) approve arrangements with the Bank for the use of the Bank's administrative facilities and services;
  (e) determine the conditions of service of the Secretary-General and of any Deputy Secretary-General;
  (f) adopt the annual budget of revenues and expenditures of the Centre;
  (g) approve the annual report on the operation of the Centre.
The decisions referred to in sub-paragraphs (a), (b), (c) and (f) above shall be adopted by a majority of two-thirds of the members of the Administrative Council.

(2) The Administrative Council may appoint such committees as it considers necessary.

(3) The Administrative Council shall also exercise such other powers and perform such other functions as it shall determine to be necessary for the implementation of the provisions of this Convention.

Article 7

(1) The Administrative Council shall hold an annual meeting and such other meetings as may be determined by the Council, or convened by the Chairman,

or convened by the Secretary-General at the request of not less than five members of the Council.

(2) Each member of the Administrative Council shall have one vote and, except as otherwise herein provided, all matters before the Council shall be decided by a majority of the votes cast.

(3) A quorum for any meeting of the Administrative Council shall be a majority of its members.

(4) The Administrative Council may establish, by a majority of two-thirds of its members, a procedure whereby the Chairman may seek a vote of the Council without convening a meeting of the Council. The vote shall be considered valid only if the majority of the members of the Council cast their votes within the time limit by the said procedure.

Article 8

Members of the Administrative Council and the Chairman shall serve without remuneration from the Centre.

Section 3   The Secretariat

Article 9

The Secretariat shall consist of a Secretary-General, one or more Deputy Secretaries-General and staff.

Article 10

(1) The Secretary-General and any Deputy Secretary-General shall be elected by the Administrative Council by a majority of two-thirds of its members upon the nomination of the Chairman for a term of service not exceeeding six years and shall be eligible for re-election. After consulting the members of the Administrative Council, the Chairman shall propose one or more candidates for each such office.

(2) The offices of Secretary-General and Deputy Secretary-General shall be incompatible with the exercise of any political function. Neither the Secretary-General nor any Deputy Secretary-General may hold any other employment or engage in any other occupation except with the approval of the Administrative Council.

(3) During the Secretary-General's absence or inability to act, and during any vacancy of the office of Secretary-General, the Deputy Secretary-General shall act as Secretary-General. If there shall be more than one Deputy Secretary-General, the Administrative Council shall determine in advance the order in which they shall act as Secretary-General.

Article 11

The Secretary-General shall be the legal representative and the principal officer of the Centre and shall be responsible for its administration, including the appointment of staff, in accordance with the provisions of this Convention and the rules adopted by the Administrative Council. He shall perform the function of registrar and shall have the power to authenticate arbitral awards rendered pursuant to this Convention, and to certify copies thereof.

Section 4   The Panels

Article 12

The Panel of Conciliators and the Panel of Arbitrators shall each consist of qualified persons, designated as hereinafter provided, who are willing to serve thereon.

Article 13

(1) Each Contracting State may designate to each Panel four persons who may but need not be its nationals.

(2) The Chairman may designate ten persons to each Panel. The persons so designated to a Panel shall each have a different nationality.

Article 14

(1) Persons designated to serve on the Panels shall be persons of high moral character and recognized competence in the fields of law, commerce, industry or finance, who may be relied upon to exercise independent judgment. Competence in the field of law shall be of particular importance in the case of persons on the Panel of Arbitrators.

(2) The Chairman, in designating persons to serve on the Panels, shall in addition pay due regard to the importance of assuring representation on the Panels of the principal legal systems of the world and of the main forms of economic activity.

Article 15

(1) Panel members shall serve for renewable periods of six years.

(2) In case of death or resignation of a member of a Panel, the authority which designated the member shall have the right to designate another person to serve for the remainder of that member's term.

(3) Panel members shall continue in office until their successors have been designated.

Article 16

(1) A person may serve on both Panels.

(2) If a person shall have been designated to serve on the same Panel by more than one Contracting State, or by one or more Contracting States and the Chairman, he shall be deemed to have been designated by the authority which first designated him or, if one such authority is the State of which he is a national, by that State.

(3) All designations shall be notified to the Secretary-General and shall take effect from the date on which the notification is received.

Section 5   Financing the Centre

Article 17

If the expenditure of the Centre cannot be met out of charges for the use of its facilities, or out of other receipts, the excess shall be borne by Contracting States which are members of the Bank in proportion to their respective subscriptions to the capital stock of the Bank, and by Contracting States which are not members of the Bank in accordance with rules adopted by the Administrative Council.

Section 6   Status, Immunities and Privileges

Article 18

The Centre shall have full international legal personality. The legal capacity of the Centre shall include the capacity
  (a) to contract;
  (b) to acquire and dispose of movable and immovable property;
  (c) to institute legal proceedings.

Article 19

To enable the Centre to fulfil its functions, it shall enjoy in the territories of each Contracting State the immunities and privileges set forth in this Section.

Article 20

The Centre, its property and assets shall enjoy immunity from all legal process, except when the Centre waives this immunity.

Article 21

The Chairman, the members of the Administrative Council, persons acting as conciliators or arbitrators or members of a Committee appointed pursuant to paragraph (3) of Article 52, and the officers and employees of the Secretariat
  (a) shall enjoy immunity from legal process with respect to acts performed by them in the exercise of their functions, except when the Centre waives this immunity;

(b) not being local nationals, shall enjoy the same immunities from immigration restrictions, alien registration requirements and national service obligations, the same facilities as regards exchange restrictions and the same treatment in respect of travelling facilities as are accorded by Contracting States to the representatives, officials and employees of comparable rank of other Contracting States.

Article 22

The provisions of Article 21 shall apply to persons appearing in proceedings under this Convention as parties, agents, counsel, advocates, witnesses or experts; provided, however, that sub-paragraph (b) thereof shall apply only in connection with their travel to and from, and their stay at, the place where the proceedings are held.

Article 23

(1) The archives of the Centre shall be inviolable, wherever they may be.

(2) With regard to its official communications, the Centre shall be accorded by each Contracting State treatment not less favourable than that accorded to other international organizations.

Article 24

(1) The Centre, its assets, property and income, and its operations and transactions authorized by this Convention shall be exempt from all taxation and customs duties. The Centre shall also be exempt from liability for the collection or payment of any taxes or customs duties.

(2) Except in the case of local nationals, no tax shall be levied on or in respect of expense allowances paid by the Centre to the Chairman or members of the Administrative Council, or on or in respect of salaries, expense allowances or other emoluments paid by the Centre to officials or employees of the Secretariat.

(3) No tax shall be levied on or in respect of fees or expense allowances received by persons acting as conciliators, or arbitrators, or members of a Committee appointed pursuant to paragraph (3) of Article 52, in proceedings under this Convention, if the sole jurisdictional basis for such tax is the location of the Centre or the place where such proceedings are conducted or the place where such fees or allowances are paid.

CHAPTER II JURISDICTION OF THE CENTRE

Article 25

(1) The jurisdiction of the Centre shall extend to any legal dispute arising directly out of an investment, between a Contracting State (or any constituent subdivision or agency of a Contracting State designated to the Centre by that State) and a national of another Contracting State, which the parties to the

dispute consent in writing to submit to the Centre. When the parties have given their consent, no party may withdraw its consent unilaterally.

(2) 'National of another Contracting State' means:

(a) any natural person who had the nationality of a Contracting State other than the State party to the dispute on the date on which the parties consented to submit such dispute to conciliation or arbitration as well as on the date on which the request was registered pursuant to paragraph (3) of Article 28 or paragraph (3) of Article 36, but does not include any person who on either date also had the nationality of the Contracting State party to the dispute; and

(b) any juridical person which had the nationality of a Contracting State other than the State party to the dispute on the date on which the parties consented to submit such dispute to conciliation or arbitration and any juridical person which had the nationality of the Contracting State party to the dispute on that date and which, because of foreign control, the parties have agreed should be treated as a national of another Contracting State for the purposes of this Convention.

(3) Consent by a constituent subdivision or agency of a Contracting State shall require the approval of that State unless that State notifies the Centre that no such approval is required.

(4) Any Contracting State may, at the time of ratification, acceptance or approval of this Convention or at any time thereafter, notify the Centre of the class or classes of disputes which it would or would not consider submitting to the jurisdiction of the Centre. The Secretary-General shall forthwith transmit such notification to all Contracting States. Such notification shall not constitute the consent required by paragraph (1).

Article 26

Consent of the parties to arbitration under this Convention shall, unless otherwise stated, be deemed consent to such arbitration to the exclusion of any other remedy. A Contracting State may require the exhaustion of local administrative or judicial remedies as a condition of its consent to arbitration under this Convention.

Article 27

(1) No Contracting State shall give diplomatic protection, or bring an international claim, in respect of a dispute which one of its nationals and another Contracting State shall have consented to submit or shall have submitted to arbitration under this Convention, unless such other Contracting State shall have failed to abide by and comply with the award rendered in such dispute.

(2) Diplomatic protection, for the purposes of paragraph (1), shall not include informal diplomatic exchanges for the sole purpose of facilitating a settlement of the dispute.

CHAPTER III   CONCILIATION

Section 1   Request for Conciliation

Article 28

(1) Any Contracting State or any national of a Contracting State wishing to

institute conciliation proceedings shall address a request to that effect in writing to the Secretary-General who shall send a copy of the request to the other party.

(2) The request shall contain information concerning the issues in dispute, the identity of the parties and their consent to conciliation in accordance with the rules of procedure for the institution of conciliation and arbitration proceedings.

(3) The Secretary-General shall register the request unless he finds, on the basis of the information contained in the request, that the dispute is manifestly outside the jurisdiction of the Centre. He shall forthwith notify the parties of registration or refusal to register.

Section 2 Constitution of the Conciliation Commission

Article 29

(1) The Conciliation Commission (hereinafter called the Commission) shall be constituted as soon as possible after registration of a request pursuant to Article 28.

(2) (a) The Commission shall consist of a sole conciliator or any uneven number of conciliators appointed as the parties shall agree.

    (b) Where the parties do not agree upon the number of conciliators and the method of their appointment, the Commission shall consist of three conciliators, one conciliator appointed by each party and the third, who shall be the president of the Commission, appointed by agreement of the parties.

Article 30

If the Commission shall not have been constituted within 90 days after notice of registration of the request has been dispatched by the Secretary-General in accordance with paragraph (3) of Article 28, or such other period as the parties may agree, the Chairman shall, at the request of either party and after consulting both parties as far as possible, appoint the conciliator or conciliators not yet appointed.

Article 31

(1) Conciliators may be appointed from outside the Panel of Conciliators, except in the case of appointments by the Chairman pursuant to Article 30.

(2) Conciliators appointed from outside the Panel of Conciliators shall possess the qualities stated in paragraph (1) of Article 14.

Section 3 Conciliation Proceedings

Article 32

(1) The Commission shall be the judge of its own competence.

    (2) Any objection by a party to the dispute that that dispute is not within the

jurisdiction of the Centre, or for other reasons is not within the competence of the Commission, shall be considered by the Commission which shall determine whether to deal with it as a preliminary question or to join it to the merits of the dispute.

Article 33

Any conciliation proceeding shall be conducted in accordance with the provisions of this Section and, except as the parties otherwise agree, in accordance with the Conciliation Rules in effect on the date on which the parties consented to conciliation. If any question of procedure arises which is not covered by this Section or the Conciliation Rules or any rules agreed by the parties, the Commission shall decide the question.

Article 34

(1) It shall be the duty of the Commission to clarify the issues in dispute between the parties and to endeavour to bring about agreement between them upon mutually acceptable terms. To that end, the Commission may at any stage of the proceedings and from time to time recommend terms of settlement to the parties. The parties shall cooperate in good faith with the Commission in order to enable the Commission to carry out its functions, and shall give their most serious consideration to its recommendations.

(2) If the parties reach agreement, the Commission shall draw up a report noting the issues in dispute and recording that the parties have reached agreement. If, at any stage of the proceedings, it appears to the Commission that there is no likelihood of agreement between the parties, it shall close the proceedings and shall draw up a report noting the submission of the dispute and recording the failure of the parties to reach agreement. If one party fails to appear or participate in the proceedings, the Commission shall close the proceedings and shall draw up a report noting that party's failure to appear or participate.

Article 35

Except as the parties to the dispute shall otherwise agree, neither party to a conciliation proceeding shall be entitled in any other proceeding, whether before arbitrators or in a court of law or otherwise, to invoke or rely on any views expressed or statements or admissions or offers of settlement made by the other party in the conciliation proceedings, or the report or any recommendations made by the Commission.

CHAPTER IV   ARBITRATION

Section 1   Request for Arbitration

Article 36

(1) Any Contracting State or any national of a Contracting State wishing to

institute arbitration proceedings shall address a request to that effect in writing to the Secretary-General who shall send a copy of the request to the other party.

(2) The request shall contain information concerning the issues in dispute, the identity of the parties and their consent to arbitration in accordance with the rules of procedure for the institution of conciliation and arbitration proceedings.

(3) The Secretary-General shall register the request unless he finds, on the basis of the information contained in the request, that the dispute is manifestly outside the jurisdiction of the Centre. He shall forthwith notify the parties of registration or refusal to register.

Section 2   Constitution of the Tribunal

Article 37

(1) The Arbitral Tribunal (hereinafter called the Tribunal) shall be constituted as soon as possible after registration of a request pursuant to Article 36.

(2) (a) The Tribunal shall consist of a sole arbitrator or any uneven number of arbitrators appointed as the parties shall agree.

   (b) Where the parties do not agree upon the number of arbitrators and the method of their appointment, the Tribunal shall consist of three arbitrators, one arbitrator appointed by each party and the third, who shall be the president of the Tribunal, appointed by agreement of the parties.

Article 38

If the Tribunal shall not have been constituted within 90 days after notice of registration of the request has been dispatched by the Secretary-General in accordance with paragraph (3) of Article 36, or such other period as the parties may agree, the Chairman shall, at the request of either party and after consulting both parties as far as possible, appoint the arbitrator or arbitrators not yet appointed. Arbitrators appointed by the Chairman pursuant to this Article shall not be nationals of the Contracting State party to the dispute or of the Contracting State whose national is a party to the dispute.

Article 39

The majority of the arbitrators shall be nationals of States other than the Contracting State party to the dispute and the Contracting State whose national is a party to the dispute; provided, however, that the foregoing provisions of this Article shall not apply if the sole arbitrator or each individual member of the Tribunal has been appointed by agreement of the parties.

Article 40

(1) Arbitrators may be appointed from outside the Panel of Arbitrators, except in the case of appointments by the Chairman pursuant to Article 38.

(2) Arbitrators appointed from outside the Panel of Arbitrators shall possess the qualities stated in paragraph (1) of Article 14.

Section 3 Powers and Functions of the Tribunal

Article 41

(1) The Tribunal shall be the judge of its own competence.

(2) Any objection by a party to the dispute that that dispute is not within the jurisdiction of the Centre, or for other reasons is not within the competence of the Tribunal, shall be considered by the Tribunal which shall determine whether to deal with it as a preliminary question or to join it to the merits of the dispute.

Article 42

(1) The Tribunal shall decide a dispute in accordance with such rules of law as may be agreed by the parties. In the absence of such agreement, the Tribunal shall apply the law of the Contracting State party to the dispute (including its rules on the conflict of laws) and such rules of international law as may be applicable.

(2) The Tribunal may not bring in a finding of *non liquet* on the ground of silence or obscurity of the law.

(3) The provisions of paragraphs (1) and (2) shall not prejudice the power of the Tribunal to decide a dispute *ex aequo et bono* if the parties so agree.

Article 43

Except as the parties otherwise agree, the Tribunal may, if it deems it necessary at any stage of the proceedings,
  (a) call upon the parties to produce documents or other evidence, and
  (b) visit the scene connected with the dispute, and conduct such enquiries there as it may deem appropriate.

Article 44

Any arbitration proceeding shall be conducted in accordance with the provisions of this Section and, except as the parties otherwise agree, in accordance with the Arbitration Rules in effect on the date on which the parties consented to arbitration. If any question of procedure arises which is not covered by this Section or the Arbitration Rules or any rules agreed by the parties, the Tribunal shall decide the question.

Article 45

(1) Failure of a party to appear or to present his case shall not be deemed an admission of the other party's assertions.

(2) If a party fails to appear or to present his case at any stage of the proceedings the other party may request the Tribunal to deal with the questions submitted to it and to render an award. Before rendering an award, the Tribunal shall notify, and grant a period of grace to, the party failing to appear or to present its case, unless it is satisfied that that party does not intend to do so.

Article 46

Except as the parties otherwise agree, the Tribunal shall, if requested by a party, determine any incidental or additional claims or counter-claims arising directly out of the subject-matter of the dispute provided that they are within the scope of the consent of the parties and are otherwise within the jurisdiction of the Centre.

Article 47

Except as the parties otherwise agree, the Tribunal may, if it considers that the circumstances so require, recommend any provisional measures which should be taken to preserve the respective rights of either party.

Section 4   The Award

Article 48

(1) The Tribunal shall decide questions by a majority of the votes of all its members.

(2) The award of the Tribunal shall be in writing and shall be signed by the members of the Tribunal who voted for it.

(3) The award shall deal with every question submitted to the Tribunal, and shall state the reasons upon which it is based.

(4) Any member of the Tribunal may attach his individual opinion to the award, whether he dissents from the majority or not, or a statement of his dissent.

(5) The Centre shall not publish the award without the consent of the parties.

Article 49

(1) The Secretary-General shall promptly dispatch certified copies of the award to the parties. The award shall be deemed to have been rendered on the date on which the certified copies were dispatched.

(2) The Tribunal upon the request of a party made within 45 days after the date on which the award was rendered may after notice to the other party decide any question which it had omitted to decide in the award, and shall rectify any clerical, arithmetical or similar error in the award. Its decision shall become part of the award and shall be notified to the parties in the same manner as the award. The periods of time provided for under paragraph (2) of Article 51 and paragraph (2) of Article 52 shall run from the date on which the decision was rendered.

Section 5   Interpretation, Revision and Annulment of the Award

Article 50

(1) If any dispute shall arise between the parties as to the meaning or scope of an award, either party may request interpretation of the award by an application in writing addressed to the Secretary-General.

(2) The request shall, if possible, be submitted to the Tribunal which rendered the award. If this shall not be possible, a new Tribunal shall be constituted in accordance with Section 2 of this Chapter. The Tribunal may, if it considers that the circumstances so require, stay enforcement of the award pending its decision.

Article 51

(1) Either party may request revision of the award by an application in writing addressed to the Secretary-General on the ground of discovery of some fact of such a nature as decisively to affect the award, provided that when the award was rendered that fact was unknown to the Tribunal and to the applicant and that the applicant's ignorance of that fact was not due to negligence.

(2) The application shall be made within 90 days after the discovery of such fact and in any event within three years after the date on which the award was rendered.

(3) The request shall, if possible, be submitted to the Tribunal which rendered the award. If this shall not be possible, a new Tribunal shall be constituted in accordance with Section 2 of this Chapter.

(4) The Tribunal may, if it considers that the circumstances so require, stay enforcement of the award pending its decision. If the applicant requests stay of enforcement of the award in his application, enforcement shall be stayed provisionally until the Tribunal rules on such request.

Article 52

(1) Either party may request annulment of the award by an application in writing addressed to the Secretary-General on one or more of the following grounds:
  (a) that the Tribunal was not properly constituted;
  (b) that the Tribunal has manifestly exceeded its powers;
  (c) that there was corruption on the part of a member of the Tribunal;
  (d) that there has been a serious departure from a fundamental rule of procedure; or
  (e) that the award has failed to state the reasons on which it is based.

(2) The application shall be made within 120 days after the date on which the award was rendered except that when annulment is requested on the ground of corruption such application shall be made within 120 days after discovery of the corruption and in any event within three years after the date on which the award was rendered.

(3) On receipt of the request the Chairman shall forthwith appoint from the Panel of Arbitrators an *ad hoc* Committee of three persons. None of the members

of the Committee shall have been a member of the Tribunal which rendered the award, shall be of the same nationality as any such member, shall be a national of the State party to the dispute or of the State whose national is a party to the dispute, shall have been designated to the Panel of Arbitrators by either of those States, or shall have acted as a conciliator in the same dispute. The Committee shall have the authority to annul the award or any part thereof on any of the grounds set forth in paragraph (1).

(4) The provisions of Articles 41–45, 48, 49, 53 and 54, and of Chapters VI and VII shall apply *mutatis mutandis* to proceedings before the Committee.

(5) The Committee may, if it considers that circumstances so require, stay enforcement of the award pending its decision. If the applicant requests a stay of enforcement of the award in his application, enforcement shall be stayed provisionally until the Committee rules on such request.

(6) If the award is annulled the dispute shall, at the request of either party, be submitted to a new Tribunal constituted in accordance with Section 2 of this Chapter.

Section 6   Recognition and Enforcement of the Award

Article 53

(1) The award shall be binding on the parties and shall not be subject to any appeal or to any other remedy except those provided for in this Convention. Each party shall abide by and comply with the terms of the award except to the extent that enforcement shall have been stayed pursuant to the relevant provisions of this Convention.

(2) For the purposes of this Section, 'award' shall include any decision interpreting, revising or annulling such award pursuant to Articles 50, 51 or 52.

Article 54

(1) Each Contracting State shall recognize an award rendered pursuant to this Convention as binding and enforce the pecuniary obligations imposed by that award within its territories as if it were a final judgment of a court in that State. A Contracting State with a federal constitution may enforce such an award in or through its federal courts and may provide that such courts shall treat the award as if it were a final judgment of the courts of a constituent state.

(2) A party seeking recognition or enforcement in the territories of a Contracting State shall furnish to a competent court or other authority which such State shall have designated for this purpose a copy of the award certified by the Secretary-General. Each Contracting State shall notify the Secretary-General of the designation of the competent court or other authority for this purpose and of any subsequent change in such designation.

(3) Execution of the award shall be governed by the laws concerning the execution of judgments in force in the State in whose territories such execution is sought.

Article 55

Nothing in Article 54 shall be construed as derogating from the law in force in any Contracting State relating to immunity of that State or of any foreign State from execution.

CHAPTER V   REPLACEMENT AND DISQUALIFICATION OF CONCILIATORS AND ARBITRATORS

Article 56

(1) After a Commission or a Tribunal has been constituted and proceedings have begun, its composition shall remain unchanged; provided, however, that if a conciliator or an arbitrator should die, become incapacitated, or resign, the resulting vacancy shall be filled in accordance with the provisions of Section 2 of Chapter III or Section 2 of Chapter IV.

(2) A member of the Commission or Tribunal shall continue to serve in that capacity notwithstanding that he shall have ceased to be a member of the Panel.

(3) If a conciliator or arbitrator appointed by a party shall have resigned without the consent of the Commission or Tribunal of which he was a member, the Chairman shall appoint a person from the appropriate Panel to fill the resulting vacancy.

Article 57

A party may propose to a Commission or Tribunal the disqualification of any of its members on account of any fact indicating a manifest lack of the qualities required by paragraph (1) of Article 14. A party to arbitration proceedings may, in addition, propose the disqualification of an arbitrator on the ground that he was ineligible for appointment to the Tribunal under Section 2 of Chapter IV.

Article 58

The decision on any proposal to disqualify a conciliator or arbitrator shall be taken by the other members of the Commission or Tribunal as the case may be, provided that where those members are equally divided, or in the case of a proposal to disqualify a sole conciliator or arbitrator, or a majority of the conciliators or arbitrators, the Chairman shall take that decision. If it is decided that the proposal is well-founded the conciliator or arbitrator to whom the decision relates shall be replaced in accordance with the provisions of Section 2 of Chapter III or Section 2 of Chapter IV.

CHAPTER VI   COST OF PROCEEDINGS

Article 59

The charges payable by the parties for the use of the facilities of the Centre shall be determined by the Secretary-General in accordance with the regulations adopted by the Administrative Council.

Article 60

(1) Each Commission and each Tribunal shall determine the fees and expenses of its members within limits established from time to time by the Administrative Council and after consultation with the Secretary-General.

(2) Nothing in paragraph (1) of this Article shall preclude the parties from agreeing in advance with the Commission or Tribunal concerned upon the fees and expenses of its members.

Article 61

(1) In the case of conciliation proceedings the fees and expenses of members of the Commission as well as the charges for the use of the facilities of the Centre, shall be borne equally by the parties. Each party shall bear any other expenses it incurs in connection with the proceedings.

(2) In the case of arbitration proceedings the Tribunal shall, except as the parties otherwise agree, assess the expenses incurred by the parties in connection with the proceedings, and shall decide how and by whom those expenses, the fees and expenses of the members of the Tribunal and the charges for the use of the facilities of the Centre shall be paid. Such decision shall form part of the award.

CHAPTER VII   PLACE OF PROCEEDINGS

Article 62

Conciliation and arbitration proceedings shall be held at the seat of the Centre except as hereinafter provided.

Article 63

Conciliation and arbitration proceedings may be held, if the parties so agree,
- (a) at the seat of the Permanent Court of Arbitration or of any other appropriate institution, whether private or public, with which the Centre may make arrangements for that purpose; or
- (b) at any other place approved by the Commission or Tribunal after consultation with the Secretary-General.

CHAPTER VIII   DISPUTES BETWEEN CONTRACTING STATES

Article 64

Any dispute arising between Contracting States concerning the interpretation or application of this Convention which is not settled by negotiation shall be referred to the International Court of Justice by the application of any party to such dispute, unless the States concerned agree to another method of settlement.

CHAPTER IX   AMENDMENT

Article 65

Any Contracting State may propose amendment of this Convention. The text of a proposed amendment shall be communicated to the Secretary-General not less than 90 days prior to the meeting of the Administrative Council at which such amendment is to be considered and shall forthwith be transmitted by him to all the members of the Administrative Council.

Article 66

(1) If the Administrative Council shall so decide by a majority of two-thirds of its members, the proposed amendment shall be circulated to all Contracting States for ratification, acceptance or approval. Each amendment shall enter into force 30 days after dispatch by the depositary of this Convention of a notification to Contracting States that all Contracting States have ratified, accepted or approved the amendment.

(2) No amendment shall affect the rights and obligations under this Convention of any Contracting State or of any of its constituent subdivisions or agencies, or of any national of such State arising out of consent to the jurisdiction of the Centre given before the date of entry into force of the amendment.

CHAPTER X   FINAL PROVISIONS

Article 67

This Convention shall be open for signature on behalf of States members of the Bank. It shall also be open for signature on behalf of any other State which is a party to the Statute of the International Court of Justice and which the Administrative Council, by a vote of two-thirds of its members, shall have invited to sign the Convention.

Article 68

(1) This Convention shall be subject to ratification, acceptance or approval by the signatory States in accordance with their respective constitutional procedures.

(2) This Convention shall enter into force 30 days after the date of deposit of the twentieth instrument of ratification, acceptance or approval. It shall enter into force for each State which subsequently deposits its instrument of ratification, acceptance or approval 30 days after the date of such deposit.

Article 69

Each Contracting State shall take legislative or other measures as may be necessary for making the provisions of this Convention effective in its territories.

Article 70

This Convention shall apply to all territories for whose international relations a Contracting State is responsible, except those which are excluded by such State by written notice to the depositary of this Convention either at the time of ratification, acceptance or approval or subsequently.

Article 71

Any Contracting State may denounce this Convention by written notice to the depositary of this Convention. The denunciation shall take effect six months after receipt of such notice.

Article 72

Notice by a Contracting State pursuant to Article 70 or 71 shall not affect the rights or obligations under this Convention of that State or of any of its constituent subdivisions or agencies or of any national of that State arising out of consent to the jurisdiction of the Centre given by one of them before such notice was received by the depositary.

Article 73

Instruments of ratification, acceptance or approval of this Convention and of amendments thereto shall be deposited with the Bank which shall act as the depositary of this Convention. The depositary shall transmit certified copies of this Convention to States members of the Bank and to any other State invited to sign the Convention.

Article 74

The depositary shall register this Convention with the Secretariat of the United Nations in accordance with Article 102 of the Charter of the United Nations and the Regulations thereunder adopted by the General Assembly.

Article 75

The depositary shall notify all signatory States of the following:
  (a) signatures in accordance with Article 67;
  (b) deposits of instruments of ratification, acceptance and approval in accordance with Article 73;

(c) the date on which this Convention enters into force in accordance with Article 68;

(d) exclusions from territorial application pursuant to Article 70;

(e) the date on which any amendment of this Convention enters into force in accordance with Article 66; and

(f) denunciations in accordance with Article 71.

DONE at Washington in the English, French and Spanish languages, all three texts being equally authentic, in a single copy which shall remain deposited in the archives of the International Bank for Reconstruction and Development, which has indicated by its signature below its agreement to fulfil the functions with which it is charged under this Convention.

(Here follow the signatures)

Administration of Justice Act 1970
(1970 c. 31)

*   *   *   *   *

4 Power of judges of Commercial Court to take arbitrations   (1) A judge of the Commercial Court may, if in all the circumstances he thinks fit, accept appointment as sole arbitrator, or as umpire, by or by virtue of an arbitration agreement within the meaning of the Arbitration Act 1950, where the dispute appears to him to be of a commercial character.

(2) A judge of the Commercial Court shall not accept appointment as arbitrator or umpire unless the Lord Chief Justice has informed him that, having regard to the state of business in the High Court and [in the Crown Court], he can be made available to do so.

(3) The fees payable for the services of a judge as arbitrator or umpire shall be taken in the High Court.

(4) Schedule 3 to this Act shall have effect for modifying, and in certain cases replacing, provisions of the Arbitration Act 1950 in relation to arbitration by judges and, in particular, for substituting the Court of Appeal for the High Court in provisions of that Act whereby arbitrators and umpires, their proceedings and awards, are subject to control and review by the court.

(5) Any jurisdiction which is exercisable by the High Court in relation to arbitrators and umpires otherwise than under the Arbitration Act 1950 shall, in relation to a judge of the Commercial Court appointed as arbitrator or umpire, be exercisable instead by the Court of Appeal.

Note: In sub-s. (2) the words in square brackets were substituted by the Courts Act 1971, s. 56(1) and Sch. 8, para. 60.

*   *   *   *   *

SCHEDULE 3

Application of Arbitration Act 1950 to Judge-Arbitrators

1 In this Schedule –

(a) 'the Act' means the Arbitration Act 1950;

   (b) 'arbitration agreement' has the same meaning as in the Act; and

   (c) 'judge-arbitrator' and 'judge-umpire' mean a judge of the Commercial Court appointed as arbitrator or, as the case may be, as umpire by or by virtue of an arbitration agreement.

2 In section 1 of the Act (authority of arbitrator to be irrevocable except by leave of the court), in its application to a judge-arbitrator or judge-umpire, the Court of Appeal shall be substituted for the High Court.

3 The power of the High Court under section 7 of the Act (vacancy among arbitrators supplied by parties) to set aside the appointment of an arbitrator shall not be exercisable in the case of the appointment of a judge-arbitrator.

4 Section 8(3) of the Act (power of High Court to order umpire to enter immediately on reference as sole arbitrator) shall not apply to a judge-umpire; but a judge-umpire may, on the application of any party to the reference and notwithstanding anything to the contrary in the arbitration agreement, enter on the reference in lieu of the arbitrators and as if he were the sole arbitrator.

5 (1) The powers conferred on the High Court or a judge thereof by section 12(4), (5) and (6) of the Act (summoning of witnesses, interlocutory orders, etc.) shall be exercisable in the case of a reference to a judge-arbitrator or judge-umpire as in the case of any other reference to arbitration, but shall in any such case be exercisable also by the judge-arbitrator or judge-umpire himself.

(2) Anything done by an arbitrator or umpire in the exercise of powers conferred by this paragraph shall be done by him in his capacity as judge of the High Court and have effect as if done by the court; but nothing in this paragraph prejudices any power vested in the arbitrator or umpire in his capacity as such.

6 Section 13(2) and (3) of the Act (extension of time for making award; provision for ensuring that reference is conducted with reasonable dispatch) shall not apply to a reference to a judge-arbitrator or judge-umpire; but a judge-arbitrator or judge-umpire may enlarge any time limited for making his award (whether under the Act or otherwise), whether that time has expired or not.

7 (1) Section 18(4) of the Act (provision enabling a party in an arbitration to obtain an order for costs) shall apply, in the case of a reference to a judge-arbitrator, with the omission of the words from 'within fourteen days' to 'may direct'.

(2) The power of the High Court to make declarations and orders for the purposes of section 18(5) of the Act (charging order for solicitor's costs) shall be exercisable in the case of an arbitration by a judge-arbitrator or judge-umpire as in the case of any other arbitration, but shall in any such case be exercisable also by the judge-arbitrator or judge-umpire himself.

(3) A declaration or order made by an arbitrator or umpire in the exercise of the power conferred by the last foregoing sub-paragraph shall be made by him in his capacity as judge of the High Court and have effect as if made by that court.

8 (1) Section 19 of the Act (power of High Court to order delivery of award on payment of arbitrators' fees into court) shall not apply with respect to the award of a judge-arbitrator or judge-umpire.

(2) A judge-umpire may withhold his award until the fees payable to the arbitrators have been paid into the High Court.

(3) Arbitrators' fees paid into court under this paragraph shall be paid out in accordance with rules of court, subject to the right of any party to the reference

to apply (in accordance with the rules) for any fee to be taxed, not being a fee which has been fixed by written agreement between him and the arbitrator.

(4) A taxation under this paragraph may be reviewed in the same manner as a taxation of the costs of an award.

(5) On a taxation under this paragraph, or on a review thereof, an arbitrator shall be entitled to appear and be heard.

9 (1) In sections [21(1) and (2)] 22 and 23 of the Act (special case, remission and setting aside of awards, etc.), in their application to a judge-arbitrator or judge-umpire, and to a reference to him and to his award thereon, the Court of Appeal shall be substituted for the High Court.

[(2) A decision of the Court of Appeal on a case stated by a judge-arbitrator or judge-umpire under section 21 of the Act (as amended by this paragraph) shall be deemed to be a judgment of that court for the purposes of section 3 of the Appellate Jurisdiction Act 1876 (appeal to House of Lords); but no appeal shall lie from any such decision without the leave of the Court of Appeal or the House of Lords.]

10 (1) Section 24(2) of the Act (removal of issue of fraud for trial in the High Court) shall not apply to an agreement under or by virtue of which a judge-arbitrator or judge-umpire has been appointed; nor shall leave be given by the High Court under that subsection to revoke the authority of a judge-arbitrator or judge-umpire.

(2) Where, on a reference of a dispute to a judge-arbitrator or judge-umpire, it appears to the judge that the dispute involves the question whether a party to the dispute has been guilty of fraud, he may, so far as may be necessary to enable that question to be determined by the High Court, order that the agreement by or by virtue of which he was appointed shall cease to have effect and revoke his authority as arbitrator or umpire.

(3) An order made by a judge-arbitrator or judge-umpire under this paragraph shall have effect as if made by the High Court.

11 Section 25 of the Act (powers of court on removal of arbitrator or revocation of arbitration agreement) shall be amended as follows: –

(a) after the words 'the High Court' where they first occur in subsection (1), where they occur for the first and second time in subsection (2), and in subsections (3) and (4), there shall be inserted the words 'or the Court of Appeal'; and

(b) after those words where they occur for the second time in subsection (1) and for the third time in subsection (2) there shall be inserted the words 'or the Court of Appeal, as the case may be'.

12 The leave required by section 26 of the Act (enforcement in High Court) for an award on an arbitration agreement to be enforced as mentioned in that section may, in the case of an award by a judge-arbitrator or a judge-umpire, be given by the judge-arbitrator or judge-umpire himself.

Note: The words in square brackets in para. 9 were repealed by s. 8(3)(c) of the Arbitration Act 1979, but continue to apply to arbitrations to which the Arbitration Act 1979 does not apply (see Introductory note to this Appendix).

Arbitration Act 1975
(1975 c. 3)

An Act to give effect to the New York Convention on the Recognition and Enforcement of Foreign Arbitral Awards.

Effect of arbitration agreement on court proceedings

1 Staying court proceedings where party proves arbitration agreement (1) If any party to an arbitration agreement to which this section applies, or any person claiming through or under him, commences any legal proceedings in any court against any other party to the agreement, or any person claiming through or under him, in respect of any matter agreed to be referred, any party to the proceedings may at any time after appearance, and before delivering any pleadings or taking any other steps in the proceedings, apply to the court to stay the proceedings; and the court, unless satisfied that the arbitration agreement is null and void, inoperative or incapable of being performed or that there is not in fact any dispute between the parties with regard to the matter agreed to be referred, shall make an order staying the proceedings.

(2) This section applies to any arbitration agreement which is not a domestic arbitration agreement; and neither section 4(1) of the Arbitration Act 1950 nor section 4 of the Arbitration Act (Northern Ireland) 1937 shall apply to an arbitration agreement to which this section applies.

(3) In the application of this section to Scotland, for the references to staying proceedings there shall be substituted references to sisting proceedings.

(4) In this section 'domestic arbitration agreement' means an arbitration agreement which does not provide, expressly or by implication, for arbitration in a State other than the United Kingdom and to which neither –
 (a) an individual who is a national of, or habitually resident in, any State other than the United Kingdom; nor
 (b) a body corporate which is incorporated in, or whose central management and control is exercised in, any State other than the United Kingdom;
is a party at the time the proceedings are commenced.

Enforcement of Convention awards

2 Replacement of former provisions Sections 3 to 6 of this Act shall have effect with respect to the enforcement of Convention awards; and where a Convention award would, but for this section, be also a foreign award within the meaning of Part II of the Arbitration Act 1950, that Part shall not apply to it.

3 Effect of Convention awards (1) A Convention award shall, subject to the following provisions of this Act, be enforceable –
 (a) in England and Wales, either by action or in the same manner as the award of an arbitrator is enforceable by virtue of section 26 of the Arbitration Act 1950;
 (b) in Scotland, either by action or, in a case where the arbitration agreement

contains consent to the registration of the award in the Books of Council and Session for execution and the award is so registered, by summary diligence;

(c) in Northern Ireland, either by action or in the same manner as the award of an arbitrator is enforceable by virtue of section 16 of the Arbitration Act (Northern Ireland) 1937.

(2) Any Convention award which would be enforceable under this Act shall be treated as binding for all purposes on the persons as between whom it was made, and may accordingly be relied on by any of those persons by way of defence, set off or otherwise in any legal proceedings in the United Kingdom; and any reference in this Act to enforcing a Convention award shall be construed as including references to relying on such an award.

4 Evidence   The party seeking to enforce a Convention award must produce –

(a) the duly authenticated original award or a duly certified copy of it; and
(b) the original arbitration agreement or a duly certified copy of it; and
(c) where the award or agreement is in a foreign language, a translation of it certified by an official or sworn translator or by a diplomatic or consular agent.

5 Refusal of enforcement   (1) Enforcement of a Convention award shall not be refused except in the cases mentioned in this section.

(2) Enforcement of a Convention award may be refused if the person against whom it is invoked proves –

(a) that a party to the arbitration agreement was (under the law applicable to him) under some incapacity; or
(b) that the arbitration agreement was not valid under the law to which the parties subjected it or, failing any indication thereon, under the law of the country where the award was made; or
(c) that he was not given proper notice of the appointment of the arbitrator or of the arbitration proceedings or was otherwise unable to present his case; or
(d) (subject to subsection (4) of this section) that the award deals with a difference not contemplated by or not falling within the terms of the submission to arbitration or contains decisions on matters beyond the scope of the submission to arbitration; or
(e) that the composition of the arbitral authority or the arbitral procedure was not in accordance with the agreement of the parties or, failing such agreement, with the law of the country where the arbitration took place; or
(f) that the award has not yet become binding on the parties, or has been set aside or suspended by a competent authority of the country in which, or under the law of which, it was made.

(3) Enforcement of a Convention award may also be refused if the award is in respect of a matter which is not capable of settlement by arbitration, or if it would be contrary to public policy to enforce the award.

(4) A Convention award which contains decisions on matters not submitted to arbitration may be enforced to the extent that it contains decisions on matters

submitted to arbitration which can be separated from those on matters not so submitted.

(5) Where an application for the setting aside or suspension of a Convention award has been made to such a competent authority as is mentioned in subsection (2)(f) of this section, the court before which enforcement of the award is sought may, if it thinks fit, adjourn the proceedings and may, on the application of the party seeking to enforce the award, order the other party to give security.

6 Saving   Nothing in this Act shall prejudice any right to enforce or rely on an award otherwise than under this Act or Party II of the Arbitration Act 1950.

General

7 Interpretation   (1) In this Act –
   'arbitration agreement' means an agreement in writing (including an agreement contained in an exchange of letters or telegrams) to submit to arbitration present or future differences capable of settlement by arbitration;
   'Convention award' means an award made in pursuance of an arbitration agreement in the territory of a State, other than the United Kingdom, which is a party to the New York Convention; and
   'the New York Convention' means the Convention on the Recognition and Enforcement of Foreign Arbitral Awards adopted by the United Nations Conference on International Commercial Arbitration on 10th June 1958.

(2) If Her Majesty by Order in Council declares that any State specified in the Order is a party to the New York Convention the Order shall, while in force, be conclusive evidence that that State is a party to that Convention.

(3) An Order in Council under this section may be varied or revoked by a subsequent Order in Council.

Note: The following States have been declared by Order in Council S.I. 1979 No. 304 to be parties to the Convention:

Australia (including all the external territories for the international relations of which Australia is responsible)
Austria
Belgium
Benin
Botswana
Bulgaria
Central African Empire
Chile
Cuba
Czechoslovakia
Denmark
Ecuador
Egypt
Finland
France (including territories of the French Republic)
Federal Republic of Germany and Berlin (West)

German Democratic Republic
Ghana
Greece
Holy See
Hungary
India
Israel
Italy
Japan
Democratic Kampuchea
Republic of Korea
Kuwait
Madagascar
Mexico
Morocco
Netherlands (including the Netherlands Antilles)
Niger
Nigeria
Norway

Philippines	Thailand
Poland	Trinidad and Tobago
Romania	Tunisia
South Africa	Union of Soviet Socialist Republics
Spain	United Republic of Tanzania
Sri Lanka	United States of America (including all the
Sweden	territories for the international relations of
Switzerland	which the United States of America is
Syrian Arab Republic	responsible)

Evidence is admissible to show that a State referred to in an Order in Council became a party to the Convention earlier than the date of the Order, or that a State not referred to in an Order in Council is in fact a party to the Convention: *Government of Kuwait v Sir Frederick Snow and Partners* [1981] 1 Lloyd's Rep 656; not overruled on this point by the Court of Appeal: [1983] 1 Lloyd's Rep 596.

8 Short title, repeals, commencement and extent   (1) This Act may be cited as the Arbitration Act 1975.

(2) The following provisions of the Arbitration Act 1950 are hereby repealed, that is to say –

(a) section 4(2);

(b) in section 28 the proviso;

(c) in section 30 the words '(except the provisions of subsection (2) of section 4 thereof)';

(d) in section 31(2) the words 'subsection (2) of section 4'; and

(e) in section 34 the words from the beginning to 'save as aforesaid'.

(3) This Act shall come into operation on such date as the Secretary of State may by order made by statutory instrument appoint.

(4) This Act extends to Northern Ireland.

Arbitration Act 1979
(1979) c. 42)

Arrangement of sections

Section

An Act to amend the law relating to arbitrations and for purposes connected therewith.

1 Judicial review of arbitration awards   (1) In the Arbitration Act 1950 (in this Act referred to as 'the principal Act') section 21 (statement of case for a decision of the High Court) shall cease to have effect and, without prejudice to the right of appeal conferred by subsection (2) below, the High Court shall not have jurisdiction to set aside or remit an award on an arbitration agreement on the ground of errors of fact or law on the face of the award.

(2) Subject to subsection (3) below, an appeal shall lie to the High Court on any question of law arising out of an award made on an arbitration agreement; and on the determination of such an appeal the High Court may by order –

(a) confirm, vary or set aside the award; or

(b) remit the award to the reconsideration of the arbitrator or umpire together with the court's opinion on the question of law which was the subject of the appeal;

and where the award is remitted under paragraph (b) above the arbitrator or umpire shall, unless the order otherwise directs, make his award within three months after the date of the order.

(3) An appeal under this section may be brought by any of the parties to the reference –

(a) with the consent of all the other parties to the reference; or

(b) subject to section 3 below, with the leave of the court.

(4) The High Court shall not grant leave under subsection (3)(b) above unless it considers that, having regard to all the circumstances, the determination of the question of law concerned could substantially affect the rights of one or more of the parties to the arbitration agreement; and the court may make any leave which it gives conditional upon the applicant complying with such conditions as it considers appropriate.

(5) Subject to subsection (6) below, if an award is made and, on an application made by any of the parties to the reference –

(a) with the consent of all the other parties to the reference, or

(b) subject to section 3 below, with the leave of the court,

it appears to the High Court that the award does not or does not sufficiently set out the reasons for the award, the court may order the arbitrator or umpire concerned to state the reasons for his award in sufficient detail to enable the court, should an appeal be brought under this section, to consider any question of law arising out of the award.

(6) In any case where an award is made without any reason being given, the High Court shall not make an order under subsection (5) above unless it is satisfied –

(a) that before the award was made one of the parties to the reference gave notice to the arbitrator or umpire concerned that a reasoned award would be required; or

(b) that there is some special reason why such a notice was not given.

(6A) Unless the High Court gives leave, no appeal shall lie to the Court of Appeal from a decision of the High Court –

(a) to grant or refuse leave under subsection 3(b) or 5(b) above; or

(b) to make or not to make an order under subsection (5) above.

(7) No appeal shall lie to the Court of Appeal from a decision of the High Court on an appeal under this section unless –

(a) the High Court or the Court of Appeal gives leave; and

(b) it is certified by the High Court that the question of law to which its decision relates either is one of general public importance or is one which for some other special reason should be considered by the Court of Appeal.

(8) Where the award of an arbitrator or umpire is varied on appeal, the award as varied shall have effect (except for the purposes of this section) as if it were the award of the arbitrator or umpire.

Note: Sub-s. (6A) was added by s. 148(2) of the Supreme Court Act 1981.

2 Determination of preliminary point of law by court   (1) Subject to subsection (2) and section 3 below, on an application to the High Court made by any of the parties to a reference –

    (a) with the consent of an arbitrator who has entered on the reference or, if an umpire has entered on the reference, with his consent, or

    (b) with the consent of all the other parties,

the High Court shall have jurisdiction to determine any question of law arising in the course of the reference.

(2) The High Court shall not entertain an application under subsection (1)(a) above with respect to any question of law unless it is satisfied that –

    (a) the determination of the application might produce substantial savings in costs to the parties; and

    (b) the question of law is one in respect of which leave to appeal would be likely to be given under section 1(3)(b) above.

(2A) Unless the High Court gives leave, no appeal shall lie to the Court of Appeal from a decision of the High Court to entertain or not to entertain an application under subsection 1(a) above.

(3) A decision of the High Court under [sub-section (1) above] shall be deemed to be a judgment of the court within the meaning of section [16 of the Supreme Courts Act 1981] (appeals to the Court of Appeal), but no appeal shall lie from such a decision unless –

    (a) the High Court or the Court of Appeal gives leave; and

    (b) it is certified by the High Court that the question of law to which its decision relates either is one of general public importance or is one which for some other special reason should be considered by the Court of Appeal.

Note: The words in square brackets were substituted by the Supreme Court Act 1981, s. 148(3) and Sch. 5. S. 148 of that Act added sub-s. (2A).

3 Exclusion agreements affecting rights under sections 1 and 2

(1) Subject to the following provisions of this section and section 4 below –

    (a) the High Court shall not, under section 1(3)(b) above, grant leave to appeal with respect to a question of law arising out of an award, and

    (b) the High Court shall not, under section 1(5)(b) above, grant leave to make an application with respect to an award, and

    (c) no application may be made under section 2(1)(a) above with respect to a question of law,

if the parties to the reference in question have entered into an agreement in writing (in this section referred to as an 'exclusion agreement') which excludes the right of appeal under section 1 above in relation to that award or, in a case falling within paragraph (c) above, in relation to an award to which the determination of the question of law is material.

(2) An exclusion agreement may be expressed so as to relate to a particular award, to awards under a particular reference or to any other description of awards, whether arising out of the same reference or not; and an agreement may be an exclusion agreement for the purposes of this section whether it is entered into before or after the passing of this Act and whether or not it forms part of an arbitration agreement.

(3) In any case where –

(a) an arbitration agreement, other than a domestic arbitration agreement, provides for disputes between the parties to be referred to arbitration, and

(b) a dispute to which the agreement relates involves the question whether a party has been guilty of fraud, and

(c) the parties have entered into an exclusion agreement which is applicable to any award made on the reference of that dispute,

then, except in so far as the exclusion agreement otherwise provides, the High Court shall not exercise its powers under section 24(2) of the principal Act (to take steps necessary to enable the question to be determined by the High Court) in relation to that dispute.

(4) Except as provided by subsection (1) above, sections 1 and 2 above shall have effect notwithstanding anything in any agreement purporting –

(a) to prohibit or restrict access to the High Court; or

(b) to restrict the jurisdiction of that court; or

(c) to prohibit or restrict the making of a reasoned award.

(5) An exclusion agreement shall be of no effect in relation to an award made on, or a question of law arising in the course of a reference under, a statutory arbitration, that is to say, such an arbitration as is referred to in subsection (1) of section 31 of the principal Act.

(6) An exclusion agreement shall be of no effect in relation to an award made on, or a question of law arising in the course of a reference under, an arbitration agreement which is a domestic arbitration agreement unless the exclusion agreement is entered into after the commencement of the arbitration in which the award is made or, as the case may be, in which the question of law arises.

(7) In this section 'domestic arbitration agreement' means an arbitration agreement which does not provide, expressly or by implication, for arbitration in a State other than the United Kingdom and to which neither –

(a) an individual who is a national of, or habitually resident in, any State other than the United Kingdom, nor

(b) a body corporate which is incorporated in, or whose central management and control is exercised in, any State other than the United Kingdom,

is a party at the time the arbitration agreement is entered into.

4 Exclusion agreements not to apply in certain cases   (1) Subject to subsection (3) below, if an arbitration award or a question of law arising in the course of a reference relates, in whole or in part, to –

(a) a question or claim falling within the Admiralty jurisdiction of the High Court, or

(b) a dispute arising out of a contract of insurance, or

(c) a dispute arising out of a commodity contract,

an exclusion agreement shall have no effect in relation to the award or question unless either –

> (i) the exclusion agreement is entered into after the commencement of the arbitration in which the award is made or, as the case may be, in which the question of law arises, or
>
> (ii) the award or question relates to a contract which is expressed to be governed by a law other than the law of England and Wales.

(2) In subsection (1)(c) above 'commodity contract' means a contract –

(a) for the sale of goods regularly dealt with on a commodity market or exchange in England or Wales which is specified for the purposes of this section by an order made by the Secretary of State; and

(b) of a description so specified.

(3) The Secretary of State may by order provide that subsection (1) above –

(a) shall cease to have effect; or

(b) subject to such conditions as may be specified in the order, shall not apply to any exclusion agreement made in relation to an arbitration award of a description so specified;

and an order under this subsection may contain such supplementary, incidental and transitional provisions as appear to the Secretary of State to be necessary or expedient.

(4) The power to make an order under subsection (2) or subsection (3) above shall be exercisable by statutory instrument which shall be subject to annulment in pursuance of a resolution of either House of Parliament.

(5) In this section 'exclusion agreement' has the same meaning as in section 3 above.

5 Interlocutory orders   (1) If any party to a reference under an arbitration agreement fails within the time specified in the order or, if no time is so specified, within a reasonable time to comply with an order made by the arbitrator or umpire in the course of the reference, then, on the application of the arbitrator or umpire or of any party to the reference, the High Court may make an order extending the powers of the arbitrator or umpire as mentioned in subsection (2) below.

(2) If an order is made by the High Court under this section, the arbitrator or umpire shall have power, to the extent and subject to any conditions specified in that order, to continue with the reference in default of appearance or of any other act by one of the parties in like manner as a judge of the High Court might continue with proceedings in that court where a party fails to comply with an order of that court or a requirement of rules of court.

(3) Section 4(5) of the Administration of Justice Act 1970 (jurisdiction of the High Court to be exercisable by the Court of Appeal in relation to judge-arbitrators and judge-umpires) shall not apply in relation to the power of the High Court to make an order under this section, but in the case of a reference to a judge-arbitrator or judge-umpire that power shall be exercisable as in the case of any other reference to arbitration and also by the judge-arbitrator or judge-umpire himself.

(4) Anything done by a judge-arbitrator or judge-umpire in the exercise of the power conferred by subsection (3) above shall be done by him in his capacity as judge of the High Court and have effect as if done by that court.

(5) The preceding provisions of this section have effect notwithstanding

anything in any agreement but do not derogate from any powers conferred on an arbitrator or umpire, whether by an arbitration agreement or otherwise.

(6) In this section 'judge-arbitrator' and 'judge-umpire' have the same meaning as in Schedule 3 to the Administration of Justice Act 1970.

6 Minor amendments relating to awards and appointments of arbitrators and umpires   (1) In subsection (1) of section 8 of the principal Act (agreements where reference is to two arbitrators deemed to include provision that the arbitrators shall appoint an umpire immediately after their own appointment) –

(a) for the words 'shall appoint an umpire immediately' there shall be substituted the words 'may appoint an umpire at any time'; and

(b) at the end there shall be added the words 'and shall do so forthwith if they cannot agree'.

(2) For section 9 of the principal Act (agreements for reference to three arbitrators) there shall be substituted the following section : –

9 'Majority award of three arbitrators   Unless the contrary intention is expressed in the arbitration agreement, in any case where there is a reference to three arbitrators, the award of any two of the arbitrators shall be binding'.

(3) In section 10 of the principal Act (power of court in certain cases to appoint an arbitrator or umpire) in paragraph (c) after the word 'are', in the first place where it occurs, there shall be inserted the words 'required or are' and the words from 'or where' to the end of the paragraph shall be omitted.

(4) At the end of section 10 of the principal Act there shall be added the following subsection : –

'(2) In any case where –

(a) an arbitration agreement provides for the appointment of an arbitration or umpire by a person who is neither one of the parties nor an existing arbitrator (whether the provision applies directly or in default of agreement by the parties or otherwise), and

(b) that person refuses to make the appointment or does not make it within the time specified in the agreement or, if no time is so specified, within a reasonable time,

any party to the agreement may serve the person in question with a written notice to appoint an arbitrator or umpire and, if the appointment is not made within seven clear days after the service of the notice, the High Court or a judge thereof may, on the application of the party who gave the notice, appoint an arbitrator or umpire who shall have the like powers to act in the reference and make an award as if he had been appointed in accordance with the terms of the agreement'.

7 Application and interpretation of certain provisions of Part I of principal Act   (1) References in the following provisions of Part I of the principal Act to that Part of that Act shall have effect as if the preceding provisions of this Act were included in that Part, namely, –

(a) section 14 (interim awards);

(b) section 28 (terms as to costs of orders);

(c) section 30 (Crown to be bound);

(d) section 31 (application to statutory arbitration); and

(e) section 32 (meaning of 'arbitration agreement').

(2) Subsections (2) and (3) of section 29 of the principal Act shall apply to determine when an arbitration is deemed to be commenced for the purposes of this Act.

(3) For the avoidance of doubts, it is hereby declared that the reference in subsection (1) of section 31 of the principal Act (statutory arbitrations) to arbitration under any other Act does not extend to arbitration under section 92 of the County Courts Act 1959 (cases in which proceedings are to be or may be referred to arbitration) and accordingly nothing in this Act or in Part I of the principal Act applies to arbitration under the said section 92.

8 Short title, commencement, repeals and extent   (1) This Act may be cited as the Arbitration Act 1979.

(2) This Act shall come into operation on such day as the Secretary of State may appoint by order made by statutory instrument; and such an order –

(a) may appoint different days for different provisions of this Act and for the purposes of the operation of the same provision in relation to different descriptions of arbitration agreement; and

(b) may contain such supplementary, incidental and transitional provisions as appear to the Secretary of State to be necessary or expedient.

(3) In consequence of the preceding provisions of this Act, the following provisions are hereby repealed, namely –

(a) in paragraph (c) of section 10 of the principal Act the words from 'or where' to the end of the paragraph;

(b) section 21 of the principal Act;

(c) in paragraph 9 of Schedule 3 to the Administration of Justice Act 1970, in sub-paragraph (1) the words '21(1) and (2)' and sub-paragraph (2).

(4) This Act forms part of the law of England and Wales only.

Arbitration Act 1979 (Commencement) Order 1979
(S.I. 1979 No. 750)

Citation and interpretation

1   (1) This Order may be cited as the Arbitration Act 1979 (Commencement) Order 1979.

(2) In this Order 'the Act' means the Arbitration Act 1979.

Appointed day

2   The Act shall come into operation on 1st August 1979 (hereinafter referred to as 'the appointed day'), but, except as provided in Article 3 of this Order, shall not apply to arbitrations commenced before that date.

3   If all the parties to a reference to arbitration commenced before the appointed day have agreed in writing that the Act should apply to that arbitration, the Act shall so apply from the appointed day or the date of the agreement whichever is the later.

Note: 'Commenced' has the meaning ascribed to it by s. 7(2) of the Act: see Interpretation Act 1978, s. 11.

Arbitration (Commodity Contracts) Order 1979
(S.I. 1979 No. 754)

1 (1) This Order may be cited as the Arbitration (Commodity Contracts) Order 1979 and shall come into operation on 1st August 1979.

(2) In this Order –

'the Act' means the Arbitration Act 1979;

'market' means a commodity market or exchange.

2 The following markets are hereby specified for the purpose of section 4 of the Act –

(a) the markets set out in Part I of the Schedule hereto;

(b) any market in which contracts for sale are subject to the rules or regulations of one or other of the associations set out in Part II of the Schedule, whether or not the market is a market on which commodities are bought and sold at a particular place.

3 The following descriptions of contract are hereby specified for the purpose of section 4 of the Act –

(a) contracts for the sale of goods on any market specified in Article 2 of this Order;

(b) contracts for the sale of goods which are subject to arbitration rules of the London Metal Exchange or of an association set out in Part II of the Schedule hereto.

SCHEDULE

Part I

Markets

The London Cocoa Terminal Market
The London Coffee Terminal Market
The London Grain Futures Market
The London Metal Exchange
The London Rubber Terminal Market
The Gafta Soya Bean Meal Futures Market
The London Sugar Terminal Market
The London Vegetable Oil Terminal Market
The London Wool Terminal Market

Part II

Markets in which contracts are subject to rules or regulations of the following Associations –

The Cocoa Association of London Limited
The Coffee Trade Federation
The Combined Edible Nut Trade Association
Federation of Oils, Seeds and Fats Associations Limited
The General Produce Brokers' Association of London
The Grain and Feed Trade Association Limited
The Hull Seed, Oil and Cake Association
The Liverpool Cotton Association Limited
London Jute Association
London Rice Brokers' Association
The National Federation of Fruit and Potato Trades Limited
The Rubber Trade Association of London
Skin, Hide and Leather Traders' Association Limited
The Sugar Association of London
The Refined Sugar Association
The Tea Brokers' Association of London
The British Wool Confederation

Limitation Act 1980
(1980 c. 58)

*   *   *   *   *

34 Application of Act and other limitation enactments to arbitrations (1) This Act and any other limitation enactment shall apply to arbitrations as they apply to actions in the High Court.

(2) Notwithstanding any term in an arbitration agreement to the effect that no cause of action shall accrue in respect of any matter required by the agreement to be referred until an award is made under the agreement, the cause of action shall, for the purposes of this Act and any other limitation enactment (whether in their application to arbitrations or to other proceedings), be deemed to have accrued in respect of any such matter at the time when it would have accrued but for that term in the agreement.

(3) For the purposes of this Act and of any other limitation enactment an arbitration shall be treated as being commenced –

(a) when one party to the arbitration serves on the other party or parties a notice requiring him or them to appoint an arbitrator or to agree to the appointment of an arbitrator; or

(b) where the arbitration agreement provides that the reference shall be to a person named or designated in the agreement, when one party to the arbitration serves on the other party or parties a notice requiring him or them to submit the dispute to the person so named or designated.

(4) Any such notice may be served either –

(a) by delivering it to the person on whom it is to be served; or

(b) by leaving it at the usual or last-known place of abode in England and Wales of that person; or

(c) by sending it by post in a registered letter addressed to that person at his usual or last-known place of abode in England and Wales:

as well as in any other manner provided in the arbitration agreement.

(5) Where the High Court –

(a) orders that an award be set aside; or

(b) orders, after the commencement of an arbitration, that the arbitration agreement shall cease to have effect with respect to the dispute referred;

the court may further order that the period between the commencement of the arbitration and the date of the order of the court shall be excluded in computing the time prescribed by this Act or by any other limitation enactment for the commencement of proceedings (including arbitration) with respect to the dispute referred.

(6) This section shall apply to an arbitration under an Act of Parliament as well as to an arbitration pursuant to an arbitration agreement.

Subsections (3) and (4) above shall have effect, in relation to an arbitration under an Act, as if for the references to the arbitration agreement there were substituted references to such of the provisions of the Act or of any order scheme, rules, regulations or byelaws made under the Act as relate to the arbitration.

(7) In this section –

(a) 'arbitration', 'arbitration agreement' and 'award' have the same meanings as in Part I of the Arbitration Act 1950; and

(b) references to any other limitation enactment are references to any other enactment relating to the limitation of actions, whether passed before or after the passing of this Act.

Supreme Court Act 1981
(1981 c. 54)

*   *   *   *   *

18 Restrictions on appeals to Court of Appeal   (1) No appeal shall lie to the Court of Appeal – . . .

(g) except as provided by the Arbitration Act 1979, from any decision of the High Court –

(i) on an appeal under section 1 of that Act on a question of law arising out of an arbitration award; or

(ii) under section 2 of that Act on a question of law arising in the course of the reference; . . . .

Civil Jurisdiction and Judgments Act 1982
(1982 c. 27)

*   *   *   *   *

25 Interim relief in England and Wales and Northern Ireland in the absence of substantive proceedings   (1) The High Court in England and Wales or Northern Ireland shall have power to grant interim relief where –

  (a) proceedings have been or are to be commenced in a Contracting State other than the United Kingdom or in a part of the United Kingdom other than that in which the High Court in question exercises jurisdiction; and

  (b) they are or will be proceedings whose subject-matter is within the scope of the 1968 Convention as determined by Article 1 (whether or not the Convention has effect in relation to the proceedings).

  (2) On an application for any interim relief under subsection (1) the court may refuse to grant that relief if, in the opinion of the court, the fact that the court has no jurisdiction apart from this section in relation to the subject-matter of the proceedings in question makes it inexpedient for the court to grant it.

  (3) Her Majesty may by Order in Council extend the power to grant interim relief conferred by subsection (1) so as to make it exercisable in relation to proceedings of any of the following descriptions, namely –

  (a) proceedings commenced or to be commenced otherwise than in a Contracting State;

  (b) proceedings whose subject-matter is not within the scope of the 1968 Convention as determined by Article 1;

  (c) arbitration proceedings.

  (4) An Order in Council under subsection (3) –

  (a) may confer power to grant only specified descriptions of interim relief;

  (b) may make different provision for different classes of proceedings, for proceedings pending in different countries or courts outside the United Kingdom or in different parts of the United Kingdom, and for other different circumstances; and

  (c) may impose conditions or restrictions on the exercise of any power conferred by the Order.

  (5) An Order in Council under subsection (3) which confers power to grant interim relief in relation to arbitration proceedings may provide for the repeal of any provision of section 12(6) of the Arbitration Act 1950 or section 21(1) of the Arbitration Act (Northern Ireland) 1937 to the extent that it is superseded by the provisions of the Order.

  (6) Any Order in Council under subsection (3) shall be subject to annulment in pursuance of a resolution of either House of Parliament.

  (7) In this section 'interim relief', in relation to the High Court in England and Wales or Northern Ireland, means interim relief of any kind which that court has power to grant in proceedings relating to matters within its jurisdiction, other than –

  (a) a warrant for the arrest of property; or

  (b) provision for obtaining evidence.

26 Security in Admiralty proceedings in England and Wales or Northern Ireland in case of stay, etc   (1) Where in England and Wales or Northern Ireland a court stays or dismisses Admiralty proceedings on the ground that the dispute in question should be submitted to arbitration or to the determination of the courts of another part of the United Kingdom or of an overseas country, the court may, if in those proceedings property has been arrested or bail or other security has been given to prevent or obtain release from arrest –

(a) order that the property arrested be retained as security for the satisfaction of any award or judgment which –

(i) is given in respect of the dispute in the arbitration or legal proceedings in favour of which those proceedings are stayed or dismissed; and

(ii) is enforceable in England and Wales or, as the case may be, in Northern Ireland; or

(b) order that the stay or dismissal of those proceedings be conditional on the provision of equivalent security for the satisfaction of any such award or judgment.

(2) Where a court makes an order under subsection (1), it may attach such conditions to the order as it thinks fit, in particular conditions with respect to the institution or prosecution of the relevant arbitration or legal proceedings.

(3) Subject to any provision made by rules of court and to any necessary modifications, the same law and practice shall apply in relation to property retained in pursuance of an order made by a court under subsection (1) as would apply if it were held for the purposes of proceedings in that court.

32 Overseas judgments given in proceedings brought in breach of agreement for settlement of disputes (1) Subject to the following provisions of this section, a judgment given by a court of an overseas country in any proceedings shall not be recognised or enforced in the United Kingdom if –

(a) the bringing of those proceedings in that court was contrary to an agreement under which the dispute in question was to be settled otherwise than by proceedings in the courts of that country; and

(b) those proceedings were not brought in that court by, or with the agreement of, the person against whom the judgment was given; and

(c) that person did not counterclaim in the proceedings or otherwise submit to the jurisdiction of that court.

(2) Subsection (1) does not apply where the agreement referred to in paragraph (a) of that subsection was illegal, void or unenforceable or was incapable of being performed for reasons not attributable to the fault of the party bringing the proceedings in which the judgment was given.

(3) In determining whether a judgment given by a court of an overseas country should be recognised or enforced in the United Kingdom, a court in the United Kingdom shall not be bound by any decision of the overseas court relating to any of the matters mentioned in subsection (1) or (2).

(4) Nothing in subsection (1) shall affect the recognition or enforcement in the United Kingdom of –

(a) a judgment which is required to be recognised or enforced there under the 1968 Convention;

(b) a judgment to which Part I of the Foreign Judgments (Reciprocal Enforcement) Act 1933 applies by virtue of section 4 of the Carriage of Goods by Road Act 1965, section 17(4) of the Nuclear Installations Act 1965, section 13(3) of the Merchant Shipping (Oil Pollution) Act 1971, [section 6 of the International Transport Conventions Act 1983], section

5 of the Carriage of Passengers by Road Act 1974 or section 6(4) of the Merchant Shipping Act 1974.

Note: Words in square brackets in sub-s. (4) were substituted by the International Transport Conventions Act 1983, s. 11(2).

33 Certain steps not to amount to submission to jurisdiction of overseas court   (1) For the purposes of determining whether a judgment given by a court of an overseas country should be recognised or enforced in England and Wales or Northern Ireland, the person against whom the judgment was given shall not be regarded as having submitted to the jurisdiction of the court by reason only of the fact that he appeared (conditionally or otherwise) in the proceedings for all or any one or more of the following purposes, namely –

(a) to contest the jurisdiction of the court;

(b) to ask the court to dismiss or stay the proceedings on the ground that the dispute in question should be submitted to arbitration or to the determination of the courts of another country;

(c) to protect, or obtain the release of, property seized or threatened with seizure in the proceedings.

(2) Nothing in this section shall affect the recognition or enforcement in England and Wales or Northern Ireland of a judgment which is required to be recognised or enforced there under the 1968 Convention.

Rules of Supreme Court

Order 73

Arbitration Proceedings

1 Arbitration proceedings not to be assigned to the Chancery Division   [*Revoked.*]

2 Matters for a judge in court   (1) Every application to the Court –

(a) to remit an award under section 22 of the Arbitration Act 1950, or

(b) to remove an arbitrator or umpire under section 23(1) of that Act, or

(c) to set aside an award under section 23(2) thereof, or

(d) [*Revoked.*]

(e) to determine, under section 2(1) of that Act, any question of law arising in the course of a reference,

must be made by originating motion to a single judge in court.

(2) Any appeal to the High Court under section 1(2) of the Arbitration Act 1979 shall be made by originating motion to a single judge in court.

(3) An application for a declaration that an award made by an arbitrator or umpire is not binding on a party to the award on the ground that it was made without jurisdiction may be made by originating motion to a single judge in court, but the foregoing provision shall not be taken as affecting the judge's power to refuse to make such a declaration in proceedings begun by motion.

3 Matters for judge in chambers or master   (1) Subject to the foregoing provisions of this Order and the provisions of this rule, the jurisdiction of the High Court under the Arbitration Act 1950 and the jurisdiction of the High Court under the Arbitration Act 1975 and the Arbitration Act 1979 may be exercised by a judge in chambers, a master or the Admiralty Registrar.

(2) Any application

(a) for leave to appeal under section 1(2) of the Arbitration Act 1979, or

(b) under section 1(5) of that Act (including any application for leave), or

(c) under section 5 of that Act,

shall be made to a judge in chambers.

(3) Any application to which this rule applies shall, where an action is pending, be made by summons in the action, and in any other case by an originating summons which shall be in Form No. 10 in Appendix A.

(4) Where an application is made under section 1(5) of the Arbitration Act 1979 (including any application for leave), the summons must be served on the arbitrator or umpire and on any other party to the reference.

4 Applications in district registries An application under section 12(4) of the Arbitration Act 1950 for an order that a writ of subpoena ad testificandum or of subpoena duces tecum shall issue to compel the attendance before an arbitrator or umpire of a witness may, if the attendance of the witness is required within the district of any district registry, be made at that registry, instead of at the Admiralty and Commercial Registry, at the option of the applicant.

5 Time-limits and other special provisions as to appeals and application under the Arbitration Acts (1) An application to the Court –

(a) to remit an award under section 22 of the Arbitration Act 1950, or

(b) set aside an award under section 23(2) of that Act or otherwise, or

(c) to direct an arbitrator or umpire to state the reasons for an award under section 1(5) of the Arbitration Act 1979,

must be made, and the summons or notice must be served, within 21 days after the award has been made and published to the parties.

(2) In the case of an appeal to the Court under section 1(2) of the Arbitration Act 1979, the notice must be served, and the appeal entered, within 21 days after the award has been made and published to the parties:

Provided that, where reasons material to the appeal are given on a date subsequent to the publication of the award, the period of 21 days shall run from the date on which the reasons are given.

(3) An application, under section 2(1) of the Arbitration Act 1979, to determine any question of law arising in the course of a reference, must be made and notice thereof served within 14 days after the arbitrator or umpire has consented to the application being made, or the other parties have so consented.

(4) For the purpose of paragraph (2) the consent must be given in writing.

(5) In the case of every appeal or application to which this rule applies, the notice of originating motion, the originating summons or the summons, as the case may be, must state the grounds of the appeal or application and, where the appeal or application is founded on evidence by affidavit, or is made with the consent of the arbitrator or umpire or of the other parties, a copy of every affidavit intended to be used, or, as the case may be, of every consent given in writing, must be served with that notice.

(6) Without prejudice to paragraph (5), in an appeal under section 1(2) of the Arbitration Act 1979 the statement of the grounds of the appeal shall specify the relevant parts of the award and reasons, and a copy of the award and reasons, or the relevant parts thereof, shall be lodged with the court and served with the notice of originating motion.

(7) Without prejudice to paragraph (5), in an application for leave to appeal under section 1(2) of the Arbitration Act 1979, any affidavit verifying the facts in support of a contention that the question of law concerns a term of a contract or an event which is not a one-off term or event must be lodged with the court and served with the notice of originating motion.

(8) Any affidavit in reply to an affidavit under paragraph (7) shall be lodged with the court and served on the applicant not less than two clear days before the hearing of the application.

(9) A respondent to an application for leave to appeal under section 1(2) of the Arbitration Act 1979 who desires to contend that the award should be upheld on grounds not expressed or not fully expressed in the award or reasons shall not less than two clear days before the hearing of the application lodge with the court and serve on the applicant a notice specifying the grounds of his contention.

Note: The reference to para. (2) in para. (4) must be a mistake for para. (3). For the application of the above rule to arbitration before a judge-arbitrator or judge-umpire: see Ord. 59, r. 14(5).

6 Applications and appeals to be heard by Commercial Judges   (1) Any matter which is required, by rule 2 or 3, to be heard by a judge, shall be heard by a Commercial Judge, unless any such judge otherwise directs.

(2) Nothing in the foregoing paragraph shall be construed as preventing the powers of a Commercial Judge from being exercised by any judge of the High Court.

7 Service out of the jurisdiction of summons, notice, etc.   (1) Subject to paragraph (1A) service out of the jurisdiction of –

(a) any originating summons or notice of originating motion under the Arbitration Act 1950 or the Arbitration Act 1979, or

(b) any order made on such a summons or motion as aforesaid, is permissible with the leave of the Court provided that the arbitration to which the summons, motion or order related is governed by English law or has been, is being, or is to be held, within the jurisdiction.

(1A) Service out of the jurisdiction of an originating summons for leave to enforce an award is permissible with the leave of the Court whether or not the arbitration is governed by English law.

(2) An application for the grant of leave under this rule must be supported by an affidavit stating the grounds on which the application is made and showing in what place or country the person to be served is, or probably may be found; and no such leave shall be granted unless it shall be made sufficiently to appear to the Court that the case is a proper one for service out of the jurisdiction under this rule.

(3) Order 11, rules 5, 6 and 8, shall apply in relation to any such summons, notice or order as is referred to in paragraph (1) as they apply in relation to notice of a writ.

8 Registration in High Court of foreign awards   Where an award is made in proceedings on an arbitration in any part of Her Majesty's dominions or other territory to which Part I of the Foreign Judgments (Reciprocal Enforcement) Act 1933 extends, being a part to which Part II of the Administration of Justice Act 1920 extended immediately before the said Part I was extended thereto, then, if the award has, in pursuance of the law in force in the place where it was made, become enforceable in the same manner as a judgment given by a court in that place, Order 71 shall apply in relation to the award as it applies in relation to a judgment given by that court, subject, however, to the following modifications: –
   (a) for references to the country of the original court there shall be substituted references to the place where the award was made; and
   (b) the affidavit required by rule 3 of the said Order must state (in addition to the other matters required by that rule) that to the best of the information or belief of the deponent the award has, in pursuance of the law in force in the place where it was made, become enforceable in the same manner as a judgment given by a court in that place.

9 Registration of awards under Arbitration (International Investment Disputes) Act 1966   [Omitted.]

10 Enforcement of arbitration awards   (1) An application for leave under section 26 of the Arbitration Act 1950 or under section 3(1)(a) of the Arbitration Act 1975 to enforce an award on an arbitration agreement in the same manner as a judgment or order may be made ex parte but the Court hearing the application may direct a summons to be issued.
   (2) If the Court directs a summons to be issued, the summons shall be an originating summons which shall be in Form No. 10 in Appendix A.
   (3) An application for leave must be supported by affidavit –
   (a) exhibiting
      (i) where the application is under section 26 of the Arbitration Act 1950, the arbitration agreement and the original award or, in either case, a copy thereof;
      (ii) where the application is under section 3(1)(a) of the Arbitration Act 1975, the documents required to be produced by section 4 of that Act,
   (b) stating the name and the usual or last known place of abode or business of the applicant (hereinafter referred to as 'the creditor') and the person against whom it is sought to enforce the award (herinafter referred to as 'the debtor') respectively,
   (c) as the case may require, either that award has not been complied with or the extent to which it has not been complied with at the date of the application.
   (4) An order giving leave must be drawn up by or on behalf of the creditor and must be served on the debtor by delivering a copy to him personally or by sending a copy to him at his usual or last known place of abode or business or in such other manner as the Court may direct.
   (5) Service of the order out of the jurisdiction is permissible without leave, and Order 11, rules 5, 6 and 8, shall apply in relation to such an order as they apply in relation to notice of a writ.

(6) Within 14 days after service of the order or, if the order is to be served out of the jurisdiction, within such other period as the Court may fix, the debtor may apply to set aside the order and the award shall not be enforced until after the expiration of that period or, if the debtor applies within that period to set aside the order, until after the application is finally disposed of.

(7) The copy of the order served on the debtor shall state the effect of paragraph (6).

(8) In relation to a body corporate this rule shall have effect as if for any reference to the place of abode or business of the creditor or the debtor there were substituted a reference to the registered or principal address of the body corporate; so, however, that nothing in this rule shall affect any enactment which provides for the manner in which a document may be served on a body corporate.

Order 59, rule 1A

(1A) For all purposes connected with appeals to the Court of Appeal, a judgment or order shall be treated as final or interlocutory in accordance with the following provisions of this rule.

*   *   *   *   *

(7) Notwithstanding anything in paragraph (3) –
   (a) orders made on an appeal to the High Court under section 1(2) of the Arbitration Act 1979 shall be treated as final orders;
   (b) all other orders made in connection with or arising out of an arbitration or arbitral award shall be treated as interlocutory orders; without prejudice to the generality of the foregoing, such orders shall include –
      (i) orders made in connection with the appointment or removal of an arbitrator or umpire;
      (ii) orders made on or in connection with applications for an extension of time for commencing arbitration proceedings;
      (iii) orders setting aside an arbitral award or remitting the matter to an arbitrator or umpire (other than orders setting aside the award or remitting the matter made on an appeal in pursuance of the said section 1(2)); and
      (iv) orders made on or in connection with applications for leave to enforce an award.

Note: Ord. 59, r. 1A was added to the Rules of the Supreme Court with effect from 1 October 1988 by S.I. 1988 No. 1340, r. 8.

Convention on the recognition and enforcement of foreign arbitral awards. Done at New York, on 10 June 1958[1]

Article I

1 This Convention shall apply to the recognition and enforcement of arbitral awards made in the territory of a State other than the State where the recognition and enforcement of such awards are sought, and arising out of differences between persons, whether physical or legal. It shall also apply to arbitral awards not considered as domestic awards in the State where their recognition and enforcement are sought.

2 The term 'arbitral awards' shall include not only awards made by arbitrators appointed for each case but also those made by permanent arbitral bodies to which the parties have submitted.

3 When signing, ratifying or acceding to this Convention, or notifying extension under article X hereof, any State may on the basis of reciprocity declare that it will apply the Convention to the recognition and enforcement of awards made only in the territory of another Contracting State. It may also declare that it will apply the Convention only to differences arising out of legal relationships, whether contractual or not, which are considered as commercial under the national law of the State making such declaration.

Article II

1 Each Contracting State shall recognize an agreement in writing under which the parties undertake to submit to arbitration all or any differences which have arisen or which may arise between them in respect of a defined legal relationship, whether contractual or not, concerning a subject matter capable of settlement by arbitration.

2 The term 'agreement in writing' shall include an arbitral clause in a contract or an arbitration agreement, signed by the parties or contained in an exchange of letters or telegrams.

3 The court of a Contracting State, when seized of an action in a matter in respect of which the parties have made an agreement within the meaning of this article, at the request of one of the parties, refer the parties to arbitration, unless it finds that the said agreement is null and void, inoperative or incapable of being performed.

---

[1] This is the English text. The Chinese, French, Russian and Spanish texts are equally authentic: Article XVI. The texts in all five languages are printed in the United Nations Treaty Series (1959) 330.

Article III

Each Contracting State shall recognize arbitral awards as binding and enforce them in accordance with the rules of procedure of the territory where the award is relied upon, under the conditions laid down in the following articles. There shall not be imposed substantially more onerous conditions or higher fees or charges on the recognition or enforecement of arbitral awards to which this Convention applies than are imposed on the recognition or enforcement of domestic arbitral awards.

Article IV

1 To obtain the recognition and enforcement mentioned in the preceding article, the party applying for recognition and enforcement shall, at the time of the application, supply:
   (a) The duly authenticated original award or a duly certified copy thereof;
   (b) The original agreement referred to in article II or a duly certified copy thereof.
2 If the said award or agreement is not made in an official language of the country in which the award is relied upon, the party applying for recognition and enforcement of the award shall produce a translation of these documents into such language. The translation shall be certified by an official or sworn translator or by a diplomatic or consular agent.

Article V

1 Recognition and enforcement of the award may be refused, at the request of the party against whom it is invoked, only if that party furnishes to the competent authority where the recognition and enforcement is sought, proof that:
   (a) The parties to the agreement referred to in article II were, under the law applicable to them, under some incapacity, or the said agreement is not valid under the law to which the parties have subjected it or, failing any indication thereon, under the law of the country where the award was made; or
   (b) The party against whom the award is invoked was not given proper notice of the appointment of the arbitrator or of the arbitration proceedings or was otherwise unable to present his case; or
   (c) The award deals with a difference not contemplated by or not falling within the terms of the submission to arbitration, or it contains decisions on matters beyond the scope of the submission to arbitration, provided that, if the decisions on matters submitted to arbitration can be separated from those not so submitted, that part of the award which contains decisions on matters submitted to arbitration may be recognized and enforced; or
   (d) The composition of the arbitral authority or the arbitral procedure was not in accordance with the agreement of the parties, or, failing such agreement, was not in accordance with the law of the country where the arbitration took place; or
   (e) The award has not yet become binding on the parties, or has been set

aside or suspended by a competent authority of the country in which, or under the law of which, that award was made.

2 Recognition and enforcement of an arbitral award may also be refused if the competent authority in the country where recognition and enforcement is sought finds that:

(a) The subject matter of the difference is not capable of settlement by arbitration under the law of that country; or

(b) The recognition or enforcement of the award would be contrary to the public policy of that country.

Article VI

If an application for the setting aside or suspension of the award has been made to a competent authority referred to in article V(1)(e), the authority before which the award is sought to be relied upon may, if it considers it proper, adjourn the decision on the enforcement of the award and may also, on the application of the party claiming enforcement of the award, order the other party to give suitable security.

Article VII

1 The provisions of the present Convention shall not affect the validity of multilateral or bilateral agreements concerning the recognition and enforcement of arbitral awards entered into by the Contracting States nor deprive any interested party of any right he may have to avail himself of an arbitral award in the manner and to the extent allowed by the law or the treaties of the country where such award is sought to be relied upon.

2 The Geneva Protocol on Arbitration Clauses of 1923 and the Geneva Convention on the Execution of Foreign Arbitral Awards 1927 shall cease to have effect between Contracting States on their becoming bound and to the extent that they become bound, by this Convention.

Article VIII

1 This Convention shall be open until 31 December 1958 for signature on behalf of any Member of the United Nations and also on behalf of any other State which is or hereafter becomes a member of any specialized agency of the United Nations, or which is or hereafter becomes a party to the Statute of the International Court of Justice, or any other State to which an invitation has been addressed by the General Assembly of the United Nations.

2 This Convention shall be ratified and the instrument of ratification shall be deposited with the Secretary-General of the United Nations.

Article IX

1 This Convention shall be open for accession to all States referred to in article VIII.

2 Accession shall be effected by the deposit of an instrument of accession with the Secretary-General of the United Nations.

Article X

1 Any State may, at the time of signature, ratification or accession, declare that this Convention shall extend to all or any of the territories for the international relations of which it is responsible. Such a declaration shall take effect when the Convention enters into force for the State concerned.

2 At any time thereafter any such extension shall be made by notification addressed to the Secretary-General of the United Nations and shall take effect as from the ninetieth day after the day of receipt by the Secretary-General of the United Nations of this notification, or as from the date of entry into force of the Convention for the State concerned, whichever is the later.

3 With respect to those territories to which this Convention is not extended at the time of signature, ratification or accession, each State concerned shall consider the possibility of taking the necessary steps in order to extend the application of this Convention to such territories, subject, where necessary for constitutional reasons, to the consent of the Governments of such territories.

Article XI

In the case of a federal or non-unitary State, the following provisions shall apply:

(a) With respect to those articles of this Convention that come within the legislative jurisdiction of the federal authority, the obligations of the federal Government shall to this extent be the same as those of Contracting States which are not federal States;

(b) With respect to those articles of this Convention that come within the legislative jurisdiction of constituent states or provinces which are not, under the constitutional system of the federation, bound to take legislative action, the federal Government shall bring such articles with a favourable recommendation to the notice of the appropriate authorities of constituent states or provinces at the earliest possible moment;

(c) A federal State Party to this Convention shall, at the request of any other Contracting State transmitted through the Secretary-General of the United Nations, supply a statement of the law and practice of the federation and its constituent units in regard to any particular provision of this Convention, showing the extent to which effect has been given to that provision by legislative or other action.

Article XII

1 This Convention shall come into force on the ninetieth day following the date of deposit of the third instrument of ratification or accession.

2 For each State ratifying or acceding to this Convention after the deposit of the third instrument of ratification or accession, this Convention shall enter into

force on the ninetieth day after deposit by such State of its instrument of ratification or accession.

Article XIII

1 Any Contracting State may denounce this Convention by a written notification to the Secretary-General of the United Nations. Denunciation shall take effect one year after the date of receipt of the notification by the Secretary-General.

2 Any State which has made a declaration or notification under article X may, at any time thereafter, by notification to the Secretary-General of the United Nations, declare that this Convention shall cease to extend to the territory concerned one year after the date of the receipt of the notification by the Secretary-General.

3 This Convention shall continue to be applicable to arbitral awards in respect of which recognition or enforcement proceedings have been instituted before the denunciation takes effect.

Article XIV

A Contracting State shall not be entitled to avail itself of the present Convention against other Contracting States except to the extent that it is itself bound to apply the Convention.

Article XV

The Secretary-General of the United Nations shall notify the States contemplated in article VIII of the following:

   (a) Signatures and ratifications in accordance with article VIII;

   (b) Accessions in accordance with article IX;

   (c) Declarations and notifications under articles I, X and XI;

   (d) The date upon which this Convention enters into force in accordance with article XII;

   (e) Denunciations and notifications in accordance with article XIII.

Article XVI

1 This Convention, of which the Chinese, English, French, Russian and Spanish texts shall be equally authentic, shall be deposited in the archives of the United Nations.

2 The Secretary-General of the United Nations shall transmit a certified copy of this Convention to the States contemplated in article VIII.

APPENDIX 3

UNCITRAL Model Law on International Commercial Arbitration

(As adopted by the United Nations Commission on
International Trade Law on 21 June 1985)

CHAPTER I GENERAL PROVISIONS

Article 1 Scope of application*

(1) This Law applies to international commercial† arbitration, subject to any agreement in force between this State and any other State or States.

(2) The provisions of this Law, except articles 8, 9, 35 and 36, apply only if the place of arbitration is in the territory of this State.

(3) An arbitration is international if:

(a) the parties to an arbitration agreement have, at the time of the conclusion of that agreement, their places of business in different States; or

(b) one of the following places is situated outside the State in which the parties have their places of business:

(i) the place of arbitration if determined in, or pursuant to, the arbitration agreement;

(ii) any place where a substantial part of the obligations of the commercial relationship is to be performed or the place with which the subject-matter of the dispute is most closely connected; or

(c) the parties have expressly agreed that the subject-matter of the arbitration agreement relates to more than one country.

(4) For the purposes of paragraph (3) of this article:

(a) if a party has more than one place of business, the place of business is that which has the closest relationship to the arbitration agreement;

(b) if a party does not have a place of business, reference is to be made to his habitual residence.

(5) This Law shall not affect any other law of this State by virtue of which certain disputes may not be submitted to arbitration or may be submitted to arbitration only according to provisions other than those of this Law.

---

* Article headings are for reference purposes only and are not to be used for purposes of interpretation.

† The term 'commercial' should be given a wide interpretation so as to cover matters arising from all relationships of a commercial nature, whether contractual or not. Relationships of a commercial nature include, but are not limited to, the following transactions: any trade transaction for the supply or exchange of goods or services; distribution agreement; commercial representation or agency; factoring; leasing; construction of works; consulting; engineering; licensing; investment; financing; banking; insurance; exploitation agreement or concession; joint venture and other forms of industrial or business co-operation; carriage of goods or passengers by air, sea, rail or road.

Article 2 Definitions and rules of interpretation

For the purposes of this Law:

    (a) 'arbitration' means any arbitration whether or not administered by a permanent arbitral institution;

    (b) 'arbitral tribunal' means a sole arbitrator or a panel of arbitrators;

    (c) 'court' means a body or organ of the judicial system of a State;

    (d) where a provision of this Law, except article 28, leaves the parties free to determine a certain issue, such freedom includes the right of the parties to authorize a third party, including an institution, to make that determination;

    (e) where a provision of this Law refers to the fact that the parties have agreed or that they may agree or in any other way refers to an agreement of the parties, such agreement includes any arbitration rules referred to in that agreement;

    (f) where a provision of this Law, other than in articles 25(a) and 32(2)(a), refers to a claim, it also applies to a counter-claim, and where it refers to a defence, it also applies to a defence to such counter-claim.

Article 3 Receipt of written communications

    (1) Unless otherwise agreed by the parties:

    (a) any written communication is deemed to have been received if it is delivered to the addressee personally or if it is delivered at his place of business, habitual residence or mailing address; if none of these can be found after making a reasonable inquiry, a written communication is deemed to have been received if it is sent to the addressee's last-known place of business, habitual residence or mailing address by registered letter or any other means which provides a record of the attempt to deliver it;

    (b) the communication is deemed to have been received on the day it is so delivered.

(2) The provisions of this article do not apply to communications in court proceedings.

Article 4 Waiver of right to object

A party who knows that any provision of this Law from which the parties may derogate or any requirement under the arbitration agreement has not been complied with and yet proceeds with the arbitration without stating his objection to such non-compliance without undue delay or, if a time-limit is provided therefor, within such period of time, shall be deemed to have waived his right to object.

Article 5 Extent of court intervention

In matters governed by this Law, no court shall intervene except where so provided in this Law.

Article 6 Court or other authority for certain functions of arbitration assistance and supervision

The functions referred to in articles 11(3), 11(4), 13(3), 14, 16(3) and 34(2) shall be performed by . . . [Each State enacting this model law specifies the court, courts or, where referred to therein, other authority competent to perform these functions.]

CHAPTER II ARBITRATION AGREEMENT

Article 7 Definition and form of arbitration agreement

(1) 'Arbitration agreement' is an agreement by the parties to submit to arbitration all or certain disputes which have arisen or which may arise between them in respect of a defined legal relationship, whether contractual or not. An arbitration agreement may be in the form of an arbitration clause in a contract or in the form of a separate agreement.

(2) The arbitration agreement shall be in writing. An agreement is in writing if it is contained in a document signed by the parties or in an exchange of letters, telex, telegrams or other means of telecommunication which provide a record of the agreement, or in an exchange of statements of claim and defence in which the existence of an agreement is alleged by one party and not denied by another. The reference in a contract to a document containing an arbitration clause constitutes an arbitration agreement provided that the contract is in writing and the reference is such as to make that clause part of the contract.

Article 8 Arbitration agreement and substantive claim before court

(1) A court before which an action is brought in a matter which is the subject of an arbitration agreement shall, if a party so requests not later than when submitting his first statement on the substance of the dispute, refer the parties to arbitration unless it finds that the agreement is null and void, inoperative or incapable of being performed.

(2) Where an action referred to in paragraph (1) of this article has been brought, arbitral proceedings may nevertheless be commenced or continued, and an award may be made, while the issue is pending before the court.

Article 9 Arbitration agreement and interim measures by court

It is not incompatible with an arbitration agreement for a party to request, before or during arbitral proceedings, from a court an interim measure of protection and for a court to grant such measure.

CHAPTER III COMPOSITION OF ARBITRAL TRIBUNAL

Article 10 Number of arbitrators

(1) The parties are free to determine the number of arbitrators.

(2) Failing such determination, the number of arbitrators shall be three.

Article 11 Appointment of arbitrators

(1) No person shall be precluded by reason of his nationality from acting as an arbitrator, unless otherwise agreed by the parties.

(2) The parties are free to agree on a procedure of appointing the arbitrator or arbitrators, subject to the provisions of paragraphs (4) and (5) of this article.

(3) Failing such agreement,

(a) in an arbitration with three arbitrators, each party shall appoint one arbitrator, and the two arbitrators thus appointed shall appoint the third arbitrator; if a party fails to appoint the arbitrator within thirty days of receipt of a request to do so from the other party, or if the two arbitrators fail to agree on the third arbitrator within thirty days of their appointment, the appointment shall be made, upon request of a party, by the court or other authority specified in article 6;

(b) in an arbitration with a sole arbitrator, if the parties are unable to agree on the arbitrator, he shall be appointed, upon request of a party, by the court or other authority specified in article 6.

(4) Where, under an appointment procedure agreed upon by the parties,

(a) a party fails to act as required under such procedure, or

(b) the parties, or two arbitrators, are unable to reach an agreement expected of them under such procedure, or

(c) a third party, including an institution, fails to perform any function entrusted to it under such procedure,
any party may request the court or other authority specified in article 6 to take the necessary measure, unless the agreement on the appointment procedure provides other means for securing the appointment.

(5) A decision on a matter entrusted by paragraph (3) or (4) of this article to the court or other authority specified in article 6 shall be subject to no appeal. The court or other authority, in appointing an arbitrator, shall have due regard to any qualifications required of the arbitrator by the agreement of the parties and to such considerations as are likely to secure the appointment of an independent and impartial arbitrator and, in the case of a sole or third arbitrator, shall take into account as well the advisability of appointing an arbitrator of a nationality other than those of the parties.

Article 12 Grounds for challenge

(1) When a person is approached in connection with his possible appointment as an arbitrator, he shall disclose any circumstances likely to give rise to justifiable doubts as to his impartiality or independence. An arbitrator, from the

time of his appointment and throughout the arbitral proceedings, shall without delay disclose any such circumstances to the parties unless they have already been informed of them by him.

(2) An arbitrator may be challenged only if circumstances exist that give rise to justifiable doubts as to his impartiality or independence, or if he does not possess qualifications agreed to by the parties. A party may challenge an arbitrator appointed by him, or in whose appointment he has participated, only for reasons of which he becomes aware after the appointment has been made.

Article 13 Challenge procedure

(1) The parties are free to agree on a procedure for challenging an arbitrator, subject to the provisions of paragraph (3) of this article.

(2) Failing such agreement, a party who intends to challenge an arbitrator shall, within fifteen days after becoming aware of the constitution of the arbitral tribunal or after becoming aware of any circumstance referred to in article 12(2), send a written statement of the reasons for the challenge to the arbitral tribunal. Unless the challenged arbitrator withdraws from his office or the other party agrees to the challenge, the arbitral tribunal shall decide on the challenge.

(3) If a challenge under any procedure agreed upon by the parties or under the procedure of paragraph (2) of this article is not successful, the challenging party may request, within thirty days after having received notice of the decision rejecting the challenge, the court or other authority specified in article 6 to decide on the challenge, which decision shall be subject to no appeal; while such a request is pending, the arbitral tribunal, including the challenged arbitrator, may continue the arbitral proceedings and make an award.

Article 14 Failure or impossibility to act

(1) If an arbitrator becomes *de jure* or *de facto* unable to perform his functions or for other reasons fails to act without undue delay, his mandate terminates if he withdraws from his office or if the parties agree on the termination. Otherwise, if a controversy remains concerning any of these grounds, any party may request the court or other authority specified in article 6 to decide on the termination of the mandate, which decision shall be subject to no appeal.

(2) If, under this article or article 13(2), an arbitrator withdraws from his office or a party agrees to the termination of the mandate of an arbitrator, this does not imply acceptance of the validity of any ground referred to in this article or article 12(2).

Article 15 Appointment of substitute arbitrator

Where the mandate of an arbitrator terminates under article 13 or 14 or because of his withdrawal from office for any other reason or because of the revocation of his mandate by agreement of the parties or in any other case of termination of his mandate, a substitute arbitrator shall be appointed according to the rules that were applicable to the appointment of the arbitrator being replaced.

CHAPTER IV JURISDICTION OF ARBITRAL TRIBUNAL

Article 16 Competence of arbitral tribunal to rule on its jurisdiction

(1) The arbitral tribunal may rule on its own jurisdiction, including any objections with respect to the existence or validity of the arbitration agreement. For that purpose, an arbitration clause which forms part of a contract shall be treated as an agreement independent of the other terms of the contract. A decision by the arbitral tribunal that the contract is null and void shall not entail *ipso jure* the invalidity of the arbitration clause.

(2) A plea that the arbitral tribunal does not have jurisdiction shall be raised not later than the submission of the statement of defence. A party is not precluded from raising such a plea by the fact that he has appointed, or participated in the appointment of, an arbitrator. A plea that the arbitral tribunal is exceeding the scope of its authority shall be raised as soon as the matter alleged to be beyond the scope of its authority is raised during the arbitral proceedings. The arbitral tribunal may, in either case, admit a later plea if it considers the delay justified.

(3) The arbitral tribunal may rule on a plea referred to in paragraph (2) of this article either as a preliminary question or in an award on the merits. If the arbitral tribunal rules as a preliminary question that it has jurisdiction, any party may request, within thirty days after having received notice of that ruling, the court specified in article 6 to decide the matter, which decision shall be subject to no appeal; while such a request is pending, the arbitral tribunal may continue the arbitral proceedings and make an award.

Article 17 Power of arbitral tribunal to order interim measures

Unless otherwise agreed by the parties, the arbitral tribunal may, at the request of a party, order any party to take such interim measure of protection as the arbitral tribunal may consider necessary in respect of the subject-matter of the dispute. The arbitral tribunal may require any party to provide appropriate security in connection with such measure.

CHAPTER V CONDUCT OF ARBITRAL PROCEEDINGS

Article 18 Equal treatment of parties

The parties shall be treated with equality and each party shall be given a full opportunity of presenting his case.

Article 19 Determination of rules of procedure

(1) Subject to the provisions of this Law, the parties are free to agree on the procedure to be followed by the arbitral tribunal in conducting the proceedings.

(2) Failing such agreement, the arbitral tribunal may, subject to the provisions of this Law, conduct the arbitration in such manner as it considers appropriate. The power conferred upon the arbitral tribunal includes the power to determine the admissibility, relevance, materiality and weight of any evidence.

Article 20 Place of arbitration

(1) The parties are free to agree on the place of arbitration. Failing such agreement, the place of arbitration shall be determined by the arbitral tribunal having regard to the circumstances of the case, including the convenience of the parties.

(2) Notwithstanding the provisions of paragraph (1) of this article, the arbitral tribunal may, unless otherwise agreed by the parties, meet at any place it considers appropriate for consultation among its members, for hearing witnesses, experts or the parties, or for inspection of goods, other property or documents.

Article 21 Commencement of arbitral proceedings

Unless otherwise agreed by the parties, the arbitral proceedings in respect of a particular dispute commence on the date on which a request for that dispute to be referred to arbitration is received by the respondent.

Article 22 Language

(1) The parties are free to agree on the language or languages to be used in the arbitral proceedings. Failing such agreement, the arbitral tribunal shall determine the language or languages to be used in the proceedings. This agreement or determination, unless otherwise specified therein, shall apply to any written statement by a party, any hearing and any award, decision or other communication by the arbitral tribunal.

(2) The arbitral tribunal may order that any documentary evidence shall be accompanied by a translation into the language or languages agreed upon by the parties or determined by the arbitral tribunal.

Article 23 Statements of claim and defence

(1) Within the period of time agreed by the parties or determined by the arbitral tribunal, the claimant shall state the facts supporting his claim, the points at issue and the relief of remedy sought, and the respondent shall state his defence in respect of these particulars, unless the parties have otherwise agreed as to the required elements of such statements. The parties may submit with

their statements all documents they consider to be relevant or may add a reference to the documents or other evidence they will submit.

(2) Unless otherwise agreed by the parties, either party may amend or supplement his claim or defence during the course of the arbitral proceedings, unless the arbitral tribunal considers it inappropriate to allow such amendment having regard to the delay in making it.

Article 24 Hearings and written proceedings

(1) Subject to any contrary agreement by the parties, the arbitral tribunal shall decide whether to hold oral hearings for the presentation of evidence or for oral argument, or whether the proceedings shall be conducted on the basis of documents and other materials. However, unless the parties have agreed that no hearings shall be held, the arbitral tribunal shall hold such hearings at an appropriate stage of the proceedings, if so requested by a party.

(2) The parties shall be given sufficient advance notice of any hearing and of any meeting of the arbitral tribunal for the purposes of inspection of goods, other property or documents.

(3) All statements, documents or other information supplied to the arbitral tribunal by one party shall be communicated to the other party. Also any expert report or evidentiary document on which the arbitral tribunal may rely in making its decision shall be communicated to the parties.

Article 25 Default of a party

Unless otherwise agreed by the parties, if, without showing sufficient cause,

(a) the claimant fails to communicate his statement of claim in accordance with article 23(1), the arbitral tribunal shall terminate the proceedings;

(b) the respondent fails to communicate his statement of defence in accordance with article 23(1), the arbitral tribunal shall continue the proceedings without treating such failure in itself as an admission of the claimant's allegations;

(c) any party fails to appear at a hearing or to produce documentary evidence, the arbitral tribunal may continue the proceedings and make the award on the evidence before it.

Article 26 Expert appointed by arbitral tribunal

(1) Unless otherwise agreed by the parties, the arbitral tribunal

(a) may appoint one or more experts to report to it on specific issues to be determined by the arbitral tribunal;

(b) may require a party to give the expert any relevant information or to produce, or to provide access to, any relevant documents, goods or other property for his inspection.

(2) Unless otherwise agreed by the parties, if a party so requests or if the arbitral tribunal considers it necessary, the expert shall, after delivery of his written or oral report, participate in a hearing where the parties have the opportunity to put questions to him and to present expert witnesses in order to testify on the points at issue.

Article 27   Court assistance in taking evidence

The arbitral tribunal or a party with the approval of the arbitral tribunal may request from a competent court of this State assistance in taking evidence. The court may execute the request within its competence and according to its rules on taking evidence.

CHAPTER VI MAKING OF AWARD AND TERMINATION OF PROCEEDINGS

Article 28   Rules applicable to substance of dispute

(1) The arbitral tribunal shall decide the dispute in accordance with such rules of law as are chosen by the parties as applicable to the substance of the dispute. Any designation of the law or legal system of a given State shall be construed, unless otherwise expressed, as directly referring to the substantive law of that State and not to its conflict of laws rules.

(2) Failing any designation by the parties, the arbitral tribunal shall apply the law determined by the conflict of laws rules which it considers applicable.

(3) The arbitral tribunal shall decide *ex aequo et bono* or as *amiable compositeur* only if the parties have expressly authorized it to do so.

(4) In all cases, the arbitral tribunal shall decide in accordance with the terms of the contract and shall take into account the usages of the trade applicable to the transaction.

Article 29   Decision making by panel of arbitrators

In arbitral proceedings with more than one arbitrator, any decision of the arbitral tribunal shall be made, unless otherwise agreed by the parties, by a majority of all its members. However, questions of procedure may be decided by a presiding arbitrator, if so authorized by the parties or all members of the arbitral tribunal.

Article 30   Settlement

(1) If, during arbitral proceedings, the parties settle the dispute, the arbitral tribunal shall terminate the proceedings and, if requested by the parties and not objected to by the arbitral tribunal, record the settlement in the form of an arbitral award on agreed terms.

(2) An award on agreed terms shall be made in accordance with the provisions of article 31 and shall state that it is an award. Such an award has the same status and effect as any other award on the merits of the case.

Article 31 Form and contents of award

(1) The award shall be made in writing and shall be signed by the arbitrator or arbitrators. In arbitral proceedings with more than one arbitrator, the signatures of the majority of all members of the arbitral tribunal shall suffice, provided that the reason for any omitted signature is stated.

(2) The award shall state the reasons upon which it is based, unless the parties have agreed that no reasons are to be given or the award is an award on agreed terms under article 30.

(3) The award shall state its date and the place of arbitration as determined in accordance with article 20(1). The award shall be deemed to have been made at that place.

(4) After the award is made, a copy signed by the arbitrators in accordance with paragraph (1) of this article shall be delivered to each party.

Article 32 Termination of proceedings

(1) The arbitral proceedings are terminated by the final award or by an order of the arbitral tribunal in accordance with paragraph (2) of this article.

(2) The arbitral tribunal shall issue an order for the termination of the arbitral proceedings when:

(a) the claimant withdraws his claim, unless the respondent objects thereto and the arbitral tribunal recognizes a legitimate interest on his part in obtaining a final settlement of the dispute;

(b) the parties agree on the termination of the proceedings;

(c) the arbitral tribunal finds that the continuation of the proceedings has for any other reason become unnecessary or impossible.

(3) The mandate of the arbitral tribunal terminates with the termination of the arbitral proceedings, subject to the provisions of articles 33 and 34(4).

Article 33 Correction and interpretation of award: additional award

(1) Within thirty days of receipt of the award, unless another period of time has been agreed upon by the parties:

(a) a party, with notice to the other party, may request the arbitral tribunal to correct in the award any errors in computation, any clerical or typographical errors or any errors of similar nature;

(b) if so agreed by the parties, a party, with notice to the other party, may request the arbitral tribunal to give an interpretation of a specific point or part of the award.

If the arbitral tribunal considers the request to be justified, it shall make the correction or give the interpretation within thirty days of receipt of the request. The interpretation shall form part of the award.

(2) The arbitral tribunal may correct any error of the type referred to in paragraph (1)(a) of this article on its own initiative within thirty days of the date of the award.

(3) Unless otherwise agreed by the parties, a party, with notice to the other party, may request, within thirty days of receipt of the award, the arbitral

tribunal to make an additional award as to claims presented in the arbitral proceedings but omitted from the award. If the arbitral tribunal considers the request to be justified, it shall make the additional award within sixty days.

(4) The arbitral tribunal may extend, if necessary, the period of time within which it shall make a correction, interpretation or an additional award under paragraph (1) or (3) of this article.

(5) The provisions of article 31 shall apply to a correction or interpretation of the award or to an additional award.

CHAPTER VII RECOURSE AGAINST AWARD

Article 34 Application for setting aside as exclusive recourse against arbitral award

(1) Recourse to a court against an arbitral award may be made only by an application for setting aside in accordance with paragraphs (2) and (3) of this article.

(2) An arbitral award may be set aside by the court specified in article 6 only if:

(a) the party making the application furnishes proof that:

(i) a party to the arbitration agreement referred to in article 7 was under some incapacity; or the said agreement is not valid under the law to which the parties have subjected it or, failing any indication thereon, under the law of this State; or

(ii) the party making the application was not given proper notice of the appointment of an arbitrator or of the arbitral proceedings or was otherwise unable to present his case; or

(iii) the award deals with a dispute not contemplated by or not falling within the terms of the submission to arbitration, or contains decisions on matters beyond the scope of the submission to arbitration, provided that, if the decisions on matters submitted to arbitration can be separated from those not so submitted, only that part of the award which contains decisions on matters not submitted to arbitration may be set aside; or

(iv) the composition of the arbitral tribunal or the arbitral procedure was not in accordance with the agreement of the parties, unless such agreement was in conflict with a provision of this Law from which the parties cannot derogate, or, failing such agreement, was not in accordance with this Law; or

(b) the court finds that:

(i) the subject-matter of the dispute is not capable of settlement by arbitration under the law of this State; or

(ii) the award is in conflict with the public policy of this State.

(3) An application for setting aside may not be made after three months have elapsed from the date on which the party making that application had received the award or, if a request had been made under article 33, from the date on which that request had been disposed of by the arbitral tribunal.

(4) The court, when asked to set aside an award, may, where appropriate

and so requested by a party, suspend the setting aside proceedings for a period of time determined by it in order to give the arbitral tribunal an opportunity to resume the arbitral proceedings or to take such other action as in the arbitral tribunal's opinion will eliminate the grounds for setting aside.

CHAPTER VIII RECOGNITION AND ENFORCEMENT OF AWARDS

Article 35 Recognition and enforcement

(1) An arbitral award, irrespective of the country in which it was made, shall be recognized as binding and, upon application in writing to the competent court, shall be enforced subject to the provisions of this article and of article 36.

(2) The party relying on an award or applying for its enforcement shall supply the duly authenticated original award or a duly certified copy thereof, and the original arbitration agreement referred to in article 7 or a duly certified copy thereof. If the award or agreement is not made in an official language of this State, the party shall supply a duly certified translation thereof into such language.*

Article 36 Grounds for refusing recognition or enforcement

(1) Recognition or enforcement of an arbitral award, irrespective of the country in which it was made, may be refused only:

(a) at the request of the party against whom it is invoked, if that party furnishes to the competent court where recognition or enforcement is sought proof that:

(i) a party to the arbitration agreement referred to in article 7 was under some incapacity; or the said agreement is not valid under the law to which the parties have subjected it or, failing any indication thereon, under the law of the country where the award was made; or;

(ii) the party against whom the award is invoked was not given proper notice of the appointment of an arbitrator or of the arbitral proceedings or was otherwise unable to present his case; or

(iii) the award deals with a dispute not contemplated by or not falling within the terms of the submission to arbitration, or it contains decisions on matters beyond the scope of the submission to arbitration, provided that, if the decisions on matters submitted to arbitration can be separated from those not so submitted, that part of the award which contains decisions on matters submitted to arbitration may be recognized and enforced; or

(iv) the composition of the arbitral tribunal or the arbitral procedure was not in accordance with the agreement of the parties or, failing such

---

* The conditions set forth in this paragraph are intended to set maximum standards. It would, thus, not be contrary to the harmonization to be achieved by the model law if a State retained even less onerous conditions.

agreement, was not in accordance with the law of the country where the arbitration took place; or

(v) the award has not yet become binding on the parties or has been set aside or suspended by a court of the country in which, or under the law of which, that award was made; or

(b) if the court finds that:

(i) the subject-matter of the dispute is not capable of settlement by arbitration under the law of this State; or

(ii) the recognition or enforcement of the award would be contrary to the public policy of this State.

(2) If an application for setting aside or suspension of an award has been made to a court referred to in paragraph (1)(a)(v) of this article, the court where recognition or enforcement is sought may, if it considers it proper, adjourn its decision and may also, on the application of the party claiming recognition or enforcement of the award, order the other party to provide appropriate security.

APPENDIX 4

Arbitration Rules

International Chamber of Commerce Rules of Conciliation and Arbitration*

Conciliation and amended Arbitration Rules in force as from 1 January 1988

Contents

Foreword

Standard ICC Arbitration Clause

Rules of Optional Conciliation

Rules of Arbitration

*Publication no 447.
COPYRIGHT c 1987.
Published by the International Chamber of Commerce, Paris.
Available from: ICC PUBLISHING SA 38, cours Albert ıer, 75008 PARIS or ICC UNITED KINGDOM, Centre Point, 103 New Oxford Street, LONDON WC1A 1QB.

STANDARD ICC ARBITRATION CLAUSE

The ICC recommends that all parties wishing to make reference to ICC arbitration in their contracts use the following standard clause:

English

'All disputes arising in connection with the present contract shall be finally settled under the Rules of Conciliation and Arbitration of the International Chamber of Commerce by one or more arbitrators appointed in accordance with the said Rules.'

French

'Tous différends découlant du présent contrat seront tranchés définitivement suivant le Règlement de Conciliation et d'Arbitrage de la Chambre de Commerce Internationale par un ou plusieurs arbitres nommés conformément à ce Règlement.'

German

'Alle aus dem gegenwärtigen Vertrage sich ergebenden Streitigkeiten werden nach der Vergleichs- und Schiedsgerichtsordnung der Internationalen Handelskammer von einem oder mehreren gemäss dieser Ordnung ernannten Schiedsrichtern endgültig entschieden.'

Spanish

'Todas las desavenencias que deriven de este contrato serán resueltas definitivamente de acuerdo con el Reglamento de Conciliatión y Arbitraje de la Cámara de Comercio Internacional por uno ó más árbitros nombrados conforme a este Reglamento.'

Arabic

جميع الخلافات التى تنشأ عن هذا العقد يتم حسمها نهائيا وفقا لنظام
المصالحة والتحكيم لغرفة التجارة الدولية بواسطة حكم او عدة حكام يتم
تعيينهم طبقا لذلك النظام .

Japanese

この契約に関連して生じるすべての紛争は，ICCの
調停および仲裁規則にしたがい，この規則にもと
づいて選定される1または2以上の仲裁人により，
最終的に解決されるものとする。

Parties are reminded that it may be desirable for them to stipulate in the arbitration clause itself the law governing the contract, the number of arbitrators and the place and language of the arbitration. The parties' free choice of the law governing the contract and of the place and language of the arbitration is not limited by the ICC Rules of Arbitration.

Attention is called to the fact that the laws of certain countries require that parties to contracts expressly accept arbitration clauses, sometimes in a precise and particular manner.

RULES OF OPTIONAL CONCILIATION

Preamble

Settlement is a desirable solution for business disputes of an international character.

The International Chamber of Commerce therefore sets out these Rules of Optional Conciliation in order to facilitate the amicable settlement of such disputes.

Article 1

All business disputes of an international character may be submitted to conciliation by a sole conciliator appointed by the International Chamber of Commerce.

Article 2

The party requesting conciliation shall apply to the Secretariat of the Court of the International Chamber of Commerce setting out succinctly the purpose of the request and accompanying it with the fee required to open the file, as set out in Appendix III hereto.

Article 3

The Secretariat of the Court shall, as soon as possible, inform the other party of the request for conciliation. That party will be given a period of 15 days to inform the Secretariat whether it agrees or declines to participate in the attempt to conciliate.

If the other party agrees to participate in the attempt to conciliate it shall so inform the Secretariat within such period.

In the absence of any reply within such period or in the case of a negative reply the request for conciliation shall be deemed to have been declined. The Secretariat shall, as soon as possible, so inform the party which had requested conciliation.

Article 4

Upon receipt of an agreement to attempt conciliation, the Secretary General of the Court shall appoint a conciliator as soon as possible. The conciliator shall inform the parties of his appointment and set a time-limit for the parties to present their respective arguments to him.

Article 5

The conciliator shall conduct the conciliation process as he thinks fit, guided by the principles of impartiality, equity and justice.

With the agreement of the parties, the conciliator shall fix the place for conciliation.

The conciliator may at any time during the conciliation process request a party to submit to him such additional information as he deems necessary.

The parties may, if they so wish, be assisted by counsel of their choice.

Article 6

The confidential nature of the conciliation process shall be respected by every person who is involved in it in whatever capacity.

Article 7

The conciliaton process shall come to an end:

(a) Upon the parties signing an agreement. The parties shall be bound by such agreement. The agreement shall remain confidential unless and to the extent that its execution or application require disclosure.

(b) Upon the production by the conciliator of a report recording that the attempt to conciliate has not been successful. Such report shall not contain reasons.

(c) Upon notification to the conciliator by one or more parties at any time during the conciliation process of an intention no longer to pursue the conciliation process.

Article 8

Upon termination of the conciliation, the conciliator shall provide the Secretariat of the Court with the settlement agreement signed by the parties or with his report of lack of success or with a notice from one or more parties of the intention no longer to pursue the conciliation process.

Article 9

Upon the file being opened, the Secretariat of the Court shall fix the sum required to permit the process to proceed, taking into consideration the nature and importance of the dispute. Such sum shall be paid in equal shares by the parties.

The sum shall cover the estimated fees of the conciliator, expenses of the conciliation, and the administrative expenses as set out in Appendix III hereto.

In any case where, in the course of the conciliation process, the Secretariat of the Court shall decide that the sum originally paid is insufficient to cover the likely total costs of the conciliation, the Secretariat shall require the provision of an additional amount which shall be paid in equal shares by the parties.

Upon termination of the conciliation, the Secretariat shall settle the total costs of the process and advise the parties in writing.

All the above costs shall be borne in equal shares by the parties except and insofar as a settlement agreement provides otherwise.

A party's other expenditures shall remain the responsibility of that party.

Article 10

Unless the parties agree otherwise, a conciliator shall not act in any judicial or arbitration proceeding relating to the dispute which has been the subject of the conciliation process whether as an arbitrator, representative or counsel of a party.

The parties mutually undertake not to call the conciliator as a witness in any such proceedings, unless otherwise agreed between them.

Article 11

The parties agree not to introduce in any judicial or arbitration proceeding as evidence or in any manner whatsoever:

(a) any views expressed or suggestions made by any party with regard to the possible settlement of the dispute;

(b) any proposals put forward by the conciliator;

(c) the fact that a party had indicated that it was ready to accept some proposal for a settlement put forward by the conciliator.

RULES OF ARBITRATION

Article 1   Court of Arbitration

1 The Court of Arbitration of the International Chamber of Commerce is the international arbitration body attached to the International Chamber of

Commerce. Members of the Court are appointed by the Council of the International Chamber of Commerce. The function of the Court is to provide for the settlement by arbitration of business disputes of an international character in accordance with these Rules.

2   In principle, the Court meets once a month. It draws up its own internal regulations.

3   The Chairman of the Court of Arbitration or his deputy shall have power to take urgent decisions on behalf of the Court, provided that any such decision shall be reported to the Court at its next session.

4   The Court may, in the manner provided for in its internal regulations, delegate to one or more groups of its members the power to take certain decisions provided that any such decision shall be reported to the Court at its next session.

5   The Secretariat of the Court of Arbitration shall be at the Headquarters of the International Chamber of Commerce.

Article 2   The arbitral tribunal

1   The Court of Arbitration does not itself settle disputes. Insofar as the parties shall not have provided otherwise, it appoints, or confirms the appointments of, arbitrators in accordance with the provisions of this Article. In making or confirming such appointment, the Court shall have regard to the proposed arbitrator's nationality, residence and other relationships with the countries of which the parties or the other arbitrators are nationals.

2   The disputes may be settled by a sole arbitrator or by three arbitrators. In the following Articles the word 'arbitrator' denotes a single arbitrator or three arbitrators as the case may be.

3   Where the parties have agreed that the disputes shall be settled by a sole arbitrator, they may, by agreement, nominate him for confirmation by the Court. If the parties fail so to nominate a sole arbitrator within 30 days from the date when the Claimant's Request for Arbitration has been communicated to the other party, the sole arbitrator shall be appointed by the Court.

4   Where the dispute is to be referred to three arbitrators, each party shall nominate in the Request for Arbitration and the Answer thereto respectively one arbitrator for confirmation by the Court. Such person shall be independent of the party nominating him. If a party fails to nominate an arbitrator, the appointment shall be made by the Court.

The third arbitrator, who will act as chairman of the arbitral tribunal, shall be appointed by the Court, unless the parties have provided that the arbitrators nominated by them shall agree on the third arbitrator within a fixed time-limit. In such a case the Court shall confirm the appointment of such third arbitrator. Should the two arbitrators fail, within the time-limit fixed by the parties or the Court, to reach agreement on the third arbitrator, he shall be appointed by the Court.

5   Where the parties have not agreed upon the number of arbitrators, the court shall appoint a sole arbitrator, save where it appears to the Court that the dispute is such as to warrant the appointment of three arbitrators. In such a case

the parties shall each have a period of 30 days within which to nominate an arbitrator.

6   Where the Court is to appoint a sole arbitrator or the chairman of an arbitral tribunal, it shall make the appointment after having requested a proposal from a National Committee of the ICC that it considers to be appropriate. If the Court does not accept the proposal made, or if said National Committee fails to make the proposal requested within the time-limit fixed by the Court, the Court may repeat its request or may request a proposal from another appropriate National Committee.

Where the Court considers that the circumstances so demand, it may choose the sole arbitrator or the chairman of the arbitral tribunal from a country where there is no National Committee, provided that neither of the parties objects within the time-limit fixed by the Court.

The sole arbitrator or the chairman of the arbitral tribunal shall be chosen from a country other than those of which the parties are nationals. However, in suitable circumstances and provided that neither of the parties objects within the time-limit fixed by the Court, the sole arbitrator or the chairman of the arbitral tribunal may be chosen from a country of which any of the parties is a national.

Where the Court is to appoint an arbitrator on behalf of a party which has failed to nominate one, it shall make the appointment after having requested a proposal from the National Committee of the country of which the said party is a national. If the Court does not accept the proposal made, or if said National Committee fails to make the proposal requested within the time-limit fixed by the Court, or if the country of which the said party is a national has no National Committee, the Court shall be at liberty to choose any person whom it regards as suitable, after having informed the National Committee of the country of which such person is a national, if one exists.

7   Every arbitrator appointed or confirmed by the Court must be and remain independent of the parties involved in the arbitration.

Before appointment or confirmation by the Court, a prospective arbitrator shall disclose in writing to the Secretary General of the Court any facts or circumstances which might be of such a nature as to call into question the arbitrator's independence in the eyes of the parties. Upon receipt of such information, the Secretary General of the Court shall provide it to the parties in writing and fix a time-limit for any comments from them.

An arbitrator shall immediately disclose in writing to the Secretary General of the Court and the parties any facts or circumstances of a similar nature which may arise between the arbitrator's appointment or confirmation by the Court and the notification of the final award.

8   A challenge of an arbitrator, whether for an alleged lack of independence or otherwise, is made by the submission to the Secretary General of the Court of a written statement specifying the facts and circumstances on which the challenge is based.

For a challenge to be admissible, it must be sent by a party either within 30 days from receipt by that party of the notification of the appointment or confirmation of the arbitrator by the Court; or within 30 days from the date when the party making the challenge was informed of the facts and circumstances on which the challenge is based, if such date is subsequent to the receipt of the aforementioned notification.

9   The Court shall decide on the admissibility, and at the same time if need be on the merits, of a challenge after the Secretary General of the Court has accorded an opportunity for the arbitrator concerned, the parties and any other members of the arbitral tribunal to comment in writing within a suitable period of time.

10   An arbitrator shall be replaced upon his death, upon the acceptance by the Court of a challenge, or upon the acceptance by the Court of the arbitrator's resignation.

11   An arbitrator shall also be replaced when the Court decides that he is prevented *de jure* or *de facto* from fulfilling his functions, or that he is not fulfilling his functions in accordance with the Rules or within the prescribed time-limits.

When, on the basis of information that has come to its attention, the Court considers applying the preceding subparagraph, it shall decide on the matter after the Secretary General of the Court has provided such information in writing to the arbitrator concerned, the parties and any other members of the arbitral tribunal, and accorded an oppportunity to them to comment in writing within a suitable period of time.

12   In each instance where an arbitrator is to be replaced, the procedure indicated in the preceding paragraphs 3, 4, 5 and 6 shall be followed. Once reconstituted, and after having invited the parties to comment, the arbitral tribunal shall determine if and to what extent prior proceedings shall again take place.

13   Decisions of the Court as to the appointment, confirmation, challenge or replacement of an arbitrator shall be final.

The reasons for decisions by the Court as to the appointment, confirmation, challenge, or replacement of an arbitrator on the grounds that he is not fulfilling his functions in accordance with the Rules or within the prescribed time-limits, shall not be communicated.

Article 3   Request for Arbitration

1   A party wishing to have recourse to arbitration by the International Chamber of Commerce shall submit its Request for Arbitration to the Secretariat of the Court, through its National Committee or directly. In this latter case the Secretariat shall bring the Request to the notice of the National Committee concerned.

The date when the Request is received by the Secretariat of the Court shall, for all purposes, be deemed to be the date of commencement of the arbitral proceedings.

2   The Request for Arbitration shall *inter alia* contain the following information :

(a)   names in full, description, and addresses of the parties,

(b)   a statement of the Claimant's case,

(c)   the relevant agreements, and in particular the agreement to arbitrate, and such documentation or information as will serve clearly to establish the circumstances of the case,

(d)   all relevant particulars concerning the number of arbitrators and their choice in accordance with the provisions of Article 2 above.

3   The Secretariat shall send a copy of the Request and the documents annexed thereto to the Defendant for his Answer.

Article 4 Answer to the Request

1 The Defendant shall within 30 days from the receipt of the documents referred to in paragraph 3 of Article 3 comment on the proposals made concerning the number of arbitrators and their choice and, where appropriate, nominate an arbitrator. He shall at the same time set out his defence and supply relevant documents. In exceptional circumstances the Defendant may apply to the Secretariat for an extension of time for the filing of his defence and his documents. The application must, however, include the Defendant's comments on the proposals made with regard to the number of arbitrators and their choice and also, where appropriate, the nomination of an arbitrator. If the Defendant fails so to do, the Secretariat shall report to the Court, which shall proceed with the arbitration in accordance with these Rules.

2 A copy of the Answer and of the documents annexed thereto, if any, shall be communicated to the Claimant for his information.

Article 5 Counter-claim

1 If the Defendant wishes to make a counter-claim, he shall file the same with the Secretariat, at the same time as his Answer as provided for in Article 4.

2 It shall be open to the Claimant to file a Reply with the Secretariat within 30 days from the date when the counter-claim was communicated to him.

Article 6 Pleadings and written statements, notifications or communications

1 All pleadings and written statements submitted by the parties, as well as all documents annexed thereto, shall be supplied in a number of copies sufficient to provide one copy for each party, plus one for each arbitrator, and one for the Secretariat.

2 All notifications or communications from the Secretariat and the arbitrator shall be validly made if they are delivered against receipt or forwarded by registered post to the address or last known address of the party for whom the same are intended as notified by the party in question or by the other party as appropriate.

3 Notification or communication shall be deemed to have been effected on the day when it was received, or should, if made in accordance with the preceding paragraph, have been received by the party itself or by its representative.

4 Periods of time specified in the present Rules or in the Internal Rules or set by the Court pursuant to its authority under any of these Rules shall start to run on the day following the date a notification or communication is deemed to have been effected in accordance with the preceding paragraph. When, in the country where the notification or communication is deemed to have been effected, the day next following such date is an official holiday or a non-business day, the period of time shall commence on the first following working day. Official holidays and non-working days are included in the calculation of the period of time. If the last day of the relevant period of time granted is an official holiday or a non-business day in the country where the notification or communication is deemed to have been effected, the period of time shall expire at the end of the first following working day.

Article 7   Absence of agreement to arbitrate

Where there is no prima facie agreement between the parties to arbitrate or where there is an agreement but it does not specify the International Chamber of Commerce, and if the Defendant does not file an Answer within the period of 30 days provided by paragraph 1 of Article 4 or refuses arbitration by the International Chamber of Commerce, the Claimant shall be informed that the arbitration cannot proceed.

Article 8   Effect of the agreement to arbitrate

1   Where the parties have agreed to submit to arbitration by the International Chamber of Commerce, they shall be deemed thereby to have submitted *ipso facto* to the present Rules.

2   If one of the parties refuses or fails to take part in the arbitration, the arbitration shall proceed notwithstanding such refusal or failure.

3   Should one of the parties raise one or more pleas concerning the existence or validity of the agreement to arbitrate, and should the Court be satisfied of the prima facie existence of such an agreement, the Court may, without prejudice to the admissibility or merits of the plea or pleas, decide that the arbitration shall proceed. In such a case any decision as to the arbitrator's jurisdiction shall be taken by the arbitrator himself.

4   Unless otherwise provided, the arbitrator shall not cease to have jurisdiction by reason of any claim that the contract is null and void or allegation that it is inexistent provided that he upholds the validity of the agreement to arbitrate. He shall continue to have jurisdiction, even though the contract itself may be inexistent or null and void, to determine the respective rights of the parties and to adjudicate upon their claims and pleas.

5   Before the file is transmitted to the arbitrator, and in exceptional circumstances even thereafter, the parties shall be at liberty to apply to any competent judicial authority for interim or conservatory measures, and they shall not by so doing be held to infringe the agreement to arbitrate or to affect the relevant powers reserved to the arbitrator.

Any such application and any measures taken by the judicial authority must be notified without delay to the Secretariat of the Court of Arbitration. The Secretariat shall inform the arbitrator thereof.

Article 9   Advance to cover costs of arbitration

1   The Court shall fix the amount of the advance on costs in a sum likely to cover the costs of arbitration of the claims which have been referred to it.

Where, apart from the principal claim, one or more counter-claims are submitted, the Court may fix separate advances on costs for the principal claim and the counter-claim or counter-claims.

2   The advance on costs shall be payable in equal shares by the Claimant or Claimants and the Defendant or Defendants. However, any one party shall be free to pay the whole of the advance on costs in respect of the claim or the counter-claim should the other party fail to pay its share.

3   The Secretariat may make the transmission of the file to the arbitrator conditional upon the payment by the parties or one of them of the whole or part of the advance on costs to the International Chamber of Commerce.

4   When the Terms of Reference are communicated to the Court in accordance with the provisions of Article 13, the Court shall verify whether the requests for the advance on costs have been complied with.

The Terms of Reference shall only become operative and the arbitrator shall only proceed in respect of those claims for which the advance on costs has been duly paid to the International Chamber of Commerce.

Article 10   Transmission of the file to the arbitrator

Subject to the provisions of Article 9, the Secretariat shall transmit the file to the arbitrator as soon as it has received the Defendant's Answer to the Request for Arbitration, at the latest upon the expiry of the time-limits fixed in Articles 4 and 5 above for the filing of these documents.

Article 11   Rules governing the proceedings

The rules governing the proceedings befor the arbitrator shall be those resulting from these Rules and, where these Rules are silent, any rules which the parties (or, failing them, the arbitrator) may settle, and whether or not reference is thereby made to a municipal procedural law to be applied to the arbitration.

Article 12   Place of arbitration

The place of arbitration shall be fixed by the Court, unless agreed upon by the parties.

Article 13   Terms of Reference

1   Before proceeding with the preparation of the case, the arbitrator shall draw up, on the basis of the documents or in the presence of the parties and in the light of their most recent submissions, a document defining his Terms of Reference. This document shall include the following particulars:

(a)   the full names and description of the parties,

(b)   the addresses of the parties to which notifications or communications arising in the course of the arbitration may validly be made,

(c)   a summary of the parties' respective claims,

(d)   definition of the issues to be determined,

(e)   the arbitrator's full name, description and address,

(f)   the place of arbitration,

(g)   particulars of the applicable procedural rules and, if such is the case, reference to the power conferred upon the arbitrator to act as amiable compositeur,

(h)   such other particulars as may be required to make the arbitral award enforceable in law, or may be regarded as helpful by the Court of Arbitration or the arbitrator.

2   The document mentioned in paragraph 1 of this Article shall be signed by the parties and the arbitrator. Within two months of the date when the file has been transmitted to him, the arbitrator shall transmit to the Court the said document signed by himself and by the parties. The Court may, pursuant to a reasoned request from the arbitrator or if need be on its own initiative, extend this time-limit if it decides it is necessary to do so.

Should one of the parties refuse to take part in the drawing up of the said document or to sign the same, the Court, if it is satisfied that the case is one of those mentioned in paragraphs 2 and 3 of Article 8, shall take such action as is necessary for its approval. Thereafter the Court shall set a time-limit for the signature of the statement by the defaulting party and on expiry of that time-limit the arbitration shall proceed and the award shall be made.

3 The parties shall be free to determine the law to be applied by the arbitrator to the merits of the dispute. In the absence of any indication by the parties as to the applicable law, the arbitrator shall apply the law designated as the proper law by the rule of conflict which he deems appropriate.

4 The arbitrator shall assume the powers of an amiable compositeur if the parties are agreed to give him such powers.

5 In all cases the arbitrator shall take account of the provisions of the contract and the relevant trade usages.

Article 14   The arbitral proceedings

1 The arbitrator shall proceed within as short a time as possible to establish the facts of the case by all appropriate means. After study of the written submissions of the parties and of all documents relied upon, the arbitrator shall hear the parties together in person if one of them so requests; and failing such a request he may of his own motion decide to hear them.

In addition, the arbitrator may decide to hear any other person in the presence of the parties or in their absence provided they have been duly summoned.

2 The arbitrator may appoint one or more experts, define their Terms of Reference, receive their reports and/or hear them in person.

3 The arbitrator may decide the case on the relevant documents alone if the parties so request or agree.

Article 15

1 At the request of one of the parties or if necessary on his own initiative, the arbitrator, giving reasonable notice, shall summon the parties to appear before him on the day and at the place appointed by him and shall so inform the Secretariat of the Court.

2 If one of the parties, although duly summoned, fails to appear, the arbitrator, if he is satisfied that the summons was duly received and the party is absent without valid excuse, shall have power to proceed with the arbitration, and such proceedings shall be deemed to have been conducted in the presence of all parties.

3 The arbitrator shall determine the language or languages of the arbitration, due regard being paid to all the relevant circumstances and in particular to the language of the contract.

4 The arbitrator shall be in full charge of the hearings, at which all the parties shall be entitled to be present. Save with the approval of the arbitrator and of the parties, persons not involved in the proceedings shall not be admitted.
5 The parties may appear in person or through duly accredited agents. In addition, they may be assisted by advisers.

Article 16

The parties may make new claims or counter-claims before the arbitrator on condition that these remain within the limits fixed by the Terms of Reference provided for in Article 13 or that they are specified in a rider to that document, signed by the parties and communicated to the Court.

Article 17   Award by consent

If the parties reach a settlement after the file has been transmitted to the arbitrator in accordance with Article 10, the same shall be recorded in the form of an arbitral award made by consent of the parties.

Article 18   Time-limit for award

1 The time-limit within which the arbitrator must render his award is fixed at six months. Once the terms of Article 9 (4) have been satisfied, such time-limit shall start to run from the date of the last signature by the arbitrator or of the parties of the document mentioned in Article 13, or from the expiry of the time-limit granted to a party by virtue of Article 13 (2), or from the date that the Secretary General of the Court notifies the arbitrator that the advance on costs is paid in full, if such notification occurs later.
2 The Court may, pursuant to a reasoned request from the arbitrator or if need be on its own initiative, extend this time-limit if it decides it is necessary to do so.
3 Where no such extension is granted and, if appropriate, after application of the provisions of Article 2(11), the Court shall determine the manner in which the dispute is to be resolved.

Article 19   Award by three arbitrators

When three arbitrators have been appointed, the award is given by a majority decision. If there be no majority, the award shall be made by the Chairman of the arbitral tribunal alone.

Article 20   Decision as to costs of arbitration

1 The arbitrator's award shall, in addition to dealing with the merits of the case, fix the costs of the arbitration and decide which of the parties shall bear the costs or in what proportions the costs shall be borne by the parties.
2 The costs of the arbitration shall include the arbitrator's fees and the

administrative costs fixed by the Court in accordance with the scale annexed to the present Rules, the expenses, if any, of the arbitrator, the fees and expenses of any experts, and the normal legal costs incurred by the parties.

3 The Court may fix the arbitrator's fees at a figure higher or lower than that which would result from the application of the annexed scale if in the exceptional circumstances of the case this appears to be necessary.

Article 21   Scrutiny of award by the Court

Before signing an award, whether partial or definitive, the arbitrator shall submit it in draft form to the Court. The Court may lay down modifications as to the form of the award and, without affecting the arbitrator's liberty of decision, may also draw his attention to points of substance. No award shall be signed until it has been approved by the Court as to its form.

Article 22   Making of award

The arbitral award shall be deemed to be made at the place of the arbitration proceedings and on the date when it is signed by the arbitrator.

Article 23   Notification of award to parties

1 Once an award has been made, the Secretariat shall notify to the parties the text signed by the arbitrator; provided always that the costs of the arbitration have been fully paid to the International Chamber of Commerce by the parties or by one of them.

2 Additional copies certified true by the Secretary General of the Court shall be made available, on request and at any time, to the parties but to no one else.

3 By virtue of the notification made in accordance with paragraph 1 of this article, the parties waive any other form of notification or deposit on the part of the arbitrator.

Article 24   Finality and enforceability of award

1 The arbitral award shall be final.

2 By submitting the dispute to arbitration by the International Chamber of Commerce, the parties shall be deemed to have undertaken to carry out the resulting award without delay and to have waived their right to any form of appeal insofar as such waiver can validly be made.

Article 25   Deposit of award

An original of each award made in accordance with the present Rules shall be deposited with the Secretariat of the Court.

The arbitrator and the Secretariat of the Court shall assist the parties in complying with whatever further formalities may be necessary.

Article 26   General rule

In all matters not expressly provided for in these Rules, the Court of Arbitration and the arbitrator shall act in the spirit of these Rules and shall make every effort to make sure that the award is enforceable at law.

APPENDIX I – STATUTES OF THE COURT

Article 1   Appointment of members

The members of the Court of Arbitration of the International Chamber of Commerce are appointed for a term of three years by the Council of that Chamber pursuant to Article 5.3i of the Constitution, on the proposal of each National Committee.

Article 2   Composition

The Court of Arbitration shall be composed of a Chairman, of eight Vice-Chairmen, of a Secretary General and of one or several Technical Advisers chosen by the Council of the International Chamber of Commerce either from among the members of the Court or apart from them, and of one member for, and appointed by, each National Committee.

The chairmanship may be exercised by two Co-Chairmen; in this case, they shall have equal rights, and the expression 'the Chairman', used in the Rules of Conciliation and Arbitration, shall apply to either of them equally.

When a member of the Court does not reside in the city where International Headquarters of the International Chamber of Commerce is situated, the Council may appoint an alternate member.

If the Chairman is unable to attend a session of the Court, he shall be replaced by one of the Vice-Chairmen.

Article 3   Function and powers

The function of the Court of Arbitration is to ensure the application of the Rules of Conciliation and Arbitration of the International Chamber of Commerce, and the Court has all the necessary powers for that purpose. It is further entrusted, if need be, with laying before the Commission on International Arbitration any proposals for modifying the Rules of Conciliation and Arbitration of the International Chamber of Commerce which it considers necessary.

Article 4   Deliberations and quorum

The decisions of the Court shall be taken by a majority vote, the Chairman having a casting vote in the event of a tie. The deliberations of the Court shall be valid when at least six members are present.

The Secretary General of the International Chamber of Commerce, the

Secretary General of the Court and the Technical Adviser or Advisers shall attend in an advisory capacity only.

APPENDIX II – INTERNAL RULES OF THE COURT OF ARBITRATION

Role of the Court of Arbitration

1 The Court of Arbitration may accept jurisdiction over business disputes not of an international business nature, if it has jurisdiction by reason of an arbitration agreement.

Confidential character of the work of the Court of Arbitration

2 The work of the Court of Arbitration is of a confidential character which must be respected by everyone who participates in that work in whatever capacity.

3 The sessions of the Court of Arbitration, whether plenary or those of a Committee of the Court, are open only to its members and to the Secretariat.

However, in exceptional circumstances and, if need be, after obtaining the opinion of members of the Court, the Chairman of the Court of Arbitration may invite honorary members of the Court and authorize observers to attend. Such persons must respect the confidential character of the work of the Court.

4 The documents submitted to the Court of Arbitration or drawn up by it in the course of the proceedings it conducts are communicated only to the members of the Court and to the Secretariat.

The Chairman or the Secretary General of the Court may nevertheless authorize researchers undertaking work of a scientific nature on international trade law to acquaint themselves with certain documents of general interest, with the exception of memoranda, notes, statements and documents remitted by the parties within the framework of arbitration proceedings.

Such authorization shall not be given unless the beneficiary has undertaken to respect the confidential character of the documents made available and to refrain from any publication in their respect without having previously submitted the text for approval to the Secretary General of the Court.

Participation of members of the Court of Arbitration in ICC arbitration

5 Owing to the special responsibilities laid upon them by the ICC Rules of Arbitration, the Chairman, the Vice-Chairmen and the Secretariat of the Court of Arbitration may not personally act as arbitrators or as counsel in cases submitted to ICC arbitration.

The members of the Court of Arbitration may not be directly appointed as co-arbitrators, sole arbitrator or Chairman of an arbitral tribunal by the Court of Arbitration. They may however be proposed for such duties by one or more of the parties, subject to confirmation by the Court.

6 When the Chairman, a Vice-Chairman or a member of the Court of Arbitration is involved, in any capacity whatsoever, in proceedings pending before the Court, he must inform the Secretary General of the Court as soon as he becomes aware of such involvement.

He must refrain from participating in the discussions or in the decisions of the Court concerning the proceedings and he must be absent from the courtroom whenever the matter is considered.

He will not receive documentation or information submitted to the Court of Arbitration during the proceedings.

Relations between the members of the Court and the ICC National Committees

7 By virtue of their capacity, the members of the Court are independent of the ICC National Committees which proposed them for nomination by the ICC Council.

Furthermore, they must regard as confidential, vis-à-vis the said National Committees, any information concerning individual disputes with which they have become acquainted in their capacity as members of the Court except when they have been requested, by the Chairman of the Court or by its Secretary General, to communicate that information to their respective National Committees.

Committee of the Court

8 In accordance with the provisions of Article 1 (4) of the ICC Rules of Arbitration, the Court of Arbitration hereby establishes a Committee of the Court composed as follows, and with the following powers.

9 The Committee consists of a Chairman and two members. The Chairman of the Court of Arbitration acts as the Chairman of the Committee. He may nevertheless designate a Vice-Chairman of the Court to replace him during a session of the Committee.

The other two members of the Committee are appointed by the Court of Arbitration from among the Vice-Chairmen or the other members of the Court. At each meeting of the Court it appoints the members who are to attend the meeting of the Committee to be held before the next plenary session of the Court.

10 The Committee meets when convened by its Chairman, in principle twice a month.

11 (a) The Committee is empowered to take any decision within the jurisdiction of the Court of Arbitration, with the exception of decisions concerning challenges of arbitrators (Arts. 2 (8) and 2 (9) of the ICC Rules of Arbitration), allegations that an arbitrator is not fulfilling his functions (Art. 2 (11) of the ICC Rules of Arbitration) and approval of draft awards other than awards made with the consent of the parties.

(b) The decisions of the Committee are taken unanimously.

(c) When the Committee cannot reach a decision or deems it preferable to abstain, it transfers the case to the next plenary session of the Court of Arbitration, making any suggestions it deems appropriate.

(d) The Committee's proceedings are brought to the notice of the Court of Arbitration at its next plenary session.

Absence of an arbitration agreement

12 Where there is no *prima facie* arbitration agreement between the parties or where there is an agreement but it does not specify the ICC, the Secretariat draws the attention of the Claimant to the provisions laid down in Article 7 of the Rules of Arbitration. The Claimant is entitled to require the decision to be taken by the Court of Arbitration.

This decision is of an administrative nature. If the Court decides that the arbitration solicited by the Claimant cannot proceed, the parties retain the right to ask the competent jurisdiction whether or not they are bound by an arbitration agreement in the light of the law applicable.

If the Court of Arbitration considers *prima facie* that the proceedings may take place, the arbitrator appointed has the duty to decide as to his own jurisdiction and, where such jurisdiction exists, as to the merits of the dispute.

Joinder of claims in arbitration proceedings

13 When a party presents a Request for Arbitration in connection with a legal relationship already submitted to arbitration proceedings by the same parties and pending before the Court of Arbitration, the Court may decide to include that claim in the existing proceedings, subject to the provisions of Article 16 of the ICC Rules of Arbitration.

Advances to cover costs of arbitration

14 When the Court of Arbitration has set separate advances on costs for a specific case in accordance with Article 9 (1) (sub-para. 2) of the ICC Rules of Arbitration, the Secretariat requests each of the parties to pay the amount corresponding to its claims without prejudice to the right of the parties to pay the said advances on costs in equal shares, if they deem it advisable.

15 When a request for an advance on costs has not been complied with, the Secretariat may set a time-limit, which must not be less than 30 days, on the expiry of which the relevant claim, whether principal claim or counter-claim, shall be considered as withdrawn. This does not prevent the party in question from lodging a new claim at a later date.

Should one of the parties wish to object to this measure, he must make a request, within the aforementioned period, for the matter to be decided by the Court of Arbitration.

16 If one of the parties claims a right to a set-off with regard to either a principal claim or counter-claim, such set-off is taken into account in determining the advance to cover the costs of arbitration, in the same way as a separate claim, insofar as it may require the arbitrators to consider additional matters.

Arbitral awards : form

17 When it scrutinizes draft arbitral awards in accordance with Article 21 of the ICC Rules of Arbitration, the Court of Arbitration pays particular attention to the respect of the formal requirements laid down by the law applicable to the proceedings and, where relevant, by the mandatory rules of the place of arbitration, notably with regard to the reasons for awards, their signature and the admissibility of dissenting opinions.

Arbitrators' fees

18   In setting the arbitrators' fees on the basis of the scale attached to the ICC Rules of Arbitration, the Court of Arbitration takes into consideration the time spent, the rapidity of the proceedings and the complexity of the dispute, so as to arrive at a figure within the limits specified or, when circumstances require, higher or lower than those limits (Art. 20 (3) of the ICC Rules of Arbitration).

APPENDIX III – SCHEDULE OF CONCILIATION AND ARBITRATION COSTS

[*Not reproduced in this work*]

UNCITRAL Arbitration Rules

Contents

GENERAL ASSEMBLY RESOLUTION 31/98
UNCITRAL ARBITRATION RULES

Correction of the award (article 36)
Additional award (article 37)
Costs (articles 38 to 40)
Deposit of costs (article 41)

Resolution 31/98 adopted by the General Assembly on 15 December 1976

31/98. Arbitration Rules of the United Nations Commission on International Trade Law

The General Assembly,

Recognizing the value of arbitration as a method of settling disputes arising in the context of international commercial relations,

Being convinced that the establishment of rules for *ad hoc* arbitration that are acceptable in countries with different legal, social and economic systems would significantly contribute to the development of harmonious international economic relations,

Bearing in mind that the Arbitration Rules of the United Nations Commission on International Trade Law have been prepared after extensive consultation with arbitral institutions and centres of international commercial arbitration,

Noting that the Arbitration Rules were adopted by the United Nations Commission on International Trade Law at its ninth session[1] after due deliberation,

1 *Recommends* the use of the Arbitration Rules of the United Nations Commission on International Trade Law in the settlement of disputes arising in the context of international commercial relations, particularly by reference to the Arbitration Rules in commercial contracts,

2 *Requests* the Secretary-General to arrange for the widest possible distribution of the Arbitration Rules.

SECTION I INTRODUCTORY RULES

Scope of application

Article 1

1 Where the parties to a contract have agreed in writing* that disputes in relation to that contract shall be referred to arbitration under the UNCITRAL

---

[1] *Official Records of the General Assembly, Thirty-first Session, Supplement No 17* (A/31/17), chap. V, sect. C.

* *MODEL ARBITRATION CLAUSE*
  Any dispute, controversy or claim arising out of or relating to this contract, or the breach,

Arbitration Rules, then such disputes shall be settled in accordance with these Rules subject to such modification as the parties may agree in writing.

2 These Rules shall govern the arbitration except that where any of these Rules is in conflict with a provision of the law applicable to the arbitration from which the parties cannot derogate, that provision shall prevail.

Notice, calculation of periods of time

Article 2

1 For the purposes of these Rules, any notice, including a notification, communication or proposal, is deemed to have been received if it is physically delivered to the addressee or if it is delivered at his habitual residence, place of business or mailing address, or, if none of these can be found after making reasonable inquiry, then at the addressee's last-known residence or place of business. Notice shall be deemed to have been received on the day it is so delivered.

2 For the purposes of calculating a period of time under these Rules, such period shall begin to run on the day following the day when a notice, notification, communication or proposal is received. If the last day of such period is an official holiday or a non-business day at the residence or place of business of the addressee, the period is extended until the first business day which follows. Official holidays or non-business days occurring during the running of the period of time are included in calculating the period.

Notice of arbitration

Article 3

1 The party initiating recourse to arbitration (hereinafter called the 'claimant') shall give to the other party (hereinafter called the 'respondent') a notice of arbitration.

2 Arbitral proceedings shall be deemed to commence on the date on which the notice of arbitration is received by the respondent.

3 The notice of arbitration shall include the following:

(a) A demand that the dispute be referred to arbitration;

(b) The names and addresses of the parties;

---

termination or invalidity thereof, shall be settled by arbitration in accordance with the UNCITRAL Arbitration Rules as at present in force.

Note – Parties may wish to consider adding:

(a) The appointing authority shall be ... (name of institution or person);

(b) The number of arbitrators shall be ... (one or three);

(c) The place of arbitration shall be ... (town or country);

(d) The language(s) to be used in the arbitral proceedings shall be ...

(c) A reference to the arbitration clause or the separate arbitration agreement that is invoked;

(d) A reference to the contract out of or in relation to which the dispute arises;

(e) The general nature of the claim and an indication of the amount involved, if any;

(f) The relief or remedy sought;

(g) A proposal as to the number of arbitrators (i.e. one or three), if the parties have not previously agreed thereon.

4 The notice of arbitration may also include:

(a) The proposals for the appointments of a sole arbitrator and an appointing authority referred to in article 6, paragraph 1;

(b) The notification of the appointment of an arbitrator referred to in article 7;

(c) The statement of claim referred to in article 18.

Representation and assistance

Article 4

The parties may be represented or assisted by persons of their choice. The names and addresses of such persons must be communicated in writing to the other party; such communication must specify whether the appointment is being made for purposes of representation or assistance.

SECTION II COMPOSITION OF THE ARBITRAL TRIBUNAL

Number of arbitrators

Article 5

If the parties have not previously agreed on the number of arbitrators (ie one or three), and if within fifteen days after the receipt by the respondent of the notice of arbitration the parties have not agreed that there shall be only one arbitrator, three arbitrators shall be appointed.

Appointment of arbitrators (articles 6 to 8)

Article 6

1 If a sole arbitrator is to be appointed, either party may propose to the other:

(a) The names of one or more persons, one of whom would serve as the sole arbitrator; and

(b) If no appointing authority has been agreed upon by the parties, the name or names of one or more institutions or persons, one of whom would serve as appointing authority.

2 If within thirty days after receipt by a party of a proposal made in

accordance with paragraph 1 the parties have not reached agreement on the choice of a sole arbitrator, the sole arbitrator shall be appointed by the appointing authority agreed upon by the parties. If no appointing authority has been agreed upon by the parties, or if the appointing authority agreed upon refuses to act or fails to appoint the arbitrator within sixty days of the receipt of a party's request therefor, either party may request the Secretary-General of the Permanent Court of Arbitration at The Hague to designate an appointing authority.

3 The appointing authority shall, at the request of one of the parties, appoint the sole arbitrator as promptly as possible. In making the appointment the appointing authority shall use the following list-procedure, unless both parties agree that the list-procedure should not be used or unless the appointing authority determines in its discretion that the use of the list-procedure is not appropriate for the case :

(a) At the request of one of the parties the appointing authority shall communicate to both parties an identical list containing at least three names;

(b) Within fifteen days after the receipt of this list, each party may return the list to the appointing authority after having deleted the name or names to which he objects and numbered the remaining names on the list in the order of his preference;

(c) After the expiration of the above period of time the appointing authority shall appoint the sole arbitrator from among the names approved on the lists returned to it and in accordance with the order of preference indicated by the parties;

(d) If for any reason the appointment cannot be made according to this procedure, the appointing authority may exercise its discretion in appointing the sole arbitrator.

4 In making the appointment, the appointing authority shall have regard to such considerations as are likely to secure the appointment of an independent and impartial arbitrator and shall take into account as well the advisability of appointing an arbitrator of a nationality other than the nationalities of the parties.

Article 7

1 If three arbitrators are to be appointed, each party shall appoint one arbitrator. The two arbitrators thus appointed shall choose the third arbitrator who will act as the presiding arbitrator of the tribunal.

2 If within thirty days after the receipt of a party's notification of the appointment of an arbitrator the other party has not notified the first party of the arbitrator he has appointed:

(a) The first party may request the appointing authority previously designated by the parties to appoint the second arbitrator; or

(b) If no such authority has been previously designated by the parties, or if the appointing authority previously designated refuses to act or fails to appoint the arbitrator within thirty days after receipt of a party's request therefor, the first party may request the Secretary-General of the Permanent Court of Arbitration at The Hague to designate the appointing authority. The first party may then request the appointing authority so designated to appoint the second arbitrator. In either case, the appointing authority may exercise its discretion in appointing the arbitrator.

3 If within thirty days after the appointment of the second arbitrator the two arbitrators have not agreed on the choice of the presiding arbitrator, the presiding arbitrator shall be appointed by an appointing authority in the same way as a sole arbitrator would be appointed under article 6.

Article 8

1 When an appointing authority is requested to appoint an arbitrator pursuant to article 6 or article 7, the party which makes the request shall send to the appointing authority a copy of the notice of arbitration, a copy of the contract out of or in relation to which the dispute has arisen and a copy of the arbitration agreement if it is not contained in the contract. The appointing authority may require from either party such information as it deems necessary to fulfil its function.

2 Where the names of one or more persons are proposed for appointment as arbitrators, their full names, addresses and nationalities shall be indicated, together with a description of their qualifications.

Challenge of arbitrators (articles 9 to 12)

Article 9

A prospective arbitrator shall disclose to those who approach him in connexion with his possible appointment any circumstances likely to give rise to justifiable doubts as to his impartiality or independence. An arbitrator, once appointed or chosen, shall disclose such circumstances to the parties unless they have already been informed by him of these circumstances.

Article 10

1 Any arbitrator may be challenged if circumstances exist that give rise to justifiable doubts as to the arbitrator's impartiality or independence.

2 A party may challenge the arbitrator appointed by him only for reasons of which he becomes aware after the appointment has been made.

Article 11

1 A party who intends to challenge an arbitrator shall send notice of his challenge within fifteen days after the appointment of the challenged arbitrator has been notified to the challenging party or within fifteen days after the circumstances mentioned in articles 9 and 10 became known to that party.

2 The challenge shall be notified to the other party, to the arbitrator who is challenged and to the other members of the arbitral tribunal. The notification shall be in writing and shall state the reasons for the challenge.

3 When an arbitrator has been challenged by one party, the other party may agree to the challenge. The arbitrator may also, after the challenge, withdraw

from his office. In neither case does this imply acceptance of the validity of the grounds for the challenge. In both cases the procedure provided in article 6 or 7 shall be used in full for the appointment of the substitute arbitrator, even if during the process of appointing the challenged arbitrator a party had failed to exercise his right to appoint or to participate in the appointment.

Article 12

1 If the other party does not agree to the challenge and the challenged arbitrator does not withdraw, the decision on the challenge will be made:

(a) When the initial appointment was made by an appointing authority, by that authority;

(b) When the initial appointment was not made by an appointing authority, but an appointing authority has been previously designated, by that authority;

(c) In all other cases, by the appointing authority to be designated in accordance with the procedure for designating an appointing authority as provided for in article 6.

2 If the appointing authority sustains the challenge, a substitute arbitrator shall be appointed or chosen pursuant to the procedure applicable to the appointment or choice of an arbitrator as provided in articles 6 to 9 except that, when this procedure would call for the designation of an appointing authority, the appointment of the arbitrator shall be made by the appointing authority which decided on the challenge.

Replacement of an arbitrator

Article 13

1 In the event of the death or resignation of an arbitrator during the course of the arbitral proceedings, a substitute arbitrator shall be appointed or chosen pursuant to the procedure provided for in articles 6 to 9 that was applicable to the appointment or choice of the arbitrator being replaced.

2 In the event that an arbitrator fails to act or in the event of the *de jure* or *de facto* impossibility of his performing his functions, the procedure in respect of the challenge and replacement of an arbitrator as provided in the preceding articles shall apply.

Repetition of hearings in the event of the replacement of an arbitrator

Article 14

If under articles 11 to 13 the sole or presiding arbitrator is replaced, any hearings held previously shall be repeated; if any other arbitrator is replaced, such prior hearings may be repeated at the discretion of the arbitral tribunal.

SECTION III ARBITRAL PROCEEDINGS

General provisions

Article 15

1 Subject to these Rules, the arbitral tribunal may conduct the arbitration in such manner as it considers appropriate, provided that the parties are treated with equality and that at any stage of the proceedings each party is given a full opportunity of presenting his case.

2 If either party so requests at any stage of the proceedings, the arbitral tribunal shall hold hearings for the presentation of evidence by witnesses, including expert witnesses, or for oral argument. In the absence of such a request, the arbitral tribunal shall decide whether to hold such hearings or whether the proceedings shall be conducted on the basis of documents and other materials.

3 All documents or information supplied to the arbitral tribunal by one party shall at the same time be communicated by that party to the other party.

Place of arbitration

Article 16

1 Unless the parties have agreed upon the place where the arbitration is to be held, such place shall be determined by the arbitral tribunal, having regard to the circumstances of the arbitration.

2 The arbitral tribunal may determine the locale of the arbitration within the country agreed upon by the parties. It may hear witnesses and hold meetings for consultation among its members at any place it deems appropriate, having regard to the circumstances of the arbitration.

3 The arbitral tribunal may meet at any place it deems appropriate for the inspection of goods, other property or documents. The parties shall be given sufficient notice to enable them to be present at such inspection.

4 The award shall be made at the place of arbitration.

Language

Article 17

1 Subject to an agreement by the parties, the arbitral tribunal shall, promptly after its appointment, determine the language or languages to be used in the proceedings. This determination shall apply to the statement of claim, the statement of defence, and any further written statements and, if oral hearings take place, to the language or languages to be used in such hearings.

2 The arbitral tribunal may order that any documents annexed to the statement of claim or statement of defence, and any supplementary documents or exhibits submitted in the course of the proceedings, delivered in their original

language, shall be accompanied by a translation into the language or languages agreed upon by the parties or determined by the arbitral tribunal.

Statement of claim

Article 18

1 Unless the statement of claim was contained in the notice of arbitration, within a period of time to be determined by the arbitral tribunal, the claimant shall communicate his statement of claim in writing to the respondent and to each of the arbitrators. A copy of the contract, and of the arbitration agreement if not contained in the contract, shall be annexed thereto.

2 The statement of claim shall include the following particulars:
 (a) The names and addresses of the parties;
 (b) A statement of the facts supporting the claim;
 (c) The points at issue;
 (d) The relief or remedy sought.

The claimant may annex to his statement of claim all documents he deems relevant or may add a reference to the documents or other evidence he will submit.

Statement of defence

Article 19

1 Within a period of time to be determined by the arbitral tribunal, the respondent shall communicate his statement of defence in writing to the claimant and to each of the arbitrators.

2 The statement of defence shall reply to the particulars (b), (c) and (d) of the statement of claim (article 18, para. 2). The respondent may annex to his statement the documents on which he relies for his defence or may add a reference to the documents or other evidence he will submit.

3 In his statement of defence, or at a later stage in the arbitral proceedings if the arbitral tribunal decides that the delay was justified under the circumstances, the respondent may make a counter-claim arising out of the same contract or rely on a claim arising out of the same contract for the purpose of a set-off.

4 The provisions of article 18, paragraph 2, shall apply to a counter-claim and a claim relied on for the purpose of a set-off.

Amendments to the claim or defence

Article 20

During the course of the arbitral proceedings either party may amend or supplement his claim or defence unless the arbitral tribunal considers it inappropriate to allow such amendment having regard to the delay in making it or prejudice to the other party or any other circumstances. However, a claim may not be amended in such a manner that the amended claim falls outside the scope of the arbitration clause or separate arbitration agreement.

Pleas as to the jurisdiction of the arbitral tribunal

Article 21

1 The arbitral tribunal shall have the power to rule on objections that it has no jurisdiction, including any objections with respect to the existence or validity of the arbitration clause or of the separate arbitration agreement.

2 The arbitral tribunal shall have the power to determine the existence or the validity of the contract of which an arbitration clause forms a part. For the purposes of article 21, an arbitration clause which forms part of a contract and which provides for arbitration under these Rules shall be treated as an agreement independent of the other terms of the contract. A decision by the arbitral tribunal that the contract is null and void shall not entail *ipso jure* the invalidity of the arbitration clause.

3 A plea that the arbitral tribunal does not have jurisdiction shall be raised not later than in the statement of defence or, with respect to a counter-claim, in the reply to the counter-claim.

4 In general, the arbitral tribunal should rule on a plea concerning its jurisdiction as a preliminary question. However, the arbitral tribunal may proceed with the arbitration and rule on such a plea in their final award.

Further written statements

Article 22

The arbitral tribunal shall decide which further written statements, in addition to the statement of claim and the statement of defence, shall be required from the parties or may be presented by them and shall fix the periods of time for communicating such statements.

Periods of time

Article 23

The periods of time fixed by the arbitral tribunal for the communication of written statements (including the statement of claim and statement of defence) should not exceed forty-five days. However, the arbitral tribunal may extend the time-limits if it concludes that an extension is justified.

Evidence and hearings (articles 24 and 25)

Article 24

1 Each party shall have the burden of proving the facts relied on to support his claim or defence.

2 The arbitral tribunal may, if it considers it appropriate, require a party to deliver to the tribunal and to the other party, within such a period of time as the arbitral tribunal shall decide, a summary of the documents and other evidence which that party intends to present in support of the facts in issue set out in his statement of claim or statement of defence.

3 At any time during the arbitral proceedings the arbitral tribunal may require the parties to produce documents, exhibits or other evidence within such a period of time as the tribunal shall determine.

Article 25

1 In the event of an oral hearing, the arbitral tribunal shall give the parties adequate advance notice of the date, time and place thereof.

2 If witnesses are to be heard, at least fifteen days before the hearing each party shall communicate to the arbitral tribunal and to the other party the names and addresses of the witnesses he intends to present, the subject upon and the languages in which such witnesses will give their testimony.

3 The arbitral tribunal shall make arrangements for the translation of oral statements made at a hearing and for a record of the hearing if either is deemed necessary by the tribunal under the circumstances of the case, or if the parties have agreed thereto and have communicated such agreement to the tribunal at least fifteen days before the hearing.

4 Hearings shall be held *in camera* unless the parties agree otherwise. The arbitral tribunal may require the retirement of any witness or witnesses during the testimony of other witnesses. The arbitral tribunal is free to determine the manner in which witnesses are examined.

5 Evidence of witnesses may also be presented in the form of written statements signed by them.

6 The arbitral tribunal shall determine the admissibility, relevance, materiality and weight of the evidence offered.

Interim measures of protection

Article 26

1 At the request of either party, the arbitral tribunal may take any interim measures it deems necessary in respect of the subject-matter of the dispute, including measures for the conservation of the goods forming the subject-matter in dispute, such as ordering their deposit with a third person or the sale of perishable goods.

2 Such interim measures may be established in the form of an interim award. The arbitral tribunal shall be entitled to require security for the costs of such measures.

3 A request for interim measures addressed by any party to a judicial authority shall not be deemed incompatible with the agreement to arbitrate, or as a waiver of that agreement.

Experts

Article 27

1 The arbitral tribunal may appoint one or more experts to report to it, in writing, on specific issues to be determined by the tribunal. A copy of the expert's terms of reference, established by the arbitral tribunal, shall be communicated to the parties.

2 The parties shall give the expert any relevant information or produce for his inspection any relevant documents or goods that he may require of them. Any dispute between a party and such expert as to the relevance of the required information or production shall be referred to the arbitral tribunal for decision.

3 Upon receipt of the expert's report, the arbitral tribunal shall communicate a copy of the report to the parties who shall be given the opportunity to express, in writing, their opinion on the report. A party shall be entitled to examine any document on which the expert has relied in his report.

4 At the request of either party the expert, after delivery of the report, may be heard at a hearing where the parties shall have the opportunity to be present and to interrogate the expert. At this hearing either party may present expert witnesses in order to testify on the points at issue. The provisions of article 25 shall be applicable to such proceedings.

Default

Article 28

1 If, within the period of time fixed by the arbitral tribunal, the claimant has failed to communicate his claim without showing sufficient cause for such failure, the arbitral tribunal shall issue an order for the termination of the arbitral proceedings. If, within the period of time fixed by the arbitral tribunal, the respondent has failed to communicate his statement of defence without showing sufficient cause for such failure, the arbitral tribunal shall order that the proceedings continue.

2 If one of the parties, duly notified under these Rules, fails to appear at a hearing, without showing sufficient cause for such failure, the arbitral tribunal may proceed with the arbitration.

3 If one of the parties, duly invited to produce documentary evidence, fails to do so within the established period of time, without showing sufficient cause for such failure, the arbitral tribunal may make the award on the evidence before it.

Closure of hearings

Article 29

1 The arbitral tribunal may inquire of the parties if they have any further proof to offer or witnesses to be heard or submissions to make and, if there are none, it may declare the hearings closed.

2 The arbitral tribunal may, if it considers it necessary owing to exceptional

circumstances, decide, on its own motion or upon application of a party, to reopen the hearings at any time before the award is made.

Waiver of rules

Article 30

A party who knows that any provision of, or requirement under, these Rules has not been complied with and yet proceeds with the arbitration without promptly stating his objection to such non-compliance, shall be deemed to have waived his right to object.

SECTION IV THE AWARD

Decisions

Article 31

1 When there are three arbitrators, any award or other decision of the arbitral tribunal shall be made by a majority of the arbitrators.

2 In the case of questions of procedure, when there is no majority or when the arbitral tribunal so authorizes, the presiding arbitrator may decide on his own, subject to revision, if any, by the arbitral tribunal.

Form and effect of the award

Article 32

1 In addition to making a final award, the arbitral tribunal shall be entitled to make interim, interlocutory, or partial awards.

2 The award shall be made in writing and shall be final and binding on the parties. The parties undertake to carry out the award without delay.

3 The arbitral tribunal shall state the reasons upon which the award is based, unless the parties have agreed that no reasons are to be given.

4 An award shall be signed by the arbitrators and it shall contain the date on which and the place where the award was made. Where there are three arbitrators and one of them fails to sign, the award shall state the reason for the absence of the signature.

5 The award may be made public only with the consent of both parties.

6 Copies of the award signed by the arbitrators shall be communicated to the parties by the arbitral tribunal.

7 If the arbitration law of the country where the award is made requires that the award be filed or registered by the arbitral tribunal, the tribunal shall comply with this requirement within the period of time required by law.

Applicable law, amiable compositeur

Article 33

1 The arbitral tribunal shall apply the law designated by the parties as applicable to the substance of the dispute. Failing such designation by the parties, the arbitral tribunal shall apply the law determined by the conflict of laws rules which it considers applicable.

2 The arbitral tribunal shall decide as *amiable compositeur* or *ex aequo et bono* only if the parties have expressly authorized the arbitral tribunal to do so and if the law applicable to the arbitral procedure permits such arbitration.

3 In all cases, the arbitral tribunal shall decide in accordance with the terms of the contract and shall take into account the usages of the trade applicable to the transaction.

Settlement or other grounds for termination

Article 34

1 If, before the award is made, the parties agree on a settlement of the dispute, the arbitral tribunal shall either issue an order for the termination of the arbitral proceedings or, if requested by both parties and accepted by the tribunal, record the settlement in the form of an arbitral award on agreed terms. The arbitral tribunal is not obliged to give reasons for such an award.

2 If, before the award is made, the continuation of the arbitral proceedings becomes unnecessary or impossible for any reason not mentioned in paragraph 1, the arbitral tribunal shall inform the parties of its intention to issue an order for the termination of the proceedings. The arbitral tribunal shall have the power to issue such an order unless a party raises justifiable grounds for objection.

3 Copies of the order for termination of the arbitral proceedings or of the arbitral award on agreed terms, signed by the arbitrators, shall be communicated by the arbitral tribunal to the parties. Where an arbitral award on agreed terms is made, the provisions of article 32, paragraphs 2 and 4 to 7, shall apply.

Interpretation of the award

Article 35

1 Within thirty days after the receipt of the award, either party, with notice to the other party, may request that the arbitral tribunal give an interpretation of the award.

2 The interpretation shall be given in writing within forty-five days after the receipt of the request. The interpretation shall form part of the award and the provisions of article 32, paragraphs 2 to 7, shall apply.

Correction of the award

Article 36

1 Within thirty days after the receipt of the award, either party, with notice to

the other party, may request the arbitral tribunal to correct in the award any errors in computation, any clerical or typographical errors, or any errors of similar nature. The arbitral tribunal may within thirty days after the communication of the award make such corrections on its own initiative.

2 Such corrections shall be in writing, and the provisions of article 32, paragraphs 2 to 7, shall apply.

Additional award

Article 37

1 Within thirty days after the receipt of the award, either party, with notice to the other party, may request the arbitral tribunal to make an additional award as to claims presented in the arbitral proceedings but omitted from the award.

2 If the arbitral tribunal considers the request for an additional award to be justified and considers that the omission can be rectified without any further hearings or evidence, it shall complete its award within sixty days after the receipt of the request.

3 When an additional award is made, the provisions of article 32, paragraphs 2 to 7, shall apply.

Costs (Articles 38 to 40)

Article 38

The arbitral tribunal shall fix the costs of arbitration in its award. The term 'costs' includes only:

(a) The fees of the arbitral tribunal to be stated separately as to each arbitrator and to be fixed by the tribunal itself in accordance with article 39;

(b) The travel and other expenses incurred by the arbitrators;

(c) The costs of expert advice and of other assistance required by the arbitral tribunal;

(d) The travel and other expenses of witnesses to the extent such expenses are approved by the arbitral tribunal;

(e) The costs for legal representation and assistance of the successful party if such costs were claimed during the arbitral proceedings, and only to the extent that the arbitral tribunal determines that the amount of such costs is reasonable;

(f) Any fees and expenses of the appointing authority as well as the expenses of the Secretary-General of the Permanent Court of Arbitration at The Hague.

Article 39

1 The fees of the arbitral tribunal shall be reasonable in amount, taking into account the amount in dispute, the complexity of the subject-matter, the time spent by the arbitrators and any other relevant circumstances of the case.

2 If an appointing authority has been agreed upon by the parties or designated by the Secretary-General of the Permanent Court of Arbitration at The Hague, and if that authority has issued a schedule of fees for arbitrators in

international cases which it administers, the arbitral tribunal in fixing its fees shall take that schedule of fees into account to the extent that it considers appropriate in the circumstances of the case.

3 If such appointing authority has not issued a schedule of fees for arbitrators in international cases, any party may at any time request the appointing authority to furnish a statement setting forth the basis for establishing fees which is customarily followed in international cases in which the authority appoints arbitrators. If the appointing authority consents to provide such a statement, the arbitral tribunal in fixing its fees shall take such information into account to the extent that it considers appropriate in the circumstances of the case.

4 In cases referred to in paragraphs 2 and 3, when a party so requests and the appointing authority consents to perform the function, the arbitral tribunal shall fix its fees only after consultation with the appointing authority which may make any comment it deems appropriate to the arbitral tribunal concerning the fees.

Article 40

1 Except as provided in paragraph 2, the costs of arbitration shall in principle be borne by the unsuccessful party. However, the arbitral tribunal may apportion each of such costs between the parties if it determines that apportionment is reasonable, taking into account the circumstances of the case.

2 With respect to the costs of legal representation and assistance referred to in article 38, paragraph (e), the arbitral tribunal, taking into account the circumstances of the case, shall be free to determine which party shall bear such costs or may apportion such costs between the parties if it determines that apportionment is reasonable.

3 When the arbitral tribunal issues an order for the termination of the arbitral proceedings or makes an award on agreed terms, it shall fix the costs of arbitration referred to in article 38 and article 39, paragraph 1, in the text of that order or award.

4 No additional fees may be charged by an arbitral tribunal for interpretation or correction or completion of its award under articles 35 to 37.

Deposit of costs

Article 41

1 The arbitral tribunal, on its establishment, may request each party to deposit an equal amount as an advance for the costs referred to in article 38, paragraphs (a), (b) and (c).

2 During the course of the arbitral proceedings the arbitral tribunal may request supplementary deposits from the parties.

3 If an appointing authority has been agreed upon by the parties or designated by the Secretary-General of the Permanent Court of Arbitration at The Hague, and when a party so requests and the appointing authority consents to perform the function, the arbitral tribunal shall fix the amounts of any deposits or supplementary deposits only after consultation with the appointing authority which may make any comments to the arbitral tribunal which it

deems appropriate concerning the amount of such deposits and supplementary deposits.

4 If the required deposits are not paid in full within thirty days after the receipt of the request, the arbitral tribunal shall so inform the parties in order that one or another of them may make the required payment. If such payment is not made, the arbitral tribunal may order the suspension or termination of the arbitral proceedings.

5 After the award has been made, the arbitral tribunal shall render an accounting to the parties of the deposits received and return any unexpended balance to the parties.

London Maritime Arbitrators' Association Terms (1987)

Preliminary

1 These Terms may be referred to as 'the L.M.A.A. Terms (1987)'.

2 (a) In these Terms, unless the context otherwise requires,

    (i) 'The Association' means the London Maritime Arbitrators' Association; 'Member of the Association' includes both full and supporting members; 'President' means the President for the time being of the Association

    (ii) 'Tribunal' includes a sole arbitrator, a tribunal or two or more arbitrators, and an umpire

    (iii) 'Original arbitrator' means an arbitrator appointed (whether initially or by substitution) by or at the request of a party as its nominee and any arbitrator duly appointed so to act following failure of a party to make its own nomination.

(b) Save where original arbitrators, having disagreed, are thereafter requested and agree to act as advocates for presentation of the dispute to an umpire, an original arbitrator will at all times act with judicial impartiality and with exactly equal duties towards both parties and is in no sense to be considered as the representative of this appointer.

3 (a) The Terms apply to all arbitration proceedings commenced on and after 1st January 1987 whenever the dispute (unless it arises under an agreement providing for application to the arbitration of other specified rules or terms) is referred to members of the Association by their appointment as sole or original arbitrators and the dispute arises out of a transaction of a kind which, if it were to have been litigated in the High Court, would have been tried in the Admiralty or Commercial Courts. The Terms likewise apply whenever a sole or original arbitrator, not being a member, expressly accepts appointment on these Terms.

(b) For the foregoing purpose arbitration proceedings shall be treated as having commenced upon acceptance of appointment (i) by a sole arbitrator or (ii) by whichever original arbitrator is first appointed.

Jurisdiction and powers

4 (a) Subject to sub-paragraph (b) below, by submitting to arbitration under these Terms the parties confer upon the tribunal the jurisdiction and powers set out in the First Schedule.

(b) A party shall be entitled to make application to the High Court, instead of to the tribunal, in relation to any interlocutory matters over which the High Court has jurisdiction; save that applications for security for costs shall be made to the High Court only with the concurrence of the other party or with leave of the tribunal.

Tribunal fees

5 Provisions regulating fees payable to the tribunal and other related matters are set out in the Second Schedule. Save as therein or herein otherwise provided, payment of the tribunal's fees and expenses is the joint and several responsibility of the parties.

Arbitrations on documents

6 If it is agreed that an arbitration is to be on documents (i.e. without an oral hearing) it is the responsibility of the parties to agree the procedure to be followed and to inform the tribunal of the agreement reached. The procedure set out in the Third Schedule should normally be adopted, with any such modifications as may be appropriate: and in default of agreement the tribunal will give appropriate directions.

7 Applications for directions should not be necessary but, if required, they should be made in accordance with paragraph 10.

Oral hearings

8 A time-table for preparation of the case for hearing should, whenever possible, be agreed between the parties and the tribunal should then be informed by the claimant of the agreement reached. In default of agreement, application for directions should be made in accordance with paragraph 10.

9 (a) A hearing date will not be fixed, save in exceptional circumstances, until the preparation of a case is sufficiently advanced to enable the duration of the hearing to be properly estimated; this will normally be after discovery has been completed.

(b) Unless the case calls for a preliminary meeting with the tribunal (see paragraph 11), it is the duty of the parties or their advisers, prior to application for a hearing date, to consult together (i) to assess the expected readiness and the likely duration of the hearing, (ii) to plan the preparatory work still to be done, and (iii) to consider whether any other directions are required from the tribunal when the hearing date is requested.

(c) Following such consultation, application for a hearing date must be made in writing, or by telex, indicating the expected date of readiness and likely duration of the hearing.

(d) Following fixture of the hearing date a booking feee will be payable in accordance with the provisions of the Second Schedule.

Interlocutory applications

10 (a) Application to the tribunal for directions should, save in special circumstances, be made only after the other party has been afforded a reasonable opportunity to agree the terms of the directions proposed.

(b) If agreement is not reached, the applicant should apply to the tribunal, setting out the terms of the directions proposed. The application must be copied to the other party, who must respond to the tribunal (copy to the applicant) stating the grounds of objection. The response must be made within 3 working days, or such further time as the tribunal may allow on the application of the respondent party.

(c) Unless either party has requested an oral hearing, the tribunal will make its order following receipt of the response or, in default of response within the time allowed, upon expiry of that time.

(d) Prior to appointment of a third arbitrator, original arbitrators shall, if in agreement, be entitled to give directions without the need to appoint a third arbitrator for that purpose.

(e) Communications regarding interlocutory matters should be made expeditiously and whenever practicable by telex.

Preliminary meetings

11 (a) In cases expected to be of more than 5 days' duration or where there are other circumstances which merit preliminary informal discussion with the tribunal, the application for a hearing date should be preceded by a discussion between the parties' representatives to review the progress of the case; to reach agreement, so far as possible, upon further preparation for, and the conduct of, the hearing; to identify matters for discussion with the tribunal; and to prepare for submission to the tribunal an agenda of matters for approval or determination by it.

(b) Following the discussion between the parties' representatives, the parties should request a preliminary meeting with the tribunal, submitting their agenda together with an updated pleadings bundle and giving their estimates of readiness for hearing and the likely duration of the hearing.

(c) The preliminary meeting with the tribunal will be informal. Its object is to secure agreement so far as possible in the conduct of the arbitration generally, and to give any such directions as the tribunal considers fit.

(d) There is set out in the Fourth Schedule a guidance document indicating topics which may be appropriate for consideration prior to and, if still outstanding, at the preliminary meeting.

Settlement

12 It is the duty of the claimant (a) to notify the tribunal immediately if the arbitration is settled or otherwise terminated and (b) to inform the tribunal of the parties' agreement as to the manner in which payment will be made of any outstanding fees and expenses of the tribunal, eg for interlocutory work not covered by any booking fee paid.

13 Any booking fee paid will be dealt with in accordance with the provisions of paragraph (B) (1) (c) of the Second Schedule. Any other fees and expenses of the tribunal shall be settled, promptly and at latest within 28 days of presentation of the relevant account(s), in accordance with the agreement of the parties or, in default of agreement, the parties shall be jointly and severally responsible for such fees and expenses.

Adjournment

14 If a case is for any reason adjourned part-heard, the tribunal will be entitled to an interim payment, payable in equal shares or otherwise as the tribunal may direct, in respect of fees and expenses already incurred, appropriate credit being given for the booking fee.

15 The provisions of paragraphs (B) (1) (d) and (e) of the Second Schedule shall apply in relation to adjournments ordered prior to the start of the hearing.

Umpires

16 An umpire who attends the principal hearing or any interlocutory application shall be entitled to remuneration accordingly for his services, irrespective of whether or not he is thereafter required to enter upon the reference, and as from the date of his appointment he shall, for the purposes of paragraphs 5 and 11–15 above, be treated as if he were a member of the tribunal.

Availability of arbitrators

17 (a) In cases where it is known at the outset that an early hearing is essential, the parties should consult and ensure the availability of the arbitrator(s) to be appointed by them.

(b) If, in cases when the tribunal has already been constituted, the fixture of an acceptable hearing date is precluded by the commitments of the original appointee(s) the provisions of the Fifth Schedule shall apply.

The award

18 The time required for preparation of an award must vary with the circumstances of the case. The award should normally be available within not more than six weeks from the close of the proceedings. In many cases, and in particular where the matter is one of urgency, the interval should be substantially shorter.

19 The members of a tribunal need not meet together for the purpose of signing their award or of effecting any corrections thereto.

20 Where the reference is to a tribunal of three arbitrators, the majority view shall prevail in relation to any head of claim or counterclaim upon which unanimity is lacking. In the event of there being no majority the view of the third arbitrator shall prevail.

21 Unless a reasoned award is requested under section 1 of the Arbitration Act 1979, the tribunal will normally supply the parties, on a confidential basis, with a document outlining the reasons for its decision. The document will not form part of the award, nor (unless the Court should otherwise direct) may it be relied upon or referred to by the parties in any proceedings relating to the award.

22 If an award has not been collected within two months of the date of publication, the claimant will be obliged to collect and pay for the award within fourteen days of being called upon to do so by the tribunal.

23 If, following the making of an interim award, outstanding matters are amicably resolved the tribunal should be promptly advised so that the file can be closed and documents disposed of.

24 If the tribunal or either party or its legal advisers should consider that an arbitration decision merits publication then, provided such publication is expressly authorised by the parties, the decision may be publicised in digest form.

The digest will be so drafted as to preserve anonymity as regards the identity of the parties and of the tribunal.

If the parties are legally represented their advisers will be responsible for arranging preparation of the digest for approval by the tribunal and, thereafter, for arranging publication as may be considered appropriate.

If the parties are not legally represented the preparation and publication of the digest will be arranged by the tribunal.

General

25 Three months after publication of any final award the tribunal will notify the parties of its intention to dispose of the documents and to close the file, and it will act accordingly unless otherwise requested within 14 days of such notice being given.

26 In relation to any matters not expressly provided for herein the tribunal shall act in accordance with the tenor of these Terms.

THE FIRST SCHEDULE

(A) Jurisdiction

The tribunal shall have jurisdiction in relation to the following matters –

(1) To determine all disputes arising under or in connection with the transaction the subject of the reference, including (so far as the tribunal considers that course to be both practicable and desirable) any further disputes arising subsequent to the commencement of the arbitration proceedings.

Provided however that, unless the parties otherwise agree, this jurisdiction shall not extend to determination of (a) a dispute as to whether the transaction was the subject of an agreement binding in law upon the parties or (b) a claim for rectification of any written agreement.

(2) To proceed to an award on any claim or counterclaim on the application of the claimant party and without the need for an oral hearing if the respondent party (a) has failed to furnish defence submissions to such claim or counterclaim within such time as the tribunal has directed by final and peremptory order, and (b) (except where an arbitration on documents only has been agreed) has declined or failed to take advantage of an opportunity to attend an oral hearing on a date offered for that purpose by the tribunal.

(3) To impose, in relation to any final and peremptory order, such terms as the tribunal considers appropriate in the event of non-compliance with the order.

(4) To make interim orders, upon the application of a respondent party to a claim or counter-claim, for the provision of security for that party's costs of the reference, with power to direct, pending provision of such security, a stay of the arbitration or such other direction as may in the circumstances be appropriate.

(5) At the request of the parties or either of them or of its own volition, to

correct any accidental mistake, omission, or error of calculation in its award, any such request to be made within 28 days of the collection of the award. Any correction shall be effected in a separate memorandum which shall become part of the award.

(B) Powers

Without derogation from all powers with which it is otherwise invested or with which it may be invested pursuant to application made to the High Court under section 5(2) of the Arbitration Act 1979, the tribunal shall have the following specific powers, to be exercised as the circumstances may require for the most efficient and expeditious conduct of the reference:

(1) To receive and act upon such oral or written evidence as it determines to be relevant, whether or not the evidence is strictly admissible in law; but this power shall not be exercisable in relation to evidence directed to any allegation of fraud that is raised against either party.

(2) To limit the number of expert witnesses, to direct that experts' reports be exchanged in advance of the hearing and, if the tribunal thinks fit, to direct that there be a 'without prejudice meeting' of such experts within such period before or after the disclosure of the reports as the tribunal may direct, for the purpose of identifying those parts of their evidence which are at issue.

(3) To direct, in appropriate circumstances, that statements of witnesses of fact be exchanged in advance of the hearing and be received as their evidence-in-chief.

(4) To appoint, upon the application of any party, an expert assessor or assessors to sit with and advise the tribunal upon any matters which are outside its own expertise; the fees of any assessor(s) so appointed to form part of the cost of the award.

(5) To direct, upon the application of any party or of its own volition, that any thing the subject of the reference be made available for inspection by the tribunal.

(C) Multi-party disputes

A tribunal shall have the following powers in relation to multi-party disputes:

(1) If the disputes have been referred to the same tribunal, the tribunal shall have power to direct that the references shall be heard concurrently and to give all such directions as to procedure as the interests of economy and expedition may require.

(2) Upon the application of any party to an existing reference, the tribunal shall have power to direct that there be joined in that reference any other party or parties who, by written consent, have indicated readiness to be so joined; and the arbitration shall then proceed as though the tribunal had been appointed to deal with all associated disputes between the respective interests on a consolidated basis.

THE SECOND SCHEDULE

Tribunal's fees

(A) Appointment fee

An appointment fee is payable on appointment by the appointing party or by the party at whose request the appointment is made. Unless otherwise agreed, the appointment fee of an umpire or third arbitrator shall in the first instance be paid by the claimant.

(B) Booking fee

(1) (a) For a hearing of *up to 10 days' duration* there shall be payable to the tribunal a booking fee of £150 per person for each day reserved. The booking fee will be invoiced to the parties in equal shares and shall be paid within 14 days of confirmation of the reservation or six months in advance of the first day reserved ('the start date'), whichever date be the later. If the fee is not paid in full by the due date the tribunal will be entitled to cancel the reservation but either party may secure reinstatement of the reservation by payment within 7 days of any balance outstanding.

(b) Where the case proceeds to an award, or is settled subsequent to the start of the hearing, appropriate credit will be given for the booking fee in calculating the cost of the award or, as the case may be, the amount payable to the tribunal upon settlement of the case.

(c) Where a hearing date is vacated prior to the start date otherwise than by adjournment the booking fee will be retained by the tribunal (i) in full if the date is vacated less than three months before the start date (ii) as to 50% if the date is vacated three months or more before the start date. Any interlocutory fees and expenses incurred will also be payable or, as the case may be, deductible from the refund under (ii).

(d) Where, on the application of either party, an adjournment is granted six weeks or more before the start date any booking fee paid is not returnable but will be credited against the fee payable for any fresh reservation in the reference.

(e) Where, on the application of either party, an adjournment is granted less than six weeks before the start date any booking fee paid is not returnable and a further booking fee will be payble on reserving a fresh hearing date.

(f) The tribunal, when giving directions as to the terms upon which an adjournment is granted under (e) above, shall be entitled to give such directions as it considers appropriate regarding the manner in which there shall be borne any booking fee forfeited and/or any further booking fee payable on reserving a fresh hearing date.

(2) For hearings estimated to be likely to occupy *more than 10 days* the booking fee arrangements will be subject to negotiation, but the reservation will be treated as provisional until terms have been agreed.

(3) An arbitrator or umpire who, following receipt of his booking fee, is for any reason replaced is, upon settlement of his fees for any interlocutory work, responsible for transfer of his booking fee to the person appointed to act in his place. In the event of death the personal representatives shall have a corresponding responsibility.

Accommodation

(1) If accommodation and/or catering is arranged by the tribunal, the cost will normally be recovered as part of the cost of the award, but where a case is adjourned part-heard or in other special circumstances, the tribunal reserves the

right to direct that the cost shall be provisionally paid by the parties in equal shares (or as the tribunal may direct) promptly upon issue of the relevant account.

(2) If accommodation is reserved and paid for by the parties and it is desired that the cost incurred be the subject of directions in the award, the information necessary for that purpose must be furnished promptly to the tribunal.

THE THIRD SCHEDULE

Arbitration on documents

Recommended procedure

If parties wish a dispute to be decided without an oral hearing the procedure set out in paragraphs 1–5 below is recommended for adoption by agreement.

When this procedure (or any modification) has been agreed, the tribunal should be so informed. The tribunal must be promptly advised if, at a later stage, the parties or either of them consider that an oral hearing is going to be necessary.

The exchange of submissions, etc., will take place directly between the parties unless the case is being handled by others (eg by lawyers or a Club) on their behalf.

Copies of all submissions, comments and documents must be supplied simultaneously to the tribunal, and all communications with the tribunal must be copied to the other party.

All documents relied on must be legibly copied and translations supplied as necessary.

(1) Claimants' written submissions, together with copies of supporting documents, to be furnished by them within 28 days after the agreement by the parties to adopt the procedure.

(2) Respondents' written submissions (including those relating to any counterclaim), together with copies of any documents relied on additional to those already provided by the claimants, to be furnished by them within 28 days after receipt of the claimants' submissions and documents.

(3) If there is no counterclaim, claimants' final comments (if any) on the claim to be furnished within 21 days after receipt of the respondents' submissions and documents.

(4) If there is a counterclaim:

(a) claimants to furnish comments and any additional documents relative to the counterclaim within 28 days after receipt of the respondents' submissions and documents;

(b) respondents' final comments (if any) on the counterclaim to be furnished within 21 days after receipt of the claimants' comments and additional documents (if any).

(5) The tribunal will then give notice to the parties of its intention to proceed to its award and will so proceed unless either party within 7 days requests, and is thereafter granted, leave to provide further submissions and/or documents.

THE FOURTH SCHEDULE

Preliminary meetings

Paragraph 11 of the Terms envisages that where the hearing of a case is expected to last more than 5 days, or if there are other special circumstances, the representatives should first review the progress of the matter and consider preparations for the hearing, and thereafter a preliminary meeting should take place with the tribunal to consider those matters (see paragraph 11 of the Terms for fuller details).

This Schedule sets out, in check-list form, topics which may be appropriate for consideration. The representatives' discussion should lead to a measure of procedural agreement, and any remaining areas for discussion with the tribunal can be identified and the scope for specific directions from the tribunal thus reduced.

In complex cases, more than one preliminary meeting may be required in order to deal with developments since, or any matters stood over at, a prior meeting.

Because cases vary so much, the procedure and matters for consideration must be flexible. Inevitably, certain matters must be left to the discretion of the parties' advisers (eg what facts can be agreed, how evidence is to be dealt with, what level of representation is required, etc.); those mentioned in the check-list are not, in all instances, matters on which the tribunal can or will rule. This makes it all the more important that the representatives first consider in a comprehensive, realistic and co-operative way all the relevant points listed, always bearing in mind the underlying object of the anticipated meetings: to achieve the speediest, cheapest and most efficient resolution of the parties' disputes.

1 Pleadings	(i) closed (including particulars)?
	(ii) amendments required?
	(iii) are all issues still alive?
2 Discovery	(i) completed?
	(ii) disputes re outstanding discovery.
3 The Hearing	
A. *General*	(i) preliminary issues appropriate for determination? (eg interpretation of contract, liability only, etc).
	(ii) any issues suitable for determination on written submissions alone?
B. *Evidence (Fact)*	(i) can some facts/figures be agreed?
	(ii) exchange lists of witnesses of fact (indicating broadly areas each will deal with)?
	(iii) presentation of some evidence-in-chief by proofs or affidavits appropriate? If so, what arrangements should be made re exchange prior to hearing?

	(iv)	admission of some evidence (perhaps formal or of marginal importance) in proof or affidavit form only?
C. Evidence (Expert)	(i)	expert(s) needed? If so, should numbers be limited, generally or by reference to specific aspects of dispute?
	(ii)	when should reports be exchanged (leaving enough time for reply reports to be supplied well before hearing)?
	(iii)	should a 'without prejudice meeting' of experts be held?
	(iv)	could tribunal deal with technical aspects on basis of reports, without need to call experts?
	(v)	could an independent assessor usefully assist tribunal?
D. Inspection		would tribunal be assisted by attending trials or experiments, or inspecting any object featuring in the dispute?
E. Documents	(i)	if possible provide agreed chronology, dramatis personae, list of telex answerbacks, agreed statement of accounts.
	(ii)	arrangement of documents (eg different bundles for different topics, or as appropriate) and dates by which bundles to be produced.
	(iii)	unnecessary inclusion of documents to be avoided.
	(iv)	when documents voluminous, consider copying only key bundles, holding other material available for reference and copying if required.
F. Advance Reading	(i)	provision of pleadings and other suitable material (eg experts' reports) to tribunal as far in advance of hearing as possible.
	(ii)	should time be set aside during hearing, after appropriate opening, for private reading of any documents by tribunal (to reduce time otherwise involved in reading documents out)?
G. Multi-Party Disputes	(i)	procedure generally.
	(ii)	consolidated, concurrent or consecutive hearings?
H. Representation		level of representation at hearing appropriate to case.

4 Hearing Dates
(The fixing of dates will, in the majority of cases, be most usefully considered after the matters covered in paragraph 3 have been reviewed, for they are

bound to have a considerable bearing on how long the hearing is likely to take, and when the parties can be ready.)

 (i) estimated duration of hearing.
 (ii) when can parties realistically be expected to be ready?
 (iii) any problems re availability of witnesses? (If so, can these be mitigated by taking evidence in advance, or using proofs/ affidavits?)
 (iv) availability of tribunal (see LMAA Terms, paragraph 17 and Fifth Schedule).
 (v) accommodation required and numbers attending.
 (vi) any special facilities required (eg transcripts, interpreters, etc).
 (vii) arrangements for accommodation, etc: who to book/pay for?

THE FIFTH SCHEDULE

Reconstitution of the tribunal

The following provisions are directed to avoiding delay which the parties or either of them consider unacceptable, but if both parties prefer to retain a tribunal as already constituted they remain free so to agree.

(1) The governing factor will be the ability of the tribunal to fix a hearing date within a reasonable time of the expected readiness date as notified by the parties on application for a date (see para. 9 (c) of the Terms), or, if they are not agreed as to the expected readiness date, within a reasonable time of whichever forecast date the tribunal considers more realistic.

(2) For hearings of up to 10 days' estimated duration, what constitutes a reasonable time will (unless the parties apply for a date further ahead) be determined by reference to the estimated length of hearing as follows –

Estimated Duration	*Reasonable Time*
(i) Up to 2 days	4 months
(ii) 3–5 days	6 months
(iii) 6–10 days	10 months

'Relevant time-scale' is used below to mean whichever of the foregoing periods is applicable and, in cases of more than 10 days' duration, such corresponding time-scale as the tribunal may consider appropriate.

(3) A sole arbitrator who is unable to offer a date within the relevant time-scale will offer to retire and, if so requested by the parties or either of them, will retire upon being satisfied that an appropriate substitute appointment has been effected by the parties; in event of their disagreement, either party may request the President to make the necessary substitute appointment.

(4) In all other cases, unless all members of the tribunal are able to offer a matching date within the relevant time-scale:

(A) The tribunal will have regard to any agreed preference of the parties, but if there is no agreed preference the tribunal will fix:
  (i) the earliest hearing date that can be given by any member(s) able to offer a guaranteed date within the relevant time-scale;
  or
  (ii) if a guaranteed date within the relevant time-scale cannot be offered by any member of the tribunal, the earliest date thereafter which can be guaranteed by any member(s) of the tribunal;
  on the basis, in either case, that any member then unable (by reason of a prior commitment) to guarantee the date so fixed will (unless that prior commitment has meanwhile cleared) retire by notice given six clear weeks prior to the start date.

(B) Upon notification of any such retirement an appropriate substitution will be effected as follows –
  (i) If an original arbitrator retires the substitute shall be promptly appointed by his appointer; or failing such appointment at least 21 days prior to the start date the substitute will then be appointed by the umpire or third arbitrator or, if an umpire or third arbitrator has not yet been appointed, the substitute will be appointed by the President;
  (ii) If an umpire or third arbitrator retires the substitute will be appointed by the original arbitrators.

(5) For the purpose of paragraph (4):

(A) 'Appropriate substitution' means appointment of a substitute able to match the hearing date established in accordance with sub-paragraph (A)

(B) 'Start date' means the first date reserved for the hearing

(C) An umpire or third arbitrator will retain power to make any necessary substitution under sub-paragraph (B) (i) notwithstanding that he may himself have given notice of retirement under sub-paragraph (A) and an original arbitrator will retain the like power under sub-paragraph (B) (ii).

(6) Applications to vacate dates fixed by implementation of this schedule will be granted only in exceptional circumstances. The convenience of counsel and/or expert witnesses will not normally be treated as justifying vacation of the date.

Rules of the London Court of International Arbitration
(Effective from 1 January 1985)

Where any agreement, submission or reference provides for arbitration under the Rules of the London Court of International Arbitration* (the LCIA), the parties shall be taken to have agreed that the arbitration shall be conducted in accordance with the following Rules, or such amended rules as the Court may have adopted to take effect before the commencement of the arbitration.

The Arbitration Court of the LCIA, in these Rules called 'The Court', has the function of ensuring the application of the Rules.

---

*Formerly called the London Court of Arbitration.

Article 1   *Request for arbitration*

Any party wishing to commence an arbitration under these Rules ('the Claimant') shall send to the Registrar of the Court ('the Registrar') a written request for arbitration ('the Request') which shall include, or be accompanied by:

   (a) the names and addresses of the parties to the arbitration;
   (b) copies of the contractual documents in which the arbitration clause is contained or under which the arbitration arises;
   (c) a brief statement describing the nature and circumstances of the dispute, and specifying the relief claimed;
   (d) a statement of any matters (such as the place or language of the arbitration, or the number of arbitrators, or their qualifications or identities) on which the parties have already agreed in relation to the conduct of the arbitration, or with respect to which the requesting party wishes to make a proposal;
   (e) if the arbitration agreement calls for party nomination of arbitrators, the name and address (and telephone and telex numbers, if known) of the Claimant's nominee;
   (f) the fee prescribed in the Schedule of Costs;
and shall confirm to the Registrar that copies have been served on the other parties. The date of receipt by the Registrar of the Request for Arbitration shall be deemed to be the date on which the arbitration has commenced.

Article 2   *Response by respondent*

2.1 For the purpose of facilitating the choice of arbitrators, within 30 days of receipt of its copy of the Request for Arbitration the Respondent may send to the Registrar a Response containing:

   (a) confirmation or denial of all or part of the claims;
   (b) a brief statement of the nature and circumstances of any envisaged counterclaims;
   (c) comment in response to any statements contained in the Request, as called for under Article 1(d), on matters relating to the conduct of the arbitration;
   (d) if the arbitration agreement calls for party nomination of arbitrators, the name and address (and telephone and telex numbers if known) of the Respondent's nominee;
and shall confirm to the Registrar that copies have been served on the other parties..

2.2 Failure to send a Response shall not preclude the Respondent from denying the claim nor from setting out a counterclaim in its Statement of Defence. However, if the arbitration agreement calls for party nomination of arbitrators, failure to send a Response or to nominate an arbitrator in it shall constitute a waiver of the opportunity to nominate an arbitrator.

Article 3   *The arbitral tribunal*

3.1 In these Rules, the expression 'the Tribunal' includes a sole arbitrator or all the arbitrators where more than one is appointed. All arbitrators (whether or not nominated by the parties) conducting an arbitration under these Rules shall be and remain at all times wholly independent and impartial, and shall not act as advocates for any party. Before appointment by the Court, if the Registrar so requests, any arbitrator shall furnish a resumé of his past and present professional positions (which will be communicated to the parties). In any event every arbitrator shall sign a declaration to the effect that there are no circumstances likely to give rise to any justified doubts as to his impartiality or independence, and that he will forthwith disclose any such circumstances to the Court and to all the parties if they should arise after that time and before the arbitration is concluded.

3.2 The Court will appoint the Tribunal to determine the dispute as soon as practicable after receipt by the Registrar of the Response, or after the expiry of 30 days following receipt by the Respondent of the Request if no Response is received, provided that the Registrar is satisfied that the Request has been properly served. A sole arbitrator will be appointed unless the parties have agreed otherwise, or unless the Court determines that in view of all the circumstances of the case a three-member tribunal is appropriate.

3.3 The Court alone is empowered to appoint arbitrators and such appointment will be made in the name of the Court by the President or any Vice President of the Court. The Court will appoint arbitrators with due regard for any particular method or criteria of selection agreed by the parties. In selecting arbitrators consideration will be given, so far as possible, to the nature of the contract, the nature and circumstances of the dispute, and the nationality, location and languages of the parties. Where the parties are of different nationalities, then unless they have agreed otherwise, sole arbitrators or chairmen are not to be appointed if they have the same nationality as any party (the nationality of parties being understood to include that of controlling shareholders or interests). If the parties have agreed that they are to nominate arbitrators themselves, or to allow two arbitrators, or a third party, to nominate an arbitrator, the Court may refuse to appoint such nominees if it determines that they are not suitable or independent or impartial. In the case of a three-member Tribunal the Court will designate the Chairman, who will not be a party-nominated arbitrator.

3.4 If the arbitration agreement calls for party nominations, and the Respondent fails to make such a nomination within the time limit established by Article 2, the Court will forthwith appoint an arbitrator in place of the arbitrator to be nominated by the Respondent. If the Request does not contain a nomination by the Claimant, and the Claimant fails to make such a nomination with the same time limit, the Court will likewise make that appointment.

3.5 In the event that the Court determines that a nominee is not suitable or independent or impartial, or if an appointed arbitrator is to be replaced, the Court shall have discretion to decide whether or not to follow the original nominating process. If it so decides any opportunity for renomination shall be waived if not exercised within 30 days, after which the Court shall appoint the replacement as soon as practicable.

3.6 If any arbitrator, after appointment, dies, refuses, or in the opinion of the Court becomes unable or unfit to act, the Court will, upon request by a party or by the remaining arbitrators, appoint another arbitrator in accordance with the provisions of Article 3.5. If in the opinion of the Court an arbitrator acts in manifest violation of these rules, or does not conduct the proceedings with reasonable diligence, he will be considered unfit.

3.7 An arbitrator may be challenged if circumstances exist that give rise to justifiable doubts as to his impartiality or independence. A party may challenge an arbitrator it has nominated, or in whose appointment it has participated, only for reasons of which it becomes aware after the appointment has been made.

3.8 A party who intends to challenge an arbitrator shall, within fifteen days of the constitution of the Tribunal or after becoming aware of any circumstances referred to in Article 3.6 or 3.7, whichever is the later, send a written statement of the reasons for the challenge to the Court. Unless the challenged arbitrator withdraws or the other party agrees to the challenge within 15 days of receipt of the written statement of challenge, the Court shall decide on the challenge.

3.9 The decision of the Court with respect to all matters referred to in this Article shall be final. Such decisions are deemed to be administrative in nature, and the Court shall not be required to give reasons for them. To the extent permitted by the law of the place of arbitration the parties shall be taken to have waived any right of appeal in respect of any such decisions to a court of law or other judicial authority. If such appeals remain possible due to mandatory provisions of the law of the place of arbitration, the Court shall, subject to the provisions of the applicable law, decide whether the arbitral proceedings are to continue notwithstanding an appeal.

Article 4   Communications between parties and the tribunal

4.1 Until the Tribunal is finally constituted and the Court determines that it would be appropriate for the parties and the Tribunal to communicate directly, all communications between parties and arbitrators shall be made through the Registrar. If and when the Court directs that communication shall take place directly between the Tribunal and the parties (with simultaneous copies to the Registrar) all further reference in these Rules to the Registrar shall thereafter be read as references to the Tribunal.

4.2 Where the Registrar, on behalf of the Tribunal, sends any communication to one party, he shall send a copy to each of the other parties.

4.3 Where any party sends any communication (including Statements under Article 6) to the Registrar, it shall include a copy for each arbitrator, and it shall also send copies to all the other parties and confirm to the Registrar in writing that it has done so.

4.4 The addresses of the parties for the purpose of all communications during the proceedings shall be those set out in the Request, or as any party may at any time notify to the Registrar and to the other parties.

Article 5   Conduct of the proceedings

5.1 The parties may agree on the arbitral procedure, and are encouraged to do so.

5.2 In the absence of procedural rules agreed by the parties or contained herein, the Tribunal shall have the widest discretion allowed under such law as may be applicable to ensure the just, expeditious, economical, and final determination of the dispute.

5.3 In the case of a three-member tribunal the Chairman may, after consulting the other arbitrators, make procedural rulings alone.

Article 6 Submission of written statements and documents

6.1 Subject to any procedural rules agreed by the parties or determined by the Tribunal under Article 5, the written stage of the proceedings shall be as set out in this Article.

6.2 Within 30 days of receipt of notification from the Court of the appointment of the Tribunal, the Claimant shall send to the Registrar a Statement of Case setting out in sufficient detail the facts and any contentions of law on which it relies, and the relief claimed.

6.3 Within 40 days of receipt of the Statement of Case, the Respondent shall send to the Registrar a Statement of Defence stating in sufficient detail which of the facts and contentions of law in the Statement of Case it admits or denies, on what grounds, and on what other facts and contentions of law it relies. Any counterclaims shall be submitted with the Statement of Defence in the same manner as claims are set out in the Statement of Case.

6.4 Within 40 days of receipt of the Statement of Defence, the Claimant may send to the Registrar a Statement of Reply which, where there are counterclaims, shall include a Defence to Counterclaims.

6.5 If the Statement of Reply contains a Defence to Counterclaims, the Respondent has a further 40 days to send to the Registrar a Statement of Reply regarding Counterclaims.

6.6 All Statements referred to in this Article shall be accompanied by copies (or, if they are especially voluminous, lists) of all essential documents on which the party concerned relies and which have not previously been submitted by any party, and (where appropriate) by any relevant samples.

6.7 As soon as practicable following completion of submission of the Statements specified in this Article, the Tribunal shall proceed in such manner as has been agreed by the parties, or pursuant to its authority under these Rules. If the Respondent fails to submit a Statement of Defence, or if at any point any party fails to avail itself of the opportunity to present its case in the manner directed by the Tribunal, the Tribunal may nevertheless proceed with the arbitration and make the award.

Article 7 Place of arbitration

7.1 The parties may choose the place of arbitration. Failing such a choice, the place of arbitration shall be London, unless the Tribunal determines in view of all the circumstances of the case that another place is more appropriate.

7.2 The Tribunal may hold hearings and meetings anywhere convenient, subject to the provisions of Article 10.2, and provided that the award shall be made at the place of arbitration.

Article 8   *Language of arbitration*

8.1 The language(s) of the arbitration shall be that of the document(s) containing the arbitration agreement, unless the parties have agreed otherwise.

8.2 If a document is drawn up in a language other than the language(s) of the arbitration, and no translation of such document is submitted by the party producing the document, The Tribunal, or if the Tribunal has not been appointed the court, may order that party to submit a translation in a form to be determined by the Tribunal or the Court.

Article 9   *Party representatives*

Any party may be represented by legal practitioners or any other representatives, subject to such proof of authority as the Tribunal may require.

Article 10   *Hearings*

10.1 Any party has the right to be heard before the Tribunal, unless the parties have agreed on documents-only arbitration.

10.2 The Tribunal shall fix the date, time and place of any meetings and hearings in the arbitration, and the Registrar shall give the parties reasonable notice thereof.

10.3 The Tribunal may in advance of hearings submit to the parties a list of questions which it wishes them to treat with special attention.

10.4 All meetings and hearings shall be in private unless the parties agree otherwise.

Article 11   *Witnesses*

11.1 Before any hearing, the Tribunal may require any party to give notice of the identity of witnesses it wishes to call, as well as the subject matter of their testimony and its relevance to the issues.

11.2 The Tribunal has discretion to allow, refuse, or limit the appearance of witnesses, whether witnesses of fact or expert witnesses.

11.3 Any witness who gives oral evidence may be questioned by each of the parties or their legal practitioners, under the control of the Tribunal. The Tribunal may put questions at any stage of the examination of the witnesses.

11.4 The testimony of witnesses may be presented in written form, either as signed statements or by duly sworn affidavits. Subject to Article 11.2 any party may request that such a witness should attend for oral examination at a hearing. If he fails to attend, the Tribunal may place such weight on the written testimony as it thinks fit, or exclude it altogether.

11.5 Subject to the mandatory provisions of any applicable law it shall be proper for any party or its legal practitioners to interview any witness or potential witness prior to his appearance at any hearing.

Article 12   Experts appointed by the Tribunal

12.1 Unless otherwise agreed by the parties, the Tribunal:

(a) may appoint one or more experts to report to the Tribunal on specific issues;

(b) may require a party to give any such expert any relevant information or to produce, or to provide access to, any relevant documents, goods or property for inspection by the expert.

12.2 Unless otherwise agreed by the parties, if a party so requests or if the Tribunal considers it necessary, the expert shall, after delivery of his written or oral report, participate in a hearing at which the parties shall have the opportunity to question him, and to present expert witnesses in order to testify on the points at issue.

Article 13   Additional powers of the Tribunal

13.1 Unless the parties at any time agree otherwise, and subject to any mandatory limitations of any applicable law, the Tribunal shall have the power, on the application of any party or of its own motion, but in either case only after giving the parties a proper opportunity to state their views, to:

(a) determine what are the rules of law governing or applicable to any contract, or arbitration agreement or issue between the parties;

(b) order the correction of any such contract or arbitration agreement, but only to the extent required to rectify any mistake which it determines to be common to all the parties and then only if and to the extent to which the rules of law governing or applicable to the contract permits such correction;

(c) allow other parties to be joined in the arbitration with their express consent, and make a single final award determining all disputes between them;

(d) allow any party, upon such terms (as to costs and otherwise) as it shall determine, to amend claims or counterclaims;

(e) extend or abbreviate any time limits provided by these Rules or by its directions;

(f) conduct such enquiries as may appear to the Tribunal to be necessary or expedient;

(g) order the parties to make any property or thing available for inspection, in their presence, by the Tribunal or any expert;

(h) order the preservation, storage, sale or other disposal of any property or thing under the control of any party;

(i) order any party to produce to the Tribunal, and to the other parties for inspection, and to supply copies of, any documents or classes of documents in their possession or power which the Tribunal determines to be relevant.

13.2 By agreeing to arbitration under these Rules the parties shall be taken to have agreed to apply only to the Tribunal, and not to any court of law or other judicial authority, for an order under paragraphs (g), (h) or (i) of Article 13.1.

Article 14   Jurisdiction of the Tribunal

14.1 The Tribunal shall have the power to rule on its own jurisdiction, including any objections with respect to the existence or validity of the arbitration agreement. For that purpose, an arbitration clause which forms part of a contract shall be treated as an agreement independent of the other terms of the contract. A decision by the Tribunal that the contract is null and void shall not entail ipso jure the invalidity of the arbitration clause.

14.2 A plea that the Tribunal does not have jurisdiction shall be raised not later than in the Statement of Defence. A plea that the Tribunal is exceeding the scope of its authority shall be raised promptly after the Tribunal has indicated its intention to decide on the matter alleged to be beyond the scope of its authority. In either case the Tribunal may nevertheless admit a late plea under this paragraph if it considers the delay justified.

14.3 In addition to the jurisdiction to exercise the powers defined elsewhere in these Rules, the Tribunal shall have jurisdiction to determine any question of law arising in the arbitration; proceed in the arbitration notwithstanding the failure or refusal of any party to comply with these Rules or with the Tribunal's orders or directions, or to attend any meeting or hearing, but only after giving that party written notice that it intends to do so; and to receive and take into account such written or oral evidence as it shall determine to be relevant, whether or not strictly admissible in law.

Article 15   Deposits and security

15.1 The Tribunal may direct the parties, in such proportions as it deems just, and subject to the confirmation of the Court that the amounts are in conformity with the Schedule of Costs, to make one or several interim or final payments on account of the costs of the arbitration. Such deposits shall be made to and held by the Court to the order of the Chairman of the Tribunal or sole arbitrator, and may be drawn from as required by the Tribunal. Interest on sums deposited, if any, shall be accumulated to the deposits.

15.2 The Tribunal shall have the power to order any party to provide security for the legal or other costs of any other party by way of deposit or bank guarantee or in any other manner the Tribunal thinks fit.

15.3 By agreeing to arbitration under these Rules the parties shall be taken to have agreed to apply only to the Tribunal, and not to any court of law or other judicial authority, for an order under Article 15.1, or for an order for security for costs under Article 15.2.

15.4 Without prejudice to the right of any party to apply to a competent court for pre-award conservatory measures (except those referred to in Articles 15.1 and 15.2), the Tribunal shall also have the power to order any party to provide security for all or part of any amount in dispute in the arbitration.

15.5 In the event that orders under paragraphs 1, 2 and 4 of this Article are not complied with, the Tribunal may disregard claims or counterclaims by the non-complying party, although it may proceed to determine claims or counterclaims by complying parties.

Article 16   The award

16.1 The Tribunal shall make its award in writing and, unless all the parties agree otherwise, shall state the reasons upon which its award is based. The award shall state its date and shall be signed by the arbitrator or arbitrators.

16.2 If any arbitrator refuses or fails to comply with the mandatory provisions of any applicable law relating to the making of the award, having been given a reasonable opportunity to do so, the remaining arbitrators shall proceed in his absence.

16.3 Where there is more than one arbitrator and they fail to agree on any issue, they shall decide by a majority. Failing a majority decision on any issue, the Chairman of the Tribunal shall make the award alone as if he were the sole arbitrator. If an arbitrator refuses or fails to sign the award, the signatures of the majority shall be sufficient, provided that the reason for the omitted signature is stated.

16.4 The sole arbitrator or chairman shall be responsible for delivering the award to the court, which shall transmit certified copies to the parties provided that the costs of the arbitration have been paid to the Court in accordance with Article 18.

16.5 Awards may be expressed in any currency, and the Tribunal may award that simple or compound interest shall be paid by any party on any sum which is the subject of the reference at such rates as the Tribunal determines to be appropriate, without being bound by legal rates of interest, in respect of any period which the Tribunal determines to be appropriate ending not later than the date upon which the award is complied with.

16.6 The Tribunal may make separate final awards on different issues at different times, which shall be subject to correction under the procedure specified in Article 17. Such awards shall be enforceable.

16.7 In the event of a settlement, the Tribunal may render an award recording the settlement if any party so requests. If the parties do not require a consent award, then on confirmation in writing by the parties to the Court that a settlement has been reached the Tribunal shall be discharged and the reference to arbitration concluded, subject to payment by the parties of any outstanding costs of the arbitration in accordance with Article 18.

16.8 By agreeing to arbitration under these Rules, the parties undertake to carry out the award without delay, and waive their right to any form of appeal or recourse to a court of law or other judicial authority, insofar as such waiver may be validly made. Awards shall be final and binding on the parties as from the date they are made.

Article 17   Correction of awards and additional awards

17.1 Within 30 days of receipt of the award, unless another period of time has been agreed upon by the parties, a party may by notice to the Registrar request the Tribunal to correct in the award any errors in computation, any clerical or typographical errors or any errors of a similar nature. If the Tribunal considers the request to be justified, it shall make the corrections within thirty days of receipt of the request. Any correction, which shall take the form of a separate memorandum, shall become part of the award.

17.2 The Tribunal may correct any error of the type referred to in Article 17.1 on its own initiative within thirty days of the date of the award.

17.3 Unless otherwise agreed by the parties, a party may, within thirty days of receipt of the award, and with notice to the other party or parties, request the Tribunal to make an additional award as to claims presented in the arbitral proceedings but not dealt with in the award. If the Tribunal considers the request to be justified, it shall make the additional award within sixty days.

17.4　The provisions of Article 16 shall apply mutatis mutandis to a correction of the award and to any additional award.

Article 18　Costs

18.1　The costs of the arbitration (other than the legal or other costs incurred by the parties themselves) shall be in accordance with the Schedule of Costs applicable to these Rules as of the date of the Request for Arbitration.

18.2　The Tribunal shall specify in the award the total amount of the costs of the arbitration, subject to the confirmation of the Court that the amount is in conformity with the Schedule of Costs. Unless the parties shall agree otherwise, the Tribunal shall determine the proportions in which the parties shall pay all or part of them to the Court. If the Tribunal has determined that all or any part of the costs of the arbitration shall be paid by any party other than a party which has already paid them to the Court, the latter shall have the right to recover the appropriate amount from the former.

18.3　The Tribunal shall have the authority to order in its award that all or a part of the legal or other costs of a party (apart from the costs of the arbitration) be paid by another party.

18.4　If the arbitration is abandoned, suspended or concluded, by agreement or otherwise, before the final award is made, the parties shall be jointly and severally liable to pay to the Court the costs of the arbitration as determined by the Tribunal, subject to the confirmation by the Court that the amount is in conformity with the Schedule of Costs. In the event that the costs so determined are less than the deposits made, there shall be a refund in such proportions as the parties may agree, or, failing agreement, in the same proportions as the deposits were made.

Article 19　Exclusion of liability

19.1　Neither the court nor any arbitrator shall be liable to any party for any act or omission in connection with any arbitration conducted under these Rules, save that arbitrators (but not the Court) may be liable for the consequences of conscious and deliberate wrongdoing.

19.2　After the award has been made and the possibilities of correction and additional awards referred to in Article 17 have lapsed or been exhausted, neither the Court nor any arbitrator shall be under any obligation to make any statement to any person about any matter concerning the arbitration, nor shall any party seek to make any arbitrator or any officer of the Court a witness in any legal proceedings arising out of the arbitration.

Article 20　General rules

20.1　A party who knows that any provision of, or requirement under, these

Rules has not been complied with and yet proceeds with the arbitration without promptly stating its objection to such non-compliance, shall be deemed to have waived its right to object.

20.2 In all matters not expressly provided for in these Rules, the Court and the Tribunal shall act in the spirit of these Rules and shall make every reasonable effort to ensure that the award is legally enforceable.

SCHEDULE OF COSTS

(effective 1 January 1985)
[*Not reproduced in this work*]

The following does not form part of the Rules but is issued by the London Court of International Arbitration.

Recommended arbitration clause

Parties to an international contract who wish to have any disputes referred to arbitration under these Rules are recommended to insert in the contract an arbitration clause in the following form:

> **'Any dispute arising out of or in connection with this contract, including any question regarding its existence, validity or termination, shall be referred to and finally resolved by arbitration under the Rules of the London Court of International Arbitration, which Rules are deemed to be incorporated by reference into this clause.'**

Parties are also reminded that difficulties and expense may be avoided if they expressly specify the law governing their contract. The parties may if they wish also specify the number of arbitrators, and the place and language of the arbitration. The following provisions may be suitable:

> **'The governing law of this contract shall be the substantive law of . . .'**

> **'The tribunal shall consist of . . . (a sole or three) arbitrator(s)'. (In the case of a three member tribunal, the following words may be added '. . . two of them shall be nominated by the respective parties').**

> **'The place of arbitration shall be . . . (city).'**

> **'The language of the arbitration shall be . . .'**

Institution of Civil Engineers'
Arbitration Procedure (1983)

This Procedure (approved February 1983) has been prepared by The Institution of Civil Engineers to be used with the ICE Conditions of Contract (fifth edition) for the settlement of disputes by arbitration under Clause 66 thereof. It replaces The ICE Arbitration Procedure (1973). This Procedure is also suitable for other engineering arbitrations.

Part A. Reference and Appointment

Rule 1 Notice to refer

1.1 A dispute of difference shall be deemed to arise when a claim or assertion made by one party is rejected by the other party and that rejection is not accepted. Subject only to Clause 66(1) of *the ICE Conditions of Contract* (if applicable) either party may then invoke arbitration by serving a *Notice to Refer* on the other party.

1.2 The Notice to Refer shall list the matters which the issuing party wishes to be referred to arbitration. Where Clause 66 of the ICE Conditions of Contract applies the Notice to Refer shall also state the date when the matters listed therein were referred to the Engineer for his decision under Clause 66(1) and the date on which the Engineer gave his decision thereon or that he has failed to do so.

Rule 2 Appointment of sole Arbitrator by agreement

2.1 After serving the Notice to Refer either party may serve upon the other a *Notice to Concur* in the appointment of an Arbitrator listing therein the names and addresses of any persons he proposes as Arbitrator.

2.2 Within 14 days thereafter the other party shall

(a) agree in writing to the appointment of one of the persons listed in the Notice to Concur, or

(b) propose a list of alternative persons.

2.3 Once agreement has been reached the issuing party shall write to the person so selected inviting him to accept the appointment enclosing a copy of the Notice to Refer and documentary evidence of the other party's agreement.

2.4 If the person so selected accepts the appointment he shall notify the issuing party in writing and send a copy to the other party. The date of posting or service as the case may be of this notification shall be deemed to be the date on which the Arbitrator's appointment is completed.

Rule 3 Appointment of sole Arbitrator by the President

3.1 If within one calendar month from service of the Notice to Concur the parties fail to appoint an Arbitrator in accordance with Rule 2 either party may then apply to the President to appoint an Arbitrator. The parties may also agree to apply to the President without a Notice to Concur.

3.2 Such application shall be in writing and shall include copies of the Notice to Refer, the Notice to Concur (if any) and any other relevant documents. The application shall be accompanied by the appropriate fee.

3.3 The Institution will send a copy of the application to the other party stating that the President intends to make the appointment on a specified date. Having first contacted an appropriate person and obtained his agreement the President will make the appointment on the specified date or such later date as may be appropriate which shall then be deemed to be the date on which the Arbitrator's appointment is completed. The Institution will notify both parties and the Arbitrator in writing as soon as possible thereafter.

Rule 4 *Notice of further disputes or differences*

4.1 At any time before the Arbitrator's appointment is completed either party may put forward further disputes or differences to be referred to him. This shall be done by serving upon the other party an additional Notice to Refer in accordance with Rule 1.

4.2 Once his appointment is completed the Arbitrator shall have jurisdiction over any issue connected with and necessary to the determination of any dispute or difference already referred to him whether or not the connected issue has first been referred to the Engineer for his decision under Clause 66(1) of the ICE Conditions of Contract.

Part B. Powers of the Arbitrator

Rule 5 *Power to control the proceedings*

5.1 The Arbitrator may exercise any or all of the powers set out or necessarily to be implied in this Procedure on such terms as he thinks fit. These terms may include orders as to costs, time for compliance and the consequences of non-compliance.

5.2 Powers under this Procedure shall be in addition to any other powers available to the Arbitrator.

Rule 6 *Power to order protective measures*

6.1 The arbitrator shall have power
  (a) to give directions for the detention storage sale or disposal of the whole or any part of the subject matter of the dispute at the expense of one or both of the parties
  (b) to give directions for the preservation of any document or thing which is or may become evidence in the arbitration
  (c) to order the deposit of money or other security to secure the whole or any part of the amount(s) in dispute
  (d) to make an order for security for costs in favour of one or more of the parties
and (e) to order his own costs to be secured.

6.2 Money ordered to be paid under this Rule shall be paid without delay into a separate bank account in the name of a stakeholder to be appointed by and subject to the directions of the Arbitrator.

Rule 7   *Power to order concurrent Hearings*

7.1 Where disputes or differences have arisen under two or more contracts each concerned wholly or mainly with the same subject matter and the resulting arbitrations have been referred to the same Arbitrator he may with the agreement of all the parties concerned or upon the application of one of the parties being a party to all the contracts involved order that the whole or any part of the matters at issue shall be heard together upon such terms or conditions as the Arbitrator thinks fit.

7.2 Where an order for concurrent Hearings has been made under Rule 7.1 the Arbitrator shall nevertheless make and publish separate Awards unless the parties otherwise agree but the Arbitrator may if he thinks fit prepare one combined set of Reasons to cover all the Awards.

Rule 8   *Powers at the Hearing*

8.1 The Arbitrator may hear the parties their representatives and/or witnesses at any time or place and may adjourn the arbitration for any period on the application of any party or as he thinks fit.

8.2 Any party may be represented by any person including in the case of a company or other legal entity a director officer employee or beneficiary of such company or entity. In particular, a person shall not be prevented from representing a party because he is or may be also a witness in the proceedings. Nothing shall prevent a party from being represented by different persons at different times.

8.3 Nothing in these Rules or in any other rule custom or practice shall prevent the Arbitrator from starting to hear the arbitration once his appointment is completed or at any time thereafter.

8.4 Any meeting with or summons before the Arbitrator at which both parties are represented shall if the Arbitrator so directs be treated as part of the hearing of the arbitration.

Rule 9   *Power to appoint assessors or to seek outside advice*

9.1 The Arbitrator may appoint a legal technical or other assessor to assist him in the conduct of the arbitration. The Arbitrator shall direct when such assessor is to attend hearings of the arbitration.

9.2 The Arbitrator may seek legal technical or other advice on any matter arising out of or in connection with the proceedings.

9.3 Further and/or alternatively the Arbitrator may rely upon his own knowledge and expertise to such extent as he thinks fit.

Part C. Procedure before the Hearing

Rule 10   *The preliminary meeting*

10.1 As soon as possible after accepting the appointment the Arbitrator shall summon the parties to a preliminary meeting for the purpose of giving such directions about the procedure to be adopted in the arbitration as he considers necessary.

10.2 At the preliminary meeting the parties and the Arbitrator shall consider whether and to what extent

(a) Part F (Short Procedure) or Part G (Special Procedure for Experts) of these Rules shall apply

(b) the arbitration may proceed on documents only

(c) progress may be facilitated and costs saved by determining some of the issues in advance of the main Hearing

(d) the parties should enter into an exclusion agreement (if they have not already done so) in accordance with s. 3 of the Arbitration Act 1979 (where the Act applies to the arbitration)

and in general shall consider such other steps as may minimise delay and expedite the determination of the real issues between the parties.

10.3 If the parties so wish they may themselves agree directions and submit them to the Arbitrator for his approval. In so doing the parties shall state whether or not they wish Part F or Part G of these Rules to apply. The Arbitrator may then approve the directions as submitted or (having first consulted the parties) may vary them or substitute his own as he thinks fit.

Rule 11 Pleadings and discovery

11.1 The Arbitrator may order the parties to deliver pleadings or statements of their cases in any form he thinks appropriate. The Arbitrator may order any party to answer the other party's case and to give reasons for any disagreement.

11.2 The Arbitrator may order any party to deliver in advance of formal discovery copies of any documents in his possession custody or power which relate either generally or specifically to matters raised in any pleading statement or answer.

11.3 Any pleading statement or answer shall contain sufficient detail for the other party to know the case he has to answer. If sufficient detail is not provided the Arbitrator may of his own motion or at the request of the other party order further and better particulars to be delivered.

11.4 If a party fails to comply with any order made under this Rule the Arbitrator shall have power to debar that party from relying on the matters in respect of which he is in default and the Arbitrator may proceed with the arbitration and make his Award accordingly. Provided that the Arbitrator shall first give notice to the party in default that he intends to proceed under this Rule.

Rule 12 Procedural meetings

12.1 The Arbitrator may at any time call such procedural meetings as he deems necessary to identify or clarify the issues to be decided and the procedures to be adopted. For this purpose the Arbitrator may request particular persons to attend on behalf of the parties.

12.2 Either party may at any time apply to the Arbitrator for leave to appear before him on any interlocutory matter. The Arbitrator may call a procedural meeting for the purpose or deal with the application in correspondence or otherwise as he thinks fit.

12.3 At any procedural meeting or otherwise the Arbitrator may give such directions as he thinks fit for the proper conduct of the arbitration. Whether or not formal pleadings have been ordered under Rule 11 such directions may include an order that either or both parties shall prepare in writing and shall serve upon the other party and the Arbitrator any or all of the following

(a) a summary of that party's case

(b) a summary of that party's evidence

(c) a statement or summary of the issues between the parties

(d) a list and/or a summary of the documents relied upon

(e) a statement or summary of any other matters likely to assist the resolution of the disputes or differences between the parties.

Rule 13 *Preparation for the Hearing*

13.1 In addition to his powers under Rules 11 and 12 the Arbitrator shall also have power

(a) to order that the parties shall agree facts as facts and figures as figures where possible

(b) to order the parties to prepare an agreed bundle of all documents relevant to the arbitration. The agreed bundle shall thereby be deemed to have been entered in evidence without further proof and without being read out at the Hearing. Provided always that either party may at the Hearing challenge the admissibility of any document in the agreed bundle.

(c) to order that any experts whose reports have been exchanged before the Hearing shall be examined by the Arbitrator in the presence of the parties or their legal representatives and not by the parties or their legal representatives themselves. Where such an order is made either party may put questions whether by way of cross-examination or re-examination to any party's expert after all experts have been examined by the Arbitrator provided that the party so doing shall first give notice of the nature of the questions he wishes to put.

13.2 Before the Hearing the Arbitrator may and shall if so requested by the parties read the documents to be used at the Hearing. For this or any other purpose the Arbitrator may require all such documents to be delivered to him at such time and place as he may specify.

Rule 14 *Summary Awards*

14.1 The Arbitrator may at any time make a *Summary Award* and for this purpose shall have power to award payment by one party to another of a sum representing a reasonable proportion of the final nett amount which in his opinion that party is likely to be ordered to pay after determination of all the issues in the arbitration and after taking into account any defence or counterclaim upon which the other party may be entitled to rely.

14.2 The Arbitrator shall have power to order the party against whom a Summary Award is made to pay part or all of the sum awarded to a stakeholder. In default of compliance with such an order the Arbitrator may order payment of the whole sum in the Summary Award to the other party.

14.3 The Arbitrator shall have power to order payment of costs in relation to a Summary Award including power to order that such costs shall be paid forthwith.

14.4 A Summary Award shall be final and binding upon the parties unless and until it is varied by any subsequent Award made and published by the same Arbitrator or by any other arbitrator having jurisdiction over the matters in dispute. Any such subsequent Award may order repayment of monies paid in accordance with the Summary Award.

Part D. Procedure at the Hearing

Rule 15 The Hearing

15.1 At or before the Hearing and after hearing representations on behalf of each party the Arbitrator shall determine the order in which the parties shall present their cases and/or the order in which the issues shall be heard and determined.

15.2 The Arbitrator may order any submission or speech by or on behalf of any party to be put into writing and delivered to him and to the other party. A party so ordered shall be entitled if he so wishes to enlarge upon or vary any such submission orally.

15.3 The Arbitrator may on the application of either party or of his own motion hear and determine any issue or issues separately.

15.4 If a party fails to appear at the Hearing and provided that the absent party has had notice of the Hearing or the Arbitrator is satisfied that all reasonable steps have been taken to notify him of the Hearing the Arbitrator may proceed with the Hearing in his absence. The Arbitrator shall nevertheless take all reasonable steps to ensure that the real issues between the parties are determined justly and fairly.

Rule 16 Evidence

16.1 The Arbitrator may order a party to submit in advance of the Hearing a list of the witnesses he intends to call. That party shall not thereby be bound to call any witness so listed and may add to the list so submitted at any time.

16.2 No expert evidence shall be admissible except by leave of the Arbitrator. Leave may be given on such terms and conditions as the Arbitrator thinks fit. Unless the Arbitrator otherwise orders such terms shall be deemed to include a requirement that a report from each expert containing the substance of the evidence to be given shall be served upon the other party within a reasonable time before the Hearing.

16.3 The Arbitrator may order disclosure or exchange of proofs of evidence relating to factual issues. The Arbitrator may also order any party to prepare and disclose in advance a list of points or questions to be put in cross-examination of any witness.

16.4 Where a list of questions is disclosed whether pursuant to an order of the Arbitrator or otherwise the party making disclosure shall not be bound to put any question therein to the witness unless the Arbitrator so orders. Where the party making disclosure puts a question not so listed in cross-examination the Arbitrator may disallow the costs thereby occasioned.

16.5 The Arbitrator may order that any proof of evidence which has been disclosed shall stand as the evidence in chief of the deponent provided that the other party has been or will be given an opportunity to cross-examine the deponent thereon. The Arbitrator may also at any time before such cross-examination order the deponent or some other identified person to deliver written answers to questions arising out of the proof of evidence.

16.6 The Arbitrator may himself put questions to any witness and/or require the parties to conduct enquiries tests or investigations. Subject to his agreement the parties may ask the Arbitrator to conduct or arrange for any enquiry test or investigation.

Part E. After the Hearing

Rule 17 The Award

17.1 Upon the closing of the Hearing (if any) and after having considered all the evidence and submissions the Arbitrator will prepare and publish his Award.

17.2 When the Arbitrator has made and published his Award (including a Summary Award under Rule 14) he will so inform the parties in writing and shall specify how and where it may be taken up upon due payment of his fee.

Rule 18 Reasons

18.1 Whether requested by any party to do so or not the Arbitrator may at his discretion state his Reasons for all or any part of his Award. Such Reasons may form part of the Award itself or may be contained in a separate document.

18.2 A party asking for Reasons shall state the purpose for his request. If the purpose is to use them for an appeal (whether under s. 1 of the Arbitration Act 1979 or otherwise) the requesting party shall also specify the points of law with which he wishes the Reasons to deal. In that event the Arbitrator shall give the other party an opportunity to specify additional points of law to be dealt with.

18.3 Reasons prepared as a separate document may be delivered with the Award or later as the Arbitrator thinks fit.

18.4 Where the Arbitrator decides not to state his Reasons he shall nevertheless keep such notes as will enable him to prepare Reasons later if so ordered by the High Court.

Rule 19 Appeals

19.1 If any party applies to the High Court for leave to appeal against any Award or decision or for an order staying the arbitration proceedings or for any other purpose that party shall forthwith notify the Arbitrator of the application.

19.2 Once any Award or decision has been made and published the Arbitrator shall be under no obligation to make any statement in connection therewith other than in compliance with an order of the High Court under s. 1 (5) of the Arbitration Act 1979.

Part F. Short Procedure

Rule 20   Short Procedure

20.1 Where the parties so agree (either of their own motion or at the invitation of the Arbitrator) the arbitration shall be conducted in accordance with the following *Short Procedure.*

20.2 Each party shall set out his case in the form of a file containing
  (a) a statement as to the orders or awards he seeks
  (b) a statement of his reasons for being entitled to such orders or awards and
  (c) copies of any documents on which he relies (including statements) identifying the origin and date of each document
and shall deliver copies of the said file to the other party and to the Arbitrator in such manner and within such time as the Arbitrator may direct.

20.3 After reading the parties' cases the Arbitrator may view the site or the Works and may require either or both parties to submit further documents or information in writing.

20.4 Within one calendar month of completing the foregoing steps the Arbitrator shall fix a day when he shall meet the parties for the purpose of
  (a) receiving any oral submissions which either party may wish to make and/or
  (b) the Arbitrator's putting questions to the parties their representatives or witnesses.
For this purpose the Arbitrator shall give notice of any particular person he wishes to question but no person shall be bound to appear before him.

20.5 Within one calendar month following the conclusion of the meeting under Rule 20.4 or such further period as the Arbitrator may reasonably require the Arbitrator shall make and publish his Award.

Rule 21   Other matters

21.1 Unless the parties otherwise agree the Arbitrator shall have no power to award costs to either party and the Arbitrator's own fees and charges shall be paid in equal shares by the parties. Where one party has agreed to the Arbitrator's fees the other party by agreeing to this Short Procedure shall be deemed to have agreed likewise to the Arbitrator's fees.

21.2 Either party may at any time before the Arbitrator has made and published his Award under this Short Procedure require by written notice served on the Arbitrator and the other party that the arbitration shall cease to be conducted in accordance with this Short Procedure. Save only for Rule 21.3 the Short Procedure shall thereupon no longer apply or find the parties but any evidence already laid before the Arbitrator shall be admissible in further proceedings as if it had been submitted as part of those proceedings and without further proof.

21.3 The party giving written notice under Rule 21.2 shall thereupon in any event become liable to pay
  (a) the whole of the Arbitrator's fees and charges incurred up to the date of such notice and
  (b) a sum to be assessed by the Arbitrator as reasonable compensation for the

costs (including any legal costs) incurred by the other party up to the date of such notice.

Payment in full of such charges shall be a condition precedent to that party's proceeding further in the arbitration unless the Arbitrator otherwise directs. Provided that non-payment of the said charges shall not prevent the other party from proceeding in the arbitration.

Part G. Special Procedure for Experts

Rule 22 Special Procedure for Experts

22.1 Where the parties so agree (either of their own motion or at the invitation of the Arbitrator) the hearing and determination of any issues of fact which depend upon the evidence of experts shall be conducted in accordance with the following *Special Procedure*.

22.2 Each party shall set out his case on such issues in the form of a file containing

(a) a statement of the factual findings he seeks

(b) a report or statement from and signed by each expert upon whom that party relies and

(c) copies of any other documents referred to in each expert's report or statement or on which the party relies identifying the origin and date of each document

and shall deliver copies of the said file to the other party and to the Arbitrator in such manner and within such time as the Arbitrator may direct.

22.3 After reading the parties' cases the Arbitrator may view the site or the Works and may require either or both parties to submit further documents or information in writing.

22.4 Thereafter the Arbitrator shall fix a day when he shall meet the experts whose reports or statements have been submitted. At the meeting each expert may address the Arbitrator and put questions to any other expert representing the other party. The Arbitrator shall so direct the meeting as to ensure that each expert has an adequate opportunity to explain his opinion and to comment upon any opposing opinion. No other person shall be entitled to address the Arbitrator or question any expert unless the parties and the Arbitrator so agree.

22.5 Thereafter the Arbitrator may make and publish an Award setting out with such details or particulars as may be necessary his decision upon the issues dealt with.

Rule 23 Costs

23.1 The Arbitrator may in his Award make orders as to the payment of any costs relating to the foregoing matters including his own fees and charges in connection therewith.

23.2 Unless the parties otherwise agree and so notify the Arbitrator neither party shall be entitled to any costs in respect of legal representation assistance or other legal work relating to the hearing and determination of factual issues by this Special Procedure.

Part H. Interim Arbitration

Rule 24 Interim Arbitration

24.1 Where the Arbitrator is appointed and the arbitration is to proceed before completion or alleged completion of the Works then save in the case of a dispute arising under Clause 63 of the ICE Conditions of Contract the following provisions shall apply in addition to the foregoing Rules and the arbitration shall be called an Interim Arbitration.

24.2 In conducting an Interim Arbitration the Arbitrator shall apply the powers at his disposal with a view to making his Award or Awards as quickly as possible and thereby allowing or facilitating the timely completion of the Works.

24.3 Should an Interim Arbitration not be completed before the Works or the relevant parts thereof are complete the Arbitrator shall within 14 days of the date of such completion make and publish his Award findings of fact or Interim Decision pursuant to Rule 24.5 hereunder on the basis of evidence given and submissions made up to that date together with such further evidence and submissions as he may in his discretion agree to receive during the said 14 days. Provided that before the expiry of the said 14 days the parties may otherwise agree and so notify the Arbitrator.

24.4 For the purpose only of Rule 24.3 the Arbitrator shall decide finally whether and if so when the Works or the relevant parts thereof are complete.

24.5 In an Interim Arbitration the Arbitrator may make and publish any or all of the following

(a) a Final Award or an Interim Award on the matters at issue therein

(b) findings of fact

(c) a Summary Award in accordance with Rule 14

(d) an Interim Decision as defined in Rule 24.6.

An Award under (a) above or a Finding under (b) above shall be final and binding upon the parties in any subsequent proceedings. Anything not expressly identified as falling under either of headings (a) (b) or (c) above shall be deemed to be an Interim Decision under heading (d). Save as aforesaid the Arbitrator shall not make an Interim Decision without first notifying the parties that he intends to do so.

24.6 An *Interim Decision* shall be final and binding upon the parties and upon the Engineer (if any) until such time as the Works have been completed or any Award or decision under Rule 24.3 has been given. Thereafter the Interim Decision may be re-opened by another Arbitrator appointed under these Rules and where such other Arbitrator was also the Arbitrator appointed to conduct the Interim Arbitration he shall not be bound by his earlier Interim Decision.

24.7 The Arbitrator in an Interim Arbitration shall have power to direct that Part F (Short Procedure) and/or Part G (Special Procedure for Experts) shall apply to the Interim Arbitration.

Part J. Miscellaneous

Rule 25 Definitions

25.1 In these Rules the following definitions shall apply.

(a) 'Arbitrator' includes a tribunal of two or more Arbitrators or an Umpire.

(b) 'Institution' means the Institution of Civil Engineers.

(c) 'ICI Conditions of Contract' means the Conditions of Contract for use in connection with Works of Civil Engineering Construction published jointly by the Institution, the Association of Consulting Engineers and the Federation of Civil Engineering Contractors.

(d) 'Other party' includes the plural unless the context otherwise requires.

(e) 'President' means the President for the time being of the Institution or any Vice-President acting on his behalf.

(f) 'Procedure' means the Institution of Civil Engineers' Arbitration Procedure (1983) unless the context otherwise requires.

(g) 'Award', 'Final Award' and 'Interim Award' have the meanings given to those terms in or in connection with the Arbitration Acts 1950 to 1979. 'Summary Award' means an Award made under Rule 14 hereof.

(h) 'Interim Arbitration' means an arbitration in accordance with Part H of these Rules. 'Interim Decision' means a decision as defined in Rule 24.6 hereof.

Rule 26   Application of the ICE Procedure

26.1 This Procedure shall apply to the conduct of the arbitration if

(a) the parties at any time so agree

(b) the President when making an appointment so directs, or

(c) the Arbitrator so stipulates at the time of his appointment.

Provided that where this Procedure applies by virtue of the Arbitrator's stipulation under (c) above the parties may within 14 days of that appointment agree otherwise in which event the Arbitrator's appointment shall terminate and the parties shall pay his reasonable charges in equal shares.

26.2 This Procedure shall not apply to arbitrations under the law of Scotland for which a separate *ICE Arbitration Procedure (Scotland)* is available.

26.3 Where an arbitration is governed by the law of a country other than England and Wales this Procedure shall apply to the extent that the applicable law permits.

Rule 27   Exclusion of liability

27.1 Neither the Institution nor its servants or agents nor the President shall be liable to any party for any act omission or misconduct in connection with any appointment made or any arbitration conducted under this Procedure.

Index

Appeal—*continued*
preliminary questions of law—*continued*
section 2, determination under,
application,
arbitrator, consent of, 623–625
consent of all parties, with, 625
decision to entertain, 622–625
generally, 622
umpire, consent of, 623–625
decision, 626
decision to invoke s 2, 621–622
discretion, 625
procedural powers, allocation of, 269–270
procedures not by way of,
judicial control, 638–640
recourse, possible methods of,
arbitrator, removal of, 645
equity clause, decision under, 648–649
generally, 640–641
intervention in equity, 644
judicial review, 646
jurisdiction, 641–643
mandate, renunciation of, 644–645
misconduct, 646–648
remission, 643–644
procedures, 363–367
questions of law, on, 26–28
RSC Order 55, 636–637
reasons,
court's power to order,
discretion, 598–599
jurisdiction, 597–598
generally, 596–597
identification of, 594–595
inferences of fact, 600
remission under s 22, 599–600
Applicable law. *See* LAW
Applicant
identity of, 471
Appointment of arbitrator. *See*
ARBITRATOR
Arbitration
acts, subject to, 50–52
agreement. *See* ARBITRATION AGREEMENT
award. *See* AWARD
clause. *See* CLAUSE
definition,
attributes which must be present,
consensual resolution of dispute, 43–44
consensual tribunal, 44
decision intended to be binding, 42
enforceable agreement to refer, 45–46
formulated dispute, 46–48
generally, 41
impartial tribunal, 44–45
parties to process, 42–43
generally, 38–40
relevant factors,
attributes which must be present, 41
choice of tribunal, 49–50
contentions, 48–49

Arbitration—*continued*
definition—*continued*
relevant factors—*continued*
evidence, 48–49
generally, 41–42
obligation to apply law, 50
summary, 41–42
wording of agreement, 49
distinctive features,
coercive powers of court, 37–38
constitution of tribunal, defects in, 37
decision of tribunal, enforcement of, 38
form of intervention, 35–36
procedural misconduct, 36–37
supervising court, intervention by,
error of fact, 34–35
incorrect view of law, 35
judicial arbitration compared with, 266–267
multiple. *See* MULTIPLE ARBITRATIONS
notice of. *See* NOTICE
other types of tribunal, relationship to, 30–32
private. *See* PRIVATE ARBITRATION
separate historical origins, 32–34
total breakdown of, 543
Arbitration Act 1979
origins, 452–458
Arbitration agreement
abandonment, 512–513
ad hoc submission, 6, 104
affirmation, 513–514
cesser of, 164–165
claim, clause requiring, 129
consent, termination by, 510–512
cross-claim,
generally, 129–130
outside clause, 131
within clause, 130–131
delay, problem of, 516–517
difference, meaning, 128–129
dispute,
clause requiring,
amendments,
claimant, by, 126–127
generally, 125–126
respondent, by, 126
appointment of arbitrator, dispute
arising after, 125
award, dispute resolved before, 128
genuine dispute, 123–124
undisputed claim, 122–123
generally, 122
meaning, 127–128
domestic, enforcement of, 7
effect of, 6–7
enforcement, 7–8, 268
equity clause as, 85–86
estoppel, 512
existence of,
certainty,
abbreviated clauses, 107
generally, 106